KU-498-192

THE GREAT IDEAS

A Syntopicon of Great Books of the Western World

MORTIMER J. ADLER, *Editor in Chief*

WILLIAM GORMAN, *General Editor*

VOLUME II

WILLIAM BENTON, *Publisher*

ENCYCLOPÆDIA BRITANNICA, INC

CHICAGO · LONDON · TORONTO · GENEVA · SYDNEY · TOKYO · MANILA

THE UNIVERSITY OF CHICAGO

The Great Books
is published with the editorial advice of the faculties
of The University of Chicago

THIRTY-SECOND PRINTING, 1990

Library of Congress Catalog Card Number: 55-10312
International Standard Book Number: ~~0-85229-476-X~~

GENERAL CONTENTS

VOLUME I

VOLUME II

CONTENTS

THE GREAT IDEAS: II

Chapters 51–102: Man *to* World

Chapter 51: MAN

INTRODUCTION

WHETHER or not the proper study of mankind is man, it is the only study in which the knower and the known are one, in which the object of the science is the nature of the scientist. If we consider every effort men have made in response to the ancient injunction "know thyself," then psychology has perhaps a longer tradition than any other science. But by a stricter conception of science, more is required than individual insight or self-consciousness. Definitions, principles, analyses applicable to all men must be established, and it has been questioned whether the method of introspection suffices for this purpose. What methods should be used by the psychologist depends in part upon the precise object and scope of his inquiry. According as different subject matters and different methods define psychology, there seem to be several disciplines bearing that name, each with its own tradition in western thought.

In one conception, psychology begins with the dialogues of Plato and with Aristotle's treatise *On the Soul*. As Aristotle's title indicates, and as the Greek roots of the word "psychology" connote, the soul rather than man is the object of the science. Anthropology, Kant later suggests, would be a more appropriate name for the science of man. The Greek inquiry into the soul extends, beyond man, to all living things. It is because "the soul is in some sense the principle of animal life," Aristotle writes, that "the knowledge of the soul admittedly contributes greatly to the advance of truth in general, and, above all, to our understanding of Nature."

Nevertheless, psychology for the Greeks is principally concerned with the study of man. The analysis of the parts or faculties of the human soul is an analysis of the properties of human nature—the powers which man has and the characteristically human acts or functions he can perform. The methods by which this analysis is developed are, for the most part, the same methods which the Greek philosophers use in physics. "The study of the soul," Aristotle writes, "falls within the science of Nature." The definitions of the psychologist, like those of the physicist, give "a certain mode of movement of such and such a body (or part or faculty of a body) by this or that cause and for this or that end." In the case of the human soul, however, the psychologist can employ a method not applicable to other things. The human intellect is able to examine itself. Mind can thus know things about mind which are not otherwise observable.

The subject matter of psychology narrows somewhat when, at a later moment in the tradition, the study of mind tends to replace the study of man. This narrowing takes place gradually. Though Descartes identifies soul with mind or intellect, he treats of the passions and the will as well as thought and knowledge. Differing from Descartes with regard to body and soul, Hobbes and Spinoza also give as much attention to the emotions as to ideas and reasoning. But with Locke, Berkeley, and Hume there is an increasing tendency to analyze the contents of consciousness and the acts of the understanding, treated exclusively as a faculty of thinking or knowing. Where in the earlier tradition the observation of human behavior and the behavior of other animals appears to be useful in psychology, here the main source of psychological knowledge seems to be introspection.

The *Principles of Psychology* by James and the writings of Freud represent a return to the broader conception of the science. According to James, "it is better . . . to let the science be as vague as its subject . . . if by so doing we can throw any light on the main business in hand."

If psychology "takes into account the fact that minds inhabit environments which act on them and on which they in turn react" and "takes mind in the midst of all its concrete relations, it is immensely more fertile than the old-fashioned 'rational psychology,' which treated the soul as a detached existent, sufficient unto itself, and assumed to consider only its nature and properties. I shall therefore feel free," James goes on to say, "to make any sallies into zoology or into pure nerve-physiology which may seem instructive for our purposes."

Though in the hands of James and Freud the scope of psychology extends no further than the range of topics Aquinas covers in his treatise on man and his treatise on human acts and passions, their return to the study of man as a whole is accompanied by an interest in or invention of new methods, experimental and clinical. "As a science," Freud writes, "psychoanalysis is characterized by the methods with which it works, not by the subject matter with which it deals." Those who distinguish between science and philosophy in terms of empirical research date the beginning of psychology from the inception of these new methods. They regard most psychological writings earlier than James and Freud as works of speculation or philosophy.

Controversy over the validity of conclusions in psychology sometimes turns on the conflicting claims of rival methods to be the *only* way of arriving at the truth; and sometimes, as with Kant, the issue of method seems to be subordinate to the issue of subject matter. Kant admits the possibility of an empirical psychology which would confine its inquiries to the phenomenal processes of thought and feeling, because with respect to such an object "we could call in aid observations on the play of our thoughts," and thence derive "natural laws of the thinking self." But, he goes on to say, "it could never be available for discovering those properties which do not belong to possible experience."

What Kant calls "rational psychology" aims at what is for him impossible, namely, knowledge of the reality or substance of the soul itself. It is impossible, he says, to make "any dogmatical affirmation concerning an object of experience beyond the boundaries of experience." Kant's critique of rational psychology thus appears to be based on the same principles which underlie his critique of metaphysical assertions concerning God's existence and the freedom of the will.

Those principles are in turn based on an elaborate theory of the human faculties, such as sense, understanding, and reason, and the role they play in the constitution of experience and knowledge. But Kant does not regard his own theory of the faculties as psychology. Writers like Locke and Hume, on the other hand, seem to make their psychology—certainly in its principal concern with how the content of the mind is acquired and formed—the basis for appraising the validity of all other knowledge. They do not question the validity of psychology itself. They seem to assume that self-knowledge has unique advantages over all other inquiries.

THESE ISSUES of the scope and validity of psychology are in one sense more relevant to the chapters on KNOWLEDGE, MIND, and SOUL than to this one. Their relevance here is limited by their connection with the main issues about the nature of man. Not merely the tradition of psychology, but the whole tradition of western thought seems to divide on the question of man's essence.

The question can be put in a number of ways. Is man a rational animal, and does that definition imply that only man has reason? Does it imply that man has free will, and that only man has free will? Like the question about the distinction between living and non-living things or the similar question about the difference between plants and animals, this question can also be asked in terms of the contrast between difference in kind and difference in degree. Does man differ essentially or in kind from other animals, or do all animals possess the same fundamental properties? Does man differ from the others only in the degree to which he possesses some of these shared qualities?

Some, like Darwin, think that "the difference in mind between man and the higher animals, great as it is, certainly is one of degree and not of kind. We have seen," he writes, "that the senses and intuitions, the various emotions and faculties, such as love, memory, attention, curiosity, imitation, reason, etc., of which man boasts, may be found in an incipient, or even sometimes in a well-developed condition, in the lower animals. They are also capable of some inherited improvement, as we see in the domestic dog compared with the wolf or jackal. If it could be proved that certain high mental powers, such as the formation of general concepts, self-consciousness, etc., were absolutely peculiar to man, which seems extremely doubtful, it is not improbable that these qualities are merely the incidental results of other highly-advanced intellectual faculties; and these again mainly the result of the continued use of a perfect language." Such a view clearly takes the position that man varies from other animals in the same way that one species of animal varies from another.

Those who take the opposite position do not always agree on the precise nature of the difference in kind. For the most part, they attribute rationality to man alone and use the word "brute" to signify that all other animals totally lack reason, no matter how acute their intelligence or the apparent sagacity of their instinctive reactions. Milton, for example, in common with many others, describes man as

> . . . a creature who not prone
> And brute as other creatures, but endued
> With sanctity of reason, might erect
> His stature, and upright with front serene
> Govern the rest, self-knowing, and from thence
> Magnanimous to correspond with heaven.

Those who find a difference in kind between man and other animals also tend to think that human society and human language are essentially different from the beehive or the ant mound, from bird calls, jungle cries, or parroting, because they are the work or expression of reason. Unlike Darwin, some of them find in human speech not the cause of man's *apparent* difference in kind from other animals, but the consequence of his *real* difference in kind—his distinctive rationality. The fact that man does certain things that no other animal does at all means to them that man possesses certain powers which no other animal shares to any degree, even the slightest. They would therefore interpret Darwin's admission that an anthropoid ape could not fashion "a stone into a tool" or "follow a train of metaphysical reasoning, or solve a mathematical problem, or reflect on God, or admire a grand natural scene," as an indication that the ape totally lacked human reason or intellect, however acute his animal intelligence. But the writers who agree that man is radically different from the brutes do not all agree in the account they give of human reason; nor do they all affirm free will as the natural accompaniment of rationality.

Locke, for example, begins his essay on *Human Understanding* with the remark that "the understanding . . . sets man above the rest of sensible beings." Men and other animals alike have the powers of sense, memory, and imagination, but, he says, "brutes abstract not. . . . The power of abstracting is not at all in them." This power of having "general ideas is that which puts a perfect distinction betwixt man and brutes, and is an excellency which the faculties of brutes do by no means attain to." But Locke denies that man has free will in the sense of a free choice among alternatives. Rousseau, on the other hand, declares that "every animal has ideas . . . and it is only in degree that man differs, in this respect, from the brute. . . . It is not, therefore, so much the understanding that constitutes the specific difference between the man and the brute, as the human quality of free agency . . . and it is particularly in his consciousness of this liberty that the spirituality of his soul is displayed."

James agrees with Locke that "it is probable that brutes neither attend to abstract characters nor have associations by similarity," but it is the latter fact which James himself makes the principal distinction between man and brute. "We may," he asserts, "consider it proven that the most elementary single difference between the human mind and that of brutes lies in this deficiency on the brute's part to associate ideas by similarity." James enumerates "other classical *differentiae* of man besides that of being the only reasoning animal." Man has been called, he says, "the laughing animal" and "the talking animal," but these distinctive traits, like human reasoning, James regards as "consequences of his unrivalled powers . . . to associate ideas by similarity."

Reason and speech are for James the effects, where for Adam Smith they are the cause, of man's peculiarly human attributes. "The propensity to truck, barter, and exchange one thing for another," Smith writes, is "common to all men, and to be found in no other race of animals." This seems to him to be a "necessary consequence of the faculties of reason and speech" which are peculiar to man. Hobbes, as we shall see presently, takes still another position, since he explains man's reasoning power in terms of his faculty of speech, a faculty which is possessed by no other animal.

Despite all these variations in theory or explanation, writers like Locke, Rousseau, James, Smith, and perhaps Hobbes seem to agree that man and brute differ in kind. On that point they agree even with writers like Plato, Aristotle, Augustine, Aquinas, Descartes, Spinoza, Kant, and Hegel who hold, as they most definitely do not, that man has a special faculty of mind, reason, or intellect. The contradictory position is, therefore, not to be found in the denial of some particular theory of reason, but rather in the denial that any faculty or attribute which man possesses warrants our calling him "rational" and other animals "brute."

THE ISSUE IS sharply drawn between these contradictory positions. Yet it is avoided by those who go no further than to see in human civilization certain distinctive features, such as the arts and sciences, or law, government, and religion. Mill, for example, discussing the sentiment of justice, finds its root in the natural impulse "to resent, and to repel or retaliate, any harm done or attempted against ourselves, or against those with whom we sympathise . . . common to all animal nature." Man differs from other animals, he writes, "first, in being capable of sympathising, not solely with their offspring, or, like some of the more noble animals, with some superior animal who is kind to them, but with all human and even with all sentient beings. Secondly, in having a more developed intelligence, which gives a wider range to the whole of their sentiments, whether self-regarding or sympathetic. By virtue of his superior intelligence, even apart from his superior range of sympathy, a human being is capable of apprehending a community of interest between himself and the human society of which he forms a part."

A view of this sort would seem to leave open the question whether such typically human developments signify the possession by man of special powers which set him apart as *different in kind*. While admitting extraordinary differences between the behavior or accomplishments of men and other animals, this view does not reject the possibility that such accomplishments may represent merely wide differences in degree of power, which give the *appearance* of differences in kind.

As we have already observed, the issue about man and brute cannot be separated from the controversy about the so-called "higher faculties" of man. Except for the view that man is a purely spiritual being, who merely inhabits or uses a physical body, no theory of human nature doubts that man, as a living organism, possesses in common with plants and animals certain bodily powers or functions. The vegetative functions which Galen calls "the natural faculties" are indispensable to human as to all other forms of corporeal life. Similarly, the powers of sensitivity and appetite or desire are obviously present in man as in other animals. To the observer, who sees only the externals of human and animal behavior, men and the higher animals appear to react to the physical stimulation of their sense organs with a similar repertoire of bodily movements, which vary only as their skeletal structure and their organs of locomotion differ. They also manifest outward signs of inner emotional disturbance sufficiently similar to warrant treating emotions like fear and rage as common to men and other animals.

On all this there seems to be little dispute in the tradition of the great books. But difficult questions arise when the inner significance of these external movements is considered. Both men and animals have the familiar sense organs and such powers as touch, taste, smell, hearing, and vision. But do sensations give rise to knowledge in the same way for both men and animals? Do the powers of memory and imagination extend an animal's range of apprehension as they do man's? Do these powers affect the perception of present objects in the same way for men and animals?

Such questions are not readily answered by observation of external behavior alone. What seems to be called for—a comparison of human and animal experience—cannot be obtained. The difficulty of the problem becomes most intense when a special faculty of knowledge or thought is attributed to man, for animal and human sense perception, imagination, or even emotion may be incommensurable if a special factor of understanding or reason enters into all human experience and is totally absent from that of animals.

In the ancient and mediaeval periods, the sensitive faculty, including the interior sensitive powers of memory and imagination, is generally distinguished from another faculty, variously called "intellect," "reason," or "mind." Writers like Plato, Aristotle, Plotinus, Lucretius, Augustine, and Aquinas have different conceptions of intellect or mind, in itself and in its relation to sense and imagination, but they do not question its existence as a separate faculty. The range of the sensitive powers does not extend to ideas or intelligible objects, nor is sensitive memory or imagination for them the same as rational thought.

Not only does it seem unquestionable in the ancient and mediaeval tradition that man has these two distinct faculties of knowledge, but it is generally assumed that other animals have to a greater or less degree, the power of the senses alone. Only men can understand as well as perceive; only men can know the universal as well as the particular; only men can think about objects which are neither sensible nor, strictly, imaginable—objects such as atoms and God, the infinite and the eternal, or the intellect itself. The affirmation of an essential difference between reason and sense seems to be inseparable from the affirmation of an essential difference between men and brutes.

DOUBTS OR DENIALS with regard to both affirmations achieve considerable prevalence in modern times. But though the two affirmations appear inseparable, they are not always denied together. Montaigne, for example, does not so much doubt that men have reason as he does that other animals lack it. He considers the matter in the light of external evidences, in terms of the comparable performances of men and animals. The light of reason seems to shine in both.

He repeats many stories from Plutarch and Pliny which supposedly reveal the comparable mentality of animals and men. One is the story of the hound who, following the scent, comes to a triple parting of the ways. After sniffing along the first and second paths and discovering no trace of the scent, the hound, without a moment's hesitation or sniffing, takes up the pursuit along the third trail. This, Montaigne suggests, is a kind of syllogizing; as if the dog reasoned thus with himself: "I have followed my master by foot to this place; he must, of necessity, be gone by one of these three ways; he is not gone this way nor that; he must then infallibly be gone this other."

It is noteworthy that Aquinas tells exactly the same story in order to make the point that such *appearances* of reasoning in animals can be explained as instinctively determined conduct. "In the works of irrational animals," he writes, "we notice certain marks of sagacity, in so far as they have a natural inclination to set about their actions in a most orderly manner through being ordained by the supreme art. For which reason, too, certain animals are called prudent or sagacious; and not because they reason or exercise any choice about things." That such behavior is not the work of reason, he claims, "is clear from the fact that all that share in one nature invariably act in the same way."

Unlike Montaigne, Machiavelli seems to imply that men and brutes are alike not in having reason, but in lacking it. The passions control behavior. Intelligence exhibits itself largely as craft or cunning in gaining ends set by the passions. Man is no less the brute in essence because in the jungle of society he often succeeds by cunning rather than by force. He may have more cunning than the fox, but without armor he also has less strength than the lion. The prince, Machiavelli remarks, "being compelled knowingly to adopt the beast, ought to choose the lion and the fox, because the lion cannot defend himself against snares and the fox cannot defend himself against wolves."

For the most part, however, the modern dissent from the ancient and mediaeval view takes the form of denying that reason and sense are distinct powers. In its most characteristic expression, this denial is accompanied by a denial of abstract ideas as in the writings of Hobbes, Berkeley, and Hume. Their position, discussed more fully in the chapter on UNIVERSAL AND PARTICULAR, is that men only give the appearance of having abstract or general ideas because they employ common names which have general significance.

Language, according to Hobbes, is the root of all other differences between man and brute. Sense and imagination are "common to man and beast." Reasoning, or the "train of thoughts," can take place in any animal which has memory and imagination. But that type of understanding which Hobbes describes as "conception caused by speech" is peculiar to man. His statement that "by the help of speech and method, the same faculties" which belong to both men and beasts "may be improved to such a height as to distinguish men from all other living creatures," would seem to imply that Hobbes regards man as superior to other animals only in degree. Yet, on the other hand, he enumerates a variety of institutions peculiar to human life, such as religion, law, and science, which imply a difference in kind.

Like Hobbes, Berkeley thinks that men use general names but do not have general or abstract ideas. But he seems much less willing than Hobbes to assert man's clear superiority, even on the basis of man's attainments through the power of speech. If the fact that "brutes abstract not," he says in reply to Locke, "be made the distinguishing property of that sort of animals, I fear a great many of those that pass for men must be reckoned into their number." Hume goes further than either Berkeley or Hobbes. Agreeing with them that man has no faculty above sense and imagination, and hence no faculty which animals do not also possess, he alone explicitly draws the conclusion which that implies.

"Animals as well as men," he writes, "learn many things from experience and infer that the same events will always follow from the same causes." Such inferences, in animals or men, are not "founded on any process of argument or reasoning." They are the result of the operation of custom and instinct. "Were this doubtful with regard to men, it seems to admit of no question with regard to the brute creation; and the conclusion being once firmly established in the one, we have a strong presumption, from all the rules of analogy, that it ought to be universally admitted, without any exception or reserve."

But if custom and instinct underlie the appearance of reasoning in both men and animals, it may be asked, says Hume, "how it happens that men so much surpass animals in reasoning, and one man so much surpasses another?" His answer seems to be entirely in terms of degree of the same factors. The same sort of difference which obtains between a superior and an inferior intelligence among men obtains between men and other animals.

All the evidence which Darwin later assembles on the characteristics of human mentality is offered by him in proof of the same point. But to those who think that man alone has an intellect or a rational faculty, over and above all his sensitive powers, such evidence remains inconclusive. As in the case of the dog, whose behavior Aquinas and Montaigne interpret differently, the same observed facts seem to be capable of quite opposite explanation by those who hold opposite theories of human and animal intelligence.

Is THERE INTERNAL evidence, obtained from man's introspective experience of his own thought, which can resolve the controversy? As Descartes sees it, the interpretation of such evidence also seems to depend on the prior assumption one makes about the sameness or difference of men and brutes.

"We cannot help at every moment experiencing within us that we think," he writes; "nor can anyone infer from the fact that it has been shown that the animate brutes can discharge all these operations entirely without thought, that he therefore does not think; unless it be that having previously persuaded himself that his actions are entirely like those of the brutes, just because he has ascribed thought to them, he were to adhere so pertinaciously to these very words, '*men and brutes operate in the same way*,' that when it was shown to him that the brutes did not think, he preferred to divest himself of that thought of his of which he could not fail to have an inner consciousness, rather than to alter his opinion that he acted in the same way as the brutes."

On the other hand, Descartes continues, those who hold "*that thought is not to be distinguished from bodily motion*, will with much better reason conclude that it is the same thing in us and in them, since they notice in them all corporeal movements as in us; they will add *that a difference merely of greater and less makes no difference to the essence*, and will infer that, though perchance they think that there is less reason in the beasts than in us, our minds are of exactly the same species."

THE ISSUE concerning the senses and the reason is more fully discussed in the chapters on MIND and SENSE, and also in the chapters on IDEA and UNIVERSAL AND PARTICULAR, where the problem of abstract ideas or universal notions is considered. The issue concerning soul in general and the human soul in particular belongs primarily to the chapter on SOUL, and also to the chapter on MIND. But like the issue about sense and intellect, its bearing on the problem of man's nature deserves brief comment here.

The question is not whether man has a soul, but whether only man has a soul; a rational soul; a soul which is, in whole or in part, immaterial; a soul capable of separate existence from the body; an immortal soul. If soul is conceived as the principle of life in all living organisms—as Aristotle conceives it—then having a soul does not distinguish man from plants or animals. If, furthermore, the rational soul is distinguished from the sensitive and vegetative soul in the same way that men are distinguished from brute animals and plants, namely, by reference to certain powers, such as intellect and will, then the statement that men alone have rational souls would seem to add nothing to the statement that men alone are rational.

But if the human soul, through being rational, confers a mode of immaterial, or spiritual, being upon man, then man's possession of such a soul sets him apart from all other physical things, even further than the special power of reason separates him from the brutes. The position of Lucretius illustrates this distinction in reverse. He does not deny that man has a soul. Unlike other living things which also have souls, man's soul includes a special part which Lucretius calls "mind." He describes it as the part "which we often call the understanding, in which dwells the directing and governing principle of life, [and] is no less part of the man than hand and foot and eyes are parts of the whole living creature."

So far as his having this special faculty is concerned, man is set apart. But for Lucretius nothing exists except atoms and void. Consequently, "the nature of the mind and soul is bodily," consisting of "seeds exceedingly round and exceedingly minute, in order to be stirred and set in motion by a small moving power." In his physical constitution man does not differ in any fundamental respect from any other composite thing. The materiality of his soul, furthermore, means that it is as perishable as any composite body.

At the other extreme from Lucretius, Descartes conceives man as a union of two substances. "I possess a body," he writes, "with which I am very intimately conjoined, yet because, on the one side, I have a clear and distinct idea of myself inasmuch as I am only a thinking and unextended thing, and as, on the other, I possess a distinct idea of body as it is only an extended and unthinking thing, it is certain that this I (that is to say, my soul by which I am what I am), is entirely and absolutely distinct from my body and can exist without it." Nevertheless, "sensations of pain, hunger, thirst, etc." lead Descartes to add: "I am not only lodged in my body as a pilot in a vessel, but . . . I am very closely united to it, and so to speak so intermingled with it that I seem to compose with it one whole."

Only man has a dual nature, thus compounded. Other living things, Descartes seems to hold, are merely bodies, having the structure and operation of complex machines. If, like the "*automata* or moving machines . . . made by the industry of man," there were "such machines, possessing the organs and outward form of a monkey, or some other animal without reason, we should not have . . . any means of ascertaining that they were not of the same nature as those animals."

It is indifferent to Descartes whether other animals are conceived as automata or whether, because they have life, sensation, and imagination, they are granted souls. "I have neither denied to the brutes," he writes, "what is vulgarly called life, nor a corporeal soul, or organic sense." What he has denied is thought, and it is this one factor which makes it impossible for a machine to imitate human speech and action. It is this one factor which also requires man's soul, unlike that of the brute, to be an incorporeal substance.

Unlike sensations and passions, acts of thought and will, according to Descartes, cannot be functions of bodily organs. "Even though I were to grant," he says, "that thought existed" in dogs and apes, "it would in nowise follow that the human mind was not to be distinguished from the body, but on the contrary rather that in other animals also there was a mind distinct from their body." When Descartes affirms man's uniqueness, he is therefore affirming more than that man alone has reason and free will. He is affirming that of all things man alone is "formed of body and soul"—not a corporeal soul, but a spiritual substance. The angels, in contrast, are simply spirits.

The remark of Plotinus, that "humanity is poised midway between the gods and the beasts," applies with somewhat altered significance to the Cartesian view. But there are other conceptions of the human constitution which, though they preserve the sense of man's dual nature, do not make him a union of two separate substances.

Spinoza, for example, gives man special status in the order of nature by conferring on him alone participation in the divine mind. "The human mind," he writes, "is a part of the infinite intellect of God." The human body, on the other hand, is "a mode which expresses in a certain and determinate manner the essence of God in so far as He is considered as the thing extended." Man is thus "composed of mind and body," but for Spinoza this duality in human nature is a duality of aspects, not a duality of substances.

There is still another way in which a certain immateriality is attributed to man. In Aristotle's theory, the soul is not a substance in its own right, but the substantial form of an organic body. This is true of all kinds of souls—whether of plants, animals, or men. But when Aristotle enumerates the various powers which living things possess—such as "the nutritive, the appetitive, the sensory, the locomotive, and the power of thinking"—he assigns to man alone, or "possibly another order like man or superior to him, the power of thinking, *i.e.*, mind." Furthermore, of all the parts or powers of the soul, thinking seems to Aristotle to afford "the most probable exception" to the rule that "all the affections of soul involve body."

Apart from thinking, "there seems to be no case," he says, "in which the soul can act or be acted upon without involving body." Whereas the sensitive powers are seated in bodily organs and cannot act except as bodily functions, the intellect is immaterial. It has no bodily organ which is comparable to the eye as the organ of vision and the brain as the organ of memory and imagination. The act of understanding is not a function of physical matter.

According to this theory, man as a whole is a single substance, composite of correlative principles of being—matter and form, or body and soul. But man differs from all other physical substances which are similarly composite in that he has a faculty and mode of activity separate from matter. In the later development of this theory by Aquinas, the immateriality of the intellect becomes the basis for arguing that the rational soul of man can exist apart from matter when the composite human substance is disintegrated by death.

As indicated in the chapters on IMMORTALITY and SOUL, this is not the only argument for the immortality of the soul. We are not here concerned, however, with the various arguments and their merits, but only with the fact that certain conceptions of man's constitution attribute to man something more than the power of rationality, namely, the distinction of having a spiritual and immortal life.

HIS FUTURE AND his past color the present life of man and alter the aspect under which he conceives his place in the general scheme of things. Immortality promises release from mutability as well as salvation from death. With an immortal soul, man belongs to eternity as well as to time. He is not merely a transient character in the universe. His stature and his dignity are not the same when man regards himself as completely dissolvable into dust.

The question of man's past or origin is, perhaps, even more critical in its bearing on man's present status. Ancient poetry and history contain many myths of man's kinship with the gods. The heroes trace their lineage back to the gods. Through them or through the progenitors of the race, man conceives himself as of divine descent or, at least, as having more affinity with the immortal gods than with all other earth-bound things.

In the *Descent of Man*, Darwin paints a different picture of human origin. Two propositions determine its general outlines. The first, already stated, is that man belongs to the animal kingdom without any differentiation except in degree. Not only in anatomy, physiology, and embryology are there marks of man's affinity with the mammals; man's behavior and mentality also show, according to Darwin, that man possesses no attribute so peculiarly human that some trace of it cannot be found in the higher forms of animal life.

The second proposition is that man's origin on earth has come about by a process of natural variation from an ancestral type, exactly as other new species of plants or animals have originated by descent with variation from a common ancestor. This theory of the origin of species is discussed in the chapter on EVOLUTION. Its special application to the human species involves the notion of a common ancestor for both man and the anthropoid apes, and the disappearance not only of the ancestral form, but of the intermediate varieties—the so-called "missing links" in the chain of variation.

These two propositions are logically interdependent. If the proposition is false that man differs from other animals only in degree, the proposition cannot be true that man originated along with the anthropoid apes by descent from a common ancestor. Conversely, if the Darwinian theory of man's origin is true, it cannot be true that men and brutes differ in kind. But though the truth of each of these two propositions implies the truth of the other, the problem of the difference between man and other animals has a certain logical priority over the problem of man's origin, simply because more evidence is available to solve it. That question calls for an examination of man as he is today in comparison with other extant species; whereas the other question necessarily requires the collection and interpretation of historical evidence, which may have some bearing on hypothetical missing links.

It should be added that if, in regard to the first question, the evidence favored the affirmation of a difference in kind, that would not entail the denial of biological evolution, though it would necessarily challenge the Darwinian theory of how such evolution took place. One alternative to the Darwinian hypothesis is the theory of emergent evolution, according to which lower forms of life may give rise to new organic forms which are not only higher but are distinct in kind.

Whether or not Christian theology and some theory of biological evolution can be reconciled, there seems to be an inescapable contradiction between Darwin's view of man's origin and the Judaeo-Christian conception of man as a special creation, special above all in the sense that "God created man in his own image."

As God is in essence a perfect intelligence and a spiritual being, man, according to Aquinas, "is said to be to the image of God by reason of his intellectual nature." In all creatures "there is some kind of likeness to God," but it is only in man that that likeness is an image. Man's finitude, imperfection, and corporeal existence make the image a remote resemblance; yet, according to the theologians, it is precisely that likeness which separates man from all other earthly creatures and places him in the company of the angels.

But man is no more an angel than he is a brute. He is separated from the one by his body as from the other by his reason. Nor does he in the present life have the spiritual existence of a disembodied and immortal soul. To these three negatives in the definition of man—*not* an angel, *not* a brute, *not* a soul—the Christian theologian adds a fourth, drawn from man's past. Man is of the race begotten by Adam, but he does not have the attributes which Adam possessed before the fall.

The dogma of man's fall from grace is discussed in the chapter on SIN. Here we are concerned only with its implications for the understanding of man's present nature, as not only being deprived of the extraordinary gifts of life and knowledge which Adam lost through disobedience, but as also being wounded in perpetuity by Adam's sin. Weakness, ignorance, malice, and concupiscence, Aquinas declares, "are the four wounds inflicted on the whole of human nature as a result of our first parent's sin." Man in the world is not only disinherited from Adam's gifts, but with the loss of grace, he also suffers, according to Aquinas, a diminution in "his natural inclination to virtue."

THERE ARE OTHER divisions in the realm of man, but none so radical as that between Eden and the world thereafter. As retold by Plato, the ancient myths of a golden age when men lived under the immediate benevolence of the gods also imply a condition of mankind quite different from the observable reality, but they do not imply a decline in human nature itself with the transition from the golden age to the present. The modern distinction between man living in a state of nature and man living in civil society considers only the external circumstances of human life and does not divide man according to two conditions of his soul. Other dichotomies—such as that between prehistoric and historic man, or between primitive and civilized man—are even less radical, for they deal even more in gradations or degrees of the same external conditions.

These considerations lead us to another phase of man's thinking about man. Where the previous problem was how man differs from everything else in the universe, here the question is how man is divided from man. If men are not equal as individuals, to what extent are their individual differences the result of the unequal endowment of the natures with which they are born, and to what extent are they the result of individual acquirement in the course of life?

The range of human differences, whether innate or acquired, may itself become the basis for a division of men into the normal and the abnormal, a division which separates the feebleminded and the insane from the competent and sane. From a moral and political point of view, this is perhaps the most fundamental of all classifications. It must be admitted, however, that traditionally the problem of the difference between men and women and the problem of the difference between the ages of man from the extreme of infancy to the extreme of senility seem to have exercised more influence on the determination of political status and moral responsibility.

One other differentiation of man from man seems to have significance for the theory of human society and the history of civilization. That is the division of men into groups, sometimes by reference to physical and mental traits which separate one race from another—whether these traits are supposed to be determined biologically as inheritable racial characteristics or are attributed to environmental influences; sometimes by reference to the customs and ideals of a culture. Both sets of criteria appear to be used in the traditional discussion of the opposition between Greek and barbarian, Jew and gentile, European and Asiatic.

THE ULTIMATE questions which man asks about himself are partly answered by the very fact of their being asked. The answer may be that man is the measure of all things; that he is sufficient unto himself or at least sufficient for the station he occupies and the part he plays in the structure of the universe. The answer may be that man is not a god overlooking the rest of nature, or even at home in the environment of time and space, but rather that he is a finite and dependent creature aware of his insufficiency, a lonely wanderer seeking something greater than himself and this whole world. Whatever answer is given, man's asking what sort of thing he is, whence he comes, and whither he is destined symbolizes the two strains in human nature—man's knowledge and his ignorance, man's greatness and his misery.

Man, writes Pascal, is "a nothing in comparison with the Infinite, an All in comparison with the Nothing, a mean between nothing and everything. Since he is infinitely removed from comprehending the extremes, the end of things and their beginning are hopelessly hidden from him in an impenetrable secret; he is equally incapable of seeing the Nothing from which he was made, and the Infinite in which he is swallowed up.

"Man," Pascal goes on, "must not think that he is on a level either with the brutes or with the angels, nor must he be ignorant of both sides of his nature; but he must know both." In recognizing both lies his wretchedness and grandeur. "Man knows that he is wretched. He is therefore wretched, because he is so; but he is really greater because he knows it."

OUTLINE OF TOPICS

1. Definitions of man: conceptions of the properties and qualities of human nature
    - *1a.* The conception of man as essentially distinct, or differing in kind, from brute animals: man's specific rationality and freedom
    - *1b.* The conception of man as distinguished from brutes by such powers or properties as abstraction or relational thought, language and law, art and science
    - *1c.* The conception of man as an animal, differing only in degree of intelligence and of other qualities possessed by other animals

2. Man's knowledge of man
    - *2a.* Immediate self-consciousness: man's intimate or introspective knowledge of himself
    - *2b.* The sciences of human nature: anthropology and psychology; rational and empirical psychology; experimental and clinical psychology
        - (1) The subject matter and scope of the science of man
        - (2) The methods and validity of psychology
        - (3) The relation of psychology to physiology: the study of organic factors in human behavior
        - (4) The place of psychology in the order of sciences: the study of man as prerequisite for other studies

3. The constitution of man
    - *3a.* Man as a unity or conjunction of matter and spirit, body and soul, extension and thought
        - (1) Man as a pure spirit: a soul or mind using a body
        - (2) Man's spirituality as limited to his immaterial powers or functions, such as reason and will
    - *3b.* Comparisons of man with God or the gods, or with angels or spiritual substances
    - *3c.* Man as an organization of matter or as a collocation of atoms

4. The analysis of human nature into its faculties, powers, or functions: the id, ego, and super-ego in the structure of the psyche
    - *4a.* Man's vegetative powers: comparison with similar functions in plants and animals
    - *4b.* Man's sensitive and appetitive powers: comparison with similar functions in other animals
    - *4c.* Man's rational powers: the problem of similar powers in other animals
    - *4d.* The general theory of faculties: the critique of faculty psychology

5. The order and harmony of man's powers and functions: contradictions in human nature; the higher and lower nature of man
    - *5a.* Cooperation or conflict among man's powers
    - *5b.* Abnormalities due to defect or conflict of powers: feeble-mindedness, neuroses, insanity, madness

REFERENCES

References are listed by volume number (in bold type), author's name, and page number. Bible references are to book, chapter, and verse of the Authorized King James version of the Bible. The abbreviation "esp" calls the reader's attention to one or more especially relevant parts of a whole reference; "passim" signifies that the topic is discussed intermittently rather than continuously in the work or passage cited. Where the work as a whole is relevant to the topic, the page numbers refer to the entire work. For general guidance in the use of *The Great Ideas*, consult the Preface.

1. Definitions of man: conceptions of the properties and qualities of human nature

5 Euripides, 260
7 Plato, 270, 649–650, 704, 723
8 Aristotle, 182, 185, 499, 659–660
9 Aristotle, 178, 182, 184–185, 201–202, 244–245, 268, 314, 397, 446, 537, 539, 682
12 Epictetus, 128
12 Aurelius, 260–261, 264, 269, 280, 288, 303
14 Plutarch, 512
17 Plotinus, 18
18 Augustine, 216
19 Aquinas, 378–440
23 Machiavelli, 24, 25–26 passim
23 Hobbes, 47, 79, 84–86
24 Rabelais, 65
25 Montaigne, 215–232, 462–463
27 Shakespeare, 43
28 Harvey, 454
31 Descartes, 51–54 passim
31 Spinoza, 376–378, 429, 433–434, 447–450
32 Milton, 354–355
33 Pascal, 195–204, 236, 240–243
35 Locke, 273–274, 304, 326–328, 344
37 Fielding, 1, 187–188
38 Montesquieu, 1–2
38 Rousseau, 329–348 passim
39 Smith, 147–148, 343
42 Kant, 284–285, 316–317, 348, 372, 400–402, 587–588
43 Federalist, 38–41 passim, 50, 65, 160, 163
43 Mill, 273, 459–464
44 Boswell, 403
46 Hegel, 122, 178–179
47 Goethe, 8, 197–198
48 Melville, 84–85, 313–314, 343, 345–347
49 Darwin, 286–287, 310–314
51 Tolstoy, 689
52 Dostoevsky, 54
53 James, 712–737 passim, 826–827
54 Freud, 684–686, 883

1*a*. The conception of man as essentially distinct, or differing in kind, from brute animals: man's specific rationality and freedom

Apocrypha: *Ecclesiasticus*, 17:1–9
7 Plato, 44–45
8 Aristotle, 499, 645, 659–660, 695
9 Aristotle, 114, 164, 343, 347–348, 357, 395, 432, 448
12 Epictetus, 121–122, 134, 146–147, 213–223, 228–229
12 Aurelius, 276, 286, 288, 292
17 Plotinus, 94–95, 323–325
18 Augustine, 120–121, 626–627
19 Aquinas, 105–107, 308–309, 368–369, 463–464, 510–513, 609–611, 672, 673–674, 682, 687–688
20 Aquinas, 350–351
21 Dante, 116
25 Montaigne, 184
31 Descartes, 56, 59–60, 89–93, 226, 276
31 Spinoza, 414–415
32 Milton, 227–229, 320–321
33 Pascal, 233–234, 243
35 Locke, 36–38, 221–222, 274–276, 295–296
38 Rousseau, 357–358
42 Kant, 291–293, 378, 420–421
43 Mill, 294–297
46 Hegel, 17, 24, 46–47, 48–49, 116, 117–118, 156, 168
49 Darwin, 319, 331–332
51 Tolstoy, 689–690

1*b*. The conception of man as distinguished from brutes by such powers or properties as abstraction or relational thought, language and law, art and science

5 Aeschylus, 44–45
7 Plato, 35, 534–536
8 Aristotle, 384
9 Aristotle, 9, 133–134, 186–187, 217–219, 328, 342–343, 414
12 Epictetus, 108, 240–242
12 Aurelius, 262–263
23 Hobbes, 52, 53, 54, 59, 100
25 Montaigne, 215–216, 218
31 Descartes, 226
32 Milton, 240–242, 259
35 Locke, 93, 144–146, 251–252, 278
35 Berkeley, 407–408
35 Hume, 452
38 Rousseau, 341
39 Smith, 6–8
42 Kant, 316–317, 479, 602

46 HEGEL, 70, 121, 136
49 DARWIN, 278–279, 294–304, 320, 349, 591–593
50 MARX, 85, 86
52 DOSTOEVSKY, 122–123, 167
53 JAMES, 85, 677, 678–686, 691, 704–706
54 FREUD, 385, 429, 616, 778

1*c*. The conception of man as an animal, differing only in degree of intelligence and of other qualities possessed by other animals

23 HOBBES, 53–54, 64
25 MONTAIGNE, 207, 215–232
30 BACON, 163–164
35 LOCKE, 271–272, 370–371
35 HUME, 487–488
38 ROUSSEAU, 334–338, 348–349
42 KANT, 199–200
43 MILL, 448–449, 469
49 DARWIN, 286–319

2. Man's knowledge of man

2*a*. Immediate self-consciousness: man's intimate or introspective knowledge of himself

7 PLATO, 7, 8, 116
8 ARISTOTLE, 661, 662
9 ARISTOTLE, 424
12 EPICTETUS, 105
12 AURELIUS, 302
18 AUGUSTINE, 72
19 AQUINAS, 465–467, 468
25 MONTAIGNE, 6–7, 69–70, 177–181, 319–320, 322–323, 388–389, 520–522
29 CERVANTES, 332
30 BACON, 54, 88–89
31 DESCARTES, 51–52, 77–81, 207, 224, 276
31 SPINOZA, 382–383
35 LOCKE, 121–123 esp 122–123, 175–176, 208, 212–213, 222
35 HUME, 454, 472–474
42 KANT, 32, 55–56, 99–101, 121–123, 307–310
43 MILL, 303
46 HEGEL, 13, 14, 21, 116–117, 257–258, 278, 304
51 TOLSTOY, 688–689, 693–694
53 JAMES, 121, 122–126, 191–197, 233
54 FREUD, 429–430, 451

2*b*. The sciences of human nature: anthropology and psychology; rational and empirical psychology; experimental and clinical psychology

8 ARISTOTLE, 631–632
25 MONTAIGNE, 261–269 passim
35 HUME, 479–480
42 KANT, 1–4, 253–254, 388, 599–600
46 HEGEL, 15
53 JAMES, 1–4
54 FREUD, 431, 451–453, 864–868

2*b*(1) The subject matter and scope of the science of man

8 ARISTOTLE, 631–632
30 BACON, 49–50, 54
35 HUME, 451–455
38 ROUSSEAU, 329–331
42 KANT, 388, 599–600
53 JAMES, 3–4, 120–121, 129, 236, 825
54 FREUD, 428–429, 452–454, 467, 550, 664–665

2*b*(2) The methods and validity of psychology

8 ARISTOTLE, 645
9 ARISTOTLE, 347
19 AQUINAS, 464–468
23 HOBBES, 47
35 HUME, 487
42 KANT, 126, 294
52 DOSTOEVSKY, 386–387
53 JAMES, 17–18, 56–66, 121–129, 235–236, 259
54 FREUD, 13–14, 548–550, 639, 661–662, 706–707

2*b*(3) The relation of psychology to physiology: the study of organic factors in human behavior

7 PLATO, 474–475
8 ARISTOTLE, 330, 642–643, 665, 696–701, 702–706 passim
9 ARISTOTLE, 175–176, 237, 239
10 HIPPOCRATES, 155–160
12 LUCRETIUS, 31–40
19 AQUINAS, 394–396, 449–451, 459–460, 798
28 HARVEY, 296, 321–322
30 BACON, 48–50
31 DESCARTES, 99
31 SPINOZA, 380–381, 451–452, 462
42 KANT, 538–539
53 JAMES, 56, 66–71 passim
54 FREUD, 154–155, 451–452, 605–606, 872

2*b*(4) The place of psychology in the order of sciences: the study of man as prerequisite for other studies

7 PLATO, 240–242, 629
9 ARISTOTLE, 595
25 MONTAIGNE, 259–260
31 DESCARTES, 77–81
33 PASCAL, 200
35 LOCKE, 87, 93–95
35 HUME, 453–454
42 KANT, 331–332, 511–512
46 HEGEL, 12–13, 16–17
54 FREUD, 868, 874, 883

3. The constitution of man

3*a*. Man as a unity or a conjunction of matter and spirit, body and soul, extension and thought

OLD TESTAMENT: *Genesis*, 2:7
NEW TESTAMENT: *Romans*, 7:14–23; 8:4–13 / *I Corinthians*, 15:36–49

7 PLATO, 93, 338–339, 686–687
8 ARISTOTLE, 559, 569–570, 640, 641, 642–644
9 ARISTOTLE, 448
12 EPICTETUS, 240–241
12 AURELIUS, 265, 283, 310
14 PLUTARCH, 29
17 PLOTINUS, 1–6, 37, 151–154, 197–198
18 AUGUSTINE, 289–295 passim, 377–378, 379–380
19 AQUINAS, 378–399, 604–607, 632–634
20 AQUINAS, 951–958
25 MONTAIGNE, 311, 432, 538–543
31 DESCARTES, 77–81, 130, 133, 152–156, 224–225, 231–232
31 SPINOZA, 376–378, 396–398
35 LOCKE, 113, 220–222, 224, 225–226, 227–228
35 HUME, 472–473
36 STERNE, 277
42 KANT, 557–558
46 HEGEL, 24, 115
53 JAMES, 84–93, 116–119, 139–140, 208, 221–226

3*a*(1) Man as a pure spirit: a soul or mind using a body

7 PLATO, 124–126, 179–180, 231–234, 250
13 VIRGIL, 230–231
17 PLOTINUS, 2–4, 97–98, 191, 323–325
18 AUGUSTINE, 367, 369–370
19 AQUINAS, 162–163, 381–382, 385–388, 393–394, 396–397
20 AQUINAS, 951–953
31 DESCARTES, 119–120, 135–136, 155–156
35 LOCKE, 220–222
35 BERKELEY, 413, 430, 440–441
40 GIBBON, 186
46 HEGEL, 21
48 MELVILLE, 28
53 JAMES, 220–226

3*a*(2) Man's spirituality as limited to his immaterial powers or functions, such as reason and will

8 ARISTOTLE, 638, 661–662
19 AQUINAS, 31–32, 379–380, 382–384, 403–404, 413–427, 428, 431–442, 451–453, 461–462

3*b*. Comparisons of man with God or the gods, or with angels or spiritual substances

OLD TESTAMENT: *Job*, 4:16–21 / *Psalms*, 8:5
NEW TESTAMENT: *Hebrews*, 2:7
7 PLATO, 476
12 EPICTETUS, 158
18 AUGUSTINE, 36, 103, 119, 283, 357, 360, 426–427, 630, 632–634
19 AQUINAS, 168–169, 269–338, 384–385, 545–553 passim, 561–562, 571–573, 597–599
20 AQUINAS, 11–12, 742–743
21 DANTE, 150–151
23 HOBBES, 183–184
32 MILTON, 160–161, 183–186, 293–294
35 LOCKE, 143, 207–208
35 BERKELEY, 428
42 KANT, 33, 350–351
47 GOETHE, 14, 16–19 passim

3*c*. Man as an organization of matter or as a collocation of atoms

7 PLATO, 567–568
8 ARISTOTLE, 633–641
10 GALEN, 172–173
12 LUCRETIUS, 31–41, 53–54, 55–56
17 PLOTINUS, 79, 191–200
19 AQUINAS, 378–379, 442–443, 447–449
23 HOBBES, 80, 251
31 DESCARTES, 226
35 LOCKE, 313–315, 350, 351–352, 353
35 BERKELEY, 431
42 KANT, 575–582
53 JAMES, 95–119

4. The analysis of human nature into its faculties, powers, or functions: the id, ego, and super-ego in the structure of the psyche

7 PLATO, 350–353
8 ARISTOTLE, 642–668
19 AQUINAS, 399–440
31 DESCARTES, 96–103 passim
42 KANT, 465–467, 475
49 DARWIN, 287–302 passim
54 FREUD, 501–504, 531–532, 701–708, 715–716, 721–722, 830–840

4*a*. Man's vegetative powers: comparison with similar functions in plants and animals

7 PLATO, 469–471
8 ARISTOTLE, 417–420, 645–647
9 ARISTOTLE, 271, 275–276, 281–282, 347–348
10 GALEN, 167–215
17 PLOTINUS, 97–98
18 AUGUSTINE, 395–396
19 AQUINAS, 407–410, 516–519, 601–603, 604–608, 692
20 AQUINAS, 959–963
21 DANTE, 91–92
24 RABELAIS, 143–144
28 HARVEY, 427–428
30 BACON, 158

4*b*. Man's sensitive and appetitive powers: comparison with similar functions in other animals

7 PLATO, 319–320, 466–467, 620–622
8 ARISTOTLE, 643, 647–661, 673–689
9 ARISTOTLE, 59–64, 235–239, 294, 357, 364–365
12 LUCRETIUS, 51–53
12 AURELIUS, 262–263
17 PLOTINUS, 151–152, 167–168, 169–171, 172–173, 206
18 AUGUSTINE, 256

5*b*. Abnormalities due to defect or conflict of powers: feeble-mindedness, neuroses, insanity, madness

6. Individual differences among men

6*a*. The cause and range of human inequalities: differences in ability, inclination, temperament, habit

6*b*. The differences between men and women: their equality or inequality

6c. The ages of man: infancy, youth, maturity, senescence

7. Group variations in human type: racial differences

7*a*. Biological aspects of racial type

7*b*. The influence of environmental factors on human characteristics: climate and geography as determinants of racial or national differences

7*c*. Cultural differences among men: Greek and barbarian, Jew and gentile, European and Asiatic

8. The origin or genealogy of man

***8a.* The race of men as descendants or products of the gods**

***8b.* God's special creation of man**

***8c.* Man as a natural variation from other forms of animal life**

9. The two conditions of man

***9a.* The myth of a golden age: the age of Kronos and the age of Zeus**

***9b.* The Christian doctrine of Eden and of the history of man in the world**

***9b(1)* The condition of man in Eden: the preternatural powers of Adam**

***9b(2)* The condition of man in the world: fallen man; corrupted or wounded human nature**

46 HEGEL, 118
50 MARX, 354
51 TOLSTOY, 275
52 DOSTOEVSKY, 125–126, 165–169

9*b*(3) The Christian view of the stages of human life in the world: law and grace

NEW TESTAMENT: *Matthew,* 5:17–44 /*John,* 1:17 / *Acts,* 10 / *Romans,* 2–8 / *II Corinthians,* 3 / *Galatians* / *Ephesians,* 2:14–15; 4:17–24 / *Philippians,* 3:8–10 / *Colossians,* 2–3 / *Hebrews* / *I Peter,* 1:1–2:10
18 AUGUSTINE, 124, 313–314, 397–507, 532, 573–574, 670
19 AQUINAS, 276–277
20 AQUINAS, 239–245, 321–330
22 CHAUCER, 526–527
32 MILTON, 136–144, 306–333
52 DOSTOEVSKY, 127–137 passim

9*c*. Secular conceptions of the stages of human life: man in a state of nature and in society; prehistoric and historic man; primitive and civilized man

4 HOMER, 230
5 AESCHYLUS, 42, 44–45
6 THUCYDIDES, 349–354
7 PLATO, 157–159, 311, 663–667
12 LUCRETIUS, 73–80
15 TACITUS, 51
23 HOBBES, 84–86, 94, 267–268
25 MONTAIGNE, 91–98, 440–443
26 SHAKESPEARE, 597–626
27 SHAKESPEARE, 465–466
31 SPINOZA, 435–436
35 LOCKE, 16, 25–28, 29, 46, 53–54
38 MONTESQUIEU, 2–3
38 ROUSSEAU, 329–366, 387–394
39 SMITH, 6, 309–311
40 GIBBON, 86–96 passim, 409–414 passim, 632–634
41 GIBBON, 86–87
42 KANT, 405–406, 408–409, 412–414, 433–434, 435–436, 450–451
43 FEDERALIST, 164
44 BOSWELL, 204–205, 221, 311, 408, 510
46 HEGEL, 65, 66, 79–80, 137, 171–172, 179–182, 196–199, 235–236, 240, 243–244, 260–261
48 MELVILLE, 9–23, 221–223
49 DARWIN, 13, 314–316, 317, 320–330 passim
50 MARX-ENGELS, 421
54 FREUD, 755–766 passim, 776–782, 788–789

10. Man's conception of himself and his place in the world

10*a*. Man's understanding of his relation to the gods or God

OLD TESTAMENT
NEW TESTAMENT
4 HOMER, 3–179, 183–322
5 AESCHYLUS, 2, 23–24, 27–39, 40–51, 52–69, 70–80, 81–91
5 SOPHOCLES, 114–130, 131–142, 143–155, 170–181, 186
5 EURIPIDES, 225–236, 258–269, 270–281, 282–297, 298–314, 324–326, 327–339, 340–352, 394–410, 411–424
5 ARISTOPHANES, 492–493, 557–558, 560–563, 629–642
6 HERODOTUS, 7–10, 20–22, 217, 279–280
6 THUCYDIDES, 506
7 PLATO, 94, 191–199, 314, 320–324, 447–477 passim, 478–485, 682–683, 686–689 passim, 757–771
8 ARISTOTLE, 501
9 ARISTOTLE, 410–411
12 LUCRETIUS, 22–23, 42–43, 63–64, 80–81
12 EPICTETUS, 110–112, 120–121, 123–124, 226–228
12 AURELIUS, 257, 258, 269–270, 272, 278, 307–308, 309
13 VIRGIL, 103–379
14 PLUTARCH, 50–51
15 TACITUS, 59–60, 189–190
17 PLOTINUS, 86–88
18 AUGUSTINE, 1–125 passim, 129–618, 624–636, 638–639
19 AQUINAS, 36–37, 128–130, 132–143, 436–438, 592–595, 609–826
20 AQUINAS, 1–378
21 DANTE, 107
22 CHAUCER, 66, 106–108, 154–155, 180–182, 236–255, 281, 353–354, 391–395, 432–448, 463–471, 495–550
23 MACHIAVELLI, 35
23 HOBBES, 54, 78–83, 113, 159–164, 260
24 RABELAIS, 265
25 MONTAIGNE, 98–99, 208–294
27 SHAKESPEARE, 53–54, 433–434, 481–482
31 DESCARTES, 81–89 passim, 89–93, 122, 123, 142, 213–214, 226–227, 229
31 SPINOZA, 365, 366, 369–372
32 MILTON, 137–138, 161–162, 186–187, 347–348, 394–395
33 PASCAL, 78–80, 243–270
35 BERKELEY, 444
35 HUME, 485–487
38 ROUSSEAU, 435–439
40 GIBBON, 292–296
41 GIBBON, 259–260
42 KANT, 278–279, 325–328, 334–335, 345, 502–503, 594
43 MILL, 296
44 BOSWELL, 394, 481–482
46 HEGEL, 158–160, 224–225, 236, 245–246, 263–265, 268–271, 291–292, 303–307, 322, 339, 349–350
47 GOETHE, 11–14
48 MELVILLE, 28–36, 380–381
49 DARWIN, 302–303
51 TOLSTOY, 196–198, 216–218, 608, 631, 675–676, 684

10*b*. Man as the measure of all things

10*c*. Man as an integral part of the universe: his station in the cosmos

10*d*. The finiteness and insufficiency of man: his sense of being dependent and ordered to something beyond himself

10*e*. Man's comparison of himself with other creatures and with the universe as a whole

11. The theological conception of man

11*a*. Man as made in the image of God

11*b*. The fatherhood of God and the brotherhood of man

53 James, 887
54 Freud, 674

11*c*. God incarnate in human form: the human nature of Christ

New Testament, *Matthew*, 1:18–25; 11:18–19; 13:54–56; 16:13–17; 17:1–9; 22:41–46; 26:63–66; 27:26–54 / *Luke*, 1–2; 5:18–26; 23:24–47; 24:2–7,36–43 / *John*, 1:1–18; 1:30–34; 5:16–47; 8:12–28; 10:22–38; 14; 19:25–34; 20:24–21:14 / *Romans*, 1:3–4; / *Galatians*, 4:4 / *Philippians*, 2:5–8 / *Colossians*, 1:12–20 / *I Timothy*, 3:16 / *Hebrews*, 1:1–6; 2:14–18; 4:14–15 / *I John*, 1:1–4; 2:18–29
18 Augustine, 47–48, 50–51, 88–89, 90, 293–294, 311, 312–313, 572–574, 627–628
19 Aquinas, 277–278
20 Aquinas, 701–846, 939–941
21 Dante, 101–102, 157
22 Chaucer, 503–505
23 Hobbes, 182
32 Milton, 1–7, 10–13, 136–144, 327–329
33 Pascal, 262, 268–270, 325
40 Gibbon, 308
41 Gibbon, 134–161
46 Hegel, 306–307
52 Dostoevsky, 127–137

12. Man as an object of laughter and ridicule: comedy and satire

5 Aristophanes, 455–469 / 470–487, 488–506, 507–525, 526–541, 542–563, 564–582, 583–599, 600–614, 615–628, 629–642
7 Plato, 629–630
12 Lucretius, 58–59
22 Chaucer, 211–223, 225–232
23 Machiavelli, 24, 25–26
23 Hobbes, 63
24 Rabelais, 1–312
25 Montaigne, 6–10 passim, 10–11, 42, 145–147, 165–167, 208–295, 300–301, 326–327, 388–395, 424–426, 478–482
26 Shakespeare, 149–169, 199–228, 254–284, 352–375, 503–531, 597–626
27 Shakespeare, 1–28, 73–102, 183, 263
36 Swift, 3–184
36 Sterne, 191–556
37 Fielding, 186–189, 274
47 Goethe, 3–4, 44–48, 79–81, 134–135

13. The grandeur and misery of man

Old Testament: *Genesis*, 11:1–9 / *I Chronicles*, 29:15 / *Job* / *Psalms*, 8:4–8; 49:12–14 / *Ecclesiastes* passim / *Isaiah*, 40:6–8
Apocrypha: *Wisdom of Solomon*, 9:1–3,13–16 / *Ecclesiasticus*, 10:9–11; 14:17–19; 17:1–4,30–32; 40:1–11
New Testament: *Romans*, 7:21–25
5 Sophocles, 110, 125, 134, 171
5 Aristophanes, 551
6 Herodotus, 224–225, 252
7 Plato, 476
12 Lucretius, 15, 30–31
12 Epictetus, 108–110, 156–158, 195–201
17 Plotinus, 93–94
18 Augustine, 343, 364, 511–516, 523–524, 529, 572–573, 606–612
22 Chaucer, 181–182, 432–448
25 Montaigne, 149
26 Shakespeare, 320–351
27 Shakespeare, 29–72, 103–141, 244–283, 393–420, 572
30 Bacon, 49
32 Milton, 309–310, 343, 354–355
33 Pascal, 195–204, 209–210, 236, 240–243, 245–247, 249–251, 264–270, 301
36 Sterne, 383–384
38 Rousseau, 363–366
40 Gibbon, 633–634
42 Kant, 300, 321–329, 345–347, 360–361, 584–586, 587–588, 591–592
44 Boswell, 94–95, 102–103, 312, 362–363, 401, 540–542
46 Hegel, 113, 120, 165–170, 280–281
47 Goethe, 1–294
48 Melville, 54–55, 88–91, 107
49 Darwin, 597
51 Tolstoy, 1–696
54 Freud, 654, 767–802

CROSS-REFERENCES

For: Other discussions of the difference between men and other animals, *see* Animal 1c–1c(2); Knowledge 7d; Memory and Imagination 1, 6b; Mind 3a–3b; Sense 2c; Will 6c.

Matters relevant to the science of psychology and its relation to other sciences, *see* Knowledge 5e; Mind 6; Soul 5a–5b.

The issues concerning matter and spirit in the constitution of man, *see* Element 5f; Matter 2d, 3a, 4c–4d; Mind 2a–2e; One and Many 3b(4); Soul 3a–3d; and for comparisons of human with angelic nature, *see* Angel 4; Soul 4d(2).

Discussions bearing on the analysis of human faculties or powers, *see* Animal 1c(1)–1c(2), 8d; Desire 3b–3b(2); Emotion 1, 1c; Habit 3; Memory and Imagination 1–1a, 1c, 5; Mind 1a–1g(3); Sense 1a–1d; Soul 2c(1)–2c(3), 4a; Will 3a, 9a.

The problem of harmony and conflict in human nature and the discussion of human abnormality, *see* EMOTION 3a, 3c; MEDICINE 6a–6c(2); MIND 8–8c; ONE AND MANY 3b(5); OPPOSITION 4–4e; WILL 9b.

Another consideration of the cycle of human life, *see* LIFE AND DEATH 6b–6c; and for the consideration of human immaturity, or childhood, *see* FAMILY 6c, 6e; MIND 4b.

The relation of men and women in the domestic community, and for the place of women in the state, *see* FAMILY 5a–5c.

Matters relevant to the problem of individual and racial differences, *see* ANIMAL 10; EVOLUTION 1b; MIND 4a.

The issue concerning the ultimate origin of man, *see* EVOLUTION 7a–7b.

Other statements of the myth of a golden age, *see* LABOR 1a; PROGRESS 1c; TIME 8b; and for the distinction between prehistoric and historic man, or for the progress of historic man, *see* ART 12; EVOLUTION 7c; TIME 8a.

The distinction between man in a state of nature and in a state of civil society, *see* LAW 4b; LIBERTY 1b; NATURE 2b; STATE 3c; and for the consideration of man as a social animal, *see* FAMILY 1; STATE 3b(1).

Other discussions of the condition of Adam before and after original sin, and of the condition of the human race as a result of Adam's sin, *see* GOD 9c; JUSTICE 1b; SIN 3–3c; VIRTUE AND VICE 8b; WILL 7e(1); and for theological doctrines concerning man's life on earth and his immortal destiny, *see* HISTORY 5a; IMMORTALITY 5d–5g; PUNISHMENT 5d; SIN 6c–6e.

The teaching of Christian theology concerning Christ, *see* GOD 9b–9b(3); ONE AND MANY 6c.

Matters relevant to man's understanding of himself, his place in the world, and his relation to God or the gods, *see* DESIRE 7b; GOD 3–3f; WORLD 2.

The tragedy or comedy of human life, *see* HAPPINESS 4b; POETRY 4b.

ADDITIONAL READINGS

Listed below are works not included in *Great Books of the Western World*, but relevant to the idea and topics with which this chapter deals. These works are divided into two groups:

I. Works by authors represented in this collection.
II. Works by authors not represented in this collection.

For the date, place, and other facts concerning the publication of the works cited, consult the Bibliography of Additional Readings which follows the last chapter of *The Great Ideas*.

I.

PLUTARCH. "That Brute Beasts Make Use of Reason," in *Moralia*
AUGUSTINE. *On Nature and Grace*
AQUINAS. *Quaestiones Disputatae, De Veritate*, Q 18
AQUINAS. *Summa Theologica*, PART II–II, QQ 161–165
DANTE. *Convivio (The Banquet)*, FOURTH TREATISE, CH 23–28
F. BACON. "Of Nature in Men," "Of Youth and Age," in *Essays*
HOBBES. *The Elements of Law, Natural and Politic*
——. *The Whole Art of Rhetoric*. BK II, CH 14–19
KANT. *Anthropologie*
J. S. MILL. *A System of Logic*, BK VI, CH 3–4
FREUD. *An Outline of Psychoanalysis*

II.

THEOPHRASTUS. *The Characters*
CICERO. *De Finibus (On the Supreme Good)*, IV–V
HORACE. *Satires*
SEXTUS EMPIRICUS. *Against the Logicians*, BK I (Concerning Man)
BOETHIUS. *Contra Eutychen (A Treatise Against Eutyches and Nestorius)*
ERIGENA. *De Divisione Naturae*, BK IV
IBN GABIROL. *The Improvement of the Moral Qualities*
ABAILARD. *Ethics (Scito Teipsum)*
BONAVENTURA. *Breviloquium*, PART II (9–11), IV
PETRARCH. *On His Own Ignorance*
ALBO. *The Book of Principles (Sefer ha-Ikkarim)*, BK III, CH 1–7
NICOLAS OF CUSA. *De Docta Ignorantia*, BK III

G. Pico della Mirandola. *Oration on the Dignity of Man*
Luther. *A Treatise on Christian Liberty*
——. *The Magnificat*
Vives. *A Fable About Man*
Calvin. *Institutes of the Christian Religion*, bk i, ch 15; bk ii, ch 1–3
Ben Jonson. *Every Man in His Humour*
Molière. *Le misanthrope* (*The Man-Hater*)
Marvell. *Dialogue Between the Soul and the Body*
Defoe. *Robinson Crusoe*
Pope. *Essay on Man*
Lamettrie. *Man a Machine*
Buffon. "On Man," in *Natural History*
Hartley. *Observations on Man, His Frame, His Duty and His Expectations*
Ferguson. *An Essay on the History of Civil Society*, part i, sect i–iv
Voltaire. *Candide*
——. "Contradictions," "Man, Woman," in *A Philosophical Dictionary*
——. *The Huron, or Pupil of Nature* (*L'ingénue*)
Goldsmith. *The Deserted Village*
Helvétius. *A Treatise on Man*
Kames. *Sketches of the History of Man*
Bentham. *An Introduction to the Principles of Morals and Legislation*, ch 7
J. G. Fichte. *The Dignity of Man*
——. *Addresses to the German Nation*, iv–viii
Schleiermacher. *The Christian Faith*, par 60–61
D. Stewart. *Elements of the Philosophy of the Human Mind*, part iii, ch 2
——. *Philosophy of the Active and Moral Powers of Man*
Gogol. *The Overcoat*
Kierkegaard. *Either/Or*
——. *Concluding Unscientific Postscript*
——. *The Sickness Unto Death*
Schopenhauer. *The World as Will and Idea*, vol i, bk iv; vol iii, sup, ch 31–32
——. *On Human Nature*
Comte. *System of Positive Polity*, vol iv, *Theory of the Future of Man*, ch i, 3–4
Lotze. *Microcosmos*, bk iv, ch 4–5; bk vi, ch 2, 4–5
Renouvier. *Essais de critique générale*, ii, part i
T. H. Huxley. *Man's Place in Nature*
——. *Methods and Results*, vii
Galton. *Inquiries into Human Faculty and Its Development*
Meredith. *Earth and Man*
C. S. Peirce. *Collected Papers*, vol vi, par 238–271
Wundt. *Outlines of Psychology*, (20–21)
Royce. *The World and the Individual*, series ii (6–7)
Santayana. *Reason in Common Sense*, ch 12
Mark Twain. *What Is Man?*
France. *Penguin Island*
Unamuno. *The Tragic Sense of Life*
Jung. *Two Essays on Analytical Psychology*
——. *Psychological Types*
Shaw. *Back to Methuselah*
Buber. *I and Thou*
Chesterton. *The Everlasting Man*
B. Russell. *What I Believe*, ch i
Frazer. *The Golden Bough*, part i; part vi, note (The Crucifixion of Christ); part vii
——. *Man, God, and Immortality*, part i–ii
Spearman. *The Abilities of Man*
J. S. Haldane. *The Sciences and Philosophy*, lect vi–x
M. R. Cohen. *Reason and Nature*, bk ii, ch 4
Jaspers. *Man in the Modern Age*
Blondel. *L'action*
Dewey. *Human Nature and Conduct*
——. *Freedom and Culture*, ch 2
Maritain. *Ransoming the Time*, ch i
Niebuhr. *The Nature and Destiny of Man*
J. S. Huxley. *Evolution, the Modern Synthesis*, ch 10
T. S. Eliot. *Four Quartets*
Cassirer. *An Essay on Man*
Lubac. *Surnaturel*
Weiss. *Nature and Man*
Sartre. *Existentialism*
Keith. *A New Theory of Human Evolution*
Wiener. *Cybernetics*
Von Weizsäcker. *The History of Nature*

Chapter 52: MATHEMATICS

INTRODUCTION

IT is necessary for us to observe the difference between problems *in* mathematics and the problem of the truth *about* mathematics. In the case of any science—in physics, logic, or metaphysics, as well as mathematics—it is one thing to examine the discourses or treatises of the scientists on the special subject matter of their field, and quite another to examine discussions of the science itself, its scope, branches, and unity, its objects, its methods and its relation to other disciplines. The chapter on QUANTITY deals with the subject matter of arithmetic, geometry, and other branches of mathematics; here we are primarily concerned with the nature of mathematical science itself.

Sometimes reflections on the nature of a science are expressed by experts in its subject matter who comment on the scientific enterprise in which they are engaged in prefaces or interspersed remarks. Sometimes such reflections are the commentary on a particular science by those who may claim to speak with competence on the processes of the human mind, the nature of knowledge or of science in general, but who claim no special competence in the particular science under consideration. This is usually the commentary of philosophers who may assert their right to make all knowledge, as well as all reality, their province. The same man may, of course, be both a mathematician and a philosopher; as, for example, Plato, Descartes, Pascal.

In the case of mathematics, the disparity between discourse *in* and *about* the science could hardly escape notice. Even if no preliminary rule of caution were laid down, we should be struck by the contrast between the agreement mathematicians have been able to reach in the solution of their problems and the disagreement of the commentators on basic questions about mathematics. To this there may be one significant exception. Mathematics is honored for the precision of its concepts, the rigor of its demonstrations, the certitude of its truth. Even its detractors—like Swift or Berkeley—concede the exactitude and brilliance of mathematics while questioning its utility; or they admit its intellectual austerity while challenging some application of its method. Its "clearness and certainty of demonstration," Berkeley writes, "is hardly anywhere else to be found."

This general agreement about the quality of mathematical thought may explain why in all epochs mathematics has been looked upon as the type of certain and exact knowledge. Sometimes it is taken as more than a model for other sciences; it is regarded as the method of pure science itself or as the universal science. Sometimes its excellences are thought to be qualified by the limited or special character of its objects; or it is contrasted with other disciplines which, employing different methods, deal with more fundamental matters no less scientifically. But always the conclusions of mathematics serve to exemplify rational truth; always the method of mathematics represents the spirit of dispassionate thought; always mathematical knowledge symbolizes the power of the human mind to rise above sensible particulars and contingent events to universal and necessary relationships.

Mathematics means this not only to mathematicians and philosophers, but also to moralists and statesmen. "The objects of geometrical inquiry," writes Alexander Hamilton, "are so entirely abstracted from those pursuits which stir and put in motion the unruly passions of the human heart, that mankind, without difficulty, adopt not only the more simple theorems of the science, but even those abstruse paradoxes which, however they may appear susceptible of demonstration, are at variance with the natural conceptions which the mind, without the aid of philosophy, would be led to entertain upon the subject. . . . But in the sciences of morals and politics, men are found far less tractable." This, Hamilton points out, is not due merely to the passionate interest in their problems. "It cannot be pretended," he says, "that the principles of moral and political knowledge have, in general, the same degree of certainty with those of mathematics."

Admiration for mathematics often extends beyond enthusiasm for its exemplary virtues or delight in its intellectual beauty to the recognition of its influence on the whole history of thought. Yet here differences of opinion begin to appear.

In the ancient world Plato and Aristotle represent opposite estimates of the importance of mathematics for the rest of philosophy. For the Platonists, Aristotle says, "mathematics has come to be identical with philosophy, though they say that it should be studied for the sake of other things." He complains of those students of science who "do not listen to a lecturer unless he speaks mathematically." They make the error of supposing that "the minute accuracy of mathematics is . . . to be demanded in all cases," whereas, according to Aristotle's own view, "its method is not that of natural science."

In the modern world, thinkers who are both mathematicians and philosophers, like Descartes and Whitehead, represent a return to the Platonic point of view; while Kant, even more than Aristotle, insists that the philosopher is grievously misled if he tries to follow the method of mathematics in his own inquiries. Whitehead charges Aristotle with having deposed mathematics from its high role "as a formative element in the development of philosophy"—a demotion which lasted until, with Descartes and others in the 17th century, mathematics recovered the importance it had for Plato.

Attempting to qualify his own enthusiasm, Whitehead admits that he would not "go so far as to say that to construct a history of thought without a profound study of the mathematical ideas of successive epochs is like omitting Hamlet from the play which is named after him. That would be claiming too much. But it is certainly analogous to cutting out the part of Ophelia. This simile is singularly exact. For Ophelia is quite essential to the play, she is very charming—and a little mad. Let us grant that the pursuit of mathematics is a divine madness of the human spirit, a refuge from the goading urgency of contingent happenings."

For Kant the madness lies not in the pursuit of mathematics itself, but in the delusion of the philosopher that he can proceed in the same way. "The science of mathematics," Kant writes, "presents the most brilliant example of how pure reason may successfully enlarge its domain without the aid of experience. Such examples are always contagious, particularly when the faculty is the same, which naturally flatters itself that it will meet with the same success in other cases which it has had in one." The expectation naturally arises that the method of mathematics "would have the same success outside the field of quantities." But philosophers who understand their own task, Kant thinks, should not be infected by the "confidence . . . of those who are masters in the art of mathematics . . . as to their ability of achieving such success" by applying its method in other fields.

"The exactness of mathematics," Kant holds, "depends on definitions, axioms, and demonstrations. . . . None of these can be achieved or imitated by the philosopher in the sense in which they are understood by the mathematician," because, according to Kant, the validity of the mathematician's definitions and demonstrations ultimately depends on the fact that he is able to *construct* the concepts he uses. The point is not that mathematics obtains its objects from reason rather than experience, but rather that it obtains them from reason by construction; as, for example, Euclid begins by constructing a triangle which corresponds with his definition of that figure.

Hence, Kant maintains, "we must not try in philosophy to imitate mathematics by beginning with definitions, except it be by the way of experiment. . . . In philosophy, in fact, the definition in its complete clearness ought to conclude rather than begin our work"; whereas in mathematics we cannot begin until we have constructed the objects corresponding to our definitions. "It follows from all this," Kant concludes, "that it is not in accordance with the very nature of philosophy to boast of its dogmatical character, particularly in the field of pure reason, and to deck itself with the titles and ribands of mathematics."

DIFFERENCES OF opinion about mathematics represent, for the most part, philosophical controversy concerning the nature of science or the objects of its knowledge. Mathematicians who engage in such controversy assume the role of philosophers in doing so, for mathematics itself is not concerned with questions of this sort. But there are some questions about mathematics which seem to call for a close study of the science itself and even for proficiency in its subject matter and operations. They are questions about the scope of mathematics and about the divisions of the science, in relation to one another and to its unity. On these issues, mathematicians disagree not only with philosophers, but among themselves and in their capacity as mathematicians.

These issues usually involve different interpretations of the history of mathematics. The problem is not one of the origin of mathematics.

The ancient opinion, found in Herodotus, Plato, and Aristotle, that the mathematical arts, especially geometry, were first developed by the Egyptians, is of interest because of the questions it raises about the circumstances of the origin of mathematics. Herodotus seems to suggest that geometry arose as an aid in the practice of surveying land. "From this practice," he says, "geometry first came to be known in Egypt, whence it passed into Greece." Aristotle, on the other hand, separating from the useful arts those which "do not aim at utility," thinks the latter arose "first in the places where men first began to have leisure. That is why the mathematical arts were founded in Egypt, for there the priestly caste was allowed to be at leisure."

The Greek development of mathematics very early distinguishes between the pure sciences of arithmetic and geometry and their useful applications in the arts of measurement. The Greeks conceived mathematics as essentially speculative rather than practical or productive. They also divorced it from empirical investigation of the sensible world. As arithmetic is concerned with numbers, not with numbered things, and geometry with figures, not with physical shapes, areas, or volumes, so Plato points out that music and astronomy belong to the mathematical sciences when they deal not with audible harmonies but with their numerical ratios, not with visible celestial motions but with their geometrical configurations.

Provoked by Glaucon's interest in the usefulness of the mathematical arts, Socrates excludes their utility as being of no interest to the philosopher. He recommends arithmetic and its sister disciplines only so far as these sciences entirely ignore the world of sensible things. The reason why the philosopher "who has to rise out of the sea of change and lay hold of true being . . . must be an arithmetician," he explains, is that arithmetic can have "a very great and elevating effect," when it compels "the soul to reason about abstract number" and rebels "against the introduction of visible or tangible objects into the argument." In the same way, only when it concerns itself with "knowledge of the eternal," not with measuring earthly distances, will geometry "draw the soul towards truth, and create the spirit of philosophy." The astronomer, like the geometer, "should employ problems, and let the heavens alone, if he would approach the subject in the right way"; and, like the astronomer, the student of harmony will work in vain, if he compares "the sounds and consonances which are heard only" and so fails to "reach the natural harmonies of number."

About the non-empirical or non-experimental character of mathematics there has been little dispute. It is seldom suggested that the growth of mathematical knowledge depends upon improvement in methods of observation. But on the relation of mathematics to physics, which raises the whole problem of pure and applied mathematics, or of mathematical and experimental physics, there has been much controversy, especially in modern times.

Bacon, for example, adopts the ancient division of mathematics into pure and mixed, the former "wholly abstracted from matter and physical axioms." Though he regards mathematics as a useful instrument in physics—"the investigation of nature" being "best conducted when mathematics are applied to physics"—he also insists upon the primacy of physics and upon its essentially experimental character. Physics has been corrupted, he says, by logic and by mathematics when these seek to dominate instead of to serve it. "It is a strange fatality that mathematics and logic, which ought to be but handmaids to physics, should boast their certainty before it, and even exercise dominion against it."

The certainty and clarity which Hume is willing to attribute to mathematics cannot, in his opinion, be extended to mathematical physics. "The most perfect philosophy of the natural kind," he thinks, "only staves off our ignorance a little longer. . . . Nor is geometry, when taken into the assistance of natural philosophy, ever able to remedy this defect, or lead us into the knowledge of ultimate causes, by all that accuracy of reasoning for which it is so justly celebrated. Every part of mixed mathematics," Hume continues, "proceeds upon the assumption that certain laws are established by nature in her operations; and abstract reasonings are employed, either to assist experience in the discovery of these laws, or to determine their influence in particular instances, where it depends upon any precise degree of distance or quantity." When mixed with physics, mathematics remains subordinate—at best an aid in the formulation and the discovery of the laws of nature.

A different view seems to be taken by the great mathematicians and physicists of the 17th century. Galileo, Descartes, and Newton tend to make mathematical analysis an integral part of physics. As the structure of the world is mathematical, so, too, must the science of nature be mathematical. Geometry, says Descartes, is "the science which furnishes a general knowledge of the measurement of all bodies." If we retain the ancient distinction between geometry and mechanics, it can only be in terms of the assumption, "confirmed by the usage" of these names, that "geometry is precise and exact, while mechanics is not."

In the preface to his *Mathematical Principles of Natural Philosophy*, Newton also says that "geometry is founded in mechanical practice, and is nothing but that part of universal mechanics which accurately proposes and demonstrates the art of measuring." What is called "rational mechanics" must not be confused with the manual arts of measurement which are imperfect and inexact; and it is therefore wrong to distinguish geometry from mechanics as that which is perfectly accurate from that which is less so. "But since the manual arts are chiefly employed in the moving of bodies, it happens that geometry is commonly referred to their magnitude, and mechanics to their motion."

Newton himself does not abide by this distinction. His aim is to subject all the phenomena of nature "to the laws of mathematics" and to cultivate mathematics as far as it relates to natural philosophy. "I offer this work as the mathematical principles of philosophy, for the whole burden of philosophy consists in this—from the phenomena of motions to investigate the forces of nature and from these forces to demonstrate the other phenomena." He regrets that he has not been able to deduce *all* the phenomena of nature "by the same kind of reasoning from mechanical principles."

Fourier goes even further. "Mathematical analysis," he says, is "as extensive as nature itself." Mathematical analysis has "necessary relations with sensible phenomena." In laying hold "of the laws of these phenomena," mathematics "interprets them by the same language as if to attest the unity and simplicity of the plan of the universe, and to make still more evident that unchangeable order which presides over all natural causes." This much had been said or implied by Descartes and Newton. But in addition to all this, Fourier, from his own experience in developing a mathematical theory of heat, comes to the conclusion that "profound study of nature is the most fertile source of mathematical discoveries." Mathematics itself benefits from its alliance with physics; it increases in analytical power and in the generality of its formulations as physical inquiries extend the range of phenomena to be analyzed and formulated.

THE RELATIONS OF mathematics to physics are considered in the chapters on ASTRONOMY, MECHANICS, and PHYSICS. Mathematical physics must be examined in the light of the opinion that mathematics and physics are separate sciences, distinct in object and method. Furthermore, whereas some of the major contributions to mathematics appear in the great books of physics or natural philosophy (*e.g.*, Archimedes, Kepler, Newton, Fourier), even more fundamental formulations of the science occur in great books devoted exclusively to mathematics: Euclid's *Elements* (on geometry), Apollonius' treatise *On Conic Sections*, Nicomachus' *Introduction to Arithmetic*, Descartes' *Geometry*, and Pascal's mathematical papers. Others belonging to this latter group are listed in the Additional Readings. The great modern advances in mathematics are exemplified by the works of Gauss, Lobachevski, Hamilton, Riemann, Boole, Dedekind, Peano, Frege, Cantor, Hilbert.

It would be both natural and reasonable to inquire about the relation between the great works of mathematics included in this set and the equally great treatises or monographs, listed in the Additional Readings, which represent for the most part the contributions of the 19th century. But since the major question which immediately confronts us in such an inquiry concerns the relation of modern to ancient mathematics, we can examine the problem in terms of the works included in this set, for they represent both the continuity and the discontinuity in the tradition of mathematical science.

Galileo and Newton are disciples of Euclid and Archimedes; Fourier is a disciple of Newton and Descartes. But Descartes is the great innovator. He seems to be quite self-conscious of his radical departure from the ancients and from the state of mathematics as he found it in his own day. Yet the truth and power of his mathematical discoveries seem so evident to him that he cannot doubt the ancients must have had some inkling of it.

"I am quite ready to believe," he writes, "that the greater minds of former ages had some knowledge of it, nature even conducting them to it. We have sufficient evidence that the ancient Geometricians made use of a certain analysis which they extended to the resolution of all problems, though they grudged the secret to posterity. At the present day also there flourishes a certain kind of Arithmetic, called Algebra, which designs to effect, when dealing with numbers, what the ancients achieved in the matter of figures. These two methods," he claims, "are nothing else than the spontaneous fruit sprung from the inborn principles of the discipline here in question."

Descartes does not regard his success as consisting in the advance of mathematical truth through discoveries based upon principles or conclusions already established. Nor would he even be satisfied to say that his use of algebra in developing analytical geometry created a new branch of mathematics. Rather, in his own view, it tended to unify all existing branches and to form a single universal method of analysis. In effect, it revolutionized the whole character of mathematics and laid the foundation for the characteristically modern development of that science since his day. "To speak freely," he writes, "I am convinced that it is a more powerful instrument of knowledge than any other that has been bequeathed to us by human agency, as being the source of all others."

One need not quite agree with Bertrand Russell that pure mathematics was not discovered until the 19th century, in order to perceive that the discoveries made in that century carry out the spirit of the Cartesian revolution. If one understands the difference between the universal mathematics of Descartes and the separate sciences of arithmetic and geometry as developed by the ancients; if one understands the difference between the theory of equations in Descartes and the theory of proportions in Euclid; if one understands how algebraic symbolism, replacing numbers by letters, frees both arithmetic and geometry from definite quantities, then the profound discontinuity between modern and ancient mathematics begins to be discernible.

There are other differences contributing to that discontinuity, such as the modern treatment of the infinite, the invention of the calculus, and the theory of functions. But what is of prime importance for the purpose of understanding the nature of mathematics, its objects, and its methods, is the perception of the discontinuity in any one or another of its manifestations. Here is a fundamental disagreement about the nature of mathematics which is not an issue between philosophers disputing the definition of the science, but rather an issue made by the actual work of mathematicians in ancient and modern times.

In his *Battle of the Books*—ancient and modern—Swift sees only the great poets and philosophers of the two epochs set against one another. The battle between the ancient and the modern books of mathematics might be as dramatically represented. In such affairs there is a natural tendency to prejudge the issue in favor of the modern contender. That prejudice has reason on its side in certain fields of knowledge where the perfection of new instruments and the discovery of new facts work to the advantage of the latecomer. But it is questionable whether in this dispute over the nature of mathematics the same advantage prevails.

When the issue is fairly explored by an examination of the differences between the great masterpieces of ancient and modern mathematics, it may be found impossible to say that truth lies more on one side than on the other, or that one conception of mathematics is more fruitful than another, because the two versions of the science may seem to be incommensurable in their aims, methods, and standards of accomplishment.

One example will illustrate this incommensurability. The ancient notion of number, as may be seen in Nicomachus' *Introduction to Arithmetic*, limits the variety of numbers. A number always numbers a number of things, even though we can deal with the number itself apart from any set of numbered things. It is always a positive and integral quantity which, excepting unity itself, "the natural starting point of all numbers," contains a multitude of discrete units.

Numbers are classified according to the way in which they are constituted of parts and according to the constitution of these parts. The primary division of numbers is into even and odd. "The even is that which can be divided into two equal parts without a unit intervening in the middle; and the odd is that which cannot be divided into two equal parts because of the aforesaid intervention of a unit."

The even numbers are capable of subdivision into the even-times-even, the odd-times-even, and the even-times-odd; and the odd into the prime and incomposite, the secondary and composite, and the number which, in itself, is secondary and composite, but relatively is prime and incomposite. The peculiarities of these types of number are explained in the chapter on Quantity. There are still further classifications of numbers into superabundant, deficient, and perfect; and of the parts of numbers in relation to the numbers of which they are parts.

Finally, numbers are considered in terms of their geometrical properties, to be observed when their units are disposed discretely in spatial patterns, and in one, two, or three dimensions. There are linear, plane, and solid numbers, and among plane numbers, for example, there are triangular, square, pentagonal, hexagonal numbers, and so on.

The arithmetic operations of addition, subtraction, multiplication, and division are performed in the production of numbers or in the resolution of numbers into their parts. But though any two numbers can be added together or multiplied, the inverse operations cannot always be performed. A greater number cannot be subtracted from a less, for subtraction consists in taking a part from the whole, and leaving a positive remainder. Since division is the decomposition of a number into its parts, a number cannot be divided by one greater than itself, for the greater cannot be a part of the less.

In short, in Nicomachus' theory of numbers what later came to be treated as negative numbers and fractions can have no place. Nicomachus will not carry out arithmetical operations in all possible directions without regard to the result obtained. He refuses to perform these operations when the results which would be obtained do not have for him the requisite mathematical reality. He does not find it repugnant to reason that subtraction and division, unlike addition and multiplication, are not possible for any two numbers; as, for example, subtracting a larger from a smaller number, or using a divisor which does not go into the dividend evenly, and so leaves a fractional remainder. On the contrary, Nicomachus finds it repugnant to reason to perform these operations in violation of their proper meaning, and to produce thereby results, such as negative quantities and fractions, which are for him not numbers, *i.e.*, which cannot number any real thing.

Understanding the nature of square numbers, Nicomachus would be able to understand a square root, but he would not see why the operation of extracting the square root should be applied to numbers which are not square. Hence another kind of modern number, the irrational fraction which is generated by such operations as the extraction of the square of positive integers which are not perfect squares, would never appear in Nicomachus' set of numbers; nor would the imaginary number, which is the result of applying the same operation to negative quantities.

When the arithmetical operations are performed algebraically, with unknowns as well as definite quantities, the solution of equations requires the employment of terms which Nicomachus would not admit to be numbers—negatives, fractions (both rational and irrational), imaginaries, and complex numbers, which are partly real and partly imaginary. Descartes finds nothing repugnant in these novel quantities. On the contrary, he would find it repugnant not to be able to perform the basic arithmetical operations without restriction. Algebra would be impossible, and with it the general method of analysis that proceeds in terms of the purely formal structure of equations from which all definite quantities have been excluded. It would also be impossible to do what Descartes thinks essential to the unity of mathematics, namely, to represent geometrical operations algebraically and to perform most algebraic operations geometrically.

Geometrical loci cannot be expressed by algebraic formulae or equations, unless there are as many numbers as there are points on a line. The number series for Nicomachus, without fractions and irrationals, is neither dense nor continuous. There are fewer numbers than there are points on a line. And without the use of zero, negative numbers, and fractions—none of which would be regarded as numbers by Nicomachus—it would be impossible for Descartes to construct a set of coordinates for the geometrical representation of equations, whereby all the points in a plane have their unique numerical equivalents.

The Cartesian synthesis of algebra and geometry, which in his view vastly increases the power of each, violates the ancient distinction between continuous and discontinuous quantities—magnitudes (like lines and planes) and multitudes (or numbers). Euclid, for example, treats the irrational or the incommensurable always as a relation of magnitudes, never of multitudes, or numbers; for him certain geometrical relationships cannot be expressed numerically. Arithmetic and geometry are not even coordinate, much less co-extensive sciences. Arithmetic is the simpler, the more elementary science, and is presupposed by geometry.

Other examples arising from the innovations of Descartes might be employed to show the chasm between the arithmetic and geometry of the ancients, and modern mathematics—such as the treatment of infinite magnitudes and numbers, the theory of functions, and the method of the calculus. But the multiplication of examples does not seem necessary to suggest that there may be no answer to the question, Is Descartes right, and Nicomachus and Euclid wrong? or to the question, Are the modern innovations improvements or corruptions of the mathematical arts and sciences?

These questions are not like questions concerning the truth or falsity of a proposition in mathematics or the validity of a proof. A given theorem in Euclid must, in the light of his definitions, axioms, and postulates, be either true or false; and accordingly Euclid's demonstrations or constructions are either cogent or fallacious. The same rules apply to Descartes. But whether Euclid's or Descartes' conception of the whole mathematical enterprise is right seems to present a choice between disparate worlds, a choice to be made by reference to principles and purposes which are themselves not mathematical.

Modern mathematics may be much more useful in its physical applications, especially in the analysis and calculation of variable notions or quantities. It may have a special elegance and simplicity, as well as greater unity and even systematic rigor. But it may also purchase these qualities at the expense of the kind of intelligibility which seems to characterize ancient mathematics as a result of the insistence that its objects have an immediately recognizable reality. Ancient mathematics never occasioned such an extreme remark as that made by Bertrand Russell about modern mathematics—that it is "the science in which we never know what we are talking about, nor whether what we are saying is true."

The question of the reality of the objects of mathematics is in part a problem for the mathematician and in part a question for the philosopher. The problem for the mathematician seems to be one of establishing the existence of the objects he defines. This can be illustrated by reference to Euclid's *Elements.*

The basic principles, as Euclid expounds the science, seem to be threefold: definitions, postulates, and axioms or common notions. The axioms are called "common notions" because they are truths common to other branches of mathematics as well as to geometry. The common notions are called "axioms" because their truth is supposed to be self-evident. In contrast, the postulates are peculiar to geometry, for they are written as rules of construction. They demand that certain operations be *assumed* possible, such as the drawing of a straight line or a circle, or the transposition of a figure from one portion of space to another without alteration of its form or quantity.

Euclid's definitions include the definition of a straight line and a circle. His first two postulates, therefore, seem to ask us to assume that space is such that these defined geometrical objects exist in it as they are defined; or, in other words, that objects corresponding to the definitions have geometrical reality. But there are many definitions—of a triangle, of an equilateral triangle, of a parallelogram—for which Euclid states no postulate demanding that we assume the geometrical reality of the object defined. Hence before he undertakes to demonstrate the properties of these figures, he finds it necessary to prove that they can be constructed. Until they are constructed, and the construction demonstrated, the definitions state only possibilities to which no geometrical realities are *known* to correspond in the space determined by Euclid's postulates.

In his first constructions, Euclid can employ only the definition of the figure itself, his axioms, and those postulates which permit him to use certain mechanical devices—the straight edge and the compass, which are the mechanical equivalents of his postulates that a straight line can be drawn between any two points and a circle described with any radius from any point upon a plane. When, for example, in the first proposition of Book I, Euclid thus demonstrates the construction of an equilateral triangle, he has proved the geometrical existence of that figure, or, in other words, its reality in the space of his postulates.

A number of questions can be asked about this and many other similar demonstrations. The postulates being assumptions, their truth can be questioned and an effort made to prove or disprove them. This type of questioning led to the development of the non-Euclidean geometries. After centuries of trying unsuccessfully to prove Euclid's postulate about parallel lines, geometers like Lobachevski and Riemann postulated other conditions concerning parallels, with consequences for the properties of other geometrical figures.

The interior angles of a Euclidean triangle, for example, equal the sum of two right angles; in certain non-Euclidean triangles, they add up to more or less than two rights. One interpretation of this situation is that the truth of conclusions in geometry is entirely dependent on arbitrary assumptions. Another is that the several variants of the parallel postulate indicate the selection of different spaces in which to construct figures; and under each set of spatial conditions postulated, there is only one body of geometrical truths concerning the properties of the figures therein constructed.

Another type of question concerns the logical, as opposed to the geometrical, conditions of geometrical proof. In his essay *On Geometrical Demonstration*, Pascal declares the geometric method to be the most perfect available to men, for it "consists not in defining or in proving everything, nor in defining or proving nothing, but in maintaining itself in the middleground of not defining things which are clear to all men and in defining all others; and not proving everything known to men, but in proving all the other things." This method, it seems, is not restricted to the subject matter of geometry; to Descartes and Spinoza, at least, it seems to be the method for demonstrating any theoretical truth. Descartes presents "arguments demonstrating the existence of God and the distinction between soul and body, drawn up in geometrical fashion"; and as its title page indicates, the whole of Spinoza's *Ethics* is set forth "in geometrical order."

It may be questioned whether the postulates

which Descartes adds to his definitions and axioms, or those which Spinoza introduces beginning with Proposition 13 of Book II, function as postulates do in geometry, *i.e.*, as rules of construction; it may similarly be questioned whether Spinoza is following the geometrical method in Book I where he proceeds without any postulates at all. But the more general question concerns the criteria for testing the consistency and the adequacy of the primitive propositions—the definitions, axioms, postulates—laid down as the foundation for all that is to be demonstrated. The investigation of this problem calls for an examination of the whole process of proof, from which has developed the modern theory of mathematical logic that challenges the universality and adequacy of the traditional logic of Aristotle, and asserts that mathematics and logic are continuous with one another—essentially the same discipline.

THE ISSUES RAISED by mathematical logic or the logic of mathematics are considered in the chapters on HYPOTHESIS, LOGIC, and REASONING. Here we must turn finally to one other question which is of interest principally to the philosopher rather than the mathematician. It concerns the objects of mathematics. It is a question about their reality or mode of existence which cannot be answered by the mathematical proof of a construction.

When, for example, Euclid constructs an equilateral triangle, the figure established cannot be the one imperfectly drawn upon paper. The postulated permission to use a ruler and compass does not remove the imperfection of these mechanical instruments or the inaccuracy in their physical use. The triangle whose properties the geometer tries to demonstrate must be perfect, as no actually drawn figure can be. The philosophical question, therefore, concerns the reality or existence of this ideal, perfect figure. The same question can be asked about pure numbers—numbers apart from all numbered things.

Are the objects of mathematics purely intelligible beings existing apart from the sensible world of material things? Or are they ideal entities—not in the sense of existing outside the mind, but in the sense of being ideas in the mind itself rather than perceptible particulars? As indicated in the chapters on BEING, FORM, and IDEA, Plato and Aristotle seem to answer these questions differently. But there are further differences among those who regard mathematical objects as having being only in the mind.

Aristotle, Aquinas, Locke, and James, for example, think of the objects of mathematics as universals formed by abstraction from the particulars of sense and imagination. "The mathematicals," such as numbers and figures, Aquinas writes, "do not subsist as separate beings." Apart from numbered things and physical configurations, numbers and figures "have a separate existence only in the reason, in so far as they are abstracted from motion and matter." Hobbes, Berkeley, and Hume, on the other hand, deny abstract ideas or universal concepts. "Let any man try to conceive a triangle in general," Hume declares, "which is neither *isosceles* nor *scalenum*, nor has any particular length or proportion of sides; and he will soon perceive the absurdity of all the scholastic notions with regard to abstraction and general ideas."

Despite these differences, there seems to be general agreement in the tradition of the great books that the truths of mathematics are rational rather than empirical; or, in the language of Kant and James, *a priori* rather than *a posteriori*. But the meaning of this agreement is not the same for those who think that truth in mathematics does not differ from truth in other sciences and those who think that mathematical truths stand alone precisely because they are not about matters of fact or real existence.

Plato, for whom all science is knowledge of purely intelligible objects, regards the mathematical sciences as inferior to dialectic in the knowledge of such objects "because they start from hypotheses and do not ascend to principles." The students of such sciences, Plato writes, "assume the odd and the even and the figures and three kinds of angles and the like in their several branches of science; these are their hypotheses, which they and everybody are supposed to know, and therefore they do not deign to give any account of them either to themselves or others; but they begin with them, and go on until they arrive at last, and in a consistent manner, at their conclusion."

For Aristotle, what differentiates mathematics from physics and metaphysics is the special character of its objects. Physics and metaphysics both deal with substances as they exist outside the mind, whereas the objects of mathematics are abstractions. Though figures and numbers "are inseparable in fact" from material substances, they are "separable from any particular kind of body by an effort of abstraction." This does not deny, for example, that physical things have perceptible figures. It merely insists that the geometer does not treat figures *as* sensible, but *as* intelligible, that is, as abstracted from matter. Nevertheless, the truths of mathematics, no less than those of physics and metaphysics, apply to reality. All three sciences are further alike in demonstrating their conclusions rationally rather than by experiment. All three employ induction to obtain their principles, though metaphysics alone attains to the first principles of all science.

For Kant, "mathematical cognition is cognition by means of the *construction* of conceptions." To explain this he cites the example of the construction of a triangle. "I construct a triangle, by the presentation of the object which corresponds to this conception, either by mere imagination (in pure intuition) or upon paper (in empirical intuition); in both cases completely *a priori* without borrowing the type of that figure from any experience. . . . We keep our eye merely on the act of the construction of the conception, and pay no attention to the various modes of determining it, for example, its size, the length of its sides, the size of its angles." The *a priori* character of such intuitions, on which rests the *a priori* character of mathematical truths, does not mean that mathematics has no relevance to experience. Arithmetic and geometry are like physics, according to Kant; they are sciences of experience or nature but like pure (as opposed to empirical) physics, they are *a priori* sciences. Since Kant holds that experience itself is constituted by *a priori* forms of perception, he can ascribe the validity which mathematics has for all possible experience to the "*a priori* intuition of the pure forms of phenomena—space and time."

Bertrand Russell rejects this "Kantian view which [asserts] that mathematical reasoning is not strictly formal, but always uses intuitions, *i.e.*, the *a priori* knowledge of space and time. Thanks to the progress of Symbolic Logic . . . this part of the Kantian philosophy," Russell holds, "is now capable of a final and irrevocable refutation." Leibnitz, before Kant, had advocated "the general doctrine that all mathematics is a deduction from logical principles," but, according to Russell, he had failed to substantiate this insight, partly because of his "belief in the logical necessity of Euclidean geometry." The same belief is, in Russell's opinion, the cause of Kant's error. "The actual propositions of Euclid . . . do not follow from the principles of logic alone; and the perception of this fact," he thinks, "led Kant to his innovations in the theory of knowledge. But since the growth of non-Euclidean geometry, it has appeared that pure mathematics has no concern with the question whether the axioms and propositions of Euclid hold of actual space or not."

Russell asserts that "by the help of ten principles of deduction and ten other premises of a general logical nature (*e.g.*, 'implication is a relation'), all mathematics can be strictly and formally deduced." He regards "the fact that all Mathematics is Symbolic Logic" as "one of the greatest discoveries of our age; and when this fact has been established, the remainder of the principles of Mathematics consists in the analysis of Symbolic Logic itself." Though this view of mathematics may not be worked out in detail except in such treatises as Russell's *Principles of Mathematics* and in the *Principia Mathematica*, on which he collaborated with Whitehead, the conception of mathematics as a purely formal science, analogous to (if not identical with) logic, does have some anticipations in the great books. For James, as for Locke and Hume, mathematics is strictly a science of the relations between ideas, not of real existences. "As regards mathematical judgments," James writes, "they are all 'rational propositions' . . . for they express results of comparison and nothing more. The mathematical sciences deal with similarities and equalities exclusively, and not with coexistences and sequences." Both James and Locke, however, differ from Hume in thinking that there are sciences other than those of number and quantity which can demonstrate their conclusions with certitude.

The foregoing discussion indicates *some* of the differences among philosophers concerning the objects of mathematics, the conditions of its truth, and its relation to other sciences. These disagreements do not seem to take the form of an opposition between ancient and modern thought, like that between ancient and modern mathematicians concerning the nature of their science. The two oppositions do not run parallel to one another.

On the contrary, the objections which modern philosophers, especially Berkeley, Hume, and Kant, raise against the notion of infinite quantities seem to favor the ancient rather than the modern tenor of mathematical thought. Though the reasons they give do not derive from the same principles as those to which Plato and Aristotle appeal, they, like the ancients, appear to insist upon a certain type of intelligibility in the objects of mathematics, which seems to have been sacrificed in the mathematical development initiated by Descartes.

OUTLINE OF TOPICS

1. The science of mathematics: its branches or divisions; the origin and development of mathematics
   - 1*a*. The distinction of mathematics from physics and metaphysics: its relation to logic
   - 1*b*. The service of mathematics to dialectic and philosophy: its place in liberal education
   - 1*c*. The certainty and exactitude of mathematical knowledge: the *a priori* foundations of arithmetic and geometry
   - 1*d*. The ideal of a universal mathesis: the unification of arithmetic and geometry

2. The objects of mathematics: number, figure, extension, relation, order
   - 2*a*. The apprehension of mathematical objects: by intuition, abstraction, imagination, construction; the forms of time and space
   - 2*b*. The being of mathematical objects: their real, ideal, or mental existence
   - 2*c*. Kinds of quantity: continuous and discrete quantities; the problem of the irrational

3. Method in mathematics: the model of mathematical thought
   - 3*a*. The conditions and character of demonstration in mathematics: the use of definitions, postulates, axioms, hypotheses
   - 3*b*. The role of construction: its bearing on proof, mathematical existence, and the scope of mathematical inquiry
   - 3*c*. Analysis and synthesis: function and variable
   - 3*d*. Symbols and formulae: the attainment of generality

4. Mathematical techniques
   - 4*a*. The arithmetic and algebraic processes
   - 4*b*. The operations of geometry
   - 4*c*. The use of proportions and equations
   - 4*d*. The method of exhaustion: the theory of limits and the calculus

5. The applications of mathematics to physical phenomena: the utility of mathematics
   - 5*a*. The art of measurement
   - 5*b*. Mathematical physics: the mathematical structure of nature

REFERENCES

References are listed by volume number (in bold type), author's name, and page number. Bible references are to book, chapter, and verse of the Authorized King James version of the Bible. The abbreviation "esp" calls the reader's attention to one or more especially relevant parts of a whole reference; "passim" signifies that the topic is discussed intermittently rather than continuously in the work or passage cited. Where the work as a whole is relevant to the topic, the page numbers refer to the entire work. For general guidance in the use of *The Great Ideas,* consult the Preface.

1. The science of mathematics: its branches or divisions; the origin and development of mathematics

6 Herodotus, 70
7 Plato, 254, 451
8 Aristotle, 119
11 Nicomachus, 831–832
16 Copernicus, 510
17 Plotinus, 250
18 Augustine, 654
23 Hobbes, 268, 269
30 Bacon, 46
31 Descartes, 6–7
35 Locke, 363
35 Hume, 458
41 Gibbon, 299
42 Kant, 17–18, 68–69, 553
46 Hegel, 122–123, 219

1*a*. The distinction of mathematics from physics and metaphysics: its relation to logic

7 Plato, 386–388, 391–398
8 Aristotle, 270, 508, 522, 547–548, 589–590, 592–593, 632
9 Aristotle, 391
16 Ptolemy, 5–6
19 Aquinas, 238–239
20 Aquinas, 424–425
23 Hobbes, 58, 59, 72, 267
28 Galileo, 190
31 Descartes, 5–7, 12–13, 70, 128–129
33 Pascal, 445
34 Newton, 1–2
35 Locke, 322–323, 360–362 passim
39 Smith, 335–337
42 Kant, 5–9, 17–19, 243–248, 311–313
53 James, 867–870

1*b*. The service of mathematics to dialectic and philosophy: its place in liberal education

7 Plato, 391–398, 633–635, 728–730
8 Aristotle, 396–399, 428–429, 503–506, 510, 622–623, 624–626
11 Nicomachus, 811–813
16 Copernicus, 510
17 Plotinus, 10–11
18 Augustine, 644–645
23 Hobbes, 56–57
24 Rabelais, 27
30 Bacon, 46
31 Descartes, 2–3, 29, 46–48
33 Pascal, 171–172
42 Kant, 15–16, 46, 215
53 James, 882–883

1*c*. The certainty and exactitude of mathematical knowledge: the *a priori* foundations of arithmetic and geometry

7 Plato, 633–634
8 Aristotle, 119, 513, 609–610
11 Nicomachus, 811–814
23 Hobbes, 59
30 Bacon, 1–106
31 Descartes, 2–3, 5–7, 43, 93–95, 128–129
33 Pascal, 430–434, 442–446
35 Locke, 317–319 passim, 325–326
35 Berkeley, 436
35 Hume, 470–471, 508–509
42 Kant, 5–8, 31, 46, 68–69, 211–218, 312, 399
43 Federalist, 103–104
43 Mill, 283–284, 445
53 James, 175–176, 879–882

1*d*. The ideal of a universal mathesis: the unification of arithmetic and geometry

7 Plato, 180–182
8 Aristotle, 9, 103, 513
11 Euclid, 30–40, 81–98
11 Nicomachus, 831–841
23 Hobbes, 58
31 Descartes, 1–40, 46–48, 295–353
33 Pascal, 447–456
42 Kant, 68–69
45 Fourier, 172–173

2. The objects of mathematics: number, figure, extension, relation, order

7 Plato, 387
8 Aristotle, 9–11
11 Euclid, 1–2
11 Nicomachus, 811–812
19 Aquinas, 33–34, 167–168
31 Descartes, 8–10, 30–33, 217, 304–306
35 Berkeley, 436–439
42 Kant, 62
53 James, 874–878

2a. The apprehension of mathematical objects: by intuition, abstraction, imagination, construction; the forms of time and space

2b. The being of mathematical objects: their real, ideal, or mental existence

2c. Kinds of quantity: continuous and discrete quantities; the problem of the irrational

3. Method in mathematics: the model of mathematical thought

3a. The conditions and character of demonstration in mathematics: the use of definitions, postulates, axioms, hypotheses

3b. The role of construction: its bearing on proof, mathematical existence, and the scope of mathematical inquiry

3c. Analysis and synthesis: function and variable

3d. Symbols and formulae: the attainment of generality

31 Descartes, 28–40, 47, 295–298, 314
35 Locke, 318–319
35 Berkeley, 436–437
42 Kant, 68–69
45 Fourier, 181, 233–240

4. Mathematical techniques

4*a*. The arithmetic and algebraic processes

8 Aristotle, 222
11 Euclid, 127–190
11 Archimedes, 448–451, 520–526
11 Nicomachus, 814–821
31 Descartes, 33–35, 36–39, 295–296
33 Pascal, 447–473, 474–487 passim
35 Berkeley, 436–437
42 Kant, 17–18, 68–69
53 James, 874–876

4*b*. The operations of geometry

7 Plato, 180–183, 387
11 Euclid, 1–80, 99–126, 301–396
11 Archimedes, 403–446, 447–451, 452–481, 482–501, 527–537, 561–568
11 Apollonius, 603–804
28 Galileo, 149–150
31 Descartes, 33–35, 36–39, 295–296, 297–298, 304–308
34 Newton, 50–75
42 Kant, 551–552
53 James, 876–878

4*c*. The use of proportions and equations

9 Aristotle, 351–352, 378–379
11 Euclid, 81–126, 134–136, 137–140, 145–146, 150–161, 163–170, 174–180, 181–183, 188–190, 195–198, 199, 201–202, 320–321, 327–332, 335–336, 338–368
11 Archimedes, 459–460
11 Apollonius, 603–804 passim
11 Nicomachus, 821–831, 841–848
16 Kepler, 1012–1014
31 Descartes, 8–10, 28–29, 36–40, 295–353
51 Tolstoy, 590

4*d*. The method of exhaustion: the theory of limits and the calculus

11 Euclid, 191–192, 339–340, 351–359, 367–368
11 Archimedes, 411–414, 424–427, 459–460, 470–471, 473–479, 492–495, 496–500, 503–504, 527–537, 569–592 passim
16 Kepler, 973–975, 979–983
28 Galileo, 193–194, 205, 224
33 Pascal, 395
34 Newton, 25–32, 168–170
45 Fourier, 177, 181, 221–248
51 Tolstoy, 695

5. The applications of mathematics to physical phenomena: the utility of mathematics

7 Plato, 403, 424–425, 453–454, 691–692
8 Aristotle, 104, 108, 333, 477–478, 480–481
9 Aristotle, 247–248
11 Archimedes, 502–519, 538–560
14 Plutarch, 252–255
16 Kepler, 964–965
18 Augustine, 27–28
23 Hobbes, 268
28 Galileo, 178–260
31 Descartes, 169–170, 322–331
34 Newton, 7–8, 15–16, 269–372
34 Huygens, 551–619
35 Hume, 460
36 Swift, 94–103
40 Gibbon, 661–662
45 Fourier, 169–173, 175, 177–251
51 Tolstoy, 694–695
53 James, 348–359

5*a*. The art of measurement

5 Aristophanes, 555
6 Herodotus, 139
7 Plato, 431, 594–595, 691–692, 695–697
8 Aristotle, 300, 303, 330–333, 579–580
11 Euclid, 81–98
11 Archimedes, 520–526
16 Ptolemy, 14–28, 38–39, 143–144, 165–176, 233–258
16 Copernicus, 532–556, 558–559, 586–621, 705–725
19 Aquinas, 348–349
28 Gilbert, 85–89, 92–95
28 Galileo, 136–137, 148–149, 164–166, 207–208
28 Harvey, 286–288
30 Bacon, 175–188
31 Descartes, 31–33
33 Pascal, 382–389
34 Newton, 20–22, 211–219, 239–246
34 Huygens, 554–557
35 Locke, 167
42 Kant, 497–498
45 Lavoisier, 14, 33–36, 41–44, 87–90, 91–95, 96–103
45 Fourier, 184–185, 249–251

5*b*. Mathematical physics: the mathematical structure of nature

7 Plato, 448–450, 453–454, 458–460
8 Aristotle, 104, 108, 270, 390–391, 510, 516, 603–604
11 Nicomachus, 812, 813–814
16 Kepler, 863–872, 1023–1080 passim
23 Hobbes, 72, 268
28 Galileo, 131–132, 245
30 Bacon, 46, 140
31 Descartes, 7, 43
33 Pascal, 195
34 Newton, 111, 371–372
35 Hume, 460
45 Fourier, 169, 172–173
45 Faraday, 831
53 James, 348–359, 876, 882–884

CROSS-REFERENCES

For: The relation of mathematics to other arts and sciences, *see* ASTRONOMY 2c; MECHANICS 3; METAPHYSICS 3b; PHILOSOPHY 1b; PHYSICS 1b, 3; SCIENCE 5c.

The quality of necessity in mathematical truth, and for the theory of the *a priori* foundations of arithmetic and geometry in the transcendental forms of space and time, *see* NECESSITY AND CONTINGENCY 4d; SENSE 1c; SPACE 4a; TIME 6c.

The controversy over the character and existence of the objects of mathematics, *see* BEING 7d(3); QUANTITY 1; SPACE 5.

The discussion of the mental processes by which mathematical objects are apprehended, *see* IDEA 1a, 2f–2g; KNOWLEDGE 6a(3), 6c(4); MEMORY AND IMAGINATION 1a, 6c(2)–6d; SENSE 5a; UNIVERSAL AND PARTICULAR 2b.

The consideration of the specific objects of mathematical inquiry, such as numbers and figures, ratios and proportions, continuous and discontinuous quantities, finite and infinite quantities, *see* INFINITY 3a–3c; QUANTITY 1b–4c, 7; RELATION 1d, 5a(3); SPACE 3a–3c.

The general theory of mathematical method or logic, *see* DEFINITION 6a; HYPOTHESIS 3; JUDGMENT 8b–8c; LOGIC 4a; REASONING 6b; TRUTH 4c; and for the particular techniques of arithmetic, geometry, algebra, and calculus, *see* MECHANICS 3b–3d; QUANTITY 1b, 6b; RELATION 5a(3); SPACE 3d.

Other discussions of applied mathematics or mathematical physics, and of the role of measurement, *see* ASTRONOMY 2c; MECHANICS 3; PHYSICS 3, 4d; QUANTITY 3d(1), 6–6a, 6c; SCIENCE 5c.

ADDITIONAL READINGS

Listed below are works not included in *Great Books of the Western World*, but relevant to the idea and topics with which this chapter deals. These works are divided into two groups:

I. Works by authors represented in this collection.
II. Works by authors not represented in this collection.

For the date, place, and other facts concerning the publication of the works cited, consult the Bibliography of Additional Readings which follows the last chapter of *The Great Ideas.*

I.

AQUINAS. *On the Trinity of Boethius,* QQ 5–6
HOBBES. *Six Lessons to the Savilian Professors of Mathematics*
NEWTON. *The Method of Fluxions and Infinite Series*
——. *Universal Arithmetic*
BERKELEY. *A Defence of Free Thinking in Mathematics*
KANT. *Prolegomena to Any Future Metaphysic,* PAR 6–13
HEGEL. *The Phenomenology of Mind,* INTRO
J. S. MILL. *A System of Logic,* BK I, CH 5
——. *An Examination of Sir William Hamilton's Philosophy,* CH 27

II.

R. BACON. *Opus Majus,* PART IV
ORÊME. *Treatise on the Breadth of Forms*
SUÁREZ. *Disputationes Metaphysicae,* IV (9), X (3), XL (3, 5–6), XLI (4), XLVII (13)
BARROW. *Lectiones Mathematicae*
——. *Thirteen Geometrical Lectures*
LEIBNITZ. *Early Mathematical Manuscripts*
SACCHERI. *Euclides Vindicatus (Vindication of Euclid)*
VOLTAIRE. "Geometry," in *A Philosophical Dictionary*
EULER. *Elements of Algebra*
CARNOT. *Réflexions sur la métaphysique du calcul infinitésimal*
GAUSS. *Untersuchungen über höhere Arithmetik*
SCHOPENHAUER. *The World as Will and Idea,* VOL II, SUP, CH 13
DE MORGAN. *On the Study and Difficulties of Mathematics*
COMTE. *The Philosophy of Mathematics*
——. *The Positive Philosophy,* BK I
LOBACHEVSKI. *Geometrical Researches on the Theory of Parallels*
WHEWELL. *The Philosophy of the Inductive Sciences,* VOL I, BK II, CH 11–12, 14
G. PEACOCK. *A Treatise on Algebra*
B. PEIRCE. *An Elementary Treatise on Curves, Functions, and Forces*

W. R. HAMILTON. *Lectures on Quaternions*
RIEMANN. *Über die Hypothesen welche der Geometrie zu Grunde liegen (The Hypotheses of Geometry)*
BOOLE. *A Treatise on Differential Equations*
——. *A Treatise on the Calculus of Finite Differences*
DEDEKIND. *Essays on the Theory of Numbers*
CLIFFORD. *Preliminary Sketch of Biquaternions*
——. *On the Canonical Form and Dissection of a Riemann's Surface*
JEVONS. *On Geometrical Reasoning*
LEWIS CARROLL. *Euclid and His Modern Rivals*
GIBBS. *Collected Works*
C. S. PEIRCE. *Collected Papers*, VOL III, par 553–562I, 609–645
FREGE. *Grundgesetze der Arithmetik*
BURNSIDE. *Theory of Groups of Finite Order*
CANTOR. *Contributions to the Founding of the Theory of Transfinite Numbers*
HILBERT. *The Foundations of Geometry*
PEANO. *Arithmetices Principia*
——. *Formulaire de mathématique*
——. *Arithmetica generale e algebra elementare*
BONOLA. *Non-Euclidean Geometry*
E. W. HOBSON. *The Theory of Functions of a Real Variable and the Theory of Fourier's Series*
O. VEBLEN and LENNES. *Introduction to Infinitesimal Analysis*
KLEIN. *Famous Problems of Elementary Geometry*
——. *Elementary Mathematics from an Advanced Standpoint*
POINCARÉ. *Science and Hypothesis*, PART II
——. *The Value of Science*, PART I, CH I; PART II
——. *Science and Method*, BK I, CH 2–3; BK II, CH 3
CASSIRER. *Substance and Function*, PART I, CH 2–3; SUP VI
E. V. HUNTINGTON. *The Continuum, and Other Types of Serial Order*
——. *The Fundamental Propositions of Algebra*
J. W. YOUNG. *Lectures on Fundamental Concepts of Algebra and Geometry*
JOURDAIN. *The Nature of Mathematics*
O. VEBLEN and YOUNG. *Projective Geometry*
B. RUSSELL. *Principles of Mathematics*, CH I
——. *Philosophical Essays*, CH 3
——. *Mysticism and Logic*, CH 4–5
——. *Introduction to Mathematical Philosophy*, CH 18
N. R. CAMPBELL. *What Is Science?*, CH 6–7
MARITAIN. *An Introduction to Philosophy*, PART II (3)
——. *Theonas, Conversations of a Sage*, VI
NICOD. *Foundations of Geometry and Induction*
WHITEHEAD. *A Treatise on Universal Algebra*
——. *An Introduction to Mathematics*
——. *Science and the Modern World*, CH 2
G. N. LEWIS. *The Anatomy of Science*, ESSAY I–II
HILBERT and ACKERMAN. *Grundzüge der theoretischen Logik*
BUCHANAN. *Poetry and Mathematics*
M. R. COHEN. *Reason and Nature*, BK II, CH I
A. E. TAYLOR. *Philosophical Studies*, CH III
GILSON. *The Unity of Philosophical Experience*, CH 5
DEWEY. *Logic, the Theory of Inquiry*, CH 20
CARNAP. *Foundations of Logic and Mathematics*
BELL. *The Development of Mathematics*
G. H. HARDY. *A Course of Pure Mathematics*
——. *A Mathematician's Apology*
KASNER and NEWMAN. *Mathematics and the Imagination*
COURANT and ROBBINS. *What Is Mathematics?*
WEYL. *The Philosophy of Mathematics and Natural Science*

Chapter 53: MATTER

INTRODUCTION

"AFTER we came out of the church," says Boswell in his *Life of Johnson*, "we stood talking for some time together of Bishop Berkeley's ingenious sophistry to prove the non-existence of matter, and that everything in the universe is merely ideal. I observed that though we are satisfied his doctrine is not true, it is impossible to refute it. I shall never forget the alacrity with which Johnson answered, striking his foot with mighty force against a large stone, till he rebounded from it, 'I refute it thus.'"

But Berkeley's argument anticipated Dr. Johnson's style of refutation. "I do not argue," he says, "against the existence of any one thing that we can apprehend either by sense or reflexion. That the things I see with my eyes and touch with my hands do exist, really exist, I make not the least question. The only thing whose existence I deny is that which *philosophers* call Matter or corporeal substance. And in doing this there is no damage done to the rest of mankind, who, I dare say, will never miss it."

The rest of mankind does need to be instructed, however, that when they use the word "matter," they speak of *nothing*. They may from careless habit suppose they are referring to the most obvious something there is in the world—the solid, massy, concrete stuff of which tangible, visible, movable, and moving things are made. Of them, Berkeley would ask how they know such stuff exists. It is not itself perceptible.

We perceive a variety of qualities—colors, shapes, temperatures, textures, sizes, or extensions—but these, Berkeley argues, have their being *in being perceived*. Even if certain of these sensible qualities, sometimes called "primary," such as figure, size, or weight, are supposed to belong to bodies when they are not actually being sensed, they are not matter, but only its properties. Matter itself is not sensible. Those who assert its existence postulate it as a substratum or support for the sensible qualities they perceive.

The question, therefore, is whether such a substratum is a necessary or an unnecessary hypothesis. Berkeley does not deny the existence of beings which cannot be directly sensed. He affirms the existence of the human spirit or mind, of minds other than his own, and the spiritual being of God. These must be inferred to exist in order to explain the phenomena of our sensible experience and the experience of our own activities in thinking, imagining, willing. If, in addition, the existence of matter or a material substance were necessary to explain the phenomena, Berkeley would not object to affirming its existence by inference, even if it could in no way be directly perceived.

His argument therefore involves, first, a denial of Locke's distinction between primary and secondary qualities. Supposing it to be generally agreed that colors, sounds, odors have no actual existence except in the perceiving mind, he denies that perceptible figure, size, or motion can exist otherwise. "It having been shown that none even of these can possibly exist otherwise than in a Spirit or Mind which perceives them, it follows that we have no longer any reason to suppose the being of Matter."

Matter is not needed as a substratum or support for the qualities we perceive. This is the second main point in Berkeley's argument. "Though we give the materialists their external bodies, they by their own confession are never the nearer knowing how our ideas are produced; since they own themselves unable to comprehend in what manner body can act upon spirit, or how it is possible it should imprint any idea in the mind. Hence it is evident that the production of ideas or sensations in our minds can be no reason why we should suppose Matter or corporeal substances, since that is acknowledged to remain equally inexplicable with or without this supposition."

BERKELEY'S ARGUMENTS against matter, which occupy the greater part of his *Principles of Human Knowledge*, may not have the same force when they are applied against different theories of matter. Berkeley seems to regard his attack on materialism as the refutation of an error at the root of skepticism, atheism, and irreligion. He also thinks materialism creates difficulties for the sciences. But are all affirmations of matter to be lumped together as materialism *in the same sense*? Are Aristotle, Plotinus, Descartes, Spinoza, and Locke materialists in the same sense as Lucretius, Hobbes, and perhaps Marx? Does it make no difference whether bodies are said to be the only real existences, or whether, in addition to bodies, immaterial substances or spiritual beings are also said to exist?

Does it make no difference how matter is conceived—whether as a self-subsistent substance in its own right, capable of existing apart from any qualities except extension and motion which belong to its very essence, or merely as one factor in the constitution of bodies, the factor of potentiality which, as will be presently explained, has no existence apart from the forms which actualize it? Are skepticism, atheism, and irreligion to be associated with all affirmations of matter, in view of the fact that theologians like Augustine and Aquinas seem to think that a sound view of matter supports the truths of religion against the errors of the materialists?

There seem to be, in short, three distinct positions to which Berkeley's blanket denial of matter stands opposed. The diametrically opposite view seems to be the blanket denial of anything except bodies, or of anything which cannot be reduced to a property or function of matter. The atomism of Lucretius, discussed in the chapter on ELEMENT, may be taken as representative of this view, though Engels would insist that materialism can be dialectical rather than atomistic or mechanical.

Between the two extremes, there appear to be two middle positions which are alike insofar as both affirm the immaterial as well as the material. Although they are alike in asserting the existence of spiritual substances, they may, of course, define the nature of these immaterial things differently, and differently interpret their relation to the realm of matter. But, as theories of matter, their principal difference consists in the way in which they conceive the being of bodies, material substances, or the bodily mode of substance.

In the conceptions of Descartes and Locke, for example, it is matter which gives actuality to sensible bodies. We have "no other idea or notion of matter," Locke writes, "but something wherein those many sensible qualities, which affect our sense, do subsist." The entire substance of sensible bodies consists of matter. All their properties derive from the essence or nature of matter. But in the conceptions of Aristotle and Plotinus, bodies would not exist at all if they were composed only of matter, for matter is no more than a capacity for being, not something which by itself actually is. Sensible bodies derive their being and all their attributes from the forms which matter assumes when its potentialities are actualized. Matter totally devoid of form is not the *nothing* Berkeley calls it, but it is so near to nothing that Plotinus says it is "more plausibly called a non-being . . . a bare aspiration towards substantial existence."

These theories of matter or corporeal being seem to be as contrary to one another as together they are contrary to Berkeley's doctrine. Yet each of the two middle positions leans toward one of the opposite extremes.

The conception of matter seems to be very much the same in the complete materialism of Lucretius and Hobbes and in the view of Descartes, Spinoza, and Locke. In the former, only bodies exist. In the latter, bodies do not comprise the whole of existence, but matter is the whole substance of bodies. The separation of body and mind, or matter and spirit, into distinct substances, or modes of substance, leaves matter the same kind of stuff that it is in a world which admits of no other reality. Atomism, furthermore, may be common to both theories, at least to the extent that it is held that the complex bodies we perceive are composed of minute and insensible particles. Unlike Lucretius, Locke may not insist upon the absolute indivisibility of the particles, or upon the eternity of the uncreated atoms of matter;

but he, like Hobbes and Newton, carries the division of the familiar bodies of sense-experience down to parts which cannot be perceived and yet have, in a way, a more ultimate reality as units of matter than the complex bodies they constitute.

"Had we senses acute enough to discern the minute particles of bodies, and the real constitution on which their sensible qualities depend," Locke writes, "I doubt not but that would produce quite different ideas in us; and that which is now the yellow color of gold, would then disappear, and instead of it we should see an admirable texture of parts, of a certain size and figure."

At the other extreme, Berkeley's complete denial of matter has less in common with the view of Aristotle, Plotinus, Augustine, and Aquinas than the theory of Descartes, Spinoza, and Locke has with the materialism of Lucretius and Hobbes. They would appear to be close enough, for one seems to hold that matter is almost non-being and the other that matter is simply nothing at all. But where Berkeley denies any role to matter, Aristotle and those who take his view affirm matter to be an indispensable factor in the constitution of physical things. They do not question the reality of bodies or their existence apart from mind. On both of these points they are as opposed to Berkeley as they would be if they were complete materialists. Nevertheless they lean toward Berkeley rather than toward the other extreme in one respect. Where Berkeley denies the existence of matter, they deny its substantiality. Where Berkeley says matter has no being, they say it has the lowest grade of being—on the very verge of not being!

IN SPITE OF ALL the differences noted, the idea of matter has a certain constant meaning throughout the tradition of the great books.

It is generally associated with the idea of quantity, and especially the basic magnitudes, such as time, space, and mass. Sometimes it is said that the essence of matter itself is extension; sometimes that bodies—not matter itself—have the property of tridimensionality. But in either case that which *is* or *has* matter in it necessarily occupies space.

The manner of that occupation is also generally agreed upon. Two bodies or two distinct quantities of matter cannot occupy the same place at the same time. A body may not be impenetrable in the sense of being indivisible, but so long as it remains the whole that it is, it offers resistance to other bodies tending to move into the place it occupies.

There is another connection between matter and quantity. To those who ask what makes two otherwise identical things two in number—or what is involved in the merely numerical difference of things alike in every other respect—the usual answer is in terms of matter. Matter is traditionally spoken of as "the principle of individuation." Aquinas, for example, holds that angels, unlike physical substances, cannot differ from one another as do numerically distinct individuals. Because they are immaterial, they can differ only as do species or kinds. "Such things as agree in species," he writes, "but differ in number, agree in form, but are distinguished materially. If, therefore, the angels be not composed of matter and form, it follows that it is impossible for two angels to be of one species; just as it would be impossible for there to be several whitenesses apart, or several humanities, since whitenesses are not several, except in so far as they are in several substances."

The way in which matter is related to individual differences can be exemplified in works of art. Two coins, stamped out of the same kind of matter by the impression of the same die, may differ in no other discernible respect than that they are *two* of the same kind. Their *twoness* seems to be somehow related to the fact that each consists of a distinct quantity of matter. But it may be asked how two units of matter have the distinction of being two while they differ in no other respect. One answer to this difficult question is that their distinction consists in their occupying different places. In the Platonic theory of the origin of many particulars all participating in the same form, diversity of place seems to play the role which matter plays for Aristotle and Aquinas.

Plato's doctrine of the receptacle, which is discussed in the chapter on FORM, is sometimes interpreted by conceiving the receptacle as space, and sometimes by conceiving it as matter. The receptacle, it is said in the *Timaeus*, is that which, "while receiving all things, never departs at all from her own nature and never in any way, or at any time, assumes a form like that of any of the things which enter into her." This, according to Plotinus, means that "its one form is an invincible formlessness."

But Plotinus, who combines Plato's doctrine of the receptacle and the forms with Aristotle's theory of potentiality and actuality, holds that it is matter, not space, which is "the receptacle and nurse of all generation." He says that "recipient and nurse" is a better description of matter than the term "mother," for that term "is used by those who think of a mother as matter to the offspring, as a container only, giving nothing to them." In his own view, matter is more than space or mere receptivity. He is willing to admit the "parallel with motherhood" only to the extent that "matter is sterile, not female to full effect, female in receptivity only, not in pregnancy."

TRADITIONALLY, the distinction between universal and particular is understood as a distinction between the intelligible and the sensible. This indicates another traditional meaning of matter or the material. The realm of sensible things is the realm of bodies. But the atoms which are the elementary bodies are also usually called "insensible particles of matter." This, however, can be interpreted to mean, not that a definite material mass or bulk is in itself absolutely *intangible* or *imponderable*, but that, because of the limitation in our senses, it is imperceptible to us. On this interpretation it would then seem possible to say that *all* bodily existence is sensible existence.

But if we ask about the sensibility of matter itself, rather than of bodies large or small, questions arise which are more difficult to solve. On one theory of matter, matter devoid of form is as insensible as it is unintelligible, yet forms which are not material, that is, not in matter, are also insensible but not unintelligible. On the contrary, they are regarded as more perfectly intelligible than embodied forms. How, then, does matter which is itself insensible cause the forms which it assumes to become sensible when they are materialized?

The theory of matter which does not regard it as a co-principle with form seems to be confronted with a different problem of sensibility. It is supposed that some of the qualities which we sense in bodies are actually in them whether we sense them or not—such properties as size, figure, weight, motion. Other sensible qualities, such as colors, odors, temperatures, or sounds, are supposed to be effects produced by the motions of material particles acting on the sensitive apparatus of animals. This distinction between what Locke calls "primary and secondary qualities"—found also in Lucretius and Descartes—is more fully considered in the chapters on QUALITY and SENSE, but here it calls attention to the problem of how matter, devoid of certain sensible qualities, causes these qualities to arise.

For Lucretius the peculiar difficulty of the problem seems to lie in the fact that the sensitive animal is itself nothing but a material system. All its powers and acts are conceived as functions of matter in motion. How, then, does moving matter within the organism generate certain qualities which do not belong to moving matter outside the organism? For Locke the problem raises a difficulty of still another sort. Secondary qualities, such as colors, sounds, odors, exist only as sensations in the mind. In corporeal substances, or bodies, such qualities, he writes, "are nothing but the powers those substances have to produce several ideas in us by our senses; which ideas are not in the things themselves, otherwise than as anything is in its cause." Though they result from the impact of moving particles on the bodily sense-organs, they do not belong to the world of matter at all, but to the realm of spirit. How, then, do the motions of matter cause effects which exist only in the immaterial domain of mind?

These questions indicate some of the problems of matter as an object, condition, or cause of knowledge. They also show how the nature of the problem varies with different conceptions of matter, both in itself and in its relation to mind. There are still other problems which confront those theories of mind which separate reason or intellect from the sensitive faculty.

In such theories the consideration of matter's relation to mind goes beyond the question of the origin of sensations. It takes sensations and images as somehow the functions of living matter—the acts of the various sense-organs and the brain. But sensations and images, because they are acts of corporeal organs, have the same limitation which belongs to everything material. As matter is said to cause the individuality or numerical diversity of bodies, so is it said to make sensations and images "particular intentions of the mind"—that is, capable of representing only particular objects, not general kinds or classes. Hence such theories face the problem of the relation of sensations and images to the "universal intentions of the mind," its general concepts or abstract ideas.

ONE MORE TRADITIONAL meaning of matter remains to be mentioned. The sciences of physics or mechanics are concerned with change or motion. They are not concerned with mutability in general, but with the kind of mutability that is manifested by material things. Material things are never conceived as unmovable or unchangeable.

The question whether matter itself is immutable has different meanings for different theories of matter. On the theory (discussed in the chapter on CHANGE) that matter and form are together principles of change in changing substances, it is neither matter nor form but the substance composite of matter and form which changes. Those who think that the motions of the physical world are without beginning and end, attribute a similar eternity to matter and conceive it as imperishable. The theologians who think that God can annihilate whatever He creates, do not hold that matter is indestructible, but they nevertheless attribute everlasting endurance to matter in God's plan. Aquinas, for example, in his treatise on the end of the world, describes the final conflagration which will purge the material universe but leave its matter in existence under the forms of the elements and the heavenly bodies. "The world will be renewed," he writes, "in such a way as to throw off all corruption and remain forever at rest." Hence nothing can be "the subject of that renewal, unless it be a subject of incorruption," such as "the heavenly bodies, the elements, and man."

On other theories of matter the fact that motion is regarded as an intrinsic property of bodies seems to be similarly consistent with the notion that matter itself is immutable or indestructible. This indestructibility may be conceived in terms of the absolute indivisibility of the atoms, as in Lucretius and Newton; or, as in Spinoza, it may be established by the uncreated and eternal nature of God. "By body," Spinoza writes, "I understand a mode which expresses in a certain and determinate manner the essence of God in so far as He is considered as the thing extended."

In the modern development of the science of mechanics the law of the conservation of matter seems to be another expression of the same insight. "We may lay it down as an incontestable axiom," Lavoisier writes, "that in all the operations of art and nature, nothing is created; an equal quantity of matter exists both before and after the experiment." What appears to be the destruction of a body is merely the transformation of its matter into another physical condition, without loss of mass unless there is an equivalent gain in energy. The total quantity of matter and energy remains constant throughout all physical changes.

But though change or motion seems to be inherent in the material world, the mutability of bodies, as well as the immutability of matter, seems to be differently conceived according to different conceptions of matter. The difference between the physics of Aristotle and the physics of Descartes can be expressed in terms of contrary definitions of motion, or divergent notions of causality, but neither of these differences is fully intelligible apart from the variance of these theories from one another on the nature of matter.

When matter is an actual substance, whose essence is extension and whose chief property is local motion, the principles of physics are mechanical. The laws of mechanics, with time, space, and mass as their fundamental variables, seem to have a universality adequate for describing all natural phenomena. All changes in material things are either the local motions of bodies or the result of the local motions of their parts. Motions are determined in their magnitude and direction by the impressed force which one body exerts upon another and the resistance of that other. Motion is itself completely actual, as matter is; and the only type of cause to which physics need appeal is the efficient cause, that is, the push or pull of one body upon another.

Physicists who share this conception of matter may not agree, as Descartes and Newton do not, in their mechanical formulations. They may or may not be atomists. They may, like Lucretius, think that local motion is an absolutely intrinsic property of the eternal particles; or, like Descartes and Newton, they may think that God first imparted motion to matter at the world's creation. They may hold that all subsequent motions issue therefrom in a continuous chain of cause and effect. But when matter is the only factor in the constitution of bodies, and one body differs from another only in its quantitative determinations, the consequence for physical theory seems to be one or another sort of mechanical formulation.

When matter is nothing more than a body's potentiality for change, and when neither what the body is nor how it changes can be explained by reference to its matter alone, physical theory seems to be constructed in other than mechanical terms. Its concepts and principles resemble those of biology. It finds natural tendencies or desires, and ends or final causes, in the motion of inert as well as animate bodies.

Central to Aristotle's physics are his theory of the four causes, discussed in the chapter on CAUSE, and his theory of the four types of change, discussed in the chapter on CHANGE. But even more fundamental is his definition of motion as the actualization of that which is potential in a respect in which it is potential. With motion so defined, the principles of physics must include the correlative factors of potentiality and actuality which Aristotle conceives in terms of matter and form.

REMOVE MATTER entirely from a thing and, according to Aristotle, you remove its capacity for physical change. Remove form, and you remove its existence, for nothing can exist without being actual or determinate in certain respects. When a thing changes physically, it loses certain determinate characteristics and acquires others. The determinations it acquires it had previously lacked, yet all the while it must have had a capacity for acquiring them. The thing is "capable both of being and of not being," Aristotle says, "and this capacity," he goes on to say, "is the matter in each." The matter of an existing substance is thus conceived as that which has certain forms (the respects in which the substance is actually determinate), and lacks certain forms which it can assume (the respects in which the substance is both indeterminate and potential).

As the chapter on ART indicates, Aristotle frequently uses artistic production to afford a simple illustration of his theory of matter and form as principles of change. When a man sets out to make a bed, he chooses material, such as wood, which can be shaped in a certain way. The same wood could have been made into a chair or a table. With respect to these various possible determinations in structure, the wood is itself indeterminate and determinable.

Before the artist has worked on it productively, the wood is in a state of both privation and potentiality with regard to the form of a bed, a chair, or a table. The transformation which the artist effects consists in his actualizing certain potentialities in the material for forms or determinations which the material at the moment lacks. When the bed is made, the wood or matter which is now actually in the form of a bed may still have the potentiality for being *remade* into a chair or table.

The wood, of course, remains actually wood throughout these artificial changes, as it does not when it suffers the natural change of combustion. This indicates that though the wood may be called matter or material by the artist, it is not matter, but a substance, a thing composite of matter and form; for when the wood is reduced to ashes by fire, the matter which had the form of wood assumes another form.

In the analysis of accidental change, which artistic production illustrates, it suffices to treat a composite substance, like wood or iron or bronze, as the material principle. But in the analysis of substantial change, when matter itself changes from being one kind of matter to being another in the coming to be or perishing of composite substances, the material principle must be pure matter—matter totally devoid of form. Where a whole substance can be regarded as the matter or substratum of accidental change (in quality, quantity, or place) the substratum of substantial change, which Aristotle calls "generation and corruption," must be matter in a condition of absolute indeterminacy and pure potentiality.

Referring to this ultimate substratum as "the

underlying nature," Aristotle says that it "is an object of scientific knowledge by analogy. For as the bronze is to the statue, the wood to the bed, so is the matter and the formless before receiving form to anything which has form, and so also is the underlying nature to substance, *i.e.*, the actually existing."

ARISTOTLE'S DEFINITION of matter as "the primary substratum of each thing, from which it comes to be without qualification, and which persists in the result" not only signifies an object which the physicist must apprehend analogically (*i.e.*, by comparison with substantially formed matter like wood and bronze), but also indicates that matter, by definition, must be in itself both unintelligible and non-existent. What Aristotle calls "the primary substratum" is later called by Plotinus "primal matter," by Augustine "formless matter," and by Aquinas "prime matter." Since they all agree that that which is without form lacks all determination and actuality, they deny that it can have existence by itself or be an object of knowledge, either by sense or reason.

Augustine and Aquinas go further. They deny even to God's omnipotence the power of creating matter without form. They speak of matter not as created, but as *concreated*, that is, united at the very instant of its creation with the forms it must assume in order to exist. God "made formless matter of absolutely nothing, and the form of the world from this formless matter," Augustine writes. Yet He "created both simultaneously, so that form came upon matter with no space of time intervening."

IN THE TRADITION of Aristotle's physics and metaphysics, especially as developed by Aquinas, matter and form become basic analytic terms, often having a significance remote from their original meaning in the analysis of change. The conception of prime (or formless) matter as the substratum of substantial change leads to the designation of the formed matter underlying accidental change as "second matter." This, in turn, is called "signate matter" when, considered as the matter of an individual substance, it is viewed as having the limiting determinations of individuality.

"Matter is twofold," Aquinas writes, "common, and signate or individual; common, such as flesh and bones; and individual, as this flesh and these bones." When the intellect forms concepts of different kinds of physical substances, it abstracts "from the individual sensible matter, but not from the common sensible matter." In defining the nature of man, for example, we abstract, Aquinas says, from "this flesh and these bones, which do not belong to the species as such, but to the individual"; but we do not abstract from the fact that man, consisting of body and soul, is a thing of flesh and bones.

To say that man consists of body and soul is to indicate that common matter enters into the definition of man as a physical substance. But in distinction from definitions of this type, which are proper to physics, mathematical and metaphysical definitions carry the abstraction from matter still further. In mathematics, Aquinas declares, the intellect abstracts "not only from individual sensible matter, but also from common sensible matter." In conceiving numbers and figures, the intellect does not, however, abstract from matter entirely, but only from individual intelligible matter. The common intelligible matter which is represented by "substance as subject to quantity" underlies all mathematical notions. "But some things," Aquinas maintains, "can be abstracted even from common intelligible matter, such as *being*, *unity*, *potency*, *act* and the like, all of which can exist without matter." Such abstraction characterizes the concepts of metaphysics. Aquinas thus differentiates the three speculative sciences of physics, mathematics, and metaphysics in terms of three grades of abstraction, each distinguished by the type of matter from which the concepts of the science are abstracted.

With one exception physical matter is not said to be of different kinds when it exists under different forms. The one exception for both Aristotle and Aquinas is the matter of terrestrial and celestial bodies.

Basing his inference on the observations available to him, Aristotle holds that the heavenly bodies are eternal—"not subject to increase or diminution, but unaging and unalterable and unmodified." Immutable in every other way, they are, however, subject to local motion. Since they are eternal, both their matter and their motion must be different from that of perishable terrestrial bodies. "All things that change have matter," Aristotle writes, "but matter of different sorts; of eternal things those which are not generable but are movable in space have matter—not matter for generation, however, but for motion from one place to another." That motion from place to place is, unlike terrestrial motion, circular; it has the appropriate characteristic of endlessness.

Kepler challenges this theory of a radical difference between celestial and terrestrial matter or motion, and as the chapter on ASTRONOMY shows, by so doing he not only gives impetus to the Copernican system, but also paves the way for Newton to frame laws of motion applicable to matter everywhere in the universe. Because their matter is the same, it is possible, Kepler insists, to explain the motion of the heavenly bodies by the same principles which account for the motion of bodies on earth.

OUTLINE OF TOPICS

1. The conception of matter as a principle of change and as one constituent of the being of changing things: the receptacle or substratum
   - *1a.* Matter and the analysis of change: prime and secondary matter; privation and form; participation and the receptacle
   - *1b.* Matter in relation to the kinds of change: substantial and accidental change; terrestrial and celestial motion
   - *1c.* Matter and the distinction between individual and universal: signate and common matter; sensible and intelligible matter
2. The conception of matter as extension, as a bodily substance, or as a mode of substance: atoms and compound bodies
   - *2a.* The properties of matter: hypotheses concerning its constitution
   - *2b.* The motions of matter or bodies
   - *2c.* Matter as the support of sensible qualities
   - *2d.* The diremption of body and mind, or matter and spirit
3. The existence of matter
   - *3a.* Matter as the sole existent: materialism, atomism
   - *3b.* Matter as the most imperfect grade of being or reality
   - *3c.* Matter as a fiction of the mind
   - *3d.* The relation of God to matter: the creation of matter and its motions
4. Matter as an object or condition of knowledge
   - *4a.* The knowability of matter: by sense, by reason
   - *4b.* The role of matter in the concepts and definitions of the several sciences: the grades of abstraction in physics, mathematics, and metaphysics
   - *4c.* The material conditions of sensation, imagination, and memory
   - *4d.* The material conditions of thought: the relation of matter to the existence and acts of the mind
5. Matter in relation to good and evil
6. Criticisms of materialism and its consequences

REFERENCES

References are listed by volume number (in bold type), author's name, and page number. Bible references are to book, chapter, and verse of the Authorized King James version of the Bible. The abbreviation "esp" calls the reader's attention to one or more especially relevant parts of a whole reference; "passim" signifies that the topic is discussed intermittently rather than continuously in the work or passage cited. Where the work as a whole is relevant to the topic, the page numbers refer to the entire work. For general guidance in the use of *The Great Ideas,* consult the Preface.

1. The conception of matter as a principle of change and as one constituent of the being of changing things: the receptacle or substratum

7 PLATO, 455–458
8 ARISTOTLE, 262–268, 505–508, 534–535, 551–552, 555–570
12 AURELIUS, 310
17 PLOTINUS, 32, 110–119, 281–285
19 AQUINAS, 31–32, 107–108, 662–663
20 AQUINAS, 15–18
35 LOCKE, 295
42 KANT, 72–76, 565

1*a*. Matter and the analysis of change: prime and secondary matter; privation and form; participation and the receptacle

7 PLATO, 455–458
8 ARISTOTLE, 262–268, 269–270, 271, 275–280, 288–289, 290–291, 297, 324–325, 360–362, 393, 403–404, 409–441, 512, 535, 549, 574–575, 594, 598–601
9 ARISTOTLE, 269–271
12 AURELIUS, 281
16 KEPLER, 1078
17 PLOTINUS, 49–60, 307–308
18 AUGUSTINE, 99–100, 102–103
19 AQUINAS, 25, 38–39, 163–164, 249–250, 399–401, 443–444, 489–491, 534–536, 564–568, 720–721
20 AQUINAS, 49–50, 498–499
28 HARVEY, 407–409, 412–415, 494–496
35 BERKELEY, 415
42 KANT, 74–76, 100–101

1*b*. Matter in relation to the kinds of change: substantial and accidental change; terrestrial and celestial motion

8 ARISTOTLE, 304–307, 359–364, 369–375, 402, 403, 409–441, 555, 576, 596–597, 598–601, 636–637
16 PTOLEMY, 5–6, 8, 10–11
16 COPERNICUS, 517–518, 519–520
16 KEPLER, 888–890, 929–930
17 PLOTINUS, 35–37, 103–104
19 AQUINAS, 261–262, 343–347
20 AQUINAS, 5–6
28 GILBERT, 110

1*c*. Matter and the distinction between individual and universal: signate and common matter; sensible and intelligible matter

8 ARISTOTLE, 517, 518, 521–522, 558–561, 578, 599–601, 618–619
12 AURELIUS, 310
17 PLOTINUS, 282
19 AQUINAS, 15–16, 84–85, 162–163, 257–258, 273–274, 292, 382–383, 384–385, 388–391, 604–607
20 AQUINAS, 711–712, 713–714

2. The conception of matter as extension, as a bodily substance, or as a mode of substance: atoms and compound bodies

12 LUCRETIUS, 2–6
17 PLOTINUS, 54–55, 64, 111, 116–119
31 DESCARTES, 28–33, 130, 153–154
31 SPINOZA, 360–361
34 NEWTON, 537, 541
35 LOCKE, 150–154 passim, 204–214 passim
35 BERKELEY, 414–416 passim, 430–431
42 KANT, 99–100, 580
45 LAVOISIER, 3–4
45 FARADAY, 850–855
53 JAMES, 882–884

2*a*. The properties of matter: hypotheses concerning its constitution

8 ARISTOTLE, 410–413, 423–425
10 GALEN, 172–173
12 LUCRETIUS, 2–12, 19–27
16 KEPLER, 936–937
23 HOBBES, 271–272
28 GILBERT, 29–30
28 GALILEO, 178–196 passim
30 BACON, 155
31 DESCARTES, 80
31 SPINOZA, 360–361
34 NEWTON, 5, 270–271, 281–282, 479–485, 531–543
34 HUYGENS, 566–569
35 LOCKE, 129–131, 134–138 passim, 152–154, 200, 204–212 passim, 239, 269, 273
35 BERKELEY, 414–416, 421–422
42 KANT, 137–140
45 LAVOISIER, 9–10, 12–13, 16

45 Faraday, 273–276, 386–390, 604–632
46 Hegel, 160
53 James, 68

2*b*. The motions of matter or bodies

8 Aristotle, 292–297
12 Lucretius, 12–14, 15–19
19 Aquinas, 585–587
23 Hobbes, 50
28 Galileo, 157–171, 197–260
30 Bacon, 162–168, 179–188
31 Descartes, 54–60, 114–115, 231
31 Spinoza, 378–380
34 Newton, 1–372
35 Locke, 178–179, 211–212
51 Tolstoy, 694–695

2*c*. Matter as the support of sensible qualities

8 Aristotle, 680, 683–684
12 Lucretius, 20–21
17 Plotinus, 52–55, 109–119, 196
23 Hobbes, 49, 57
30 Bacon, 170–173
31 Descartes, 229–230
35 Locke, 134–138 passim, 204–205
35 Berkeley, 414–417, 419, 422, 427
35 Hume, 505–506
42 Kant, 15, 100
53 James, 331, 503

2*d*. The diremption of body and mind, or matter and spirit

17 Plotinus, 1–6, 297, 299–300
19 Aquinas, 393–394
30 Bacon, 48–50
31 Descartes, 51–52, 77–81, 96–103, 133, 153–155, 224–225, 231–232, 248
31 Spinoza, 373–375, 376–378, 396–398, 451–452
35 Locke, 205, 227–228, 322, 351–354 passim
53 James, 84–93, 115–119, 139–140, 221–226

3. The existence of matter

3*a*. Matter as the sole existent: materialism, atomism

8 Aristotle, 394, 410–413, 423–425, 501–503, 506–507, 606
12 Lucretius, 2–8
12 Aurelius, 297
17 Plotinus, 50, 52, 192–193, 265–268
18 Augustine, 43–44, 45
19 Aquinas, 256–257, 378–379
23 Hobbes, 269–272
53 James, 95–98, 671, 882–884

3*b*. Matter as the most imperfect grade of being or reality

7 Plato, 423–424
12 Aurelius, 294–295
17 Plotinus, 51, 56–57, 59–60, 113–116
19 Aquinas, 20–21, 93–94, 528–529

3*c*. Matter as a fiction of the mind

35 Berkeley, 413–431 passim, 439–440
35 Hume, 506
42 Kant, 85–91
44 Boswell, 134

3*d*. The relation of God to matter: the creation of matter and its motions

Old Testament: *Genesis*, 1–2
7 Plato, 448–449, 450–451, 466
8 Aristotle, 606
12 Lucretius, 63
18 Augustine, 90–91, 102–103, 104–107, 108–110, 123, 124, 334–335
19 Aquinas, 93–94, 99, 239–240, 242–244, 250–252, 256–257, 341–342, 343–349, 382–383, 484–488, 491, 538–540, 565–566, 598–599
20 Aquinas, 182–184
21 Dante, 116, 126, 150
22 Chaucer, 209
30 Bacon, 17
31 Descartes, 54–56
31 Spinoza, 375
32 Milton, 150–151, 185–186, 187–188, 218–231
34 Newton, 541–543
35 Locke, 351–354
35 Berkeley, 426–428 passim, 430–431
46 Hegel, 156–157

4. Matter as an object or condition of knowledge

4*a*. The knowability of matter: by sense, by reason

7 Plato, 228–229
8 Aristotle, 563–564, 661–662
12 Lucretius, 16
17 Plotinus, 53, 54–55
18 Augustine, 99–100
19 Aquinas, 269–270, 295, 440–464, 465–466
30 Bacon, 114–115
31 Descartes, 75–81 passim, 96–103 passim
35 Locke, 208–212, 313–317 passim, 320–322 passim, 335–336
35 Berkeley, 416–417, 423
35 Hume, 506
42 Kant, 186
46 Hegel, 25
53 James, 140–145, 502–503 passim

4*b*. The role of matter in the concepts and definitions of the several sciences: the grades of abstraction in physics, mathematics, and metaphysics

8 Aristotle, 270–271, 493–494, 547–548, 558–561, 563–564, 565–568, 569–570, 585–586, 609, 632
16 Ptolemy, 5
19 Aquinas, 3–4, 16, 270–272, 381–382
20 Aquinas, 424–425

30 BACON, 43–44, 111, 140
31 DESCARTES, 19, 169–170
35 BERKELEY, 436–439

4c. The material conditions of sensation, imagination, and memory

8 ARISTOTLE, 632, 656, 661, 696
12 LUCRETIUS, 24–26, 44–47, 51–54
19 AQUINAS, 379–381, 394–396, 410–411, 447–449, 450–451
23 HOBBES, 49–51, 62, 172, 258
31 DESCARTES, 18–25 passim
31 SPINOZA, 380–382
34 NEWTON, 518–519
35 LOCKE, 127, 133, 142, 143, 234, 249
35 BERKELEY, 417–418
45 LAVOISIER, 14
49 DARWIN, 85–87, 568–569
53 JAMES, 2–3, 13–19, 26–42, 49–50, 98–106 passim, 348–359, 367–373, 427–433, 455–457, 459–479 passim, 497–501, 520–521
54 FREUD, 351–352, 646–648

4d. The material conditions of thought: the relation of matter to the existence and acts of the mind

8 ARISTOTLE, 638, 661–662, 663–664
12 LUCRETIUS, 31–32, 53–54
17 PLOTINUS, 195
19 AQUINAS, 14–15, 76–77, 289–290, 385–399, 416–417, 440–473, 598–599
20 AQUINAS, 1025–1032
23 HOBBES, 52, 54
31 DESCARTES, 18–20, 53
42 KANT, 23–24, 34, 36, 45–46, 48–49, 63–64, 69–72, 81–83, 85–91, 95, 115, 117–119, 173–174, 281–282, 349–350, 542–543, 570–572, 604
49 DARWIN, 288
53 JAMES, xiii-xiv; 8–67, 69–73, 84–93, 116–119, 151–153, 291–295, 367–373, 455–456, 690, 758–759, 827–835, 856–858
54 FREUD, 367, 382, 384–385, 431

5. Matter in relation to good and evil

7 PLATO, 224–226, 231–234, 452–453, 474, 587–589
8 ARISTOTLE, 267–268
12 EPICTETUS, 114–116
12 AURELIUS, 260
17 PLOTINUS, 27–34, 57, 250, 334–336
18 AUGUSTINE, 32–33, 43–45, 49–50, 334–335
21 DANTE, 107
41 GIBBON, 330

6. Criticisms of materialism and its consequences

7 PLATO, 567–568
8 ARISTOTLE, 633–641
9 ARISTOTLE, 163–164
10 GALEN, 172–173, 185, 188–191
17 PLOTINUS, 78, 79, 194–197
19 AQUINAS, 440–442
28 HARVEY, 355, 495–496
35 BERKELEY, 419, 422, 429–430, 431, 441
42 KANT, 558–559, 582
51 TOLSTOY, 469–472, 589–590, 609, 678, 689–690
53 JAMES, 84–119, 291–295, 655–656, 745, 823–525
54 FREUD, 882–884

CROSS-REFERENCES

For: Other considerations of matter as a principle of change, *see* ART 2b; BEING 7b(5); CHANGE 2a; FORM 1d(1)–1d(2); and for the theory of celestial and terrestrial matter as distinct in kind, *see* ASTRONOMY 8a; BEING 7b(3); CHANGE 7c(4); WORLD 6a.

The conception of matter as potentiality in relation to form as actuality, and for the theory of physical substances as composite of matter and form, *see* BEING 7b(2), 7c(3); FORM 2c(1)–2c(3); INFINITY 4c; MAN 3a; MIND 2b; ONE AND MANY 3b(4); SOUL 3c.

Considerations relevant to the doctrine that matter is the source of numerical diversity or the principle of individuality in material things, *see* SAME AND OTHER 1a; UNIVERSAL AND PARTICULAR 3.

For: The conception of matter or extension as a substance, or as a mode of substance, *see* BEING 7b(4); FORM 2d; MAN 3a; MIND 2d; SOUL 3c.

Atomism as a theory of matter and as a materialistic philosophy of nature, *see* ELEMENT 5a–5h; MIND 2e; and for discussions bearing on materialism as a philosophy of nature, society, and history, *see* ELEMENT 5; HISTORY 4a(2); MAN 3c; WILL 5c.

Matter in relation to mind, or body in relation to soul, *see* MAN 3a; MIND 2a–2e; SOUL 3c, 3e; and for the discussion of immaterial substances, spirits, or beings which exist apart from matter, *see* ANGEL 2, 3b; BEING 7b(2); ETERNITY 4a; FORM 2a, 2d; GOD 4c; MAN 3a(1); MIND 2a; SOUL 3a–3c.

The theological problems of matter, its creation and conservation, *see* GOD 7a; WORLD 4e–4e(1).

The physical properties of matter or bodies and the laws of their motion, *see* ASTRONOMY 8c(3); MECHANICS 4a, 5a–5f(2), 6a–6e; QUANTITY 5d–5e; SPACE 1a–1d; and for the problem of the infinity of matter or of an infinite body, *see* INFINITY 4a–4b.

Matter as an object of knowledge, *see* KNOWLEDGE 5a(2).

Matter in relation to sensation and to sensible qualities, *see* ELEMENT 5e; MECHANICS 4b; QUALITY 1; SENSE 3c(3).

Matter in relation to thought, abstract ideas, or definitions, *see* DEFINITION 6a; FORM 3c; IDEA 2g; MEMORY AND IMAGINATION 6c(1); MIND 1a(2); SENSE 5a; UNIVERSAL AND PARTICULAR 4c.

ADDITIONAL READINGS

Listed below are works not included in *Great Books of the Western World*, but relevant to the idea and topics with which this chapter deals. These works are divided into two groups:

I. Works by authors represented in this collection.
II. Works by authors not represented in this collection.

For the date, place, and other facts concerning the publication of the works cited, consult the Bibliography of Additional Readings which follows the last chapter of *The Great Ideas*.

I.

AQUINAS. *On Being and Essence*
——. *On the Power of God*, Q 4
——. *De Natura Materiae et Dimensionibus Interminalis*
DESCARTES. *The Principles of Philosophy*, PART I, 7–8, 11–12, 62–65; PART II, 22–23; PART III, 48–102; PART IV, 1–27, 31–48
HOBBES. *Concerning Body*, PART II, CH 8
BERKELEY. *Three Dialogues Between Hylas and Philonous*
KANT. *Metaphysical Foundations of Natural Science*
J. S. MILL. *An Examination of Sir William Hamilton's Philosophy*, CH 12–13
ENGELS. *Ludwig Feuerbach and the Outline of Classical German Philosophy*

II.

EPICURUS. *Letter to Herodotus*
ERIGENA. *De Divisione Naturae*
JUDAH HA-LEVI. *Kitab al Khazari*
CRESCAS. *Or Adonai*, PROPOSITIONS 10–12, 16, 19–24
SUÁREZ. *Disputationes Metaphysicae*, V (3), X (3), XII (3), XIII–XV, XVI (1), XXVI (2), XXVII, XXX (4), XXXI (8, 10, 13), XXXIV (5–6), XXXV (3, 6), XXXVI
JOHN OF SAINT THOMAS. *Cursus Philosophicus Thomisticus, Philosophia Naturalis*, PART I, QQ 2–3, 9, 11
DIGBY. *The Nature of Bodies*
MALEBRANCHE. *De la recherche de la vérité*, BK III (II), CH 8 (2)
LEIBNITZ. *New Essays Concerning Human Understanding*, APPENDIX, CH I
VOLTAIRE. "Matter," in *A Philosophical Dictionary*
HOLBACH. *The System of Nature*
J. PRIESTLEY and PRICE. *A Free Discussion of the Doctrine of Materialism and Philosophical Necessity*
SCHOPENHAUER. *The World as Will and Idea*, VOL III, SUP, CH 24
BÜCHNER. *Force and Matter*
HELMHOLTZ. *Popular Lectures on Scientific Subjects*, VII
LANGE. *The History of Materialism*
B. STEWART. *The Conservation of Energy*
MAXWELL. *Matter and Motion*
LOTZE. *Metaphysics*, BK II, CH 5–6
PLANCK. *Das Prinzip der Erhaltung der Energie*
C. S. PEIRCE. *Collected Papers*, VOL VI, par 238–286
PEARSON. *The Grammar of Science*, CH 8
MACH. "On the Principle of the Conservation of Energy," in *Popular Scientific Lectures*
BERGSON. *Matter and Memory*, CH 4
PLEKHANOV. *In Defense of Materialism*
——. *Essays in the History of Materialism*

MCTAGGART. *The Nature of Existence*, CH 34
STOUT. *Mind and Matter*
BROAD. *The Mind and Its Place in Nature*, CH 4
DESCOQS. *Essai critique sur l'hylémorphisme*
G. N. LEWIS. *The Anatomy of Science*, ESSAY IV
MEYERSON. *Identity and Reality*, CH 4–5, 7–8
LENIN. *Materialism and Empiriocriticism*
CASSIRER. *Substance and Function*, SUP IV
WEYL. *Space—Time—Matter*
WHITEHEAD. *An Enquiry Concerning the Principles of Natural Knowledge*, CH 15
B. RUSSELL. *Principles of Mathematics*, CH 53
——. *The Problems of Philosophy*, CH 2–4
——. *Mysticism and Logic*, CH 7
——. *The Analysis of Matter*, CH 1–14
MCDOUGALL. *Modern Materialism and Emergent Evolution*
SANTAYANA. *Scepticism and Animal Faith*, CH 19–20
——. *The Realm of Matter*, CH 2–3, 10
LENZEN. *The Nature of Physical Theory*, PART IV, CH 15
KONINCK. *Le problème de l'indéterminisme*

Chapter 54: MECHANICS

INTRODUCTION

MECHANICS, taken as the name for just one of the physical sciences, would merit no place on a small list of basic, focal terms. But the word "mechanics" means more than that. In the tradition of western thought it signifies a whole philosophy of nature, and it connotes a set of fundamental principles under which, it has been thought, all the physical sciences can be unified.

The principles of mechanics have been applied not only in statics and dynamics, which are concerned with the action and reaction of bodies at rest or in motion, but also in acoustics and optics and the sciences of heat, magnetism, and electricity. They have been extended to astronomical phenomena to constitute what is called "celestial mechanics." They have been thought to govern the action or motion of invisible particles or waves as well as the familiar bodies of ordinary experience. In the range and variety of the phenomena it covers, mechanics would seem to be co-extensive with physics. Such at least appears to be its scope at one stage in the development of natural science.

We shall presently consider the dissatisfaction with the mechanical point of view which causes scientists in our own day to hail the replacement of "classical mechanics" by the "new physics" as a great advance in science. The intellectual significance of this change can be compared with that earlier revolution in the 17th century when the new natural science founded on the achievements of Galileo, Huygens, and Newton replaced the physics of Aristotle which had long reigned as the traditional philosophy of nature. What Einstein calls "the rise and decline of the mechanical point of view" thus seems to provide an apt title for the story of three stages in the history of science, in only one of which does the whole of physics appear to be dominated by mechanics.

One way, then, of understanding the importance of mechanics is in terms of that story. Other chapters, such as ASTRONOMY, CHANGE, ELEMENT, MATTER, PHYSICS, SPACE, and TIME—and perhaps also CAUSE and HYPOTHESIS—tell part of that story, especially the part which turns on the differences between Aristotle's physics (which is neither experimental nor mathematical) and modern physics (which is both). This chapter focuses on issues which fall largely within modern physics—issues belonging to that part of the story which, in the great books, begins with Galileo, Huygens, and Newton and runs to Fourier and Faraday. The story itself does not end there, but the point to which Faraday carries it suggests the sequel in Clerk Maxwell and Einstein, just as Galileo's point of departure reflects antecedents in Aristotle. The great books state the issues sufficiently well, though they do not tell the whole story. That can be fully documented only by a host of supplementary scientific classics in various fields, such as the works listed in the Additional Readings.

IN MODERN TIMES it is accepted that physics should be both experimental and mathematical. No one questions the ideal of unifying the physical sciences and finding the unity in nature's laws. But the question is whether that unification can be achieved under the aegis of mechanics; and the issue is whether physics should gather its experimental findings together under purely mathematical formulations or should also try to give those mathematical formulae a mechanical interpretation.

The issue involves more than a question of scientific method. It concerns the ultimate aim of natural science and the kind of concepts it should employ to fulfill this aim. Should the scientist seek to do no more than describe the phenomena of nature in terms of the simplest and most universal mathematical relations? Or should he go beyond description to an explanation of the phenomena in terms of their causes?

When the issue is thus stated as a choice between being content with description or striving for explanation, it appears to be broader than the question whether physics should or should not be mechanical. Even granted that explanation is desirable, does it necessarily follow that physical explanation must employ the principles and concepts of mechanics? Aristotle's physics, it can be argued, provides a negative answer. His various physical treatises represent a natural science which tries to explain the phenomena without doing so mechanically, just as it tries to describe the phenomena without doing so mathematically.

That the connection of these two features of Aristotle's physics is not accidental seems to be indicated by the conjunction of their opposites in modern physics. When in the 17th century the physicist describes natural phenomena in mathematical terms, he explains them—if he tries to explain them at all—in mechanical terms. "The laws of Mechanics," writes Descartes, "are the laws of Nature." Huygens opens his *Treatise on Light* by referring to optics as the kind of science "in which Geometry is applied to matter"; but he at once expresses the desire to advance this branch of mathematical physics by investigating "the origin and the causes" of the truths already known, in order to provide "better and more satisfactory explanations." Such explanations, he thinks, will be found only if we conceive "the causes of all natural effects in terms of mechanical motions." He declares it his opinion that "we must necessarily do this, or else renounce all hopes of ever comprehending anything in Physics."

Galileo and Newton, as will be noted, do not unqualifiedly share Huygens' view that it is proper for the mathematical physicist to inquire about causes. But they would agree that if any explanation is to be given for laws of nature expressed in mathematical form, one or another type of mechanical hypothesis would be required to state the causes. Postponing for the moment the consideration of whether the investigation of causes belongs to mathematical physics, let us examine what is involved in giving a mechanical explanation of anything and why this type of explanation tends to occur in the causal interpretation of mathematically formulated laws of nature.

Two points seem to constitute the essence of mechanical theory. Both are fundamental notions and both are philosophical in the sense that they do not seem to result from the findings of experimental research. The first point is an exclusive emphasis upon efficient causes, which means the exclusion of other types of causes, especially final and formal causes, from mechanical explanation. As the chapter on CAUSE indicates, efficient causality consists in *one thing acting on another*. But not every sort of action by which one thing affects another is mechanical. According to the doctrine, an efficient cause is mechanical only if it consists in a moving body acting on another by impact, or if it consists in a force exerted by one body to cause motion in another or to change its quantity or direction. The notion of a force which does not work through the impact of one moving thing upon another raises the problem of action-at-a-distance to which we shall return subsequently.

The second fundamental point is an exclusive emphasis upon quantities. Mechanical explanation makes no references to qualities or other attributes of things. Paradoxically this point is sometimes expressed in terms of a distinction between primary and secondary *qualities*; but, as the chapters on QUANTITY and QUALITY point out, the primary qualities are all quantities. According to Locke, they are "solidity, extension, figure, motion or rest, and number"; according to Newton, "the universal qualities of all bodies whatsoever" are "extension, hardness, impenetrability, mobility, and inertia." Others, like Galileo and Descartes, give still different enumerations, but the point remains that the only attributes of bodies which have mechanical significance are measurable quantities. Such secondary qualities, for example, as colors and tones belong to the physical world (as it is mechanically conceived) only by reduction to the local motion of particles or waves having certain velocities, lengths, or other quantitative attributes.

We need not be concerned here with what sort of reality is assigned to secondary qualities, or how their presence in experience is accounted for. These problems are discussed in other chapters, such as QUALITY and SENSE. However they are solved, the philosophy of mechanism excludes from the physical world whatever does not consist in, or cannot be reduced to, quantities of matter (or mass), motion, or force, and such related quantities as those of time and space (or distance).

The two points of mechanical theory are obviously connected, for the kind of cause which mechanical explanation employs to the exclusion of all others consists in a quantity of motion or of force. Just as obviously, mechanical explanation, dealing only in quantities and in causes which are quantitatively measurable, is precisely the type of explanation which would seem to be appropriate if one felt called upon to give an interpretation of the mathematical relationships which the mathematical physicist formulates as laws of nature. These mathematical laws are after all statements of the relations among physical quantities which have been subjected to experimental determination or measurement.

AS A PHILOSOPHICAL theory the mechanical view of nature antedates modern physical science. The atomistic conception of the world, which Lucretius expounds, contains both of the fundamental points of mechanism—the doctrine of primary and secondary qualities and the doctrine that all effects in nature are produced by efficient moving causes.

The controversy over mechanism is also ancient. Aristotle denies both points of doctrine in his criticism of the Greek atomists, Democritus and Leucippus; and in the exposition of his own physical theories he states an opposite view. To qualities and qualitative change he assigns physical reality. He explains change in terms of four types of causes, not one. He does not exclude the mechanical type of cause in his explanation of local motion. On the contrary, with respect to local motion his theory that a body in motion must be directly acted upon by a moving cause throughout the period of its motion, seems to be more mechanical than the modern theory that no cause need be assigned for the continuing uniform motion of a body along a straight line but only for a change in its direction or velocity.

What is new in modern times is not the philosophical doctrine of mechanism, but the introduction of mechanical explanation into experimental and mathematical physics, and the controversy about whether it belongs there or can be defended as useful. The so-called rise and decline of the mechanical view in modern physics is connected with experimental discoveries and mathematical formulations. It is not an alternation between success and failure on the level of philosophical argument concerning the ultimate truth of mechanical conceptions. When these conceptions are rejected, it is not for the sake of returning to opposite notions in physical theory, such as those of Aristotle, but rather because, as Einstein says, "science did not succeed in carrying out the mechanical program convincingly, and today no physicist believes in the possibility of its fulfillment."

There is a touch of prophecy in the conversation Swift imagines taking place between Aristotle and the physicists of the 17th century. According to Swift, when Aristotle was confronted with Descartes and Gassendi, he "freely acknowledged his own mistakes in natural philosophy, because he proceeded in many things upon conjecture, as all men must do; and he found that Gassendi, who had made the doctrine of Epicurus as palatable as he could, and the *vortices* of Descartes, were equally exploded. He predicted the same fate to *attraction*, whereof the present learned are such zealous asserters. He said that new systems of nature were but new fashions, which would vary in every age; and even those who pretend to demonstrate them from mathematical principles, would flourish but a short period of time, and be out of vogue when that was determined."

BOTH GALILEO and Descartes re-state the philosophical doctrine which first appears in ancient atomism, but both re-state it in a way that suggests its utility for an experimental investigation of nature. It is significant that Galileo's statement occurs in the context of his concern with the nature and causes of heat. He wishes to explain, he writes in *Il Saggiatore*, why he thinks that "motion is the cause of heat." To do this he finds it necessary to question a prevalent notion "which is very remote from the truth"—the belief that "there is a true accident, affection, or quality, really inherent in the substance by which we feel ourselves heated." He denies the physical reality of heat as an inherent quality of bodies on the same ground that he denies the physical reality of other qualities. "I do not believe," he declares, "that there exists anything in external bodies for exciting tastes, smells, and sounds, but size, shape, quantity, and motion, swift or slow; and if ears, tongues, and noses were removed, I am of the opinion that shape, quantity, and motion would remain, but there would be an end of smells, tastes, and sounds, which, apart from the living creature, I regard as mere words."

Descartes' statement of the doctrine is bolder, perhaps, in its suggestion of a mechanical program for physical research. "Colors, odors, savors, and the rest of such things," he writes, are "merely sensations existing in my thought." They differ from the real properties of bodies just as much as "pain differs from the shape and motion of the instrument which inflicts it." The true physical properties, such as "gravity, hardness, the power of heating, of attracting and purging" consist, in Descartes' opinion, "solely in motion or its absence, and in the configuration and situation of [bodily] parts."

As a philosophical doctrine, the mechanical view is not necessarily tied to atomism. Descartes opposes atomism as plainly as does Aristotle. Furthermore, Newton, who is an atomist, disagrees with both Descartes and the Greek atomists on one fundamental point in mechanical theory. The ancient atomists make the actual motion of one particle in collision with another the indispensable cause of a change of motion in the latter. Descartes likewise requires one motion to be the cause of another and explains gravity in terms of actual bodily motions. Newton rejects Descartes' mechanical hypothesis of material vortices as the cause of gravitation. He seems to have this in mind, and to put Descartes in the same class with Aristotle, when he says that "hypotheses, whether metaphysical or physical, whether of occult qualities or mechanical, have no place in experimental philosophy."

The force of gravity, according to Newton, is a power of attraction which one body exercises on another without the first being in motion or coming into contact with the second. Newton acknowledges the problem of action-at-a-distance which his theory raises. For the most part he lets it stand as a problem which does not affect the mathematical results of his work. But in the Queries he attaches to his *Optics* he suggests, by way of solution, the hypothesis of an ether as the continuous medium through which gravitational force is exerted. In the opinion of later physicists, Newton's hypothesis is no less mechanical than Descartes'. Nor does there seem to be any philosophical grounds for preferring one hypothesis to the other.

But Newton's quarrel with Descartes is not on a philosophical issue. It turns on which mechanical conception, if any at all is to be offered, fits best with the mathematical laws of terrestrial and celestial motion which Newton had succeeded in formulating as universal laws of nature. Those mathematical laws, moreover, had the merit of fitting the observed phenomena and so, of realizing the scientific ideal of accurate description stated in the most generalized form. Newton's triumph over Descartes, then, is a triumph in mathematical and experimental physics, not a triumph in philosophy.

Pope's couplet

Nature and Nature's Laws lay hid in Night,
God said, Let Newton be, and all was light

records that triumph, and celebrates the illumination of nature by the mechanical as well as the mathematical principles of Newton's physics. Newton's picture of the world dominates the mind of a century and controls its science. Locke speaks of "the incomparable Mr. Newton" and of "his never enough to be admired book"; Hume refers to him as the philosopher who, "from the happiest reasoning . . . determined the laws and forces, by which the revolutions of the planets are governed and directed"; and even Berkeley, who challenges his theories of space, time, and attraction, regrets that he must take issue with "the authority of so great a man," a man "whom all the world admires" as the author of "a treatise on Mechanics, demonstrated and applied to nature."

Newton's achievement is to have accomplished an extraordinary synthesis of all that was good in previous scientific work, and a sweeping criticism of all that was considered stultifying. That so many and such varied phenomena should be organized mathematically by a theory as simple as Newton's, is altogether impressive. Equally astonishing is the predictive power of Newton's laws and the explanatory power of his mechanics, not to mention the technological fruits of the latter in mechanical engineering and the invention of machinery of all sorts. Whatever difficulties are implicit in the Newtonian mechanics—subsequently to become, with new discoveries, more and more perplexing—the scope and grandeur of Newton's book gives mechanics a commanding position with respect to the future of science for at least two centuries.

In the century between the publication of Newton's *Mathematical Principles* and the publication in 1787 of Lagrange's *Mécanique analytique*, "the notion of the mechanical explanation of all the processes of nature," writes Whitehead, "finally hardened into a dogma of science." In the next century, the mechanical dogma spreads from physics and chemistry throughout the whole domain of natural science—into biology and psychology—and even beyond that, into economics and sociology. Books bear such titles as *The Mechanistic Conception of Life*, *The Mechanism of Human Behavior*, *Social Statics*, *Social Dynamics*. At the end of the 19th century, James notes the conquests which are being made on all sides by the mechanical idea. "Once the possibility of *some* kind of mechanical interpretation is established," he writes, "Mechanical Science, in her present mood, will not hesitate to set her brand of ownership upon the matter."

James himself testifies to the persuasiveness and success of the mechanical dogma, though not without some resentment. "The modern mechanico-physical philosophy, of which we are so proud," he says, "because it includes the nebular cosmogony, the conservation of energy, the kinetic theory of heat and gases, etc., etc., begins by saying that the *only* facts are collocations and motions of primordial solids, and the only laws the changes in motion which changes in collocation bring. The ideal which this philosophy strives after," he continues, "is a mathematical world-formula, by which, if all the collocations and motions at a given moment were known, it would be possible to reckon those of any wished-for future moment, by simply considering the necessary geometrical, arithmetical, and logical implications."

Laplace had in fact pictured a lightning calculator who, given the total configuration of the world at one instant, would be able to bring the whole future "present to his eyes." And James quotes Helmholtz to the effect that the whole problem of physical science is "to refer natural phenomena back to unchangeable attractive and repulsive forces whose intensity depends wholly upon distance. The solubility of this problem is the condition of the complete comprehensibility of nature."

In commenting on this, James admits that "the world grows more orderly and rational to the mind, which passes from one feature of it to another by deductive necessity, as soon as it conceives it as made up of so few and so simple phenomena as bodies with no properties but number and movement to and fro." But he also insists that it is "a world with a very minimum of rational *stuff*. The sentimental facts and relations," he complains, "are butchered at a blow. But the rationality yielded is so superbly complete in *form* that to many minds this atones for the loss, and reconciles the thinker to the notion of a purposeless universe, in which all the things and qualities men love . . . are but illusions of our fancy attached to accidental clouds of dust which will be dissipated by the eternal cosmic weather as careless as they were formed."

With the 20th century a change occurs. The dogma of mechanism may continue to spread in other sciences and gain even wider acceptance as a popular philosophical creed, but within the domain of the physical sciences, certain mechanical conceptions become suspect and a wholesale rejection of classical mechanics (which becomes identified with Newtonian physics) is called for.

Einstein, for example, quotes the passage from Helmholtz that James had cited, in which Helmholtz goes on to say that the vocation of physics "will be ended as soon as the reduction of natural phenomena to simple forces is complete." This "*mechanical view*, most clearly formulated by Helmholtz," Einstein concedes, "played an important role in its time"; but, he adds, it "appears dull and naive to a twentieth century physicist."

Einstein reviews the assumptions which physicists had to make in order to construct a mechanical theory of light, gravitation, and electricity. "The artificial character of all these assumptions," he says, "and the necessity for introducing so many of them all quite independent of each other, was enough to shatter the belief in the mechanical point of view. . . . In the attempt to understand the phenomena of nature from the mechanical point of view," he continues, "throughout the whole development of science up to the twentieth century, it was necessary to introduce artificial substances like electric and magnetic fluids, light corpuscles, or ether." According to Einstein, "attempts to construct an ether in some simple way" have been "fruitless"; but what is more important in his opinion, such failures "indicate that the fault lies in the fundamental assumption that it is possible to explain all events in nature from a mechanical point of view."

Does this mean that the contemporary physicist has found another and better way of explaining nature? Is there a non-mechanical way of explaining the phenomena, which fits the mathematical laws of experimental physics; or does discarding mechanics mean relinquishing all efforts to explain nature?

Eddington suggests an answer. "One of the greatest changes in physics between the nineteenth century and the present day," he writes, "has been the change in our ideal of scientific explanation. It was the boast of the Victorian scientist that he would not claim to understand a thing until he could make a model of it; and by a model he meant something constructed of levers, geared wheels, squirts, and other appliances familiar to the engineer. Nature in building the universe was supposed to be dependent on just the same kind of resources as any human mechanic. . . . The man who could make gravitation out of cogwheels would have been a hero in the Victorian age." Today, however, Eddington continues, "we do not encourage the engineer to build the world for us out of his material, but we turn to the mathematician to build it out of his material."

We may turn to the mathematician's construction of the world in his terms; but in the tradition of western thought, mathematically formulated laws of nature are not, with the single exception perhaps of the Pythagoreans, regarded as explanations of why things behave as they do or how they work. The change from the 19th to the 20th century with respect to "our ideal of scientific explanation" cannot, then, be the substitution of the mathematical for the mechanical account of why and how. The shift from mechanics to mathematics is rather a shift from explanation as the scientific ideal to the statement of laws which, while having maximum generality, remain purely descriptive. What Eddington means by building the world out of the material of mathematics seems to be the same as what Galileo means, four centuries earlier, when he says that the book of nature "is written in mathematical language." The materials are such symbols as "triangles, circles, and other geometrical figures." Without the help of these, Galileo writes to Kepler, nature "is impossible to comprehend."

But does the mathematical comprehension of nature mean a causal explanation of it? More explicitly than Eddington, Galileo insists that explanation—at least in the sense of stating the causes—is not the business of the mathematical physicist. In a passage which cannot be read too often or examined too closely, he names three opinions which the philosophers have expressed about "the cause of the acceleration of natural motion." Some, he says, "explain it by attraction to the center, others to repulsion between the very small parts of the body, while still others attribute it to a certain stress in the surrounding medium which closes in behind the falling body and drives it from one of its positions to another. Now all of these fantasies," he continues, "and others too, ought to be examined, but it is not really worthwhile."

They ought to be examined by philosophers, perhaps, but debating them is not worthwhile in "those sciences where mathematical demonstrations are applied to natural phenomena." Perfectly defining the program of mathematical physics, Galileo sets himself a limited task:

"merely to investigate and to demonstrate some of the properties of accelerated motion (whatever the cause of this acceleration may be)." It should be noted that of the three opinions about causes which Galileo mentions, the first, which anticipates Newtonian attraction, is no less summarily dismissed than the third, which summarizes the Aristotelian theory.

"What I call Attraction," Newton later writes, "may be performed by impulse or by some other means unknown to me. I use that word here to signify only in general any force by which bodies tend towards one another, whatsoever be the cause." It is well known, he asserts in the same passage of the *Optics*, "that bodies act one upon another by the attractions of gravity, magnetism, and electricity"; but, he goes on, "how these attractions may be performed I do not here consider."

Newton's attitude toward causes and explanation would seem to be identical with Galileo's. Galileo calls opinions about causes "fantasies" and dismisses them; Newton calls them "hypotheses" and seems to banish them as resolutely. "Hypotheses are not to be regarded in experimental philosophy," he declares in one place; and in another, having just referred to predecessors who feigned hypotheses "for explaining all things mechanically," he says that, on the contrary, "the main business of natural philosophy is to argue from phenomena without feigning hypotheses."

The task of the physicist who is both experimental and mathematical in his method, Newton plainly states, is "to derive two or three general principles of motion from phenomena, and afterwards to tell us how the properties and actions of all corporeal things follow from those manifest principles. [This] would be a very great step in philosophy, though the causes of those principles were not yet discovered. And therefore," he says of his own work, "I scruple not to propose the principles of motion above mentioned, they being of very general extent, and leave their causes to be found out."

The two or three principles of motion mentioned in this passage from the *Optics* are the foundation of Newton's other great work, the *Mathematical Principles of Natural Philosophy*. Its title indicates the clearly conceived intention of its author to limit himself to the program of mathematical physics on which both he and Galileo seem to agree. He will not try to define "the species or physical qualities of forces"; he will only investigate "the quantities and mathematical proportions of them." In the General Scholium with which the *Mathematical Principles* concludes, Newton disavows once more any knowledge of the cause of gravity. "To us it is enough," he says, "that gravity does really exist, and acts according to the laws which we have explained, and abundantly serves to account for all the motions of the celestial bodies, and of our sea." Admitting that he has "not been able to discover the causes . . . of gravity from phenomena," Newton flatly reiterates his policy: "I frame no hypotheses."

In view of this policy, how does the name of Newton come to be associated with the triumph of the mechanical point of view in physics? Why do contemporary scientists like Einstein identify Newtonian physics with classical mechanics? If a mathematical physicist, like Newton or Galileo, refrains from guessing at or asserting causes, how can he be charged with having indulged in the impurity of a mechanical explanation of the phenomena, and with having foisted a mechanical conception of the universe upon mankind?

The answer to these questions, so far as Newton is concerned, may be partly found in his own writings. He did not, it seems, entirely disavow an inquiry into the cause of attractive force, as in itself either misguided or irrelevant to science. "We must learn from the phenomena of nature," he tells us, "what bodies attract one another, and what are the laws and properties of the attraction, before we enquire the cause by which the attraction is performed." This statement postpones, but does not exclude, an inquiry into causes. In another statement, Newton even gives us a reason for the postponement. "In mathematics," he says, "we are to investigate the quantities of force with their proportions consequent upon any conditions supposed; then, when we enter upon physics, we compare those proportions with the phenomena of nature, that we may know the several kinds of attractive bodies. And this preparation being made, we argue more safely concerning the physical species, causes, and proportions of the forces."

These remarks of Newton do not give the whole answer. For the other and perhaps more important part of it, we must go to the actual development of physical science in the 17th century. The steps in this development—largely discoveries and formulations made by Galileo, Huygens, and Newton—lead to crises from which the scientists could not extricate themselves without discussing causes—the causes of gravity and of the propagation of light. We may thus be able to understand why Newton could not abandon the search for causes; and why, in the Queries he appended to the *Optics*, he proposes a mechanical hypothesis in order to explain how the attractive force of gravity exerts itself across great distances, and also defends his mechanical theory of light against the equally mechanical but different hypothesis of Huygens.

It might well be argued that, though Galileo's pure position initiated modern mathematical physics, it was the persistence of impurity in the worrying about causes, or even the inescapability of such concern, which caused great scientific advances to be made. The concern about causes seems to provide, time and time again, the pivot for new discoveries. The causes are not found, but new hypotheses are made, and these, when employed, lead to wider, more general results in the form of more inclusive, unifying laws. We see this happen not only in the study of gravitation and light, but also in the investigation of heat and electricity. The concern of Faraday, for example, to explain electrical attraction and repulsion in terms of the action of contiguous particles, and to establish the existence of physical lines of force, leads to Maxwell's theory of the electro-magnetic field; and his field equations, combined with Faraday's speculations concerning the relation between electrical and gravitational attraction, lead to the attempt, on the part of contemporary physics, to construct a unified field theory covering all physical phenomena.

Physics may return in the 20th century to the purely mathematical character it had at the beginning of its modern development. But as may be seen in any introduction to recent physics written for the layman, it is necessary to mark the influence of mechanical conceptions upon scientific discovery and thought, in order to understand the difference between the unifying mathematical laws of the 17th and the 20th centuries. As we retrace the steps we see how fertile is the interplay between mathematical insights and mechanical hypotheses.

AS FOURIER TELLS the story of "rational mechanics," the "discoveries of Archimedes" begin the science. "This great geometer," he says, "explained the mathematical principles of the equilibrium of solids and fluids. About eighteen centuries elapsed before Galileo, the originator of dynamical theories, discovered the laws of motion of heavy bodies." Statics and dynamics are related as the two parts of mechanics when that is conceived narrowly as the science which treats of the local motions of inert or inanimate bodies. The rest or equilibrium of bodies, which is the subject of statics, can be thought of as a limiting case of their motions, to which the principles of dynamics apply.

In the eighteen centuries between Archimedes and Galileo, little progress is made in mechanics. So far as statics is concerned, Archimedes, according to Galileo, by the "rigor of his demonstration" established the science in all its essentials; "since upon a single proposition in his book on Equilibrium depends not only the law of the lever but also those of most other mechanical devices." Pascal may later enlarge statics, by showing in his treatise *On the Equilibrium of Liquids* that "a vessel full of water is a new principle of Mechanics, a new machine which will multiply force to any degree we choose"; in other works Pascal extends these conceptions further, as in his treatment of the pressure of air. But at the time of Galileo, it could be said that although Archimedes had offered an exemplary model of mathematical physics, no progress was made until the work of Galileo's immediate predecessors.

Not without assistance from certain predecessors like Stevin, Galileo founds the science of dynamics. It may be wondered why, with the start made by Archimedes, no earlier application of his principles and method had been made. The answer may be found in the physics of Aristotle. His theory of the four elements carried with it a doctrine of natural motions to different natural places, drawn from the observation of fire rising, stones dropping, air bubbling up through water. Such a doctrine would prevent the search for laws of motion applicable to all bodies; and the general character of Aristotle's physics, treating qualities as well as quantities, seems to have discouraged the application of mathematics even to the study of local motions.

The mathematical expression of the laws of motion is Galileo's objective. His interest in the new astronomy which affirmed the motion of the earth led him, he told Hobbes, to the careful study of movements on the earth. His aim is simply to describe with precision the motions to be found in a child's play—stones dropped and stones thrown, the one the natural motion of free fall, the other the violent motion of a projectile. It is clear to observation that the motion of a freely falling body is accelerated. But though, as a mathematical physicist, Galileo refrains from asking why this is so, he is not satisfied to know simply that it is so. He wants to know the properties of such acceleration. What is the relation of the rate of increase in velocity to the durations and distances of the fall? How much increase in velocity is acquired and how fast? What is the body's velocity at any given point in the fall? Similarly, when Galileo turns to projectiles, he wants to know, not merely that their trajectory is consistently curvilinear, but precisely what curve the path of the projectile describes.

Galileo succeeds in answering all these questions without being perturbed by any of the philosophical perplexities connected with space and time; nor does he allow questions about the forces involved in these motions to distract him from his purpose to "demonstrate everything by mathematical methods." With mathematical demonstration he combines observation and experiment and uses the latter to determine which mathematical conclusions can be applied to nature—which principles can be empirically verified as well as mathematically deduced.

One of Galileo's principles, however, seems to outrun ordinary experience and to defy experimental verification. In the interpretation of his experiments on inclined planes, Galileo expresses an insight which Newton later formulates as the first law of motion, sometimes called the "law of inertia." It declares that "every body continues in its state of rest, or of uniform motion in a right line, unless it is compelled to change that state by forces impressed upon it." Though Newton describes his method as one of "making experiments and observations, and in drawing general conclusions from them by induction," the law of inertia seems to be an exception; for it is difficult to say, as Hume does, that "we find by experience that a body at rest or in motion continues forever in its present state"—that is, *unless* it is acted on by some new force.

The condition introduced by "unless" raises Poincaré's question: "Have there ever been experiments on bodies acted on by no forces?" If not, and if they are impossible, then James may be right in saying that "the elementary laws of mechanics" are "never matters of experience at all, but have to be disengaged from under experience by a process of elimination, that is, by ignoring conditions which are always present." Because "the idealized experiment [which it calls for] can never be performed," the law of inertia, according to Einstein, can be derived "only by speculative thinking consistent with observation."

In any case, the first law of motion initiates a new departure in physics. So far as local motion is concerned, Aristotle and his followers look for the cause which keeps a moving body in motion or a stationary body at rest. According to Galileo and Newton, uniform motion continues naturally without cause. Only a change in the velocity or direction of that motion requires a cause, such as a force impressed upon it.

How radical this innovation is may be judged from its consequences in celestial mechanics, which in turn lead to a completely unified dynamics for both celestial and terrestrial motions. These advances are the work of Newton's mathematical genius, but the ground for them had been laid by the investigations of Galileo. Galileo had resolved the curvilinear motion of a projectile into the imparted rectilinear motion and the deflecting pull of gravity. This composition of forces—sometimes called the "parallelogram law"—explains why the path of the projectile is a parabola. The path of the planets in their orbits, Kepler had previously shown, is another conical curve—an ellipse. But Kepler, lacking the first law of motion, could theorize physically about the cause of the planetary orbits only by looking for a force, projected outward from the sun, which would sweep around to keep the planets moving in their paths. On the other hand, a follower of Galileo, as Whitehead points out, would seek "for normal forces to deflect the direction of motion along the curved orbit." He would look for a force pulling the planet off its own rectilinear course inward toward the sun.

That is precisely what Newton did. When the problem, which others had been able to formulate, was put to Newton, he simply went to his study for the solution. He had solved that problem some years before. He had found the law of the force which, attracting the planets to the sun, would produce their elliptical paths and the other proportionalities stated in Kepler's purely descriptive laws.

With that single discovery, Galileo's terrestrial dynamics becomes a celestial one, too; and the traditional separation of the heavens from the earth is overcome. Newton goes even further. He guesses, and then shows by arithmetic, that the force deflecting the planets around the sun and the moon around the earth, is the same force which makes apples fall and stones heavy in the hand. He generalizes this insight in his famous inverse-square law: "Every particle of matter attracts every other particle of matter with a force proportional to the mass of each and to the inverse square of the distance between them."

Accordingly, the world can be pictured as one in which material particles each have position in absolute space and a determinate velocity. The velocity of each particle causes the change of its position, and changes in velocity are caused by forces, the amounts of which are determined by positions. From his laws of motion and this simple law of force Newton is able, by mathematical deduction, to account for the perturbations of the moon, the oblateness of the earth, the precession of the equinoxes, the solar and lunar tides, and the paths of the comets.

But is Newton's law of force as simple as it appears to be at first? Its mathematical meaning is plain enough, and its application to measured phenomena reveals its descriptive scope. When we ask, however, about its physical significance, we raise difficult questions concerning the nature of this attractive force and how it operates. To call it the "force of gravity" and to point out that this is a familiar force which everyone experiences in his own person hardly answers the question.

GALILEO WOULD NOT have tried to answer it. In his *Dialogues Concerning the Two Great Systems of the World*, one of the characters, Simplicio, refers to that manifest cause which "everyone knows is gravity." To this Salviati replies: "You should say that everyone knows it is *called* gravity. I do not question you about the name," he continues, "but about the essence of the thing"; and that, he concludes, is precisely what cannot be defined.

A physicist like Huygens, who expects the explanation of natural effects to be expressed in the familiar mechanical terms of bodily impact, has other objections. "I am not at all pleased," he writes to Leibnitz about Newton, "with any theories which he builds on his principle of attraction, which seems to me absurd." What shocks Huygens is a scandal that Newton himself cannot avoid facing. It is the scandal of action-at-a-distance—of the force of gravity being propagated instantaneously across great distances and producing effects at some remote place but no effects along the way. Newton recognizes the strangeness of such a force. In a letter to Bentley, he echoes Huygens' protest to Leibnitz. "That gravity should be innate, inherent and essential to matter," he says, "so that one body may act on another at a distance through a vacuum, without the mediation of anything else, by and through which their action and force may be conveyed from one to another, is to me so great an absurdity, that I believe no man who has in philosophical matters a competent faculty of thinking, can ever fall into it."

The absurdity of action-at-a-distance seems to be recognized by common sense and philosophy alike. "No action of an agent," Aquinas remarks, "however powerful it may be, acts at a distance except through a medium"; and

Kant, who regards Newtonian physics as the model of a rational science of nature, speaks of "*a force of attraction without contact*" as a "chimerical fancy" which "we have no right to assume." How can Newton avoid this absurdity without violating his rule of method in mathematical physics—not to frame hypotheses?

Newton's dilemma can perhaps be stated in the following alternatives: *either* the inverse-square law of gravitational attraction is to be treated as a purely mathematical, and hence a purely descriptive, proposition of great simplicity and generality; *or* it must be given physical meaning by a causal explanation of how gravitational force operates. On the first alternative, Newton can avoid framing hypotheses, but the physical meaning of the concepts he employs to state the mathematical law is then left dark. On the second alternative, he can solve the mechanical problem created by such words in his law as "attracts" and "force," but only by going beyond mathematical physics into the realm of mechanical hypotheses.

Newton seems to take the first alternative in his *Mathematical Principles of Natural Philosophy*, and the second in his *Optics*. There he proposes the hypothesis of an ethereal medium to explain the attractive force of gravity. "Is not this medium," he asks, "much rarer within the dense bodies of the sun, stars, planets, and comets, than in the empty celestial spaces between them? And in passing from them to great distances, doth it not grow denser and denser perpetually, and thereby cause the gravity of those great bodies towards one another, and of their parts towards the bodies; every body endeavoring to go from the denser parts of the medium towards the rare? . . . And though this increase of density may at great distances be exceeding slow, yet if the elastic force of this medium be exceeding great, it may suffice to impel bodies from the denser parts of the medium towards the rarer, with all that power which we call gravity."

The hypothesis fits the law of gravitation if, as Maxwell points out, "the diminution of pressure [in the ether] is inversely as the distance from the dense body." Newton recognized, according to Maxwell, that it then becomes necessary "to account for this inequality of pressure in this medium; and as he was not able to do this, he left the explanation of the cause of gravity as a problem for succeeding ages. . . . The progress made towards the solution of the problem since the time of Newton," Maxwell adds, "has been almost imperceptible."

The problem of the mechanical properties of an ethereal medium occurs in another form in the field of optics. Here it is complicated by the rivalry between two theories of light—Newton's corpuscular theory and Huygens' undulatory or wave theory. Each involves a mechanical hypothesis—one concerning the motion of particles emitted from the light source, and one concerning the wave-like propagation of the light impulse through a medium. Both theories involve the motion of particles. In their explanation of the oar which appears bent in the water, both appeal to the action of the particles in the refracting medium on the light corpuscles or the light waves.

Both theories, furthermore, are expressed by their authors in a mathematical form which permits the deduction of quantitative facts like the equality of the angles of incidence and of reflexion, the bending of the light ray in refraction according to the law of sines, and the recently discovered fact of the finite velocity of light. Huygens' book gives prominence to the explanation of the strange phenomena of double refraction found in "a certain kind of crystal brought from Iceland"—Iceland spar. But both theories seem to be equally competent in dealing with the established facts of reflexion and refraction, and the new facts about dispersion.

For a century at least, their rivalry resembles that between the Ptolemaic and Copernican theories at a time when they seemed equally tenable so far as accounting for the phenomena was concerned. Later, new discoveries, such as those by Young and Fresnel, tend to favor the wave theory of light; but the rivalry continues right down to the present day. It remains unresolved, at least to an extent which prompts Eddington, in reviewing contemporary controversy about the nature of light and electricity, to suggest the invention of the word "wavicle" to signify the complementary use of both particles and waves in the modern theory of radiation.

Unlike the rivalry between the Ptolemaic and Copernican systems, which seemed for a while to be entirely a matter of different mathematical descriptions of the same phenomena, the conflict between these two theories of light involves from the very beginning an issue between diverse mechanical hypotheses to explain the phenomena. That issue is argued not only with respect to the adequacy of either theory to explain such phenomena as the rectilinear propagation of light and its different behavior in different mediums; but it is also debated in terms of the underlying mechanical conceptions. As gravitational force acting at a distance raises a mechanical problem which Newton's ether is not finally able to solve, so Huygens' ether as the medium through which light is propagated in waves raises mechanical problems which, if insoluble (as they seem to be), contribute even more heavily to the general scientific scandal of mechanics.

The two authors take different attitudes toward hypotheses and mechanical explanation. Huygens, as we have seen, begins his book with the express intention to "investigate . . . the causes" and to express them "in terms of mechanical motions." Newton, on the other hand, begins his with a reiteration of his disavowal of hypotheses. "My design in this book," he writes, "is not to explain the properties of light by hypotheses, but to propose and prove them by reason and experiments." Nevertheless, Newton's explanation of how the prism produces from white light the band of colors in the spectrum seems to require the assumption of a distinct kind of light corpuscle for each color; and, in addition, the assumption that, although all light particles have the same velocity when they travel together making white light, separate particles for different colors are differently refrangible, that is, differently susceptible to the action of the particles in the refracting medium of the glass.

Perhaps only in Newton's somewhat artificially restricted sense of the word "hypothesis" could these assumptions escape that denomination. In any case, the existence of Huygens' rival theory prevented his escaping a controversy about hypotheses. In the Queries attached to his *Optics*, he engages in that controversy with an acumen which shows another side of his genius.

HUYGENS' WAVE THEORY requires what anybody would have to call an hypothesis and requires it from the very start. "It is inconceivable," he writes, "to doubt that light consists in the motion of some sort of matter." He immediately rejects the notion that light rays consist in the "transport of matter coming to us from the [luminous] object, in the way in which a shot or an arrow traverse the air"—if for no other reason, because "the rays traverse one another without hindrance." The similarity between the phenomena of light and the phenomena of sound suggests to him the "way that light spreads," and causes him to extend the mechanics of sound—conceived as a wave motion—to light.

"We know that by means of air, which is an invisible and impalpable body," Huygens argues, "sound spreads around the spot where it has been produced, by a movement which is passed on successively from one part of air to another; and that the spreading of this movement, taking place equally on all sides, ought to form spherical surfaces ever enlarging and which strike our ears. Now there is no doubt at all that light also comes from the luminous body to our eyes by some movement impressed on the matter which is between the two. . . . If, in addition, light takes time for its passage . . . it will follow that this movement, impressed on the intervening matter, is successive; and consequently it spreads, as sound does, by spherical surfaces and waves; for I call them waves from their resemblance to those which are seen to be formed in water when a stone is thrown into it."

Huygens is aware, however, that the analogy between light and sound is far from perfect. "If one examines," he says, "what this matter may be in which the movement coming from the luminous body is propagated, one will see that it is not the same that serves for the propagation of sound. . . . This may be proved," he goes on, "by shutting up a sounding body in a glass vessel from which the air is withdrawn." An alarm clock beating its bell in a jar without air makes no sound, but a jar without air is no less transparent than one with air. Since when "the air is removed from the vessel the light does not cease to traverse it as before," and since waves have to be waves of something, and light waves cannot be waves of air, they must be waves of a substance, says Huygens, "which I call ethereal matter."

This ether, a transparent medium permeating the whole universe, proves to be what Einstein calls the *enfant terrible* in the family of hypothetical physical substances. Postulated by Huygens in order to explain light mechanically, it in turn calls for a mechanical account of its own extraordinary properties. Huygens does not avoid this new problem, but neither does he undertake to solve it completely.

Suppose "one takes a number of spheres of equal size, made of some very hard substance, and arranges them in a straight line, so that they touch one another." Then, says Huygens, "one finds, on striking with a similar sphere against the first of these spheres, that the motion passes as in an instant to the last of them, which separates itself from the row, without one's being able to perceive that the others have been stirred." This type of motion in the ether would account for "the extreme velocity of light" and yet "this progression of motion is not instantaneous," as the motion of light also is not.

"Now in applying this kind of movement to that which produces light," Huygens continues, "there is nothing to hinder us from estimating the particles of the ether to be of a substance as nearly approaching to perfect hardness and possessing a springiness as prompt as we choose." Beyond this Huygens does not go. "It is not necessary to examine here," he says, "the causes of this hardness, or of that springiness. . . . Though we shall ignore the true cause of springiness we still see that there are many bodies which possess this property; and thus there is nothing strange in supposing that it exists also in little invisible bodies like the particles of the ether."

But difficulties which Huygens did not foresee make his ether more than a strange supposition—almost a mechanical impossibility. Huygens had thought that light waves are transmitted in the ether in the way that sound waves are in the air, that is, longitudinally, the direction in which the individual particles vibrate being the same as the direction of the wave motion itself. But when, in the 19th century, it was found that the phenomena of the polarization of light could not be explained by the corpuscular theory, but only by the wave theory (thus shifting the scales decisively in favor of the latter), it was also found that the wave theory could explain polarization *only* on the assumption that the motion of the ether particles which produce the light waves is not longitudinal, but transverse, that is, in a direction perpendicular to the waves produced by the vibration of the particles.

As Fresnel pointed out at the time, "the supposition that the vibrations were transverse was contrary to the received ideas on the nature of the vibration of elastic fluids." They had all involved, as in the case of air as the medium for sound, a longitudinal transmission. The character of the ether is changed by the requirement that its particles vibrate transversely. It ceases to be an air-like ether and must be imagined as a jelly-like ether.

The task which Huygens had postponed—that of giving a mechanical explanation of the ether he had posited in order to state the mechanics of light—becomes in consequence far more difficult, if not impossible. In their efforts to construct "the ether as a jelly-like mechanical substance, physicists," according to Einstein, had to make so many "highly artificial and unnatural assumptions," that they finally decided to abandon the whole program of mechanical explanation.

Of Newton's two objections to the wave theory of light, the second by itself seems to create an insuperable difficulty for Huygens' ether, even before the realization that it must be a jelly-like medium.

Newton's first objection is that any wave theory is inconsistent with the fact of the rectilinear propagation of light. "If light consisted in pression or motion, propagated either in an instant or in time, it would bend into the shadow; for," he points out, "pression or motion cannot be propagated in a fluid in right lines, beyond an obstacle which stops part of the motion, but will bend and spread every way into the quiescent medium which lies beyond the obstacle. . . . The waves, pulses or vibrations of the air, wherein sound consists, bend manifestly, even though not so much as the waves of water."

This objection loses its force when, in the

19th century, light's bending is experimentally discovered. But Newton's other objection gains force when, two centuries after he made it, a jelly-like density is imposed upon the ether by the experimental facts of polarization. This second objection does not point to the inadequacy of the wave theory with respect to the phenomena which must be described, but rather calls attention to its inconsistency with celestial mechanics.

Light travels through inter-stellar space. But so also do the planets. Newton's astronomy accounts for the motion of the planets with great precision, *only on the supposition of no resistance from a medium*. "To make way for the regular and lasting motions of the planets and comets," he writes, "it is necessary to empty the heavens of all matter, except perhaps . . . such an exceedingly rare ethereal medium as we described above." Here he refers to the ether he himself had posited as a possible cause of gravitational attraction. Its resistance, he thinks, is "so small as to be inconsiderable." The "planets and comets and all gross bodies [can] perform their motions more freely in this ethereal medium than in any fluid, which fills all space adequately without leaving any pores." Such "a dense fluid . . . serves only to disturb and retard the motions of those great bodies, and make the frame of nature languish." Since it "hinders the operations of nature," and since "there is no evidence for its existence," Newton concludes that "it ought to be rejected."

The next conclusion follows immediately. "If it be rejected, the hypotheses that light consists in pression or motion, propagated through such a medium, are rejected with it." Newton would seem entitled to draw these conclusions because, no matter how slight the density of ethereal matter, the use of the ether in the wave theory of light involves some interaction between the particles of ether and the particles of matter. Unless such interaction takes place, no explanation can be given of the change in the velocity of light when it enters a medium like glass or water. Since in Newton's universe there is no difference between terrestrial and celestial matter, Newton cannot accept an ether which interacts with the matter of glass or water, but does not interact with the matter of the planets.

This objection of Newton's, pointing to an inconsistency between the kind of ether required by the wave theory of light and the unretarded motion of the heavenly bodies, appears not to have been answered, but only waived, at the time of the wave theory's ascendancy. The famous Michelson-Morley experiment on ether drift later re-opens Newton's penetrating query about the ether. But this occurs at a time when physicists are prepared to give up not only the ether, but also with it the mechanical explanations of gravity and light which it had brought into conflict with one another.

BEFORE THE MECHANICAL dogma runs its course, it has a career in other fields of physical inquiry. The phenomena of heat, magnetism, and electricity are explored and explained under its inspiration. The history of these subjects is marked by a very rash of hypotheses. Each time mechanical explanation is attempted for a new domain of phenomena, new substances are added.

The postulated entities—calorific, magnetical, and electric fluids—are unobservable and without weight. In Newton's terms, they are "occult"; though, it must be added, they are no more occult than the ether Newton himself postulated to explain gravity or the ether Huygens postulated to explain light. In fact, each of these new substances seems to resemble the aeriform or fluid ether, just as each is conceived, as the gravitational or optical ether was earlier conceived, in the context of the issue of action-at-a-distance as opposed to action-by-contact. They would seem to be unavoidable in a mechanical account of the radiations of heat, magnetism, and electricity.

The phenomena of heat, Lavoisier writes, are "difficult to comprehend . . . without admitting them as the effects of a real and material substance, or very subtle fluid. . . . Wherefore," he continues, "we have distinguished the cause of heat, or that exquisitely elastic fluid which produces it, by the term of caloric." Lavoisier declares himself "unable to determine whether light be a modification of caloric, or if caloric be, on the contrary, a modification of light." But in terms of observed effects he does attribute ether-like properties to caloric. "This subtle matter," he says, "penetrates through the pores of all known substances"; for "there are no vessels through which it cannot escape."

The theory of caloric serves its purpose before it gives way to the theory of heat as molecular motion, a conception which can be integrated with the molecular, or kinetic, theory of gases. "The development of the kinetic theory of matter," writes Einstein, "is one of the greatest achievements directly influenced by the mechanical view." It is all the more striking, therefore, that in the opening pages of Fourier's *Analytical Theory of Heat*—wherein he reviews the triumphs of explanation achieved by Newton and his successors—Fourier should so flatly assert: "But whatever may be the range of mechanical theories, they do not apply to the effects of heat. These make up a special order of phenomena which cannot be explained by the principles of motion and equilibrium."

It is equally striking that Lavoisier seems to have anticipated not only the mechanical theory of heat, but the possibility of a purely mathematical treatment of the phenomena. "We are not obliged to suppose [caloric] to be a real substance," he writes; it is sufficient "that it be considered as the repulsive cause, whatever that may be, which separates the particles of matter from each other, so that we are still at liberty to investigate its effects in an abstract and mathematical manner."

The second of these two things is precisely what Fourier proposes to undertake, but he disavows any interest in the first, namely, the explanation of heat in terms of the mechanical separation of particles by repulsion. In language which resembles Newton's disavowal of concern with the cause of attraction, Fourier declares that "primary causes are unknown to us, but are subject to simple and constant laws, which may be discovered by observation."

In another place he writes: "Of the nature of heat only uncertain hypotheses could be formed, but the knowledge of the mathematical laws to which its effects are subject is independent of all hypothesis." Fourier's aim, therefore, with respect to "the very extensive class of phenomena, not produced by mechanical forces, but resulting simply from the presence and accumulation of heat," is "to reduce the physical questions to problems of pure analysis" and "to express the most general conditions of the propagation of heat in differential equations." He expresses his indebtedness to Descartes for "the analytical equations" which that mathematician "was the first to introduce into the study of curves and surfaces," but "which are not restricted to the properties of figures, and those properties which are the object of rational mechanics." These equations, he insists, "extend to all general phenomena," and "from this point of view, mathematical analysis is as extensive as nature itself."

This strongly worded statement affirms the mathematical character of nature as the support and justification for a purely mathematical physics. If Fourier's remarks about causes and hypotheses are reminiscent of Newton in his mathematical mood, how much more is Fourier's faith in pure mathematical analysis reminiscent of Galileo. Like Galileo, and unlike Newton, Fourier never deviates from his indifference to causes and never softens his judgment of the incompetence and irrelevance of mechanics to the subject he is investigating. His trust in mathematical analysis, which is able by itself to yield and organize physical discoveries, not only revives the spirit of Galileo, but also seems to have inspired Clerk Maxwell to turn from a mechanical to a mathematical theory of electricity.

Certain of Fourier's mathematical achievements, such as his theory of dimensions, prove useful to Maxwell. More important, perhaps, is the fact that Maxwell's predictions about the propagation of electro-magnetic waves, later experimentally verified by Hertz, are the result of mathematical analysis. With such a demonstration of the power of mathematics to work fruitfully with experiment, *and without any aid from mechanical hypotheses*, Maxwell gives up the attempt to formulate a mechanics for his equations describing the electro-magnetic field. He is quite content to let his field theory state the mathematical structure of the phenomena.

Between Fourier and Maxwell comes Faraday. One of the greatest experimenters in the whole tradition of science, Faraday discovers the phenomena whose mathematical structure Maxwell later develops. He prepares the way for Maxwell's application to electricity and magnetism of the method Fourier had practiced. His speculations concerning the relation of electrical and gravitational force point ahead, beyond Maxwell, to the possibility of a field theory which might unify all physical phenomena under a single set of mathematical laws.

Faraday sees no incompatibility between experimentation and speculation. On the contrary he says that "as an experimentalist I feel bound to let experiment guide me into any train of thought which it may justify; being satisfied that experiment, like analysis, must lead to strict truth, if rightly interpreted; and believing also that it is in its nature far more suggestive of new trains of thought and new conditions of natural power." Faraday's faith seems to have been amply justified. His experiments not only discovered a stunning number of new facts, but the speculations to which they led transformed the whole mode of thinking about electricity and magnetism, and, to some extent, the whole of physics.

The Elizabethan Gilbert, with his bold and brilliantly handled thesis that the earth is a magnet, had made magnetism appear something more than a random phenomenon occasionally met with in nature. But not until Faraday's discovery of diamagnetism, announced in a memoir *On the Magnetic Condition of All Matter*, would anyone have dared to say that "all matter appears to be subject to the magnetic force as universally as it is to the gravitating, the electric and the chemical or cohesive forces." Of electricity, he can only predict, as the result of his protracted experimental investigations, that "it is probable that every effect depending upon the powers of inorganic matter . . . will ultimately be found subordinate to it."

These remarks indicate the controlling theme of Faraday's researches, namely, the convertibility and unity of natural forces. It seems to have been suggested to him by the discovery that both electrical and magnetic forces obey the same simple inverse-square law as the force of gravitational attraction. The fact that certain forces obey the same law or that their action can be described by the same equations, would not of itself reveal whether one of these forces is primary or all are derivative from some other primary force. But it would suggest questions to be asked by experiment.

Gilbert compares magnetism and electricity but he is not able to convert one into the other. Oersted, before Faraday, is the first to establish one aspect of their convertibility. He shows that an electric current has a magnetic effect. Faraday succeeds in showing the reverse—that a magnetic current has electrical power. He expresses his fascination with such reversibilities in his remarks on the electrical torpedo fish. "Seebeck," he writes, "taught us how to commute heat into electricity; and Peltier has more lately given us the strict converse of this, and shown us how to convert electricity into heat. . . . Oersted showed how we were to convert electric into magnetic forces, and I had the delight of adding the other member of the full relation, by reacting back again and converting magnetic into electric forces. So perhaps in these organs, where nature has provided the apparatus by means of which the fish can exert and convert nervous into electric force, we may be able, possessing in that point of view a power far beyond that of the fish itself, to reconvert the electric into the nervous force."

Faraday demonstrates still another such reversibility in nature. The nature of his discovery is indicated by the titles of the papers in which he announces it: *On the Magnetization of Light and the Illumination of Magnetic Lines of Force* and *The Action of Electric Currents on Light*. These papers, in his opinion, "established for the first time, a true, direct relation and dependence between light and the magnetic and electric forces"; and he concludes them with an explicit statement of the central theme of all his researches and speculations.

"Thus a great addition is made," he writes, "to the facts and considerations which tend to prove that all natural forces are tied together and have one common origin. It is no doubt difficult in the present state of our knowledge to express our expectation in exact terms; and, though I have said that another of the powers of nature is, in these experiments, directly related to the rest, I ought, perhaps, rather to say that another form of the great power is distinctly and directly related to the other forms."

One form of the "great power" remained to be connected with such "other forms" as those of light, heat, electricity, and magnetism. That was the power of gravitational force. Faraday comes to this last stage of his speculations concerning the unity of nature's powers in terms of his conception of "lines of force" and of what later came to be called "the field of force."

The earliest theories of electricity and magnetism, in an orthodox atomistic vein, had conceived them as exerting an influence by means of the effluvia which they emitted. Newton, for example, speculates on "how the effluvia of a magnet can be so rare and subtle, as to pass through a plate of glass without any resistance or diminution of their force, and yet so potent as to turn a magnetic needle beyond the glass." When electrical conduction is later discovered, effluvia are replaced by fluids, on the analogy of caloric as the fluid conductor of heat. But when Faraday finds that he can induce from one current to another, he becomes interested in the dielectric, non-conducting medium around the circuits. He is strongly averse to any theory which involves action-at-a-distance, and so he argues that induction takes place by the action of contiguous particles. To support that argument he shows experimentally that electrical induction can "turn a corner."

From his study of all the phenomena of magnetism, Faraday forms the conception of "lines of force" and concludes that there is "a center of power surrounded by lines of force which are physical lines essential both to the existence of force within the magnet and to its conveyance to, and exertion upon, magnetic bodies at a distance." He says of this "idea of lines of force" that "all the points which are experimentally established with regard to [magnetic] action, *i.e.*, all that is not hypothetical, appear to be well and truly represented by it"; and he adds: "Whatever idea we employ to represent the power ought ultimately to include electric forces, for the two are so related that one expression ought to serve for both."

Subsequently Faraday satisfies himself as to the physical reality of electrical lines of force in addition to the magnetic lines. The compulsion of his interest in the unity of nature then drives him to speculate about gravitational force. He begins by admitting that, "in the case of gravitation, no effect sustaining the idea of an independent or physical line of force is presented to us; as far as we at present know, the line of gravitation is merely an ideal line representing the direction in which the power is exerted." But encouraged, perhaps, by Newton's repeated references to "the attractions of gravity, magnetism, and electricity," and by Newton's letter to Bentley which he interprets as showing Newton to be "an unhesitating believer in physical lines of gravitating force," Faraday goes to work experimentally.

The report of these researches *On the Possible Relation of Gravity to Electricity* opens with the re-statement of Faraday's central theme. "The long and constant persuasion that all the forces of nature are mutually dependent, having one origin, or rather being different manifestations of one fundamental power, has made me often think of establishing, by experiment, a connexion between gravity and electricity, and so introducing the former into the group, the chain of which, including also magnetism, chemical force and heat, binds so many and such varied exhibitions of force together by common relations." His experiments, he tells us, unfortunately "produced only negative results," but that does not shake his "strong feeling of the existence of a relation between gravity and electricity."

Though Faraday fails to prove "that such a relation exists," he does bequeath, as a legacy to 20th century physics, the problem of a field theory which would embrace both gravitational and electrical force. But whereas Faraday conceives the problem mechanically in terms of the physical reality, as well as unity, of all lines of force, in which contiguous particles act on one another, those who inherit the problem from him cease to concern themselves with the physical existence of "lines of force" and their mechanical basis in the action and reaction of bodies. Influenced by the amazing generality implicit in Maxwell's field equations, they proceed to search for a purely mathematical statement of nature's structure.

In the judgment of the 20th century physicist mathematics may at last succeed in doing precisely what mechanics, from Newton to Faraday, kept promising but forever failing to do. If the unity of nature can be expressed in a single set of laws, they will be, according to Einstein, laws of a type radically different from the laws of mechanics. Taking the form of Maxwell's equations, a form which appears "in all other equations of modern physics," they will be, he writes, "laws representing the *structure* of the field."

In saying that "Maxwell's equations are structure laws" and that they provide "a new pattern for the laws of nature," Einstein means to emphasize their non-mechanical character. "In Maxwell's theory," he writes, "there are no material actors." Whereas "Newton's gravitational laws connect the motion of a body here and now with the action of a body at the same time in the far distance," Maxwell's equations "connect events which happen now and here with events which will happen a little later in the immediate vicinity." Like the equations which describe "the changes of the electromagnetic field, our new gravitational laws are," according to Einstein, "also structure laws describing the changes of the gravitational field."

The heart of the difference between a "structure law" and a mechanical law seems to be contained in Einstein's statement that "all space is the scene of these laws and not, as for mechanical laws, only points in which matter or changes are present." This contrast between matter and space brings to mind the difference between physics and geometry. Yet Einstein's repeated reference to "changes" in these space-structures also reminds us that the electrical and gravitational fields are not purely geometrical, but physical as well.

The structure laws of the new physics may be geometrical in form, but if they are to have any physical meaning, can they entirely avoid some coloring by the mechanical conceptions which have been traditionally associated with the consideration of matter and motion? At least one contemporary physicist appears to think that mechanics survives to bury its undertakers. After describing the development in which geometry progressively "swallowed up the whole of mechanics," Eddington observes that "mechanics in becoming geometry remains none the less mechanics. The partition between mechanics and geometry," he continues, "has broken down and the nature of each of them has diffused through the whole"; so that "besides the geometrisation of mechanics, there has been a mechanisation of geometry."

According to this view, it is not mechanics, but *classical* mechanics, which the new physics has abandoned. The character of the mechanics seems to have altered with the character of the mathematical formulations. Field theory, dealing with contiguous areas and successive events, avoids the problem of action-at-a-distance and also apparently that problem's classical solution in terms of the action of contiguous particles. But another sort of mechanics may be implicit in the field equations which connect events in one area with events in the immediate vicinity. If those equations had been available to him, Newton might have expressed his theory of a variably dense ether—analogous to the modern conception of a variably filled or variably curved space—in terms of structure laws describing the gravitational field.

WE ARE LEFT with a number of questions. Is the story of mechanics the story of its rise and decline or the story of its changing role—now dominant, now subordinate; now more manifest, now more concealed—at all stages in the development of a physics which is committed to being both mathematical and experimental? Do the status and character of mechanical conceptions change with changes in the form of the mathematical laws which describe the phenomena? Can physics be totally devoid of mechanical insight and yet perform experiments which somehow require the scientist to act on bodies and to make them act on one another? Could a pure mathematical physics have yielded productive applications in mechanical engineering without the intermediation of mechanical notions of cause and effect?

Whichever way these questions are answered, we face alternatives that seem to be equally unsatisfactory. *Either* experimental physics is purely mathematical and proclaims its disinterest in as well as its ignorance of causes; *or* physics cannot be experimental and mathematical without also being mechanical, and without being involved in a search for causes which are never found.

To the layman there is something mysterious

about all this. He stands in awe of the physicist's practical mastery of matter and its motions, which he naively supposes to depend upon a scientific knowledge of the causes, while all the time the scientists protest that the causes remain unknown to an experimental and mathematical physics. Mechanical explanations may be offered from time to time, but the various "forces" they appeal to can be understood only from their effects, and are nothing more than verbal shorthand for the formulae or equations which express the mathematical laws. Yet they remain cause-names, and seem to stimulate advances in science—both experimental and mathematical—almost as a consequence of the exasperating elusiveness of these hidden causes.

Certain philosophers hold a view which suggests that the clue to the mystery may lie in the word "hidden." Causes exist and we can control them to build machines and explode bombs, but we cannot with our senses catch them in the very act of causing, or perceive the inwardness of their operation. If the fact that they are thus unobservable means that they are occult, then all causes are occult—not least of all the mechanical type of cause which consists in the impact of one body upon another. In the century in which physicists tried to avoid the scandal of forces acting at a distance by postulating mechanical mediums through which one body acted directly on another, philosophers like Locke and Hume express their doubts that such causal action is any less occult than Newton had said Aristotle's causes were.

"The passing of motion out of one body into another," Locke thinks, "is as obscure and unconceivable, as how our minds move or stop our bodies by thought. . . . The increase of motion by impulse, which is observed or believed sometimes to happen, is yet harder to understand. We have by daily experience, clear evidence of motion produced both by impulse and by thought; but the manner how, hardly comes within our comprehension; we are equally at a loss in both." In Locke's judgment we will always remain "ignorant of the several powers, efficacies, and ways of operation, whereby the effects, which we daily see, are produced." If scientific knowledge is knowledge of causes, then "how far soever human industry may advance useful and experimental philosophy in physical things, scientifical will still be out of our reach."

When we try to observe efficient causes at work, what do we see? Hume answers that we only see one thing happening after another. "The impulse of one billiard-ball is attended with motion in the second. This is the whole that appears to the *outward* senses." Nor can we form any "*inward* impression" of what takes place at the moment of impact. "We are ignorant," he writes, "of the manner in which bodies operate on each other"; and we shall always remain so, for "their force or energy is entirely incomprehensible."

As the chapter on CAUSE indicates, Aristotle holds an opposite view of the matter. What takes place in efficient causation may be imperceptible, but it is not incomprehensible. All causes may be occult so far as the senses are concerned, but they are not obscure to the intellect. But Aristotle would also insist that the action of efficient causes cannot be understood if they are totally isolated from other causes—material, formal, final. A purely mechanical physics, in his opinion, defeats itself by its basic philosophical tenets, which exclude all properties that are not quantitative and all causes except the efficient. Only a different metaphysics —one which conceives physical substances in terms of matter and form, or potentiality and actuality—can yield a physics which is able to deal with causes and explain the phenomena; but such an Aristotelian physics, from the modern point of view, stands condemned on other grounds. It is not experimental. It is not productive of useful applications. It is not mathematical; nor is it capable of comprehending all the phenomena of nature under a few simple, universal laws.

OUTLINE OF TOPICS

1. The foundations of mechanics

   1*a*. Matter, mass, and atoms: the primary qualities of bodies

   1*b*. The laws of motion: inertia; the measure of force; action and reaction

   1*c*. Space and time in the analysis of motion

2. The logic and method of mechanics

   2*a*. The role of experience, experiment, and induction in mechanics

   2*b*. The use of hypotheses in mechanics

   2*c*. Theories of causality in mechanics

3. The use of mathematics in mechanics: the dependence of progress in mechanics on mathematical discovery

   3*a*. Number and the continuum: the theory of measurement

   3*b*. The geometry of conics: the motion of planets and projectiles

   3*c*. Algebra and analytic geometry: the symbolic formulation of mechanical problems

   3*d*. Calculus: the measurement of irregular areas and variable motions

4. The place, scope, and ideal of the science of mechanics: its relation to the philosophy of nature and other sciences

   4*a*. Terrestrial and celestial mechanics: the mechanics of finite bodies and of particles or atoms

   4*b*. The explanation of qualities and qualitative change in terms of quantity and motion

   4*c*. The mechanistic account of the phenomena of life

5. The basic phenomena and problems of mechanics: statics and dynamics

   5*a*. Simple machines: the balance and the lever

   5*b*. The equilibrium and motion of fluids: buoyancy, the weight and pressure of air, the effects of a vacuum

   5*c*. Stress, strain, and elasticity: the strength of materials

   5*d*. Motion, void, and medium: resistance and friction

   5*e*. Rectilinear motion

      (1) Uniform motion: its causes and laws

      (2) Accelerated motion: free fall

   5*f*. Motion about a center: planets, projectiles, pendulum

      (1) Determination of orbit, force, speed, time, and period

      (2) Perturbation of motion: the two and three body problems

6. Basic concepts of mechanics

   6*a*. Center of gravity: its determination for one or several bodies

   6*b*. Weight and specific gravity: the relation of mass and weight

   6*c*. Velocity, acceleration, and momentum: angular or rectilinear, average or instantaneous

   6*d*. Force: its kinds and its effects

      (1) The relation of mass and force: the law of universal gravitation

      (2) Action-at-a-distance: the field and medium of force

      (3) The parallelogram law: the composition of forces and the composition of velocities

   6*e*. Work and energy: their conservation; perpetual motion

7. The extension of mechanical principles to other phenomena: optics, acoustics, the theory of heat, magnetism, and electricity

   7*a*. Light: the corpuscular and the wave theory

      (1) The laws of reflection and refraction

      (2) The production of colors

      (3) The speed of light

      (4) The medium of light: the ether

   7*b*. Sound: the mechanical explanation of acoustic phenomena

   7*c*. The theory of heat

      (1) The description and explanation of the phenomena of heat: the hypothesis of caloric

      (2) The measurement and the mathematical analysis of the quantities of heat

   7*d*. Magnetism: the great magnet of the earth

      (1) Magnetic phenomena: coition, verticity, variation, dip

      (2) Magnetic force and magnetic fields

   7*e*. Electricity: electrostatics and electrodynamics

      (1) The source of electricity: the relation of the kinds of electricity

      (2) Electricity and matter: conduction, insulation, induction, electrochemical decomposition

      (3) The relation of electricity and magnetism: the electromagnetic field

      (4) The relation of electricity to heat and light: thermoelectricity

      (5) The measurement of electric quantities

REFERENCES

References are listed by volume number (in bold type), author's name, and page number. Bible references are to book, chapter, and verse of the Authorized King James version of the Bible. The abbreviation "esp" calls the reader's attention to one or more especially relevant parts of a whole reference; "passim" signifies that the topic is discussed intermittently rather than continuously in the work or passage cited. Where the work as a whole is relevant to the topic, the page numbers refer to the entire work. For general guidance in the use of *The Great Ideas,* consult the Preface.

1. The foundations of mechanics

1*a*. Matter, mass, and atoms: the primary qualities of bodies

8 ARISTOTLE, 394, 410–413, 423–425
10 GALEN, 173
12 LUCRETIUS, 2–5, 7–8, 19–22
19 AQUINAS, 585–587
23 HOBBES, 172, 269
28 GILBERT, 29–34
28 GALILEO, 134–153 passim
30 BACON, 114–115
31 DESCARTES, 78
34 NEWTON, 270–271, 281–282, 479–485, 528, 531–543
34 HUYGENS, 558–560, 601–603
35 LOCKE, 129–131, 134–138 passim, 150–154 passim, 209–212, 295
35 BERKELEY, 414–416 passim, 422
45 LAVOISIER, 3–4, 9–15 passim, 16
45 FARADAY, 850–855
53 JAMES, 68
54 FREUD, 400–401

1*b*. The laws of motion: inertia; the measure of force; action and reaction

8 ARISTOTLE, 354
9 ARISTOTLE, 233–235, 243–244
12 LUCRETIUS, 17–18
16 KEPLER, 894–895, 905–906
23 HOBBES, 50
28 GALILEO, 209–210, 224–225
30 BACON, 162–168 passim, 179–188
34 NEWTON, 5, 14–24, 246, 541–542
35 LOCKE, 178–179
35 BERKELEY, 434
35 HUME, 475–476
51 TOLSTOY, 695

1*c*. Space and time in the analysis of motion

8 ARISTOTLE, 312–325
28 GALILEO, 201–202
30 BACON, 176–179
33 PASCAL, 434–439
34 NEWTON, 8–13, 542–543
35 BERKELEY, 434–436
42 KANT, 24–29, 74–76, 160–163
51 TOLSTOY, 469

2. The logic and method of mechanics

28 GALILEO, 200
30 BACON, 105–106, 116–117, 120–121, 127, 132, 137–195, 210–214
31 DESCARTES, 12–13
33 PASCAL, 355–358 passim, 365–366
34 NEWTON, 270–271, 531
34 HUYGENS, 551–552
35 LOCKE, 321–323 passim
35 HUME, 459–460
42 KANT, 17–18, 69–72
45 FOURIER, 169–170
45 FARADAY, 758–759
49 DARWIN, 239
53 JAMES, 882–884
54 FREUD, 412

2*a*. The role of experience, experiment, and induction in mechanics

28 GILBERT, 1, 6–7
28 GALILEO, 207–208
30 BACON, 33–34, 42
31 DESCARTES, 61–62
34 NEWTON, 130–131, 271, 371–372, 543
35 LOCKE, 317, 360–362
35 BERKELEY, 424, 433–434
35 HUME, 460
42 KANT, 6, 227
45 LAVOISIER, 1–2
45 FARADAY, 440, 607, 659, 774–776
53 JAMES, 864

2*b*. The use of hypotheses in mechanics

28 GALILEO, 240–241
33 PASCAL, 367–370
34 NEWTON, 528, 543
35 LOCKE, 362
35 BERKELEY, 433
42 KANT, 227
45 FOURIER, 184
45 FARADAY, 467, 777–778
49 DARWIN, 239

2*c*. Theories of causality in mechanics

12 LUCRETIUS, 67–68
31 DESCARTES, 59
34 NEWTON, 7–8, 369–372, 528–529, 531, 541–542

34 Huygens, 553–554
35 Locke, 321
35 Berkeley, 422–423 passim, 424–426
35 Hume, 459–460, 474, 475, 478
45 Fourier, 183
53 James, 885–886

3. The use of mathematics in mechanics: the dependence of progress in mechanics on mathematical discovery

8 Aristotle, 104, 108
11 Archimedes, 502–519, 538–560, 569–592
14 Plutarch, 252–255
28 Galileo, 131–132, 178–260
30 Bacon, 46
31 Descartes, 169–170
34 Newton, 32–50, 76–157, 159–267, 269
35 Hume, 460
45 Fourier, 169, 172–173, 175, 182–184, 249
45 Faraday, 831

3*a*. Number and the continuum: the theory of measurement

11 Euclid, 81–98, 191–193, 195–198
11 Archimedes, 448–451, 458–460
28 Galileo, 197–200, 205–206
31 Descartes, 31–33, 295–296
34 Newton, 25
51 Tolstoy, 469

3*b*. The geometry of conics: the motion of planets and projectiles

11 Archimedes, 527–537
11 Apollonius, 603–804
16 Kepler, 975–979
28 Galileo, 191–195, 238–240
31 Descartes, 298–314
34 Newton, 42–75, 286, 337–338
34 Huygens, 583–598, 607–611
42 Kant, 551–552

3*c*. Algebra and analytic geometry: the symbolic formulation of mechanical problems

31 Descartes, 30–33, 295–353
34 Newton, 57–58
45 Fourier, 177–251

3*d*. Calculus: the measurement of irregular areas and variable motions

11 Archimedes, 527–537
16 Kepler, 973–975, 979–983
28 Galileo, 205, 224
33 Pascal, 434–435
34 Newton, 25–32, 168–170
45 Fourier, 181, 221–248

4. The place, scope, and ideal of the science of mechanics: its relation to the philosophy of nature and other sciences

23 Hobbes, 72
30 Bacon, 16, 33–34, 118
31 Descartes, 8, 59
34 Newton, 1–2
35 Hume, 454
36 Swift, 94–103
42 Kant, 69–72, 563–564
45 Fourier, 169
53 James, 882–886, 889–890

4*a*. Terrestrial and celestial mechanics: the mechanics of finite bodies and of particles or atoms

9 Aristotle, 234–235
16 Kepler, 888–905 passim, 929–933, 940–941, 959–960
28 Galileo, 245
30 Bacon, 138–139, 165–166, 178, 186
34 Newton, 281–282, 539–542
51 Tolstoy, 694–696

4*b*. The explanation of qualities and qualitative change in terms of quantity and motion

8 Aristotle, 680
10 Galen, 167–168
12 Lucretius, 20–21, 24–28
23 Hobbes, 49
31 Descartes, 231
34 Newton, 431–455
35 Locke, 134–138, 200, 206–207, 239, 311–312, 316, 322
35 Berkeley, 432–433

4*c*. The mechanistic account of the phenomena of life

7 Plato, 240–242
8 Aristotle, 680
9 Aristotle, 163–164, 236–239, 243–252, 275, 282
10 Galen, 172–195
12 Lucretius, 31–41, 71–72
23 Hobbes, 47
28 Harvey, 355, 495–496
31 Descartes, 56–60
34 Newton, 428, 518–519
35 Locke, 140, 143, 145–146, 321
38 Rousseau, 337–338
42 Kant, 571–572, 575–582
45 Faraday, 440, 540–541
51 Tolstoy, 689–690
53 James, 5–6, 9–17, 44–52, 68–71, 95–98
54 Freud, 412–414, 651–657, 659–661

5. The basic phenomena and problems of mechanics: statics and dynamics

5*a*. Simple machines: the balance and the lever

8 Aristotle, 339
11 Archimedes, 502–503
14 Plutarch, 252
16 Kepler, 933–934
28 Galileo, 178–180, 258
33 Pascal, 390–394
34 Newton, 15–16, 23–24
50 Marx, 181

5*b*. The equilibrium and motion of fluids: buoyancy, the weight and pressure of air, the effects of a vacuum

5*c*. Stress, strain, and elasticity: the strength of materials

5*d*. Motion, void, and medium: resistance and friction

5*e*. Rectilinear motion

5*e*(1) Uniform motion: its causes and laws

5*e*(2) Accelerated motion: free fall

5*f*. Motion about a center: planets, projectiles, pendulum

5*f*(1) Determination of orbit, force, speed, time, and period

5*f*(2) Perturbation of motion: the two and three body problems

6. Basic concepts of mechanics

6*a*. Center of gravity: its determination for one or several bodies

6*b*. Weight and specific gravity: the relation of mass and weight

6*c*. Velocity, acceleration, and momentum: angular or rectilinear, average or instantaneous

6*d*. Force: its kinds and its effects

8 Aristotle, 333, 353–354
16 Kepler, 938–939, 969–971
19 Aquinas, 541–542
28 Gilbert, 26–40 passim
34 Newton, 5–8, 11–13, 37–38, 281, 371–372
45 Faraday, 514–532, 646–655, 670–674, 817–818, 819
54 Freud, 400–401

6*d*(1) The relation of mass and force: the law of universal gravitation

28 Gilbert, 51–52
30 Bacon, 170–173
31 Descartes, 231–232
34 Newton, 130–152, 276–282, 531–543
35 Berkeley, 433
45 Faraday, 850–855

6*d*(2) Action-at-a-distance: the field and medium of force

8 Aristotle, 354
16 Kepler, 897–905, 906
28 Gilbert, 10, 26–40, 42–43, 51, 54–55, 102–104
30 Bacon, 168–169, 176–177
31 Descartes, 15
34 Newton, 6–8, 507–516, 520–522, 531–542 passim
35 Hume, 475
45 Faraday, 441–442, 451–454, 463–465, 513–514, 521–524, 528–532, 648, 685–686, 816–819, 832, 840–842

6*d*(3) The parallelogram law: the composition of forces and the composition of velocities

16 Kepler, 969–970
28 Galileo, 224–225, 243–249 passim
34 Newton, 15–16
45 Faraday, 691–692, 788–793
53 James, 105

6*e*. Work and energy: their conservation; perpetual motion

31 Descartes, 27
33 Pascal, 392–394
34 Newton, 15–16, 23–24
45 Faraday, 582–584, 837–840

7. The extension of mechanical principles to other phenomena: optics, acoustics, the theory of heat, magnetism, and electricity

7*a*. Light: the corpuscular and the wave theory

8 Aristotle, 649–650
16 Kepler, 896, 901–903
17 Plotinus, 183–189
19 Aquinas, 283–284, 349–354
20 Aquinas, 1025–1032
28 Gilbert, 43
30 Bacon, 167, 185
31 Descartes, 54–55
34 Newton, 152–157, 377–544
34 Huygens, 551–619
35 Locke, 261, 311–312
45 Faraday, 595–607

7*a*(1) The laws of reflection and refraction

7 Plato, 454–455
8 Aristotle, 476–482
12 Lucretius, 47–48
20 Aquinas, 972–974
31 Descartes, 12–13
34 Newton, 152–153, 154–157, 379–423, 485–495, 522–530 passim
34 Huygens, 563–619

7*a*(2) The production of colors

7 Plato, 465
12 Lucretius, 24–25
30 Bacon, 154
34 Newton, 379–506 passim
48 Melville, 144–145

7*a*(3) The speed of light

12 Lucretius, 46–47, 82
28 Galileo, 148–149
30 Bacon, 178
34 Newton, 379, 488–492
34 Huygens, 554–557, 570–575

7*a*(4) The medium of light: the ether

8 Aristotle, 676–678, 684–685
12 Lucretius, 67
33 Pascal, 366–367
34 Newton, 520–522, 525–529
34 Huygens, 553–560

7*b*. Sound: the mechanical explanation of acoustic phenomena

7 Plato, 471
8 Aristotle, 650–652
9 Aristotle, 328–330
12 Lucretius, 51–52
17 Plotinus, 186
28 Galileo, 172–177
30 Bacon, 178, 185
31 Descartes, 25
34 Newton, 247–259 passim
34 Huygens, 554–558 passim
45 Faraday, 485–486

7*c*. The theory of heat

7*c*(1) The description and explanation of the phenomena of heat: the hypothesis of caloric

7 Plato, 533
8 Aristotle, 380
12 Lucretius, 82–84, 91–92
30 Bacon, 140–153, 161, 168, 184–185, 190–192
34 Newton, 516–518, 520
42 Kant, 545–546

45 LAVOISIER, 9–16
45 FOURIER, 169–251
45 FARADAY, 812, 813–815, 857–858

7c(2) The measurement and the mathematical analysis of the quantities of heat

45 LAVOISIER, 14, 33–36, 99–103
45 FOURIER, 184–185

7d. Magnetism: the great magnet of the earth

10 GALEN, 177–178
12 LUCRETIUS, 92–94
28 GILBERT, 23–25, 106–121
30 BACON, 166–167, 176, 183
36 SWIFT, 100–102
45 FARADAY, 286–294, 697–757

7d(1) Magnetic phenomena: coition, verticity, variation, dip

7 PLATO, 144
16 KEPLER, 897–898, 935–936
28 GILBERT, 3–105 passim
30 BACON, 155, 163, 174
45 FARADAY, 607–669, 673–757, 855–866

7d(2) Magnetic force and magnetic fields

16 KEPLER, 941–942
28 GILBERT, 26–43, 45–47, 102–105
30 BACON, 169
34 NEWTON, 202–203, 281
45 FARADAY, 298–301, 528–532, 690–697, 758–795, 816–824, 830–848
48 MELVILLE, 376–379

7e. Electricity: electrostatics and electrodynamics

28 GILBERT, 26–34
34 NEWTON, 372, 531, 542
45 FARADAY, 514–528

7e(1) The source of electricity: the relation of the kinds of electricity

45 FARADAY, 269–273, 277–316, 386–422, 433–440, 532–539, 541–594, 824–830
49 DARWIN, 89

7e(2) Electricity and matter: conduction, insulation, induction, electrochemical decomposition

30 BACON, 181
45 FARADAY, 265–269, 273–277, 309–313, 319–345, 361–432, 440–514, 522–532, 541–584, 824–830, 848–855

7e(3) The relation of electricity and magnetism: the electromagnetic field

28 GILBERT, 26–34
34 NEWTON, 282
45 FARADAY, 269–302, 307–309, 520–521, 528–532, 615–619, 658–667, 685–686, 759–788, 795–813, 816–819

7e(4) The relation of electricity to heat and light: thermoelectricity

34 NEWTON, 516–517
45 FARADAY, 404–405, 476–506, 561–569, 580–582, 595–607

7e(5) The measurement of electric quantities

45 FARADAY, 277–279, 316–318, 366–371, 377–390, 444–451, 465–467, 768–773, 778–788

CROSS-REFERENCES

For: Considerations relevant to the basic concepts and laws of mechanics, *see* CHANGE 7d; QUANTITY 5a–5e; SPACE 2a; TIME 1.

Discussions of the role of experiment, induction, and hypotheses in physical science, *see* EXPERIENCE 5a–5c; HYPOTHESIS 4b–4d; INDUCTION 5; LOGIC 4b; PHYSICS 4a–4d; SCIENCE 5a–5e; and for the physicist's treatment of causes, *see* CAUSE 2, 5b, 6; NATURE 3c(3); PHYSICS 2b; SCIENCE 4c.

The general theory of applied mathematics or mathematical physics, *see* ASTRONOMY 2c; MATHEMATICS 5b; PHYSICS 1b, 3; SCIENCE 5c.

Other discussions of the mathematical ideas or operations which are applied in mechanics, *see* MATHEMATICS 4a–4d; QUANTITY 3d(1), 4c, 6b.

The relation of mechanics to the philosophy of nature and to other natural sciences, *see* PHILOSOPHY 1c; PHYSICS 2; SCIENCE 1c.

Other treatments of the problem of qualitative change, *see* CHANGE 6a–6b; QUALITY 3a, 3c; QUANTITY 1a.

Mechanism as a philosophy of nature, man, and history, *see* ANIMAL 1e; ELEMENT 5e–5g; HISTORY 4a(2); MAN 3c; MIND 2e; WILL 5c; WORLD 1b.

Other discussions of motion and its laws, *see* ASTRONOMY 8c–8c(3); CHANGE 7–7d; MATTER

2b; and for the related consideration of the void and action-at-a-distance, *see* ASTRONOMY 3b; ELEMENT 5c; SPACE 2b(2)–2c.

Another discussion of mass and weight, *see* QUANTITY 5d; for another discussion of velocity, acceleration, and momentum, *see* QUANTITY 5c; for another discussion of force, *see* QUANTITY 5e; and for another discussion of the composition of forces, *see* OPPOSITION 3d.

ADDITIONAL READINGS

Listed below are works not included in *Great Books of the Western World*, but relevant to the idea and topics with which this chapter deals. These works are divided into two groups:

I. Works by authors represented in this collection.
II. Works by authors not represented in this collection.

For the date, place, and other facts concerning the publication of the works cited, consult the Bibliography of Additional Readings which follows the last chapter of *The Great Ideas*.

I.

KEPLER. *Dioptrik*
DESCARTES. *The Principles of Philosophy*, PART II, 6–7, 19, 24–27, 48–64; PART III, 48–102, 121–125; PART IV, 20–27, 133–187
HOBBES. *Concerning Body*, PART IV, CH 30
——. *Examinatio et Emendatio Mathematicae Hodiernae*
——. *Dialogus Physicus*
HUYGENS. *Travaux divers de statique et de dynamique de 1659 à 1666*
——. *Percussion*
——. *L'horloge à pendule*
——. *Sur la cause de la pesanteur*
——. *Force centrifuge*
——. *Question de l'existence et de la perceptibilité du mouvement absolu*
BERKELEY. *De Motu*
KANT. *Metaphysical Foundations of Natural Science*
GOETHE. *Beiträge zur Optik*
——. *Theory of Colours*
HEGEL. *Science of Logic*, VOL II, SECT II, CH I
FARADAY. *The Various Forces of Matter and Their Relations to Each Other*

II.

EPICURUS. *Letter to Pythocles*
R. BACON. *Opus Majus*, PART V
NICOLAS OF CUSA. *The Idiot*, BK IV
STEVIN. *L'art ponderaire, ou la statique*
BOYLE. *New Experiments Physico-Mechanical*
——. *A Defence of the Doctrine Touching the Spring and Weight of the Air . . . Against the Objections of Franciscus Linus*
WALLIS. *Mechanica: sive, De Motu*
GUERICKE. *Experimenta Nova*
LEIBNITZ. *Discourse on Metaphysics*, XV–XXII
——. *Philosophical Works*, CH 20 (*On Nature in Itself*)
——. *New Essays Concerning Human Understanding*, APPENDIX, CH 4–5
VOLTAIRE. *Letters on the English*, XIV–XVII
EULER. *Mechanik*
D'ALEMBERT. *Traité de dynamique*
FRANKLIN. *Experiments*
J. PRIESTLEY. *Experiments and Observations on Different Kinds of Air*
——. *Experiments and Observations Relating to Various Branches of Natural Philosophy*
CARNOT. *Principes fondamentaux de l'équilibre et du mouvement*
LAGRANGE. *Mécanique analytique*
GALVANI. *De Viribus Electricitatis in Motu Musculari Commentarius*
RUMFORD. *An Experimental Inquiry Concerning the Source of Heat*
LAPLACE. *Mécanique céleste* (*Celestial Mechanics*)
POINSOT. *Élémens de statique*
T. YOUNG. *Miscellaneous Works*, VOL I, NUMBER III, VII, IX–X, XVII–XVIII
FRESNEL. *Théorie de la lumière*
PONCELET. *Cours de mécanique*
AIRY. *Gravitation*
W. R. HAMILTON. *Dynamics*
WHEWELL. *The Philosophy of the Inductive Sciences*, VOL I, BK III, CH 5–10
JOULE. *Scientific Papers*
HELMHOLTZ. *Popular Lectures on Scientific Subjects*, VII
W. THOMSON and TAIT. *Treatise on Natural Philosophy*

TYNDALL. *Light and Electricity*
REULEAUX. *The Kinematics of Machinery*
MAXWELL. *Theory of Heat.*
——. *A Treatise on Electricity and Magnetism*
——. *Matter and Motion*
RAYLEIGH. *The Theory of Sound*
STALLO. *Concepts and Theories of Modern Physics*, CH 2–6, 9–12
CLIFFORD. *The Common Sense of the Exact Sciences*, CH V
BALL. *A Treatise on the Theory of Screws*
GIBBS. *Collected Works*
C. S. PEIRCE. *Collected Papers*, VOL VI, par 35–87
KELVIN. *Lectures on Molecular Dynamics and the Wave Theory of Light*
——. *Popular Lectures and Addresses*
PEARSON. *The Grammar of Science*
APPELL. *Traité de mécanique rationnelle*
HERTZ. *The Principles of Mechanics*
MACH. *History and Root of the Principle of the Conservation of Energy*
——. *The Science of Mechanics*
——. "On the Principle of the Conservation of Energy," in *Popular Scientific Lectures*
BOLTZMANN. *Principe der Mechanik*
B. RUSSELL. *Principles of Mathematics*, CH 54, 56–59
PAINLEVÉ. *Les axiomes de la mécanique*
SANTAYANA. *Reason in Science*, CH 3
DUHEM. *L'évolution de la mécanique*
——. *Les origines de la statique*
——. *Études sur Léonard de Vinci*
ENRIQUES. *Problems of Science*, CH 5–6
HEAVISIDE. *Electromagnetic Theory*
MEYERSON. *Identity and Reality*, CH 2–3, 10
POINCARÉ. *Science and Hypothesis*, PART III; PART IV, CH 12–13
——. *Science and Method*, BK III
CASSIRER. *Substance and Function*, PART I, CH 4; SUP VII
CURIE. *Traité de radioactivité*
E. T. WHITTAKER. *A Treatise on the Analytical Dynamics of Particles and Rigid Bodies*
——. *A History of the Theories of Aether and Electricity*
RUTHERFORD. *Radio-active Substances and Their Radiations*
EDDINGTON. *Space, Time, and Gravitation*
EINSTEIN. *Relativity: The Special and the General Theory*
——. *Sidelights on Relativity*
——. *The Meaning of Relativity*
LEVI-CIVITA. *Fragen der klassischen und relativistischen Mechanik*
PLANCK. *Das Prinzip der Erhaltung der Energie*
——. *Treatise on Thermodynamics*
——. "The Place of Modern Physics in the Mechanical View of Nature," in *A Survey of Physics*
WHITEHEAD. *Science and the Modern World*, CH I–IV
BRIDGMAN. *The Logic of Modern Physics*, CH 3
SCHRÖDINGER. *Collected Papers on Wave Mechanics*
——. *Four Lectures on Wave Mechanics*
BOHR. *Atomic Theory and the Description of Nature*
BROGLIE. *An Introduction to the Study of Wave Mechanics*
DIRAC. *The Principles of Quantum Mechanics*
HEISENBERG. *The Physical Principles of the Quantum Theory*
NAGEL. *On the Logic of Measurement*
M. R. COHEN. *Reason and Nature*, BK II, CH 2–3
C. G. DARWIN. *The New Conceptions of Matter*
LENZEN. *The Nature of Physical Theory*, PART I, III
BERGSON, *Time and Free Will*
——. *Creative Evolution*, CH I, 4
——. *Two Sources of Morality and Religion*, CH 4
WIENER. *Cybernetics*

Chapter 55: MEDICINE

INTRODUCTION

MEDICINE is the name of an art, of a science or group of sciences, and of a learned profession whose members are proficient in these sciences and experienced in the practice of the art. By derivation it is also the name for curative drugs, physics, or other remedies prescribed by the physician. The archaic usage of the English word "physic" as the name for the art, practice, and profession of what is now generally called "medicine" suggests what the word's Greek root signifies, namely, that the physician, no less than the physicist, is a student of nature.

There is one other historic use of "medicine" which indicates its scope and connections in the western tradition. When mediaeval institutions first shaped the university, the basic divisions of learning then embodied in its structure reflected different uses of learning as well as differences in subject matter. The three faculties of medicine, law, and theology not only disciplined their students in different branches of knowledge, but also trained them for distinct applications of knowledge to practice.

The faculty of medicine represented all the natural sciences, especially those which have come to be called "biological sciences," just as the faculty of law or jurisprudence represented all the moral sciences and their later offshoots, now called "social sciences." The doctor of medicine was concerned with knowledge bearing on the relation of man to nature, as the doctor of laws was concerned with knowledge bearing on the relation of man to man, and the doctor of theology with knowledge bearing on the relation of man to God.

It is a curious accident that the word "doctor," which in origin signified the competence to teach others who might practice in each of these great fields of learning, has come in popular usage to designate, not the teacher, but the practitioner, and chiefly the practitioner in only one of the learned professions. Medicine may not deserve the implied emphasis upon the learning of its practitioners, but there would be some truth in granting it the distinction of being the oldest of the professions in the sense that it comprises a group of men who not only share a common training in the relevant sciences and arts, but who also have adopted a code of practice and obligated themselves to perform a service to their fellow men.

The Hippocratic Oath, sworn to in the name of "Apollo the physician and Aesculapius, and Health . . . and all the gods and goddesses," is the first explicit formulation of a professional ideal. In the collection of writings attributed to Hippocrates, *The Law* explicitly indicates as *The Oath* implies that there are intellectual as well as moral conditions to be fulfilled by those who would dedicate themselves to the service of health. Only those who have satisfied all requisites for the study of medicine and by diligent application have acquired a true knowledge of it shall be "esteemed physicians not only in name but in reality."

The same high conception of medicine appears in the Bible. We read in Ecclesiasticus: "Honor the physician for the need thou hast of him: for the most High hath created him. For all healing is from God, and he shall receive gifts of the king. The skill of the physician shall lift up his head, and in the sight of great men he shall be praised. The most High hath created medicines out of the earth, and a wise man will not abhor them. . . . The virtue of these things is come to the knowledge of men, and the most High hath given knowledge to men, that he may be honored in his wonders. By these he shall cure and shall allay their pains, and of these the apothecary shall make sweet confections, and shall make up ointments of health, and of his works there shall be no end. For the peace of God is over all the face of the earth."

FIVE OF THE authors of the great books—Hippocrates, Galen, Gilbert, Harvey, and Freud—belonged to the profession of medicine. They were major figures in its history. Practitioners of its arts, they were also contributors to the sciences concerned with health and disease. Three others combined medicine with other pursuits. Copernicus studied medicine at Padua and devoted considerable time to its practice; Locke was Lord Shaftesbury's personal physician; James took a medical degree at Harvard after years spent in the biological sciences. Still another, Rabelais, not only studied and practiced medicine, but also edited the *Aphorisms* of Hippocrates and Galen's little treatise on the medical art. His knowledge of medicine and his observation of its contemporary practices can be readily discerned in his comic exaggerations of anatomical and physiological detail, and of regimens of diet or exercise.

The discussion of medicine in the great books is not limited to its professors or practitioners. Montaigne has many doubts about medical diagnosis and the possibility of charting the causes of disease or the remedies which cure. The patient's ignorance permits the physician to claim credit for his successes and to blame fortune for his failures.

Montaigne, characteristically, delights in observing that the doctors disagree. He offers, as "one example of the ancient controversy in physics," the following: "Herophilus lodges the original cause of all disease in the humours; Erasistratus, in the blood of the arteries; Asclepiades, in the invisible atoms of the pores; Alcmaeon, in the exuberance or defect of our bodily strength; Diocles, in the inequality of the elements of which the body is composed, and in the quality of the air we breathe; Strato, in the abundance, crudity, and corruption of the nourishment we take; and Hippocrates lodges it in the spirits." There is no great danger, he adds, "in our mistaking the height of the sun, or the fraction of some astronomical computation; but here where our whole being is concerned, 'tis not wisdom to abandon ourselves to the mercy of the agitation of so many contrary winds."

Such commentary as this bears more on the history of medicine than on the abiding problems of its science or art, which, from Hippocrates to Freud, have been more generally agreed upon than the theories proposed for their solution. Of similar historical significance are the passages in the great works of history which describe the phenomena of disease as they appeared to contemporary observers, the plagues which ravaged Athens, Rome, and London, or the maladies which afflicted eminent individuals. Poetry, as well as history and biography, contributes to this record. The novels of Tolstoy and Fielding, the plays of Shakespeare, the tales of Cervantes and Chaucer, the Greek tragedies, and the Homeric epics furnish evidence of both the constant and the changing elements in the conception of disease, the vocation of medicine, and the social acceptance of the physician.

The history of medicine is an epitome of the history of the natural sciences. The researches of the Hippocratic school inititate specific methods of empirical investigation, such as the systematic collection and comparison of observations and the painstaking record of individual case histories. The fundamental concepts of medical theory reflect the philosophy of nature and of man. Conflicting notions of the causes of disease focus major issues in biology, such as the controversy in which Galen engages with Asclepiades and Erasistratus in the defense of what he supposes to be Hippocrates' and Aristotle's organic view of nature against mechanism and atomism.

Medicine, moreover, provides some of the clearest examples of the interdependence of theory and practice, for the rules of the healing art put theories to work and to the test; and as the rules are refined or altered by the accumulated experience of particular cases, inductive insight leads to new theoretical generalizations. As the work of Dr. Harvey illustrates, biological science is both the source and the reflection of medical knowledge. Medicine also affords Bacon and Descartes the prime example of a useful application of the knowledge gained by the new methods they propose.

More than engineering or the invention of mechanical utilities, medicine represents for them knowledge in the service of mankind.

That science shall bear fruit in technology "is not merely to be desired," writes Descartes, "with a view to the invention of an infinity of arts and crafts . . . but principally because it brings about the preservation of health, which is without doubt the chief blessing and the foundation of all other blessings in this life . . . It is true that the medicine which is now in vogue contains little of which the utility is remarkable; but, without any intention of decrying it, I am sure that there is no one, even among those who make its study a profession, who does not confess that all that men know is almost nothing in comparison with what remains to be known."

The subsequent history of medicine, some of the great documents of which are cited in the list of Additional Readings under the names of Jenner, Bichat, Virchow, Claude Bernard, and Koch, seems to substantiate Descartes' prophecy. But it also seems to be true that the major problems of medical practice are not greatly altered or diminished by the tremendous increase in our knowledge of the causes of specific diseases and our vast store of well tested remedies.

What sort of art medicine is; to what extent the physician should let nature run its course; with what restraint or prudence the physician should apply general rules to particular cases; whether health is better served by the general practitioner treating the whole man or by a specialist treating a special organ; how the relation of the physician to his patient is itself a therapeutic factor and underlies the effectiveness of his skill in all other respects; to what extent mind and body interact both in the origin and in the cure of disease—these are the problems of medicine concerning which Hippocrates and Galen can converse with Osler and Freud almost as contemporaries.

The distinction made in the chapter on Art between the simply productive and the cooperative arts associates medicine with agriculture and teaching, and separates these arts, which merely help a natural result to come about, from the arts which produce an effect that would never occur without the work of the artist. Plants grow and reproduce without the help of farmers. The mind can discover some truth without the aid of teachers. Animals and men can preserve and regain their health without the care of physicians. But without shoemakers or house builders, shoes and houses would not be produced.

The art of medicine does not produce health in the sense in which the shoemaker produces a shoe, or the sculptor a statue. These other arts imitate nature by embodying natural forms or functions in materials wherein they do not naturally arise. An art like medicine seems to imitate nature by cooperating with natural processes. It follows the course of nature itself and, by working with it, enables the natural result to eventuate more surely than it might if art made no attempt to overcome the factors of chance.

Socrates expresses this understanding of the physician's art when he uses the metaphor of midwifery to characterize his own method of teaching. As it is the mother who labors and gives birth, so it is the student who is primarily active in the process of learning. The teacher, like the midwife, merely assists in a natural process which might be more painful, and might possibly fail, without such help. "The teacher," writes Aquinas, "only brings exterior help as does the physician who heals; just as the interior nature is the principal cause of the healing, so the interior light of the intellect is the principal cause of knowledge.

"Health," he continues, "is caused in a sick man, sometimes by an exterior principle, namely, by the medical art; sometimes by an interior principle, as when a man is healed by the force of nature. . . . Just as nature heals a man by alteration, digestion, rejection of the matter that caused the sickness, so does art. . . . The exterior principle, art, acts not as a primary agent, but as helping the primary agent, which is the interior principle, and by furnishing it with instruments and assistance, of which the interior principle makes use in producing the effect. Thus the physician strengthens nature, and employs food and medicine, of which nature makes use for the intended end."

The subordination of the medical art to nature seems to be the keystone of the whole structure of Hippocratic medicine. It is implied in the emphasis which Hippocrates places on the control of the patient's regimen, especially the elements of his diet, the exercise of his body, and the general circumstances of his life. Even in the treatment of acute diseases, Hippocrates looks to the regimen first, prescribing changes or special articles of diet.

Medicines or drugs perform an auxiliary function. Surgery is always a last resort, to be used primarily in the treatment of injuries, and not to be employed in diseases which will yield to a course of regimen and medication. There is an element of violence in surgery which puts it last among the means of an art which should work by cooperating with nature rather than by operating on it. And among medicines, those are preferable which, like ptisan, a special preparation of barley water, derive their efficacy from properties similar to those of normal nutriment.

According to Hippocrates, the control of regimen is not only the primary factor in therapy, but also the original principle of medicine. In the treatise *On Ancient Medicine*, he points out that "the art of medicine would not have been invented at first, nor would it have been made the subject of investigation (for there would have been no need for it), if when men are indisposed, the same food and other articles of regimen which they eat and drink when in good health were proper for them, and if no other were preferable to these. . . . The diet and food which people in health now use would not have been discovered, provided it suited man to eat and drink in like manner as the ox, the horse, and all other animals. . . . What other object, then, has he in view who is called a physician, and is admitted to be a practitioner of the art, who found out the regimen and diet befitting the sick, than he who originally found out and prepared for all mankind that kind of food which we all now use, in place of the former savage and brutish mode of living?"

THE SAME CONCEPTION of medicine's relation to nature seems to be fundamental in Galen's thought. He attributes to Hippocrates his own reformulation of the insight that the art of healing consists in imitating the health-giving and healing powers of nature itself. The medical doctrines which he criticizes were based on the atomism of Epicurus. They regarded the body as a complex piece of machinery. When it gets out of order, it needs a mechanic and mechanical remedies to fix it. On the contrary, it seems to him, the living body is an organic unity, not an aggregation of atoms, or a system of interlocking parts.

"Nature is not posterior to the corpuscles, but a long way prior to them," Galen writes. "Therefore it is nature which puts together the bodies both of plants and animals; and this she does by virtue of certain faculties which she possesses—these being, on the one hand, attractive and assimilative of what is appropriate, and, on the other, expulsive of what is foreign. Further, she skillfully moulds everything during the stage of genesis; and she also provides for the creatures after birth, employing here other faculties again."

Nature, according to Galen, works not by the external impact of part upon part, but by its faculties or powers for the performance of natural functions and the production of natural effects. Galen's polemic against the mechanists thus leads him to reverse the usual statement. Where Hippocrates looks upon nature as the model for art to follow, Galen calls Nature the artist, in order to set his view in sharp contrast to all mechanical conceptions. "Instead of admiring Nature's artistic skill," he declares, "they even go so far as to scoff and maintain that . . . things have been made by Nature for no purpose!" Nature, Galen holds, produces effects according to its powers and in conformity to its needs. It seems to work with intelligence and for an end, not blindly and by chance. The true art of medicine, therefore, borrows its method from "Nature's art."

The conception of nature as an artist may be taken metaphorically or literally, but the insight controlling the practice of medicine remains the same. The physician is a servant, not a master, of nature. Aristotle's doctrine of final causes, summarized in the maxim Galen so often repeats—that "nothing is done by Nature in vain"—furnishes a principle for physiological research, as well as the rules of medical art. Whether because of faulty observation on his part, or because of a failure to apply his own principle, Galen leaves to Harvey one of the great discoveries which can be credited to close attention to final causes. Always observant of the relation between structure and function, always questioning the purpose which bodily organs serve, Harvey establishes the fact that the blood circulates, and finds therein the reason for the structure of the heart, its motions, and its relation to the lungs.

It may also be possible for a principle to be carried to excess. Montaigne, for example, expresses his distrust of medical theory and the physician's remedies by an unqualified trust in nature's own resourcefulness. Drugs, especially purgatives, do violence to nature. "Men disturb and irritate the disease by contrary oppositions; it must be the way of living that must gently dissolve, and bring it to an end. The violent gripings and contest betwixt the drug and the disease are ever to our loss, since the combat is fought within ourselves, and that the drug is an assistant not to be trusted, being in its own nature an enemy to our health, and by trouble having only access into our condition. Let it alone a little; the general order of things that takes care of fleas and moles, also takes care of men, if they will have the same patience that fleas and moles have, to leave it to itself."

Nor is there any need for an art of medicine when nature can do better by herself. "We ought to grant free passage to diseases; I find they stay less with me, who let them alone; and I have lost some, reputed the most tenacious and obstinate, by their own decay, without help and without art, and contrary to its rules. Let us a little permit Nature to take her own way; she better understands her own affairs than we." The Hippocratic doctrine seems to occupy a middle ground between this view of nature as an unerring artist and the opposite extreme which permits all sorts of tampering and tinkering with the machinery of the body.

THE ART OF MEDICINE "consists in three things," writes Hippocrates: "the disease, the patient, and the physician. The physician is the servant of the art, and the patient must combat the disease along with the physician." With regard to diseases, the physician must "have two special objects in view . . . to do good, and to do no harm."

This celebrated summary indicates the two kinds of knowledge which the physician should possess. He should know about disease in general, so that he can classify diseases according to their special causes, their symptoms, and the typical course each seems to take. Such knowledge underlies the doctor's diagnosis of the patient's malady. That in turn determines his prognosis of the stages through which the illness will run, from its onset through various crises or turning points to its *sequelae* or consequences. Upon the accuracy of his diagnosis and the certainty of his prognosis may depend the effectiveness of any remedy the physician prescribes in the individual case.

But individual cases are seldom completely alike. The physician must therefore know the patient as an individual, and all the relevant circumstances of his life as well as the particular characteristics of this instance of the disease; even though its general characteristics are familiar to him from much experience in the treatment of similar cases. The *Book of Prognostics* and the treatise *Of the Epidemics* in the Hippocratic collection seem to combine both these kinds of knowledge. They enumerate the symptoms by which diseases can be recognized and their future foretold. They also set forth individual case histories from which such generalizations can be drawn.

The practice of medicine thus appears to require more than scientific knowledge of health and disease in general, and more than general rules of art. It requires the sort of experience which can be gained only from actual practice. Without prudence born of experience, general rules can be misapplied, for no general rule, in medicine as in law, fits all cases alike. The most famous of Hippocratic aphorisms conveys a sense of the hazards of medical practice: "Life is short, and Art long; the crisis fleeting; experiment perilous, and decision difficult. The physician must not only be prepared to do what is right himself, but also to make the patient, the attendants, and the externals cooperate."

To persuade the patient to cooperate is the first maxim governing the physician's relation to his patient. Plato contrasts the right and wrong relation between doctor and patient by comparing the practice of the physicians who treated slaves and those who treated free men. "The slave-doctor," he says, "prescribes what mere experience suggests, as if he had exact knowledge, and when he has given his orders, like a tyrant, he rushes off with equal assurance to some other servant who is ill. . . . But the other doctor, who is a freeman, attends and practices upon freemen; and he carries his enquiries far back, and goes into the nature of the disorder; he enters into discourse with the patient and with his friends, and is at once getting information from the sick man, and also instructing him as far as he is able, and he will not prescribe for him until he has first convinced him; at last, when he has brought the patient more and more under his persuasive influences and set him on the road to health, he attempts to effect a cure."

In the treatment of mental diseases, as Freud points out, the proper development and management of the relationship between patient and physician is itself a major factor in psychotherapy. "It presupposes a profound interest for psychological incidents, as well as a personal sympathy for the patient," he writes. "It requires the full consent and the attention of the patients, but above all, their confidence, for the analysis regularly leads to the inmost and most secretly guarded psychic processes." Since fears, anxieties, or other temperamental dispositions on the part of the patient may affect the course of an organic ailment, the patient's confidence in the physician and, even more generally, his emotional response to the physician's character play an important role in the successful treatment of bodily ills as well as of mental or functional disorders.

Hippocrates recommends that the physician cultivate prognosis, not only for the guidance of his own actions, but also for the sake of the patient. "By foreseeing and foretelling, in the presence of the sick, the present, the past, and the future, and explaining the omissions which patients have been guilty of, he will be the more readily believed to be acquainted with the circumstances of the sick; so that men will have confidence to entrust themselves to such a physician."

THE RELATION OF physician and patient raises a question about the organization of the practice of medicine, to which opposite answers have been given in both ancient and modern times. Herodotus reports a high degree of medical specialization in Egypt. "Medicine is practised among them on a plan of separation," he writes; "each physician treats a single disorder, and no more: thus the country swarms with medical practitioners, some undertaking to cure diseases of the eye, others of the hand, others again of the teeth, others of the intestines, and some those which are not local." The fact that the next paragraph begins a discussion of funerals can hardly be taken as revealing the attitude of Herodotus toward specialization, though his comment on the Egyptian practice does imply a contrast to Greek medicine.

One sentence in the Hippocratic Oath—"I will not cut persons laboring under the stone, but will leave this to be done by men who are practitioners of this work"—indicates some division of labor in the organization of Greek medicine. But apart from the special tasks and skills of surgery, the Hippocratic conception of the physician's work favors the practice of general medicine rather than specialization. The man, not the disease, is to be treated, and to treat him well the physician must examine the man as a whole, not merely the organ or bodily part in which the disorder seems to be located. The Hippocratic formula for getting a case history calls for an inquiry into the background of the individual's life, his antecedents, his occupation, his temperament, "the patient's habits, regimen, and pursuits; his conversation, manners, taciturnity, thoughts, sleep, or absence of sleep, and sometimes his dreams, what they are and when they occur; his picking and scratching; his tears." From these as well as from the symptoms, says Hippocrates, "we must form our judgment."

The defense of general practice against specialization is part of Galen's argument with his adversaries. Treatment of the disordered part as if it could be isolated from the living unity of the whole man is, to Galen, one of the deplorable consequences in medical practice of atomism or mechanism in medical theory.

This issue is argued again and again in the history of medicine, with each side pressing the advantages in its favor. Montaigne, for example, states the case for the specialist by analogy with the advantages of specialization in other arts. "As we have doublet and breeches makers, distinct trades, to clothe us, and are so much the better fitted, seeing that each of them meddles only with his own business, and has less to trouble his head with than the tailor who undertakes them all; and as in matter of diet, great persons, for their better convenience, have cooks for the different offices . . . so also as to the cure of our maladies." With Freud and the development of a greater awareness of the psychological origin of many bodily disorders, a new factor enters into the argument. It tends to favor the general practitioner who, from his acquaintance with the patient as a person, may be better able than the specialist to detect hidden psychological causes.

THE CONCEPTION of disease is usually determined by the conception of health. The abnormality is judged and measured as a deviation from the norm. Hippocrates uses the outward appearance of man in a healthy condition as the standard for discerning the visible signs of illness. The physician, he says, "should observe . . . first the countenance of the patient, if it be like those of persons in health, and more so, if like itself, for this is the best of all; whereas the most opposite to it is the worst." He should also take note when he finds the patient reclining in a posture which resembles the normal disposition of the healthy body. "To find the whole body lying in a relaxed state" is a more favorable sign than to find him "upon his back, with the hands, neck, and the legs extended."

The history of medicine, especially on the side of its science and theory, if not so much with regard to its art and practice, can be told in terms of refinements in the classification of diseases and progressive discovery of their specific causes, both internal and external, predisposing and exciting. But the analysis of diseases according to their aetiology and by reference to the typical picture of the disease process leaves unanswered the general question about the nature of disease as a loss of health.

Apart from its causes and its symptoms, its modes and its patterns, what is disease? This is the question of major speculative interest in the tradition of the great books. The answers given have a certain uniformity in spite of the varying terms in which they are expressed.

The humoural hypothesis of ancient medical theory, for example, conceives health as that condition of the body in which the physiological elements are in a proper proportion or balance, and in which the various parts or powers function harmoniously with one another. As health is harmony or good order in the body, so disease consists in imbalance and disharmony—an excess or defect with consequent disproportion of the elements, or the disorder of conflicting bodily processes.

In the *Timaeus*, Plato first states this theory in terms of the four physical elements. "There are four natures out of which the body is compacted, earth and fire and water and air, and the unnatural excess or defect of these, or the change of any of them from its own natural place into another . . . produces disorders and diseases." He then considers the diseases which result from excess or defect of one or another of the four humours—blood, phlegm, black and yellow bile.

The humoural hypothesis, which Hippocrates and Galen share with Plato and Aristotle, undergoes many transformations in the history of medicine. The four elements or humours are replaced by other physiological factors, such as the hormones or internal secretions, or the elements of modern biochemistry. But constant throughout these changing formulations is the conception of health as an equilibrium, and of disease as its loss through disorder and disproportion.

This broad conception of health and disease seems to apply to mental as well as bodily ills. There is not only a basic continuity between Plato's and Freud's discussion of the bodily origin of mental disorders and the psychic origin of physical ailments; but the Freudian emphasis upon conflict and disintegration in the neurotic character—milder forms of the schizophrenia or "split personality" which characterizes insanity—also appeals to harmony as the principle of health. The language of modern psychiatry which refers to "the integrated personality" or "the well-balanced and adjusted individual" defines the norm or the ideal of mental health.

The various kinds and degrees of mental disorder, especially those which seem to be entirely functional rather than organic, represent abnormalities which, though they differ in cause, symptom, and tendency, have in common some excess or defect in the psychic structure or some unresolved conflict in the nature of man. Freud's psychoanalytic method in the treatment of mental ills places psychotherapy in the main tradition of medical practice; for in addition to insisting that the patient shall help to cure himself, it is directed toward the resolution of conflict, restoring the harmony which is health.

OUTLINE OF TOPICS

1. The profession of medicine, its aims and obligations: the relation of physician to patient; the place of the physician in society

2. The art of medicine

  2a. The scientific foundations of the art of medicine: the contrast between the empiric and the artist in medicine

  2b. The relation of art to nature in healing: imitation and cooperation

  2c. The comparison of medicine with other arts and professions

3. The practice of medicine

  3a. The application of rules of art to particular cases in medical practice

  3b. General and specialized practice: treating the whole man or the isolated part

  3c. Diagnosis and prognosis: the interpretation of symptoms; case histories

  3d. The factors in prevention and therapy

    (1) Control of regimen: climate, diet, exercise, occupation, daily routine

    (2) Medication: drugs, specifics

    (3) Surgery

4. The concept of health: normal balance or harmony

5. The theory of disease

  5a. The nature of disease

  5b. The classification of diseases

  5c. The disease process: onset, crisis, after-effects

  5d. The causes of disease: internal and external factors

    (1) The humoural hypothesis: temperamental dispositions

    (2) The psychogenesis of bodily disorders

  5e. The moral and political analogues of disease

6. Mental disease or disorder: its causes and cure

  6a. The distinction between sanity and insanity: the concept of mental health and the nature of madness

  6b. The classification of mental diseases

  6c. The process and causes of mental disorder

    (1) Somatic origins of mental disease

    (2) Functional origins of mental disease

  6d. The treatment of functional disorders: psychotherapy as a branch of medicine

7. The historical record on disease and its treatment: epidemics, plagues, pestilences

REFERENCES

References are listed by volume number (in bold type), author's name, and page number. Bible references are to book, chapter, and verse of the Authorized King James version of the Bible. The abbreviation "esp" calls the reader's attention to one or more especially relevant parts of a whole reference; "passim" signifies that the topic is discussed intermittently rather than continuously in the work or passage cited. Where the work as a whole is relevant to the topic, the page numbers refer to the entire work. For general guidance in the use of *The Great Ideas,* consult the Preface.

1. The profession of medicine, its aims and obligations: the relation of physician to patient; the place of the physician in society

APOCRYPHA: *Ecclesiasticus,* 38:1–15
6 HERODOTUS, 117–118
7 PLATO, 7, 10–11, 22–23, 261, 268–270, 303–304, 335–338, 745
9 ARISTOTLE, 479, 485–486
10 HIPPOCRATES, xiii, 26–27, 46, 131, 144
10 GALEN, 178–179, 207
13 VIRGIL, 364
22 CHAUCER, 166–167
24 RABELAIS, 232–233, 234
25 MONTAIGNE, 365–379
28 HARVEY, 267–268
29 CERVANTES, 345–346
30 BACON, 52–53
37 FIELDING, 33–34, 86, 161–162
38 MONTESQUIEU, 266
44 BOSWELL, 13, 261
47 GOETHE, 47–48, 180
51 TOLSTOY, 225–227, 307, 374, 464
52 DOSTOEVSKY, 356–359
54 FREUD, 64, 71–72, 78–81, 125–127, 623–625, 866

2. The art of medicine

2*a*. The scientific foundations of the art of medicine: the contrast between the empiric and the artist in medicine

7 PLATO, 280–281, 287–288, 337
8 ARISTOTLE, 499, 673, 726
9 ARISTOTLE, 358, 435, 536
10 HIPPOCRATES, 1–3, 7–9, 49, 59, 70, 94
10 GALEN, 175–177, 191–199
19 AQUINAS, 595–597
25 MONTAIGNE, 377, 523–524
28 HARVEY, 289–292
30 BACON, 50–51, 52, 53, 56–57, 114–115
31 DESCARTES, 61, 66–67
54 FREUD, 123–125, 128–130, 549–550, 606, 871

2*b*. The relation of art to nature in healing: imitation and cooperation

7 PLATO, 155–156, 475
8 ARISTOTLE, 269–270, 277
10 HIPPOCRATES, 7, 74–76, 96–97, 132
20 AQUINAS, 12–13
25 MONTAIGNE, 52, 368–369
28 HARVEY, 305, 438
30 BACON, 53
51 TOLSTOY, 372–373
54 FREUD, 746

2*c*. The comparison of medicine with other arts and professions

7 PLATO, 136–137, 260–262, 289, 298–299, 515–517, 599–602, 803–804
8 ARISTOTLE, 189, 267, 268–269, 555
9 ARISTOTLE, 161–162, 342, 347, 390, 435–436
10 HIPPOCRATES, 1
14 PLUTARCH, 726
17 PLOTINUS, 250–251
18 AUGUSTINE, 651
19 AQUINAS, 679
24 RABELAIS, 186
25 MONTAIGNE, 450–451
30 BACON, 5–6, 77–78
37 FIELDING, 86, 90
39 SMITH, 44

3. The practice of medicine

3*a*. The application of rules of art to particular cases in medical practice

7 PLATO, 599, 600, 684–685
9 ARISTOTLE, 596
10 HIPPOCRATES, 4, 9, 59
12 EPICTETUS, 159
30 BACON, 52–53
36 STERNE, 372–373
42 KANT, 60
54 FREUD, 32

3*b*. General and specialized practice: treating the whole man or the isolated part

6 HERODOTUS, 65
7 PLATO, 2–3
10 HIPPOCRATES, 7, 49
25 MONTAIGNE, 373
44 BOSWELL, 350
51 TOLSTOY, 372–373
52 DOSTOEVSKY, 340
54 FREUD, 451–452

3c. Diagnosis and prognosis: the interpretation of symptoms; case histories

OLD TESTAMENT: *Leviticus*, 13–14
6 HERODOTUS, 44–45
6 THUCYDIDES, 399–400
9 ARISTOTLE, 130
10 HIPPOCRATES, 13–14, 19–26, 38–40, 49–56, 59–63, 65–67, 69, 76–77, 94–95, 99–100, 109, 111–112, 122–126 passim, 131, 132–134 passim, 135–144 passim
19 AQUINAS, 67–68
24 RABELAIS, 197
25 MONTAIGNE, 370, 372–373, 531–532
30 BACON, 49–50
36 SWIFT, 114, 156–157
37 FIELDING, 145–146, 157–158
51 TOLSTOY, 524–525
54 FREUD, 1–2, 31, 38–40, 50, 54–56, 60–62, 87–90, 124, 128–129, 151, 550–557, 605–607, 872–873

3d. The factors in prevention and therapy

3d(1) Control of regimen: climate, diet, exercise, occupation, daily routine

APOCRYPHA: *Ecclesiasticus*, 31:19–22; 37:29–31
6 HERODOTUS, 64
7 PLATO, 50, 334–337
9 ARISTOTLE, 114, 129, 535, 541, 544
10 HIPPOCRATES, 4–6, 9–14, 15, 16–17, 26–44, 45, 47, 56–57, 77–78, 88–89, 111, 112–113, 120, 131–132, 133, 134, 138, 160
10 GALEN, 191–195
14 PLUTARCH, 34, 40–42, 583–584
22 CHAUCER, 450
24 RABELAIS, 26–29, 68–69, 134–135, 152–153, 188–191
25 MONTAIGNE, 66–67, 374–375, 524, 527–528
30 BACON, 47, 53–54, 201, 211–212
37 FIELDING, 145–146
38 ROUSSEAU, 335
39 SMITH, 293–294
44 BOSWELL, 171
49 DARWIN, 356–357
50 MARX, 324–325
51 TOLSTOY, 215

3d(2) Medication: drugs, specifics

4 HOMER, 25–26, 81
6 HERODOTUS, 143, 157
9 ARISTOTLE, 129, 131
10 HIPPOCRATES, 26, 27–29, 32–34, 39–40, 43–44, 114–115, 145, 146–149, 150–152
10 GALEN, 176–177, 179
24 RABELAIS, 96, 124–125, 225, 226, 246–247, 310–311
25 MONTAIGNE, 369–370
27 SHAKESPEARE, 147–148, 149–150
28 GILBERT, 19–21, 35
28 HARVEY, 297
30 BACON, 26, 53
36 SWIFT, 108–109, 161–162
36 STERNE, 372–373
37 FIELDING, 63, 76
44 BOSWELL, 257
51 TOLSTOY, 38

3d(3) Surgery

7 PLATO, 601–602
9 ARISTOTLE, 157
10 HIPPOCRATES, 43, 67–130, 149–150, 152–154
25 MONTAIGNE, 373
28 HARVEY, 376–377, 438
37 FIELDING, 70–71
38 ROUSSEAU, 336–337
51 TOLSTOY, 464–465

4. The concept of health: normal balance or harmony

7 PLATO, 155–157, 282–283, 334–337, 355, 472, 474–475, 690
8 ARISTOTLE, 637
9 ARISTOTLE, 45–46, 176, 177–179, 602
10 HIPPOCRATES, 4–7
12 LUCRETIUS, 37
18 AUGUSTINE, 610–611
20 AQUINAS, 2–5, 6–7, 8–9, 15–18, 22–23
24 RABELAIS, 137–139
25 MONTAIGNE, 233–236
28 HARVEY, 493
30 BACON, 50–51, 72
36 STERNE, 412–417
38 ROUSSEAU, 336
54 FREUD, 635

5. The theory of disease

5a. The nature of disease

7 PLATO, 472–474
8 ARISTOTLE, 329–330
9 ARISTOTLE, 326
10 HIPPOCRATES, 5–7
10 GALEN, 195–196, 208–209
17 PLOTINUS, 74
20 AQUINAS, 105–106, 966–967
25 MONTAIGNE, 528–529
32 MILTON, 309–311
51 TOLSTOY, 372
53 JAMES, 799–807

5b. The classification of diseases

7 PLATO, 472–474
9 ARISTOTLE, 127–131
10 HIPPOCRATES, 9–11, 49–50, 134–135
10 GALEN, 193–194
36 SWIFT, 155–157
54 FREUD, 87

5c. The disease process: onset, crisis, after-effects

6 THUCYDIDES, 399–400
10 HIPPOCRATES, 22–24, 35, 38–40, 44–63, 69, 86–87, 116–117, 131, 132–133, 136–137

5*d*. The causes of disease: internal and external factors

5*d*(1) The humoural hypothesis: temperamental dispositions

5*d*(2) The psychogenesis of bodily disorders

5*e*. The moral and political analogues of disease

6. Mental disease or disorder: its causes and cure

6*a*. The distinction between sanity and insanity: the concept of mental health and the nature of madness

6*b*. The classification of mental diseases

6*c*. The process and causes of mental disorder

5 EURIPIDES, 212–224, 340–352, 371–374, 394–398
6 HERODOTUS, 95–98, 199–201
8 ARISTOTLE, 704
9 ARISTOTLE, 399 passim
10 HIPPOCRATES, 155–156, 159
19 AQUINAS, 590–591, 664–665, 742, 785–786, 824–826
23 HOBBES, 68–71
26 SHAKESPEARE, 370–371
27 SHAKESPEARE, 42, 55–56, 59–60, 61, 264–266, 272, 274–277, 306–307
29 CERVANTES, 1–429
31 DESCARTES, 75
35 LOCKE, 146
40 GIBBON, 598
44 BOSWELL, 127, 214
48 MELVILLE, 122–124, 135–138, 232–235
51 TOLSTOY, 616–617
52 DOSTOEVSKY, 5, 62–63, 337–348 passim, 364–365, 376–377
53 JAMES, 132–138, 244–252, 258, 533–538, 753–754, 828–829
54 FREUD, 1–19, 25–106, 110–118, 402–404, 440–443, 451–452, 546–623, 641, 648–650, 690–691, 695–696, 712–715, 716–717, 720–752, 774, 798–799, 830–832, 866–867

6*c*(1) Somatic origins of mental disease

6 HERODOTUS, 96
7 PLATO, 474
10 HIPPOCRATES, 155–160
12 LUCRETIUS, 36
19 AQUINAS, 449–450
28 HARVEY, 347
31 SPINOZA, 436–438
49 DARWIN, 318
51 TOLSTOY, 524–527
53 JAMES, 2–3, 23–26, 35–37, 40–41
54 FREUD, 90–97, 111–115, 604–606, 744–745, 773

6*c*(2) Functional origins of mental disease

54 FREUD, 1–20, 25–106, 364–365, 380–382, 406–410, 425–427, 434–436, 546–623, 690–691, 699, 720–752

6*d*. The treatment of functional disorders: psychotherapy as a branch of medicine

12 LUCRETIUS, 30–31, 80
19 AQUINAS, 786–789
24 RABELAIS, 188–191
25 MONTAIGNE, 37–39, 401–406
27 SHAKESPEARE, 306–307, 308
30 BACON, 77–78
44 BOSWELL, 284, 297–298
48 MELVILLE, 357–358
51 TOLSTOY, 614, 616–618
52 DOSTOEVSKY, 21–23
53 JAMES, 132, 135
54 FREUD, 1–20, 26, 30–81, 106–111, 123–127, 449–452, 545–550, 560–561, 563–566, 623–638, 748, 864–873

7. The historical record on disease and its treatment: epidemics, plagues, pestilences

4 HOMER, 25–26
6 HERODOTUS, 117–118, 135
6 THUCYDIDES, 399–401, 438
7 PLATO, 335–336
9 ARISTOTLE, 128, 484
10 HIPPOCRATES, 44–63, 154–155, 160
12 LUCRETIUS, 36, 95–97
14 PLUTARCH, 26–27, 138–140, 179–180, 212, 386, 575–576, 812
15 TACITUS, 239, 292–293
23 HOBBES, 69–71
24 RABELAIS, 124
25 MONTAIGNE, 365–368, 371–372, 529–537 passim
30 BACON, 50–53
38 MONTESQUIEU, 106–107
38 ROUSSEAU, 336, 364
40 GIBBON, 114
41 GIBBON, 70–71, 298–300, 355
44 BOSWELL, 13–14
51 TOLSTOY, 225–227
54 FREUD, 6, 550–551

CROSS-REFERENCES

For: Discussions bearing on learned professions or professional education, *see* EDUCATION 5a, 6; LAW 9; RHETORIC 6.

The general theory of art which underlies the consideration of medicine as an art, *see* ART 3, 9a; EXPERIENCE 3a; KNOWLEDGE 8a.

The theory of signs involved in the interpretation of symptoms, *see* LANGUAGE 10; SIGN AND SYMBOL 4e; and for other matters relevant to medical diagnosis and prognosis, *see* HYPOTHESIS 4b, 4d.

Another discussion of health and disease, *see* LIFE AND DEATH 5a, 5c; and for the special problems of mental disease and the methods of psychopathology, *see* EMOTION 3a, 3c–3d; MAN 5b; MEMORY AND IMAGINATION 2e(3)–2e(4), 5c; MIND 2c(2), 8a–8c; WILL 9b.

Discussions relevant to the comparison of mental health or sanity with happiness, *see* HAPPINESS 2a; JUSTICE 1b.

ADDITIONAL READINGS

Listed below are works not included in *Great Books of the Western World*, but relevant to the idea and topics with which this chapter deals. These works are divided into two groups:

I. Works by authors represented in this collection.

II. Works by authors not represented in this collection.

For the date, place, and other facts concerning the publication of the works cited, consult the Bibliography of Additional Readings which follows the last chapter of *The Great Ideas*.

I.

PLUTARCH. "Rules for the Preservation of Health," in *Moralia*

GALEN. *On Medical Experience*

——. *Opera Omnia*

F. BACON. "Regimen of Health," in *Essays*

DOSTOEVSKY. *The Idiot*

FREUD. *The Dynamics of the Transference*

——. *The Employment of Dream-Interpretation in Psycho-Analysis*

——. *Recommendations for Physicians on the Psycho-Analytic Method of Treatment*

——. *An Outline of Psychoanalysis*

II.

CELSUS. *De Medicina (On Medicine)*

AVICENNA. *The Canon of Medicine*, BK I

MAIMONIDES. *Regimen Sanitatis*

BARTHOLOMAEUS ANGLICUS. *On Medicine*

R. BACON. *On the Errors of Physicians*

BOCCACCIO. *Decameron*, PROEM

PARACELSUS. *The Diseases That Deprive Man of His Reason*

——. *On the Miners' Sickness and Other Miners' Diseases*

——. *Seven Defensiones*

VESALIUS. *The Epitome*

BURTON. *The Anatomy of Melancholy*

MOLIÈRE. *Le médecin malgré lui (The Mock-Doctor)*

——. *Le malade imaginaire (The Hypochondriac)*

RAMAZZINI. *De Morbis Artificum (The Diseases of Workers)*

VOLTAIRE. "Physicians," in *A Philosophical Dictionary*

JENNER. *An Inquiry into the Causes and Effects of the Variolae Vaccinae*

BICHAT. *General Anatomy, Applied to Physiology and Medicine*

HAHNEMANN. *Organon of the Rational Art of Healing*

LAËNNEC. *Mediate Auscultation*

VIRCHOW. *Cellular Pathology*

O. W. HOLMES. *Currents and Counter-Currents in Medical Science*

BERNARD. *Introduction to Experimental Medicine*

KOCH. *The Aetiology of Tuberculosis*

S. W. MITCHELL. *Doctor and Patient*

CHEKHOV. *Ward No. 6*

OSLER. *Aequanimitas*

P. M. JANET. *The Major Symptoms of Hysteria*

ROMAINS. *Doctor Knock*

MANN. *The Magic Mountain*

S. LEWIS. *Arrowsmith*

CROOKSHANK. *Individual Diagnosis*

SHAW. *Doctors' Delusions*

E. ALLEN. *Sex and Internal Secretions*

CANNON. *The Wisdom of the Body*

GIBSON. *The Physician's Art*

B. RUSSELL. *Religion and Science*, CH 4

ZILBOORG. *The Medical Man and the Witch During the Renaissance*

BEST and TAYLOR. *The Physiological Basis of Medical Practice*

BUCHANAN. *The Doctrine of Signatures*, CH 3–6

FEARING. *The Hospital*

Chapter 56: MEMORY AND IMAGINATION

INTRODUCTION

CONCERNING memory and imagination, the tradition of western thought seems to be involved in less dispute than it is on other aspects of human and animal life. There are, as we shall see, points of difficulty and debatable theories. But these arise only within the framework of certain fundamental insights which are widely, if not universally, shared. Here at least we can begin without having to deal with verbal ambiguities. Unlike many of the words which are the traditional bearers of the great ideas, "memory" and "imagination" have a constant core of meaning in almost everyone's discourse.

It is understood that memory and imagination depend upon sense-perception or upon previous experience. Except for illusions of memory, we do not remember objects we have never perceived or events in our own life, such as emotions or desires, that we have not experienced. The imagination is not limited in the same way by prior experience, for we can imagine things we have never perceived and may never be able to.

Yet even when imagination outruns perception, it draws upon experience for the materials it uses in its constructions. It is possible to imagine a golden mountain or a purple cow, though no such object has ever presented itself to perception. But, as Hume suggests, the possibility of combining a familiar color and a familiar shape depends upon the availability of the separate images to be combined.

"When we think of a golden mountain," Hume writes, "we only join two consistent ideas, *gold* and *mountain*, with which we were formerly acquainted . . . All this creative power of the mind amounts to no more than the faculty of compounding, transposing, augmenting, or diminishing the materials afforded us by the senses and experience." A congenitally color-blind man who lived entirely in a world of grays would not be able to imagine a golden mountain or a purple cow, though he might be able to imagine things as unreal as these.

Because of their dependence on sense-perception, memory and imagination are usually regarded as belonging to the same general faculty as the external senses. Not all writers, however, conceive of a generic power of sense, which they then divide into the exterior senses such as sight, hearing, and touch, and the interior senses such as memory and imagination. Some, like Hobbes, treat imagination as "nothing but decaying sense," and use the word "memory" to "express the decay, and signify that the sense is fading, old, and past."

The image, whether it is a memory-image or fancy-free, *re-produces* or *re-presents* sensory material. It may be less vivid, less sharp in outline, and less definite in detail than the sensation or perception from which it is derived. But in one important respect the image does not differ from the original sense-impression. That is the respect in which ideas or concepts do differ from sense-impressions—at least according to those who hold that ideas or concepts have a certain universality and abstractness which is not found in sensations and sensory images. Those who, like Berkeley and Hume, call sensations or images "ideas" deny the existence of abstract ideas or universal notions precisely because they, too, agree that sense-impressions or sensory images are always particular in their content and meaning.

THE FUNDAMENTAL controversy about what an idea is and the verbal confusion occasioned by the ambiguity of the word (which appears in the chapter on IDEA) do not seem to affect the understanding of the nature of images or their role in the activities of memory and imagination. As William James points out, in discussing the "blended" or "generic" image which is somehow associated with abstract or universal meaning, "a blurred thing is just as particular as a sharp thing, and the generic character of either sharp image or blurred image depends on its being felt *with its representative function*." He speaks of this function as "the mysterious *plus*, the understood meaning," but he denies the possibility of universal or abstract *images*, whatever may be the truth about ideas which are not images at all. Certainly those who deny the presence of anything abstract or universal in the understanding do so on the ground that the content of the mind is basically sensory, whether the mind is perceiving or remembering, imagining or thinking.

The controversy about the nature of the mind does not seem to affect the conception of memory or imagination. As neither is confused with sense-perception, so neither is confused with rational thought. This remains the case whether the theory of mind looks upon the intellect as a faculty separate from the sensitive faculty (including memory and imagination), or conceives the understanding as a single faculty which is active in judgment and reasoning as well as in perceiving, remembering, and imagining.

This and related issues are considered in the chapter on MIND. Except for one point, perhaps, such issues can be ignored here. Sensation is attributed to both animals and men—to all organisms which give evidence of having sense-organs or some sort of sensitive apparatus. Whether all animals, even those which have the most rudimentary sensorium, also have memory and imagination may be disputed; but no one doubts that the higher animals, with central nervous systems and brain structures resembling those of men, can remember and imagine as well as perceive.

All agree, furthermore, that memory and imagination require bodily organs, though the assignment of these two functions to the brain as their organic seat is more uniformly a tenet of modern than of ancient physiology, and can be more clearly expounded as the result of modern researches in neurology. But the question whether the memory or imagination of men and other animals differs more than their bodies do, elicits opposite answers from those who affirm that man alone has reason and those who deny that man has powers of knowing or thinking not possessed by other animals to some degree.

Nevertheless, if man alone is considered, the nature of memory and imagination is clear. The object remembered or imagined need not be physically present to the senses like the object perceived. The object imagined need not be located in the past like the object remembered; nor, for that matter, need it have any definite location in time and space. It need have no actual existence. It may be a mere possibility, unlike the object which cannot be known without being known to exist. As the object of memory is an event which no longer exists, so the object of imagination may be something which has never existed and never will.

Thus memory and imagination greatly enlarge the world of human experience. Without them, man would live in a confined and narrow present, lacking past and future, restricted to what happens to be actual out of the almost infinite possibilities of being. Without memory and imagination, man could be neither a poet nor an historian; and unless he had an angelic sort of intellect which in no way depended on sense-experience, he would be impeded in all the work of science, if memory and imagination did not extend the reach of his senses.

THE PSYCHOLOGICAL analysis of memory usually divides it into a number of separate acts or phases. Recollection presupposes the retention of the material to be recalled. The ingenious experiments of Ebbinghaus that James reports—using the memorization of nonsense syllables to isolate the factors influencing memory—seem to show that retention is affected by the strength of the original associations. But retention is also affected by the interval between the time of learning and the time of revival. The amount of forgetting seems to be a function of two separate factors: the force with which the material to be recalled is originally committed to memory, and the lapse of time.

That retention is not the same as recall may be seen from Ebbinghaus' experimental discovery of the fact that forgetting is never complete. Material which lies below the threshold of recall is nevertheless retained, and manifests its presence by its effect on attempts to relearn the material which *appears* to have been forgotten.

Nothing can be utterly forgotten if, as Augustine suggests, what seems to be forgotten remains in the memory. He considers the effort men make to remember a forgotten name. "Where does that name come back from," he asks, "except from the memory? For even when it is through being reminded of something else that we recognize someone's name, it is still by memory that we do it, for we do not hold it as some new thing learned, but by memory we are sure that this is what the name was. But, were the name utterly blotted out of mind," Augustine argues, "we should not remember it even if we were reminded. For if we had utterly forgotten it, we should not even be able to think of looking for it."

Freud considers forgetting from another point of view. He describes the psychoanalytic method at its inception as a "talking cure" involving efforts in reminiscence. The things which we have put out of mind, he claims, are "hindered from becoming conscious, and forced to remain in the unconscious by some sort of force." He calls this "repression." Freud observed that it occurred when" a wish had been aroused, which was in sharp opposition to the other desires of the individual, and was not capable of being reconciled with the ethical, aesthetic, and personal pretensions of the patient's personality. . . . The end of this inner struggle was the repression of the idea which presented itself to consciousness as the bearer of this irreconcilable wish. This was repressed from consciousness and forgotten."

On this view things which have been put out of mind because we find them unpleasant to contemplate, things which are repressed in order to avoid conflict, are not forgotten when they cannot be consciously remembered. Nor are they below the threshold of recall in the sense that our retention of them has been so weakened by time that no effort at recollection can revive them. On the contrary, they may be capable of quite vivid revival when the emotional obstacles to recollection are removed. Freud applies his theory of the "obliviscence of the disagreeable" to such everyday occurrences as the forgetting of familiar names as well as to the repression of memories connected with the emotional traumas of early life.

Recollection is distinct not only from retention, but also from recognition. The illusion known as *déjà vu* consists in the experience of intense familiarity with a place or scene that, so far as one can recall, has never been witnessed before. In contrast, normal recognition depends upon previous acquaintance with the object being cognized again, *i.e.*, *re-cognized*. The fact, noted by many observers, that recognition may or may not be accompanied by recollection of the previous circumstances, indicates the separation of recall and recognition as acts of memory. Whereas recollection is remembering through the recall of images, recognition consists in remembering at the very moment of perceiving. Both, however, depend upon what seems to be memory's fundamental act —retention.

WITH REGARD TO retention, there are two problems which have been the subject of inquiry throughout the whole tradition. The first concerns what is usually called "the association of ideas." From Aristotle through Hobbes and Hume to James and Freud, there have been various formulations of the laws of association and various interpretations of what such laws signify about the mind. Ebbinghaus, for example, used nonsense syllables in order to measure the effect upon retention of the associations formed by repetition of a series of sounds. All meaning had been removed in order to avoid the influence upon recollection of associations resulting from meaningful connections of the sort which exists among ordinary words. The repetition of nonsense syllables in pairs or series illustrates association by contiguity or succession. According to most writers, the elements of experience become associated through other modes of relation also, such as their similarity or contrast with one another in any significant respect.

It is not the association itself which is remembered. Rather it is through the association of one part of experience with another that memory seems to work, one particular tending to recall others with which it has been associated in one or more ways. Recollection seems to occur through activating connections which have been formed and retained. The modern differentiation of controlled and free association indicates two ways in which this can happen—either by a purposeful pursuit of the past or by the apparently chance recall of one thing by another. The ancients make a parallel distinction between reminiscence and reverie. The former is a process in which recollection resembles reasoning in proceeding step by step through a series of related terms; the latter is more like daydreaming or spontaneous fantasy.

The second problem can be stated, perhaps, as the mystery of retention itself. In describing the capacity of the memory to hold the innumerable things which are not now in mind but can be recalled, the ancients speak of memory as "the storehouse of images." Every variety of thing which can be perceived can be "stored up in the memory," says Augustine, and "called up at my pleasure. . . . When I speak of this or that," he goes on, "the images of all the things I mention are at hand from the same storehouse of memory, and if the images were not there I could not so much as speak of the things . . . The things themselves are not brought into the memory; it is only their images which are seized with such marvellous speed, and stored away marvellously as if in cabinets, and as marvellously brought forth again when we remember."

The marvel of memory deepens into a mystery when we ask what the metaphor of the storehouse literally means. Where actually are the images when they are not actually in mind? If an image is by its nature an act of consciousness, whereby we apprehend objects not immediately present to our senses, how do images exist outside of consciousness during intervals when they do not function in remembering, imagining, or other acts of knowing? Their return to consciousness seems to imply that they have been retained, but where and how is the problem not solved by the metaphor of things stored away in a capacious barn.

The physical storehouse does not require any fundamental transformation in the being of the things it holds between periods when they are actually in use. The memory does. This problem of the nature and causes of retention William James seems to think can be solved only in terms of the retentive power of nervous tissue—what he calls "physiological retentiveness"—though in the view of others the problem becomes no easier (and may even be more complicated) when it is transferred from mind to matter. On either view, there seems to be no question that changes in the brain are somehow causally connected with the activity of memory and imagination, especially retention and recall. Aquinas, for example, observes that the imagination and memory may be "hindered by a lesion of the corporeal organ . . . or by lethargy," an observation many times extended by more recent investigations of the brain pathology underlying amnesia and aphasia.

James' treatment of retention as somehow based on pathways traced in the brain, with recall the result of a retracing of these paths, tends to emphasize the affinity between memory and habit. His theory, discussed in the chapter on Habit, that the plasticity of matter, certainly living matter, underlies learning or habit formation, while the inertia or retentiveness of matter, especially the neural matter of the brain, explains memory or the persistence of habits during periods of disuse, seems almost to identify habit and memory. Ice skating after many years of absence from the sport is as much remembering how to ice skate as reciting a poem committed to memory in youth is the exercise of an old habit.

Not all conceptions of habit and memory permit this fusion of the two—or even their affinity as related aspects of the same phenomenon. Aquinas, for example, restricts memory to an act of knowledge. The performance popularly called "reciting from memory" would not be for him an act of memory, though it might involve memory if the recitation were accompanied by knowledge of the time or place and occasion when the poem was first learned. Such knowledge would be a memory, but the recitation itself would not be, any more than ice skating is. These performances represent the exercise of habits of skill or art.

In view of this, Aquinas raises the question whether the act of knowledge, of the sort involved in reconsidering a geometric proof learned at some earlier moment and now recalled to mind, is an act of memory. The knowledge of the proof which is retained by the intellect during periods when it is not actually exercised, he would call an intellectual habit or habit of knowledge. But should the recollection of this retained knowledge, or the activation of this intellectual habit, also be called an act of memory? Aquinas answers No, on the ground that no reference to the past need be involved in reworking a geometrical problem solved at some earlier time. But if the individual also happens to recall *when* he first solved the problem, that is another matter. Even so, Aquinas claims that "if in the notion of memory we include its object as something past, then the memory is not in the intellectual, but only in the sensitive part." The intellect is said to remember only in the sense of recalling a truth retained by habit, and "not in the sense that it understands the past as something here and now."

Memory is considered in still another way in relation to speculative truths about scientific or philosophical matters. The question is one of the origin of such knowledge. In the usual conception of memory as knowledge of past particulars, one traditional view, found in Aristotle, holds that "out of sense-perception comes to be what we call memory, and out of frequently repeated memories of the same thing develops experience"—the generalized experience which gives rise to induction and the apprehension of the universal. But in the tradition of the great books we also find a more radical and, perhaps, less familiar conception of memory as the chief source of knowledge.

This is Plato's doctrine of reminiscence, in which all learning is a kind of remembering of knowledge already present in the soul. All teaching takes the form of helping the learner to recollect things he may not be aware he knows, by reminding him through a process of questioning which awakens the knowledge already latent in him.

In the *Meno*, Meno asks Socrates, "What do you mean by saying that we do not learn, and that what we call learning is only a process of recollection?" Socrates undertakes to show Meno what he means by taking a slave boy who appears not to know the solution of a certain geometrical problem and merely by questioning him, without ever giving him a single answer, getting the slave boy to find the right solution for himself. Meno assures Socrates that the slave boy had never been taught geometry. Since the boy was not told the answer, he must have always known it, and needed only some reminding to remember what he knew. Socrates suggests the explanation that the boy's soul always possessed this knowledge, bringing it from another life.

Before he undertook the demonstration with the slave boy, Socrates had proposed this hypothesis. "The soul, being immortal, and having been born again many times, and having seen all things that exist . . . has knowledge of them all; and it is no wonder that it should be able to call to remembrance all that it ever knew about virtue, and about everything; for as all nature is akin, and the soul has learned all things, there is no difficulty in her eliciting, or as men say learning, out of a single recollection all the rest, if a man is strenuous and does not faint; for all enquiry and all learning is but recollection."

Though he differs from Plato in his conception of the soul and the origin of the knowledge which it innately possesses, Augustine seems to hold a similar view. As he examines his own memory, it appears to contain much that has not been implanted there by sense-experience. Certain things, referred to by words he understands, he says, "I never reached with any sense of my body, nor ever discerned them otherwise than in my mind; yet in my memory have I laid up not their images, but themselves. How they entered into me, let them say if they can; for I have gone over all the avenues of my flesh, but cannot find by which they entered." If the seeds of learning are in the soul at its creation, memory can draw from these "seminal reasons" the full fruit of knowledge.

THE DOCTRINE OF reminiscence changes the meaning of both learning and memory at the same time. When learning consists in remembering knowledge not acquired in this life, then the activity of memory cannot be, as it is usually conceived, a recollection of knowledge previously acquired in this life by learning. In order to understand a doctrine in which familiar meanings are so profoundly altered, it is perhaps necessary to understand the problem it tries to solve.

That problem exists only for those who make an absolute distinction between particular sensory images and universal ideas or abstract concepts. Those who, like Hobbes, Berkeley, or Hume, deny universals or abstractions as any part of the mind's content, see no special problem in the origin of that part of the mind's content which is not received as sense-impressions. The original impressions are somehow externally caused, and all the rest of the mind's content—its images and memories and all constructions of the sort Locke calls "complex ideas"—then arise by natural derivation from the original sense-impressions.

But those who, on the contrary, maintain that ideas or concepts are *not* images of any sort, cannot avoid the problem of how the mind comes by its ideas. One solution of this problem attributes existence to ideas as intelligible objects, and attributes to the mind the power to apprehend them by direct intuition, just as the senses directly apprehend sensible objects. But if ideas, whether or not they exist outside the mind, cannot be apprehended intuitively, then what is the origin of the ideas whereby the mind understands intelligible objects?

To this question, the doctrine of reminiscence is one answer. Another answer is the doctrine of abstraction, as formulated by Aristotle and Aquinas. Locke and James also seem to recognize a distinction in kind between abstractions and other mental content, but they do not appear to find any need for a special power to perform the act of abstracting general ideas or universal concepts from the sensory particulars of perception and imagination. Aquinas, however, thinks that a special faculty called "the active intellect" must be postulated to account for the mind's possession of the ideas or concepts whereby it actually understands what it cannot perceive or imagine.

THESE THEORIES are considered in the chapters on IDEA and MIND. But just as the doctrine of reminiscence is relevant here for its bearing on the discussion of memory, so the doctrine of abstraction which posits an active intellect is relevant to the discussion of imagination.

"Imagination," writes Aristotle, "is different from either perceiving or discursive thinking, though it is not found apart from sensation or judgment without it. That this activity is not the same kind of thinking as judgment is obvious. For imagining lies within our own power whenever we wish (*e.g.*, we can call up a picture, as in the practice of mnemonics by the use of mental images), but in forming opinions we are not free; we cannot escape the alternatives of falsehood or truth."

The point is not that images cannot be false. They frequently are, as (according to Aristotle) sensations never are. But the falsity of our imaginations involves a judgment that things really are as we imagine them to be. If imagination is not accompanied by judgment, the question of truth or falsity does not arise, for in pure imagination we are not concerned with the way things actually exist, but with the possible, *i.e.*, the imaginary rather than the real. "Everyone knows the difference," says James, "between imagining a thing and believing in its existence."

Conceiving imagination as an activity depending upon the prior activity of the senses, Aristotle holds that imagination is "incapable of existing apart from sensation." In this he does not differ from other psychologists. But he also holds that rational thought, which for him is quite distinct from imagination, cannot exist apart from imagination. "To the thinking soul images serve as if they were the contents of perception. . . . That is the why the soul never thinks without an image."

Aristotle is here saying more than that a special faculty of mind or intellect abstracts the universal form—or what Aquinas calls "the intelligible species"—from the sensory matter of the image, or what Aquinas calls "the phantasm." Aristotle is, in addition, insisting that the act of understanding is always accompanied by imaginative activity. The kind of thinking which depends upon the abstraction of ideas from imagery also depends upon the presence of images when the thinking takes place. "The faculty of thinking," says Aristotle, "thinks the forms in the images"; or, as Aquinas expresses it, "for the intellect to understand actually, not only when it acquires new knowledge, but also when it uses knowledge already acquired, there is need for the act of imagination. . . It must of necessity turn to the phantasms in order to perceive the universal nature existing in the individual." The cooperation of the imagination with the intellect is shown, furthermore, by the fact that "when the act of imagination is hindered by a lesion of the corporeal organ . . . we see that a man is hindered from understanding actually even those things of which he had a previous knowledge."

Augustine, on the contrary, refers to things "which we know within ourselves without images." When we consider numbers, for example, "it is not their images which are in [our] memory, but themselves." The question of imageless thought—of thinking abstractly without the use of images—seems to be peculiarly insistent in sciences like mathematics, metaphysics, and theology, in which the conceivable may not be imaginable. The objects peculiar to these sciences seem to require the scientist to do without imagery, or, as Aquinas says, "to rise above his imagination."

This may be true even in physics. Atoms, according to Lucretius, are conceivable, but they are no more imaginable than they are perceptible. If we need images to think of them, we must use imagery in a metaphorical way, picturing the atom as the smallest particle imaginable—only more so! To the objection that there must be imageless thought if we can think of incorporeal beings, of which there can be no images or phantasms, Aquinas replies that we do so "by comparison with sensible bodies of which there are phantasms."

ARISTOTLE'S THEORY that the operations of thinking are always dependent on (though not reducible to) acts of imagination, does not imply that imagination is always accompanied by abstract or rational thought. Normally, human thinking and knowing is a work which combines both sense and intellect, both reason and imagination, but sometimes even in man imagination may be active without judgment or reasoning. Brute animals, according to Aristotle, are largely guided by their imaginations "because of the non-existence in them of mind." But when imagination takes the place of thought in men, it is "because of the temporary eclipse of their minds by passion or disease or sleep."

Dreaming seems to be the striking case of imagination divorced from reason's judgment or control. It has long been suspected that animals also dream, but the question whether they can distinguish their dreams from their waking perceptions may prove forever unanswerable. Philosophers and psychologists have, however, asked themselves whether there is any way of being certain of the difference between waking thought and the phantasmagoria of dreams.

Descartes, for example, asks, "How do we know that the thoughts that come in dreams are more false than those that we have when we are awake, seeing that often enough the former are not less lively and vivid than the latter?" It seems to him that "there are no certain indications by which we may clearly distinguish wakefulness from sleep." Even as he writes these words, he can almost persuade himself that he is dreaming. Yet he does find one probable sign whereby to tell dreaming from waking. "Our memory," he observes, "can never connect our dreams with one another, or with the whole course of our lives, as it unites events which happen to us while we are awake."

Aquinas finds other evidences of the difference. When a man is fully asleep, he does not dream at all, for his imagination is inactive as well as his senses and his mind. But as sleep passes gradually into waking, his faculties begin to act again, not merely the imagination, but the reason also, so that "a man may judge that what he sees is a dream, discerning, as it were, between things and their images. Nevertheless, the common sense remains partly suspended, and therefore, although it discriminates some images from reality, yet it is always deceived in some particular. Even while a man is asleep, his sense and imagination may be to some extent free, and similarly the judgment of his intellect may be unfettered, though not entirely. Consequently, if a man syllogizes while asleep, when he wakes up he invariably recognizes a flaw in some respect."

APART FROM QUESTIONS of truth and falsity, or reality and illusion, the nature and causes of dreaming are perennial themes in the tradition of western thought. As different suppositions are made concerning the cause of dreams, so different interpretations are given of their content.

When it is supposed that the dream is inspired by the gods or is a divine visitation, it becomes a medium of divination or prophecy—a way of foretelling the future, or of knowing what the gods intend in general, or for the guidance of some particular man. In the great books of ancient poetry and history, and in the Old Testament as well, dreams, like oracles, are interpreted as supernatural portents, and figure as one of the major sources of prophecy. Aristotle discounts both the fulfillment of dreams and their non-fulfillment, "for coincidences do not occur according to any universal or general law." Regarding prophetic dreams as mere coincidences, he does not find it surprising that "many dreams have no fulfillment." From the fact that "certain of the lower animals also dream," he thinks "it may be concluded that dreams are not sent by God, nor are they designed for the purpose of revealing the future."

Instead, Aristotle proposes natural causes for the origin of dreams. Slight stimulations of the sense-organs awaken the dream process and determine its content. "Dreamers fancy that they are affected by thunder and lightning, when in fact there are only faint ringings in their ears . . . or that they are walking through fire and feeling intense heat, when there is only a slight warmth affecting certain parts of the body." Lucretius similarly explains dreams by natural causes, but attributes their content to events which have dominated the thought of waking life.

"On whatever things we have before spent much time," he writes, "so that the mind was more strained in the task than is its wont, in our sleep we seem mostly to traffic in the same things; lawyers think that they plead their cases and confront law with law, generals that they fight and engage in battles, sailors that they pass a life of conflict waged with winds." This is true even of animals. "Strong horses, when their limbs are lain to rest," Lucretius continues, "yet sweat in their sleep, and pant forever, and strain every nerve as though for victory. . . . And hunters' dogs often in their soft sleep yet suddenly toss their legs, and all at once give tongue, and again and again sniff the air with their nostrils, as if they had found and were following the tracks of wild beasts."

In the tradition of the great books, modern writers like their ancient forebears appeal thus to sensation and memory as the natural causes of the origin and content of dreams. But, except for daydreams or waking fantasy, they do not observe that dreaming may be even more profoundly a product of desire. If Freud's extraordinary insight on this point is supported by all the evidences he assembles in his great work, the *Interpretation of Dreams*, then the lateness of this discovery may be thought even more extraordinary than the theory itself.

The theory is not simply that the content of dreams is determined by desires. When Oedipus tells Jocasta of his fear that in taking her to wife he has unwittingly married his mother, she tells him to fear not, for "many men ere now have so fared in dreams also." If that is so, then such dreams do not call for the interpretation which Freud gives. If there are men who suffer from what Freud calls "the Oedipus complex," involving repressed incestuous desires, then the expression of those desires in dreaming will not take the form of imagining them to be actually fulfilled.

On the contrary, Freud's theory of dream symbolism holds that "the dream as remembered is not the real thing at all, but a distorted substitute." Beneath what he calls "the manifest dream-content"—the actual moving images which occupy the dreaming consciousness—lie "the latent dream-thoughts" which are distorted in the actual dream. This distortion "is due to the activities of censorship, directed against the unacceptable unconscious wish-impulses . . . invariably of an objectionable nature, offensive from the ethical, aesthetic, or social point of view, things about which we do not dare to think at all, or think of only with abhorrence." The repressed desires or wishes, the loves or fears, which the dreamer refuses to acknowledge consciously must, therefore, appear in dreams in a disguised form. The imagery of dreams seems to Freud to be a kind of language in which the repressed materials of thought and feeling employ a special symbolism to express what the moral censor will not permit us to express in the ordinary language of our conscious thought or social conversation.

As ordinary language contains symbols conventionally agreed upon, so Freud finds that the recurrence again and again of certain images in the dreams of neurotic patients, and of normal persons as well, gives them the character of conventional symbols. "The number of things which are represented symbolically in dreams is," according to Freud, "not great." They are, he says, "the human body as a whole, parents, children, brothers and sisters, birth, death, nakedness—and one thing more. The only typical, that is to say, regularly occurring, representation of the human form as a whole is that of a *house*. . . . When the walls are quite smooth, the house means a man; when there are ledges and balconies which can be caught hold of, a woman. Parents appear in dreams as *emperor* and *empress*, *king* and *queen*, or other exalted personages . . . Children and brothers are less tenderly treated, being symbolized by little *animals* or *vermin*. Birth is almost invariably represented by some reference to *water*. . . . For dying we have setting out upon a *journey* or *travelling* by train. *Clothes* and *uniforms* stand for nakedness." The one thing more, which Freud mentions in his enumeration, comprises the sexual organs and acts. In contrast to all the others, these, he says, "are represented by a remarkably rich symbolism. . . . An overwhelming majority of symbols in dreams are sexual symbols."

Freud points out why it would be a mistake to treat dream symbols like the words of an ordinary language. "Their object is not to tell anyone anything; they are not a means of communication; on the contrary, it is important to them not to be understood." Wresting their secret from such symbols is a remarkable achievement. Aristotle's remark, which Freud quotes, that "the most skilful interpreter of dreams is he who has the faculty of observing resemblances," seems to be borne out in the Freudian method of discovering the latent content of the dream symbolism. But Freud's therapeutic use of what can thus be discovered makes the psychoanalytic method a thing totally unanticipated by any of his predecessors.

OUTLINE OF TOPICS

1. The faculties of memory and imagination in brutes and men
    - 1*a*. The relation of memory and imagination to sense: the *a priori* grounds of possible experience in the synthesis of intuition, reproduction, and recognition
    - 1*b*. The physiology of memory and imagination: their bodily organs
    - 1*c*. The distinction and connection of memory and imagination: their interdependence
    - 1*d*. The influence of memory and imagination on the emotions and will: voluntary movement
2. The activity of memory
    - 2*a*. Retention: factors influencing its strength
    - 2*b*. Recollection: factors influencing ease and adequacy of recall
    - 2*c*. The association of ideas: controlled and free association; reminiscence and reverie
    - 2*d*. Recognition with or without recall
    - 2*e*. The scope and range of normal memory: failure or defect of memory and its causes
        - (1) Forgetting as a function of the time elapsed
        - (2) The obliviscence of the disagreeable: conflict and repression
        - (3) Organic lesions: amnesia and the aphasias
        - (4) False memories: illusions of memory; *déjà vu*

3. Remembering as an act of knowledge and as a source of knowledge

3a. Reminiscence as the process of all learning: innate ideas or seminal reasons

3b. Sensitive and intellectual memory: knowledge of the past and the habit of knowledge

3c. The scientist's use of memory: collated memories as the source of generalized experience

3d. Memory as the muse of poetry and history: the dependence of history on the memory of men

4. The contribution of memory: the binding of time

4a. Memory in the life of the individual: personal identity and continuity

4b. Memory in the life of the group or race: instinct, legend, and tradition

5. The activity of imagination, fancy, or fantasy: the nature and variety of images

5a. The distinction between reproductive and creative imagination: the representative image and the imaginative construct

5b. The image distinguished from the idea or concept: the concrete and particular as contrasted with the abstract and universal

5c. The pathology of imagination: hallucinations, persistent imagery

6. The role of imagination in thinking and knowing

6a. Imagination as knowledge: its relation to possible and actual experience

6b. The effect of intellect on human imagination: the imaginative thinking of animals

6c. The dependence of rational thought and knowledge on imagination

(1) The abstraction of ideas from images: the image as a condition of thought

(2) The schema of the imagination as mediating between concepts of the understanding and the sensory manifold of intuition: the transcendental unity of apperception

6d. The limits of imagination: imageless thought; the necessity of going beyond imagination in the speculative sciences

7. Imagination and the fine arts

7a. The use of imagination in the production and appreciation of works of art

7b. The fantastic and the realistic in poetry: the probable and the possible in poetry and history

8. The nature and causes of dreaming

8a. Dreams as divinely inspired: their prophetic portent; divination through the medium of dreams

8b. The role of sensation and memory in the dreams of sleep

8c. The expression of desire in daydreaming or fantasy

8d. The symbolism of dreams

(1) The manifest and latent content of dreams: the dream-work

(2) The recurrent use of specific symbols in dreams: the dream-language

8e. Dream-analysis as uncovering the repressed unconscious

REFERENCES

References are listed by volume number (in bold type), author's name, and page number. Bible references are to book, chapter, and verse of the Authorized King James version of the Bible. The abbreviation "esp" calls the reader's attention to one or more especially relevant parts of a whole reference; "passim" signifies that the topic is discussed intermittently rather than continuously in the work or passage cited. Where the work as a whole is relevant to the topic, the page numbers refer to the entire work. For general guidance in the use of *The Great Ideas*, consult the Preface.

1. The faculties of memory and imagination in brutes and men

7 PLATO, 538–541
8 ARISTOTLE, 690–692
17 PLOTINUS, 154–158
18 AUGUSTINE, 74–80
23 HOBBES, 50
30 BACON, 55
31 SPINOZA, 381, 382
35 LOCKE, 141–143
42 KANT, 58
49 DARWIN, 291–292, 412, 480–481
53 JAMES, 421–433, 484–501
54 FREUD, 352

1*a*. The relation of memory and imagination to sense: the *a priori* grounds of possible experience in the synthesis of intuition, reproduction, and recognition

7 PLATO, 523–524
8 ARISTOTLE, 136, 660–661
9 ARISTOTLE, 237
17 PLOTINUS, 157, 161–162, 189–191
19 AQUINAS, 411–413
23 HOBBES, 49–50, 52, 258
28 HARVEY, 332–335
31 DESCARTES, 19–20, 130
31 SPINOZA, 391, 458
35 LOCKE, 98–99, 118–119, 128, 148, 213–214, 355–356
35 BERKELEY, 418–419, 420
35 HUME, 455–457, 477–478
42 KANT, 48–55, 61–64, 85–89 passim, 115, 552–553
53 JAMES, 324, 422–424, 453–456, 480, 483–484, 497–501
54 FREUD, 700–701

1*b*. The physiology of memory and imagination: their bodily organs

8 ARISTOTLE, 703–706
19 AQUINAS, 447–450
23 HOBBES, 172
31 DESCARTES, 96–97, 208–209
31 SPINOZA, 380–382
35 LOCKE, 227–228, 249
53 JAMES, 13, 15–17, 32–37, 70–71, 367–373
54 FREUD, 646–647

1*c*. The distinction and connection of memory and imagination: their interdependence

8 ARISTOTLE, 690–692
17 PLOTINUS, 156–158
18 AUGUSTINE, 77
19 AQUINAS, 496–498
23 HOBBES, 50
31 DESCARTES, 10
31 SPINOZA, 382
35 LOCKE, 142–143
35 HUME, 466–467
42 KANT, 194–195
53 JAMES, 424–427

1*d*. The influence of memory and imagination on the emotions and will: voluntary movement

4 HOMER, 176
9 ARISTOTLE, 235–237, 239, 613–614
12 LUCRETIUS, 55
13 VIRGIL, 115–116
18 AUGUSTINE, 79
19 AQUINAS, 430–431, 690–692
20 AQUINAS, 782–783
23 HOBBES, 61
25 MONTAIGNE, 36–40
27 SHAKESPEARE, 225–227, 289
29 CERVANTES, 57–58
30 BACON, 67
31 SPINOZA, 400–415 passim, 426–428
35 LOCKE, 248–251
38 ROUSSEAU, 345–346
53 JAMES, 704–705, 759–760, 767–792
54 FREUD, 353, 363–364, 377–378

2. The activity of memory

7 PLATO, 538–541
8 ARISTOTLE, 690–695
17 PLOTINUS, 190–191
18 AUGUSTINE, 74–80
23 HOBBES, 53
31 SPINOZA, 382
35 LOCKE, 141–143, 175
53 JAMES, 421–451
54 FREUD, 527

2*a*. Retention: factors influencing its strength

7 PLATO, 446

8 Aristotle, 691
17 Plotinus, 161–162
18 Augustine, 74–75
20 Aquinas, 8–9
30 Bacon, 61–62
35 Locke, 234
53 James, 421–424, 427–441, 448–450
54 Freud, 27–28, 145, 155–157, 769–770

2*b*. Recollection: factors influencing ease and adequacy of recall

7 Plato, 165–166, 621
8 Aristotle, 692–695
18 Augustine, 77–80
30 Bacon, 59, 156–157
31 Descartes, 208–209
31 Spinoza, 456
35 Locke, 118–119
51 Tolstoy, 422
53 James, 163, 382–385, 427–431, 433–434, 438–440
54 Freud, 32–33, 156–157, 485–486, 488–489

2*c*. The association of ideas: controlled and free association; reminiscence and reverie

8 Aristotle, 693–695
23 Hobbes, 52–53, 67
26 Shakespeare, 349–350
29 Cervantes, 1–3, 50–52
31 Descartes, 143
31 Spinoza, 400–402
35 Locke, 248–251
35 Hume, 457–458
36 Sterne, 193–194, 319–320
42 Kant, 51, 493
49 Darwin, 292–293
51 Tolstoy, 82, 146–148, 293–295, 443–444, 464–465, 608
53 James, 360–395
54 Freud, 65–67, 74–79, 347–350, 375–376, 486–489

2*d*. Recognition with or without recall

7 Plato, 538–541
18 Augustine, 78
35 Locke, 118–119
53 James, 163, 384, 440–441
54 Freud, 33, 79

2*e*. The scope and range of normal memory: failure or defect of memory and its causes

4 Homer, 230
7 Plato, 138–141
17 Plotinus, 157
18 Augustine, 74–80
21 Dante, 106, 156–157
25 Montaigne, 15–16, 316–317, 465–466
35 Locke, 141–142, 254–255
36 Sterne, 234–236
51 Tolstoy, 129–130
53 James, 216, 240–258, 443–450
54 Freud, 155–156, 453–456, 526–527

2*e*(1) Forgetting as a function of the time elapsed

18 Augustine, 75–76
20 Aquinas, 1076–1077
23 Hobbes, 50
25 Montaigne, 404
35 Locke, 142
53 James, 438

2*e*(2) The obliviscence of the disagreeable: conflict and repression

25 Montaigne, 177–180
51 Tolstoy, 200, 355–356, 616–617, 630
54 Freud, 6–8, 13, 65–66, 82, 343–345, 378–380, 422–425, 464–467, 472–475, 566–567, 720

2*e*(3) Organic lesions: amnesia and the aphasias

8 Aristotle, 695
19 Aquinas, 449–450
49 Darwin, 299
53 James, 25–26, 32–34, 35–37, 241–258, 448, 490–493 passim
54 Freud, 561–562

2*e*(4) False memories: illusions of memory; *déjà vu*

8 Aristotle, 692
51 Tolstoy, 293–295, 393
53 James, 241, 442
54 Freud, 597–599

3. Remembering as an act of knowledge and as a source of knowledge

7 Plato, 124–126, 228–230
8 Aristotle, 499
17 Plotinus, 159–166
18 Augustine, 640, 643
19 Aquinas, 419–421, 443–444
20 Aquinas, 896–897
23 Hobbes, 53
30 Bacon, 61–62
31 Descartes, 17–18, 95
35 Locke, 141, 308–309
53 James, 396–397, 424–427, 450–451
54 Freud, 484–486

3*a*. Reminiscence as the process of all learning: innate ideas or seminal reasons

7 Plato, 179–183, 228–230, 515–517
8 Aristotle, 136, 511
10 Galen, 173
12 Epictetus, 150
17 Plotinus, 8, 160–161
18 Augustine, 269, 627
19 Aquinas, 295, 300–301, 311, 444–446, 447–449, 595–597
25 Montaigne, 264–265
28 Harvey, 333–334
31 Descartes, 5, 8–9, 13, 77–81 passim, 83, 88, 120, 215, 224–225

31 SPINOZA, 458
35 LOCKE, 90–91, 95–121 passim, 121, 122, 139
35 HUME, 457
42 KANT, 113–115, 352–353
53 JAMES, 851–862

3*b*. Sensitive and intellectual memory: knowledge of the past and the habit of knowledge

7 PLATO, 538–544
8 ARISTOTLE, 174, 662, 692
18 AUGUSTINE, 618
19 AQUINAS, 419–421
20 AQUINAS, 14–15
23 HOBBES, 60, 65
31 DESCARTES, 17–18
31 SPINOZA, 458
35 LOCKE, 308–309, 357, 366–367
53 JAMES, 424–427

3*c*. The scientist's use of memory: collated memories as the source of generalized experience

8 ARISTOTLE, 499–500
28 GILBERT, 1–2
28 HARVEY, 332–335
30 BACON, 105–106, 107–136
31 DESCARTES, 10–12 passim, 33–35
33 PASCAL, 355–358
53 JAMES, 385, 677–678

3*d*. Memory as the muse of poetry and history: the dependence of history on the memory of men

4 HOMER, 183, 226–227
6 THUCYDIDES, 353–354
7 PLATO, 443–444
13 VIRGIL, 254
14 PLUTARCH, 128–129
15 TACITUS, 66
21 DANTE, 2
23 HOBBES, 71
25 MONTAIGNE, 41–42, 199, 305–306
30 BACON, 13–14, 34, 38–39
40 GIBBON, 354, 413
41 GIBBON, 337, 501–503
44 BOSWELL, 3–4
46 HEGEL, 153–154, 181–182, 239–240
47 GOETHE, 1
51 TOLSTOY, 134

4. The contribution of memory: the binding of time

4*a*. Memory in the life of the individual: personal identity and continuity

7 PLATO, 138–140
9 ARISTOTLE, 636, 637
12 LUCRETIUS, 38, 40–41
13 VIRGIL, 229–231
17 PLOTINUS, 154–158 passim
18 AUGUSTINE, 93–98
20 AQUINAS, 997–998
21 DANTE, 100–105 passim
25 MONTAIGNE, 236–237, 316–317
31 DESCARTES, 103
35 LOCKE, 222–227
40 GIBBON, 544–545
48 MELVILLE, 19–20
49 DARWIN, 297
52 DOSTOEVSKY, 411–412
53 JAMES, 213–259, 396–397, 412–413
54 FREUD, 760, 769–770

4*b*. Memory in the life of the group or race: instinct, legend, and tradition

OLD TESTAMENT: *Exodus*, 12:14–20; 13:1–16 / *Numbers*, 15:38–41 / *Deuteronomy*, 4:32–40; 6; 8:2–6; 16:1–12 / *Joshua*, 3:14–4:9 / *Esther*, 9:25–32
APOCRYPHA: *I Maccabees*, 14:16–49
NEW TESTAMENT: *Mark*, 14:3–9 / *I Corinthians*, 11:23–25
7 PLATO, 716, 717–718
13 VIRGIL, 149–152
26 SHAKESPEARE, 556
33 PASCAL, 286
40 GIBBON, 88, 97–98, 398, 627
41 GIBBON, 527–528
43 MILL, 424–425
46 HEGEL, 113, 186–190, 230–231, 261, 263–266
49 DARWIN, 318, 570–571
53 JAMES, 717–719, 722–725, 853–858
54 FREUD, 509–513, 686–689, 692–693, 706–708, 763, 795–796, 800

5. The activity of imagination, fancy, or fantasy: the nature and variety of images

7 PLATO, 577, 623–624
8 ARISTOTLE, 659–661, 666
17 PLOTINUS, 158
19 AQUINAS, 58–59
21 DANTE, 78–79
23 HOBBES, 49–52, 172, 262
26 SHAKESPEARE, 370–371
31 DESCARTES, 79, 96–97
31 SPINOZA, 388
32 MILTON, 177
35 LOCKE, 147–149, 154, 160–162 passim, 165, 168–169, 303, 324
35 BERKELEY, 406–407, 414
35 HUME, 455–456
42 KANT, 528–529
46 HEGEL, 219–221, 254
49 DARWIN, 292
51 TOLSTOY, 105–106, 294–295, 523–524, 601–602
53 JAMES, 480–501
54 FREUD, 597–599

5*a*. The distinction between reproductive and creative imagination: the representative image and the imaginative construct

12 LUCRETIUS, 53–54

19 Aquinas, 447–449
30 Bacon, 112–113
31 Descartes, 76, 82–83
31 Spinoza, 393
35 Locke, 201
35 Berkeley, 413
35 Hume, 466–467
42 Kant, 89, 173–174, 211–212, 493–495
54 Freud, 270–271

5*b*. The image distinguished from the idea or concept: the concrete and particular as contrasted with the abstract and universal

7 Plato, 108–111, 113–114, 534–536, 809–810
8 Aristotle, 111, 120, 136, 508, 518, 648
18 Augustine, 75–76
19 Aquinas, 289–290, 380–381, 430–431, 440–442, 447–450, 451–455, 461–462
20 Aquinas, 896–897
31 Descartes, 80–81, 98–99, 136–137, 211–212
31 Spinoza, 389–390, 391–392
35 Locke, 244–245, 277–278
35 Berkeley, 405–410 passim, 417–418, 430, 440–441
38 Rousseau, 341–342
42 Kant, 15–16, 23–24, 34, 542–543, 570–572
46 Hegel, 155, 230–231, 254
53 James, 305–311, 480–484
54 Freud, 442–443

5*c*. The pathology of imagination: hallucinations, persistent imagery

7 Plato, 520–522
8 Aristotle, 704
14 Plutarch, 816–817
19 Aquinas, 102, 570–571
20 Aquinas, 21–22
23 Hobbes, 51–52, 258
25 Montaigne, 36–41
27 Shakespeare, 290–291, 298–299
29 Cervantes, 4, 18–22, 44–46, 134–136, 285–288
31 Descartes, 22–23, 75–77
31 Spinoza, 437–438
44 Boswell, 13, 114–115
47 Goethe, 110–114
48 Melville, 148–150, 232–235
51 Tolstoy, 109–110, 524–527, 616–617
52 Dostoevsky, 337–348
53 James, 490–493, 506–507, 515–520, 527–538, 662–663, 842–844
54 Freud, 3, 86, 102–106, 115–117, 176, 354–355, 551–552, 597–600

6. The role of imagination in thinking and knowing

6*a*. Imagination as knowledge: its relation to possible and actual experience

7 Plato, 575–577
8 Aristotle, 659–661
19 Aquinas, 250–252
23 Hobbes, 50–54
30 Bacon, 55
31 Descartes, 28, 79–81
31 Spinoza, 384, 387–388, 389–390, 424–425
42 Kant, 72–88, 227–230
53 James, 285–287, 617–625

6*b*. The effect of intellect on human imagination: the imaginative thinking of animals

8 Aristotle, 666–667
19 Aquinas, 442–443, 451–453, 690–692
23 Hobbes, 52
25 Montaigne, 229–230
31 Descartes, 96–97
35 Locke, 145–146
42 Kant, 479
49 Darwin, 292–294, 296–297
53 James, 665–666, 678–686

6*c*. The dependence of rational thought and knowledge on imagination

7 Plato, 333, 383–398
8 Aristotle, 632
19 Aquinas, 380–381, 459–460, 469–471, 473–475, 477–478
20 Aquinas, 15–18
23 Hobbes, 66–67
31 Descartes, 10, 13, 14, 30–31, 79, 136–137
42 Kant, 14–108
53 James, 158–161, 301–302, 328–331, 677–678
54 Freud, 442–443

6*c*(1) The abstraction of ideas from images: the image as a condition of thought

8 Aristotle, 194–195, 663–664
19 Aquinas, 289–290, 383–384, 385–388, 417–418, 447–451, 461–462, 748–749
31 Descartes, 53
35 Locke, 98–99, 145, 147, 339
35 Berkeley, 408–409, 431–432
35 Hume, 505, 506–507
38 Rousseau, 341–342
46 Hegel, 254
53 James, 305–308, 330–331

6*c*(2) The schema of the imagination as mediating between concepts of the understanding and the sensory manifold of intuition: the transcendental unity of apperception

42 Kant, 14–108, 319–320
53 James, 232–235 passim

6*d*. The limits of imagination: imageless thought; the necessity of going beyond imagination in the speculative sciences

7 Plato, 167, 388–398, 595
8 Aristotle, 690
12 Lucretius, 4–5, 16, 19
18 Augustine, 323, 626

7. Imagination and the fine arts

7*a*. The use of imagination in the production and appreciation of works of art

7*b*. The fantastic and the realistic in poetry: the probable and the possible in poetry and history

8. The nature and causes of dreaming

8*a*. Dreams as divinely inspired: their prophetic portent; divination through the medium of dreams

8*b*. The role of sensation and memory in the dreams of sleep

205–237, 250–251, 297–298, 351–356, 478–483, 497–499, 526–527

8*c*. The expression of desire in daydreaming or fantasy

7 Plato, 361
23 Hobbes, 69
25 Montaigne, 14–15, 37, 177, 405–406
26 Shakespeare, 349–350
29 Cervantes, 18–19, 50–52, 134–135
33 Pascal, 186–189
47 Goethe, 245
51 Tolstoy, 125, 146–148, 497–499, 601–602, 615–617
54 Freud, 115–116, 333, 483, 599

8*d*. The symbolism of dreams

8*d*(1) The manifest and latent content of dreams: the dream-work

4 Homer, 294–295
5 Aeschylus, 17, 75
6 Herodotus, 28–29, 47
7 Plato, 213, 221–222
14 Plutarch, 329, 398–399, 548–549, 702–703, 727
21 Dante, 81–82, 95
22 Chaucer, 143–144, 147–148
26 Shakespeare, 36–37, 114–117, 291
27 Shakespeare, 488
32 Milton, 176–178
46 Hegel, 263–265
51 Tolstoy, 249–250, 481–482, 673–674
54 Freud, 178–205, 252–340, 356–373 passim, 489–504, 513–526, 532–544, 809–810, 812–814, 816–818

8*d*(2) The recurrent use of specific symbols in dreams: the dream-language

54 Freud, 173–174, 178–179, 230–231, 265–272, 277–298, 504–513, 516–518, 523–526, 815–817

8*e*. Dream-analysis as uncovering the repressed unconscious

54 Freud, 11–13, 178–205, 319–320, 340–387, 483–494, 501–504, 519–524 passim, 531–532, 538–539, 808–813

CROSS-REFERENCES

For: The discussion of memory and imagination in relation to the faculties of sense and understanding, desire and will, *see* Desire 5a; Idea 1c, 2e–2f; Sense 3b(2), 3d(2).

The controversy over the distinction between image and idea, *see* Idea 2f–2g; Mind 1a(1); Sense 1d, 5a; Universal and Particular 4d.

Other discussions of the association of ideas, and of reverie or daydreaming, *see* Desire 5a; Idea 5e; Relation 4f.

The consideration of memory as knowledge of the past, *see* Knowledge 6b(2); Time 6e; Truth 3a(2); and for the distinction between memory and intellectual habit, *see* Habit 1, 5d; Mind 4c.

The doctrine of reminiscence which identifies learning with remembering, or for the doctrine of innate ideas, *see* Idea 2b; Knowledge 6c(3); Mind 4d(2).

The role of memory in science, history, and poetry, *see* Experience 2a–2b; History 1; Induction 2; Poetry 2.

The problem of personal identity, *see* Same and Other 1b; Soul 1d.

The theory of racial memory in relation to instinct and tradition, *see* Habit 3e; Language 3c; Poetry 3.

For: The function of imagination in thinking and knowing, *see* Mind 1a(2); Reasoning 1c; and for the doctrine that universal concepts are abstracted from sensory images, *see* Idea 2g; Sense 5a; Universal and Particular 4c.

The theory of the transcendental unity of apperception, to which memory or imagination contributes, *see* Knowledge 6b(4); One and Many 4b; Sense 1c, 3c(5).

The imagination as a factor in art, *see* Art 5; and for another discussion of the probable and the possible in poetry, *see* Poetry 8a(2).

Other discussions of dreams, their causes and meaning, *see* Desire 5a, 6c; Language 10; Prophecy 3c; Sign and Symbol 6a; and for the theory of conflict, censorship, and repression involved in the Freudian interpretation of dreams, *see* Desire 4a–4d, 6b.

Matters relevant to the psychopathology of memory and imagination, *see* Desire 5a–5b; Emotion 3a–3b; Man 5b; Mind 8b; Sense 4d(2); Truth 3a(2).

ADDITIONAL READINGS

Listed below are works not included in *Great Books of the Western World*, but relevant to the idea and topics with which this chapter deals. These works are divided into two groups:

I. Works by authors represented in this collection.
II. Works by authors not represented in this collection.

For the date, place, and other facts concerning the publication of the works cited, consult the Bibliography of Additional Readings which follows the last chapter of *The Great Ideas*.

I.

HOBBES. *The Elements of Law, Natural and Politic*, PART I, CH 3
HUME. *A Treatise of Human Nature*, BK I, PART I, SECT III; PART III, SECT V–VII
FREUD. *The Psychopathology of Everyday Life*, CH 1–7
——. *Wit and Its Relation to the Unconscious*
——. *Leonardo da Vinci*

II.

CICERO. *Academics*, II
ALBERTUS MAGNUS. *De Memoria et Reminiscentia*
G. F. PICO DELLA MIRANDOLA. *On the Imagination*
MALEBRANCHE. *De la recherche de la vérité*, BK II
LEIBNITZ. *New Essays Concerning Human Understanding*, BK II
——. *Monadology*, par 26–28
HARTLEY. *Observations on Man, His Frame, His Duty and His Expectations*, VOL I, INTRO; PROPOSITION 8–14, 79–94
VOLTAIRE. "Imagination," in *A Philosophical Dictionary*
T. REID. *Essays on the Intellectual Powers of Man*, III
BLAKE. *Songs of Innocence*
——. *Songs of Experience*
COLERIDGE. *Biographia Literaria*, CH 13
BROWN. *Lectures on the Philosophy of the Human Mind*, VOL II, pp 354–405
DE QUINCEY. *Confessions of an English Opium-Eater*
LAMB. "Dream-Children," in *The Essays of Elia*
J. MILL. *Analysis of the Phenomena of the Human Mind*, CH 7, 10
W. HAMILTON. *Lectures on Metaphysics and Logic*, VOL I (30–33)
BAIN. *The Senses and the Intellect* (Intellect)
SPENCER. *The Principles of Psychology*, VOL I, PART II, CH 5–8; PART IV, CH 6; VOL II, PART IX, CH 3
EMERSON. *Natural History of Intellect*
HERING. *Memory*
TAINE. *On Intelligence*
TYNDALL. *Scientific Use of the Imagination*
LEWIS CARROLL. *Alice's Adventures in Wonderland*
——. *Through the Looking-Glass and What Alice Found There*
S. BUTLER. *Unconscious Memory*
SULLY. *Illusions*, CH 10
GALTON. *Inquiries into Human Faculty and Its Development* (Mental Imagery, Associations, Psychometric Experiments, Anti-Chamber of Consciousness, Visionaries, Number Forms)
ROMANES. *Mental Evolution in Animals*
EBBINGHAUS. *Memory*
C. S. PEIRCE. *Collected Papers*, VOL VI, par 494–504
STEVENSON. "A Chapter on Dreams," in *Across the Plains*
HODGSON. *The Metaphysic of Experience*, VOL I, CH 2 (3–4, 6), 3 (3–4), 7 (5), 8 (4); VOL III, CH I (2 (c)), 2, 3 (5), 4 (3), 5
STOUT. *Analytic Psychology*, CH 11
——. *Manual of Psychology*, BK IV, CH I
RIBOT. *Diseases of Memory*
——. *Essay on the Creative Imagination*
WOODWORTH. *Psychological Issues*, CH 4, 7
TITCHENER. *Lectures on the Experimental Psychology of the Thought-Processes*
BRADLEY. *Collected Essays*, VOL I (13, 18)
——. *Essays on Truth and Reality*, CH 3, 12–13
BERGSON. *Matter and Memory*
——. *Dreams*
——. *Mind-Energy*, CH 4–5
JUNG. *Instinct and the Unconscious*
PROUST. *Remembrance of Things Past*
B. RUSSELL. *The Analysis of Mind*, LECT 8–9
BROAD. *The Mind and Its Place in Nature*, CH 5
SANTAYANA. *Soliloquies in England and Later Soliloquies*, CH 29
——. *Scepticism and Animal Faith*, CH 17
JAENSCH. *Eidetic Imagery and Typological Methods of Investigation*
LOWES. *The Road to Xanadu*
JONES. *Nightmare, Witches, and Devils*
JOYCE. *Ulysses*
——. *Finnegans Wake*
WERTHEIMER. *Productive Thinking*

Chapter 57: METAPHYSICS

INTRODUCTION

IN this chapter, as in MATHEMATICS, we must distinguish controversies about the science we are considering from controversies in it. But here the situation is complicated by many ambiguities. In the tradition of western thought, the name of science has never been denied to mathematics, no matter how its subject matter has been defined or what conception of science has prevailed. But controversies about metaphysics often begin, in modern times at least, by questioning our right to use the word "science" when we speak of metaphysical inquiry or speculation. The challenge usually implies that metaphysics cannot be regarded as a body of valid knowledge because the peculiar objects it has chosen to investigate are not susceptible to scientific inquiry.

If experimentation were the *sine qua non* of scientific knowledge, it would follow, of course, that a discipline which could not perform experiments or even less rigorous types of empirical research could not be called a science. But by that standard mathematics would also be ruled out. It does not seem to be the case, however, that mathematics and metaphysics stand or fall together.

Hume, for example, admits the one and excludes the other. If we are persuaded of his principles concerning science, what havoc, he says, must we make when we run over our libraries. "If we take in our hand any volume; of divinity or school metaphysics, for instance; let us ask, *Does it contain any abstract reasoning concerning quantity or number?* No. *Does it contain any experimental reasoning concerning matter of fact and existence?* No. Commit it then to the flames; for it can contain nothing but sophistry and illusion."

Nor does Kant make experimentation or empirical research indispensable to valid and certain knowledge. On the contrary, pure, as opposed to empirical, physics is for him like mathematics in having the superior status of *a priori* knowledge. They are both sciences in the highest sense of the term because they consist of valid synthetic judgments *a priori*. Kant, therefore, does not exclude metaphysics from the ranks of science because he thinks that "metaphysic, according to its proper aim, consists merely of synthetic propositions *a priori*." Not the method of metaphysics, nor the form of its propositions, but the character of its objects seems to be the cause of its frustration, reducing it to what Kant calls an "illusory dialectic" rather than a valid science.

It might be supposed that those who take the opposite view—that metaphysics is a science, even, perhaps, the highest of the sciences—would agree in defining its objects or the scope of its inquiry. This does not seem to be the case, any more than it seems to be true that all those who criticize metaphysics conceive its subject matter in the same way.

Following what he takes to be the traditional conception of metaphysics in the mediaeval schools, which appears to him to be continued in the writings of Descartes, Leibnitz, and Wolff, Kant says that "metaphysic has for the proper object of its inquiries only three grand ideas: God, Freedom, and Immortality." This also seems to be at least part of what Hume has in mind when he refers to "school metaphysics" and associates it with "divinity," by which he means theology, natural or sacred. Yet we find William James saying that "Hume is at bottom as much of a metaphysician as Thomas Aquinas," because he is engaged in speculations concerning the relation or lack of relation, the identity or lack of identity, in the discrete elements of immediate experience. Here the question seems to be not about God, freedom, and immortality, but about the existence of enduring substances underlying all perceptible qualities, or about a fixed order of reality behind the sequence of phenomena in experience. According to James, "the whole question of interaction and influence between things is a metaphysical question, and cannot be discussed at all by those who are unwilling to go into matters thoroughly."

In the Preface to his *Principles of Psychology*, James declares his plan to limit his own inquiries to what can be known by the empirical methods of the natural sciences. Psychology like physics must assume certain data. The discussion of these assumptions, he says, "is called metaphysics and falls outside the province of this book. . . . The data assumed by psychology, just like those assumed by physics and the other natural sciences, must sometime be overhauled. The effort to overhaul them clearly and thoroughly is metaphysics; but metaphysics can only perform her task well when distinctly conscious of its great extent." The implication seems to be not that metaphysics is impossible but rather that metaphysics, as James conceives it, does not yet exist in any mature or satisfactory development. "Only a metaphysics alive to the weight of her task," he writes, can hope to be successful. "That will perhaps be centuries hence."

WE CANNOT FULLY explore the issue concerning the objects of metaphysics without observing that other names are used in the tradition of the great books to designate the discipline which, rightly or wrongly, claims to be the highest human science. The Greeks initiated the conception of a discipline which should be preeminent because it deals with first principles and highest causes. It not only searches for wisdom about the ultimate realities; it also lays the foundations for all other sciences. But the Greeks do not have one name for this discipline, nor is "metaphysics" even among the various names they use.

Aristotle, whose *Metaphysics* is the first great book to have this word in its title, never uses the word to refer to the science which he is trying to define and establish. In the opening chapters, he speaks of it under the name of wisdom, for "all men suppose what is called Wisdom to deal with the first causes and the principles of all things." There are other theoretical sciences, such as physics and mathematics, which investigate causes or deal with principles, but they do not reach to the highest causes or first principles, nor do they take all things in their most universal aspect as the object of their inquiry.

Though "physics also is a kind of Wisdom," says Aristotle, "it is not the first kind"; and elsewhere he says that "both physics and mathematics must be classed as *parts* of Wisdom." Physics deals only with material things in motion; and "the mathematician investigates abstractions"—objects which, except as abstracted, cannot exist apart from matter and motion. "If there is something which is eternal and immovable and separated from matter, clearly the knowledge of it belongs to a theoretical science —not, however, to physics nor to mathematics, but to a science prior to both." It is that science which is the highest part of wisdom.

Aristotle gives two names to the supreme form of human wisdom or the highest of the theoretical sciences. He denominates it both from the position it occupies in relation to all other disciplines and also in terms of the kind of substance which it alone investigates. If there is "no substance other than those which are formed by nature, natural science (*i.e.*, physics) will be the first science, but if there is an immovable substance, the science of this must be prior and must be first philosophy." But this highest science also deserves to be called "theology" as well as "first philosophy." There are, Aristotle says, "three theoretical philosophies, mathematics, physics, and what we may call theology, since it is obvious that if the divine is present anywhere, it is present in things of this sort," *i.e.*, the eternal, immutable, immaterial.

THERE IS STILL another name for the highest speculative discipline in the Greek conception of the order of the sciences. "Dialectic" is the name which Plato gives to the search for first principles and for the knowledge of the most intelligible realities. As appears in the chapter on DIALECTIC, Aristotle contrasts the dialectician and the philosopher as respectively concerned with opinion and knowledge, but Plato regards the dialectician as preeminently the philosopher. Not only does dialectic belong to the realm of knowledge rather than opinion, but in the realm of knowledge, mathematics occupies the lower, dialectic the upper part. The mathematical sciences build upon hypotheses which they do not and cannot establish. Dialectic uses hypotheses only "as steps and points of departure into a world which is above hypotheses, in order that she may soar beyond them to the first principle of the whole; and . . . by successive steps she descends again without the aid of any sensible object from ideas, through ideas, and in ideas she ends."

Despite all the relevant differences between Plato and Aristotle concerning being and becoming, reason and sense, the intelligible and the sensible, it seems possible to compare the knowledge which Plato calls "dialectic" with what Aristotle calls "first philosophy" or "theology."

Both, for example, proceed from first principles and establish the foundations of the inferior sciences. On its downward path, dialectic, according to Plato, brings the light of reason to bear on the understanding of the hypotheses which are the principles of mathematics. Though Aristotle thinks that mathematics rests on axioms or self-evident truths, he also says that "it must be the business of first philosophy to examine the principles of mathematics" because the mathematician only uses them in a special application without investigating their general truth. Furthermore, the question concerning how the objects of mathematics exist is a question for the first philosopher, not the mathematician.

In the *Sophist*, Plato, to illustrate the difference between the sophist and the dialectician or philosopher, develops an analysis of such terms as being and non-being, true and false, same and other, one and many, rest and motion. These, it seems, are the fundamental concepts in the philosopher's knowledge of the ultimate reality. But these are also the fundamental concepts in Aristotle's *Metaphysics*. In the mediaeval period when "metaphysics" generally replaces "dialectic" as the name for the first philosophy, the so-called transcendental terms—such as *being, essence, other, one, true, good*—are treated as the basic metaphysical concepts; and what is characteristic of them as abstractions helps to characterize the nature of metaphysics as a science.

The word "metaphysics" comes into use as a result of the title supposedly given by the Alexandrian librarians to the work in which Aristotle treats the problems of the first philosophy. The word is short for "the books which come after the books on physics." Plotinus uses the word and connects it with the Platonic meaning of "dialectic. "In the training of the metaphysician he says, dialectic is the ultimate study.

Dialectic, according to Plotinus, "is the method, or discipline, that brings with it the power of pronouncing with final truth upon the nature and relation of things—what each is, how it differs from others, what common quality all have, to what kind each belongs and in what rank each stands in its kind and whether its being is real-being, and how many beings there are, and how many non-beings to be distinguished from beings." But we must not think of dialectic, Plotinus declares, "as the mere tool of the metaphysician." It goes beyond metaphysics as vision or contemplative wisdom goes beyond discursive reasoning and demonstration. "It leaves to another science all that coil of premises and conclusions called the art of reasoning."

THE QUESTION which Plotinus raises—whether there is a higher science or form of knowledge than metaphysics—is naturally considered by the great Christian theologians. In part their answer resembles that of Plotinus; in part it differs. Where Plotinus speaks of dialectic as "the most precious part of philosophy" because it transcends reasoning and argument and reaches the sort of immediate apprehension of reality which cannot be expressed in words, theologians recognize the supremacy of mystical knowledge—a foretaste in this life of what the vision of God will be like in the life to come. But, unlike Plotinus, they do not think such knowledge, here or hereafter, is natural wisdom. Rather it is supernatural knowledge, the divine gift to man of a contemplative wisdom to which his nature cannot attain by its own unaided powers.

The subordination of metaphysical science to knowledge which is both supernatural and nonscientific (*i.e.*, neither discursive nor analytical nor demonstrative) is considered in the chapters on THEOLOGY and WISDOM. Another subordination of metaphysics, considered there also, must be mentioned here as well. That is the subordination of metaphysics to theology. Both metaphysics and theology may be conceived as sciences which are engaged in reasoning and argument and in trying to demonstrate conclusions from principles. But one is merely a human science working with the principles of reason, whereas the other is what Aquinas calls "sacred doctrine," in order to signify that its principles are articles of religious faith.

In the hierarchy of human sciences, metaphysics remains supreme—the first philosophy. It suffers only by comparison with theology insofar as the latter rests upon divine revelation and, since it enjoys the certainty of faith, escapes the insecurity of reason. Though metaphysics and theology differ in their principles and somewhat in their methods, they do not differ entirely in their subject matter. Both, for example, may treat of God and of the existence of immaterial and imperishable beings. Aquinas, therefore, must face the objection that there is no need for any knowledge in addition to metaphysics because "everything that is, is treated of in philosophical science—even God Himself, in that part of philosophy called theology, or the divine science, by Aristotle." To this he replies by giving two reasons for sacred theology.

It is necessary, he says, "for the salvation of man that certain truths which exceed human reason should be made known to him by divine revelation. Even as regards those truths about God which human reason could have discovered, it was necessary that man should be taught by a divine revelation; because the truth about God such as reason could discover, would only be known by a few, and that after a long time, and with the admixture of many errors." Furthermore, he continues, there is no reason "why those things which may be learnt from philosophical science, so far as they can be known by natural reason, may not also be taught us by another science so far as they fall within revelation. Hence the theology included in sacred doctrine differs in kind from that theology which is a part of philosophy."

These two kinds of theology are traditionally distinguished as natural and sacred. When Francis Bacon divides the sciences "into theology and philosophy," he adds that "in the former we do not include natural theology." Natural theology is the divine part of philosophy, yet it is clearly distinct from sacred theology or what Bacon calls "inspired divinity."

This distinction, in whatever language it is made, raises two problems. The first concerns the relation of natural to sacred theology, especially with regard to the scope of natural theology and the precise nature of its independence of sacred doctrine. On this question there seems to be considerable difference between such writers as Augustine and Aquinas, or Bacon and Descartes. As already noted, the various issues involved are reserved for discussion in the chapter on THEOLOGY. The second problem is directly pertinent to metaphysics alone. The question is whether metaphysics and natural theology are identical in subject matter or scope, or whether natural theology is only a part of metaphysics.

Aristotle seems to answer this question when he suggests that "first philosophy" and "theology" are interchangeable designations for the highest branch of speculative knowledge. To the extent that he declares this science to be an inquiry concerning the existence and nature of immaterial and imperishable substances, his definition of the object of metaphysics would seem to justify the title of theology.

Descartes, who also separates metaphysics from physics by reference to the immateriality and materiality of the substances which are their objects, even more explicitly seems to give the whole of metaphysics a theological character. In the Preface to his *Meditations on the First Philosophy*, he says that he is concerned to treat of "God and the human soul"; for, as he explains to the professors of Sacred Theology of the Sorbonne, "I have always considered that the two questions respecting God and the soul were the chief of those that ought to be demonstrated by philosophical rather than theological argument."

Though he adds the freedom of the human will to the existence of God and the immortality of the soul, Kant's definition of the objects of metaphysical speculation similarly makes metaphysics an inquiry into things which lie outside the realm of physics and associates it with the traditional subject matter of theology, at least in the sense that here reason tries to prove propositions which are the main tenets of religious faith. In his Preface to the first edition of the *Critique of Pure Reason*, Kant remarks that when reason "finds itself compelled to have recourse to principles which transcend the region of experience," it "falls into confusion and contradictions. . . . The arena of these endless contests is called Metaphysic."

If nothing immaterial exists, if there are no beings apart from the changing things of sense-experience, or if, although such things exist, they cannot be known by reason proceeding in the manner of speculative science, does it follow that metaphysics must also be denied existence, at least as a speculative science? The answer seems to be clear. If the declared objects of a science do not exist, or if those objects are unknowable by the methods which that science proposes to follow, then it seems difficult to defend its claims to be a valid science against those who challenge them. The controversy over the validity of metaphysics would thus appear to turn on the truth or falsity of the two "ifs" just mentioned.

But the matter cannot be so resolved if natural theology does not exhaust the whole of metaphysics; that is, if metaphysics considers objects other than the immaterial, and if it inquires into their nature rather than their existence. Aristotle's definition of the subject matter of the first philosophy seems to contain an alternative conception of metaphysics, one which may be quite consistent with the conception of it as theology, but which, however, gives it problems to solve in the realm of physical things.

"There is a science," Aristotle writes, "which investigates being as being and the attributes which belong to being in virtue of its own nature." This definition of the first philosophy seems to differentiate it from mathematics and physics as sharply as the other definition in terms of immaterial and imperishable substances. The other sciences, according to Aristotle, do not treat of "being *qua* being universally." The properties of anything which is "in so far as it has being, and the contraries in it *qua* being, it is the business of no other science to investigate; for to physics one would assign the study of things not *qua* being, but rather *qua* sharing in movement"; and mathematics is concerned with the attributes of things insofar as they are "quantitative and continuous." These sciences "mark off some particular kind of being, some genus, and inquire into this, but not being simply, nor *qua* being. . . . Similarly, these sciences omit the question whether the genus with which they deal exists or does not exist, because it belongs to the same kind of thinking to show what it is and that it is."

Only the first philosophy "does not inquire about particular subjects in so far as each has some attribute or other, but speculates about being, in so far as each particular thing is." Its subject matter, then, includes *all* existing things as existing, and involves not only the question how anything which exists exists (*i.e.*, the properties of being), but also the question whether certain things, whose existence can be questioned, do in fact exist. Whatever truths hold good for all things *qua* being—such as the principle that the same thing cannot both be and not be in the same respect at the same time —belong to the first philosophy, even though, as in this case Aristotle points out, the law of contradiction may also belong to logic as the principle of demonstration.

This broader conception of the first philosophy explains, as its restriction to natural theology could not explain, why the central books in Aristotle's *Metaphysics* treat of sensible, physical substances; their nature as substances; the distinction between substance and accident, form and matter, potentiality and actuality, as principles of the composite nature of changing substances; and the properties of such existences in virtue of their having being, *e.g.*, their unity and divisibility, their sameness and otherness.

Aristotle does not inquire whether such substances exist. He seems to take their existence as unquestionable, for he frequently refers to physical things as "the readily recognized substances." But in addition to the question "how sensible substances exist," there are such questions as "whether there are or are not any besides sensible substances. . . and whether there is a substance capable of separate existence, apart from sensible substances, and if so why and how." These latter questions lead to the concluding books of the *Metaphysics* which inquire into the existence of the non-sensible, the immaterial, the immutable. If Aristotle's theology begins here, then theology is only a part—the crowning part, perhaps—of a larger science whose object is not a special realm of being, but all of being.

Hobbes and Bacon go further than Aristotle in the direction of opposing the identification of metaphysics with theology. Where Aristotle seems to admit theological subject matter as a part of the first philosophy, they exclude it entirely.

Hobbes does not use the word "metaphysics" in his own classification of the sciences; he employs it only as a term of derogation to refer to scholastic doctrines which he repudiates. His own classification makes *philosophia prima* that branch of natural philosophy which is prior to the mathematical and mechanical sciences. The latter deal with determinate quantity and motion. The antecedent science deals with "quantity and motion *indeterminate*." These "being the principles or first foundation of philosophy," the science which deals with them "is called *Philosophia Prima*."

Bacon distinguishes between first philosophy and metaphysics and between metaphysics and natural theology. First philosophy, he says, is "the common parent of sciences." It is concerned with "axioms, not peculiar to any science, but common to a number of them" and also with "the adventitious or transcendental condition of things, such as little, much, like, different, possible, impossible, entity, nonentity, etc." Natural theology, which is the divine part of philosophy because it inquires about "God, unity, goodness, angels, and spirits," is separate from the rest of natural philosophy.

"But to assign the proper office of metaphysics, as contra-distinguished from primary philosophy and natural theology," Bacon writes, "we must note that as physics regards the things which are wholly immersed in matter and movable, so metaphysics regards what is more abstracted and fixed; that physics supposes only existence, motion, and natural necessity, whilst metaphysics supposes also mind and idea. . . . As we have divided natural philosophy into the investigation of causes and the production of effects, and referred the investigation of causes to theory, which we again divide into physical and metaphysical, it is necessary that the real difference of these two be drawn from the nature of the causes they inquire into." Physics, according to Bacon, inquires into efficient and material causes; metaphysics, into formal and final causes; and as mechanics is the practical application of physical theory, so what Bacon calls "magic" is the practical doctrine that corresponds to the metaphysical theory of forms.

AGREEMENT OR disagreement concerning the subject matter and problems of that which claims to be the highest human science, however named, does not seem to be uniformly accompanied by agreement or disagreement concerning the status and development of the discipline in question.

There seems to be some similarity, for example, between Plato's dialectic as an inquiry into forms and Bacon's notion of metaphysics as concerned with formal causes—a similarity which Bacon himself observes. But where Plato seems to think that dialectic exists, to be taught and learned, Bacon's judgment is that this part of metaphysics, if not the part dealing with final causes, has not yet been developed because the right method has not been employed.

Again, Aristotle's conception of metaphysics as concerned with the primary axioms, the universal principles applicable to all existence, and the transcendental properties of being, seems to bear some resemblance to Bacon's primary philosophy. But Bacon writes as if Aristotle's *Metaphysics* had not been written, or at least as if it had not succeeded, as Aristotle might have supposed it had, in establishing the science which Bacon finds for the most part in a defective or undeveloped condition.

If we turn to natural theology, either as a part of metaphysics (with Aristotle), or as separate from metaphysics (with Bacon), or as identical with metaphysics (with Descartes), we find the same situation. Aside from some verbal and some real differences concerning the objects of the inquiry, Aristotle, Bacon, and Descartes think that the existence of beings apart from the sensible world of matter and change can be demonstrated and that something can be known of their nature—whether they are called immaterial substances, spirits, and intelligences, or God, angels, and souls.

With some alterations in language and thought, Plato and Plotinus, Augustine and Aquinas, Spinoza and Locke can be added to this company. They are theologians in that sense of "theology" which implies a rational knowledge—without religious faith, and either by intuition or demonstration—of beings which really exist, yet are not sensible or material or mutable or finite. Spinoza, for example, does not use the word "metaphysics," but he holds that "the human mind possesses an adequate knowledge of the eternal and infinite essence of God." Although Locke's use of the word "metaphysics" is derogatory, and though the purpose of his *Essay Concerning Human Understanding* is to prevent human inquiries from extending beyond man's capacities, he attributes greater certainty to our knowledge of God and the soul than to our knowledge of bodies, and finds no greater difficulty in our speculations about spirits than about particles of matter.

"Experimenting and discovering in ourselves knowledge, and the power of voluntary motion, as certainly as we experiment, or discover in things without us, the cohesion and separation of solid parts, which is the extension and motion of bodies," Locke writes, "we have as much reason to be satisfied with our notion of immaterial spirit, as with our notion of body, and the existence of the one as well as the other. . . . But whichever of these complex ideas be clearest, that of body, or immaterial spirit, this is evident, that the simple ideas that make them up are no other than what we have received from sensation or reflection; and so is it of all our other ideas of substances, even of God himself."

As we have already seen, Hume and Kant deny metaphysics (so far as it is identified with what is traditionally natural theology) the status of a valid theoretical science. For them it is incapable of taking its place beside physics and mathematics. Hume, in addition, denies validity to metaphysical speculation concerning causes and substances in the natural order. Unlike Hume, who simply removes metaphysical problems from the realm of questions worth thinking about, Kant does not reject the problems but rather offers alternative methods of stating and solving them. He hopes thereby to accomplish a reformation rather than an abolition of metaphysical inquiry.

The existence of God, freedom, and immortality must be affirmed, Kant thinks, in the order of practical, not speculative reason. They are indispensable "conditions of the necessary object of our will . . . . that is to say, conditions of the practical use of pure reason." Yet, he adds, "we cannot affirm that we *know* and *understand*, I will not say the actuality, but even the possibility, of them."

Furthermore, by redefining metaphysics to mean "any system of knowledge *a priori* that consists of pure conceptions," Kant not only gives his fundamental treatises in morals and ethics a metaphysical character, but sees the possibility of a genuine metaphysic emerging from the *Critique of Pure Reason*. Once "the dogmatism of metaphysic" has been removed, "that is, the presumption that it is possible to achieve anything in metaphysic without a previous criticism of pure reason. . . . it may not be too difficult to leave a bequest to posterity in the shape of a systematical metaphysic, carried out according to the critique of pure reason."

Kant's transcendental philosophy, and especially what he calls "the architectonic of pure reason," is in a sense that metaphysic already begun. In subject matter, if not in its method or conclusions, it resembles the traditional inquiry concerning the universal principles and transcendental properties of being. The objects of natural theology are, of course, excluded as being beyond the power of reason to know in a speculative manner.

Metaphysics as a possible science is for Kant "nothing more than the inventory of all that is given us by *pure reason*, systematically arranged. . . . Such a system of pure speculative reason," he says in his original preface to the *Critique*, "I hope to be able to publish under the title of *Metaphysic of Nature*." And in the last pages of the *Critique*, wherein he criticizes all speculative efforts in the sphere of natural theology, Kant reaffirms "the speculative and the practical use of pure reason" to constitute "a Metaphysic of Nature and a Metaphysic of

Ethics." The former, he says, is "what is commonly called Metaphysic in the more limited sense." Both together "form properly that department of knowledge which may be termed, in the truest sense of the word, philosophy. The path which it pursues is that of science, which, when it has once been discovered, is never lost, and never misleads."

CONTROVERSIES ABOUT metaphysics can be distinguished from metaphysical controversies—that is, disputes within the field of metaphysical thought. We have confined our attention to the former throughout this chapter. But it may not be possible to judge, much less to resolve, the issues about the scope, methods, and validity of metaphysics without engaging in, or at least facing, issues which are themselves metaphysical.

The only way to escape this would be to suppose that psychology (as an analysis of the powers of the mind) or epistemology (as a theory of the criteria of valid knowledge) could determine in advance of any examination of metaphysical discussion whether the matters to be discussed fall within the range of questions concerning which the human mind has the power to find and validate answers. But if this supposition is untenable in itself; or if it is untenable because psychology and epistemology, when they are treated as the first philosophy, themselves presuppose a metaphysics or conceal their metaphysical presuppositions; then no alternative remains but to judge metaphysics directly by its fruits.

In that case, the issues surveyed in this chapter require an examination of the metaphysical discussions to be found in such chapters as GOD, ANGEL, IDEA, SOUL, IMMORTALITY, WILL (which are relevant particularly to the problems of natural theology); and (as relevant to other parts or problems of metaphysics) such chapters as BEING, CAUSE, FORM, MATTER, ONE AND MANY, RELATION, SAME AND OTHER.

OUTLINE OF TOPICS

1. Conceptions of the highest human science: dialectic, first philosophy, metaphysics, natural theology, transcendental philosophy

2. The analysis of the highest human science: the character of dialectical, metaphysical, or transcendental knowledge

   2*a*. The distinctive objects or problems of the supreme science

   2*b*. The nature of the concepts, abstractions, or principles of the highest science

   2*c*. The method of metaphysics: the distinction between empirical and transcendental methods

   2*d*. The distinction between a metaphysic of nature and a metaphysic of morals: the difference between the speculative treatment and the practical resolution of the metaphysical problems of God, freedom, and immortality

3. Metaphysics in relation to other disciplines

   3*a*. The relation of metaphysics to theology

   3*b*. The relation of metaphysics to mathematics, physics or natural philosophy, psychology, and the empirical sciences

   3*c*. The relation of metaphysics to logic and dialectic

4. The criticism and reformation of metaphysics

   4*a*. The dismissal or satirization of metaphysics as dogmatism or sophistry

   4*b*. Reconstructions of metaphysics: critical philosophy as a propaedeutic to metaphysics

REFERENCES

References are listed by volume number (in bold type), author's name, and page number. Bible references are to book, chapter, and verse of the Authorized King James version of the Bible. The abbreviation "esp" calls the reader's attention to one or more especially relevant parts of a whole reference; "passim" signifies that the topic is discussed intermittently rather than continuously in the work or passage cited. Where the work as a whole is relevant to the topic, the page numbers refer to the entire work. For general guidance in the use of *The Great Ideas,* consult the Preface.

1. Conceptions of the highest human science: dialectic, first philosophy, metaphysics, natural theology, transcendental philosophy

7 PLATO, 167, 486–511, 561–574, 585, 633–635
8 ARISTOTLE, 499–501, 511–512, 522–525, 587–590, 592–593
9 ARISTOTLE, 390
17 PLOTINUS, 10–12
19 AQUINAS, 7–8
23 HOBBES, 269–272
30 BACON, 40–48, 140
31 DESCARTES, 51–54
31 SPINOZA, 458–463
35 HUME, 451–455 passim
42 KANT, 115–117, 120, 172–174, 243–250, 365–366, 551–552
46 HEGEL, 165
51 TOLSTOY, 197
53 JAMES, 95
54 FREUD, 874

2. The analysis of the highest human science: the character of dialectical, metaphysical, or transcendental knowledge

2*a*. The distinctive objects or problems of the supreme science

7 PLATO, 7–13, 368–373, 396–398, 476, 634–635
8 ARISTOTLE, 271, 390, 499–532, 547–551, 587–593
11 NICOMACHUS, 811–813
19 AQUINAS, 24–25, 47–48
30 BACON, 42–46
31 DESCARTES, 75–81
31 SPINOZA, 390–391
35 HUME, 509
42 KANT, 6, 19, 388, 603–607
51 TOLSTOY, 694
53 JAMES, 89–90, 258–259

2*b*. The nature of the concepts, abstractions, or principles of the highest science

7 PLATO, 383–398, 564–574, 809–810
8 ARISTOTLE, 176–177, 537–538, 589, 599–601
19 AQUINAS, 46–47, 66–67, 96–97, 260–261, 451–453
20 AQUINAS, 36–37
23 HOBBES, 269–272
31 DESCARTES, 128–129
31 SPINOZA, 388
35 BERKELEY, 405–406
42 KANT, 6, 215–216, 245–249, 270, 467–468
53 JAMES, 884–886

2*c*. The method of metaphysics: the distinction between empirical and transcendental methods

7 PLATO, 134, 139–140, 396–398, 491, 551–579, 580–608, 610–613
8 ARISTOTLE, 525, 573–574, 590, 592, 631
30 BACON, 44–45
31 DESCARTES, 5–7, 46–47, 128–129, 130–131, 206–207, 237–238, 239–240, 242–244, 245–246
31 SPINOZA, 390, 458–459
42 KANT, 121, 349–250, 277–279, 298–332, 349–351

2*d*. The distinction between a metaphysic of nature and a metaphysic of morals: the difference between the speculative treatment and the practical resolution of the metaphysical problems of God, freedom, and immortality

42 KANT, 33, 124–128, 143–145, 152–153, 164–177, 177–179, 200–209, 234–240, 241–242, 246–250, 253, 263–264, 277–287, 291–293, 301–302, 307–314, 331–337, 340–342, 344–349, 353–354, 386–388, 390–391, 568–570, 588–613 passim

3. Metaphysics in relation to other disciplines

3*a*. The relation of metaphysics to theology

18 AUGUSTINE, 264–273
19 AQUINAS, 3–10, 60–62, 175–178, 209–213, 253–255, 446–447
20 AQUINAS, 392–394, 598–603 passim
23 HOBBES, 163, 165, 269–271
25 MONTAIGNE, 155
30 BACON, 4, 15–16, 39–40, 41, 95–101
31 DESCARTES, 69–71, 125–126, 283–284
33 PASCAL, 266
40 GIBBON, 307–310 passim, esp 308–309, 670

42 KANT, 177–192, 238–240, 346–347, 351–352, 600–601, 604–606, 607–609
46 HEGEL, 158–160, 308–309

3b. The relation of metaphysics to mathematics, physics or natural philosophy, psychology, and the empirical sciences

7 PLATO, 634–635
8 ARISTOTLE, 275, 510, 513–516, 587–588, 598, 603, 632
11 NICOMACHUS, 812–813
16 PTOLEMY, 5–6
20 AQUINAS, 36–37, 598–599
23 HOBBES, 72
30 BACON, 140
39 SMITH, 335–337
42 KANT, 17–19, 211–218, 245–246, 295, 311–313, 330–332
43 MILL, 445

3c. The relation of metaphysics to logic and dialectic

8 ARISTOTLE, 237, 515, 524–525, 589–590
30 BACON, 43–46
38 ROUSSEAU, 341–342
42 KANT, 36–37
46 HEGEL, 182–183
53 JAMES, 881–886

4. The criticism and reformation of metaphysics

4a. The dismissal or satirization of metaphysics as dogmatism or sophistry

23 HOBBES, 52, 54, 56, 59–60, 71, 267–272, 274
25 MONTAIGNE, 240–246, 257–264
30 BACON, 57–58, 60, 113–114, 117
35 LOCKE, 291–292, 293–295
35 BERKELEY, 409–410, 431–432, 441
35 HUME, 478
36 STERNE, 329–336, 421–422
41 GIBBON, 526–527
42 KANT, 1–4, 109, 120–121, 129–130, 187–188, 192
47 GOETHE, 46
48 MELVILLE, 115–117, 255
53 JAMES, 227, 235

4b. Reconstructions of metaphysics: critical philosophy as a propaedeutic to metaphysics

23 HOBBES, 269
31 DESCARTES, 46–48, 75–77, 267–277
35 BERKELEY, 405–412 passim, 439–440
35 HUME, 453–455, 503–504
42 KANT, 1–13, 15–16, 19–22, 101–102, 133–134, 146–149, 157, 196–197, 292–293, 296, 307, 567–568

CROSS-REFERENCES

For: Statements in other contexts concerning the highest human science, *see* DIALECTIC 2a, 4; PHILOSOPHY 2b; SCIENCE 1a(2); THEOLOGY 3a; WISDOM 1a.

Discussions relevant to the objects, problems, and concepts of metaphysics or the highest human science, *see* BEING 2, 3, 4–4a, 7a–7b, 7c, 7d, 7e, 8a–8b; CAUSE 5a, 5d; GOD 2b–2c, 6b; GOOD AND EVIL 1a–1b; IDEA 1f; IMMORTALITY 2; KNOWLEDGE 6a(1), 6a(4); LIBERTY 4a; MIND 10f; NECESSITY AND CONTINGENCY 1, 2a–2b; ONE AND MANY 1–1b; RELATION 3; SAME AND OTHER 1, 2c, 2e; SOUL 4b; TRUTH 1b–1c.

Considerations relevant to the nature of metaphysical concepts or abstractions, *see* BEING 1; DEFINITION 6a; IDEA 1d, 2g, 4b(4); MEMORY AND IMAGINATION 6d; SIGN AND SYMBOL 3d.

The method or character of metaphysical thought, *see* KNOWLEDGE 6c(4); LOGIC 4d; PHILOSOPHY 3a–3b; REASONING 6a; TRUTH 4c.

The relation of metaphysics to theology, *see* KNOWLEDGE 6c(5); THEOLOGY 2, 3a, 4a; WISDOM 1a, 1c; and for the relation of metaphysics to mathematics and physics, *see* MATHEMATICS 1a; NATURE 4b; PHILOSOPHY 2b; PHYSICS 1a; SCIENCE 1a(2).

The problem of principles common to metaphysics and logic, *see* PRINCIPLE 1c; and for the statement of the law of contradiction, *see* OPPOSITION 2a.

Criticisms of metaphysics, and for the substitution of psychology or epistemology for metaphysics as the first philosophy, *see* DIALECTIC 2c, 3c, 6; KNOWLEDGE 5d–5e; MAN 2b(4); PHILOSOPHY 3d, 6b; SOUL 5a; THEOLOGY 5.

Considerations relevant to a metaphysic of morals, and for the solution therein of the problems of God, freedom, and immortality, *see* GOD 2d; IMMORTALITY 3a; NECESSITY AND CONTINGENCY 4b; PHILOSOPHY 2a; WILL 5b(4).

ADDITIONAL READINGS

Listed below are works not included in *Great Books of the Western World*, but relevant to the idea and topics with which this chapter deals. These works are divided into two groups:

I. Works by authors represented in this collection.
II. Works by authors not represented in this collection.

For the date, place, and other facts concerning the publication of the works cited, consult the Bibliography of Additional Readings which follows the last chapter of *The Great Ideas*.

I.

AQUINAS. *On the Trinity of Boethius*, QQ 5–6
HUME. *A Treatise of Human Nature*, BK I, PART IV, SECT III–IV
KANT. *De Mundi Sensibilis (Inaugural Dissertation)*, SECT V
——. *Prolegomena to Any Future Metaphysic*, par 1–5, 40–60; SCHOLIA
——. *Metaphysical Foundations of Natural Science*
HEGEL. *Science of Logic*, VOL I, BK I
W. JAMES. *Some Problems of Philosophy*, CH 2–3

II.

MAIMONIDES. *The Guide for the Perplexed*, PART I, CH 33–36
BONAVENTURA. *Itinerarium Mentis in Deum (The Itinerary of the Mind to God)*
SUÁREZ. *Disputationes Metaphysicae*, esp I
MALEBRANCHE. *Dialogues on Metaphysics and Religion*
LEIBNITZ. *Philosophical Works*, CH 11 (*On the Reform of Metaphysics and on the Notion of Substance*)
VOLTAIRE. "Metaphysics," in *A Philosophical Dictionary*
SCHOPENHAUER. *The World as Will and Idea*, VOL II, SUP, CH 17
COMTE. *The Positive Philosophy*, INTRO
LOTZE. *Metaphysics*, INTRO
C. S. PEIRCE. *Collected Papers*, VOL VI, par 318–394
A. E. TAYLOR. *Elements of Metaphysics*
BERGSON. *The Creative Mind*, CH 6
SANTAYANA. *Dialogues in Limbo*, CH 10
HEIDEGGER. *Was ist Metaphysik?*
WHITEHEAD. *Process and Reality*, PART I, CH 3 (2); PART II, CH 9 (4)
T. WHITTAKER. *Prolegomena to a New Metaphysic*
MARITAIN. *The Degrees of Knowledge*, INTRO; CH 4
——. *A Preface to Metaphysics*, LECT II–III
CARNAP. *The Unity of Science*
——. *Philosophy and Logical Syntax*, I
GILSON. *The Unity of Philosophical Experience*, CH 12
B. RUSSELL. *Mysticism and Logic*, CH 5
——. *An Inquiry into Meaning and Truth*, CH 25

Chapter 58: MIND

INTRODUCTION

IN the tradition of the great books, the word "mind" is used less frequently than "reason," "intellect," "understanding," or "soul." There are still other words, like "intelligence," "consciousness," and even "spirit" or "psyche," which often carry some part of the connotation of the word "mind." Certain authors use "mind" as a synonym for one or another of these words, and give it the meaning which other writers express exclusively in terms of "reason" or "understanding." Some discuss mind without reference to soul, some identify mind with soul or spirit, and some conceive mind as only a part of soul or spirit.

For the purpose of assembling in a single chapter references to all discussions which fall within the area of meaning common to all these terms, it was necessary to adopt some single covering word. Our choice of "mind" is partly the result of its present currency, partly the result of the fact that it is somewhat more neutral than the others and therefore less prejudicial to the conflicting theories which are juxtaposed in this chapter.

Words like "reason" or "intellect" usually imply a sharper distinction between the functions or faculties of sensation and thought than does the word "mind." Imagination and memory, for example, are attributed to the understanding in the writings of Locke and Hume, whereas, in the analytical vocabulary of Aristotle and Aquinas, imagination and memory belong to sense, not to reason or intellect. Similarly, words like "soul" or "spirit" usually connote a substantial as well as an immaterial mode of being, whereas "mind" can have the meaning of a faculty or a power to be found in living organisms.

The adoption of the word "mind" is purely a matter of convenience. It begs no questions and decides no issues. The relations between what is here discussed and the matters considered in the chapters on SOUL, SENSE, MEMORY AND IMAGINATION, remain the same as they would be if "reason" or "intellect" were used in place of "mind." Different formulations of these relationships are not affected by the words used, but by different theories of what the mind is, however it is named.

Before we consider the diverse conceptions of the human mind which are enumerated under the seven main divisions of the first section in the Outline of Topics, it may be useful to examine the elements of meaning more or less common to the connotation of all the words which "mind" here represents. Even here we must avoid begging the question whether mind is a peculiarly human possession. Other animals may have minds. Mind may be, as it is on one theory, a universal property of matter. According to another theory, there may be superhuman minds or intelligences, or a single absolute mind, a transcendent intelligence.

What, then, does the universe contain because there is mind in it, which would be lacking if everything else could remain the same with mind removed? The facts we are compelled to mention in answering this question should give us some indication of the elements of meaning common to "mind" and all its synonyms.

FIRST IS THE FACT of thought or thinking. If there were no evidence of thought in the world, mind would have little or no meaning. The recognition of this fact throughout the tradition accounts for the development of diverse theories of mind. None of the great writers denies the phenomenon of thought, however differently each may describe or explain it; none, therefore, is without some conception of mind.

It may be supposed that such words as "thought" or "thinking" cannot, because of their own ambiguity, help us to define the sphere of mind. But whatever the relation of thinking to sensing, thinking seems to involve more—for almost all observers—than a mere reception of impressions from without. This seems to be the opinion of those who make thinking a consequence of sensing, as well as of those who regard thought as independent of sense. For both, thinking goes beyond sensing, either as an elaboration of the materials of sense or as an apprehension of objects which are totally beyond the reach of the senses. To the extent that this insight is true, the elements or aspects of thought discussed in the chapters on IDEA, JUDGMENT, and REASONING have an obvious relevance to the various theories of mind discussed in this chapter.

THE SECOND FACT which seems to be a root common to all conceptions of mind is that of knowledge or knowing. This may be questioned on the ground that if there were sensation without any form of thought, judgment, or reasoning, there would be at least a rudimentary form of knowledge—some degree of consciousness or awareness by one thing of another. Granting the point of this objection, it nevertheless seems to be true that the distinction between truth and falsity, and the difference between knowledge, error, and ignorance, or knowledge, belief, and opinion, do not apply to sensations in the total absence of thought. The chapter on KNOWLEDGE reports formulations of these distinctions or differences. Any understanding of knowledge which involves them seems to imply mind for the same reason that it implies thought.

There is a further implication of mind in the fact of self-knowledge. Sensing may be awareness of an object and to this extent it may be a kind of knowing, but it has never been observed that the senses can sense or be aware of themselves. Take, for example, definitions of sense, or theories of sensation and the objects of sense. Such definitions and theories must be regarded as works of reflective thought; they are not products of sensation.

Thought seems to be not only reflective, but reflexive, that is, able to consider itself, to define the nature of thinking and to develop theories of mind. This fact about thought—its reflexivity—also seems to be a common element in all the meanings of "mind." It is sometimes referred to as "the reflexivity of the intellect" or as "the reflexive power of the understanding" or as "the ability of the understanding to reflect upon its own acts" or as "self-consciousness." Whatever the phrasing, a world without self-consciousness or self-knowledge would be a world in which the traditional conception of mind would probably not have arisen.

THE THIRD FACT is the fact of purpose or intention, of planning a course of action with foreknowledge of its goal, or working in any other way toward a desired and foreseen objective. As in the case of sensitivity, the phenomena of desire do not, without further qualification, indicate the realm of mind. According to the theory of natural desire, for example, the natural tendencies of even inanimate and insensitive things are expressions of desire. But it is not in that sense of desire that the fact of purpose or intention is here taken as evidence of mind.

It is rather on the level of the behavior of living things that purpose seems to require a factor over and above the senses, limited as they are to present appearances. It cannot be found in the passions which have the same limitation as the senses, for unless they are checked they tend toward immediate emotional discharge. That factor, called for by the direction of conduct to future ends, is either an element common to all meanings of "mind" or is at least an element associated with mind.

It is sometimes called the faculty of will—rational desire or the intellectual appetite. Sometimes it is treated as the act of willing which, along with thinking, is one of the two major activities of mind or understanding; and sometimes purposiveness is regarded as the very essense of mentality. Considerations relevant to this aspect of mind are discussed in the chapter on WILL.

THESE THREE OR FOUR FACTS—thought, knowledge or self-knowledge, and purpose—seem to be common to all theories of mind. More than that, they seem to be facts which require the development of the conception. They are, for the most part, not questioned in the tradition of the great books; but they are not always seen in the same light. They are not always related in the same way to one another and to other relevant considerations. From such differences in interpretation and analysis arise the various conflicting conceptions of the human mind.

The conflict of theories concerning *what* the human mind is, what *structure* it has, what *parts* belong to it or what *whole* it belongs to, does not comprise the entire range of controversy on the subject. Yet enough is common to all theories of mind to permit certain other questions to be formulated.

How does the human mind operate? How does it do whatever is its work, and with what intrinsic excellences or defects? What is the relation of mind to matter, to bodily organs, to material conditions? Is mind a common possession of men and animals, or is whatever might be called mind in animals distinctly different from the human mind? Are there minds or a mind in existence apart from man and the whole world of corporeal life?

Such questions constitute the major topics of this chapter. Other topics which appear here, such as the moral and political aspects of mind, are reserved for discussion in the many other chapters devoted to the great ideas of moral and political thought. Still others, like the problem of insanity—the loss or derangement of mind—are obviously relevant here even though the more general consideration of psychopathology belongs elsewhere, *e.g.*, in the chapter on MEDICINE.

The intelligibility of the positions taken in the dispute of the issues which are here our major concern depends to some degree on the divergent conceptions of the human mind from which they stem. It seems necessary, therefore, to examine the seven notions of mind which appear in the great books. This will at least provide the general context for the reader's further explorations, even if it is not possible to trace the implications each of these notions may have for the great controversial issues.

Seven is, of course, a fiction of analysis. There are, from one point of view, more—perhaps as many as there are, among the great authors, thinkers who have dwelt at length on the subject. From another point of view, there may be fewer than seven, for when the lines are drawn according to certain basic differences, several of these theories appear to be variants of a single doctrine.

"THAT IN THE SOUL which is called mind," Aristotle writes, is "that whereby the soul thinks and judges." For him, as for Plato, the human intellect or reason is a part or power of the soul of man, distinct from other parts or faculties, such as the senses and the imagination, desire and the passions. Though the human soul is distinguished from the souls of other living things by virtue of its having this part or power, and is therefore called by Aristotle a "rational soul," these writers do not identify mind and soul. As soul is the principle of life and all vital activities, so mind is the subordinate principle of knowledge and the activities of thinking, deliberating, deciding.

Within the general framework of this theory, many differences exist between Plato and Aristotle and between them and others who share their views. These differences arise not only with respect to the soul of which the intellect is a part, but also with respect to the power or activity of the intellect itself. For example, the distinction which Aristotle initiates, between mind as an active and as a passive power, is more explicitly formulated by Aquinas in his theory of the active intellect and the intellect as potential.

The human intellect, Aquinas writes, "is in potentiality to things intelligible, and is at first *like a clean tablet on which nothing is written*, as the Philosopher says. This is made clear from the fact that at first we are only in potentiality towards understanding, and afterwards we are made to understand actually. And so it is evident that with us to understand is *in a way to be passive*." But the forms of things, or what Aquinas calls their "intelligible species," are not actually intelligible as they exist in material things. He therefore argues that in addition to the "power receptive of such species, which is called the *possible intellect* by reason of its being in potentiality to such species," there must also be another intellectual power, which he calls the active or "agent" intellect.

Nothing, he says, can be "reduced from potentiality to act except by something in act" or already actual. "We must therefore assign on the part of the intellect some power to make things actually intelligible, by the abstraction of the species from material conditions. Such is the necessity for positing an agent intellect."

The more explicit formulation which Aquinas gives of the distinction between the active and the possible intellects as distinct powers has further consequences for the analysis of three states of the passive or possible intellect distinguished by Aristotle. The intellectual power which is receptive of the intelligible species may either be in complete potentiality to them, as it is when it has not yet come to understand certain things. Or it may be described as in habitual possession of the intelligible species when it has previously acquired the understanding of certain things, but is not now actually engaged in understanding them. In the third place, the potential intellect may also be actual or in act whenever it is actually exercising its habit of understanding or is for the first time actually understanding something.

In this traditional theory of mind, many other distinctions are made in the sphere of mental activity, but none is thought to require a division of the mind into two distinct powers, or even to require the discrimination of several states of the same power. Just as Plato regards the intuition or direct apprehension of intelligible objects as an activity of the same intelligence which is able to reason discursively about the ideas it can contemplate, so Aristotle and Aquinas assign three different activities to the intellectual power which apprehends intelligible objects, not by intuition, but only as the result of the abstraction of forms from matter by the active intellect.

Once the possible intellect is actualized by the reception of the abstracted species, it can act in three ways. It can express in concepts the species which have been impressed upon it. This—the first act of the intellect—is conception. Its second and third acts—of judgment and of reasoning—consist in forming propositions out of concepts and in seeing how one proposition follows from others in inference or proof.

Unlike abstraction and conception, which Aquinas assigns to the active and the possible intellect respectively, conception, judgment, and reasoning do not, in his opinion, require distinct powers. Nor do the two kinds of thought or reasoning which Aquinas calls "speculative" and "practical." The speculative and practical intellects, he maintains, "are not distinct powers," for they differ only in their ends. The speculative intellect "directs what it apprehends, not to operation, but to the sole consideration of truth"; the practical intellect "directs what it apprehends to operation" or action. But to the nature of intellect as a power of apprehension, "it is accidental whether it be directed to operation or not."

Not all the foregoing distinctions are made, or made in the same way, by Plato, Aristotle and other authors like Plotinus, Augustine, or Aquinas, who stand together in regarding mind as only a part of the human soul. Lucretius belongs with them on this point, though he differs radically from them on the issue of mind and matter. Mind, for him, is only "the directing principle" of the soul, "the head so to speak, and reigns paramount in the whole body." It is only the thinking or deciding part of the soul. But Plato, Aristotle, and their followers make a distinction in kind between sensations or images and universal ideas or abstract concepts. Sense and intellect are for them distinct faculties of knowing and have distinct objects of knowledge. For Lucretius, on the other hand, thinking is merely a reworking of the images received by the senses. In this one respect at least, Lucretius is more closely associated with the theory of mind to be found in Hobbes, Locke, and Hume.

In the consideration of mind, agreement on one point seems everywhere to be accompanied by disagreement on another. Locke does not agree with Lucretius or Hobbes about the materiality of mind; and though he agrees with Berkeley that mind is a spiritual entity, he does not agree with him, any more than he agrees with Hobbes and Hume, about the abstraction of general concepts from particular sense-impressions. Plato and Aristotle agree that the senses and the intellect or reason are quite distinct, but they do not agree about the relation of these faculties, especially not on the extent to which the mind can act independently of sense and imagination. Augustine seems to share Plato's doctrine of reminiscence as an account of how the senses recall actively to mind ideas it has always somehow possessed. Aquinas adopts Aristotle's doctrine of abstraction as the quite contrary account of the role the senses play in providing the materials on which the mind works to obtain ideas. But Augustine and Aquinas come together on another point in which they depart alike from Aristotle and Plato. They distinguish with precision between the intellect and will as separate faculties of the soul, whereas Plato and Aristotle treat thinking and willing (or knowing and loving) as merely diverse aspects of mental life.

THE SAME SITUATION prevails with respect to the other theories of mind which we must now consider in their own terms. Descartes, for example, resembles Plato and Augustine on the point on which we have seen that they together differ from Aristotle and Aquinas, namely, the relation of mind or reason to the senses or imagination. Yet he is also closer to Aristotle and Plato in a respect in which they together differ from Augustine and Aquinas, namely, in regarding thinking and willing as acts of the mind rather than as belonging to completely separate faculties.

These agreements and differences occur in the context of a basic opposition between Descartes and all the other writers so far mentioned. Unlike all of them, he *identifies* the human mind with the rational soul of man. In the dual nature of man, he says, "there are certain activities, which we call corporeal, *e.g.*, magnitude, figure, motion, and all those that cannot be thought of apart from extension in space; and the substance in which they exist is called *body*. . . . Further, there are other activities, which we call *thinking* activities, *e.g.*, understanding, willing, imagining, feeling, etc., which agree in falling under the description of thought, perception, or consciousness. The substance in which they reside we call a *thinking thing* or *the mind*, or any other name we care, provided only we do not confound it with corporeal substance, since thinking activities have no affinity with corporeal activities, and thought, which is the common nature in which the former agree, is totally different from extension, the common term for describing the latter." Descartes denies that brutes possess thought, but "even though I were to grant," he says, "that thought existed in them, it would in nowise follow that the human mind was not to be distinguished from the body, but on the contrary that in other animals also there was a mind distinct from their body."

The two components of human nature are, according to Descartes, each of them substances —a *res cogitans* or a thinking substance and a *res extensa* or an extended substance. Descartes uses the phrases "rational soul" and "mind" interchangeably. Reason or intellect—the capacity to think—is not a power of the soul. Nor is thinking an act which the soul sometimes performs, sometimes does not. It is the very essence of the soul itself, even as extension is the essence of body. Just as bodies cannot exist without actually having three dimensions, so the mind cannot exist without thinking.

Though it is literally translated into English by "I think, therefore I am," Descartes' *cogito, ergo sum* can be rendered by "Thinking is; therefore, the mind is," or by the strictly equivalent statement, "The mind exists; therefore, there is thinking." It is precisely this equation of the mind's existence with the activity of thought which Locke challenges. "We know certainly, by experience," he writes, "that we sometimes think, and thence draw this infallible consequence, that there is something in us that has the power to think; but whether that substance perpetually thinks or not, we can be no farther assured than experience informs us. . . . I grant that the soul in a waking man is never without thought, because it is the condition of being awake: but whether sleeping, without dreaming, be not an affection of the whole man, mind as well as body, may be worth a waking man's consideration. . . . Methinks every drowsy nod shakes their doctrine, who teach that the soul is always thinking."

What is striking about this disagreement is that Locke and Descartes agree in their conception of man as a union of two distinct substances—the union of a material substance or body with a spiritual substance, a mind or soul. It is not surprising, however, that Berkeley should hold the Cartesian view against Locke. Considering the flow of time in terms of the succession of ideas, Berkeley affirms it to be "a plain consequence that the soul always thinks." To try to "abstract the *existence* of a spirit from its cogitation" is, he adds modestly, "no easy task." He might have said it is impossible, for since he holds that bodies do not exist and that man consists of mind or spirit alone, he need not hesitate to assert that the mind cannot cease to think without ceasing to be. Neither he nor Descartes is, in James' opinion, "free to take the appearances for what they seem to be, and to admit that the mind, as well as the body, may go to sleep."

Despite these differences, Descartes, Locke, and Berkeley seem to agree on the range of activities within the sphere of mind. The mind is a thinking substance for Descartes, yet it also senses and imagines, suffers passions, and exercises acts of will. What Descartes says in terms of acts, Locke says in terms of powers. Mind has many distinct powers, among which Locke includes all the cognitive faculties (not only the powers of abstract thought and reasoning, but also those of sense and imagination), and such voluntary faculties as choosing and willing. Berkeley also includes the whole range of psychological phenomena—sensation, imagination, memory, the passions, reasoning, and choice.

Hume takes a similar view, though in his case one basic qualification must be added. He does not conceive the mind as a soul or a spirit or any other sort of substance. He even has some difficulty with the notion of its continuity or identity from moment to moment in the flow of experience. Yet, he says, "it cannot be doubted that the mind is endowed with several powers and faculties, that these powers are distinct from each other. . . . There are many obvious distinctions of this kind, such as those between will and understanding, the imagination and the passions, which fall within the comprehension of every human creature." What the mind is or how it exists, we may not be able to say; but Hume thinks that "if we can go no farther than this mental geography, or delineation of the distinct parts and powers of the mind, it is at least a satisfaction to go so far."

Descartes' theory of mind seems to serve as a point of departure in another direction from that taken by Locke. Spinoza agrees that the mind is a thinking thing. He agrees that man consists of an individual body united with an individual mind. But he differs from Descartes on the meaning of substance. By its very nature, substance is infinite; and because it is infinite, there can be only one substance, which is God. Finite individual things, whether bodies or minds, do not exist as substances, but as modes of the divine attributes.

"The human mind is a part of the infinite intellect of God, and therefore," Spinoza declares, "when we say that the human mind perceives this or that thing, we say nothing less than that God has this or that idea." He includes love and desire, as well as perception and imagination, among the affections of the mind, even calling them "modes of thought." He adds, however, that these do not exist apart from the idea of the thing loved or desired, "though the idea may exist although no other mode of thinking exist."

Of the remaining three of the seven conceptions of mind here being considered, two bear certain resemblances to theories already mentioned.

Hegel's view of the human mind as a phase or dialectical moment of the Absolute Mind or Spirit seems comparable to Spinoza's conception of the human mind as a part of God's infinite intellect. The Hegelian theory of mind, developed in such works as the *Phenomenology of Mind* and the *Philosophy of Mind*, is reflected in his *Philosophy of History* and in his *Philosophy of Right*. The expression of his view of mind appears, therefore, in the chapters on History and State, as well as here.

There seems to be similar justification for associating the views of William James with those of Locke and Hume. Willing to posit a soul "influenced in some mysterious way by the brain states and responding to them by conscious affections of its own," James goes on to say that "the bare phenomenon, however, the immediately known thing which on the mental side is in apposition with the entire brain-process is the state of consciousness and not the soul itself."

What the soul is and whether it exists belong to metaphysics. So far as psychological observation and analysis are concerned, the phenomena of mind are to be found in the stream of thought or consciousness. States of mind are states of consciousness. James uses the words "feeling" or "thought" to cover every type of mental operation, every state of mind, every form of consciousness, including sensations and emotions, desires and wishes, as well as conception and reasoning.

Locke and Hume distinguish powers of the mind according to different types of mental operation. James tends rather to analyze the mind in terms of its diverse states according to different types of mental content. But he also lays great stress on the dynamic interconnection of the various elements of consciousness in the continuous flow of the stream of thought.

Freud too presents an analysis of different types of mental content, and accompanies it by a theory of the different layers of mind—or psychic structure. He holds, for example, that "we have two kinds of unconscious—that which is latent but capable of becoming conscious, and that which is repressed and not capable of becoming conscious in the ordinary way. . . . That which is latent, and only unconscious in the descriptive and not in the dynamic sense, we call *preconscious*; the term unconscious we reserve for the dynamically unconscious repressed, so that we have three terms, conscious (Cs), preconscious (Pcs), and unconscious (Ucs)."

Like James, Freud is concerned with the dynamic interaction of various mental operations or contents. In addition, a further point of similarity exists between them. James says that "the pursuance of future ends and the choice of means for their attainment are . . . the mark and criterion of the presence of mentality . . . No actions but such as are done for an end, and show a choice of means, can be called indubitable expressions of Mind." Freud goes further in the same direction. By identifying "psychic energy in general" with what he calls "libido," he implies that mind in its most primitive form has entirely the aspect of desire or seeking. It expresses itself in "two fundamentally different kinds of instincts, the sexual instincts in the widest sense of the word . . . and the aggressive instincts, whose aim is destruction."

FINALLY, THERE IS the theory in which mind is neither one of the faculties of the soul, nor itself a thinking substance; nor is it a soul or spirit with a diversity of powers. "All our knowledge," Kant writes, "begins with sense, proceeds thence to understanding, and ends with reason beyond which nothing higher can be discovered in the human mind for elaborating the matter of intuition and subjecting it to the highest unity of thought." These three faculties have distinct functions for Kant. The sensitive faculty is a faculty of intuition. The faculty of understanding is a faculty of judgment and scientific knowledge. The faculty of reason, when properly employed, performs a critical and regulative function in the realm of thought, but when employed beyond the province of its power leads thought into blind alleys or dialectical frustrations.

Mind is not one of these faculties, nor is it the being in which these faculties inhere. The notion of mind seems to have significance, for Kant, primarily in a collective sense. It represents the unity and order of the triad of cognitive faculties. The faculties of feeling and will—which Kant adds to these in his enumeration of "the higher faculties"—belong to the "transcendental ego," but they do not fall within that part of the transcendental structure which is mind. Kant's distinction between the speculative and the practical use of reason, and his distinction between the moral and the aesthetic judgment, involve different relationships between mind—or its triad of faculties—and these other faculties.

THE FOREGOING SURVEY of conceptions of the human mind gives some indication of the way in which other questions about mind are answered.

With regard to the relation of mind and matter, for example, the theories of Descartes, Spinoza, Locke, and James seem to affirm a duality of substances, or of modes of substance, or at least of realms—the physical and the mental. They are confronted by the problem of the relation which obtains between the two —their independence or interaction.

"Mental and physical events," writes James, "are, on all hands, admitted to present the strongest contrast in the entire field of being.

The chasm which yawns between them is less easily bridged over by the mind than any interval we know. Why, then, not call it an absolute chasm," he asks, "and say not only that the two worlds are different, but that they are independent?"

James thinks that to urge this theory of the complete independence of mind and body "is an *unwarrantable impertinence in the present state of psychology.*" He prefers the common-sense theory that each acts on the other somehow. But earlier writers who consider body and mind as distinct substances, find grave difficulties in the way of conceiving their interaction. "How our minds move or stop our bodies by thought, which we every moment find they do," is, according to Locke, "obscure and inconceivable." According to Hume, there is no "principle in all nature more mysterious than the union of soul with body." He interprets one consequence of the union to be that "a supposed spiritual substance acquires such an influence over a material one, that the most refined thought is able to actuate the grossest matter. Were we empowered by a secret wish, to remove mountains, or control planets in their orbit; this extensive authority," Hume thinks, "would not be more extraordinary, nor more beyond our comprehension."

Denying that bodies exist, Berkeley nevertheless argues that even if they did, they could exert no influence upon mind. "Though we give the materialists their external bodies," he says, "they by their own confession are never the nearer knowing how our ideas are produced; since they own themselves unable to comprehend in what manner body can act upon spirit, or how it is possible that it should imprint any idea in the mind. Hence it is evident that the production of ideas or sensations in our minds can be no reason why we should suppose matter or corporeal substances, since that is acknowledged to remain equally inexplicable with or without this supposition."

Those who deny the existence of matter, like Berkeley, or the existence of anything immaterial, like Lucretius or Hobbes, are confronted by problems of their own. Berkeley must explain the mind's perception of bodies or why the mind thinks of matter. Lucretius must explain perception, thought, and choice as functions of material particles in motion.

The reduction of mind to matter raises a question which leads in the opposite direction. Why may it not be supposed that thought and feeling are present in the universe wherever matter is—an atom of mind inseparably conjoined with every atom of matter, as in the "mind-stuff" or "mind-dust" theory which William James considers and criticizes? Still another formulation of the relation of mind to matter is found in the theory of Aristotle and Aquinas, according to whom the rational soul is "the substantial form of an organic body," but the intellect—one of its powers—is not united to matter in any way. Mind is said to be immaterial in that understanding or thought does not require a bodily organ.

The angelic intellect, according to Aquinas, is a "cognitive power which is neither the act of a corporeal organ, nor in any way connected with corporeal matter." The human mind is not so completely divorced from matter, for, though man's intellect "is not the act of an organ, yet it is a power of the soul, which is the form of the body." Among all bodily forms, the human soul alone has the distinction of possessing "an operation and a power in which corporeal matter has no share whatever." But Aquinas also maintains that "the body is necessary for the action of the intellect, not as its organ of action, but on the part of the object" —the phantasm or image produced by the sensitive faculty. He conceives this dependence in the following manner. "For the intellect to understand actually . . . there is need for the act of the imagination and of the other powers" that are acts of bodily organs. "When the act of the imagination is hindered by a lesion of the corporeal organ, for instance, in a case of frenzy, or when the act of the memory is hindered, as in the case of lethargy, we see that a man is hindered from understanding actually even those things of which he had a previous knowledge."

The problem of body and mind is discussed more fully in the chapter on MATTER. Other problems involved in the theory of mind similarly occur in other chapters as well as in this one, *e.g.*, the problem of mind in animals and men (in the chapters on ANIMAL and MAN); the problem of the existence of minds superior to that of man (in the chapters on ANGEL and

GOD); the problem of the origin of ideas in the human mind (in the chapters on IDEA and MEMORY AND IMAGINATION). It should be noted, however, that agreement or disagreement on the nature of the human mind does not always determine agreement or disagreement with respect to these other questions.

Sharing the view that the mind is a spiritual substance, Locke and Descartes do not agree about innate ideas or principles. Locke tends to agree with Aristotle when he says that the mind is a *tabula rasa*, "void of all characters, without any ideas. How comes it to be furnished?" he asks. "Whence has it all the *materials* of reason and knowledge? To this I answer in one word, from *Experience*. In that all our knowledge is founded; and from that it ultimately derives itself. Our observation employed either about external sensible objects, or about the internal operations of our own minds, is that which supplies our understandings with all the *materials* of thinking."

But Locke does not accept Aristotle's sharp distinction between the faculties of sense and reason, nor does he find it necessary to adopt Aristotle's notion of an active intellect to explain how the mind abstracts general ideas from the particulars of sense-perception. So far as his theory attributes to mind the power of sense, Locke has more affinity with Berkeley and Hume than with Aristotle; yet on the question of abstract ideas or the distinction between men and brutes, he is as much opposed to them as they are to Aristotle.

These few observations may be taken as a sample of the many intricately crossing lines of thought which make the complex pattern of the traditional discussion of mind. With few exceptions, almost any other choice of authors and topics would provide similar examples. That fact, combined with the fact that almost every major topic in this chapter leads into the discussion of other great ideas, tends to make the chapter on MIND a kind of focal point for perspective on the whole world of thought. It is not surprising that this should be the case, for on any theory, mind is somehow the place of ideas or, as Aristotle says, "the form of forms."

OUTLINE OF TOPICS

1. Diverse conceptions of the human mind

 1*a*. Mind as intellect or reason, a part or power of the soul or human nature, distinct from sense and imagination

  (1) The difference between the acts of sensing and understanding, and the objects of sense and reason

  (2) The cooperation of intellect and sense: the dependence of thought upon imagination and the direction of imagination by reason

  (3) The functioning of intellect: the acts of understanding, judgment, and reasoning

  (4) The distinction of the active and the possible intellect in power and function

 1*b*. Mind as identical with thinking substance

  (1) The relation of the mind as thinking substance to sense and imagination

  (2) Thinking and willing as the acts of the thinking substance

 1*c*. Mind as a particular mode of that attribute of God which is thought

  (1) The origin of the human mind as a mode of thought

  (2) The properties of the human mind as a mode of thought

 1*d*. Mind as soul or spirit, having the power to perform all cognitive and voluntary functions

  (1) The origin of the mind's simple ideas: sensation and reflection

  (2) The activity of the understanding in relating ideas: the formation of complex ideas

1e. Mind as a triad of cognitive faculties: understanding, judgment, reason

(1) The relation of understanding to sense or intuition: its application in the realm of nature; conformity to law

(2) The relation of judgment to pleasure and displeasure: its application in the realm of art; aesthetic finality

(3) The relation of reason to desire or will: its application in the realm of freedom; the *summum bonum*

1f. Mind as intelligence or self-consciousness, knowing itself as universal: the unity of intellect and will

1g. Mind as the totality of mental processes and as the principle of meaningful or purposive behavior

(1) The nature of the stream of thought, consciousness, or experience: the variety of mental operations

(2) The topography of mind

(3) The unity of attention and of consciousness: the selectivity of mind

2. The human mind in relation to matter or body

2a. The immateriality of mind: mind as an immaterial principle, a spiritual substance, or as an incorporeal power functioning without a bodily organ

2b. The potentiality of intellect or reason compared with the potentiality of matter or nature

2c. The interaction of mind and body

(1) The physiological conditions of mental activity

(2) The influence of mental activity on bodily states

2d. The parallelism of mind and body

2e. The reduction of mind to matter: the atomic explanation of its processes, and of the difference between mind and soul, and between mind and body

3. Mind in animals and in men

3a. Mind, reason, or understanding as a specific property of human nature: comparison of human reason with animal intelligence and instinct

3b. Mentality as a common property of men and animals: the differences between human and animal intelligence in degree or quality

3c. The evolution of mind or intelligence

4. The various states of the human mind

4a. Individual differences in intelligence: degrees of capacity for understanding

4b. The mentality of children

4c. The states of the possible intellect: its potentiality, habits, and actuality

4d. The condition of the mind prior to experience

(1) The mind as completely potential: the mind as a *tabula rasa*

(2) The innate endowment of the mind with ideas: instinctive determinations

(3) The transcendental or *a priori* forms and categories of the mind

4e. The condition of the human mind when the soul is separate from the body

4f. Supernatural states of the human intellect: the state of innocence; beatitude; the human intellect of Christ

5. The weakness and limits of the human mind

  5*a.* The fallibility of the human mind: the causes of error

  5*b.* The natural limits of the mind: the unknowable; objects which transcend its powers; reason's critical determination of its own limits or boundaries

  5*c.* The elevation of the human mind by divine grace: faith and the supernatural gifts

6. The reflexivity of mind: the mind's knowledge of itself and its acts

7. The nature and phases of consciousness: the realm of the unconscious

  7*a.* The nature of self-consciousness

  7*b.* The degrees or states of consciousness: waking, dreaming, sleeping

  7*c.* The conscious, pre-conscious, and unconscious activities of mind

8. The pathology of mind: the loss or abeyance of reason

  8*a.* The distinction between sanity and madness: the criterion of lucidity or insight

  8*b.* The causes of mental pathology: organic and functional factors

  8*c.* The abnormality peculiar to mind: systematic delusion

9. Mind in the moral and political order

  9*a.* The distinction between the speculative and practical intellect or reason: the spheres of knowledge, belief, and action

  9*b.* The relation of reason to will, desire, and emotion

  9*c.* Reason as regulating human conduct: reason as the principle of virtue or duty

  9*d.* Reason as the principle of free will: rationality as the source of moral and political freedom

  9*e.* Reason as formative of human society: the authority of government and law

  9*f.* The life of reason, or the life of the mind, as man's highest vocation: reason as the principle of all human work

10. The existence of mind apart from man

  10*a.* The indwelling reason in the order of nature

  10*b.* *Nous* or the intellectual principle: its relation to the One and to the world-soul

  10*c.* The realm of the pure intelligences: the angelic intellect

  10*d.* The unity and separate existence of the active or the possible intellect

  10*e.* Mind as an immediate infinite mode of God

  10*f.* Absolute mind: the moments of its manifestations

    (1) The unfolding of mind or spirit in world history

    (2) The concrete objectification of mind in the state

  10*g.* The divine intellect: its relation to the divine being and the divine will

REFERENCES

References are listed by volume number (in bold type), author's name, and page number. Bible references are to book, chapter, and verse of the Authorized King James version of the Bible. The abbreviation "esp" calls the reader's attention to one or more especially relevant parts of a whole reference; "passim" signifies that the topic is discussed intermittently rather than continuously in the work or passage cited. Where the work as a whole is relevant to the topic, the page numbers refer to the entire work. For general guidance in the use of *The Great Ideas,* consult the Preface.

1. Diverse conceptions of the human mind

1*a*. Mind as intellect or reason, a part or power of the soul or human nature, distinct from sense and imagination

7 PLATO, 386–388, 392–393, 421
8 ARISTOTLE, 659–664
12 LUCRETIUS, 31–32
17 PLOTINUS, 216–217
18 AUGUSTINE, 74–80
19 AQUINAS, 413–427
42 KANT, 248–250

1*a*(1) The difference between the acts of sensing and understanding, and the objects of sense and reason

7 PLATO, 224–225, 383–398, 457–458, 565–569, 634–635
8 ARISTOTLE, 120, 159–160, 499–500, 518, 559, 648
12 LUCRETIUS, 48–51
12 EPICTETUS, 110–111
17 PLOTINUS, 3–4, 153–154, 189–190
18 AUGUSTINE, 269
19 AQUINAS, 52–53, 105–106, 295–297, 388–391, 418–420, 440–443, 447–455, 461–462, 748–749
20 AQUINAS, 896–897

1*a*(2) The cooperation of intellect and sense: the dependence of thought upon imagination and the direction of imagination by reason

7 PLATO, 228–230, 333, 535–536, 809–810
8 ARISTOTLE, 136–137, 632, 663–664, 683
19 AQUINAS, 380–381, 417–418, 430–431, 443–446, 459–460, 469–472, 486–487
20 AQUINAS, 8–10

1*a*(3) The functioning of intellect: the acts of understanding, judgment, and reasoning

7 PLATO, 392–394, 537–538
8 ARISTOTLE, 39, 550, 577–578, 636–637, 662–663
12 LUCRETIUS, 50–51
17 PLOTINUS, 107
18 AUGUSTINE, 120–121, 651–652
19 AQUINAS, 81–82, 301–303, 306–307, 421–424, 434–435, 440–480, 612–613, 636–637, 683–684
20 AQUINAS, 205–206, 417, 613–614, 773–774
30 BACON, 59–61

1*a*(4) The distinction of the active and the possible intellect in power and function

8 ARISTOTLE, 661–662
19 AQUINAS, 287–288, 289–290, 414–419, 465–466
20 AQUINAS, 10, 82–83, 765–767, 776–777
31 SPINOZA, 366–367

1*b*. Mind as identical with thinking substance

31 DESCARTES, 51–52, 98, 133, 135–136, 152–156, 208, 248, 249–250, 261, 276
35 LOCKE, 123–127
35 BERKELEY, 432, 440–441
53 JAMES, 130–131, 221–226

1*b*(1) The relation of the mind as thinking substance to sense and imagination

31 DESCARTES, 14, 18, 20, 28–33, 53, 77–81, 96–103, 130, 136–137, 215, 218, 229–230
35 BERKELEY, 440

1*b*(2) Thinking and willing as the acts of the thinking substance

31 DESCARTES, 3–5, 17–18, 81–93, 162
35 BERKELEY, 418, 440

1*c*. Mind as a particular mode of that attribute of God which is thought

31 SPINOZA, 366–367, 374, 377–378, 382, 396

1*c*(1) The origin of the human mind as a mode of thought

31 SPINOZA, 373–394

1*c*(2) The properties of the human mind as a mode of thought

31 SPINOZA, 380–382, 387–388, 391–394, 396, 398, 399–401

1*d*. Mind as soul or spirit, having the power to perform all cognitive and voluntary functions

35 LOCKE, 123, 138–141, 143–147, 179–180
35 BERKELEY, 414, 418, 430

53 JAMES, 8–52, 84–94, 116–119, 208, 288–289, 450–451, 742–755, 758–759, 827–835
54 FREUD, 402–404, 412–414, 451–452, 605–606, 639–640, 646–651, 700–703, 829

2*c*(1) The physiological conditions of mental activity

8 ARISTOTLE, 330, 702–706
10 HIPPOCRATES, 159
12 LUCRETIUS, 53–54
19 AQUINAS, 449–450
31 DESCARTES, 19–20
31 SPINOZA, 380–381, 384, 462
35 BERKELEY, 416–417
49 DARWIN, 288
53 JAMES, 9–73, 152–153, 166–167, 367–373, 413–420, 427–430, 455–456, 497–501, 520–521, 533–538, 690–691
54 FREUD, 351–352, 378–382, 586

2*c*(2) The influence of mental activity on bodily states

7 PLATO, 474–475
9 ARISTOTLE, 237, 239
12 LUCRETIUS, 31–32
19 AQUINAS, 106–107
25 MONTAIGNE, 36–40, 332–333
28 HARVEY, 296, 321–322
35 LOCKE, 354
35 HUME, 472–473, 475–476
51 TOLSTOY, 350–354, 567–568, 617, 618
53 JAMES, 64–67, 132–134, 694–699, 767–794, 827–835, 841–848
54 FREUD, 1–6, 25–59, 403, 572, 718–719, 728–729, 852

2*d*. The parallelism of mind and body

31 SPINOZA, 380–384, 396–398, 399–401, 452
53 JAMES, 84–90, 116–119

2*e*. The reduction of mind to matter: the atomic explanation of its processes, and of the difference between mind and soul, and between mind and body

7 PLATO, 567–568
8 ARISTOTLE, 633–641 passim
12 LUCRETIUS, 26–27, 53–54, 55–56
17 PLOTINUS, 78, 79, 195–196
19 AQUINAS, 447–449
23 HOBBES, 49, 52
31 DESCARTES, 224–226, 261
35 LOCKE, 313–315, 350, 351–352, 353
35 BERKELEY, 431
53 JAMES, 95–107, 115–118

3. Mind in animals and in men

3*a*. Mind, reason, or understanding as a specific property of human nature: comparison of human reason with animal intelligence and instinct

5 SOPHOCLES, 134
7 PLATO, 452–454
8 ARISTOTLE, 499, 644, 659–660, 695
9 ARISTOTLE, 9, 347–348, 397, 423–424, 433, 537
12 EPICTETUS, 110–112, 114–116, 233
12 AURELIUS, 276, 286
17 PLOTINUS, 4–6, 94–95, 97–98, 213–214, 323–325
18 AUGUSTINE, 256, 337–338, 610
19 AQUINAS, 105–106, 394–396, 418–419, 421–422, 463–464, 486–487, 510–511, 589–590, 609–610, 664–665, 672, 673–674, 687–688
20 AQUINAS, 8–9, 350–351, 951–953
21 DANTE, 91–92
23 HOBBES, 59, 100
28 HARVEY, 454
31 DESCARTES, 41, 56, 71, 156
31 SPINOZA, 415
32 MILTON, 240–241
33 PASCAL, 233–234, 236, 357–358
35 LOCKE, 36–37, 144–146, 223
36 SWIFT, 151–152, 159–160
38 MONTESQUIEU, 1–2
38 ROUSSEAU, 336, 341
42 KANT, 199–200, 264–265, 316–317, 584–585, 587–588, 602
43 MILL, 294–295
46 HEGEL, 83–84, 136, 168, 304–305
49 DARWIN, 319, 331–332
51 TOLSTOY, 689–690
53 JAMES, 85, 678–686, 691
54 FREUD, 429

3*b*. Mentality as a common property of men and animals: the differences between human and animal intelligence in degree or quality

9 ARISTOTLE, 114, 138, 218
12 LUCRETIUS, 74–75
23 HOBBES, 52, 53, 54, 64, 79
25 MONTAIGNE, 215–232
30 BACON, 163–164
31 DESCARTES, 226
32 MILTON, 240
35 LOCKE, 221–222, 271–272 esp 272, 273–274, 370–371
35 HUME, 487–488
43 MILL, 448–449, 469
49 DARWIN, 287–303
51 TOLSTOY, 689–690
53 JAMES, 47–51 passim, 85, 676–677, 704–706, 873
54 FREUD, 385

3*c*. The evolution of mind or intelligence

38 ROUSSEAU, 337–342, 348–349
49 DARWIN, 281, 286–288, 299, 320–330 esp 320–321
53 JAMES, 51–52, 95–98, 851–861 esp 857–858, 890–897
54 FREUD, 413, 591–592, 647–648, 707–708

4. The various states of the human mind

4*a*. Individual differences in intelligence: degrees of capacity for understanding

4*b*. The mentality of children

4*c*. The states of the possible intellect: its potentiality, habits, and actuality

4*d*. The condition of the mind prior to experience

4*d*(1) The mind as completely potential: the mind as a *tabula rasa*

4*d*(2) The innate endowment of the mind with ideas: instinctive determinations

4*d*(3) The transcendental or *a priori* forms and categories of the mind

4*e*. The condition of the human mind when the soul is separate from the body

4*f*. Supernatural states of the human intellect: the state of innocence; beatitude; the human intellect of Christ

5. The weakness and limits of the human mind

5*a*. The fallibility of the human mind: the causes of error

7*b*. The degrees or states of consciousness: waking, dreaming, sleeping

7*c*. The conscious, pre-conscious, and unconscious activities of mind

8. The pathology of mind: the loss or abeyance of reason

8*a*. The distinction between sanity and madness: the criterion of lucidity or insight

8*b*. The causes of mental pathology: organic and functional factors

8*c*. The abnormality peculiar to mind: systematic delusion

9. Mind in the moral and political order

9*a*. The distinction between the speculative and practical intellect or reason: the spheres of knowledge, belief, and action

9*b*. The relation of reason to will, desire, and emotion

9*c*. Reason as regulating human conduct: reason as the principle of virtue or duty

9*d*. Reason as the principle of free will: rationality as the source of moral and political freedom

9*e*. Reason as formative of human society: the authority of government and law

9*f*. The life of reason, or the life of the mind, as man's highest vocation: reason as the principle of all human work

30 BACON, 18, 27, 69–76
31 DESCARTES, 41–42, 49–50
31 SPINOZA, 431, 447, 448, 458–462
33 PASCAL, 233–234
35 HUME, 452–453
36 SWIFT, 94–99
40 GIBBON, 645
42 KANT, 256–257, 268–270, 337–338, 591–592, 596–597
43 MILL, 448–450, 451
54 FREUD, 779–780

10. The existence of mind apart from man

10*a*. The indwelling reason in the order of nature

12 AURELIUS, 253–310

10*b*. *Nous* or the intellectual principle: its relation to the One and to the world-soul

7 PLATO, 93, 101–102, 455–456, 567–569, 618–619
8 ARISTOTLE, 281, 334, 506, 507
13 VIRGIL, 89
17 PLOTINUS, 66, 129–136, 165–166, 208–251, 278–280, 328–334, 339–342, 351–352
46 HEGEL, 158

10*c*. The realm of the pure intelligences: the angelic intellect

8 ARISTOTLE, 603–605
16 KEPLER, 890–895, 897, 914, 930, 932–933, 1080–1085
17 PLOTINUS, 103–104
18 AUGUSTINE, 103, 299–300, 586–587
19 AQUINAS, 269–275, 284–288, 289–290, 292–294, 297–298, 334–335, 384–385, 465–466, 467–468
20 AQUINAS, 11–13
21 DANTE, 107, 118, 148–150, 151
32 MILTON, 185–186
35 LOCKE, 320, 321–322

10*d*. The unity and separate existence of the active or the possible intellect

8 ARISTOTLE, 662
19 AQUINAS, 388–391, 417–419, 444–446, 595–597
20 AQUINAS, 9–10

10*e*. Mind as an immediate infinite mode of God

31 SPINOZA, 360, 364–365, 366–367, 374–375, 376–377

10*f*. Absolute mind: the moments of its manifestations

46 HEGEL, 18, 19, 82, 83–84, 133, 141, 156–157, 160–162, 177–178, 179, 186–188, 189–190

10*f*(1) The unfolding of mind or spirit in world history

46 HEGEL, 110–114, 153–369

10*f*(2) The concrete objectification of mind in the state

46 HEGEL, 57, 80–82, 84–89, 92, 97, 141, 142, 144, 170–176

10*g*. The divine intellect: its relation to the divine being and the divine will

8 ARISTOTLE, 605
17 PLOTINUS, 65–66
18 AUGUSTINE, 113, 333, 353–354
19 AQUINAS, 14–15, 75–79, 82–83, 97–98, 108–109, 110–112, 291, 457–458, 467–468, 496–500, 540–541, 705
20 AQUINAS, 741–742
21 DANTE, 128–129
31 DESCARTES, 228
31 SPINOZA, 362–363, 367–369, 373–374
42 KANT, 303–304, 612

CROSS-REFERENCES

For: Matters relevant to the conception of reason or intellect as a faculty distinct from sense and imagination and also from will, *see* BEING 8a–8b; IDEA 2b; KNOWLEDGE 6c(3); MAN 1a, 4b–4c; MEMORY AND IMAGINATION 5b, 6b–6c; SENSE 1a–1d; SOUL 2c(2)–2c(3); WILL 1, 5a(1); and for the further distinction of the various intellectual powers and acts, *see* EXPERIENCE 2b; IDEA 1b, 2g; JUDGMENT 1; MEMORY AND IMAGINATION 6c(1); SENSE 5a; UNIVERSAL AND PARTICULAR 2b, 4c–4d.

Matters relevant to the conception of the human mind as a thinking substance, *see* BEING 7b(4); FORM 2d; IDEA 2b; MAN 3a(1); SOUL 1c.

Matters relevant to the conception of the human mind as a finite mode of an attribute of God, *see* BEING 7b(4); IDEA 1e; MAN 3a; NATURE 1b.

Matters relevant to the conception of the human mind as soul or spirit performing all psychological functions, *see* IDEA 1c, 2c–2f; MAN 3a; ONE AND MANY 4a; SENSE 1d, 5a.

Matters relevant to the conception of the human mind as a triad of cognitive faculties, *see*

Idea 1d, 2b; Judgment 1–4, 8d; Knowledge 6b(4); Memory and Imagination 6c(2); One and Many 4b; Principle 2b(3); Sense 3c(5); Soul 1d; Will 5a(4); and for the consideration of its transcendental or *a priori* forms and categories, *see* Experience 2c–2d; Quality 1; Quantity 1; Relation 4c; Sense 1c; Space 4a; Time 6c.

For: Matters relevant to the conception of the human mind as self-consciousness, *see* History 4a(3); Idea 1f; Soul 1d.

Matters relevant to the conception of the mind as consciousness or as a psychic structure including conscious and unconscious processes, *see* Desire 2a, 5a–5c; Experience 1, 2a; Man 4; One and Many 4a; Soul 2b; Will 3b.

The general problem of the relation of body and mind, or matter and spirit, *see* Element 5e; Man 3a–3a(2), 3c; Matter 4c–4d; Soul 3c–3d; and for the condition of the human mind when the soul is separated from the body, *see* Soul 4d.

The distinction between real and intentional existence, or being in nature and being in mind, *see* Being 7d, 7d(2); Form 2a; Idea 6a–6b; Knowledge 1; and for the difference between change in matter and change in mind, *see* Change 6d.

Other comparisons of human and animal mentality, *see* Animal 1c, 1c(2); Evolution 7b(3); Language 1; Man 1a–1c; Sense 2c; and for the relation of reason and instinct, *see* Habit 3c.

The mind's knowledge of itself in relation to the nature and method of psychology, *see* Idea 2d; Knowledge 5a(6); Man 2a–2b(4); Soul 5a–5b.

Other discussions of the weakness and limits of the human mind, *see* Knowledge 5a–5e; Truth 3d–3d(1), 7a; and for the consideration of the training of mind, habits of mind, intellectual virtues, and supernatural gifts, *see* Education 5a–5f; God 6c(2); Habit 5c–5d; Knowledge 6c(5); Prudence 1; Religion 1a; Science 1a(1); Virtue and Vice 2a(2), 8e; Wisdom 1c, 2a.

Other discussions of sleep and dreams, *see* Desire 5a; Life and Death 5b; Memory and Imagination 8a–8e; Sign and Symbol 6a; and for matters relevant to the theory of the repressed unconscious, *see* Desire 3b(2), 6c; Memory and Imagination 2e(2); Opposition 4c; Sign and Symbol 6a.

Other discussions of psychopathology and the causes and cure of mental disorder, *see* Emotion 3c–3d; Man 5b; Medicine 6a–6d; Memory and Imagination 5c.

Matters relevant to the distinction between the speculative and practical intellect, or the pure and practical reason, *see* Judgment 2; Knowledge 6e(1); Philosophy 2a; Prudence 2a–2b; Science 3a; Truth 2c; Wisdom 1b; and for the bearing of this distinction, and the bearing of reason's relation to will and desire, on the differentiation of knowledge, belief, and opinion, *see* Desire 5b; Emotion 3b; God 2d; Immortality 3a; Knowledge 4b; Metaphysics 2d; Opinion 2a–2b; Will 3b–3b(1), 3b(3), 5b(4).

The moral and political aspects of mind, *see* Desire 6a; Emotion 4a–4a(2); Law 1b; Liberty 3b; Slavery 7; State 1a; Tyranny 5d; Virtue and Vice 5b.

The consideration of the existence of mind, reason, or intellect apart from man, *see* Angel 2, 3d; God 5f; Idea 1e; Nature 3a; Soul 1a; Will 4a; World 6c.

ADDITIONAL READINGS

Listed below are works not included in *Great Books of the Western World*, but relevant to the idea and topics with which this chapter deals. These works are divided into two groups:

I. Works by authors represented in this collection.
II. Works by authors not represented in this collection.

For the date, place, and other facts concerning the publication of the works cited, consult the Bibliography of Additional Readings which follows the last chapter of *The Great Ideas.*

I.

PLUTARCH. "That Brute Beasts Make Use of Reason," in *Moralia*
AUGUSTINE. *On the Trinity*, BK X
AQUINAS. *Summa Contra Gentiles*, BK II, CH 73–78
——. *On Spiritual Creatures*, AA 9–10
——. *Quaestiones Disputatae, De Veritate*, QQ 10, 15; *De Anima*, AA 3–5
——. *The Unicity of the Intellect*, III–VII
DANTE. *Convivio* (*The Banquet*), THIRD TREATISE, CH 2, 3 (3), 4 (11)
DESCARTES. *The Principles of Philosophy*, PART I, 7–8, 11–12, 52–53, 62–65; PART IV, 196–197
HUME. *A Treatise of Human Nature*, BK I, PART III, SECT XVI
KANT. *De Mundi Sensibilis* (*Inaugural Dissertation*)
HEGEL. *The Phenomenology of Mind*, V
——. *The Philosophy of Mind*, SECT I

II.

PETER LOMBARD. *The Four Books of Sentences*, BK I, DIST 3
MAIMONIDES. *The Guide for the Perplexed*, PART I, CH 31–32; PART II, CH 37
ALBERTUS MAGNUS. *On the Intellect and the Intelligible*
BONAVENTURA. *Itinerarium Mentis in Deum* (*The Itinerary of the Mind to God*)
DUNS SCOTUS. *Opus Oxoniense*, BK I, DIST 2, Q 3
PETRARCH. *On His Own Ignorance*
FICINO. *Five Questions Concerning the Mind*
PARACELSUS. *The Diseases That Deprive Man of His Reason*
SUÁREZ. *Disputationes Metaphysicae*, XXX (14–15), XXXV, XLIV (4)
BURTON. *The Anatomy of Melancholy*, PART I, SECT I, MEMB II, SUB-SECT 9–11
JOHN OF SAINT THOMAS. *Cursus Philosophicus Thomisticus, Philosophia Naturalis*, PART IV, QQ 9–11
MALEBRANCHE. *De la recherche de la vérité*, BK I, CH I (1); BK III (1), CH 1–4
LEIBNITZ. *New Essays Concerning Human Understanding*
——. *Monadology*
VAUVENARGUES. *Introduction à la connaissance de l'esprit humain*
VOLTAIRE. "Wit," "Spirit," "Intellect," "Mind (Limits of Human)," in *A Philosophical Dictionary*
T. REID. *Essays on the Intellectual Powers of Man*, I, CH 5–8
D. STEWART. *Elements of the Philosophy of the Human Mind*
COLERIDGE. *Biographia Literaria*, CH 5–8
SCHOPENHAUER. *The World as Will and Idea*, VOL I, BK I; VOL II, SUP, CH 15; VOL III, SUP, CH 22
BROWN. *Lectures on the Philosophy of the Human Mind*
J. MILL. *Analysis of the Phenomena of the Human Mind*, CH 16
BAIN. *The Senses and the Intellect*
E. HARTMANN. *Philosophy of the Unconscious*
TAINE. *On Intelligence*
CLIFFORD. "Body and Mind," in VOL II, *Lectures and Essays*
LOTZE. *Microcosmos*, BK V
——. *Metaphysics*, BK III, CH 5
ROMANES. *Animal Intelligence*
T. H. GREEN. *Prolegomena to Ethics*, BK II, CH 2
C. S. PEIRCE. *Collected Papers*, VOL VI, par 238–286
FRAZER. *The Golden Bough*, PART VII
C. L. MORGAN. *Animal Life and Intelligence*
WUNDT. *Outlines of Psychology*, (15–17, 22)
LOEB. *Comparative Physiology of the Brain and Comparative Psychology*
P. M. JANET. *The Major Symptoms of Hysteria*
HOLT. *The Concept of Consciousness*
BERGSON. *Matter and Memory*, CH 3
——. *Creative Evolution*, CH 3–4
——. *Mind-Energy*, CH I, 7
MARITAIN. *Réflexions sur l'intelligence et sur la vie propre*
——. *Theonas: Conversations of a Sage*, I, III
STOUT. *Mind and Matter*
BOSANQUET. *Three Chapters on the Nature of Mind*
BROAD. *The Mind and Its Place in Nature*, CH 3, 7–10, 13–14
PIÉRON. *Thought and the Brain*
DEWEY. *Experience and Nature*, CH 2, 6–8
G. N. LEWIS. *The Anatomy of Science*, ESSAY VIII
WOODBRIDGE. *Nature and Mind*
——. *The Realm of Mind*
JUNG. *Two Essays on Analytical Psychology*
——. *Instinct and the Unconscious*
——. *Mind and the Earth*
SPEARMAN. *The Abilities of Man*
LASHLEY. *Brain Mechanisms and Intelligence*
C. I. LEWIS. *Mind and the World Order*
WHITEHEAD. *The Function of Reason*
R. M. and A. W. YERKES. *The Great Apes*
SHERRINGTON. *The Brain and Its Mechanism*
BLONDEL. *La pensée*
THURSTONE. *The Vectors of Mind*
BLANSHARD. *The Nature of Thought*
SANTAYANA. *Reason in Common Sense*, CH 5–6
——. *The Realm of Spirit*
B. RUSSELL. *The Analysis of Mind*
——. *Human Knowledge, Its Scope and Limits*, PART I, CH 6; PART II, CH 7

Chapter 59: MONARCHY

INTRODUCTION

Of all the traditionally recognized forms of government, monarchy is the easiest to define and to identify. As the word indicates, it is government by one man. It is indifferent whether that man is called king or prince, Caesar or Czar. Of all such titles, "king" is the most frequent; and in consequence monarchy is often called kingship or referred to as the royal form of government.

When monarchy is thus defined in terms of the principle of *unity*, other forms of government, such as aristocracy or oligarchy and democracy, tend to be characterized as government by the few or the many. But the numerical criterion by itself is obviously inadequate. To those who distinguish between aristocracy and oligarchy, it makes a difference whether the few who rule are selected for their pre-eminence in virtue or in wealth. A tyranny, like a monarchy, may be government by one man. Hence those who wish to use the word "monarch" or "king" eulogistically cannot be satisfied with a definition that fails to distinguish between king and tyrant.

It has been said—by Aristotle, for example—that the perversion of, or "deviation from, monarchy is tyranny; for both are forms of one-man rule. But," he adds, "there is the greatest difference between them; the tyrant looks to his own advantage, the king to that of his subjects." Both Aristotle and Plato also say that as tyranny is the worst form of government, so monarchy at the opposite extreme is the best. But though in their opinion tyranny is *always* the worst form of government, Aristotle at least does not seem to think that monarchy is always—*under all conditions*—best.

Further complications appear when other views are taken into consideration. The chapters on CITIZEN, CONSTITUTION, and GOVERNMENT discuss the basic opposition between absolute and limited government in the various terms in which that opposition is traditionally expressed: royal as opposed to political, despotic as opposed to constitutional government; or government by men as opposed to government by law. That opposition seems to be relevant to the theory of monarchy, certainly to any conception of monarchy which tends to identify it with absolute rule, or which sees some affinity between royal and despotic government.

The word "despotic" is, of course, sometimes used in a purely descriptive rather than a disparaging sense. Used descriptively, it designates the absolute rule exercised by the head of a household over children and slaves, neither of whom have any voice in their own government. Aristotle sometimes characterizes the royal government of a political community as despotic to signify its resemblance to the absolute rule of the father or master. He expresses the same comparison in reverse when he says that "the rule of a father over his children is royal."

The derogatory sense of "despotic" would seem to apply to those cases in which grown men are ruled as if they were children, or free men as if they were slaves. The great issue concerning monarchy, therefore, is whether royal government is despotic in this sense. Always, or only under certain conditions? And if despotic, is it also tyrannical? Is monarchy in principle the foe of human liberties? To all these questions there are opposite answers in the great books of political theory. Where Hegel says that "public freedom in general and an hereditary monarchy guarantee each other," others, like Rousseau and Mill, identify the freedom of citizenship with republican or representative government.

This central issue is complicated not only by

the various meanings of "despotism" (discussed in the chapter on TYRANNY), but also by variations in the meaning of the word "monarchy" as it is used by different writers. The word is even used by the same writer in a number of senses. Rousseau, for example, says in one place that "every legitimate government is republican," and in another that "monarchical always ranks below republican government." But he also treats monarchy or royal rule as one form of legitimate government. He describes the king, in whose hands all political power is concentrated, as only having "the right to dispose of it in accordance with the laws." He distinguishes not only between king and tyrant, but also between king and despot.

To avoid what may be only verbal difficulties here, Kant suggests the use of the word "autocrat" to signify "one who has *all* power" and who in his own person "*is* the Sovereign." In contra-distinction "monarch" should signify the king or chief magistrate (sometimes called "president") who "merely represents the sovereignty" or the people who "are themselves sovereign."

SOME POLITICAL theorists distinguish between absolute and limited (or constitutional) monarchy. This in turn raises new problems of definition and evaluation.

Is absolute government always monarchical in form, so that absolute government and absolute monarchy can be treated as identical? Hobbes, who seems to think that government by its very nature must be absolute, nevertheless treats aristocracy and democracy along with monarchy as forms of absolute government. Furthermore, as Rousseau points out, "the Roman Empire saw as many as eight emperors at once, without it being possible to say that the Empire was split up." The absolutism of the government was not diminished by the fact that two or more Caesars often held power at the same time. The triumvirates were also absolute dictatorships.

It would seem, therefore, that the principle of absolute government can be separated from the principle of monarchy. But can monarchy as a form of government be separated from absolute rule?

The question is not whether, in a republic, the monarchical principle is present in the sense that *one* man may hold the office of chief executive. On the issue of a single as opposed to a plural executive, Hamilton and Madison—and with them Jefferson—emphatically favor the principle of unity in the executive branch of the government. "Energy in government," according to *The Federalist*, "requires not only a certain duration of power, but the execution of it by a single hand." The qualities essential to a good executive, such as "decision, activity, secrecy, and dispatch," Hamilton says, "will generally characterize the proceedings of one man in a much more eminent degree than the proceedings of any greater number; and in proportion as the number is increased, these qualities will be diminished."

Yet the authors of *The Federalist*, and Jefferson too, are equally emphatic in insisting upon the difference in kind, not degree, between the power granted the President of the United States and that enjoyed by the King of Great Britain. For them, monarchies and republics are fundamentally opposed in the spirit of their institutions. Despotism is inherent in the nature of monarchy—not only absolute, but even limited monarchy.

If the Constitution of the United States does not set up a constitutional monarchy, even though it provides for one man as chief executive, then a constitutional monarchy must have some other principle in it which distinguishes it from a republic. That may be hereditary succession to the throne; or it may be a certain symbolic identification of the king with the state. But in a monarchy, no matter how attenuated, so long as it does not become purely and simply constitutional government, the king also seems to retain some degree of despotic power—the absolute power exercised by a sovereign person who is free from the supervision of law.

Aristotle takes a similar view. Enumerating five types of kingly rule, he sets one form apart from all the rest—the form in which one man "has the disposal of everything. . . . This form corresponds to the control of a household. For as household management is the kingly rule of a family, so kingly rule is the household management of a city or of a nation." The other forms are all, in one way or another, kingships according to law. Of these, most clearly exemplified in the Spartan constitution, Aristotle says that "the so-called limited monarchy, or kingship according to law . . . is not a distinct form of government, for under all governments, as for example, in a democracy or aristocracy, there may be a general holding office for life, and one person is often made supreme over the administration of a state."

Whether or not there is a supreme commander or a chief magistrate, elected or hereditary, the government is not distinctively royal if the man called "king" is subject to the laws and if the other men in the state are not his subjects but his fellow citizens. For somewhat different reasons, Hobbes agrees with the view that only absolute monarchy is monarchy. When the king is limited in power, he says, the sovereignty is always "in that assembly which had the right to limit him; and by consequence the government is not monarchy, but either democracy or aristocracy; as of old time in Sparta, where the kings had a privilege to lead their armies, but the sovereignty was in the *Ephori*." Hobbes uses the government of one people over another people—the mother country over colonies, or the conqueror over a subjugated nation—to illustrate what he means by absolute monarchy. This suggests a significant parallelism between the problems of monarchy and the problems of empire.

IF THERE WERE universal agreement on the point that only absolute monarchy is truly monarchy, the issue concerning monarchy could be readily translated into the basic opposition between rule by men and rule by law. But such agreement seems to be wanting, and the problems of monarchy are, in consequence, further complicated.

Plato, for example, distinguishes in the *Statesman* between three forms of government according to established laws, of which one is monarchy. Monarchy is better than aristocracy and democracy, obviously not with respect to the principle of the supremacy of law, but simply because government by one seems to be more efficient than government by a few or many; just as tyranny is the worst form of government because, in violating or overthrowing the laws, one man can succeed in going further than a multitude, which is "unable to do either any great good or any great evil."

But all these forms of government, good and bad, better and worse, are compared by Plato with a form of government which he says "excels them all, and is among States what God is among men." It seems to be monarchical in type, but, though not lawless like tyranny, it is entirely above the need of written or customary rules of law. "The best thing of all," Plato writes, "is not that the law should rule, but that a man should rule, supposing him to have wisdom and royal power." Whether such government can ever exist apart from divine rule, or perhaps the advent of the "philosopher king," the point remains that Plato seems to conceive monarchy in two quite distinct ways—both as an absolute rule and also as one of the legally limited forms of government.

Montesquieu separates monarchy from absolute government entirely. At the same time, he distinguishes it from republics, whether aristocracies or democracies. According to him, monarchy is as much a government by law, as much opposed to despotism or absolute government, as are republics. Monarchies and republics are the two main kinds of constitutional government, just as aristocracies and democracies are the two main kinds of republic.

Where Aristotle holds that constitutional monarchy is not a distinct type of government, Montesquieu holds that absolute monarchy does not deserve the name of "monarchy," but should be called "despotism" instead. He criticizes Aristotle's fivefold classification of kingships, saying that "among the number of monarchies, he [Aristotle] ranks the Persian empire and the kingdom of Sparta. But is it not evident," he asks, "that the one was a despotic state and the other a republic?" Since Montesquieu's own view of monarchy involves, in addition to a king, a body of nobles in whom intermediate and subordinate powers are vested, he thinks no true notion of monarchy can be found in the ancient world.

Hegel agrees with Montesquieu that constitutional monarchy is the very opposite of despotism, but he goes much further than Montesquieu in the direction of identifying monarchy with constitutional government. For him constitutional monarchy is the ultimately true form of government. "The development of the state to constitutional monarchy is the achievement of the modern world." He thinks Montesquieu was right in recognizing that the ancient world knew only the patriarchal type of monarchy, a kind of transference of familial government to larger communities still organized on the domestic pattern. But according to Hegel, Montesquieu himself, in stressing the role of the nobility, shows that he understands, not the type of monarchy which is "organized into an objective constitution" and in which "the monarch is the absolute apex of an organically developed state," but only "feudal monarchy, the type in which the relationships recognized in its constitutional law are crystallized into the rights of private property and the privileges of individuals and corporations."

It may be questioned, however, whether Hegel's theory of constitutional monarchy avoids the issue raised by republicans who think that monarchy is inseparable from some form of absolutism, or that monarchy, if entirely devoid of absolutism, has no special character as a form of government. In spite of his acceptance of the traditional distinction between constitutional government and despotism, Hegel seems to regard the sovereignty of the state as absolute in relation to its own subjects at home—no less absolute than is its sovereignty in external affairs *vis-à-vis* foreign states. The crown is the personification of the absolute sovereignty of the state at home. The absolute power of the state comes into existence only in the person of a monarch who has the final decision in all matters.

"The sovereignty of the people," writes Hegel, "is one of the confused notions based on the wild idea of the 'people.' Taken without its monarchy and the articulation of the whole which is the indispensable and direct concomitant of monarchy, the people is a formless mass and no longer a state." Hegel thus dismisses the notion of popular sovereignty (which to Rousseau, Kant, and the Federalists is of the essence of republican government) as inconsistent with "the Idea of the state in its full development." A profound opposition, therefore, exists between Hegel's theory of constitutional monarchy and republican theories of constitutional government. Even though the issue cannot be stated in terms of government by men *vs.* government by laws, a monarchy as opposed to a republic still seems to represent the principle of absolutism in government.

THERE IS STILL another conception of a type of government which is neither a pure republic nor an absolute monarchy. What the mediaeval writers call a "mixed regime" is not a constitutional monarchy in the Hegelian sense, nor is it what Aristotle means when he uses that term. The mediaeval mixed regime is a combination of two distinct principles of government—the *royal principle*, according to which absolute power is vested in the sovereign personality of an individual man; and the *political principle*, according to which the supremacy of law reflects the sovereignty of the people, who have the power of making laws either directly or through their representatives.

This conception of a mixed regime—of government which is *both royal and political*—appears at first to be self-contradictory. In Aristotle's terms, it would seem impossible to combine the supremacy of law, which is the essence of constitutional government, with the supremacy of a sovereign person, which is the essence of royal government. The mixed regime would also seem to be impossible in terms of Hobbes' theory of the indivisibility of sovereignty. Impossible in theory, the mixed regime nevertheless existed as a matter of historic fact in the typical mediaeval kingdom, which derived its character from the feudal conditions under which it developed.

Does not the fact of its historic existence refute the incompatibility of the principles which the mixed regime combines? The answer may be that, like a mixture of oil and water, royal and political government can only exist as a mixture in unstable equilibrium. Originating under feudal conditions, the mixed regime tends toward dissolution as these conditions disappear with the rise of the modern nation-state. It first tends to be supplanted by a movement toward absolute monarchy. Then, in the course of re action and revolution, it tends toward constitutional monarchies or republics through added limitations on the power of the throne.

These historic developments seem to indicate that the principles of the mixed regime are ultimately as irreconcilable in fact as they are in theory.

Montesquieu's remark that the ancients "had not a clear idea of monarchy" can be interpreted to mean that they did not have the conception of a mixed regime. Before the accidents of history brought it into existence, it is unlikely that anyone would have conceived of a government both royal and political. Montesquieu does not adopt the mediaeval description of a mixed regime, which, as stated by Aquinas, is "partly kingdom, since there is one at the head of all; partly aristocracy, in so far as a number of persons are set in authority; and partly democracy, *i.e.*, government by the people, in so far as the rulers can be chosen by the people, and the people have the right to choose their rulers." Yet Montesquieu's theory of monarchy seems to be determined by characteristics peculiar to the mediaeval kingdom.

This seems to be the point of Hegel's observation, already quoted, that Montesquieu's theory of monarchy identifies it with the feudal kingdom. The point is confirmed in another way by the fact that Montesquieu's ideal of monarchy is the government of England at the end of the 17th century, which, he says, "may be justly called a republic, disguised under the form of a monarchy." Locke's conception of the English government in his own day tends to clarify this point.

The form of a government, says Locke, "depends upon the placing of the supreme power, which is the legislative." When the power of making laws is placed in the hands of one man, then it is a monarchy. But, according to Locke, "the legislative and executive power are in distinct hands . . . in all moderated monarchies and well-framed governments."

What Locke here calls a "moderated monarchy" (intending to describe the government of England), seems to be the mixed regime, the form of government which Fortescue had earlier called a "political kingdom," and Bracton a *regimen regale et politicum*. The legislative power is in the hands of the people or their representatives. If it belonged exclusively to the king as a right vested in his sovereign person, and not merely as the people's representative —or, in the language of Aquinas, their vicegerent—the government would be in form an absolute monarchy. If, on the other hand, the king were merely a representative, the government would be a republic.

The sovereign character of the king in a mixed regime seems to stem from his unique relation to the laws of the land. In one way, he is above the laws, and has certain powers not limited by law; in another way, his whole power is limited by the fact that he does not have the power to make laws in his own right or authority. When a people are free and able to make their own laws, Aquinas writes, "the consent of the whole people expressed by custom counts far more in favor of a particular observance, than does the authority of the sovereign, who has not the power to frame laws, except as representing the people." But Aquinas also says that the sovereign is "*exempt from the law*, as to its coercive power; since, properly speaking, no man is coerced by himself, and law has no coercive power save from the authority of the sovereign."

The coercive power of the law belongs to the sovereign as executive, not legislator. Admitting the king to a share in legislative power, Locke conceives his essential function—that which belongs to him alone—as executive. The absoluteness of this executive power Locke defines in terms of the royal prerogative, that "being nothing but a power in the hands of the prince to provide for the public good in such cases which, depending upon unforeseen and uncertain occurrences, certain and unalterable laws could not safely direct." Prerogative, he then goes on to say, is the power "to act according to discretion for the public good without the prescription of law, and sometimes even against it."

Locke thus gives us a picture of the mixed regime in which the king's sovereign power is limited to the exercise of an absolute prerogative in performing the executive functions of government. In the executive sphere, the king's power is absolute, yet his sovereignty is not absolute; for in the legislative sphere, he either has no voice at all where ancient customs prevail, or, in the making of new laws, he can count himself merely as one representative of the people among others.

The extent of the prerogative permitted the king depends upon the extent to which matters are explicitly regulated by law. When in the infancy of governments the laws were few in number, "the government was almost all prerogative," as Locke sees it. He thinks that "they have a very wrong notion of government who say that the people have encroached upon the prerogative when they have got any part of it to be defined by positive laws. For in so doing they have not pulled from the prince anything that of right belonged to him, but only declared that that power which they indefinitely left in his or his ancestors' hands, to be exercised for their good, was not a thing they intended him, when he used it otherwise."

Here we see the seed of conflict between sovereign king and sovereign people in the combination of incompatible principles that constitute a mixed regime. As the king, jealous of his prerogative, tries to maintain or even extend his power, royal and political government tends toward absolute monarchy. As the people, jealous of their sovereignty, try to safeguard their legislative power from royal usurpations, the mixed regime tends to dissolve in the other direction. This happens as it moves toward republican government through various stages of limited or constitutional monarchy in which the sovereignty of the king becomes more and more attenuated.

When the king's prerogative includes the power of calling parliament into session, nothing short of revolution may resolve the issue; for, as Locke observes, "between an executive power in being, with such a prerogative, and a legislative that depends upon his will for their convening, there can be no judge on earth."

IN THE DISCUSSION of monarchy, as in the discussion of democracy or other forms of government, the fundamental terms and issues do not have the same meaning in the various epochs of western thought. The continuity of discussion in the tradition of the great books must be qualified, especially in the field of political theory, by reference to the differing historic institutions with which their authors are acquainted and concerned. Ancient and modern controversies over the merits of monarchy in relation to other forms of government seem to be comparing institutions of government as different as the ancient and modern forms of the democratic constitution.

In the ancient world, the choice between purely royal and purely political government underlies the meaning and evaluation of monarchy. In the modern world, with its heritage from the feudal institutions of the Middle Ages, either the mixed regime or constitutional monarchy is thought to offer a third alternative. The praise of monarchy may therefore be the corollary of a justification of absolute government or the absolute state, as with Hobbes and Hegel; it may be accompanied by an attack on absolute or despotic power, as with Locke and Montesquieu; or in defense of purely republican principles, monarchy may be attacked, as by Rousseau and the Federalists, without differentiation between its absolute and limited forms.

This does not mean that there is no continuity between ancient and modern discussion. It seems to exist with respect to both elements in the idea of monarchy—the unification of government through its having one head, and the rightness of absolute power. On the point of unity, Plato's argument that monarchy is the most efficient of the several forms of government which are otherwise equally just, seems to be paralleled by modern arguments for a unified executive in the constitution of a republic. It is also reflected in the reasoning of Montesquieu and Rousseau concerning the greater competence of monarchies to govern extensive territories. On the point of absolute power, there is some continuity between ancient and modern discussions of government by men versus government by law. But here there seems to be greater similarity between ancient and modern arguments against giving sovereignty to an individual human being than there is between the modern defense of monarchy and ancient speculations concerning royal government.

Taking different shape in Hobbes and Hegel, the argument for the *necessity* of absolute government seems to be peculiarly modern. It is not simply the point made by the ancients, that under certain circumstances it may be right for the man of superior wisdom to govern his inferiors in an absolute manner, as a father governs children, or a god men. The point is rather that the very nature of government and the state requires a unified repository of absolute power. Hobbes does not ask whether the monarch in whose hands such power is placed deserves this by reason of personal superiority to his subjects. Hegel explicitly repudiates the relevance of any consideration of the monarch's particular character. Neither Hobbes nor Hegel argues for the divine right of kings, or their divine appointment; though Hegel does insist that the constitution itself, which establishes the supremacy of the crown, is not something made by man, but "divine and constant, and exalted above the sphere of things that are made."

That kings have absolute power by divine right is another peculiarly modern argument for absolute monarchy. "Not all the water from the rough rude sea," says Shakespeare's Richard II, "can wash the balm off from an anointed king. The breath of worldly men cannot depose the deputy elected by the Lord." According to the theory of divine right, the king is God's vicar, not, as Aquinas thinks, the vicegerent of the people. The theory of the divine right of kings does not seem to be a mediaeval doctrine. It appears later in such tracts as those by Barclay and Filmer, which Locke undertakes to answer.

The controversy involves its adversaries in dispute over the interpretation of Holy Writ. The anointing of Christian kings is supposed to draw its significance from the establishment of this practice among the ancient Hebrews. But the story of the origin of the Hebrew kingship can be given an opposite interpretation.

The people of Israel, after the leadership of Moses and Aaron, first submitted their affairs to the government of judges, and "there was no king in Israel, but every one did that which seemed right to himself." Later they went to Samuel, their judge, saying: "Make us a king to judge us like all the nations." This displeased Samuel. Samuel prayed unto the Lord, and the Lord said unto Samuel: "Hearken to the voice of the people in all that they say unto thee; for they have not rejected thee, but they have rejected me, that I should not reign over them." The Lord then describes the tribulations the people will suffer at the hands of an earthly ruler with absolute power, a punishment they deserve for wanting to be ruled by a king, instead of by God and God's law, administered for them by judges.

The great poems and histories of ancient Greece and Rome would seem to indicate that the divinity of kings is not a modern notion. The deification of emperors and kings certainly appears to be a common practice. But the assumption of divinity by kings is not supposed to signify divine appointment, or election by the gods; nor do the rulers of the ancient world justify their absolute power as a god-given right.

Furthermore, in the political theory of Plato and Aristotle, the analogy between royal rule and divine government works in the opposite direction. According to their view, the right to absolute government depends upon a radical inequality between ruler and ruled. If a god were to rule men on earth, as in the myth retold in Plato's *Statesman*, he would govern them absolutely, deciding everything by his wisdom and without recourse to written laws or established customs. If there were a god-like man, or if a true philosopher were to become king, he too would deserve to be an absolute monarch. It would be unjust, says Aristotle, to treat the god-like man merely as a citizen, and so to treat him as no more than "the equal of those who are so far inferior to him in virtue and in political capacity." It would also seem to be unjust for a man who does not have great superiority over his fellow men to rule them like a king, instead of being merely a citizen entitled to hold public office for a time.

Aristotle frequently refers to royal government as the divine sort of government, but he does not justify its existence except when one man stands to others as a god to men. Though some of the historic kingships which Aristotle classifies are absolute monarchies, none is royal government of the divine sort. That seems to remain for Aristotle, as for Plato, a purely hypothetical construction.

Actual royal government has a patriarchal rather than a divine origin. It is the kind of government which is appropriate to the village community rather than to the city-state. The kingly form of government prevails in the village because it is an outgrowth of the family. That is why, says Aristotle, "the Hellenic states were originally governed by kings; the Hellenes were under royal rule before they came together, as the barbarians still are."

In thinking that absolute or despotic government befits the servile Asiatics, but not the free men of the Greek city-states, Aristotle takes a position which has a certain counterpart in the views of Montesquieu and Mill. These modern opponents of absolute monarchy do not assert that constitutional government is unconditionally better than despotism. For certain peoples, under certain conditions, self-government may not be possible or advantageous. "A rude people," Mill writes, "though in some degree alive to the benefits of civilized society, may be unable to practice the forbearance which it demands: their passions may be too violent, or their personal pride too exacting, to forego private conflict, and leave to the laws the avenging of their real or supposed wrongs. In such a case, a civilized government, to be really advantageous to them, will require to be in a considerable degree despotic; to be one over which they do not themselves exercise control, and which imposes a great amount of forcible restraint upon their actions." Montesquieu seems further to suppose that different races—largely as a result of the climate in which they live—are by nature inclined toward freedom or servitude. The Asiatics are for him a people whose spirit perpetually dooms them to live under despotism.

In contrast, Mill's conditional justification of absolute government demands that despotism serve only a temporary purpose. It must seek not merely to keep order, but by gradual steps to prepare the people it rules for self-government. "Leading-strings are only admissible," he says, "as a means of gradually training the people to walk alone." When they have reached that stage of development where they are able to govern themselves, the despotic ruler must either abdicate or be overthrown.

There is a deeper contrast between Mill on the one hand, and Aristotle and Plato on the other, one which goes to the very heart of the issue concerning royal and political government. Both Aristotle and Plato seem to be saying that if the superior or god-like man existed, then royal government would be better than the best republic, even for the civilized Greeks. In calling royal rule the divine form of government, they imply that it is the ideal, even if it can never be realized. This Mill most emphatically denies.

The notion that "if a good despot could be ensured, despotic monarchy would be the best form of government, I look upon," he writes, "as a radical and most pernicious conception of what good government is." The point at issue is not whether the good despot—the god-like ruler or philosopher king—can be found. Suppose him to exist. The point then to be made is that the people ruled by "one man of superhuman mental activity" would of necessity have to be entirely passive. "Their passivity is implied in the very idea of absolute power. . . . What sort of human beings," Mill asks, "can be formed under such a regimen?" Men must actually engage in self-government in order to pass from political infancy to maturity. Whenever it is possible, representative or constitutional government is therefore better than absolute monarchy.

OUTLINE OF TOPICS

1. The definition of monarchy and the classification of the types of kingship

   1*a*. The distinction between royal and political government

   (1) Absolute or personal rule contrasted with constitutional government or rule by law

   (2) The theory of absolute government: the nature of absolute power; the rights and duties of the monarch; the radical inequality between ruler and ruled in absolute government

   1*b*. Modifications of absolute monarchy: other embodiments of the monarchical principle

   (1) The combination of monarchy with other forms of government: the mixed regime

(2) Constitutional or limited monarchy

(3) The monarchical principle in the executive branch of republican government

1c. The principle of succession in monarchies

2. The theory of royalty

2a. The divinity of kings

2b. The analogy between divine government and rule by the best man: the philosopher king

2c. The divine institution of kings: the theory of the divine right of kings

2d. The myth of the royal personage: the attributes of royalty and the burdens of monarchy

3. The use and abuse of monarchical power

3a. The good king and the benevolent despot in the service of their subjects: the education of the prince

3b. The exploitation of absolute power for personal aggrandizement: the strategies of princes and tyrants

4. Comparison of monarchy with other forms of government

4a. The patriarchical character of kingship: absolute rule in the family or tribe, and paternalism in the state

4b. The line which divides monarchy from despotism and tyranny

4c. The differences between kingdoms and republics with respect to unity, wealth, and extent of territory

4d. The defense of monarchy or royal rule

(1) The necessity for absolute government

(2) Monarchy as the best or most efficient of the several good forms of government

(3) The preference for the mixed regime: defense of royal prerogatives as absolute in their sphere

4e. The attack on monarchy or absolute government

(1) The paternalistic or despotic character of monarchy: the rejection of benevolent despotism; the advantages of constitutional safeguards

(2) The justification of absolute rule or benevolent despotism for peoples incapable of self-government

(3) The illegitimacy of absolute monarchy: the violation of the principle of popular sovereignty

(4) The illegality of royal usurpations of power in a mixed regime: the limitations of royal prerogative in a constitutional monarchy

5. The absolute government of colonies, dependencies, or conquered peoples

5a. The justification of imperial rule: the rights of the conqueror; the unifying and civilizing achievements of empire

5b. The injustice of imperialism: exploitation and despotism

6. The history of monarchy: its origin and developments

REFERENCES

References are listed by volume number (in bold type), author's name, and page number. Bible references are to book, chapter, and verse of the Authorized King James version of the Bible. The abbreviation "esp" calls the reader's attention to one or more especially relevant parts of a whole reference; "passim" signifies that the topic is discussed intermittently rather than continuously in the work or passage cited. Where the work as a whole is relevant to the topic, the page numbers refer to the entire work. For general guidance in the use of *The Great Ideas,* consult the Preface.

1. The definition of monarchy and the classification of the types of kingship

7 PLATO, 598–604
9 ARISTOTLE, 483–484
23 MACHIAVELLI, 14–16
23 HOBBES, 106–107
38 MONTESQUIEU, 7, 75–76
40 GIBBON, 24
46 HEGEL, 91

1*a*. The distinction between royal and political government

1*a*(1) Absolute or personal rule contrasted with constitutional government or rule by law

5 EURIPIDES, 261–262
6 HERODOTUS, 107, 233
7 PLATO, 670–676, 680–682, 805
9 ARISTOTLE, 448, 449, 453–454, 484–487
14 PLUTARCH, 638–639
15 TACITUS, 51, 61–62
20 AQUINAS, 233–234
23 HOBBES, 131–132
35 LOCKE, 44–46, 55–58
38 MONTESQUIEU, 8, 29–31, 36–37, 54
38 ROUSSEAU, 323–324, 358
40 GIBBON, 24–28 passim, 51
41 GIBBON, 73–75
42 KANT, 547
43 MILL, 267–268, 339–340
44 BOSWELL, 195
46 HEGEL, 146, 213–214, 262, 301–302

1*a*(2) The theory of absolute government: the nature of absolute power; the rights and duties of the monarch; the radical inequality between ruler and ruled in absolute government

6 HERODOTUS, 195–196
7 PLATO, 679–680
9 ARISTOTLE, 447–448, 453–455 passim, 482–487
23 HOBBES, 47–283
26 SHAKESPEARE, 342–344
33 PASCAL, 231–232
35 LOCKE, 28–30, 55–58
38 MONTESQUIEU, 12–13, 15, 26–31, 33–34, 39–40, 137
38 ROUSSEAU, 388–389
40 GIBBON, 27, 50, 153–155 passim
41 GIBBON, 173, 219–220, 317
42 KANT, 438
43 MILL, 341–344 passim
44 BOSWELL, 120
48 MELVILLE, 107

1*b*. Modifications of absolute monarchy: other embodiments of the monarchical principle

1*b*(1) The combination of monarchy with other forms of government: the mixed regime

5 AESCHYLUS, 5–6
7 PLATO, 671–672, 699–700
9 ARISTOTLE, 461, 466–467, 469–470
14 PLUTARCH, 34–35
15 TACITUS, 72
19 AQUINAS, 430–431
20 AQUINAS, 229–230, 307–309
23 MACHIAVELLI, 27
23 HOBBES, 103–104, 151–152
35 LOCKE, 55, 59–60, 62–64, 74–76
38 MONTESQUIEU, 7–8, 75–78
38 ROUSSEAU, 414–415
41 GIBBON, 81, 217–219
43 FEDERALIST, 70, 213
43 MILL, 351
44 BOSWELL, 178, 390
46 HEGEL, 342, 356–357

1*b*(2) Constitutional or limited monarchy

7 PLATO, 598–604, 667
9 ARISTOTLE, 483, 484, 485, 515–516
23 HOBBES, 106–107
35 LOCKE, 46
40 GIBBON, 622–623
42 KANT, 439–440
46 HEGEL, 90–92, 96–97, 145–146

1*b*(3) The monarchical principle in the executive branch of republican government

38 MONTESQUIEU, 72
43 FEDERALIST, 118–119, 203–205
43 MILL, 356–357, 409–413 passim

1*c*. The principle of succession in monarchies

OLD TESTAMENT: *I Kings*

APOCRYPHA: *I Maccabees*, 9:28–30
6 HERODOTUS, 167–168, 194–195, 196–199, 214, 252–253
14 PLUTARCH, 49–52, 363–366, 480–482
15 TACITUS, 98, 193–194
23 HOBBES, 106, 107, 108–109
26 SHAKESPEARE, 13–14, 43–44, 70–71, 534–537
33 PASCAL, 229–230
38 MONTESQUIEU, 28, 222
38 ROUSSEAU, 413–414
40 GIBBON, 30, 61, 68–69
41 GIBBON, 204–205, 212–213, 223
46 HEGEL, 94–95, 96–97

2. The theory of royalty

2*a*. The divinity of kings

APOCRYPHA: *Wisdom of Solomon*, 14:16–21
5 AESCHYLUS, 21–22
13 VIRGIL, 16–18, 37–38, 110–111, 232, 262–263
14 PLUTARCH, 28–29, 50–52
15 TACITUS, 73
26 SHAKESPEARE, 343–344
40 GIBBON, 28

2*b*. The analogy between divine government and rule by the best man: the philosopher king

7 PLATO, 310–401, 586–590, 679–681
9 ARISTOTLE, 482, 486–487, 537
14 PLUTARCH, 47–48, 59–60, 605, 784–785
30 BACON, 20–21, 74–75
35 LOCKE, 63–64
36 SWIFT, 28–29
40 GIBBON, 338–339

2*c*. The divine institution of kings: the theory of the divine right of kings

OLD TESTAMENT: *Deuteronomy*, 17:14–20 / *I Samuel*, 9:15–10:13; 12:12–14; 16:1–13; 24:4–10; 26:7–12 / *II Samuel*, 5:12; 7:11–16; 12:7; 23:1 / *II Kings*, 9:1–7,12 / *I Chronicles*, 28:1–10 / *Isaiah*, 45:1–6
APOCRYPHA: *Ecclesiasticus*, 47:11
14 PLUTARCH, 50–51
23 HOBBES, 111–112, 225
26 SHAKESPEARE, 338, 342–344
35 LOCKE, 51
40 GIBBON, 292–293
41 GIBBON, 209
46 HEGEL, 93
51 TOLSTOY, 680

2*d*. The myth of the royal personage: the attributes of royalty and the burdens of monarchy

APOCRYPHA: *Wisdom of Solomon*, 7:1–6 / *Ecclesiasticus*, 11:5
4 HOMER, 20–21
5 SOPHOCLES, 104
5 EURIPIDES, 428–429
6 HERODOTUS, 7–8, 85–86, 281–282
7 PLATO, 669–674
9 ARISTOTLE, 413, 517–518
12 AURELIUS, 253–256
14 PLUTARCH, 540–576 passim, 661, 678, 732, 835, 847
15 TACITUS, 73–74, 193
23 MACHIAVELLI, 1
24 RABELAIS, 58–59
25 MONTAIGNE, 126–131, 327–329, 443–446
26 SHAKESPEARE, 81–82, 320–351, 427, 453, 482–483, 494, 499
27 SHAKESPEARE, 53, 244–283, 289, 311–350
28 HARVEY, 267
30 BACON, 1–2, 20–25, 205–207
32 MILTON, 120–121
33 PASCAL, 196–199, 228
35 LOCKE, 72
38 MONTESQUIEU, 15, 26–29, 39, 42, 43, 94–95
38 ROUSSEAU, 358–359
39 SMITH, 356
40 GIBBON, 154–155, 156–157, 547, 572
41 GIBBON, 39–40, 194, 297, 317–321
43 FEDERALIST, 203
43 MILL, 341–342, 363
44 BOSWELL, 125, 251
46 HEGEL, 95–96
47 GOETHE, 52–53, 118–121, 254–255
48 MELVILLE, 93–94, 107–109
51 TOLSTOY, 1–2, 87, 135–137, 147–150, 157–161, 230–234, 342–346, 348–349, 382–388, 405–406, 444–450, 456–459, 465–468, 497–499, 518, 536–537

3. The use and abuse of monarchical power

3*a*. The good king and the benevolent despot in the service of their subjects: the education of the prince

OLD TESTAMENT: *Exodus*, 18:21–26 / *I Samuel*, 15:10–35 / *I Kings*, 4:29–34; 11:26–40; 14:1–20 / *II Chronicles*, 1:7–12 / *Psalms*, 72 / *Proverbs*, 8:15–16; 16:10–15; 20:26,28; 25:2–5; 29:2,4,12,14 / *Ecclesiastes*, 10:16–17
APOCRYPHA: *Ecclesiasticus*, 10:1–4,14 / *I Maccabees*, 14
4 HOMER, 57–58
5 AESCHYLUS, 23
5 SOPHOCLES, 99, 132, 136–137
5 EURIPIDES, 261
7 PLATO, 316–356, 383–401, 598–608, 806
9 ARISTOTLE, 413, 483–485
12 AURELIUS, 253–256
14 PLUTARCH, 32–48, 64–77, 80–81, 129–141, 542–544, 782–788
15 TACITUS, 125–126, 215, 290
21 DANTE, 63–64, 68, 126
23 HOBBES, 153–159
24 RABELAIS, 26–30
25 MONTAIGNE, 131–132, 386–388, 436–439
26 SHAKESPEARE, 434–466, 467–502, 533, 552–554
27 SHAKESPEARE, 303–304

3*b*. The exploitation of absolute power for personal aggrandizement: the strategies of princes and tyrants

4. Comparison of monarchy with other forms of government

4*a*. The patriarchical character of kingship: absolute rule in the family or tribe, and paternalism in the state

4*b*. The line which divides monarchy from despotism and tyranny

4*c*. The differences between kingdoms and republics with respect to unity, wealth, and extent of territory

4*d*. The defense of monarchy or royal rule

4*d*(1) The necessity for absolute government

4*d*(2) Monarchy as the best or most efficient of the several good forms of government

37 Fielding, 268–269
38 Montesquieu, 25
38 Rousseau, 412–414
41 Gibbon, 74–75, 81
43 Mill, 341–344
44 Boswell, 120, 255
46 Hegel, 95, 96, 98, 100, 145–146, 174–175, 368

4*d*(3) The preference for the mixed regime: defense of royal prerogatives as absolute in their sphere

7 Plato, 671–672
15 Tacitus, 72
20 Aquinas, 229–230
23 Hobbes, 228
35 Locke, 59–60, 62–64
38 Montesquieu, 69–75, 142–146
38 Rousseau, 414–415
43 Mill, 353–354
44 Boswell, 178

4*e*. The attack on monarchy or absolute government

4*e*(1) The paternalistic or despotic character of monarchy: the rejection of benevolent despotism; the advantages of constitutional safeguards

5 Euripides, 261–262
7 Plato, 671–674, 681–682, 754
9 Aristotle, 382, 484–486
35 Locke, 44–46, 63
38 Montesquieu, 69–84
38 Rousseau, 408, 412–414
40 Gibbon, 32–34, 68–69, 522–523
42 Kant, 450
43 Federalist, 153–156
43 Mill, 348–349
46 Hegel, 148

4*e*(2) The justification of absolute rule or benevolent despotism for peoples incapable of self-government

15 Tacitus, 290
35 Locke, 48–50
38 Montesquieu, 110–111, 122–123, 124
38 Rousseau, 324, 402–403
43 Federalist, 47
43 Mill, 329, 338–341, 351–353, 436–442 passim, esp 436–437
46 Hegel, 198–199, 300–301

4*e*(3) The illegitimacy of absolute monarchy: the violation of the principle of popular sovereignty

35 Locke, 44–46, 48–51 passim, 55–58 passim, 65, 71–72
38 Rousseau, 356–359, 387–391
42 Kant, 137, 439–441, 450–452
43 Declaration of Independence, 1–3
46 Hegel, 93–94

4*e*(4) The illegality of royal usurpations of power in a mixed regime: the limitations of royal prerogative in a constitutional monarchy

9 Aristotle, 515
35 Locke, 50–51 passim, 62–64, 70–71
38 Montesquieu, 7–9
38 Rousseau, 418–419, 424
40 Gibbon, 24–28
41 Gibbon, 74
42 Kant, 445
43 Declaration of Independence, 1–3
43 Federalist, 157, 252–253
46 Hegel, 96–97

5. The absolute government of colonies, dependencies, or conquered peoples

Old Testament: *Joshua,* 9 / *I Kings,* 9:20–23 / *II Kings,* 23:30–35; 24:12–16; 25:5–30
Apocrypha: *I Maccabees,* 1:41–64; 8:1–13 / *II Maccabees,* 5:11–7:42
6 Herodotus, 16–20, 30–31, 37–40, 109–111, 186–191
6 Thucydides, 353, 403–404, 425–428, 504–507, 579–580
7 Plato, 698
9 Aristotle, 528–529
14 Plutarch, 47–48
15 Tacitus, 122, 149, 162–163
23 Machiavelli, 3–14, 30–31
23 Hobbes, 107, 119, 126–127
24 Rabelais, 131–133
35 Locke, 65–70 passim
36 Swift, 102–103
38 Montesquieu, 83–84, 170–171
38 Rousseau, 380
39 Smith, 239–279, 288
40 Gibbon, 14–15, 245–246, 518–519
41 Gibbon, 216
46 Hegel, 299

5*a*. The justification of imperial rule: the rights of the conqueror; the unifying and civilizing achievements of empire

5 Aeschylus, 24
6 Thucydides, 358–360, 367–369, 402–404, 530–532
13 Virgil, 14–15, 233–234, 278
14 Plutarch, 302–313
15 Tacitus, 106, 139–140, 191–192, 286–287, 290, 301
18 Augustine, 216–218
23 Hobbes, 110–111, 279–281
38 Montesquieu, 63
40 Gibbon, 12–24, 255, 608–609, 638–639
43 Mill, 353–354
46 Hegel, 112, 241–250
51 Tolstoy, 466, 498–499

5*b*. The injustice of imperialism: exploitation and despotism

6 Thucydides, 424–429, 504–507, 529–533

9 ARISTOTLE, 538
14 PLUTARCH, 409–410, 480–499
15 TACITUS, 39–40, 82–83, 122, 149
18 AUGUSTINE, 196–197
25 MONTAIGNE, 440–443
35 LOCKE, 65–70
36 SWIFT, 182–183
36 SWIFT, 182–183
38 MONTESQUIEU, 62–63, 109–110
38 ROUSSEAU, 355, 389–390
39 SMITH, 253–255
40 GIBBON, 23, 33–34, 631–633
41 GIBBON, 420, 505
42 KANT, 413, 454–455
43 DECLARATION OF INDEPENDENCE, 1–3
43 MILL, 436–442 passim
44 BOSWELL, 179
46 HEGEL, 146
50 MARX, 372–374, 379–383 passim

6. The history of monarchy: its origin and developments

OLD TESTAMENT: *I Samuel*, 8–31 / *II Samuel* / *I Kings* / *II Kings*
6 HERODOTUS, 23–24, 152–153
6 THUCYDIDES, 391
7 PLATO, 672–674
9 ARISTOTLE, 466–468, 469–470, 512–515, 553–554, 558–560
14 PLUTARCH, 20–28, 32–48, 77–86, 480–499, 600–603, 657–663
15 TACITUS, 1–2
21 DANTE, 113–114
23 HOBBES, 150–151, 275–278
26 SHAKESPEARE, 1–32, 33–68, 69–104, 105–148, 320–351, 376–405, 434–466, 467–502, 532–567
27 SHAKESPEARE, 549–585
35 LOCKE, 48–51
38 MONTESQUIEU, 69–78, 269–315
40 GIBBON, 1–671 passim
41 GIBBON, 1–598 passim
43 FEDERALIST, 92, 252–253
43 MILL, 267–269, 340–341
46 HEGEL, 261–263, 293–294, 301–302, 324–327, 342–345, 355–358
50 MARX, 356
51 TOLSTOY, 675–683

CROSS-REFERENCES

For: Discussions relevant to the distinction between royal and political government, *see* CITIZEN 2b; CONSTITUTION 1; GOVERNMENT 1b; LAW 7a; SLAVERY 6b; TYRANNY 5.

Other considerations of the mixed regime and its distinction from the mixed constitution, *see* CONSTITUTION 3a, 5b; DEMOCRACY 3b; GOVERNMENT 2b.

Monarchy in relation to other forms of government, *see* ARISTOCRACY 2a; DEMOCRACY 3c; GOVERNMENT 2–2e; OLIGARCHY 2; STATE 6a; TYRANNY 2a, 4a; and for the comparison of monarchy with domestic or despotic government, *see* FAMILY 2b; GOVERNMENT 1b; TYRANNY 4b.

Another discussion of government in relation to the wealth and territorial extent of the state, *see* STATE 4a–4c; WEALTH 9f.

Matters relevant to the theory of the royal prerogative, *see* GOVERNMENT 3e; LAW 7e.

The controversy concerning the legitimacy or justice of absolute monarchy, and for the statement of the issue in terms of the doctrine of natural rights and popular sovereignty, *see* CONSTITUTION 3b; DEMOCRACY 4b; GOVERNMENT 1g(1)–1g(3); JUSTICE 9c–9d; LAW 6b, 7b; LIBERTY 1d, 1g; STATE 2c; TYRANNY 5a–5c.

Matters relevant to the justification of absolute rule when it takes the form of a benevolent despotism, *see* DEMOCRACY 4d; GOVERNMENT 2c; PROGRESS 4b; SLAVERY 6b–6c; TYRANNY 4b.

The issues concerning imperialism as a form of absolute rule, *see* GOVERNMENT 5b; LIBERTY 6c; REVOLUTION 7; SLAVERY 6d; STATE 10b; TYRANNY 6.

ADDITIONAL READINGS

Listed below are works not included in *Great Books of the Western World*, but relevant to the idea and topics with which this chapter deals. These works are divided into two groups:

I. Works by authors represented in this collection.
II. Works by authors not represented in this collection.

For the date, place, and other facts concerning the publication of the works cited, consult the Bibliography of Additional Readings which follows the last chapter of *The Great Ideas*.

I.

PLUTARCH. "Of the Three Sorts of Government—Monarchy, Democracy and Oligarchy," in *Moralia*
AQUINAS. *On the Governance of Rulers*
DANTE. *On World-Government or De Monarchia*
F. BACON. "Of the True Greatness of Kingdoms and Estates," in *Essays*
MILTON. *The Tenure of Kings and Magistrates*
——. *Defence of the People of England*
HOBBES. *Behemoth*
SPINOZA. *Tractatus Politicus (Political Treatise)*, CH 6–7
BERKELEY. *Passive Obedience*

II.

DEMOSTHENES. *Philippics*
——. *De Corona (On the Crown)*
BRACTON. *De Legibus et Consuetudinibus Angliae (On the Laws and Customs of England)*
MARSILIUS OF PADUA. *Defensor Pacis*
WYCLIFFE. *Tractatus de Officio Regis*
FORTESCUE. *Governance of England*
ERASMUS. *The Education of a Christian Prince*
CASTIGLIONE. *The Book of the Courtier*
LA BOÉTIE. *Anti-Dictator, the Discours de la servitude volontaire*
BODIN. *The Six Bookes of a Commonweale*
BELLARMINE. *The Treatise on Civil Government (De Laicis)*
MARLOWE. *Edward the Second*
HOOKER. *Of the Laws of Ecclesiastical Polity*
MARIANA. *The King and the Education of the King*
W. BARCLAY. *De Regno*
JAMES I. *The Trew Law of Free Monarchies*
——. *An Apologie for the Oath of Allegiance*
——. *A Premonition to all Christian Monarches, Free Princes and States*
——. *A Defence of the Right of Kings, Against Cardinall Perron*
CAMPANELLA. *A Discourse Touching the Spanish Monarchy*
CORNEILLE. *Cinna*
PRYNNE. *The Soveraigne Power of Parliaments and Kingdomes*
HUDSON. *The Divine Right of Government*
FILMER. *The Anarchy of a Limited or Mixed Monarchy*
——. *Patriarcha*
SÉVIGNÉ. *Letters*
BARROW. *A Treatise of the Pope's Supremacy*
BOSSUET. *Politique tirée des propres paroles de l'Écriture Sainte*
A. SIDNEY. *Discourses Concerning Government*
VOLTAIRE. "King," in *A Philosophical Dictionary*
BURKE. *Reflections on the Revolution in France*
PAINE. *Common Sense*, II
——. *Rights of Man*, PART I
MAISTRE. *Du pape*
PUSHKIN. *Boris Godunov*
BAGEHOT. *The English Constitution*
FRAZER. *The Golden Bough*, PART I; PART II, CH I; PART III, CH 2–5
FIGGIS. *Theory of the Divine Right of Kings*
MAURRAS. *Enquête sur la monarchie*
HOCART. *Kingship*
B. RUSSELL. *Power*, CH 5
A. J. CARLYLE. *Political Liberty*

Chapter 60: NATURE

INTRODUCTION

NATURE is a term which draws its meaning from the other terms with which it is associated by implication or contrast. Yet it is not one of a fixed pair of terms, like necessity and contingency, one and many, universal and particular, war and peace. When things are divided into the natural and the artificial, or into the natural and the conventional, the opposite of the natural does not represent a loss or violation of nature, but rather a transformation of nature through the addition of a new factor. The unnatural, on the other hand, seems to be merely a deviation, a falling away from, or sometimes a transgression of nature.

Most of the terms which stand in opposition to nature represent the activity or being of man or God. As appears in the chapter on MEDICINE, Galen thinks of nature as an artist. Harvey later develops this notion. But with these two exceptions, the traditional theory of art conceives it not as the work of nature, but of man. Despite other differences in the great books on the theory of art, especially with regard to art's imitation of nature, there seems to be a common understanding that works of art are distinguished from productions of nature by the fact that man has added something to nature. A world which man left exactly as he found it would be a world without art or any trace of the artificial in it.

The ancient authors who contrast the natural and the conventional and the modern authors who distinguish man's life in a state of nature from his life in civil society seem to imply that without something done by man there would be nothing conventional or political. Locke appears to be an exception here. He thinks that there is a natural as well as a civil, or political, society. Natural society is the society of "men living together according to reason without a common superior on earth, with authority to judge between them." Unlike Hobbes or Kant or Hegel, Locke does not think that the state of nature is necessarily a state of war. But this difference between Locke and others does not affect the point that the political institutions of civil society are things of man's own devising.

There may be, among the social insects, natural organizations such as the bee-hive and the ant-mound. It may even be, as Locke supposes, that in a state of nature, "men living together according to reason" would constitute a society. But in neither case does the society we call "a state" result. States differ from one another in many features of their political organization. In this sense the state or political community is conventional rather than natural; its institutions are humanly contrived.

The social contract theory of the origin of the state is not necessarily involved in the recognition that the state is partly conventional. Aristotle, for example, who regards the state as natural—he speaks of it as "a creation of nature"—does not think of the political community as natural in the sense in which a bee-hive is natural. That men should form political communities is, in his view, the result of a natural desire, a tendency inherent in the nature of man as a political animal. But what form the political community will take is at least partly determined by the particular arrangements men voluntarily institute. Man-made laws are conventional, but so also are other institutions which vary from state to state or change from time to time.

THE ISSUES IN political theory raised by any consideration of what is and is not natural about society or the state are discussed in other chapters, *e.g.*, FAMILY and STATE. What is true in this connection is likely to be true of each of the other fundamental oppositions in which the notion of nature is involved. The issues raised by the relation of art to nature are, for example, considered in the chapter on ART; those raised by the distinction between nature and nurture are considered in the chapter on HABIT, and so on. Here we are concerned not with the theoretical consequences of different conceptions of nature, but with the various meanings of the term itself as it is used in different contexts.

Common to all meanings is the notion that the natural is that which man's doing or making has not altered or enlarged. The distinction between nature and nurture confirms this. Man's activities are the source of modifications in his own nature as well as in the nature of other things. The human nature man is born with undergoes transformations in the course of life: the acquirement of knowledge, the formation of habits (which are often called "second nature"), the modification of instincts. The sum of these changes represents what nurture adds to nature.

When changes of this sort are looked at collectively they give rise to the notions of culture or civilization—two more terms which present a contrast to nature. In Rousseau and others we meet the feeling that man may have lost, not gained, by exchanging the natural for the civilized life. The ideal of a return to nature involves more than a return to the soil, or an exodus from the city to the country. In its most radical form, this ideal calls upon man to divest himself of all the artifices and conceits with which he has thought to improve on nature—"by renouncing its advances," Rousseau says, "in order to renounce its vices."

But why, it may be asked, is the whole world which man creates not as natural as the materials which man finds to work with—the resources of physical nature and the native equipment which is man's nature at birth? If man himself is a natural entity, and if all human activities are somehow determined by human nature, then why are not the works of art and science, the development of political institutions, the cultivation of human beings by education and experience, and all other features of civilization—why are not all these just as natural as the falling stone, the flourishing forest, or the bee-hive? Why, in short, should there by any contrast between the works of nature and the works of man?

THIS QUESTION points to one of the fundamental issues in the traditional discussion of nature. Those who uphold the validity of the contrast defend its significance in terms of something quite special about human nature. If man were entirely a creature of instinct—if everything man did were determined by his nature so that no choices were open to him and no deviation from the course of nature possible—then the human world would seem to fade into the rest of nature. Only on the supposition that man is by nature rational and free do those human works which are the products of reason or the consequences of free choice seem to stand in sharp contrast to all other natural existences or effects of natural causes.

Of these two factors—rationality and freedom—the element of freedom is usually the one most emphasized. The line is drawn between that which natural causes determine and that which man determines by his own free choice. The laws of nature are often conceived as expressing an inherent rationality in nature itself, but they also state the uniformity of nature's operations. Such maxims of nature as 'nature does nothing in vain,' 'nature abhors a vacuum,' or 'nature does nothing by jumps' are usually interpreted as describing nature's invariable way of doing things. Aristotle's distinction between things which happen naturally and those which happen by chance turns on the regularity of the events which result from causes in the very nature of things. The natural is that which happens either always or for the most part.

Hence, even if there is rationality of some sort in the structure of nature, that supposition does not seem to affect the position of those who connect human reason with human freedom and who, in consequence, divide the things which happen as a result of man's free choice from everything else which happens in the course of nature. This may be exemplified by the Greek understanding of the difference between nature and convention. The laws of Persia vary from the laws of Greece, the political institutions of the city-states vary from those of the Homeric age, customs and constitutions differ from city to city. Unlike such conventions, "that which is by nature," Aristotle writes, "is unchangeable and has everywhere the same force, as fire burns both here and in Persia." The conventional is the variable, the natural the uniform. The variability of conventions, moreover, seems to suggest that they are products of freedom or choice.

The difference between the bee-hive and the human city is that one is *entirely* a creation of nature, a social organization entirely determined by the instincts of the bees, so that wherever bees form a hive, it is formed in the same way; whereas the human city involves something more than a natural desire of men, since when these political animals associate in different places, they set up different forms of government and different kinds of law. The same comparison can be made between the spider's web or the beaver's dam and such products of human art as cloth and houses. The variability of the works of reason, as opposed to the uniformity of instinctive productions of all sorts, implies the factor of choice in reason's work.

THE CONCEPTION OF nature which tries to separate the natural from what man contributes thus seems to depend upon the conception of man. Controversies concerning man's difference from other animals, especially the dispute about human freedom (considered in such chapters as MAN and WILL), bear directly on the issue of the naturalness of the things which result from man's doing and making.

Spinoza, for example, in holding that human actions constitute no exception to the reign of necessity throughout nature, removes any ground for distinguishing the effects of human operation from other effects. Man exercises no freedom of choice; nor does man in any other way introduce a new principle into the order or process of nature. Hobbes and Locke concur in the denial of free will, but they separate the inventions of man's mind or his social institutions from what happens without human contrivance in the realm of thought or action. The difference between simple and complex ideas for Locke seems to parallel the ancient distinction between nature and art.

At the other extreme from Spinoza, Kant separates the order of nature and the order of freedom into worlds as radically asunder as the Cartesian realms of matter and mind. The world of nature is the system or order of the objects of sense—"the sum total of phenomena insofar as they . . . are connected with each other throughout." For Kant this means two things which are strictly correlative. Nature is the object of the theoretic sciences and it is also the realm of time, space, and causality. Like Spinoza, Kant identifies the order of nature with the order of causal necessity. But, unlike Spinoza, Kant places the moral and political life of man in an order unconditioned by time, space, and causality. This realm of freedom is the sphere of the moral or practical sciences. The natural or theoretic sciences do not extend to what Kant calls the "supersensible" or the "noumenal" order—the world of things lying outside the range of sense-experience.

There is an alternative to Spinoza's location of all events within the order of nature and to Kant's separation of the realm of nature from the domain of freedom. It takes the form of Aristotle's or Aquinas' distinction between the natural and the voluntary. The voluntary is in one sense natural, in another not. It is natural in the sense that what happens voluntarily in the realm of animal and human motions proceeds from causes as natural as those responsible for the motions of inert bodies. A voluntary act, according to Aquinas, comes from "an intrinsic principle," just as the falling of a stone proceeds from "a principle of movement in the stone." But among the factors responsible for voluntary acts is "knowledge of the end"—knowledge of the object being sought. The sphere of the voluntary can therefore be equated with the sphere of conscious desire, *i.e.*, with desire aroused by an object known, whether known by sense or reason. The natural in the sense in which it is distinguished from the voluntary is the sphere of motions in line with natural desire, *i.e.*, with tendencies founded in the very nature of a body or organism and unaccompanied by any awareness of the goal toward which it is thus inclined to move.

Aristotle's distinction between natural and violent motion (which Galileo and other physicists adopt) seems to throw light on a double use of the term 'natural' here. Galileo treats the motion of a freely falling body as natural, in contrast to the motion of a projectile. In the former case, it is the nature of heavy bodies to gravitate toward the earth; whereas in the latter case, in addition to the motion of gravitation, another motion is imparted to the body when it is shot from a gun—a motion which does not proceed from the body's own nature but is caused by the motions of other bodies. In terms of this distinction, voluntary motions are natural rather than violent. In fact, the violent is sometimes thought to be even more opposed to the voluntary than to the natural, in the sense that a man acting contrary to his will under external coercion suffers violence. When he does what he wishes, his conduct is not only voluntary but natural, *i.e.*, free from the violence of external forces.

It is necessary to consider the additional distinction between the voluntary and the free. Animals acting from desires caused by the perception of certain objects act voluntarily, but, in the theory of Aristotle and Aquinas, only men freely choose among alternative objects of desire or between means for accomplishing an end. The effects of voluntary action differ from other natural events only because knowledge enters into their determination. But that which happens as the result of man's free choice is determined neither by his nature nor by his knowledge. Hence whatever comes into existence through man's choice stands apart from all that is naturally determined to exist.

One other matter bears on this consideration of the natural in relation to the voluntary and the free. Spinoza excludes the operation of final causes, as well as free choice, from the order of nature. Purposes or ends are not principles of nature. Aristotle, on the other hand, thinks that final causes are operative in every part of nature. He finds them in the sphere of inert bodies which naturally tend toward certain results. He finds them in the sphere of animal and human motions, where the final cause or end may be an object of conscious desire.

So far as the search for causes is concerned, nature presents the same kind of problems to the physicist as to the biologist or psychologist. In only one sense are final causes peculiarly present in human conduct; that is the sense in which the change effected is not the ultimate end, but only a means to some further end desired. Here there is an extrinsic final cause as well as a final cause intrinsic to the change itself. It may be with regard to this special sense that Bacon says of final causes that they are "more allied to man's own nature than to the system of the universe." Yet Bacon, far from denying their presence in the scheme of things, assigns the investigation of final causes to metaphysics (as a branch of natural philosophy) rather than to physics. For him the ascertainment of final causes does not discover a purpose in the nature of things. Rather it looks to God's plan and providence.

We have so far dealt with that consideration of nature which opposes the natural to the works of man. The discussion of nature also moves on a theological plane. Here, on one traditional view, the natural is not opposed to, but rather identified with the work of God. "Things which are said to be made by nature," Plato writes, "are the work of divine art." Those who conceive the universe as God's creation, and think of God alone as uncreated being, tend to use the word "nature" collectively for the whole world of creatures and distributively for each type of thing which has its being from God.

The distinction between the supernatural and the natural has many interpretations in Christian theology, but none more basic than that which divides all being into the uncreated and the created. On this view, the order of nature includes more than the world of physical, sensible things. It includes the spiritual creation—angels and souls—as well. Immaterial beings are no more supernatural than bodies. They, too, are created natures. Only God is uncreated being.

Those who do not have or who deny a doctrine of creation use the word "nature" in a *less* and in a *more* comprehensive sense. The Greek philosophers, for example, seem to restrict the natural to the physical, *i.e.*, to the realm of material, sensible, changing things. Change is an element in the connotation of the Greek word *phüsis*, of which *natura* is the Latin equivalent. As Greek scientists conceive the study of nature, it is the business of physics to investigate the principles, causes, and elements of change.

Things which are thought to be untouched by change, such as the objects of mathematics, self-subsistent ideas, or separate forms; or things which are thought to be eternal and immutable, such as immaterial substances or intelligences, do not belong to the realm of physics or *natural* science. In Aristotle's classification of the sciences such beings are the objects of mathematics and metaphysics, or theology. Since, for him, whatever is both sensible and mutable is also material, the realm of nature includes no more than the whole material universe, celestial as well as terrestrial.

The *more* comprehensive sense of nature appears in Spinoza's identification of nature with the infinite and eternal substance of God. "Besides God," says Spinoza, "no substance can be nor be conceived. . . . Whatever is, is in God, and nothing can either be or be conceived without God." All finite things are modes of the divine substance or, more precisely, of the attributes of God, such as extension and thought. Nature, therefore, is the totality of finite things, both material and immaterial. But nature exceeds even this totality, for the infinite substance of God is greater than the sum of its parts.

To make this clear, Spinoza employs the distinction between *natura naturans* and *natura naturata*. "By *natura naturans* we are to understand that which is in itself and is conceived through itself, or those attributes of substance which express eternal and infinite essence; that is to say, God in so far as He is considered as a free cause. But by *natura naturata* I understand everything which follows from the necessity of the nature of God, or of any one of God's attributes in so far as they are considered as things which are in God, and which without God can neither be nor be conceived."

Viewed under the aspect of time rather than eternity, the order of nature (*i.e.*, *natura naturata*) is as much an order of ideas as it is an order of things. "The order and connection of ideas is the same as the order and connection of things," Spinoza writes. "Whether we think of nature under the attribute of extension or under the attribute of thought, or under any other attribute whatever, we shall discover one and the same order, or one and the same connection of causes."

Except perhaps for the Stoics, like Marcus Aurelius and Epictetus, Spinoza seems to stand alone in this conception of nature as all-embracing. The Stoics too regard nature as the system of the universe, with man a part of its cosmic structure, and with God or divinity inherent in nature as the rational principle governing all things. But with or without reference to God and creation, thinkers like Descartes and Hume tend to identify nature not with the totality of finite things, but with the world of bodies in motion or changing sensible things.

For Descartes, nature does not include the realm of thought or thinking substances, though these, like bodies, are finite and dependent creatures of God. For Hume, nature seems to be that which lies outside experience—in a way, the reality which underlies appearances. Where Spinoza thinks that the system of ideas is as much a part of nature as the system of bodies in motion, Hume speaks of "a kind of pre-established harmony between the course of nature and the succession of our ideas."

Hume's distinction between knowledge of the relation between our own ideas and knowledge of matters of fact or real existence seems furthermore to imply that nature is the reality known (however inadequately) when we assert certain things to be matters of fact. Here we perceive another meaning of nature, defined by another basic opposition, this time between the real and the ideal or the imaginary. It is in this sense that mediaeval writers oppose *entia naturae*, *i.e.*, natural or real beings, to *entia rationis*, or things which have their being in the mind.

THIS DISTINCTION, like most of the others in which nature is concerned, does not have universal acceptance. Kant, as we have seen, far from making nature the reality which exists independently of our experience or knowledge, conceives the realm of nature as identical with all possible experience. "We possess two expressions," Kant writes, "*world* and *nature*, which are generally interchanged. The first denotes the mathematical total of all phenomena and the totality of their synthesis. . . . And the world is termed nature, when it is regarded as a dynamical whole—when our attention is not directed to the aggregation in space and time . . . but to the unity in the *existence* of phenomena."

On quite different principles of analysis, Berkeley also treats as natural things the ideas or sensations which "are not produced by, or dependent on, the wills of men." Natural beings do not exist apart from the mind, but unlike imaginary ones, natural beings are those ideas which are not subject to our will or the human mind's own constructive activities. Such ideas are produced in our minds immediately by God.

To the question whether "Nature hath no share in the production of natural things," Berkeley answers: "If by *Nature* is meant the visible series of effects or sensations imprinted on our minds, according to certain fixed and general laws, then it is plain that Nature, taken in this sense, cannot produce anything at all. But, if by *Nature* is meant some being distinct from God, as well as from the laws of nature, and things perceived by sense, I must confess that word is to me an empty sound without any intelligible meaning annexed to it. Nature, in this acceptation, is a vain chimera, introduced by those heathens who had not just notions of the omnipresence and infinite perfection of God."

Berkeley's view represents one extreme position on a theological issue of the utmost difficulty. According to him God is not only the creator or first cause, but the sole cause of everything which happens in the course of nature. There are no natural causes. Nature has no productive power. Everything is the work of God or the work of man—nothing the work of nature.

Within the limits of this issue, the other extreme consists in denying not the creativity of God, but the role of divine causality in the production of natural effects. It relegates them entirely to the efficacy of natural causes. Lucretius, of course, denies both the creation of the world and the intervention of the gods in the processes of nature. But others, like Descartes, seem to say that once God has created the physical world, once He has formed matter into bodies and given them their initial impetus, their motions henceforward need only the laws of nature which God laid down for them to follow. For everything that happens in the course of nature, natural causes, operating under these laws, suffice.

There is a third position which distinguishes between the work of God in the creation of nature, and the work of nature in the production of effects of all sorts, such as the natural motions of bodies or the propagation of animals. But though it ascribes efficacy to natural agents or second causes in the production of natural effects, it also regards natural causes as instrumental to the hand of God, the first or principal cause of everything which happens as well as of everything which is. Aquinas seems to hold that God acts alone only in the original creation of things; whereas in the preservation of created natures and in their causal interaction, God works through secondary, or natural, causes.

"Some have understood God to work in every agent," Aquinas writes, "in such a way that no created power has any effect in things, but that God alone is the immediate cause of everything wrought; for instance, that it is not fire that gives heat, but God in the fire, and so forth. But this is impossible. First, because the order of cause and effect would be taken away from created things, and this would imply a lack of power in the Creator. . . . Secondly, because the operative powers which are seen to exist in things would be bestowed on things to no purpose, if things produced nothing through them. . . . We must therefore understand that God works in things in such a manner that things have also their proper operation."

In other words, according to Aquinas, "God is the cause of action in every agent." Furthermore, "God not only moves things to operate . . . but He also gives created agents their forms and preserves them in being." With regard to the being of things, Aquinas holds that God "established an order among things, so that some depend on others, by which they are conserved in being, though He remains the principal cause of their conservation."

WITH REGARD TO NATURE itself this theological doctrine raises two sorts of problems. The first concerns the efficacy of natural causes, which are sufficient for the scientist to appeal to in explaining natural phenomena, yet are insufficient by themselves for the production of natural effects. The second concerns the distinction between the natural and the supernatural, now not in terms of the created and the uncreated, but in terms of what happens naturally (or even by chance) as opposed to what happens as a result of God's intervention in the course of nature.

Miracles, for example, are supernatural rather than natural events. They are not produced by natural causes; nor do they happen by accident. They are attributed by the theologian to divine causality, yet not in such a way that violence is done to nature. "The term *miracle*," Aquinas explains, "is derived from admiration, which arises when an effect is manifest, whereas its cause is hidden. . . . A miracle is so called as being full of wonder; in other words, as having a cause absolutely hidden from all. This cause is God. Therefore those things which God does outside the causes which we know are called miracles."

The miraculous is that which is beyond the power of nature to accomplish. "A thing is said to be above the ability of nature," Aquinas writes, "not only by reason of the substance of the thing done, but also because of the manner and the order in which it is done"; and "the more the power of nature is surpassed, the greater the miracle." Aquinas distinguishes three grades of miracles.

The first, he says, surpasses nature "in the substance of the deed; as, for example, if two bodies occupy the same place, or if the sun goes backwards, or if a human body is glorified. Such things nature is absolutely unable to do; and these hold the highest rank among miracles. Secondly, a thing surpasses the power of nature, not in the deed, but in that wherein it is done; as the raising of the dead, and giving sight to the blind, and the like. For nature can give life, but not to the dead, and it can give sight, but not to the blind. Such hold the second rank in miracles. Thirdly, a thing surpasses nature's power in the measure and order in which it is done; as when a man is cured of a fever suddenly by God, without treatment or the usual process of nature. . . . These hold the lowest place in miracles."

Though "each of these kinds has various degrees, according to the different ways in which the power of nature is surpassed," no miracle, according to Aquinas, transgresses the order of nature in the sense of accomplishing the impossible. Unlike the impossible, which would destroy nature, the improbable can be elicited by God's power within the general framework of nature.

Hume, on the other hand, thinks that "a miracle is a violation of the laws of nature." And since, in his view, a firm and unalterable experience has established these laws, the proof against a miracle, from the nature of the fact, is as entire as any argument from experience can be. "Why is it more than probable," he asks, "that all men must die; that lead cannot, of itself remain suspended in the air; that fire consumes wood, and is extinguished by water; unless it be, that these events are found agreeable to the laws of nature, and there is required a violation of these laws, or in other words, a miracle to prevent them?

"Nothing is esteemed a miracle," Hume continues, "if it ever happens in the common course of nature. . . . There must, therefore, be a uniform experience against every miraculous event, otherwise the event would not merit that appellation. And as a uniform experience amounts to proof, there is here a direct and full *proof*, from the nature of the fact, against the existence of any miracle; nor can such a proof be destroyed, or the miracle rendered credible, but by an opposite proof which is superior."

Hume does not think that miracles can be proved against our uniform experience of the order of nature. But he also thinks that they are "dangerous friends or disguised enemies to the *Christian religion*" who would try to defend its beliefs "by the principles of human reason. . . . The *Christian religion* not only was at first attended with miracles," he declares, "but even at this day cannot be believed by any reasonable person without one. Mere reason is insufficient to convince us of its veracity: and whoever is moved by *Faith* to assent to it, is conscious of a continued miracle in his own person . . . which gives him a determination to believe what is most contrary to custom and experience."

One other traditional conception of nature, implicit in much of the foregoing, should be noted. The various senses of the term so far explicitly considered are alike in this: that they justify the use of the word "Nature" with a capital N and in the singular. This other sense of the term appears when we speak of each thing as having a nature of its own, and of the world as containing a vast plurality and radical diversity of natures.

In this sense we attribute a nature even to things which are contrasted with Nature and the natural. We speak of the nature of God and the nature of freedom, the nature of art, the nature of reason, the nature of ideas, the nature of the state, the nature of customs and habits. This could, of course, imply a theory that things which are not completely natural, nevertheless have a natural basis, as art, the state, or habit. Another meaning, however, seems to be involved.

The phrase "nature of" appears almost as frequently in the great books as the word "is," and frequently it is unaccompanied by any explicit theory of Nature or the natural. The discussion of the *nature of* anything seems, for the most part, to be a discussion of *what* it is. To state the nature of anything is to give its definition; or if for any reason definition in a strict sense cannot be given, then the attempt to state the nature of the thing consists in trying to say what characterizes this thing or kind of thing, in distinction from everything else or all other kinds.

Enumerating the senses of the term 'nature,' Aristotle gives this as the fifth meaning. The first four comprise senses which distinguish the natural from the artificial or the immutable, and which indicate that the natural or the physical has an immanent principle of movement in itself and involves matter or potency. The fifth sense is that in which 'nature' means "the *essence* of natural objects"; and, as he goes on to say, this implies the presence in them of form as well as matter. "By an extension of meaning from this sense of 'nature' every essence in general has come to be called a 'nature,' because the nature of a thing is one kind of essence." This is the sixth and most general sense, according to which the nature or essence of anything is the object of definition.

Does each individual thing have a nature peculiarly its own, even if it cannot be defined? Or is a nature or essence always something common to a number of individuals, according to which they can be classified into kinds, and the kinds ordered as species and genera? Do John and James, for example, have individual natures in addition to the common nature which they share through belonging to the human species; and does their human nature entail certain properties which are generic rather than specific, *i.e.*, which seem to be determined by their having the generic nature common to all animals as well as the specific nature common to all men?

Such questions about individual, specific, and generic natures raise problems of definition and classification which are discussed in the chapter on Evolution. They also raise problems about the existence or reality of the *kinds* which men define and classify. Are they merely what Locke calls "nominal essences," or do our definitions signify real essences, *i.e.*, the natures of things as they really are? Is the real world one which, as William James says, "plays right into logic's hands"? Does Nature consist of a *hierarchy* of natures or distinct kinds; or is it a *continuum* of things all having the same nature and differing from each other only individually or accidentally, but not essentially? These problems are discussed elsewhere, in such chapters as Animal, Definition, Evolution, Life and Death, and Same and Other.

OUTLINE OF TOPICS

1. Conceptions of nature

1*a*. Nature as the intrinsic source of a thing's properties and behavior

(1) The distinction between essential and individual nature: generic or specific properties, and individual, contingent accidents

(2) Nature or essence in relation to matter and form

1b. Nature as the universe or the totality of things: the identification of God and nature; the distinction between *natura naturans* and *natura naturata*

1c. Nature as the complex of the objects of sense: the realm of things existing under the determination of universal laws

2. The antitheses of nature or the natural

2a. Nature and art: the imitation of nature; cooperation with nature

2b. Nature and convention: the state of nature and the state of society

2c. Nature and nurture: the innate or native and the acquired; habit as second nature

2d. Natural and violent motion

2e. The natural and the unnatural or monstrous: the normal and the abnormal

2f. The order of nature and the order of freedom: the phenomenal and the noumenal worlds; the antithesis of nature and spirit

3. The order of nature

3a. The rationality of nature: the maxims and laws of nature

3b. Continuity and hierarchy in the order of nature

3c. Nature and causality

(1) The distinction between the regular and the chance event: the uniformity of nature

(2) The determinations of nature distinguished from the voluntary or free

(3) Teleology in nature: the operation of final causes

(4) Divine causality in relation to the course of nature: the preservation of nature; providence; miracles

4. Knowledge of nature or the natural

4a. Nature or essence as an object of definition

4b. Nature in relation to diverse types of science: the theoretic and the practical sciences; natural philosophy or science, mathematics, and metaphysics

4c. Nature as an object of history

5. Nature or the natural as the standard of the right and the good

5a. Human nature in relation to the good for man

5b. Natural inclinations and natural needs with respect to property and wealth

5c. The naturalness of the state and political obligation

5d. The natural as providing a canon of beauty for production or judgment

6. Nature in religion and theology

6a. The personification and worship of nature

6b. Nature and grace in human life

REFERENCES

References are listed by volume number (in bold type), author's name, and page number. Bible references are to book, chapter, and verse of the Authorized King James version of the Bible. The abbreviation "esp" calls the reader's attention to one or more especially relevant parts of a whole reference; "passim" signifies that the topic is discussed intermittently rather than continuously in the work or passage cited. Where the work as a whole is relevant to the topic, the page numbers refer to the entire work. For general guidance in the use of *The Great Ideas,* consult the Preface.

1. Conceptions of nature

1*a*. Nature as the intrinsic source of a thing's properties and behavior

8 ARISTOTLE, 259, 268–270, 534–535, 540, 645–646
10 GALEN, 167, 172–173
19 AQUINAS, 106–107, 162–163, 203–204, 311, 587–588
20 AQUINAS, 710–711, 808–809
28 HARVEY, 384–390 passim, 428
31 DESCARTES, 60, 83, 90, 93, 99–100, 126–127
35 LOCKE, 287–288
42 KANT, 133
46 HEGEL, 165
49 DARWIN, 9–10 passim

1*a*(1) The distinction between essential and individual nature: generic or specific properties, and individual, contingent accidents

8 ARISTOTLE, 100–101, 123–124, 182, 517–518, 536–537, 538–539, 547, 558–564, 581, 587–588
9 ARISTOTLE, 7, 320–321
19 AQUINAS, 16, 39–40, 71–72, 203–204, 604–607, 619–620
20 AQUINAS, 2–4, 12–13, 182–184, 711–712, 966
35 LOCKE, 255–260, 277–278
38 ROUSSEAU, 341–342
49 DARWIN, 28–29

1*a*(2) Nature or essence in relation to matter and form

8 ARISTOTLE, 270–271, 276, 277–278, 513, 535, 547–548, 555–561, 564–570, 585–586, 592, 599, 632, 645–646
9 ARISTOTLE, 163–164
10 GALEN, 169, 185–186
12 AURELIUS, 281
17 PLOTINUS, 146–149
19 AQUINAS, 106–109, 163–164, 249–250, 611–612
20 AQUINAS, 182–184, 959–963
30 BACON, 137–138
42 KANT, 186

1*b*. Nature as the universe or the totality of things: the identification of God and nature; the distinction between *natura naturans* and *natura naturata*

12 LUCRETIUS, 6–7, 12–14
12 EPICTETUS, 120–121
12 AURELIUS, 257, 267, 273, 277–278, 280, 281, 292, 310
17 PLOTINUS, 90–91, 129–131, 178–179
31 DESCARTES, 99
31 SPINOZA, 355, 356–357, 358, 359–362, 365–367, 373–375, 376–377, 422–424, 425, 447
42 KANT, 564–565, 566, 580
46 HEGEL, 220–221, 245–246
48 MELVILLE, 115–117
51 TOLSTOY, 216–218, 608, 631

1*c*. Nature as the complex of the objects of sense: the realm of things existing under the determination of universal laws

42 KANT, 25–26, 29–33, 49–51, 88–91, 109–110, 195, 200–209, 281–282, 285, 387, 550–551, 562–563, 574–577

2. The antitheses of nature or the natural

2*a*. Nature and art: the imitation of nature; cooperation with nature

5 AESCHYLUS, 44–45
5 SOPHOCLES, 134
7 PLATO, 320–334, 427–434, 478, 561, 577–578, 660–662
8 ARISTOTLE, 270–271, 437, 555–558, 568, 592, 599, 642
9 ARISTOTLE, 388, 545–546, 654–655, 682, 695–696
10 HIPPOCRATES, 73, 74–76
10 GALEN, 189–190
12 LUCRETIUS, 78–79
12 AURELIUS, 259–260, 303
13 VIRGIL, 37–99
17 PLOTINUS, 174–175, 239–240
18 AUGUSTINE, 651
19 AQUINAS, 106–107, 242–244, 486–487, 493, 528–529, 534–536
20 AQUINAS, 956–958
21 DANTE, 16, 67–68

46 HEGEL, 171, 236
51 TOLSTOY, 688–694
53 JAMES, 84–94, 291–295, 704–706, 820–825
54 FREUD, 453–467

3c(3) Teleology in nature: the operation of final causes

7 PLATO, 447–448
8 ARISTOTLE, 270–271, 275–278, 493–494, 506, 512–513, 514–515, 605–606, 652, 667–668 passim, 698
9 ARISTOTLE, 161–162, 164–165, 170–229 passim, 249, 255, 257–260 passim, 283, 285–286, 320–321, 330–331
10 GALEN, 167–215
12 LUCRETIUS, 55, 62
12 AURELIUS, 269–270
16 KEPLER, 857–860, 863–887 passim, 915–916, 925–928, 932–933
17 PLOTINUS, 40–41, 242–243
18 AUGUSTINE, 610–611
19 AQUINAS, 25–26, 241, 340–341, 407–409, 486–487, 488–489, 528–534, 610–611, 614, 615
28 HARVEY, 271–273, 309, 355, 401, 418, 439–440, 442–443, 447, 461, 462
30 BACON, 43, 45–46
31 SPINOZA, 369–372
34 NEWTON, 528–529
35 LOCKE, 124–125
35 HUME, 469, 501
42 KANT, 127–128, 205–209, 467–470, 473–474, 550–613
46 HEGEL, 161–162
49 DARWIN, 40–42, 60–61, 95–97, 593
51 TOLSTOY, 650
53 JAMES, 4–6, 671
54 FREUD, 651–654

3c(4) Divine causality in relation to the course of nature: the preservation of nature; providence; miracles

OLD TESTAMENT: *Genesis*, 1–2; 7–8; 11:1–9; 17:15–21 / *Exodus*, 3–4; 7–12; 14:19–31; 16:1–17:7 / *Numbers*, 16–17; 20:1–13; 21:4–9; 22:21–34 / *Joshua*, 3; 6:1–20; 10:12–14 / *I Kings*, 17–19 / *Nehemiah*, 9 / *Job*, 36:24–42:2 / *Psalms*, 8; 18:6–17; 19:1–6; 65; 78; 89:8–12; 104; 106–107; 136; 147:7–20 / *Amos*, 8:8–12 / *Jonah*
APOCRYPHA: *Ecclesiasticus*, 43
NEW TESTAMENT: *Matthew*, 1:18–25; 6:25–34; 8–9; 14:14–36; 15:30–39 / *Luke*, 1:5–66; 5:4–15 / *John*, 2:1–11; 9:1–34; 11:1–45 / *Acts*, 3:1–16
7 PLATO, 757–771 passim
8 ARISTOTLE, 438, 645
10 HIPPOCRATES, 17–18, 154–160
12 LUCRETIUS, 17, 29, 63–64, 76–77, 80–81, 85
12 EPICTETUS, 110–112, 121–122, 191–192, 195–201
12 AURELIUS, 308
16 KEPLER, 1049–1050, 1061
18 AUGUSTINE, 333–334, 344–345, 518–520, 562–568
19 AQUINAS, 12–14, 34–38, 82–83, 111–113, 127–133, 238–255, 279–280, 310–311, 313–314, 378–379, 480–491, 504–505, 528–608, 665–666
20 AQUINAS, 369–370, 978–980, 1016–1025
21 DANTE, 108–109, 126, 148
22 CHAUCER, 209–210
23 HOBBES, 51–52, 160, 183–187 passim, 188–191, 241–242
28 HARVEY, 406–407, 416, 426–429, 443, 490–493
30 BACON, 2, 4
31 DESCARTES, 90, 214–215
31 SPINOZA, 362–363, 365–366, 367–372, 422–424
32 MILTON, 354–355
33 PASCAL, 284–290, 328–341
34 NEWTON, 369–371, 542–543
35 LOCKE, 371
35 BERKELEY, 417–419 passim, 422–423, 424–428 passim, 429, 431, 442–444
35 HUME, 474–475, 488–503 passim
40 GIBBON, 189–191, 206, 292–296, 409, 465–467
42 KANT, 187–190, 239–240, 334–335, 560–562, 572–578, 581–582, 588–592
44 BOSWELL, 126
46 HEGEL, 246, 361
49 DARWIN, 239, 243
51 TOLSTOY, 675–677, 684
52 DOSTOEVSKY, 171–177 passim

4. Knowledge of nature or the natural

4a. Nature or essence as an object of definition

7 PLATO, 104–105, 763, 809–810
8 ARISTOTLE, 122–128, 131–133, 493–494, 513, 514–515, 552–555, 558–562, 563–564, 566–568, 569–570, 631–632, 642–645 passim
9 ARISTOTLE, 163–164, 165–167
19 AQUINAS, 17–18, 84–85, 102–103, 163–164, 461–462
20 AQUINAS, 402–403
23 HOBBES, 270–271
31 DESCARTES, 14
31 SPINOZA, 356–357, 373
35 LOCKE, 204–206, 240–243, 246–247, 257–260, 268–283, 287–290, 295–297, 331–336 passim
35 BERKELEY, 432–433
53 JAMES, 185, 669–671

4b. Nature in relation to diverse types of science: the theoretic and the practical sciences; natural philosophy or science, mathematics, and metaphysics

7 PLATO, 447–477
8 ARISTOTLE, 259–260, 270–271, 278, 334, 337,

389–390, 397, 510, 547–548, 560, 589–590, 592–593
9 ARISTOTLE, 161–165, 168–170
16 PTOLEMY, 5–6
18 AUGUSTINE, 265–267, 268–269, 336
19 AQUINAS, 3–4, 90–91, 450–453
23 HOBBES, 268
28 HARVEY, 331–332
30 BACON, 40, 42, 43, 114–115
31 DESCARTES, 61–62, 66–67
31 SPINOZA, 369–372
34 NEWTON, 270–271
35 LOCKE, 270–271, 360–362, 394–395
35 BERKELEY, 418–419, 424–426, 432–434
35 HUME, 478–480
39 SMITH, 335–337
42 KANT, 5–13, 15–16, 190–191, 291–292, 297, 300, 307–314, 329–337, 461–475, 578, 596–598
46 HEGEL, 361
51 TOLSTOY, 694
53 JAMES, 862–866, 882–886

4*c*. Nature as an object of history

18 AUGUSTINE, 650–651
23 HOBBES, 71
28 HARVEY, 338, 473
30 BACON, 32–34
38 ROUSSEAU, 333–334
46 HEGEL, 156–164, 190–201
48 MELVILLE, 221–224, 243–249, 267–271, 335–341
49 DARWIN, 152–166

5. Nature or the natural as the standard of the right and the good

5*a*. Human nature in relation to the good for man

6 THUCYDIDES, 368, 461–462, 504–507
7 PLATO, 155–157, 282–284, 309–310, 350–355, 410, 421–425, 474–476
8 ARISTOTLE, 329–330, 499–501 passim
9 ARISTOTLE, 343, 360, 431–432 passim, 446, 537
12 LUCRETIUS, 15, 43–44, 75
12 EPICTETUS, 116–118, 121, 175–180, 185–187, 230–235
12 AURELIUS, 259, 261, 265, 266, 267–268, 269, 271, 283, 285, 291, 295–296
18 AUGUSTINE, 17, 385–388, 507–513
19 AQUINAS, 609–643, 662–663
20 AQUINAS, 24–25, 63–64, 106–107, 178–184, 208–209, 220–226
21 DANTE, 15–16, 79–80
24 RABELAIS, 65
25 MONTAIGNE, 71–73, 424–426, 502–504, 508–512, 528–529, 538–543
27 SHAKESPEARE, 115
30 BACON, 70–71
31 SPINOZA, 429–431, 462–463
35 LOCKE, 90, 191–193, 230–231
37 FIELDING, 38–39
38 ROUSSEAU, 329–366, 367–385 passim
42 KANT, 253–254, 327–329
43 MILL, 448–455, 464–465
44 BOSWELL, 413
49 DARWIN, 310–319, 592
50 MARX, 301
54 FREUD, 623–625, 758–759, 785–789 esp 786–787, 800–801

5*b*. Natural inclinations and natural needs with respect to property and wealth

5 EURIPIDES, 306–307, 382
7 PLATO, 409–410
9 ARISTOTLE, 446–453, 536–537
14 PLUTARCH, 285
15 TACITUS, 31
19 AQUINAS, 615–616
20 AQUINAS, 224–225
22 CHAUCER, 422–424
25 MONTAIGNE, 489–490
27 SHAKESPEARE, 261
31 SPINOZA, 450
35 LOCKE, 30–36 passim
38 MONTESQUIEU, 44
38 ROUSSEAU, 352, 363–366, 393–394
39 SMITH, 6–8, 27–37 passim, 42–50, 63, 70–71, 147–148, 163–164, 383
44 BOSWELL, 124–125
50 MARX, 71–72, 251–255
54 FREUD, 787–788

5*c*. The naturalness of the state and political obligation

7 PLATO, 316–319
9 ARISTOTLE, 382, 445–446, 447–449, 475–476, 511–512, 530, 537
12 AURELIUS, 264, 280, 293, 297, 303
20 AQUINAS, 227–228
23 HOBBES, 100, 101, 164
30 BACON, 94–95
31 SPINOZA, 433–436
35 LOCKE, 42–53
38 MONTESQUIEU, 1–2, 3, 39
38 ROUSSEAU, 329–366, 368–369, 387–400, 419
42 KANT, 433–434, 435–436, 437
43 DECLARATION OF INDEPENDENCE, 1
43 MILL, 327–328
46 HEGEL, 94–95
54 FREUD, 780

5*d*. The natural as providing a canon of beauty for production or judgment

7 PLATO, 427–431, 660–661
9 ARISTOTLE, 168–169, 654–655, 685, 695–696
21 DANTE, 67–68
29 CERVANTES, 184–187, 189–193, 212–215
33 PASCAL, 176
42 KANT, 476–479, 494–495, 502–503, 521–524, 546, 557–558
48 MELVILLE, 277, 335
49 DARWIN, 576–577

6. Nature in religion and theology

6*a*. The personification and worship of nature

OLD TESTAMENT: *Deuteronomy*, 4:16–19; *II Kings*, 23:4–5,11 / *Jeremiah*, 8:1–2
APOCRYPHA: *Wisdom of Solomon*, 13:1–9
NEW TESTAMENT: *Romans*, 1:23–25
6 HERODOTUS, 31
8 ARISTOTLE, 604–605
12 LUCRETIUS, 1, 22–23
18 AUGUSTINE, 192–193
27 SHAKESPEARE, 253, 262–263
40 GIBBON, 81, 93
42 KANT, 504–505
46 HEGEL, 196–197, 220–221, 228, 244–245, 252–255, 263–265, 268–271
47 GOETHE, 12–15, 26–28, 116–117
48 MELVILLE, 367–372
50 MARX, 35
54 FREUD, 876–877

6*b*. Nature and grace in human life

NEW TESTAMENT: *John*, 1:12–13; 3; 6:22–27 / *Romans* / *I Corinthians*, 2–3; 12; 15:42–50 / *II Corinthians*, 5:14–17 / *Galatians*, 5:3–4,19–26 / *Ephesians* / *Colossians* / *James*, 4:1–10 / *I John* passim
18 AUGUSTINE, 51–52, 397–399, 438–439, 572–573
19 AQUINAS, 7–8, 11–12, 51–52, 60–62, 317–325, 501–523
20 AQUINAS, 65–66, 87–96, 158, 338–378, 392–394, 720–721, 745–763, 771–772, 858–864
21 DANTE, 99–100, 115–116, 155
22 CHAUCER, 504–505, 508
23 HOBBES, 192–193, 250–251, 253–254
25 MONTAIGNE, 212–215, 267–268
31 DESCARTES, 125–126
32 MILTON, 133, 136–144 esp 138, 299, 304–305, 347
33 PASCAL, 248–250, 263–264, 290–291, 295, 296–297
46 HEGEL, 354
42 KANT, 238
52 DOSTOEVSKY, 127–137 passim

CROSS-REFERENCES

For: Terms or discussions relevant to the conception of the nature of a thing as its essence, *see* BEING 8c–8e; DEFINITION 1a; FORM 2c(2), 3c; IDEA 4b(3); ONE AND MANY 3b–3b(1); SAME AND OTHER 3a–3a(1).

Terms or discussions relevant to the conception of nature as the totality of things or as the whole of sensible reality, *see* EXPERIENCE 1; GOD 11; ONE AND MANY 1b; WORLD 3–3b.

Other considerations of the distinction between nature and art, *see* ART 2a–2c, 9a; and for the distinction between the natural and the conventional in language, law, and justice, *see* CUSTOM AND CONVENTION 1; JUSTICE 6b, 10a; LANGUAGE 2a–2b; LAW 2, 4f; SIGN AND SYMBOL 1a–1f; SLAVERY 2, 3.

For: The distinction between the state of nature and the state of civil society, and for the problem of the naturalness of the family and the state, *see* FAMILY 1; LAW 4b; LIBERTY 1b; NECESSITY AND CONTINGENCY 5b–5d; STATE 1–1a, 3b–3c; WAR AND PEACE 1.

Another consideration of the distinction between nature and nurture, *see* HABIT 1, 3d.

Other treatments of natural and violent motion, *see* CHANGE 7b; MECHANICS 5e(2)–5f.

The distinction between the natural, the voluntary, and the free, *see* CAUSE 3; LIBERTY 4b; WILL 3a(1)–3a(2), 6c.

The distinction between the natural and the supernatural, *see* GOD 6b–6c(4), 10; HABIT 5e(1)–5e(3); HAPPINESS 7c; KNOWLEDGE 6c(5); RELIGION 6f; THEOLOGY 2; VIRTUE AND VICE 2b, 8d–8e; WISDOM 1a, 1c.

Discussions bearing on the rationality or order of nature, *see* MIND 10a; RELATION 5b; WORLD 6c; and for the special problem of continuity or hierarchy in the order of nature, *see* ANIMAL 1b–1c; EVOLUTION 4a, 4c; LIFE AND DEATH 2, 3a; MAN 1a, 1c; WORLD 6b.

The reign of causality and the uniformity of nature, *see* CHANCE 2a; FATE 5; NECESSITY AND CONTINGENCY 3c; WILL 5c; and for the problem of final causes in nature, *see* CAUSE 6.

Other considerations of divine causality in relation to the order of nature, *see* CAUSE 7b–7d; GOD 7e.

Nature in relation to the various sciences, *see* METAPHYSICS 2a, 3b; PHILOSOPHY 2a–2b; PHYSICS 1–1b; SCIENCE 3a; TRUTH 2c.

The nature of man as a standard in ethics, economics, and politics, *see* CITIZEN 8; DEMOCRACY 4b; DESIRE 3a; GOOD AND EVIL 3a; NECESSITY AND CONTINGENCY 5e; SLAVERY 2d, 3d; STATE 3b(1); WEALTH 10b.

The theological discussion of nature and grace in human life, *see* GOD 7d; HABIT 5e(1); HAPPINESS 7a; MAN 9b(1)–9b(2); SIN 3a, 3c, 7; VIRTUE AND VICE 8b.

ADDITIONAL READINGS

Listed below are works not included in *Great Books of the Western World*, but relevant to the idea and topics with which this chapter deals. These works are divided into two groups:

I. Works by authors represented in this collection.
II. Works by authors not represented in this collection.

For the date, place, and other facts concerning the publication of the works cited, consult the Bibliography of Additional Readings which follows the last chapter of *The Great Ideas.*

I.

EPICTETUS. *The Manual*
AUGUSTINE. *On Nature and Grace*
AQUINAS. *Summa Contra Gentiles*, BK III, CH 99–103
ROUSSEAU. *Eloisa* (*La nouvelle Héloïse*)
KANT. *Prolegomena to Any Future Metaphysic*, par 14–39
GOETHE. *Zur Natur- und Wissenschaftslehre*
HEGEL. *The Phenomenology of Mind*, V, A (a)
J. S. MILL. *A System of Logic*, BK III, CH 12–14, 22, 24
——. "Nature," in *Three Essays on Religion*
TOLSTOY. *The Cossacks*
ENGELS. *Dialectics of Nature*

II.

EPICURUS. *Letter to Herodotus*
ERIGENA. *De Divisione Naturae*
MAIMONIDES. *The Guide for the Perplexed*, PART II, CH 17, 19–20
BRUNO, *De la causa, principio, e uno*
SUÁREZ. *Disputationes Metaphysicae*, XXXIV, XLIII (4), XLVII (2)
BOYLE. *A Free Inquiry into the Vulgarly Received Notion of Nature*
LEIBNITZ. *Philosophical Works*, CH 4 (*Extract from a Letter to Bayle*)
J. BUTLER. *The Analogy of Religion*
VOLTAIRE. "Nature," in *A Philosophical Dictionary*
——. *The Ignorant Philosopher*, CH 36
——. *The Study of Nature*
SCHELLING. *Ideen zu einer Philosophie der Natur*
CHATEAUBRIAND. *René*
WORDSWORTH. *Tintern Abbey*
——. *Michael*
——. *The Prelude*
SCHOPENHAUER. *The World as Will and Idea*, VOL III, SUP, CH 23
EMERSON. *Nature*
WHEWELL. *The Philosophy of the Inductive Sciences*, VOL I, BK X, CH 3
THOREAU. *A Week on the Concord and Merrimack Rivers*
——. *Walden*
TYNDALL. *The Belfast Address*
LOTZE. *Microcosmos*, BK I, CH 1–2; BK IV, CH 1–3
——. *Logic*, BK II, CH 8
——. *Metaphysics*, BK II, CH 7–8
C. S. PEIRCE. *Collected Papers*, VOL VI, par 88–101, 395–427
NIETZSCHE. *The Will to Power*, BK III (2)
FRAZER. *The Golden Bough*, PART I, CH 3–6; PART VII, CH 13
BRADLEY. *Appearance and Reality*, BK I, CH 11–12; BK II, CH 13–15, 22
WARD. *Naturalism and Agnosticism*

ROYCE. *The World and the Individual*, SERIES II (5)
C. READ. *The Metaphysics of Nature*
BERGSON. *Creative Evolution*, CH 3
B. RUSSELL. *Philosophical Essays*, CH 2
HENDERSON. *The Order of Nature*
DEWEY. "Nature and Its Good, A Conversation," in *The Influence of Darwin on Philosophy*
——. *Experience and Nature*, CH 3–7, 9
BRIDGMAN. *The Logic of Modern Physics*, CH 4
EDDINGTON. *The Nature of the Physical World*, CH 13
LENZEN. *The Nature of Physical Theory*, PART II
LÉVY-BRUHL. *Primitives and the Supernatural*
SANTAYANA. *Reason in Common Sense*, CH 3–5
——. *Scepticism and Animal Faith*, CH 22
——. *The Genteel Tradition at Bay*, CH 2–3
MARITAIN. *The Degrees of Knowledge*, CH 3
LOVEJOY. *The Great Chain of Being*, CH 10
COLLINGWOOD. *The Idea of Nature*
PLANCK. "The Unity of the Physical Universe," in *A Survey of Physics*
——. *The Philosophy of Physics*, CH 2
WHITEHEAD. *The Concept of Nature*, CH 1–2
——. *Process and Reality*, PART II, CH 3–4
——. *Adventures of Ideas*, CH 7–8
——. *Modes of Thought*, LECT VII–VIII
SHERRINGTON. *Man on His Nature*, I–II, XII
WOODBRIDGE. *An Essay on Nature*
KELSEN. *Society and Nature*
CASSIRER. *Substance and Function*, PART II, CH 6
—— *The Myth of the State*, PART II (9)
VON WEIZSÄCKER. *The History of Nature*

Chapter 61: NECESSITY AND CONTINGENCY

INTRODUCTION

THE basic meaning of the words *necessity* and *contingency* is made known to us by the fact that we can substitute for them the familiar words *must* and *may*. "Is there any being which *must* exist?" asks the same question as, "Does anything exist of *necessity*?" "Are all things of the sort which *may* or *may not* exist, or are they divided into those which *must* exist and those which *may* or *may not* exist?" means the same as, "Is everything *contingent* in being or do some things exist *necessarily* and some *contingently*?"

The great issues which involve the opposition between necessity and contingency are concerned with more than questions about being or existence. They also deal with cause and effect, judgment and reasoning, happenings or events, the actions and decisions of men, human history and social institutions. In each case, the problem is formulated by such questions as: Does everything which happens in nature or history happen necessarily? Is everything contingent? Or are some events necessary and others contingent? Is the relation between cause and effect a necessary connection, or do some causes produce their effects contingently?

Are there some propositions which the mind *must* affirm because their truth is necessary? Or are all propositions such that they *may* or *may not* be true, our affirmation or denial of them being contingent upon factors which lie outside the propositions themselves? In reasoning, does the conclusion always follow by necessity from the premises if it follows at all? And are all conclusions which follow necessarily from their premises necessarily true, or may some be necessary truths and some contingent?

Are men necessitated in all their acts, or are certain actions contingent upon the exercise of their will and in this sense free? Does human liberty consist merely in the freedom of a man's action from the external necessity of coercion or constraint; or does it consist in a man's being able to choose whatever he chooses, freely rather than necessarily? Is every act of the will necessarily determined, or are some acts of the will acts of free choice?

Are certain human institutions, such as the family and the state, necessary? Are men compelled to live socially or can they choose the solitary life? If domestic and political society are necessary, are the ways in which they are organized also necessary, or are such things as monogamy in the family and monarchy in the state contingent? Are such things as war, slavery, poverty, and crime necessary features of human society, or are they the result of circumstances which are contingent and which can therefore be remedied?

These questions indicate the range of subject matters in which issues are raised concerning the necessary and the contingent. They also indicate that the other ideas to which necessity and contingency have relevance are too manifold to permit an enumeration of all the other chapters in which some aspect of necessity and contingency is discussed. This chapter stands to the others as a kind of summary of the theme of necessity and contingency. It assembles in one place the various topics, problems, or subject matters which traditionally engage the human mind with that theme.

Two chapters alone demand specific mention as, in a sense, being concerned with ideas that seem to be inseparable from the notions of necessity and contingency. They are FATE and CHANCE. Though they stand opposed to one another as the necessary to the contingent, they do not cover every application of this opposition. They are largely concerned with necessity and contingency in the realm of change, in the causation of the events of nature or the happenings of history. They do not deal, at least not directly, with necessity and contingency in being or existence, in thought or knowledge, in human acts and social institutions.

THE NECESSARY AND the contingent do not seem to be opposed in exactly the same way in each of the four areas—namely, being, change, thought, and action—in which they raise basic issues.

In the sphere of human action, for example, writers like Hobbes, Locke, and Hume substitute the notion of liberty for contingency as the opposite of necessity. The meaning of necessity alters in consequence. Liberty, according to these authors, implies the absence not of all necessity, but only of external necessity in the form of compulsion. An internal necessity, they think, is quite compatible with complete freedom.

Hume therefore dismisses the supposed conflict between liberty and necessity as groundless. "By liberty," he writes, "we can only mean *a power of acting or not acting, according to the determinations of the will*; that is, if we choose to remain at rest, we may; if we choose to move, we also may. Now this hypothetical liberty is universally allowed to belong to everyone who is not a prisoner and in chains.... Liberty, when opposed to necessity, not to constraint, is the same thing with chance; which is universally allowed to have no existence."

Similarly, Locke defines liberty as a man's power "to do or forbear doing any particular action, according as its doing or forbearance has the actual preference in the mind, which is the same thing as to say, according as he himself wills it." Liberty in this sense, he adds, belongs not to the will, the acts of which are necessitated by their causes, but to the man who is under no external necessity, in the form of compulsion, to do what is contrary to his will or to refrain from doing what he wills.

Hobbes seems to go even further along the same line of thought. Holding that liberty is destroyed only by external impediments to action, he uses "necessity" in a sense which makes it consistent with liberty, or inseparable from it. "The actions which men voluntarily do," he says, "because they proceed from their will, proceed from *liberty*; and yet, because every act of man's will, and every desire, and inclination, proceeds from some cause, and that from another cause, in a continual chain (whose first link is in the hand of God, the first of all causes), they proceed from *necessity*."

Yet if what Hobbes means by "external impediments" represents the same nullification of liberty which others call "compulsion" or "restraint," then there is at least one meaning of "necessity" which stands opposed to liberty. Enumerating the meanings of "necessary," Aristotle lists as one sense "the compulsory or compulsion, *i.e.*, that which impedes or tends to hinder, that which is contrary to impulse or purpose . . . or to the movement which accords with purpose and with reasoning." It is in a related sense that Plato opposes necessity to intelligence. Necessity represents for him those resistant factors in nature which the mind of man or God must overcome, or persuade to give way, if reason or purpose is to prevail in the coming to be of anything. In this sense, necessity like chance is opposed to purpose. Blind necessity and blind chance both exclude the operation of final causes; both exclude the possibility that the events of nature are directed toward an end.

WE SEEM TO HAVE found almost universal agreement on the point that there is one sense in which necessity conflicts with liberty. But this agreement does not affect the issue whether liberty is more than freedom from external coercion. There are those, like Aquinas, who think that man's will is free in its acts of choice with regard to "particular contingent means." Aquinas agrees that what is called "necessity of coercion" is "altogether repugnant to the will." The same act cannot be absolutely coerced and voluntary. But the question is whether the will's acts are necessarily determined by causes operating within the sphere of the will itself.

Aquinas names two modes of necessity which operate *within* the sphere of the will and restrict its freedom. One is the natural necessity that the will should desire an ultimate end, such as the complete good or happiness. If a man wills any object at all as the ultimate goal of his life, he cannot will anything other or less than that which can satisfy all his natural desires. The other necessity is that which concerns the use of those means which are absolutely indispensable conditions for reaching the end being sought. This may be an absolute or a conditional necessity. When the end is itself necessary (*e.g.*, happiness), whatever means are necessary thereto necessitate the will absolutely. When a certain end is not necessary, but has been freely adopted (*e.g.*, a certain destination), and when *only one* means is available (*e.g.*, one mode of transportation), then it becomes necessary to choose that means. But this necessity is conditional since it remains in force only on the condition that we continue to have a certain end in view—an end we can relinquish at any time as freely as we adopted it.

According to Aquinas, this leaves a great many acts of the will which are in no way necessitated: those in which there is no necessary connection between the means and a given end, and those in which a given means is necessary only on the condition that a certain end is sought. If the end need not be sought, then the will is free not to choose the means of achieving it; and if, when the end is necessarily sought, alternative means are available, then the will is free to choose one rather than another.

According to this theory, liberty consists in the absence of internal as well as external necessity. Furthermore, liberty seems to be related positively to contingency, insofar as freedom of choice depends on a contingent connection between means and ends, or upon the contingent, *i.e.*, the conditional, character of the end. On the other hand, those who hold that the will is never free from internal necessity insist that the act of choice, even with respect to contingent means, is always caused. If being caused is equivalent to being determined—which seems to be the view of Hobbes, Locke, and Hume—then whether or not we know what causes a particular choice, our wills are so determined that we could not have chosen otherwise.

The problem of the freedom of the will in relation to the causes which determine its acts is considered in the chapter on Will. The foregoing discussion suffices here for the purpose of throwing light on the meaning of necessity. If now we shift from human action to the realm of becoming, change, or motion, we face the question of the relation between necessity and causation in its most general form.

In the realm of nature the alternatives to necessity are referred to as "chance" and as "contingency." The significance of these alternatives depends on the theory of causation. According to one opinion, every effect is necessarily determined by its causes, and every cause necessarily produces certain effects. Given the causal chain of past events leading up to the present, every future event is necessarily determined. Nothing that ever happens could happen otherwise. Nothing happens contingently or by chance. This theory of causation is accordingly a doctrine of universal necessity or absolute determinism in the realm of change.

"In nature," writes Spinoza, "there is nothing contingent, but all things are determined from the necessity of the divine nature to exist and act in a certain manner." Though nothing which exists or happens is contingent, "God alone exists from the necessity of His own nature and acts alone from the necessity of His own nature." The divine necessity is therefore different from the necessity of everything else which follows from the divine nature. One is the necessity of freedom or self-determination, the other the necessity of compulsion, or determination by another. "That thing is called free," says Spinoza, "which exists from the necessity of its own nature alone, and is determined to action by itself alone. That thing, on the other hand, is called necessary, or rather compelled, which by another is determined to existence and action in a fixed and prescribed manner."

Hume's statement that there is "no such thing as *Chance* in the world," would appear to agree with Spinoza's denial of contingency. But Hume also seems to deny the perception of any necessary connection between cause and effect. This is not to say that events happen without cause, but only that "our ignorance of the real cause of any event has the same influence on the understanding" as if nothing were necessarily determined by its causes.

"We are never able," Hume thinks, "to discover any power or necessary connexion, any quality, which binds the effect to the cause, and renders the one an infallible consequence of the other. . . . One event follows another; but we never can observe any tie between them. They seem *conjoined*, but never *connected*. . . . Our idea, therefore, of necessity and causation arises entirely from the uniformity observable in the operations of nature, where similar objects are constantly conjoined together, and the mind is determined by custom to infer the one from the appearance of the other. These two circumstances form the whole of that necessity, which we ascribe to matter. Beyond the constant *conjunction* of similar objects, and the consequent *inference* from one to the other, we have no notion of any necessity or connexion."

But the question remains whether in the order of nature itself particular events are necessarily determined or happen contingently. The fact that we may be ignorant of real necessities does not, as Hume seems to admit, imply their non-existence. Our saying it is only probable that the sun will rise tomorrow may reflect our inadequate knowledge of causes rather than a real indeterminacy in the order of nature. On the other hand, to say as Hume does that chance has no place in nature, may mean only that "nothing exists without a cause of its existence," rather than that whatever happens is necessarily determined by its causes.

AS INDICATED IN the chapter on CHANCE, two things must be distinguished here: the absolutely uncaused—the spontaneous or fortuitous—and the contingently caused, or that which depends upon the coincidence of a number of independent causes. A given condition may be necessary to produce a certain result, as, for example, oxygen may be necessary for combustion. But by itself it may not be sufficient for the production of that effect. If the maxim, "nothing exists without a cause of its existence," requires a cause or causes adequate to produce the effect, then the maxim is equivalent to the principle of sufficient reason. Whenever two or more causes, each of which may be necessary, are not sufficient in separation, the existence of the effect depends upon their combination; and the effect is contingent if the required combination of causes is itself not necessarily caused.

The issue concerning contingency in nature thus seems to be more sharply stated when there is no reference to our knowledge or ignorance of causes. On this issue, Aristotle and Spinoza appear to be more clearly opposed to one another than Hume is to either.

If things do not take place of necessity, "an event," according to Aristotle, "might just as easily not happen as happen; for the meaning of the word 'fortuitous' with regard to present or future events is that reality is so constituted that it may issue in either of two opposite directions." For example, "a sea-fight must either take place tomorrow or not, but it is not necessary that it should take place tomorrow, neither is it necessary that it should not take place, yet it is necessary that it either should or should not take place tomorrow." Though Aristotle holds that "one of the two propositions in such instances must be true and the other false," he also insists that "we cannot say determinately that this or that is false, but must leave the alternative undecided."

Aristotle's view with regard to propositions about future particular events is that our judgments cannot be either true or false, not because of insufficient knowledge on our part, but because future particulars are in themselves always contingent. Nothing in the nature of things or causes—existent in the past or present—necessarily determines them to happen. They will occur only if independent causes happen to coincide. Since these causes are independent—not determined to combination by their natures—the coincidence will be a matter of chance, not of necessity.

This theory of contingency in the realm of change—involving an affirmation of the real existence of contingent events—raises problems for the theologian concerning God's knowledge and will. Does the fact that nothing happens contrary to God's will imply that whatever happens happens necessarily? Aquinas answers that "God wills some things to be done necessarily, some contingently. . . . Therefore, to some effects, He has attached necessary causes that cannot fail; but to others defectible and contingent causes, from which arise contingent effects . . . it being His will that they should happen contingently."

Similarly, the fact that God knows all things

infallibly does not seem to Aquinas to be inconsistent with the real contingency of some things. He explains that "whoever knows a contingent effect in its causes only, has merely a conjectural knowledge of it." But "God knows all contingent things not only as they are in their causes, but also as each one of them is actually in itself. . . . Hence it is manifest that contingent things are infallibly known by God, inasmuch as they are subject to the divine sight in their presentiality; yet they are future contingent things in relation to their own causes."

This has a bearing on the difference between human and divine apprehension of future contingent things. "Things reduced to actuality in time," Aquinas declares, "are known by us successively in time, but by God they are known in eternity, which is above time. Whence to us they cannot be certain, since we know future contingent things only as contingent futures; but they are certain to God alone, Whose understanding is in eternity above time. Just as he who goes along the road does not see those who come after him; whereas he who sees the whole road from a height sees at once all those travelling on it. Hence," Aquinas continues, "what is known by us must be necessary, even as it is in itself; for what is in itself a future contingent cannot be known by us. But what is known by God must be necessary according to the mode in which it is subject to the divine knowledge . . . but not absolutely as considered in its proper causes." It does not follow, therefore, that *everything known by God must necessarily be*; for that statement, according to Aquinas, "may refer to the thing or to the saying. If it refers to the thing, it is divided and false; for the sense is, *Everything which God knows is necessary.* If understood of the saying, it is composite and true, for the sense is, *This proposition, 'that which is known by God is,' is necessary.*"

With regard to human knowledge, Aquinas makes another distinction in answering the question whether man can have scientific or certain knowledge of contingent things. If, as Aristotle seems to hold, the objects of knowledge are necessary, not contingent things, then the realm of contingency belongs to opinion, conjecture, or probability. Insofar as the particular events of nature are contingent, they cannot be objects of scientific knowledge. But, according to Aquinas, "contingent things can be considered in two ways: either as contingent or as containing some element of necessity, since every contingent thing has in it something necessary; for example, that Socrates runs is in itself contingent; but the relation of running to motion is necessary, for it is necessary that Socrates moves if he runs."

The contingency that Socrates *may* or *may not* run does not alter the hypothetical necessity that *if* he runs, he *must* move. In its concern with contingent things, natural science is concerned only with such hypothetical necessities. Unlike physics, other sciences may deal with absolutely necessary things. That the objects of mathematics are of this sort seems to be an opinion shared by James and Kant, Hume and Descartes, Plato and Aristotle. But they do not agree on whether the necessities of mathematics belong to reality or have only ideal existence, *i.e.*, whether they exist apart from or only in the human mind. This issue is connected with another major issue concerning necessity and contingency, namely, whether any reality has necessary existence.

As WE HAVE SEEN, those who discuss necessity and contingency in the domain of human acts and natural events seem to construe these alternatives differently, according as they conceive liberty and chance in terms of different theories of causation. With regard to being or real existence, however, there seems to be a common understanding of the alternatives, even among those who do not agree that God alone is a necessary being because they think that this world is also determined to exist as a necessary consequence of God's existence.

In the preceding discussions, one meaning of contingency has repeatedly appeared. The contingent is that which can be otherwise. "That which cannot be otherwise is necessarily as it is," writes Aristotle, "and from this sense of 'necessary' all its other meanings are somehow derived." This insight is sometimes expressed by the statement that the opposite of the necessary is the impossible, whereas the contingent—which is neither necessary nor impossible—includes contrary possibilities.

In logical analysis what is called the "modality of necessity" is attributed to judgments the contradictories of which are self-contradictory; *e.g.*, if the proposition 'the whole is *not* greater than any of its parts' represents an impossible judgment, then the contradictory proposition 'the whole *is* greater than any of its parts' represents a necessary judgment. In contrast, as Hume points out, "*that the sun will not rise to-morrow* is no less intelligible a proposition, and implies no more contradiction than the affirmation *that it will rise*." These two propositions represent contrary possibilities. No matter which turns out to be true, the event could have been otherwise.

In logical analysis some complication seems to arise from the fact that the necessary has two opposites: the impossible on the one hand, and the possible or contingent on the other. This is usually clarified by the recognition that the possible is the opposite of the impossible as well as of the necessary. In that sense of "possible" which excludes only the impossible, the necessary is, of course, possible, for what is necessary cannot be impossible. But in that sense of "possible" which implies contrary possibilities, the possible excludes the necessary as well as the impossible.

"From the proposition 'it may be' it follows," according to Aristotle, "that it is not impossible, and from that it follows that it is not necessary; it comes about therefore that the thing which must necessarily be need not be; which is absurd. But again, the proposition 'it is necessary that it should be' does not follow from the proposition 'it may be,' nor does the proposition 'it is necessary that it should not be.' For the proposition 'it may be' implies a two-fold possibility, while, if either of the two former propositions is true, the twofold possibility vanishes. For if a thing may be, it may also not be, but if it is necessary that it should be or that it should not be, one of the two alternatives will be excluded. It remains, therefore, that the proposition 'it is not necessary that it should not be' follows from the proposition 'it may be.' For this is true also of that which must necessarily be."

Of the same thing we can say that it *may* be and that it *may not* be; but we cannot say of the same thing both that it *may* be and that it *must* be, or that it *may not* be and that it *cannot* be. As Aristotle traces the implications of these modes of 'to be,' we see that *may-be* implies *may-not-be*, which contradicts *must-be*; and similarly that *may-not-be* implies *may-be*, which contradicts *cannot-be*.

When we pass from the analysis of propositions or judgments to the consideration of being or existence, the situation is simpler. Since the impossible is that which cannot exist, whatever does exist must either be necessary or possible. Here the necessary and the possible are generally understood to exclude one another. The necessary is that which *cannot* not be, the possible that which *can* not be.

IN SPITE OF THIS common understanding of the alternatives, there are basic differences among the authors of the great books in regard to the analysis or demonstration of necessary being.

Aristotle, for example, tends to identify the possible with the perishable—with that which both comes into being and passes away. Those substances are necessary, in contrast, which are not subject to generation and corruption. Holding that the matter of the celestial bodies differs from that of terrestrial bodies with respect to the potentiality for substantial change, Aristotle seems to regard the heavenly bodies as necessary beings, eternal in the sense of always existing, even though changeable in regard to place, *i.e.*, subject to local motion. The changing things of this earth are all contingent in being, for the mutability to which their matter inclines them includes coming to be and passing away.

This analysis of necessity and contingency in terms of matter's potentialities leads to another conception of necessary being—that of a totally immutable being which has necessary existence because it lacks matter entirely and, since it consists of form alone, is purely actual. Whether or not there are for Aristotle substances other than the prime mover which are necessary because they are immaterial beings, he attributes pure actuality only to that one necessary being which is an *unmoved* mover.

Aquinas seems to adopt both of Aristotle's senses of "necessary being." He treats the celestial bodies and the angels as having necessity to the extent that they are immutable. But their immutability is limited in his opinion to the fact that they are by nature imperishable—the celestial bodies because of their matter; the angels because they are simple substances, not composed of matter and form. Since they are creatures they cannot be altogether immutable. "All creatures," Aquinas writes, "before they existed, were possible"—and in this sense contingent as regards their being, not necessary. "As it was in the Creator's power to produce them before they existed in themselves," he continues, "so likewise is it in the Creator's power when they exist in themselves to bring them to nothing." Furthermore, at every moment of their existence, their contingent being depends upon God's power. God preserves them in being, Aquinas says, "by ever giving them existence," for "if He took away His action from them, all things would be reduced to nothing."

In the strict sense then of "necessary being," no creature, but only God, the uncreated being, is truly a necessary being—because in God alone existence is identical with essence. Only a being whose very essence it is to exist is incapable of not existing; only such a being is necessary in the sense of being purely actual. All created things must be contingent, for if in their case to exist belonged to their very natures, God could not have created them by causing their natures to exist, nor when they did exist would His power be necessary to sustain them in being.

Where Aquinas defines God's necessity in terms of the *identity* of essence and existence, Descartes and Spinoza tend to conceive God as necessary because his essence is such that his existence *follows from* it. The difference may affect the meaning with which it is said that God is uncaused or that God is self-caused. "If its existence is caused," Aquinas writes, "nothing can be the sufficient cause of its own existence." According to Descartes, to say that God is "cause of His own existence . . . merely means that the inexhaustible power of God is the cause or reason why he needs no cause."

Descartes' position seems to be that that which is self-caused in the sense of having its existence determined by its own nature or essence, is also uncaused in the sense that its existence is not caused by anything outside itself. "Existence," he writes, "is involved in the essence of an infinite being, no less than the equality of its angles to two right angles is involved in that of a triangle." But though this suggests the notion of God's existence following from His essence, Descartes also says that "in God existence is not distinguished from essence."

For Descartes as for Aquinas the basic point remains that that which does not depend for its being upon any external cause, exists necessarily. Descartes, furthermore, associates the necessary existence of an independent being with that being's infinity or perfection of nature. That which is conceived as infinite or perfect cannot be conceived as lacking existence. "The notion of possible or contingent existence," he says, "belongs only to the concept of a limited thing."

Like Descartes, Spinoza conceives God as the only infinite and immutable being which exists necessarily in the sense of being "that whose essence involves existence." But unlike him Spinoza also attributes necessity in another sense to every finite and mutable thing which God causes to exist; for in his view, God not only exists necessarily but, acting from the necessity of His own nature, God also necessitates whatever follows as a consequence of His action. No other world than this is possible. "Things could be produced by God," Spinoza writes, "in no other manner and in no other order than that in which they have been produced." Furthermore, since whatever is in God's power "necessarily follows from it, and consequently exists necessarily," it is impossible for this world not to have existed. The existence of this particular world is as inseparable from God's existence as God's own existence is inseparable from His essence or nature.

In the tradition of western thought, there is, perhaps, no deeper theological issue than that which opposes the freedom of God's will to the necessity of God's acting according to His nature; and which, in consequence, sets the possibility of other worlds (or even of no world at all) against the necessity that, if God exists, this particular world inevitably follows.

Taking the other side on both points, Aquinas, for example, argues that "since the goodness of God is perfect, and can exist without other things inasmuch as no perfection can accrue to Him from them, it follows that His willing things apart from Himself is not absolutely necessary." As for the particular features of this world, Aquinas says that "since God does not act from natural necessity" nor from a will that is "naturally or from necessity determined" to the things which exist, it follows that "in no way at all is the present course of events produced by God from any necessity, so that other things could not happen. . . . Wherefore, we must simply say that God can do other things than those He has done." Other, and even better, worlds than this are possible, for "God could make other things, or add something to the present creation; and then there would be another and a better universe."

Nor does the Christian theologian admit that the divine nature is subject to any necessity. "We do not put the life of God or the foreknowledge of God under necessity," writes Augustine, "if we should say that it is necessary that God should live forever, and foreknow all things; as neither is His power diminished when we say that He cannot die or fall into error—for this is in such a way impossible to Him, that if it were possible for Him, He would be of less power. But assuredly He is rightly called omnipotent, though He can neither die nor fall into error. For He is called omnipotent on account of His doing what He wills, not on account of His suffering what He wills not; for if that should befall him, He would by no means be omnipotent. Wherefore, He cannot do some things for the very reason that He is omnipotent."

ONE OTHER TRADITIONAL issue is raised by the conception of God as a necessary being; or, more strictly, as the only necessary being in the sense of having a nature which involves existence. It is formed by opposite views of the validity of the so-called "ontological" or *a priori* argument for God's existence.

Both Descartes and Spinoza argue, like Anselm and others before them, that since God cannot be conceived as not existing, it is impossible in fact for God not to exist. Those who reject such reasoning do not deny that it is unintelligible or self-contradictory to think of God as merely possible rather than necessary, *i.e.*, as requiring a cause outside Himself in order to exist. Kant, for example, admits that existence must be included in the conception of God as *ens realissimum*—the most real and perfect being. But he denies that the real existence of the object so conceived is implied by the logical necessity of the conception itself.

This amounts to saying that it is possible for a being we cannot conceive except as existing, not to exist. Aquinas seems to make the same critical point when he says that even if everyone understood by the word "God" something than which nothing greater can be conceived, and therefore a being necessarily existing, still it would not follow that "he understands that what the word signifies actually exists, but only mentally."

Stated in its most general form, the problem is whether that which is inconceivable by the human mind is impossible in reality; or whether that which is logically necessary, or necessary in thought, is also necessary in fact or existence. However that issue is resolved, it must be noted that among the so-called *a posteriori* demonstrations of God's existence, or arguments from the existence of certain effects to the existence of their cause, one mode of reasoning turns upon the distinction between contingent and necessary being.

If contingent beings exist (as it is evident they do, from the mutability and perishability of physical things), *and if* each contingent being is by definition incapable of causing its own existence, *and if* one contingent being cannot cause the existence of another, *and if* everything which exists must have a cause for its existence, either in itself or in another; *then* from all these premises it would seem to follow that a necessary being exists.

Here the conclusion may follow with logical necessity from the premises, but whether it is necessarily true depends upon the truth of the premises. That in turn seems to depend upon the understanding of what it means for anything to be contingent or necessary in being. It may also depend on whether or not the reasoning escapes Kant's criticism of all *a posteriori* arguments for the existence of a necessary being, namely, that such reasoning always implicitly contains the ontological argument, and is thereby invalidated.

OUTLINE OF TOPICS

1. The meaning of necessity and contingency: the possible and the impossible

2. Necessary and contingent being or existence

   2*a*. The independent or unconditioned as the necessarily existent: the uncaused or self-caused; the identity of essence and existence

   2*b*. The argument for the existence of a necessary being: the problem of logical and ontological necessity

   2*c*. Mutability in relation to necessity in being

   2*d*. The necessary and contingent with respect to properties, accidents, and modes

3. Necessity and contingency in the realm of change: chance and determinism

   3*a*. The distinction between the essential and the accidental cause: the contingent effect; contingency and chance

   3*b*. The necessity of contingent events: absolute and hypothetical or conditional necessity; necessitation by efficient or material and final or formal causes

   3*c*. The grounds of contingency in the phenomenal order: real indeterminacy or ignorance of causes

4. Necessity and contingency in the realm of thought

   4*a*. The necessary as the domain of knowledge, the contingent as the object of opinion: certainty, doubt, and probability; necessary truths

   4*b*. Practical necessity as a cause of belief

   4*c*. The truth of judgments concerning future contingents

   4*d*. Mathematical necessity: necessity in the objects of mathematics and in mathematical reasoning

   4*e*. Necessity and contingency in logical analysis

   (1) The modality of propositions or judgments: modal opposition

   (2) Modality in reasoning: the logical necessity of inference; the necessity and contingency of premises and conclusions

5. Necessity and contingency in human life and society

   5*a*. Liberty and necessity in human conduct: the voluntary and the compulsory

   (1) The necessitation of the will: the range of its freedom

   (2) Categorical and hypothetical imperatives as expressing necessary and contingent obligations

   (3) Human freedom as knowledge or acceptance of necessity

   5*b*. The necessity of family and state: the contingency of their forms and institutions

   5*c*. Necessity and contingency in relation to the natural and conventional in law

   5*d*. The necessity or inevitability of slavery, poverty, war, or crime

   5*e*. Economic necessities or luxuries

   5*f*. Necessity and contingency in history

REFERENCES

References are listed by volume number (in bold type), author's name, and page number. Bible references are to book, chapter, and verse of the Authorized King James version of the Bible. The abbreviation "esp" calls the reader's attention to one or more especially relevant parts of a whole reference; "passim" signifies that the topic is discussed intermittently rather than continuously in the work or passage cited. Where the work as a whole is relevant to the topic, the page numbers refer to the entire work. For general guidance in the use of *The Great Ideas,* consult the Preface.

1. The meaning of necessity and contingency: the possible and the impossible

7 PLATO, 103–104
8 ARISTOTLE, 33–35, 48–49, 372–375, 535–536, 541, 572–573
9 ARISTOTLE, 234–235, 639–640
17 PLOTINUS, 203
19 AQUINAS, 83, 110–111, 137–138, 145–147, 218–219, 221–222, 250–252, 431–432, 463, 629–630
20 AQUINAS, 883–884
31 SPINOZA, 355, 367, 424
35 HUME, 469–478
42 KANT, 85–88, 90–91, 95, 107, 129–145, 186, 550–578

2. Necessary and contingent being or existence

2*a*. The independent or unconditioned as the necessarily existent: the uncaused or self-caused; the identity of essence and existence

OLD TESTAMENT: *Exodus,* 3:13–14
7 PLATO, 762–765
8 ARISTOTLE, 281, 340–346, 536, 601–603
12 LUCRETIUS, 7–8
17 PLOTINUS, 345–353
18 AUGUSTINE, 3, 48–50, 272, 633
19 AQUINAS, 16–17, 19, 20–23, 29–30, 41–42, 49–50, 73–74, 158–160
20 AQUINAS, 218, 724
31 DESCARTES, 81–89, 108–115, 130, 217–218
31 SPINOZA, 355, 359–360, 362–363, 365, 369
42 KANT, 140–145, 164–167, 177–182, 291–292, 587
46 HEGEL, 156–157, 161–162

2*b*. The argument for the existence of a necessary being: the problem of logical and ontological necessity

7 PLATO, 758–765
8 ARISTOTLE, 334–346, 575–577
18 AUGUSTINE, 43–45, 268–269, 626–627
19 AQUINAS, 10–14, 34–35, 112–113, 339–343, 534–537
31 DESCARTES, 51–53, 84–87, 93–96, 126–127, 131–132, 158–162
31 SPINOZA, 356–359, 363–364
33 PASCAL, 256
35 LOCKE, 349–352
35 BERKELEY, 417–419, 442
35 HUME, 497–503
42 KANT, 85–93, 152–153, 177–192, 205, 310–311, 334–337, 568–570, 600–603, 606–609

2*c*. Mutability in relation to necessity in being

8 ARISTOTLE, 334–346, 360–362, 375–376, 439–441, 586, 603
17 PLOTINUS, 347–348
18 AUGUSTINE, 23–24, 103, 351–352
19 AQUINAS, 44–45, 274–275, 345–347
20 AQUINAS, 1017–1020
21 DANTE, 126
31 DESCARTES, 113–114
31 SPINOZA, 358–359, 365–366, 367–369, 373
42 KANT, 74–76

2*d*. The necessary and contingent with respect to properties, accidents, and modes

7 PLATO, 244–246
8 ARISTOTLE, 100–101, 178–179, 182, 261, 547, 548–549, 561–562, 586, 593, 625–626 esp 626
12 LUCRETIUS, 6–7
19 AQUINAS, 18–19, 39–40, 286–287, 399–401, 404–405, 619–620
20 AQUINAS, 711–712
30 BACON, 161, 164–169
31 DESCARTES, 152, 231
31 SPINOZA, 358, 362, 363
35 LOCKE, 268–283, 315–317, 332–336 passim, 360–361
42 KANT, 131, 566, 580
53 JAMES, 668–671

3. Necessity and contingency in the realm of change: chance and determinism

5 AESCHYLUS, 45
7 PLATO, 438–439, 587–589
8 ARISTOTLE, 28–29, 129, 157–158, 401, 434–435, 555, 573
9 ARISTOTLE, 612
12 LUCRETIUS, 17–19, 66
12 AURELIUS, 293–294
17 PLOTINUS, 78–82, 150, 176

19 Aquinas, 86–88, 116, 128–130, 131–132, 147, 528–529, 533–534
31 Descartes, 55–56
31 Spinoza, 355, 362, 369, 377–379, 395, 425, 447
35 Berkeley, 433
35 Hume, 469–470
38 Montesquieu, 1
42 Kant, 72–85, 171–172, 331–333
46 Hegel, 160–190
53 James, 823–825

3*a*. The distinction between the essential and the accidental cause: the contingent effect; contingency and chance

7 Plato, 455–456, 465–466
8 Aristotle, 263–264, 271–275, 535–536, 593
12 Aurelius, 257
19 Aquinas, 49, 128–130, 297–298, 531–532, 591–593, 594–595
42 Kant, 311–314, 550–551, 553–555
46 Hegel, 10–11

3*b*. The necessity of contingent events: absolute and hypothetical or conditional necessity; necessitation by efficient or material and final or formal causes

8 Aristotle, 277–278, 439–441, 529, 556, 591, 667–668, 698
9 Aristotle, 161–165, 170–171, 191, 320–321, 331
18 Augustine, 610–611
19 Aquinas, 110–111, 114–115
30 Bacon, 45–46
31 Spinoza, 362–363, 364–366, 367–369
42 Kant, 262–279, 491–492, 581–582, 584
46 Hegel, 158
51 Tolstoy, 563, 650, 679

3*c*. The grounds of contingency in the phenomenal order: real indeterminacy or ignorance of causes

8 Aristotle, 28–29, 272–275
19 Aquinas, 131–132, 463
23 Hobbes, 272
31 Spinoza, 384–385, 395, 396–398
35 Hume, 480–481, 484
42 Kant, 164–172, 387
46 Hegel, 107
49 Darwin, 37, 593
51 Tolstoy, 646–647

4. Necessity and contingency in the realm of thought

4*a*. The necessary as the domain of knowledge, the contingent as the object of opinion: certainty, doubt, and probability; necessary truths

7 Plato, 384–388
8 Aristotle, 8–9, 97–99, 100–104, 119, 121–122, 563–564, 577–578
9 Aristotle, 358, 388
19 Aquinas, 86–88, 110–111, 256–257, 422–423, 432–433
20 Aquinas, 223–224
31 Descartes, 2–3, 21–22, 75–77, 95–96, 124–125
31 Spinoza, 389–390
35 Locke, 315–317 esp 316, 322–323, 332–336 passim, 349, 360–361, 365, 371–372, 378–379
35 Hume, 458, 462, 508–509 passim
42 Kant, 1–4, 194, 240–243
51 Tolstoy, 365
53 James, 851–890

4*b*. Practical necessity as a cause of belief

31 Descartes, 48–50, 126
33 Pascal, 205–217
35 Hume, 507–508
42 Kant, 124–128, 236–243 esp 239–240, 279–287, 314–321, 344–349, 351–352, 588–607, 608–611
53 James, 223–225, 653

4*c*. The truth of judgments concerning future contingents

8 Aristotle, 28–29
19 Aquinas, 86–88, 297–298, 463–464
21 Dante, 132
22 Chaucer, 107
32 Milton, 137–138
51 Tolstoy, 441–442, 584–585, 685

4*d*. Mathematical necessity: necessity in the objects of mathematics and in mathematical reasoning

8 Aristotle, 277
31 Descartes, 3, 47
35 Locke, 317–319, 325, 338
35 Hume, 458
42 Kant, 15–16, 17–18, 68–69, 211–218, 398–399 esp 399
53 James, 874–878

4*e*. Necessity and contingency in logical analysis

4*e*(1) The modality of propositions or judgments: modal opposition

8 Aristotle, 32–35, 40
42 Kant, 14–15, 39–41

4*e*(2) Modality in reasoning: the logical necessity of inference; the necessity and contingency of premises and conclusions

8 Aristotle, 45–57
9 Aristotle, 596–597
12 Epictetus, 112–113
18 Augustine, 651–653
19 Aquinas, 675–677
23 Hobbes, 65–71
42 Kant, 110–111, 194

5. Necessity and contingency in human life and society

5*a*. Liberty and necessity in human conduct: the voluntary and the compulsory

4 HOMER, 3–179
5 AESCHYLUS, 53–54
6 THUCYDIDES, 506
7 PLATO, 56, 59–64, 439–441
9 ARISTOTLE, 355–359, 596–597, 611–613
12 LUCRETIUS, 18
12 AURELIUS, 253–310
15 TACITUS, 91
17 PLOTINUS, 81–82
18 AUGUSTINE, 55–56, 207–216, 513–515, 649–650
19 AQUINAS, 132–141, 436–438, 644–666
21 DANTE, 77–78, 117–118
22 CHAUCER, 106–108, 209–210
23 HOBBES, 59, 86, 112–113, 163–164
25 MONTAIGNE, 216–219
27 SHAKESPEARE, 249
31 SPINOZA, 395, 425
32 MILTON, 137–138
33 PASCAL, 331–332
35 LOCKE, 180–184, 193, 198–199
35 HUME, 478–487
38 ROUSSEAU, 337–338
42 KANT, 133, 190, 234–235, 279–287, 292–293, 307–314, 400–402
44 BOSWELL, 392–393
46 HEGEL, 35–36, 42–43, 118, 128, 158–159, 160–190
48 MELVILLE, 1–420
51 TOLSTOY, 221, 275–276, 303–304, 343, 688–694
53 JAMES, 84–94, 796–798, 820–827
54 FREUD, 453–476 passim, esp 454, 486–488 esp 486–487

5*a*(1) The necessitation of the will: the range of its freedom

9 ARISTOTLE, 359–361
12 EPICTETUS, 105–245
12 AURELIUS, 253–310
18 AUGUSTINE, 215–216, 346
19 AQUINAS, 117–118, 311–312, 431–433, 438, 613–614, 642–643, 674–677, 690
21 DANTE, 79–80
31 DESCARTES, 132, 141, 215–216, 228
31 SPINOZA, 362–363, 367, 391–394
42 KANT, 164–165, 234–236, 259–260, 264–267, 268, 286–287, 296, 325–326
46 HEGEL, 14–17, 130
53 JAMES, 291–295, 821–822

5*a*(2) Categorical and hypothetical imperatives as expressing necessary and contingent obligations

42 KANT, 253–287, 297–314, 386–387, 390–391, 392–393, 397–398, 571–572, 595, 605–606
46 HEGEL, 46–47, 129

5*a*(3) Human freedom as knowledge or acceptance of necessity

12 EPICTETUS, 118–120, 213–223, 225–228
31 SPINOZA, 453–454
46 HEGEL, 14–17, 55, 132, 142

5*b*. The necessity of family and state: the contingency of their forms and institutions

7 PLATO, 311–312
9 ARISTOTLE, 445–446
12 LUCRETIUS, 74
18 AUGUSTINE, 520–523
19 AQUINAS, 488–489, 516–517
20 AQUINAS, 318–321
23 HOBBES, 84–87, 91, 96, 99–101
25 MONTAIGNE, 462–463
31 SPINOZA, 429, 447–450
32 MILTON, 240–241
33 PASCAL, 228
35 LOCKE, 16, 28, 36–43, 53–54
38 MONTESQUIEU, 2–3, 187–188
38 ROUSSEAU, 387–392
42 KANT, 433–434
43 DECLARATION OF INDEPENDENCE, 1
43 MILL, 327–332 passim, 460–461
44 BOSWELL, 120
46 HEGEL, 84–89, 135, 143–144, 173–175, 262
49 DARWIN, 579–581
50 MARX-ENGELS, 427–428
54 FREUD, 781–782

5*c*. Necessity and contingency in relation to the natural and conventional in law

9 ARISTOTLE, 382
18 AUGUSTINE, 17
20 AQUINAS, 224–226, 227–228, 229–231, 238–239, 247–248
23 HOBBES, 115, 131, 136–137
31 SPINOZA, 435–436
35 LOCKE, 27–28, 55–56
38 MONTESQUIEU, 1, 219–221
38 ROUSSEAU, 399
43 MILL, 470–471
46 HEGEL, 71, 138

5*d*. The necessity or inevitability of slavery, poverty, war, or crime

5 ARISTOPHANES, 633–636
6 THUCYDIDES, 427–428, 436–437
7 PLATO, 640–641
9 ARISTOTLE, 447–449
18 AUGUSTINE, 172–173, 515, 521
19 AQUINAS, 512–513
23 MACHIAVELLI, 21, 32
23 HOBBES, 76, 94
24 RABELAIS, 30–41
32 MILTON, 307–318
35 LOCKE, 25–30, 65
36 SWIFT, 154–155
38 MONTESQUIEU, 61–62, 109–111
38 ROUSSEAU, 356–358, 389–390

39 Smith, 309
42 Kant, 457–458, 586–587
43 Federalist, 33–44, 85–89, 96, 110, 132–135
43 Mill, 339–340
46 Hegel, 109
50 Marx, 303–307, 315–321
50 Marx-Engels, 419–420, 425, 428
54 Freud, 755–757, 766, 787–788

5*e*. Economic necessities or luxuries

7 Plato, 316–319, 409–410
8 Aristotle, 164–165
9 Aristotle, 451–452, 536
14 Plutarch, 36–37, 285, 291–292
15 Tacitus, 31
19 Aquinas, 615–616
25 Montaigne, 110, 131–132, 489–490
27 Shakespeare, 261
31 Spinoza, 450
33 Pascal, 91–94
35 Locke, 30–36
38 Montesquieu, 44
38 Rousseau, 352–353, 364, 365–366, 393–394
39 Smith, 27–37 passim, 70–71, 74–75, 163–164, 383
40 Gibbon, 22
44 Boswell, 124–125, 389–390
46 Hegel, 66–67, 68, 136
50 Marx, 16–17, 81, 218–219, 253–254, 261–262, 280–283, 292–296

5*f*. Necessity and contingency in history

6 Herodotus, 21–22, 291
7 Plato, 679
14 Plutarch, 18, 20, 195–213, 698–699
15 Tacitus, 91
18 Augustine, 150–151, 206, 207–208, 216–230, 397–398, 472–473
21 Dante, 10
23 Machiavelli, 35–36
41 Gibbon, 590
46 Hegel, 110–114, 156–201, 241–242, 274–275, 281–282, 283–284, 285, 300–301, 368–369
50 Marx, 6, 7, 10–11, 378
50 Marx-Engels, 421–422
51 Tolstoy, 342–344, 389–391, 469–472, 563–587, 588–590, 609–613, 618–621, 626–630, 645–650, 675–696
54 Freud, 882–884

CROSS-REFERENCES

For: Matters relevant to the distinction between necessary and contingent being, *see* Being 7a, 7b(3); Change 15c; Eternity 3, 4b; God 2b, 4a; and for the application of this distinction to properties, accidents, and modes, *see* Being 7b(5)–7b(6), 8c–8e; Nature 1a(1).

Matters relevant to the distinction between necessity and contingency in the realm of change, *see* Cause 1–1a; Chance 1a, 2a; Fate 3; Nature 3c(1).

Other discussions of the distinction between knowledge and opinion, and of the difference between certainty and probability, *see* Chance 4; Judgment 3, 9; Knowledge 4b, 6d(1)–6d(2); Opinion 1, 3b; Truth 2e; Will 3b(1).

The moral certainty of the things in which it is practically necessary to believe, *see* God 2d; Immortality 3a; Metaphysics 2d; Will 5b(4).

Other discussions of the truth of propositions about future contingents, *see* Time 6f; Truth 3b(2).

Necessity and contingency in logical analysis and in mathematical reasoning, *see* Judgment 6c; Mathematics 1c; Opposition 1d(2); Principle 2b(2), 5; Reasoning 3d; Truth 3b(3)–3c, 7a.

For: The opposition between necessity and liberty in the sphere of human life and history, *see* Cause 3; Fate 2–3, 5–6; History 4a(1); Liberty 1c, 4a; Nature 2f, 3c(2); Prudence 4a; Wealth 11; Will 5a(1)–5a(4), 5c, 6a, 7b; and for the related problem of divine providence in relation to human freedom, *see* Fate 4; God 7b; History 5a; Liberty 5a–5b; Will 7c.

The necessary and contingent, or the natural and the conventional, with respect to the family and the state, and also in language and law, *see* Custom and Convention 1; Family 1; Justice 10a; Law 4f, 5e; Nature 2b, 5c; Punishment 4c; State 3b–3c.

The consideration of the inevitability or necessity of certain social institutions or phenomena, such as slavery, poverty, or war, *see* LAW 4h; NATURE 5b; OPPOSITION 5c; SLAVERY 2, 3; WAR AND PEACE 7; WEALTH 9g, 10b.

Another discussion of the distinction of the necessary, the possible, and the probable in poetry, *see* POETRY 8a(2).

ADDITIONAL READINGS

Listed below are works not included in *Great Books of the Western World*, but relevant to the idea and topics with which this chapter deals. These works are divided into two groups:

I. Works by authors represented in this collection.
II. Works by authors not represented in this collection.

For the date, place, and other facts concerning the publication of the works cited, consult the Bibliography of Additional Readings which follows the last chapter of *The Great Ideas.*

I.

AQUINAS. *Summa Contra Gentiles*, BK II, CH 29–31; BK III, CH 64–83

HUME. *A Treatise of Human Nature*, BK I, PART III, SECT XIV; BK II, PART III, SECT I

KANT. *Introduction to Logic*, IX

HEGEL. *Science of Logic*, VOL I, BK II, SECT III, CH 2

J. S. MILL. *A System of Logic*, BK III, CH 17; BK VI, CH 2

W. JAMES. "The Dilemma of Determinism," in *The Will to Believe*

II.

EPICURUS. *Letter to Menoeceus*

CICERO. *De Fato (On Fate)*

ANSELM OF CANTERBURY. *De Potestate et Impotentia; Possibilitate et Impossibilitate; Necessitate et Libertate*

MAIMONIDES. *The Guide for the Perplexed*, PART II, CH 21

SUÁREZ. *Disputationes Metaphysicae*, XIX, XXVIII–XXIX, XXXI (14)

LEIBNITZ. *Philosophical Works*, CH 28 (*Letter on Necessity and Contingency*), 34 (*The Principles of Nature and of Grace*)

——. *Monadology*, par 33–37

J. BUTLER. *The Analogy of Religion*, PART I, CH 6

J. PRIESTLEY and PRICE. *A Free Discussion of the Doctrine of Materialism and Philosophical Necessity*

T. REID. *Essays on the Intellectual Powers of Man*, VI, CH 5–6

VOLTAIRE. "Necessary-Necessity," "Power-Omnipotence," in *A Philosophical Dictionary*

——. *Candide*

GODWIN. *An Enquiry Concerning Political Justice*, BK IV, CH 5–6

SCHOPENHAUER. *On the Fourfold Root of the Principle of Sufficient Reason*

LAPLACE. *A Philosophical Essay on Probabilities*

WHEWELL. *On the Philosophy of Discovery*, CH 29

BOUTROUX. *The Contingency of the Laws of Nature*

BRADLEY. *Ethical Studies*, I

——. *The Principles of Logic*, BK I, CH 7

C. S. PEIRCE. *Collected Papers*, VOL VI, par 35–65

BERGSON. *Time and Free Will*

BRIDGMAN. *The Logic of Modern Physics*, CH 4

DEWEY. *The Quest for Certainty*

HEISENBERG. *The Physical Principles of the Quantum Theory*

KONINCK. *Le problème de l'indéterminisme*

BLANSHARD. *The Nature of Thought*, CH 28–32

MARITAIN. *Scholasticism and Politics*, CH V

WEISS. *Nature and Man*, CH I

HARTSHORNE. *The Divine Relativity*

Chapter 62: OLIGARCHY

INTRODUCTION

IN the great books of political theory the word "oligarchy" is usually listed along with "monarchy" and "democracy" among the traditional names for the forms of government. According to the meaning of their Greek roots, "oligarchy" signifies the rule of the few as "monarchy" signifies the rule of one and "democracy" the rule of the people—or the many. These verbal meanings are somewhat altered, however, when we consider the actual conflict between oligarchy and democracy in Greek political life. It involved an opposition, not simply between the few and the many, but between the wealthy and the working classes. The contest between these factions for political power dominated more than a century of Greek history around the Periclean age; and that fact justifies Aristotle's remark that oligarchy and democracy are the two principal conflicting forms of government.

We would not so describe the political struggle of our time. We would not speak of oligarchy as one of the principal forms of government in the world today. Instead we tend to think in terms of the conflict between democracy and dictatorship or despotism. Even when we look to the background of present issues, it is the age-old struggle between absolute and constitutional government—or between monarchies and republics—which seems to supply the obvious historical parallels for the contemporary conflict between the principles of arbitrary and legal government. The traditional terms of political theory, with the exception of oligarchy, thus appear to have a certain liveliness in the consideration of current problems. But though it does not have such frequency in our speech or familiarity in our thought, oligarchy may be much more relevant to the real issues of our day than appears on the surface.

Certainly within the framework of constitutional government oligarchical and democratic principles are the opposed sources of policy and legislation. In modern as in ancient republics the division of men into political parties tends to follow the lines of the division of men into economic factions. The ancient meanings of oligarchy and democracy, especially for those observers like Thucydides and Aristotle who see the rich and the poor as the major rivals for constitutional power, indicate the fusion of political and economic issues.

The difference between oligarchy and democracy, says Aristotle, is not well-defined by reference to the few and the many, unless it is understood that the few are also the rich and the many the poor. The issue is not whether the few are wiser than the many, or whether it is more efficient to have the government in the hands of the few rather than the many. Such issues have been debated in the history of political thought, but they are more appropriate to the alternatives of aristocracy and democracy than to the conflict between oligarchy and democracy.

The historic struggle between oligarchs and democrats—whether described as a struggle between rich and poor, nobility and bourgeoisie, landed gentry and agrarian peons, owners and workers, classes and masses—is a struggle over the political privileges of wealth, the rights of property, the protection of special interests. In the tradition of the great books, Marx and Engels may be the first to call this struggle "the class war," but they are only the most recent in a long line of political and economic writers to recognize that the economic antagonism of rich and poor generates the basic political conflict in any state. "Any city, however small," says Socrates, "is in fact divided into two, one the city of the poor, the other of the rich: these are at war with one another."

OLIGARCHY IS NOT always defined as the rule of the wealthy, nor is it always conceived as the opponent of democracy on constitutional questions. In the *Statesman*, for example, Plato first divides the forms of government into "monarchy, the rule of the few, and the rule of the many," and then divides "the rule of the few into aristocracy, which has an auspicious name, and oligarchy." Here aristocracy and oligarchy seem to be regarded as opposites, the one a government in which the few rule according to the laws, the other lawless government by the few. In both, the few are the wealthy; hence wealth is no more characteristic of oligarchy than of aristocracy.

Some political theorists make no reference to wealth at all in the discussion of oligarchy. Hobbes divides the forms of government according to whether the sovereign power is in the hands of one or more; and if in the hands of more than one, then whether it is held by some or all. He calls the several forms of government monarchy (one), aristocracy (some), and democracy (all). There are "other names of government in the histories and books of policy," he adds, such as "*tyranny* and *oligarchy*. But they are not the names of other forms of government, but of the same forms misliked. For they that are discontented under *monarchy* call it *tyranny*, and they that are displeased with *aristocracy* call it *oligarchy*." Like Hobbes, both Locke and Rousseau use no criterion except numbers to distinguish the forms of government, Locke calling government by the few "oligarchy" and Rousseau calling it "aristocracy."

Barely outlined in this way, the alternatives of monarchy, aristocracy *or* oligarchy, and democracy seem to raise issues only of expediency or efficiency rather than of justice. Whether oligarchy is intrinsically a good or bad form of government tends to become a question only when other factors are considered; when, for example, the distinction between aristocracy and oligarchy is made to turn on whether the few are men of virtue or men of property, or when, in the comparison of oligarchy with democracy, the emphasis is not upon numbers but on the principles of wealth and liberty.

Nevertheless, the numerical criterion does not seem to be totally irrelevant to the comparison. "Oligarchy and democracy," Aristotle writes, "are not sufficiently distinguished merely by these two characteristics of wealth and freedom." Though the "real difference between democracy and oligarchy is poverty and wealth," and though "wherever men rule by reason of their wealth, whether they be few or many, that is an oligarchy," Aristotle does not seem to think we can neglect the political significance of what he calls the "accidental fact that the rich everywhere are few, and the poor numerous."

With regard to aristocracy and oligarchy, the chief question does not seem to be one of principle, but of fact. Plato in the *Republic* and Aristotle in the *Politics* define aristocracy as government by the few best men, or the most virtuous. They also place it next to what is for them the ideal government by the supremely wise man—the rule of the philosopher king, or what Aristotle calls "the divine sort of government." In this context, oligarchy represents a perversion of aristocracy, as tyranny represents a corruption of monarchy.

Plato describes oligarchy as arising when "riches and rich men are honored in the State" and when the law "fixes a sum of money as the qualification for citizenship" and allows "no one whose property falls below the amount fixed to have any share in the government." But according to Socrates, wealth does not qualify men to rule, as virtue and wisdom do. "Just think what would happen," he says, "if pilots were to be chosen according to their property, and a poor man were refused permission to steer, even though he were a better pilot." To which Adeimantus agrees that in government, as in navigation, the probable result would be shipwreck.

But though there may be no question of the superiority of aristocracy over oligarchy in principle, the critics of aristocracy question whether any historic state in which the few hold political power is not in fact an oligarchy. It may not always be the case that the power of the few rests directly on wealth. The privileged class may be a military clique or an hereditary nobility. Yet these distinctions are seldom unaccompanied by the control of land or other forms of wealth, so that indirectly at least the oligarchical factor is thought to be operative.

The criticism of aristocracies as masked oligarchies is discussed in the chapter on Aristocracy. The critical point seems to be that nothing except superior virtue or talent justifies a political inequality between the few and the many. The meaning of oligarchy is generalized in consequence to include any government in which the special privileges or powers held by the few cannot be justified, whether it is wealth or some other title to pre-eminence that is substituted for superiority in virtue or talent. When it is so understood, the word "oligarchical" tends to become like "tyrannical," a term of reproach.

In describing different forms of democracy, Aristotle observes that their common principle is to give a share in the government to all who meet whatever minimum qualification is set by law. "The absolute exclusion of any class," he says, "would be a step towards oligarchy." To the same effect is Mill's comment on the steps away from oligarchy accomplished by English constitutional reforms in the 19th century.

"In times not long gone by," Mill writes, "the higher and richer classes were in complete possession of the government. . . . A vote given in opposition to those influences . . . was almost sure to be a good vote, for it was a vote against the monster evil, the over-ruling influence of oligarchy." But now that the higher classes are no longer masters of the country, now that the franchise has been extended to the middle classes, a diminished form of oligarchy still remains. "The electors themselves are becoming the oligarchy"—in a population where many are still disfranchised. "The present electors," Mill continues, "and the bulk of those whom any probable Reform Bill would add to the number, are the middle class; and have as much a class interest, distinct from the working classes, as landlords or great manufacturers. Were the suffrage extended to all skilled laborers, even those would, or might, still have a class interest distinct from the unskilled."

Oligarchy remains, according to Mill, so long as there is any unjustifiable discrimination among classes in the population. It is not in his view limited to discrimination based on the extremes of wealth and poverty, as he plainly indicates by his remarks on the special interests of different parts of the working class, or their relation as a whole to the lower middle classes. He makes this even plainer by what he has to say on political discrimination as between the sexes. Suppose the suffrage to be extended to all men, he writes, "suppose that what was formerly called by the misapplied name of universal suffrage, and now by the silly title of manhood suffrage, became the law; the voters would still have a class interest, as distinguished from women."

The oligarchical defect in representative government which Mill is here criticizing seems to have little or no basis in economic class divisions. The exclusion of any class in the population from a voice in government renders that government oligarchical with respect to them. The excluded class may even be a minority. So conceived, oligarchy no longer means the rule of either the rich or the few.

When the meaning of oligarchy is generalized in this way, the discussion of oligarchy seems to presuppose the typically modern conception of democracy. As indicated in the chapter on Democracy, the distinguishing feature of the modern democratic constitution is universal suffrage. By this criterion, the conflict between the democrats and the oligarchs of the ancient world appears to be a conflict between two forms of the oligarchical constitution—one in which the wealthier few and one in which the poorer many have political rights, but in neither of which membership in the political community includes all normal adult human beings in the population.

Where ancient political theory could conceive of a mixed constitution—somehow combining oligarchical and democratic principles—the modern conception of democracy seems to make any compromise with oligarchy impossible. Certain modern writers, notably Mosca, Michels, and Pareto, seem to insist, on the contrary, that oligarchy is present in all forms of government, and is especially prevalent in representative democracies where the actual conduct of government—the effective power—is in the hands of a bureaucracy or an elite, whether popularly chosen or self-appointed. But the contradiction may be more verbal than real if on one side the word "oligarchy" means some degree of restriction in the franchise or citizenship, and, on the other, it applies to any situation in which the whole people are not directly active in all the affairs of government and, consequently, a small number of men administers the state. Understood in the latter sense, the oligarchical principle does not seem to be incompatible with representative democracy. Those who use the word in this sense merely call attention to an inevitable characteristic of representative government. A representative democracy may also have an aristocratic aspect when it follows the principle that the men best qualified by virtue or talent for public office should be chosen by the suffrage of all their fellow-citizens.

FULLER DISCUSSION of these aspects of oligarchy is found in the chapters on ARISTOCRACY and DEMOCRACY. Here we are primarily concerned with political issues which have their source in the opposition of economic classes in the state, primarily that extreme division of men into those who live by their labor and those who live on their property and the labor of others. It is in terms of this extreme division between men of leisure and working men that the conflict between oligarchy and democracy takes place in the ancient world.

At a time when citizenship meant a much more active and frequent participation in government than it does under the modern institutions of the ballot box and the representative assembly, the ancient defenders of oligarchy could argue that only men of wealth had the leisure requisite for citizenship. Oligarchy could be further defended on the ground that, in many of the Greek city-states, public officials were either not compensated at all or at least not substantially. Only men of sizeable property could afford to hold public office.

Aristotle weighs the arguments for and against oligarchy. On the point of leisure, for example, he holds that "nothing is more absolutely necessary than to provide that the highest class, not only when in office, but when out of office, should have leisure." Yet "even if you must have regard to wealth in order to secure leisure," it is "surely a bad thing," he thinks, "that the greatest offices, such as those of kings and generals, should be bought. The law which allows this abuse makes wealth of more account than virtue."

Aristotle seems to regard democratic and oligarchical claims as complementary half-truths. "Both parties to the argument," he says, "are speaking of a limited and partial justice, but imagine themselves to be speaking of absolute justice." According to an adequate conception of political justice, it is as unjust to treat equals unequally as it is to treat unequals equally. The oligarch violates the first of these principles, the democrat the second. "Democracy arises out of the notion that those who are equal in any respect are equal in all respects; because men are equally free, they claim to be absolutely equal. Oligarchy is based on the notion that those who are unequal in one respect are in all respects unequal; being unequal, that is, in property, they suppose themselves to be unequal absolutely."

Both forms of government have "a kind of justice, but, tried by an absolute standard, they are faulty; and, therefore, both parties, whenever their share in the government does not accord with their preconceived ideas, stir up revolution. . . . In oligarchies the masses make revolution under the idea that they are unjustly treated, because . . . they are equals and have not an equal share; and in democracies, the notables revolt, because they are not equal, and yet have only an equal share."

What can cure this situation in which perpetual revolution seems to be inevitable, as democracy succeeds oligarchy, or oligarchy democracy, in the government of the Greek cities? Aristotle describes many forms of oligarchy and democracy, but none seems to remove the cause of revolution. When, in an attempt to preserve their position, the wealthier families turn to the more extreme forms of oligarchical constitution, that tendency eventually leads to a kind of despotic government which Aristotle calls "dynasty," or the lawless rule of powerful families.

To establish a stable government which shall be less subject to revolution in favor of a contrary principle of government, and which shall resist the tendency toward lawless rule, by either the masses or the powerful few, Aristotle proposes the mixed constitution, which shall combine the elements of both democratic and oligarchical justice. But this will not work in actual practice, he thinks, unless the middle class "is large, and stronger if possible than both the other classes. . . . . Great then is the good fortune of a state in which the citizens have a moderate and sufficient property; for where some possess much, and the others nothing, there may arise an extreme democracy, or a pure oligarchy; or a tyranny may grow out of either extreme. . . . . These considerations will help us to understand why most governments are either democratical or oligarchical. The reason is that the middle class is seldom numerous in them, and whichever party, whether the rich or the common people, transgresses the mean and predominates, draws the constitution its own way, and thus arises either oligarchy or democracy."

From the point of view which sees no justice in granting any special privileges to property, Aristotle's position on oligarchy seems open to question. For one thing, in admitting a partial justice in the principle that those who are unequal in wealth should be treated unequally in the distribution of political power, Aristotle appears to affirm that the possessors of wealth *deserve* a special political status. For another thing, in his own formulation of an ideal polity, Aristotle advocates the exclusion of the working classes from citizenship. "The citizens must not lead the life of mechanics or tradesmen, for such a life is ignoble and inimical to virtue. Neither must they be husbandmen, since leisure is necessary both for the development of virtue and the performance of political duties." All these classes of men are necessary for the existence of the state, but they are to be no part of it in the sense of political membership. "The best form of state will not admit them to citizenship," though it will include as necessary "the slaves who minister to the wants of individuals, or mechanics and laborers who are the servants of the community."

Some of the great speeches in Thucydides' *History*, which deal with domestic issues as well as the issues of war and peace, eloquently argue the opposite side of the case. Debating with Hermocrates before the Syracusan assembly, Athenagoras answers those who say that "democracy is neither wise nor equitable, but that the holders of property are the best fitted to rule. I say, on the contrary, first, that the word *demos*, or people, includes the whole state, oligarchy only a part; next, that if the best guardians of property are the rich, and the best counsellors the wise, none can hear and decide so well as the many, and that all these talents, severally and collectively, have their just place in a democracy. But an oligarchy gives the many their share of the danger, and not content with the largest part, takes and keeps the whole of the profit."

In modern political thought, the discussion of oligarchy seems to occur on two levels. There is a controversy on the level of constitutional principles with regard to suffrage and representation and the qualifications for public office. Here the issues concern the justice of the fundamental laws of republican or popular government. There is also a consideration of the way in which men of property or corporate concentrations of wealth are able to exert influence upon the actual course of government. Here the problem becomes, not so much the justice of the constitution or of the laws, but the weight which wealth seems able to throw onto the scales of justice.

The great modern defense of the oligarchical constitution does not seem to be as plainly or forcefully made in any of the great books as in the speeches of Edmund Burke, especially those in opposition to the suffrage reform measures proposed by Charles James Fox, wherein Burke argues for the principle of *virtual* representation. It is unnecessary, he claims, for the franchise to be extended to the working classes if their economic betters—who also happen to be their superiors in talent and education—deliberate on what is for the common good of all.

The Federalists seem to take an opposite view. Reflecting on the system of British representation in their day, they observe that, for the eight millions of people in the kingdoms of England and Scotland, "the representatives . . . in the House of Commons amount to five hundred and fifty-eight." But, they go on, "of this number one ninth are elected by three hundred and sixty-four persons and one half by five thousand seven hundred and twenty-three persons. It cannot be supposed," they argue, "that the half thus elected and who do not even reside among the people at large, can add anything either to the security of the people against the government, or to the knowledge of their circumstances and interests in the legislative councils. On the contrary, it is notorious that they are more frequently the representatives and instruments of the executive magistrate than the guardians and advocates of the popular rights." Nevertheless, they do not condemn such an oligarchical system of representation as entirely inimical to the virtues of parliamentary government. "It is very certain," they declare, "not only that a valuable portion of freedom has been preserved under all these circumstances, but that the defects in the British code are chargeable, in a very small proportion, on the ignorance of the legislature concerning the circumstances of the people."

Some of the American constitutionalists may be influenced by Burke's defense of oligarchy in terms of the virtues of an aristocracy, but they state their own position in terms which are more plainly oligarchical. They argue for poll tax clauses and property qualifications for public office on the ground that the country should be run by the people who own it. Furthermore, those who are not economically independent are not in a position to exercise political liberty. "Power over a man's subsistence," Hamilton declares, "amounts to power over his will."

Facing the issue which had been raised on the floor of the constitutional convention, Madison remarks that "the most common and durable source of factions has been the various and unequal distribution of property. Those who hold and those who are without property have ever formed distinct interests in society." He proposes a representative—or what he calls a "republican"—system of government to avoid the excessive factionalism of the pure or direct democracies of Greek city-states.

"Theoretic politicians, who have patronized this species of government," Madison writes, "have erroneously supposed that by reducing mankind to perfect equality in their political rights, they would, at the same time, be perfectly equalized and assimilated in their possessions, their opinions, and their passions." By a weighted system of representation, the power of sheer numbers may be counter-balanced by the power given to other factors, thus preventing the "accomplishment of the secret wishes of an unjust and interested majority. . . . . A rage for paper money, for an abolition of debts, for an equal division of property, or for any other improper or wicked project, will be less apt to pervade the whole body of the Union than a particular member of it."

In another paper, the Federalists answer the charge that the constitution is oligarchical, because "the House of Representatives . . . . will be taken from that class of citizens which will have least sympathy with the mass of the people and be most likely to aim at an ambitious sacrifice of the many to the aggrandizement of the few." This objection, they say, while "leveled against a pretended oligarchy," in principle "strikes at the very root of republican government."

The method of election provided for by the Constitution aims "to obtain for rulers men who possess most wisdom to discern, and most virtue to pursue, the common good of the society. . . . Who are to be the electors of the federal representatives? Not the rich, more than the poor; not the learned, more than the ignorant; not the haughty heirs of distinguished names, more than the humble sons of obscurity and unpropitious fortune. . . . . Who are to be the objects of popular choice? Every citizen whose merit may recommend him to the esteem and confidence of the country. No qualification of wealth, of birth, of religious faith, or of civil profession, is permitted to fetter the judgment or disappoint the inclination of the people."

WHETHER THE AMERICAN Constitution in its original formulation is an oligarchical document has long been a matter of dispute. Whether the Federalists favor devices for protecting the rights of property or repudiate oligarchical restrictions in favor of the rights of man has also been the subject of controversy. That this is so may indicate at least a certain ambiguity in their position. But on the question of the oligarchical influences on government—the political pressures exerted by propertied classes to serve their special interests—the opinion of the modern authors of the great books seems much clearer.

The most extreme statement of this opinion is, of course, to be found in the *Communist Manifesto*. There government, in fact the state itself, is regarded as an instrument which the economic oppressors wield against the oppressed. The final step in the bourgeois revolution, according to Marx and Engels, occurred when the bourgeoisie "conquered for itself, in the modern representative State, exclusive political sway." In the bourgeois state, legislation is nothing but the will of this one class made into a law for all. One aim of the communist revolution, beyond the temporary dictatorship of the proletariat, is the withering away of that historic formation of the state in which "political power . . . is merely the organized power of one class for oppressing another."

Though much less radical in intention than Marx, Smith and Mill make statements which seem to be no less radical in their criticism of the oligarchical influences on modern parliamentary government. It has been said, Smith observes, that "we rarely hear . . . of combinations of masters, though frequently of those of workmen. But whoever imagines, upon this account, that masters rarely combine, is as ignorant of the world as of the subject. Masters are always and everywhere in a sort of tacit, but constant and uniform combination, not to raise the wages of labor above their actual rate . . . . Masters too sometimes enter into particular combinations to sink the wages of labor even below this rate." Furthermore, the parties to the conflict do not have equal access to legislative protection. "Whenever the legislature attempts to regulate the differences between masters and their workmen, its counsellors are always the masters."

Almost a century later, Mill writes in a similar vein concerning "the persevering attempts so long made to keep down wages by law . . . . Does Parliament," he asks, "ever for an instant look at any question with the eyes of a working man? . . . . On the question of strikes, for instance, it is doubtful if there is so much as one among the leading members of either House who is not firmly convinced that the reason of the matter is unqualifiedly on the side of the masters, and that the men's view of it is simply absurd." The remedy for this inequity, according to Mill, is not communism, but constitutional reforms in the direction of universal suffrage which will no longer leave the working classes "excluded from all direct participation in the government."

OUTLINE OF TOPICS

1. The oligarchical constitution: the principles and types of oligarchy

2. The relation of oligarchy to monarchy, aristocracy, and democracy

3. The instability of oligarchical government

   3*a*. The revolutionary changes to which oligarchy is subject: the change to despotism or democracy

   3*b*. The preservation of oligarchies against revolution

4. The defense of oligarchy: the political rights and privileges of property

5. The attack on oligarchy and on the political power of wealth

   5*a*. The objection to property as a basis for privilege with regard to citizenship or public office

   5*b*. The character of the oligarch: the man of property; the capitalist

   5*c*. Economic status and power as a political instrument: oligarchy in relation to the class war

6. Historical observations of oligarchy: the rise and fall of oligarchies

REFERENCES

References are listed by volume number (in bold type), author's name, and page number. Bible references are to book, chapter, and verse of the Authorized King James version of the Bible. The abbreviation "esp" calls the reader's attention to one or more especially relevant parts of a whole reference; "passim" signifies that the topic is discussed intermittently rather than continuously in the work or passage cited. Where the work as a whole is relevant to the topic, the page numbers refer to the entire work. For general guidance in the use of *The Great Ideas*, consult the Preface.

1. The oligarchical constitution: the principles and types of oligarchy

6 HERODOTUS, 107–108
6 THUCYDIDES, 579–581
7 PLATO, 405–408
9 ARISTOTLE, 461, 488–494, 502, 519, 524–526, 566
23 MACHIAVELLI, 14–15
38 MONTESQUIEU, 52
39 SMITH, 165–166
43 FEDERALIST, 176–179
46 HEGEL, 277

2. The relation of oligarchy to monarchy, aristocracy, and democracy

6 HERODOTUS, 107–108
6 THUCYDIDES, 520, 575–576, 587
7 PLATO, 402, 598–604, 680
9 ARISTOTLE, 412, 413, 461, 469–470, 475, 476–483, 488–494, 498–502, 508, 524–526, 608
20 AQUINAS, 229–230
23 HOBBES, 104–105, 273
35 LOCKE, 55
38 ROUSSEAU, 419
39 SMITH, 309–310
42 KANT, 450
43 FEDERALIST, 181, 228–229
43 MILL, 363–364, 393–395

3. The instability of oligarchical government

3*a*. The revolutionary changes to which oligarchy is subject: the change to despotism or democracy

6 THUCYDIDES, 436–438, 569–585 esp 582, 587–590
7 PLATO, 408–409
9 ARISTOTLE, 470, 484–485, 492, 496, 507–508, 518–519, 568–572
14 PLUTARCH, 68–71, 444–445, 521, 581–582, 657–663, 708
15 TACITUS, 224–225
23 HOBBES, 149–152
38 MONTESQUIEU, 51–52
46 HEGEL, 300–301
50 MARX, 377–378
50 MARX-ENGELS, 421–425, 429

3*b*. The preservation of oligarchies against revolution

6 THUCYDIDES, 463–465, 482–483, 580, 582–583, 587–589
9 ARISTOTLE, 470, 496–498, 509–512
14 PLUTARCH, 35, 117–121, 176–184, 674–681
39 SMITH, 239–240
50 MARX, 305
50 MARX-ENGELS, 432

4. The defense of oligarchy: the political rights and privileges of property

6 THUCYDIDES, 590
7 PLATO, 695, 699–700
9 ARISTOTLE, 475, 478–479, 480–483, 493–494, 495–497, 502–503
14 PLUTARCH, 34–35, 70–71, 176–184
15 TACITUS, 32, 35
23 MACHIAVELLI, 8
35 LOCKE, 44, 46, 53–54, 56–58
38 MONTESQUIEU, 25, 45–46, 71–72
38 ROUSSEAU, 377, 412
39 SMITH, 309–311
41 GIBBON, 81–82, 94
42 KANT, 436–437
43 FEDERALIST, 50, 113–114, 186, 194–195
43 MILL, 366, 383–387
46 HEGEL, 102, 148

5. The attack on oligarchy and on the political power of wealth

6 THUCYDIDES, 519–520, 575–576
7 PLATO, 342–344, 733–734
9 ARISTOTLE, 495–496, 497, 502, 503, 511–512
14 PLUTARCH, 34–37, 180
23 HOBBES, 140
38 MONTESQUIEU, 23–25
38 ROUSSEAU, 353–358 passim
40 GIBBON, 501
42 KANT, 441–443
43 FEDERALIST, 176–179
50 MARX-ENGELS, 415–434

5*a*. The objection to property as a basis for privilege with regard to citizenship or public office

6 THUCYDIDES, 520
7 PLATO, 405–407

CROSS-REFERENCES

For: The general discussion of constitutional government, *see* Constitution 1–3b; Law 7a; Monarchy 1a–1a(1).

Other considerations of the relation of oligarchy to aristocracy and democracy, *see* Aristocracy 2d; Democracy 2b, 3a–3b; Government 2a, 2c; and for the theory of the mixed constitution as a compromise between democracy and oligarchy, *see* Aristocracy 2b; Constitution 5b; Democracy 3a; Government 2b.

For: The tyrannical and despotic extremes to which oligarchy can go, *see* Tyranny 2b.

The revolutions generated by oligarchy, *see* Aristocracy 3; Revolution 3c(2).

Other discussions of property rights, *see* Democracy 4a(2); Justice 8a; Labor 7b; Wealth 7a.

The general issues of economic and political justice in the conflict between democracy and oligarchy concerning the qualifications for citizenship and the extension of the suffrage, *see* Citizen 2c–3; Constitution 5a; Democracy 4a(1); Justice 9e; Labor 7d, 7f; Liberty 2d; Slavery 5a–5b; Wealth 9h.

Other discussions of capitalism, and of the class war, *see* Democracy 4a(2); Labor 7c–7c(3); Opposition 5b; Revolution 4a, 5a–5c; War and Peace 2c; Wealth 6a, 9h.

ADDITIONAL READINGS

Listed below are works not included in *Great Books of the Western World*, but relevant to the idea and topics with which this chapter deals. These works are divided into two groups:

I. Works by authors represented in this collection.
II. Works by authors not represented in this collection.

For the date, place, and other facts concerning the publication of the works cited, consult the Bibliography of Additional Readings which follows the last chapter of *The Great Ideas.*

I.

PLUTARCH. "Of the Three Sorts of Government—Monarchy, Democracy and Oligarchy," in *Moralia*

DANTE. *Convivio (The Banquet)*, FOURTH TREATISE, CH 10–14

II.

J. ADAMS. *A Defense of the Constitutions of Government of the United States of America*

BURKE. *Thoughts on the Cause of the Present Discontents*

——. *On the Reform of the Representation in the House of Commons*

——. *An Appeal from the New to the Old Whigs*

BURKE. *Letter to Sir Hercules Langrishe*

MOSCA. *The Ruling Class*

MICHELS. *Political Parties*

B. ADAMS. *The Theory of Social Revolutions*

BEARD. *An Economic Interpretation of the Constitution of the United States*

——. *Economic Origins of Jeffersonian Democracy*

PARETO. *The Mind and Society*, VOL III, CH 11

T. VEBLEN. *The Theory of Business Enterprise*

——. *The Vested Interests and the State of the Industrial Arts*

BRYCE. *Modern Democracies*, PART III, CH 74–75

TAWNEY. *Equality*

BRINTON. *The Anatomy of Revolution*, CH II, VII

BURNHAM. *The Machiavellians*

Chapter 63: ONE AND MANY

INTRODUCTION

IN *Pragmatism* and in his unfinished last work, *Some Problems of Philosophy*, William James uses the problem of the one and the many as one of the crucial tests of the philosophical mind. In his famous table of doctrines or "isms" he aligns monism with rationalism and idealism in the column headed "tender-minded," and in the other column, headed "tough-minded," he places their opposites—pluralism, empiricism, and materialism. But as his own theories show, "isms" like monism and pluralism tend to oversimplify the issues.

Whoever emphasizes the oneness of the world, for example, may also acknowledge its manyness and recognize that it is somehow a pluriverse as well as a universe. Some, like Bradley, may qualify this view by regarding the unity as ultimate reality, the plurality as appearance or illusion. Whoever finds the multiplicity of things the primary fact may, nevertheless, find some unity in the order and connection of things. Some, like James himself, may insist that the connection is a loose concatenation of relatively independent parts of reality, rather than an interpenetration of each part with every other in the solid whole which James calls the "block universe."

There may be another oversimplification in James' consideration of the problem of the one and the many. He seems to be concerned largely, if not exclusively, with the alternatives of the block and the concatenated universe as conceptions of the structure of reality. But, as some of the great books of antiquity make evident, that is only one of the problems of the one and the many. Perhaps it should be said, not that there are many problems of the one and the many, but that there is one problem having many aspects or applications, for in every statement of the problem there is at least this singleness of theme; that the one and the many are opposed, that the one is *not* a many and the many *not* a one. Yet even that does not seem to be quite accurate for, as Socrates tells Protarchus in the *Philebus*, it may also be said that the one is a many and the many a one. These are "wonderful propositions," he says, wonderful because "whoever affirms either is very open to attack."

At this early moment in the recorded tradition of western thought, the dialogues of Plato, so thorough in their exploration of the problems of the one and many, make no claim to having discovered or invented them. They were ancient even then. They seem to hang in the very atmosphere of thought, usually befogging those who try to see the truth about anything else without first clearing away their obscurities.

Socrates refers to "the common and acknowledged paradoxes of the one and the many . . . that everybody has by this time agreed to dismiss as childish and obvious and detrimental to the true course of thought." These aside, some genuine perplexities remain. Protarchus asks Socrates to instruct him about "those other marvels connected with this subject which," as Socrates seems to have implied, "have not yet become common and acknowledged."

Socrates begins by calling his attention, not to the unity of *this* man or *this* ox, but to the sense in which it is said that "man is one, or ox is one, or beauty one, or the good one." It is necessary to ask, he says, first, whether such unities exist; then, such unities being always the same, and admitting neither generation nor destruction, how each is itself alone, is not only one but *this* one; finally, how these unities can be conceived as dispersed and multiplied in the world of things which come to be and pass away. This last question seems to be the most difficult because it asks about the *being* of the same and one as it *becomes* in the one and many.

Protarchus is impatient to begin clearing up these problems. Willing to undertake what he calls "this great and multifarious battle, in which such various points are at issue," Socrates is also anxious to let Protarchus and the other youths know the intellectual perils which lie ahead for novices who enter upon this inquiry. "The one and many," he tells them, "become identified by thought . . . They run about together, in and out of every word which is uttered . . . This union of them will never cease, and is not now beginning, but is . . . an everlasting quality of thought itself, which never grows old."

That is why, he explains, "any young man, when he first tastes these subtleties, is delighted, and fancies that he has found a treasure of wisdom; in the first enthusiasm of his joy, he leaves no stone, or rather no thought, unturned, now rolling up the many into the one, and kneading them together, now unfolding and dividing them; he puzzles himself first and above all, and then he proceeds to puzzle his neighbors, whether they are older or younger or of his own age—that makes no difference; neither father nor mother does he spare; no human being who has ears is safe from him, hardly even his dog; and a barbarian would have no chance of escaping him, if an interpreter could only be found."

WHETHER IT IS full of exasperating subtleties or is a treasure of true wisdom, the discussion of the one and the many—in itself and in relation to being and becoming, the intelligible and the sensible, the definite and the infinite, the same and other, universals and particulars, wholes and parts, the simple and the complex, the indivisible and the continuous—is a discussion which seems unavoidable to the ancients. In the dialogues of Plato and in Aristotle's treatises, especially his *Metaphysics*, the one and the many are connected with the basic terms of philosophical thought.

For Plato, the distinction between the one and the many enters into the analysis of almost any object—such as pleasure or virtue or knowledge. Anything, viewed under the aspect of its being or its becoming, its definite sameness or its indefinite otherness and variety, must be discussed both as a one and as a many. The motion of Plato's dialectic may be from the one to the many or from the many to the one; or it may be on the level of the many as an intermediate stage through which analysis must go in proceeding from the infinite to the one. Those who pass at once from unity to infinity, says Socrates, do not recognize "the difference between the mere art of disputation and true dialectic."

For Aristotle, first philosophy or metaphysics, concerned as it is with "being *qua* being and the attributes which belong to anything *qua* being," also investigates unity. Unity is the first property of being. The meanings of one or unity are as various as the meanings of 'to be.' If there is a difference between essential and accidental being, there is a parallel difference between essential and accidental unity. If natural and artificial things differ in substance or being, so too must they differ in unity. "Being and unity are the same," Aristotle says, "and are one thing in the sense that they are implied in one another as are principle and cause." Unity is nothing apart from being, and nothing can be without being one in some sense of unity which is determined by the way in which the thing exists. Aristotle's analysis of any subject matter, proceeding as it does by reference to contraries, always appeals to the one and the many. "All contraries," he says, "are reducible to being and non-being and to unity and plurality, as for instance, rest belongs to unity and movement to plurality . . . And everything else is evidently reducible to unity and plurality. . . . For all things are either contraries or composed of contraries, and unity and plurality are the principles of all contrariety."

THE PROBLEMS IN whose analysis one and many seem to be involved recur in every period of western thought. The question, for example, whether there is an irreducible duality in the relation of knower and known, or whether, in the act of knowledge, knower and known are one, is discussed by Hobbes and William James as well as Plotinus and Aristotle. The question whether the state—which is a multitude somehow united for a common life—has, or should have, the same degree of unity as the family, is discussed by Locke and Hegel as well as Plato and Aristotle.

The earlier controversy over the indivisibility of sovereignty becomes at a later stage the central issue of federal union, to which *e pluribus unum* is the solution offered by the Federalists. Questions concerning the simple and the complex, or wholes and parts, as objects of knowledge, or questions concerning the unity and divisibility of time, space, or matter, engage the attention of inquirers and analysts no less in modern than in ancient times.

But there are certain problems which are treated with unusual speculative vigor by the ancients alone. Unlike the problems just mentioned, which deal with applications of the contrast between unity and multiplicity, these are questions about the One itself—what it is, whether it exists, whether it is identical with Being, whether it is itself a substance or the substance of all things.

The sustained inquiry into such matters in antiquity seems to testify to the extraordinary power exerted upon ancient thought by Parmenides of Elea. The person called "the Eleatic Stranger" represents his theories in such dialogues of Plato as the *Sophist* and the *Statesman*. Parmenides, or his disciple Zeno, is probably the source of many of the paradoxes and riddles which Socrates, in the *Philebus*, dismisses as no longer worthy of serious attention. One whole dialogue, named *Parmenides* because of his part in the discussion, exhibits the Eleatic demonstration that 'all is one.' It abounds in the subtleties of the various arguments which try to defend the reality of the many or try to reduce that position to absurdity.

Questioned by Socrates concerning his paradoxes, Zeno says that his writings "were meant to protect the arguments of Parmenides against those who make fun of him and seek to show the many ridiculous and contradictory results which they suppose to follow from the affirmation of the one." When he addresses himself to the partisans of the many, Zeno says that he returns "their attack with interest by retorting upon them that their hypothesis of the being of many, if carried out, appears to be still more ridiculous than the hypothesis of the being of one."

Aristotle also deals with the Eleatic arguments. In the *Physics*, he says first that inquiring about whether being is one, cannot contribute to the study of nature. He then adds that such inquiry anyway would be "like arguing against any other position maintained for the sake of argument . . . or like refuting a merely contentious argument." This description, he says, "applies to the arguments both of Melissus and Parmenides: their premises are false and their conclusions do not follow . . . Accept one ridiculous proposition and the rest follows—a simple enough proceeding." Aristotle's treatment of Parmenides and Zeno in the *Metaphysics* seems to be no more sympathetic, though it tacitly admits the relevance of the Eleatic speculations to the study of being, if not to the study of change and the principles of nature. Nevertheless, many of the questions concerning the one and the many which both Plato and Aristotle deem worthy of discussion appear to have some connection with the perplexities propounded by Parmenides and his school.

THOSE WHO DO NOT deny either the unity of being or its multiplicity tend to make the primary fact about reality either its oneness or its manyness. This may seem at first to be of slight significance, but if the two views of the world which result from this difference are examined, it may be found that the disagreement on this single point changes the perspective on everything else. The philosophers who magnify either the one or the many behold universes more radically dissimilar than the same object looked at from opposite ends of a telescope. But that is not all. Almost every other fundamental conception—of God and man, of the mind and knowledge, of matter and motion, of cause and necessity—seems also to be altered.

Spinoza, for example, criticizes those who attribute to finite things, of which there are necessarily many, the properties which belong to the infinite being, of which there can be only one. This man, this stone, or any comparable individual thing, is not a substance, having the power to exist in and of itself; it consists merely "of certain modifications of the attributes of God," the one infinite substance in which everything else "both is and is conceived." According to Spinoza, those who suppose that the finite many are substances "have not observed a proper order of philosophic study."

They begin with the objects of sense which have the least reality and come last to the divine nature, the infinite one, which "ought to be studied first because it is first in the order of knowledge and in the order of things . . . Hence it has come to pass," Spinoza continues, "that there was nothing of which men thought less than the divine nature while they have been studying natural objects, and when they afterwards applied themselves to think about God, there was nothing of which they could think less than those prior fictions upon which they had built their knowledge of natural things, for these fictions could in no way help to the knowledge of the divine nature."

Starting with the definition of substance as that which exists in itself and is conceived through itself, and with the definition of God as absolutely infinite being, "that is to say, substance consisting of infinite attributes," Spinoza undertakes to prove that there cannot be two or more substances having the same nature or attributes, that substance is necessarily infinite, and hence that it is impossible for more than one substance to exist. Since he regards it as axiomatic that "everything which is, is either in itself or in another," it follows for Spinoza that if anything at all exists, God (or substance) must necessarily exist—as that which alone exists in itself and as that in which everything else has its finite being as a mode or affection of the attributes of God.

Certain other consequences seem to follow. The one infinite substance is indivisible: it is not a whole made up of parts which can have independent existence, as the parts of a quantitative whole seem able to exist when the quantity is divided. Furthermore, God, according to Spinoza, "is the immanent, and not the transitive, cause of all things." God causes them not as one thing acting on another when both are independent in existence, but rather as the being *in which* all things are. God is not present in the world, as other theologians seem to think, in the manner in which a cause exists in an effect that depends upon it. Rather the whole world is in God as an effect which can in no way be separated from the existence of the cause, any more than an aspect can be separated from that of which it is an aspect.

For Spinoza, the unity and totality of being can be called "nature," as well as "infinite substance" or "God." His distinction between *natura naturans* and *natura naturata*, discussed in the chapter on NATURE, seems to permit him to distinguish between the infinite or eternal and the finite or temporal—the one and the many—without implying a real separation between God and the world. Since God is immanent in the world, and since God not only exists necessarily but also acts from the necessity of His own nature, it follows (as is indicated in the chapter on NECESSITY AND CONTINGENCY) that every finite and temporal aspect of nature is necessarily determined. Nothing is contingent. Nothing could be otherwise than it is.

THIS EXAMINATION of a doctrine in which the primacy of the one absorbs as well as subordinates the many, serves to exemplify the point that making the one primary is more than a matter of emphasis. It also shows that almost every fundamental question is affected. It presents a picture of what William James appears to mean when he speaks of the block universe, though he himself usually seems to have in mind Hegel's Absolute rather than Spinoza's God.

Aristotle advances a contrary doctrine. Like Spinoza he uses the term 'substance.' Like Spinoza he defines substance as that which exists in itself, not as an accident (a quality, for example) which exists in another, *e.g.*, the redness in the rose. But for him substance is not necessarily infinite, nor is it indivisible. A rose or a man is a substance. Every physical thing which has a natural unity is a substance.

Each is a finite whole, or rather each is a whole in a number of different senses. Insofar as it has essential unity, it is a whole composed of matter and form which, according to Aristotle, are represented in the formulation of a definition by the genus and the differentia. Insofar as it is composed of matter, it also has the unity of a quantitative whole in virtue of which it moves as one thing or uniquely occupies a place. Since quantitative unity involves continuity, and continuity entails divisibility, a substance remains one only so long as it is not divided into its quantitative parts, just as it remains one essentially only so long as its matter and form are not separated.

A substance is individual not because it is absolutely indivisible—as for Lucretius the atom is because it is simple rather than composite. Its individuality rather consists, first, in its being divided from other substances in such a way that it can perish without necessarily destroying them, or they can perish without destroying it; and, second, in the fact that, though divisible into parts, it is one whole when these parts remain undivided. Yet as one substance it has more unity than a mere collection of things.

The difference between a man and a machine, according to Aristotle's differentiation between the unity of natural substances and of artificial things, is that a man is not composed of substances (though the parts of a living organism may come to exist as substances when it is decomposed or they are separated from it), whereas a machine, made up of separate pieces of metal, is nothing but a number of individual substances arranged in a certain way. The unity of man does not appear to be the same, therefore, when soul and body are conceived by Descartes as two substances and by Aristotle not as distinct substances but as form and matter which through their union constitute a single substance.

Unity, in short, belongs essentially to the individual natural substance. Because each individual substance is necessarily a one among a many, Aristotle, unlike Spinoza, cannot affirm the unity of substance without also affirming a plurality of substances. Not itself a substance, but only an aggregation of substances, the world is primarily a many rather than a one. The unity it possesses derives from the order and connection of the substances which are its component parts; and that in turn largely derives from the way in which distinct substances causally interact.

Since, according to Aristotle, causality includes contingency and chance, the causal interdependence of substances, with respect to their generation and their motions, does not lock them together into a solid block. To use James' imagery again, a vast plurality of individual substances, causally yet also contingently related, constitutes a loosely-knit world, a concatenated universe.

THE RELATION OF the world as a whole to God does give it greater unity, if the supposition of a plurality of finite individual substances remains the fundamental feature of the world God creates. The Christian doctrine of creation may attribute to the world a greater unity than that possessed by any work of human art, in proportion as the infinitely greater wisdom of the divine plan orders the separate things of nature with an infinitely greater perfection than man can achieve in putting things together or in ordering them to his purpose. But if, according to the theologian, God in creating the world creates not one substance, but many substances, forming a single whole through the pattern of their connection with one another, then in a sense the world has less unity than each of its component substances.

For Aquinas, one kind of substance may have greater unity than another. The immaterial has more than the material; and God more than any finite substance, since each of these is composed of matter and form, or essence and accidents, or at least of essence and existence, whereas the infinite being of God is absolutely simple. The divine nature is without matter, without accidents; its attributes are identical with its essence, and its essence with its existence.

This cardinal point about the divine nature is crucial to the conception of God, and of the world's relation to God. In the formation of Christian theology, God's absolute simplicity seems to exclude all but one resolution of the issue concerning the Trinity. According to the position Augustine takes in criticizing the Arian heresy, the position which is expressed in the Nicene Creed, God is not a trinity of substances, but a trinity of persons—aspects of, or relations within, one substance. The plurality of things which constitutes the world puts the world entirely outside the divine substance. Immanent only as a cause, the simple being of God transcends the complex whole of the created world.

This transcendence seems, furthermore, to imply for theologians like Augustine and Aquinas a fundamental duality in the realm of existence. God and the world are two, not one. Infinite being is absolutely prior to and independent of finite beings. The one can exist without the many. Though the many are said to participate in being, when they do exist, they do not enter into the being of the one, or share it in any way.

The being they have is not only separate from the being of God, but even their mode of being is only analogical to the divine being.

The doctrine that each thing has its own being, and that, as Aquinas says, "being is common to all things only in an analogical sense," seems to put diversity above unity in the structure of reality, and to leave the ultimate plurality of this world unaffected either by the fact that it was created as one or by the fact of its relation to a transcendent One.

IN THE TRADITION of the great books, the problem of the one and the many is often stated without using the notion of substance as the pivotal term.

It appears in Plato's consideration of being and becoming. It is sometimes present in his treatment of the relation between intelligible forms and sensible things—between the universal ideas and the particulars which resemble them through some manner of imitation or participation. It even runs through the discussion of the realm of ideas itself; for the idea of the one is one idea among many, and yet each of the many ideas is in some way one.

The problem of the one and the many appears in Hume's consideration of the absolute distinctness of each unit of experience from every other, accompanied as it is by his skepticism concerning our ability to discover any connections which might tie these units together into a real unity. It appears in Kant's theory of the transcendental unity of apperception, which reduces the sensory manifold to a unity of order; and in Hegel's theory of the one Absolute Idea which contains within itself all the variety that becomes manifest as the Idea unfolds in the processes of nature or history.

The substitution of one set of terms for another does not seem to alter the fundamental issue. Nor does it enable the mind to escape taking sides with those who give primacy to the one or to the many, except perhaps by trying to balance them as correlatives. Among the great books, however, the *Enneads* of Plotinus develops a theory of the One which, putting it above being and beyond knowing, seems to transfigure all the traditional terms of analysis.

The One of Parmenides is, after all, Being; and this identification of Being with One raises a question of the reality of the many. But, according to Plotinus, "there exists a Principle which transcends Being; this is The One, whose nature we have sought to establish so far as such matters lend themselves to proof. Upon The One follows immediately the Principle, which is at once Being and the Intellectual-Principle. Third comes the Principle, Soul." These are what Plotinus calls the three hypotases. He finds some analogy for his trinity in a doctrine he ascribes to Plato's *Parmenides*, in which he finds a threefold distinction "between the Primal One, a strictly pure Unity, and a secondary One which is a One-Many, and a third which is a One-and-Many."

The One, according to Plotinus, not only transcends being; it also transcends intelligence. Knowing or thinking requires an object. The relation of knower and known entails a duality which would fracture the utter simplicity of The One. Even the complete reflexivity of The One knowing only itself is excluded. The super-essential is for Plotinus also the supra-cogitative. "What stands above Being stands above intellection," he says; "it is no weakness in it not to know itself, since as pure unity it contains nothing which it needs to explore." Multiplicity begins with the effort of the Intellectual-Principle to know the Transcendent. "It knows the Transcendent in its very essence but, with all its efforts to grasp that prior as pure unity, it goes forth amassing successive impressions, so that, to it, the object becomes multiple . . . The Intellectual-Principle is established in multiplicity."

What is the All of which The One is not all, since the Intellectual-Principle and the Soul also belong to it? Plotinus answers that "The One is all things and no one of them. The source of all things is not all things . . . It is precisely because there is nothing within the One that all things are from it." Everything else in the totality of which the Transcendent is the source emanates from it.

"Seeking nothing, possessing nothing, lacking nothing," Plotinus declares, "The One is perfect and, in our metaphor, has overflowed, and its exuberance has produced the new: this product has turned again to its begetter and has filled and has become its contemplator and so an Intellectual-Principle . . . It is simultaneously Intellectual-Principle and Being; and, attaining resemblance in virtue of this vision, it repeats the act of the One in pouring forth a vast power. This second outflow is a Form or Idea representing the Divine Intellect as the Divine Intellect represented its own prior, The One. This active power sprung from essences (from the Intellectual-Principle considered as Being) is Soul. Soul arises as the idea and act of the motionless Intellectual-Principle. . . . It takes fullness by looking toward its source; but it generates its image by adopting another, a downward, movement. This image of Soul is Sense and Nature, the vegetal principle."

Nothing, writes Plotinus, "is completely severed from its prior. Thus the human Soul appears to reach as far down as to the vegetal order." In these successive emanations "all that is not One is conserved by virtue of the One, and from the One derives its characteristic nature." Everything except the One is a one-many. "If it had not attained such unity as is consistent with being made up of multiplicity, we could not affirm its existence." The Transcendent alone is "a really existent One, wholly and truly One, while its sequent, poured down in some way from the One, is all, a total which has participation in unity and whose every member is similarly all and one."

If reason cannot fully grasp the Transcendent One, that may be because discursive reason is itself a thing of multiplicity. The unity of an all-embracing vision may be required to apprehend the ineffable unity of the Transcendent. But the mysteriousness of unity is not confined to the Transcendent One. It confronts the mathematician as well as the philosopher. It challenges Nicomachus and Euclid as well as Plotinus.

"Unity," writes Nicomachus, "occupying the place and character of a point, will be the beginning of intervals and numbers, but is not itself an interval or a number." What, then, is unity or a unit in itself? Euclid answers with this definition: "A unit is that by virtue of which each of the things that exist is called one." Unity is not only the measure of existence, but also of numbers; for, according to Euclid, "a number is a multitude composed of units." In mathematics no less than in metaphysics or in theology the relation of unity to number seems to be the heart of the problem of the one and the many.

"Number," according to Locke, "applies itself to men, angels, actions, thoughts; everything that either does exist, or can be imagined." Unity or *one* is, in his view, not only the simplest of all our ideas, but the most omnipresent. "Every object our senses are employed about; every idea in our understandings; every thought of our minds, brings this idea along with it. And therefore it is . . . in its agreement to all other things, *the most universal idea we have.*"

OUTLINE OF TOPICS

1. The transcendental one: the Absolute; the unity of being, of nature, of the universe

   1*a*. The relation of the one and the many: emanation of the many from the one

   1*b*. The unity or duality of God and the world: the immanence and transcendence of God

   1*c*. The one and the many in relation to the universal and the particular: the abstract and the concrete universal

2. The modes of unity: comparison of numerical, essential, and divine unity

   2*a*. Numerical unity or identity: the number *one*

   2*b*. The unity of the indivisible or the simple: the individual thing, the point, the atom, the quality

   2*c*. The complex unity of a whole composed of parts: the distinction between the indivisible and the undivided

3. Kinds of wholes or complex unities

3*a*. Quantitative wholes: oneness in matter or motion

(1) The continuity of a quantitative whole

(2) The unity and divisibility of a motion

(3) The unity and divisibility of matter

(4) The unity and divisibility of time and space

3*b*. Natural or essential wholes: the oneness of a being or a nature

(1) The distinction between essential and accidental unity

(2) The comparison of the unity of natural things with man-made compositions or aggregations: artificial wholes

(3) The unity of a substance and of substantial form

(4) The unity of man as composite of body and soul, matter and spirit, extension and thought

(5) The unity of the human person or the self: the order of man's powers; the split personality

4. Unity in the realm of mind: unity in thought or knowledge

4*a*. The unity of mind or intellect, the cognitive faculties, or consciousness

4*b*. The unity of sense-experience: the unity of attention; the transcendental unity of apperception

4*c*. Unity in thinking or understanding: the unity of complex ideas and definitions; the unity of the term, the judgment, and the syllogism

4*d*. The unity of science: the unity of particular sciences

4*e*. The one and the many, or the simple and the complex, as objects of knowledge: the order of learning with respect to wholes and parts

4*f*. The unity of knower and known, or of subject and object

5. Unity in moral and political matters

5*a*. The unity of virtue and the many virtues

5*b*. The unity of the last end: the plurality of intermediate ends or means

5*c*. The unity of subjective will and objective morality in the ethical realm

5*d*. The unity of the family and the unity of the state: the limits of political or social unification

5*e*. The unity of sovereignty: its divisibility or indivisibility; the problem of federal union

6. Unity in the supernatural order

6*a*. The unity and simplicity of God

6*b*. The unity of the Trinity

6*c*. The unity of the Incarnation

REFERENCES

References are listed by volume number (in bold type), author's name, and page number. Bible references are to book, chapter, and verse of the Authorized King James version of the Bible. The abbreviation "esp" calls the reader's attention to one or more especially relevant parts of a whole reference; "passim" signifies that the topic is discussed intermittently rather than continuously in the work or passage cited. Where the work as a whole is relevant to the topic, the page numbers refer to the entire work. For general guidance in the use of *The Great Ideas,* consult the Preface.

1. The transcendental one: the Absolute; the unity of being, of nature, of the universe

7 Plato, 491–511
8 Aristotle, 235, 259–262, 367–370, 409–410, 423–424, 501–502, 504–507, 517, 519–520, 522–524, 527, 559–560, 580, 588, 605–606, 620, 642
12 Lucretius, 28–29
12 Aurelius, 266, 267, 277–278, 292, 297, 310
17 Plotinus, 46–47, 222–226, 230–237, 300–301, 305–310
19 Aquinas, 258–259, 500–501, 530
23 Hobbes, 172
31 Spinoza, 355–372, 395
35 Locke, 154, 165
42 Kant, 44–45, 550–551, 564–565

***1a.* The relation of the one and the many: emanation of the many from the one**

7 Plato, 486–511, 561–574
8 Aristotle, 505–506, 583–584, 619, 622
17 Plotinus, 46, 70, 126, 137, 142–144, 163–164, 202–207, 209–215, 226–228, 238–239, 242–243, 268–273, 299
19 Aquinas, 98, 167–175, 238–250, 256–259, 404–405, 460–461, 688–689
31 Spinoza, 355–362, 364–366
42 Kant, 43–44, 74–76, 173–177

***1b.* The unity or duality of God and the world: the immanence and transcendence of God**

9 Aristotle, 234–235
12 Epictetus, 120–121
12 Aurelius, 280
18 Augustine, 1–2, 73–74, 100–101, 195–196, 261, 358–359
19 Aquinas, 30, 34–38, 107–108, 238–240, 277–278, 480–481, 528–545
21 Dante, 107, 109, 135, 148–150
31 Descartes, 54–56, 110–112, 158–159
31 Spinoza, 355–372
32 Milton, 185–186
34 Newton, 370–371
35 Locke, 271–272
35 Berkeley, 442–443
35 Hume, 475
42 Kant, 342, 351–352, 566, 580, 592
46 Hegel, 156–157, 220–221, 227–228, 237–238, 245–246
51 Tolstoy, 608, 631
52 Dostoevsky, 153

***1c.* The one and the many in relation to the universal and the particular: the abstract and the concrete universal**

7 Plato, 32–33, 174–175, 383–388, 486–489, 610–613
8 Aristotle, 5, 105–106, 116, 117, 369, 505–506, 520, 534, 537, 558–559, 563–564, 578–580, 618–619
19 Aquinas, 15–16, 49, 80–81, 170–171, 257–258, 399–401, 418–419, 500–501, 662–663, 688–689
23 Hobbes, 55
28 Harvey, 332–333
31 Spinoza, 387–388
35 Locke, 145, 251–252, 254–256 passim, 277–278
35 Berkeley, 406–410
35 Hume, 507
42 Kant, 197–198, 211–213
46 Hegel, 13–14, 17–18, 64, 112–114, 158–159, 176–177
53 James, 308–311

2. The modes of unity: comparison of numerical, essential, and divine unity

8 Aristotle, 260, 504–505, 536–537
17 Plotinus, 205–206
19 Aquinas, 492
20 Aquinas, 719–720, 806–809
31 Descartes, 224–225
53 James, 215–216

2a.* Numerical unity or identity: the number *one

7 Plato, 392–394
8 Aristotle, 8–9, 303–304, 520, 537, 604, 611–618, 620
11 Nicomachus, 821
17 Plotinus, 230, 273–275, 310–321
19 Aquinas, 45–49, 167–170
28 Galileo, 146–147
35 Locke, 113, 218–228, 307
35 Berkeley, 415
42 Kant, 99–101

2*b*. The unity of the indivisible or the simple: the individual thing, the point, the atom, the quality

7 PLATO, 506–507
8 ARISTOTLE, 285–286, 297–298, 411–413, 534
11 NICOMACHUS, 832
12 LUCRETIUS, 7–8
19 AQUINAS, 35–36, 40–41, 49–50, 270–272, 279–282, 460–461
20 AQUINAS, 978–980
31 DESCARTES, 20–21
31 SPINOZA, 359–361
34 NEWTON, 541
35 LOCKE, 127–128, 263
42 KANT, 120–133, 137–140, 158–159

2*c*. The complex unity of a whole composed of parts: the distinction between the indivisible and the undivided

7 PLATO, 495–497, 505–506, 566
8 ARISTOTLE, 204–206, 285, 289, 536–537
12 LUCRETIUS, 8
17 PLOTINUS, 206–207
19 AQUINAS, 204–205, 455–457
20 AQUINAS, 953–955
28 GALILEO, 145–146, 150–151
34 NEWTON, 270–271
35 LOCKE, 201, 266
46 HEGEL, 145
53 JAMES, 104–106

3. Kinds of wholes or complex unities

8 ARISTOTLE, 545, 578–580
17 PLOTINUS, 142–143
19 AQUINAS, 35–36, 397–399
20 AQUINAS, 955–956
42 KANT, 161–163

3*a*. Quantitative wholes: oneness in matter or motion

8 ARISTOTLE, 9, 420–421, 426–428, 541
19 AQUINAS, 47–48, 604–607
31 DESCARTES, 114–115
31 SPINOZA, 373, 379–380
42 KANT, 129–159

3*a*(1) The continuity of a quantitative whole

8 ARISTOTLE, 260, 284–286, 307–308, 312, 315, 535, 598, 662–663
11 ARCHIMEDES, 527
19 AQUINAS, 32–33, 350–351, 397–399
28 GALILEO, 139–153 passim
42 KANT, 69–72

3*a*(2) The unity and divisibility of a motion

8 ARISTOTLE, 308–310, 312–325, 347–352, 536, 541, 578
9 ARISTOTLE, 428–429
17 PLOTINUS, 123–125
19 AQUINAS, 32–33
28 GALILEO, 201–202
30 BACON, 173–174
33 PASCAL, 434–439 passim
34 NEWTON, 31
42 KANT, 26–27, 74–76
51 TOLSTOY, 469

3*a*(3) The unity and divisibility of matter

7 PLATO, 456–457
8 ARISTOTLE, 284–286, 411–413, 423–428, 683–684
10 GALEN, 172–173
17 PLOTINUS, 52
19 AQUINAS, 99, 258–259, 270–272
20 AQUINAS, 951–953
28 GALILEO, 147–148
35 LOCKE, 170, 212, 237
35 BERKELEY, 421–422
42 KANT, 137–140
43 FEDERALIST, 103
45 FARADAY, 850–855

3*a*(4) The unity and divisibility of time and space

7 PLATO, 450–451
8 ARISTOTLE, 312–325 passim, 439
17 PLOTINUS, 123–129
18 AUGUSTINE, 93–99
31 DESCARTES, 213
33 PASCAL, 434–439 passim
35 LOCKE, 151, 164
35 BERKELEY, 432
42 KANT, 24–26, 130–133, 160–163
53 JAMES, 398–399, 420, 547–548, 631

3*b*. Natural or essential wholes: the oneness of a being or a nature

8 ARISTOTLE, 536–537
10 GALEN, 189–190
19 AQUINAS, 35–36, 71–72
31 DESCARTES, 224–225
35 LOCKE, 268–271, 334–335

3*b*(1) The distinction between essential and accidental unity

8 ARISTOTLE, 536–537, 552–555, 561–562
19 AQUINAS, 45–46, 603–604, 740–741
20 AQUINAS, 710–711, 716–718
35 LOCKE, 268–271

3*b*(2) The comparison of the unity of natural things with man-made compositions or aggregations: artificial wholes

19 AQUINAS, 688–689
20 AQUINAS, 953–955
42 KANT, 557–558

3*b*(3) The unity of a substance and of substantial form

8 ARISTOTLE, 288, 369, 565–566, 569–570, 641–644
19 AQUINAS, 15–16, 163–164, 365–367
20 AQUINAS, 728–729, 806–809
31 DESCARTES, 152–155

31 Spinoza, 356–361
35 Locke, 204–205, 213–214, 219–221, 273, 334–335
42 Kant, 15, 63–64, 74–76, 81–83, 91–93, 95, 131, 137–140, 162–163, 556–558, 559, 575–576

3*b*(4) The unity of man as composite of body and soul, matter and spirit, extension and thought

7 Plato, 231–234, 686–687
8 Aristotle, 559, 567, 569–570, 606, 632, 640, 641–644
12 Lucretius, 31–32, 34–35
12 Epictetus, 240–242
12 Aurelius, 292
17 Plotinus, 1–6, 151–154, 191, 197–198, 323–325
18 Augustine, 289–295 passim, 367, 369–370, 377–380
19 Aquinas, 379–382, 385–399, 600–607, 632–634
20 Aquinas, 715–716, 728–729, 951–955, 968–992
25 Montaigne, 311, 432, 540–543
31 Descartes, 51–52, 77–81, 98–99, 119–120, 133, 135–136, 170, 224–225, 231–232
31 Spinoza, 377–378, 396–398, 451–452
33 Pascal, 262
35 Locke, 220–222, 224
35 Hume, 472–473
36 Sterne, 277
46 Hegel, 24, 115
53 James, 1–4, 84–93, 116–119, 139–140, 222–223

3*b*(5) The unity of the human person or the self: the order of man's powers; the split personality

New Testament: *Romans*, 6:12–14; 7–8; 13:13–14
7 Plato, 165–166, 346–355
8 Aristotle, 662–667
12 Epictetus, 118–120, 203–210
12 Aurelius, 280, 283, 285
17 Plotinus, 166–167
18 Augustine, 55–56, 58–60
19 Aquinas, 399–407, 492–523
20 Aquinas, 145–147, 162–174, 530–533, 816–818, 893–895
25 Montaigne, 105–107, 159–162, 273–276, 326–327, 388–389
31 Descartes, 89–93
35 Locke, 123–124, 126, 218–228
42 Kant, 120–129, 200–204, 584–585
47 Goethe, 26–28
51 Tolstoy, 554–555
53 James, 130–139 passim, 147–149, 154–155, 188–259
54 Freud, 6–9, 81–83, 430, 589–593, 615–616, 633–635, 640, 689–690, 701–707, 712–716, 721–722, 767–768, 830–840, 843–845

4. Unity in the realm of mind: unity in thought or knowledge

4*a*. The unity of mind or intellect, the cognitive faculties, or consciousness

8 Aristotle, 636, 656–662
17 Plotinus, 143
19 Aquinas, 388–391, 417–419, 469–471
20 Aquinas, 9–10
42 Kant, 55–56, 99–101, 110–112, 121–124, 126–128, 185, 193–200, 329, 463–475, 570–572
46 Hegel, 110–111
53 James, 154–157, 159–161

4*b*. The unity of sense-experience: the unity of attention; the transcendental unity of apperception

7 Plato, 534–535
8 Aristotle, 654–659, 685–689
19 Aquinas, 410–413
21 Dante, 57
35 Berkeley, 432
42 Kant, 48–59
48 Melville, 244–245
53 James, 232–238, 261–269, 315–318, 469–471, 502–503, 570–572

4*c*. Unity in thinking or understanding: the unity of complex ideas and definitions; the unity of the term, the judgment, and the syllogism

7 Plato, 32–33, 174–179, 514–515, 534–536, 545–547
8 Aristotle, 6, 7, 26, 27–28, 31–32, 115–116, 126, 128, 133, 152, 171, 177, 194, 196, 202–206, 208, 552–555, 558–562, 565–566, 569–570, 644–645, 662–663
9 Aristotle, 166–167
19 Aquinas, 301, 457, 460–461
30 Bacon, 59
35 Locke, 147, 148, 201, 214, 263–268, 276–278 passim
35 Berkeley, 413
42 Kant, 44–45, 107, 193–200, 550–551
46 Hegel, 220
53 James, 178–184, 213–214

4*d*. The unity of science: the unity of particular sciences

7 Plato, 10–11, 397–398
8 Aristotle, 103, 104, 119, 121, 155, 234, 513–516, 522–525, 547–548, 587–590, 592–593
17 Plotinus, 137
19 Aquinas, 4–5
20 Aquinas, 40–41
23 Hobbes, 71, 72
30 Bacon, 13, 15–16, 44–45
31 Descartes, 1–2
42 Kant, 193–200, 560–561
51 Tolstoy, 197

4e. The one and the many, or the simple and the complex, as objects of knowledge: the order of learning with respect to wholes and parts

7 PLATO, 231–232, 368–373, 486–511, 537, 594–595
8 ARISTOTLE, 136–137, 186–187, 259, 565, 594–596, 657, 662–663
9 ARISTOTLE, 161
17 PLOTINUS, 159
19 AQUINAS, 57–59, 79–81, 210–213, 455–457
30 BACON, 105–106, 108–109, 137–139, 157–158, 162–164
31 DESCARTES, 14–15, 18–25, 46–48
35 LOCKE, 277–278, 334–335
35 HUME, 454–455
42 KANT, 49–51, 110–111, 193–200, 294
53 JAMES, 315–319, 327–331, 452–453, 547–548, 551–552

4f. The unity of knower and known, or of subject and object

7 PLATO, 809–810
8 ARISTOTLE, 152, 605, 639–641, 657–658, 661–662, 664, 685, 691–692
17 PLOTINUS, 136, 221–222, 235
18 AUGUSTINE, 75–78
19 AQUINAS, 76–77, 80–81, 153–154, 595–597
42 KANT, 23–24, 52–53, 88–91
46 HEGEL, 19–20, 55–56
53 JAMES, 142–143, 147, 176–178, 232–238, 309–311

5. Unity in moral and political matters

5a. The unity of virtue and the many virtues

7 PLATO, 32–37, 48–50, 58–64, 174–190, 605–607, 795–797
9 ARISTOTLE, 377–378, 394
17 PLOTINUS, 9–10
20 AQUINAS, 49–50, 56–58, 70–75, 485–489
30 BACON, 80–81
33 PASCAL, 175
42 KANT, 377

5b. The unity of the last end: the plurality of intermediate ends or means

8 ARISTOTLE, 666
9 ARISTOTLE, 339–341
12 AURELIUS, 271, 278
17 PLOTINUS, 14–19
18 AUGUSTINE, 270–271
19 AQUINAS, 613–615
20 AQUINAS, 390–409
42 KANT, 234–240, 266–267, 271–279, 286–287, 307, 317, 327–329, 337–355, 594–597
43 MILL, 448, 461–463

5c. The unity of subjective will and objective morality in the ethical realm

46 HEGEL, 14, 20, 54, 57, 64, 80–83, 112–114, 133, 136

5d. The unity of the family and the unity of the state: the limits of political or social unification

7 PLATO, 356–365, 605–608
9 ARISTOTLE, 420–421, 445–446, 455–461, 530, 532–533
18 AUGUSTINE, 357, 520–523
23 HOBBES, 99–101, 111, 121
35 LOCKE, 42–43
38 MONTESQUIEU, 3, 64–65, 140
38 ROUSSEAU, 367–369, 392–393, 425–427
43 FEDERALIST, 30–32, 60–62
43 MILL, 352–353, 460–461
46 HEGEL, 58, 61, 63, 84–89, 143, 170–178, 211–212, 222, 236
50 MARX-ENGELS, 421, 427–428
54 FREUD, 785–788, 799–800

5e. The unity of sovereignty: its divisibility or indivisibility; the problem of federal union

23 HOBBES, 97–98, 100–105, 151–152
38 MONTESQUIEU, 58–60
38 ROUSSEAU, 395–396, 406–410, 422
42 KANT, 437, 439–441, 455–456
43 CONSTITUTION OF THE U.S., 11–20
43 FEDERALIST, 29–62 passim, 71–78 passim, 105–107, 126–128, 146–147, 242–244
43 MILL, 428–433
46 HEGEL, 92–93, 95, 106–107, 342, 355

6. Unity in the supernatural order

6a. The unity and simplicity of God

OLD TESTAMENT: *Deuteronomy,* 5:6–10; 6:4 / *Isaiah,* 45:5–6
APOCRYPHA: *II Maccabees,* 1:24–25
NEW TESTAMENT: *Mark,* 12:29–34 / *I Corinthians,* 8:1–6; 12:1–13
8 ARISTOTLE, 353–355, 603
17 PLOTINUS, 353–360
18 AUGUSTINE, 3, 43–44, 48–50, 268–269
19 AQUINAS, 14, 29–32, 46–50, 62–63, 73–76, 153–154, 213–214, 694
20 AQUINAS, 724
21 DANTE, 151, 157
31 DESCARTES, 52, 81–89
31 SPINOZA, 355–372
35 LOCKE, 116, 213, 271
40 GIBBON, 307
41 GIBBON, 229–230
42 KANT, 192, 205
46 HEGEL, 322

6b. The unity of the Trinity

NEW TESTAMENT: *John,* 1:1–5
18 AUGUSTINE, 113, 312–313, 327–328, 335–338, 625–626
19 AQUINAS, 153–175, 210–213, 224–230
20 AQUINAS, 807–809
21 DANTE, 143–144
22 CHAUCER, 155, 467

23 Hobbes, 207–208
30 Bacon, 100
32 Milton, 1, 329–331
40 Gibbon, 307–313
46 Hegel, 306

6c. The unity of the Incarnation

New Testament: *John*, 1:9–14; 14:10–11 / *Philippians*, 2:5–7 / *Colossians*, 2:9
18 Augustine, 293–295, 316–318
20 Aquinas, 701–846 esp 709–723, 1045–1046
21 Dante, 108
33 Pascal, 262
40 Gibbon, 308
41 Gibbon, 134–138 esp 136, 140, 145, 150–151
46 Hegel, 306–307

CROSS-REFERENCES

For: Other discussions of the problem of the one and the many in relation to the order of being, nature, or reality, *see* Being 2–2a; God 5d–5e; Nature 1b; Opposition 2b, 2e; Relation 3; World 3a–3b.

Problems closely related to that of the one and the many, *see* Relation 1d; Same and Other 2b, 2e; Universal and Particular 1.

The dialectical significance of the problem of the one and the many, *see* Dialectic 3a, 3d; Opposition 2b.

Other discussions of numerical unity or identity, or the unity of the individual or the indivisible, *see* Element 5a–5b; Infinity 4b; Mathematics 2c; Quantity 2, 6a; Same and Other 1a–1b.

Discussions relevant to the unity and divisibility of matter, motion, time, and space, *see* Change 5b; Element 5b; Infinity 4b; Quantity 2; Space 3a; Time 1.

The problem of essential and accidental unity, *see* Same and Other 3a.

The problem of the unity of substantial form, *see* Form 2c(3).

The problem of the unity of man, or of unity in the human personality, *see* Man 3a, 5–5a; Opposition 4–4b, 4d; Soul 4a.

Considerations of unity in the faculties or operations of thought or knowledge, *see* Definition 1d; Memory and Imagination 6c(2); Mind 1g(3); Same and Other 4c; Sense 3c(5).

For: The one and the many, or the simple and the complex, as objects of knowledge and in relation to the order of learning, *see* Idea 5d; Knowledge 5b.

The unity and diversity of knower and known, *see* Knowledge 1; Same and Other 4a.

The controversy over the unity of virtue and the plurality of virtues, *see* Courage 4; Prudence 3b; Temperance 1a; Virtue and Vice 1b, 3b.

Other discussions of the order of means and ends, *see* Good and Evil 5c; Principle 4a; Relation 5a(2).

Unity as an aesthetic or an artistic principle, *see* Art 7b; Beauty 1c; Poetry 8a(1).

Matters bearing on the unity of the family and the state, and relevant to the process and limits of social unification, *see* Citizen 8; Family 2a; Government 1b; State 1b, 10a–10f; War and Peace 11a, 11d.

Considerations germane to the divisibility or indivisibility of sovereignty, *see* Government 1g, 5d; State 9d.

Other discussions of the uniqueness and simplicity of God, and of the mysteries of the Trinity and the Incarnation, *see* God 4b, 9a–9b; Man 11c; Relation 2.

ADDITIONAL READINGS

Listed below are works not included in *Great Books of the Western World*, but relevant to the idea and topics with which this chapter deals. These works are divided into two groups:

I. Works by authors represented in this collection.
II. Works by authors not represented in this collection.

For the date, place, and other facts concerning the publication of the works cited, consult the Bibliography of Additional Readings which follows the last chapter of *The Great Ideas.*

I.

AQUINAS. *On the Trinity of Boethius*, Q 4
DANTE. *On World-Government or De Monarchia*, BK I, CH 14–15
DESCARTES. *The Principles of Philosophy*, PART I, 60–65
HEGEL. *The Phenomenology of Mind*
——. *Science of Logic*, VOL I, BK I, SECT I, CH 3(B); BK II, SECT II, CH 3(A)
W. JAMES. *Memories and Studies*, CH 8
——. *Pragmatism*, LECT IV
——. *A Pluralistic Universe*
——. *Some Problems of Philosophy*, CH 7–8

II.

SEXTUS EMPIRICUS. *Against the Physicists*, BK I (Concerning Whole and Part)
PROCLUS. *The Elements of Theology*, (A, H)
ERIGENA. *De Divisione Naturae*
ALBO. *The Book of Principles (Sefer ha-Ikkarim)*, BK II, CH 8, 10–13
G. PICO DELLA MIRANDOLA. *Of Being and Unity*
BRUNO. *De la causa, principio, e uno*
SUÁREZ. *Disputationes Metaphysicae*, III–VI, XV (10), XXX (10), XXXIV, XLIV (11), XLVI (1), XLVII (11, 14–15, 17)
SUÁREZ. *On the Various Kinds of Distinctions (Disputationes Metaphysicae*, VII)
JOHN OF SAINT THOMAS. *Cursus Philosophicus Thomisticus, Ars Logica*, PART II, Q 27; *Philosophia Naturalis*, PART III, Q 9
LEIBNITZ. *Monadology*, par 1–9, 56–90
SCHELLING. *Von der Weltseele*
SCHOPENHAUER. *The World as Will and Idea*, VOL I, BK IV (56)
FECHNER. *Über die physikalische und philosophische Atomenlehre*
LOTZE. *Metaphysics*, BK I, CH 6
——. *Outlines of Metaphysic*, DIV I, esp CH 3, 5; DIV II
C. S. PEIRCE. *Collected Papers*, VOL VI, par 373–383
BRADLEY. *The Principles of Logic*, Terminal Essays, IV–V
——. *Appearance and Reality*
ROYCE. *The World and the Individual*, SERIES I(4, 9–10); Supplementary Essay
B. RUSSELL. *Principles of Mathematics*, CH 16–17
H. ADAMS. *Mont-Saint-Michel and Chartres*
MEYERSON. *Identity and Reality*
BLOOD. *Pluriverse*
MCTAGGART. *The Nature of Existence*, BK III
BROAD. *The Mind and Its Place in Nature*, CH I
WHITEHEAD. *Science and the Modern World*, CH 10

Chapter 64: OPINION

INTRODUCTION

THE noble Houyhnhnms are paragons of reason. They have no conceptions or ideas of what is evil in a rational nature. "Their grand maxim," according to Swift, their creator, "is to cultivate reason and to be wholly governed by it. Neither is reason among them a point problematical as with us, where men can argue with plausibility on both sides of the question; but strikes you with immediate conviction, as it needs must do where it is not mingled, obscured, or discolored by passion and interest."

What Captain Gulliver finds most striking in the contrast between men and this noble race of horses is that the perfect rationality of the Houyhnhnms lifts them entirely above the vagaries and vicissitudes of opinion. "I remember it was with extreme difficulty," he says, "that I could bring my master to understand the meaning of the word *opinion*, or how a point could be disputable; because reason taught us to affirm or deny only where we are certain, and beyond our knowledge we cannot do either. So that controversies, wranglings, disputes, and positiveness in false and dubious propositions, are evils unknown among the Houyhnhnms."

Among men it is not the meaning of "opinion" but of "knowledge" which causes trouble. If men had no conception of knowledge at all, as the Houyhnhnms seem to have no conception of opinion, they would find themselves disagreeing about many matters of opinion, but probably not about the nature of opinion itself. The great controversies concerning opinion in the tradition of western thought all relate to its distinction from knowledge, both with regard to the difference in their respective objects and with regard to the way in which the mind works when it knows and when it opines.

Only when something better than opinion is proposed as attainable do the characteristics of opinion come to be questioned. That something may stand in relation to opinion as certainty to probability, as fact to conjecture, as adequate to inadequate knowledge, as demonstration to persuasion. The chief source of disagreement about the nature of opinion seems to be the meaning of the other term in the comparison. Yet a few commonly recognized features of knowledge—if that is taken as the contrasting term—throw some light on the characteristics of opinion. Certain things which are never said about knowledge seem to be generally said of opinion.

AN OPINION, it is said, may be either true or false. But knowledge is never said to be false. For a great many writers, though not for all, doubt and belief are attitudes of mind which accompany the holding of opinions, but not the possession of knowledge. It is possible to opine and doubt at the same time, but not to know and doubt. Belief overcomes doubt with respect to opinion, but in those matters in which the mind is convinced of the truth of its judgments, an act of belief does not seem to be necessary.

In the sense in which belief implies a willingness to assent where assent might reasonably be withheld, belief seems to be appropriate to opinion but incompatible with knowledge. The opposite of an opinion may be reasonably maintained, whereas the opposite of that which is known must be error or falsehood, and therefore untenable. The traditional distinction between axioms and postulates (or assumptions) exemplifies this difference between knowledge and opinion. If a proposition is axiomatic, its contrary must be false. But if something is proposed as an assumption to be taken for granted, then its opposite can also be postulated, and probably will be postulated by those who are unwilling to grant what has been proposed.

This last point in the comparison of knowledge and opinion appears to have political significance. It is not merely that men are accustomed to expect more disagreement in the sphere of politics than in science; they take a different attitude toward scientific and political controversy, largely because one is supposed to occur in the domain of knowledge and the other in the realm of opinion. Men speak of having a right to their own opinions, which includes a right to persist in them despite the conflicting opinions of others. The notion of a right to a certain obstinacy in differing from one's fellow men seems to follow from the nature of opinion and to accord with its distinction from knowledge. With regard to matters concerning which it is supposed that knowledge rather than opinion is possible, disagreement may of course occur, but never without the expectation that reasonable men should be able to reach agreement on the disputed point by re-examining the facts.

The differences between men which we appeal to a consensus to resolve are differences of opinion, not knowledge. Sometimes conflicts of opinion cannot be settled in any other manner, and for practical purposes it may be necessary to accept the opinion of the majority. The theory of majority rule raises many questions on which the great books take opposite views, but for the most part they restrict the application of the theory to matters of opinion. Disputed issues in mathematics or other theoretic sciences are seldom, if ever, settled by counting heads. The weight of numbers seems to be peculiarly relevant to measuring the worth of conflicting opinions.

The traditional consideration of opinion naturally divides, therefore, into two major lines of discussion. The first deals with the theoretical problem of the difference between knowledge and opinion, and involves such related terms as doubt, belief, faith, certitude, and probability. The second assumes that distinction for the most part, and deals with the problems of decision and responsibility in the sphere of opinion—the problem of liberty of conscience, of freedom of thought and expression, of majorities and minorities, and of individual judgment in difficult cases of conscience.

THE DISTINCTION between knowledge and opinion is sometimes made in terms of a difference in their objects, and sometimes in terms of a difference in the way the mind works when it knows and when it opines. These two modes of differentiation may, of course, supplement one another—the object of opinion being such that the mind must operate in a certain way with respect to it. The same authors usually treat the matter both ways. But not all the great books in which these things are discussed use the words "knowledge" and "opinion" to signify the basic opposition.

Locke, for example, says that "the mind has two faculties conversant about truth and falsehood: first, knowledge, whereby it certainly *perceives* and is undoubtedly satisfied of the agreement or disagreement of any ideas; secondly, judgment, which is the putting ideas together, or separating them from one another in the mind, when their certain agreement or disagreement is not perceived, but *presumed* to be so." To the faculty of judgment belongs "belief, assent, or opinion, which is the admitting or receiving of any proposition for true, upon arguments or proofs that are found to persuade us to receive it as true, without certain knowledge that it is so."

As demonstration is to persuasion, as certainty is to probability, so for Locke knowing or perceiving stands to judging or presuming. Others, like Hume, tend to use the term 'belief' in the place of 'opinion' as the opposite of 'knowledge'; or, like Spinoza, to assign opinion along with imagination to the domain of inadequate as opposed to adequate knowledge. But such differences in vocabulary do not seem to obscure the fact that these authors are making distinctions which, if not identical, are at least analogous.

A certain parallelism or analogy exists between different statements of the objects of knowledge and opinion. The knowable seems to have the properties of necessity and immutability, of universality, clarity, and distinctness. That which is contingent and variable, or confused and obscure, is usually regarded as the object of opinion.

Plato, for example, says that that which is apprehended by intelligence and reason "always is, and has no becoming," whereas "that which is conceived by opinion with the help of sensation and without reason, is always in a process of becoming and perishing and never really is." As understanding and reason divide the realm of knowledge, whose object is the immutable being of the intelligible forms, so fancy and perception divide the realm of opinion, whose objects are the sensible things which come to be and perish.

According to Aristotle, the object of science is the essential and the necessary, the object of opinion the accidental and the contingent. To whatever extent sensible particulars involve contingent accidents of all sorts, they belong to opinion, while the intelligible essences of things, universal in the sense of being common to many individuals, belong to science. The parallel which so far seems to be present between Plato's and Aristotle's statements of the objects of knowledge and opinion does not continue when we consider the consequences of their analyses.

For Aristotle, it is possible to have scientific knowledge as well as probable opinion about the changing things of the physical world, to the extent that these things are both intelligible and sensible, and have aspects both of necessity and contingency. But for Plato the realm of becoming belongs exclusively to opinion, as the quite separate realm of being belongs exclusively to knowledge. In consequence, Aristotle's enumeration of the sciences includes physics along with mathematics and theology, whereas the study of the physical world does not yield a science, according to Plato, but only, as he says in the *Timaeus*, "a likely story"—a plausible composition of probable opinions.

At first glance, Hume seems to provide a closer parallel to Plato. "All the objects of human reason or enquiry may naturally be divided into two kinds," he writes, "*relations of ideas*, and *matters of fact*." Objects of the first sort are capable of demonstratively certain knowledge, *e.g.*, the mathematical sciences. Matters of fact, which include questions concerning the real existence of anything or the causal connection of one thing with another, do not permit demonstration. They are objects of belief or opinion.

It would seem, therefore, that Hume, like Plato, regards the objects of knowledge and opinion, or science and belief, as belonging to altogether distinct realms. They even seem to agree that physics cannot be classified as a science, though the probabilities it establishes may be quite sufficient for action. But this agreement must be qualified by the fact that the realm of ideas is for Plato the reality which changing things image, while for Hume ideas have no reality at all. They exist only in the mind, which obtains them from the impressions of sense-experience.

A parallel between Hume and Aristotle might also be drawn, at least insofar as both connect opinion with the contingent—that which can be otherwise. If the opposite of a proposition is not impossible or does not lead to self-contradiction, then the proposition and its contrary are matters of opinion. This criterion, in Aristotle's terms, excludes all self-evident and demonstrable propositions. Such propositions, for both Hume and Aristotle, express knowledge, not opinion. Yet Aristotle, unlike Hume, does not seem to think that the real existence even of immaterial beings is indemonstrable, or that no necessary connections can be discovered between cause and effect.

THESE EXAMPLES might be extended to include similar observations concerning Locke, Spinoza, Kant, James—in fact, almost every writer who distinguishes between knowledge and opinion by reference to characteristically different objects. In the tradition of western thought the major controversies concerning the objects of knowledge and opinion occur with regard to the kind of being or reality assigned to each type of object; and, in consequence, with regard to applications of the distinction. One writer treats as knowledge what another, by apparently the same criterion, calls opinion. The term 'opinion' gets its skeptical impact from this circumstance. The skeptic never denies that men can form opinions about a given subject; he denies that the topic can be a matter of certain or unquestionable knowledge.

Skepticism approaches its limit when it is maintained that everything is a matter of opinion. At the furthest extreme, it is sometimes said that nothing is either true or false, though

Aristotle and others argue that such skepticism is self-destructive since the proposition 'nothing is true or false' is inconsequential if it is false, and self-contradictory if it is true. But the proposition 'everything is a matter of opinion' can itself be an opinion, and its opposite an opinion also.

The position which Montaigne takes in the *Apology for Raimond de Sebonde* is not the provisional skepticism of universal doubt in order to discover the foundations of certain knowledge. It is rather a resolute skepticism which reduces all human judgments to the status of equally tenable opinions and gives man no hope that he will ever be able to do better than adopt opinions on insufficient grounds or else suspend judgment entirely. No axioms, according to Montaigne, have ever won the universal consent of mankind; no demonstrations have ever escaped the need to assume their initial premises. Unless men beg the question in this way, they cannot avoid an infinite regress in reasoning. There is no proposition about which men have not disagreed or changed their minds. Illusions and hallucinations suggest the pervasive unreliability of the senses, as errors of judgment and reasoning suggest the radical infirmity of the mind.

"How variously do we judge of things?" Montaigne asks. "How often do we alter our opinions? What I hold and believe today," he continues, "I hold and believe with my whole belief. . . .I could not embrace nor preserve any truth with greater assurance than I do this; but has it not befallen me, not only once but a thousand times, and every day, to have embraced some other thing with the same instruments, and in the same condition, which I have since judged to be false? A man must, at least, become wise at his own expense; if I have often found myself betrayed under this color, if my touch prove ordinarily false and my balance unequal and unjust, what assurance can I now have more than at other times? . . . We ought to remember that whatever we receive into the understanding, we often receive things that are false; and that it is by the same instruments that so often give themselves the lie, and are so often deceived."

MONTAIGNE EXEMPTS religious faith from the uncertainty of all beliefs or opinions which man arrives at through the unaided efforts of his senses and his reason. Though we must "accompany our faith with all the reason we have," we must do so "always with this reservation, not to fancy that it is upon us that it depends, nor that our arguments and endeavors can arrive at so supernatural and divine a knowledge." Faith is distinguished from ordinary belief, according to Montaigne, only "if it enter into us by an extraordinary infusion."

What is an article of faith to one man may, however, be merely a matter of opinion to another. This seems to be generally recognized by all who differentiate religious faith from secular belief. The difference lies not in the object, but in the causes of belief.

Those who distinguish between knowledge and opinion also admit that a difference in the way the mind judges, is able to produce either knowledge or opinion concerning the same object. It is impossible, according to Aristotle, for the same mind with regard to the same object to know and opine at the same time. A given individual, for example, cannot hold a proposition of geometry to be true *both* as a matter of knowledge and of opinion. But this does not prevent the individual who once held the proposition to be true merely on the authority of his teacher—and thus as a matter of opinion—from subsequently learning the reasons for its truth and thus coming to know what formerly he merely opined. Two individuals may likewise assert the same truth in different ways, the one as knowledge, the other as opinion.

The traditional account of the difference in the activity of the mind when it knows and when it opines appears to involve two related points. The point which both Plato and Aristotle emphasize is that the man who knows does not merely assert something to be true, but has adequate reasons for doing so. The truth of right opinion is no less true than the truth of knowledge. It differs, as the discussion in Plato's *Meno* and *Theaetetus* seems to show, in that the man of right opinion cannot explain why what he asserts is true. He cannot give the causes of its truth, or trace its connections with other truths which help to demonstrate it. The fact that an opinion is true does not prevent its being overturned or given up, since without adequate reasons it is insecure against attack. Unsupported by reasons, opinion is not only unstable as compared with knowledge, but it is also unteachable in the sense in which knowledge can be learned and taught. The man of right opinion, unable to explain satisfactorily why he thinks as he does, cannot help others understand the rightness of his opinions.

The other characterization of the mind's activity in forming opinions seems to follow from the preceding observation. If reasons do not determine the mind to think *this* rather than *that*, what is the cause of its judgment? If the mind is not compelled by the object under consideration to think of it in a certain way, what does move the mind in its act of assent or dissent to that which is proposed? To such questions, the traditional answer seems to be wish or desire, whether an act of free choice on the part of the will or an inclination determined by the driving power of the emotions.

Pascal makes this point when he observes that there are two ways in which men come to think as they do. The more natural way "is that of the understanding, for one should only agree to demonstrated truths; but the more usual... is that of the will; for all men are nearly always led to believe, not by proof, but by inclination." Hobbes similarly differentiates knowledge, which rests upon definitions and demonstrations, from the opinions or beliefs which the mind adopts, not as the result of reasoning, but by an act of will.

The assent of reason is not, according to Aquinas, subject to command by the will in respect to all matters on which the reason can judge. If "that which the reason apprehends is such that it naturally assents thereto, *e.g.*, first principles, it is not in our power to assent to it or to dissent. For in such cases," he holds, "assent follows naturally, and consequently, properly speaking, is not subject to our command. But some things which are apprehended do not convince the intellect to such an extent as not to leave it free to assent or dissent, or at least suspend its assent or dissent for some cause or other; and in such things, assent or dissent is in our power, and is subject to our command." Knowledge, it would seem, consists in those judgments wherein the mind is moved to assent solely by the matter being considered, whereas all matters about which we are free to make up our minds one way or the other are matters of opinion.

Though they vary in the terms of their analyses, Descartes, Locke, and Hume seem also to agree that when the mind is moved to assent by the relations it perceives between ideas, especially when these are clear and distinct, it knows beyond doubt or the possibility of error. But when the mind, lacking such intuitive or rational grounds, nevertheless forms a judgment concerning what is not evident, then the result is opinion entertained as merely probable, accompanied by doubt, and subject to error.

For Descartes, the will, freely exercised, moves the mind to such fallible judgments. Except when it is so moved the mind, responding to its object alone, is naturally infallible. For Hume, the mind is free to imagine whatever it pleases, but its beliefs are determined by a sentiment or feeling of instinctive origin, "which depends not on the will, nor can be commanded at pleasure." The issue between those who connect opinion with free will and those who deny that beliefs are voluntarily formed is discussed in the chapter on WILL. It does not seem to affect the fairly general agreement on the point that opinion is an act of the mind caused by *something other than the object itself* which the mind is considering.

DOES THIS DISTINCTION between knowledge and opinion exhaustively divide all the acts of the mind? As we have seen, Montaigne appears to reject both alternatives and substitutes instead supernatural faith and ordinary belief. Aquinas, on the other hand, accepts knowledge and opinion as exhaustive on the plane of the mind's natural operations and makes religious faith a supernatural alternative to both.

He calls faith a mean or intermediate between science and opinion because he conceives it as having some of the characteristics of each. "To believe," he says, "is an act of the intellect assenting to the truth at the command of the will." In this faith resembles opinion. The act of faith is due to the will rather than to the rational evidence of the object. Faith is "the evidence of things unseen." But faith also resembles science because the affirmations of faith have the certitude or freedom from doubt which characterizes knowledge. According to Aquinas, faith has greater certitude than natural knowledge, since, as intellectual virtues, "science, wisdom, and understanding . . . are based upon the natural light of reason, which falls short of the certitude of God's word, on which faith is founded." Faith differs from knowledge in that the object of faith exceeds the intellect's comprehension. That is why faith requires an act of the will to move the intellect to assent; but whereas ordinary opinions are adopted by a man's own volition, Aquinas attributes faith to God. "Faith," he writes, "as regards the assent which is the chief act of faith, is from God moving man inwardly by grace."

Just as skepticism with respect to science takes the form of reducing all human judgments to opinion, so skepticism with respect to religion takes the form of attributing all belief to purely natural causes. If Freud is correct that all beliefs are the product of wishful thinking, then it is difficult to separate religion from superstition or prejudice—or even, perhaps, to separate science from religion.

James finds the will to believe in science as well as religion. Like Freud, he explains belief in terms of emotion and desire. "Will and Belief, meaning a certain relation between objects and the Self," he writes, "are two names for one and the same *psychological* phenomenon." Except for those necessary truths which concern only ideal relationships, the mind in thinking about reality is free to choose between alternative theories, in the sphere of science as well as in religion. To believe is to attribute reality to a theory. Though the operation of the will to believe is not for James entirely independent of objective criteria, neither is it mainly determined thereby.

"That theory will be most generally believed," he says, "which, besides offering us objects able to account for our sensible experience, also offers those which are most interesting, those which appeal most urgently to our aesthetic, emotional, and active needs. . . .So-called 'scientific' conceptions of the universe have so far gratified the purely intellectual interests more than the mere sentimental conceptions have. But. . .they leave the emotional and active interests cold. *The perfect object of belief would be a God or 'Soul of the World,' represented both optimistically and moralistically (if such a combination could be), and withal so definitely conceived as to show us why our phenomenal experiences should be sent to us by Him in just the very way in which they come.*"

OPINION RAISES moral and political as well as psychological issues of liberty. One of them is the problem of freedom of discussion. This problem has aspects which belong to other chapters—freedom in scientific inquiry to SCIENCE, freedom in artistic or poetic expression to ART and POETRY, freedom of conscience and worship to RELIGION, freedom in teaching to EDUCATION, and the general issue of freedom of thought and speech to the chapter on LIBERTY. Yet what is common to all these related questions seems to be determined by the nature of opinion, particularly in its distinction from knowledge.

None of the books which argue for freedom of expression—Milton's *Areopagitica*, Locke's *Letter Concerning Toleration*, or Mill's essay *On Liberty*—defends the right to disseminate error or falsehood *knowingly*. All of them argue that the individual who claims the right to be heard is morally bound by the duty to speak the truth as it appears to him. Nor do those, like Plato and Hobbes, who recommend political censorship seek thereby to fortify the state by suppressing truth. In saying that the sovereign should "judge of what opinions and doctrines are averse, and what conducing to peace," Hobbes observes that "though in matters of doctrine, nothing ought to be regarded but the truth, yet this is not repugnant to regulating the same by peace. For doctrine repugnant to peace can no more be true, than peace and concord can be against the law of nature."

Since knowledge as distinct from opinion has the character of incontrovertible truth, the issue of freedom or censorship cannot be stated in terms of knowledge. But what some men hold to be knowledge others regard as opinion. The issue of free expression applies therefore to the entire range of human thought on the supposition that *no* proposition or doctrine is exempt from controversy, and no human judgment secure from contradiction. This supposition does not abolish the distinction between knowledge and opinion; nor does it flout the law of contradiction by treating opposite answers to the same question as in fact equally true.

"If all mankind minus one were of one opinion, and only one person were of the contrary opinion, mankind," according to Mill, "would be no more justified in silencing that one person, than he, if he had the power, would be justified in silencing mankind. . . . The peculiar evil of silencing the expression of an opinion is, that it is robbing the human race; posterity as well as the existing generation; those who dissent from the opinion, still more than those who hold it. If the opinion is right, they are deprived of the opportunity of exchanging error for truth; if wrong, they lose, what is almost as great a benefit, the clearer perception and livelier impression of truth produced by its collision with error."

Mill advances four distinct reasons for recognizing "the necessity to the mental well-being of mankind (on which all their other well-being depends) of freedom of opinion, and freedom of the expression of opinion. . . . First, if any opinion is compelled to silence, that opinion may, for aught we can certainly know, be true. To deny this is to assume our own infallibility. Secondly, though the silenced opinion be an error, it may, and very commonly does, contain a portion of truth; and . . . it is only by the collision of adverse opinions that the remainder of the truth has any chance of being supplied. Thirdly, even if the received opinion be not only true, but the whole truth; unless it is suffered to be, and actually is vigorously and earnestly contested, it will, by most of those who receive it, be held in the manner of a prejudice, with little comprehension or feeling of its rational grounds. And not only this, but, fourthly, the meaning of the doctrine itself will be in danger of being lost, or enfeebled."

The aim is not to perpetuate controversy; nor is it to keep all doctrines perpetually on the level of debatable opinion. "As mankind improve," Mill writes, "the number of doctrines which are no longer disputed or doubted will be constantly on the increase; and the well-being of mankind may almost be measured by the number and gravity of the truths which have reached the point of being uncontested. The cessation, on one question after another, of serious controversy, is one of the necessary incidents of the consolidation of opinion; a consolidation as salutary in the case of true opinions, as it is dangerous and noxious when the opinions are erroneous."

As Mill argues the case for freedom of thought and discussion, it appears to be based on the hypothesis that the public debate of all matters, carried on without any restriction except those minimum restraints needed to prevent violence, serves the end of separating true from false opinion and, by the clarification of opinion as well as the correction of error, discovering the reasons which turn opinion into knowledge. It is not to multiply opinions but to advance knowledge, not to encourage skepticism but to invigorate the search for truth, that Mill advocates the submission of all matters to open dispute so long as any disagreement remains.

His fundamental principle, like that of Locke, consists in divorcing political from logical criteria. Logically, the disputants may stand opposed to each other as one who knows and one who merely opines, or as one who holds a true and one a false opinion, or even as one who enjoys God's gift of supernatural faith and one who lacks such light; but considered politically, the opponents represent a conflict of opinion, with each party equally deserving the benefit of the doubt that it may have the truth on its side. If the state were to intervene, it would be deciding a disputed question, not by reason, but by force, in an area to which force is inapplicable.

"The business of laws," Locke writes, "is not to provide for the truth of opinions, but for the safety and security of the commonwealth, and for every particular man's goods and person. And so it ought to be. For the truth certainly would do well enough if she were once left to shift for herself. . . .She is not taught by laws, nor has she any need of force to procure her entrance into the minds of men. Errors indeed prevail by the assistance of foreign and borrowed succours. But if Truth makes not her way into the understanding by her own light, she will be but the weaker for any borrowed force violence can add to her."

Those who argue that state censorship is justified, whether the matters whose debate is prohibited are speculative or practical, moral, political, or theological, appear to extend the safeguarding of the common good beyond security from immediate peril of violence; or to proceed upon the hypothesis of sufficient wisdom in the rulers to discriminate unerringly between truth and falsehood. Those who distinguish between church and state with regard to censorship tend to limit the application of ecclesiastical authority to questions of faith and morals, on which the church is supposed to have supernatural guidance in deciding what is true or sound.

THE PRINCIPLE OF majority rule in matters of opinion seems to be opposite to the principle that the voice of a minority should be heard. To settle a difference of opinion by taking a vote gives a decisive weight to numbers which, it may be thought, is as illegitimate as resolving a debate by force. But when it is necessary to legislate or to act, debate must be terminated and issues resolved.

On speculative questions, which may be answerable by knowledge rather than by opinion, and with respect to which agreement may be possible, the end of truth seems to be served by permitting discussion to go on as long as reason opposes reason. But if the discussion is for the sake of determining action and if, in addition, the subject under discussion is strictly a matter of opinion concerning which it is possible for reasonable men perpetually to disagree, then it may be necessary to appeal to some principle other than reason.

Traditional political theory appears to offer only two solutions. One principle of decision is to follow the opinion of a single man—an absolute monarch or an elected chief magistrate—whether or not that one man also has the wisdom commensurate with such responsibility. The other principle is to accept the opinion of the majority. According to Aristotle, this second principle is operative in every form of government except absolute monarchy. It is not only in democracy, he says, that "the greater number are sovereign, for in oligarchy, and indeed in every government, the majority rules." It is characteristic of every form of constitutional state that "whatever seems good to the majority of those who share in the government should have authority."

Considered in this way, the principle of majority rule leaves open the question whether the majority should be a preponderance of the many or the few. Should it be a democratic majority or, according to some aristocratic standard, the majority of the few who are wiser, more expert, or more virtuous than the many? With regard to some questions, Aristotle suggests, the multitude may be a better judge than any individual, even the most expert. "If the people are not utterly degraded, although individually they may be worse judges than those who have special knowledge, as a body they are as good or better."

The opposing claims of the greater number and the more competent, as well as the possibility of combining the merits of both, are discussed in the chapters on DEMOCRACY and ARISTOCRACY. The problem of majority rule also appears in those chapters as a factor in the theory of representation, especially the question considered by Mill—whether the representative shall exercise his own judgment or act on the opinion of the majority of his constituents.

Mill tries to separate those problems of government which should be submitted to representative assemblies and decision by majorities from those which should be solved by experts. But even on matters subject to deliberation by representatives of the people, Mill advocates such measures as plural voting and minority representation to offset the sheer weight of numbers and prevent its being the decisive force in settling political differences and determining action.

Such qualifications of the principle of majority rule do not seem necessary to those who, like Rousseau, think that "the general will is found by counting votes." What Rousseau says of any individual opinion applies to minority opinions as well, namely, that when a contrary opinion prevails, it proves that what the minority "thought to be the general will was not so." On the question of how large a majority should be decisive, he thinks that "the more grave and important the questions discussed, the nearer should the opinion that is to prevail approach unanimity. . . .The more the matter in hand calls for speed, the smaller the prescribed difference in the number of votes may be allowed to become."

There is, according to Rousseau, only one political decision which requires unanimity, and that is the decision to enter upon the social contract, to set up popular government under which individual liberty endures as long as "the qualities of the general will still reside in the majority." When the principle of majority rule is unanimously adopted, each individual agrees to substitute the general will for his own particular opinion.

OUTLINE OF TOPICS

1. The different objects of knowledge and opinion: being and becoming; universal and particular; the necessary and the contingent

2. The difference between the acts and sources of knowing and opining

2a. The influence of the emotions on the formation of opinion: wishful thinking, rationalization, prejudice

2b. The will as cause of assent in acts of opinion

2c. Reasoning and argument concerning matters of opinion: comparison of demonstration and persuasion, principles and assumptions, axioms and postulates

2d. Reason, experience, and authority as sources of opinion

3. Opinion, knowledge, and truth

3a. The truth of knowledge and of right opinion: their difference with respect to manner of acquisition, stability, and teachability

3b. Certain and probable, adequate and inadequate knowledge: degrees of certitude; modes of assent

3c. The skeptical reduction of human judgments to opinion

4. Opinion, belief, and faith

4a. Comparison of supernatural or religious faith with science and opinion

4b. Criticism of superstitious or dogmatic belief as opinion without foundation or warrant

5. Freedom in the sphere of opinion

5a. Rights and duties with respect to the expression of opinion

5b. Advantages and disadvantages of freedom of discussion

6. Opinion in the realm of morals

6a. Good and evil as matters of opinion: moral standards as customs or conventions reflecting prevalent opinion

6b. The inexactitude of moral principles as applied to particular cases

7. The social and political significance of public opinion

7a. The value of the majority opinion: the distinction between matters to be determined by the expert or by a consensus

7b. Majority rule, its merits and dangers: protections against the false weight of numbers

REFERENCES

References are listed by volume number (in bold type), author's name, and page number. Bible references are to book, chapter, and verse of the Authorized King James version of the Bible. The abbreviation "esp" calls the reader's attention to one or more especially relevant parts of a whole reference; "passim" signifies that the topic is discussed intermittently rather than continuously in the work or passage cited. Where the work as a whole is relevant to the topic, the page numbers refer to the entire work. For general guidance in the use of *The Great Ideas,* consult the Preface.

1. The different objects of knowledge and opinion: being and becoming; universal and particular; the necessary and the contingent

7 PLATO, 113–114, 368–373, 383–398, 532–536, 559–561
8 ARISTOTLE, 97–98, 121–122, 169
9 ARISTOTLE, 343–344, 357–358, 392, 396–398 passim, 652–653
17 PLOTINUS, 249
19 AQUINAS, 422–423, 463–464
31 DESCARTES, 1–5, 8–10, 93, 229–230
31 SPINOZA, 376–377, 388–390
35 LOCKE, 371–372
35 HUME, 458–462
42 KANT, 240–243, 601, 603–604
46 HEGEL, 1–7, 46–47

2. The difference between the acts and sources of knowing and opining

7 PLATO, 182–183, 370–373, 450, 457, 536–549, 575–577
8 ARISTOTLE, 666–667
9 ARISTOTLE, 395–398, 593–675
18 AUGUSTINE, 339
19 AQUINAS, 422–423, 436–438
20 AQUINAS, 14–15, 391–392
23 HOBBES, 65–66
31 DESCARTES, 41, 124–125, 167
32 MILTON, 406
35 LOCKE, 119–120, 364–365
36 SWIFT, 165
42 KANT, 194, 202–203
54 FREUD, 882

2*a*. The influence of the emotions on the formation of opinion: wishful thinking, rationalization, prejudice

6 THUCYDIDES, 402–404, 427–428, 474, 506, 507
9 ARISTOTLE, 401–402, 485–486, 593–594, 622–636, 659–660, 668–670
12 LUCRETIUS, 59
18 AUGUSTINE, 675–676
20 AQUINAS, 145–148
21 DANTE, 126
23 HOBBES, 57–58, 128, 129
24 RABELAIS, 154–156, 159–163
25 MONTAIGNE, 210–212, 272–276, 288–290, 404–406, 446–450, 490–491
26 SHAKESPEARE, 425–426, 583–586
28 HARVEY, 268
30 BACON, 16, 27, 79–80, 90, 109, 111
31 SPINOZA, 369–372, 408, 411–412
33 PASCAL, 186–189, 191–193
35 LOCKE, 195–196, 248–251, 384–388, 392
35 BERKELEY, 427
35 HUME, 453, 491–492
40 GIBBON, 296
42 KANT, 221–222
43 FEDERALIST, 29–30, 118, 162
48 MELVILLE, 317–321
51 TOLSTOY, 134, 238, 358–365, 505–511, 645–646, 686–687
53 JAMES, 652–659
54 FREUD, 125–126, 682, 760–761, 819

2*b*. The will as cause of assent in acts of opinion

9 ARISTOTLE, 357–358
19 AQUINAS, 690
20 AQUINAS, 382–384, 398–399
31 DESCARTES, 89–93
31 SPINOZA, 391–394
33 PASCAL, 191, 439–442
53 JAMES, 636, 660–661

2*c*. Reasoning and argument concerning matters of opinion: comparison of demonstration and persuasion, principles and assumptions, axioms and postulates

7 PLATO, 187–189, 383–398
8 ARISTOTLE, 111, 143–223, 227–253
9 ARISTOTLE, 389, 396–398, 593–675
12 EPICTETUS, 150–151
19 AQUINAS, 56–57, 253–255, 432–433, 560–561
20 AQUINAS, 765–766
23 HOBBES, 65
30 BACON, 56–59, 61, 65
31 DESCARTES, 48–51
34 HUYGENS, 551–552
35 LOCKE, 3–4, 365–366, 378–380
35 HUME, 458–463, 469–470, 508–509
36 STERNE, 227–228
42 KANT, 215–218, 376, 600–603
43 MILL, 274–293 passim

44 BOSWELL, 299
48 MELVILLE, 272–276
51 TOLSTOY, 661–662, 668–669

2*d*. Reason, experience, and authority as sources of opinion

7 PLATO, 517–518, 522–523, 525–527
8 ARISTOTLE, 143
9 ARISTOTLE, 340, 433–434
19 AQUINAS, 3–4, 7–8
20 AQUINAS, 409
23 HOBBES, 56, 58–61, 78, 128–129, 282
25 MONTAIGNE, 65–66, 259–261, 524–525
28 HARVEY, 279–280, 306, 319, 364–365
30 BACON, 12–15, 47–48
31 DESCARTES, 168
33 PASCAL, 220–221, 355–358
35 LOCKE, 366–371, 380–388, 394
35 BERKELEY, 410–411
35 HUME, 458–470, 488–497, 499
42 KANT, 15–16, 146–149, 260–261
43 MILL, 269–270, 275–277, 283–288
51 TOLSTOY, 170–171, 260
54 FREUD, 125

3. Opinion, knowledge, and truth

3*a*. The truth of knowledge and of right opinion: their difference with respect to manner of acquisition, stability, and teachability

7 PLATO, 163, 527, 536–549, 564, 622–626
8 ARISTOTLE, 8–9, 102–104, 563–564, 577–578
9 ARISTOTLE, 339–340, 349, 357–358, 388, 390–393, 594
19 AQUINAS, 99–100
20 AQUINAS, 19–21, 383–384
31 DESCARTES, 43, 49, 63–64
31 SPINOZA, 388–389
42 KANT, 240–243
43 MILL, 283–288
46 HEGEL, 115

3*b*. Certain and probable, adequate and inadequate knowledge: degrees of certitude; modes of assent

7 PLATO, 383–398, 633–635
8 ARISTOTLE, 28–29, 48, 91, 97–99, 524–525
9 ARISTOTLE, 388, 596–597
10 HIPPOCRATES, 144
12 AURELIUS, 264
16 COPERNICUS, 505–506
18 AUGUSTINE, 32, 266, 336–337, 523
19 AQUINAS, 86–88, 297–298, 305–306
20 AQUINAS, 382–384
28 HARVEY, 333
31 DESCARTES, 51–53, 72, 74–82, 95–103 passim, 130–131, 152–153
31 SPINOZA, 384–390, 401–402
33 PASCAL, 213–217
35 LOCKE, 93–95, 307, 312, 324–326, 331–336, 356–357, 360–363 passim, 364–371
35 HUME, 488–491
39 SMITH, 334–336
42 KANT, 1–4, 14–15, 39–41, 211–218, 228, 230–233, 600–603
46 HEGEL, 19–20, 131
54 FREUD, 463, 661–662

3*c*. The skeptical reduction of human judgments to opinion

7 PLATO, 86, 107–109, 236–238, 400, 517–532 passim
8 ARISTOTLE, 99, 528–531, 590–592
12 LUCRETIUS, 50
12 EPICTETUS, 164–166
19 AQUINAS, 440–442
25 MONTAIGNE, 80–82, 208–294, 318–319, 497–502
30 BACON, 115–116
31 DESCARTES, 46, 272–273
33 PASCAL, 238–239
35 BERKELEY, 405, 429–430
35 HUME, 460–466, 477, 503–509
42 KANT, 224–227, 311–313
43 MILL, 274–293 passim
44 BOSWELL, 121
50 MARX-ENGELS, 428
54 FREUD, 881–882

4. Opinion, belief, and faith

7 PLATO, 256, 447
8 ARISTOTLE, 660
18 AUGUSTINE, 36–37, 588–590, 655–656
19 AQUINAS, 7–8
20 AQUINAS, 83–84, 381–383, 402–403, 464–465, 747–748
23 HOBBES, 65–66, 165–166, 238, 241–242
25 MONTAIGNE, 98–99, 150–151, 209, 238–239, 267–268, 271–273
30 BACON, 95–96
31 DESCARTES, 69, 125–126
35 LOCKE, 380–384
35 HUME, 466–467
42 KANT, 240–243, 353–354, 601–609
46 HEGEL, 55–56, 349–350
48 MELVILLE, 360–361
52 DOSTOEVSKY, 11

4*a*. Comparison of supernatural or religious faith with science and opinion

18 AUGUSTINE, 1, 589–590, 638–639
19 AQUINAS, 5–7, 61–62, 175–178, 446–447
20 AQUINAS, 380–381, 393–394, 398–399, 422–424
21 DANTE, 108–109 passim
23 HOBBES, 65–66, 163, 267
30 BACON, 2–4, 41, 55, 96–97
33 PASCAL, 221–225, 248–250, 342–343, 440
35 LOCKE, 340, 357, 371
40 GIBBON, 308–309
42 KANT, 604–606
46 HEGEL, 158–160
51 TOLSTOY, 196–198

4*b*. Criticism of superstitious or dogmatic belief as opinion without foundation or warrant

6 THUCYDIDES, 353–354
18 AUGUSTINE, 20, 45–47, 129–322 passim esp 207–212, 647–649
19 AQUINAS, 589–590, 592–593, 660–662
23 HOBBES, 51–52, 56, 68–69, 79–84, 151, 165–166, 172–177, 192–195, 247–267, 269–271, 272, 274
25 MONTAIGNE, 80–82, 500
28 HARVEY, 331–332
30 BACON, 114, 124
35 LOCKE, 4–5, 119–120, 390–394 passim
35 BERKELEY, 423, 437–438
35 HUME, 499–500
40 GIBBON, 189–191, 200–201, 308–309, 465–467
41 GIBBON, 333–334
42 KANT, 129–130, 187–188, 218–222
43 MILL, 278
46 HEGEL, 85, 86, 143–144
50 MARX, 36
54 FREUD, 874–875, 877–880, 883–884

5. Freedom in the sphere of opinion

5*a*. Rights and duties with respect to the expression of opinion

5 SOPHOCLES, 135, 137
6 THUCYDIDES, 402
7 PLATO, 200–212, 789–790
12 AURELIUS, 254
14 PLUTARCH, 632, 636–637
15 TACITUS, 21
22 CHAUCER, 59–60
25 MONTAIGNE, 7, 240–242, 381–388
26 SHAKESPEARE, 467–468
32 MILTON, 381–412
35 LOCKE, 1–22, 367–368
37 FIELDING, 223
38 MONTESQUIEU, 89–90
43 FEDERALIST, 29–31
43 MILL, 274–293, 302–312 passim, 370–389 passim, 392–399 passim, 401–406 passim
44 BOSWELL, 300–301, 402
46 HEGEL, 104–107, 149
51 TOLSTOY, 307–309

5*b*. Advantages and disadvantages of freedom of discussion

6 HERODOTUS, 216–218
6 THUCYDIDES, 397, 425, 427
7 PLATO, 601–602
15 TACITUS, 57, 72–73
23 HOBBES, 102–103, 114–115, 129–130, 149–151, 155–156
25 MONTAIGNE, 270–271, 324–326
30 BACON, 118–119
31 DESCARTES, 60–61, 283–284
32 MILTON, 381–412
35 LOCKE, 18–21
38 MONTESQUIEU, 89–90
40 GIBBON, 669–670
41 GIBBON, 161–162, 334–335
42 KANT, 220–221, 223
43 FEDERALIST, 49–53 passim
43 MILL, 274–275, 293–294, 318–319, 361–362, 410–412
44 BOSWELL, 221–224, 512
46 HEGEL, 84–89 passim, 104
51 TOLSTOY, 384–388
54 FREUD, 757

6. Opinion in the realm of morals

6*a*. Good and evil as matters of opinion: moral standards as customs or conventions reflecting prevalent opinion

5 ARISTOPHANES, 499–502
6 HERODOTUS, 97–98
7 PLATO, 193–194, 215, 271–274, 311–312, 525–528, 531–532, 759–760
9 ARISTOTLE, 344, 382
12 EPICTETUS, 179–180
18 AUGUSTINE, 16, 661–662
23 HOBBES, 78, 96, 140, 149
25 MONTAIGNE, 46–47, 102–103, 115–119, 124–125, 143–144, 278–284
27 SHAKESPEARE, 114, 274–275
30 BACON, 94
31 DESCARTES, 48–51 passim
31 SPINOZA, 371–372, 399, 411–412, 423, 426, 429, 431, 443–444
33 PASCAL, 349–350
35 LOCKE, 105–106, 111, 230–231, 303–304, 317–319, 325–326
38 ROUSSEAU, 362, 434–435
39 SMITH, 346–347
42 KANT, 263, 270–271, 278, 320–321, 330–331, 387–388, 397–398
43 MILL, 269–270, 296, 300, 307–312, 457–461, 471–476
46 HEGEL, 46–47, 49–54, 115
49 DARWIN, 305, 317
51 TOLSTOY, 214–215, 304–305, 645–649
52 DOSTOEVSKY, 33–34
53 JAMES, 190–191, 886–887

6*b*. The inexactitude of moral principles as applied to particular cases

9 ARISTOTLE, 339–340, 349, 354–357, 389, 395–398
19 AQUINAS, 651–655
20 AQUINAS, 209–210, 223–224
26 SHAKESPEARE, 11–12
30 BACON, 94–95
31 DESCARTES, 126, 237
33 PASCAL, 27–44
42 KANT, 278–279, 357–360, 398–399
43 MILL, 456–457
44 BOSWELL, 219
46 HEGEL, 74–76, 140
53 JAMES, 887–888

7. The social and political significance of public opinion

7*a*. The value of the majority opinion: the distinction between matters to be determined by the expert or by a consensus

6 Herodotus, 107–108
6 Thucydides, 520
7 Plato, 29, 43–45, 213–219, 258, 286–287, 377–379, 598–599, 653–662
9 Aristotle, 420–421, 479–480, 484, 486
14 Plutarch, 792–802
15 Tacitus, 238
22 Chaucer, 401–432
23 Hobbes, 58, 78
25 Montaigne, 303–304
26 Shakespeare, 568–569
33 Pascal, 231, 232
35 Locke, 76
38 Montesquieu, 84, 85
38 Rousseau, 371–372, 396, 425–428
43 Federalist, 98, 192–193, 205, 214–215
43 Mill, 274–302, 330, 332, 343–344, 350–351, 355–409, 410–412, 422–423, 425, 437–442 passim esp 439
44 Boswell, 86
46 Hegel, 100–103, 149, 272–273
51 Tolstoy, 482–484, 503–511

7*b*. Majority rule, its merits and dangers: protections against the false weight of numbers

5 Euripides, 261–262
5 Aristophanes, 470–487, 512–513
6 Herodotus, 180
6 Thucydides, 425, 515–516, 520
7 Plato, 409–413
9 Aristotle, 470, 476–477, 481–483, 491, 496, 498–499, 511–512, 520–522
14 Plutarch, 34–35, 648–649
23 Hobbes, 152
25 Montaigne, 147–148
27 Shakespeare, 351–353, 361–362, 383–384
33 Pascal, 227, 345
35 Locke, 46–47
38 Montesquieu, 4–6, 35–36, 51–52, 71, 73
38 Rousseau, 369, 391, 411
40 Gibbon, 91
43 Articles of Confederation, 5–6
43 Federalist, 47, 49–53, 82–83, 120, 181, 189, 232
43 Mill, 268–271, 307–312, 350–355 passim, 355–392, 401–409
44 Boswell, 261
46 Hegel, 103–104, 172–173, 175

CROSS-REFERENCES

For: Other discussions of the distinction between knowledge and opinion in terms of their objects, *see* Being 8e; Knowledge 4b; Necessity and Contingency 4a; Principle 3c(2); Time 6f; Truth 3b(2); and for other discussions of this distinction in terms of psychological causes, *see* Custom and Convention 9a; Desire 5b; Emotion 3b; Will 3b(1).

The logic of argumentation in the sphere of opinion, *see* Dialectic 2b–2b(2); Reasoning 5c–5d; Rhetoric 4c–4c(3).

The consideration of opinion in relation to truth and falsity, to certainty and probability, and to adequate and inadequate knowledge, *see* Judgment 9; Knowledge 6d(1)–6d(3); Necessity and Contingency 4a; Truth 2e.

Other statements of the extreme skeptical position that everything is a matter of opinion, *see* Custom and Convention 9b; Knowledge 5c; Principle 5; Relation 6b; Truth 7a–7b; Universal and Particular 7a.

The more limited skepticism which treats philosophy as opinion in contrast to science, *see* Metaphysics 4a; Philosophy 6b; Science 7a; and for still another variety of skepticism which treats all moral or aesthetic judgments as matters of opinion, *see* Beauty 5; Custom and Convention 5a; Good and Evil 6d; Relation 6c; Universal and Particular 7b.

The special problem of applying moral principles or legal rules to particular cases, *see* Justice 10d; Law 5g; Reasoning 5e–5e(3); Universal and Particular 6c.

The conception of supernatural faith as distinguished from both science and opinion, *see* God 6c–6c(2); Knowledge 6c(5); Religion 1a; Theology 2, 4b; Truth 4a; Will 3b(3); and for the treatment of religious faith as ordinary belief or as the result of the will to believe, *see* God 13; Religion 6f; Science 7a; Theology 5; Will 3b(1), 3b(3).

Other considerations of the problem of freedom in the sphere of opinion, *see* Knowledge 9b; Liberty 2a; Progress 6e; Truth 8d.

Other considerations of the value of the majority opinion, the principle of majority rule, and the problem of minority opinions, *see* ARISTOCRACY 6; CONSTITUTION 9–9a; DEMOCRACY 2a, 3b, 5b(1); GOVERNMENT 1h; STATE 8d(3); TYRANNY 2c.

ADDITIONAL READINGS

Listed below are works not included in *Great Books of the Western World*, but relevant to the idea and topics with which this chapter deals. These works are divided into two groups:

I. Works by authors represented in this collection.
II. Works by authors not represented in this collection.

For the date, place, and other facts concerning the publication of the works cited, consult the Bibliography of Additional Readings which follows the last chapter of *The Great Ideas*.

I.

AUGUSTINE. *On the Profit of Believing*
——. *On Faith in Things Unseen*
F. BACON. *Of the Colours of Good and Evil*
LOCKE. *Conduct of the Understanding*
HUME. *A Treatise of Human Nature*, BK I, PART IV, SECT I–IV
KANT. *Introduction to Logic*, IX
J. S. MILL. *A System of Logic*, BK III, CH 25
W. JAMES. *The Will to Believe*

II.

SEXTUS EMPIRICUS. *Outlines of Pyrrhonism*, BK I–II
NICOLAS OF CUSA. *De Docta Ignorantia*
BROWNE. *Pseudodoxia Epidemica* (*Vulgar Errors*)
SANDERSON. *De Obligatione Conscientiae* (*On the Obligations of Conscience*)
J. TAYLOR. *Ductor Dubitantium*
GLANVILL. *The Vanity of Dogmatizing*
VOLTAIRE. "Opinion," "Sect," in *A Philosophical Dictionary*
BEATTIE. *An Essay on the Nature and Immutability of Truth*
T. REID. *Essays on the Active Powers of the Human Mind*, III, PART II, CH 8
HAZLITT. *Table Talk*, VII
DE MORGAN. *A Budget of Paradoxes*
J. H. NEWMAN. "Private Judgment," in VOL II, *Essays and Sketches*
——. *An Essay in Aid of a Grammar of Assent*
VENN. *On Some of the Characteristics of Belief, Scientific and Religious*
MORLEY. *On Compromise*
CLIFFORD. "The Ethics of Belief," in VOL II, *Lectures and Essays*
C. S. PEIRCE. *Collected Papers*, VOL V, par 358–410
A. SIDGWICK. *Distinction and the Criticism of Beliefs*
BALFOUR. *The Foundations of Belief*
BOSANQUET. *Science and Philosophy*, 3
HODDER. *The Adversaries of the Sceptic*
DICEY. *The Relation Between Law and Public Opinion in England During the Nineteenth Century*
BRADLEY. *Essays on Truth and Reality*, CH 2
T. VEBLEN. *The Vested Interests and the State of the Industrial Arts*, CH I
B. RUSSELL. *The Analysis of Mind*, LECT 12
LIPPMANN. *Public Opinion*
KIRK. *Ignorance, Faith and Conformity*
LAIRD. *Knowledge, Belief and Opinion*
GILL. *The Necessity of Belief*

Chapter 65: OPPOSITION

INTRODUCTION

CERTAIN words in the vocabulary of common speech, used at almost every turn of discourse, indicate ideas so indispensable to human thought that they are often employed without analysis. The word "is" is one of these, signifying the idea of being or existence. The word "not" and the pair of words "either. . . . or" have the same character. Taken together, "not" and "either. . . .or" signify the idea of opposition. The quality of redness is *not* the same as the quality of hotness, yet this negative relation by itself does not make them opposite, for something can be red-hot. It is only when a thing can have *either* one quality *or* another, but *not* both, that the qualities are said to be opposed. Opposites are more than merely distinct; they exclude one another.

Opposition seems to be as pervasive as the familiar words which signify it. Even if it were not itself one of the great ideas, it would be manifest in all the other basic notions which come in antithetical pairs, *e.g.*, good and evil, life and death, war and peace, universal and particular, pleasure and pain, necessity and contingency, same and other, one and many, virtue and vice. Each of these notions seems to imply its opposite and to draw its meaning from the opposition. There are other terms in the list of great ideas which, though not paired in the same chapter, stand opposed to one another: art to nature, chance to fate, liberty to slavery, time to eternity, knowledge to opinion, matter to form, democracy to oligarchy and similarly other forms of government. Still other terms cannot be discussed without reference to their opposites, even though we have not explicitly listed them, such as being and non-being, truth and falsity, love and hate, justice and injustice, wealth and poverty.

The enumeration might extend to include every fundamental notion, except for the inconvenience in certain cases of not having readily familiar names to designate the opposites. In some instances, moreover, the opposition seems to involve more than a pair of terms, as, for example, is the case with poetry, history, and science; or physics, mathematics, and metaphysics.

In the tradition of the great books we not only find the opposition of one idea to another, but we also find opposite points of view, conflicting theories or doctrines, in the discussion of almost every basic topic under the heading of these ideas. We find the same word used with contrary meanings, the same proposition affirmed and denied. We find reasoning opposed to reasoning. The same conclusion is reached from apparently opposite principles, or opposite conclusions are drawn from premises apparently the same.

But though opposition seems to be inherent in the realm of ideas and in the life of thought, the idea of opposition is not itself explicitly thought about in many of the great books. This does not mean that in the consideration of other matters the significance and consequences of opposition go unnoted. On the contrary, all the chapters dealing with the nature and conduct of man, or with the institutions and history of society, give evidence of the general recognition—by poets and historians, by scientists and philosophers—that opposition in the form of active conflict characterizes the phenomena. The fact of warring opposites not only enters into descriptions of the way things are, but also poses problems for psychologists, moralists, economists, and statesmen to solve.

The study of nature, as well as of man and society, discovers opposition at the root of change. The physics of antiquity, for example, defines the elements or the bodily humours in terms of contrary qualities; according to Aristotle, contraries are among the ultimate principles of nature—the terms of change. The cosmology of Lucretius makes the conflict of opposites the principle of growth and decay in the universe. Destruction struggles against creativity; life against death. "The death-dealing motions," the poet writes, "cannot keep the mastery always nor entomb existence for evermore, nor on the other hand can the birth and increase-giving motions of things preserve them always after they are born. Thus the war of first-beginnings waged from eternity is carried on with dubious issue: now here, now there, the life-bringing elements of things get the mastery and are overmastered in turn."

Modern mechanics deals with action and reaction in the impact of bodies and the resolution of forces tending to produce opposite results. The theory of evolution pictures the world of living organisms as engaged in the struggle for survival, organism competing with organism or against an adverse environment for the means of subsistence or reproduction.

These indications of the prevalence of conflict in the realm of thought itself, or as a fundamental conception in man's thinking about nature and society, do not alter the point that only in logic or metaphysics is opposition abstracted from special subject matters, to become itself the object of thought. Even so, not all of the great speculative works develop an explicit theory of opposition—classifying its types, analyzing its structure, formulating it as a universal principle of being, mind, or spirit.

Four authors especially treat opposition as a primary theme, though not out of the context of such other notions as being, relation, one and many, same and other, or identity and difference. They are Plato, Aristotle, Kant, and Hegel. It should not be surprising that the same authors are the principal figures in the chapter on DIALECTIC. Their disagreement about the nature or meaning of dialectic has a parallel here in their conflicting theories of opposition.

SOCRATES ARGUES, in the *Protagoras*, for the unity of virtue by using the principle that "everything has one opposite and not more than one." If wisdom is the opposite of folly, and if it also appears that folly is opposed by temperance, then either wisdom and temperance are the same, or a thing may have more than one opposite. Protagoras reluctantly accepts the first alternative; he is apparently unwilling to re-open the question concerning the pairing of opposites. But the question is reopened by others. It is one of the great problems in the theory of opposition, relevant to the distinction of different kinds of opposites.

The problem can most readily be stated in terms of the logical processes of division and definition. On the hypothesis that opposites always come in pairs, every class can be divided into two sub-classes which not only exclude each other, but also exhaust the membership of the divided class. Such division is called dichotomy. Many of the Platonic dialogues—notably the *Sophist* and the *Statesman*—exemplify the method of dichotomous division, used as a device for constructing definitions. The object to be defined, the character of the statesman or the sophist, is finally caught in the net of classification when, division after division having been made, two sub-classes are reached which leave no other possibilities open. The thing is either one or the other.

In the *Sophist* a preliminary exercise is undertaken in the method of division as preparation for the use of this method to define the sophist. It will serve us here as an example of dichotomy. All the arts are first divided into two kinds, the productive and the acquisitive; then the acquisitive arts are divided into those making voluntary exchanges and those which obtain goods by coercion; the coercive divides into fighting and hunting according to the alternatives of open or secret attack; hunting into the hunting of the lifeless and the living; hunting of the living into hunting of swimming or walking animals; the hunting of swimming animals into the hunting of winged animals and the hunting of water animals; the hunting of water animals into opposite methods of catching fish, with further sub-divisions made until the art of angling can be defined as an acquisitive art which, being coercive, is a form of hunting, distinguished from other forms of hunting by the character of its object—animals which swim in water rather than air—and by the method used to catch them—hooks or barbs rather than nets or baskets.

Aristotle objects to this process of division as a way of defining things. "Some writers," he says, "propose to reach the definitions of the ultimate forms of animal life by bipartite division. But this method is often difficult, and often impracticable." For one thing, it tends to associate or dissociate natural groups arbitrarily, *e.g.*, the classification of birds with water animals, or of some birds with fish and some birds with land animals. "If such natural groups are not to be broken up, the method of dichotomy cannot be employed, for it necessarily involves such breaking up and dislocation."

Aristotle also calls attention to the fact that the method of dichotomy often uses negative terms in order to make an exhaustive division into two and only two sub-classes. But the class which is formed by a negative characterization cannot be further sub-divided. "There can be no specific forms of a negation, of featherless for instance or of footless, as there are of feathered and of footed." It is impossible, Aristotle says, to "get at the ultimate specific forms of animal life by bifurcate division." He therefore proposes a method of defining by genus and difference, according to which it is possible in biological classification to sub-divide a genus into more than two species. To avoid sub-division into two and only two, that which differentiates each species from the others within the same genus must be some positive characteristic.

As ALTERNATIVE methods of definition, dichotomous division and the differentiation of species within a genus are discussed in the chapter on DEFINITION. Here we are concerned with the problem of the number of opposites produced by the exhaustive division of a class or kind. For example, how many species of color are there? If the primary colors are more than two, it would appear that each primary color has more than one opposite, since the same object at the same time and in the same respect cannot be both red and yellow, red and green, green and yellow. But Aristotle seems to restrict the notion of contrariety to pairs of opposite qualities. "Red, yellow, and such colors, though qualities, have no contraries," he says. Whether or not he would have regarded them as contraries if he had been acquainted with the chromatic series of the spectrum, remains a conjecture.

To find a single opposite for red, it is necessary to employ the negative term 'not-red.' But then another difficulty arises which Aristotle recognizes when he calls the negative term "indefinite" and which Kant discusses when he treats the infinity of the negative. The not-red includes more than other colors which are not red, such as green and yellow. It includes everything in the universe, colored or colorless, which is *not* red, *e.g.*, happiness or atoms or poetry.

Perfect dichotomy can be achieved by using positive and negative terms as opposites, or what Aristotle sometimes calls "contradictory terms"—such as man and not-man or just and not-just. But the class which is thus divided is absolutely indeterminate. It is the universe, everything, the infinite. It is necessary, furthermore, to distinguish between the opposition of 'just' and 'not-just' and the opposition of 'just' and 'unjust.' The term 'unjust' is the contrary rather than the contradictory of 'just,' for these opposites apply only to men, or laws, or acts; only certain kinds of things are either just or unjust, and that is why it is said that contraries are always opposites within a genus or a definite kind. In contrast, 'not-just' is the contradictory rather than the contrary of 'just,' for these opposites apply to everything in the universe; everything is either the kind of thing to which just and unjust apply or it is the kind of thing to which neither of these terms apply, and so it is the not-just.

In addition to separating contraries (both of which are positive terms) from contradictory opposites (one of which is a positive, the other a negative term), Aristotle distinguishes two sorts of contraries. On the one hand, such contraries as odd and even exhaustively divide a limited class (*e.g.*, integral numbers): on the other hand, such contraries as white and black represent the extremes of a continuous series of shades, in which any degree of grayness can be considered as the opposite of either extreme or of a darker or a lighter gray.

There are still other kinds of opposite pairs, according to Aristotle, such as the terms 'double' and 'half,' which have the peculiarity of implying each other; or the terms 'blindness' and 'sight,' which are opposite conditions of the same subject. In this last case, one of the opposites naturally belongs to a certain kind of thing, and the other represents a loss of that natural property or trait. It is therefore called a "privation."

Considering these various modes of opposition, Aristotle proposes a fourfold classification of opposite terms: *correlative* opposites, like double and half; *contrary* opposites, like odd and even, white and black, just and unjust; the opposites of *possession* and *privation*, such as sight and blindness; the opposites of *affirmation* and *negation*, such as man and not-man, or just and not-just. He discusses the special characteristics of each type of opposition, but it is only contrariety which he thinks requires further subdivision.

Even though both are always positive terms, some contraries, like odd and even, exhaust a definite class, just as positive and negative opposites exhaust the infinite. They admit of no intermediate terms and hence they differ from contraries like white and black. White and black are extreme limits of a continuous series and thus permit an indefinite number of intermediates which fall between them. Things which differ only in degree are like the sort of contraries which find their place in a continuous series. Things which differ in kind are like the sort of contraries between which no intermediates are possible.

One of the great problems of classification, especially with respect to living organisms, is whether the diverse species which fall within a single genus differ in kind or only in degree. The answer would seem to depend on whether the several species are related by one or the other sort of contrariety. As the chapter on EVOLUTION indicates, the basic meaning of the word "species" changes when the possibility of "intermediate forms" is rejected or admitted. When a class is divided by contraries without intermediates, the genus can have only two species, as for example, the division of animals into brutes and men. When a genus is divided into more than two sub-classes, (*e.g.*, the division of vertebrates into fish, amphibians, reptiles, birds, and mammals), it would seem to follow that the species are like points in a continuous series and admit the possibility of intermediate types.

According to Darwin's conception of species, their contrariety always tends to take the latter form. Aristotle, on the other hand, seems to use the word "species" in two distinct senses which correspond to the two kinds of contrariety—with and without intermediates. "A thing's difference from that from which it differs in species," he writes, "must be a contrariety." But though contrariety is always a "complete difference," the fact that "contraries are so-called in several senses" leads him to observe that "their modes of completeness will answer to the various modes of contrariety which attach to the contraries."

THE LOGICAL OPPOSITION of propositions or judgments depends in part on the opposition of terms or concepts. If contrary things are said about the same subject of discourse (*i.e.*, if the same number is called odd and even, or the same act is called cowardly and courageous, or the same animal is called a bird and a mammal), pairs of contrary statements are made, of which both cannot be true. But it does not seem to follow that one of the two statements must be true. Both can be false. In the examples given, the number may be a fraction and neither odd nor even; the act may be foolhardy and neither courageous nor cowardly; the animal may be a reptile and neither bird nor mammal.

This characteristic of contrary statements—the impossibility of their both being true combined with the possibility of their both being false—can also be found, according to Aristotle, in propositions which have the same subject and do not contain contrary terms as predicates. The propositions 'All men are white' and 'No men are white' cannot both be true, but they can both be false. The contrariety of these two statements, which can be taken as typifying the opposition of all universal affirmations and negations, does not depend on contrary predicates, but on the opposed meanings of 'all are' and 'none is.'

Keeping the terms constant and varying only the quality and quantity of the propositions, Aristotle formulates two other typical modes of opposition between pairs of statements. When both statements are particular or limited, but one is affirmative and the other negative, both cannot be false though both can be true, *e.g.*, 'Some men are white' and 'Some men are not white.' This pair of opposites Aristotle calls "sub-contraries." When one statement is universal and affirmative and the other is particular and negative—or when one is universal and negative, the other particular and affirmative—the two propositions are, according to Aristotle, contradictory. Contradiction is the most complete type of opposition, for contradictory statements are opposite in both quality and quantity. Of a pair of contradictories, both cannot be true and both cannot be false. One must be true and the other false, *e.g.*, it must be true either that all men are white or that some men are not white.

The formal scheme of opposite statements, traditionally known as "the square of opposition," appears to exhaust all possibilities. It indicates, moreover, that every statement may have two opposites, a contradictory and either a contrary or a sub-contrary; for example, 'All men are white' is contradicted by 'Some men are not white' and opposed in a merely contrary fashion by 'No men are white.' The latter is a weaker form of opposition since it permits the dilemma to be avoided by the truth of a third statement, that some men are white and some are not. The dilemma set up by a contradiction cannot be avoided in this way.

The propositions 'God exists' and 'God does not exist,' or 'The world had a beginning' and 'The world did not have a beginning,' constitute contradictions from which there seems to be no escape. It would seem to make a difference, therefore, in facing the great controversies in the tradition of western thought, to know whether the opposite views which men have taken on fundamental issues are genuine contradictions, requiring everyone to take sides, or whether they are merely contrary positions. In the latter alternative, the inconsistency of the theories prevents us from agreeing with both parties to the dispute, but it does not require us to agree with either, for contrary doctrines never exhaust the possibilities. Between such extreme positions, for example, as that everything is in flux and nothing changes, both of which cannot be true, the truth may lie in the doctrine that some elements of permanence are involved in all change; or it may be in the theory of a realm of becoming that lacks permanence and a realm of being that is free from change.

One of the basic controversies in the tradition of the great books concerns opposition itself. Is the principle of contradiction the ultimate test of the truth of judgments and reasoning? Is the truth of indemonstrable propositions or axioms certified by the self-contradiction of their contradictories? For example, is the truth of the proposition 'The whole is greater than the part' made necessary by the impossibility of the contradictory statement 'The whole is *not* greater than the part,' on the theory that this latter statement is impossible because it is self-contradictory? And when a conclusion is demonstrated by propositions which seem to be necessarily true, must not the contradictory of this conclusion be false—or at least be incapable of demonstration by propositions which are also necessarily true?

On both these questions Kant and Aristotle seem to be opposed. According to Aristotle, no truths are necessary or axiomatic unless their contradictories are self-contradictory. But Kant makes a distinction between analytical and synthetical propositions (discussed in the chapter on Judgment) and in terms of it he restricts the principle of contradiction to serving as a criterion of truth for analytical judgments alone. "In an analytical judgement," he writes, "whether negative or affirmative, its truth can always be tested by the principle of contradiction." But though we must admit, Kant continues, that "the principle of contradiction is the general and altogether sufficient principle of all analytical knowledge, beyond this its authority and utility, as a sufficient criterion of truth, must not be allowed to extend." In "the synthetical part of our knowledge, we must no doubt take great care never to offend against that inviolable principle, but we ought never to expect from it any help with regard to the truth of this kind of knowledge."

The reason, Kant explains, is that "in forming an analytical judgement I remain within a given concept, while predicating something of it. If what I predicate is affirmative, I only predicate of that concept what is already contained in it; if it is negative, I only exclude from it the opposite of it." For example, if the meaning of the concept 'whole' involves 'being greater than a part,' self-contradiction results from denying that the whole is greater than a part.

"In forming synthetical judgements, on the contrary, I have to go beyond a given concept, in order to bring something together with it, which is totally different from what is contained in it. Here," Kant declares, "we have neither the relation of identity nor of contradiction, and nothing in the judgement itself by which we can discover its truth or its falsehood"; for example, the judgment that everything which happens has a cause. The truth of such synthetical judgments, according to Kant, is as necessary and as *a priori* as the truth of analytical judgments, but the principle of contradiction does not provide their ground or validation.

For Aristotle, in contrast, those propositions which do not derive necessity from the principle of contradiction belong to the sphere of opinion rather than to the domain of knowledge. They can be asserted as probable only, not as true or false. In the domain of knowledge, it is impossible to construct valid arguments for contradictory conclusions, for if one must be true and the other false, one can be validly demonstrated and the other cannot be demonstrated at all. But in the sphere of opinion, dialectical opposition is possible. Because the contradictory of a probable statement is itself also probable, probable arguments can be constructed on the opposite sides of every dialectical issue.

For Kant dialectical issues do not consist in a conflict of opposed probabilities. Far from setting probable reasoning against probable reasoning, dialectical opposition consists in what appear to be *demonstrations* of contradictory propositions. For example, in that part of the *Critique of Pure Reason* devoted to the Transcendental Dialectic, Kant presents opposed arguments which look like demonstrations of contradictory propositions—such as the thesis that "the world has a beginning in time" and its antithesis that "the world has no beginning"; or the thesis that "there exists an absolutely necessary being" and its antithesis that "there nowhere exists an absolutely necessary being." These are two of the four issues which Kant calls the "antinomies of a transcendental dialectic."

Such issues, Aristotle would agree with Kant, do not belong to the sphere of opinion or probability. But Kant would not agree with Aristotle that such issues belong to the domain of science or certain knowledge. The problem of the world's beginning or eternity, for example, is one which Aristotle treats in his *Physics* and appears to think is solved by the demonstration that motion can have neither beginning nor end. The problem of the existence of a necessary being is one which Aristotle treats in his *Metaphysics* and which he also appears to think is capable of a demonstrative solution. For him, therefore, both are problems to which scientific answers can be given. But for Kant the demonstration of the antitheses, or contradictory propositions, in both cases is as cogent as the demonstrations of the theses; and therefore, since we know that both of a pair of contradictory propositions cannot be validly demonstrated, we must conclude that the arguments advanced are only counterfeit demonstrations, or as Kant says, "illusory." He calls these demonstrations "dialectical," and the issues they attempt to resolve "antinomies," precisely because he thinks the reasoning goes beyond the limits of scientific thought and because he thinks the issues are problems reason cannot ever solve.

With respect to conclusions affirming or denying matters beyond experience, the antinomies can be interpreted either as showing that contradictory arguments are equally sound or as showing that they are equally faulty. On either interpretation, Kant and Aristotle seem to be opposed on the applicability of the principle of contradiction to conflicting arguments and conclusions (except, of course, those which are merely probable). This difference between them accords with the difference in their conceptions of science and dialectic, and in their theories of the scope and conditions of valid knowledge.

THE OPPOSITION between Kant and Aristotle may not present the only alternatives. Hegel's theory of the dialectical process seems to offer a third. Where Aristotle appears to think that all contradictions must be resolved in favor of one of the opposites, and where Kant appears to think that some contradictions cannot be resolved at all, Hegel proposes the resolution of all contradictions, not by a choice between them, but by a synthesis uniting the opposites and reconciling their differences.

According to Aristotle, opposites exclude one another in existence as well as in thought. A thing cannot both exist and not exist at the same time; nor in any particular respect can it simultaneously both be and not be of a certain sort. Only with the passage of time and in the course of change can opposites be realized, when a thing passes from being to non-being, or gives up one attribute in order to assume its contrary.

The difference for Aristotle between becoming and being (or between change and complete actuality) seems to be that the one includes and the other excludes opposites. Change cannot occur except as one opposite comes into existence *while* the other passes away. But opposites cannot co-exist with complete actuality. So far as reality consists of co-existent actualities, it is limited by the principle of contradiction—as a principle of being—to those which are not contradictory. All possibilities cannot, therefore, be simultaneously realized, for, as Leibnitz states the principle, all possibilities are not "compossible."

According to Hegel, every finite phase of reality—everything except the Absolute Idea itself—has its contradictory, as real as itself, and co-existent with it. Contradictories imply one another and require each other, almost as correlative opposites do. Whatever is partial and incomplete presupposes something which is partial and incomplete in an opposite respect. The opposition between them can therefore be overcome by a synthesis which includes them both, and which complements each by uniting it with the other.

For example, the category of being is opposed by non-being. These opposites both exclude and imply one another. They are in a sense even identical with one another, insofar as the notion of being contains the notion of non-being, and, conversely, the notion of non-being, the notion of being. Except for the Absolute, everything which is also is not, and everything which is not also is. The apparent contradiction involved in this simultaneous application of opposite categories to the same thing is overcome by a third category, becoming, which is the synthesis of being and non-being. Being and non-being are united in becoming.

This reconciling of opposites, by their union in a more inclusive whole embracing both, typifies the Hegelian dialectic of thesis, antithesis, and synthesis. The motion repeats itself as the synthesis of one contradiction faces its own opposite and requires a higher synthesis to overcome the contradiction it has generated. Thus every opposition in reality or thought is a phase in the progressive realization of the Absolute, wherein all contradictions are resolved.

In Hegel's *Philosophy of History* and in his theory of the development of the state in the *Philosophy of Right*, the dialectical process is exemplified at every stage of progress. The conflict of interdependent opposites—of opposite classes or forces in society, of opposite political institutions or principles—calls for a resolution which shall unite rather than exclude the opposites.

Considering the division of labor, for example, Hegel writes: "When men are dependent on one another and reciprocally related in their work and the satisfaction of their needs, subjective self-seeking turns into a contribution to the satisfaction of the needs of everyone else. That is to say, by a dialectical advance, subjective self-seeking turns into the mediation of the particular through the universal, with the result that each man in earning, producing, and enjoying on his own account is *eo ipso* producing and earning for the enjoyment of everyone else." The opposition between the particular good of each individual and the universal good of all is thus overcome by that advance in social organization which is the division of labor.

Each of the stages of world history is, according to Hegel, "the presence of a necessary moment in the Idea of the world mind." But the world mind itself is a synthesis, a resolution of the conflicting opposites—of the various national minds "which are wholly restricted on account of their particularity. Their deeds and destinies in their reciprocal relations to one another are the dialectic of the finitude of these minds, and out of it arises the universal mind, the mind of the world, free from all restrictions, producing itself as that which exercises its right —and its right is the highest right of all—over these finite minds in the 'history of the world which is the world's court of judgment.'"

OUTLINE OF TOPICS

1. Opposition in logic

 1*a*. Kinds of opposition among terms: correlation, contrariety, privation, negation

 1*b*. The analysis of contrariety: the kinds of terms which can be contrary; contrariety with and without intermediates between extremes

 1*c*. The exclusiveness of opposites as a principle of logical division

  (1) Dichotomous division: positive and negative terms

  (2) Division of a genus by differentia: the contrariety of species

 1*d*. The opposition of propositions or judgments

  (1) The square of opposition: contradictories, contraries, subcontraries

  (2) Modal opposition: the necessary and the contingent

 1*e*. Opposition in reasoning and proof: the conflict of dialectical arguments; the antinomies of a transcendental dialectic

2. The metaphysical significance of opposition

 2*a*. Opposition as limiting coexistence: noncontradiction as a principle of being

 2*b*. Opposites in the realm of being, mind, or spirit: the one and the many; the dialectical triad of thesis, antithesis, and synthesis

 2*c*. Nonbeing as the opposite of being

 2*d*. The opposition of good and evil in the world and in relation to God

 2*e*. The reconciliation of opposites in the divine nature: the synthesis of all contraries in the Absolute

3. Opposition in the realm of physical nature

 3*a*. The contraries as principles of change

 3*b*. Contrariety of quality in the theory of the elements or humours

 3*c*. The opposition of motion and rest, and of contrary motions

 3*d*. The opposition of physical forces and its resolution

 3*e*. The struggle for existence: the competition of species

4. Opposition or conflict in the psychological and moral order

 4*a*. The conflict of reason and the passions

 4*b*. Conflicting emotions, humours, instincts, or habits

 4*c*. Conflict as the cause of repression and as a factor in neurotic disorders

 4*d*. The conflict of loves and loyalties, desires and duties

 4*e*. Conflict in human life: opposed types of men and modes of life

5. Conflict in society and history

 5*a*. Competition in commerce and the rivalry of factions in politics

 5*b*. The class war: the opposition of the rich and the poor, the propertied and the propertyless, capital and labor, producers and consumers

 5*c*. The inevitability of civil strife and war between states

 5*d*. Opposition or strife as a productive principle or source of progress

REFERENCES

References are listed by volume number (in bold type), author's name, and page number. Bible references are to book, chapter, and verse of the Authorized King James version of the Bible. The abbreviation "esp" calls the reader's attention to one or more especially relevant parts of a whole reference; "passim" signifies that the topic is discussed intermittently rather than continuously in the work or passage cited. Where the work as a whole is relevant to the topic, the page numbers refer to the entire work. For general guidance in the use of *The Great Ideas,* consult the Preface.

1. Opposition in logic

1*a*. Kinds of opposition among terms: correlation, contrariety, privation, negation

7 PLATO, 49–50, 242–245
8 ARISTOTLE, 16–19, 70–71, 159–160, 173, 187–188, 201–202, 523–524, 539, 582
19 AQUINAS, 103–104, 699–700
23 HOBBES, 57

1*b*. The analysis of contrariety: the kinds of terms which can be contrary; contrariety with and without intermediates between extremes

7 PLATO, 21–22, 83–84, 163, 350–351
8 ARISTOTLE, 8, 10, 15, 17, 19, 158–159, 201, 531–532
9 ARISTOTLE, 407
17 PLOTINUS, 292–293
19 AQUINAS, 721–722
24 RABELAIS, 12–13

1*c*. The exclusiveness of opposites as a principle of logical division

1*c*(1) Dichotomous division: positive and negative terms

7 PLATO, 134, 552–561, 577–608 esp 595, 610–613
8 ARISTOTLE, 64–65, 125
9 ARISTOTLE, 165–167
42 KANT, 43–44

1*c*(2) Division of a genus by differentia: the contrariety of species

7 PLATO, 548–549
8 ARISTOTLE, 5, 7–8, 132–133, 171–172, 177, 178, 196–199, 261–262, 539, 546, 561–562, 568–570, 585–586
9 ARISTOTLE, 165–168
17 PLOTINUS, 285–286, 291
19 AQUINAS, 17–18, 257–258, 381–382, 611–612, 697–702, 746, 774–775
20 AQUINAS, 15–18, 54–55, 115–118, 479–480, 710–711
42 KANT, 193–200
53 JAMES, 344–345

1*d*. The opposition of propositions or judgments

1*d*(1) The square of opposition: contradictories, contraries, subcontraries

8 ARISTOTLE, 19, 26, 29–31
20 AQUINAS, 68–69
42 KANT, 64–65, 156–157, 174

1*d*(2) Modal opposition: the necessary and the contingent

8 ARISTOTLE, 32–35
31 DESCARTES, 22
42 KANT, 39–41, 193–200
53 JAMES, 861

1*e*. Opposition in reasoning and proof: the conflict of dialectical arguments; the antinomies of a transcendental dialectic

7 PLATO, 65–84, 226–227, 350–351, 491–511, 558, 571–574
8 ARISTOTLE, 84–85, 148, 234
9 ARISTOTLE, 645, 647–648
19 AQUINAS, 477–478
20 AQUINAS, 765–766
25 MONTAIGNE, 446–449
31 DESCARTES, 2
35 LOCKE, 369
35 HUME, 488–491
42 KANT, 120–173, 174–177, 187–192, 200–209, 219–220, 231–232, 260–261, 283–284, 291–292, 296, 302, 331–337, 340–342, 540–542, 562–578
43 MILL, 274–293 passim
54 FREUD, 545

2. The metaphysical significance of opposition

2*a*. Opposition as limiting coexistence: noncontradiction as a principle of being

7 PLATO, 244–246, 504
8 ARISTOTLE, 34–35, 515, 524–532, 577, 587, 590–592
19 AQUINAS, 613–614
20 AQUINAS, 221–223
31 SPINOZA, 398, 399
35 LOCKE, 316–317
42 KANT, 99–101, 179–182
53 JAMES, 302

2*b*. Opposites in the realm of being, mind, or spirit: the one and the many; the dialectical triad of thesis, antithesis, and synthesis

7 PLATO, 368–373, 392–394, 486–511, 534–536, 561–577, 615–617
8 ARISTOTLE, 34–35, 522–524, 581–586, 589, 619, 620
17 PLOTINUS, 91–92, 119–129, 136–138, 208–251, 310–312, 353–355
19 AQUINAS, 47–48
31 DESCARTES, 51–54, 77–81, 98, 130, 133, 152–155, 231–232
42 KANT, 7–8, 173–177
46 HEGEL, 18, 41, 112–114, 156–157, 279–280, 286–287, 333–334
53 JAMES, 238

2*c*. Nonbeing as the opposite of being

7 PLATO, 507–511, 561–577
8 ARISTOTLE, 268, 522
17 PLOTINUS, 50–57, 109–111
18 AUGUSTINE, 343
19 AQUINAS, 68–70, 83, 96, 537

2*d*. The opposition of good and evil in the world and in relation to God

7 PLATO, 322, 530–531
8 ARISTOTLE, 503
12 EPICTETUS, 118–120, 129–131, 134–138
17 PLOTINUS, 27–34, 85–86, 88–89
18 AUGUSTINE, 25, 32–33, 44–45, 47–50, 331–332, 343–348
19 AQUINAS, 259–268, 780–781
20 AQUINAS, 137–138
21 DANTE, 64–65, 126
23 HOBBES, 160–161
32 MILTON, 33–56, 188–195, 262–264
40 GIBBON, 81
42 KANT, 316–317
46 HEGEL, 237–238
47 GOETHE, 284–288
48 MELVILLE, 1–420
52 DOSTOEVSKY, 120–126, 308–309, 341–345

2*e*. The reconciliation of opposites in the divine nature: the synthesis of all contraries in the Absolute

19 AQUINAS, 14–20
21 DANTE, 157
31 SPINOZA, 360–361, 373–374
46 HEGEL, 156–160, 245, 306

3. Opposition in the realm of physical nature

3*a*. The contraries as principles of change

7 PLATO, 165–166, 226–228, 243–246, 519–520, 762–764
8 ARISTOTLE, 8–9, 18–19, 263–268, 297, 306–307, 316–317, 361, 364, 368, 399–405, 413–423, 428–433, 512, 531, 569, 584, 596, 598–599, 646, 710–711
9 ARISTOTLE, 264
11 NICOMACHUS, 839–840
14 PLUTARCH, 482
17 PLOTINUS, 293–294
19 AQUINAS, 305–306, 322–323, 699–700, 724–725
28 HARVEY, 408
31 SPINOZA, 431–434
42 KANT, 27, 76–83, 91–93
46 HEGEL, 178

3*b*. Contrariety of quality in the theory of the elements or humours

7 PLATO, 155–157, 462–464
8 ARISTOTLE, 428–431, 435–436, 507, 674–689 passim
9 ARISTOTLE, 177–179, 306–308
10 HIPPOCRATES, 4–7
10 GALEN, 191–199
12 LUCRETIUS, 66
19 AQUINAS, 345–347, 484–485
28 HARVEY, 435
30 BACON, 114–115

3*c*. The opposition of motion and rest, and of contrary motions

7 PLATO, 350–351, 453, 460, 567–574, 587–589 esp 587
8 ARISTOTLE, 21, 310–312, 362
10 GALEN, 167
16 COPERNICUS, 517–520
17 PLOTINUS, 295–297
19 AQUINAS, 104–105, 283–284, 371, 644–646, 799–800
23 HOBBES, 50
30 BACON, 163
31 SPINOZA, 378–379
34 NEWTON, 5, 14

3*d*. The opposition of physical forces and its resolution

11 ARCHIMEDES, 502–504
16 KEPLER, 696–972
20 AQUINAS, 985–989
28 GILBERT, 11–12, 38–39, 52–54, 59, 65–67
28 GALILEO, 209–210, 224–225, 243–249 passim
34 NEWTON, 15–16, 111–130
45 LAVOISIER, 9–12
45 FARADAY, 691–692, 788–793, 817

3*e*. The struggle for existence: the competition of species

6 HERODOTUS, 112–113
7 PLATO, 44–45
9 ARISTOTLE, 134–136
36 SWIFT, 79–80
38 ROUSSEAU, 334–337, 348–349
39 SMITH, 34
49 DARWIN, 32–39 esp 32–33, 49–53, 182, 233–234, 596
54 FREUD, 791

4. Opposition or conflict in the psychological and moral order

4*a*. The conflict of reason and the passions

7 Plato, 120, 128–129, 224–226, 346–355, 416, 425–427, 735–738
8 Aristotle, 666
9 Aristotle, 239, 348, 395–406
12 Epictetus, 161–162
12 Aurelius, 257–261, 269–270, 283–284
13 Virgil, 167–186
18 Augustine, 40–43, 55–60, 376, 380, 385–387
19 Aquinas, 430–431, 507–508, 658–659, 664–665, 690–692, 767–769, 824–825
20 Aquinas, 56–57, 144–152, 160–161, 627–628
21 Dante, 2–4, 7–8
22 Chaucer, 503–504
23 Hobbes, 58, 141
25 Montaigne, 20–22, 36–41, 165–167, 200–205, 273–276, 350–354, 486–495
26 Shakespeare, 408
27 Shakespeare, 49, 113–115, 212, 264–266
30 Bacon, 55, 67
31 Spinoza, 442–447, 450, 452–458
32 Milton, 243–246, 321
33 Pascal, 242–243
35 Locke, 192, 392
36 Sterne, 239–243
42 Kant, 282–283, 303–304
46 Hegel, 312–313, 321
47 Goethe, 79–82, 93–103
52 Dostoevsky, 50–62
53 James, 799–808, 816–819
54 Freud, 702, 715–716, 800–801, 838–839, 843–845

4*b*. Conflicting emotions, humours, instincts, or habits

9 Aristotle, 351–355, 623–636 passim
12 Lucretius, 58
18 Augustine, 379–385
19 Aquinas, 724–725, 758–759, 774–777
20 Aquinas, 19–21, 105–107
24 Rabelais, 8
25 Montaigne, 105–107
26 Shakespeare, 304
31 Spinoza, 401–402, 411–412, 424–429, 449
46 Hegel, 118
47 Goethe, 11–12, 26–28, 32–41
49 Darwin, 311–314, 318–319
50 Marx, 293–294
51 Tolstoy, 235–238, 292–296, 560–562
52 Dostoevsky, 95–100, 200–201
53 James, 704–706, 717–718, 734–735
54 Freud, 414–421, 590–593, 615–616, 640, 651–654, 659, 677–678, 708–712, 789–791, 846–851

4*c*. Conflict as the cause of repression and as a factor in neurotic disorders

54 Freud, 6–9, 81–84, 117, 377–382, 406–407, 422–427, 566–569, 589–591, 593–594, 611–624, 633–635, 690–691, 712–715 passim, 718–754

4*d*. The conflict of loves and loyalties, desires and duties

Old Testament: *Genesis,* 22:1–12 / *Judges,* 11:30–40 / *Ruth,* 1 / *II Samuel,* 11–13 / *I Kings,* 11:1–13
Apocrypha: *Susanna,* 19–24
New Testament: *Matthew,* 10:34–37 / *Romans,* 6:12–14; 7–8; 13:13–14 / *Galatians,* 5:16–26 / *James,* 1:12–17; 4:1–2
4 Homer, 43–45
5 Aeschylus, 38–39, 54, 78–79
5 Sophocles, 131–142, 182–195
5 Euripides, 392–393
5 Aristophanes, 583–599
6 Herodotus, 197, 201–202, 223
7 Plato, 153–157
12 Epictetus, 223–224
13 Virgil, 176–177
14 Plutarch, 77–79, 152, 196–198
17 Plotinus, 100–101
20 Aquinas, 499–500
21 Dante, 68
22 Chaucer, 88–120, 351–366
23 Hobbes, 240, 245–246
25 Montaigne, 381–388, 467–470
26 Shakespeare, 238, 239, 268–272, 285–319, 348–349, 583–584
27 Shakespeare, 103–141, 210–211, 289, 311–350, 377–379
29 Cervantes, 120–137
32 Milton, 358
33 Pascal, 193
37 Fielding, 77–80
48 Melville, 394–397
49 Darwin, 310–314, 318–319
51 Tolstoy, 273–274, 301–302, 327–329, 490–493, 520–521
52 Dostoevsky, 282–283, 402–404
53 James, 199–201, 293, 791–798
54 Freud, 467–476 passim, 694–695, 757–759, 764–766, 780–781, 783–789, 792–802 passim

4*e*. Conflict in human life: opposed types of men and modes of life

Old Testament: *Genesis,* 4:1–8
Apocrypha: *Ecclesiasticus,* 33:10–15
New Testament: *Matthew,* 5–7; 25 / *Mark,* 4:1–20 / *Ephesians* / *I Thessalonians,* 3:11–4:12 / *II Timothy,* 3 / *I Peter,* 2:1–5:11
5 Euripides, 225–236, 287–288
5 Aristophanes, 499–502
6 Herodotus, 232–233, 264
6 Thucydides, 366–367
7 Plato, 223–225, 340–341, 401–427, 528–531, 605–639, 690
9 Aristotle, 340–341, 350, 431–434, 636–639
10 Hippocrates, 14–19
12 Lucretius, 15, 30–31, 40–44, 75

12 EPICTETUS, 108, 150–151, 190–191, 195–201, 235–237
14 PLUTARCH, 254–256
17 PLOTINUS, 10–11, 246–247
18 AUGUSTINE, 663
19 AQUINAS, 512–513, 655–656, 815–816
20 AQUINAS, 506, 531–532, 570–584, 606–607, 1063–1064
22 CHAUCER, 159–174, 413–414
23 MACHIAVELLI, 25
23 HOBBES, 84, 279
24 RABELAIS, 62–63, 189–191
25 MONTAIGNE, 43–47, 91–98, 150–151, 159–162, 167–169, 278–279, 281–284, 406–408, 492–493, 524
26 SHAKESPEARE, 254–256, 406–466, 467–502, 506–507, 569–572, 603, 617
27 SHAKESPEARE, 8–11, 29–72, 103–141, 208–213, 311–350, 395–396, 413–415
29 CERVANTES, 1–429
30 BACON, 18, 69–77, 109, 111–112
31 SPINOZA, 395–450 passim
33 PASCAL, 195–204
38 ROUSSEAU, 416–417
40 GIBBON, 191–194, 409–410, 593–599, 632–633
43 MILL, 290–291, 293–302, 346–348
40 HEGEL, 48–49, 137, 192–194, 318–319
47 GOETHE, 2–12, 15–16, 128–130
48 MELVILLE, 1–420
50 MARX-ENGELS, 415–434
51 TOLSTOY, 131–135, 238–243, 260–262, 358–365, 403–406, 426–430, 480–482, 515–521, 577–578
52 DOSTOEVSKY, 1–88, 146–170, 337–346
53 JAMES, 199–204
54 FREUD, 246–247, 501–504, 697–717, 771–802, 830–853

5. Conflict in society and history

5*a*. Competition in commerce and the rivalry of factions in politics

6 THUCYDIDES, 434–438, 458–459, 502–504, 564–593
9 ARISTOTLE, 420–421, 511–512
14 PLUTARCH, 68, 126, 482
15 TACITUS, 97, 224–225
23 HOBBES, 121, 148–151
25 MONTAIGNE, 42
26 SHAKESPEARE, 1–148, 434–502
27 SHAKESPEARE, 108–109
38 MONTESQUIEU, 142–143
39 SMITH, 23–27, 51–62, 192–201, 225–228, 269–271, 420
40 GIBBON, 652–655
41 GIBBON, 572
43 FEDERALIST, 42–43, 49–51, 185–187
43 MILL, 312–313, 366–370, 376
46 HEGEL, 102, 275
50 MARX, 130, 171–176, 308–311, 316–317, 371–377, 379–383

5*b*. The class war: the opposition of the rich and the poor, the propertied and the propertyless, capital and labor, producers and consumers

5 EURIPIDES, 260
6 THUCYDIDES, 463–465, 467, 482–483, 520, 524–525, 533, 564–593
7 PLATO, 343, 405–416
9 ARISTOTLE, 461–463, 465, 478–479, 489–491, 495–497, 506–508, 519, 553–555
14 PLUTARCH, 36–37, 68–71, 117–121, 176–184, 648–656, 674–689
23 MACHIAVELLI, 14
27 SHAKESPEARE, 351–353
36 SWIFT, 154–155
38 MONTESQUIEU, 77–83
38 ROUSSEAU, 381–382, 429
39 SMITH, 28, 61–62, 239–240, 279–288, 309–311
40 GIBBON, 144, 501–502
41 GIBBON, 574–582
43 FEDERALIST, 113–115
43 MILL, 345–346, 369–370
46 HEGEL, 140–141, 250, 287–288, 295–297, 335–336, 356–357
50 MARX, 6–11, 63, 111–146, 209–215, 262, 282–286, 294–295, 354–368
50 MARX-ENGELS, 415–434
52 DOSTOEVSKY, 165–166
54 FREUD, 882

5*c*. The inevitability of civil strife and war between states

5 ARISTOTLE, 526–541
6 THUCYDIDES, 384–386, 436–438, 518–520
7 PLATO, 640–641, 732
9 ARISTOTLE, 531, 535, 538
23 MACHIAVELLI, 21, 32
23 HOBBES, 84–86, 114
36 SWIFT, 76–78
38 MONTESQUIEU, 61–62
38 ROUSSEAU, 355
42 KANT, 452–458
43 FEDERALIST, 33–53 passim, 110, 132–135
46 HEGEL, 278–279
51 TOLSTOY, 342–344
54 FREUD, 755–757, 766, 787–788

5*d*. Opposition or strife as a productive principle or source of progress

18 AUGUSTINE, 129–618
23 HOBBES, 100
38 ROUSSEAU, 338–339
39 SMITH, 170–173
40 GIBBON, 633
43 MILL, 387
46 HEGEL, 107, 178–179, 187–188, 274–275, 279–281, 321, 333–334, 346
49 DARWIN, 320–323, 328, 350–351
50 MARX, 377–378
50 MARX-ENGELS, 419–425
54 FREUD, 654, 882–884

CROSS-REFERENCES

For: Other considerations of the opposition of terms and propositions, or of opposition in reasoning and argument, *see* DIALECTIC 3b–3d; IDEA 4c; JUDGMENT 7a; NECESSITY AND CONTINGENCY 4e(1); REASONING 5c; SAME AND OTHER 3a(2).

The distinction between dichotomous division and the differentiation of a genus as methods of definition, *see* DEFINITION 2a–2b.

Discussions of the law of contradiction as a principle of thought and of being, *see* LOGIC 1a; METAPHYSICS 3c; PRINCIPLE 1c; TRUTH 3c; and for the various ways in which dialectic is concerned with opposition, *see* DIALECTIC 3a–3d.

The opposition of being and nonbeing, one and many, same and other, *see* BEING 1; DIALECTIC 3a; ONE AND MANY 1a, 1c; SAME AND OTHER 2e; UNIVERSAL AND PARTICULAR 1.

The theory of synthesis or the reconciliation of opposites, *see* DIALECTIC 3d; HISTORY 4a(3); IDEA 1f; LIBERTY 6a; MIND 1f, 10f–10f(2); PROGRESS 1a; STATE 2a(3).

The role of opposition in nature, *see* CHANGE 2b, 4; ELEMENT 3b; EVOLUTION 5a; MECHANICS 6d(3); QUALITY 4a–4b.

Conflict in human nature and the life of man, *see* DESIRE 3d, 4a; DUTY 6, 8; EMOTION 4a; LOVE 3c; MAN 5–5a; MIND 9b; ONE AND MANY 3b(5); and for conflict in society and history, *see* DEMOCRACY 5b(4); LABOR 7c–7c(1); NECESSITY AND CONTINGENCY 5d; PROGRESS 1a; REVOLUTION 5a; STATE 5d–5d(2); WAR AND PEACE 2c, 7; WEALTH 4f.

ADDITIONAL READINGS

Listed below are works not included in *Great Books of the Western World*, but relevant to the idea and topics with which this chapter deals. These works are divided into two groups:

I. Works by authors represented in this collection.
II. Works by authors not represented in this collection.

For the date, place, and other facts concerning the publication of the works cited, consult the Bibliography of Additional Readings which follows the last chapter of *The Great Ideas*.

I.

KANT. *Prolegomena to Any Future Metaphysic*, par 2 (b, c)
HEGEL. *Science of Logic*, VOL I, BK II, SECT I, CH 2
——. *Logic*, CH 8, par 115–122
MARX. *The Poverty of Philosophy*

II.

ERIGENA. *De Divisione Naturae*, BK I
NICOLAS OF CUSA. *De Docta Ignorantia*
SUÁREZ. *Disputationes Metaphysicae*, IV (6), VI (9–10), XXVI (6), XLII (6), XLV
JOHN OF SAINT THOMAS. *Cursus Philosophicus Thomisticus, Ars Logica*, PART I, Q 7
J. G. FICHTE. *The Science of Knowledge*, PART III, A–D
W. HAMILTON. *Lectures on Metaphysics and Logic*, VOL II (14)
EMERSON. "Compensation," in *Essays*, I
PROUDHON. *The Philosophy of Misery*
LOTZE. *Logic*, BK I, CH 2 (c)
C. S. PEIRCE. *Collected Papers*, VOL I, par 322–336, 457–461
BOSANQUET. *Logic*, VOL I, CH 7
——. *Science and Philosophy*, 5
CROCE. *Logic as the Science of Pure Concept*, PART I, SECT I (6)
ROYCE. *The Principles of Logic*
BRADLEY. *Appearance and Reality*
——. *Essays on Truth and Reality*, CH 7–9
SHELDON. *Strife of Systems and Productive Duality*
M. R. COHEN. *Reason and Nature*, BK I, CH 4 (5)
OGDEN. *Opposition*
DEWEY. *Logic, the Theory of Inquiry*, CH 10
B. RUSSELL. *Introduction to Mathematical Philosophy*, CH 14
——. *An Inquiry into Meaning and Truth*, CH 20

Chapter 66: PHILOSOPHY

INTRODUCTION

THE difficulties which attend the consideration of any great idea—by philosophers or others—appear with peculiar force in the traditional discussion of philosophy itself. The word "philosophy" not only varies in its descriptive significance, now designating one part of learning, now another, and sometimes even an attitude of mind or a way of life; but it also varies as a term of evaluation. It is seldom used without expressing either praise or dispraise of the methods and accomplishments of philosophy, or of the calling and character of the philosopher.

On the descriptive side the meaning of the word ranges from a conception of philosophy which covers *all* branches of scientific knowledge and which contrasts philosophy with poetry, history, and religion, to a conception of philosophy in which the primary point is its contrast to science and its association with poetry and religion as works of vision, speculation, or belief rather than of knowledge.

On its evaluative side, the word "philosophy" sometimes eulogizes the love and search for truth, the pursuit and even the attainment of wisdom. At the other extreme, it derogates vain learning, idle disputation, and the dogmatism of unsupported opinion. At one time, the good name of the philosopher stands in contrast to the questionable reputation of the sophist. At another, "philosopher" carries almost the same invidious connotation as "sophist." The dismissal of philosophy as useless, or at best ornamental, in the practical affairs of society is sharply opposed to the vision of an ideal state which can come to pass only if philosophers are kings, or kings philosophers.

THESE SHIFTS IN the meaning of the words "philosophy" and "philosopher" record crises in the history of western thought. They reflect the characteristic formations of our culture in its major epochs.

The great books of antiquity, for example, seem to give no intimation of a division between science and philosophy. Particular bodies of knowledge, such as physics or mathematics, are indifferently regarded as sciences or branches of philosophy. The crown of knowledge is wisdom, approached as one rises in the hierarchy of knowledge to the highest science or the first philosophy. Aristotle and Plato may disagree in naming or defining the type of knowledge which deserves to be called wisdom, yet for both it is the ultimate attainment of philosophical inquiry or scientific work.

The differences between Plato and Aristotle discussed in the chapters on DIALECTIC and METAPHYSICS—the one using "dialectic" as the name for the supreme form of knowledge, the other using "theology" to name the summit of the sciences—do not affect their agreement that the philosopher is a man of knowledge, not opinion, and that his ultimate goal is wisdom.

If there is any distinction in antiquity between science and philosophy, it seems to find expression in the sense in which Socrates speaks of philosophy as the love of wisdom, implying thereby its pursuit rather than its attainment. A man would not be called a scientist in a particular field—mathematics, let us say—unless he actually had some mathematical knowledge; but a man who is not actually wise can be called a philosopher by virtue of his effort to become wise. Apart from this point of distinction, the Greeks tend to identify philosophy with the fundamental sciences, which somehow yield speculative or practical wisdom.

Considering the whole of human learning, all its arts and disciplines, we see that the things the ancients distinguish from philosophy are poetry, history, and the particular productive arts or crafts. Here again Plato and Aristotle do not make the distinction in the same terms. Plato compares the poet unfavorably with the philosopher in the *Republic*. The poet is an imitator of imitations and moves on the level of images and beliefs, whereas the philosopher rises above the imagination to the level of ideas which are the only true objects of knowledge. Aristotle, on the other hand, seems to pay poetry a compliment when in the *Poetics* he says that it is more philosophical than history because it deals with the universal rather than the particular. These attitudes toward poetry in relation to philosophy are somewhat reversed by the fact that for Plato myth and poetry provide materials from which philosophical insights can sometimes be distilled, whereas for Aristotle sense-experience is the source from which, by induction, the principles or axioms of philosophical knowledge are obtained. Despite these differences their accord on the supremacy of the philosopher remains unaffected.

More than poetry and history—and all the knowledge that can be applied productively —philosophy represents the highest use of man's faculties. On this Aristotle and Plato seem to be agreed, even though Aristotle distinguishes the philosophical from the political life and assigns the most perfect happiness to the contemplative activity of the philosopher, whereas Plato —in the *Republic* at least—brings the philosopher back to the shadows of the cave after he has seen the light of truth itself, so that he can put his wisdom to practice in the government of his less fortunate fellow man.

The practice of philosophy seems to become, for the Roman writers, more important than the content of philosophy as a body of doctrine. "What is that which is able to conduct a man?" asks Marcus Aurelius. "One thing and only one, philosophy." It keeps the inner man "free from violence and unharmed, superior to pains and pleasures, doing nothing without a purpose." It enables him to "accept all that happens and all that is allotted . . . and finally to wait for death with a cheerful mind, as being nothing else than a dissolution of the elements of which every living being is compounded." To Aurelius his imperial court is like a stepmother to whom one must be dutiful, philosophy like a mother from whom one gains solace and help. "Return to philosophy frequently and repose in her," he tells himself, so that "what thou meetest with in the court appears to thee tolerable, and thou tolerable in the court."

The Stoic conception of philosophy as a moral discipline and as a consolation creates that sense of the word in which the familiar injunction to a person in distress—"Be philosophical"—carries the same meaning as "Be stoical." Philosophy provides only peace of mind, not worldly riches or external power. "Philosophy does not promise to secure to man anything outside himself," says Epictetus. Nor does it fulfill its promise of inner strength without stern resolution to withdraw desire from the goods of fortune.

"Do you suppose that you can be a philosopher if you do as you do now?" Epictetus asks. "Do you suppose that you can eat and drink as you do now, and indulge your anger and displeasure just as before? No, you must sit up late, you must work hard, conquer some of your desires. . . When you have carefully considered these drawbacks, then come to us . . . if you are willing to pay this price for peace of mind, freedom, tranquility." Do not try to be "first a philosopher, then a tax-collector, then an orator, then one of Caesar's procurators. These callings do not agree . . . You must be busy either with your inner man, or with things outside, that is, you must choose between the position of a philosopher and that of an ordinary man."

There seems to be no difference between the Stoic and Epicurean conception of philosophy. Lucretius praises Epicurus, "thanks to whom sweet solaces of life soothe the mind," for as soon as his philosophy "begins to proclaim aloud the nature of things, the terrors of the mind fly away."

But for Lucretius philosophy achieves this boon not merely by curbing the passions and quieting desires, but also, and primarily, by the truth of its teachings about the constitution of the world and the causes of things. Nor is it merely that the philosophical mind is able "to dwell in the calm high places, firmly embattled on the heights by the teaching of the wise, whence you can look down on others, and see them wandering hither and thither, going astray as they seek the way of life." Philosophy provides a more specific remedy for the deepest of human ills by "freeing the mind from the close bondage of religion."

Men fear the thunderbolts of the gods, their intervention in the course of nature and human affairs, and the punishments of the after-life. Before Epicurus taught them the mortality of the soul and the atomic determination of all things, "the life of man lay foul to see and grovelling upon the earth, crushed by the weight of religion." His teaching concerning "what can come to be and what cannot, and in what way each thing has its power limited," rids the mind of the terrors fostered by religion. This "darkness of mind must needs be scattered . . . by the outer view and the inner law of nature."

EXCEPT FOR Lucretius, the triumph of philosophy over religion does not seem to be central to ancient conceptions of philosophy's contribution to the mind and life of man. In the pagan world, religious belief is either combined with philosophy to constitute the worship of the gods, which seems to be Plato's view in the *Laws*; or it represents the superstitions of the ignorant as opposed to the sophistication of the educated. Gibbon describes the rift between religion and philosophy not as a matter of intellectual controversy, but as a division of society into classes lacking or having the benefits of education—or, what is the same in the ancient world, instruction in philosophy.

But in the mediaeval world, the distinction between philosophy and religion seems to be essential to the consideration of the nature and value of philosophy. The importance of the distinction appears alike in the great books of the Christian tradition and in the great writings of the Mohammedan and Jewish cultures—in Augustine and Aquinas, Avicenna, Averroës, and Maimonides—though the problem of philosophy's relation to religion and theology may be quite differently solved by each. In all three religious communities secular learning and sacred doctrine are set apart by their origin—the one from the efforts of human reason, the other from the word of God as revealed to the faithful. Even when it is held in highest esteem as the best achievement of secular learning, philosophy is for the most part regarded as inferior to the teachings of religion.

There are those—the simply religious, the devout, the mystical—who abominate the pretensions of reason and the vanity of philosophers who claim either merit or need for any knowledge beyond the truths which God himself has revealed. This position is expressed by such Christian writers as Tertullian, Peter Damian, Bernard of Clairvaux; or, in the Arabic tradition, by Al-Ghazzali's *The Destruction of Philosophy*. Al-Ghazzali is answered by Averroës in his *Destruction of the "Destruction"* which asserts the supremacy of philosophy. Averroës reserves philosophy for men of requisite intellectual strength and relegates theology and religion to those who must substitute opinion and imagination for reason.

Neither Augustine nor Aquinas goes to these extremes. They do not dismiss philosophy as useless learning or as dangerous folly, subversive of the wisdom of faith; but neither do they admit the sufficiency of philosophy for knowledge of God—the mysteries of the divine nature, God's providence and His gracious gift of salvation to man.

Quoting St. Paul's warning to "beware lest any man spoil you through philosophy and vain deceit according to the tradition of men and the rudiments of the world, and not according to Christ," Augustine defends his praise of the Platonic philosophy which in his judgment comes nearest to the Christian faith, on the ground that the Apostle also said to the gentiles that "that which is known of God is manifest among them, for God has manifested it to them." Yet he adds that "the Christian man who is ignorant of their writings . . . is not, therefore, ignorant that it is from the one true and supremely good God that we have that nature in which we are made in the image of God, and that doctrine by which we know Him and ourselves, and that grace with which, by cleaving to Him, we are blessed."

Philosophy, according to Augustine, can thus be dispensed with in all the major concerns of knowledge, love, or action. But Augustine does not argue that it should therefore be discarded. "If those who are called philosophers," he says, "and especially the Platonists, have said aught that is true and in harmony with our faith, we are not only not to shrink from it, but to claim it for our own use from those who have unlawful possession of it," even as the spoils of the Egyptians belong to the Jews.

Though Augustine and Aquinas conceive the relation of faith and reason differently, they seem to share a conception of philosophy as the handmaiden of theology when faith seeks understanding. For Aquinas this does not appear to imply lack of dignity or even the loss of a certain autonomy on the part of philosophy. On the contrary, so highly does he regard the demonstrations of Aristotle, whom he calls "the philosopher," that he opens the *Summa Theologica* with the question "Whether, besides the philosophical sciences, any further doctrine is required."

He answers that "it was necessary for the salvation of man that certain truths which exceed human reason should be made known to him by divine revelation. Even as regards those truths about God which human reason can investigate, it was necessary that man be taught by a divine revelation. For the truth about God, such as reason can know it, would only be known by a few, and that after a long time, and with the admixture of many errors; whereas man's whole salvation, which is in God, depends upon the knowledge of this truth. . . . It was, therefore, necessary that besides the philosophical sciences investigated by reason, there should be a sacred science by way of revelation." That sacred science is theology—not the theology which is a part of philosophy, but the theology whose principles come from faith rather than from reason.

"There is no reason," Aquinas writes, "why those things which are treated by the philosophical sciences, so far as they can be known by the light of natural reason, may not also be treated by another science so far as they are known by the light of the divine revelation." On this view, sacred theology may treat of certain things, such as the mystery of the Trinity, which do not belong properly to the philosopher because they exceed the power of reason to demonstrate; but other matters concerning nature, man, and God may belong both to the philosopher and to the theologian, who consider them according to their different lights. Since a truth cannot conflict with a truth, though reason sponsors one and faith the other, there can be no conflict between philosophy and theology.

Some modern philosophers, like Bacon and Locke, seem to agree with mediaeval theologians about the subordination of philosophy to theology. But for the most part the modern tendency, increasingly evident in the writings of Descartes, Spinoza, Kant, and Hegel, is to insist upon the complete autonomy of philosophy.

Hegel, for example, challenges "the imputation against Philosophy of being shy of noticing religious truths, or of having occasion to be so," and the insinuated "suspicion that it has anything but a clear conscience in the presence of these truths. So far from this being the case," Hegel remarks, "the fact is that in recent times Philosophy has been obliged to defend the domain of religion against the attacks of several theological systems."

The diverse aspects of the problem of the relation of philosophy to theology, and of theology to faith, are discussed in the chapters on Metaphysics, Theology, and Religion. The problem which is more characteristic of the modern consideration of philosophy concerns its relation to science.

To state the problem some distinction between the two is necessary, and making this distinction represents a novel departure, both in thought and language. As we have seen, philosophy and science are almost identified throughout the ancient and mediaeval tradition. Insofar as the word "science" means knowledge rather than opinion, the result of philosophical inquiry is science, and philosophy as a whole is divided into a number of sciences. There may be, as ancient writings seem to suggest, sciences which aim at useful productions rather than at speculative or practical wisdom, and fall below the level of philosophy; or there may be, as some Christian theologians hold, a sacred science superior in its wisdom to all the philosophical sciences. But these exceptions to the identity of philosophy and science merely confirm the point that in the ancient or mediaeval view philosophy is scientific and consists of sciences, even though there may be sciences which are not philosophical.

This use of the words "science" and "philosophy" persists well into modern times. Hobbes, for example, presents his classification of the types of knowledge under the heading "science, that is, Knowledge of Consequences, which is also called Philosophy." Bacon proposes to "divide sciences into theology and philosophy." Descartes uses the words "science" and "philosophy" interchangeably. "Among the different branches of Philosophy," he says, "I had in my younger days to a certain extent studied Logic; and in those of Mathematics, Geometrical Analysis and Algebra—three arts or sciences which seemed as though they ought to contribute to the design I had in view." In the Prefatory Letter to his *Principles of Philosophy*, he likens "philosophy as a whole" to "a tree whose roots are metaphysics, whose trunk is physics, and whose branches, which issue from this trunk, are all the other sciences. These reduce themselves to three principal ones, *viz.*, medicine, mechanics, and morals."

Even as near the end of the eighteenth century as Hume, the word "philosophy" continues to be the general name for the particular sciences. It covers the experimental study of natural phenomena as well as what are for Hume the non-experimental sciences of mathematics and psychology. But it excludes divinity or theology, insofar as "its best and most solid foundation is *faith* and divine revelation"; metaphysics, which is "nothing but sophistry and illusion"; and all inquiries into particular as opposed to general facts, such as "history, chronology, geography, and astronomy."

Nor is this use of terms confined to what readers today would call books of philosophy. The authors of the books which are today regarded as among the foundations of modern science—Galileo, Newton, Huygens and, in the eighteenth century, Lavoisier and Fourier—refer to themselves as philosophers and to the science in which they are engaged, *e.g.*, mathematics, mechanics, physics, chemistry, as parts or aspects of natural philosophy. They do, however, indicate an awareness of how they differ from ancient and mediaeval scientists (who also called themselves philosophers) by calling their own work "experimental philosophy."

In this phrase lies the root of the distinction between philosophy and science as that distinction is generally understood by writers since the eighteenth century. The word "experimental" applied to philosophy signifies a radical difference in the method of inquiry and even in the objects to be investigated, for certain objects can be known only by experimental or empirical research. Kant appears to be the first (in the great books at least) to make a sharp separation between the investigation of either nature or mind by what he calls "empirical" as opposed to "rational" methods. He still uses the name "science" for both sorts of investigation, but he appears to restrict "philosophy" to the latter—the pure, the *a priori*, the rational sciences.

Two other innovations must be noted. Though Kant regards it as a rational discipline, he excludes mathematics entirely from philosophy and criticizes its misleading influence upon those philosophers who have tried to imitate mathematical thought. And though he sometimes uses "metaphysic" narrowly to designate the critical examination of pure reason itself, he also says that "this name of metaphysic may be given to the whole of pure philosophy . . . excluding all that belongs to the empirical and the mathematical employment of reason." Considering that it has only two objects, nature and freedom—that which *is* and that which *ought to be*—Kant divides philosophy into the speculative and the practical use of pure reason, which gives rise to a *metaphysic of nature* and a *metaphysic of morals*. "Metaphysic, therefore, that of nature as well as that of morals, and particularly the criticism of our adventurous reason which forms the introduction to and preparation for it, constitute together," Kant writes, "what may be termed philosophy in the true sense of the word. Its only goal is wisdom, and the path to it, science."

Kant's innovations in vocabulary plainly announce the separation of philosophy from mathematics and experimental science, which is only intimated by earlier modern writers. But Kant still uses the word "science" for both the philosophical and the empirical sciences. The final step is taken in the nineteenth century when the word "science" is restricted to mathematics and to such knowledge of nature, man, and society as can be obtained by the methods of experimental or empirical research. William James, for example, stresses the fact that he is trying to expound psychology as one of the natural sciences, and to that end he tries to separate the problems which are capable of empirical investigation from those which belong to philosophical speculation. For Freud that separation is an accomplished fact, and one which leaves to philosophy no problem that can be solved by science.

According to Freud, "it is inadmissible to declare that science is one field of human intellectual activity, and that religion and philosophy are others, at least as valuable, and that science has no business to interfere with the other two." On the contrary, Freud thinks it is right for scientific research to look "on the whole field of human activity as its own," and to criticize the unscientific formulations of philosophy. The trouble with philosophy is that "it behaves itself as if it were a science . . . but it parts company with science, in that it clings to the illusion that it can produce a complete and coherent picture of the universe." It is this illusion which science continually punctures, since, in Freud's opinion, "that picture must needs fall to pieces with every new advance in our knowledge."

When science and philosophy are set apart at last, it is possible to make sense of the typically modern questions concerning philosophy. How does it stand in relation to science? Does it consist of verifiable knowledge comparable to that which can be obtained in the natural and social sciences? If not, what is the standard of truth in philosophy? Does it consist of definitions and postulates leading to rigorously demonstrated conclusions in a manner comparable to mathematics, especially in its modern construction? If not, must it not be regarded as opinion or speculation rather than as knowledge in any strict sense? Or if philosophical thought can be compared with mathematics, does not the diversity of definitions and postulates employed by different philosophers reduce philosophy to a collection of competing "systems" rather than a single discipline in which philosophers work cooperatively as do scientists and mathematicians?

However the foregoing questions are answered, there are still others. Does philosophy have distinct branches, divided according to their objects of study like the natural sciences, or is philosophy to be identified with metaphysics? If, in addition to metaphysics, there is a philosophy of nature, how are its principles and conclusions related to the findings of the natural sciences which appear to study the same object? Similarly, if psychology is a branch of philosophy, how is it related to experimental or clinical psychology? What is the relation of moral and political philosophy to the empirical social sciences concerned with describing, not judging or regulating, human conduct and social institutions? Is economics a science or is it a branch of moral philosophy; or, if it is both, how are the two related?

What is the use of philosophy, especially in its theoretic branches, if, unlike science, it cannot be applied to the mastery of physical nature and the production of utilities, whether bridges or bombs? What, finally, at the end of its long history, does philosophy come to if, in such marked contrast to the continuously accelerated progress of the sciences, it cannot claim any signal advance on which all philosophers are agreed, but instead must admit that most of its problems seem to be perennially debated, now as in every preceding century?

Some of these questions, as well as certain answers to them, are considered in other chapters: the comparison of empirical research and philosophical thought as constituting different types of science, in the chapter on Science; the distinction and relation between natural philosophy and natural science, in the chapter on Physics; the difference between philosophical and scientific psychology, in the chapter on Man; the function of definitions, hypotheses, postulates, or axioms in the foundation and method of philosophy and science, in the chapter on Principle; the difference between the practical use of philosophy in the sphere of morals and the use of science in the sphere of the productive arts, in the chapter on Knowledge; the accumulation of truth as measuring advances in science and philosophy, in the chapter on Progress.

Here we must observe that such answers to these questions as tend to subordinate philosophy to science originate exclusively with modern views of the nature of knowledge, of the criteria of truth, and of the capacities of the human mind, especially the power of reason. Even those modern authors who write at a time when the words "science" and "philosophy" are, for the most part, interchangeable tend in this direction. The points they make about the nature, aim, and method of what they call either science or philosophy have the effect of giving the status of *knowledge* only to mathematics and the empirical sciences, and of reducing philosophical speculation to the status of *opinion.*

Bacon's insistence, for example, that genuine knowledge gives us power over nature and generates productions, seems to have this effect, certainly upon any part of traditional philosophy which cannot meet this test. Hume's insistence upon experimental reasoning with respect to all matters of fact seems to eliminate not only metaphysics, but any science or philosophy of nature which is not experimental. The methodological reforms in philosophy which these philosophers and others, like Hobbes, Descartes, and Spinoza, propose seem to be reforms which eliminate whatever in philosophy cannot become either experimental science or a quasi-mathematical system of thought.

Among the modern reformers of philosophy, Kant represents the exception. By his critical method he hopes to establish philosophy above and independent of all the empirical sciences; and to institute metaphysics as a science which neither imitates mathematics nor accepts it as an equal in the scale of reason's accomplishments. Yet even Kant seems to betray the typically modern attitude toward philosophy. The intellectual revolution which he projects as the philosophical parallel to the Copernican revolution in astronomy is motivated by his desire to secure for philosophy a stability and development comparable to that enjoyed by mathematics and the empirical sciences.

"IN THE PROGRESS of society," writes Adam Smith, "philosophy or speculation becomes, like every other employment, the principal or sole trade and occupation of a particular class of citizens. Like every other employment too, it is subdivided into a great number of different branches, each of which affords occupation to a peculiar tribe or class of philosophers; and this subdivision of employment in philosophy, as well as in every other business, improves dexterity and saves time. Each individual becomes more expert in his own peculiar branch, more work is done upon the whole, and the quantity of science is considerably increased by it."

Despite his use of the word "philosophy," it seems likely that Adam Smith is describing the division of labor in scientific research and the specialization of scientists. Though philosophy has divisions, and though the distinction and order of its parts are discussed by the great philosophers, their own work exhibits a spirit opposed to specialization. In fact, one measure of the greatness of a philosopher is the comprehensiveness of his thought, the range of subject matters and the scope of the problems with which he deals.

Those philosophers, like Aristotle, Bacon, Hobbes, or Kant, who show great interest in the divisions of philosophy seem to be largely concerned with distinguishing the different objects of philosophical thought and differentiating the concepts or principles peculiarly relevant to each. Other chapters deal with subject matters, sciences, or disciplines that have been regarded, by one philosopher or another, as major divisions of philosophy, *e.g.*, LOGIC, METAPHYSICS, THEOLOGY, DIALECTIC, MATHEMATICS, PHYSICS, and psychology (in the chapter on MAN). But one group of sciences or disciplines is not discussed elsewhere and must be briefly noted here. Traditionally within the province of the philosopher, they are sometimes expanded to his whole domain. They come nearer to what the ordinary man means by "philosophy" when he speaks of having a philosophy of life—an over-all yet personal view of the human situation, illuminated by a sense of the values which should direct conduct.

The disciplines in question are traditionally called ethics and politics, or moral philosophy. Socrates is credited with having accomplished the first great reform in philosophy when he turned to such subjects and away from the inquiries of his predecessors. "I do not mean to speak disparagingly of the students of natural philosophy," he says at his trial, "but the simple truth is, O Athenians, that I have nothing to do with physical speculations." Subsequently he tells his judges that he "will never cease from the practice and teaching of philosophy"—reproaching those whom he questions with "under-valuing the greater and over-valuing the less," enjoining them not to take thought of their persons or their properties, "but first and chiefly to care about the greatest improvement of the soul." He will not foreswear philosophy even to save his life. "I cannot hold my tongue," he says. "Daily discourse about virtue . . . is the greatest good of man," for "the unexamined life is not worth living."

The conception of ethics and politics and of their relation to other branches of philosophy seems to depend upon the acceptance or rejection of a fundamental principle in the division of philosophy. Aristotle and Kant, for example, divide the philosophical sciences into the theoretic or speculative and the practical or moral, according as they consider what *is* (the nature and causes of things) or what *ought to be* (the objects of choice, the ends and means, in the conduct of life and the institutions of society). According to this conception of the practical, the practical sciences are ethics and politics, and with them economics and jurisprudence; or in another statement of the same divisions, the parts of practical philosophy are moral philosophy, the philosophy of right, the philosophy of law. They are all conceived as normative, prescriptive, or regulative disciplines, determining what is good and evil or right and wrong, and directing action in the sphere of human freedom.

Hobbes proceeds on a different principle. He separates natural philosophy (including *philosophia prima*) from civil philosophy, or the theory of the body politic. But he includes ethics and poetics under natural philosophy as part of the theoretic study of human nature. The distinction between the theoretic and the practical seems to be here ignored, or even implicitly denied insofar as Hobbes would reject the basis of the distinction—the difference between natural necessity and human freedom. Necessity governs the motions of the human body and of the body politic as much as it does the bodies studied by the physicist, and so ethics, politics, and physics are alike sciences of determined consequences.

Still another view seems to be taken by Bacon who separates natural from human and civil philosophy and divides natural philosophy into two main speculative branches (physics and metaphysics) and two main practical branches (mechanics and magic). Psychology, logic, and ethics belong to human philosophy; politics and jurisprudence to civil philosophy. But with respect to all of these Bacon does not apply the distinction between the speculative and the practical which seems to him of the utmost importance in natural philosophy. The reason seems to be that Bacon uses the word "practical" to mean the production of effects resulting from the knowledge of causes, rather than actions to be performed by men as the result of choice. His practical sciences correspond, therefore, to what Aristotle conceives as arts, or productive sciences—the sphere of making or poetics in general—not to what Aristotle means by the practical, the sphere of doing rather than of making, of prudence rather than of art. These matters are discussed in the chapters on ART and POETRY.

The problem of the relation of science to art becomes, if restated in Bacon's terms, the problem of the relation of the theoretic to the practical (*i.e.*, productive) sciences. But in terms of Aristotle, Aquinas, or Kant, the problem of the relation between the speculative and practical branches of philosophy becomes the quite different problem of how knowledge of being or nature relates to knowledge of what should be sought or ought to be done. In Hobbes' terms the problem shifts in still another direction to the consideration of the bearing of physics upon psychology, ethics, and politics.

How, on any of the foregoing views, do speculations concerning the nature of things affect the theory of human life and society, or the practical principles by which man tries to lead a good life and organize a good society? What relation do the truths of physics and metaphysics, or the major philosophical issues in these fields, bear to the truths and issues in psychology, ethics, and politics? Or, as William James puts the question, must not any man who has a philosophy of life also have, implicitly at least, a metaphysics?

Upon the answers to such questions depends the varying esteem in which philosophy is held in the great periods of western culture. Unlike supernatural religion and empirical science, and especially when separated from them, philosophy does not promise eternal salvation or earthly prosperity. The uses of philosophy, as compared with religion and science, must somehow be assessed in the terms which, from the beginning of philosophy, are of its essence—the love of wisdom, and through it the search for a human wisdom which shall be at once speculative and practical.

OUTLINE OF TOPICS

REFERENCES

References are listed by volume number (in bold type), author's name, and page number. Bible references are to book, chapter, and verse of the Authorized King James version of the Bible. The abbreviation "esp" calls the reader's attention to one or more especially relevant parts of a whole reference; "passim" signifies that the topic is discussed intermittently rather than continuously in the work or passage cited. Where the work as a whole is relevant to the topic, the page numbers refer to the entire work. For general guidance in the use of *The Great Ideas*, consult the Preface.

1. The definition and scope of philosophy

7 Plato, 74–76, 383–398, 633–635
8 Aristotle, 499–550, 587–590, 592–593
12 Epictetus, 150–151, 158–161
18 Augustine, 14–15
23 Hobbes, 267–272
30 Bacon, 39–46, 48–49, 126
31 Descartes, 1–5
35 Hume, 451–455, 508–509
42 Kant, 1–13, 211–218, 243–250, 365–366
46 Hegel, 1–7, 116
54 Freud, 874

1*a*. The relation of philosophy to theology or religion

7 Plato, 797–798
8 Aristotle, 501
12 Lucretius, 1–2, 30–31, 61–62
14 Plutarch, 435
18 Augustine, 264–273, 493–494, 655–656
19 Aquinas, 3–10, 112–113, 209–213, 446–447
20 Aquinas, 110–111, 469–470, 598–603
23 Hobbes, 65–66, 137, 163, 247, 269–271
25 Montaigne, 155, 208–209, 212, 238–239, 271–273
30 Bacon, 4, 12–13, 16, 39–48, 55, 95–101, 114, 124
31 Descartes, 69–71, 125–126, 162–165, 168–169, 283–284
33 Pascal, 205–210, 218–220, 266
35 Hume, 497–503
40 Gibbon, 12–13, 159, 186, 307–309, 670
42 Kant, 177–192, 236–240, 346–347, 349–353, 588–613
43 Mill, 455
46 Hegel, 158–160, 177, 308–309
54 Freud, 875

1*b*. The relation of philosophy to mathematics

7 Plato, 633–635, 728–730
8 Aristotle, 270–271, 510, 547–548, 589–590
9 Aristotle, 391
11 Nicomachus, 811–813
23 Hobbes, 58, 268–269
30 Bacon, 120
31 Descartes, 5–7, 29, 46–47
34 Newton, 1–2
35 Hume, 470–471
42 Kant, 15–19, 211–218, 551–552

1*c*. The relation of philosophy to experimental or empirical science

7 Plato, 240–242, 391–398
8 Aristotle, 411
10 Hippocrates, 7
30 Bacon, 42–43, 46–47, 105–106, 111, 113–115, 140
31 Descartes, 43
34 Newton, 371–372, 542–543
42 Kant, 5–13, 387, 561–562, 578
46 Hegel, 182–183
51 Tolstoy, 694
53 James, 882–886 passim
54 Freud, 873–875

1*d*. The relation of philosophy to myth, poetry, and history

7 Plato, 57, 138–140, 142–148, 319–334, 586–589
25 Montaigne, 41–42
30 Bacon, 38–39
35 Hume, 452–453, 479
40 Gibbon, 345–346
46 Hegel, 10–12, 156–190
51 Tolstoy, 690
54 Freud, 239–240, 246–248 passim

2. The divisions of philosophy

2*a*. The distinction between theoretic or speculative and practical or moral philosophy: the distinction between natural and civil philosophy

8 Aristotle, 149, 499–501, 512, 527–528, 547
9 Aristotle, 162, 343–344, 349–351, 358, 387–391, 393–394
12 Epictetus, 131–132, 181–182
16 Ptolemy, 5–6
19 Aquinas, 90–91, 424–425, 450–451
20 Aquinas, 39–40, 223–224, 772–773, 780–781
23 Hobbes, 72
30 Bacon, 16–17, 40, 42, 55, 65–66
31 Descartes, 126, 206–207, 237
35 Locke, 94–95, 103–105

35 HUME, 451–455
42 KANT, 5–13, 190–191, 234–235, 253, 260–261, 291–297, 307–314, 319–321, 329–337, 388, 461–475, 596–598
43 MILL, 445
46 HEGEL, 115

2*b*. The branches of speculative philosophy: the divisions of natural philosophy

7 PLATO, 388–398, 634–635
8 ARISTOTLE, 270–271, 275, 523, 547–548, 592–593, 598
17 PLOTINUS, 11–12
18 AUGUSTINE, 266–267, 336
19 AQUINAS, 3–4, 451–453
30 BACON, 39–48, 55–61
31 DESCARTES, 1–3, 5–7, 46–48
35 LOCKE, 394–395
35 BERKELEY, 432
39 SMITH, 335–337
42 KANT, 1–13, 34–37, 253, 463–467, 476–479, 488–495

2*c*. The nature and branches of practical or moral philosophy: economics, ethics, politics, jurisprudence; poetics or the theory of art

7 PLATO, 427–434, 604–608
9 ARISTOTLE, 339–340, 343–344, 434–436, 487–488, 681–699
18 AUGUSTINE, 270
21 DANTE, 80
23 HOBBES, 95–96, 128–129, 164
30 BACON, 81–95
35 LOCKE, 303–304, 317–319, 325–326, 360, 394–395
35 HUME, 508–509
38 ROUSSEAU, 329–334
41 GIBBON, 75–80
42 KANT, 264, 271, 283–287, 291–296, 307–321, 327, 329–337, 366–368, 370–372, 374, 383, 388, 390–391, 398–399, 463–467, 523–524, 596–598
43 MILL, 445–447 passim
46 HEGEL, 1–7
50 MARX, 6–11, 178–179, 265–266
51 TOLSTOY, 680–684
54 FREUD, 800–801

3. The method of philosophy

3*a*. The foundations of philosophy in experience and common sense

8 ARISTOTLE, 64, 111, 120, 136–137, 259, 397, 411, 499–500, 673–674
12 LUCRETIUS, 6, 9
23 HOBBES, 267
28 HARVEY, 331–335
30 BACON, 16, 57–58, 108
31 DESCARTES, 53, 75–77
35 HUME, 508
42 KANT, 263, 271, 281–282, 329–330, 387–388, 562–563, 604
43 MILL, 445–446
53 JAMES, 655–659

3*b*. The philosopher's appeal to first principles and to definitions

7 PLATO, 383–398
8 ARISTOTLE, 97–137, 143, 513, 515, 589–592, 643–645
9 ARISTOTLE, 340, 389–390, 392–393
19 AQUINAS, 4
23 HOBBES, 56, 269
31 DESCARTES, 21, 51–54, 69–72, 130–131, 206–207
33 PASCAL, 430–434
42 KANT, 179–182, 215–217
43 FEDERALIST, 103–104
46 HEGEL, 9–10

3*c*. The processes of philosophical thought: induction, intuition, definition, demonstration, reasoning, analysis, and synthesis

7 PLATO, 50–52, 65–84, 134, 139–140, 179–183, 383–398, 486–511, 525–526, 570–574, 580–613
8 ARISTOTLE, 97–137, 211, 259–260, 275–278, 397, 515–516, 522–525, 547, 589, 610, 631–633
9 ARISTOTLE, 388
17 PLOTINUS, 270–271
18 AUGUSTINE, 265–270 passim
19 AQUINAS, 11–12, 175–178
23 HOBBES, 58–60, 65
24 RABELAIS, 101–106
30 BACON, 56–59, 105–195
31 DESCARTES, 1–27, 119–120, 128–129
33 PASCAL, 442–443
34 NEWTON, 270–271
35 LOCKE, 93–94, 120
35 HUME, 453–455, 457, 503–504
38 ROUSSEAU, 341–342
42 KANT, 1–13, 16, 109–112, 119, 193–200, 211–218
43 MILL, 274–293 passim
53 JAMES, 674–675

3*d*. The methodological reformation of philosophy

30 BACON, 11–17 esp 12–13, 30, 40, 47–48, 65, 105–195
31 DESCARTES, 1–27, 41–67, 69–71, 130–134, 167, 237–238, 267–277
35 LOCKE, 358–363
35 BERKELEY, 405–412, 439–440
35 HUME, 471
42 KANT, 1–13, 19–22, 133–134, 146–149, 157, 196–197, 218–227, 248–250, 292–296, 311–313, 331–332, 492, 567–568
54 FREUD, 875

4. The uses of philosophy: diverse conceptions of its aim, function, and value

4*a*. The philosophic mode of life: contemplation and happiness

7 PLATO, 122–128, 167, 200–212, 368–401, 609–639
8 ARISTOTLE, 602–603
9 ARISTOTLE, 344, 431–434, 527–530
12 LUCRETIUS, 15, 80–81
12 EPICTETUS, 108–110, 121, 132–133, 153–155, 180–181, 185–187, 190–191
12 AURELIUS, 261–262, 269–270, 298
13 VIRGIL, 65
17 PLOTINUS, 14–19
18 AUGUSTINE, 267–268, 299–300
19 AQUINAS, 57–58, 150–151, 625–627
20 AQUINAS, 79–80
22 CHAUCER, 164
25 MONTAIGNE, 107–112, 231–246, 503–504, 508–512, 538–543
30 BACON, 69–76
31 DESCARTES, 41–42, 49–50
31 SPINOZA, 447, 451–463
42 KANT, 591–592
43 MILL, 451
46 HEGEL, 368–369

4*b*. Philosophy as a moral discipline: the consolation of philosophy

7 PLATO, 69–71, 183–184, 222–226, 231–234, 476, 528–531
12 LUCRETIUS, 34, 40–44, 61
12 EPICTETUS, 105–245
12 AURELIUS, 253–310
18 AUGUSTINE, 266, 270
25 MONTAIGNE, 28–36, 69–75, 240–242, 283–284, 529–530
30 BACON, 26
31 SPINOZA, 444–447, 458–463
35 HUME, 463–464
36 STERNE, 388–417
37 FIELDING, 182
38 ROUSSEAU, 373–374
40 GIBBON, 644–646
42 KANT, 261
46 HEGEL, 303

4*c*. The social role of philosophy: the philosopher and the statesman; the philosopher king

7 PLATO, 83, 207–208, 272–273, 291–292, 368–383, 390–391, 398–401, 528–531, 598–608
9 ARISTOTLE, 390–391, 434–436
12 LUCRETIUS, 75
14 PLUTARCH, 32–48, 64–77, 122–123, 156–158, 543–544, 571–572, 717, 782–788
15 TACITUS, 153–155, 172–173
24 RABELAIS, 127–131
25 MONTAIGNE, 55–62
30 BACON, 20–26
38 MONTESQUIEU, 202–203
40 GIBBON, 32, 284, 338–339, 669
41 GIBBON, 40–41, 76–77
42 KANT, 360–361
46 HEGEL, 279–281, 363–364

5. The character and training of the philosopher: the difficulty of being a philosopher

7 PLATO, 125–126, 163–172, 200–212, 273, 368–401, 491
8 ARISTOTLE, 500–501
9 ARISTOTLE, 431–432
12 EPICTETUS, 113–114, 134–142, 146–148, 158–161, 192–201, 230–232
12 AURELIUS, 270
17 PLOTINUS, 10–12, 246
25 MONTAIGNE, 60, 70–72, 451
28 HARVEY, 268, 331–332
30 BACON, 26–27
31 DESCARTES, 41–67
37 FIELDING, 81–82
40 GIBBON, 31–32, 644–646
41 GIBBON, 526–527
47 GOETHE, 17–18, 44–48

6. Praise and dispraise of the philosopher and his work

6*a*. The philosopher as a man of science or wisdom: the love and search for truth

7 PLATO, 200–212, 222–224, 280–294, 319–320 368–401, 569–571
8 ARISTOTLE, 499–501
9 ARISTOTLE, 390, 528
10 GALEN, 207
12 LUCRETIUS, 30, 61
12 EPICTETUS, 167–170, 172–174, 184–185, 193–201, 228–230
17 PLOTINUS, 10–12, 246
18 AUGUSTINE, 266, 271
25 MONTAIGNE, 70–72, 446–450
28 HARVEY, 268
30 BACON, 1–28
31 DESCARTES, 50–51, 60–67
35 HUME, 452–455

6*b*. The philosopher and the man of opinion: sophistry and dogmatism, idle disputation, perpetual controversy

5 ARISTOPHANES, 488–506
7 PLATO, 42–43, 65–84, 271–273, 300–301, 551–579
9 ARISTOTLE, 417, 435–436
10 GALEN, 174–175, 177–179, 199
12 EPICTETUS, 129–132, 162–166, 177–178, 193–195
14 PLUTARCH, 287–288, 566–567
23 HOBBES, 57, 59–60, 71, 267–274
24 RABELAIS, 18–24, 197–200
25 MONTAIGNE, 55–62, 74–77, 239–294, 517–519
30 BACON, 1–28, 57–58, 66–67, 112–114, 117

31 DESCARTES, 43–44, 64
33 PASCAL, 231
35 LOCKE, 89, 284–285, 291–295, 323, 341, 347–348
35 BERKELEY, 409–410, 430–432, 441
35 HUME, 478
36 STERNE, 227–228, 318–321, 329–336, 421–422
41 GIBBON, 299, 526–527
42 KANT, 36–37, 120–121, 187–188, 221–222, 260–261, 607–608
46 HEGEL, 2–4
47 GOETHE, 45–46
53 JAMES, 227
54 FREUD, 874–875

6c. The philosopher as a man of reason: the limits of reason; its supplementation by experience or faith

16 PTOLEMY, 5–6
18 AUGUSTINE, 26–28, 36–37, 507–513
19 AQUINAS, 3–4, 11–12, 60–61, 175–178, 253–255
21 DANTE, 56, 143
25 MONTAIGNE, 208–294
30 BACON, 2–4, 96–97
31 DESCARTES, 13–14
33 PASCAL, 205–217 passim, 217–219, 221–225, 248–251, 272–273, 277, 440
35 BERKELEY, 405
35 HUME, 451–455 passim, 460, 503–504, 508
37 FIELDING, 380
40 GIBBON, 186, 200–201, 308–309
42 KANT, 129–173, 219–220, 227–235, 285–287, 296, 337–355, 551–552, 570–572, 588–607
47 GOETHE, 11–14, 17–21
51 TOLSTOY, 242–243
52 DOSTOEVSKY, 337–346

6d. The philosopher as a man of theory or vision: neglect of the practical; withdrawal from the affairs of men and the marketplace

7 PLATO, 200–212, 375–376
9 ARISTOTLE, 351, 453
12 EPICTETUS, 127–128, 131–132, 195–201, 213–223, 235–237
14 PLUTARCH, 130, 255
25 MONTAIGNE, 63–75, 327, 478–482, 538–543
30 BACON, 2–17, 73–74
35 BERKELEY, 431–432
35 HUME, 451–452
39 SMITH, 335–337
42 KANT, 187–188
43 MILL, 346–347
46 HEGEL, 5–6
48 MELVILLE, 116–117
50 MARX-ENGELS, 430–432
51 TOLSTOY, 361–365
53 JAMES, 271
54 FREUD, 722

7. Observations on the history of philosophy: the lives of the philosophers in relation to their thought

7 PLATO, 54–55, 564–568, 800–814
8 ARISTOTLE, 253, 259–268, 501–512, 606, 633–641
9 ARISTOTLE, 341–342
10 GALEN, 207
12 LUCRETIUS, 30
12 EPICTETUS, 151–152, 177–178, 193–201
14 PLUTARCH, 65, 252–255, 381, 420, 705, 720
18 AUGUSTINE, 264–273, 507–511
19 AQUINAS, 239–240, 342–347, 385–388, 391–393, 440–449, 453–455, 469–471
23 HOBBES, 164, 267–269, 274
25 MONTAIGNE, 65–66
28 HARVEY, 279–280
30 BACON, 1–101, 109–128
31 DESCARTES, 41–67, 278–293
33 PASCAL, 355–358
35 LOCKE, 260–261, 293–295, 373
35 BERKELEY, 409–410, 429–430
35 HUME, 451–509
38 MONTESQUIEU, 169, 202–203
38 ROUSSEAU, 329–334, 373–374
39 SMITH, 5–6, 335–339
40 GIBBON, 23–24, 31–32, 159, 186, 204–206, 364, 644–646, 668–671
41 GIBBON, 299, 326–327, 522–528
42 KANT, 1–8, 100–102, 224–227, 248–250, 311–313, 339
43 MILL, 274–293 passim
46 HEGEL, 2–5, 158–159, 218, 229, 279–281, 341–342
50 MARX, 25, 190, 301, 305–306
53 JAMES, 221–239, 305–312, 627–635, 879–882

CROSS-REFERENCES

For: Another discussion of the nature of philosophical science, *see* SCIENCE 1a, 1c; and for various conceptions of the highest philosophical knowledge, *see* DIALECTIC 2a; KNOWLEDGE 6c(4); METAPHYSICS 1; WISDOM 1a.

The relation of philosophy to theology and religion, *see* RELIGION 6g; SCIENCE 2a; THEOLOGY 2, 4a; TRUTH 4a.

The relation between philosophy and mathematics, *see* MATHEMATICS 1a–1b; PHYSICS 1b.

The relation of the philosophical to the experimental and empirical sciences, *see* PHYSICS 2–2b; PROGRESS 6b; SCIENCE 1c.

The comparison of philosophy, poetry, and history, *see* HISTORY 1; POETRY 5b; SCIENCE 2b.

Discussions relevant to the distinction between theoretic and practical philosophy, *see* JUDGMENT 2; KNOWLEDGE 6e(1); MIND 9a; PRUDENCE 2a; SCIENCE 3a; THEOLOGY 3b, 4d; TRUTH 2c; WISDOM 1b.

Other treatments of the branches of speculative or natural philosophy and their relation to one another, *see* DIALECTIC 4; LOGIC 1; MAN 2b, 2b(4); MATHEMATICS 1a; METAPHYSICS 3a–3c; PHYSICS 1–1a; SCIENCE 1a(2); THEOLOGY 3a; TRUTH 4c.

Other treatments of the branches of practical, moral, or civil philosophy, *see* KNOWLEDGE 6e(2), 8a–8c; LOGIC 4e; POETRY 8; SCIENCE 3a; STATE 8d; WEALTH 9.

Discussions relevant to the method of philosophy, *see* DEFINITION 6a–6c; EXPERIENCE 2c, 4a–4b; INDUCTION 1a, 3; KNOWLEDGE 6c(4); LOGIC 4d; METAPHYSICS 2c, 4b; PRINCIPLE 3–4; REASONING 6a, 6c–6d.

The uses of philosophy in the conduct of life and the organization of society, *see* HAPPINESS 2b(7); WISDOM 2c.

The conception of the philosopher as a man of wisdom or as seeking wisdom, *see* TRUTH 8e; WISDOM 3; and for the comparison of philosophical with supernatural wisdom, *see* THEOLOGY 2; WISDOM 1d.

The association or contrast of the philosopher with the sophist, the rhetorician, or the dogmatist, *see* DIALECTIC 6; METAPHYSICS 4a; OPINION 4b; RHETORIC 1a; WISDOM 3.

The comparison of progress in philosophy and science, and for the conditions of progress in philosophy, *see* PROGRESS 6b–6c.

ADDITIONAL READINGS

Listed below are works not included in *Great Books of the Western World*, but relevant to the idea and topics with which this chapter deals. These works are divided into two groups:

I. Works by authors represented in this collection.
II. Works by authors not represented in this collection.

For the date, place, and other facts concerning the publication of the works cited, consult the Bibliography of Additional Readings which follows the last chapter of *The Great Ideas*.

I.

AUGUSTINE. *Soliloquies*, BK I, CH 7
——. *Divine Providence and the Problem of Evil*, BK II, CH XVIII
AQUINAS. *On the Trinity of Boethius*, QQ 2, 5–6
DANTE. *Convivio* (*The Banquet*), SECOND TREATISE, CH 12–16; THIRD TREATISE, CH 11–15; FOURTH TREATISE, CH 1
DESCARTES. *The Principles of Philosophy*, PREF
HOBBES. *Concerning Body*, PART I, CH I
GIBBON. *An Essay on the Study of Literature*, XLIV–LV
KANT. *Introduction to Logic*, III–IV, X
HEGEL. *The Phenomenology of Mind*, PREF
——. *The Philosophy of Mind*, SECT III, SUBSECT C
——. *Lectures on the History of Philosophy*
ENGELS. *Herr Eugen Dühring's Revolution in Science*, PART I
W. JAMES. *Pragmatism*, LECT I–II
——. *A Pluralistic Universe*, LECT I
——. *Some Problems of Philosophy*, CH I

II.

TERTULLIAN. *On Idolatry*
——. *Apology*
CICERO. *De Oratore* (*On Oratory*), III, CH XV–XVI
DIOGENES. *Lives of Eminent Philosophers*
PHILOSTRATUS. *Lives of the Sophists*
BOETHIUS. *De Fide Catholica* (*On the Catholic Faith*)
AL-GHAZZALI. *The Destruction of Philosophy*
ABAILARD. *Ethics* (*Scito Teipsum*)
JUDAH HA-LEVI. *Kitab al Khazari*
JOHN OF SALISBURY. *Metalogicon*
AVERROËS. *The Destruction of the "Destruction"*
R. BACON. *Opus Majus*, PART II
DUNS SCOTUS. *Oxford Commentary*, BK I, DIST 3, Q 4
THOMAS À KEMPIS. *The Imitation of Christ*, BK I, CH 1–5; BK III, CH 43–45

ERASMUS. *The Praise of Folly*
GLANVILL. *The Vanity of Dogmatizing*
VOLTAIRE. "Philosopher," "Sophist," "Philosophy," in *A Philosophical Dictionary*
COLERIDGE. *Biographia Literaria*, CH 9
HEINE. *Religion and Philosophy in Germany*
COMTE. *The Positive Philosophy*, INTRO, CH 1
W. HAMILTON. *Discussions on Philosophy and Literature, Education and University Reform*
——. *Lectures on Metaphysics and Logic*, VOL I (1–7)
WHEWELL. *The Philosophy of the Inductive Sciences*, VOL I, BK I, CH 2
LOTZE. *Outlines of Encyclopedia of Philosophy*, SECT I–II
C. S. PEIRCE. *Collected Papers*, VOL I
NIETZSCHE. *Beyond Good and Evil*, CH I
——. *The Will to Power*, BK II (2–3)
H. SIDGWICK. *Philosophy, Its Scope and Relations*
BOSANQUET. *Science and Philosophy*, I
T. VEBLEN. *The Place of Science in Modern Civilization*, pp 56–179
BERGSON. *An Introduction to Metaphysics*, pp 75–92
DEWEY *et al.* "The Need for a Recovery of Philosophy," in *Creative Intelligence*
SANTAYANA. *Soliloquies in England and Later Soliloquies*, CH 48
B. RUSSELL. *The Problems of Philosophy*, CH 14–15
——. *Mysticism and Logic*, CH 6
BEARD. *The Economic Basis of Politics*
CROCE. *Politics and Morals*
DEWEY. *Reconstruction in Philosophy*, CH 1
——. *The Quest for Certainty*, CH 11
J. S. HALDANE. *The Sciences and Philosophy*, LECT X–XI
M. R. COHEN. *Reason and Nature*, BK III, CH 5
TENNANT. *Philosophy of the Sciences*
WHITEHEAD. *Science and the Modern World*, CH 9
——. *Process and Reality*, PART I
——. *Adventures of Ideas*, CH 9–10
CARNAP. *Philosophy and Logical Syntax*
MARITAIN. *The Degrees of Knowledge*, CH I
——. *De la philosophie chrétienne*
——. *Science and Wisdom*, pp 137–220
——. *Scholasticism and Politics*, CH 2
GILSON. *Christianisme et philosophie*
——. *The Unity of Philosophical Experience*
——. *History of Philosophy and Philosophical Education*
JASPERS. *The Perennial Scope of Philosophy*

Chapter 67: PHYSICS

INTRODUCTION

CONCERNING the subject matter of physics, one thing seems to be traditionally taken for granted. The object of its study is the sensible world of changing things or matter in motion. When Plato, for example, conceives astronomy as dealing not with the actual and observable motions of the heavenly bodies, but with the possible forms of the motions of solids, he gives it the character of a mathematical rather than a physical science. He associates it with geometry, as for a similar reason he associates music—divorced from concern with audible harmonies—with arithmetic. In anyone's view, if a science does not investigate sensible realities, if it does not undertake to account for the motions of actual bodies, or, stated most generally, if it has no concern with the phenomena of change, then it does not have the character of physical or natural science.

The early Greek physicists, the pre-Socratics, to whom Plato and Aristotle refer, inaugurate the study of change with speculations about ultimate origins, the underlying principles or causes of natural phenomena. Sometimes they are called philosophers and sometimes scientists—or, at least, precursors of empirical science. But there seems to be no difference of opinion about their title as physicists. Their undisputed claim to this title derives, not from the method they employ, but from the object they study—change. In that primary meaning of the word "nature" which comes from the Latin *natura*—the equivalent of *phüsis* in Greek—they can be called "naturalists" or "physicists" indifferently. The realm of nature is the realm of change.

It is for this reason that Aristotle, considering the theories of his predecessors in the opening chapters of his *Physics*, sets Parmenides apart from all the rest. Parmenides' affirmation of the unity of being, which leads to his denial of the reality of change or motion, cannot be treated as a physical theory. On the contrary, it is, according to Aristotle, a complete negation of the subject matter of physics. No matter what other points physicists may dispute among themselves, they must all at least agree in taking a stand against Parmenides. Aristotle does not even seem to think that a book on physics is the proper place to argue against Parmenides. That argument belongs to another part of philosophy. The reality of change seems to him sufficiently evident to assure the physicist that he has a subject matter to investigate.

THE QUESTION whether the early physicists were scientists or philosophers calls attention to different methods of investigating natural phenomena. Agreement on the subject matter of physics may prevail, therefore, only in very general terms. When, in a manner to accord with the method employed, the object of physical inquiry is more specifically defined, there seem to be two physics, not one—a philosophical and a scientific physics, a philosophy of nature and a natural science, or, to use Kant's phrasing, a rational or pure physics and an empirical or experimental physics.

Though Newton may call his work a philosophy of nature, he also refers to it as an experimental philosophy, in order to distinguish it from the work of earlier natural philosophers who did not perform experiments. The difference between the physics of Newton and that of Aristotle seems, however, to involve more than a divergence in method. The problems which Newton and Aristotle try to solve indicate a difference in subject matter as well. Nevertheless, this difference falls within what, in the most general terms, must be conceived as the domain of physics. For all their differences, both are physicists, though both are not philosophers or scientists in the same sense.

There are other sources of variation in the definition of physics. The problem of the relation of physics to other disciplines—whether these are other branches of philosophy or other fields of empirical research—raises issues about the object and scope of physics. Aristotle, Bacon, Descartes, and Kant, for example, do not seem to have a common understanding of the relation of physics to mathematics and metaphysics. In consequence they conceive physics itself differently.

On the level of empirical research, physics is sometimes regarded as just one of the natural sciences and sometimes as the whole group of natural sciences. In the latter case it includes such fields as astronomy, mechanics, optics, acoustics, thermodynamics, magnetism, and electricity; and sometimes chemistry, biology, and even psychology are included under the head of physical or natural sciences, contrasted in the broadest terms to the social sciences. The conception of physics obviously changes when its scope is determined by a boundary line which separates it from chemistry, or from biology and psychology, or from the study of society.

The separation of these other sciences from physics does not necessarily imply a discontinuity in nature or the natural sciences. The biologist and the psychologist, for example, consider the physical bases of life and the physical conditions or correlates of mental phenomena. Hybrid sciences like biophysics and psychophysics have developed. Even the study of society draws upon physics to the extent that the laws of matter in motion and considerations of space and time must be appealed to for an understanding of the physical foundations of economic and political life.

OTHER CHAPTERS DEAL with specific physical sciences, *e.g.*, ASTRONOMY and MECHANICS. The latter tries to cover the various branches of mechanics and related fields of study, such as dynamics, optics, the theory of heat, magnetism, and electricity; particularly so far as these are represented in the work of Galileo, Newton, Huygens, Gilbert, Fourier, and Faraday. The basic concepts of mechanics and its branches or affiliates are also treated in that chapter. Still other chapters deal with fundamental terms representing concepts or problems in the larger domain of physics, philosophical or scientific, *e.g.*, CAUSE, CHANGE, ELEMENT, INFINITY, MATTER, PRINCIPLE, QUANTITY, SPACE, and TIME—not to mention NATURE and WORLD, terms which represent in the most comprehensive way the reality studied by the physicist.

Our discussion here can therefore be restricted to the problems raised in the great books concerning the conception of physics, its subject matter and method, its relation to other sciences or other parts of philosophy. It will lead to such questions as whether physics is supreme among the sciences studying reality or the nature of things and, at the other extreme, whether physics is at all possible as a science, whether there can be scientific knowledge of bodies in motion or of the whole realm of change and becoming.

The problem of the distinction between philosophical and scientific physics would appear to be only a special case of the distinction between philosophy and science in general. But it is more than that. It is the case which tests the main distinction itself, since here both philosopher and scientist claim to be expounding the same subject matter or at least to be dealing with the same general field of phenomena.

Mathematics and metaphysics bear on the distinction between philosophy and science in a different way. If, for example, we take experimentation or empirical research to be characteristic of science in distinction from philosophy, then mathematics would seem to resemble philosophy rather than science. On no understanding of the nature of mathematical knowledge is mathematics ever divided into two kinds which are capable of being described as empirical and rational. The possibility of metaphysical knowledge may be challenged, but no one has ever proposed an experimental metaphysics to challenge the metaphysics of the philosophers.

But physics seems to permit both an experimental and a philosophical treatment. Whether they are to be regarded as in conflict with one another depends on whether they are attacking the same problems by different methods or whether they represent something like a division of labor. In the latter view, each would deal, according to its method, with different problems and tend to supplement rather than to exclude the other. Psychology is another subject matter which seems to receive a dual treatment—philosophical and experimental—in the tradition of the great books. It raises issues similar to those just mentioned. They are considered in the chapter on MAN.

As the chapters on PHILOSOPHY and on SCIENCE indicate, the discussion of their difference from and relation to one another is complicated by the double use of both terms. The word "science," for example, is used for both the philosophical and the experimental sciences throughout the greater part of the tradition. Similarly, until quite recently, the name of philosopher is taken by those who experiment as well as by those who do not.

It is impossible, therefore, to speak without confusion of a scientific and a philosophical physics unless the verbal ambiguities are resolved by some convention, such as the understanding that when the context indicates that the words "science" and "philosophy" are being used as opposites rather than as synonyms, then "science" shall signify the experimental and "philosophy" the non-experimental mode of treatment. Beyond this, it is necessary to proceed as if the chapters on PHILOSOPHY and SCIENCE formed a background for some of the matters to be discussed here. Otherwise the consideration of natural philosophy and natural science would tend to become a general discussion of philosophy and science.

THE GREAT BOOKS of experimental physics seem to have three characteristics in common. First, and most naturally, they insist upon experimentation as either the indispensable source or the ultimate test of scientific formulations. Second, they tend to rely upon mathematics as much as upon experiment, both for the formulation of nature's laws and for the demonstration of the consequences or corollaries of the primary laws. Third, though experiments and observations multiply as science develops, they seek to bring all the phenomena of nature under the smallest number of generalizations, which have the utmost simplicity in mathematical statement.

On the second and third points, Newton's declarations seem to be most explicit. "Nature," he says, "is pleased with simplicity and affects not the pomp of superflous causes." Accordingly, Newton directs his efforts toward the simplest statement of the laws of motion, and these he seeks to give the universality requisite for covering every type of natural phenomenon. At the opening of the third book of the *Mathematical Principles of Natural Philosophy*, he explains that in the preceding books, he has "laid down the principles of philosophy, principles not philosophical but mathematical; such, namely, as we may build our reasonings upon in philosophical inquiries. These principles are the laws and conditions of certain motions, and powers or forces." From these same principles, he will now undertake to "demonstrate the frame of the System of the World."

In the Preface to the first edition of this work, Newton describes the third book as one in which he derives "from the celestial phenomena the forces of gravity with which bodies tend to the sun and the several planets. Then from these forces, by other propositions which are also mathematical," he goes on, "I deduce the motions of the planets, the comets, the moon, the sea." But he does not consider his work to have attained the goal of physics—the comprehension of all natural phenomena by a few simple mathematical formulae.

His confession of failure may also be read as a prognostication of what an experimental physics based on mathematical principles might some day be able to achieve. "I wish we could derive the rest of the phenomena of nature by the same kind of reasoning," he writes, "for I am induced by many reasons to suspect that they may all depend upon certain forces by which the particles of bodies, by some causes hitherto unknown, are either mutually impelled towards one another, and cohere in regular figures, or are repelled and recede from one another." Einstein's unified field equations, covering both gravitational phenomena on the astronomical scale and the electrical attractions and repulsions of sub-atomic particles, seem to realize, or at least closely to approximate, the ideal Newton has in mind.

Midway between Newton and Einstein, Fourier also bears testimony to the ideal of physics as a science at once simple in its principles and universal in the scope of their application. The successors of Newton and Galileo, he writes, "have extended their theories and given them an admirable perfection; they have taught us that the most diverse phenomena are subject to a small number of universal laws which are reproduced in all the acts of nature. It is recognized that the same principles regulate all the movements of the stars, their form, the inequalities of their courses, the equilibrium and the oscillations of the seas, the harmonic vibrations of air and sonorous bodies, the transmission of light, capillary actions, the undulations of fluids, in fine the most complex effects of all natural forces. Thus has the thought of Newton been confirmed," he concludes, referring to Newton's praise of geometry, whose glory it is that the few mathematical principles it provided for use in physics should have been "able to produce so many things."

ON THE EXPERIMENTAL SIDE, the great works of physical science seem to contain diverse notions of the purposes served by experimentation, accompanied by a fairly uniform recognition of the dependence of natural science upon experiment. In the field of magnetism, for example, Gilbert sets aside as unscientific all those authors who "have written about amber and jet as attracting chaff . . . but with never a proof from experiments. . . . These writers deal only in words. . . . Such philosophy bears no fruit." The fruitfulness of experiments on the vacuum, the equilibrium of fluids, and the weight of air leads Pascal to conclude that the secrets of nature remain hidden until "the experiments which supply us with knowledge about it" can be performed and multiplied.

"We ought never to search for truth but by the natural road of experiment and observation," writes Lavoisier; and Faraday describes himself as "an experimentalist" who feels "bound to let experiment guide me into any train of thought which it may justify." The science of electricity, he finds, "is in that state in which every part of it requires experimental investigation, not merely for the discovery of new effects," but ultimately for "the more accurate determination of the first principles of action of the most extraordinary and universal power in nature."

Methods of experimentation necessarily differ in different fields of physical research. Newton's optical experiments with mirrors and prisms were adapted to the phenomena of light, as Galileo's experiment with the inclined plane, Pascal's experiment on the equilibrium of fluids, or Faraday's experiments with induction coils were adapted to the phenomena of dynamics, hydrostatics, and electricity. The materials employed, the apparatus or instruments devised, the factors controlled or isolated from irrelevant circumstances, and the units of measurement in which the results are recorded, naturally vary with the phenomena under observation. Yet one thing is common to the variety of experiments described in the great books of physical science. They all involve the construction of an artificial physical system which permits more accurate and refined observation than does nature uncontrolled or untampered with.

The student of nature must observe in any case, no matter whether he is a philosopher or a scientist. To say that philosophical physics is non-experimental does not mean for Aristotle that knowledge of nature is possible without observation or induction from experience. But the experimentalists insist upon the distinction between the kind of observations which men normally make in the course of everyday experience and the kind which involve the special experience enjoyed only by those who observe and, in addition, measure the results of specially contrived experiments.

This point of distinction seems to be strikingly illustrated by a passage in Galileo's *Two New Sciences*. One of the persons in the dialogue, Simplicio, declares "everyday experience to show the propagation of light to be instantaneous." He explains that "when we see a piece of artillery fired at a great distance, the flash reaches our eyes without lapse of time; but the sound reaches the ear only after a noticeable interval." Sagredo replies that this familiar bit of experience permits him to infer only that "sound, in reaching our ear, travels more slowly than light." It does not inform us, he says, "whether the coming of light is instantaneous or whether, although extremely rapid, it still occupies time." The choice between these alternatives could not be determined by ordinary experience. An experiment had to be constructed in order to measure the velocity of light.

Recourse to experimentation to find by observation and measurement the answers which ordinary experience fails to yield does not exhaust the uses of experiment. The great experimental physicists indicate at least three distinct uses to which experiments can be put in addition to a merely exploratory use for "the discovery of new effects."

In natural philosophy as in mathematics, writes Newton, "the method of analysis ought ever to precede the method of composition" or synthesis. In physics, the method of analysis "consists in making experiments and observations, and in drawing conclusions from them by induction." In contrast, the synthetic method begins with the principles *assumed*, therefrom "explaining the phenomena . . . and proving the explanations."

Here experiments perform a probative rather than an inductive function. As Huygens observes, proof in physics does not have the certitude of mathematical demonstration, but it can have an extremely high degree of probability —"very often scarcely less than complete proof"—as a result of the experimental confirmation of a conclusion deduced from the assumed principles. This occurs "when things which have been demonstrated by the principles that have been assumed, correspond perfectly to the phenomena which experiment has brought under observation, especially when there are a great number of them." A single crucial experiment, so perfect in construction that all relevant factors have been controlled, makes unnecessary the multiplication of experiments to establish the conclusion.

A third use of experiment is illustrated by Galileo when he measures the velocity of a ball rolling down an inclined plane, in order to decide whether a certain mathematical definition of uniformly accelerated motion describes the acceleration "which one meets in nature in the case of falling bodies." The persons in the dialogue seem to be satisfied with some mathematical reasoning which shows that the velocity increases with the units of time elapsed rather than with the intervals of space traversed. But when Simplicio asks for an experiment to show that the mathematical conclusion has physical reality, in the sense of describing observable phenomena, Salviati replies that this request "is a very reasonable one, for this is the custom —and properly so—in those sciences where mathematical demonstrations are applied to natural phenomena" and "where the principles once established by well-chosen experiments become the foundations of the entire superstructure." Here experiment does not confirm conclusions. It establishes principles, not by inductive generalization but by comparing actual measurements with mathematical expectations.

Without experiment but not without inductions from experience, without measurements but not without recourse to observation, Aristotle's *Physics*—and with it such physical treatises as his works *On the Heavens* and *On Generation and Corruption*—represents a philosophy of nature. In Aristotle's meaning of the term 'science,' these treatises expound sciences, but they also constitute one part of philosophy, to be distinguished from mathematics and from what Aristotle regards as the first or highest part of philosophy, *i.e.*, the science of metaphysics.

Aristotle's tripartite division of the theoretic sciences or speculative philosophy into physics, mathematics, and metaphysics raises a question concerning his numerous biological works, and perhaps also his treatise *On the Soul*. Are these to be classified as physical sciences or parts of natural philosophy? The fact that Aristotle distinguishes between the forms and properties of living and non-living matter does not seem to affect the answer. By his criteria of physical inquiry—namely, that it investigates what neither exists nor can be conceived apart from matter and motion, and that it is concerned with every type of change—all these works belong to the domain of physics. Accordingly even such apparently psychological studies as those dealing with sensation, memory, dreams, justify the title under which they have been traditionally grouped—*Parva Naturalia*, *i.e.*, short physical treatises.

For all these more specialized considerations of natural phenomena the *Physics* seems to serve as a general introduction, as well as being in its own right an exposition of the most fundamental science in the sphere of natural philosophy. It tries to define change and to state the principles underlying every type of change. It tries to classify the types of change, separating coming to be and passing away simply (or generation and corruption), from coming to be in a special respect (or change in quality, quantity, and place) which Aristotle usually calls "motion" in distinction from "becoming" or "generation." It undertakes to analyze the conditions or causes of change or motion, to distinguish what happens by chance from what happens of necessity, to discriminate between natural and unnatural or violent motions, to treat the relation of mover and moved, to deal with the continuity and divisibility of motions, to consider place and time as conditions or aspects of motion, and to ask about the infinity of body and of change, and about the eternity of motion or the whole order of becoming, the natural world of things in motion.

Aristotle's physics thus seems to stand in sharp contrast to the physics of the experimentalists, not merely in method, but in the questions it tries to answer and in the principles to which it appeals. The effort to define change in general and to state the principles and causes operative in every type of change might appear to correspond to the search for formulae of maximum generality to cover all natural phenomena. But where Newton and Fourier hope thereby to reduce nature's variety to the simplest terms—a few laws of motion comprehending the whole framework of nature—Aristotle tends on the contrary to insist upon an irreducible variety of types of motion, kinds of matter, and causes of change.

Furthermore, the principles to which Aristotle appeals are not mathematical. He criticizes the discussion of becoming which takes place in Plato's *Timaeus*, on the ground that it tries to substitute mathematical for physical terms in the analysis of change. "Physical bodies contain surfaces and volumes, lines and points," he writes, "and these are the subject matter of mathematics"; but the mathematician is not concerned with these things as the attributes of physical bodies, but only as separated, in thought at least, from matter and motion. There are sciences which represent mixtures of mathematics and physics, such as optics and harmonics, but the existence of these mixed sciences—the equivalent of what is later called "mathematical physics"—seems to Aristotle to imply rather than deny the separation of pure physical science from pure mathematics.

Where Newton (who can be taken as the exemplary author of a physics which is at once mathematical and experimental) goes to mathematics for the principles of natural philosophy, Aristotle seems to think that physics has its own proper principles. If any deeper understanding of these principles is sought, it is not to be found in mathematics, but in metaphysics, or what Aristotle calls "the first philosophy."

For example, matter, form and privation, are proposed by Aristotle as the basic physical principles. In such terms he is able to state his insight that all change involves a substratum (or *that which* changes) and contraries (or that *from which* and that *to which* the change occurs). But the analysis of matter and form in terms of potentiality and actuality as modes of being, and the consideration of form and privation in terms of being and non-being, belong to metaphysics rather than physics.

Furthermore, Aristotle as a physicist deals with bodies in motion and with the difference between the generation of bodies and their alteration, increase and decrease, or change of place. But he leaves to metaphysics—to the books which come after the books on physics—the discussion of physical bodies as substances composite of matter and form, and the distinction of substance and accident which bears on the difference between substantial and accidental change (*i.e.*, generation and corruption as opposed to the change in quality, quantity, or place).

Though for Aristotle physics is as separate from metaphysics as it is from mathematics in subject matter, physics depends upon metaphysics, as it does not upon mathematics, for the establishment as well as the elucidation of its principles. It is in this sense that metaphysics is logically prior to physics. But there may also be a sense in which philosophical physics is logically prior to experimental natural science. To the extent that the experimentalist employs physical as opposed to mathematical principles, he may have to derive these from a philosophy of nature. Galileo, for example, investigates the properties of natural and violent motions in the Third and Fourth Day of his *Two New Sciences* (*i.e.*, the motions of freely falling bodies and of projectiles). The problem of establishing the reality of this distinction and of defining the natural and the non-natural types of motion seems to be a matter of philosophical analysis rather than of experimental investigation.

Bacon and Kant appear to agree with Aristotle about the separation of physics from mathematics. Rational (or pure, as opposed to empirical) physics is, according to Kant, "entirely separate from mathematics." It is not to be confused with "what is commonly called *physica generalis*, which is mathematics rather than a philosophy of nature." Criticizing the natural philosophy of the ancients because it is corrupted by logic in the school of Aristotle and by mathematics in the school of Plato, Bacon says that mathematics should "terminate natural philosophy rather than generate or create it. We may hope for better results," he adds, "from pure and unmixed natural philosophy."

Bacon elsewhere observes that "the investigation of nature is best conducted when mathematics are applied to physics." He does not deny "the great use of mathematics in physics," but rather insists that mathematics be regarded as "an appendage or auxiliary" of natural philosophy, not its master. He is writing against the mathematicians "who would have their science preside over physics."

But to whatever extent Aristotle, Bacon, and Kant are in agreement concerning the relation of physics and mathematics, their theories of the scope and subject matter of physics seem to be at variance. For Bacon, physics is only one of the theoretic parts of natural philosophy; the other is metaphysics. Both are sciences of nature or the physical world, though one investigates material and efficient, the other formal and final causes. Both studies, moreover, can be conducted experimentally and can yield practical fruits (in mechanics and what Bacon calls "magic") through the production of effects by the application of a knowledge of causes.

For Kant, the whole body of theoretical knowledge which is rational and *a priori*, not empirical and *a posteriori*, is the metaphysic of nature, of which one part is rational physics, and the other rational psychology. "The metaphysic of corporeal nature," he writes, "is called *physic*, or, because it must contain the principles of an *a priori* knowledge of nature only, *rational physic*." Here physics and metaphysics do not have distinct objects as they do for Aristotle; nor does Kant's conception of physics as purely *a priori* knowledge of nature seem to agree with Aristotle's conception of physics as inductive and empirical, if not experimental.

These issues concerning the relation of physics to mathematics and metaphysics have significance for the experimental as well as the philosophical study of nature. If, for example, following the position taken by Hume, metaphysical inquiry is dismissed as incapable of yielding knowledge, and mathematical knowledge is restricted to the realm of ideal entities, then natural science, which for Hume consists in experimental reasoning about matters of fact, becomes the only knowledge of reality. Even though Hume looks upon the conclusions of experimental reasoning as at best probable, it remains the case that questions about nature which cannot be answered by physics cannot be answered scientifically.

The effect is the same as that achieved by Hobbes, who makes physics the primary science of reality on the ground that nothing exists except bodies in motion. The assertion of the primacy of physics, in short, may be due *either* to the denial that immaterial objects can be known by us, *or* to the denial that such objects have any real existence. Of quite opposite tenor is the view that only immaterial and eternal things can be scientifically known, and that the sensible world of things which come to be, pass away, and are forever undergoing change, belongs to the realm of probability and opinion, not knowledge.

For Plato, mathematics and dialectic can be, respectively, science and wisdom because they study the intelligible reality of being in its immutable forms. But the physicists who try to give an account of becoming in all its changing sensible appearances can do no better than "adduce probabilities as likely as any others." On such matters, Timaeus says, "we ought to accept a tale which is probable and inquire no further." After discoursing at length of physical matters, Timaeus apologizes for the merely conjectural character of his account of natural phenomena, saying that "a man may sometimes set aside meditations about eternal things, and for recreation turn to consider the truths of becoming which are probable only; he will thus gain a pleasure not to be repented of, and secure for himself a wise and moderate pastime."

This view goes further than Hume's in depreciating physics by contrasting its probability with the certitude of mathematics. It praises mathematics and dialectic, as Hume's theory does not, for something more than their certitude—for their being knowledge of reality rather than of appearances.

Furthermore, Hume, unlike Plato, does not think the probability of physics detracts from its utility, the sort of utility which Bacon magnifies more eloquently than Hume—the invention of machines and the technical applications of physics whereby man extends his dominion over nature. In the traditional discussion of the dignity and value of physics, Plato and Bacon seem to represent attitudes as far apart as are the theories of Aristotle and Newton in the discussion of the subject matter and method of physics.

OUTLINE OF TOPICS

1. Physics as the general theory of becoming and the order of nature or change: philosophical physics, the philosophy of nature, pure or rational physics

   1*a*. The relation of the philosophy of nature to metaphysics and dialectic

   1*b*. The relation of the philosophy of nature to mathematics: mathematical method and mathematical principles in natural philosophy

2. Experimental physics and the empirical natural sciences: the relation of experimental and philosophical physics

   2*a*. The derivation of definitions, distinctions, and principles from the philosophy of nature: the metaphysics of the scientist

   2*b*. The treatment of causes in philosophical and empirical physics: description and explanation, theory and prediction

3. The role of mathematics in the natural sciences: observation and measurement in relation to mathematical formulations

4. The experimental method in the study of nature

   4*a*. The distinction between simple observation and experimentation: the art of creating ideal or isolated physical systems

   4*b*. Experimental discovery: inductive generalization from experiment; the role of theory or hypothesis in experimentation

   4*c*. Experimental testing and verification: the crucial experiment

   4*d*. Experimental measurement: the application of mathematical formulae

5. The utility of physics: the invention of machines; the techniques of engineering; the mastery of nature

REFERENCES

References are listed by volume number (in bold type), author's name, and page number. Bible references are to book, chapter, and verse of the Authorized King James version of the Bible. The abbreviation "esp" calls the reader's attention to one or more especially relevant parts of a whole reference; "passim" signifies that the topic is discussed intermittently rather than continuously in the work or passage cited. Where the work as a whole is relevant to the topic, the page numbers refer to the entire work. For general guidance in the use of *The Great Ideas,* consult the Preface.

1. Physics as the general theory of becoming and the order of nature or change: philosophical physics, the philosophy of nature, pure or rational physics

7 Plato, 447–477
8 Aristotle, 259–260, 268, 270–271, 275–278, 337, 359, 362, 390, 547–548, 589–590, 592–593
9 Aristotle, 161–165
16 Ptolemy, 5–6
18 Augustine, 265–266
19 Aquinas, 3–4
23 Hobbes, 271
30 Bacon, 40
31 Descartes, 61–62
35 Locke, 394
35 Berkeley, 432–436
42 Kant, 5–13
53 James, 882–886

1*a*. The relation of the philosophy of nature to metaphysics and dialectic

7 Plato, 240–242, 385–388
8 Aristotle, 259–260, 268, 282, 334, 507–508, 560, 589, 632
16 Ptolemy, 5–6
19 Aquinas, 451–453
23 Hobbes, 72
30 Bacon, 33–34, 42–43
42 Kant, 351–352, 561–562,
51 Tolstoy, 693–694
53 James, 862–866

1*b*. The relation of the philosophy of nature to mathematics: mathematical method and mathematical principles in natural philosophy

7 Plato, 391–398, 449–450, 458–460
8 Aristotle, 270–271, 277, 390–391, 510, 513, 589–590, 603–604, 609–610
11 Nicomachus, 812
19 Aquinas, 32–33
23 Hobbes, 72, 268
28 Galileo, 252
31 Descartes, 7, 169–170
34 Newton, 1–2
42 Kant, 5–13, 17–19, 211–218

2. Experimental physics and the empirical natural sciences: the relation of experimental and philosophical physics

8 Aristotle, 397, 411
9 Aristotle, 162
28 Gilbert, 1
28 Galileo, 202–203
30 Bacon, 30–31, 42–43, 46–47, 105–106, 111, 113–115, 120, 126, 128–129, 137–140
31 Descartes, 61–62
34 Newton, 270–271, 542–543
35 Locke, 320–323, 360–362 passim
35 Berkeley, 424
35 Hume, 459–460, 508–509
39 Smith, 336
42 Kant, 5–13, 253
45 Lavoisier, 1–2
53 James, xiii–xiv, 883
54 Freud, 545, 873–875

2*a*. The derivation of definitions, distinctions, and principles from the philosophy of nature: the metaphysics of the scientist

8 Aristotle, 397, 673
10 Hippocrates, 1
28 Gilbert, 104–105, 109
28 Galileo, 135–136, 197, 200
33 Pascal, 366–368
34 Newton, 270–271, 369–372, 540, 541–542
34 Huygens, 553–554
42 Kant, 387
45 Lavoisier, 41
45 Fourier, 172
45 Faraday, 582–584, 824, 837
53 James, 84–119, 889–890
54 Freud, 400–401, 412

2*b*. The treatment of causes in philosophical and empirical physics: description and explanation, theory and prediction

7 Plato, 240–246, 383–398, 455
8 Aristotle, 97–137 passim, 271, 275–278, 499–500, 514–515, 565, 569
9 Aristotle, 165, 255
12 Lucretius, 67–68
16 Kepler, 959–960
19 Aquinas, 175–178, 297–298

28 GILBERT, 6–7
28 HARVEY, 319, 335–336
30 BACON, 42, 45–46, 110–111, 127, 137
31 DESCARTES, 15, 131, 215
31 SPINOZA, 369–372
34 NEWTON, 7–8, 270, 371–372
35 LOCKE, 322–323
35 BERKELEY, 418–419, 422–423, 424–426 passim, 432–434 passim
35 HUME, 454–455, 460, 475–476, 477, 480–481
42 KANT, 46–47, 311–314, 557–558, 564, 581–582
49 DARWIN, 239–240
51 TOLSTOY, 344, 470, 563, 650, 694–696
53 JAMES, 89–90, 882–884, 885–886

3. The role of mathematics in the natural sciences: observation and measurement in relation to mathematical formulations

8 ARISTOTLE, 104, 108, 333
9 ARISTOTLE, 247–248
11 ARCHIMEDES, 538–560, 569–592
14 PLUTARCH, 252–255
16 KEPLER, 964–965
18 AUGUSTINE, 27–28
20 AQUINAS, 424–425
23 HOBBES, 268
28 GALILEO, 245
30 BACON, 46, 140
31 DESCARTES, 43
34 NEWTON, 7–8
35 HUME, 460
36 SWIFT, 94–103
42 KANT, 551–552
45 LAVOISIER, 33–36, 41–44, 96–103
45 FOURIER, 169, 172–173, 182–184, 249
45 FARADAY, 831
51 TOLSTOY, 469
53 JAMES, 348–359

4. The experimental method in the study of nature

4*a*. The distinction between simple observation and experimentation: the art of creating ideal or isolated physical systems

28 GALILEO, 166–167
53 JAMES, 126–127
54 FREUD, 815

4*b*. Experimental discovery: inductive generalization from experiment; the role of theory or hypothesis in experimentation

10 HIPPOCRATES, 1–3
28 GILBERT, 1, 27–28
28 GALILEO, 131–138, 157–171 passim, 203–205, 207–208
28 HARVEY, 273, 331–333
30 BACON, 56–59, 105–136, 140–148
31 DESCARTES, 61–62
33 PASCAL, 359–365, 390–403 passim
34 NEWTON, 386–404, 424–440, 450–453, 457–478, 496–516
34 HUYGENS, 551–552
35 LOCKE, 281–282
45 LAVOISIER, 2, 10–12, 17–20 esp 17, 22–24, 29–33
45 FARADAY, 265–273, 277–300, 319–330, 347–351, 362–366, 371–377, 774–775, 851
49 DARWIN, 136–139 passim
53 JAMES, 126–127, 265–268, 341–344, 348–357 passim, 385

4*c*. Experimental testing and verification: the crucial experiment

10 GALEN, 173–177, 199–200, 205–207
21 DANTE, 108
28 GALILEO, 148–149, 207–208
28 HARVEY, 268–273, 286–304, 311–312
30 BACON, 164–168
31 DESCARTES, 61–62, 66
33 PASCAL, 368–370, 382–389, 404–405, 425–429
34 NEWTON, 408–410, 412–416, 453–455
35 LOCKE, 362
45 LAVOISIER, 32–33
45 FARADAY, 300–316, 334–335, 377–383, 388–389, 440, 830–832
49 DARWIN, 12
53 JAMES, 882–884
54 FREUD, 815, 818–819

4*d*. Experimental measurement: the application of mathematical formulae

28 GILBERT, 85–89, 92–93
28 GALILEO, 136–137, 164–166
28 HARVEY, 286–288
34 NEWTON, 20–22, 211–219, 239–246
45 LAVOISIER, 33–36, 87–90, 91–95, 96–103
45 FOURIER, 175, 184–185
45 FARADAY, 316–318, 366–371, 444–451, 465–467, 768–773, 778–793
53 JAMES, 56–66, 341–344, 348–359

5. The utility of physics: the invention of machines; the techniques of engineering; the mastery of nature

14 PLUTARCH, 252–255
28 GILBERT, 75, 100–101
28 GALILEO, 191–193
30 BACON, 34, 120, 134–135, 170, 175–194, 210–214
31 DESCARTES, 60–67
34 NEWTON, 412–423
36 SWIFT, 99–112
40 GIBBON, 661–663
41 GIBBON, 291–292, 509–510
45 LAVOISIER, 41–44
45 FARADAY, 433–440
50 MARX, 170, 180–188
54 FREUD, 778–779

CROSS-REFERENCES

For: The general discussion of the distinction between philosophy and science, relevant to the difference between a philosophical and an experimental physics, *see* Knowledge 6c(4); Philosophy 1c; Science 1c.

The relation of physics as a philosophy of nature to mathematics and to metaphysics, *see* Mathematics 1a; Matter 4b; Metaphysics 3b; Nature 4b; Philosophy 2b; Science 1a(2).

The relation of mathematics to experimental physics, and for the nature of mathematical physics, *see* Astronomy 2c; Mathematics 5b; Mechanics 3; Science 5c.

Other discussions relevant to the treatment of causes in philosophical and scientific physics, *see* Astronomy 3a–3b; Cause 5b; Science 4c; and for other treatments of problems or concepts fundamental to physics, *see* Chance 1a–1b; Change 2–2b, 5a–5b, 6a–6b, 7a–7d; Element 3–3d, 5; Infinity 3d–3e, 4a–4b; Matter 1–1b, 2a–2b; Mechanics 1a–1c, 6a–6e; Nature 3a–3c(3); Quantity 5a–5e; Space 1–2c, 3b; Time 1.

The logic of the experimental method in the study of nature, *see* Induction 5; Logic 4b; Mechanics 2a; Reasoning 6c; and for the theory of experimentation and the use of hypotheses and measurements, *see* Astronomy 2a–2b; Experience 5a–5c; Hypothesis 4–4d; Mathematics 5a; Mechanics 2b, 3a; Quantity 6–6c; Science 5a–5b, 5d–5e.

Other considerations of the utility of physics or natural science generally, *see* Knowledge 8a; Science 1b(1).

The various branches of physics, such as astronomy, statics, dynamics, optics, acoustics, hydrodynamics, magnetism, and electricity, *see* Astronomy 8a–9f; Mechanics 1b, 5a–5f(2), 6a–6e, 7a, 7b–7c, 7d, 7e.

Discussions relevant to the distinction between physics and biology or psychology, *see* Animal 4a; Change 6c–6d, 9a–9b, 10a–10b; Life and Death 2; Mechanics 4b–4c; Mind 2e; and for the treatment of one aspect of psychophysics, *see* Sense 3c(2).

ADDITIONAL READINGS

Listed below are works not included in *Great Books of the Western World*, but relevant to the idea and topics with which this chapter deals. These works are divided into two groups:

I. Works by authors represented in this collection.
II. Works by authors not represented in this collection.

For the date, place, and other facts concerning the publication of the works cited, consult the Bibliography of Additional Readings which follows the last chapter of *The Great Ideas*.

I.

AQUINAS. *On the Trinity of Boethius*, QQ 5–6
HOBBES. *Concerning Body*, PART IV, CH 27
NEWTON. *Letters on Various Subjects in Natural Philosophy*
KANT. *Prolegomena to Any Future Metaphysic*, par 14–39
——. *Metaphysical Foundations of Natural Science*
HEGEL. *Science of Logic*, VOL II, SECT II, CH 2

II.

SUÁREZ. *Disputationes Metaphysicae*, I (4), XV (11)
BOYLE. *New Experiments Physico-Mechanical*
——. *The Sceptical Chymist*
——. *The Origin of Forms and Qualities, According to the Corpuscular Philosophy*
——. *Experiments, Notes, etc. About the Mechanical Origine or Production of Divers Particular Qualities*
VOLTAIRE. *Letters on the English*, XIV–XVII
BLACK. *Experiments upon Magnesia Alba, Quicklime, and Some Other Alcaline Substances*
J. PRIESTLEY. *Experiments and Observations on Different Kinds of Air*
CAVENDISH. *Experiments of Factitious Air*
——. *Electrical Researches*
——. *Experiments on Air*
SCHELLING. *Ideen zu einer Philosophie der Natur*
T. YOUNG. *Lectures on Natural Philosophy and the Mechanical Arts*
DAVY. *Elements of Chemical Philosophy*
DALTON. *A New System of Chemical Philosophy*
COMTE. *The Positive Philosophy*, BK III–IV
WHEWELL. *The Philosophy of the Inductive Sciences*, VOL I, BK V–VI
TYNDALL. *On the Study of Physics*
HELMHOLTZ. *Popular Lectures on Scientific Subjects*, I
HERSCHEL. *A Preliminary Discourse on the Study of Natural Philosophy*
——. *Familiar Lectures on Scientific Subjects*, VI–VIII, XIII
MENDELEYEV. *The Principles of Chemistry*
W. THOMSON and TAIT. *Treatise on Natural Philosophy*
——. *Elements of Natural Philosophy*
LOTZE. *Grundzüge der Naturphilosophie*
MAXWELL. *Matter and Motion*
CLIFFORD. *The Common Sense of the Exact Sciences*, CH 2, 5
OSTWALD. *Natural Philosophy*
POINCARÉ. *The Value of Science*, PART II
DUHEM. *La théorie physique, son objet—sa structure*
MEYERSON. *Identity and Reality*
CASSIRER. *Substance and Function*, PART I, CH 4; SUP VII
BROAD. *Perception, Physics, and Reality*
N. R. CAMPBELL. *Physics; the Elements*
PAULI. *Relativitätstheorie*
LORENTZ. *Lectures on Theoretical Physics*
——. *Problems of Modern Physics*
WHITEHEAD. *The Concept of Nature*, CH 9
——. *The Principle of Relativity with Applications to Physical Science*
——. *Science and the Modern World*, CH 7–8
BRIDGMAN. *The Logic of Modern Physics*
WEYL. *Space—Time—Matter*
——. *Philosophy of Mathematics and Natural Science*
BOHR. *Atomic Theory and the Description of Nature*
HEISENBERG. *The Physical Principles of the Quantum Theory*
SANTAYANA. *The Realm of Matter*, CH I
M. R. COHEN. *Reason and Nature*, BK II, CH 2
LENZEN. *The Nature of Physical Theory*
EINSTEIN. *Relativity: The Special and the General Theory*
——. *Sidelights on Relativity*
——. *The Meaning of Relativity*
——. *On the Method of Theoretical Physics*
CARNAP. *The Unity of Science*
——. *Philosophy and Logical Syntax*, III (5–9)
MARITAIN. *An Introduction to Philosophy*, PART II (3)
——. *The Degrees of Knowledge*, CH 3
——. *Science and Wisdom*, pp 34–69
GILSON. *The Unity of Philosophical Experience*, CH 9
EINSTEIN and INFELD. *The Evolution of Physics*
WATSON. *On Understanding Physics*
D'ABRO. *Decline of Mechanism in Modern Physics*
EDDINGTON. *The Mathematical Theory of Relativity*
——. *The Philosophy of Physical Science*
RIEZLER. *Physics and Reality*
P. FRANK. *Between Physics and Philosophy*
B. RUSSELL. *Our Knowledge of the External World*, III–IV
——. *The Analysis of Matter*, CH 1–26, 37
——. *Human Knowledge, Its Scope and Limits*, PART I, CH 3; PART II, CH 4
PLANCK. *A Survey of Physics*
——. *The Philosophy of Physics*, CH I
——. *Scientific Autobiography*
SCHLICK. *Philosophy of Nature*

Chapter 68: PLEASURE AND PAIN

INTRODUCTION

PLEASURE and pain, writes Locke, "like other simple ideas, cannot be described, nor their names defined; the way of knowing them is . . . only by experience." That pleasure and pain are elementary experiences, attributed to animals as well as enjoyed or suffered by men, is attested by poets and physiologists alike, by economists and theologians, by historians and moralists. Yet in the tradition of western thought, few of the great writers are content to leave the nature or meaning of pleasure and pain to the intuitions of experience alone.

Conflicting definitions are proposed. Psychologists disagree about the conditions under which the feelings of pleasure and pain occur, their causes and consequences, their relation to sensation, to desire and emotion, to thought, volition, and action. Moralists dispute whether pleasure is the only good and pain the only evil, whether pleasure is only one good among others to be assessed according to its worth in the scale of goods, whether pleasure and pain are morally indifferent, whether some pleasures are good, others bad, or all are intrinsically evil.

Not only in the theory of good and evil, but also in the theories of beauty and truth, pleasure and pain are fundamental terms. They are affected by all the difficulties which belong to these great themes; and also with the difficulties attendant on the ideas of virtue, sin, and punishment, of duty and happiness, into the consideration of which pleasure and pain traditionally enter.

The traditional use of the words "pleasure" and "pain" is complicated by more than the variety of definitions which have been given. Other words are frequently substituted for them, sometimes as synonyms and sometimes to express only one part or aspect of their meaning. Locke, for example, uses "pleasure" or "delight," "pain" or "uneasiness," and he observes that "whether we call it satisfaction, delight, pleasure, happiness, etc., on the one side, or uneasiness, trouble, pain, torment, anguish, misery, etc., on the other, they are still but different degrees of the same thing." Other writers use "joy" and "sorrow" or "grief" as synonyms for "pleasure" and "pain."

The words "pleasure" and "pain" are closely associated in meaning with "pleasant" and "unpleasant," though Freud sometimes uses "unpleasure" (*unlust*) to signify an opposite of pleasure which is not the same as ordinary pain (*schmerz*). The pleasant is often called "agreeable," "enjoyable," or "satisfying." In the language of Shakespeare, the words "like" and "dislike" have currency as the equivalents of "please" and "displease." A person who is displeased by something says of it that "it likes me not."

THE PROBLEM OF what pleasure and pain are seems logically to precede the ethical consideration of their relation to good and evil, happiness and misery, virtue and duty. But in the tradition of the great books, the psychological questions about pleasure and pain are usually raised in moral or political treatises, and sometimes in connection with discussions of rhetoric. What pleasure is, how it is caused, and the effects it produces are seldom considered apart from whether pleasures should be sought or avoided, whether some pleasures should be preferred to others, and whether pleasure is the sole criterion of the good. Sometimes, as with Marcus Aurelius and Epictetus, the ethical point—that pleasure and pain are in one sense morally indifferent—is made without any psychological account of the nature and origin of these experiences. More frequently, as in Plato's *Philebus* and Aristotle's *Ethics*, or in the writings of Hobbes, Spinoza, Locke, and Mill, the psychological discussion is imbedded in an ethical or political context.

Even Lucretius and William James do not seem to be complete exceptions. James' theory that the feeling of pleasure accompanies activity which is unimpeded, whereas pain attends arrested activity, seems to be a purely psychological observation, and one which can be readily divorced from moral considerations on the ground that it makes no difference to the occurrence of pleasure and pain whether the activity in question is ethically good or bad. Yet James makes this observation the basis for arguing against those whom he calls "the pleasure-philosophers"—those who make pleasure the only motive or goal of conduct. They confuse, he thinks, the pursuit of pleasure itself with the pleasure which accompanies the successful achievement of other things which may be the goals of activity.

"A *pleasant act*," he writes, "and an act *pursuing a pleasure* are in themselves two perfectly distinct conceptions, though they coalesce in one concrete phenomenon whenever a pleasure is deliberately pursued . . . Because a pleasure of achievement *can* become a pursued pleasure upon occasion, it does not follow that everywhere and always that pleasure must be pursued." One might as well suppose that "because no steamer can go to sea without incidentally consuming coal, and because some steamers may occasionally go to sea to *try* their coal, that therefore no steamer *can* go to sea for any other motive than that of coal-consumption."

Psychological observations of this sort have an obvious relevance to Aristotle's theory of good and bad pleasures, as well as to Locke's and Mill's position that pleasure is the only good or the only object of desire. They reveal an ethical strain even in the psychologist's view of pleasure and pain. The same point can be made with regard to James' observation that "pleasures are generally associated with beneficial, pains with detrimental, experiences."

Lucretius appears to give a purely physiological account of pleasure and pain in terms of the effect upon the sense-organs of various atomic configurations. "Those things which can touch the senses pleasantly are made of smooth and round bodies, but those which seem to be bitter and harsh are made up of particles more hooked, and for this reason are wont to tear a way into our senses . . . Hot fires and cold frost have particles fanged in different ways to prick the senses." But Lucretius is concerned to point out not only the basis of pain in the atomic nature of things, but also the natural tendency of all sensible things to avoid pain as the one besetting evil. "Nature cries aloud for nothing else but that pain may be kept far sundered from the body, and that, withdrawn from care and fear, she may enjoy in mind the sense of pleasure."

Without giving any psychological explanation of the pleasures of the mind, Lucretius sets them above the pleasures of the body because the latter—as his diatribe against love makes clear—seem to be inevitably followed by bodily torments or even to be admixed with them. The first maxim of nature, then, is not to seek pleasure, but to avoid pain; and among pleasures to seek only the unmixed or pure, the pleasures of knowledge and truth. The distinction between different qualities of pleasure (pleasures of the body and of the mind, mixed and pure pleasures), which is made by Plato and Mill as well as by Lucretius, inevitably tends to have at once both moral and psychological significance.

If, in the great books, there is any purely psychological theory of pleasure and pain, divorced from moral considerations, it is probably to be found in Freud. The pleasure-principle, according to him, automatically regulates the operation of the mental apparatus. "Our entire psychical activity," he writes, "is bent upon *procuring pleasure* and *avoiding pain*." Though pleasure and pain are for him primary elements of mental life, Freud admits the difficulty they present for psychological analysis. "We should like to know," he writes, "what are the conditions giving rise to pleasure and pain, but that is just where we fall short. We may only venture to say that pleasure is *in some way* connected with lessening, lowering, or extinguishing the amount of stimulation in the mental apparatus; and that pain involves a heightening of the latter. Consideration of the most intense pleasure of which man is capable, the pleasure in the performance of the sexual act, leaves little doubt upon this point."

Yet for Freud the pleasure-principle is not the only regulator of mental life. In addition to the sexual instincts, which aim at gratification and pleasure, there are the ego-instincts which, "under the influence of necessity, their mistress, soon learn to replace the pleasure-principle by a modification of it. The task of avoiding pain becomes for them almost equal in importance to that of gaining pleasure; the ego learns that it must inevitably go without immediate satisfaction, postpone gratification, learn to endure a degree of pain, and altogether renounce certain sources of pleasure. Thus trained, the ego becomes 'reasonable,' is no longer controlled by the pleasure-principle, but follows the reality-principle, which at bottom also seeks pleasure—although a delayed and diminished pleasure, one which is assured by its realization of fact, its relation to reality."

This recognition of a conflict between pleasure and reality, with a consequent attenuation or redirection of the pleasure-principle, is not amplified by Freud into a moral doctrine. It does, however, bear a striking resemblance to the theories of moralists like Kant who oppose duty to pleasure; and also to the teachings of those who, like Aristotle and Aquinas, conceive virtue as the foregoing of certain pleasures and the endurance of certain pains, through a reasonable and habitual moderation of these passions.

If pleasure and pain were simply sensations, like sensations of color or sound, they would pose a problem for the physiological psychologist no different from the problems which arise in the fields of vision and audition. Modern physiological research claims to have discovered differentiated nerve-endings for pain which, together with the specific sense-organs for pressure, heat, and cold, make up the cutaneous senses. But whether there are special cells for the reception of pain stimuli or whether cutaneous pain results from the too intense stimulation of the pressure and thermal nerve-endings, there seems to be no evidence of organs sensitized to pleasure as, for example, the nerve cells of the retina are sensitized to light. The feeling of pleasure, it would seem to follow, is not a sensation. This seems to be confirmed by the traditional observation that every type of sensation, including the sensation of pain, can be pleasant.

Even if pain, unlike pleasure, is found to be a specific mode of sensation with a special sense-organ of its own, all other types of sensation—visual, auditory, olfactory, etc.—might still have painfulness or a feeling of unpleasantness as an attribute. That such is the case seems to be a matter of traditional observation. Locke, for example, says that "delight or uneasiness, one or the other of them, join themselves to almost all our ideas of sensation and reflection: there is scarce any affection of our senses from without . . . which is not able to produce in us pleasure or pain." So understood, pleasure and pain—or the pleasant and the unpleasant—are not opposite sensations, as are hot and cold, but contrary attributes with which every sort of sensation *can* be affected. All *need* not be. Some sensations may be neutral with respect to what psychologists call "affective tone" or "affective quality."

The kind of pleasure and pain which is called "bodily" or "sensuous" would thus be sensuous because it is an attribute of sensations, and bodily because sensations involve bodily organs. But in almost every great discussion of pleasure and pain, other types are recognized: intellectual delights, the pleasures and pains of learning, aesthetic pleasure in contemplating beauty with the mind as well as with the senses, and the pain of loss, the grief accompanying deprivation, which is so different from the torment of a painful affliction of the senses. The human suffering with which the great poems deal is much more often a torment of the spirit than of the flesh.

To cover these other types of pleasure and pain, we must go beyond sensation to two other terms traditionally connected with the psychological analysis of pleasure and pain. One is emotion, the other desire, the latter to be understood broadly as including both the sensitive and the rational appetites—both the passions and the will. Aquinas, for example, treats joy and sorrow as specific emotions which represent the appetite in a state of satisfaction or frustration. So, too, the will as an appetite can come to rest in the attainment of its object and, with fruition, be in a state of joy.

As conditions of the appetite, pleasure and

pain (or joy and sorrow) can be either passions and, like all other emotions, bodily states; or they can be acts of the will and, according to Aquinas at least, spiritual states. But either way pleasure and pain seem to represent the satisfaction or frustration of desire rather than objects desired or averted. To be pleased by the attainment of an object desired, such as food and drink or knowledge, is not the same as to desire pleasure itself, as, for example, the pleasant sensations which may be involved in eating or drinking.

Aquinas talks about the desire for pleasure and the aversion to pain, as well as the pleasure and pain of satisfied and unsatisfied desires. Since the same words are almost always used to express both meanings, the two senses of pleasure and displeasure may go unnoticed unless by context or by explicit mention the author refers to pleasure as an object of desire or identifies it with the satisfaction of any desire, whether for pleasure or for some other object. As a passage already quoted from James indicates, and as we shall presently see more fully, the distinction between these two senses of pleasure has a critical bearing on the dispute between those who think that pleasure is the only good, and those who think that pleasure is one good among others.

The generally recognized difference between two kinds of pain—the pain of sense and the pain of loss or deprivation—parallels the distinction which most writers acknowledge between sensuous pleasure and the pleasure of possession or satisfaction. Plato's example of the pleasure involved in the relief of itching by scratching seems to catch both meanings, and, in addition, to show that bodily pleasures may be either sensual *objects* or sensual *satisfactions*. In contrast, the pleasures of the mind are satisfactions of intellectual desire, as in the contemplation of beauty or the knowledge of truth.

Aristotle deals with pleasure and pain as *objects* when he defines temperance as a moderate pursuit of bodily pleasures, and courage as controlling the fear of pain and its avoidance. But he also conceives pleasure as that which completes any activity, whether of the senses and the body or of thought and the mind. "Without activity," he writes, "pleasure does not arise, and every activity is completed by the attendant pleasure." This meaning of pleasure seems to be analogous to, if not identical with, pleasure as satisfaction, at least insofar as the satisfaction of a desire is that which completes the activity springing therefrom. There can be as many different kinds of pleasure as there are kinds of activity; the quality of the pleasure is determined by the character of the activity it accompanies.

Though Mill refers to pleasure and freedom from pain as "the only things desirable as ends," he admits many other objects of desire, in the attainment of which men find pleasure or satisfaction. It is wrong to suppose that human beings, he writes, are "capable of no pleasures except those of which swine are capable." Precisely because "human beings have faculties more elevated than the animal appetites," they have sources of pleasure or gratification not open to swine. Here as before two meanings of pleasure seem to be involved. In pointing out that "money, in many cases, is desired in and for itself," Mill is naming an object of desire which, like health, knowledge, power, or fame, is not pleasure, yet which, through being desired, is a source of pleasure (*i.e.*, satisfaction) when achieved. Like other objects of desire, sensual or bodily pleasures may also be sources of satisfaction.

THESE TWO MEANINGS of pleasure are most in need of clear distinction when the relation of pleasure to happiness is being discussed. If happiness, as Aristotle and Mill seem to say, consists in having all desires satisfied, then the content of the happy life can be described either in terms of the goods which the happy man possesses—the objects of desires fulfilled—or in terms of the pleasures which accompany the goods possessed, that is, the pleasures which are satisfactions of desire. If pleasure in the other meaning, especially sensual or bodily pleasure, is only one object of normal desire, then lack or deficiency of pleasure may, like loss of health or fortune, impair a man's happiness. But the pursuit of pleasure in this sense cannot be identified with the pursuit of happiness. A life including every sort of bodily pleasure and free from every sort of bodily pain, if it lacked other things men normally desire, would be marred by many dissatisfactions inconsistent with happiness.

Talking to Don Quixote of the island he would like to govern, Sancho Panza says: "The first thing I would do in my government, I would have nobody to control me, I would be absolute . . . Now he that's absolute, can do what he likes; he that can do what he likes, can take his pleasure; he that can take his pleasure, can be content, and he that can be content, has no more to desire." Here, it would seem, Sancho conceives happiness as the sum of pleasures in the sense of satisfactions—all desires come to rest through the possession of their objects.

Dr. Johnson seems to make the opposite point about pleasure and happiness. Boswell asks him whether abstention from wine would be "a great deduction from life." "It is a diminution of pleasure to be sure," Johnson replies, "but I do not say a diminution of happiness." But, Boswell asks, "if we could have pleasure always, should we not be happy?" Johnson explains his negative answer by saying that "when we talk of pleasure, we mean sensual pleasure. When a man says, he had pleasure with a woman, he does not mean conversation, but something of a different nature. Philosophers tell you that pleasure is contrary to happiness."

This last observation does not seem to describe the position taken by those philosophers who make happiness the greatest good or ultimate end of human striving. Both Aristotle and Mill distinguish the life of pleasure, the bestial or swinish life, from one which employs the higher faculties peculiar to man. In this sense, perhaps, the life of pleasure can be regarded as contrary or opposed to what Johnson, along with Aristotle and Mill, calls "the rational life." But pleasure itself, far from being inimical to happiness, either represents the state of satisfaction which is identical with happiness, or one of the things a man desires and hence a constituent of the happy life.

Hobbes and Locke seem to go further in the direction of identifying pleasure with happiness or the good. "Pleasure," writes Hobbes, "is the appearance or sense of Good . . . and Displeasure, the appearance or sense of Evil." Similarly, Locke says that "things are good or evil only in reference to pleasure or pain. That we call *good* which is apt to cause or increase pleasure or to diminish pain in us . . . And, on the contrary, we name that *evil* which is apt to produce or increase any pain, or diminish any pleasure in us." As for happiness, it is, according to Locke, "the utmost pleasure we are capable of, and misery the utmost pain; and the lowest degree of what can be called happiness is so much ease from all pain, and so much present pleasure, as without which anyone cannot be content."

In which sense of the term is Locke identifying pleasure with happiness? Not sensual pleasure, nor even pleasure as an object of desire, it would seem, for he says: "Let one man place his satisfaction in sensual pleasure, another in the delight of knowledge; though each of them cannot but confess there is great pleasure in what the other pursues, yet neither of them making the other's delight a part of *his* happiness, their desires are not moved, but each is satisfied without what the other enjoys." Yet his understanding of happiness as consisting in the pleasures or satisfactions accompanying the possession of things desired leads him to criticize "the philosophers of old" who "did in vain inquire whether the *summum bonum* consisted in riches, or bodily delights, or virtue, or contemplation; they might have as reasonably disputed whether the best relish were to be found in apples, plums, or nuts, and have divided themselves into sects upon it. For as pleasant tastes depend not on the things themselves, but on their agreeableness to this or that particular palate, wherein there is great variety; so the greatest happiness consists in the having those things which produce the greatest pleasure . . . These, to different men, are very different things."

The difference between Locke's position and that of Mill seems, therefore, not to lie in a different conception of the relation of pleasure—as object or as satisfaction of desire—to happiness, but rather in Locke's conception of degrees of happiness as being determined only by larger and smaller quantities of pleasure, whereas Mill insists upon diverse qualities of pleasure, and upon the possibility of ordering pleasures as higher and lower. In consequence, Mill can say what Locke would seem unable to approve, namely, that "it is better to be a human being dissatisfied than a pig satisfied; better to be Socrates dissatisfied than a fool satisfied."

Locke's denial that happiness is the same

for all men explicitly takes issue with Aristotle's contrary view. It also involves an issue about pleasure. For Locke, as apparently for Hobbes and Mill, the good and the pleasant are inseparable. Nothing which satisfies a desire can be evil. Whether, as in Locke's view, one satisfaction is as good as another, and the only thing which matters is the amount or number of satisfactions; or whether, as in Mill's view one pleasure may be better than another, in no case is a pleasure bad so long as some one desires it, or desires the thing which produces satisfaction when possessed.

But, for Aristotle, desires themselves can be good or bad, and consequently there can be good and bad pleasures, as well as pleasures which vary in quality and in degree of goodness. "Since activities differ in respect of goodness and badness, and some are worthy to be chosen, others to be avoided, and others neutral, so, too," Aristotle writes, "are the pleasures; for to each activity there is a proper pleasure. The pleasure proper to a worthy activity is good, and that proper to an unworthy activity bad; just as the appetites for noble objects are laudable, those for base objects culpable."

Pleasure and pain, in Aristotle's judgment, are measured by virtue, not what is good and evil by pleasure and pain. Pleasure and pain are elements common to the good life and the bad, but only the pleasures which the good man enjoys, and the pains he willingly suffers, can be called good. That is why "in educating the young we steer them by the rudders of pleasure and pain . . . for to enjoy the things we ought and to hate the things we ought has the greatest bearing on virtue or character." Virtue is possessed only by those who habitually take pleasure in the right things.

AS INDICATED IN THE chapters on HAPPINESS and DUTY, the moralists who make duty rather than virtue the spring of right conduct, and who make the goodness of anything depend upon its rightness according to the moral law, see little difference among the various theories of pleasure and happiness as the ultimate good and the standard of conduct.

The most eloquent tribute which Kant can pay to the idea of duty is that it "embraces nothing charming or insinuating." Reason, he says, "will never let itself be brought around" to the view that "there is any intrinsic worth in the real existence of a man who merely lives for enjoyment . . . even when in so doing he serves others." Admitting that "the greatest aggregate of the pleasures of life, taking duration as well as number into account," would appear to merit "the name of a true, nay, even of the highest good," Kant adds that "reason sets its face against this, too." The line of duty is always set against the seductions of pleasure or any calculations of utility, whether in terms of the means to achieving happiness or the ways of augmenting life's satisfactions.

According to Stoics like Marcus Aurelius, "pleasure is neither good nor useful," nor is pain an evil, for when we are "pained by any external thing," we should remember that "it is not this thing which disturbs us, but our own judgment about it." Pleasure and pain are morally indifferent, for like death and life, honor and dishonor, pain and pleasure are things which "happen equally to good men and bad" and therefore "make us neither better nor worse . . . and are neither good nor evil."

From the same observation, that pleasure is enjoyed by good and bad men, Aristotle and Plato seem to draw the conclusion, not that it is morally indifferent, but, as we have seen, that there are good and bad pleasures. Plato uses pleasure and wisdom to typify fundamentally different kinds of good. Wisdom is always true and good, but like opinion, which can be either true or false, there are true and false pleasures, good and evil pleasures. Furthermore, wisdom or knowledge represents the kind of good which is definite or intrinsically measured, whereas pleasure, like wealth, is an indefinite good, requiring something external to itself, something like wisdom, to measure it and limit its quantity.

If wisdom be allowed to choose among pleasures, Socrates suggests in the *Philebus*, it will choose those associated with itself in the activities of the mind, not the bodily pleasures which are always mixed with pain. So far as pleasure belongs to the realm of change or becoming, it is, again like opinion, inferior to knowledge and wisdom, which draw their goodness from the realm of immutable being. Yet Plato does not seem to think that knowledge and wisdom are the only goods. The argument against those who think so seems to be as conclusive as against those who think that pleasure is the only good.

Each of the simple lives—the life of pleasure or the life of wisdom—is deficient. Only the mixed life, the life which combines both pleasure and wisdom, is the complete life. Like the happy life in Aristotle's view, it includes every kind of good; and the difficult problem, for Plato as for Aristotle, seems to be finding the principle which determines the goodness of the mixture or the right order and proportion in which the variety of goods should be combined.

THE MORAL ISSUES which have been raised here with respect to pleasure and pain are more broadly considered in the chapters on GOOD AND EVIL and on VIRTUE, TEMPERANCE, and SIN, as well as in the chapters on HAPPINESS and DUTY. Other issues are reserved entirely for discussion elsewhere, such as the role of pleasure in the perception of beauty and in judgments of taste (the chapter on BEAUTY), or the role of pain in relation to the government of men (the chapter on PUNISHMENT).

Two special problems which involve pleasure and pain remain to be briefly mentioned. The first concerns the contrast between asceticism and self-indulgence or even profligacy.

In the tradition of western thought and culture, and in the ancient as well as in the modern world, those who worship pleasure, though perhaps only as a minor deity to be celebrated in bacchic revels, stand opposed to those who turn away from pleasure, as from the world, the flesh, and the devil, even mortifying the flesh and sanctifying themselves with pain. In their less extreme forms these contrasting attitudes generate the traditional issue concerning the place of worldly recreations in man's life and in the state. Is the pleasure of play a necessary and proper relief from the pain of work, or is it always an indulgence which provides occasions for sin? Are the enjoyment of the theatre, of music and poetry, the gaiety of public festivals, and the diversions of games or sports things to be promoted or prohibited by the state?

Man's avidity for amusements and diversions of all sorts leads Pascal to say, "How hollow and full of ribaldry is the heart of man!" The fact that "men spend their time in following a ball or a hare" and that "it is the pleasure even of kings," indicates to him how deep is the misery from which men try to escape through play and pleasure. "If man were happy," Pascal suggests, "he would be the more so, the less he was diverted." But "so wretched is man that he would weary, even without any cause of weariness, from the peculiar state of his disposition; and so frivolous is he, that, though full of a thousand reasons for weariness, the least thing, such as playing billiards or hitting a ball, is sufficient to amuse him." Men need such diversions in order to "prevent them from thinking of themselves."

Men indulge in pastimes for another reason, according to Aristotle. They "need relaxation because they cannot work continuously" and "amusement is a sort of relaxation." But "happiness does not lie in amusement. It would, indeed, be strange," he says, "if the end were amusement, and one were to take trouble and suffer hardship all one's life in order to amuse one's self." It is true that "pleasant amusements" resemble happiness in having the nature of an end, because we engage in playful activity "not for the sake of other things," whereas we do serious work for some end beyond itself. But in Aristotle's opinion "a virtuous life requires exertion" and since "the happy life is thought to be virtuous," it follows that "serious things are better than laughable things and those connected with amusement."

These reflections on work and play, and the pains and pleasures they involve, lead us to the second of the two problems mentioned above. That concerns pleasure and pain in the life of learning. Here there seems to be no fundamental issue, for the tradition speaks with an almost unanimous voice of the pleasure all men find in knowing and the pain none can avoid in the process of seeking the truth. The problem is rather a practical and personal one which the great books put to their readers, to solve in their individual lives. Their invitation to learning should not be accepted, nor their promise of pleasure relied upon, by those unwilling to take the pains which, however great initially, gradually diminish as the mind, in the very process of learning, learns how to learn.

OUTLINE OF TOPICS

1. The nature of pleasure and pain

2. The causes of pleasure and pain

3. The effects or concomitants of pleasure and pain

4. The kinds of pleasure and pain: different qualities of pleasure

 4*a*. The pleasant and unpleasant in the sphere of emotion: joy and sorrow, delight and grief

 4*b*. Sensuous pleasure: the affective quality of sensations

 4*c*. Intellectual pleasure: the pleasures of reflection and contemplation

  (1) Pleasure in the beauty of nature or art: disinterested pleasure

  (2) The pleasure and pain of learning and knowledge

 4*d*. The pleasures of play and diversion

 4*e*. The kinds of pain: the pain of sense and the pain of loss or deprivation

5. The quantity of pleasure: the weighing of pleasures; the limits of pleasure

6. Pleasure and the good

 6*a*. Pleasure as the only good or as the measure of goodness in all other things

 6*b*. Pleasure as one good among many: pleasure as one object of desire

 6*c*. Good and bad pleasures: higher and lower pleasures

 6*d*. Pleasure as the accompaniment of goods possessed: the satisfaction of desire

 6*e*. Pleasure as intrinsically evil or morally indifferent

7. Pleasure and happiness: their distinction and relation

 7*a*. Pleasure and pain in relation to love and friendship

 7*b*. The life of pleasure contrasted with other modes of life: the ascetic life

8. The discipline of pleasure

 8*a*. Pleasure and pain in relation to virtue: the restraints of temperance and the endurance of courage

 8*b*. The conflict between pleasure and duty, or the obligations of justice: the pleasure principle and the reality principle

 8*c*. Perversions or degradations in the sphere of pleasure and pain: sadism and masochism

9. The regulation of pleasures by law

10. The social utility of pleasure and pain

 10*a*. The employment of pleasure and pain by parent or teacher in moral and mental training

 10*b*. The use of pleasure and pain by orator or statesman in persuasion and government

REFERENCES

References are listed by volume number (in bold type), author's name, and page number. Bible references are to book, chapter, and verse of the Authorized King James version of the Bible. The abbreviation "esp" calls the reader's attention to one or more especially relevant parts of a whole reference; "passim" signifies that the topic is discussed intermittently rather than continuously in the work or passage cited. Where the work as a whole is relevant to the topic, the page numbers refer to the entire work. For general guidance in the use of *The Great Ideas,* consult the Preface.

1. The nature of pleasure and pain

7 PLATO, 221, 609–639, 748
9 ARISTOTLE, 399, 403–406, 426–430 esp 428–429, 613
12 AURELIUS, 282, 287–289
17 PLOTINUS, 167
18 AUGUSTINE, 54–55, 389–390
19 AQUINAS, 263–264, 752–759, 772–780
25 MONTAIGNE, 531
31 SPINOZA, 416–417
35 LOCKE, 131–132
42 KANT, 293, 385–386
53 JAMES, 829–830
54 FREUD, 663

2. The causes of pleasure and pain

7 PLATO, 422–425, 463–464, 619–633
8 ARISTOTLE, 330
9 ARISTOTLE, 398–399, 404, 612–615
12 LUCRETIUS, 33
12 AURELIUS, 289
18 AUGUSTINE, 13–14, 76–77
19 AQUINAS, 759–765, 770–771, 780–783, 786–789
20 AQUINAS, 897–900
23 HOBBES, 62
31 SPINOZA, 399–415 passim
32 MILTON, 171–173
35 LOCKE, 135, 176, 197–198
41 GIBBON, 234
42 KANT, 314–318, 470–471
48 MELVILLE, 39–40
53 JAMES, 812
54 FREUD, 403–404, 413, 422, 639–640, 648–649, 701, 753–754, 772–773

3. The effects or concomitants of pleasure and pain

7 PLATO, 474, 628, 637
8 ARISTOTLE, 644
9 ARISTOTLE, 365–366, 400, 421
19 AQUINAS, 761–762, 765–768, 783–789
21 DANTE, 80
24 RABELAIS, 8
31 SPINOZA, 416–422
35 LOCKE, 186, 192–194
42 KANT, 375, 385–386
46 HEGEL, 220
49 DARWIN, 308–309
53 JAMES, 94, 526–527, 725–726, 808–814
54 FREUD, 377–380, 402–404, 419–427, 639–663, 701, 711–712, 737–741, 753, 843–846

4. The kinds of pleasure and pain: different qualities of pleasure

7 PLATO, 220–221, 277–280, 409–410, 421–425, 609–610
9 ARISTOTLE, 364–365, 404–406, 427–430, 613–615
12 LUCRETIUS, 31
19 AQUINAS, 619–620, 754–758, 772–780
23 HOBBES, 62
25 MONTAIGNE, 432, 537–543
32 MILTON, 17–21, 205–206
33 PASCAL, 441–442
35 LOCKE, 176–178, 192–193
43 MILL, 447–450
50 MARX, 292–295
51 TOLSTOY, 577–578, 630–631
53 JAMES, 754–758, 812–813

4*a*. The pleasant and unpleasant in the sphere of emotion: joy and sorrow, delight and grief

7 PLATO, 628–630
8 ARISTOTLE, 175
9 ARISTOTLE, 363–366, 399, 400, 419–420, 613–614, 623–636
12 AURELIUS, 257–258
14 PLUTARCH, 184
17 PLOTINUS, 172–173
18 AUGUSTINE, 21, 81
19 AQUINAS, 752–792, 822–823
23 HOBBES, 63
29 CERVANTES, 217–218
35 LOCKE, 176–178, 187–188
44 BOSWELL, 103
53 JAMES, 197, 730
54 FREUD, 418–421, 422–425, 641–643, 720–721, 736–740, 752–754, 843–846

4*b*. Sensuous pleasure: the affective quality of sensations

7 PLATO, 295–296, 463–464, 474, 619–620, 627–628

8 ARISTOTLE, 644, 652, 658, 679–682
9 ARISTOTLE, 268, 340–341, 364–365, 404–406, 429–431
12 LUCRETIUS, 20–21, 48, 52–53, 57–58
19 AQUINAS, 486–487, 619–620
22 CHAUCER, 256–259
27 SHAKESPEARE, 320–321
31 DESCARTES, 97–98
35 LOCKE, 188–189
42 KANT, 477–478
44 BOSWELL, 409
47 GOETHE, 93–103, 247–248
48 MELVILLE, 307–308
53 JAMES, 650–651, 755–756
54 FREUD, 15–16, 119–120, 403, 574–576, 578–579, 648, 701, 737, 847–849

4c. Intellectual pleasure: the pleasures of reflection and contemplation

7 PLATO, 167, 420–425, 620–621
8 ARISTOTLE, 499, 602–603
9 ARISTOTLE, 429–434
12 LUCRETIUS, 15, 80
12 EPICTETUS, 185–187
12 AURELIUS, 261–262, 270
17 PLOTINUS, 17, 336
18 AUGUSTINE, 68
19 AQUINAS, 625–626, 629–631, 770–771, 775–777, 788–789
20 AQUINAS, 614–616, 1014–1016
21 DANTE, 99–102, 156
25 MONTAIGNE, 69–72
30 BACON, 27
31 SPINOZA, 413, 415–416, 460–461
32 MILTON, 21–25
35 LOCKE, 176
40 GIBBON, 645
42 KANT, 551–552, 586–587
47 GOETHE, 29, 79
53 JAMES, 755–758
54 FREUD, 773–774

4c(1) Pleasure in the beauty of nature or art: disinterested pleasure

7 PLATO, 266–267, 630–631, 653–656
9 ARISTOTLE, 168–169, 364, 404, 543–546, 682
12 AURELIUS, 259–260
19 AQUINAS, 25–26, 737, 764–765
21 DANTE, 67–68
26 SHAKESPEARE, 431
29 CERVANTES, 184
32 MILTON, 337–338
37 FIELDING, 1–2, 49–50
42 KANT, 471–473, 476–483, 485–486, 495–496, 516–518, 525–527, 534–539
46 HEGEL, 267–268
47 GOETHE, 224, 274–275
49 DARWIN, 95, 301–302, 568–571, 577
51 TOLSTOY, 235–238 passim, esp 237–238, 450–451, 497–498
54 FREUD, 600–601, 756, 775

4c(2) The pleasure and pain of learning and knowledge

5 AESCHYLUS, 53–54
7 PLATO, 515–517
9 ARISTOTLE, 168–169, 429, 543
12 LUCRETIUS, 12, 44
12 EPICTETUS, 153–155, 201–203
18 AUGUSTINE, 4–7
19 AQUINAS, 759–761, 767, 783–784
21 DANTE, 111–112
22 CHAUCER, 164
23 HOBBES, 79–80
24 RABELAIS, 26–27, 29–30
25 MONTAIGNE, 70–74, 111, 244–246
26 SHAKESPEARE, 255
28 HARVEY, 331–332
29 CERVANTES, 146
30 BACON, 3–4, 6–7
31 SPINOZA, 413, 415
35 LOCKE, 87, 188–189, 250
35 HUME, 453
41 GIBBON, 523–527 passim
42 KANT, 532
43 MILL, 451
44 BOSWELL, 15, 135–136
47 GOETHE, 11–19
53 JAMES, 524–525, 729–730
54 FREUD, 779–780

4d. The pleasures of play and diversion

4 HOMER, 164–170, 222–228
5 EURIPIDES, 340–341, 343, 441, 444–445
6 HERODOTUS, 86
7 PLATO, 149–173, 644–663
9 ARISTOTLE, 375, 405–406, 431, 541, 544–546, 614–615
14 PLUTARCH, 572
18 AUGUSTINE, 13–14
22 CHAUCER, 172–173
24 RABELAIS, 1–3, 7–8, 97–99
25 MONTAIGNE, 538–540
29 CERVANTES, 186–187
33 PASCAL, 195–204
37 FIELDING, 265–266
39 SMITH, 346–347
40 GIBBON, 502–503, 583–584
42 KANT, 537–539
44 BOSWELL, 287, 309
46 HEGEL, 291–292
51 TOLSTOY, 16–18, 37, 254–260, 278–287, 296–298, 303–305
52 DOSTOEVSKY, 220–235
53 JAMES, 727–729
54 FREUD, 641–643, 651

4e. The kinds of pain: the pain of sense and the pain of loss or deprivation

4 HOMER, 130–131, 139–140, 159–160, 171–179
5 AESCHYLUS, 56–57
5 SOPHOCLES, 157–158
5 EURIPIDES, 221, 244–245, 328

7 PLATO, 619–633
9 ARISTOTLE, 404–406, 430
12 LUCRETIUS, 36
13 VIRGIL, 108, 145–146, 291–292, 325, 328–329
18 AUGUSTINE, 388–390
19 AQUINAS, 337, 772–780
20 AQUINAS, 792–793, 1068–1070
21 DANTE, 5, 7–8, 19–20, 88–89
22 CHAUCER, 120–155, 401–402
23 HOBBES, 195
26 SHAKESPEARE, 285–319, 323, 325–326, 331, 343–344
27 SHAKESPEARE, 32, 211, 344–345
31 SPINOZA, 413–414
32 MILTON, 94–95, 122–125, 204–205, 352–343
35 LOCKE, 176–178
46 HEGEL, 245
51 TOLSTOY, 109–110, 551–554, 614–618
52 DOSTOEVSKY, 160–163, 169–170, 398
54 FREUD, 736–740, 743–744, 752–754

5. The quantity of pleasure: the weighing of pleasures; the limits of pleasure

7 PLATO, 225–226, 618, 625–631
9 ARISTOTLE, 364–365 passim, 427, 452
12 LUCRETIUS, 42, 79
19 AQUINAS, 755–757, 759–760, 766–767, 782–783, 785–786
20 AQUINAS, 528–529, 1037–1039
25 MONTAIGNE, 128–129, 326–327
35 LOCKE, 188
42 KANT, 584–585
43 MILL, 448–450
51 TOLSTOY, 660–661
54 FREUD, 639–663, 771–776

6. Pleasure and the good

6*a*. Pleasure as the only good or as the measure of goodness in all other things

7 PLATO, 57–62, 275–280, 609–639
9 ARISTOTLE, 404–405, 426–427
17 PLOTINUS, 74–75
18 AUGUSTINE, 225–226, 310
19 AQUINAS, 770–771
25 MONTAIGNE, 28
30 BACON, 71–72
31 SPINOZA, 426, 450
35 LOCKE, 185–190, 229
42 KANT, 298–300, 478–479
43 MILL, 445–476
53 JAMES, 808–814
54 FREUD, 418–420, 574, 592–593, 772

6*b*. Pleasure as one good among many: pleasure as one object of desire

7 PLATO, 275–280, 609–639
8 ARISTOTLE, 172–173, 359, 403–406, 426–427
18 AUGUSTINE, 507–513 passim
19 AQUINAS, 27–28, 614–615
21 DANTE, 100–101
25 MONTAIGNE, 109–112, 527–528
43 MILL, 461–464
44 BOSWELL, 404
49 DARWIN, 316–317
53 JAMES, 808–814

6*c*. Good and bad pleasures: higher and lower pleasures

7 PLATO, 227–280, 409–410, 421–427, 635–639, 698–690
9 ARISTOTLE, 364–366, 398–399, 428, 430, 543
17 PLOTINUS, 334
18 AUGUSTINE, 42–43, 54–55
19 AQUINAS, 768–771
25 MONTAIGNE, 28, 424–426
30 BACON, 73–74
31 SPINOZA, 414–415
42 KANT, 298–300
43 MILL, 461–464

6*d*. Pleasure as the accompaniment of goods possessed: the satisfaction of desire

7 PLATO, 275–278, 423–424
9 ARISTOTLE, 344, 403–405, 427–430
18 AUGUSTINE, 37–38, 625
19 AQUINAS, 629–631, 666–669, 751–752, 768–772
20 AQUINAS, 527–533
21 DANTE, 109–110
23 HOBBES, 76
42 KANT, 341–342
49 DARWIN, 308
53 JAMES, 725–726, 812–813
54 FREUD, 377, 412–413, 711–712

6*e*. Pleasure as intrinsically evil or morally indifferent

7 PLATO, 60–61, 224–226, 233–234
9 ARISTOTLE, 404–405, 426–427
12 EPICTETUS, 151, 203–210
12 AURELIUS, 257–258, 275, 284, 287–289, 291, 301
18 AUGUSTINE, 287–288, 381–383
19 AQUINAS, 768–769, 790–792
25 MONTAIGNE, 118–122, 124–125, 165–169, 432, 541–542
31 SPINOZA, 437
40 GIBBON, 192–193
42 KANT, 238, 256–257, 262–263, 297–318, 325–327, 338–355
44 BOSWELL, 393

7. Pleasure and happiness: their distinction and relation

5 SOPHOCLES, 140–141
7 PLATO, 275–284, 635–639, 657–658
9 ARISTOTLE, 344–345, 423–424, 430–431, 545, 600–601
12 EPICTETUS, 162–164
17 PLOTINUS, 12–13, 15–16, 19
19 AQUINAS, 151–152, 625–626, 629–631, 642–643, 770–771
20 AQUINAS, 176–178, 966–967, 1048–1066

21 DANTE, 79, 81–94, 99–102
22 CHAUCER, 374–382
24 RABELAIS, 60–66
25 MONTAIGNE, 200–205, 235–237, 394–395, 406–408, 527–529
30 BACON, 71–72
33 PASCAL, 195–204
35 LOCKE, 188–190, 192–193
42 KANT, 298–300, 314–318, 478–479
43 MILL, 447–457, 461–464
44 BOSWELL, 378
46 HEGEL, 118
47 GOETHE, 41–42
51 TOLSTOY, 577–578, 605
52 DOSTOEVSKY, 1–7, 54–58
54 FREUD, 771–776

7*a*. Pleasure and pain in relation to love and friendship

4 HOMER, 130–131, 155–156, 176–179, 280
5 EURIPIDES, 274–276, 279–281
7 PLATO, 120–122
9 ARISTOTLE, 373–374 passim, 407–410, 414, 419–421 passim, 423–425, 428, 626–627
12 LUCRETIUS, 57–60
12 EPICTETUS, 167–170, 223–224
13 VIRGIL, 174–186, 245–247, 370
18 AUGUSTINE, 12–13, 513–514, 516
19 AQUINAS, 636, 760–764, 782–783, 786–787, 788
20 AQUINAS, 527–530, 534–535
21 DANTE, 7–8, 79–80
22 CHAUCER, 1–155, 174–211
25 MONTAIGNE, 398–399, 426–427, 431–433
26 SHAKESPEARE, 242, 285–319, 353–355, 524–525, 582–583
27 SHAKESPEARE, 51, 126, 128–129, 267, 314–315, 393–420, 586–609 passim
29 CERVANTES, 73–89
31 SPINOZA, 402–404, 406–410
32 MILTON, 243–245
37 FIELDING, 126–127, 235–238
38 ROUSSEAU, 345–346
49 DARWIN, 308–313
51 TOLSTOY, 30–31, 140–142, 167, 203, 276–277, 323–324, 340–341, 615
52 DOSTOEVSKY, 32–36, 58–59, 69–70, 95–100, 200–201, 324, 402–408
54 FREUD, 418–421, 782–783

7*b*. The life of pleasure contrasted with other modes of life: the ascetic life

OLD TESTAMENT: *Numbers*, 6:1–5 / *Ecclesiastes*, 2:1–11; 5:18–20 / *Isaiah*, 5:11–12; 22:12–13
APOCRYPHA: *Wisdom of Solomon*, 2 / *Ecclesiasticus*, 18:30–32; 19:1–2; 23:5–6
NEW TESTAMENT: *Luke*, 1:13–17; 16:19–25 / *Romans*, 1:18–32; 8:1–13; 13:13–14 / *I Corinthians*, 5:9–13; 6:13–7:9 / *Galatians*, 5:16–25 / *Colossians*, 3:5–8 / *I Thessalonians*, 4:3–7 / *I Timothy*, 4:1–10 / *II Timothy*, 3 / *James*, 4:1–6 / *I Peter*, 4:1–5
5 EURIPIDES, 244
5 ARISTOPHANES, 551–553, 633–636
7 PLATO, 223–225, 635–639, 656–658, 801
9 ARISTOTLE, 340–341, 434
12 LUCRETIUS, 15
12 EPICTETUS, 195–201, 225–228, 230–232
12 AURELIUS, 262–263, 269–270
14 PLUTARCH, 732–733, 747, 755–758, 780
17 PLOTINUS, 14–19
18 AUGUSTINE, 9–10, 60, 139–140
19 AQUINAS, 614–615
20 AQUINAS, 607, 652–657
21 DANTE, 99–102
22 CHAUCER, 256–259
23 HOBBES, 155–156
24 RABELAIS, 46–49, 65–66, 126
25 MONTAIGNE, 162–167, 406–408
26 SHAKESPEARE, 254–256, 435–436
30 BACON, 69–74
32 MILTON, 21–25
40 GIBBON, 192–193, 593–599
43 MILL, 296, 448–449
51 TOLSTOY, 273–274, 321–322, 329–333
52 DOSTOEVSKY, 1–412
54 FREUD, 624–625, 772–774

8. The discipline of pleasure

8*a*. Pleasure and pain in relation to virtue: the restraints of temperance and the endurance of courage

OLD TESTAMENT: *Proverbs*, 7:6–27
4 HOMER, 183–322
5 SOPHOCLES, 182–195
7 PLATO, 120–122, 275–285, 347–348, 644–645, 653, 657–658, 669–670, 689–690
9 ARISTOTLE, 340–341, 344, 349–350, 354–355, 359, 361–366, 373–374, 398–404, 426, 430–431, 545
12 EPICTETUS, 194, 203–210
12 AURELIUS, 257–258, 261, 272, 280, 291
14 PLUTARCH, 139–140
19 AQUINAS, 762–763, 768–769, 771–772, 777–778, 790–791
20 AQUINAS, 47–48, 53–54, 57–58, 134–136, 453–454, 562–570
21 DANTE, 7–11, 77, 81–94, 99–102
23 HOBBES, 163–164
24 RABELAIS, 234–240
25 MONTAIGNE, 162–167, 200–205, 350–351, 353–354, 365–367, 394–395, 406–408, 474, 537–543
31 SPINOZA, 437–447
35 LOCKE, 186, 193–194
37 FIELDING, 9
38 ROUSSEAU, 343–345
40 GIBBON, 596–597
43 MILL, 461–464
49 DARWIN, 315–317
51 TOLSTOY, 122, 201, 248–250, 321–322, 369, 481–482
54 FREUD, 793–794

8*b*. The conflict between pleasure and duty, or the obligations of justice: the pleasure principle and the reality principle

Old Testament: *Proverbs,* 5:1–13; 6:23–35; 23:20–21, 29–35
Apocrypha: *Ecclesiasticus,* 18:30–32; 19:1–5; 31:12–31
5 Euripides, 228
7 Plato, 311–315, 748
12 Epictetus, 108, 150–151, 177–178
12 Aurelius, 274, 283, 287–288
33 Pascal, 64–67
42 Kant, 234–240, 253–287, 291–361, 365–379, 387–388, 478–479, 584–588, 591–592, 594–596
43 Mill, 452–456 passim, 457–461 passim, 464–476 passim
47 Goethe, 79–82
49 Darwin, 208–314 passim
54 Freud, 452, 599, 624–625, 768, 784, 799–800, 837–839

8*c*. Perversions or degradations in the sphere of pleasure and pain: sadism and masochism

Old Testament: *Genesis,* 19:4–11
New Testament: *Romans,* 1:26–32
5 Euripides, 340–352
7 Plato, 645–646, 735–738
9 Aristotle, 399–400
14 Plutarch, 783–784
15 Tacitus, 86, 107, 145–147, 166, 265
18 Augustine, 664–666
19 Aquinas, 757–758
21 Dante, 15–16, 21–23, 25–26
25 Montaigne, 89–90, 118–122, 166–167
27 Shakespeare, 606
31 Spinoza, 421
32 Milton, 269–272
40 Gibbon, 38, 60, 138–139, 389
41 Gibbon, 169, 174–175
51 Tolstoy, 188–190, 271–273, 505–511
52 Dostoevsky, 4, 121–127, 307–310
53 James, 718–720
54 Freud, 415–418, 570–572, 577–579 passim, 790–791, 847–850 passim

9. The regulation of pleasures by law

Old Testament: *Deuteronomy,* 5:18,21; 21:18–21
5 Euripides, 340–352
7 Plato, 283–285, 326–328, 432–434, 643–663, 675–676, 713–716, 718–720, 731–738
9 Aristotle, 465–466, 541
14 Plutarch, 32–48, 61–62
15 Tacitus, 31, 57–58
20 Aquinas, 255–257
21 Dante, 77–78
25 Montaigne, 131–132
27 Shakespeare, 174–204
30 Bacon, 54
32 Milton, 390, 393–395
35 Locke, 8
38 Montesquieu, 44–50, 105–106
38 Rousseau, 434–435
39 Smith, 149–150
40 Gibbon, 100–101, 484
41 Gibbon, 93–94
43 Mill, 302–312, 314–316
44 Boswell, 301

10. The social utility of pleasure and pain

10*a*. The employment of pleasure and pain by parent or teacher in moral and mental training

Old Testament: *Proverbs,* 13:24; 19:18; 23:13–14
Apocrypha: *Ecclesiasticus,* 30:1–12
5 Aristophanes, 504–506
7 Plato, 46, 653–663, 713–716
9 Aristotle, 350, 434
18 Augustine, 4–7, 521–522
20 Aquinas, 226–227
24 Rabelais, 26–30
25 Montaigne, 16, 70–74, 185
31 Spinoza, 419
42 Kant, 357–360
44 Boswell, 191, 199–200
51 Tolstoy, 47–48, 306
53 James, 290–291
54 Freud, 759, 876

10*b*. The use of pleasure and pain by orator or statesman in persuasion and government

7 Plato, 45, 640–652
9 Aristotle, 434, 623–636
14 Plutarch, 125–130, 578–579
15 Tacitus, 269–270
20 Aquinas, 250–251
23 Hobbes, 82, 145–147
25 Montaigne, 176, 181–183
30 Bacon, 23–26
33 Pascal, 440–442
40 Gibbon, 139–140
42 Kant, 535
51 Tolstoy, 245

CROSS-REFERENCES

For: The relation of pleasure and pain to sensations and emotions, *see* EMOTION 1a; SENSE 3c(2).

The discussion of intellectual pleasure with respect to beauty and truth, *see* BEAUTY 4; EDUCATION 5e; KNOWLEDGE 8b(4).

Another discussion of the kinds of pain, *see* PUNISHMENT 1a.

The aspect of infinity in the desire for pleasure, *see* DESIRE 7a(1).

The problem of pleasure and pain in relation to good and evil, *see* GOOD AND EVIL 3d, 4a, 4c; and for the conception of pleasure as an object of desire and as the satisfaction of desire, *see* DESIRE 2b, 2d.

The problem of pleasure in relation to happiness, *see* HAPPINESS 2b(2).

Other discussions of pleasure and pain in relation to moral virtue, *see* COURAGE 1, 3; PUNISHMENT 3a; TEMPERANCE 1, 2; VIRTUE AND VICE 5a; and for the consideration of asceticism and pleasure-seeking, *see* TEMPERANCE 6a–6b.

The conflict between duty and pleasure, *see* DUTY 8; and for the basic issue between an ethics of duty and an ethics of happiness, *see* DUTY 2; HAPPINESS 3.

Pleasure and pain in relation to friendship and love, *see* LOVE 1b.

Another discussion of pleasure in relation to law, *see* TEMPERANCE 5c.

The role of pleasure and pain in moral training, *see* PUNISHMENT 3a; VIRTUE AND VICE 4d(2).

ADDITIONAL READINGS

Listed below are works not included in *Great Books of the Western World*, but relevant to the idea and topics with which this chapter deals. These works are divided into two groups:

I. Works by authors represented in this collection.

II. Works by authors not represented in this collection.

For the date, place, and other facts concerning the publication of the works cited, consult the Bibliography of Additional Readings which follows the last chapter of *The Great Ideas.*

I.

DESCARTES. *The Passions of the Soul*

HUME. *An Inquiry Concerning the Principles of Morals*

J. S. MILL. *An Examination of Sir William Hamilton's Philosophy*, CH 25

FREUD. *Wit and Its Relation to the Unconscious*, CH 1–5

——. *Mourning and Melancholia*

II.

EPICURUS. *Letter to Menoeceus*

CICERO. *De Finibus (On the Supreme Good)*, I–II

——. *Tusculan Disputations*, II

TERTULLIAN. *De Spectaculis*

T. MORE. *Utopia*, BK II

MALEBRANCHE. *De la recherche de la vérité*, BK IV, CH 5–13

LEIBNITZ. *New Essays Concerning Human Understanding*, BK II, CH 20

FRANKLIN. *Dissertation on Liberty and Necessity, Pleasure and Pain*

HUTCHESON. *An Essay on the Nature and Conduct of the Passions and Affections*

BENTHAM. *An Introduction to the Principles of Morals and Legislation*, CH 1–5

LAMB. *Hospita on the Immoderate Indulgences of the Pleasures of the Palate*

DE QUINCEY. *Confessions of an English Opium-Eater*

ALIBERT. *Physiologie des passions*

LEOPARDI. *Essays, Dialogues, and Thoughts*

Coleridge. *The Pains of Sleep*
J. Mill. *Analysis of the Phenomena of the Human Mind*. ch 17–23
W. Hamilton. *Lectures on Metaphysics and Logic*, vol i (41–46)
Emerson. "Compensation," in *Essays*, i
Whewell. *The Elements of Morality*, bk ii, ch 25
Schopenhauer. "On the Sufferings of the World," "On the Vanity of Existence," in *Studies in Pessimism*
Bain. *The Emotions and the Will*
Hinton. *The Mystery of Pain*
E. Hartmann. *Philosophy of the Unconscious*, iii
H. Sidgwick. *The Methods of Ethics*, bk i, ch 4; bk ii, ch 1–6; bk iii, ch 14; bk iv
Spencer. *The Principles of Ethics*, part i, ch 7
T. H. Green. *Prolegomena to Ethics*, bk iii, ch 4(a)
Avebury. *The Pleasures of Life*
Frazer. *The Golden Bough*, part vi, ch 8
Ribot. *The Psychology of the Emotions*
Wundt. *Outlines of Psychology*, (7)
Bradley. *Ethical Studies*, iii
——. *Collected Essays*, vol i(14)
Titchener. *Lectures on the Elementary Psychology of Feeling and Attention*, ii–iv, viii
Moore. *Principia Ethica*, ch 2–3
——. *Ethics*, ch 1–2
Ellis. *Studies in the Psychology of Sex*, vol i, part ii, pp 66–188
Proust. *Remembrance of Things Past*
A. H. Allen. *Pleasure and Instinct*
Powys. *In Defence of Sensuality*
Beebe-Center. *The Psychology of Pleasantness and Unpleasantness*
Bertrand. *The Art of Suffering*
C. S. Lewis. *The Problem of Pain*

Chapter 69: POETRY

INTRODUCTION

THE spirit in which the great poets have read their predecessors differs remarkably from the attitude toward the past which prevails in other fields. The philosophers and scientists frequently feel assured that they can improve upon their predecessors. The poets, for the most part, wish only to do as well. Virgil's admiration for Homer; Dante's accolade to Virgil; Milton's praise of Aeschylus, Sophocles, and Euripides as "the three tragic poets unequall'd yet by any"; the tributes which Cervantes and Fielding pay to the poets of antiquity—these testify that there is no battle between the modern and the ancient books of poetry.

Contemporary novelists and dramatists—especially those who are proud of their innovations in the forms or materials of poetry—may constitute an exception. But they would still be the exception to a rule which can be verified for almost all the great books of poetry. Part of the reason for such unusual accord may be that, in the tradition of the great books, one book enjoys the unique distinction of having founded the science of poetry. More than that, it seems to have gained from the poets a large measure of approval, and even adherence to its principles, during a period of more than 2000 years.

Not that Aristotle's *Poetics* is without sources. They exist in Plato's comments on the kinds of poetry; in Aristophanes' critical weighing of Aeschylus and Euripides; and, of course, in the original inventions of Homer and the great dramatic poets, both tragic and comic. Not that the acceptance of Aristotle's theory of poetry is unaccompanied by some dissent, as, for example, in Fielding's quarrel with the rules about the unities of time and place. But Fielding, like Cervantes who is another close student of the *Poetics*, more frequently adopts than rejects Aristotle's basic insights. His most rebellious protest—that the originality of creative genius cannot be bound by the laws of art or held accountable to any established critical standards—would certainly receive sympathetic consideration from the man who formulated the rules of poetry and its measures of excellence by the study of the productions of Greek genius.

One way in which later poets have expressed their disagreement with the *Poetics* confirms Fielding's insight. Those who have violated its rules and yet produced great poems have been men of exceptional genius. Where the genius has been lacking to create new forms, the violation of the rules has usually resulted in formlessness. But it is not only in the creative work of the poets that Aristotle's principles have been put to use and tested. His influence also appears in the comments which the poets make on the nature and purpose of poetry. The terms and distinctions of the *Poetics* are reflected in the writings of Dante, Chaucer, Shakespeare, Milton, Goethe, and Melville, as well as in many essays in criticism from Horace and Demetrius to Boccaccio, Boileau, Dryden, and Pope.

Socrates once complained of the wisdom of the poets. Those whom he asked about their poetry were tongue-tied. They finally resorted to the mystery of inspiration or the inscrutability of genius. "There is hardly a person present," he tells his judges in the *Apology*, "who would not have talked better about their poetry than they did themselves." The poets of a later age were, through benefit of Aristotle, better able to discourse analytically of their art.

IF WE TURN FROM the poets themselves, or rather from their poems, to the analysis of poetry—by poets or others—we find a number of major issues. On what poetry is and on the end it serves, the tradition does not seem to be either unified or harmonious. Basic disagreements begin with the ancients.

On the question, for example, whether the poets have the same obligation to speak the truth—and the same kind of truth—as do philosophers or scientists, Plato and Aristotle seem to be opposed. On the question whether the art of poetry lies in its use of language or is primarily the craft of fiction, Aristotle's *Poetics* and Horace's *Art of Poetry* represent the opposite answers which have been points of departure for divergent discussions of poetry throughout the whole tradition of western thought.

With regard to the second of these two questions, it may be wondered whether we are in the presence of the sort of disagreement which requires us to take one side rather than the other. The fact that Aristotle, in his *Rhetoric*, writes about poetry in a vein contrary to the theory he advances in his *Poetics*, would suggest the possibility of different but not inconsistent points of view about poetry. Unless Aristotle unwittingly contradicts himself, the rhetorical consideration of poetry is simply a different way of conceiving what is poetic.

In the *Advancement of Learning*, Bacon records this difference in the meaning of poetry, which had become traditional by his time. He treats it, moreover, as the sort of difference which does not require the rejection of either alternative as incorrect. Poetry, he writes, can be "taken in two senses: in respect of words or matter. In the first sense it is but a character of style, and belongeth to the arts of speech, and is not pertinent for the present. In the latter it is (as hath been said) one of the principal portions of learning, and is nothing else but feigned history, which may be styled as well in prose as in verse."

When Bacon says that the conception of poetry as a literary style—as an art of writing in verse rather than prose— "is not pertinent for the present," he does not reject that alternative entirely. He merely postpones it for the later section of his work in which he treats of grammar and rhetoric. The other alternative —poetry as "feigned history"—is germane to his present consideration of the kinds of learning. Just as Aristotle does not set his *Rhetoric* against his *Poetics* on the nature of poetry, so Bacon does not exclude one of these conceptions in favor of the other when he observes how different are the principles and considerations appropriate to each.

These two points of view about the nature of poetry are not always treated in this way. Sometimes one or the other is taken as the primary or even the only way of approaching the subject, and then a genuine issue ensues—either with those who take the excluded point of view or with those who find it possible to embrace both. The Alexandrian and Roman critics seem to create such an issue by considering poetry largely in terms of style. Modern criticism, especially since the beginning of the 19th century, goes even further in the direction of identifying poetry with verse.

When Wordsworth discusses the art of poetry in his preface to *Lyrical Ballads*, he is concerned largely with its language. His definition of poetry as "emotion recollected in tranquility" indicates his emphasis upon the lyrical aspect of even narrative poetry. When Edgar Allen Poe writes his *Poetic Principle* and Mathew Arnold his *Essays in Criticism*, each is concerned almost exclusively with lyric poetry, with that kind of poetry which is written in verse rather than prose. The poet tends to become more and more a composer of verses—so much so that the free-verse movement can appear to be a great revolution in poetry. In the *Brothers Karamazov*, Smerdyakov says, "Poetry is rubbish." At Maria's protest that she is very fond of poetry, he adds: "So far as it's poetry, it's essentially rubbish. Consider yourself, whoever talks in rhyme?"

Just as the word "art" has come in popular usage to mean only painting and sculpture, so its sister-word "poetry" has also narrowed in significance. Contemporary readers who are accustomed to think of poems as lyrics and of poetry as verse may be surprised to learn that according to the significance of its Greek root, the word "poetry" can cover all the forms of art or human productivity; they are just as likely to be surprised by the reference to novels and plays, written in prose, as poems. Yet, in the tradition of the great books, novelists like Cervantes, Fielding, and Melville call themselves poets. The great books consider poetry primarily as narrative rather than lyrical, as story rather than song.

This does not mean that they exclude the

other consideration of poetry. Fielding, for example, says in one place that "poetry . . . demands numbers or something like numbers" (*i.e.*, metre), but for the most part he insists that the art of the novelist or romancer lies mainly in the invention of good stories, not in the mastery of rules of prosody which apply only to poems of the lyric sort, written in verse. Speaking of "the sweet influence which melody and rhythm by nature have," Plato may observe "what a poor appearance the tales of the poets make when stripped of the colors which music puts upon them and recited in simple prose"; but for Plato as for Aristotle the poet is a teller of tales, either in prose or in verse.

Aristotle does not ignore the devices of language. In the third book of the *Rhetoric*, where he considers problems of style in all sorts of compositions, he distinguishes "poetic" from "prosaic" writing; and in the *Poetics* also he devotes a few chapters to style. But when in the latter case he deals with the language of poetry, he is not concerned with the style of any sort of composition, but only of dramatic and epic narratives. Except for a brief mention of the form of verse known as the "dithyramb," Aristotle does not discuss the isolated lyric as a kind of poetry. He treats song and spectacle merely as embellishments of the drama. In the *Poetics* his emphasis is not upon the devices of language or the sentiments of the poet, but upon the construction of plot, the development of character, the diction and thought of the characters—in short, upon the subject matter of the poem rather than upon the feelings of the poet and the eloquence with which he expresses them.

Because he regards plot as the "soul of tragedy"—and, by extension, the primary principle of all narrative poetry— Aristotle insists that "the poet or 'maker' should be the maker of plots rather than of verses." He is therefore led to criticize the confusion—apparently prevalent in his day as in ours—which he thinks results from identifying the art of poetry with skill in writing verse. "Even when a treatise on medicine or natural science is brought out in verse," he writes, "the name of poet is given by custom to the author; and yet Homer and Empedocles have nothing in common except the metre, so that it would be better to call the one poet, the other physicist rather than poet." Just as Bacon later remarks that "a true narrative may be delivered in verse and a feigned one in prose," so Aristotle says that "the poet and the historian differ not by writing in verse or in prose. The work of Herodotus might be put into verse, and it would still be a species of history, with metre no less than without it."

That the difference between prose and verse may affect the style of writing but not the essence of storytelling is a point which has wide acceptance among writers who call themselves poets. In the Prologue to Melibeus, Chaucer's host commands him to leave off rhyming and "tell a tale in prose—you might do worse—wherein there's mirth or doctrine good and plain." Thinking of his *History of Don Quixote* as a species of epic poetry, Cervantes declares that "epics may be as well written in prose as in verse."

The use, by Cervantes and Fielding, of the word "history" in the title of their novels indicates the acceptance of the other point in the conception of poetry by reference to its subject matter rather than to its linguistic style. The great poets recognize that, as narratives, their works resemble histories, but they also know that the stories poets tell are, in the words of Bacon, "imaginary history." Just as Fielding writes at length in mock justification of himself as an historian, so Melville touches upon "the plain facts, historical and otherwise," of whale fishery, lest someone "scout at Moby Dick as a monstrous fable, or still worse and more detestable, a hideous and intolerable allegory." In his chapter on the Leviathan's tail, he says, "Other poets have warbled the praise of the soft eye of the antelope, and the lovely plumage of the bird that never alights; less celestial, I celebrate a tail."

THE CONCEPTION of poetry as feigned or imaginary history seems to have a direct bearing on the question of the poet's obligation to speak the truth. We shall return subsequently to other aspects of the comparison of poetry with history and philosophy. For the present we are concerned with the issue in the theory of poetry which arises from applying the standards of knowledge to the inventions of the poet.

Bacon, like Aristotle, denies that such standards are applicable. Though he treats poetry as "a part of learning," he holds that it is only restrained "in measure of words"; "in all other points," it is "extremely licensed, and doth truly refer to the imagination; which, being not tied to the laws of matter, may at pleasure join that which nature hath severed, and sever that which nature hath joined." Kant, on the other hand, like Plato, judges poetry in terms of its contribution to knowledge. A thing of the imagination, poetry, he maintains, serves the understanding, for it conducts "a free play of the imagination as if it were a serious business of the understanding."

Though "the *poet* promises merely an entertaining *play* with ideas," Kant continues, "yet for the understanding there enures as much as if the promotion of its business had been his one intention." He achieves a certain "combination and harmony of the two faculties of cognition, sensibility and understanding, which, though doubtless indispensable to one another, do not readily permit of being united without compulsion and reciprocal abatement." In so doing, the poet, in Kant's opinion, "accomplishes something worthy of being made a serious business, namely, the using of play to provide food for the understanding, and the giving of life to its concepts by means of the imagination."

Yet Kant and Plato do not agree in their judgment of the poet. Regarding "the poet's promise" as "a modest one"—"a mere play with ideas is all he holds out to us"—Kant praises him for achieving more in actual performance than he promises. Plato, on the contrary, seems to think the poet promises more and achieves less. He seems to regard the poet not as assisting, but as competing with the philosopher. The reason why the poet must fail in this attempt is that he tries to do on the level of the imagination what the philosopher is better able to do on the level of reason.

Both are engaged in a process of imitation—for all knowledge is imitation—but whereas the notions of the philosopher imitate the reality of the Ideas, the images of the poet imitate sensible appearances, which are themselves imitations of the Ideas or eternal Forms. Even when it is accurate or truthful, poetry must, therefore, be an inferior form of knowledge. In Plato's terms, it is on the level of opinion, along with fancy and belief. In any case, it must submit to being judged by the same standards of accuracy as anything else which claims to be knowledge or right opinion. "Imitations," he writes, "are not to be judged of by pleasure and false opinion. . . . They are to be judged of by the standard of truth, and by no other whatever." The competent judge of poetry must, therefore, "possess three things: he must know, in the first place, of what the imitation is; secondly, he must know that it is true; and thirdly, that it has been well executed in words and melodies and rhythms."

The issue concerning poetry and truth can be most sharply drawn between Plato and Aristotle, precisely because Aristotle thinks that poetry is a form of imitation, but that knowledge does not have the character of imitation at all. Since poetry is not a kind of knowledge, the same standards do not apply to both. "There is not the same kind of correctness," he insists, "in poetry as in politics"—or "in medicine or any other special science." The poet's art is at fault if he "meant to describe the thing correctly but failed through lack of power of expression." But if a technical error in physiology enters into his description because he meant to describe the thing "in some incorrect way (*e.g.*, to make the horse in movement have both right legs thrown forward)," then, according to Aristotle, "his error in that case is not in the essentials of the poetic art." The poet's obligation is not to be truthful in such particulars but to make his whole story seem plausible. Aristotle summarizes his position in the statement of his famous rule concerning the probable and the possible. "For the purposes of poetry," he says, "a convincing impossibility is preferable to an unconvincing possibility."

Connected with this issue concerning the kind of truth to be expected from the poet is the controversy over the purpose of poetry—to instruct or to delight, or to do both. This in turn relates to the moral problem of the influence poetry can have on human character or virtue; and to the political problem of the regulation of poetry by the state or the right of poetry to be free from such censorship. It is not surprising that Plato, conceiving poetry as he does, should banish poets from the ideal state described in the *Republic*; or that he should lay down specific regulations for the content of poetry in the *Laws*.

At the opposite extreme are those who, like Milton and Mill, attack the principle of censorship itself—as applied to poetry as well as to other forms of communication. But the traditional defense of poetry, in essays bearing that title from the pen of Sidney and Shelley or in the writings of Chaucer, Montaigne, and Cervantes, usually tries to answer Plato by praising poetry as an instrument of moral instruction as well as of delight. Waiving the question of its effect upon morals, some, like Adam Smith, answer the sort of criticism Augustine levels against pagan poetry and theatrical presentations by holding the theatre to be a legitimate, a lawful, even a necessary means of recreation.

SOME OF THESE issues touch on considerations dealt with in other chapters. The problem of censorship is discussed in the chapters on ART and LIBERTY; and the theory of imitation as applied to the arts in general, useful as well as fine, is discussed in the chapter on ART. Here we are concerned with the bearing of that theory upon the nature of poetry. The difference we have observed between Plato and Aristotle concerning imitation itself does not seem to affect their use of this notion in treating works of fine art, and more particularly poetry. What Hamlet tells the players is the purpose of their play—"to hold, as 'twere, the mirror up to nature"—Aristotle says is the aim of such arts as poetry, sculpture, painting, music, and the dance, which give both instruction and delight through imitation.

Within the sphere of the fine arts, the distinction of poetry from the others is usually made in terms of the medium of imitation. Poetry, according to Aristotle, imitates through the medium of language; painting and sculpture through lines, planes, colors, and shapes; music through rhythm and harmony. Whether Aristotle's statement that "the objects of imitation are men in action" applies to poetry alone or to all the fine arts, is a question of interpretation to which opposite answers have been given. Some commentators seem to think that human action as the object of imitation specifically defines poetry, whereas music and sculpture have distinct objects as well as distinct mediums of imitation. Others hold that human action is the object of imitation common to all the arts.

However this issue is resolved, the differentiation of the kinds of poetry can be made neither in terms of the object nor the medium of imitation, but only in terms of the manner. "The medium being the same and the object the same," Aristotle writes, "the poet may imitate by narration—in which case he can either take another personality as Homer does, or speak in his own person, unchanged—or he may present all his characters as living and moving before us."

Plato makes the same distinction, pointing out that the Homeric type of poetry combines both the discourse of the poet and the discourse of his characters in dialogue. He calls stage plays pure imitations in the sense that the author never speaks directly, but tells his story entirely through the actions and speeches of the characters; whereas the type of poetry which he calls narrative as opposed to imitative may combine both methods of storytelling or may, in some extreme instances, never resort to dialogue at all.

Since all storytelling is narration, and since all poetry is imitation, it seems slightly confusing to call the two major types of poetry "narration" and "imitation," as Plato sometimes does, or "narrative" and "dramatic," as Aristotle sometimes does. Bacon also speaks of "narrative" and "dramatic" or "representative" poetry. He defines narrative poetry as "such an exact imitation of history as to deceive, did it not often carry things beyond probability," and dramatic poetry as "a kind of visible history, giving the images of things as if they were present, whilst history represents them as past."

The difficulties of language seem to be removed by other terms which both Plato and Aristotle use to express the main distinction. The manner of storytelling, exemplified by Homer, which either employs direct narration without dialogue or combines both, is *epic* poetry. That which uses dialogue alone, is *dramatic*.

These words—"epic" and "dramatic"—may have their difficulties, too, especially for the contemporary reader, unless a number of things are remembered. First, epics and dramas may be written either in prose or verse. Second, the arts of theatrical representation are auxiliary to the art of the dramatic poet. The writing of a play is completely independent of its acting, "the production of spectacular effects depending," as Aristotle says, "more on the art of the stage machinist than on that of the poet." Third, epic poetry differs from dramatic poetry in other respects than the use of indirect discourse as well as dialogue.

On this last point, Aristotle observes that all the elements of epic poetry are found in drama, whereas the dramatic form may include the embellishments of song and spectacle in addition to plot, character, thought, and diction. Even more important is his distinction of the two in terms of the unities of time, place, and action. Because it need not be limited at all in time and place, epic narration may have a much more complicated plot structure or even, as Aristotle says, "a multiplicity of plots."

With this understanding of the distinction between the two major types of storytelling, we can see why the great novels of Cervantes, Melville, Tolstoy, and Dostoevsky should be classified as epic poems, and were apparently so conceived by their authors, at least in the cases of Cervantes and Melville. As measured by the magnitude of its plot—its reach in time, and its scene the whole universe "from Heaven, through the world, to Hell"—Goethe's *Faust*, even though dramatic in manner, seems to be no less epic in its structure and proportions than the poems of Homer, Virgil, Dante, and Milton. The story of a single white whale can be epic in its immensity if the storyteller, like Melville, makes it "include the whole circle of the sciences, and all the generations of whales, and men, and mastodons, past, present, and to come, with all the revolving panoramas of empire on earth, and throughout the whole universe, not excluding its suburbs."

Another traditional division in the kinds of poetry is that between the tragic and the comic. This distinction is variously expressed. Fielding sees the difference in terms of the misery or happiness to which the poet brings his principal characters in the end. Speaking of tragedy alone, Milton says that it has ever been held "the gravest, moralest, and most profitable of all other poems." In similar vein, Marcus Aurelius praises tragedy "for reminding men of the things which happen to them and that it is according to nature for things to happen so." He does not admit comedy to be of equal worth, though he does look with some favor upon the older forms of comedy which were "useful in reminding men to beware of insolence."

According to Aristotle, "comedy represents men as worse, tragedy as better than in actual life." He describes the action which tragic poetry imitates as serious, adding that tragedies "through pity and fear effect the proper purgation of these emotions." Whether comedies also arouse and purge certain emotions Aristotle does not say, for his promise to speak more fully of comic poetry is not fulfilled in the *Poetics*. Concerning the meaning of the tragic catharsis, there are questions enough.

Augustine asks: "How is it that a man wants to be made sad by the sight of tragic sufferings that he could not bear in his own person? . . . The more a man feels such sufferings in himself, the more he is moved by the sight of them on the stage. Now when a man suffers himself, it is called misery; when he suffers in the suffering of another, it is called pity. But how can the unreal sufferings of the stage possibly move pity?"

Boswell begs Dr. Johnson to explain Aristotle's doctrine of the purging of the passions as the purpose of tragedy. "Why, Sir," Johnson replies, "you are to consider what is the meaning of purging in the original sense. It is to expel impurities from the body. The mind is subject to the same imperfections. The passions are the great movers of human actions; but they are mixed with such impurities, that it is necessary they should be purged or refined by means of terror and pity. For instance, ambition is a noble passion; but by seeing upon the stage, that a man who is so excessively ambitious as to raise himself by injustice is punished, we are terrified by the fatal consequences of such a passion. In the same manner a certain degree of resentment is necessary; but if we see that a man carries it too far, we pity the object of it, and are taught to moderate that passion." Johnson's interpretation seems to be more specific than Milton's notion that to purge the passions by tragedy is "to temper and reduce them to just measure with a kind of delight, stirr'd up by reading or seeing those passions well imitated."

It may be arguable whether the difference between tragedy and comedy is well defined by reference to the nobility or vulgarity of the leading characters; by the contrast between the pride of the tragic and the wit of the comic hero; by the seriousness or lightness of the tragic and comic themes and by the passions appropriate to each. In any case it seems clear that this division of poetry crosses the other division into epic and dramatic writing. The plays of Sophocles and the *Iliad* of Homer, Aristotle observes, are tragic poetry, yet dramatic and epic respectively in manner; but from another point of view, Sophocles is to be compared with Aristophanes, for though the one writes tragedies and the other comedies, both are dramatists. In the tradition of the great books, there are comic as well as tragic epics—Chaucer's *Troilus and Cressida*, Rabelais' *Gargantua and Pantagruel*, Cervantes' *Don Quixote*, Sterne's *Tristram Shandy*, and Fielding's *Tom Jones*—just as there are tragic and comic plays. The examination of these suggests that talk rather than action is the essence of comedy.

The chief thing which Aristodemus remembers of Socrates' discourse the morning after the banquet, in Plato's *Symposium*, is Socrates' success in compelling Aristophanes and Agathon "to acknowledge that the genius of comedy was the same as that of tragedy, and that the true artist in tragedy was an artist in comedy also. To this they were constrained to assent, being drowsy, and not quite following the argument." Precisely what they assented to has never been entirely clear. On one interpretation of Socrates' remark, examples of his point are difficult to find in the great books—except, perhaps, for the plays of Shakespeare which, in the sphere of dramatic poetry, seem to represent an equal genius for tragic and comic writing. In the sphere of epic poetry, we have only Aristotle's reference to a lost poem of Homer's—the *Margites*—which he says "bears the same relation to comedy that the *Iliad* and *Odyssey* do to tragedy."

According to another interpretation the insight of Socrates is that the totality of the great tragic vision tends to approximate the totality of the great comic vision. The same poem may be both tragic and comic because the poet has been able to see far enough into the nature of things to reveal a world which is at once dreadful and ridiculous. In this sense *Moby Dick* may be both a tragedy and a comedy. "Though in many of its aspects," Melville writes, "this visible world seems formed in love, the invisible spheres were formed in fright"; but he also remarks that "there are certain queer times and occasions . . . when a man takes this whole universe for a vast practical joke."

IN THE SCIENCE of poetics, certain principles or rules seem to apply to all the major forms of poetry, where others relate specifically to epic or dramatic writing, or to tragedy or comedy. Aristotle implies that his most general formulations hold not only for long poems, but for dithyrambic poetry as well. If that is so, they should be capable of extension to other forms of lyric poetry, such as, for example, the sonnets of Shakespeare and Milton, and Milton's odes and elegies. Yet the two principal elements in Aristotle's analysis of poetry—plot and character—seem, superficially at least, to belong peculiarly to narrative poems, long or short. Whether they are present in any comparable manner in the structure of a lyric, or whether the form and content of lyric poetry requires an analysis peculiar to itself, are among the most difficult questions in the theory of poetry.

In the tradition of the great books, there seems to be, as already observed, general agreement about the basic rules for writing narrative poetry. Since these rules aim to direct the artist toward the achievement of excellence, they are also the basic principles of criticism. The science of poetics is at once an organon of production and a canon of criticism.

The simple rules such as those of plot construction afford an example. A well constructed plot must have a beginning, middle, and end. It must observe certain unities (at least of action, if not of time and place). Certain effects, it is held, can best be produced by the use of recognition scenes and reversals of fortune. Whether the events narrated are possible or impossible, the poet must at least invest them with plausibility or verisimilitude. Such rules, formulated by Aristotle and discussed by Cervantes, Fielding, and others, provide standards for judging whether a poem is skillfully made, as well as give directions for the attainment of skill by the poet.

It may be held, of course, that the great poet works by inspiration, by a divine madness rather than by rule; that, as Theseus says in *A Midsummer-Night's Dream*, "the lunatic, the lover, and the poet are of imagination all compact . . . The poet's eye, in a fine frenzy rolling, doth glance from heaven to earth, from earth to heaven; and as imagination bodies forth the forms of things unknown, the poet's pen turns them to shapes, and gives to airy nothing a local habitation and a name." But if there is an art of poetry, then like any other art it is a thing of rules, whether or not genius needs their guidance or can be regulated by them.

The pivotal question here is, Which takes precedence, the creative or the critical faculty? Does Aristotle's rule concerning the primacy of plot derive from the greatest poems of antiquity in which he found this principle observed? Does it set up an infallible measure of excellence in narration or, on the other hand, do certain modern novels have an impeccable greatness despite their violation of this rule by the emphasis they place on the development of character rather than on the action in which the characters are involved? The rule of probability and necessity may, on the other hand, be inviolable. Not even the most original genius may be able to tell a good story without giving it poetic truth, according to the necessities of the characters he has created and the probabilities of the situations in which he places them.

On the side of language, poetic theory seems to draw much from the art of rhetoric. The relation of rhetoric to poetics, the nature of rhetorical devices such as metaphor and simile, the choice among existing words or the invention of new ones, are matters dealt with in the chapter on Rhetoric as well as here. Aristotle's treatment of these problems both in his *Rhetoric* and his *Poetics* lays the foundation for the traditional association of these two disciplines. In both, for example, he discusses the various modes of metaphor and their utility in achieving an expansion of meaning combined with a contraction of speech.

This, in turn, relates to his general maxim of style which directs the writer "to be clear without being ordinary. The clearest style," he says, "is that which uses only current or proper words," but in order to avoid being commonplace or ordinary, it must be admixed with lofty diction—"raised above the commonplace by the employment of unusual words. . . . Nothing contributes more to produce a clearness of diction that is remote from commonness than the lengthening, contraction, and alteration of words. . . . Phrases which are not part of current idiom give distinction to style. . . . But the greatest thing by far is to have a command of metaphor. This alone cannot be imparted by another; it is the mark of genius for to make good metaphors implies an eye for resemblances."

One part of Aristotle's theory of style seems to be amplified by Pascal's observation that a certain perfection is achieved by the use of those words which, if altered, would spoil the discourse. In these terms, prosaic as opposed to poetic writing does not result from the lack of a fixed metre but rather from commonplaceness or lack of distinction in language. This standard of style does not apply to poetry alone; for just as history and philosophy may be written in prose or verse, so also may they be written poetically or prosaically.

Dr. Johnson's point that poetry cannot be translated, that "the beauties of poetry cannot be preserved in any language except that in which it was originally written," may be capable of the widest generalization. It may be extended to mean that writing which is poetic cannot be translated into any other form of words, even in the same language. A poetic sentence in English is untranslatable in this absolute sense when no alternative English phrasing is truly its equivalent. For example, it seems impossible to re-state, without loss or ruin, Shakespeare's "Life is a tale told by an idiot, full of sound and fury, signifying nothing" or Hobbes' "Life in a state of nature is solitary, poor, nasty, brutish, and short."

The other part of Aristotle's theory of style, that concerning metaphors, seems to be converted by William James into a general distinction between poetic and philosophic thought, or what he calls "the splendid and the analytic" types of intellect. Poetic thought tends to develop the implications of an analogy without giving an explication of its grounds. This, in James' view, explains "the abrupt transitions in Shakespeare's thought," which "astonish the reader by their unexpectedness, no less than delight him by their fitness." Quoting a passage from Homer, unfathomably rich in metaphor, he says that "a man in whom all the accidents of an analogy rise up as vividly as this, may be excused for not attending to the ground of the analogy." The two types of intellect are rarely found in conjunction—Plato, according to James, being one of the few exceptions "whose strangeness proves the rule."

ON THE LEVEL of thought and knowledge, as opposed to that of language, poetry is traditionally contrasted to philosophy and history. As indicated in the chapter on HISTORY, historians like Herodotus, Thucydides, and Plutarch emphasize the difference rather than the similarity; the historian is a reporter of fact, the poet a creator of fables or fictions. The one gains credence by his display of evidence and reasons; the other, by the intrinsic plausibility of his tale. "In a good poem," writes Hobbes, "whether it be epic or dramatic . . . both judgment and fancy are required, but the fancy must be more eminent . . . In a good history, the judgment must be eminent, because the goodness consists in the method, in the truth . . . Fancy has no place but only in adorning the style."

Bacon associates poetry most intimately with history, both being concerned with "individuals, circumscribed by time and place," and differing only as one employs the imagination, the other the memory. Aristotle, on the other hand, finds poetry and philosophy more alike, at least to the extent that poetry, unlike history, "tends to express the universal," by which he means "how a person of a certain type will on occasion speak or act, according to the law of probability or necessity." Even if the poet "chances to take an historical subject, he is none the less a poet; for there is no reason why some events that have actually happened should not conform to the law of the probable and possible, and in virtue of that quality in them he is their poet or maker." In this sense the historian also may turn poet. Referring to the speeches in his history, Thucydides tells us that it was his habit "to make the speakers say what was in my opinion demanded of them by the various occasions, of course adhering as closely as possible to the general sense of what they really said."

Some of the great poems, notably the *Divine Comedy*, *Paradise Lost*, and *Faust*, are frequently called philosophical for what appear to be other reasons: either because the discourse of their characters is weighted with doctrine, or because the poet himself is expressing a doctrine, not in particular speeches, nor by argument, but in the symbolism of the poem as a whole. By these criteria, Lucretius' *On the Nature of Things* is a philosophical work, but not a philosophical poem. It is argumentative throughout, not narrative at all; it aims to be a literal rather than an allegorical statement of the truth. Bacon's definition of allegorical poetry—as that "which represents intellectual things to the senses"—seems to characterize both the poetic aspect of philosophy and a distinctively philosophical type of poetry.

Yet Aristotle's point, that poetry and philosophy are alike, may remain valid. All poetry, certainly all the great narrative poems, the great epics and dramas, novels and plays, deal with the abiding problems of human action and the perennial themes of human thought. It is not this moral or metaphysical content, however, which makes poetry more philosophical than history. It is the poet's treatment of such matters. In the persons and events of his story he succeeds in giving the universal a concrete embodiment. Precisely because these are only imaginary, not real particulars, they permit the abstract universal to be readily disengaged.

Poets like Chaucer and Cervantes, who insist that their function is to instruct as well as to delight, do not assume the role of pedagogues or preachers. They teach, not dogmatically, but as experience does, by affording the mind the materials or occasions for insight and inference. As an artistic imitation, poetry may be better than the experience it represents. It may improve upon experience as a teacher, because, born of the poet's mind, it is already impregnated with ideas.

OUTLINE OF TOPICS

1. The nature of poetry: its distinction from other arts
   - 1*a*. The theory of poetry as imitation: the enjoyment of imitation
   - 1*b*. The object, medium, and manner of imitation in poetry and other arts

2. The origin and development of poetry: the materials of myth and legend

3. The inspiration or genius of the poet: the influence of the poetic tradition

4. The major kinds of poetry: their comparative excellence
   - 4*a*. Epic and dramatic poetry
   - 4*b*. Tragedy and comedy

5. Poetry in relation to knowledge
   - 5*a*. The aim of poetry to instruct as well as to delight: the pretensions or deceptions of the poet as teacher
   - 5*b*. Poetry contrasted with history and philosophy: the dispraise and defense of the poet

6. Poetry and emotion
   - 6*a*. The expression of emotion in poetry
   - 6*b*. The arousal and purgation of the emotions by poetry: the catharsis of pity and fear

7. The elements of poetic narrative
   - 7*a*. Plot: its primacy; its construction
   - 7*b*. The role of character: its relation to plot
   - 7*c*. Thought and diction as elements of poetry
   - 7*d*. Spectacle and song in drama

8. The science of poetics: rules of art and principles of criticism
   - 8*a*. Critical standards and artistic rules with respect to narrative structure
     - (1) The poetic unities: comparison of epic and dramatic unity
     - (2) Poetic truth: verisimilitude or plausibility; the possible, the probable, and the necessary
     - (3) The significance of recognitions and reversals in the development of plot
   - 8*b*. Critical standards and artistic rules with respect to the language of poetry: the distinction between prose and verse; the measure of excellence in style
   - 8*c*. The interpretation of poetry

9. The moral and political significance of poetry
   - 9*a*. The influence of poetry on mind and character: its role in education
   - 9*b*. The issue concerning the censorship of poetry

REFERENCES

References are listed by volume number (in bold type), author's name, and page number. Bible references are to book, chapter, and verse of the Authorized King James version of the Bible. The abbreviation "esp" calls the reader's attention to one or more especially relevant parts of a whole reference; "passim" signifies that the topic is discussed intermittently rather than continuously in the work or passage cited. Where the work as a whole is relevant to the topic, the page numbers refer to the entire work. For general guidance in the use of *The Great Ideas,* consult the Preface.

1. The nature of poetry: its distinction from other arts

7 PLATO, 142–148
9 ARISTOTLE, 681–699
17 PLOTINUS, 250
25 MONTAIGNE, 482
27 SHAKESPEARE, 594
29 CERVANTES, 251–252
30 BACON, 38–39, 55
33 PASCAL, 176
42 KANT, 524, 532–536
44 BOSWELL, 254
47 GOETHE, 4, 235–240
54 FREUD, 643

1*a*. The theory of poetry as imitation: the enjoyment of imitation

5 ARISTOPHANES, 601–602
7 PLATO, 105, 320–334, 427–434, 654, 660–662
9 ARISTOTLE, 696–698
12 LUCRETIUS, 79
19 AQUINAS, 764–765
29 CERVANTES, xiii
33 PASCAL, 176
37 FIELDING, 121–123
54 FREUD, 643

1*b*. The object, medium, and manner of imitation in poetry and other arts

7 PLATO, 654–662, 726–728
9 ARISTOTLE, 545–546, 681–682
12 AURELIUS, 303
23 HOBBES, 262
26 SHAKESPEARE, 532
27 SHAKESPEARE, 393–394
30 BACON, 38–39
36 SWIFT, 169
42 KANT, 527–528, 557–558
44 BOSWELL, 196–197
48 MELVILLE, 335
54 FREUD, 265

2. The origin and development of poetry: the materials of myth and legend

4 HOMER, 3, 183
5 ARISTOPHANES, 476
6 HERODOTUS, 5
7 PLATO, 324–328
9 ARISTOTLE, 682–684, 687–688
12 AURELIUS, 302–303
13 VIRGIL, 19–21, 103
14 PLUTARCH, 128–129
18 AUGUSTINE, 478–479
21 DANTE, 156–157
24 RABELAIS, 190–191
25 MONTAIGNE, 362–363
32 MILTON, 247–248, 337–338
37 FIELDING, 357
40 GIBBON, 23–24, 94, 158–159, 476–477, 544–545, 627
41 GIBBON, 225, 325–328, 522–528
46 HEGEL, 229–230, 239–240, 263–265
48 MELVILLE, xi–xx
49 DARWIN, 569–571
54 FREUD, 483, 692–693

3. The inspiration or genius of the poet: the influence of the poetic tradition

4 HOMER, 14–15
5 ARISTOPHANES, 477, 491–492, 559, 600–601, 630–631
7 PLATO, 144–145, 160–161, 166–167, 202, 684
9 ARISTOTLE, 653–654, 682–683
12 LUCRETIUS, 12
21 DANTE, 6, 47, 53, 85–87, 93–94, 98, 106, 107, 120, 140
22 CHAUCER, 21–22
24 RABELAIS, 2–3
25 MONTAIGNE, 52–53, 166–167, 195–197, 309, 512
26 SHAKESPEARE, 370–371
27 SHAKESPEARE, 601–602
29 CERVANTES, xi–xiii
30 BACON, 55
32 MILTON, 93–94, 135–136, 217–218
37 FIELDING, 246–247, 273–274
40 GIBBON, 345, 476–477
41 GIBBON, 527–528, 573–574
42 KANT, 525–532, 542–543
44 BOSWELL, 455
47 GOETHE, 1–6, 137–138
53 JAMES, 686–688, 863
54 FREUD, 181, 239–240, 383, 600–601

4. The major kinds of poetry: their comparative excellence

4*a*. Epic and dramatic poetry

7 Plato, 328–331
9 Aristotle, 681–682, 683–684, 695–696, 698–699
29 Cervantes, 185
30 Bacon, 39
52 Dostoevsky, 127–128
54 Freud, 692

4*b*. Tragedy and comedy

7 Plato, 173, 281–282, 329, 431, 629–630, 655, 727–728
9 Aristotle, 681–699
12 Epictetus, 133–134
12 Aurelius, 302–303
21 Dante, 152
22 Chaucer, 153–154
29 Cervantes, 237
32 Milton, 337–338
37 Fielding, 357
44 Boswell, 308
46 Hegel, 263
48 Melville, 84–85, 107
54 Freud, 246–248, 581–582

5. Poetry in relation to knowledge

7 Plato, 138–140, 142–148, 383
9 Aristotle, 682, 696–697
18 Augustine, 6, 16
20 Aquinas, 267–268
21 Dante, 1–2, 133
25 Montaigne, 258–259
30 Bacon, 38–39
31 Descartes, 43
37 Fielding, 296–298
41 Gibbon, 300
42 Kant, 528–530, 532

5*a*. The aim of poetry to instruct as well as to delight: the pretensions or deceptions of the poet as teacher

5 Aristophanes, 460–461, 462–463, 495, 564–582
7 Plato, 140, 281–282, 320–339, 427–434, 653–663
9 Aristotle, 544–546, 547–548
12 Lucretius, 44
14 Plutarch, 33–34, 121–122
18 Augustine, 479
22 Chaucer, 550
24 Rabelais, 168–169
29 Cervantes, xi-xvi
32 Milton, 337–338
37 Fielding, 1–2, 35
40 Gibbon, 494–495
41 Gibbon, 40–41
42 Kant, 534–539
47 Goethe, 2–6
52 Dostoevsky, 127–128

5*b*. Poetry contrasted with history and philosophy: the dispraise and defense of the poet

5 Aristophanes, 581–582
6 Herodotus, 72–73, 127
7 Plato, 19–20, 57, 122–123, 140, 280–282, 320–333, 684
9 Aristotle, 686
14 Plutarch, 140
17 Plotinus, 10–11
18 Augustine, 202–203
23 Hobbes, 67
25 Montaigne, 62, 194–201 passim
26 Shakespeare, 451
29 Cervantes, 212–215
30 Bacon, 32, 38–39
33 Pascal, 173–174, 177
35 Hume, 452–453
37 Fielding, 19–20, 49–50
40 Gibbon, 88, 186, 345–346
44 Boswell, 120, 307
46 Hegel, 153, 259
53 James, 686–689

6. Poetry and emotion

6*a*. The expression of emotion in poetry

Old Testament: *Exodus*, 15:1–21 / *II Samuel*, 1:17–27 / *Psalms* passim / *Lamentations*
Apocrypha: *Judith*, 16 / *Song of Three Children*, 28–68
New Testament: *Luke*, 1:42–55,67–79
7 Plato, 654
9 Aristotle, 544–546, 659–660, 671
13 Virgil, 115–116
25 Montaigne, 399–401, 410
27 Shakespeare, 597–599
32 Milton, 17–25
44 Boswell, 53
54 Freud, 246–248, 773–774

6*b*. The arousal and purgation of the emotions by poetry: the catharsis of pity and fear

4 Homer, 186, 227
6 Herodotus, 189
7 Plato, 145, 325–326, 431–434, 628–630
9 Aristotle, 547–548, 687–689, 690, 691–692
18 Augustine, 7, 13–14, 83–84
21 Dante, 55
25 Montaigne, 104–105
26 Shakespeare, 245
27 Shakespeare, 46
30 Bacon, 78
40 Gibbon, 94
42 Kant, 509
44 Boswell, 308
49 Darwin, 570–571
54 Freud, 239–240, 246–247, 581–582, 762

7. The elements of poetic narrative

5 Aristophanes, 534–535, 573–582
9 Aristotle, 684–685, 687

32 MILTON, 337–338
36 STERNE, 335–336

7*a*. Plot: its primacy; its construction

9 ARISTOTLE, 684, 685–691, 695–696
36 STERNE, 228–231
37 FIELDING, 204–205

7*b*. The role of character: its relation to plot

9 ARISTOTLE, 681–682, 684–685, 687–688, 689
12 EPICTETUS, 133–134
17 PLOTINUS, 91–92
37 FIELDING, 152–155, 204–205
44 BOSWELL, 157–158
54 FREUD, 247–248

7*c*. Thought and diction as elements of poetry

7 PLATO, 52–57
9 ARISTOTLE, 681, 684–685, 691–695, 697–698
22 CHAUCER, 40–41, 171–172
27 SHAKESPEARE, 45
30 BACON, 63
32 MILTON, 59–60
53 JAMES, 687–688
54 FREUD, 458–459

7*d*. Spectacle and song in drama

7 PLATO, 331–333
9 ARISTOTLE, 681, 685, 691
46 HEGEL, 263–265

8. The science of poetics: rules of art and principles of criticism

5 ARISTOPHANES, 573–582
7 PLATO, 142–148, 654–662
9 ARISTOTLE, 681–699
36 STERNE, 287–289, 344–345
37 FIELDING, 1–2, 35, 73–75, 152–155, 189–191, 223–225, 246–247, 273–274, 338, 357
41 GIBBON, 300, 526
42 KANT, 513–514, 524–527
46 HEGEL, 185

8*a*. Critical standards and artistic rules with respect to narrative structure

5 ARISTOPHANES, 534–535
9 ARISTOTLE, 685–691
33 PASCAL, 176
36 STERNE, 193–194, 195, 209–210, 228–231, 335–336, 344–345
37 FIELDING, 189–191
41 GIBBON, 300
44 BOSWELL, 513

8*a*(1) The poetic unities: comparison of epic and dramatic unity

7 PLATO, 133
9 ARISTOTLE, 685–686, 695, 699
27 SHAKESPEARE, 505
29 CERVANTES, 186
36 STERNE, 245–246
37 FIELDING, 19–20, 73–75

8*a*(2) Poetic truth: verisimilitude or plausibility; the possible, the probable, and the necessary

6 HERODOTUS, 72
7 PLATO, 142–148, 320–324, 427–434
9 ARISTOTLE, 686–687, 696–698
14 PLUTARCH, 189
21 DANTE, 36–38, 42–43, 102, 106–107
22 CHAUCER, 41
27 SHAKESPEARE, 49
29 CERVANTES, 184–186, 189–190, 208–209, 386–388
30 BACON, 38–39
31 DESCARTES, 43
37 FIELDING, 49–50, 152–155
40 GIBBON, 345, 471
44 BOSWELL, 282, 446–447
47 GOETHE, 181–182

8*a*(3) The significance of recognitions and reversals in the development of plot

9 ARISTOTLE, 686–687, 688–690
22 CHAUCER, 433
37 FIELDING, 379
54 FREUD, 246

8*b*. Critical standards and artistic rules with respect to the language of poetry: the distinction between prose and verse; the measure of excellence in style

5 ARISTOPHANES, 504–505, 559, 573–582
7 PLATO, 52–57
9 ARISTOTLE, 653–667, 681, 694–695, 697–698
18 AUGUSTINE, 97–98, 331–332, 638, 686–696 passim
21 DANTE, 41, 93–94, 102
22 CHAUCER, 295–296, 351, 491, 494
25 MONTAIGNE, 195–197, 309–310, 422–423, 455
27 SHAKESPEARE, 589, 597–598, 606
29 CERVANTES, xi-xiii, 251–252
32 MILTON, 59–61, 65–66
33 PASCAL, 174, 175–177
37 FIELDING, 1–2, 246–247
40 GIBBON, 494–495
41 GIBBON, 327
42 KANT, 513–514
44 BOSWELL, 59–61, 167–170 passim, 202, 381–382
54 FREUD, 277

8c. The interpretation of poetry

NEW TESTAMENT: *Matthew*, 13:3–50; 21:28–44 / *Luke*, 16:1–13
7 PLATO, 52–57, 142–148
9 ARISTOTLE, 697–698
18 AUGUSTINE, 640–642, 644–645, 659–660, 666–674
19 AQUINAS, 8–10
21 DANTE, 104–105
24 RABELAIS, 1–3, 66–67
25 MONTAIGNE, 104–105, 285, 362–363
40 GIBBON, 346

9. The moral and political significance of poetry

9*a*. The influence of poetry on mind and character: its role in education

9*b*. The issue concerning the censorship of poetry

CROSS-REFERENCES

For: The comparison of poetry with history, philosophy, and science, *see* HISTORY 1; KNOWLEDGE 4c; PHILOSOPHY 1d; SCIENCE 2b; TRUTH 4b.

The consideration of the fine arts in general, *see* ART 7a; and for standards of critical judgment with respect to the beauty or excellence of works of fine art, *see* ART 7b; BEAUTY 2, 5.

Another discussion of the theory of art as imitation, and for related doctrines, *see* ART 3; FORM 1d(1).

The elements of inspiration, emotion, and tradition in the formation of poetry, *see* ART 8; MEMORY AND IMAGINATION 3d.

Other aspects of the distinction between tragedy and comedy, *see* HAPPINESS 4b.

Matters related to the theory of emotional purgation, *see* ART 8; DESIRE 4d.

The place of poetics among the sciences, *see* PHILOSOPHY 2c.

The discussion of poetic truth and probability, *see* MEMORY AND IMAGINATION 7b; TRUTH 4b.

Other considerations of the problem of style, *see* LANGUAGE 9; RHETORIC 2–2b.

Matters bearing on the interpretation of poetry, *see* RHETORIC 2d.

The role of poetry and other fine arts in education, *see* ART 10a; EDUCATION 4d; VIRTUE AND VICE 4d(4).

Other discussions of the problem of censorship, or of the political regulation of artistic expression, *see* ART 10b; EDUCATION 8c; EMOTION 5e; LIBERTY 2a.

ADDITIONAL READINGS

Listed below are works not included in *Great Books of the Western World*, but relevant to the idea and topics with which this chapter deals. These works are divided into two groups:

I. Works by authors represented in this collection.
II. Works by authors not represented in this collection.

For the date, place, and other facts concerning the publication of the works cited, consult the Bibliography of Additional Readings which follows the last chapter of *The Great Ideas.*

I.

PLUTARCH. "How a Young Man Ought to Hear Poems," in *Moralia*
AUGUSTINE. *On Music*
DANTE. *De Vulgari Eloquentia*
——. *Epistle to Can Grande della Scala*
HUME. *Of the Standard of Taste*
——. *Of Tragedy*
GIBBON. *An Essay on the Study of Literature*, I–XLIII
A. SMITH. "Of the Affinity Between Music, Dancing and Poetry," in *Essays Philosophical and Literary*
GOETHE. *Poetry and Truth*
——. *Conversations with Eckermann*
J. S. MILL. "Thoughts on Poetry and Its Varieties," in VOL I, *Dissertations and Discussions*
TOLSTOY. *What Is Art?*
FREUD. *Wit and Its Relation to the Unconscious*, CH 5–7

II.

HORACE. *The Art of Poetry*
LONGINUS. *On the Sublime*
DEMETRIUS. *On Style*
BOCCACCIO. *On Poetry*
P. SIDNEY. *An Apology for Poetry*
CORNEILLE. *Examens*
——. *Trois discours sur l'art dramatique*
MOLIÈRE. *La critique de l'école des femmes* (*The School for Wives Criticised*)
BOILEAU-DESPRÉAUX. *The Art of Poetry*
DRYDEN. *An Essay of Dramatic Poesy*
——. *Of Heroic Plays*
——. *A Discourse Concerning . . . Satire*
POPE. *Essay on Criticism*
VICO. *The New Science*, BK II–III
J. HARRIS. *Three Treatises. The First Concerning Art. The Second Concerning Music, Painting, and Poetry. The Third Concerning Happiness*
——. *Upon the Rise and Progress of Criticism*
BURKE. *Hints for an Essay on the Drama*
——. *A Philosophical Enquiry into the Origin of Our Ideas of the Sublime and Beautiful*, PART V
GRAY. *The Progress of Poesy*
KAMES. *Elements of Criticism*
VOLTAIRE. *Letters on the English*, XVIII–XX
——. "Art of Poetry," "Poets," in *A Philosophical Dictionary*

LESSING. *Laocoön*
BEATTIE. *An Essay on Poetry and Music*
S. JOHNSON. *Lives of the English Poets*
BLAIR. *Lectures on Rhetoric and Belles Lettres*
SCHILLER. *The Stage as a Moral Institution*
——. *On Simple and Sentimental Poetry*
WORDSWORTH. *Preface to the Lyrical Ballads*
A. W. SCHLEGEL. *Lectures on Dramatic Art and Literature*
COLERIDGE. *Biographia Literaria*, CH 4, 14–20
SCHOPENHAUER. *The World as Will and Idea*, VOL III, SUP, CH 37
T. L. PEACOCK. *Four Ages of Poetry*
SHELLEY. *A Defense of Poetry*
HAZLITT. *Lectures on the English Poets*
——. *My First Acquaintance with Poets*
STENDHAL. *Racine et Shakespeare*
HUGO. *Préface de 'Cromwell'*
DE QUINCEY. *The Literature of Knowledge and the Literature of Power*
T. CARLYLE. *On Heroes, Hero-Worship and the Heroic in History*, LECT III
EMERSON. "The Poet," in *Essays*, II
HUNT. *An Essay in Answer to the Question "What Is Poetry?"*
KIERKEGAARD. *Either/Or*
——. *The Point of View*
POE. *The Poetic Principle*
TAINE. *Essais de critique et d'histoire*
NIETZSCHE. *The Birth of Tragedy*
ARNOLD. *Essays in Criticism*
MEREDITH. *An Essay on Comedy and the Uses of the Comic Spirit*
FRAZER. *The Golden Bough*, PART III, CH 3
CHEKHOV. *Letters on the Short Story, the Drama and Other Literary Topics*
BERGSON. *Laughter*
CLAUDEL. *Poetic Art*
DILTHEY. *Das Erlebnis und die Dichtung*
SHAW. *Dramatic Opinions and Essays*
H. JAMES. *The Art of the Novel*
BABBITT. *The New Laokoön*
KALLEN. *The Book of Job as Greek Tragedy*
MARITAIN. *Art and Scholasticism* (Frontiers of Poetry)
JUNG. *On the Relations of Analytical Psychology to Poetic Art*
ABERCROMBIE. *The Theory of Poetry*
RICHARDS. *Principles of Literary Criticism*
——. *Science and Poetry*
FORSTER. *Aspects of the Novel*
LOWES. *The Road to Xanadu*
ROUTH. *God, Man, and Epic Poetry*
MUIR. *The Structure of the Novel*
BUCHANAN. *Poetry and Mathematics*
H. E. READ. *Form in Modern Poetry*
CROCE. *Aesthetic as Science of Expression*
——. *The Defense of Poetry*
T. S. ELIOT. *The Sacred Wood*
——. "The Function of Criticism," "Rhetoric and Poetic Drama," "A Dialogue on Dramatic Poetry," in *Selected Essays*
——. *The Use of Poetry and the Use of Criticism*
HOUSMAN. *The Name and Nature of Poetry*
TATE. *Reactionary Essays on Poetry and Ideas*
YEATS. *Letters on Poetry*
SANTAYANA. *Interpretations of Poetry and Religion*, CH 2, 7, 10
——. *Reason in Art*, CH 6
——. *Soliloquies in England and Later Soliloquies*, CH 32–33, 37
——. *The Realm of Truth*, CH 7
RANSOM. *The World's Body*
VALÉRY. *Variety*
——. *Introduction à la poétique*
CASSIRER. *The Myth of the State*, PART I
VAN DOREN. *The Noble Voice*
SARTRE. *What Is Literature?*

Chapter 70: PRINCIPLE

INTRODUCTION

OF the three ways in which principles are considered in the tradition of the great books, the most familiar sense of the word is the one in which we speak of moral principles, principles of action, or political principles. The connotation of the word in this usage seems to be twofold. We think of principles as rules of conduct and we think of them as standards by which to measure and judge human acts or political events. Either conception attributes a certain generality to principles. Just as rules apply to an indefinite number of particular cases, so any principle we appeal to in order to decide a practical problem or to weigh the merits of an action undertaken, can be applied again and again in other circumstances.

In addition to this characteristic of generality, principles seem to have the quality of *underlying* or being the *source of* other things. In jurisprudence the search for principles consists in the attempt to discover those few most fundamental precepts from which the more detailed rules of law can be derived. The constitution of a state provides the principles which underlie its particular laws and sets the standards by which their legality is to be measured. Governments are judged by the principles they attempt to apply as well as by their success in putting these principles into practice. To say of a government that its acts are *unprincipled* is not to condemn the particular acts as wrong, but to accuse the government of having no uniform policy to serve as a foundation for its acts.

This aspect of the meaning of principle—as the source from which a set of consequences follows—seems to be more characteristic of the idea of principle than the aspect of generality. According to its Latin derivation and the equivalent root in Greek, "principle" means a beginning or a foundation. Sometimes it means that which comes first absolutely, in the sense of being before everything else; sometimes it means that which comes first only relatively, taking precedence over some things, but having others prior to itself. Since priority may be either absolute or relative—first without qualification or first only in a certain respect—the traditional phrase "first principle" does not have the redundancy of "first first" or "beginning beginning."

If there are absolutely first beginnings, to which nothing else can be prior, they can legitimately be called "first principles" to distinguish them from principles which come first only in a certain respect. Only if there are first principles can regression to infinity be avoided in the search for origins. The propositions which lie at the foundation of a science may, for example, constitute its principles, but they may also be derived in turn from some prior science. Only the principles of a science which is prior to or independent of all others can be truly first principles.

THE FOREGOING example brings us to the other meaning of principle that is popularly recognized. It is the sense in which men speak of principles in relation to conclusions, or of principles as the foundations of a science.

The priority which belongs to principles in the domain of thought need not be temporal. Principles may or may not be first in the order of learning. But if they are not first in the temporal order, they must be first logically, as premises are logically prior to a conclusion, or, as in Euclid's *Elements*, his principles—his definitions, postulates, and axioms—are logically prior to all the theorems he demonstrates by means of them.

It may be asked whether, among propositions related as premises and conclusions, the logical priority of one proposition to another is sufficient to make the prior proposition a principle. Can a proposition be a principle if, even though it is used as a premise in reasoning, it lacks generality? For example, is the particular proposition—that this bottle contains poison—a principle underlying the practical conclusion that its contents should not be swallowed?

Aristotle answers affirmatively. In the order of practical thinking, he holds, we deliberate neither about the end to be sought nor about the particular facts on which a choice of the means depends. "The end cannot be a subject of deliberation," he writes, "but only the means; nor indeed can the particular facts be a subject of it, as whether this is bread or has been baked as it should; for these are matters of perception." The perceived particulars thus function as principles along with the most general of all practical propositions, namely, what the end should be. Calling the faculty which apprehends first principles "intuitive reason," Aristotle says that "the intuitive reason involved in practical reasonings grasps the last and variable fact, *i.e.*, the minor premise. For these variable facts are the starting-points for the apprehension of the end, since the universals are reached from the particulars; of these therefore we must have perception, and this perception is intuitive reason."

Perception, at least in the form of *sense*-perception, seems to be only one of the two ways in which we apprehend the particular facts which are principles in practical reasoning. Like Aristotle, Aquinas uses the judgment, that *this is bread or iron*, as an example of "facts received through the senses" which are "principles . . . accepted in the inquiry of counsel." But the moral quality inherent in particular acts does not seem to be perceptible by the senses alone; and such particular moral judgments are also involved in moral reasoning. Aristotle suggests that habit (*i.e.*, the moral habits or virtues) are the immediate source of such judgments, which can be called "perceptions of the particular" even though they are not simply sense-perceptions.

"Of first principles," Aristotle explains, "we see some by induction, some by perception, some by a certain habituation." By induction we see the general truths; by sense-perception, the sensible particulars; and by habituation, the moral particulars. Hence Aristotle insists that "anyone who is to listen intelligently to lectures about what is noble and just and, generally, about the subjects of political science must have been brought up in good habits. For the fact is the starting-point, and if this is sufficiently plain to him, he will not at the start need the reason as well; for the man who has been well brought up has or can easily get the starting-points."

The word "principle" is used by Kant in a much more restricted sense. He reserves the status of principle to the general propositions which serve as the major premises in reasoning. In both the theoretic and the practical sciences, principles express reason's understanding of universal and necessary relationships.

Kant differs from Aristotle in other respects. He differentiates between ordinary general propositions which merely serve as major premises in reasoning and the propositions he classifies as "synthetic judgements *a priori*." He regards the former as principles only in a relative sense and treats the latter alone as principles absolutely. He also distinguishes between those principles of the *understanding* which he thinks are "constitutive of experience," and those principles of the *reason* which should be used in what he calls a "regulative," not a constitutive manner. They determine the direction and goals of thought beyond experience. But such differences concerning the nature and kinds of principles do not affect the commonly accepted meaning of principle as that from which, in the temporal order of learning, knowledge develops or that upon which, in the logical order, knowledge rests.

THE THIRD AND relatively unfamiliar sense in which principles are discussed in the great books does not refer to the sources of man's moral decisions, political acts, or scientific conclusions. The discussion in question refers to reality apart from man. Just as men try to discover the elements of matter, or the causes of motion, so they try to discover the principles of existence and of change. The issues which arise from this concern with the principles of reality are discussed in such chapters as BEING, CAUSE, CHANGE, FORM, NATURE, and MATTER.

If the word "principle" always connotes a beginning, every special sense of principle should involve some kind of priority. As we have already observed, principles may be either prior in time or prior logically. But the principles of the universe or the principles of change are not usually thought to be prior in either of these ways. For them Aristotle specifies another kind of priority—priority in nature—to explain the primacy of those principles which constitute the nature of a thing. In his view, for example, matter and form are the principles of a physical substance. Since a substance composite of matter and form cannot exist until its matter and its form coexist, matter and form are not prior to the substance they compose. Their priority to substance consists only in the fact that that which has the nature of a composite substance *results* from the union of matter and form as its natural components. Because the substance is the *natural resultant*, matter and form can properly be called its *natural principles*.

This way of considering principles at once suggests a close relationship among principles, elements, and causes; and also indicates the connection between the present chapter and the chapters on CAUSE and ELEMENT. The ultimate parts into which a whole can be divided may be its principles as well as its elements. The form or matter of a substance may be, in Aristotle's theory, not only one of its principles, but also a cause—a formal or a material cause. Among the great authors Aristotle and Aquinas alone seem to dwell upon the relationship of these three terms. They give instances in which the same thing is principle, element, and cause, as well as instances in which a principle is neither a cause nor an element, *e.g.*, privation. In the sphere of human conduct, an end is both a principle and a final cause, but not an element. The last end is the highest final cause and the first principle—first in intention though last in attainment.

THE TRADITIONAL issues concerning this idea differ according to the general context in which the question of principles is raised. The main controversy, for example, with regard to principles in the order of reality is over their number and order.

Aristotle argues against an infinite number of principles as incompatible with the very notion of principle itself. In his analysis of change or motion, he tries to prove that no more than three principles are necessary, and no less will do. These are, as the chapter on CHANGE explains, matter, form, and privation. Considering the principles of the universe as a whole, Plotinus also enumerates three and tries to prove that none can be added or subtracted. But whereas Aristotle treats the three principles of change as coordinate, Plotinus places the cosmic principles in the absolute order of first, second, and third.

"We need not go seeking any other Principles," writes Plotinus. "This—the One and the Good—is our First, next to it follows the Intellectual Principle, the Primal Thinker, and upon this follows Soul. Such is the order in nature. The intellectual realm allows no more than these and no fewer. Those who hold to fewer Principles must hold the identity of either Intellectual Principle and Soul, or of Intellectual Principle and The First . . . To increase the Primals by making the Supreme Mind engender the Reason-Principle, and this again engender in the Soul a distinct power to act as mediator between Soul and the Supreme Mind, this is to deny intellection to the Soul, which would no longer derive its Reason from the Intellectual Principle, but from an intermediate. . . . Therefore, we must affirm no more than these three Primals."

In the sense in which Plotinus conceives the three primals, they are not only principles in the order of reality, but are themselves the ultimate grades or modes of reality. Similarly for Plato soul is not only the principle of life and thought in the universe, but it also has its own existence in the realm of being. For Aristotle, in contrast, the principles of change do not have existence in and of themselves. Matter, form, and privation are not substances, but aspects of substance. They are present in every changing substance and in every change, but they are only the principles *of* mutable being; they are not mutable beings in themselves.

Lucretius states two principles as the basic laws of nature. The first is that nothing comes into being out of nothing; the second, that nothing is ever completely reduced to nothingness. The word "principle" is obviously not being used in the same sense here as when it designates The One for Plotinus, soul for Plato, matter for Aristotle, or the atoms which Lucretius calls the "first beginnings." Here it does not refer to an entity, or even to an aspect of some real being, but rather to a law—the statement of a universal and necessary condition which governs all that is or happens. It is in this sense that the proposition traditionally called "the law of contradiction"—that the same thing cannot both be and not be in the same respect at the same time—is said by Aristotle to be the first principle of being as well as of thought.

The conception of the law of contradiction and the related laws of identity and excluded middle as principles of thought raises problems about logical principles in general—whether they are axioms or postulates, whether they are merely rules of reasoning and demonstration or are themselves premises from which conclusions can be deduced. If, for example, the law of contradiction is *only* a rule of thought, which forbids the mind to affirm and deny the same proposition, then it is not a principle of knowledge in the sense in which the definitions and axioms of geometry function as premises in the demonstration of theorems. No conclusion can be drawn from it concerning the nature of things. But if, in addition to being a rule of thought, it is a metaphysical axiom, which states the most fundamental fact about existence, then like the axioms in geometry it may be the source of conclusions in metaphysics.

On this second point Locke seems to differ sharply from Aristotle and Aquinas. He denies that the laws of identity and contradiction are fruitful principles of knowledge. "These magnified maxims," he writes, "are not the principles and foundations of all our other knowledge." Nor have they been, he adds, "the foundations whereon any science hath been built. There is, I know, a great deal of talk, propagated from scholastic men, of sciences and the maxims on which they are built; but it has been my ill luck, never to meet with any such sciences, much less any one built upon these two maxims, 'what is, is' and 'it is impossible for the same thing to be and not to be.'"

We shall presently consider the issue concerning axioms or postulates—whether the principles of the sciences are self-evident truths or are only provisional assumptions. Those who are willing to admit the existence of axioms do not all agree, however, that such truths refer to reality. Hume, for example, limits the content of axioms to knowledge of the relations between our own ideas. They are not truths about real existence or matters of fact.

Locke also grants self-evidence only to perceptions of the agreement or disagreement between ideas. "Concerning the real existence of all other beings" except ourselves and God, we have, he writes, "not so much a demonstrative, much less a self-evident, knowledge; and therefore concerning these there are no maxims." But Locke does think that our demonstrative knowledge of God's existence depends upon an intuitive knowledge of our own existence; and in addition to knowing our own existence directly or without proof, he also thinks we have through our senses an equally direct knowledge of the existence of other things. Such intuitive and sensitive knowledge of particular existences is, like the truth of axioms, immediate—that is, something known directly or without proof, without any appeal to prior propositions. Hence Locke is not denying that we know some immediate truths about reality, but only that such truths consist exclusively of propositions about particular existences. Since axioms, or what Locke calls "maxims," are always general propositions, the self-evident truths which they express do not apply to reality.

William James uses the word "intuitive"—in a different sense from Locke—to characterize propositions that state "the necessary and eternal relations" which the mind "finds between certain of its ideal conceptions." Intuitive propositions are for him, therefore, what maxims are for Locke; and like Locke, James also denies that such axioms of reason hold for reality. "Only *hypothetically*," he says, "can we affirm intuitive truths of real things—by supposing, namely, that real things exist which correspond exactly with the ideal subject of the intuitive propositions . . . The intuitive propositions of Locke leave us as regards outer reality none the better for their possession. We still have to 'go to our senses' to find what the reality is.

"The vindication of the intuitionist position," James continues, "is thus a barren victory. The eternal verities which the very structure of our mind lays hold of do not necessarily themselves lay hold on extramental being, nor have they, as Kant pretended later, a legislating character for all possible experience. They are primarily interesting only as subjective facts. They stand waiting in the mind, forming a beautiful ideal network; and the most we can say is that we *hope* to discover outer realities over which the network may be flung so that ideal and real may coincide."

The opposite view seems to be taken by Plato, Aristotle, Aquinas, Bacon, Descartes, Spinoza, and Kant. Though they are far from being in complete agreement concerning the principles of knowledge, the propositions which they call axiomatic, self-evident, intuitive, or *a priori* synthetic judgments, are not restricted by them to the mind's perception of the relations between *its own* ideas. There are self-evident or immediate truths in physics and metaphysics, as well as in mathematics and logic. Whether these are inductions from experience or innate possessions of the mind, whether they are intuitive apprehensions of intelligible being or *a priori* judgments having a transcendental origin, these propositions are held to describe the world of experience, or the nature and existence of things outside the human mind.

THERE SEEM TO BE two degrees of skepticism with regard to principles in the order of knowledge. Complete skepticism would consist in denying principles in every sense. That would be the same as denying any beginning or basis for even the opinions which men hold. No one seems to go that far.

The issue with respect to the foundations of knowledge or opinion is therefore not between those who affirm and those who deny principles, but between different views of what the starting points are. It is sometimes said, for example, that sensations are the principles or beginnings of all human learning. This view is shared both by those who think that all our ideas or concepts are abstracted from the materials provided by the senses and by those who account for all the other contents of the mind —its memories and imaginations, its complex formations—in terms of the simple impressions originally received by the senses.

Concepts, as distinct from sense-perceptions, are also sometimes regarded as principles of knowledge by those who think that concepts originate by abstraction from sensory materials, as well as by those who think that ideas are primary principles, *i.e.*, having no origin in any prior apprehensions. On either view, ideas or concepts function as principles insofar as they are the simples from which the more complex acts of the mind develop, such as the acts of judgment and reasoning. Just as on the level of language, words are the principles of all significant speech, out of which sentences and paragraphs are formed; just as, in the logical order, terms are said to be the principles of propositions and syllogisms; so concepts are the principles of judgments and reasonings. The definitions of Euclid, for example, state the notions of point, line, triangle, etc. which underlie his theorems and demonstrations.

One common characteristic of either sensations or concepts as principles of knowledge seems to be simplicity. Nothing more elementary, out of which they can be formed, is prior to them. Another characteristic is that they are principles of knowledge or opinion without being themselves acts of knowledge or opinion. This point is made by all who hold that only propositions—whether statements of opinion or of knowledge—can be true or false.

The terms which express the simple apprehensions of the mind—its sensations or concepts—cannot be true or false, because, unlike propositions, which are composed of terms, they do not assert anything. If sensations and concepts cannot be true or false in the sense in which propositions or judgments are, then they lack the distinctive property of knowledge or opinion. In contrast, propositions or judgments —which are supposed to be principles, whether axioms or assumptions—can be treated as themselves expressions of knowledge or opinion, not merely as its starting points or sources.

THE TWO DEGREES of skepticism previously mentioned apply only to those principles of knowledge which are themselves capable of being regarded as knowledge or opinion and hence as either true or false.

We have already considered the skepticism of those who, admitting that the truth of some propositions can be immediately recognized by the mind, nevertheless deny that such self-evident truths describe reality. This may or may not be accompanied by a further depreciation of axioms on the ground that they are merely analytical propositions and hence trifling, uninstructive, or tautological.

The chapter on JUDGMENT considers the issue which revolves around the derogatory use of such words as "tautology" or "truism" to designate self-evident truths. Though the invidious connotation of the word "truism" does not make the truth to which this epithet is applied any less true, the dignity of a truth does seem to be affected by the refusal to regard it as a statement of reality. Furthermore, a certain degree of skepticism results from such refusal. Hume exemplifies this. He holds that self-evident truths are possible only in mathematics, which deals not with matters of fact, but with the relations between our own ideas. In consequence, he denies to the study of nature the certitude or demonstrative character which he finds in mathematical science. Since physics is concerned with real existences, no axioms or self-evident principles are available to it; and so, according to Hume, it cannot demonstrate its conclusions, but must advance them as probabilities.

A more thorough-going skepticism seems to consist in holding that there are absolutely no matters at all about which men have axiomatic knowledge. This appears to be the position of Montaigne. No truths are self-evident. None commands the universal assent of mankind; none belongs to the nature of the mind so that all men must agree to it. Montaigne almost holds it to be axiomatic that there are no axioms, for if there were, he says, "there would be some one thing to be found in the world . . . that would be believed by men with an universal consent; but this, that there is no one proposition that is not debated and controverted amongst us, or that may not be, makes it very manifest that our natural judgment does not very clearly comprehend what it embraces."

If it is objected that, in the absence of such principles, there is no starting point or foundation for science, Montaigne seems willing to accept the consequence. He does not flinch from an infinite regression of reasons. "No reason," he writes, "can be established but upon the foundation of another reason; and so run back to all infinity." To those who say that there is no disputing with persons who deny principles, he replies that "men can have no principles, if not revealed to them by the Divinity; of all the rest, the beginning, the middle, and the end are nothing but dream and vapor."

If, however, for practical purposes, a beginning must be made somewhere, Montaigne suggests that it can be done by taking things for granted and then getting others to grant our presuppositions. "It is very easy," he writes, "upon granted foundations to build whatever we please . . . By this way, we find our reason well-grounded and discourse at a venture; for our masters prepossess and gain beforehand as much room in our belief as is necessary for them towards concluding afterwards what they please, as geometers do by their postulates; the consent and approbation we allow them giving them power to draw us to the right and left, and to whirl us about at their own pleasure."

IF THE ONLY principles upon which reasoning can be based or from which conclusions can be drawn are assumptions, postulates, or hypotheses rather than axioms, then everything is a matter of opinion and probability; nothing can have the certitude of knowledge. As indicated in the chapters on KNOWLEDGE and OPINION, one theory of that distinction makes knowledge an act of the mind independent of our wishes or will and treats opinion as a judgment voluntarily accepted or rejected. Accordingly, assumptions or postulates are perfectly representative of opinion, and axioms express the very essence of knowledge. To assume or postulate anything is to take it for granted—voluntarily! A postulate neither compels assent, nor does it ever exclude the possibility of taking the opposite for granted. Where men make postulates, there dispute is possible. But to assert something as an axiom is to command assent on the ground that its opposite can be immediately recognized as impossible. No proposition can be regarded as an axiom if its acceptance or rejection is in any way a matter of choice.

For Aristotle the area in which men can dispute with some reason on both sides belongs to what he calls "dialectic," whereas what he calls "science" is the area from which dispute is excluded by demonstrations which rest on self-evident truths. One is the area of probability and opinion; the other, of certainty and knowledge. Contrary assumptions are the starting point of dialectical argument, whereas science begins with axioms. These may be the first principles which Aristotle and Bacon call "common notions" because they are common to diverse sciences; or they may be the axioms peculiar to a single subject matter.

The word "dialectic" is used by Plato in a quite different sense. It names the highest science. Whereas the mathematical sciences start from hypotheses which require further support, dialectic—in the conception of Plato—rises to the first principles of all knowledge. In the hierarchical ordering of the sciences, Plato's dialectic, Aristotle's metaphysics, and Bacon's *philosophia prima* seem to occupy respectively the same primary position and to perform the same function in virtue of being the discipline which contemplates or considers the absolutely first or most universal principles. For Bacon, as for Aquinas, the only higher science is sacred theology, whose principles are articles of supernatural faith, not axioms of reason.

These matters are more fully discussed in the chapters on DIALECTIC, METAPHYSICS, and THEOLOGY; questions concerning different kinds of principles or the principles of different sciences are considered in HYPOTHESIS and LOGIC. The chapter on INDUCTION, furthermore, discusses the inductive origin of axioms, as well as the disagreement between Bacon and Aristotle on the point of whether the highest axioms or first principles are immediately intuited from the particulars of experience, or are reached only through intermediate stages of generalization.

Since axioms are indemonstrable, they cannot be derived by reasoning as conclusions from any truths prior to themselves. Their indemonstrability is regarded by Aristotle and Pascal as a virtue rather than a defect, for if they were demonstrable, they could not be the principles or starting points of demonstration. If there were no axioms, then nothing could be demonstrated, because everything in turn would require proof in an endless regression.

To the ancient counterparts of the skeptical Montaigne, Aristotle replies that unless the law of contradiction is an indisputable axiom, any form of reasoning, even probable reasoning from assumptions, is impossible. The principle which underlies all disputation cannot itself be disputed. To those who, with skeptical intent, insist upon having everything demonstrated before they will accept it, Aristotle offers an indirect defense of the law of contradiction by asking the questioner to try denying that self-evident principle without reducing himself to absurdity.

Those who acknowledge the existence of axioms generally agree that they are indemonstrable truths, but some, like Descartes and Kant, do not agree that they are inductions from experience. The alternatives seem to be that axioms are innate possessions of the intellect or that they are transcendental *a priori* principles of pure reason, independent of experience. Yet Locke, who denies innate ideas and principles, or anything prior to experience, does not treat what he calls self-evident maxims as inductions from experience. They are rather direct perceptions of agreement or disagreement among the ideas we have acquired through experience.

Aquinas, who, no less than Locke, denies innate ideas and insists upon sense-experience as the source of all human knowledge, refers to the assent we give first principles as a *natural habit* of the mind—the intellectual virtue he calls "understanding," equivalent to what Aristotle calls "intuitive reason." As the chapter on HABIT indicates, axioms are called "natural" truths, not in the sense of being innate, instinctive, or congenital, but only in the sense that if the human reason functions naturally or normally it will come to recognize these truths. Again, like Locke, Aquinas seems to be saying that the truth of axioms is perceived by the human understanding as soon as their terms are known, but he does not concur with Locke in thinking that therefore such truths hold only for relations between our own ideas.

THE THEORY OF the possession of principles by natural habit has, for Aquinas, more than a verbal connection with the theory of natural law. Of the various meanings of the phrase "natural law" which are distinguished in the chapter on LAW, we are here concerned with what both Kant and Aquinas conceive as the moral law whose precepts are the fundamental principles of human conduct. Both also speak of the precepts of the natural law or the moral law as the first principles of man's practical reason.

For Aquinas, these principles are primary in the order of practical truth and the moral sciences, as metaphysical first principles are primary in the order of speculative truth and the theoretic sciences. "The precepts of the natural law," he writes, "are to the practical reason what the first principles of demonstration are to the speculative reason, because both are self-evident principles." As the proposition that "*the same thing cannot be affirmed and denied at the same time*" is the first principle of the speculative reason, so "the first precept of law, that *good is to be done, and evil is to be avoided*," is the first principle of the practical reason.

For Kant, the principles of the pure practical reason, which legislate *a priori* for the realm of freedom, play an analogous role to the principles of the pure speculative reason, which legislate *a priori* for the realm of nature or experience. It is this parallelism between the two sets of principles which Kant seems to have in mind when he conceives a *metaphysic of nature* and a *metaphysic of morals* as twin disciplines founded on the speculative and the practical employment of the transcendental principles of pure reason.

The same fundamental issues which we have considered in connection with the axioms of theoretic knowledge occur here in connection with the first principles of moral knowledge. Aquinas and Kant disagree, for example, about the way in which we come into possession of these principles. For Kant, the principles of mortality, like the principles of nature, belong to the transcendental structure of pure reason itself. For Aquinas, as already suggested, the precepts of the natural law are known in the same way as the axioms of the speculative reason. As the truth of the principle of contradiction is known when we understand the meaning of 'is' and 'not,' so the truth of the first command of natural law—'Seek the good'—is known when we understand the meaning of 'seek' and 'good.' We hold such truths by the natural habit of our minds, which in the case of the natural law is given the special name of *synderesis*.

Just as we find a certain skepticism with regard to the principle of contradiction and other axioms, so we find doubts about the existence of natural law, or about indisputable and universally acceptable principles of morality. Referring to those who think that there are some laws "first, perpetual, and immutable, which they call natural that are imprinted in mankind by the condition of their own proper being," Montaigne declares that "the only sign by which they can argue or infer some laws to be natural is the universality of approbation"; and he adds: "Let them produce me but one of this condition."

The consequences of skepticism are here the same as before. Without first principles, moral science either fails entirely or is reduced to systems of belief based upon one set of assumptions or another. In either case, moral judgments express, not knowledge, but opinion. As John Stuart Mill observes, the utilitarians must, despite all other differences, agree with Kant that if there is to be a science of ethics, "mortality must be deduced from principles," and ultimately from one first principle, for "if there be several, there should be a determinate order of precedence among them."

What Mill says concerning the self-evidence of the first principle of morality—which he formulates as a statement of the ultimate end of human conduct—closely resembles what Aristotle says about the self-evidence of the law of contradiction. "Questions of ultimate ends are not amenable to direct proof," Mill writes. "To be incapable of proof by reasoning is common to all first principles: to the first premises of our knowledge, as well as to those of our conduct."

OUTLINE OF TOPICS

1. Principles in the order of reality

  1a. The differentiation of principle, element, and cause

  1b. The being, number, and kinds of principles in the order of reality

  1c. The metaphysical significance of the principles of thought

2. The kinds of principles in the order of knowledge

  2a. The origin of knowledge in simple apprehensions

    (1) Sensations or ideas as principles
    (2) Definitions as principles
    (3) Indefinables as principles of definition

  2b. Propositions or judgments as principles

    (1) Immediate truths of perception: direct sensitive knowledge of appearances; evident particular facts
    (2) Immediate truths of understanding: axioms or self-evident truths; *a priori* judgments as principles
    (3) Constitutive and regulative principles: the maxims of reason

3. First principles or axioms in philosophy, science, dialectic

  3a. Principles and demonstration

    (1) The indemonstrability of axioms: natural habits of the mind
    (2) The indirect defense of axioms
    (3) The dependence of demonstration on axioms: the critical application of the principles of identity and contradiction

  3b. Principles and induction: axioms as intuitive inductions from experience; stages of inductive generalization

  3c. Axioms in relation to postulates, hypotheses, or assumptions

    (1) The distinction between first principles in general, or common notions, and the principles of a particular subject matter or science
    (2) The difference between axioms and assumptions, hypotheses and principles, as a basis for the distinction between knowledge and opinion, or science and dialectic
    (3) The distinction and order of the sciences according to the character of their principles

4. First principles in the practical order: the principles of action or morality; the principles of the practical reason

  4a. Ends as principles, and last ends as first principles: right appetite as a principle in the practical order

  4b. The natural moral law and the categorical imperative

5. The skeptical denial of first principles or axioms: the denial that any propositions elicit the universal assent of mankind

REFERENCES

References are listed by volume number (in bold type), author's name, and page number. Bible references are to book, chapter, and verse of the Authorized King James version of the Bible. The abbreviation "esp" calls the reader's attention to one or more especially relevant parts of a whole reference; "passim" signifies that the topic is discussed intermittently rather than continuously in the work or passage cited. Where the work as a whole is relevant to the topic, the page numbers refer to the entire work. For general guidance in the use of *The Great Ideas,* consult the Preface.

1. Principles in the order of reality

1*a*. The differentiation of principle, element, and cause

8 Aristotle, 429, 517, 533–534, 565–566, 598–601
19 Aquinas, 180–181, 543–544
45 Lavoisier, 3–4

1*b*. The being, number, and kinds of principles in the order of reality

7 Plato, 240–246, 455–458, 564–574, 610–613, 615–617
8 Aristotle, 259–268, 281, 318–319, 359–360, 393–396, 501–514, 516–522, 534–535, 550–626, 634–635
10 Galen, 168–169
12 Lucretius, 2–4, 6
17 Plotinus, 65–66, 198, 209–210, 226–228, 252–297
19 Aquinas, 12–14, 18–19, 84–85, 143–144, 153–157, 225–227, 264–268, 378–379, 404–405, 442–443, 587–588
31 Descartes, 61–62
34 Newton, 1–2, 14, 541–542
42 Kant, 66–93, 108–112, 467–470, 565, 575–578
45 Fourier, 169
53 James, 882–884

1*c*. The metaphysical significance of the principles of thought

8 Aristotle, 34–35, 515, 524–525
31 Descartes, 130–132
31 Spinoza, 376–377, 386–388
35 Locke, 339–342
42 Kant, 15–16, 59–107, 600–601
53 James, 302, 671–672, 862–866, 873–874, 881–886

2. The kinds of principles in the order of knowledge

2*a*. The origin of knowledge in simple apprehensions

2*a*(1) Sensations or ideas as principles

7 Plato, 228–230, 392–393, 517–536
8 Aristotle, 111
12 Lucretius, 48–51
19 Aquinas, 60–61, 105–106, 450–451, 680–681
28 Harvey, 332–335
35 Locke, 121–123, 127–128, 148–149, 160–162, 173–174, 202–203, 252
35 Berkeley, 405–412
35 Hume, 455–457, 471
42 Kant, 14–22, 66–72, 101–107
53 James, 452–459

2*a*(2) Definitions as principles

7 Plato, 134, 174–179, 544–549, 809–810
8 Aristotle, 97–137, 214–215, 515, 532, 610, 631–632
19 Aquinas, 303–304
23 Hobbes, 56, 58–59, 269
33 Pascal, 430–431
35 Locke, 288–289, 303–304
42 Kant, 215–217
46 Hegel, 9–10
54 Freud, 412

2*a*(3) Indefinables as principles of definition

7 Plato, 544–547
8 Aristotle, 513
33 Pascal, 431–434, 442–443
35 Locke, 133, 147–148, 262–263
44 Boswell, 82

2*b*. Propositions or judgments as principles

2*b*(1) Immediate truths of perception: direct sensitive knowledge of appearances; evident particular facts

8 Aristotle, 115–116, 136–137, 397, 511, 530, 591
9 Aristotle, 340, 397
12 Lucretius, 50–51
19 Aquinas, 680–681
28 Harvey, 332–335
31 Descartes, 229–230
35 Locke, 98–102, 307, 309, 337–338, 342, 354–358
35 Hume, 465–466
42 Kant, 66–72
53 James, 867–868

2b(2) Immediate truths of understanding: axioms or self-evident truths; *a priori* judgments as principles

8 ARISTOTLE, 99–100, 109, 128, 515
19 AQUINAS, 10–11, 612–613
20 AQUINAS, 36–37, 221–224, 417
30 BACON, 61
31 DESCARTES, 4, 5, 8–9, 13, 51–52, 95–96, 123, 125
33 PASCAL, 171–172
35 LOCKE, 95–121, 310–311, 337–344, 349, 358–360, 363, 378–379, 390–392
42 KANT, 31, 64–93, 211–218, 225–227, 295, 329–330
43 FEDERALIST, 103–104
43 MILL, 445–447
53 JAMES, 319–320, 869–879

2b(3) Constitutive and regulative principles: the maxims of reason

42 KANT, 72–74, 109–112, 199–209, 349–355, 550–551, 562, 570–572, 578

3. First principles or axioms in philosophy, science, dialectic

3a. Principles and demonstration

3a(1) The indemonstrability of axioms: natural habits of the mind

8 ARISTOTLE, 85, 99–100, 525
9 ARISTOTLE, 388, 389
19 AQUINAS, 98, 102–103
20 AQUINAS, 19–21, 36–37
35 LOCKE, 97–98, 119–120, 354–357
42 KANT, 66–72, 211–218
43 MILL, 445–447, 461, 465
53 JAMES, 851–890

3a(2) The indirect defense of axioms

8 ARISTOTLE, 525–532, 590–592

3a(3) The dependence of demonstration on axioms: the critical application of the principles of identity and contradiction

7 PLATO, 72–73, 350–351
8 ARISTOTLE, 97–100, 103, 105–106, 111–116, 214–215, 530
9 ARISTOTLE, 389
19 AQUINAS, 194–195, 443–444, 458–459, 612–613
30 BACON, 56–59
31 DESCARTES, 46–47, 82, 95–96
31 SPINOZA, 386–391
35 LOCKE, 337–344
42 KANT, 17–18, 64–65, 68–69, 174, 211–218
43 FEDERALIST, 103–104

3b. Principles and induction: axioms as intuitive inductions from experience; stages of inductive generalization

8 ARISTOTLE, 90, 136–137
9 ARISTOTLE, 388
28 HARVEY, 334
30 BACON, 56–59, 96–97, 105–195
31 DESCARTES, 167
35 HUME, 451, 460
42 KANT, 66–72
46 HEGEL, 361

3c. Axioms in relation to postulates, hypotheses, or assumptions

3c(1) The distinction between first principles in general, or common notions, and the principles of a particular subject matter or science

7 PLATO, 383–388
8 ARISTOTLE, 104–106, 120–121, 397
9 ARISTOTLE, 597–598
30 BACON, 40–48
35 BERKELEY, 436

3c(2) The difference between axioms and assumptions, hypotheses and principles, as a basis for the distinction between knowledge and opinion, or science and dialectic

7 PLATO, 396–398
8 ARISTOTLE, 97–99, 214–215, 336
9 ARISTOTLE, 597–598
19 AQUINAS, 56–57, 432–433
20 AQUINAS, 83–84, 765–766
23 HOBBES, 65
25 MONTAIGNE, 260–261
30 BACON, 56–59
31 DESCARTES, 2–3
34 HUYGENS, 551–552
35 LOCKE, 371–372
42 KANT, 240–243, 600–604

3c(3) The distinction and order of the sciences according to the character of their principles

7 PLATO, 386–388, 391–398
8 ARISTOTLE, 547, 589–590, 592, 609
9 ARISTOTLE, 343–344
19 AQUINAS, 4, 5–6
23 HOBBES, 71
30 BACON, 39–41
31 DESCARTES, 2–3, 76, 304
35 HUME, 458
42 KANT, 15–19, 215–217, 351–352, 388
53 JAMES, 884–886
54 FREUD, 400–401

4. First principles in the practical order: the principles of action or morality; the principles of the practical reason

7 PLATO, 262–263
9 ARISTOTLE, 339–340 passim, 389 passim, 392–393
12 EPICTETUS, 127–128, 177–178
12 AURELIUS, 285

18 Augustine, 270, 507–530 passim
20 Aquinas, 209–210
23 Hobbes, 86–96, 140, 153–154
31 Spinoza, 429
35 Locke, 103–121
38 Rousseau, 330–331
42 Kant, 190, 234–240, 253–287, 291–361, 365–366, 369–373, 383–394
43 Mill, 445–476
49 Darwin, 316–317, 592
53 James, 886–888
54 Freud, 592–593, 639–640, 662–663, 772

4a. Ends as principles, and last ends as first principles: right appetite as a principle in the practical order

7 Plato, 280, 383–398
8 Aristotle, 514–515, 555, 575–576, 605–606
9 Aristotle, 161–162, 235–236, 339–340, 358–359, 387–388, 391–392, 397, 430–434, 602–607
12 Epictetus, 188–190
18 Augustine, 625
19 Aquinas, 106–107, 109–110, 112–113, 147–149, 311, 431–433, 609–615, 656, 667–668, 670–672, 674–675, 678, 682–683, 685–686, 770–772
20 Aquinas, 31–32, 38–40, 43, 44–45, 72–73, 524–525, 617–618
23 Hobbes, 76, 272
31 Spinoza, 369–372, 422–424
35 Locke, 191–192, 194
42 Kant, 234–240, 257, 260, 266–267, 271–279, 318–321, 327–329, 338–355, 478–479, 584–588, 591–592, 594–595
43 Mill, 456–457, 461–464, 475
51 Tolstoy, 586–587

4b. The natural moral law and the categorical imperative

12 Aurelius, 262, 264, 283
19 Aquinas, 425–426
20 Aquinas, 208–209, 220–228
23 Hobbes, 86–87, 95–96
30 Bacon, 96
38 Rousseau, 343–345
42 Kant, 190, 253–254, 260–261, 268–270, 273–287 esp 277–279, 282–287, 297–314 esp 307–314, 321–329, 390–393, 400–402, 604–606
43 Mill, 458–459, 469–470
46 Hegel, 19, 47, 129
49 Darwin, 304

5. The skeptical denial of first principles or axioms: the denial that any propositions elicit the universal assent of mankind

7 Plato, 532
8 Aristotle, 99, 528–531, 590–592
12 Epictetus, 164
18 Augustine, 523
25 Montaigne, 259–261, 271–272, 281–284
30 Bacon, 57–58
35 Berkeley, 405
35 Hume, 503–509
42 Kant, 224–227, 294–295

CROSS-REFERENCES

For: Another discussion of principle in relation to element and cause, *see* Element 2.

The consideration of the laws of identity and contradiction as both logical and metaphysical principles, *see* Logic 1a; Metaphysics 3c; Opposition 2a; Truth 3c; and for the treatment of contraries as principles, *see* Change 2b; Dialectic 3d; Opposition 2b, 3a.

Discussions bearing on sensations, ideas, and definitions as principles of knowledge, *see* Definition 1c, 5; Idea 1c, 2f; Knowledge 3; Memory and Imagination 1a; Sense 5a.

The analysis of evident or self-evident truths, or of immediate as opposed to demonstrated propositions, *see* Judgment 8a; Knowledge 6c(2); Sense 4b; Truth 3b(3); and for the distinction between analytic and synthetic judgments *a priori*, and between constitutive and regulative principles, *see* Idea 1d; Judgment 8b–8d.

The conception of axiomatic knowledge as a natural habit of the mind and as one of the intellectual virtues, *see* Habit 5c; Virtue and Vice 2a(2).

The dependence of demonstration on axioms or self-evident truths, *see* Infinity 2c; Reasoning 5b(1); Truth 3c; and for the nature of *reductio ad absurdum* arguments in defense of axioms, *see* Reasoning 4d.

Induction as the source of axioms, *see* Induction 3.

Other discussions of the distinction between axioms and postulates, hypotheses, or assumptions, and for the bearing of this distinction on the difference between knowledge and opinion, or science and dialectic, *see* DIALECTIC 2a(2), 4; HYPOTHESIS 3–4; KNOWLEDGE 4b; MATHEMATICS 3a; OPINION 2c; TRUTH 4c; WILL 3b(1).

The principles of the several theoretic sciences, *see* ASTRONOMY 2b; DEFINITION 6a; LOGIC 1a; MATHEMATICS 3a; MECHANICS 2b; METAPHYSICS 2b, 3c; PHILOSOPHY 3b; PHYSICS 1b, 2a; TRUTH 4c.

The consideration of ends as principles in the practical order or in moral and political science, *see* GOOD AND EVIL 5c; GOVERNMENT 1c; HAPPINESS 3; MIND 9a; NECESSITY AND CONTINGENCY 5a(2); ONE AND MANY 5b; RELATION 5a(2); TRUTH 2c; and for other discussions of the natural moral law or the categorical imperative as the first principle of the practical reason, *see* DUTY 5; LAW 4b–4c; MIND 9a; NECESSITY AND CONTINGENCY 5a(2); PRUDENCE 2c, 3a; WILL 8d.

Other statements of the skepticism which results from denying first principles or axioms, *see* OPINION 3c; TRUTH 7a.

ADDITIONAL READINGS

Listed below are works not included in *Great Books of the Western World*, but relevant to the idea and topics with which this chapter deals. These works are divided into two groups:

I. Works by authors represented in this collection.
II. Works by authors not represented in this collection.

For the date, place, and other facts concerning the publication of the works cited, consult the Bibliography of Additional Readings which follows the last chapter of *The Great Ideas*.

I.

AUGUSTINE. *Answer to Skeptics*
AQUINAS. *Super Boethium de Hebdomadibus*
DESCARTES. *The Principles of Philosophy*, PREF
HEGEL. *Science of Logic*, VOL I, BK II, SECT I, CH 2
J. S. MILL. *A System of Logic*, BK II, CH 6

II.

SEXTUS EMPIRICUS. *Outlines of Pyrrhonism*
DUNS SCOTUS. *Tractatus de Primo Principio* (*A Tract Concerning the First Principle*)
BRUNO. *De la causa, principio, e uno*
SUÁREZ. *Disputationes Metaphysicae*, XII (1), XXII (2)
ARNAULD. *Logic or the Art of Thinking*, CH 6–7
LEIBNITZ. *Discourse on Metaphysics*, XXVI
——. *New Essays Concerning Human Understanding*, BK IV, CH 7–8
——. *Monadology*, par 31–37
T. REID. *Essays on the Intellectual Powers of Man*, I, CH 2; VI, CH 4–7
SCHOPENHAUER. *On the Fourfold Root of the Principle of Sufficient Reason*
W. HAMILTON. *Lectures on Metaphysics and Logic*, VOL II (5–6)
WHEWELL. *The Philosophy of the Inductive Sciences*, VOL I, BK I, CH 4, 6
——. *On the Philosophy of Discovery*, CH 28
HELMHOLTZ. *Popular Lectures on Scientific Subjects*, II
J. H. NEWMAN. *An Essay in Aid of a Grammar of Assent*, CH 4
LOTZE. *Logic*, BK III, CH 5
BRADLEY. *The Principles of Logic*, BK I, CH 5
BOSANQUET. *Logic*, VOL II, CH 7
E. HARTMANN. *Kategorienlehre*
W. E. JOHNSON. *Logic*, PART I, CH 14
RUEFF. *From the Physical to the Social Sciences*
SANTAYANA. *The Realm of Truth*, CH I
DEWEY. *Logic, the Theory of Inquiry*, CH 17
B. RUSSELL. *The Problems of Philosophy*, CH 7–8, 11
——. *Human Knowledge, Its Scope and Limits*, PART VI

Chapter 71: PROGRESS

INTRODUCTION

LIKE the idea of evolution, with which it has some affinity, the idea of progress seems to be typically modern. Anticipations of it may be found in ancient and mediaeval thought, sometimes in the form of implicit denials of the idea. But in explicit formulation, in emphasis and importance, progress, like evolution, is almost a new idea in modern times. It is not merely more prominent in modern discussion; it affects the significance of many other ideas, and so gives a characteristic color or tendency to modern thought.

The idea of evolution affects our conceptions of nature and man. But the theory of evolution is itself affected by the idea of progress. Since it was a major theme at least two centuries before Darwin, progress does not depend for its significance upon the theory of biological evolution. The reverse relationship seems to obtain. The idea of evolution gets some of its moral, social, even cosmic significance from its implication that the general motion in the world of living things, perhaps in the universe, is a progress from lower to higher forms.

Darwin thinks "Von Baer has defined advancement or progress in the organic scale better than anyone else, as resting on the amount of differentiation and specialization of the several parts of a being"—to which Darwin adds the qualification that the organisms must be judged when they have arrived at maturity. "As organisms have become slowly adapted to diversified lines of life, their parts will have become more and more differentiated and specialized for various functions from the advantage gained by the division of physiological labor. The same part appears often to have been modified first for one purpose, and then long afterwards for some other and quite distinct purpose; and thus all the parts are rendered more and more complex. . . . In accordance with this view," Darwin writes, "it seems, if we turn to geological evidence, that organization on the whole has advanced throughout the world by slow and interrupted steps. In the kingdom of the Vertebrata it has culminated in man."

Whether strictly biological evolution has a single or uniform direction may be disputed in the light of evidences of regression and the multiplication of lower as well as higher forms. But Darwin seems to think that since "natural selection works solely by and for the good of each being, all corporeal and mental endowments will tend to progress toward perfection." Whatever the evidence may be, the popular notion of evolution, especially when applied by writers like Herbert Spencer to human society or civilization, connotes progress—the gradual yet steady march toward perfection.

APART FROM THIS APPLICATION of the idea of evolution to man's world, progress seems to be the central thesis in the modern philosophy of history. In the minds of some, the philosophy of history is so intimately connected with a theory of progress that the philosophy of history is itself regarded as a modern development. There seems to be some justification for this view in modern works on the tendency of history which have no ancient counterparts, such as the writings of Vico, Condorcet, Kant, Proudhon, Comte, J. S. Mill, Hegel, and Marx.

These writers do not all define or explain progress in the same way. Nor do they all subscribe to an inviolable and irresistible law of progress which has the character of a divine ordinance, replacing or transforming less optimistic views of providence. But for the most part the moderns are optimists. They either believe in man's perfectibility and in his approach to perfection through his own efforts freely turned toward the realization of ideals; or they see in the forces of history—whether the manifestations of a world spirit or the pressure of material (*i.e.*, economic) conditions—an inevitable development from less to more advanced stages of civilization, according to a dialectical pattern of conflict and resolution, each resolution necessarily rising to a higher level.

As opposed to the optimism of expecting a continual improvement in all things or an irreversible ascent to new heights, the pessimistic view denies that progress is either the law or the hope of history. It believes rather that everything which goes up must come down. As indicated in the chapter on HISTORY, the theory of cycle after cycle of rise and decline—or even the notion that the golden age is past, that it is never to be regained, and that things are steadily getting worse—prevails more in the ancient than in the modern world.

The modern exceptions to optimism in the philosophy of history are notably Spengler and, to a much less extent, Toynbee. But modern pessimism never seems to reach the intensity of the Preacher's reiteration in Ecclesiastes that "there is no new thing under the sun" and that "all is vanity and vexation of spirit." Nor does the modern theory of cycles of civilization, even in Vico, seem to be as radical as that of the ancients. In his vision of cosmic cycles Lucretius sees the whole world crumbling into atomic dust to be reborn again. Herodotus does not relieve the gloom of his observation that, in the life of cities, prosperity "never continues long in one stay." The eternity of the world means for Aristotle that "probably each art and each science has often been developed as far as possible and has again perished."

LEAVING TO THE chapter on HISTORY the discussion of progress so far as it concerns an explicit philosophy of history, we shall here deal with considerations of progress as they occur in economics, in political theory, in the history of philosophy and the whole intellectual tradition of the arts and sciences.

In this last connection, the great books play a dual role. They provide the major evidence which, on different interpretations, points toward opposite answers to the question whether or not there has been progress in the tradition of western thought. Whatever their readers may think on this subject, the great authors, having read the works of their predecessors, offer their own interpretations of the intellectual tradition. In many cases, especially among the modern writers, their point of departure—even the conception they entertain of the originality and worth of their own contribution—stems from their concern with a deplorable lack of progress, for which they offer new methods as remedies.

Before we enter upon the discussion of economic, political, or intellectual progress, it seems useful to distinguish between the *fact* and the *idea* of progress. When men examine the fact of progress, they look to the past and find there evidence for or against the assertion that a change for the better has taken place in this or that respect. Two things are involved: a study of the changes which have occurred and the judgment—based on some standard of appraisal—that the changes have been for the better. But when men entertain the idea of progress, they turn from the past and present and look to the future. They regard the past merely as a basis for prophecy, and the present as an occasion for making plans to fulfill their prophecies or hopes. The fact of progress belongs to the record of achievement; the idea of progress sets a goal to be achieved.

This distinction seems to be exemplified by the difference between ancient and modern considerations of progress. The ancients observe the *fact* of progress in some particulars—almost never universally. Thucydides, for example, in the opening chapters of his *History*, contrasts the power and wealth of the modern city-states of Greece with "the weakness of ancient times." "Without commerce, without freedom of communication either by land or sea, cultivating no more of their territory than the exigencies of life required, destitute of capital, never planting their land (for they could not tell when an invader might not come and take it all away, and when he did come they had no walls to stop him), thinking that the necessities of daily sustenance could be supplied at one place as well as another, they cared little for shifting their habitation, and consequently neither built large cities nor attained to any other form of greatness."

But Thucydides does not seem to draw from these observations any general idea of progress. He does not concretely imagine a future excelling the Periclean age in the magnitude of its wars and the magnificence of its wealth, as that period dwarfs antiquity. He does not infer that whatever factors worked to cause the advance from past to present may continue to operate with similar results. It might almost be said that he does not think about the future; certainly he does not think of it as rich in promise. "Knowledge of the past." he writes, is "an aid to the interpretation of the future, which in the course of human things must resemble if it does not reflect it."

Adam Smith's thinking about economic progress represents the contrasting modern emphasis upon the future. In one sense, both Thucydides and Smith measure economic progress in the same way, though one writes of the wealth of cities, the other of the wealth of nations. Both Smith and Thucydides judge economic improvement in terms of increasing opulence, the growth of capital reserves, the expansion of commerce, and the enlarged power in war or peace which greater wealth bestows. But Smith, in the spirit of Francis Bacon, seeks to analyze the causes of prosperity in order to make them work for further progress. He is the promoter of progress, not merely the historian who witnesses the beneficial effect on productivity of an increasingly refined division of labor and of the multiplication of machinery.

To know how these things have operated to bring about the opulence of modern nations as compared with the miserable poverty of primitive tribes or even the limited property of ancient cities is to know how to formulate policies which shall still further expand the wealth of nations. For Smith the study of the means and methods by which economic progress has been made serves to determine the policy which is most likely to ensure even greater increments of progress in the future.

Marx appears to measure economic progress by a different standard. The transition from the slave economies of antiquity through feudal serfdom to what he calls the "wage-slavery" of the industrial proletariat may be accompanied by greater productivity and vaster accumulations of capital stock. But the essential point for him about these successive systems of production is their effect upon the status and conditions of labor. The *Communist Manifesto* notes respects in which, under the capitalist system, the supposedly free workingman is worse off than were his servile ancestors. But if economic progress is conceived as the historically determined approach to the final liberation of labor from its oppressors, then capitalism represents both an advance over feudalism and a stage in the march to communism.

Each successive economic revolution brings mankind nearer to the goal of the ideal or classless economy. Capitalism creates the proletariat—the revolutionary class which is to be that system's own undoing. The overthrow of the landed aristocracy by the bourgeoisie thus prepares the way for the dictatorship of the proletariat, as that in turn liquidates the obstacles to the realization of the perfect communist democracy.

We are not here concerned with the details of this history and prophecy but only with the theory of progress which it involves. In the first place, it seems to set an ultimate goal to progress, while at the same time it makes progress a necessary feature of what is for Marx, as it is for Hegel, the "dialectic of history." Those who think that the inevitability of progress ought to render progress as interminable as history itself, find some inconsistency in this tenet of dialectical materialism, as well as in Hegel's notion of the necessary dialectical stages by which the Absolute Idea reaches perfect realization in the German state. *Can progress be the inner law of history and yet reach its goal before the end of time?*

There may be some answer to this question in a second aspect of the theory of progress which goes with a dialectic of history. The progress which the successive stages of history represent resides in the quality of human institutions rather than in the nature of man. If more economic justice or greater political liberty is achieved, it is not because the later generations of men are born with a nature more disposed to goodness or virtue, but because better institutions have evolved from the conflict of historical forces. Furthermore, according to Marx, man's nature is only partly determined at birth. Part remains to be determined by the social and economic circumstances of his life—by the system of production under which he lives. Hence though institutional progress may arrive at its historical goal with the establishment of the ideal economy, it may be possible for further progress to be made throughout the rest of time by the improvement of men themselves, when at last their natures can develop under ideal circumstances.

WE HAVE NOTED TWO great issues in the characteristically modern discussion of progress. Is the goal of progress definitely attainable, or is its goal an ideal progressively approximated but never realized? Is progress accomplished by the betterment of human institutions or by improvements in the nature of man?

The second question has a critical bearing on the first, especially for those who conceive man as infinitely perfectible. It also relates to the problem of the evolutionist: whether a higher form of life on earth will evolve from man or whether the future belongs to the progressive development of human nature—biologically or culturally. Darwin is unwilling to admit that "man alone is capable of progressive improvement," but he does affirm that man "is capable of incomparably greater and more rapid improvement than is any other animal."

Rousseau, on the other hand, claims that "the faculty of self-improvement" is one distinction between man and brute "which will admit of no dispute." But he also thinks that this faculty is the cause of human decline as well as progress. "A brute, at the end of a few months," he writes, "is all he will ever be during his whole life, and his species, at the end of a thousand years, exactly what it was the first year of that thousand . . . .While the brute, which has acquired nothing and has therefore nothing to lose, still retains the force of instinct, man, who loses, by age or accident, all that his *perfectibility* had enabled him to gain, falls by this means lower than the brutes themselves."

One other issue concerning progress remains to be stated. It raises the question of freedom or necessity in history. Is progress inevitable in the very nature of the case, or does it occur only when men plan wisely and choose well in their efforts to better themselves or the conditions of their lives?

In his *Idea of a Universal History* and his *Principle of Progress,* Kant finds the possibility of progress in man's potentialities for improvement. He regards the realization of this possibility as a work of freedom rather than a manifestation of historical necessity. Political progress may have an ultimate goal—the world republic or federation of states. But this, according to Kant's conclusion in the *Science of Right,* is an impracticable idea, and serves only the regulative purpose of "promoting a continuous *approximation* to Perpetual Peace." Hegel's theory of the progressive realization of the idea of the state in history seems to represent the contrary position on both points. Progress is an historical necessity, and it reaches an historic consummation.

THE CONTRAST BETWEEN ancients and moderns with respect to political progress seems to be the same as that which we observed between Thucydides and Adam Smith with regard to wealth. The ancients assert the superiority of the present over the past, and even trace the stages by which advances have been made from primitive to civilized conditions. But they do not extend the motion they observe into the future. The moderns look to the future as to a fulfillment without which present political activity would be undirected.

According to Aristotle, for example, the state is the last stage in the development of social life which begins with the family. "When several families are united, and the association aims at something more than the supply of daily needs, the first society to be formed is the village." The village or tribal community, in turn, becomes the unit out of which a larger and more truly political community is formed. "When several villages are united in a single complete community, large enough to be nearly or quite self-sufficing, the state comes into existence."

Aristotle sees this development not merely as a progress from smaller and weaker societies to larger and more powerful ones, but also as an advance toward the realization of man's political nature. Absolute or despotic government by the eldest, natural to the family, still persists in the tribe. "This is the reason why the Hellenic states were originally governed by kings; because the Hellenes were under royal rule before they came together, as the barbarians still are." Not until the domestic or tribal form of government is replaced by political or constitutional government—not until kings and subjects are replaced by statesmen and citizens—is the state or political community fully realized.

But Aristotle does not conceive the development he describes as one continuing into the future. He does not imagine a larger political unity than the city-state, as Kant is able to envisage a world state as the ultimate formation toward which the progressive political unification of mankind should tend. Though Aristotle recognizes that new institutions have been invented and old ones perfected, his political theory, unlike Mill's, does not seem to measure the goodness of the best existing institutions by their devotion to further progress.

Considering the criterion of a good form of government, Mill criticizes those who separate the maintenance of order, or the preservation of existing institutions, from the cultivation of progress. "Progress includes Order," he writes, "but Order does not include Progress." Order "is not an additional end to be reconciled with Progress, but a part and means of Progress itself. If a gain in one respect is purchased by a more than equivalent loss in the same or in any other, there is not Progress. Conduciveness to Progress, thus understood, includes the whole excellence of government."

Progress fails to define good government, Mill adds, unless we understand by the term not merely "the idea of moving onward," but "quite as much the prevention of falling back. The very same social causes . . . are as much required to prevent society from retrograding, as to produce a further advance. Were there no improvement to be hoped for, life would not be the less an unceasing struggle against causes of deterioration; as it even now is. Politics, as conceived by the ancients, consisted wholly in this . . . Though we no longer hold this opinion; though most men in the present age profess a contrary creed, believing that the tendency of things, on the whole, is toward improvement; we ought not to forget that there is an incessant and everflowing current of human affairs toward the worse."

According to Mill, the ideally best polity is representative government on democratic principles. By a just distribution of political rights and by the fullest grant of liberties, it serves better than any other form of government "to promote the virtue and intelligence of the people themselves." This is the ultimate end of political progress. Inferior forms of government, such as despotic monarchy, may be justified for people as yet unfit for self-government, but only if they also work for progress, *i.e.*, "if they carry those communities through the intermediate stages which they must traverse before they can become fit for the best form of government."

The whole theory of good government is thus for Mill a theory of progress in which we must take "into account, not only the next step, but all the steps which society has yet to make; both those which can be foreseen and the far wider indefinite range which is at present out of sight." We must judge the merits of diverse forms of government by that ideal form "which, if the necessary conditions existed for giving effect to its beneficial tendencies, would, more than all others, favour and promote not some one improvement, but all forms and degrees of it."

In the field of the arts and sciences or culture generally, the modern emphasis upon progress seems to be even more pronounced than in the spheres of economics and politics. Lack of progress in a science is taken to indicate that it has not yet been established on the right foundations or that the right method for discovering the truth has not yet been found. Lack of agreement in a particular field is the chief symptom of these defects.

The fact that philosophy "has been cultivated for many centuries by the best minds that have ever lived, and that nevertheless no single thing is to be found in it which is not a subject of dispute, and in consequence which is not dubious," leads Descartes to propose his new method. He hopes this may ensure progress in philosophy, of the same sort which the new method has, in his view, accomplished in mathematics. The *Novum Organum* of Bacon seems to be dedicated to the same end of progressively augmenting knowledge in all those fields in which, according to the inventory made in the *Advancement of Learning* of the present state of the sciences, no or little progress has been made since antiquity. Similarly, Locke, Hume, and Kant insist that a study of the human mind should precede all other studies in order to save men from fruitless disputes concerning matters beyond their capacities for knowledge; they hope thereby to encourage research in areas where progress can be made.

The comparison of different disciplines or subject matters with respect to their progress leads to the condemnation of those which lag behind. The great scientific advances of the 17th century tend to intensify the complaint about philosophy, especially metaphysics. The progress which has been made from the beginning in mathematics and more recently in physics means to Kant that each of these disciplines has found the "safe way" or the "secure path" of a science. By comparison, metaphysics has not yet even made a beginning. A hundred years later, William James is still to say that, by comparison with the progress of knowledge in the natural sciences, metaphysics belongs to the future.

The notion that any field of learning has attained its full maturity seems to Bacon to be the presumption of those philosophers who, seeking "to acquire the reputation of perfection for their own art," try to instill the "belief that whatever has not yet been invented and understood can never be so hereafter." Whenever such belief prevails, learning languishes. "By far the greatest obstacle to the advancement of the sciences, and the undertaking of any new attempt or departure, is to be found in men's despair and the idea of impossibility."

THOUGH THE ANCIENTS do not evidence this presumption of perfection in their arts and sciences, neither do they fret about lack of progress. Nor does the disagreement of minds seem to them to signify an unhealthy condition which requires new and special methods to cure.

"The investigation of the truth is in one way hard, in another easy," writes Aristotle. "An indication of this is found in the fact that no one is able to attain the truth adequately, while, on the other hand, we do not collectively fail, but everyone says something true about the nature of things, and while individually we contribute little or nothing to the truth, by the union of all a considerable amount is amassed." Aristotle puts the intellectual tradition to use by adopting the policy of calling "into council the views of those of our predecessors who have declared any opinion" on whatever subject is being considered, "in order that we may profit by whatever is sound in their suggestions and avoid their errors."

But, in the opinion of the moderns, the intellectual tradition can also be the greatest impediment to the advancement of learning if it is received uncritically and with undue reverence for the authority of the ancients. "The respect in which antiquity is held today," Pascal says, "has reached such extremes in those matters in which it should have the least preponderance, that one can no longer present innovations without danger." This is the common complaint of Hobbes, Bacon, Descartes, and Harvey. "The reverence for antiquity and the authority of men who have been esteemed great in philosophy have," according to Bacon, "retarded men from advancing in science, and almost enchanted them."

Harvey agrees with Bacon that philosophers or scientists should not "swear such fealty to their mistress Antiquity, that they openly, and even in sight of all, deny and desert their friend Truth." Harvey has a much higher opinion than Bacon of the achievements of antiquity. "The ancient philosophers," he writes, "whose industry even we admire, went a different way to work, and by their unwearied labor and variety of experiments, searching into the nature of things, have left us no doubtful light to guide us in our studies. In this way it is that almost everything we yet possess of note or credit in philosophy, has been transmitted to us through the industry of ancient Greece."

His admiration for the ancients does not, however, lead Harvey to rest on their achievements. "When we acquiesce in the discoveries of the ancients, and believe (which we are apt to do through indolence) that nothing farther remains to be known," then, in his opinion, "we suffer the edge of our ingenuity to be taken off, and the lamp which they delivered us to be extinguished. No one of a surety," he continues, "will allow that all truth was engrossed by the ancients, unless he be utterly ignorant (to pass by other arts for the present) of the many remarkable discoveries that have lately been made in anatomy."

In his own anatomical researches, Harvey adopts an attitude toward the work of his predecessors, both ancient and recent, which remarkably resembles the attitude expressed by Aristotle toward his scientific forebears. "As we are about to discuss the motion, action, and use of the heart and arteries, it is imperative on us," Harvey declares, "first to state what has been thought of these things by others in their writings, and what has been held by the vulgar and by tradition, in order that what is true may be confirmed, and what is false set right by dissection, multiplied experience, and accurate observation." It is precisely this attitude which Bacon expressly condemns.

Bacon sees no genuine method of science, but merely a cultivation of opinion, in those who prepare themselves for discovery by first obtaining "a full account of all that has been said on the subject by others." Those who begin in this way, it is the judgment of Descartes, seldom go further. Particularly the followers of Aristotle "would think themselves happy," he says, "if they had as much knowledge of nature as he had, even if this were on the condition that they should never attain to any more. They are like the ivy that never tries to mount above the trees which give it support, and which often even descends again after it has reached the summit; for it appears to me that such men also sink again—that is to say, somehow render themselves more ingnorant than they would have been had they abstained from study altogether. For, not content with knowing all that is intelligibly explained in their author, they wish in addition to find in him the solution of many difficulties of which he says nothing, and in regard to which he possibly had no thought at all."

Pascal takes a more moderate view. We can profit, he thinks, from a limited respect for the ancients. "Just as they made use of those discoveries which have been handed down to them only as a means for making new ones and this happy audacity opened the road to great things, so," Pascal suggests, "must we accept those which they found for us and follow their example by making them the means and not the end of our study, and thus try to surpass them by imitating them. For what would be more wrong than to treat the ancients with more caution than they did those who preceded them, and to have for them this inviolable respect which they only deserve from us because they did not feel a similar respect for those who had the same advantage over them?"

Modern writers seem to conceive the law of intellectual progress by an analogy between the mind of the race and the individual mind. Where Aquinas says merely that "it seems natural to human reason to advance gradually from the imperfect to the perfect," adding, in the past tense, that hence the imperfect teaching of early philosophers "was afterwards perfected by those who succeeded them," Pascal generalizes the insight and gives it future significance. "Not only does each man progress from day to day in the sciences, but all men combined make constant progress as the universe ages, because the same thing happens in the succeeding generations of men as in the different ages of each particular man. So that the whole succession of men, in the course of so many centuries, should be regarded as the same man who exists always and learns continually."

At this point Pascal applies his metaphor to effect a reversal of the relation between the moderns and the ancients. "Since old age is the time of life most distant from childhood, who does not realize that old age in this universal man should not be sought in the times closest to his birth, but in those which are farthest away from it? Those whom we call ancients were really novices in all things, and actually belonged to the childhood of man; and as we have added to their knowledge the experience of the centuries which followed them, it is in ourselves that may be found this antiquity which we revere in others."

Whether by accident or borrowing, this characteristically modern view of the advantage progress confers upon modernity is expressed in similar language by Hobbes and Bacon. "Though I reverence those men of ancient times," writes Hobbes, "who either have written truth perspicuously or have set us in a better way to find it out for ourselves; yet to the antiquity itself I think nothing due; for if we will reverence age, the present is the oldest." "Antiquity, as we call it," writes Bacon, "is the young state of the world; for those times are ancient when the world is ancient; and not those we vulgarly account ancient by computing backwards; so that the present time is the real antiquity."

To secure a sound, not specious, progress in all things of the mind, Bacon recommends the avoidance of two extremes, the affectations of antiquity and novelty, for "antiquity envies new improvements, and novelty is not content to add without defacing." Since "antiquity deserves that men should stand awhile upon it, to view around which is the best way," the great books of the past can lay the foundations for progress, but only if they are properly read. "Let great authors, therefore, have their due," Bacon declares, "but so as not to defraud time, which is the author of authors, and the parent of truth."

OUTLINE OF TOPICS

1. The idea of progress in the philosophy of history

 1*a*. Providence and necessity in the theory of progress: the dialectical development of Spirit or matter; conflict as a source of progress

 1*b*. Optimism or meliorism: the doctrine of human perfectibility

 1*c*. Skeptical or pessimistic denials of progress: the golden age as past; the cyclical motion of history

2. The idea of progress in the theory of biological evolution

3. Economic progress

 3*a*. The increase of opulence: the division of labor as a factor in progress

 3*b*. The improvement of the status and conditions of labor: the goals of revolution and reform

 3*c*. Man's progressive conquest of the forces of nature through science and invention

4. Progress in politics

 4*a*. The invention and improvement of political institutions: the maintenance of political order in relation to progress

 4*b*. The progressive realization of the idea of the state

 4*c*. The growth of political freedom: the achievement of citizenship and civil rights

5. Forces operating against social progress: emotional opposition to change or novelty; political conservatism

6. Intellectual or cultural progress: its sources and impediments

 6*a*. Progress in the arts

 6*b*. Progress in philosophy and in the sciences

 6*c*. The use and criticism of the intellectual tradition: the sifting of truth from error; the reaction against the authority of the past

 6*d*. Plans for the advancement of learning and the improvement of method in the arts and sciences

 6*e*. Freedom of expression and discussion as indispensable to the progressive discovery of the truth

REFERENCES

References are listed by volume number (in bold type), author's name, and page number. Bible references are to book, chapter, and verse of the Authorized King James version of the Bible. The abbreviation "esp" calls the reader's attention to one or more especially relevant parts of a whole reference; "passim" signifies that the topic is discussed intermittently rather than continuously in the work or passage cited. Where the work as a whole is relevant to the topic, the page numbers refer to the entire work. For general guidance in the use of *The Great Ideas,* consult the Preface.

1. The idea of progress in the philosophy of history

1*a*. Providence and necessity in the theory of progress: the dialectical development of Spirit or matter; conflict as a source of progress

7 Plato, 44–45
18 Augustine, 124, 307–308, 397–507, 618
38 Rousseau, 338–339
43 Mill, 376, 387
46 Hegel, 20, 110–114, 156–190, 203–206, 368–369
49 Darwin, 321, 328, 596
50 Marx, 6–7, 10–11
50 Marx-Engels, 419–425
50 Tolstoy, 645–650, 676–677, 679–680
54 Freud, 882–883

1*b*. Optimism or meliorism: the doctrine of human perfectibility

38 Rousseau, 338
40 Gibbon, 633–634
42 Kant, 586–587
43 Mill, 460–461
46 Hegel, 110–111, 178–179
49 Darwin, 294–295, 317–319, 328–330, 596–597
54 Freud, 654, 781, 801–802

1*c*. Skeptical or pessimistic denials of progress: the golden age as past; the cyclical motion of history

Old Testament: *Ecclesiastes,* 1:1–15
7 Plato, 443–446, 479–485, 586–589, 681
12 Lucretius, 79
12 Aurelius, 258, 279, 293–294, 299
13 Virgil, 267–268
14 Plutarch, 372
15 Tacitus, 57–58
18 Augustine, 350
25 Montaigne, 103–104
27 Shakespeare, 595
29 Cervantes, 27–28
36 Swift, 79–80, 118–121
37 Fielding, 268
38 Rousseau, 329–334, 342–345, 347–348, 362–366
40 Gibbon, 32–33
43 Federalist, 41
43 Mill, 335–336
46 Hegel, 183–184
47 Goethe, 8
48 Melville, 316
54 Freud, 776–777

2. The idea of progress in the theory of biological evolution

38 Rousseau, 334
47 Goethe, 202–203
49 Darwin, 1–3, 41–42, 60–62, 63–64, 96–103, 176–178, 243, 294–295, 340–341
53 James, 95
54 Freud, 651–654, 768–769

3. Economic progress

3*a*. The increase of opulence: the division of labor as a factor in progress

5 Aristophanes, 629–642
6 Thucydides, 352
35 Locke, 34–35
36 Swift, 154–155
38 Rousseau, 352–353, 365–366
39 Smith, 3–6, 30, 38, 55, 71, 75–76, 105, 142–151, 163, 190–191, 291–295
40 Gibbon, 23, 642, 655–658
42 Kant, 253
43 Federalist, 56
43 Mill, 452
46 Hegel, 67, 263
50 Marx, 16, 31–37, 157–180, 218–219, 308–311
50 Marx-Engels, 421

3*b*. The improvement of the status and conditions of labor: the goals of revolution and reform

9 Aristotle, 554–555
14 Plutarch, 36–37, 68–70, 671–689
15 Tacitus, 132
38 Montesquieu, 111
39 Smith, 27–37, 51–62, 165–175, 200–201
40 Gibbon, 16–17, 144
43 Mill, 339–340
50 Marx, 8–9, 111–146, 209–215, 231–248, 295, 367–368, 377–378

50 MARX-ENGELS, 415–416, 423–425, 432–434
51 TOLSTOY, 211–213
54 FREUD, 787–788, 883–884

3c. Man's progressive conquest of the forces of nature through science and invention

5 AESCHYLUS, 44–45
5 SOPHOCLES, 134
12 LUCRETIUS, 77–78
13 VIRGIL, 40–41
28 GILBERT, 100–101
30 BACON, 107, 120, 133, 169–170, 188–194, 210–214
31 DESCARTES, 60–67
36 SWIFT, 106–107
38 MONTESQUIEU, 126, 191
38 ROUSSEAU, 348–353, 365–366
39 SMITH, 5–6
46 HEGEL, 195, 243–244, 267
50 MARX, 86, 170, 180–188, 253–255, 299
54 FREUD, 778–779

4. Progress in politics

4a. The invention and improvement of political institutions: the maintenance of political order in relation to progress

6 THUCYDIDES, 366–367
7 PLATO, 316–318, 344, 663–666
9 ARISTOTLE, 445–446, 464–465, 533–534, 553–584
12 LUCRETIUS, 74, 75–76
13 VIRGIL, 110–111
14 PLUTARCH, 32–48, 64–77
20 AQUINAS, 236
23 MACHIAVELLI, 36–37
23 HOBBES, 164
38 MONTESQUIEU, 16–17, 75, 170
38 ROUSSEAU, 323–325, 354–355, 356, 367–385, 391–392, 400–406, 423–424
41 GIBBON, 71–80, 202
42 KANT, 450–452, 456–458
43 FEDERALIST, 47–49, 62, 117–125, 153–165 passim, 165–167, 193–194
43 MILL, 272, 289, 300–302, 327–336, 350–355 passim, 370–380
44 BOSWELL, 172, 204–205
46 HEGEL, 147, 203–206, 258, 318, 335–336
51 TOLSTOY, 238–243
54 FREUD, 780–781

4b. The progressive realization of the idea of the state

46 HEGEL, 79–80, 82–83, 84–89, 110–114, 119–120, 141, 144–145, 170–178, 180–183, 230–231

4c. The growth of political freedom: the achievement of citizenship and civil rights

6 HERODOTUS, 171–175
6 THUCYDIDES, 396–397
9 ARISTOTLE, 470–471, 505–506, 571–572
13 VIRGIL, 231–234, 275–278
14 PLUTARCH, 9
15 TACITUS, 51–52, 106
35 LOCKE, 46, 47–51, 63–64
38 MONTESQUIEU, 75–78
39 SMITH, 170–173, 269–271
40 GIBBON, 14, 15, 521–523
41 GIBBON, 403–404
43 FEDERALIST, 47, 92–94, 252
43 MILL, 267–268, 328–332, 367, 381–382, 394–396
46 HEGEL, 275–276, 342–346
50 MARX-ENGELS, 423–425
51 TOLSTOY, 10

5. Forces operating against social progress: emotional opposition to change or novelty; political conservatism

5 ARISTOPHANES, 542–563, 623–625
7 PLATO, 654–655, 678–679, 717–718
14 PLUTARCH, 648–656
15 TACITUS, 151–152
20 AQUINAS, 236–237
21 DANTE, 128–132
23 MACHIAVELLI, 9
25 MONTAIGNE, 47–51, 131–132, 281–282, 318–319, 462–465, 504–506
30 BACON, 90, 109–110, 124–125, 205–207
33 PASCAL, 225–226, 230–231
35 LOCKE, 61–62, 76–77
38 MONTESQUIEU, 104, 137–140
38 ROUSSEAU, 324, 419–420, 437–438
39 SMITH, 27–37, 40, 96–97, 109–110, 201
43 FEDERALIST, 62
43 MILL, 293–302 passim, 335–336, 344, 346–348, 357, 377–378
44 BOSWELL, 189–190
46 HEGEL, 112–113, 145, 235–236, 257, 280–281, 302, 351–353
50 MARX, 174, 234–236, 239–240
50 MARX-ENGELS, 426–428, 429–433
51 TOLSTOY, 303–305, 403, 666–669
53 JAMES, 79
54 FREUD, 759–761, 776–777, 780–781, 783–791, 799–802

6. Intellectual or cultural progress: its sources and impediments

10 GALLEN, 207
23 HOBBES, 274
24 RABELAIS, 81–82
25 MONTAIGNE, 271
28 GALILEO, 166, 203
28 HARVEY, 268, 285
30 BACON, 1–101, 121–122, 134–135, 203–207
31 DESCARTES, 45–46
32 MILTON, 384
33 PASCAL, 355–358
35 LOCKE, 293–294 passim
38 ROUSSEAU, 336–337, 348–353, 362–363

6*a*. Progress in the arts

6*b*. Progress in philosophy and in the sciences

6*c*. The use and criticism of the intellectual tradition: the sifting of truth from error; the reaction against the authority of the past

6*d*. Plans for the advancement of learning and improvement of method in the arts and sciences

10 GALEN, 207
28 HARVEY, 331–337
30 BACON, 1–101, 105–195, 199–214
31 DESCARTES, 1–40, 41–67, 48, 295–353
33 PASCAL, 430–434, 442–443
35 LOCKE, 328, 358–363
35 BERKELEY, 411–412, 439–440
36 SWIFT, 106–115
39 SMITH, 331–356
42 KANT, 1–4, 5–13, 15–16, 19–22
45 LAVOISIER, 6–7

6e. Freedom of expression and discussion as indispensable to the progressive discovery of the truth

12 AURELIUS, 254
31 DESCARTES, 283
32 MILTON, 381–412
35 LOCKE, 15, 319
35 HUME, 497
40 GIBBON, 668–671
42 KANT, 223
43 MILL, 274–293, 297–299

CROSS-REFERENCES

For: The general discussion of the philosophy of history, *see* DIALECTIC 2d; HISTORY 4a(2)–4a(3), 4b; and for the consideration of fate, fortune, and freedom in relation to progress, *see* CHANCE 2b; FATE 3; HISTORY 4a(1); LIBERTY 4a; NECESSITY AND CONTINGENCY 3.

The religious aspects of optimism and pessimism, *see* GOD 7h, 8e, 9f; HISTORY 5a; PROPHECY 4c–4d.

The notion of progress in the theory of biological evolution, *see* EVOLUTION 4d.

Other discussions of the myth of a golden age, *see* LABOR 1a; MAN 9a; TIME 8b.

Discussions relevant to the theme of economic progress, *see* LABOR 4a, 5a–5d, 7c(2), 7f; LIBERTY 6b; REVOLUTION 4a, 5c; SLAVERY 3c, 5b; WEALTH 9b, 12.

Discussions relevant to the theme of political progress, *see* CONSTITUTION 10; DEMOCRACY 4d, 7; GOVERNMENT 6; LIBERTY 6a–6c; MONARCHY 4e(2); SLAVERY 5b; STATE 2a(3); TYRANNY 8; and for the distinction between utopian and practical ideals as goals of political progress, *see* CITIZEN 8; STATE 6, 10f; WAR AND PEACE 11d.

Attitudes toward change which have a bearing on progress, *see* CHANGE 12b; CUSTOM AND CONVENTION 8; TIME 7.

Evidences of progress in the arts and sciences, and for the comparative progress of different fields of learning, *see* ART 12; KNOWLEDGE 10; PHILOSOPHY 7.

The conditions on which intellectual progress depends, *see* KNOWLEDGE 9b; LANGUAGE 6; OPINION 5b; SCIENCE 6a–6b; SIGN AND SYMBOL 4c; TRUTH 6, 8d.

ADDITIONAL READINGS

Listed below are works not included in *Great Books of the Western World*, but relevant to the idea and topics with which this chapter deals. These works are divided into two groups:

I. Works by authors represented in this collection.
II. Works by authors not represented in this collection.

For the date, place, and other facts concerning the publication of the works cited, consult the Bibliography of Additional Readings which follows the last chapter of *The Great Ideas.*

I.

SWIFT. *The Battle of the Books*
HUME. *Of the Rise and Progress of the Arts and Sciences*
ROUSSEAU. *Discourse on the Arts and Sciences*
KANT. *The Idea of a Universal History on a Cosmo-Political Plan*
——. *The Principle of Progress*
HEGEL. *The Phenomenology of Mind*, VI, B (II)

J. S. MILL. "Civilization," in VOL I, *Dissertations and Discussions*

II.

VICO. *The New Science*
VOLTAIRE. *Candide*
——. "Optimism," in *A Philosophical Dictionary*
FERGUSON. *An Essay on the History of Civil Society*, PART III
LESSING. *Nathan the Wise*
——. *The Education of the Human Race*
HERDER. *Outlines of a Philosophy of the History of Man*
CONDORCET. *Outlines of an Historical View of the Progress of the Human Mind*
MALTHUS. *An Essay on Population*, BK III
PROUDHON. *The Philosophy of Misery*
RENAN. *The Future of Science*
TENNYSON. *Locksley Hall*
——. *In Memoriam*
SCHOPENHAUER. *Studies in Pessimism*
COMTE. *The Positive Philosophy*, BK VI
——. *System of Positive Polity*, VOL III, *Social Dynamics*
LOTZE. *Microcosmos*, BK VIII
J. H. NEWMAN. *An Essay on the Development of Christian Doctrine*
——. *Callista*
SPENCER. *Progress: Its Law and Cause*
BAGEHOT. *Physics and Politics*
S. BUTLER. *Erewhon*
GEORGE. *Progress and Poverty*
T. H. HUXLEY. *Methods and Results*, I–II
MAINE. *Ancient Law*
——. *Popular Government*, III
BELLAMY. *Looking Backward*
FRAZER. *The Golden Bough*, PART I, CH 3, 5; PART II, CH 7; PART VII
SUMNER. *The Absurd Effort to Make the World Over*
JENSEN. *The Long Journey*
SOREL. *Les illusions du progrès*
B. RUSSELL. *Proposed Roads to Freedom*, CH 4–8
SPENGLER. *The Decline of the West*
BURY. *The Idea of Progress*
WHITEHEAD. *Science and the Modern World*, CH 13
WELLS. *The World of William Clissold*
DAWSON. *Progress and Religion*
MACIVER. *Society; Its Structure and Changes*
SHAW. *Back to Methuselah*
——. *Doctors' Delusions*
A. J. TOYNBEE. *A Study of History*
MARITAIN. *Theonas, Conversations of a Sage*, VII–VIII, X
——. *True Humanism*
——. *Scholasticism and Politics*, CH 9
SIMON. *Community of the Free*, CH 3

Chapter 72: PROPHECY

INTRODUCTION

THE name of prophet signifies, throughout a great part of the western tradition, an eminence and dignity not shared by the scientist, the philosopher, the statesman, or even the sage. The soothsayer and the seer in pagan antiquity and the prophet of the Lord in Israel do not claim to speak from a merely human wisdom or to declare truths they have learned by inquiry or reflection. Nor are their utterances concerned with the nature of things. The prophet claims to know what men cannot know by any exercise of human powers. He enjoys special gifts. He is divinely inspired. He is instructed by God or has in some way been admitted to the secrets of the gods. His knowledge is not only of supernatural origin; it deals with supernatural matters.

Prophecy is more than a prediction of the future. It unveils what Fate holds in store for men; it foretells the course of providence. In most cases, the future predicted has deep moral significance, expressing the pleasure or displeasure of the gods with individuals or nations, or manifesting God's justice in the rewards promised those who keep His commandments, and the punishments awaiting those who break them. The prophet's foresight discerns more than the future; it discovers what men can hope for or must fear according to their merits, not in the eyes of men but in the sight of God.

This understanding of prophecy seems to be involved in the major issues which the great books raise about prophets. For example, the problem of distinguishing between true and false prophets goes beyond the mere truth or falsity of a prophet's utterances to the validity of his claim to special sources of knowledge or a supernaturally inspired understanding of dreams and visions, omens and portents. The false prophet is not like the mistaken scientist or philosopher—just a person in error. He is either a deceiving impostor or a self-deceived victim of his own pathology.

Similarly, the Christian theologians who criticize the pagan cult of oracles and all forms of divination which seek to pry into divine mysteries, seem to imply that the seers and soothsayers of Greece and Rome, unlike the Hebrew prophets, did not have the gift of prophecy. The acceptance or rejection of prophets and of ways of foreseeing what has been planned in Heaven cannot, it seems, be separated from a whole system of religious beliefs. In this respect, prophets are like miracles. Without faith, both are incredible. "There be two marks," writes Hobbes, "by which together, not asunder, a true Prophet is to be known. One is the doing of miracles; the other is the not teaching any other religion than that which is already established." In Hobbes' view, that there be a religion already established among a people is the one indispensable condition for their reception of prophets or their experience of miracles.

Issues concerning prophecy may, therefore, occur within a single religious community, or be relative to differences between religious communities, as, for example, the opposition between the Jewish and Christian interpretation of the messianic prophecies in the Old Testament. Necessarily, then, there is an issue between the unbelievers and the religious of any faith. Those who deny the existence of God or the gods, or divine agency in the temporal affairs of men, and certainly those who deny the credentials of revelation, cannot but regard prophets as misled and misleading and those who accept prophecy as gullible or superstitious. In the pagan tradition, a philosopher like Aristotle may, however, be critical of divination, and an historian like Thucydides may cast doubt on oracles, without discrediting all other religious beliefs or being themselves atheists.

Some who reject religious prophecy do not concede that man's natural desire to peer into the future need be completely balked. But the secular substitutes for religious prophecy appear to alter the meaning of prophecy. Scientific predictions of the future of the world or of life on this planet (as, for example, those which occur in the writings of Lucretius or Darwin) may be accompanied by attributions of moral qualities to Nature, but usually they connote Nature's sublime indifference to man's welfare. They are seldom, if ever, read as promises or threats of what man deserves to have befall him.

Similarly, historians turned prophets, or philosophers of history who, like Spengler, prophesy decline and doom, do not exhort men to avert disaster, as do the prophets of the Old Testament. Nor do those who, like Hegel and Marx, foresee the ultimate goal toward which events inevitably march, urge men to prepare themselves for it as do the prophecies of the New Testament, which speak of the second coming of Christ. Secular prophecies which bespeak the inevitable operation of necessary causes are, in this respect, like pagan previsions of Fate. At most, they leave man only the illusion of free choice. Jewish and Christian prophecy, in contrast, addresses man as a responsible agent, who, even when he knows something of God's will, remains free to will good or evil for himself. If, according to the theologians, divine providence or predestination does not abolish human freedom, neither does prophetic knowledge of the divine plan.

These matters are discussed elsewhere—secular prophecy in the chapters on History and Progress, and the problem of foreknowledge and freedom in the chapters on Fate and Necessity and Contingency.

In pagan antiquity, prophecy does not seem to be confined to men especially appointed by the gods. The gods themselves foretell the future to men. When people wish to know the future, they go or send emissaries to the temple at Delphi over which a goddess, the Pythoness, presides. The institution of the oracles, of which Delphi is perhaps the most illustrious example, leaves foresight in the hands of the gods; for, as most of the anecdotes in Herodotus and Thucydides show, only the Pythoness herself knows unequivocally the meaning of her oracular utterances.

To men is left the task of interpreting what the oracle means. The pagan unlike the Hebrew prophet seems to be a man of skill in penetrating the secrets of the gods—a skill which may itself be divinely bestowed—but he is not a man to whom the gods have spoken plainly, so that he may in turn unerringly advise others. "No man, when in his wits," according to Plato, "attains prophetic truth and inspiration."

There are passages in the Greek poets and historians which seem to suggest that the gods begrudge men too clear a vision of the future, and may even on occasion mislead them or at least permit them to be misled. In Aeschylus' play, Prometheus declares that "because he gave to men gifts claimed by the gods," he is "bound in durance here." He gave them radiant fire, the mechanical arts; he "took from men the expectancy of Death"; he gave them medicines and healing drugs. Last in his own enumeration and in a sense most significant, he endowed men with the divine gift of foresight.

"I drew clear lines for divination," Prometheus says, "and discerned (before all others) what from dreams is sure to come to pass in waking. I disclosed the mysteries of omen-bringing words, and pathway tokens, and made plain the flight of taloned birds, both of good augury and adverse . . . I cleared the way for mortals to an art hard of discernment, and made bright and clear fire-auguries, heretofore obscure and blind." The chorus questions whether "the power of creatures creeping for an hour" shall by wisdom overpass the bounds set for their little lives by "the mind of Zeus." Does the wisdom of foreknowledge, gained through the arts of divination, give men strength to resist the will of the gods or to struggle against them?

Prometheus himself is the answer to the question. The power he wields over Zeus, which Zeus tries to wrest from him by bribes and threats and by the infliction of titanic pain, is the foreknowledge which Prometheus possesses of the doom to befall the son of Kronos. No threat of Zeus will get him to divulge it,

Prometheus says, because "nought can surprise me who foreknow . . . Nought in his power shall bend me to reveal whom Fate prepares to work his overthrow."

A myth which Socrates relates in the *Gorgias* appears to contain a sequel to the legend as told by Aeschylus. It also seems to confirm the point that foresight is a divine privilege in which men should not share, lest they become too god-like. According to the myth, Zeus, in order to prevent men from evading the divine judgment, says: "In the first place, I will deprive men of the foreknowledge of death; this power which they have, Prometheus has already received my orders to take from them."

The oracles never make the future so plain that men can act with a foreknowledge equal to that possessed by the gods, but sometimes oracular utterances seem to be contrived not merely to veil the future, but to lead men astray. Herodotus tells the story of Miltiades who, on the advice of Timo, a priestess of the goddesses of the underworld, acted in a way which brought him to grief. When the Parians sent to Delphi to ask whether Timo should be punished for this, the Pythoness forbade them, saying, "Timo was not at fault; 'twas decreed that Miltiades should come to an unhappy end; and she was sent to lure him to his destruction."

There is also the story, told by Thucydides, of Cyclon who, inquiring at Delphi, was told to seize the Acropolis of Athens on the grand festival of Zeus. This, too, turned into a disastrous misadventure, apparently because, as Thucydides observes, "whether the grand festival that was meant was in Attica or elsewhere was a question he never thought of, and which the oracle did not offer to solve."

For the most part, however, the calamities which befall men who seek guidance from the oracle seem to be due to their own misinterpretation of the Delphic deliverance, itself always admittedly difficult to understand. Herodotus and Thucydides abound with such stories, and also with instances in which the same oracular statement is given conflicting interpretations, one of which must be wrong. Nevertheless, Herodotus declares himself unwilling "to say that there is no truth in prophecies," and he is certainly not willing to question "those which speak with clearness." Giving an example of a clear prediction, he adds, "When I look to this, and perceive how clearly Bacis spoke, I neither venture myself to say anything against prophecies, nor do I approve of others impugning them."

Thucydides appears to take a contrary view. He singles out one example as "an instance of faith in oracles being for once justified by the event." He puts into the speech of the Athenians at the Melian Conference the warning not to "be like the vulgar, who, abandoning such security as human means may still afford, when visible hopes fail them in extremity, turn to invisible, to prophecies and oracles, and other such inventions that delude men with hopes to their destruction."

THE PROBLEM OF THE reliability of prophecies, and of the faith or credulity of those who rely upon them, applies not only to oracles, but also to dreams or visions, and to omens and portents of all sorts. Two stories about Croesus, told by Herodotus, show that oracles and dreams can be equally ambiguous and are equally liable to misinterpretation. Croesus dreamed that his son Atys would die by the blow of an iron weapon. Subsequently when Atys wished to go boar hunting with Adrastus, he persuaded Croesus that the dream could not have been a warning against this undertaking because a boar does not have hands to strike with, nor does it wield iron weapons. But during the hunt Atys was killed by the spear which Adrastus intended for the boar.

On another occasion, Croesus inquired of Delphi how long his kingdom would last. The Pythoness answered, in effect, until "a mule is monarch in Media." This not only pleased him because "it seemed incredible to him that a mule should ever become king of the Medes," but also gave him confidence when he engaged in war with the Medes and Persians, led by Cyrus. The war ended in his defeat and capture but, according to Herodotus, he had no right to complain of the oracle because "he had misunderstood the answer which had been given him about the mule. Cyrus was that mule; for the parents of Cyrus were of different races and of different kinds"—his mother a Median princess, his father a Persian subject.

The attitude of the ancients toward these

various instruments of prophecy or divination does not seem to be consistent or constant. Herodotus reports at one place how Xerxes, "despising the omens," carried out his plans against their forebodings; and at another how an eclipse of the moon, being interpreted as of good omen, rejoiced Xerxes who, "thus instructed, proceeded on his way with great gladness of heart." And again, when Xerxes reports to Artabanus the advice—concerning his war against the Greeks—which he received from a dream apparition, Artabanus scoffs, saying, "Such things, my son, have of truth nothing divine in them . . . Whatever a man has been thinking of during the day, is wont to hover round him in the visions of his dreams at night." But when Artabanus himself experiences the same apparition which had occurred to Xerxes in his dream and, in addition to giving the same advice, the vision threatens him, Artabanus changes his mind about dreams and reverses his policy with regard to the expedition against Greece.

"As to the divination which takes place in sleep, and is said to be based on dreams," Aristotle writes, "we cannot lightly either dismiss it with contempt or give it implicit confidence." Nevertheless, he himself seems to conclude that most so-called prophetic dreams are "to be classed as mere coincidences"; and that "dreams are not sent by God, nor are they designed for this purpose," *i.e.*, foretelling the future. One proof that they are not sent by God is, in his opinion, the fact that the persons having them "are not the best and wisest but merely commonplace persons." The fact that "the power of foreseeing the future and of having vivid dreams is found in persons of inferior type implies that God does not send them."

The Christian theologians, distinguishing between prophecy and divination, condemn the latter as a kind of presumption or impiety. Though their criticism seems to be directed especially against astrology, it applies to the interpretation of terrestrial as well as celestial signs. Augustine refers to "the lying divinations and impious dotages of the astrologers," and Aquinas explains how the astrologers are able to foretell things in a general way without attributing to them any genuinely prophetic power.

In his consideration of the difference between true and false religion, Hobbes goes further than the theologians in condemning "the innumerable other superstitious ways of divination," such as "the ambiguous or senseless answers of the priests at Delphi, Delos, Ammon, and other famous oracles," or "the prediction of witches that pretended conference with the dead, which is called necromancy, conjuring, and witchcraft, and is but juggling and confederate knavery," or, in general, the recourse to omens, portents, and dreams for purposes of prognostication.

That the things Hobbes calls superstitious are not confined to pagan antiquity is manifest in Shakespeare's *Macbeth.* The witches and the omens there are like the soothsayers and the portents in *Julius Caesar;* and Macbeth's misunderstanding of "'til Birnam Forest come to Dunsinane" is as fatal as Croesus' reliance on "until a mule is monarch in Media."

In one other respect, pagan and Christian cultures seem to exhibit a certain parallelism with regard to the belief in supernatural foreknowledge. The spirits of the departed, in the *Odyssey* and the *Aeneid*, are able to inform the visitor to the underworld of coming events on earth. They speak plainly and with perfect prescience. The veil which hides the future from mortal eyes has been lifted. So, too, the damned souls and the blessed foretell future things to Dante, no less accurately though less extensively than, in *Paradise Lost*, the archangel Michael unfolds to Adam the whole future history of mankind.

But so far as the foreknowledge of mortal men is concerned, the Hebrew prophets seem to be unique. Unlike pagan diviners or soothsayers, they do not probe the future in order to help men anticipate the turns of fortune or the lines of fate. They do not have to employ arts or devices for penetrating divine secrets. God speaks to them directly and, through them, to the Chosen People. For the most part their prophetic speeches, unlike those of the oracles, seem to be unambiguous. At least the intention seems to be to reveal, not to conceal, God's plan on such matters as He Himself wishes men to foresee the course of providence.

Where pagan prognosticators may claim to be divinely inspired in the sense of having special powers of interpretation, the Hebrew prophets speak from a different kind of supernatural inspiration. They are the vessels through which the Lord Himself speaks. They are interpreters only in that they make known to others what God has made known to them.

The content of the divine communication is seldom exclusively a foretelling of the future. It is often accompanied by instruction concerning the actions to be performed by the Jewish people—the direction of their conduct toward the Promised Land or the rebuilding of the Temple. Sometimes when the prophecy is one of doom rather than of hope, as in the case of the destruction of Jerusalem, the Babylonian captivity, or the dispersion of Israel, the prediction of the future is accompanied by moral instruction of another sort—the lessons of the Law which the Jews have forsaken, meriting thereby the punishments the prophets foresee.

Mere prognostication does not seem to be the chief purpose of Hebrew prophecy. Just as the Covenant which God makes with Abraham, Isaac, and Jacob consecrates the Jewish people to a special mission; just as the Law which God hands down through Moses sets them apart from the Gentiles and prescribes for them the way of righteousness and sanctity; so the revelations of God's providence through the prophets tend to remind the Chosen People of the meaning of the Covenant and the Law as well as to disclose their destiny as a nation.

The prophets speak not only of the future, but of the present and the past. They are divinely appointed teachers, no less than the patriarchs and Moses. Yet they may rank below Moses (who is sometimes also regarded as a prophet) by reason of the manner in which they are addressed by God. As Hobbes points out, "God himself in express words declareth that to other prophets he spake in dreams and visions, but to his servant Moses, in such manner as a man speaketh to his friend"—face to face.

The content of Hebrew prophecy, in short, seems to be continuous with the rest of God's revelation of Himself to His Chosen People. The difference between the prophets as the instruments of God's teaching and the pagan philosophers as merely human teachers seems to Augustine plainly shown by the agreement of the prophets with one another and by their continuity with Moses and the patriarchs; whereas Augustine can find nothing but disagreement and dissension among even the best teachers of the pagans. Among them, false teachers or prophets seem to be accorded the same recognition and to attract the same following as true.

"But that nation," Augustine writes, "that people, that city, that republic, these Israelites, to whom the oracles of God were entrusted, by no means confounded with similar license false prophets with the true prophets; but, agreeing together, and differing in nothing, acknowledged and upheld the authentic authors of their sacred books. These were their philosophers, these were their sages, divines, prophets, and teachers of probity and piety. Whoever was wise and lived according to them was wise and lived, not according to men, but according to God who hath spoken to them."

Hobbes also conceives the prophets of the Old Testament as more than foretellers of the future. "The name of prophet," he writes, "signifies in Scripture sometimes *prolocutor*; that is, he that speaketh from God to man, or from man to God; and sometimes *predictor*, or a foreteller of things to come." In addition to their being divinely appointed teachers, the prophets, according to Hobbes, seem to perform a political function. They check the power of the kings, or seek to awaken their consciences to the dictates of justice and mercy. "Through the whole history of the kings, as well of Judah as of Israel, there were prophets that always controlled the kings for transgressing the religion; and sometimes also for errors of state."

A secular view of the Hebrew prophets seems to give prominence to their political role in the theocratic community of the Jews. Comparing the Jewish state with other sacerdotal societies, Mill observes that "neither their kings nor their priests ever obtained, as in those other countries, the exclusive moulding of their character. Their religion . . . gave existence to an inestimably precious unorganized institution—the Order (if it may be so termed) of the Prophets. Under the protection, generally though not always effectual, of their sacred character, the Prophets were a power in the nation, often more than a match for kings and priests, and kept up, in that little corner of the earth, the antagonism of influences which is the only real security for continued progress."

As THERE IS A BODY of prophetic doctrine in the Old Testament, so the religion of the Gospels contains a number of prophetic beliefs peculiar to Christian doctrine. Such, for example, is the prophecy of the second coming of Christ, the prophecy of the Last Judgment on that occasion, and the prophecy of a final conflagration to cleanse the world, which will precede the resurrection of the body as that in turn precedes the general judgment of souls.

Aquinas discusses the various signs which will foretell the imminence of these events. He also raises the question whether the time of the end of the world and of the resurrection can be known exactly. On this he agrees with Augustine that "that time is hidden from men." It cannot be calculated by natural reason, nor is it revealed. "Of that day and hour," it is written in Matthew, "no one knoweth, no, not the angels of heaven." When the apostles asked Christ about His second coming, He answered, according to Saint Paul, "It is not for you to know the times or moments which the Father hath put in His own power."

What Christ refused to tell the apostles, Aquinas adds, "He will not reveal to others. Wherefore all those who have been misled to reckon the aforesaid time have so far proved to be untruthful; for some, as Augustine says, stated from our Lord's ascension to His last coming 400 years would elapse, others 500, others 1,000. The falseness of these calculators is evident, as will likewise be the falseness of those who even now cease not to calculate."

The single greatest prophecy in the Judaeo-Christian tradition is, perhaps, the messianic prophecy—the foretelling of a Messiah or of a messianic age. The prediction of a Messiah or Saviour, who shall be born of the house of David and shall be king of the Jews, runs throughout the prophetic books of the Old Testament, though with different degrees of explicitness and varying imagery in Daniel and Jeremiah, in Isaiah and Ezekiel.

"The Lord himself shall give you a sign," says Isaiah. "Behold a virgin shall conceive and bear a son, and shall call his name Immanuel. . . . For unto us a child is born, unto us a son is given," Isaiah goes on, "and the government shall be upon his shoulder, and his name shall be called Wonderful, Counsellor, The mighty God, The Everlasting Father, The Prince of Peace. Of the increase of his government and peace, there shall be no end, upon the throne of David and upon his kingdom, to order it and to establish it with justice from henceforth even for ever." And Jeremiah tells his people, "Behold the days come, saith the Lord, that I will raise unto David a righteous Branch and a King shall reign and prosper and shall execute judgment and justice in the earth. In his days, Judah shall be saved, and Israel shall dwell safely."

Two of the great issues between the Jewish and Christian faiths concern these messianic prophecies in the Old Testament. One arises from opposite interpretations of the event predicted—a messianic age in which the kingdom of the Jews will be established on earth in perpetual righteousness and glory, or the coming to earth of God's only begotten son, incarnate in human form, for the salvation of all mankind. The other arises from opposite answers to the question whether the prediction—on either interpretation—has been fulfilled.

It is, of course, the Christian view that the prophets foretold the coming of Christ and that their prophecy has been fulfilled. But more than that, Christian apologists and theologians seem to make the fulfillment of Hebrew prophecies, interpreted as foreshadowing the truths of the Christian religion, a source of verification for these truths.

The difference between Jesus Christ and Mahomet, according to Pascal, is that "Mahomet was not foretold; Jesus Christ was foretold. I see many contradictory religions, and consequently all false save one," he writes. "Each wants to be believed on its own authority, and threatens unbelievers. I do not therefore believe them. Everyone can say this; everyone can call himself a prophet. But I see the Christian religion wherein prophecies are fulfilled; and that is what everyone cannot do."

And in another place Pascal declares that "the prophecies are the strongest proof of Jesus Christ. . . . If one man alone had made a book of predictions about Jesus Christ, as to the time and manner, and Jesus Christ had come in conformity to these prophecies, this fact would have infinite weight. But there is much more here. Here is a succession of men during four thousand years, who, consequently and without variation, come, one after another, to foretell this same event."

Centuries earlier Augustine writes in a similar vein. The Hebrew people as a whole are chosen to perform this prophetic function—to foretell, "sometimes through men who understood what they spake, and sometimes through men who understood not, all that has transpired since the advent of Christ until now, and all that will transpire." Not only the explicit "prophecies which are contained in words," but all the rituals and ceremonies, the offices and institutions, of the Jewish religion prefigure Christianity, signifying and fore-announcing "those things which we who believe in Jesus Christ unto eternal life believe to have been fulfilled, or behold in process of fulfillment, or confidently believe shall yet be fulfilled."

OUTLINE OF TOPICS

REFERENCES

References are listed by volume number (in bold type), author's name, and page number. Bible references are to book, chapter, and verse of the Authorized King James version of the Bible. The abbreviation "esp" calls the reader's attention to one or more especially relevant parts of a whole reference; "passim" signifies that the topic is discussed intermittently rather than continuously in the work or passage cited. Where the work as a whole is relevant to the topic, the page numbers refer to the entire work. For general guidance in the use of *The Great Ideas,* consult the Preface.

1. The nature and power of prophecy

1*a*. Prophecy as the reading of fate, the foretelling of fortune, the beholding of the future

4 HOMER, 121, 131, 292
5 AESCHYLUS, 41, 49–50
5 SOPHOCLES, 149, 171
5 EURIPIDES, 338–339, 422
6 HERODOTUS, 201–202, 248, 270–271, 273, 276–277
7 PLATO, 123, 210–211
9 ARISTOTLE, 620
13 VIRGIL, 14–15, 109–111, 275–278
14 PLUTARCH, 20, 679–680
23 HOBBES, 183
27 SHAKESPEARE, 285–287, 300–302
47 GOETHE, 197–198
48 MELVILLE, 364–365

1*b*. Prophecy as supernaturally inspired foresight into the course of providence

OLD TESTAMENT: *Exodus,* 4:10–17 / *Numbers,* 11:16–17, 24–30; 22:35–23:26 passim / *I Samuel,* 28:15–20 / *II Samuel,* 7:4–16 / *I Kings,* 14:1–16; 16:1–4; 17:13–16; 19:15–18; 20:13–14,22,28,35–42; 21:17–24,28–29 / *II Kings,* 1–2; 8:1,7–15; 9:30–10:17; 19:1–7,20–21,28–33,37; 20:1–6,14–19; 22:14–20 / *I Chronicles,* 17:7–15 / *II Chronicles,* 18:4–16,31–34; 20:14–16,37; 21:12–20; 34:22–28 / *Isaiah* passim / *Jeremiah* passim, 7:25–26 / *Ezekiel,* 1–39 passim / *Daniel,* 4:4–8,24–37; 5:25–31; 7–8; 9:20–27; 11–12 / *Joel,* 2–3 / *Amos* passim / *Jonah,* 3 / *Micah* passim / *Nahum* passim / *Habakkuk* passim / *Zephaniah* passim / *Haggai,* 2 / *Zechariah* passim / *Malachi* passim
APOCRYPHA: *Ecclesiasticus,* 48:22–25
NEW TESTAMENT: *Luke,* 1:67–79 / *John,* 1:6–8,15–27
7 PLATO, 467
8 ARISTOTLE, 708
18 AUGUSTINE, 313–314, 324
23 HOBBES, 176–177, 183–186
32 MILTON, 299–333
40 GIBBON, 189

1*c*. Prophecy as the instrument of providence: prophets as moral teachers and political reformers

OLD TESTAMENT: *Exodus,* 3:6–15, 7–12 passim; 24; 31:18; 34:1–4 / *Deuteronomy,* 4:14–29; 7–11 passim; 18:15–19; 28–30 / *Joshua,* 23–24 / *I Samuel,* 2:27–36; 8:10–18, 10:1–8; 12:6–25; 13:11–14 / *II Samuel,* 12:1–14 / *I Kings,* 17–19; 22:1–23 / *II Kings,* 5:1–19; 9:1–10; 19:1–7,20–37; 20; 17:9–14,23 / *I Chronicles,* 17:3–15; 21:9–13,18–19 / *II Chronicles,* 15:1–8; 21:12–15; 28:8–15; 34:22–33 / *Ezra,* 9:10–11 / *Isaiah* passim, 6:1–13, 56:1 / *Isaias* passim, 5:8–13, 5:20–25, 6:1–13, 38:4–8, 49:1–12, 56:1 / *Jeremiah* / *Ezekiel,* 1–39 / *Hosea* / *Joel* / *Amos* / *Johah,* 3 / *Micah* passim / *Nahum* passim / *Habakkuk* passim / *Zephaniah* passim / *Haggai* / *Zechariah,* 1:1–6; 7:8–14 / *Malachi*
NEW TESTAMENT: *Luke,* 11:48–50 / *Acts,* 9:3–16; 26:13–18 / *I Corinthians,* 14
18 AUGUSTINE, 449–472
20 AQUINAS, 845–846
23 HOBBES, 160, 182–183, 188–189
32 MILTON, 313–315
41 GIBBON, 229–233, 306
48 MELVILLE, 35–36

1*d*. The religious significance of the fulfillment of prophecy

NEW TESTAMENT: *Matthew* / *Mark,* 1:1–8 / *Luke,* 4:16–21 / *John,* 1:19–27, 7:25–52; 12:37–41 / *Acts,* 2:1–36; 3:12–26; 8:26–40; 13:16–52; 15:13–21; 28:16–29 / *Romans,* 9–11 / *Hebrews*
18 AUGUSTINE, 319–322, 419–420, 422–423, 444–448, 450–451, 477, 483–493, 498–507, 525, 532, 556–560, 588
23 HOBBES, 160, 165–167, 187, 244, 248, 251–252
32 MILTON, 1, 139, 313–317, 324, 326
33 PASCAL, 273–276, 278–279, 282–283, 289–291, 293, 295, 297–299, 319, 322, 323, 333–335
35 HUME, 497
40 GIBBON, 181, 297
52 DOSTOEVSKY, 127–137

2. The vocation of prophecy: the possession of foreknowledge

2a. The foreknowledge possessed by the spirits in the afterworld

OLD TESTAMENT: *I Samuel,* 28:6–20
4 HOMER, 161–162, 241, 244
5 AESCHYLUS, 23–24
5 SOPHOCLES, 194–195
13 VIRGIL, 231–235
21 DANTE, 8–9, 13–14, 21–22, 35–36, 69–70, 73–74, 83–84, 90, 104–105, 118–120, 132–133, 139, 147–148, 153

2b. The political office of prophecy: priests, soothsayers, oracles

4 HOMER, 3–4
5 SOPHOCLES, 102–103, 126–128, 139–140, 187, 194
5 EURIPIDES, 385–387
6 HERODOTUS, 13, 135–136, 150–153, 167–168, 171–172, 177, 194–195, 197–198, 241–242, 246, 284–285
6 THUCYDIDES, 355
7 PLATO, 345–346, 597–598
9 ARISTOTLE, 620
13 VIRGIL, 157–160
14 PLUTARCH, 52, 399, 541–542, 552, 594
15 TACITUS, 91, 103–104
22 CHAUCER, 114–115
23 HOBBES, 185–188, 199–204
26 SHAKESPEARE, 569
27 SHAKESPEARE, 312–313
38 ROUSSEAU, 401–402
40 GIBBON, 457–458
43 MILL, 341
46 HEGEL, 217

2c. The Hebraic conception of the prophetic vocation: the law and the prophets; Christ as prophet

OLD TESTAMENT: *Exodus,* 3:1–4:17; 20:18–21; 24:1–2,9–18; 33:9–11,17–23 / *Numbers,* 12:1–9 / *Deuteronomy,* 13:1–11 / *Joshua,* 3:7–8 / *Judges,* 4 / *I Samuel,* 8:10–18,22; 10:1–13,24 / *I Kings,* 17–18; 19:16–21; 20; 37–42; 21:17–24; 22:14–22 / *II Kings,* 1–2; 3:9–20; 4–6; 8:1–15; 9:1–10; 20 / *II Chronicles,* 18:4–26; 34:14–28; 36:15–16 / *Isaiah,* 6:8–12; 8:11–18; 20; 21–35; 49:1–12; 61:1–3 / *Jeremiah,* 1; 6:27; 18:18–23; 20; 26; 28; 36–38; 42:1–43:3 / *Ezekiel,* 2:1–5:4; 12; 33:30–33 / *Daniel,* 2; 4–6 / AMOS, 7:14–17 / *Jonah*
APOCRYPHA: *Ecclesiasticus,* 39:1–11; 45–46; 48–49 / *Bel and Dragon,* 33–39 / *II Maccabees,* 2:1–7
NEW TESTAMENT: *Matthew,* 5:17–18; 10; 11:20–24; 12:36–45; 13:53–57; 19:27–30; 23–25 / *Luke,* 16:14–16 / *John,* 1:15–27; 8:52–53 / *Acts,* 3:22–26
18 AUGUSTINE, 262, 449–451
20 AQUINAS, 750–751
23 HOBBES, 69–70, 169–170, 182–188, 201, 269
32 MILTON, 321–325
43 MILL, 341
54 FREUD, 793

3. The varieties of prophecy and the instruments of divination

3a. The institution of oracles: the interpretation of oracular or prophetic utterances

5 AESCHYLUS, 35, 72–73, 81
5 SOPHOCLES, 99–110 / 117–118
5 EURIPIDES, 422
5 ARISTOPHANES, 593, 629–630
6 HERODOTUS, 10, 11, 14–15, 20–22, 60–61, 70–71, 77, 101–103, 151–153, 178–180, 189, 199–202, 239–240, 255, 263, 295–298, 308
6 THUCYDIDES, 380, 392, 442–443
7 PLATO, 201–203
12 EPICTETUS, 122–124, 175–176
13 VIRGIL, 127, 150–152, 212–213, 238–239
14 PLUTARCH, 268, 363–367, 698–699
15 TACITUS, 37, 214–215
18 AUGUSTINE, 483–485
23 HOBBES, 81–82
27 SHAKESPEARE, 488, 495–497
33 PASCAL, 298–301
40 GIBBON, 121
46 HEGEL, 252–253, 264–265, 273

3b. Omens and portents: celestial and terrestrial signs; signs as confirmations of prophecy

OLD TESTAMENT: *Genesis,* 9:8–17; *Exodus,* 4:1–9; 29–31; 7:8–13; 17:2–7; 33:9–10; 34:29–30 / *Numbers,* 9:15–23; 12 / *Judges,* 6:17–22, 36–40 / *I Samuel,* 10:2–16 / *I Kings,* 1:1–6; 17:12–24; 18:16–39 / *II Kings,* 1:8–17; 2:9–15,19–22; 5:1–19 / *Isaiah,* 38:1–8 / *Jeremiah,* 1:11–16; 13:1–11; 18:1–10; 24 / *Ezekiel,* 37:1–19 / *Daniel,* 5 / *Amos,* 7:1–9
NEW TESTAMENT: *Matthew,* 16:1–4; 24 / *Mark,* 13:4–30 / *Luke* / *John,* 2:18–22 / *I Corinthians,* 1:22–24
4 HOMER, 13, 84, 189–190, 267, 271, 297
5 AESCHYLUS, 17, 45, 53
5 SOPHOCLES, 127–128, 175–176
5 ARISTOPHANES, 551–552
6 HERODOTUS, 12, 17, 18, 39–40, 106, 124–125, 190, 200–201, 204, 212–213, 223–227, 248, 266, 285–286, 289–290, 313–314
9 ARISTOTLE, 47
12 LUCRETIUS, 85
13 VIRGIL, 128–130, 143–144, 161–162, 216, 237–238, 273, 360–361
14 PLUTARCH, 19–20, 82, 94, 103–104, 123–124, 141–142, 198–207, 259–260, 339, 371–372, 404–405, 429–430, 435, 568, 575–576, 615, 789–790, 818, 822, 866–867, 871
15 TACITUS, 95–96, 124, 141, 144, 149, 168–169, 212–213, 235
17 PLOTINUS, 44–45, 80–81

18 AUGUSTINE, 45–47, 207–213, 263–264
23 HOBBES, 81–82
24 RABELAIS, 146–150, 175–178, 268–269, 277–279
25 MONTAIGNE, 223–224
26 SHAKESPEARE, 103–104, 334, 572–574
27 SHAKESPEARE, 249, 294
35 LOCKE, 388
40 GIBBON, 547, 571, 614
41 GIBBON, 232
46 HEGEL, 263–265
47 GOETHE, 122–123
48 MELVILLE, 175–176
51 TOLSTOY, 298–300, 340–341, 377–379
54 FREUD, 467

3*c*. Dreams, visions, visitations

OLD TESTAMENT: *Genesis,* 16:7–13; 18:1–15; 19:12–22; 20:3–7; 22:11–19; 28:10–22; 32:24–32; 35:9–13; 37:1–11; 40–41 / *Numbers,* 22:15–35 / *Deuteronomy,* 13:1–5 / *Judges,* 6:11–23; 7:13–15; 13 / *I Kings,* 3:5–15 / *I Chronicles,* 21:15–20,28–30 / *Job,* 33:14–16 / *Isaiah,* 6 / *Jeremiah* / *Ezekiel,* 1–3; 8–11; 37:1–11; 40–48 / *Daniel,* 2; 4; 7–12 passim / *Joel,* 2:28–29 / *Zechariah,* 1:7–6:15
APOCRYPHA: *Rest of Esther,* 10:4–11:12 / *Wisdom of Solomon,* 18:14–19 / *Ecclesiasticus,* 34:1–7 / *Bel and Dragon,* 33–39
NEW TESTAMENT: *Matthew,* 1:20–25; 2:12–13, 19–23; 17:1–8; 28:1–7 / *Luke,* 1:11–38; 2:8; 24:1–10 / *Acts,* 10 / *II Corinthians,* 12:1–4 / *Revelation*
4 HOMER, 207, 294–295
5 AESCHYLUS, 17, 46–47, 63–66, 75
5 SOPHOCLES, 159–160, 161
5 EURIPIDES, 272–274, 353, 411
5 ARISTOPHANES, 483
6 HERODOTUS, 8–10, 25–31, 47, 78–79, 116, 155, 218–220
7 PLATO, 213
8 ARISTOTLE, 707–709
13 VIRGIL, 182–183, 245–249, 259–261
14 PLUTARCH, 98–99, 185–186, 239–240, 398–399, 473, 483, 514–515, 534–535, 548–549, 601–604, 721–722, 816–817
15 TACITUS, 101, 112–113, 293–294
18 AUGUSTINE, 18–19
19 AQUINAS, 463–464
21 DANTE, 49–50, 66, 81–82, 95
22 CHAUCER, 143–144, 147–149, 452–455
23 HOBBES, 51–52, 184–187, 281–282
24 RABELAIS, 150–156, 278
26 SHAKESPEARE, 36–37, 40–41, 291, 578–579, 591
27 SHAKESPEARE, 29–31, 299, 481–482
32 MILTON, 176–178, 185–186, 238–239, 303–333
40 GIBBON, 294–296
47 GOETHE, 277
51 TOLSTOY, 561–562
54 FREUD, 11, 137–138, 178, 179, 477

3*d*. Prophecy by the direct word of God

OLD TESTAMENT: *Genesis,* 2:16–17; 3:8–19; 4:6–15; 7:1–4; 9:1–17; 12:1–8; 13:14–18; 15; 17; 26:1–5,24; 35:9–13 / *Exodus,* 3:4–22; 7–12; 19:3–20:22; 32:9–14,30–34; 33:1–34:27 / *Numbers,* 14:11–12,20–35 / *Deuteronomy,* 4:10–15,36; 5; 31:14–21 / *Joshua,* 1:1–9; 6:1–5 / *I Samuel,* 3; 16:1–13 / *I Kings,* 19:9–18 / *Isaiah,* 6; 48:2–5 / *Jeremiah,* 1 / *Ezekiel,* 1–39 / *Hosea,* 1–3 / *Amos,* 7–9
NEW TESTAMENT: *Acts,* 26:13–18
18 AUGUSTINE, 323
23 HOBBES, 165–166
32 MILTON, 321–322, 323–325
52 DOSTOEVSKY, 127–137

4. Particular prophecies of hope and doom

4*a*. The Convenant and the Promised Land

OLD TESTAMENT: *Genesis,* 12:1–7; 15; 17–18; 22:1–19; 35:9–13 / *Exodus,* 2:23–3:22; 6:2–8; 19:4–6; 20:1–17; 33:1–3 / *Leviticus,* 26:40–45 / *Numbers,* 32; 34:1–12 / *Deuteronomy,* 1:7–8,19–31; 4:12–13,23–40; 5; 6:1–3,10–11,18–19; 8:7–10,18–20; 9:1–6,23–29; 11; 26:1–11; 27–32; 34:1–4 / *Judges,* 2:1–6 / *I Chronicles,* 16:13–22 / *Nehemiah* / *Psalms,* 78:1–7,52–55; 105:6–44; 132 / *Isaiah,* 54:1–10; 61:7–9 / *Jeremiah,* 11:1–10; 31:31–34; 34:12–18 / *Ezekiel,* 16:60–63; 37:26–28 / *Hosea,* 6:4–7
APOCRYPHA: *Ecclesiasticus,* 44:19–23
NEW TESTAMENT: *Luke,* 1:71–75 / *Acts* / *Romans,* 9:1–9; 11:25–27 / *Galatians,* 3:13–18; 4:22–31 / *Hebrews,* 8:6–9:28; 10:14–17
18 AUGUSTINE, 433–445, 588
23 HOBBES, 177–180
32 MILTON, 321–325
43 PASCAL, 296–297

4*b*. The destruction of Jerusalem and the dispersion of Israel: the restoration of Israel and the rebuilding of the Temple

OLD TESTAMENT: *Leviticus,* 26:27–39 / *Deuteronomy,* 4:25–31; 28:15–30:10; 31:16–18 / *II Kings,* 17; 20:12–21; 21:10–15; 22; 12–20; 24:1–4,10–20; 25 / *II Chronicles,* 7:19–22; 34:21–33; 36:15–23 / *Psalms,* 78:58–72; 79 / *Isaiah,* 1–10; 14:1–3; 22; 28; 32; 36–37; 39; 42–43; 49; 51–52; 60–63 / *Jeremiah,* 1–45 passim; 49–52 passim / *Lamentations* / *Ezekiel,* 4–7; 9; 11–24; 28:20–26; 33–48 / *Hosea,* 2; 3:4–5; 5–11 / *Joel,* 2,3 / *Amos* passim / *Obadiah* passim / *Micah* / *Nahum* passim / *Habakkuk* / *Zephaniah* / *Zechariah* passim
APOCRYPHA: *Ecclesiasticus,* 49:4–50:2 / *Baruch,* 5
NEW TESTAMENT: *Mark,* 13:1–2 / *Luke,* 21:5–6; 19:41–44
18 AUGUSTINE, 458–459, 500
23 HOBBES, 179, 244
33 PASCAL, 304–315

4*c*. The coming of a Messiah: Hebraic and Christian readings of messianic prophecy

OLD TESTAMENT: *Genesis,* 3:15; 49:10–12,22–26 / *Numbers,* 24:15–25 / *Deuteronomy,* 18:15–19 / *Job,* 19:25–27 / *Psalms,* 6–7; 16:10; 21–22; 40:1–8; 45:7; 50:1–3; 68; 72; 85; 89:19–29,36–37; 110; 39:1–8; 44:7; 49 / *Isaiah,* 7:10–16; 9:6–7; 11:1–5; 22:20–25; 28:16–29; 32; 40:1–11; 41:2–3,8–14,25; 42:1–7; 49:1–13,22–23; 52–55; 59–66; 41:2–3,8–14,25; 42:1–7; 45; 46; 11–12; 59–66 passim / *Jeremiah,* 23:5–6; 30:7–9; 31:31–33; 33:10 / *Ezekiel,* 17:22–24; 34; 37:21–26 / *Daniel,* 2:44; 7:13–14; 9:24–27 / *Hosea,* 1:11; 14:5–7 / *Micah,* 5:2–5; / *Zechariah,* 3:8–9; 6:12–14; 9:9–11 / *Malachi,* 3:1–3; 4:5

APOCRYPHA: *Wisdom of Solomon,* 2:12–22

NEW TESTAMENT: *Matthew,* 3:1–12 / *Luke,* 2:25–34; 3:1–6 / *John,* 1:19–25,40–45; 7:26–31 / *Acts,* 2:29–36; 3:18–26

18 AUGUSTINE, 319–322, 419–420, 422–423, 449–472, 486–487, 490–491, 498, 500
20 AQUINAS, 327–329
23 HOBBES, 179, 187, 204–207, 243
32 MILTON, 12–13, 325–326
33 PASCAL, 280, 282–285, 293–294, 300–322
40 GIBBON, 206, 207, 308

4*d*. The second coming of the Lord: the Day of Judgment, the end of the world, and the millenium

OLD TESTAMENT: *Job* / *Psalms,* 50; 72; 96:10–13; 97–98 / *Ecclesiastes,* 3:16–17; 11:9–10 / *Isaiah,* 2–4; 11; 24; 26:1–28:15; 30; 34–35; 65:17–25; 66 / *Daniel,* 7:21–27; 11–12 / *Joel,* 1:14–2:11 / *Micah* / *Zephaniah* / *Zechariah* / *Malachi,* 3–4

APOCRYPHA: *Tobit,* 13:9–14:15 / *Judith,* 16:17

NEW TESTAMENT: *Matthew,* 11:20–24; 12:34–36; 13:24–50; 24–25 / *Mark,* 13:4–37 / *Luke,* 17:20–37; 19:11–28; 21 / *John,* 12:48 / *Acts,* 1:9–11 / *I Corinthians,* 15:23–28 / *I Thessalonians,* 1:9–10; 4:12–5:11 / *II Thessalonians,* 1–2 / *II Timothy,* 3 / *Hebrews,* 9:26–28 / *II Peter* / *I John,* 2:18–29 / *Jude,* 14–25 / *Revelation*

18 AUGUSTINE, 504–505, 530–560, 628
20 AQUINAS, 922–926, 945–946, 1000–1004, 1016–1017
21 DANTE, 9, 136
22 CHAUCER, 498–499
23 HOBBES, 244, 248, 251–252, 254
32 MILTON, 4–5, 13, 141–143, 300–301, 329, 331
40 GIBBON, 187–188
41 GIBBON, 233–234
52 DOSTOEVSKY, 127–137

5. The criticism and rejection of prophecy: the distinction between true and false prophecy; the condemnation of astrology and divination as impiety or superstition

OLD TESTAMENT: *Deuteronomy,* 13:1–5; 18:15–22 / *I Kings,* 13:11–34; 18:17–40; 22:5–25 / *II Chronicles,* 18 / *Isaiah,* 8:18–22; 30:9–11; 41:21–29; 47:12–13 / *Jeremiah,* 2:8; 5:12–14,31; 14:13–16; 23:9–40; 27:9–18; 28; 29:8–9,29–32; 36–38 / *Ezekiel,* 13; 22:23–31 / *Daniel,* 2:1–23; 4:1–27; 5:5–17 / *Micah,* 3:5–12

NEW TESTAMENT: *Matthew,* 7:15–23; 13:54–57; 23:29–39 / *Mark,* 6:1–5 / *II Peter,* 2:1–3 / *I John,* 4:1–6

4 HOMER, 84, 189–190
5 AESCHYLUS, 54, 64–65
5 SOPHOCLES, 105–106
5 EURIPIDES, 305, 416, 433–434
5 ARISTOPHANES, 471–472, 481–483, 537–539, 554–555
6 HERODOTUS, 10, 86, 116, 273
7 PLATO, 466–467
8 ARISTOTLE, 707–709
12 LUCRETIUS, 2
12 EPICTETUS, 145–146
14 PLUTARCH, 123–124, 138, 816–817
15 TACITUS, 91, 121, 195
18 AUGUSTINE, 45–47, 207–213, 263–264, 496, 525–528, 647–649
19 AQUINAS, 589–592, 660–662
21 DANTE, 28–29
22 CHAUCER, 127, 522
23 HOBBES, 81–82, 165–167, 186–188
24 RABELAIS, 66–67, 158–171, 173–175, 215–219
25 MONTAIGNE, 18–20, 94–95, 98–99, 284–285
27 SHAKESPEARE, 249
29 CERVANTES, 381
30 BACON, 54–55
33 PASCAL, 203–204, 330–331
35 HUME, 492–493
36 STERNE, 332–334
40 GIBBON, 121, 225
46 HEGEL, 263–265, 273
48 MELVILLE, 232–235
54 FREUD, 387, 822–825

CROSS-REFERENCES

For: Other discussions of man's knowledge of the future by natural or supernatural means, *see* FATE 5–6; KNOWLEDGE 5a(5); NECESSITY AND CONTINGENCY 4c; TIME 6f; TRUTH 3b(2).

Another consideration of the religious significance of prophecy and its fulfillment, *see* RELIGION 1b(3).

Other discussions of the interpretation of oracles, omens, portents, and visions, *see* LANGUAGE 10; MEMORY AND IMAGINATION 8a; SIGN AND SYMBOL 5b; and for other treatments of dreams and their meaning, *see* LANGUAGE 10; MEMORY AND IMAGINATION 8d–8d(2); SIGN AND SYMBOL 6a.

The religious dogmas related to particular prophecies in Judaism and Christianity, *see* GOD 7h, 8b, 8e, 9f; WORLD 8.

ADDITIONAL READINGS

Listed below are works not included in *Great Books of the Western World*, but relevant to the idea and topics with which this chapter deals. These works are divided into two groups:

I. Works by authors represented in this collection.
II. Works by authors not represented in this collection.

For the date, place, and other facts concerning the publication of the works cited, consult the Bibliography of Additional Readings which follows the last chapter of *The Great Ideas.*

I.

PLUTARCH. "Wherefore the Pythian Priestess Now Ceases to Deliver Her Oracles in Verse," "Why the Oracles Cease to Give Answers," in *Moralia*

AUGUSTINE. *De Genesi ad Litteram*, BK XII, CH 9

——. *On the Spirit and the Letter*

AQUINAS. *Quaestiones Disputatae, De Veritate*, Q 12

——. *Summa Theologica*, PART II–II, QQ 171–175

F. BACON. "Of Prophecies," in *Essays*

SPINOZA. *Tractatus Theologico-Politicus (Theological-Political Treatise)*, CH 1–3, 11

NEWTON. *Daniel and the Apocalypse*

II.

CICERO. *De Divinatione (On Divination)*

TERTULLIAN. *The Prescription Against Heretics*

SAADIA GAON. *The Book of Beliefs and Opinions*, TREATISE III, VIII

MAIMONIDES. *Eight Chapters on Ethics*, CH 7

——. *The Guide for the Perplexed*, PART II, CH 32–47

CALDERÓN. *Life Is a Dream*

J. TAYLOR. *A Discourse of the Liberty of Prophesying*

FONTENELLE. *Histoire des oracles*

LEIBNITZ. *New Essays Concerning Human Understanding*, BK IV, CH 19

VOLTAIRE. "Prophecies," "Prophets," in *A Philosophical Dictionary*

PAINE. *The Age of Reason*, PART I

J. H. NEWMAN. *Lectures on the Prophetical Office of the Church*

KIERKEGAARD. *Of the Difference Between a Genius and an Apostle*

COMTE. *System of Positive Polity*, VOL IV, *Theory of the Future of Man*

W. R. SMITH. *The Prophets of Israel and Their Place in History*

FRAZER. *Psyche's Task*

LODS. *The Prophets and the Rise of Judaism*

Chapter 73: PRUDENCE

INTRODUCTION

OF the qualities or virtues attributed to the intellect, prudence seems to be least concerned with knowledge and most concerned with action. When we call a man a scientist or an artist, or praise the clarity of his understanding, we imply only that he has a certain kind of knowledge. We admire his mind, but we do not necessarily admire him as a man. We may not even know what kind of man he is or what kind of life he leads. It is significant that our language does not contain a noun like "scientist" or "artist" to describe the man who possesses prudence. We must use the adjective and speak of a prudent man, which seems to suggest that prudence belongs to the whole man, rather than just to his mind.

Prudence seems to be almost as much a moral as an intellectual quality. We would hardly call a man prudent without knowing his manner of life. Whether he behaved temperately would probably be much more relevant to our judgment of his prudence than whether he had a cultivated mind. The extent of his education or the depth of his learning might not affect our judgment at all, but we probably would consider whether he was old enough to have learned anything from experience and whether he had actually profited from experience to become wise.

These observations not only express the ordinary sense of the word "prudence," but also give a summary indication of the idea for which that word stands in the great books. Like other fundamental traits of mind or character, prudence is considered by the poets and historians in terms of precept and example. For the definition of the term or for an analysis of its relation to other fundamental ideas, such as virtue and happiness, desire and duty, one must go to the great works of moral and political theory or of theology.

Even there, however, the conception of prudence is used more frequently than it is expounded. Plato, Aristotle, Aquinas, Hobbes, and Kant seem to be the exceptions, and of these only Aristotle and Aquinas offer an extended analysis—Aristotle in his book on intellectual virtue in the *Ethics*, Aquinas in certain questions of his Treatise on Habits in the *Summa Theologica*, but more extensively in his Treatise on Prudence (see the questions from the *Summa Theologica* cited in the list of Additional Readings).

THAT PRUDENCE IS NOT knowledge in the ordinary sense of the term—that it is a product of experience and a possession of reason which, unlike science or art, cannot be expressed in propositions—seems to be clearly implied by Hobbes. "When the thoughts of a man, that has a design in hand, running over a multitude of things, observes how they conduce to that design, or what design they may conduce to; if his observations are such as are not easy or usual; this wit of his is called Prudence, and depends on much experience and memory of the like things, and their consequences heretofore."

Whereas science can achieve some certainty, the judgments of prudence are, according to Hobbes, all uncertain, "because to observe by experience and remember all circumstances that may alter the success, is impossible." It is the opposition between experience and science which seems to lead Hobbes to distinguish prudence from wisdom. "As much experience is prudence, so is much science sapience. For though we usually have one name of wisdom for them both, yet the Latins did always distinguish between *prudentia* and *sapientia*, ascribing the former to experience, the latter to science."

The Greeks also had two words—*phronesis*

and *sophia*—both of which are sometimes translated in English by "wisdom." But Aristotle, like Hobbes, insists upon the distinction between the wisdom which is the ultimate fruit of the speculative sciences or philosophy and the wisdom which belongs to the sphere of moral and political action. Wishing to preserve Aristotle's sense that *phronesis* and *sophia* have something in common which deserves the eulogistic connotation of "wisdom," his translators usually render these words in English by the phrases "practical wisdom" or "political wisdom" (for *phronesis*), and "speculative wisdom" or "philosophical wisdom" (for *sophia*). The English rendering of Aquinas, on the other hand, usually translates his *prudentia* by "prudence," and his *sapientia* by "wisdom."

Whether it is permissible to use "prudence" and "practical wisdom" as synonyms may be more than a question of verbal equivalence; for there is a fundamental issue in theory concerning the unity of wisdom, on which Plato differs from both Aristotle and Aquinas. The question about the relation of knowledge and virtue may be differently answered according to the view of wisdom which denies its division into speculative and practical, and according to the view which conceives the possibility that a man may be wise in one way without being wise in the other. In the language of Aquinas, a man may have acquired wisdom through science and understanding without having the moral character of a prudent man.

"That practical wisdom is not scientific knowledge is evident," Aristotle declares. This is confirmed, he adds, "by the fact that while young men become geometricians and mathematicians and wise in matters like these, it is thought that a young man of practical wisdom cannot be found. The reason is that such wisdom is concerned not only with universals but with particulars, which become familiar from experience, but a young man has no experience, for it is length of time that gives experience."

Hobbes and Aristotle seem to agree that experience is important for the development of prudence or practical wisdom precisely because "it is practical and practice is concerned with particulars." But though both also agree that this explains the distinction between prudence and scientific knowledge—which is concerned not with action but with the nature of things—Aristotle alone raises a further question about the distinction between practical wisdom and art.

In making something, the artist also deals with particulars. In this sense, art is also practical. But, according to Aristotle, the word "productive" should be used in distinction from "practical" to signify the difference between making and doing—two kinds of human activity which, though alike as compared with scientific knowing, represent knowledge differently applied. The knowledge which the artist possesses can, furthermore, be formulated in a set of rules. An individual can acquire the skill of an art by practicing according to its rules. What a man knows when he is prudent seems to be much less capable of being communicated by precept or rule. What he knows is how to deliberate or calculate well about things to be done.

This, in Aristotle's view, marks prudence off from all other virtues. That prudence is a quality of mind seems to follow from the fact that it involves deliberation, a kind of thinking about variable and contingent particulars of the same sort which belong to the realm of opinion. That prudence is also a moral quality, an aspect of character, seems to follow no less from Aristotle's statement that prudence is not deliberation about the means to any sort of end, but only about those "which conduce to the good life in general."

PRUDENCE IS NOT ALWAYS described as skill of mind in deliberating about alternative courses of action, nor is it always regarded as entirely praiseworthy or admirable—inseparable from virtue and the good life.

It is, for example, sometimes identified with foresight or even conjecturing about the future. So conceived, prudence does not seem to require rational power so much as memory and imagination, in order to project past experience into the future. In this sense, Aristotle admits it may be said that "even some of the lower animals have practical wisdom, *viz.*, those which are found to have a power of foresight with regard to their own life."

Identifying prudence with foresight, Hobbes conceives perfect prudence as belonging only to God. When the event answers expectations, the prediction is attributed to prudence, yet human foresight being fallible, "it is but presumption. For the foresight of things to come, which is Providence, belongs only to him by whose will they are to come." Aquinas gives a quite different reason for saying that "prudence or providence may suitably be attributed to God." It is that the ordering of things toward their ultimate end is "the chief part of prudence, to which two other parts are directed —namely, remembrance of the past, and understanding of the present; inasmuch from the remembrance of what is past and the understanding of what is present, we gather how to provide for the future."

Prudence is sometimes described, not as a virtue of the mind, or even as the power of foresight, but as a temperamental trait, an emotional disposition. It is associated with timidity or caution in those who are fearful of risks or unwilling to take chances. It is in this sense that Bacon seems to oppose hopefulness to prudence, "which is diffident upon principle and in all human matters augurs the worst." The cautiousness of the over-deliberate man may involve thought as well as fear. Hamlet thinks too much and on too many sides of every action. His action being "sicklied o'er by the pale cast of thought," he is irresolute. He laments his misuse of reason. "Whether it be bestial oblivion, or some craven scruple of thinking too precisely on the event—a thought, which quartered, hath but one part wisdom and ever three parts coward—I do not know why yet I live to say 'this thing's to do,' since I have cause, and will, and strength, and means to do it."

When prudence is conceived as excessive caution, its opposite is usually described as rashness, precipitateness, or impetuosity. Thucydides portrays these opposites in the persons of Nicias and Alcibiades. Their speeches to the Athenian assembly on the question of the Sicilian expedition do not merely present an opposition of reasons for and against the undertaking, but also represent an opposition of types of human character. Both come to grief: Nicias, the overcautious leader of the expedition, who earns a not inevitable defeat by his ever-delaying tactics, and Alcibiades, who does not stop at treachery or treason when the moment seems ripe for action which, if quickly taken, may succeed.

Aristotle and Aquinas would use such facts to argue against what, in their view, is the misconception of the prudent man as the opposite of the impetuous. The prudent man, in their opinion, does not stand at the other extreme of undue caution. In their theory of the virtues as means between extremes of excess and defect, prudence, like courage or temperance, represents a mean consisting in neither too much nor too little. As cowardice and foolhardiness are the opposite vices of too much and too little fear—and as both are opposed to the mean of courage which involves a moderation of fear—so excessive caution and impetuosity are the vices opposed to prudence as well as to each other.

Nor are prudence and imprudence simply matters of temperament. Men may differ in their temperamental dispositions; but, according to Aristotle and Aquinas, these are not to be confused with virtues and vices. One man may be by nature more fearful or fearless than another, but regardless of these differences in emotional endowment, either may become courageous, by forming the habit of controlling fear for the right reasons. So, too, one man may be naturally more impulsive or more circumspect than another, but either can acquire prudence through learning to take sufficient counsel and to deliberate enough before action, while also forming the habit of resolving thought into action by reaching decisions and commanding their execution. Failing to satisfy these conditions of prudence, either may develop the vices of imprudence, becoming, like Hamlet or Nicias, irresolute; or, like Alcibiades, impatient of counsel or ill advised, lacking care in deliberation and soundness in judgment.

THE CONCEPTION OF prudence as itself the extreme of caution, whether temperamental or habitual, is not the only challenge to the Aristotelian theory of prudence as a virtue. Other moralists, especially those who take a different view of virtue generally, do not seem to look upon prudence as wholly admirable. Even when they do not condemn prudence as an indisposition to act promptly or decisively enough, they seem to give prudent deliberation the invidious connotation of cold and selfish calculation.

A suggestion of this appears in Mill's contrast between duties to ourselves and duties to others, wherein he remarks that "the term duty to oneself, when it means anything more than prudence, means self-respect and self-development." It would seem to be implied that prudence means something less—something more selfish—than a proper and justifiable self-interest, the violation of which involves "a breach of duty to others, for whose sake the individual is bound to have care for himself."

Kant, more explicitly than Mill, associates prudence with expediency and self-seeking, and separates it from action in accordance with duty under the categorical imperative of the moral law. Prudence has meaning only in relation to a hypothetical imperative "which expresses the practical necessity of an action as a means to the advancement of happiness." Granted that a man seeks his individual happiness, then "skill in the choice of means to his own greatest well-being may be called *prudence.*" Consequently, "the imperative which refers to the choice of means to one's happiness, *i.e.*, the precept of prudence, is still always hypothetical; the action is not commanded absolutely, but only as a means to another purpose," or, as Kant says elsewhere, "the maxim of self-love (prudence) only *advises*; the law of morality *commands.*" Furthermore, he holds that "what *duty* is, is plain of itself to everyone; but what it is to bring true durable advantage, such as will extend to the whole of one's existence, is always veiled in impenetrable obscurity, and much prudence is required to adapt the practical rule founded on it to the ends of life, even tolerably, by making exceptions."

In terms of Kant's division of the imperatives of conduct into the pragmatic and the moral, according as they refer to welfare and happiness or duty and law, prudence is merely pragmatic. It does not belong to morality. The pragmatic imperative of prudence is more like the technical imperative of art, which is also conditional and concerned with determining means to an end—in this case, the thing to be produced by skill. "If it were only equally easy to give a definite conception of happiness, the imperatives of prudence would correspond exactly with those of skill."

As Kant sees it, "the sole business of reason in the moral philosophy of prudence is to bring about a union of all the ends, which are aimed at by our inclinations, into one ultimate end—that of *happiness*, and to show the agreement which should exist among the means of attaining that end. In this sphere, accordingly, reason cannot present to us any more than *pragmatical* laws of free action, for our guidance towards the aims set up by the senses, and is incompetent to give us the laws which are pure and determined completely *a priori.*" Hence the precepts of prudence "are used by reason only as counsels, and by way of counterpoise against seductions to an opposite course."

The issue between Kant and Aristotle (or Aquinas) with respect to prudence thus appears to be part of the larger issue between them on the fundamental principles of morality, discussed in the chapters on DUTY and HAPPINESS. In Kant's view, Aristotle and Aquinas, no less than Mill, are pragmatists rather than moralists. They are all utilitarians in the sense that they regard happiness as the first principle of human conduct and concern themselves with the ordering of means to this end. Since the consideration of means necessarily involves the weighing of alternatives as more or less expedient, prudence becomes indispensable to the pursuit of happiness. The choice of the best means is second in importance only to the election of the right end.

Kant admits that those who live for happiness require a great deal of prudence, in order to adapt practical rules to variable circumstances and to make the proper exceptions in applying them. None is required by those who live according to the moral law. "The moral law commands the most punctual obedience from everyone; it must, therefore, not be so difficult to judge what it requires to be done, that the commonest unpracticed understanding, even without worldly prudence, should fail to apply it rightly." That "the principle of *private* happiness" is "the direct opposite of the principle of morality" Kant seems to think is evident from the questionable worth of prudence; "for a man must have a different criterion when he is compelled to say to himself: I am a *worthless* fellow, though I have filled my purse; and when he approves himself, and says: I am a *prudent* man, for I have enriched my treasure."

Kant does not limit his criticism of prudence as pragmatic—or practical rather than moral—to the fact that it serves what he calls "private happiness." It may serve the public welfare. "A history is composed pragmatically," he writes, "when it teaches *prudence, i.e.*, instructs the world how it can provide for its interests better." But he also distinguishes between worldly and private prudence. "The former is a man's ability to influence others so as to use them for his own purposes. The latter is the sagacity to combine all these purposes for his own lasting benefit." Nevertheless, the prudence which aims at individual happiness is primary, for "when a man is prudent in the former sense, but not in the latter, we might better say of him that he is clever and cunning, but, on the whole, imprudent."

THOSE WHO TAKE THE view that happiness is the first principle of morality would still agree with Kant that the man who is skillful in exercising an influence over other men so as to *use* them for his own purposes, is clever or cunning rather than prudent. Hobbes, for example, says that if you permit to prudence "the use of unjust or dishonest means . . . you have that Crooked Wisdom, which is called Craft." Aristotle goes even further in his insistence that "it is impossible to be practically wise without being good," or, as the same point is made in the language of Aquinas, "one cannot have prudence unless one has the moral virtues; since prudence is right reason about things to be done, to which end man is rightly disposed by moral virtue."

"To be able to do the things that tend towards the mark we have set before ourselves" is, according to Aristotle, to be clever. "If the mark be noble, the cleverness is laudable, but if the mark be bad, the cleverness is mere smartness." Hence the man of prudence has a certain cleverness, but the clever man who is merely smart cannot be called practically wise. By this criterion the clever thief who plans and executes a successful robbery, the shrewd businessman who, without regard to justice, calculates well how to maximize his profits, or Machiavelli's prince who exercises cunning to get or keep his power, exhibits, not prudence, but its counterfeits. In some cases, the cleverness or shrewdness may simulate prudence without involving the knavery of craft or cunning. Some men have what Aquinas conceives as artistic (or technical) rather than moral prudence. Those who are "good counsellors in matters of warfare or seamanship are said to be prudent officers or pilots, but not simply prudent. Only those are simply prudent who give good counsel about all the concerns of life."

Aristotle and Aquinas make the relation between prudence and moral virtue reciprocal. The moral virtues depend, for their formation and endurance, as much upon prudence as prudence depends upon them. "Virtue makes us aim at the right end," Aristotle writes, "and practical wisdom makes us take the right means." The rightness of the means requires not merely that they be adapted to an end, but that the end itself be right. The right end cannot be achieved unless the means to it be rightly chosen. Hence no skill of mind in deliberating about and choosing means is truly the intellectual virtue of prudence unless the man who habitually calculates well is also habitually inclined by the moral virtues to choose things for the right end, whether that be happiness or the common good of society.

Conversely, the moral virtues depend upon prudence because, in Aristotle's view, they are formed by the making of right choices. His definition of moral virtue names prudence as an indispensable cause. Since the mean between extremes, in which the virtues consist, is in most cases subjective or relative to the individual, it cannot be determined by objective measurements. Reason must determine it by a prudent consideration of the relevant circumstances.

The interdependence of prudence and the moral virtues seems to be the basis, for both Aristotle and Aquinas, of the insight that it is impossible to have one moral virtue without having all. On this basis, Aristotle says, we can "refute the dialectical argument . . . that the virtues exist in separation from one another."

As no moral virtue can exist apart from practical wisdom, so with it, all must be present.

Aquinas mentions another intellectual virtue as indispensable to the moral virtues, namely, the virtue of understanding which consists in knowing the first principles in practical as well as speculative matters. The first principles of the practical reason (*i.e.*, the precepts of the natural law) underlie prudence as well as the moral virtues. Just as sound reasoning in speculative matters "proceeds from naturally known principles . . . so also does prudence which is right reason about things to be done." Nevertheless, though prudence and the moral virtues depend upon it, Aquinas does not include understanding—as he does not include art, science, and wisdom—in his enumeration of the four cardinal virtues, cardinal in the sense of being the virtues indispensable to a good human life.

THESE MATTERS, especially the interconnection of the virtues and the theory of the cardinal virtues, are discussed in the chapter on VIRTUE. The problem of the relative worth of the moral and the intellectual virtues is also considered there and in the chapter on WISDOM, where the contributions to happiness of prudence and wisdom—or of practical and speculative wisdom—are specifically compared.

Here there remains to be considered the Socratic conception of the relation between knowledge and virtue, for there seems to be an issue between his theory of this matter and the foregoing view of the relation between prudence and the moral virtues.

In the *Meno*, Socrates argues that whatever a man desires or chooses he either knows or deems to be good. The man who chooses something evil for himself does not do so knowingly, but only through the mistake of deeming that which is in fact evil to be advantageous or good. Except for such mistakes, "no man," says Socrates, "wills or chooses anything evil." Apart from error or ignorance, evil is never voluntarily chosen. Hence, if virtue consists "in willing or desiring things which are good, and in having the power to gain them," it would seem to follow that knowledge of the good is closely related to its practice.

Subsequently, Socrates suggests that "if there be any sort of good which is distinct from knowledge, virtue may be that good; but if knowledge embraces all good, then we shall be right in thinking that virtue is knowledge." To test these hypotheses, he proceeds to consider the various things which—whether or not they are the same as virtue—are like virtue in being advantageous to men. None of these things, such as courage or temperance, seems to profit men unless accompanied by what, in English translations, is sometimes called "wisdom" and sometimes "prudence."

Socrates points out that "everything the soul attempts, when under the guidance of wisdom"—or prudence—"ends in happiness; but in the opposite when under the guidance of folly"—or imprudence. "If then," he says, "virtue is a quality of the soul, and if it be of necessity always advantageous, then virtue must be wisdom or prudence, since none of the things of the soul are either advantageous or hurtful in themselves, but they are all made advantageous or hurtful by the addition to them of prudence or imprudence"—wisdom or folly. From this, says Socrates, we can conclude that "prudence is virtue, either the whole of virtue or some part of it at least"—or, as this is sometimes translated, "virtue is either wholly or partly wisdom."

In the light of his own view that all the moral virtues depend on practical wisdom, Aristotle criticizes the Socratic position. "Socrates in one respect was on the right track while in another he went astray. In thinking that all the virtues were forms of practical wisdom he was wrong, but in saying that they implied practical wisdom he was right . . . Socrates thought the virtues were rules or rational principles . . . while we think they involve a rational principle." Similarly, in considering the question whether there can be moral without intellectual virtue, Aquinas writes: "Although virtue be not right reason, as Socrates held, yet not only is it *according to right reason*, insofar as it inclines a man to do that which is in accord with right reason as the Platonists maintained; but it also needs to be *joined with right reason*, as Aristotle declares."

Aquinas furthermore interprets the opinion that "every virtue is a kind of prudence," which he attributes to Socrates, as meaning that when "a man is in possession of knowledge, he cannot sin, and that everyone who sins does so through ignorance." This, he says, "is based on a false supposition, because the appetitive faculty obeys the reason, not blindly, but with a certain power of opposition." Nevertheless, "there is some truth in the saying of Socrates that so long as a man is in possession of knowledge he does not sin; provided that this knowledge involves the use of reason in the individual act of choice."

Whether those who criticize the position of Socrates accurately perceive his intention and state the issue fairly are problems of interpretation as difficult as the question of where in this matter the truth lies. If Socrates is saying that a man will do good if he knows the good, what sort of knowledge is implied—knowledge of the good in general or knowledge of what is good in a particular case? Do both types of knowledge of the good lead as readily or surely to good or virtuous action?

Whether or not, in addition to knowledge, a good will or right desire is essential, it may be held that prudence is required to apply moral principles—aiming at the good in general—to particular cases. "There exists no moral system," writes Mill, "under which there do not arise unequivocal cases of conflicting obligation. These are the real difficulties, the knotty points, both in the theory of ethics and in the conscientious guidance of personal conduct. They are overcome practically, with great or less success, according to the intellect and virtue of the individual." Mill seems to imply that both prudence and virtue are essential to good action on the level of particulars, and that without them the kind of knowledge which is expressed in moral principles does not necessarily lead a man to act well.

ONE OTHER PROBLEM OF INTERPRETATION must be mentioned. It occurs with respect to Aristotle's statement concerning diverse modes of prudence.

"Political wisdom and practical wisdom are the same state of mind," he writes, "but their essence is not the same. Of the wisdom concerned with the city, the practical wisdom which plays a controlling part is legislative wisdom, while that which is related to this as particulars to their universal is known by the general name of 'political wisdom' . . . Practical wisdom also is identified especially with that form of it which is concerned with the individual man, and this is known by the general name 'practical wisdom.' Of the other kinds, one is called domestic, another legislative, a third political; and of this last, one part is called deliberative and the other judicial."

Does this mean that skill of mind in determining the best means to an end is different according to differences in the end—whether the happiness of an individual or the common good of a society? Does it mean, furthermore, that the prudence involved in managing a household is different from the prudence concerned with political affairs; and that, in the state, the prudence of the ruler (prince or statesman) is different from the prudence of the ruled (subject or citizen), because the one moves on the level of general laws, the other on the level of particular acts in compliance with law? Within the sphere of jurisprudence, or the prudence of laws, is the prudence of the legislator or lawmaker different from the prudence of the judge who applies the law?

In his Treatise on Prudence, Aquinas answers these questions affirmatively. He distinguishes between private, domestic, and political prudence, and within the political sphere places special emphasis upon what he calls "reignative prudence," the sort of prudence Dante calls "a kingly prudence," which sets the prince apart from ordinary men. Hobbes, on the other hand, asserts that "to govern well a family and a kingdom, are not different degrees of prudence, but different sorts of business; no more than to draw a picture in little, or as great, or greater than life, are different degrees of art."

This issue is intimately connected with the problem of the forms of government. If only a few men are fitted by nature to acquire the special mode of prudence which is reignative or legislative, would not government by the few or by the one seem to be naturally best? If, however, in a republic, those who are citizens rule and are ruled in turn, should not each citizen have the prudence requisite for both tasks, whether it be the same or different? Finally, if the democratic theory is that all men are capable of being citizens—though not all, perhaps, are equally eligible for the highest public offices—must not political prudence be conceived as attainable by all men?

The question remains open whether those who deserve the highest magistracies have a special mode of reignative prudence; or merely a higher degree of the same prudence by which they govern their private lives and their domestic establishments; or, as Hobbes suggests, have other abilities whereby they can apply the same prudence to a different kind of business.

OUTLINE OF TOPICS

1. The nature of prudence: as practical wisdom, as a virtue or quality of the deliberative mind

2. The place of prudence among the virtues of the mind

   2*a*. Practical or political wisdom distinguished from speculative or philosophical wisdom

   2*b*. Prudence distinguished from art: action or doing contrasted with production or making

   2*c*. The relation of prudence to intuitive reason or to the understanding of the natural law: the moral perception of particulars

3. The interdependence of prudence and the moral virtues: the parts played by deliberation, will, and emotion in human conduct

   3*a*. Moral virtue as determining the end for which prudence makes a right choice of means: right desire as the standard of practical truth

   3*b*. Prudence as a factor in the formation and maintenance of moral virtue: the determination of the relative or subjective mean

   3*c*. Shrewdness or cleverness as the counterfeit of prudence: the abuses of casuistry

   3*d*. Prudence, continence, and temperance

   3*e*. The vices of imprudence: precipitance and undue caution

4. The sphere of prudence

   4*a*. The confinement of prudence to the things within our power: the relation of prudence to free will, choice, and deliberation

   4*b*. The restriction of prudence to the consideration of means rather than ends

5. The nature of a prudent judgment

   5*a*. The conditions of prudent choice: counsel, deliberation, judgment

   5*b*. The acts of the practical reason in matters open to choice: decision and command, leading to execution or use

   5*c*. The maxims of prudence

6. Prudence in relation to the common good of the community

   6*a*. Political prudence: the prudence of the prince or statesman, of the subject or citizen

   6*b*. Jurisprudence: prudence in the determination of laws and the adjudication of cases

REFERENCES

References are listed by volume number (in bold type), author's name, and page number. Bible references are to book, chapter, and verse of the Authorized King James version of the Bible. The abbreviation "esp" calls the reader's attention to one or more especially relevant parts of a whole reference; "passim" signifies that the topic is discussed intermittently rather than continuously in the work or passage cited. Where the work as a whole is relevant to the topic, the page numbers refer to the entire work. For general guidance in the use of *The Great Ideas*, consult the Preface.

1. The nature of prudence: as practical wisdom, as a virtue or quality of the deliberative mind

APOCRYPHA: *Ecclesiasticus*, 34:9–10
6 THUCYDIDES, 383–384
7 PLATO, 188–189
9 ARISTOTLE, 389, 390, 609
12 EPICTETUS, 228–230
12 AURELIUS, 258, 270, 273, 289
20 AQUINAS, 42–44
22 CHAUCER, 401–432
23 HOBBES, 53–54, 67–68
25 MONTAIGNE, 520
30 BACON, 81–95
42 KANT, 266, 267, 361
53 JAMES, 13–15

2. The place of prudence among the virtues of the mind

2*a*. Practical or political wisdom distinguished from speculative or philosophical wisdom

7 PLATO, 581–582
9 ARISTOTLE, 344, 387–388, 390–391, 393–394, 615
19 AQUINAS, 6–7
20 AQUINAS, 79–80
23 HOBBES, 60–61, 84, 267
25 MONTAIGNE, 327
30 BACON, 16–17, 55
31 DESCARTES, 44
35 LOCKE, 94–95
35 HUME, 451–453
42 KANT, 60, 190–191, 260–261, 271, 291–296, 319–321, 329–330, 388, 390–391
43 MILL, 346–347
46 HEGEL, 4–7

2*b*. Prudence distinguished from art: action or doing contrasted with production or making

7 PLATO, 5–6, 633–635
9 ARISTOTLE, 388–389
19 AQUINAS, 768–769
20 AQUINAS, 38–39, 42–43, 70–72
30 BACON, 42
42 KANT, 515, 523–524

2*c*. The relation of prudence to intuitive reason or to the understanding of the natural law: the moral perception of particulars

9 ARISTOTLE, 343–344, 358–359, 389, 392–393, 397
20 AQUINAS, 31–32, 38–40

3. The interdependence of prudence and the moral virtues: the parts played by deliberation, will, and emotion in human conduct

4 HOMER, 183–322
5 AESCHYLUS, 40–51
5 SOPHOCLES, 182–195
5 EURIPIDES, 228
6 THUCYDIDES, 370
7 PLATO, 48–50, 58–64, 174–176, 183–184
9 ARISTOTLE, 349, 351–352 passim, 393–394, 402–403
12 AURELIUS, 257
20 AQUINAS, 44–45, 54–59
25 MONTAIGNE, 20–22, 159–162
27 SHAKESPEARE, 59
30 BACON, 86–95
31 DESCARTES, 48–51
35 LOCKE, 189–192
37 FIELDING, 395–396
42 KANT, 260, 266–267, 305–307, 318, 339, 341–342
46 HEGEL, 42, 166
49 DARWIN, 310–313
51 TOLSTOY, 211–213
53 JAMES, 794–808

3*a*. Moral virtue as determining the end for which prudence makes a right choice of means: right desire as the standard of practical truth

9 ARISTOTLE, 349, 387–388, 389, 391–392, 394, 536
14 PLUTARCH, 121–122
19 AQUINAS, 576
20 AQUINAS, 31–33, 39–40, 44–45, 70–73, 617–618
25 MONTAIGNE, 52–53
42 KANT, 235, 256, 259–260, 271–279, 357–360
43 MILL, 456–457
46 HEGEL, 49–54

3*b*. Prudence as a factor in the formation and maintenance of moral virtue: the determination of the relative or subjective mean

7 Plato, 61–62, 226, 439, 643
9 Aristotle, 352, 354–355, 385, 389, 391–392
12 Epictetus, 187–188
12 Aurelius, 275
18 Augustine, 287–288
20 Aquinas, 39–40, 42–43, 44
29 Cervantes, 256
31 Descartes, 48–51
33 Pascal, 235, 238
42 Kant, 305–307, 365, 376–377, 387–388
46 Hegel, 49–54

3*c*. Shrewdness or cleverness as the counterfeit of prudence: the abuses of casuistry

6 Herodotus, 95–96, 279–280
6 Thucydides, 575, 584–585
9 Aristotle, 393–394, 403
20 Aquinas, 219–220
23 Machiavelli, 25
27 Shakespeare, 212–213
33 Pascal, 27–127
41 Gibbon, 532–533
51 Tolstoy, 204–206, 228–230, 476–480

3*d*. Prudence, continence, and temperance

7 Plato, 59–62
9 Aristotle, 366, 389, 391–392, 395–398, 399–400, 401–403
18 Augustine, 512
20 Aquinas, 43–44
25 Montaigne, 312–314
32 Milton, 310–311

3*e*. The vices of imprudence: precipitance and undue caution

Old Testament: *Genesis,* 25:29–34 / *Proverbs,* 7:6–27; 14:16; 29:11 / *Ecclesiastes,* 5:2–3
Apocrypha: *Ecclesiasticus,* 4:29; 6:7–8; 8:19; 21:25–26; 28:11
New Testament: *Matthew,* 13:19–23
4 Homer, 234, 252–254
5 Aeschylus, 15–26, 27–39, 42–44, 50–51
5 Sophocles, 99–113, 131–142, 143–155, 156–169, 182–195
5 Euripides, 203–211, 262, 340–352, 381–383
6 Herodotus, 94, 97, 216–218, 225
6 Thucydides, 370, 393, 402–404, 449, 507
7 Plato, 62–64
9 Aristotle, 399–400, 402, 636–638
13 Virgil, 252
14 Plutarch, 232–233, 244–245, 423–438, 690–691
15 Tacitus, 205–206, 252
20 Aquinas, 334–336
21 Dante, 38–39
22 Chaucer, 60, 450–460, 491–493
23 Hobbes, 77, 79
25 Montaigne, 22–23, 174
26 Shakespeare, 304–306, 437–440, 443–444, 451–452
27 Shakespeare, 29–72, 124–125, 205–243, 244–283, 393–420, 551
29 Cervantes, 8–10, 116–117, 252–257, 291
30 Bacon, 125
33 Pascal, 203
36 Sterne, 203–207
48 Melville, 148–150
51 Tolstoy, 15–18, 139, 321–322, 328–333, 336–337, 569–570, 596, 603–604
52 Dostoevsky, 273
53 James, 799–807

4. The sphere of prudence

4*a*. The confinement of prudence to the things within our power: the relation of prudence to free will, choice, and deliberation

9 Aristotle, 357–359
12 Epictetus, 105–106, 124–125, 134–138, 142–144, 148–150, 177–178, 192, 213–223
12 Aurelius, 259, 280, 286, 301, 307
19 Aquinas, 675–677
23 Machiavelli, 35
25 Montaigne, 100–101, 136–139, 451–452
30 Bacon, 76–78
35 Locke, 190–192
42 Kant, 266–267, 318–321
53 James, 199–201

4*b*. The restriction of prudence to the consideration of means rather than ends

9 Aristotle, 385, 389
19 Aquinas, 678, 682–683
20 Aquinas, 44
42 Kant, 266–267

5. The nature of a prudent judgment

5*a*. The conditions of prudent choice: counsel, deliberation, judgment

Old Testament: *Proverbs,* 11:14; 13:10,16; 15:22; 20:5, 18
Apocrypha: *Ecclesiasticus* passim
5 Aeschylus, 5–7
5 Sophocles, 136–137
5 Euripides, 381–383, 384, 428
6 Herodotus, 219, 258, 269–270
7 Thucydides, 397, 427
7 Plato, 337–338, 439–441
9 Aristotle, 340, 357–359, 390, 391–393
12 Aurelius, 264
14 Plutarch, 197–198
15 Tacitus, 234
19 Aquinas, 436–439, 672–673, 674–675, 677–681, 808
20 Aquinas, 38–39, 40–41
22 Chaucer, 12–13, 401–432

23 HOBBES, 64, 65, 66–68
25 MONTAIGNE, 393–394, 520–522
27 SHAKESPEARE, 113–115
33 PASCAL, 238
35 LOCKE, 190, 193, 196–197
35 HUME, 465
42 KANT, 318–321, 357–360
43 FEDERALIST, 32
43 MILL, 276–277, 456–457
46 HEGEL, 74
53 JAMES, 794–798
54 FREUD, 624–625

5*b*. The acts of the practical reason in matters open to choice: decision and command, leading to execution or use

8 ARISTOTLE, 665–666
9 ARISTOTLE, 357–359, 387–388, 393–394, 395–396, 403
19 AQUINAS, 127–128, 686–693
20 AQUINAS, 40–41, 56–57
42 KANT, 260, 265–267, 314–321
46 HEGEL, 21
51 TOLSTOY, 411–412, 459–461, 488–489, 584–585, 586–587
53 JAMES, 794–798

5*c*. The maxims of prudence

OLD TESTAMENT: *Proverbs* / *Ecclesiastes*
APOCRYPHA: *Ecclesiasticus*, 1–43 passim
NEW TESTAMENT: *Matthew*, 6:19–34 / *Luke*, 12:13–32 / *I Corinthians*, 7:29–35 / *Ephesians*, 5:15–16
5 AESCHYLUS, 34–35, 49, 50–51
5 SOPHOCLES, 157–159, 163–164
6 THUCYDIDES, 507
22 CHAUCER, 14–16, 18–19, 85
25 MONTAIGNE, 51–55
26 SHAKESPEARE, 535–536
27 SHAKESPEARE, 35
29 CERVANTES, 331–333
30 BACON, 81–95
31 DESCARTES, 48–51
31 SPINOZA, 438
43 MILL, 345, 410

6. Prudence in relation to the common good of the community

6*a*. Political prudence: the prudence of the prince or statesman, of the subject or citizen

OLD TESTAMENT: *Genesis*, 41:33–41 / *I Kings*, 3:16–28 / *Proverbs*, 29:12; 31:4–5
APOCRYPHA: *Ecclesiasticus*, 10:1–3
4 HOMER, 3–8, 57–58
5 AESCHYLUS, 5–7, 15–26
5 SOPHOCLES, 99–103, 131–132, 136–137, 182–195
5 EURIPIDES, 203–211, 259–263, 342, 400–401, 425–439
5 ARISTOPHANES, 460–461, 470–487, 572, 581–582
6 HERODOTUS, 41, 216–218, 225–226
6 THUCYDIDES, 365–367, 389–391, 436–438, 451, 474, 483–485, 511–516, 569–570
7 PLATO, 604–608, 669–670, 754, 813–814
9 ARISTOTLE, 434–436, 473–475, 479–480, 498–499, 509–518, 528–530
12 EPICTETUS, 182–184
12 AURELIUS, 261, 264, 280, 293, 303
13 VIRGIL, 336–340
14 PLUTARCH, 129–141, 540–576, 604–605, 689–691, 824–826
15 TACITUS, 193, 211–212
21 DANTE, 126
23 MACHIAVELLI, 1–37
25 MONTAIGNE, 51–55, 381–388, 488–489, 490–491
26 SHAKESPEARE, 453, 472–474, 576, 587
27 SHAKESPEARE, 318, 351–392
30 BACON, 4–6, 20–26, 74, 81–82, 94–95
35 LOCKE, 61–62
36 SWIFT, 28–29, 112–115
38 ROUSSEAU, 368, 373–374
39 SMITH, 109–110
40 GIBBON, 1–2, 50, 331–332, 609–610
43 FEDERALIST, 130–132, 190–191
43 MILL, 334
44 BOSWELL, 255–256
46 HEGEL, 145, 271–272
51 TOLSTOY, 9–10, 65–66, 421–426, 440–442

6*b*. Jurisprudence: prudence in the determination of laws and the adjudication of cases

5 AESCHYLUS, 85–89
5 ARISTOPANES, 507–525
6 HERODOTUS, 32
7 PLATO, 200–212, 544, 599–603, 744, 784, 792
9 ARISTOTLE, 385–386, 464, 480, 484, 593
14 PLUTARCH, 70–71
15 TACITUS, 61–62
18 AUGUSTINE, 514–515
20 AQUINAS, 209–210, 223–224, 226–227, 227–229, 235, 236–237, 238–239, 309–316
23 HOBBES, 123, 134–136
24 RABELAIS, 85–92
25 MONTAIGNE, 283, 516–517
26 SHAKESPEARE, 425–430
27 SHAKESPEARE, 178–184
29 CERVANTES, 340–343, 353–356, 360–361
33 PASCAL, 27–62, 90–99, 102–117
36 SWIFT, 152–154
38 MONTESQUIEU, 33–35, 214–215
40 GIBBON, 244–245, 343
41 GIBBON, 75–78
42 KANT, 397, 399–400
43 FEDERALIST, 198–200, 231–232
46 HEGEL, 71, 73–75, 138
48 MELVILLE, 292–295
52 DOSTOEVSKY, 348–401

CROSS-REFERENCES

For: The distinction between prudence and wisdom, or between practical and speculative wisdom, *see* KNOWLEDGE 6e(1); MIND 9a; PHILOSOPHY 2a; WISDOM 1b.

The relation of prudence to the other intellectual virtues, *see* ART 1; HABIT 5d; KNOWLEDGE 6e(2), 8b(3); LAW 4a; SCIENCE 1a(1); VIRTUE AND VICE 2a(2); WISDOM 2a.

The relation of prudence to the moral virtues, *see* COURAGE 4; KNOWLEDGE 8b(1); PRINCIPLE 4a; TEMPERANCE 1b; TRUTH 2c; VIRTUE AND VICE 1c, 3b, 5b.

The relevance of freedom and of the distinction between means and ends to the operations of prudence, *see* GOOD AND EVIL 5c; NECESSITY AND CONTINGENCY 5a(1)–5a(2); WILL 2c(1)–2c(3), 5b(2).

The elements which enter into the making of a prudent judgment, *see* EXPERIENCE 6a; JUDGMENT 3; OPINION 6b; REASONING 5e(3); WILL 2c(3), 5b(2).

Considerations of the prudence of the statesman or citizen, and of the legislator or jurist, *see* CITIZEN 5; GOVERNMENT 3d; LAW 5d, 5g; MONARCHY 3a; STATE 8d.

ADDITIONAL READINGS

Listed below are works not included in *Great Books of the Western World*, but relevant to the idea and topics with which this chapter deals. These works are divided into two groups:

I. Works by authors represented in this collection.
II. Works by authors not represented in this collection.

For the date, place, and other facts concerning the publication of the works cited, consult the Bibliography of Additional Readings which follows the last chapter of *The Great Ideas*.

I.

AUGUSTINE. *On the Morals of the Catholic Church*, CH I, XXIV

AQUINAS. *Summa Theologica*, PART II–II, QQ 47–56, 155–156

F. BACON. "Of Counsel," in *Essays*

A. SMITH. *The Theory of Moral Sentiments*, PART VI, SECT I

KANT. *Lectures on Ethics*

J. S. MILL. *A System of Logic*, BK VI, CH 12

II.

HORACE. *Epistles*

PERKINS. *The Whole Treatise of the Cases of Conscience*

GRÁCIAN Y MORALES. *The Art of Worldly Wisdom*

SANDERSON. *De Obligatione Conscientiae* (*On the Obligations of Conscience*)

J. TAYLOR. *Ductor Dubitantium*

MOLIÈRE. *L'école des femmes* (*The School for Wives*)

SHAFTESBURY. *Characteristics of Men, Manners, Opinions, Times*, TREATISE IV

J. BUTLER. *Fifteen Sermons upon Human Nature*

CHESTERFIELD. *Letters to His Son*

S. JOHNSON. *History of Rasselas*

BENTHAM. *An Introduction to the Principles of Morals and Legislation*

EMERSON. *The Conduct of Life*

MAURICE. *The Conscience*

HODGSON. *The Theory of Practice*

H. SIDGWICK. *The Methods of Ethics*, BK II

SPENCER. *The Principles of Ethics*, PART I, CH I, 13

L. STEPHEN. *The Science of Ethics*, CH 6 (4), 9 (5)

BONAR. *The Intellectual Virtues*

DEWEY. *The Study of Ethics*, CH 5–6

LECKY. *The Map of Life*, CH 6, 8–9, 11

SANTAYANA. *Reason in Common Sense*, CH 9

ADLER. *Art and Prudence*, PART III, CH 12

Chapter 74: PUNISHMENT

INTRODUCTION

THE problem of punishment divides into a number of questions. In what does punishment consist? What purpose should punishment serve, or what should be its principle or reason? Who has the authority to punish and under what conditions shall this authority be exercised? Who shall be punished and who shall be exempt from punishment? What are the forms or kinds of punishment? Are any of these reprehensible either in principle or for their consequences? Should there be a proportion between the severity of punishment and the gravity of the offense? Can a person punish himself? Do men desire to be punished?

These questions apply, though not with equal emphasis, to the three major types of wrongdoing in relation to which men discuss the nature and the need of punishment, its justice or its expediency. Punishment is traditionally considered in relation to vice, to crime, and to sin. According to the type of wrongdoing being considered, the punitive agent may be the wrongful individual himself or his family, his state, his church or God.

The lines which separate these areas of the problem of punishment cannot be sharply drawn in all cases, for as certain acts simultaneously violate the moral, the civil, and the divine law, they may also cause a person to be simultaneously subject to punishment from diverse sources. The wrong or injury which punishment is supposed to redress may in some cases fall under none of these headings, as, for example, acts of war or rebellion. It is sometimes questioned whether the theory of punishment remains the same when punitive steps are taken by one state against some or all the people of another; or again, when a government applies penalties for a rebellion engaged in by members of its own community.

In this chapter, we shall deal with the problem of punishment in its most general terms, for the most part considering the foregoing questions without regard to the distinction of sin, crime, and vice; or to the differences between divine and human punishment, or between punishment by the state and in the family (*i.e.*, punishment as involved in the enforcement of law and punishment as an instrument of education or training). These more specialized topics belong to other chapters: *e.g.*, punishment as affecting the formation of character to the chapters on EDUCATION and VIRTUE AND VICE; punishment as administered by parents to the chapter on FAMILY; divine rewards and punishments to the chapters on IMMORTALITY and SIN.

The basic ideas in terms of which any discussion of punishment proceeds are, of course, the subjects of the chapters on JUSTICE and LAW. One other chapter—PLEASURE AND PAIN—is of peculiar relevance to the question about the nature of punishment. Concerning the nature of punishment there seems to be no great difference of opinion in the tradition of western thought. Punishment is generally conceived as the infliction of pain, though some writers distinguish between corporeal and spiritual punishment according as the pain inflicted is the pain of sense or the pain of deprivation and loss. Imprisonment, for example, always entails the pain of loss—the loss of freedom—but it may also carry with it the suffering of physical hardships or even tortures. The torment of the damned is, according to some theologians, both corporeal and spiritual—the agony of hell-fire and the anguish of the soul deprived of God's love and presence.

IF THERE IS LITTLE DISPUTE about the nature of punishment, the opposite situation prevails concerning its purpose. Why men should be punished is one of the most controversial questions in the field of moral and political thought, and in psychology and theology as well.

The major opposition in the tradition of the great books is between those who think that punishment need only be inherently just, and those who think it cannot be justified without reference to its utility or expediency. While this debate goes on, for more than twenty centuries, punishments in actual practice—whether in accordance with the law or uncontrolled by it—tend generally to be severe and often fiendish or ferocious. Not until Beccaria in the 18th, and Bentham in the 19th century, does the discussion of punishment lead to major reforms in the spirit and provisions of the penal codes. But the opposite positions in the debate across the centuries are never without practical significance for penal institutions and punitive measures, even when theory is not immediately reflected in practice. The speculative significance of the issue is, however, always immediately apparent. Although justice and law are more fundamental and comprehensive ideas than punishment, this one problem of punishment—the question of its purpose—critically tests the meaning of anyone's theory of law and justice.

It may be that the issue cannot be fairly stated in terms of *purpose*. To use that word may beg the question, since one of the basic positions in the controversy appears to be that punishment has no purpose in the sense of *serving some end beyond itself*, or producing some desired consequence *in the future*. This is the theory—shared by Kant and Hegel—that punishment should be purely retributive.

According to this view the effect of the punishment upon the wrongdoer, or upon others whose conduct may be affected by punishments meted out or threatened, must not be taken into account at all. Nothing should be sought except the preservation of the balance sheet of justice, by seeing that every wrong is duly requited by a proportionate measure of punishment. Nor is the requital purely retributive if it considers any person except the wrongdoer himself. That punishment of the transgressor may assuage the feelings of those he has injured, or even satisfy a desire for revenge, should have no motivating force. The only pleasure the spectacle of punishment should yield, the only desire it should satisfy, is that of seeing the moral law upheld. We should punish only because we have, under the moral law, a duty to do so.

Kant castigates as utilitarian every theory of punishment which directs it to the service of anything besides strict justice—such as the reformation of the criminal, the deterrence of others, the welfare of society, or the slaking of the thirst for vengeance. "Juridical punishment," he says, "can never be administered merely as a means for promoting another good, either with regard to the Criminal himself, or to Civil Society, but must in all cases be imposed only because the individual on whom it is inflicted *has committed a Crime*. . . . The Penal Law is a Categorical Imperative; and woe to him who creeps through the serpent-windings of Utilitarianism to discover some advantage that may discharge him from the Justice of Punishment, or even from the due measure of it."

What shall determine the mode and measure of punishment? Kant answers: "It is just the Principle of Equality by which the pointer of the Scale of Justice is made to incline no more to one side than the other. It may be rendered by saying that the undeserved evil which anyone commits on another, is to be regarded as perpetrated on himself. . . . This is the Right of Retaliation (*ius talionis*); and properly understood it is the only Principle which . . . can definitely assign both the quality and the quantity of a just penalty. All other standards are wavering and uncertain; and on account of other considerations involved in them, they contain no principle conformable to the sentence of pure and strict Justice."

RETRIBUTIVE PUNISHMENT or retaliation seems to express the principle of justice or fairness in exchange. The Mosaic injunction that "thou shalt give life for life, eye for eye, tooth for tooth, burning for burning, wound for wound, stripe for stripe," occurs in the context of other passages which declare the compensation in goods which an injured party shall receive for the loss of or damage to his chattel. But it is also accompanied by ordinances which impose the death penalty for wrongs other than the taking of a life.

"You have heard," Christ declares in the Sermon on the Mount, "that it hath been said, An eye for an eye, and a tooth for a tooth. But I say unto you, That ye shall resist not evil; but whosoever shall smite thee on thy right cheek, turn to him the other also. And if any man will sue thee at the law, and take away thy coat, let him have thy cloak also." This passage has sometimes been taken to mean that all punishment is simply vengeance; and that instead of returning injury for injury, the Christian should love his enemies and forgive them. "If you think someone has wronged you," Princess Mary says to Prince Andrew in *War and Peace*, "forget it and forgive! We have no right to punish."

But the Christian view of punishment may not be the same when the punishment of the evildoer is a question for the state rather than for the individual. "Avenge not yourselves," St. Paul commands; "for it is written, Vengeance is mine, I will repay, saith the Lord." The individual need not avenge himself, for God punishes the wicked; not only God, but the ruler of the earthly state who, St. Paul says, "is the minister of God to thee for good. But if thou do that which is evil, be afraid; for he beareth not the sword in vain; for he is the minister of God, a revenger to execute wrath upon him that doeth evil."

A life for a life appears to be the symbolic statement of the *lex talionis* in the Greek as well as the Hebrew tradition. "Justice claims aloud her debt," the Chorus explains in the *Choephoroe* of Aeschylus. "Who in blood hath dipped the steel, deep in blood her meed shall feel. . . . Whoso'er shall take the sword, shall perish by the sword." But as Aristotle points out—and similarly Aquinas in his comment on the *lex talionis* of the Old Testament—simple reciprocity does not determine the mode of retribution. "People *want* even the justice of Rhadamanthus to mean this: Should a man suffer what he did, right justice would be done." Yet, Aristotle points out, "in many cases, reciprocity and rectificatory justice are not in accord, *e.g.*, if an official has inflicted a wound, he should not be wounded in return, and if someone has wounded an official, he ought not to be wounded only but punished in addition." Retaliation consists in reciprocity only if it is "in accordance with a proportion, and not on the basis of a precisely equal return."

Punishment as retaliation may seem to be inseparable from revenge. Yet, according to Lucretius, the surrender of primitive freedom for the restrictions of civilized life is motivated by the desire to substitute equitable retribution for unlimited vengeance. "Mankind, tired out with a life of brute force, lay exhausted from its feuds; and therefore the more readily it submitted of its own free will to laws and stringent codes. As each man moved by anger took measures to avenge himself with more severity than is now permitted by equitable laws, for this reason men grew sick of the life of brute force."

Hegel tries to clarify what he regards as a popular confusion of retribution with revenge. "In that condition of society," he writes, "when there are neither magistrates nor laws, punishment always takes the form of revenge; revenge remains defective inasmuch as it is the act of a subjective will." It is understandable that retribution should be objected to on the ground that "it looks like something immoral, *i.e.*, like revenge, and that thus it may pass for something personal. Yet it is not something personal but the concept itself which carries out retribution. 'Vengeance is mine, saith the Lord,' as the Bible says. . . . The Eumenides sleep, but crime awakens them, and hence it is the very act of crime itself which vindicates itself."

The apparent contradiction in the identity and difference of retribution and revenge can, in Hegel's opinion, be resolved. On the one hand, it can be said that "the annulment of crime is retribution insofar as retribution in *conception* is an 'injury of the injury.'" On the other hand, it can be said that "the annuling of crime in this sphere where right is immediate is principally revenge, which is just in its content insofar as it is retributive." The demand that this contradiction be resolved "is the demand for justice not as revenge but as punishment."

Hegel's resolution seems to be in terms of a distinction between the particular and the universal. "When the right against crime has the form of revenge, it is only right implicit, not right in the form of right, *i.e.*, no *act* of revenge is justified. Instead of the injured party, the injured *universal* now comes on the scene, and this has its proper actuality in the court of law. It takes over the pursuit and the avenging of crime, and this pursuit consequently ceases to be the subjective and contingent retribution of revenge, and is transformed into the genuine reconciliation of right with itself, *i.e.*, into punishment."

On this conception of punishment, Hegel like Kant decries every utilitarian purpose for punishment. Such misconceptions of punishment arise, he says, from the supposition that both crime and its annulment are "unqualified evils," which makes it seem "quite unreasonable to will an evil merely because 'another evil is there already.' To give punishment this superficial character of an evil is, amongst the various theories of punishment, the fundamental presupposition of those which regard it as a preventive, a deterrent, a threat, as reformative, etc., and what on these theories is supposed to result from punishment is characterized equally superficially as a good. But . . . the precise point at issue is wrong and the righting of it. If you adopt that superficial attitude toward punishment, you brush aside the objective treatment of the righting of wrong."

THE ISSUE WOULD SEEM to be a conflict between justice and expediency, with the utilitarians identifying retribution with revenge and demanding that punishment serve some good or mitigate some evil. But sometimes the question is whether justice and expediency are compatible.

In the debate on the treatment of the Mytilenians, which Thucydides reports, Cleon calls upon the Athenians to show no mercy to their rebellious subjects. "Their offence," he says, "was not involuntary, but of malice and deliberate," and they deserve to be punished. "If you follow my advice, you will do what is just towards the Mytilenians, and at the same time expedient. . . . For if they were right in rebelling, you must be wrong in ruling. However, if, right or wrong, you determine to rule, you must carry out your principle and punish the Mytilenians as your interest requires."

Diodotus objects to the policy of putting the Mytilenians to death on the ground that it is not a question of justice but of expediency. "We are not in a court of justice," he says, "but in a political assembly; and the question is not justice, but how to make the Mytilenians useful to Athens. . . . I consider it far more useful for the preservation of our empire to put up with injustice, than to put to death, however justly, those whom it is our interest to keep alive. As for Cleon's idea that in punishment the claims of justice and expediency can both be satisfied, facts do not confirm the possibility of such a combination."

In the chapter on justice in *Utilitarianism*, Mill seems to place justice above expediency, but he also seems to reduce retribution to revenge and call it just. "The sentiment of justice," which includes as "one of its elements . . . the desire to punish," Mill identifies with "the natural feeling of retaliation or vengeance." Retribution, or the giving of "evil for evil," he says, "becomes closely connected with the sentiment of justice and is universally included in the idea." The principle of "giving to each what they deserve," he adds, "that is, good for good as well as evil for evil, is not only included within the idea of Justice as we have defined it, but is a proper object of that intensity of sentiment, which places the Just, in human estimation, above the simply Expedient."

Other writers seem to think that the utility of punishment is not incompatible with its retributive justice. The great theologians, for example, considering the difference between the eternal punishment of the damned in Hell, and the cleansing punishment of the repentant in Purgatory, do not find it impossible for divine justice to include both absolute retribution and punishment which may be remedial as well as retributive. Purely retributive punishment seems justifiable to them, but they do not think that punishment can ever be justified simply by its utility—by the good it achieves—without any reference to the retaliation of evil for evil.

In the context of saying that the institution of slavery among men is a just punishment for Adam's sin, and that "God knows how to award fit punishments for every variety of offence," Augustine observes that "we must not only do harm to no man, but also restrain him from sin or punish his sin, so that either the man himself who is punished may profit by his experience or others be warned of his example." Here there seems to be no thought that retribution excludes a reformative or deterrent use of punishment. Aquinas even more explicitly combines the remedial and the deterrent utility of punishment with the function of punishment to preserve the order of justice by meting out an equitable retribution.

In willing justice, God wills punishment, according to Aquinas. "The order of justice belongs to the order of the universe; and this requires that penalty should be dealt out to sinners." But just retribution is not the only reason for punishment. Sometimes it is "for the good of those who are punished," sometimes "for the amendment of others." These reasons for punishment apply to human as well as to divine law. "When a thief is hanged, this is not for his own amendment, but for the sake of others, who at least may be deterred from crime through fear of punishment." Punishment is a proper effect of human law, not merely because justice requires it, but because "the law makes use of the fear of punishment in order to ensure obedience."

In discussing the proportion between the severity of the penalty and the gravity of the fault in the punishment of sin under the Mosaic law, Aquinas explains that in addition to the reason of justice (that "a greater sin, other things being equal, deserves a greater punishment"), there is the purpose of reformation ("since men are not easily cured of habitual sin except by severe punishments") and the purpose of prevention ("for men are not easily deterred from such sins unless they be severely punished"). Here three reasons for punishment are stated side by side. But in the opinion of Aquinas retribution is more than the primary, it is the one indispensable reason; for punishment cannot be justified except as doing the work of justice.

THE VIEW OF KANT AND Hegel that retribution or retaliation is *the only basis* for punishment—not merely the primary or the indispensable reason—meets its exact opposite in what appears to be the completely utilitarian theory of punishment to be found in the writings of Plato, Hobbes, Locke, and Rousseau.

In the *Protagoras*, arguing for the proposition that virtue can be taught, Protagoras insists that "no one punishes the evil-doer for the reason that he has done wrong—only the unreasonable fury of a beast acts in that manner. But he who desires to inflict rational punishment does not retaliate for a past wrong which cannot be undone. He has regard to the future, and is desirous that the man who is punished, and he who sees him punished, may be deterred from doing wrong again. He punishes for the sake of prevention, thus clearly implying that virtue is capable of being taught."

Plato himself seems to adopt the opinion of Protagoras. In the *Laws*—wherein he sets forth the provisions of a penal code in a detail equalled, in the tradition of the great books, only by the proposals of Hobbes—Plato says no man is to be punished "because he did wrong, for that which is done can never be undone, but in order that, in the future times, he, and those who see him corrected, may utterly hate injustice, or at any rate abate much of their evil-doing." Yet he also goes on to say that the law "should aim at the right measure of punishment, and in all cases at the deserved punishment." This qualification seems, in turn, to be balanced by his remarks on the death penalty which he thinks should be imposed only on the incurable who cannot profit from punishment and whose execution "would be an example to other men not to offend."

The notion of desert in Plato's theory of punishment appeals to justice without implying any separation between retribution and reform. In the *Gorgias*, Socrates says that "to suffer punishment is another name for being justly corrected when you do wrong." A wrongdoer who escapes punishment suffers a greater evil than one who is punished, for he "who is punished and suffers retribution, suffers justly." Thereby justice is restored to his soul. The judge who prescribes just punishments cures the soul, as the physician who prescribes the right remedies cures the body. The criminal who, having been unjust, goes unpunished "has no deliverance from injustice."

The fact that just punishments are deserved does not seem to be the reason why men should be punished. Considering the penalties imposed by gods and men, in the next world or in this, Socrates summarizes his argument by saying that "the proper office of punishment is twofold: he who is rightly punished ought either to become better and profit by it, or he ought to be made an example to his fellows, that they may see what he suffers, and fear and become better. Those who are improved when they are punished by gods and men, are those whose sins are curable; and they are improved, as in this world so also in another, by pain and suffering."

Like Plato, Hobbes places the reason for punishment in the future rather than in the past—in its utility to procure certain effects rather than in its effecting retaliation. He states it as a law of nature that "in revenges (that is, retribution of evil for evil), *men look not at the greatness of the evil past, but the greatness of the good to follow*. Whereby we are forbidden to inflict punishment with any other design than for the correction of the offender, or the direction of others." Anything else he calls "an act of hostility."

The chief aim of punishment, in securing the reformation and the deterrence of criminals, Hobbes thinks, is to maintain public peace. "A punishment is an evil inflicted by public authority" on those who have transgressed the law, "to the end that the will of men may thereby the better be disposed to obedience." A law, without a penalty attached, is "not a law, but vain words." It fails to achieve the end of law, which is the same as the end of punishment. The worst offenses—those to be prevented by the most severe penalties—are crimes, not against individuals, but those that "are of most danger to the public."

Locke also derives from natural law the right to punish those who transgress that law, "for restraint and preventing the like offence," to which he adds that "each transgression may be punished to that degree, and with so much severity as to make it an ill bargain to the offender, give him cause to repent, and terrify others from doing the like." This theory of punishment applies not only to man living in a state of nature, but in civil society as well.

Though Rousseau describes the wise statesman as one who knows how, by punishing crimes, to prevent them, he lays greater emphasis on the other motive for punishment—the reformation of the criminal. "There is not a single ill-doer who could not be turned to some good. The State has no right to put to death, even for the sake of making an example, anyone whom it can leave alive without danger." Or, as Fetyukovitch says in his address to the jury in the *Brothers Karamazov*: "The Russian court does not exist for punishment only, but also for the salvation of the criminal. Let other nations think of retribution and the letter of the law, we will cling to the spirit and the meaning—the salvation and the reformation of the lost."

THIS GREAT ISSUE CONCERNING the reason for or purpose of punishment seems to affect most of the other questions which men raise about the penalties to be imposed for wrongdoing—whether the wrong is a sin, a crime, or a vicious act, and whether it is God or the state, nature or the individual himself, who inflicts the pain. The reverse also seems to be true. These other questions raise difficulties or issues which test the conflicting theories that punishment should be a just retaliation *exclusively*, or should be justified *only* by its consequences, or should somehow be a *combination* of awarding just deserts and securing good effects.

For example, the question of how the various modes and measures of punishment should be determined and assigned to diverse acts of wrongdoing does not seem to be answerable in the same way when the principle is simply retribution and when the purpose of punishment is reformation and deterrence. On the principle of retribution the gravity of the offence appears to be the only determinant of the severity of the punishment. The punishment should fit the crime, not the nature of the criminal as someone capable of being benefitted by punishment.

Kant and Hegel do not think that the justification of the death penalty, for example, depends on the curability or incurability of the offender. Nor do they think that the taking of the criminal's life should be motivated, as Aquinas and Locke seem to suggest, by the desire to protect society from his future depredations. It is sufficient that he has taken a life, or committed some equally serious injury, which ought to be repaid by a proportionate requital.

"What is involved in the action of the criminal," Hegel writes, "is not only the concept of crime, the rational aspect in crime as such whether the individual wills it or not, the aspect which the state has to vindicate, but also the abstract rationality of the individual's *volition.* Since that is so," Hegel argues, "punishment is regarded as containing the criminal's right and hence by being punished he is as honored as a rational being. He does not receive this due of honor unless the concept and measure of his punishment are derived from his own act. Still less does he receive it if he is treated either as a harmful animal who has to be made harmless, or with a view to deterring or reforming him."

On these grounds, Hegel criticizes Beccaria's unqualified opposition to the death penalty. In addition, he rejects Beccaria's theory that "it could not be presumed that the readiness of individuals to allow themselves to be executed was included in the social contract." Rousseau takes the diametrically opposite view. He argues for the death penalty on the ground that "we consent to die if we ourselves turn assassins" in order to protect ourselves from falling victims to assassins. In making this consent a part of the social contract, Rousseau holds that "we think only of securing [our own lives], and it is not to be assumed that any of the parties then expects to get hanged."

Hegel disagrees with both Beccaria and Rousseau. According to him, the state is not based upon a social contract; nor does he admit that "its fundamental essence [involves] the unconditional protection and guarantee of the life and property of members of the public as individuals. On the contrary," he holds, "it is that higher entity"—the state—"which even lays claim to this very life and property and demands its sacrifice."

The state, therefore, according to Hegel, cannot be denied the right of inflicting capital punishment. Hegel admits that "Beccaria's requirement that men should give their consent to being punished is right enough," but he adds that "the criminal gives his consent already by his very act. The nature of the crime, no less than the private will of the individual, requires that the injury initiated by the criminal should be annulled. However that may be," he continues, "Beccaria's endeavor to have capital punishment abolished has had beneficial effects." Because of the efforts made by Joseph II and Napoleon to abolish it, "we have begun to see," Hegel thinks, "which crimes deserve the death penalty and which do not. Capital punishment has in consequence become rare, as in fact should be the case with this most extreme punishment."

The attitude toward the death penalty as well as toward all other punishments is different when the *only* purpose of punishment is the welfare of society and the improvement of individuals, whether they are actual or potential offenders. The modes and degrees of punishment must then be determined by considering their effectiveness as means to the ends in view. Montesquieu discusses the penal codes in various systems of law entirely in terms of their success in preventing crime. Though he does not seem to think that punishment can improve the character of the individual, he believes that a certain proportion between the penalty and the offense may tend to reduce the extent and gravity of crimes. "In Russia," he says, "where the punishment of robbery and murder is the same, they always murder."

In general, Montesquieu is opposed to unduly severe punishments, and especially to cruel and unusual punishments, not so much on the grounds of injustice as for the protection of liberty and public morals. Hobbes, Locke, and Rousseau similarly discuss the severity of punishment with reference to its utility, and, like Montesquieu, they face the problem that the same measure or degree of punishment may not be equally effective for the purposes of reformation and deterrence. Severe penalties, for example, may have a greater deterrent effect upon potential offenders than milder forms of punishment, but they may also tend to harden criminals instead of reforming them.

The conflict of principles in the determination of punishments seems to be even more marked in the case of those who try to combine retribution with utility. If, for example, the death penalty is the just desert for murder, should it be applied on the grounds of retribution, even though a particular murderer can be reformed by milder treatment? If heavy penalties were to prove highly effective as deterrents, should they be applied to minor offenses, which deserve less severe retaliations, in order to reduce the amount of crime?

There seems to be agreement for the most part on who shall have the authority to punish and who shall be subject to punishment, in the relation of men to one another, to the state, and to God. Punishment seems to be annexed to law, as indispensable for its enforcement, so that whoever has the authority to set rules of conduct for another also has the authority to impose penalties for their violation. Yet the notion that punishment is a necessary sanction for law—which is apparently shared by those who take the retributive and those who take the utilitarian view of punishment—does not seem to fit both views equally well, at least not to the extent that the end of law and its enforcement is the common good or the public welfare.

Again, it seems to be generally agreed that moral responsibility on the part of offenders is an indispensable condition of just punishment for their misdeeds. Unless the sinful or the criminal act is voluntary, unless it is intentional rather than accidental—or if negligent, capable of being attributed to a willful error of judgment—the act is without fault and the agent without guilt. But although those who make punishment retributive and those who make it reformative or deterrent seem to agree upon responsibility as prerequisite, this principle does not seem to be equally consistent with both theories—at least not to the extent that the exemplary punishment may deter others quite apart from the responsibility of the person punished.

The question of responsibility raises other difficulties, *e.g.*, the metaphysical issue about personal identity, on which Locke takes the stand that unless the human individual is an enduring substance, he cannot deserve subsequent punishment for his prior acts; and the issue of free will and causality, on which Hume's position seems to be that unless human actions are subject to causal necessity, a man cannot be blamed for his acts or "become the object of punishment or vengeance."

Finally, there is the problem of a natural need for punishment and of the penalties which nature itself imposes for wrongdoing to fulfill this need. The familiar statement that virtue is its own reward and vice its own punishment, is sometimes interpreted to mean that virtue and vice are intrinsically good and evil, and sometimes to mean that through their natural consequences they heap benefit or injury on their possessor.

Augustine, for example, says that by the sins which he committed God did justly punish him, for "every disorder in the soul is its own punishment"; and Kant distinguishes juridical from natural punishment "in which Crime as Vice punishes itself, and does not as such come within the cognizance of the Legislator." The other interpretation seems to be represented by Hobbes' theory that "intemperance is naturally punished with diseases . . . injustice with the violence of enemies . . . cowardice with oppression." In the chain of consequences started by any action, he discerns the pains which are "the natural punishments of those actions that are the beginning of more harm than good."

But according to Freud it is the craving for punishment rather than the punishment which is natural, *i.e.*, psychologically determined. Individuals punish themselves or seek to be punished for what is either real or fancied guilt. "The unconscious need for punishment plays a part in every neurotic disease," Freud writes. "It behaves like a part of the conscience, like the prolongation of conscience into the unconscious; and it must have the same origin as conscience; that is to say, it will correspond to a piece of aggressiveness which has been internalized and taken over by the super-ego. If only the words were less incongruous, we should be justified . . . in calling it 'an unconscious sense of guilt.'"

Whatever its psychological validity, Freud's theory does not resolve the moral issue concerning the justice or utility of punishment. Nor does it eliminate the possibility of other motives for submitting to punishment voluntarily. Socrates in the *Crito* explains that he refuses to escape from the death penalty he thinks he does not deserve, in order to uphold the law which is itself just even though in his own case it has been unjustly applied by men. Thoreau and Gandhi refuse to obey laws their consciences cannot approve, but do not resist the state's demand that they be punished for the law's infraction. In an unjust society, going to prison is for them the necessary fulfillment of the revolution begun by civil disobedience.

OUTLINE OF TOPICS

1. The general theory of punishment
   - 1a. The nature of punishment: the pain of sense and the pain of loss
   - 1b. The retributive purpose of punishment: the *lex talionis*; retaliation and revenge; the righting of a wrong
   - 1c. Punishment for the sake of reforming the wrongdoer
   - 1d. The preventive use of punishment: the deterrence of wrongdoing
2. Personal responsibility as a condition of just punishment: the problem of collective responsibility
   - 2a. Free will in relation to responsibility and punishment: voluntariness in relation to guilt or fault; the accidental, the negligent, and the intentional
   - 2b. Sanity, maturity, and moral competence in relation to responsibility
3. Punishment in relation to virtue and vice
   - 3a. Rewards and punishments as factors in the formation of moral character
   - 3b. Vice its own punishment
   - 3c. Guilt, repentance, and the moral need for punishment
4. Crime and punishment: punishment as a political instrument
   - 4a. Punishment for lawbreaking as a necessary sanction of law
   - 4b. The forms of punishment available to the state
     - (1) The death penalty: its justification
     - (2) Exile or ostracism: imprisonment or incarceration
     - (3) Enforced labor or enslavement
     - (4) Torture: cruel and unusual punishments
   - 4c. The justice of legal punishment: the conventionality of the punishments determined by positive law
   - 4d. Grades of severity in punishment: making the punishment fit the crime
5. The punishment for sin
   - 5a. The origin and fulfillment of curses
   - 5b. The wages of sin: the punishment of original sin
   - 5c. The pain of remorse and the torment of conscience: the atonement for sin
   - 5d. The modes of divine punishment: here and hereafter, temporal and eternal
   - 5e. The justice of divine punishment
     - (1) The justification of eternal suffering in Hell or Hades
     - (2) The necessity of expiation in Purgatory
6. Pathological motivations with respect to punishment: abnormal sense of sin or guilt; perverse desires to inflict or suffer punishment

REFERENCES

References are listed by volume number (in bold type), author's name, and page number. Bible references are to book, chapter, and verse of the Authorized King James version of the Bible. The abbreviation "esp" calls the reader's attention to one or more especially relevant parts of a whole reference; "passim" signifies that the topic is discussed intermittently rather than continuously in the work or passage cited. Where the work as a whole is relevant to the topic, the page numbers refer to the entire work. For general guidance in the use of *The Great Ideas,* consult the Preface.

1. The general theory of punishment

1*a*. The nature of punishment: the pain of sense and the pain of loss

4 Homer, 248–249
12 Lucretius, 42–43
13 Virgil, 227
18 Augustine, 519–520
19 Aquinas, 792, 816–817
20 Aquinas, 186–187
21 Dante, 7–8, 88–89
23 Hobbes, 145–147
25 Montaigne, 90–91
35 Locke, 26–28
42 Kant, 306, 446
46 Hegel, 37–38

1*b*. The retributive purpose of punishment: the *lex talionis;* retaliation and revenge; the righting of a wrong

Old Testament: *Genesis,* 9:6; 34 / *Exodus,* 21:12–34 / *Leviticus,* 19:18; 24:16–21 / *Numbers,* 35:10–34 / *Deuteronomy,* 19:11–13,21; 32:35,41–43 / *Judges,* 16:21–30 / *Psalms,* 58; 79:10–12 / *Proverbs,* 6:34–35; 20:22; 24:29 / *Isaiah,* 59:17–19 / *Jeremiah,* 9:1–11; 46:10; 50:13,28 / *Ezekiel,* 25 / *Nahum,* 1:2–3
Apocrypha: *Judith,* 2:1–12 / *Ecclesiasticus,* 5:1–7; 39:28–30 / *I Maccabees,* 2:67–68; 9:33–42 / *II Maccabees,* 6:14–15
New Testament: *Matthew,* 5:38–48 / *Luke,* 17:3–4 / *Romans,* 3:5–6; 12:17–21 / *Hebrews,* 10:29–30
4 Homer, 195, 301–311
5 Aeschylus, 68–80, 81–91 esp 86–87
5 Sophocles, 143–155, 156–169
5 Euripides, 212–224, 327–339, 353–364, 371, 394–410
6 Herodotus, 29–30, 91, 99–100, 116–117, 177, 218, 237–239, 278–279, 305
6 Thucydides, 556–557
9 Aristotle, 379–380
18 Augustine, 388–390
19 Aquinas, 266, 818
20 Aquinas, 334–336
21 Dante, 28, 41–43, 68
22 Chaucer, 224–232, 413–422
25 Montaigne, 334–335
26 Shakespeare, 74–76, 78–79, 108, 170–198, 419, 425–429
27 Shakespeare, 54, 60–62, 216, 226–227, 238–243, 419–420
29 Cervantes, 68–73
35 Locke, 26–28
37 Fielding, 20–21
38 Montesquieu, 43
38 Rousseau, 351
40 Gibbon, 617
41 Gibbon, 91–93, 224–225
43 Mill, 469–470, 472, 474
46 Hegel, 73, 126
48 Melville, 118–122
51 Tolstoy, 505–511
52 Dostoevsky, 398–399

1*c*. Punishment for the sake of reforming the wrongdoer

Old Testament: *Job,* 5:17–18 / *Proverbs,* 3:11–12; 13:24; 17:10; 19:18,25; 20:30; 23:13–14 / *Jeremiah,* 5:3 / *Zephaniah,* 3:1–13 / *Malachi,* 3
Apocrypha: *Judith,* 8:25–27 / *Wisdom of Solomon,* 12; 16:2–12 / *Ecclesiasticus,* 30:1–2,12–13; 22:6 / *Baruch,* 4
New Testament: *Hebrews,* 12:5–11
5 Aristophanes, 504–506
7 Plato, 45, 267–270, 293–294, 426–427, 485
18 Augustine, 521–522
20 Aquinas, 158–159, 309–316, 550–558
23 Hobbes, 94, 157–158
35 Locke, 1–2
37 Fielding, 267–268
38 Montesquieu, 39–40
42 Kant, 446–447
43 Mill, 302–312, 471–472
44 Boswell, 7–8, 199–200
52 Dostoevsky, 30–32, 395–401

1*d*. The preventive use of punishment: the deterrence of wrongdoing

Old Testament: *Deuteronomy,* 13:10–11
New Testament: *I Corinthians,* 10:5–11
5 Aeschylus, 81–91
5 Sophocles, 157–158
5 Euripides, 214–215, 398–400

6 THUCYDIDES, 400–401
7 PLATO, 45, 743–744, 747
9 ARISTOTLE, 434–435
15 TACITUS, 49–50, 57, 151–152
20 AQUINAS, 186–188
23 HOBBES, 140, 143
27 SHAKESPEARE, 177–184
31 SPINOZA, 444
35 LOCKE, 65
38 MONTESQUIEU, 37–40
38 ROUSSEAU, 371
40 GIBBON, 175, 199
43 MILL, 271–272, 313–316, 334–335
44 BOSWELL, 301, 344
46 HEGEL, 37–38, 139
49 DARWIN, 314
52 DOSTOEVSKY, 398–401
54 FREUD, 787

2. Personal responsibility as a condition of just punishment: the problem of collective responsibility

OLD TESTAMENT: *Numbers,* 14:18 / *II Samuel,* 21:1–9 / *II Kings,* 14:5–6 / *Jeremiah,* 31:29–30 / *Ezekiel,* 18
APOCRYPHA: *Baruch,* 3:7–8
NEW TESTAMENT: *Romans,* 5:12–19 / *I Corinthians,* 15:21–22
5 AESCHYLUS, 27–39, 52–91
5 SOPHOCLES, 99–142, 156–169
5 EURIPIDES, 378–410
6 HERODOTUS, 306–307
7 PLATO, 746–751, 785–786
9 ARISTOTLE, 359–361
18 AUGUSTINE, 366
20 AQUINAS, 162–167
21 DANTE, 80
22 CHAUCER, 506–507
23 HOBBES, 118
26 SHAKESPEARE, 553
32 MILTON, 141–143
33 PASCAL, 249
35 LOCKE, 225–226
35 HUME, 485
40 GIBBON, 451
42 KANT, 169–170
43 FEDERALIST, 202–203
43 MILL, 471–472
46 HEGEL, 42–43, 46–47
51 TOLSTOY, 606–607
52 DOSTOEVSKY, 168–169

2*a*. Free will in relation to responsibility and punishment: voluntariness in relation to guilt or fault; the accidental, the negligent, and the intentional

NEW TESTAMENT: *I Timothy,* 1:12–13
5 AESCHYLUS, 66–69, 80, 87–89
5 SOPHOCLES, 111–112, 123, 176
5 EURIPIDES, 376
6 HERODOTUS, 8:10
7 PLATO, 204, 688–689, 746–751
9 ARISTOTLE, 355–357, 359–361, 383–384, 386–387, 399–400
12 EPICTETUS, 124–125
12 AURELIUS, 263, 308
18 AUGUSTINE, 385–390 passim
19 AQUINAS, 335–336, 718
20 AQUINAS, 129–130, 142–144, 152–156, 159–167, 173
21 DANTE, 15–16, 40–41, 77, 111
23 HOBBES, 139–140
32 MILTON, 137–138, 180, 347–348
35 LOCKE, 193, 227
42 KANT, 169, 391–392
43 MILL, 474
46 HEGEL, 42–43, 126–128, 165–166
51 TOLSTOY, 686–687

2*b*. Sanity, maturity, and moral competence in relation to responsibility

18 AUGUSTINE, 573–574
21 DANTE, 49–50
23 HOBBES, 132, 142
27 SHAKESPEARE, 70
35 LOCKE, 36–38
42 KANT, 169–170
43 MILL, 302–312
46 HEGEL, 46–47
51 TOLSTOY, 690
52 DOSTOEVSKY, 348, 401
54 FREUD, 241

3. Punishment in relation to virtue and vice

3*a*. Rewards and punishments as factors in the formation of moral character

OLD TESTAMENT: *Proverbs,* 23:13–14
APOCRYPHA: *Ecclesiasticus,* 30:1–13
5 AESCHYLUS, 88
5 ARISTOPHANES, 504–506
7 PLATO, 283–285, 313, 556–557
9 ARISTOTLE, 434–435
14 PLUTARCH, 41–42
18 AUGUSTINE, 4–7
20 AQUINAS, 226–227
25 MONTAIGNE, 73–74
31 SPINOZA, 419
35 LOCKE, 105 passim, 107–108
35 HUME, 485
36 SWIFT, 28
37 FIELDING, 41, 380–381
38 MONTESQUIEU, 37–38, 139
43 MILL, 306–307, 458, 464
44 BOSWELL, 199–200
54 FREUD, 758–759, 792–795, 876

3*b*. Vice its own punishment

APOCRYPHA: *Ecclesiasticus,* 14:5–10
7 PLATO, 262–267, 417–418, 436–441, 689–690
12 EPICTETUS, 134, 149, 206–208, 228–230
12 AURELIUS, 259, 290, 292
18 AUGUSTINE, 17
20 AQUINAS, 178–185

23 Hobbes, 163–164
25 Montaigne, 389
42 Kant, 374
52 Dostoevsky, 381
53 James, 83
54 Freud, 793–794

3*c*. Guilt, repentance, and the moral need for punishment

Old Testament: *Leviticus,* 26:40–43 / *I Kings,* 8:46–51 / *Psalms,* 6; 32; 38; 51; 102; 130; 143
Apocrypha: *Wisdom of Solomon,* 12:10
New Testament: *Luke,* 16:27–31
6 Herodotus, 9–10
7 Plato, 267–270, 293–294
15 Tacitus, 255
18 Augustine, 343–344
20 Aquinas, 550–558
25 Montaigne, 388–395 passim
27 Shakespeare, 184, 481
32 Milton, 339–378
38 Rousseau, 372
40 Gibbon, 54–55
43 Mill, 458–459
52 Dostoevsky, 50–54, 369–373, 380–386, 404–408 passim
54 Freud, 792–793, 795–798

4. Crime and punishment: punishment as a political instrument

6 Herodotus, 191
6 Thucydides, 424–428
7 Plato, 743–757
9 Aristotle, 379–380, 501, 525–526, 576–577, 579–580, 615–617, 619
14 Plutarch, 710–712
15 Tacitus, 151–152
20 Aquinas, 553–555
23 Machiavelli, 14
23 Hobbes, 138–148, 281
26 Shakespeare, 49–50
35 Locke, 3–6, 14–15, 65
38 Montesquieu, 37–43, 85–92
38 Rousseau, 351, 398–399
40 Gibbon, 198–200, 215–216, 225–229, 387–388
41 Gibbon, 91–94
42 Kant, 446–448
43 Mill, 304–305, 313
46 Hegel, 35–39, 72, 139
51 Tolstoy, 223–232, 547–551
52 Dostoevsky, 30–32

4*a*. Punishment for lawbreaking as a necessary sanction of law

5 Aeschylus, 86–87
5 Sophocles, 136–137
6 Herodotus, 164
7 Plato, 747, 757, 769–770, 792–793
9 Aristotle, 434–435, 525–526
18 Augustine, 514–515
20 Aquinas, 233–234, 309–316
22 Chaucer, 418–419
23 Hobbes, 131, 145–148, 157–158
26 Shakespeare, 44, 539–541
29 Cervantes, 68–73
31 Spinoza, 439
35 Locke, 3, 25, 44, 53–54, 229–231
35 Hume, 485
38 Rousseau, 398–399
42 Kant, 446
43 Federalist, 65, 78
43 Mill, 302–303, 329–330, 467–468, 471–472
46 Hegel, 73, 125
52 Dostoevsky, 348–401

4*b*. The forms of punishment available to the state

7 Plato, 209–210, 771–784 passim, 784–786
9 Aristotle, 576–577 passim, 578–580 passim
18 Augustine, 570
20 Aquinas, 309–316
23 Hobbes, 146–147
26 Shakespeare, 429
35 Locke, 25, 230
36 Swift, 28–29, 35–37
38 Montesquieu, 37–38
41 Gibbon, 91–94
42 Kant, 446–449
43 Federalist, 65
46 Hegel, 214–216
50 Marx, 364–367

4*b*(1) The death penalty: its justification

Old Testament: *Genesis,* 9:6 / *Exodus,* 21:12–29; 22:18–20 / *Leviticus,* 20:9–18,27; 24:16–21 / *Numbers,* 35:16–31 / *Deuteronomy,* 19:11–13; 21:18–23; 22:21–27 / *I Kings,* 21:10–13 / *Esther,* 4:11–5:2; 7:7–10
Apocrypha: *II Maccabees,* 13:5–8
5 Euripides, 399–400
6 Herodotus, 87, 135–136, 149
6 Thucydides, 424–429
7 Plato, 743–744, 784, 791
14 Plutarch, 54–55, 70
18 Augustine, 142–143
20 Aquinas, 187–188, 259–261, 309–316, 504–505, 993–994
23 Hobbes, 146
25 Montaigne, 23–24, 205–206
26 Shakespeare, 334–335, 540–541
27 Shakespeare, 182–183, 371–373, 406–408, 558–559
33 Pascal, 108–109
35 Locke, 27–28, 30
36 Swift, 122–123
38 Montesquieu, 39–40, 86–91 passim
38 Rousseau, 398–399
40 Gibbon, 175–176, 216–219
41 Gibbon, 91–92, 95–96
42 Kant, 446–449
46 Hegel, 37–38
51 Tolstoy, 547–551

4b(2) Exile or ostracism: imprisonment or incarceration

5 EURIPIDES, 214–215
7 PLATO, 607, 690–691, 743–744, 769–770
9 ARISTOTLE, 482–483, 562–563
14 PLUTARCH, 97–101, 107, 160, 162–171, 179–184, 265–266, 428–429
15 TACITUS, 152–153
20 AQUINAS, 309–316, 1078–1081
21 DANTE, 132–133
22 CHAUCER, 179–182
23 HOBBES, 146–147
26 SHAKESPEARE, 242, 245–246, 324–325
27 SHAKESPEARE, 375–377
38 MONTESQUIEU, 222–223, 263
41 GIBBON, 93
42 KANT, 450

4b(3) Enforced labor or enslavement

6 HERODOTUS, 78
15 TACITUS, 132
32 MILTON, 339–378
38 MONTESQUIEU, 109, 110
42 KANT, 445–446
44 BOSWELL, 385
50 MARX, 364–366
51 TOLSTOY, 606–607

4b(4) Torture: cruel and unusual punishment

OLD TESTAMENT: *Deuteronomy*, 25:1–3,5–12
4 HOMER, 307–308
6 HERODOTUS, 28, 92–93, 159
14 PLUTARCH, 384–385, 851–852
23 HOBBES, 90
25 MONTAIGNE, 4–5, 176, 338–339, 349
26 SHAKESPEARE, 392–394
27 SHAKESPEARE, 267–269
36 SWIFT, 35–37
36 STERNE, 265–266
38 MONTESQUIEU, 42, 90, 212–213, 239, 240
40 GIBBON, 212, 232, 389, 604, 651
41 GIBBON, 91–92, 94, 167, 193, 501–503
46 HEGEL, 355
51 TOLSTOY, 429, 505–511
52 DOSTOEVSKY, 122–125

4c. The justice of legal punishment: the conventionality of the punishments determined by positive law

5 AESCHYLUS, 38–39
5 SOPHOCLES, 131–142
5 EURIPIDES, 392–393
7 PLATO, 213–219, 267–270, 743–757
9 ARISTOTLE, 379–380
17 PLOTINUS, 150
20 AQUINAS, 334–336
23 HOBBES, 101, 140–141, 145
25 MONTAIGNE, 519
26 SHAKESPEARE, 498–499
27 SHAKESPEARE, 178–179
29 CERVANTES, 68–73
31 SPINOZA, 435–436
35 LOCKE, 16, 65
38 MONTESQUIEU, 49–50, 267–268
38 ROUSSEAU, 398–399
42 KANT, 433–434, 446, 448
43 MILL, 271–272, 302–312, 467–470
46 HEGEL, 36–38, 138–139
52 DOSTOEVSKY, 348–401

4d. Grades of severity in punishment: making the punishment fit the crime

7 PLATO, 209–210, 754–756, 769–771, 782
9 ARISTOTLE, 379–380, 619
15 TACITUS, 57, 152–153
18 AUGUSTINE, 570–571
20 AQUINAS, 309–316
21 DANTE, 7, 10, 16–17, 20, 41–43, 68–69, 71–73, 82–83
23 HOBBES, 145, 157–158
27 SHAKESPEARE, 372–373
36 SWIFT, 28
37 FIELDING, 399
38 MONTESQUIEU, 37–43, 85–91, 264–266
38 ROUSSEAU, 371
41 GIBBON, 83, 91–94
42 KANT, 446–448
43 FEDERALIST, 221–222
43 MILL, 472
46 HEGEL, 72

5. The punishment for sin

5a. The origin and fulfillment of curses

OLD TESTAMENT: *Genesis*, 4:8–16; 9:21–27 / *Numbers*, 22–24 / *Deuteronomy*, 27:15–26; 28:15–68; 29:18–29 / *II Samuel*, 16:5–13 / *II Kings*, 2:23–24; 9:10,30–37 / *II Chronicles*, 21:12–20; 36 / *Zechariah*, 5:1–4 / *Malachi*, 2
APOCRYPHA: *Ecclesiasticus*, 41:8–10
NEW TESTAMENT: *Galatians*, 3:10–14
5 AESCHYLUS, 27–39, 52–69, 70–91
5 SOPHOCLES, 99–130
6 THUCYDIDES, 380
20 AQUINAS, 504–505
26 SHAKESPEARE, 107–108, 126–127, 136–138, 342–343, 583
32 MILTON, 297–298, 302–305, 309–310
36 STERNE, 281–289, 466–467

5b. The wages of sin: the punishment of original sin

OLD TESTAMENT: *Genesis*, 3:9–24
APOCRYPHA: *Wisdom of Solomon*, 2:23–24
NEW TESTAMENT: *Romans*, 5:12–21; 6:23; 7 / *I Corinthians*, 15:21–22 / *Ephesians*, 2:1–5
18 AUGUSTINE, 360–366, 372–376, 387–397, 416, 521, 529–530, 571
19 AQUINAS, 692–693
20 AQUINAS, 162–174, 178–204, 499–500
21 DANTE, 115–116
23 HOBBES, 112
32 MILTON, 141–143, 264–298, 308–327
33 PASCAL, 245–253

5c. The pain of remorse and the torment of conscience: the atonement for sin

OLD TESTAMENT: *Leviticus,* 16:29–34 / *II Samuel,* 12:9–23 / *I Kings,* 8:31–50 / *II Chronicles,* 6:24–42; 7:12–14; 33:12–19 / *Psalms,* 32; 51; 102:1–12 / *Daniel,* 9:3–20 / *Joel,* 1:1–2:17 / *Johah,* 3
APOCRYPHA: *Wisdom of Solomon,* 5:1–13; 17 / *Ecclesiasticus,* 14:1–2 / *I Maccabees,* 6:1–15
NEW TESTAMENT: *Matthew,* 3:1–12; 11:20–21; 27:3–5 / *Luke,* 7:36–50; 14:11–21 / *John,* 8:1–11 / *II Corinthians,* 7:8–12 / *James,* 4:8–10
5 AESCHYLUS, 80
5 SOPHOCLES, 141–142, 148–149
5 EURIPIDES, 322, 375–377, 394–398, 419
12 LUCRETIUS, 76
15 TACITUS, 87
18 AUGUSTINE, 9, 12–14, 22–23, 381–383
20 AQUINAS, 191–192, 1073–1074
21 DANTE, 45–46, 55–56, 58, 65–96, 99–102
22 CHAUCER, 495–506, 547–550
25 MONTAIGNE, 14, 174–176
26 SHAKESPEARE, 114–117, 145, 351
27 SHAKESPEARE, 46, 53–56, 238–243, 291–292, 296–299, 306–307, 479
31 SPINOZA, 440
32 MILTON, 153–154, 270–273, 350–353
36 STERNE, 257–266
37 FIELDING, 267
40 GIBBON, 54–55, 199, 452
42 KANT, 306–307, 333, 379, 593
46 HEGEL, 354
47 GOETHE, 92–93, 277–280
49 DARWIN, 312–314
51 TOLSTOY, 321, 606–607
52 DOSTOEVSKY, 24, 30–32, 46–47, 159–163, 184–188, 395–398
54 FREUD, 581, 797–798, 831

5d. The modes of divine punishment: here and hereafter, temporal and eternal

OLD TESTAMENT: *Genesis,* 3:9–19; 4:8–15; 6–8; 18:20–19:29 / *Exodus,* 7–12; 22:22–24; 32 / *Leviticus,* 10:1–3; 18:24–30; 26 / *Numbers,* 12–14; 15:30–31; 16; 21:5–9; 25 / *Deuteronomy,* 27–30 passim; 32 / *Joshua,* 7 / *Judges* / *I Samuel,* 15 / *II Samuel,* 6:6–8; 24 / *I Kings,* 9:6–9; 11:9–13,29–39; 13; 14:7–17; 16:1–7,18–19; 21:19–29 / *II Kings,* 5:20–27; 9:1–10:11; 17:6–18:12 / *I Chronicles,* 10:13–14; 13:9–11; 21 / *II Chronicles,* 6:24–42; 12; 21:12–20; 26:16–21; 36 / *Ezra* / *Job* / *Psalms,* 9:16–17; 11; 18; 21:8–12; 34; 37; 78–79 passim; 89:28–33; 94; 112 / *Isaiah,* 1; 2:5–3:26; 5; 9:13–10:27; 13–24; 28–32; 33:7–14; 34; 42:13–25; 47; 63:1–6; 65–66 / *Jeremiah,* 1; 4–9; 11; 13:9–14:12; 15:1–9; 16; 17:27–19:13; 21–29; 34; 44; 46–52 / *Lamentations* / *Ezekiel,* 5–7; 9; 11; 13–18; 20–39 / *Daniel,* 4; 5:17–30 / *Hosea,* 4–13 / *Joel* passim / *Amos* / *Obadiah* / *Micah* passim / *Nahum* / *Habakkuk* / *Zephaniah* / *Zechariah,* 7:8–14; 11:1–9,17; 12–14 / *Malachi,* 2
APOCRYPHA: *Wisdom of Solomon,* 12:1–8; 16–19 / *Ecclesiasticus,* 7:16–17; 21:9–10 / *I Maccabees,* 6:1–16 / *II Maccabees*
NEW TESTAMENT: *Matthew,* 10:14–15,28; 11:20–24; 13:41–42,49–50; 24:41–46 / *Mark,* 9:42–48 / *Luke,* 16:19–26 / *Acts,* 12:20–23; 13:4–12 / *II Thessalonians,* 1:7–9 / *Hebrews,* 10:26–31 / *II Peter,* 2 / *Jude,* 5–16 / *Revelation,* 9; 14:9–11; 20:9–10,12–15
4 HOMER, 3–6, 252–254
5 AESCHYLUS, 15–26, 40–51, 55–56, 75–76, 81–91
5 SOPHOCLES, 99–101, 143–155
5 EURIPIDES, 340–352
6 HERODOTUS, 103, 159, 173–174, 199, 203, 211–213, 308
7 PLATO, 246–247, 313–314, 806
12 LUCRETIUS, 42–43
13 VIRGIL, 218–227
17 PLOTINUS, 154
18 AUGUSTINE, 334–335, 360–380 esp 360–366, 372–376, 530–618, 629
19 AQUINAS, 333–338, 581–582, 692–693
20 AQUINAS, 178–192, 556–557, 897–900, 932–935, 992–996, 1016–1085
21 DANTE, 1–157
22 CHAUCER, 374–382, 434–448, 499–502
23 HOBBES, 191–198, 244, 253–258
24 RABELAIS, 119–122
32 MILTON, 309–310, 339–378
33 PASCAL, 205–209
35 LOCKE, 198, 230
35 HUME, 500, 503
37 FIELDING, 20–21, 75
40 GIBBON, 187–189
41 GIBBON, 233–234
44 BOSWELL, 363, 482
48 MELVILLE, 30–36
52 DOSTOEVSKY, 10–11, 185

5e. The justice of divine punishment

OLD TESTAMENT: *Ezra,* 9:10–15 / *Job* / *Psalms,* 28:3–4 / *Proverbs,* 11:31; 24:12 / *Isaiah,* 59:16–19; 65:6–7
APOCRYPHA: *Wisdom of Solomon,* 12; 14:27–31; 14:18–16:1; 19:4,13 / *Ecclesiasticus,* 11:26 / *II Maccabees,* 4:38; 7:36–38; 9
NEW TESTAMENT: *Romans,* 2:5–11; 3:5–6 / *II Corinthians,* 5:10 / *Hebrews,* 2:1–4
5 AESCHYLUS, 75–76
5 SOPHOCLES, 182–195
5 EURIPIDES, 365–377
6 HERODOTUS, 237–239
7 PLATO, 125–126, 292–293, 436–441
17 PLOTINUS, 150
18 AUGUSTINE, 361, 366, 388–390, 419, 571–572, 633
19 AQUINAS, 126–127, 819–820
20 AQUINAS, 465–474, 997–1016

21 DANTE, 4, 5, 18–19, 26–27, 43, 84, 114, 128
23 HOBBES, 160–161
27 SHAKESPEARE, 263, 270–271, 502–503
32 MILTON, 137–139, 277–279, 354–355, 364–365
35 LOCKE, 194
36 STERNE, 282–287
44 BOSWELL, 482, 539–540
52 DOSTOEVSKY, 337–346
54 FREUD, 878

5*e*(1) The justification of eternal suffering in Hell or Hades

OLD TESTAMENT: *Psalms*, 21:8–12 / *Isaiah*, 14:4–23; 33:10–14
APOCRYPHA: *Judith*, 16:17 / *Wisdom of Solomon*, 4:16–5:14 / *Ecclesiasticus*, 7:16–17
NEW TESTAMENT: *Matthew*, 11:20–24; 13:41–42,49–50; 25:41–46 / *Mark*, 9:42–48; 16:16 / *Luke*, 16:19–26 / *James*, 5:1–6 / *Jude*, 6–13 / *Revelation*, 9; 19:17–21; 20:9–10,12
5 ARISTOPHANES, 565–566
7 PLATO, 249–250, 437–438, 767–768
18 AUGUSTINE, 360–361, 529–530, 570–571, 576–579
20 AQUINAS, 1040–1042, 1066–1085
21 DANTE, 1–52
23 HOBBES, 254
26 SHAKESPEARE, 115
44 BOSWELL, 363, 514–515
52 DOSTOEVSKY, 169–170, 337–346

5*e*(2) The necessity of expiation in Purgatory

APOCRYPHA: *II Maccabees*, 12:43–45
18 AUGUSTINE, 554–555, 571–572, 577–579
20 AQUINAS, 886–887, 891–893, 1066
21 DANTE, 53–105
23 HOBBES, 251, 255–258
44 BOSWELL, 173

6. Pathological motivations with respect to punishment: abnormal sense of sin or guilt; perverse desires to inflict or suffer punishment

6 HERODOTUS, 95–97
9 ARISTOTLE, 373, 419–420
15 TACITUS, 14–15, 168
26 SHAKESPEARE, 170–198
27 SHAKESPEARE, 306–308
40 GIBBON, 55, 216, 389
51 TOLSTOY, 174, 183–186, 188–190, 271–274, 349–350, 505–511
52 DOSTOEVSKY, 122–125, 317–320, 324–329 passim
54 FREUD, 204, 328, 712–715, 730–731, 743–744, 831–832, 851–852

CROSS-REFERENCES

For: Another discussion of the distinction between the pain of sense and the pain of loss, *see* PLEASURE AND PAIN 4e.

The general problem of the justice or utility of punishment, *see* JUSTICE 10c; LAW 6e(2).

Responsibility as a condition of just punishment, *see* LIBERTY 3c; SIN 6a–6b; VIRTUE AND VICE 5c; WILL 5b(4).

Rewards and punishments as factors in moral training, *see* EDUCATION 4; FAMILY 6d; PLEASURE AND PAIN 8a, 10a; VIRTUE AND VICE 4d(2).

The discussion of punishment as a sanction of law, *see* LAW 6a; and for the general theory of crime and its punishment, *see* JUSTICE 10c; LAW 6e–6e(3).

Another consideration of the penal use of labor, *see* LABOR 1c; SLAVERY 3a.

The sacramental aspect of the punishment of sin, *see* SIN 4e; and for the nature and justice of divine punishment, *see* GOD 5i; HAPPINESS 7c(3); IMMORTALITY 5d–5e; JUSTICE 11a; SIN 6c–6e.

Other discussions of the sense of sin and of repentance, and of the desire or need for punishment, *see* PLEASURE AND PAIN 8c; SIN 5.

ADDITIONAL READINGS

Listed below are works not included in *Great Books of the Western World*, but relevant to the idea and topics with which this chapter deals. These works are divided into two groups:

I. Works by authors represented in this collection.
II. Works by authors not represented in this collection.

For the date, place, and other facts concerning the publication of the works cited, consult the Bibliography of Additional Readings which follows the last chapter of *The Great Ideas.*

I.

AQUINAS. *Summa Contra Gentiles*, BK III, CH 139–145
——. *Quaestiones Disputatae, De Malo*, Q 5
FIELDING. *Jonathan Wild*
A. SMITH. *The Theory of Moral Sentiments*, PART II, SECT I
KANT. *Lectures on Ethics*, pp 47–70
DOSTOEVSKY. *The House of the Dead*
——. *Crime and Punishment*
TOLSTOY. *Anna Karenina*
——. *Resurrection*
FREUD. *Totem and Taboo*

II.

SAADIA GAON. *The Book of Beliefs and Opinions*, TREATISE IX
ANSELM OF CANTERBURY. *Cur Deus Homo?*
BONAVENTURA. *Breviloquium*, PART VII
T. MORE. *Utopia*, BK I
DEFOE. *Moll Flanders*
J. BUTLER. *The Analogy of Religion*, PART I, CH 2–5
BECCARIA. *Crimes and Punishments*
VOLTAIRE. "Crimes or Offences," "Criminal," in *A Philosophical Dictionary*
HOWARD. *The State of the Prisons*
GODWIN. *An Enquiry Concerning Political Justice*, BK VII, CH I
COLERIDGE. *The Rime of the Ancient Mariner*
BENTHAM. *An Introduction to the Principles of Morals and Legislation*, CH 12–17
——. *The Theory of Legislation*
——. *The Rationale of Punishment*
——. *The Rationale of Reward*
DICKENS. *Oliver Twist*
——. *Nicholas Nickleby*
HAWTHORNE. *The Scarlet Letter*
HUGO. *Les Misérables*
R. BROWNING. *The Ring and the Book*
S. BUTLER. *Erewhon*
MAUDSLEY. *Responsibility in Mental Disease*
T. HARDY. *The Return of the Native*
T. H. GREEN. *The Principles of Political Obligation*, (K)
S. M. GREEN. *Crime: Its Nature, Causes, Treatment and Prevention*
IBSEN. *Ghosts*
——. *Hedda Gabler*
SALEILLES. *The Individualisation of Punishment*
BRADLEY. *Collected Essays*, VOL I (7)
PIRANDELLO. *The Outcast*
WHARTON. *Ethan Frome*
FAUCONNET. *La responsabilité*
MALINOWSKI. *Crime and Custom in Savage Society*
EWING. *The Morality of Punishment*
ROSS. *The Right and the Good*, II (I)
O'NEILL. *Emperor Jones*
——. *Mourning Becomes Electra*
SHAW. *Crude Criminology*

Chapter 75: QUALITY

INTRODUCTION

IT is sometimes supposed that the fundamental categories in terms of which men think they are describing reality or their experience merely reflect the conventions of their language. Substance and attribute—and among attributes, quality and quantity—happen to be fundamental categories in western thought, it is held, only because the group of languages which the western cultures use all have a grammatical structure that involves a distinction between noun and adjective and between different kinds of adjectives. It is said, for example, that Aristotle's enumeration of the categories is merely a verbal classification based on Greek grammar. When he says that the basic terms of discourse represent substances, qualities, quantities, relations, and so forth, he is recognizing the grammatical difference between such words as "man" and "white," or between "white" and "six feet tall" and "double." The lineaments of reality, the varieties of being, or the modes of experience are not, it is held, thereby finally described.

In the tradition of the great books, another interpretation generally prevails. Even those who disagree in one way or another about the basic categories do not regard them as conventional or of linguistic origin. Kant, for example, disagrees with Aristotle's listing of the categories. He makes substance a mode of relation rather than coordinate with quality, quantity, and relation. He calls his categories "transcendental" to indicate that they are not drawn from experience and that, as *a priori* forms of thought, they determine the structure of all possible experience. Aristotle, on the other hand, draws his categories from experience. He thinks that they represent fundamental modes of being and that they are, therefore, the basic concepts in terms of which thought apprehends reality. Despite all these differences, Kant and Aristotle agree that the categories signify real—not verbal—distinctions. Their agreement on this point seems to be shared even by those, like Hume, who question our ability to know whether substances exist; or those, like Berkeley, who question the validity of the distinction between quality and quantity.

In one sense, no one questions the existence of qualities, as they do the existence of substances—the enduring things, material or otherwise, in which qualities are supposed to inhere. Everyone somehow acknowledges the hot and the cold, the light and the dark, the moist and the dry, the hard and the soft. But such acknowledgement does not preclude a number of basic questions about quality on which much disagreement exists.

Are qualities attributes? Do they exist, that is, only as *qualifiers*, only as belonging to something else? Or do they exist independently, in and of themselves? If qualities are attributes, do they belong to things quite apart from our experience of them, or do they belong to things only as experienced and have no separate reality? Do things have in reality certain attributes that cause in us the experience of other traits which we then attribute to the things themselves?

Are all the attributes of things, whether in or apart from experience, to be conceived as qualities, and if so, are there different kinds of qualities? Or is quality only one kind of attribute, and if so, how is quality related to other kinds of attributes? Is quality, for example, distinct from quantity, dependent on quantity, reducible to quantity, affected by quantity?

These questions appear to be related in ways which make the issues they raise dependent on one another. If, in addition, their presuppositions and implications are observed, it will be seen that they cannot be fully discussed without entering into matters considered in other chapters, such as the notions of substance and accident in the chapter on Being; the theory of experience and the various accounts of sense-perception and the objects of sense in the chapters on Experience and Sense; and, of course, some of the principal topics considered in the closely related chapter on Quantity.

Spinoza distinguishes between substance and mode as that which exists in itself and that which exists in another thing. He lays down as an axiom that "everything which is, is either in itself or in another." Whether or not qualities are modes of substance, it seems to be clear that Spinoza would not call them substances. The notion of qualities existing in themselves, and not as the qualities *of* anything, seems to be self-contradictory. As Descartes points out, to assert "the existence of real accidents," by which he means the existence of qualities or quantities apart from substances, is to deny the distinction between substance and accident. "Substance," he writes, "can never be conceived after the fashion of accidents, nor can it derive its reality from them"; whereas "no reality can be ascribed to [accidents], which is not taken from the idea of substance."

Anyone who acknowledges the distinction between substance and accident also conceives qualities as accidents or attributes, *i.e.*, as existing in the things they qualify. Spinoza, Descartes, Locke, and Aristotle do not conceive substance in the same way, nor do they all use the word "accident" to name the characteristics which inhere in substance. Locke, for example, uses the word "quality" with almost the same generality that Spinoza gives to the word "mode," or Descartes and Aristotle to "accident." And the word "substance" Locke uses in a sense that is nearer to Aristotle's meaning for the word "matter," when, in trying to conceive bare substance as the underlying "I know not what," Locke defines this substratum as that which supports qualities. Apart from its qualities, substance has no positive characteristics.

Nevertheless, such differences in theory leave untouched the point of agreement that qualities do not float freely—without any support—in either reality or experience. Even Berkeley's denial of matter, or of bodies existing apart from their being perceived, does not turn qualities into substances, for qualities *as perceived* are the qualities of bodies *as perceived*, and both together have their existence *in* the perceiver.

The contrary view—that qualities exist in and of themselves—does not seem to receive clear or explicit expression in the tradition of the great books. It may be implied in the conception of experience which Hume develops more fully in the *Treatise on Human Nature* than in the *Enquiry*. There it seems to be supposed that each element of experience has the same reality as any other; that each stands by itself without any perceptible dependence upon any other; and that it has no existence beyond its momentary appearance. On this view no enduring substances exist. In addition, it is as appropriate to call the elements of experience "qualities" as it is to call them anything else. Experience can be described as nothing but qualities and relations—or as qualities related by succession and contiguity.

The notion that experience is a continual flux in which nothing has a continuing identity from moment to moment, seems to be basic to any theory which denies substances and affirms the independent reality of qualities. The theory of qualities which Plato attributes to Heraclitus or his followers illustrates this. "Their first principle," Socrates tells Theaetetus, "is that all is motion, and upon this all the affections of which we were just now speaking are supposed to depend; there is nothing but motion, which has two forms, one active and the other passive, both in endless number; and out of the union and friction of them is generated a progeny endless in number, having two forms, sense and the object of sense."

For example, "when the eye and the appropriate object meet together and give birth to whiteness and the sensation connatural with it . . . then, while the sight is flowing from the eye, whiteness proceeds from the object which combines in producing the color. . . . This is true of all sensible objects, hard, warm, and the like, which are similarly to be regarded not as having any absolute existence, but as being all of them generated by motion in their intercourse with one another . . . for the agent has no existence until united with the patient, and the patient has no existence until united with the agent. . . .

And from all these considerations," Socrates says, "there arises a general reflection that there is no self-existent thing, but everything is becoming and in relation."

Socrates explains that, for those who assert a universal flux, qualities are not only the products of motion, but also are themselves in motion—"not even white continues to flow white, and whiteness itself is a flux or change which is passing into another color." There is no need to refute this doctrine, Socrates thinks, since it refutes itself by its unintelligibility or, worse, its inability to say anything definite in consequence of denying that words can have a constant meaning from moment to moment.

Aristotle concurs in this attitude toward "the most extreme view of the professed Heracliteans," but goes on to remark that "not even at different times does one sense disagree about the quality, but only about that to which the quality belongs. I mean, for instance, that the same wine might seem, if either it or one's body changed, at one time sweet and at another time not sweet; but at least the sweet, such as it is when it exists, has never yet changed." The sweet thing may become sour, either in itself or to us, but sweetness itself never becomes sourness.

THAT QUALITIES DO NOT change into one another, whereas substances undergoing alteration change from one quality to another, seems to Aristotle to distinguish quality from substance. "The most distinctive mark of substance," he writes, "appears to be that, while remaining numerically one and the same, it is capable of having contrary qualities. . . . Thus, one and the same color cannot be white and black. . . . But the same individual person is at one time white, at another black, at one time warm, at another cold, at one time good, at another bad." The qualities do not change, but the substance in changing, passes from one quality to its contrary. (The difference between change of quality, or alteration, and the other types of change which substances can undergo, is discussed in the chapter on CHANGE.)

Aristotle suggests another mark of distinction between substance and quality. One substance, he says, never stands to another as its contrary, in the way in which qualities are contrary to one another, like hot and cold, white and black, good and bad. A quality may have a correlative as well as a contrary, *e.g.*, if knowledge is a quality of mind, the object known is its correlative, whereas ignorance of the object is the contrary of knowledge. In some cases, the contrary qualities may be the extremes or limits of a continuous series of intermediates, *e.g.*, white and black with all the intermediate greys. In some cases, as with knowledge and ignorance, the contrary qualities have no intermediates. (Contrariety and correlation, most frequently exemplified by qualities, are considered in the chapter on OPPOSITION.)

Still another mark of distinction between substance and quality, according to Aristotle, is that qualities *do* and substances *do not* admit of variation in degree. "One man cannot be more man than another," he writes, "as that which is white may be more or less white than some other white object. . . . The same quality, moreover, is said to subsist in a thing in varying degrees at different times. A white body is said to be whiter at one time than it was before, or a warm body is said to be warmer or less warm than at some other time."

This observation raises a number of questions. Does variation in the degree of a quality from time to time imply that qualities themselves undergo change, just as substances undergo change in quality? Do they remain one and the same in kind while varying in degree? Is this change which qualities undergo as they increase or decrease in intensity, a change in quantity? Furthermore, does the fact that something white can become more or less white, mean that a quality can have a certain quantity even as a body can? Aquinas suggests an answer by distinguishing between what he calls the "dimensive quantity" of bodies and the "virtual quantity" of qualities. Virtual quantity is the degree or intensity which non-quantitative attributes may possess—such personal qualities as virtues and habits, or such corporeal qualities as colors and textures.

But this still seems to leave a very difficult question to be answered. How can qualities have the attribute of quantity without becoming substances? On the principle which both Aristotle and Aquinas accept—that accidents exist only in substances—how can one kind of accident (quantity) exist in another (quality)? The view which William James holds, namely, that variation in intensity creates differences in color as much as variation in hue, would solve the problem, or rather it would dismiss the problem as not genuine by denying Aristotle's thesis that a color can remain the same while varying in degree.

However handled, the problem is not peculiar to qualities. Actions and passions, Aristotle points out, also vary in degree. Nor are qualities distinguished from everything else in the world by having contraries. Correlatives can also have contraries, as can actions and passions. Furthermore, not all qualities have contraries. Not all admit of variation in degree. Shape, like triangular or square, which Aristotle regards as a kind of quality, cannot vary in this way. The square thing cannot become more or less square. In view of all this, Aristotle concludes that there is one characteristic alone which differentiates quality not only from substance, but also from everything else. Quality is the basis for saying that things are like or unlike, similar or dissimilar, as quantity is the basis for saying that things are equal or unequal.

Other contrasts between quality and quantity, especially those bearing on the reduction of quality to quantity, are discussed in the chapter on QUANTITY. Here it may be illuminating to apply the foregoing distinction between quality and quantity to shapes or figures. Shape or figure is a curious mixture of quality and quantity. It is a quantified quality or a qualified quantity or, as Aquinas says, "a quality about quantity, since the nature of shape consists in fixing the bounds of magnitude." This seems to be evident in the fact that shapes, like quantities, do not admit of variation in degree. But it may also be seen in the fact that Euclid deals quite separately with problems concerning the *equality* of triangles and problems concerning their *similarity*.

EXCEPT FOR THE QUESTION of whether qualities subsist by themselves or are the attributes of substances, most of the problems of quality seem to concern its distinction from or relation to quantity. As we have seen, the question of the degree or amount of a quality involves the notion of quantity. Even more explicitly a problem of how qualities and quantities are related, is the question of the order of these two attributes. Can it be said that quantities are the more fundamental attributes of things and that they somehow precede or underlie qualities? Is it the reverse? Or are qualities prior in certain respects and quantities in other respects?

Aristotle's theory of the elements seems to give absolute primacy to quality in the realm of material things. The four elements of matter are characterized by combinations of two pairs of contrary qualities, the hot and the cold, the dry and the moist. On the other hand, the atomic theory of Lucretius appears to make quantities, such as size and weight, the primary properties of matter. Newton's enumeration of what he calls "the universal qualities of all bodies whatsoever," including, of course, their "least particles," lists "extension, hardness, impenetrability, mobility, and inertia." As indicated in the chapter on QUANTITY, the very reason Newton gives for calling these qualities "universal" would seem to justify calling them "quantities" rather than qualities. In any case, Newton's view, like that of the ancient atomists, seems to be opposed to the theory of the *elementary* and *contrary* qualities.

But Aristotle himself also appears to hold a view which makes quantity prior to quality. Considering the way in which the quality *white* is in a body, he says that it is in the body in virtue of the body's extended surface. If surface or extension is interpreted as a physical quantity, then it would seem to follow that this quantity underlies a body's possession of visible and perhaps other qualities. Aquinas, for example, says that "quantity is the proximate subject of the qualities that cause alteration, as surface is of color," and, again, that "quantity is in substance before sensible qualities are."

This last statement can be interpreted to mean that quantity is universally prior to quality among the attributes of substance. Or it can be understood to mean that quantity is prior only to *sensible* qualities and then only among the physical attributes of bodies. Which interpretation is chosen depends in part on whether *all* qualities are sensible.

It would seem that all qualities are not sensible, according to Aristotle and Aquinas, and therefore quantity is not prior to every kind of quality among the accidents of substance. Natural qualities, Aquinas writes, "may be in the intellectual part or in the body and its powers." Certainly the qualities inherent in the intellectual part of man's nature are not sensible; nor are the first two of the four species of quality which both Aristotle and Aquinas enumerate.

In their enumeration, human qualities—the habits or dispositions of a man, such as knowledge and virtue, or beauty and health—are the first sort. The powers or inborn capacities whereby men and other animals act to develop their natures are a second type of quality; *e.g.*, the power of sensitivity in animals, the power of rationality in men, are qualities proper to these species and are, therefore, sometimes called "properties." This second type of quality does not seem to be restricted to living things. Inanimate bodies also have, among their properties, certain fundamental powers of action or reaction. The third and fourth types of quality differ from the first two in that both are sensible, *i.e.*, capable of affecting the senses directly and, therefore, sometimes called "affective qualities." Of these, the third type—shape or figure—has already been discussed. The fourth type—colors, sounds, textures, odors, tastes, and such thermal qualities as hot and cold—are, more than shape or figure, regarded as the principal affective or sensible qualities.

The fact that Aristotle regards certain qualities, such as hot and cold, or hard and soft, as being dispositions or powers as well as being affective qualities, need not invalidate his fourfold classification. His classification of the same attribute under two distinct species of quality seems to imply that it can be considered from two points of view. The elementary qualities, for example, are affective or sensible qualities but they are also the active qualities or powers —the properties—of the elements.

In view of this classification of qualities, it does not seem to be the case that quantities are prior to *all* the qualitative attributes of substance. On the conception of living things as composite of soul and body, the qualities which are vital powers are usually regarded as properties which the thing has in virtue of having a soul. They are certainly not founded upon the quantitative attributes of the organism's body. The moral and spiritual qualities of men seem to afford another example of qualities either prior to, or at least independent of, quantities. Even in the case of inanimate bodies, it may be that certain fundamental properties or powers are essentially qualitative rather than quantitative. The proposition that in substances, quantities are prior to qualities—or that qualities inhere in substances in virtue of their quantities—may apply only to sensible qualities, as, for example, colors in relation to surfaces.

ONE OF THE GREAT ISSUES in the tradition of western thought concerns our perception or knowledge of qualities. If certain characteristics which are not directly sensible are to be called "qualities," then the problem of how we know such qualities does not differ from the problem of how we know anything else that cannot be apprehended by our senses. We may, for example, be able to infer such qualities as habits or powers from the sensible evidences of a thing's behavior, even as in turn we infer the thing's nature or essence from its proper qualities or properties. With regard to sensible qualities, the problem does not seem to be *how* we know them—for the fact that they are sensible means that they are knowable by the senses. The question is rather one of the mode of existence—the objectivity or subjectivity—of the qualities sensed.

Locke's famous distinction between primary and secondary qualities states the problem. It is preceded by his distinction between the qualities of things and the ideas in our minds. "A snow-ball," he writes, has "the power to produce in us the idea of white, cold, and round. The powers to produce those ideas in us, as they are in the snow-ball, I call qualities; and as they are sensations or perceptions in our understandings, I call them ideas; which ideas, if I speak of them sometimes as in the things themselves, I would be understood to mean those qualities in the objects which produce them in us."

The primary qualities of bodies are those which are utterly inseparable from body—such as "sense constantly finds in every particle of matter which has bulk enough to be perceived, and the mind finds inseparable from every particle of matter, though less than to make itself singly perceived by our senses." Locke's enumeration of these "original or primary qualities of body, which we may observe to produce simple ideas in us, *viz.*, solidity, extension, figure, motion or rest, and number," closely resembles Newton's list of the universal qualities of perceptible bodies and of their "least particles" or atoms.

In contrast, the secondary qualities, such as colors, sounds, tastes, etc., are "nothing in the objects themselves, but powers to produce various sensations in us by their primary qualities, *i.e.*, by the bulk, figure, texture, and motion of their insensible parts. . . . From whence," Locke declares, "I think it is easy to draw this observation, that the ideas of primary qualities of bodies, are resemblances of them, and their patterns do really exist in the bodies themselves, but the ideas produced in us by these secondary qualities, have no resemblance of them at all. There is nothing like our ideas existing in the bodies themselves. They are in the bodies we denominate from them, only a power to produce those sensations in us: what is sweet, blue, or warm, in idea, is but the certain bulk, figure and motion of the insensible parts in the bodies which we call so."

Locke thinks the sensation of pain confirms this insight. As the piece of steel which by its corporeal properties has the power to produce pain in us, does not itself have the quality of pain, so it does not have anything corresponding to the ideas of blueness or coldness which it produces in us, except the power to produce these ideas through the action of its primary qualities on our senses. Yet Locke maintains that all our simple ideas of quality—not only of primary, but also of secondary qualities—"agree with the reality of things." By *agreement* he does not mean *resemblance* in the sense of copying; and therefore he thinks he can, without inconsistency, deny any *resemblance* between sensations of color or taste and the secondary qualities of bodies, while saying that "if sugar produces in us the ideas we call whiteness and sweetness, we are sure there is a power in sugar to produce those ideas in our minds, or else they could not have been produced by it."

Locke's point, however, is sometimes given exactly the opposite implication. Earlier thinkers who do not speak of primary and secondary qualities attribute to bodies only the characteristics which Locke calls primary, and give what he calls secondary qualities no reality at all, that is, no existence outside the mind. The secondary qualities are not qualities of things, but of sensations or images. Descartes, for example, says that nothing belongs "to the nature or essence of body except . . . length, breadth and depth, admitting of various shapes and various motions. . . . On the other hand, colors, odors, savours, and the rest of such things are merely sensations existing in my thought, and differing no less from bodies than pain differs from the shape and motion of the instrument which inflicts it."

Hobbes similarly regards the various sensible qualities as feelings in us—the seemings or fancies of sense. All these "qualities called sensible are in the object that causes them, nothing but so many several motions of the matter. . . . The object is one thing, the fancy is another." One type of "absurd assertion," in the opinion of Hobbes, consists in giving "the names of the accidents of bodies without us, to the accidents of our own bodies, as they do that say, *the color is in the body, the sound is in the air*, etc."

The attributes or accidents which Descartes and Hobbes assign to bodies seem to be quantities rather than qualities. Accordingly, whereas Locke attributes both primary and secondary *qualities* to bodies, Hobbes and Descartes seem to be saying that bodies differ from one another only quantitatively, and that qualities or qualitative differences occur only in the realm of sense or thought. Expounding the atomism of Democritus and Epicurus, Lucretius appears to make precisely this point when he says that the first-beginnings or atoms are characterized only by size, weight, shape, and motion. "The bodies of matter," he writes, "have no color at all." They are bereft not only of color; "they are also sundered altogether from warmth and cold, and fiery heat, and are carried along barren of sound and devoid of taste." These qualities, caused by the blows of the atoms upon the sense-organs of animals, are the qualities of sensations, not of things.

THE CRITICISM OF THIS THEORY—whether in the formulation of Locke or in that of Descartes,

Hobbes, and Lucretius—seems itself to take two forms. Aristotle, for example, criticizes Democritus and the atomists for treating perceptible qualities differently from perceptible quantities. According to his own theory of the objects of sense, some, like colors, sounds, odors, flavors—which Locke calls "secondary qualities" and the others simply "qualities"—are the proper objects of the special senses, such as sight, hearing, smell, taste. In contrast to these "proper sensibles," each exclusively perceived by one and only one sense, there are the "common sensibles," such as size and shape, number, movement and rest, which can be perceived commonly by several senses, *e.g.*, shape is visible and tangible, motion is visible and audible. Such sensible attributes of body, which Locke calls "primary qualities," Aristotle, no less than Hobbes or Lucretius, regards as quantities, not qualities. Reporting his view, Aquinas writes that "the common sensibles are all reducible to quantity."

Aristotle's critical point seems to be that the atomists "reduce the proper to the common sensibles, as Democritus does with white and black; for he asserts that the latter is a mode of the rough and the former a mode of the smooth, while he reduces savours to the atomic figures." The atomists sometimes make the opposite error of representing "all objects of sense as objects of touch." But in either case they have no ground, in Aristotle's opinion, for giving to certain sensible attributes—whether these be tangible qualities or the commonly sensible quantities—an objective reality they deny to other sensible traits, like colors, sounds, and odors.

Aristotle's theory of sensation and the sensible is discussed more fully in the chapter on SENSE. According to it, the qualities, no less than the quantities, perceptible by sense have real or actual existence as the attributes of bodies. On this score Aristotle does not differentiate between qualities (the proper sensibles) and quantities (the common sensibles). Just as a body actually has the shape we perceive it to have, so it actually has the color we perceive it to have, on the supposition, of course, that our perception is accurate in both cases. If the senses are fallible at all, we are less prone to make errors, Aristotle thinks, in the field of the proper than of the common sensibles, *e.g.*, the stick in water which looks bent to the eye feels straight to the hand.

PRECISELY THE OPPOSITE direction seems to be taken by Berkeley and Hume. Where Aristotle criticizes the atomists for treating quantities (or common sensibles) as objective, and qualities (or proper sensibles) as subjective, Berkeley criticizes Locke for treating primary and secondary qualities differently. Where Aristotle's own theory assigns the same reality to all objects of sense, granting them an actuality apart from perception, Berkeley makes the actuality of the primary as well as the secondary qualities dependent upon their being perceived.

"Some there are," writes Berkeley, "who make a distinction betwixt *primary* and *secondary* qualities. By the former they mean extension, figure, motion, rest, solidity or impenetrability and number; by the latter they denote all other sensible qualities, as colors, sounds, tastes and so forth. The ideas we have of these they acknowledge not to be the resemblances of anything existing without the mind or unperceived, but they will have our ideas of the primary qualities to be patterns or images of things which exist without the mind, in an unthinking substance which they call Matter."

Berkeley then argues that the so-called primary qualities are incapable of being separated, in reality or thought, from the secondary qualities, and that, therefore, the one like the other exists only in the mind. "In short, let anyone consider those arguments which are thought manifestly to prove that colors and tastes exist only in the mind, and he shall find they may with equal force be brought to prove the same thing of extension, figure, and motion." His own arguments, he thinks, "plainly show it to be impossible that any color or extension at all, or other sensible quality whatsoever, should exist in any unthinking subject without the mind, or in truth, that there should be any such thing as an outward object."

Hume professes to adopt Berkeley's reasoning. "It is universally allowed by modern enquirers," he writes, "that all the sensible qualities of objects, such as hard, soft, hot, cold, white, black, etc., are merely secondary, and exist not in the objects themselves, but are perceptions of the mind, without any external archetype or model which they represent. If this be allowed, with regard to secondary qualities, it must also follow with regard to the supposed primary qualities of extension and solidity.... The idea of extension is entirely acquired from the senses of sight and feeling; and if all the qualities, perceived by the senses, be in the mind, not in the object, the same conclusion must reach the idea of extension. . . . Nothing can save us from this conclusion, but the asserting that the ideas of those primary qualities are attained by *Abstraction*, an opinion, which, if we examine it accurately, we shall find to be unintelligible, and even absurd."

One fundamental point about sensible qualities may, however, remain unaffected by this long and many-sided controversy. No one denies that sensible qualities are the elements of human experience. That they are "the original, innate, or *a priori* properties of our subjective nature," James declares, must be allowed by "all schools (however they otherwise differ). . . . This is so on either of the two hypotheses we may make concerning the relation of the feelings to the realities at whose touch they become alive."

OUTLINE OF TOPICS

1. The nature and existence of qualities: the relation of quality to substance or matter; the transcendental categories of quality

2. The kinds of quality
    - 2*a*. Sensible and nonsensible qualities: habits, dispositions, powers or capacities, and affective qualities
    - 2*b*. Primary and secondary qualities: the related distinction of proper and common sensibles

3. Quality and quantity
    - 3*a*. The distinction between quality and quantity: its relation to the distinction between secondary and primary qualities
    - 3*b*. Shape or figure as qualified quantity
    - 3*c*. The degrees or amounts of a quality: intensity and extensity; the quantitative conditions of variation in quality
    - 3*d*. The priority of quality or quantity in relation to form, matter, or substance

4. The relation of qualities to one another
    - 4*a*. Qualities which imply correlatives
    - 4*b*. The contrariety of qualities: with or without intermediate degrees
    - 4*c*. The similarity of things with respect to quality: likeness and unlikeness in quality

5. Change of quality: the analysis of alteration

6. Qualities as objects of knowledge
    - 6*a*. Quality in relation to definition or abstraction
    - 6*b*. The perception of qualities
    - 6*c*. The objectivity of sense-qualities: the comparative objectivity of primary and secondary qualities

REFERENCES

References are listed by volume number (in bold type), author's name, and page number. Bible references are to book, chapter, and verse of the Authorized King James version of the Bible. The abbreviation "esp" calls the reader's attention to one or more especially relevant parts of a whole reference; "passim" signifies that the topic is discussed intermittently rather than continuously in the work or passage cited. Where the work as a whole is relevant to the topic, the page numbers refer to the entire work. For general guidance in the use of *The Great Ideas*, consult the Preface.

1. The nature and existence of qualities: the relation of quality to substance or matter; the transcendental categories of quality

7 PLATO, 462–466
8 ARISTOTLE, 7–8, 13–16, 113–114, 541–542, 600–601
12 LUCRETIUS, 20–21
17 PLOTINUS, 30–31, 52–53, 60–62, 111–113, 173–174, 257–259, 267–268, 276–277, 284, 291–293
18 AUGUSTINE, 328
19 AQUINAS, 351–352, 436–438, 451–453, 588–589
20 AQUINAS, 21
23 HOBBES, 172
31 DESCARTES, 100, 164–165
35 LOCKE, 133–138, 152, 204–205, 241–243, 268–270, 316
35 BERKELEY, 403–444
35 HUME, 505–506
42 KANT, 29–33
53 JAMES, 546–547

2. The kinds of quality

2*a*. Sensible and nonsensible qualities: habits, dispositions, powers or capacities, and affective qualities

8 ARISTOTLE, 13–15, 543–544
17 PLOTINUS, 258–259, 289–292
20 AQUINAS, 2–6
35 LOCKE, 178–180, 214, 245–246

2*b*. Primary and secondary qualities: the related distinction of proper and common sensibles

7 PLATO, 464–465
8 ARISTOTLE, 648–649, 657, 673–674
10 GALEN, 169
12 LUCRETIUS, 51–53
19 AQUINAS, 410–413
20 AQUINAS, 1032–1034
31 DESCARTES, 162–165
34 NEWTON, 270–271
35 LOCKE, 131, 200, 238, 245–246, 263, 315–316, 322
35 BERKELEY, 414–416
53 JAMES, 503, 651

3. Quality and quantity

3*a*. The distinction between quality and quantity: its relation to the distinction between secondary and primary qualities

8 ARISTOTLE, 614
12 LUCRETIUS, 32–33, 51–53
17 PLOTINUS, 55, 196
23 HOBBES, 49
31 DESCARTES, 19
35 LOCKE, 134, 206, 311–312, 316
35 BERKELEY, 417–418, 427, 432–433
42 KANT, 66–72, 211–213
46 HEGEL, 122–123
50 MARX, 149

3*b*. Shape or figure as qualified quantity

8 ARISTOTLE, 15, 16, 541
11 NICOMACHUS, 831–841
17 PLOTINUS, 288–289
19 AQUINAS, 31
20 AQUINAS, 710–711
31 DESCARTES, 295–353
33 PASCAL, 455–456
42 KANT, 212
53 JAMES, 548–552

3*c*. The degrees or amounts of a quality: intensity and extensity; the quantitative conditions of variation in quality

7 PLATO, 615–616
8 ARISTOTLE, 8, 15–16, 166, 297, 531, 584–585, 589
9 ARISTOTLE, 114, 173–174, 427
12 LUCRETIUS, 53
18 AUGUSTINE, 328
19 AQUINAS, 35–36, 224–225, 721–722
20 AQUINAS, 6–7, 15–22, 412–413, 491–498, 754–755
28 GALILEO, 200–202, 205
30 BACON, 145–148
34 NEWTON, 431–443, 458–460, 466–467, 472–474, 482–485
35 LOCKE, 165–166, 169, 311–312
42 KANT, 68–72
45 LAVOISIER, 99–103
45 FOURIER, 169–172, 177–193

45 Faraday, 411–412
53 James, 319–322, 540–547
54 Freud, 403–404

3*d*. The priority of quality or quantity in relation to form, matter, or substance

8 Aristotle, 260, 683–684, 688–689
17 Plotinus, 55, 196, 289
19 Aquinas, 451–453
20 Aquinas, 976–978
31 Descartes, 18–19, 162–165
35 Locke, 178, 206
35 Berkeley, 414–416
42 Kant, 41–45
46 Hegel, 28

4. The relation of qualities to one another

4*a*. Qualities which imply correlatives

8 Aristotle, 11, 16, 329–330

4*b*. The contrariety of qualities: with or without intermediate degrees

7 Plato, 226–227, 243–244
8 Aristotle, 8–9, 15, 17, 428–431, 504, 539, 619
9 Aristotle, 376
10 Hippocrates, 4–7
10 Galen, 191–199 passim
17 Plotinus, 291–293
22 Chaucer, 13
48 Melville, 39–40
53 James, 327–328, 363–364

4*c*. The similarity of things with respect to quality: likeness and unlikeness in quality

7 Plato, 493–494
8 Aristotle, 10–11, 538–539, 581
9 Aristotle, 7
17 Plotinus, 7, 206
19 Aquinas, 22–23, 738–739
20 Aquinas, 885–886, 1025–1032
42 Kant, 602–603
53 James, 344–348, 378–379

5. Change of quality: the analysis of alteration

7 Plato, 226–227, 509–510, 533–534
8 Aristotle, 20–21, 198, 325, 328–330, 346, 409–410, 416–417, 544, 647–648, 685
9 Aristotle, 235–237, 264
10 Galen, 167–169, 203–204
12 Lucretius, 8–12, 64–66
17 Plotinus, 111–113
19 Aquinas, 262–263
20 Aquinas, 15–18, 971–972
30 Bacon, 114–115, 139–140
34 Newton, 541
35 Locke, 178, 203, 217
35 Berkeley, 417–419
45 Lavoisier, 103
53 James, 68

6. Qualities as objects of knowledge

6*a*. Quality in relation to definition or abstraction

8 Aristotle, 177–178, 196–199, 541
17 Plotinus, 60–61, 257–259, 289–292
19 Aquinas, 774–775
35 Locke, 145, 147, 260–263
35 Berkeley, 414–416, 432
35 Hume, 505
42 Kant, 73–74
53 James, 185, 305–308, 329–331, 668–673

6*b*. The perception of qualities

7 Plato, 177, 462–466, 519–522, 533
8 Aristotle, 12–13, 647–659, 661, 664, 673–689, 703–704
12 Lucretius, 4, 44–47, 50, 92
19 Aquinas, 410–411
20 Aquinas, 971–974
23 Hobbes, 49
31 Descartes, 18–19, 100
34 Newton, 428
35 Locke, 93, 127–128, 138–140 passim, 270–271
42 Kant, 15, 23–24, 29–33
48 Melville, 144–145
53 James, 98–105, 327–341, 452–471, 502–505, 520–521, 526–527, 540–635
54 Freud, 384–385

6*c*. The objectivity of sense-qualities: the comparative objectivity of primary and secondary qualities

7 Plato, 462–466
8 Aristotle, 530, 683–684
10 Galen, 167
12 Lucretius, 24–26
23 Hobbes, 57, 62, 258, 262
31 Descartes, 19, 162–165, 211, 228–231
34 Newton, 270–271, 428
35 Locke, 134–138, 205–208, 238–239, 245–246, 311–312, 314, 322, 324, 355–357
35 Berkeley, 413–431
35 Hume, 504–506
42 Kant, 15, 23–24, 29–33, 69–72, 385
50 Marx, 31
53 James, 127–128, 150–151, 176–177, 457–479, 650–651, 851–852

CROSS-REFERENCES

For: Discussions relevant to the problem of the existence of qualities and of their relation to substance, matter, or experience, *see* BEING 7b, 7b(5)–7b(6); EXPERIENCE 1; MATTER 2c.

Discussions relevant to the conception of the categories as transcendental concepts of the understanding, *see* FORM 1c; JUDGMENT 8c–8d; MEMORY AND IMAGINATION 6c(2); MIND 1e(1); PRINCIPLE 2b(3).

The consideration of such non-sensible qualities as habits, dispositions, and powers, *see* BEING 7c(2); HABIT 1; LIFE AND DEATH 2; MAN 4d; NATURE 1a(1); SOUL 2a, 2c.

The distinction between proper and common sensibles, and the related distinction between primary and secondary qualities, *see* SENSE 3c(2)–3c(4).

Other discussions of the relation of quantity to quality, *see* MECHANICS 4b; QUANTITY 1a; and for the problem of the variation of qualities in degree or intensity, *see* SAME AND OTHER 3c; SENSE 3c(2).

The contrariety and correlation of qualities, *see* OPPOSITION 1a–1b.

The conception of similarity as likeness in quality, *see* SAME AND OTHER 3c.

The distinction of alteration, or change in quality, from other kinds of change, *see* CHANGE 6, 9.

The general theory of sensitive knowledge and its bearing on the objectivity of sensible qualities, *see* KNOWLEDGE 6b(1); SENSE 4–4c.

ADDITIONAL READINGS

Listed below are works not included in *Great Books of the Western World*, but relevant to the idea and topics with which this chapter deals. These works are divided into two groups:

I. Works by authors represented in this collection.
II. Works by authors not represented in this collection.

For the date, place, and other facts concerning the publication of the works cited, consult the Bibliography of Additional Readings which follows the last chapter of *The Great Ideas.*

I.

BERKELEY. *Three Dialogues Between Hylas and Philonous*

KANT. *Metaphysical Foundations of Natural Science*, DIV II

——. *Introduction to Logic*, VIII

HEGEL. *Logic*, CH 7, par 91–98

II.

ORÊME. *Treatise on the Breadth of Forms*

SUÁREZ. *Disputationes Metaphysicae*, XIV, XVI, XVIII (3–6), XXXIX, XL (2), XLII–XLVI, LIII

JOHN OF SAINT THOMAS. *Cursus Philosophicus Thomisticus, Philosophia Naturalis*, PART III, Q 10

BOYLE. *The Origin of Forms and Qualities, According to the Corpuscular Philosophy*

LEIBNITZ. *New Essays Concerning Human Understanding*, BK II, CH 8

W. HAMILTON. *Lectures on Metaphysics and Logic*, VOL I (24)

C. S. PEIRCE. *Collected Papers*, VOL I, par 300–321, 422–426

BRADLEY. *Appearance and Reality*, BK I, CH 1, 3

BERGSON. *Matter and Memory*, CH 2, 4

J. C. WILSON. *Statement and Inference*, PART V (6, 12)

HUSSERL. *Ideas: General Introduction to Pure Phenomenology*, par 15, 40–41, 52, 124, 129, 133

W. E. JOHNSON. *Logic*, PART II, CH 7

WHITEHEAD. *The Concept of Nature*, CH 2

——. *Process and Reality*, PART III, CH 1–2

BORING. *The Physical Dimensions of Consciousness*, CH 6

Chapter 76: QUANTITY

INTRODUCTION

As indicated in the chapter on QUALITY, the traditional consideration of that fundamental notion involves questions concerning the relation of quality and quantity and the priority of one or the other in the nature of things. According to one theory of the elements, difference in quality rather than in quantity seems to be the defining characteristic. Certain kinds of qualities, it is thought, inhere in substances directly and without being based upon their quantitative aspects. But it is seldom if ever suggested that quality takes universal precedence over quantity.

In the tradition of western thought, the opposite view—that quantities are primary—seems to occur with some frequency, at least so far as the realm of material things is concerned. It is held that bodies have only quantitative attributes. Such sensible qualities as colors, odors, tastes, textures are thought to have no reality apart from experience; or, as it is sometimes put, red and blue, hot and cold, sweet and sour are the qualities of sensations, not of things.

Those who think that bodies can exist without being perceived, also tend to think that bodies can exist totally bereft of qualities, but never without the dimensions of quantity. The notions of matter and quantity seem to be inseparably associated. For matter to exist without existing in some quantity seems to be as inconceivable as for experience to exist without qualitative diversity. "As if there could be matter," says Hobbes, "that had not some determined quantity, when quantity is nothing else but determination of matter; that is to say, of body, by which we say that one body is greater or less than another by thus or thus much."

The use of the word "quality" where quantity appears to be meant only slightly obscures this point. Newton refers to "extension, hardness, impenetrability, mobility, and inertia" as "the qualities of bodies" which "are to be esteemed the universal qualities of all bodies whatsoever." Following him, Locke calls our simple ideas of "solidity, extension, figure, motion or rest, and number" ideas of "the original or primary qualities of bodies," and says that even if bodies are divided "till their parts become insensible, they must retain still each of them all those qualities. For division . . . can never take away either solidity, extension, figure, or mobility from any body, but only makes two or more distinct separate masses of matter, of that which was one before."

Though Locke uses the word "quality" for those attributes which belong to bodies even when they are not sensed or are not even sensible, he also appears to recognize that number, extension, and figure are, as the traditional objects of the mathematical sciences, traditionally regarded as quantities rather than qualities. "It has been generally taken for granted," he writes, "that mathematics alone are capable of demonstrative certainty; but to have such an agreement or disagreement as may intuitively be perceived, being, as I imagine, not the privilege of the ideas of number, extension, and figure alone, it may possibly be the want of due method and application in us . . . that demonstration has been thought to have so little to do in other parts of knowledge." Yet, he adds, "in other simple ideas, whose modes and differences are made and counted by degrees, and not quantity, we have not so nice and accurate a distinction of their differences as to perceive, or find ways to measure, their just equality."

Newton also gives some indication that his "universal qualities" are quantities. He restricts them to attributes "which admit neither intensification nor remission of degrees." One difference between quantity and quality, according to an ancient opinion, is that qualities are subject to variation in degree, quantities not. One thing may be white or hot to a greater or less degree than another, Aristotle observes, but "one thing cannot be two cubits long in a greater degree than another. Similarly with regard to number: what is 'three' is not more truly three than what is 'five' is five . . . Nor is there any other kind of quantity, of all that have been mentioned, with regard to which variation in degree can be predicated."

GRANTED THAT WHAT Newton and Locke call "qualities" are not qualities, except in the sense in which the word "quality" means attribute, difficult questions remain concerning their enumeration of the *universal* or *primary* attributes of bodies. Do extension, hardness, impenetrability, motion and rest, figure and number constitute an exhaustive enumeration? Are these *all* the corporeal quantities, or only the basic ones from which others can be derived? Are they all of the same kind and, among them, are some more fundamental than others?

Descartes, for example, seems to make extension the one primary attribute of bodies. "I observed," he writes, "that nothing at all belonged to the nature or essence of bodies, except that it was a thing with length, breadth, and depth, admitting of various shapes and various motions. I found also that its shape and motions were only modes, which no power could make to exist apart from it . . . Finally, I saw that gravity, hardness, the power of heating, of attracting, and of purging, and all other qualities which we experience in bodies, consisted solely in motion or its absence, and in the configuration and situation of their parts."

With motion and figure modes of extension, and all the other properties of bodies the result of their motions or configurations, the three dimensions of extension (or spatial magnitude) become almost identical with body itself. Considering the statement *body possesses extension*, Descartes points out that, though "the meaning of *extension* is not identical with that of *body*, yet we do not construct two distinct ideas in our imagination, one of body, the other of extension, but merely a single image of extended body; and from the point of view of the thing it is exactly as if I had said: *body is extended*, or better, *the extended is extended*."

But, Descartes adds, when we consider the expression *extension is not body*, "the meaning of the term *extension* becomes otherwise than as above. When we give it this meaning there is no special idea corresponding to it in the imagination." It becomes a purely abstract entity, which may properly be the object of the geometer's consideration; but then it should be treated as an abstraction and not as if it had independent reality.

Aquinas also distinguishes between physical and mathematical quantities, or the quantities which inhere in bodies and the quantities abstracted therefrom. "Quantities, such as number, dimension, and figure, which are the terminations of quantity, can be considered apart from sensible qualities, and this is to abstract them from sensible matter. But they cannot be considered without understanding the substance which is subject to quantity"—that is, corporeal or material substance. Like a body, a mathematical solid has three dimensions, but, as Aquinas points out, lacking matter, this three-dimensional object does not occupy space or fill a place. The three spatial dimensions are not for him, however, the only primary quantities of either the physical or the mathematical body. Number and figure are as fundamental.

Still another enumeration of corporeal quantities is given by Lucretius in his description of the properties of atoms. According to him, atoms vary in size, weight, and shape. Each of these attributes is a distinct quantity, not reducible to the others. In addition, atoms have the property which Newton calls "impenetrability" and Locke "solidity." But whereas atoms may be unequal in size and weight, and different in shape or configuration, they are all equal in their solidity, being absolutely indivisible through lack of void or pores.

THE DISTINCTION BETWEEN mathematical and physical quantity and the enumeration or ordering of diverse quantities seem to require the consideration of two prior questions. What is the nature of quantity? What are the kinds or modes of quantity?

Terms like quantity and quality do not appear to be susceptible of definition. Quantity is, perhaps, *the* fundamental notion in the mathematical sciences, yet neither it nor such terms as magnitude, figure, and number are defined in the great books of geometry or arithmetic. In Aristotle's theory of the categories as the highest genera, such terms as substance, quantity, quality, and relation are strictly indefinable, if to define a term is to give its genus and differentia.

With quite a different theory of the categories, Kant also treats them as indefinable. As indicated in the chapter on QUALITY, they are for him the transcendental concepts of the understanding. He uses such terms as quantity, quality, and relation, with modality as a coordinate fourth, to represent the four major groupings of the categories. In his table of the categories, Kant's treatment of quantity, under which he lists the concepts of unity, plurality, and totality, parallels the treatment of quantity in his table of judgments, according to which judgments are classified as universal, particular, and singular. All these considerations of quantity belong to what Kant calls his "transcendental logic." So far as Kant considers quantity in its mathematical or physical (rather than logical) significance, he discusses it in connection with the transcendental forms of space and time which provide, according to him, the *a priori* foundations of geometry and arithmetic—the sciences of magnitude and number. But in none of these connections are quantity and its principal modes, magnitude and number, defined.

Though indefinable, quantity can, according to Aristotle, be characterized by certain distinctive marks. As we have already observed, where qualities admit of variation in degree, quantities do not. With few exceptions, each quality has a contrary, whereas definite quantities such as an extent or a number are not opposed by contrary quantities. Aristotle considers the possibility that such apparently quantitative terms as 'large' and 'small' may also appear to be contrary to one another, as hot is to cold, or white is to black. But, he argues, these terms represent quantities only relatively, not absolutely. When things are compared with respect to size, one may be judged to be both larger and smaller than others, but the sizes of each of two things unequal in size are not contrary to one another.

These two characteristics (lack of contrariety and of variation in degree) do not, however, satisfy Aristotle's search for a distinctive mark of quantity. They apply to substances, such as tree or man, as well as to figures and numbers. This fact could have some bearing on the issue whether the objects of mathematics have a separate existence comparable to that of substances, but in Aristotle's view at least, quantities are not substances. Physical quantities are the attributes of bodies; the objects of mathematics consist of quantities abstracted from sensible matter.

Conceiving quantity as one of the attributes of substance, Aristotle says that "the most distinctive mark of quantity is equality and inequality." Only when things are compared quantitatively can they be said to be equal or unequal; and, conversely, in whatever respect things are said to be equal or unequal, in that respect they are determined in quantity.

"How far is it true," Plotinus asks, "that equality and inequality are characteristic of quantity?" It is significant, he thinks, that triangles and other figures are said to be similar as well as equal. "It may, of course, be the case that the term 'similarity' has a different sense here from that understood in reference to quality"; or another alternative, Plotinus adds, may be that "similarity is predicable of quantity only insofar as quantity possesses [qualitative] differences." In any case, comparison, whether in terms of equality or likeness, seems to generate the relationships fundamental to the mathematical treatment of quantities.

Euclid does not define magnitude in itself, but only the relation of magnitudes to one another. The first four definitions in the fifth book of his *Elements* illustrate this. "1. A magnitude is a *part* of a magnitude, the less of the greater, when it measures the greater. 2. The greater is a *multiple* of the less when it is measured by the less. 3. A *ratio* is a sort of relation in respect of size between two magnitudes of the same kind. 4. Magnitudes are said to *have a ratio* to one another, which are capable, when multiplied, of exceeding one another."

Archimedes also states his understanding of the distinction between kinds of magnitudes—without defining these kinds—by reference to their comparability. Assuming that any given magnitude can, by being multiplied, exceed any other magnitude of the same kind, he is able to know that magnitudes are of the same kind if, by being multiplied, they can exceed one another. It follows that an indivisible point and a finite or divisible magnitude, such as a line, are not of the same kind, for they cannot have a ratio to one another. For the same reason, the length of a line, the area of a plane, and the volume of a solid are not magnitudes of the same kind. Since they bear no ratio to one another, they are quantitatively incomparable.

THE EMPHASIS UPON ratios has some significance for a controversial point in the definition of the subject matter of mathematics. In the tradition of the great books, mathematicians and philosophers seem to agree that arithmetic and geometry have as their objects the two principal species of quantity—number and magnitude. This is the opinion of Euclid, Nicomachus, Descartes, and Galileo; it is the opinion of Plato, Aristotle, Aquinas, Bacon, Hume, and Kant. But writers like Russell and Whitehead, who reflect developments in mathematics since the 19th century, reject the traditional opinion as unduly narrowing the scope of mathematics.

To give adequate expression to the universality of mathematics, they sometimes propose that it should be conceived as the science not merely of quantity, but of relations and order. In view of the fact that the great books of mathematics deal with quantities largely in terms of their relationship or order to one another, the broader conception seems to fit the older tradition as well as more recent developments. Whether there is a genuine issue here concerning the definition of mathematical subject matter may depend, therefore, on whether the fundamental terms which generate the systems of relationship and order are or are not essentially quantitative. To this question the traditional answer seems to be that the mathematician studies not relations of any sort, but the relation of quantities.

The problem of the kinds of quantity seems to appeal for solution to the principle of commensurability. For example, Galileo's observation that finite and infinite quantities cannot be compared in any way, implies their utter diversity. But he goes further and says that "the attributes 'larger,' 'smaller,' and 'equal' have no place either in comparing infinite quantities with each other or in comparing infinite with finite quantities." If the notion of quantity entails the possibility of equality or inequality between two quantities *of the same kind*, then either infinite quantities are not quantities, or each infinite quantity belongs to a kind of its own.

The principle of incommensurability seems to be applied by mathematicians to distinguish quantities which are different species of the same generic kind. For example, the one-dimensional, two-dimensional, and three-dimensional quantities of a line, a plane, and a solid, are incommensurable *magnitudes*. The number of days in a year and the number of years in infinite or endless time are incommensurable *multitudes*.

The distinction between magnitude and multitude (or number) as two modes of quantity appears to be based upon another principle, that of continuity and discontinuity. Yet the question can be raised whether magnitudes are commensurable with numbers, at least to the extent of being measured by numbers. It may be necessary, however, to postpone answering it until we have examined the fundamental difference between magnitude and multitude as generic kinds of quantity.

What if magnitude and multitude, or continuous and discontinuous quantity, do not divide quantity into its ultimate kinds? Aquinas, for example, proposes that the two basic kinds are dimensive and virtual quantity. "There is quantity of *bulk* or dimensive quantity," he writes, "which is to be found only in corporeal things, and has, therefore, no place in God. There is also quantity of *virtue*, which is measured according to the perfection of some nature or form." It is in the latter sense, according to Aquinas, that Augustine writes: "In things which are great, but not in bulk, to be greater is to be better."

Just as dimensive quantities can be incommensurable with one another, so with respect to virtual quantities, God's infinite perfection makes him incommensurable with finite creatures. But a dimensive quantity cannot be either commensurable or incommensurable with a virtual quantity. The standard of measurement by which dimensive quantities are compared, and the standard by which virtual quantities are ordered, represent utterly diverse principles of commensurability. Euclid's statement that "those magnitudes are said to be commensurable which are measured by the same measure, and those incommensurable which cannot have a common measure," cannot be extended to cover dimensive and virtual quantities, for the very meaning of "measure" changes when we turn from the dimensions of a body to the perfections of a being.

The distinction which Aquinas makes between dimensive and virtual magnitudes has its parallel in the distinction he makes between two kinds of number, for both depend on the difference between *material* and *formal* quantity. "Division is twofold," he writes. "One is material, and is division of the continuous; from this results number, which is a species of quantity. Number in this sense is found only in material things which have quantity. The other kind of division is formal, and is effected by opposite or diverse forms; and this kind of division results in a multitude, which does not belong to a genus, but is transcendental in the sense in which being is divided by one and many. Only this kind of multitude is found in immaterial things." According to the example suggested in the context, such is the multitude which is the number of persons in the Trinity.

THE MATERIAL quantities of physics and mathematics seem to fall under the two main heads of magnitude and multitude. "Quantity is either discrete or continuous," writes Aristotle. "Instances of discrete quantities are number and speech; of continuous, lines, surfaces, solids, and, besides these, time and place." Nicomachus explains the two kinds of quantity by examples. "The unified and continuous," he says, is exemplified by "an animal, the universe, a tree, and the like, which are properly and peculiarly called 'magnitudes' "; to illustrate the discontinuous, he points to "heaps of things, which are called 'multitudes,' a flock, for instance, a people, a chorus, and the like."

The principle of this distinction appears to be the possession or lack of a common boundary. To take Aristotle's example of speech as a quantity, the letters of a written word or the syllables of vocal utterance comprise a multitude rather than a continuum or magnitude "because there is no common boundary at which the syllables join, each being separate and distinct from the rest." The continuity of magnitudes can be readily seen, according to Aristotle, in the possibility of finding a common boundary at which the parts of a line join or make contact. "In the case of a line," he says, "this common boundary is the point; in the case of a plane, it is the line. . . . Similarly, you can find a common boundary in the case of the parts of a solid, namely, either a line or a plane."

Accepting the principle of the distinction, Plotinus insists that "number and magnitude are to be regarded as the only true quantities." All others, like space and time, or motion, are quantities only in a relative sense, that is, insofar as they can be measured by number or involve magnitude. Galileo raises another sort of difficulty. The Aristotelian conception of magnitudes as continuous quantities implies their infinite divisibility. This means, in his terms, that "every magnitude is divisible into magnitudes" and that "it is impossible for anything continuous to be composed of indivisible parts." Galileo acknowledges the objections to "building up continuous quantities out of indivisible quantities" on the ground that "the addition of one indivisible to another cannot produce a divisible, for if this were so it would render the indivisible divisible." Suppose a line to comprise an odd number of indivisible points. Since such a line can, in principle, be cut into two equal parts, we are required to do the impossible, namely, "to cut the indivisible which lies exactly in the middle of the line."

To this and other objections which seem to him of the same type, Galileo replies that "a divisible magnitude cannot be constructed out of two or ten or a hundred or a thousand indivisibles, but requires an infinite number of them. . . . I am willing," he says, "to grant to the Peripatetics the truth of their opinion that a continuous quantity is divisible only into parts which are still further divisible, so that however far the division and subdivision be continued, no end will be reached; but I am not so certain that they will concede to me that none of these divisions of theirs can be a final one, as is surely the fact, because there always remains 'another'; the final and ultimate division is rather one which resolves a continuous quantity into an infinite number of indivisible quantities."

The question remains whether these indivisible units, an infinite number of which constitute the continuity of a finite magnitude, can properly be called quantities. At least they are not magnitudes, as is indicated by Euclid's definition of a point as "that which has no part," or by Nicomachus' statement that "the point is the beginning of dimension, but is not itself a dimension." If, in addition to having position, a point had size or extent, a finite line could not contain an infinite number of points. This problem of infinite and infinitesimal quantities is more fully discussed in the chapter on INFINITY.

WITHIN EACH OF THE two main divisions of quantity—magnitude and number—further sub-divisions into kinds are made. Relations of equality and inequality, or proportions of these ratios, may occur between quantities different in kind—different plane figures, for example. But the great books of mathematics indicate other problems in the study of quantity than those concerned with the ratios and proportions of quantities. The classification of lines and figures results in the discovery of the properties which belong to each type. Possessing the same properties, all lines or figures of a certain type are similar in kind, not equal in quantity. In addition to developing the properties of such straight lines as perpendiculars and parallels, or such curved lines as circles and ellipses, parabolas and hyperbolas, the geometer defines the different types of relationship in which straight lines can stand to curves, *e.g.*, tangents, secants, asymptotes.

As there are types of lines and figures, both plane and solid, so there are types of numbers. Euclid and Nicomachus divide the odd numbers into the prime and the composite—into those which are divisible only by themselves and unity, such as 5 and 7, and those which have other factors, such as 9 and 15. The composite are further differentiated into the variety which is simply secondary and composite and "the variety which, in itself, is secondary and composite, but relatively is prime and incomposite." To illustrate the latter, Nicomachus asks us to compare 9 with 25. "Each in itself," he writes, "is secondary and composite, but relatively to each other they have only unity as a common measure, and no factors in them have the same denominator, for the third part in the former does not exist in the latter nor is the fifth part in the latter found in the former."

The even numbers are divided by Nicomachus into the even-times-even (numbers like 64 which can be divided into equal halves, and their halves can again be divided into equal halves, and so on until division must stop); the even-times-odd (numbers like 6, 10, 14, 18 which can be divided into equal halves, but whose halves cannot be divided again into equal halves); and the odd-times-even (numbers like 24, 28, 40 which can be divided into equal parts, whose parts also can be so divided, and perhaps again these parts, but which cannot be divided in this way as far as unity). By another principle of classification, the even numbers fall into the superabundant, the deficient, and the perfect. The factors which produce superabundant or deficient numbers, when added together, amount to more or less than the number itself; but a number is perfect, Nicomachus writes, when, "comparing with itself the sum and combination of all the factors whose presence it will admit, it neither exceeds them in multitude nor is exceeded by them." It is "equal to its own parts"; as, for example, 6, "for 6 has the factors half, third, and sixth, 3, 2, and 1, respectively, and these added together make 6 and are equal to the original number." At the time of Nicomachus only four perfect numbers were known—6, 28, 496, 8128; since his day seven more have been discovered.

The further classification of numbers as linear, plane, and solid, and of plane numbers as triangular, square, pentagonal, etc., assigns properties to them according to their configurations. The analysis of figurate numbers by Nicomachus or Pascal represents one of the great bridges between arithmetic and geometry, of which the other, in the opposite direction, is the algebraic rendering of geometrical loci in Descartes' analytical geometry.

In either direction of the translation between arithmetic and geometry, discontinuous and continuous quantities seem to have certain properties in common, at least by analogy. Euclid, for example, proposes numerical ratios as the test for the commensurability of magnitudes. "Commensurable magnitudes have to one another," he writes, "the ratio which a number has to a number." With the exception of infinite numbers, all numbers are commensurable and so provide the criterion for determining whether two magnitudes are or are not commensurable.

Introducing the notion of dimensionality into the discussion of figurate numbers, Nicomachus observes that "mathematical speculations are always to be interlocked and to be explained one by means of another." Though the dimensions by which linear, plane, and solid numbers are to be distinguished "are more closely related to magnitude . . . yet the germs of these ideas are taken over into arithmetic as the science which is the mother of geometry and more elementary than it." The translation does not seem to fail in any respect. The only non-dimensional number, unity, finds its geometrical analogue in the point, which has position without magnitude.

When diverse magnitudes are translated into numbers, the diversity of the magnitudes seems to be effaced by the fact that their numerical measures do not have a corresponding diversity. The numbers will appear to be commensurable though the magnitudes they measure are not, as magnitudes, comparable. As Descartes points out, it is necessary, therefore, to regard each order of magnitude as a distinct dimension.

"By dimension," Descartes writes, "I understand nothing but the mode and aspect according to which a subject is considered to be measurable. Thus it is not merely the case that length, breadth, and depth are dimensions; but weight also is a dimension in terms of which the heaviness of objects is estimated. So, too, speed is a dimension of motion, and there are an infinite number of similar instances. For that very division of the whole into a number of parts of identical nature, whether it exist in the real order of things or be merely the work of the understanding, gives us exactly that dimension in terms of which we apply number to objects."

The theory of dimensions can be illustrated by the choice of clocks, rules, and balances as the fundamental instruments for the measurement of physical quantities. They represent the three dimensions in the fundamental equations of mechanics—time, distance, and mass.

Additional dimensions may be introduced in electricity or thermodynamics. In developing the theory of heat, Fourier, for example, enumerates five quantities which, in order to be numerically expressed, require five different kinds of units, "namely, the unit of length, the unit of time, that of temperature, that of weight, and finally the unit which serves to measure quantities of heat." To which he adds the remark that "every undetermined magnitude or constant has one *dimension* proper to itself, and that the terms of one and the same equation could not be compared, if they had not the same *exponent of dimension*."

A fuller discussion of the basic physical quantities, their definition, measurement, and their relation to one another, belongs to the chapter on MECHANICS. The consideration of time and space as quantities, or physical dimensions, occurs in the chapters devoted to those subjects.

OUTLINE OF TOPICS

1. The nature and existence of quantity: its relation to matter, substance, and body; the transcendental categories of quantity

    1*a*. The relation between quantity and quality: reducibility of quality to quantity

    1*b*. The relation of quantities: equality and proportion

2. The kinds of quantity: continuous and discontinuous

3. The magnitudes of geometry: the relations of dimensionality

    3*a*. Straight lines: their length and their relations; angles, perpendiculars, parallels

3*b*. Curved lines: their kinds, number, and degree
- (1) Circles
- (2) Ellipses
- (3) Parabolas
- (4) Hyperbolas

3*c*. The relations of straight and curved lines: tangents, secants, asymptotes

3*d*. Surfaces
- (1) The measurement and transformation of areas
- (2) The relations of surfaces to lines and solids

3*e*. Solids: regular and irregular
- (1) The determination of volume
- (2) The relations of solids: inscribed and circumscribed spheres; solids of revolution

4. Discrete quantities: number and numbering

4*a*. The kinds of numbers: odd-even, square-triangular, prime-composite

4*b*. The relations of numbers to one another: multiples and fractions

4*c*. The number series as a continuum

5. Physical quantities

5*a*. Space: the matrix of figures and distances

5*b*. Time: the number of motion

5*c*. The quantity of motion: momentum, velocity, acceleration

5*d*. Mass: its relation to weight

5*e*. Force: its measure and the measure of its effect

6. The measurements of quantities: the relation of magnitudes and multitudes; the units of measurement

6*a*. Commensurable and incommensurable magnitudes

6*b*. Mathematical procedures in measurement: superposition, congruence; ratio and proportion; parameters and coordinates

6*c*. Physical procedures in measurement: experiment and observation; clocks, rules, balances

7. Infinite quantity: the actual infinite and the potentially infinite quantity; the mathematical and physical infinite of the great and the small

REFERENCES

References are listed by volume number (in bold type), author's name, and page number. Bible references are to book, chapter, and verse of the Authorized King James version of the Bible. The abbreviation "esp" calls the reader's attention to one or more especially relevant parts of a whole reference; "passim" signifies that the topic is discussed intermittently rather than continuously in the work or passage cited. Where the work as a whole is relevant to the topic, the page numbers refer to the entire work. For general guidance in the use of *The Great Ideas,* consult the Preface.

1. The nature and existence of quantity: its relation to matter, substance, and body; the transcendental categories of quantity

7 Plato, 616
8 Aristotle, 8–11, 262, 270, 503–504, 508–511, 516, 520–521, 541, 568, 600–601, 607–610, 638–639
17 Plotinus, 53–55, 116–118, 253–254, 276, 286–289
19 Aquinas, 31, 35–36, 46–47, 451–453
20 Aquinas, 951–953, 963–964, 978–980
23 Hobbes, 269–272
31 Descartes, 29–30
35 Locke, 134
42 Kant, 15, 41–45, 74–76, 137–140

1*a*. The relation between quantity and quality: reducibility of quality to quantity

7 Plato, 458–460, 462–465
8 Aristotle, 411, 578–580, 614, 683–684, 687–689
11 Euclid, 127
12 Lucretius, 20–21, 24–26, 44–47, 51–53
17 Plotinus, 55, 196
19 Aquinas, 224–225, 410–411
20 Aquinas, 2–4, 15–19, 491–498
23 Hobbes, 172
31 Descartes, 19, 162–165, 228–229, 231
34 Newton, 450–453
35 Locke, 134–138, 200, 206–207, 311–312, 316
35 Berkeley, 414–416, 427
35 Hume, 505
42 Kant, 23–24, 68–72, 211–213
46 Hegel, 122–123
53 James, 319–322, 346–348
54 Freud, 403–404

1*b*. The relation of quantities: equality and proportion

7 Plato, 228–229, 494, 500–502, 508, 518–519
8 Aristotle, 542, 583–584, 620
9 Aristotle, 351–352, 378–381 passim
11 Euclid, 2, 4, 6–7, 16–17, 81–98, 117, 191–300
11 Archimedes, 484, 527
11 Nicomachus, 821–831, 841–848
16 Kepler, 1012–1014, 1078–1080
17 Plotinus, 289
19 Aquinas, 68–70, 224–225
28 Galileo, 142–145
31 Descartes, 295–298, 332–341
34 Newton, 25, 159
42 Kant, 497–498
50 Marx, 19–25
53 James, 551, 874–878

2. The kinds of quantity: continuous and discontinuous

7 Plato, 499–500
8 Aristotle, 9, 307–308, 312–315, 411–413, 519–520, 536–537, 578, 597–598
11 Euclid, 191–192
11 Archimedes, 404
17 Plotinus, 139–140
19 Aquinas, 32–34, 47–48
20 Aquinas, 491–492, 754–755
28 Galileo, 139–153 passim
31 Descartes, 32–33
34 Newton, 31–32
35 Berkeley, 437–439
35 Hume, 506–507
42 Kant, 66–72, 135–140
51 Tolstoy, 469

3. The magnitudes of geometry: the relations of dimensionality

8 Aristotle, 9, 359, 378, 608
11 Euclid, 1, 301
11 Nicomachus, 832
16 Kepler, 865
17 Plotinus, 287–289
19 Aquinas, 460–461
31 Descartes, 29–32, 52–53, 216–217
35 Locke, 149
42 Kant, 25
53 James, 876–878

3*a*. Straight lines: their length and their relations; angles, perpendiculars, parallels

8 Aristotle, 101–102, 203
11 Euclid, 1–21, 73–74, 99, 100–112, 124–125, 191–300 passim, 301, 302–319, 321–323, 332–334, 372–381

11 ARCHIMEDES, 405
16 PTOLEMY, 26–28
16 COPERNICUS, 543–545
34 NEWTON, 53–54, 67, 71–72
42 KANT, 110, 212

3*b*. Curved lines: their kinds, number, and degree

11 ARCHIMEDES, 404, 490–501
31 DESCARTES, 298–332, 341–353
34 NEWTON, 50–78, 102–105, 189–190, 338–339

3*b*(1) Circles

8 ARISTOTLE, 477, 480–481
11 EUCLID, 1, 41–80, 125–126, 339–340
11 ARCHIMEDES, 405–408, 447–451, 485–488
11 APOLLONIUS, 603–804
16 PTOLEMY, 26–28
16 COPERNICUS, 545–556
28 GALILEO, 155–156
34 NEWTON, 138

3*b*(2) Ellipses

11 ARCHIMEDES, 459–467
11 APOLLONIUS, 618, 791–796
16 KEPLER, 975–984
31 DESCARTES, 308–313
34 NEWTON, 50–75, 78–81
34 HUYGENS, 604–606

3*b*(3) Parabolas

11 ARCHIMEDES, 458–459, 528–529, 531–536, 537, 571–572
11 APOLLONIUS, 615, 793–796
28 GALILEO, 193–195, 238–239
31 DESCARTES, 308–310
34 NEWTON, 45, 50–76

3*b*(4) Hyperbolas

11 ARCHIMEDES, 464–465
11 APOLLONIUS, 616, 792–798
31 DESCARTES, 306–312
34 NEWTON, 50–75

3*c*. The relations of straight and curved lines: tangents, secants, asymptotes

11 EUCLID, 41–80, 338–339, 362–363, 375–381
11 ARCHIMEDES, 405, 418–419, 448–451, 485–488, 490–495, 561–568
11 APOLLONIUS, 604, 621–668, 682–783, 792–798
16 PTOLEMY, 14–24, 26–28
16 COPERNICUS, 532–542
16 KEPLER, 973–975
28 GALILEO, 149–150, 229–230
31 DESCARTES, 298–331
34 NEWTON, 27, 29–30, 50–75

3*d*. Surfaces

8 ARISTOTLE, 378
11 EUCLID, 1, 301
11 ARCHIMEDES, 404
11 APOLLONIUS, 604
11 NICOMACHUS, 832–833

3*d*(1) The measurement and transformation of areas

7 PLATO, 180–182
8 ARISTOTLE, 236
11 EUCLID, 21–41, 99–100, 109–123, 197–198, 200–203, 206–207, 209–211, 235, 242, 338–340, 369–373
11 ARCHIMEDES, 406–414, 419–420, 422–425, 427–432, 437, 441–446, 495–501, 535–537, 562–564
28 GALILEO, 153–154, 193–194, 239–240
34 NEWTON, 25–28, 64–65, 140–142

3*d*(2) The relations of surfaces to lines and solids

8 ARISTOTLE, 510
11 EUCLID, 301–314, 319–320, 336–337
11 ARCHIMEDES, 455, 464–468, 538
11 APOLLONIUS, 604–621
28 GALILEO, 142–143

3*e*. Solids: regular and irregular

11 EUCLID, 301–302, 381–396
11 ARCHIMEDES, 452–455
11 APOLLONIUS, 604
11 NICOMACHUS, 832, 836
16 KEPLER, 863–868, 1011–1012

3*e*(1) The determination of volume

11 EUCLID, 320–321, 323–332, 334–337, 341–362, 367–368
11 ARCHIMEDES, 421–429, 433–446, 464, 468–481, 572–576, 579–580, 583–592
28 GALILEO, 154–155

3*e*(2) The relations of solids: inscribed and circumscribed spheres; solids of revolution

8 ARISTOTLE, 378
11 EUCLID, 301, 302, 363–367, 381–393
11 ARCHIMEDES, 419–424, 427–431, 452–455, 468–469
33 PASCAL, 395
34 HUYGENS, 603–604

4. Discrete quantities: number and numbering

7 PLATO, 496
8 ARISTOTLE, 9, 285–286, 300, 568, 581, 584, 611–626
11 ARCHIMEDES, 520–526
11 NICOMACHUS, 811–814
17 PLOTINUS, 230–231, 253–254, 310–321
18 AUGUSTINE, 654
19 AQUINAS, 169–170
33 PASCAL, 455–456
35 LOCKE, 165–167
53 JAMES, 874–876

4*a*. The kinds of numbers: odd-even, square-triangular, prime-composite

7 PLATO, 244, 515
8 ARISTOTLE, 131
11 EUCLID, 127–128, 139–144, 154–155, 157–176, 182–190, 213–214
11 NICOMACHUS, 814–821, 831–841
28 GALILEO, 144
33 PASCAL, 470–473

4*b*. The relations of numbers to one another: multiples and fractions

8 ARISTOTLE, 542
11 EUCLID, 127–183
11 ARCHIMEDES, 455–456, 488–489, 520–526
11 NICOMACHUS, 821–831, 841–848
38 PASCAL, 447–454, 456–460, 468–473, 477–478, 484–486
42 KANT, 212–213

4*c*. The number series as a continuum

11 EUCLID, 81, 127
31 DESCARTES, 295–353
34 NEWTON, 168–169
45 FOURIER, 169–251 passim

5. Physical quantities

5*a*. Space: the matrix of figures and distances

7 PLATO, 456–458
8 ARISTOTLE, 287–297
12 LUCRETIUS, 6, 12–13
31 DESCARTES, 28–33
33 PASCAL, 370, 372–373, 434–439
34 NEWTON, 8–13
35 BERKELEY, 434–436
42 KANT, 23–26, 28–33
53 JAMES, 399, 548–552, 626

5*b*. Time: the number of motion

7 PLATO, 450–451, 504–505
8 ARISTOTLE, 297–304, 439, 694–695
12 AURELIUS, 275
16 KEPLER, 905–907, 979–985
17 PLOTINUS, 119–129, 260–261
18 AUGUSTINE, 92–99, 325
19 AQUINAS, 32–33, 40–41, 43–46, 283–284
20 AQUINAS, 366–367
28 GALILEO, 201–202
30 BACON, 177–179
33 PASCAL, 432–433
34 NEWTON, 8–13, 32–35, 42, 272–275
35 LOCKE, 155–165
35 BERKELEY, 431–432
36 STERNE, 292–293
42 KANT, 26–33, 72–76, 130–133
53 JAMES, 398–408

5*c*. The quantity of motion: momentum, velocity, acceleration

8 ARISTOTLE, 295, 309, 312–315, 330–333, 348–352
12 LUCRETIUS, 18–19
17 PLOTINUS, 260–261
19 AQUINAS, 144–145
28 GALILEO, 166–168, 197, 200–207, 209–210, 224–225, 243–249
30 BACON, 163, 179–188
34 NEWTON, 5, 14, 31–33, 540–541
34 HUYGENS, 558–563 passim
35 LOCKE, 174
35 HUME, 460

5*d*. Mass: its relation to weight

7 PLATO, 462–463
8 ARISTOTLE, 296–297, 364–365, 392–393, 399–401
12 LUCRETIUS, 16, 18
16 KEPLER, 970
17 PLOTINUS, 62–64
28 GALILEO, 158
30 BACON, 163, 166, 171–172
34 NEWTON, 203–204, 279–283, 291–194
45 FARADAY, 632

5*e*. Force: its measure and the measure of its effect

8 ARISTOTLE, 333, 353–354, 393–393
9 ARISTOTLE, 234
16 KEPLER, 938–939, 969–971
19 AQUINAS, 541–542
20 AQUINAS, 985–989
28 GILBERT, 26–40 passim, 54–55
31 DESCARTES, 231–232
34 NEWTON, 5–8, 11–24, 28–29, 32–50, 131–152, 276–284 esp 281, 371–372, 531, 541–542
45 FARADAY, 514–532, 646–655, 670–673, 817–818

6. The measurements of quantities: the relation of magnitudes and multitudes; the units of measurement

8 ARISTOTLE, 300, 303, 579–580
9 ARISTOTLE, 380–381
17 PLOTINUS, 253–254
19 AQUINAS, 348–349
30 BACON, 176–179
31 DESCARTES, 31–33
35 LOCKE, 167
39 SMITH, 14
42 KANT, 497–498
45 FOURIER, 249–251
45 FARADAY, 820–821
50 MARX, 44
53 JAMES, 346–347, 400–408, 567–570

6*a*. Commensurable and incommensurable magnitudes

7 PLATO, 515, 729
8 ARISTOTLE, 58, 330–333
11 EUCLID, 191–300
11 ARICHIMEDES, 503–504
16 KEPLER, 1012

6b. Mathematical procedures in measurement: superposition, congruence; ratio and proportion; parameters and coordinates

11 EUCLID, 81–100, 102–105, 128–130, 146–149, 193–195
11 ARCHIMEDES, 502–509, 538–542
16 PTOLEMY, 14–24, 26–28
16 COPERNICUS, 532–556
28 GALILEO, 178–179
31 DESCARTES, 332–341
34 NEWTON, 76–81

6c. Physical procedures in measurement: experiment and observation; clocks, rules, balances

6 HERODOTUS, 70, 139
6 THUCYDIDES, 421
16 PTOLEMY, 24–26, 34–39, 77–86, 104–107, 143–144, 165–176
16 COPERNICUS, 558–559, 567–576, 586–589, 646–652, 672–674, 705–714
28 GILBERT, 85–89, 92–95
28 GALILEO, 136–137, 148–149, 164–166, 207–208
28 HARVEY, 286–288
30 BACON, 170, 175–188 passim
33 PASCAL, 382–389
34 NEWTON, 211–219, 239–246, 333–337
34 HUYGENS, 554–557
35 LOCKE, 158–159
45 LAVOISIER, 14, 22–24, 33–36, 41–44, 87–103
45 FOURIER, 184–185
45 FARADAY, 277–279, 316–318, 366–371, 444–451, 465–467, 768–773, 778–788
53 JAMES, 56–57, 348–355

7. Infinite quantity: the actual infinite and the potentially infinite quantity; the mathematical and physical infinite of the great and the small

7 PLATO, 495–497
8 ARISTOTLE, 260, 280–286, 362–367, 414, 574, 594–595, 603
11 EUCLID, 183–184, 191–192
11 ARCHIMEDES, 520–526, 569–592
11 NICOMACHUS, 812
12 LUCRETIUS, 7–8, 12–14
17 PLOTINUS, 311–312, 319–320
18 AUGUSTINE, 324–325, 354
19 AQUINAS, 31–34
20 AQUINAS, 769–771
28 GALILEO, 139–153
31 DESCARTES, 112
31 SPINOZA, 360–361
33 PASCAL, 213–214, 434–439
34 NEWTON, 25–32, 168–169, 370
35 LOCKE, 149, 160–163, 167–174, 237–238
35 BERKELEY, 437–439
42 KANT, 135–137, 158–163, 498–501
43 FEDERALIST, 103
46 HEGEL, 119
51 TOLSTOY, 695

CROSS-REFERENCES

For: Discussions relevant to the problem of the existence of quantities and of their relation to matter, substance, and body, *see* BEING 7b, 7b(5)–7b(6); MATTER 2a; QUALITY 3d.

Discussions relevant to the conception of the categories as transcendental concepts of the understanding, *see* FORM 1c; JUDGMENT 8c–8d; MEMORY AND IMAGINATION 6c(1); MIND 1e(1); PRINCIPLE 2b(3).

Other considerations of the relation between quantity and quality, *see* MECHANICS 4b; QUALITY 3a.

The conception of equality and inequality as the basic relation between quantities, *see* SAME AND OTHER 3d; and for the general theory of ratios and proportions, *see* MATHEMATICS 4c; RELATION 5a(3); SAME AND OTHER 3b.

The division of quantities into magnitudes and multitudes, or continuous and discontinuous quantities, *see* MATHEMATICS 2c; ONE AND MANY 3a(2)–3a(4); and for the conception of space and time as magnitudes, *see* MECHANICS 3a; SPACE 1a; TIME 1.

Other discussions of magnitudes and numbers as the objects of geometry and arithmetic, *see* MATHEMATICS 2; ONE AND MANY 2a; SPACE 3b–3c; TIME 6c.

Other discussions of such physical quantities as space, time, motion, mass, and force, *see* ASTRONOMY 7; CHANGE 5a–5b; MECHANICS 5d–5e(2), 6b–6e; SPACE 3d; TIME 4.

The general theory of measurement, *see* MATHEMATICS 5a; MECHANICS 3a; PHYSICS 4d.

Other discussions of infinite quantity, *see* INFINITY 1b, 3a–3e; SPACE 3a; TIME 2b

ADDITIONAL READINGS

Listed below are works not included in *Great Books of the Western World*, but relevant to the idea and topics with which this chapter deals. These works are divided into two groups:

I. Works by authors represented in this collection.
II. Works by authors not represented in this collection.

For the date, place, and other facts concerning the publication of the works cited, consult the Bibliography of Additional Readings which follows the last chapter of *The Great Ideas*.

I.

AUGUSTINE. *On Music*
DESCARTES. *The Principles of Philosophy*, PART II, 8–9
HOBBES. *Concerning Body*, PART II, CH 12, 14; PART III, CH 17–20, 23–24
NEWTON. *The Method of Fluxions and Infinite Series*
——. *Universal Arithmetic*
BERKELEY. *A Defence of Free Thinking in Mathematics*
KANT. *Metaphysical Foundations of Natural Science*, DIV I
HEGEL. *Science of Logic*, VOL I, BK I, SECT II–III

II.

SEXTUS EMPIRICUS. *Against the Physicists*, BK II, CH 4
ORÊME. *Treatise on the Breadth of Forms*
SUÁREZ. *Disputationes Metaphysicae*, IV (9), XIII (14), XIV, XVI, XVIII (3–6), XXVIII (1), XXXIX–XLI
LEIBNITZ. *New Essays Concerning Human Understanding*, BK II, CH 16
T. REID. *An Essay on Quantity*
VOLTAIRE. "Number," "Numbering," in *A Philosophical Dictionary*
GAUSS. *General Investigations of Curved Surfaces*
WHEWELL. *The Philosophy of the Inductive Sciences*, VOL I, BK II, CH 9–10
RIEMANN. *Über die Hypothesen welche der Geometrie zu Grunde liegen* (*The Hypotheses of Geometry*)
JEVONS. *On a General System of Numerically Definite Reasoning*
DEDEKIND. *Essays on the Theory of Numbers*
CLIFFORD. *The Common Sense of the Exact Sciences*, CH I, 3
HELMHOLTZ. *Counting and Measuring*
BOSANQUET. *Logic*, VOL I, CH 3–4
C. S. PEIRCE. *Collected Papers*, VOL III, par 252–288, 554–562
MCLELLAN and DEWEY. *The Psychology of Number*
POINCARÉ. *Science and Hypothesis*, PART I
CASSIRER. *Substance and Function*, PART I, CH 2; SUP I
L. W. REID. *The Elements of the Theory of Algebraic Numbers*
WHITEHEAD and RUSSELL. *Principia Mathematica*, PART III, SECT A, B; PART VI
B. RUSSELL. *Principles of Mathematics*, CH 11–12, 14–15, 19–22, 29–36
——. *Our Knowledge of the External World*, V
——. *Introduction to Mathematical Philosophy*, CH 1–2, 7–8, 10–11
N. R. CAMPBELL. *Physics; the Elements*, PART II
W. E. JOHNSON. *Logic*, PART II, CH 7
G. N. LEWIS. *The Anatomy of Science*, ESSAY I
J. B. S. HALDANE. "On Being the Right Size," in *Possible Worlds and Other Essays*
EDDINGTON. *The Nature of the Physical World*, CH 12
DICKSON. *Introduction to the Theory of Numbers*
WHITEHEAD. *An Introduction to Mathematics*, CH 6–17
——. *An Enquiry Concerning the Principles of Natural Knowledge*, CH 9–12
——. *The Principle of Relativity with Applications to Physical Science*, CH 3
——. *Process and Reality*, PART IV
NAGEL. *On the Logic of Measurement*
TARSKI. *Introduction to Logic*, PART II

Chapter 77: REASONING

INTRODUCTION

IN the tradition of western thought, certain verbal expressions have become shorthand for the fundamental ideas in the discussion of which they happen to be so often repeated. This may be due to the influence of the text-books used in the schools, which copy one from another and hand down an easily recited jargon from generation to generation. In most cases the great books themselves are probably the original source, though they have usually suffered over-simplification or distortion when their insights are thus transmitted.

"Featherless biped" and "rational animal" are, for example, stock phrases to illustrate the idea that a definition consists of genus and differentia—the class to which man, in this instance, belongs and the attribute which differentiates him from other members of this class. Statements such as "the whole is greater than the part" or "two plus two equals four" similarly serve to represent axioms or at least statements which, whether or not they can be proved, are usually accepted as true without proof. In the field of reasoning, the familiar verbal landmark is "All men are mortal, Socrates is a man; therefore, Socrates is mortal." Even those who have never heard of syllogisms, or who are throughly innocent of the age-old controversies about the theory of the syllogism and the difference between deduction and induction, might offer this sequence of statements if, pressed to say what reasoning is, they tried to answer by giving an example.

The example, shopworn though it is and far from being the perfect paradigm, does convey certain insights into the nature of reasoning which are generally undisputed.

The word "therefore," which connects the third statement with the first two, signifies a relationship which is sometimes described in terms of cause and effect, as by Aristotle, and sometimes in terms of antecedent and consequent, as by Hobbes. The premises (*i.e.*, the statements which precede the "therefore") cause the conclusion, it is said. We know that Socrates is mortal *because* we know that Socrates is a man and that all men are mortal. The premises are the cause in the sense of the *reason why* the conclusion may be regarded as true.

The conclusion is also said to *follow from* the premises, or the premises are said to *imply* or *yield* the conclusion. *If* the premises are true, *then* the truth of the conclusion can be inferred or proved. The relationship between the premises and the conclusion seems to be the same whether the act of reasoning is called "proof" or "inference." The distinction in meaning between these two words seems to be one of direction. We speak of "proving" a conclusion when we look toward the premises as the foundation for its truth; we speak of "inferring" a conclusion when we look toward it as something which can be drawn from the premises.

The words "if" and "then" indicate that reasoning is a motion of the mind from one statement to another. Sometimes the inference is immediate, as when we argue that if all men are mortal, then some mortals are men. Here only two propositions are involved, one of which is simply the converse of the other. Those who deny that immediate inference is truly inference (because a proposition and its converse are merely two ways of stating the same fact), insist that, implicitly or explicitly, reasoning always involves *at least* three statements. In any case, a single statement like "Socrates is a man," or even a pair of statements connected by "and" rather than "if-then"—*e.g.*, "Socrates is a man and Socrates is mortal"—does not express what is commonly recognized as reasoning. The motion of reasoning does, however, appear in this sequence of statements, "If Socrates is a man, then Socrates is mortal," even though it omits a statement that may be necessary to the validity of the reasoning, namely, "All men are mortal."

Thus, the familiar grammatical distinctions of word (or phrase), sentence, and paragraph do not seem to provide a perfect parallel for the distinctions which the logicians make between terms, propositions, and syllogisms. But this much is clear. Just as a single word or phrase, like "man" or "rational animal," can never express a proposition, but only a term, so a simple sentence expresses only a proposition, and never a syllogism; and a compound sentence, one made up of a number of sentences, expresses a syllogism only if its verbal construction somehow indicates that they form a sequence in which one *follows* from the others, or if they are related in such a way that the truth of one is caused by the truth of the others.

The chapter on Idea (and perhaps also the chapter on Definition) deals with that content or act of the mind—whether a percept or a concept, an image or an abstraction—which is verbally expressed in words or phrases and of which the *term* is the logical representative. The chapter on Judgment (and perhaps also the chapter on Principle) deals with the mental act or content that requires a sentence for its expression and is logically represented by the *proposition*. Here we are concerned with mental activity which involves not only two or more ideas, but also two or more judgments so connected that the mind passes from one to another.

Whether the logical structure that Aristotle calls a "syllogism" represents all forms of the mental activity called reasoning, is one of the great traditional issues. Hume suggests, for example, that animals reason without making use of syllogisms; and Descartes and Locke seem to hold that the highest forms of thinking, such as occur in mathematics or philosophy, cannot be reduced to syllogisms, except perhaps by a *tour de force*.

We face a different sort of problem when we compare reasoning with other acts of the mind—with conception (or the having of ideas) and with judgment (or the connecting of ideas with one another in the manner which mediaeval writers call "composition and division"). No one denies that reasoning is thinking, nor does anyone deny that there are forms of thinking which are not reasoning, since conceiving and judging are generally regarded as kinds of thinking or modes of thought. Reasoning is merely that mode of thought which is a *process*—the going step by step from one statement to another.

The problem which arises from the comparison of reasoning with other modes of thought turns on the question whether the mind can learn anything without having to think rationally. Can certain things be known by insight or instinct, by induction or intuition, rather than by reasoning? Are there truths which cannot be known by reasoning at all, but only by some other mode of thought? These questions in turn raise the problem of the priority or superiority of such modes of thought as do not consist in reasoning. The theory discussed in the chapter on Induction—that induction is prior to reasoning because intuitive generalization from experience must provide the starting-points for demonstration—indicates one solution of the problem. Our present concern, however, goes beyond the issue concerning induction and deduction to the most general contrast between the intuitive and the rational.

For Plotinus any form of thinking—not merely reasoning—signifies a deficiency or weakness. In the scale of intellectual beings man occupies the lowest rank because he reasons. But even the pure intelligences, which know intuitively, rank below the One, because even the simplest act of thought involves some duality of subject and object. The One, according to Plotinus, transcends thought even as it transcends being. "The super-essential," he says, "is the supra-cogitative." The One "has no need for intellection, being always self-sufficing."

Other writers do not go as far as this. Christian theologians do, however, contrast the human mind with the angelic intellect and the mind of God by saying that the latter are supra-rational, *i.e.*, above the need to reason. They do not, like Plotinus, hold that the transcendent being transcends thought itself—certainly not insofar as they discuss the divine ideas. But the kind of thinking which is not an instantaneous act of vision or an immediate intuition involves the mind in a process of thought, somehow akin to change or motion; and this, the theologians hold, cannot take place in any immutable being—the angels or God.

The human intellect, according to Aquinas, gradually comes to know the truth "by a kind of movement and discursive intellectual operation . . . by advancing from one thing known to another. But if from the knowledge of a known principle [men] were straightway to perceive as known all its consequent conclusions, then there would be no place for discursiveness in the human intellect. Such is the condition of the angels, because in the truths which they know naturally, they at once behold all things whatsoever that can be known in them."

That, says Aquinas, is why the angels "are called *intellectual* beings" and men "are called *rational*." Recourse to reasoning on the part of men betrays "the feebleness of their intellectual light. For if they possessed the fullness of intellectual light, like the angels, then in the first grasping of principles they would at once comprehend all that they implied, by perceiving at once whatever could be reasoned out of them."

The type of intuitive apprehension which the angels enjoy is even more perfectly exemplified in God's knowledge. "In the divine knowledge," according to Aquinas, "there is no discursiveness"—no succession, neither the turning from one thought to another, nor the advance from the known to the unknown by reasoning from principles to conclusion. The divine knowledge, Aquinas explains, is a single all-embracing act of vision, in which "God sees all things in one thing alone, which is Himself," and therefore "sees all things together and not successively." Apart from participation in the vision of God through supernatural light, all human thinking on the natural plane is discursive. Even the conception and the judgment are discursive in the sense that the one involves an act of abstraction or definition and the other involves a composition or division of concepts. But though it is always discursive, human thinking is not, according to Aquinas, always involved in the *motion* of reasoning, that is, the transition from one thought to another. "Reasoning," he says, "is compared to understanding"—*i.e.*, the act of judgment by which we affirm or deny a single proposition—"as movement is to rest, or acquisition to possession."

DESCARTES USES THE word "intuition" to name the way in which we know certain truths immediately and with certitude. He distinguishes "intuition from deduction by the fact that into the conception of the latter there enters a certain movement or succession, into that of the former there does not. . . . The first principles are given by intuition alone, while, on the contrary, the remote conclusions are furnished only by deduction." But while deduction, which Descartes says he understands to be "all necessary inference from other facts that are known with certainty," supplements intuition, it is never at any stage of the reasoning process independent of intuition.

Not only does intuition, according to Descartes, supply the first principles or ultimate premises of reasoning, but it also certifies each step in the process. He asks us to "consider this consequence: 2 and 2 amount to the same as 3 and 1. Now we need to see intuitively not only that 2 and 2 make 4, and that likewise 3 and 1 make 4, but further that the third of the above statements is a necessary conclusion from these two."

If in addition to knowing the premises by intuition, the drawing of a conclusion from them is, as Descartes says, itself "effected by intuition"—if the act of inference rests on the intuition that the conclusion follows logically from the premises—in what way does deduction or reasoning supplement intuition? To this question, Descartes replies that though the mind "has a clear vision of each step in the process," it cannot comprehend in one intuition all the connections involved in a long chain of reasoning. Only by taking the steps one after another can we "know that the last link in a long chain is connected with the first, even though we do not take in by means of one and the same act of vision all the intermediate links on which that connection depends, but only remember that we have taken them successively under review."

Like Descartes, Locke contrasts intuition and reasoning, or intuitive and demonstrative knowledge. "Sometimes the mind perceives the agreement or disagreement of two ideas immediately by themselves, without the intervention of any other: and this," says Locke, "we may call intuitive knowledge. ... When the mind cannot so bring its ideas together, as by their immediate comparison ... to perceive their agreement or disagreement, it is fain by the intervention of other ideas ... to discover the agreement or disagreement which it searches; and this is that which we call reasoning."

Again like Descartes, Locke asks, "What need is there of reason?" It is necessary, he thinks, "both for the enlargement of our knowledge and regulating our assent ... Sense and intuition reach but very little of the way. The greatest part of our knowledge depends upon deductions and intermediate ideas; and in those cases where we are fain to substitute assent instead of knowledge, and take propositions for true without being certain they are so, we have need to find out, examine, and compare the grounds of their probability." But though reasoning enlarges our knowledge beyond what can be known intuitively, reasoning produces certain knowledge, according to Locke, only if "every step in reasoning ... has intuitive certainty. ... To make anything a demonstration, it is necessary to perceive the immediate agreement of the intervening ideas, whereby the agreement or disagreement of the two ideas under examination (whereof the one is always the first, and the other the last, in the account) is found."

On this view of reasoning, nothing can be known demonstratively or by proof unless some things can be known intuitively, *i.e.*, without inference or proof. Locke and Descartes seem to agree with Aquinas and Aristotle that demonstration depends upon indemonstrable truths, whether these are called axioms, immediate propositions, first principles, or self-evident maxims. Locke and Descartes, on the one hand, stress the point that in reasoning the logical connection between premises and conclusion is also indemonstrable and must be intuitively perceived. Aquinas and Aristotle, on the other, repeatedly observe that the truth of the conclusion is implicitly contained in the truth of the premises, so that the advance which reasoning appears to make from the known to the unknown consists in coming to know actually what is already potentially known. Nevertheless they, unlike Descartes and Locke, maintain that reasoning extends knowledge, even though it may not be the method of initial discovery.

A somewhat contrary view seems to be taken by Hume. If the objects under consideration are matters of fact rather than the relations between our own ideas, the kind of reasoning which goes from premises to conclusion avails not at all. The beliefs we hold about such matters, according to Hume, result from mental operations which are "a species of natural instinct ... which no reasoning or process of thought is able either to produce or to prevent." What he calls "experimental reasoning" or "reasoning concerning matters of fact" is founded, he says, "on a species of Analogy, which leads us to expect from any cause the same events which we have observed to result from similar causes."

Not only men, but also animals reason in this way. But Hume thinks "it is impossible that this inference of the animal can be founded on any process of argument or reasoning by which he concludes that like events must follow like objects. ... The experimental reasoning itself, which we possess in common with beasts, and on which the whole conduct of life depends, is nothing but a species of instinct or mechanical power, that acts in us unknown to ourselves; and in its chief operations is not directed by any such relations or comparisons of ideas, as are the proper objects of our intellectual faculties."

THE FOREGOING considerations indicate how diverse theories of the role of reasoning arise from diverse theories of the nature and kinds of knowledge in animals, men, angels, and God. According as various distinctions are made between human knowledge and opinion, or between the way in which different objects can be known, or between speculative and practical interests, so, too, different formulations are given of the nature of reasoning.

Aristotle's distinction, for example, between scientific and dialectical or rhetorical reasoning turns upon his understanding of the difference between the objects of certain knowledge and the objects of probable opinion. This difference, he says, makes it "equally foolish to accept probable reasoning from a mathematician and to demand from a rhetorician scientific proofs."

Hume's distinction between *a priori* and *a posteriori* reasoning—*i.e.*, between reasoning from principles and reasoning from experience—depends upon his understanding of what matters must be submitted to experience and of the manner in which experience generates belief. The distinction which Aquinas makes between demonstrations *propter quid* and demonstrations *quia*—*i.e.*, between proving *what* something is from its causes and proving *that* it is from its effects—depends upon his understanding of the difference between essence and existence as objects of rational knowledge.

To take an example in the opposite vein, Locke's theory that the same type of demonstration is possible in both mathematics and the moral sciences, seems to rest upon his view that all knowledge consists in the comparison of ideas. In contrast to this, other theories, which hold that the mode of reasoning differs in different disciplines (especially in mathematics and morals, or in metaphysics and the natural sciences), seem to arise from the contrary view that, in these different fields of inquiry, the objects and conditions of knowledge are different.

Sometimes a distinction in the modes of reasoning is based upon the same considerations, but the distinction itself is expressed by different writers in different terms. The role of causes in reasoning appears to underlie Aquinas' distinction between *a priori* and *a posteriori* reasoning, or reasoning from cause to effect as opposed to reasoning from effect to cause. "Demonstration can be made in two ways," he writes; "one is through the cause and is called *a priori*, and this is to argue from what is prior absolutely. The other is through the effect, and is called a demonstration *a posteriori*; this is to argue from what is prior relatively only to us." Descartes appears to make a parallel distinction, though he makes it in different terms. "The method of proof is twofold," he says, "one being analytic, the other synthetic. Analysis shows the true way by which a thing was methodically discovered, as it were effect from cause. . . . Synthesis employs an opposite procedure, one in which the search goes as it were from effect to cause." For both mathematical and metaphysical reasoning, Descartes prefers the analytic to the synthetic method.

According to Newton, the method of analysis, in natural science as well as mathematics, consists in going from effects to causes, while the method of synthesis goes from causes to effects. Newton relates the difference between analysis and synthesis to the difference between inductive and deductive reasoning. This way of distinguishing between inductive and deductive reasoning, in terms of going from effects to causes or from causes to effects, would also seem to be related to the distinction Aquinas makes between demonstration *quia* (*i.e.*, reasoning which proves only *that* something exists) and demonstration *propter quid* (*i.e.*, reasoning which proves *what* something is—its nature or properties). The proof that God exists is, according to Aquinas, a demonstration *quia*; it is also *a posteriori* reasoning or reasoning from effect to cause. But he would not call it "inductive." In one passage at least, he seems to regard induction as the method whereby we can come to some knowledge of what God is. "From natural things," he writes, "one does not come by a demonstration of reason to know non-natural things, but by the induction of reason one may know something above nature, since the natural bears a certain resemblance to the supernatural."

This sense of the word "induction," however, is like that in which Aristotle opposes induction to reasoning, not like that in which he distinguishes between inductive and deductive reasoning according to the order of terms in the inductive and deductive syllogism. In the ordinary deductive syllogism, the middle term establishes the connection between the two extreme terms (for example, 'being a man' establishes the connection between 'Socrates' and 'being mortal'). But "the syllogism which springs out of induction," according to Aristotle, establishes "a relation between one extreme and the middle by means of the other extreme, *e.g.*, if B is the middle term between A and C, it consists in proving through C that A belongs to B." Starting from C (particular cases of long-lived animals, such as man, horse, mule), we can argue inductively from the fact that these long-lived animals are bileless, to the general connection between B (being bileless) and A (being long-lived). Such reasoning is valid, Aristotle adds, only if we can treat C "as made up of all the particulars; for induction proceeds through an enumeration of all the cases."

Different theories of definition also affect the place which is assigned to definition in reasoning. Hobbes, for example, regards reasoning as a kind of calculation with names, which wholly depends upon the determination of their meanings. The operations of addition and subtraction when done with words rather than with numbers are, he thinks, equivalent to "conceiving of the consequence of the names of all the parts, to the name of the whole; or from the names of the whole and one part, to the name of the other part." It is "nothing but *reckoning* (that is, adding and subtracting) of the consequences of general names agreed upon." Aristotle, with the theory that definitions state the essential natures of things, not just the meanings of words, holds that a definition may be "the conclusion of a demonstration giving essential nature," as well as "an indemonstrable statement of essential nature." In the latter case, the definition functions as a principle in demonstration.

According to William James, reasoning, like definition, is "a selective activity of the mind" which serves an individual's interest or purpose. "My thinking," he says, "is first, last, and always for the sake of my doing. . . . Reasoning is always for a subjective interest, to attain some particular conclusion, or to gratify some special curiosity." It makes no difference whether the interest is practical or the curiosity speculative. The process of reasoning will be the same, though the element which provides a solution to the problem in any emergency will be called a " 'reason' if the emergency be theoretical, a 'means' if it be practical."

Those writers who, like Aristotle and Aquinas, regard the speculative and the practical as distinct though related orders of thought and knowledge, seem to think that practical reasoning has its own syllogistic form. Practical deliberations for them are different from theoretic demonstrations. The conclusion of theoretic reasoning is an assertion that something is either true or false, whereas the conclusion of practical deliberation is a judgment that something is good or evil, and therefore should either be done or avoided. According to Aristotle, practical reasoning of the sort which ends in a decision that leads to action, takes the form of a syllogism which has one universal and one particular premise. The major premise is a general rule of conduct, the minor premise a particular perception of fact. In the example Aristotle gives of the practical syllogism, the major premise is the rule that *everything sweet ought to be tasted*, and the minor premise is the perception that *this particular thing is sweet*. These two premises lead to the practical conclusion that *this particular thing ought to be tasted*.

Not all practical reasoning, however, is concerned with reaching decisions or prompting action in particular cases. The rules of conduct which decisions and actions apply may themselves be the products of practical reasoning. The process by which general rules are derived from even more general principles—the precepts of law or morality—involves, according to Aquinas, a form of thinking distinctly different from the theoretic or speculative sort. He points out in his Treatise on Law that we are able to formulate certain practical rules only by making particular determinations of universal principles, not by drawing deductions from them. "Something may be derived from the natural law in two ways," he writes: "first, as a conclusion from premises; secondly, by way of determination of certain generalities. The first way is like that by which, in the speculative sciences, demonstrated conclusions are drawn from the principles; while the second mode is likened to that whereby, in the arts, general forms are particularized as to details." Of these two ways of thinking in the field of law, it would appear that it is only the second type which is peculiar to the practical as opposed to the speculative order.

The discussion of reasoning in relation to knowledge, opinion, and action, or in relation to different disciplines and sciences, usually presupposes a theory of the form which reasoning takes regardless of its subject matter or use. This fact is most explicitly attested by the order of three great books concerned with reasoning. Aristotle's *Posterior Analytics* deals with the theory of demonstration in the sciences. His *Topics* deals with the theory of probable argument or reasoning in the sphere of opinion.

Both are preceded by his *Prior Analytics* which treats of the syllogism in terms of its purely formal structure and its various forms. In the later tradition, the distinction between the problems of the *Prior* and the *Posterior Analytics* comes to be represented by the separation between what are called "formal" and "material" logic.

The formal analysis of reasoning centers on the problem of its cogency. Quite apart from any consideration of the truth of its premises or conclusions, reasoning is true or false according as it is valid or invalid on purely logical grounds. From premises which are in fact false, a conclusion, which may be either true or false, can be truly inferred if the structure of the reasoning is formally valid—that is, if the form of the premises stands in a certain logically prescribed relation to the form of the conclusion. The logical problem, then, is to prescribe the formal relationships among propositions which permit valid inference from certain propositions to others, without regard to the content of the propositions or their truth in fact.

Defining a syllogism as "discourse in which, certain things being stated, something other than what is stated follows of necessity from their being so," Aristotle says, "I call that a perfect syllogism which needs nothing other than what has been stated to make plain what necessarily follows; a syllogism is imperfect, if it needs either one or more propositions which are indeed the necessary consequences of the terms set down, but have not been expressly stated as premises." Using the letters S and P to symbolize the subject and predicate of the conclusion, and the letter M to symbolize the middle term, the term which appears in the premises but not in the conclusion, Aristotle states the form of a perfect syllogism in the following manner: "All M is P, all S is M; therefore all S is P."

The first of these propositions, the one which contains the predicate of the conclusion, is called the major premise; the second, the one which contains the subject of the conclusion, the minor premise; the subject of the conclusion is called the minor term, the predicate the major term. Aristotle classifies syllogisms into three figures, or formal types, according to the position of the middle term, either as subject of the major premise and predicate of the minor in the first figure, or as predicate in both or as subject in both in the second and third figures respectively. Then according to whether the premises are universal propositions or particular ('All M is P' or 'Some S is M'), and each is either affirmative or negative ('All M is P' or 'Some S is not M'), he further distinguishes within each figure a number of valid moods, or formally correct patterns of inference.

For example, in no figure can a valid mood be constructed with two particular or two negative premises. No conclusion can be drawn from the two particular statements that some poisons are liquids and that some liquids are indispensable to life; nor can any conclusion be drawn from the two negative statements that no triangles are parallelograms and no rhomboids are parallelograms. In the first figure, the minor premise can be particular and must be affirmative, the major can be negative and must be universal. In this figure the following combinations of premises—"some figures are not rectangular" with "all rectangular figures are parallelograms," or "all prime numbers are odd" with "some odd numbers are squares"—yield no conclusions. In the second figure, one premise must be negative. Here it is impossible to draw a valid conclusion from two affirmative premises. Nothing follows from the two affirmative statements that all fish swim and all whales swim. In the third figure, only a particular conclusion can be drawn from a pair of premises both of which are universal. From the proposition that no men are wise and the proposition that all men are mortal, we can conclude only that some mortals are not wise.

From these examples it will be seen that Aristotle's rules of the syllogism are rules concerning the quantity and quality of the premises required in each figure to permit a valid inference; and as in the third figure these rules permit only a particular conclusion to be drawn, so for all figures they determine the character of the conclusion which can be drawn from premises of a certain quantity and quality. If one premise is negative, the conclusion must be negative. If one premise is particular, the conclusion must be particular.

There seems to be one universal principle of the syllogism which underlies all these specific rules for the valid moods in different figures.

"When one thing is predicated of another," Aristotle says, "all that which is predicable of the predicate will be predicable also of the subject." The negative aspect of this principle is immediately obvious. What cannot be predicated of a predicate, cannot be predicated of its subject. In the tradition of formal logic, this principle is sometimes stated in terms of the relation of classes rather than in terms of subjects and predicates: if one class is included in a second, and that second class is included in a third, the first is included in the third; and if one class excludes another, the classes which it includes are also excluded from that other.

The principle of the syllogism is traditionally called the *dictum de omni et nullo*. The *dictum de omni*, which Kant in his *Introduction to Logic* calls "the supreme principle of affirmative syllogisms," is thus expressed by him: "Whatever is universally affirmed of a concept is also affirmed of everything contained under it." The *dictum de nullo*, according to Kant, states that "whatever is universally denied of a concept is also denied of everything that is contained under it." Kant appears to think that both these rules follow from even more general principles: that "an attribute of an attribute is an attribute of the thing itself" and that "whatever is inconsistent with the attribute of a thing is inconsistent with the thing itself."

James also attempts to make a more general formulation of the *dictum de omni et nullo*. This law of thought, he says, is "*only the result of the function of comparison* in the mind which has come by some lucky variation to apprehend a series of more than two terms at once." As James states what he calls the "principle of mediate comparison," it appears to be broader than the principle of the syllogism. It applies to any series of related terms—to the relation of equal and unequal quantities in mathematics, as well as to the relation of subjects and predicates in the logic of predication or classes.

James' principle of mediate comparison itself depends on what in mathematical logic and the logic of relations is called the "transitivity" of relations. The relation of *larger than*, for example, is transitive; for if one thing is larger than a second, and the second is larger than a third, it follows that the first is larger than the third. As stated in mathematical logic, the principle of the syllogism is merely a special case of transitivity as it appears in the relation of implication; for if P implies Q, and Q implies R, then P implies R.

James recognizes this when he writes that "*the principle of mediate predication or subsumption* is only the axiom of skipped intermediaries applied to a series of successive predications. It expresses the fact that any earlier term in the series stands to any later term, in the same relation in which it stands to any intermediate term; in other words, that *whatever has an attribute has all the attributes of that attribute*; or more briefly still, that *whatever is of a kind is of that kind's kind*." Along with "the *axiom of mediate equality*, 'equals of equals are equal,' " the rule of mediate predication or subsumption is, according to James, a special case of the law that "skipping intermediary terms leaves relations the same. This AXIOM OF SKIPPED INTERMEDIARIES OR OF TRANSFERRED RELATIONS . . . seems to be on the whole the broadest and deepest law of man's thought."

JAMES' ATTEMPT TO state a law of thought or principle of reasoning which relegates all the rules of the syllogism to the status of a special case represents one type of attack on the syllogism. Whether, for instance, the sample of reasoning which Descartes asks us to consider—that if 2 and 2 make 4, and 3 and 1 make 4, then 2 and 2 amount to the same as 3 and 1—can be reduced to the syllogistic form of subject and predicate, or must be formulated under a more general principle of "transferred relations," illustrates the basic issue here between subject-predicate logic and relational or mathematical logic. Other aspects of that issue are discussed in the chapters on LOGIC, JUDGMENT, and RELATION.

Another type of criticism of the traditional theory of the syllogism accepts the syllogism as the form of *all* reasoning, but objects, as Kant does, to what he calls "the mistaken subtilty" of the classification of syllogisms according to figures and moods. But Kant does not deny all distinctions among syllogisms. On the contrary, he says that syllogisms are "threefold, like all judgements, differing from each other in the manner in which they express the relation of knowledge in the understanding, namely, categorical, hypothetical, and disjunctive." Whether the hypothetical and disjunctive syllogisms are distinct types of reasoning, or only special cases which it would be a mistaken subtlety to treat as having principles of their own, is a problem considered in the chapter on HYPOTHESIS.

Of all criticisms, the most severe is that which either rejects the syllogism entirely as of no use in reasoning, or regards the deductive syllogism as useful only in argumentation or debate, not in the process of inquiry or discovery, where inductive reasoning alone is fruitful or instructive. From the conclusion of a syllogism, according to Mill, one learns nothing more than one already knew in the premises; whereas in inductive reasoning, Mill, like Bacon, thinks that the mind goes beyond anything contained in the premises and genuinely discovers a new truth.

It seems to be Descartes' opinion that "the syllogistic forms are of no aid in perceiving the truth about objects." Locke makes the same point more extensively. Admitting that "all right reasoning may be reduced to [Aristotle's] forms of syllogism," he denies that they are "the best way of reasoning for the leading of those into truth who are willing to find it and desire to make the best use of their reason for the attainment of knowledge.... The rules of syllogism," he writes, "serve not to furnish the mind with those intermediate ideas that may show the connexion of remote ones. This way of reasoning discovers no new proofs, but is the art of marshalling and ranging the old ones we have already. The forty-seventh proposition of the first book of Euclid, is very true; but the discovery of it, I think, not owing to any rules of common logic. A man knows first, and then he is able to prove syllogistically; so that syllogism comes after knowledge, and then a man has little or no need of it.... Syllogism, at best, is but the art of fencing with the little knowledge we have, without making any addition to it."

It may be that the critics of the syllogism attribute to its exponents claims they do not make. Aristotle, for example, seems to present the syllogism as a method of expounding arguments rather than of discovering them, and of testing the validity of reasoning rather than of learning the truth about things. "All instruction given or received by way of argument," he writes, "proceeds from pre-existent knowledge. This becomes evident upon a survey of all the species of instruction. The mathematical sciences, and all other speculative disciplines, are acquired in this way, and so are the two forms of dialectical reasoning, syllogistic and inductive; for each of these latter makes use of old knowledge to impart new, the syllogism assuming an audience that accepts its premises, induction exhibiting the universal as implicit in the clearly known particular."

OUTLINE OF TOPICS

1. Definitions or descriptions of reasoning: the process of thought

   1*a*. Human reasoning compared with the reasoning of animals

   1*b*. Discursive reasoning contrasted with immediate intuition

   1*c*. The role of sense, memory, and imagination in reasoning: perceptual inference, rational reminiscence, the collation of images

2. The rules of reasoning: the theory of the syllogism

   2*a*. The structure of a syllogism: its figures and moods

   (1) The number of premises and the number of terms: the middle term in reasoning

   (2) Affirmation, negation, and the distribution of the middle term: the quantity and the quality of the premises

   2*b*. The kinds of syllogism: categorical, hypothetical, disjunctive, modal

   2*c*. The connection of syllogisms: sorites, pro-syllogisms and epi-syllogisms

REFERENCES

References are listed by volume number (in bold type), author's name, and page number. Bible references are to book, chapter, and verse of the Authorized King James version of the Bible. The abbreviation "esp" calls the reader's attention to one or more especially relevant parts of a whole reference; "passim" signifies that the topic is discussed intermittently rather than continuously in the work or passage cited. Where the work as a whole is relevant to the topic, the page numbers refer to the entire work. For general guidance in the use of *The Great Ideas*, consult the Preface.

1. Definitions or descriptions of reasoning: the process of thought

7 PLATO, 244–245, 383–398, 537–538, 570–577, 594–595
8 ARISTOTLE, 143, 227–228
12 EPICTETUS, 112–113
17 PLOTINUS, 164
19 AQUINAS, 421–424, 443–444
20 AQUINAS, 391–392, 417
23 HOBBES, 58
31 DESCARTES, 7–12, 15–25, 28–29
35 LOCKE, 371–380
38 ROUSSEAU, 337–342
42 KANT, 34–35, 108–209, 224–227, 570–572
49 DARWIN, 292–293
53 JAMES, 146–187, 360–362, 664–693
54 FREUD, 363–364, 384–385, 700–701

1*a*. Human reasoning compared with the reasoning of animals

8 ARISTOTLE, 695
12 AURELIUS, 292
19 AQUINAS, 411–413, 510–511, 673–674
20 AQUINAS, 8–9
23 HOBBES, 52, 57, 59, 100
25 MONTAIGNE, 215–223
31 DESCARTES, 59–60, 156
32 MILTON, 227–229, 240–242
35 LOCKE, 145–146, 221–222
35 BERKELEY, 407–408
35 HUME, 487–488
36 SWIFT, 151–152
38 ROUSSEAU, 337–338, 341–342
42 KANT, 199–200
49 DARWIN, 292–297, 400
53 JAMES, 665–666, 676–677, 679–686

1*b*. Discursive reasoning contrasted with immediate intuition

7 PLATO, 386–388, 809–810
8 ARISTOTLE, 605
17 PLOTINUS, 151, 159, 216–217, 231–232, 235–237
18 AUGUSTINE, 296–297, 323, 339, 614
19 AQUINAS, 81–82, 301–303, 457–458, 683–684
30 BACON, 149
31 DESCARTES, 17–18, 123
31 SPINOZA, 388, 459
32 MILTON, 185–186
33 PASCAL, 171–173, 222–224
35 LOCKE, 119–120, 309, 349, 378–379
42 KANT, 33, 350–351, 572–574

1*c*. The role of sense, memory, and imagination in reasoning: perceptual inference, rational reminiscence, the collation of images

7 PLATO, 179–183, 228–230, 383–398
8 ARISTOTLE, 136–137, 632, 663–664, 673–674, 695
12 LUCRETIUS, 48–51
18 AUGUSTINE, 73–74, 75–76, 78–81
19 AQUINAS, 430–431
23 HOBBES, 52–54, 60
28 HARVEY, 332–335
31 DESCARTES, 18, 20, 28–33, 229–230
38 ROUSSEAU, 341–342
42 KANT, 23–24, 34, 54–64
53 JAMES, 381–385, 525–526, 667–674, 676–686

2. The rules of reasoning: the theory of the syllogism

8 ARISTOTLE, 39–93
18 AUGUSTINE, 651–653
23 HOBBES, 56–60
30 BACON, 56–58, 107–108, 157–161
31 DESCARTES, 1–40
33 PASCAL, 430–434
35 LOCKE, 372–377
36 STERNE, 318–319
42 KANT, 59–108, 110–112, 601–602
53 JAMES, 868–873, 878–879

2*a*. The structure of a syllogism: its figures and moods

8 ARISTOTLE, 39–60
30 BACON, 59–60
35 LOCKE, 373–375, 377
42 KANT, 110–111

2*a*(1) The number of premises and the number of terms: the middle term in reasoning

8 ARISTOTLE, 58–59, 65
30 BACON, 59–60
35 LOCKE, 374–375
42 KANT, 110–112, 118

4*f*. Reasoning by analogy: arguments from similarity

7 PLATO, 350, 383–391
8 ARISTOTLE, 90–91, 152–153
9 ARISTOTLE, 597, 640–641
20 AQUINAS, 938–939
35 LOCKE, 370–371
35 BERKELEY, 433
35 HUME, 487, 502
42 KANT, 547–548, 600–603
53 JAMES, 677–678, 686–690

5. Reasoning in relation to knowledge, opinion, and action

5*a*. The fact and the reasoned fact: mere belief distinguished from belief on rational grounds

7 PLATO, 188–189, 370–373
8 ARISTOTLE, 103, 107–108, 122–123
9 ARISTOTLE, 388
20 AQUINAS, 765–766
35 HUME, 458–469
36 SWIFT, 165
42 KANT, 228, 240–243, 601–607
43 MILL, 283–288
46 HEGEL, 156–160
53 JAMES, 689–690

5*b*. Scientific reasoning: the theory of demonstration

7 PLATO, 174–190, 386–388, 486–511 esp 491, 610–613
8 ARISTOTLE, 97–137, 563–564
9 ARISTOTLE, 388, 389
23 HOBBES, 58, 60, 65
28 HARVEY, 332–337
30 BACON, 42, 56–59, 105–106, 107–136
31 DESCARTES, 1–27, 60–67
33 PASCAL, 365–366, 368–369, 430–434, 442–443
34 NEWTON, 270–271
35 LOCKE, 309–312, 340–341, 360–362, 371–376, 378–379
35 HUME, 458
42 KANT, 1–13, 211–218, 463–467, 542–543
43 MILL, 445
53 JAMES, 674–675, 862–865

5*b*(1) The indemonstrable as a basis for demonstration

8 ARISTOTLE, 39, 99–100, 105–106, 111–116, 511, 515, 525
9 ARISTOTLE, 283–284, 389
19 AQUINAS, 102–103, 612–613
20 AQUINAS, 221–223
28 HARVEY, 333–334
30 BACON, 97
31 DESCARTES, 2–3, 76, 123, 224
35 LOCKE, 310–311, 313
42 KANT, 307–310
43 FEDERALIST, 103–104
43 MILL, 461–462, 475
44 BOSWELL, 82

5*b*(2) Definitions used as means in reasoning: definitions as the end of reasoning

8 ARISTOTLE, 68, 104, 105, 121–122, 123–128, 209–210, 214–215, 525–527, 590, 631–632
9 ARISTOTLE, 161–165
19 AQUINAS, 11–12, 17–18, 458–459
23 HOBBES, 56–60
33 PASCAL, 430–434
35 LOCKE, 303–304
35 HUME, 484
42 KANT, 211–218
51 TOLSTOY, 690
54 FREUD, 412

5*b*(3) *A priori* and *a posteriori* reasoning: from causes or from effects; from principles or from experience; analysis and synthesis

7 PLATO, 242–243
8 ARISTOTLE, 259, 411, 552
9 ARISTOTLE, 340, 391
10 GALEN, 177–178
19 AQUINAS, 680
28 HARVEY, 332–335
30 BACON, 128
31 DESCARTES, 5–8, 128–129
35 LOCKE, 360–362
35 BERKELEY, 417
35 HUME, 458, 464–466, 497–503
42 KANT, 14–20, 34–36, 135–173, 192, 193–200, 211–218, 253–254, 262–287, 307–308, 309, 329–330
43 MILL, 445–446
46 HEGEL, 182–183
53 JAMES, 91–94

5*b*(4) The role of causes in demonstration and scientific reasoning

7 PLATO, 455
8 ARISTOTLE, 128–136, 275, 514–515, 565, 569
9 ARISTOTLE, 161–165, 343–344
19 AQUINAS, 84–85, 112–113, 238–239
28 GALILEO, 202–203
28 HARVEY, 319, 335–336, 393
30 BACON, 45–47, 110–111
31 DESCARTES, 61–62, 66, 108–112, 120–122
31 SPINOZA, 356–357, 369–372, 422–423
34 NEWTON, 371–372, 541–542
35 HUME, 477, 509
42 KANT, 46–47, 164–171, 310–311, 574, 578
45 LAVOISIER, 9–10
45 FOURIER, 183–184
49 DARWIN, 239–240
50 MARX, 10–11
53 JAMES, 668–671

5*b*(5) Demonstration in relation to essence and existence: demonstrations *propter quid* and *quia*

8 ARISTOTLE, 547

6c. Inductive and deductive inference in the philosophy of nature and the natural sciences

8 ARISTOTLE, 275–278, 379, 397
10 HIPPOCRATES, 1–3
10 GALEN, 199–200
19 AQUINAS, 3–4
28 GALILEO, 207–208
28 HARVEY, 280, 285, 332–335, 336
30 BACON, 16, 42, 56–59, 105–195
31 DESCARTES, 60–67
33 PASCAL, 365–371
34 NEWTON, 371–372, 543
35 LOCKE, 123, 321–323, 360–362
35 BERKELEY, 434
35 HUME, 454–455, 460
42 KANT, 578–582
50 MARX, 6
51 TOLSTOY, 469
53 JAMES, 126–127 passim, 295, 674–675, 862–865, 882–884 passim
54 FREUD, 400–401, 483–485, 502–503, 879

6d. Induction and demonstration in the moral sciences

9 ARISTOTLE, 339–340, 395
23 HOBBES, 130–136, 153–154
35 LOCKE, 103–105, 303–304, 317–319, 325, 360
35 HUME, 465, 509
42 KANT, 265–266, 307–310, 317–318, 320–321, 372, 376, 397, 398–399
43 FEDERALIST, 103–104, 257–258
43 MILL, 445–447
46 HEGEL, 74
53 JAMES, 886–888

CROSS-REFERENCES

For: Other comparisons of human and animal intelligence, *see* ANIMAL 1c(2); LANGUAGE 1; MAN 1a–1c; MEMORY AND IMAGINATION 6b; MIND 3a–3b.

Another discussion of the distinction between the intuitive and the discursive or rational, *see* KNOWLEDGE 6c(1); and for the consideration of supra-rational knowledge, *see* EXPERIENCE 7; GOD 6c(3)–6c(4); HAPPINESS 7c(1).

The distinction and relation between reasoning and other acts of the mind, *see* DEFINITION 5; IDEA 5a–5b, 5e; INDUCTION 1a; JUDGMENT 1, 7c; KNOWLEDGE 6c(2); MEMORY AND IMAGINATION 6c; SENSE 1c–1d.

Other discussions bearing on the theory of the syllogism, *see* HYPOTHESIS 5; IDEA 5a–5b; JUDGMENT 7c; LOGIC 1a; OPPOSITION 1d(1); UNIVERSAL AND PARTICULAR 5d.

The problems of truth and falsity, necessity and contingency, and certainty and probability in reasoning, *see* NECESSITY AND CONTINGENCY 4e(2); OPPOSITION 1d(2); SIGN AND SYMBOL 4e; TRUTH 3b(3).

An examination of immediate inference, *see* JUDGMENT 7b; and for the distinction between inductive and deductive reasoning, and *a priori* and *a posteriori* reasoning, *see* EXPERIENCE 2d; INDUCTION 1b; SCIENCE 5d.

The elements of scientific reasoning, *see* BEING 8d, 8f; CAUSE 5b; DEFINITION 5; INFINITY 2c; PHILOSOPHY 3c; PRINCIPLE 3a(2)–3a(3); SCIENCE 5d–5e.

The analysis of dialectical and rhetorical reasoning, *see* DIALECTIC 2b, 2c(2), 3b–3c; OPINION 2c; OPPOSITION 1e; RHETORIC 4c, 4c(2).

Other discussions relevant to the study of practical reasoning, *see* GOOD AND EVIL 5c; JUDGMENT 2; KNOWLEDGE 6e(1)–6e(2); LAW 5g; LOGIC 4e; OPINION 6b; PRUDENCE 5a, 6b.

The character of reasoning in the various disciplines, *see* BEING 8f; GOD 2b–2c; IMMORTALITY 2; LOGIC 4a, 4c, 4e; MATHEMATICS 3a, 3c; MECHANICS 2; MEDICINE 3c; METAPHYSICS 2c; PHILOSOPHY 3c; THEOLOGY 4c; WILL 5c.

The general problem of the rationality of the universe, *see* MIND 10a; NATURE 3a; WORLD 6c.

ADDITIONAL READINGS

Listed below are works not included in *Great Books of the Western World*, but relevant to the idea and topics with which this chapter deals. These works are divided into two groups:

I. Works by authors represented in this collection.
II. Works by authors not represented in this collection.

For the date, place, and other facts concerning the publication of the works cited, consult the Bibliography of Additional Readings which follows the last chapter of *The Great Ideas.*

I.

AQUINAS. *De Fallaciis*
SPINOZA. *Of the Improvement of the Understanding*
HOBBES. *Concerning Body,* PART I, CH 4
HOBBES. *Six Lessons to the Savilian Professors of Mathematics,* II–V
——. *The Art of Sophistry*
LOCKE. *Conduct of the Understanding*
KANT. *Introduction to Logic,* XI
HEGEL. *Science of Logic,* VOL II, SECT I, CH 3
J. S. MILL. *A System of Logic,* BK II, V
FARADAY. *Observations on the Education of the Judgment*
W. JAMES. "The Sentiment of Rationality," in *The Will to Believe*

II.

QUINTILIAN. *Institutio Oratoria (Institutes of Oratory),* BK V, CH 10–14; BK VII, CH 8
SEXTUS EMPIRICUS. *Against the Logicians,* BK II, CH 3–6
——. *Outlines of Pyrrhonism,* BK I–II
PETRUS HISPANICUS. *Summulae Logicales (Logical Treatises)*
SUÁREZ. *Disputationes Metaphysicae,* XIX (5–6), XXIX, XXX (2, 8)
JOHN OF SAINT THOMAS. *Cursus Philosophicus Thomisticus, Ars Logica,* PART I, QQ 6, 8; PART II, QQ 24–25
ARNAULD. *Logic or the Art of Thinking,* PART III–IV
LEIBNITZ. *New Essays Concerning Human Understanding,* BK II, CH 19
EULER. *Letters to a German Princess*
T. REID. *Essays on the Intellectual Powers of Man,* VII
MAINE DE BIRAN. *The Influence of Habit on the Faculty of Thinking*
SCHOPENHAUER. *The World as Will and Idea,* VOL II, SUP, CH 10
BROWN. *Lectures on the Philosophy of the Human Mind,* VOL II, pp 497–525
BENTHAM. *Rationale of Judicial Evidence*
——. *The Book of Fallacies*
WHATELY. *Elements of Logic,* BK I, CH 3; BK IV
W. HAMILTON. *Lectures on Metaphysics and Logic,* VOL II (15–23)
WHEWELL. *The Philosophy of the Inductive Sciences,* VOL I, BK I; VOL II, BK XI, XIII
COURNOT. *Essai sur les fondements de nos connaissances et sur les charactères de la critique philosophique*
MANSEL. *Prolegomena Logica. An Inquiry into the Psychological Character of Logical Processes*
G. C. LEWIS. *A Treatise on the Methods of Observation and Reasoning in Politics*
BOOLE. *An Investigation of the Laws of Thought*
DE MORGAN. *Formal Logic,* CH 5–6
——. *A Budget of Paradoxes*
TAINE. *On Intelligence*
SIGWART. *Logic,* PART I, CH 3; PART III, CH 3–4
JEVONS. *The Substitution of Similars*
——. *The Principles of Science,* CH 4, 6–7, 11
CLIFFORD. *Seeing and Thinking*
LOTZE. *Logic,* BK I, CH 3; BK II, CH 4–7
——. *Outlines of Logic,* DIV I, CH 3
VENN. *Symbolic Logic*
C. S. PEIRCE. *Collected Papers,* VOL II, par 435–618; VOL IV, par 21–79; VOL V, par 151–212
A. SIDGWICK. *Fallacies*
——. *The Use of Words in Reasoning*
J. C. WILSON. *Statement and Inference,* PART I, III
DEWEY *et al. Studies in Logical Theory,* I–IV
WHITEHEAD and RUSSELL. *Principia Mathematica,* PART I, SECT A
BRADLEY. *The Principles of Logic,* BK II–III; Terminal Essays, I
——. *Appearance and Reality,* BK II, CH 15
——. *Collected Essays,* VOL I(12)
——. *Essays on Truth and Reality,* CH 12
DEWEY. *How We Think*
——. *Essays in Experimental Logic,* II–VI
PARETO. *The Mind and Society,* VOL I–III
BOSANQUET. *Logic,* VOL II, CH 1–2, 6–7
——. *Implication and Linear Inference*
W. E. JOHNSON. *Logic,* PART I, CH 14; PART II, CH 1–6
J. M. KEYNES. *A Treatise on Probability,* PART II, CH 12–14
SANTAYANA. *Scepticism and Animal Faith,* CH 13
MEYERSON. *Du cheminement de la pensée*
B. RUSSELL. *Introduction to Mathematical Philosophy,* CH 14
——. *An Inquiry into Meaning and Truth,* CH 24

Chapter 78: RELATION

INTRODUCTION

LIKE quantity and quality, relation is generally recognized as a basic term or category. But its meaning, like theirs, cannot be defined. Relation is, perhaps, the prototype of an indefinable notion. As Bertrand Russell points out, it seems to be impossible to make any statement of what relation is without using the notion of relation in doing so.

Any term which is essentially relative seems also to be incapable of definition. Its meaning cannot be stated without referring to its correlative; and since the meaning of the latter reciprocally involves the former as *its* correlative, each member of a pair of correlative terms draws upon the other for its meaning. A part is a part of a whole; a whole, a whole of parts. Similarly, the meaning of parent involves the notion of child and the meaning of child the notion of parent.

Plato applies this maddening fact about correlative terms to all comparatives which presuppose the correlation of more and less. "Comparatives such as the hotter and the colder," he writes, "are to be ranked in the class of the infinite." They cannot be measured or defined. Terms like 'much' and 'little,' 'great' and 'small' look like quantities, but, according to Aristotle, they are "not quantities, but relatives, for things are not great or small absolutely; they are so called rather as the result of an act of comparison."

Concerning quantities and qualities, the ancients ask how they exist. The alternatives seem to be either that they exist in and of themselves, or that they exist as the attributes of substances such as stones and trees. But with regard to relations, the question seems to be whether they exist rather than how they exist.

The supposition that a relation cannot exist apart from the terms it relates may be thought to imply that the relation does exist when the terms it relates exist. The ancients, however, do not appear to regard the relation as something having a reality distinguishable from the reality of the correlative terms. It seems to be significant that both Plato and Aristotle discuss relative terms, rather than relations as such. For the most part, they signify relations by using a pair of words which name things standing in a certain relation to one another.

Thus in the *Categories*, Aristotle refers to 'double' and 'half,' 'master' and 'slave,' 'greater' and 'less,' or 'knowledge' and 'object known' as examples of correlative terms. "All relatives," he says, "have a correlative." Sometimes it is necessary to find the precise word, or even to invent the right word, for in order to indicate that a given term is relative, its correlative must be appropriately named. "Concubine," says Locke, "is, no doubt, a relative name, as well as wife; but in languages where this, and like words, have not a correlative term, there people are not so apt to take them to be so, as wanting that evident mark of relations which is between correlatives, which seem to explain one another, and not to be able to exist but together."

When "reciprocity of correlation does not appear to exist," Aristotle suggests that it may be the result of our failure to use words carefully. If we wish to use the term 'rudder' as relative, we cannot call its correlative a 'boat,' for "there are boats which have no rudders." Since there is no existing word, it would be "more accurate," Aristotle thinks, "if we coined some word like 'ruddered' to name the correlative of 'rudder.'" Similarly, in the case of 'slave' as a relative term, its correlative is not 'man' understood in any sense, but only man understood as 'master.'

The things which are designated by a pair of reciprocally relative terms must, according to

Aristotle, coexist. One man cannot be called a master unless another man exists who can be called his slave; something cannot be called larger unless something coexistent with it can be called smaller. Aristotle considers possible exceptions to this principle of the simultaneity or coexistence of correlatives; as, for example, in the case of knowledge and the knowable. It seems possible, he thinks, for the knowable to exist before anyone has actual knowledge of it. But the exception may be due to an improper naming of the correlatives. If the correlative of knowledge is the known rather than the knowable, then knowledge and its object may be said to be necessarily coexistent, for nothing comes to be an object actually known, except simultaneously with someone's coming actually to know it.

THE COEXISTENCE OF things which are correlative to one another still leaves a question concerning the existence of the relation between them. When conceived as an attribute, a quality or a quantity can be said to exist in the thing it somehow modifies. In the language of Aristotle, such accidents *inhere in* substances, and accordingly have reality as long as the substances in which they inhere exist. But a relation does not seem to inhere in *a* substance. It cannot be the attribute of a single thing. It somehow lies between two things, inhering in neither, for if it belonged to either one alone it could have some reality if that one existed and the other did not. The question, therefore, is whether relations really exist at all, or are only in the mind of him who compares things or considers them relative to one another.

"A sign that the relative is least of all a substance and a real thing," writes Aristotle, "is the fact that it alone has no proper generation or destruction or movement; as in respect of quantity there is increase and diminution, in respect of quality alteration, in respect of place locomotion, in respect of substance simple generation and destruction. In respect to relation there is no proper change; for, without changing, a thing will be now greater and now less or equal, if that with which it is compared has changed in quantity."

Plotinus also questions the reality of relations. "Has relation—for example, that of right and left, double and half—any actuality? . . . What can be the meaning of correlatives apart from our conception of their juxtaposition? 'Greater' may refer to very different magnitudes; 'different' to all sorts of objects. The comparison is ours; it does not lie in the things themselves." In the case of certain space and time relations he maintains that "right and left are in our conception, nothing of them in the things themselves. Before and after are merely two things; the relation is again of our making."

Yet Plotinus seems unwilling to say that "we do not mean anything by relation, but are victims of words," or that "none of the relations mentioned can exist." Recognizing what he calls "the elusive character of relation," he is willing to affirm the reality of relations "when the actuality of the relationships is derived from no other source than relation itself." He thinks that one quantity may be the double of another, "quite apart from our speech or thought." The fact that one quantity is the double of another is an additional fact about the two quantities over and above all their other properties. "In all the conditions in which we assert relation," Plotinus declares, "the mutual relation exists over and above the objects; we perceive it as already existent; our knowledge is directed upon a thing, there to be known—a clear testimony to the reality of relation."

The problem thus seems to become one of distinguishing between relations which have independent reality and those which exist only in the mind. "Some have said that relation is not a reality but only an idea. But this," Aquinas declares, "is plainly seen to be false from the very fact that things themselves have a mutual order and relation." Not all relations are real, however. "Relations which result in the things understood from the operation of the intellect alone are logical relations only, inasmuch as reason observes them as existing between two understood things." For example, "the relation of a thing to itself is not a real relation," for "reason, by apprehending one thing twice, regards it as two; and thus it apprehends a certain relation of a thing to itself . . . The same is true of those relations that follow upon an act of reason, as genus and species, and the like."

Aquinas offers, in contrast, "other relations which are realities with regard to both extremes; as when a relation exists between two things according to some reality that belongs to both. This is clear of all relations consequent upon quantity, great and small, double and half, and the like; for there is quantity in both extremes."

This distinction between real and logical relations seems to be qualified by the intermediate case of a relation which is partly logical and partly real; for, according to Aquinas, "sometimes a relation in one extreme may be a reality, while in the other extreme, it is only an idea. This happens whenever the two extremes are not of one order . . . Since God is outside the whole order of creation and all creatures are ordered to Him, and not conversely, it is manifest that creatures are really related to God Himself; whereas in God there is no real relation to creatures, but a relation only in idea, inasmuch as creatures are related to Him."

In the *Charmides*, Socrates raises some doubts about the admissibility of reflexive relations, or the relations of things to themselves. Others have questioned the partly real and partly logical relation, according to which one thing is related to another but the second is not related to the first. But the more important issues, in the tradition of western thought, seem to be whether there are both real and logical relations, *i.e.*, relations both in nature and in the mind, and whether, in either case, relations enter into the very nature of the things related or are merely external, so that the character of a thing is unaffected by the relations in which it stands.

As indicated in the chapters on Judgment, Reasoning, and Logic, relation tends to displace predication in certain typically modern theories of the proposition and of inference. What is currently called "relational logic" is set against "subject-predicate logic." Relations themselves, without regard to the character of the terms related, become the primary object of logical analysis. It is said, for example, that the proposition 'John hit James' has the form 'aRb' or 'R(a,b),' and that the proposition 'John went to school with James' has the form 'R(a,b,c,).' The first is a dyadic relation, the second a triadic relation.

Relations are classified not only with respect to the number of the terms they relate, but also with respect to such formal properties as symmetry, transitivity, reflexivity. The relation of parent and child, for example, is asymmetrical. It cannot be said, if A is the parent of B, that B is also the parent of A; whereas the relation of brotherhood is symmetrical. Statements of symmetrical relationship are convertible. If we say that A is the brother of B, we can also say that B is the brother of A.

The type of relationship remains the same regardless of the character of the terms. Unequal quantities are asymmetrically related, equal quantities symmetrically; 'to-the-right-of' is an asymmetrical spatial relation, 'next-to' is symmetrical; in time, 'simultaneous-with' is symmetrical and 'prior-to' asymmetrical. The distinction between transitive and intransitive relations similarly holds for all kinds of terms. The relation of father to son or of 'standing-next-to' in space is intransitive, for if A is the father of B, and B the father of C, A is not the father of C; whereas the spatial relation of 'standing-to-the-right-of' is transitive, for if A is to the right of B, and B to the right of C, then A is to the right of C.

The modern analysis of propositions as relational structures which differ in type according to the character of the relations, not the character of the terms, has an antecedent in Locke's analysis of judgments as acts of comparison which look to the relation between ideas rather than to the ideas themselves. Both analyses lead to a theory of inference which is based on the *convertibility* of symmetrical relations and on the *transitivity* of certain relationships and the intransitivity of others. As indicated in the chapter on Reasoning, the factor of transitivity appears in William James' discussion of the "principle of mediate comparison." He states this in the formula "*more than the more is more than the less.*" Then he explains that "such a formula would cover all possible cases; as, earlier than early is earlier than late, worse than bad is worse than good, east of east is east of west; etc., etc., *ad libitum*. Symbolically, we might write it as $a<b<c<d$ . . . and say that any number of intermediaries may be ex-

punged without obliging us to alter anything in what remains written."

James thus formulates what he regards as the most fundamental law of thought. For series of "homogeneously related terms," the law is that "*skipping intermediary terms leaves the relations the same.*" The factor of transitivity enters the picture when James distinguishes between relations which are and relations which are not *transferable*. "All skipping of intermediaries and transfer of relations occurs within homogeneous series," he writes. "But not all homogeneous series allow of intermediaries being skipped. It depends on which series they are, on what relations they contain. Let it not be said that it is a mere matter of verbal association, due to the fact that language sometimes permits us to transfer the *name* of a relation over skipped intermediaries, and sometimes does not; as where we call men 'progenitors' of their remote as well as of their immediate posterity, but refuse to call them 'fathers' thereof. There are relations which are *intrinsically* transferable, whilst others are not. The relation of *condition*, *e.g.*, is intrinsically transferable. What conditions a condition conditions what it conditions—'cause of cause is cause of effect.' The relations of negation and *frustration*, on the other hand, are not transferable: what frustrates a frustration does not frustrate what it frustrates. No changes in terminology would annul the intimate difference between these two cases."

The foregoing passages from James reflect the general tenor of the theory of the calculus of relations. He himself does not systematically expound it. Its elaboration is to be found in the writings of Boole, Couturat, and De Morgan, of Jevons, Pierce, Bradley, Royce, Russell and Whitehead (whose works are cited in the Additional Readings). Is this relational logic more general than the subject-predicate logic that is traditionally called "Aristotelian," or is the reverse the case?

The modern answer insists upon the greater generality of relational logic. Royce, for example, defining "subsumption" as a non-symmetrical, transitive relation which obtains between two classes when one includes the other, declares that "the entire traditional 'theory of the syllogism' can be expressed as a sort of comment upon, and relatively simple application of, the transitivity of the subsumption relation." According to Royce, William James' axiom of skipped intermediaries represents a step in the right direction, but it fails to achieve complete generality.

Russell disposes of the traditional theory of the proposition in the same fashion that Royce disposes of the traditional theory of the syllogism. Traditional logic, he writes, "believed that there was only one form of simple proposition (*i.e.*, of proposition not stating a relation between two or more other propositions), namely, the form which ascribes a predicate to a subject." It is, therefore, "unable to admit the reality of relations; all relations, it maintains, must be reduced to properties of the apparently related terms." Russell insists, on the contrary, that "propositions stating that two things have a certain relation have a different form from subject-predicate propositions." This can be most easily seen, he thinks, in the case of asymmetrical relations. The proposition which states that A and B are related by the symmetrical relation of equality, can be interpreted to mean that A and B both possess a common property. "But when we come to asymmetrical relations, such as before and after, greater and less, etc., the attempt to reduce them to properties becomes," in Russell's opinion, "obviously impossible." The relational theory of the proposition, therefore, includes the subject-predicate theory as a special case.

A defense of the subject-predicate logic would not make the counterclaim that relational logic can be treated as a special case. Rather it would insist that the two logics are radically different in principle—that the one belongs to a philosophy of nature and a metaphysics, in which substance is the primary concept; whereas the other belongs to the empirical sciences and to modern mathematics, in which the concept of relation supplants substance. Whichever side of the controversy is taken, the undeniable difference between a relational and a subject-predicate logic represents one of the great differences between modern and ancient thought.

It is not only in logic that the modern emphasis seems to be upon relations rather than upon things related—on relations denuded of their terms rather than on terms treated as correlatives. The same tendency appears in modern mathematics, in algebra, in the calculus, and especially in the theory of equations and functions, of sets and series. It also appears in modern physics where, according to Cassirer, the great conceptual revolution consists in displacing substance by function, and the casual interaction of substances by functional relationships and systems of order. Such substitutions obviously parallel the shift in logic—from the consideration of terms related as subjects and predicates, to the consideration of relations without regard to differences in the terms related.

In the tradition of the great books, this conceptual revolution seems to be announced by the treatment which Hume and Kant accord to the notion of substance. Hume appears to conceive of experience as a series of events related, as he says, by "only three principles of connexion . . . namely, *Resemblance*, *Contiguity* in time or place, and *Cause or Effect*." These relations make up the fabric of experience. So long as it consisted in such connections, our experience would be the same whether or not there were enduring things or substances.

"Nature has established connexions among particular ideas," Hume writes, so that "no sooner does one idea occur to our thoughts than it introduces its correlative." All our knowledge of matters of fact depends upon the association of ideas, or the relations of resemblance, contiguity, and causation among the elements of experience. All other knowledge has for its object those relations between ideas which do not connect them causally or place them in a spatial or temporal order. In either case, relations of all sorts, rather than things and their properties (or substances and their attributes), seem to be the prime constituents of nature and of knowledge.

Kant presents a fourfold classification of judgments according to their quantity, quality, relation, and modality. Under the head of relation, he distinguishes the categorical, the hypothetical, and the disjunctive according to the following criteria: "*a*. Relation of the predicate to the subject. *b*. Relation of the cause to its effect. *c*. Relation of subdivided knowledge, and of the collected members of the subdivision to each other." These are, he writes, "all the relations of thought in judgements."

Pointing out that he borrows the term from Aristotle, Kant calls the pure concepts of the understanding "categories" and constructs a table of categories which runs parallel to his table of judgments; because, as he explains, "the same function which imparts unity to various representations in one judgement imparts unity likewise to the mere synthesis of various representations in one intuition, which in a general way may be called the pure concept of understanding." Kant's categories, in contrast to Aristotle's, afford a striking example of the shift from substance to relation.

Where for Aristotle substance is the primary category and all other categories signify the accidents of substance, among which relation seems to have least reality in the nature of things, Kant makes relation one of the four major groups of categories, and under relation places subsistence and inherence (or substance and accident) along with causality and dependence (or cause and effect) and community (or reciprocity between the active and the passive). It is not substance, but the relation of substance and accident, which is for Kant a transcendental category.

THE ISSUE CONCERNING substance and relation takes another form in the problem whether relations exist *in* the very nature of things, as belonging to their essence, or only exist as connections *between* things. In the latter alternative, there is still the question whether relations between things are externally affixed to them or are internally inherent in them and affect the natures of the things related.

According to the Christian doctrine of the Trinity, there are real relations *in* God, each really distinct from the others, yet each identical with the divine essence. These relations are the persons of the Trinity—the relations Aquinas calls "paternity, filiation, spiration and procession," the relation of the Father and the Son, and of the Holy Spirit to them both. "Relation in God," he writes, "is not as an accident in a subject, but is the divine essence itself; and so it is subsistent, for the divine essence is subsistent. Therefore, as the Godhead is God, so the divine paternity is God the Father, Who is a divine person. Therefore, a divine person signifies a relation as subsisting."

Since the three persons of the Trinity are of the same essence, the principle of their real distinction must be found elsewhere. Denying that "there can be discerned between them a real distinction in respect of the divine essence," Descartes does not reject the possibility of a distinction "in respect of their relation to one another." Aquinas considers "two principles of difference among the divine persons . . . *origin* and *relation*," but thinks it is "better to say that the persons or hypostases are distinguished by relations rather than by origin"; for, among other reasons, "when a relation is an accident, it presupposes the distinction of subjects; but when the relation is subsistent, it does not presuppose, but brings about, distinction."

It would seem to follow that, except in God, relations are not subsistent. In Aristotle's theory of corporeal substances, for example, the matter and the form which constitute a physical thing are united, not related. Though matter and form are conceived as really distinct principles in the composition of a composite substance—as essence and existence are also sometimes said to be really distinct principles in the being of all things except God—their real distinction does not imply that they are subsistent, as are the persons of the Trinity, nor that they are relations, or in relation to one another. If real as opposed to logical relations occur only between things which somehow really subsist, then those principles which must be united in order for a thing to subsist cannot be really related to one another.

With a somewhat different analysis, Locke seems to exclude relations from the constitution of what he calls "the complex idea of substance." All complex ideas, according to Locke, "are either modes, substances, or relations." The complex idea of substance is a "collection of those several simple ideas of sensible qualities, which we . . . . find united in the thing called horse or stone; yet because we cannot conceive how they should subsist alone, nor one in another, we suppose them existing in, and supported by some common subject; which support we denote by the name substance, though it be certain we have no clear or distinct idea of that thing we suppose a support."

The various simple ideas of qualities which, together with the indistinct notion of a supporting substratum, constitute the complex idea of a particular substance, are, in Locke's theory, compounded, not related. Relation is itself a complex idea, consisting in "the consideration and comparing of one idea with another." The ideas related may be either simple or complex, but the relations are *between* ideas, not *in* them—certainly not in simple ideas, nor in complex ideas of modes and substances, which are combinations, not relations, of simple ideas.

The exception is, of course, a complex idea of relation, which involves several distinct ideas and, in addition, the idea of a relation between them which, Locke says, "it gets from their comparison one with another. . . . Since any idea, whether simple or complex, may be the occasion why the mind thus brings two things together . . . any of our ideas may be the foundation of relation"; but, Locke adds, "there must always be in relation two ideas, or things, either in themselves really separate, or considered as distinct, and then ground or occasion for their comparison."

Locke's theory of relations not only seems to exclude them from the interior constitution of substances, but also seems to make them entirely extrinsic to the natures of the things related. "Ideas of relation," Locke says, "may be the same in men who have far different ideas of the things that are related or that are thus compared." The relation is unaffected by the things it relates, as they in turn are unaffected by it, for they are "not contained in the real existence of things, but [are] something extraneous and super-induced."

Berkeley and Hume also seem to agree that relations are entirely external. "Relations are distinct from the ideas or things related," writes Berkeley, "inasmuch as the latter may be perceived by us without our perceiving the former." To Hume, "all events seem entirely loose and separate. One event follows another; but we can never observe any tie between them. They seem *conjoined*, but never *connected*." So far as our understanding goes, nothing in the nature of one event necessarily leads the mind to the consideration of another, as it would if the event could not be understood by us except as intrinsically related or connected with that other.

In the tradition of western thought, the issue concerning the internality or externality of relations has profound implications for man's conception of the order of nature or the structure of the world. The difference, discussed in the chapter on CHANCE, between what William James calls the "block" and the "concatenated" universe presupposes not only different views of causality, but also different positions with respect to the internality or externality of relations, as is indicated by James' criticism of Hegel and Bradley.

The relation of part and whole, and of one part to another in the structure of an organic whole, seems to be the prime example of internal relationship. Each part is thought to be constituted, both in its being and nature, by the being and nature of the whole to which it belongs and by the other parts which comprise that whole. This may be seen in Spinoza's theory of God or Nature as the one and only substance, in and through which everything else both is and is conceived. All things are locked together in a system of internal relationships—the finite parts with one another through the infinite whole which determines each to be what it is, in itself and in relation to all others.

RELATION SEEMS TO BE the principle of order. At least it can be said that the various conceptions of order which appear in the great books involve the idea of relation and of different kinds of relationship.

The order of the universe or of nature, for example, seems to be differently conceived according as things are causally related to one another, related as lower and higher species in a hierarchy of grades of being, or as the parts of one all-embracing whole. In each case, it makes a difference, as we have already observed, whether the relations involved are thought to be real or logical, and internal or external to the things related.

Relation similarly enters into conceptions of psychological, political, and moral order—the order of the parts of the soul, the order of classes or functions in the state, the order of goods, of means and ends, of duties, of loves. Just as the status of each thing in nature is affected by whether the universe is conceived as a whole of internally related parts or as a set of externally related wholes, so the status of the individual in society is affected by whether the state is conceived as an organic whole or merely as a political order formed by the free association of individuals.

The consideration of the various types of order occurs in other chapters, such as NATURE, WORLD, SOUL, STATE, GOOD AND EVIL, and BEAUTY. Particular types of relationship are also discussed in chapters concerned with the terms between which such relationships hold—the relation of cause and effect in the chapter on CAUSE; spatial and temporal relationships in the chapters on SPACE and TIME; the relation of species and genus in the chapters on EVOLUTION and IDEA; relations of equality and inequality in the chapter on QUANTITY; and relations of similarity and dissimilarity in the chapter on QUALITY.

This last type of relationship, more broadly conceived as including not merely likeness in quality, but the sameness or similitude of things in every sort of respect, is the main consideration of the chapter on SAME AND OTHER. The theory of analogy is discussed there also, for though it is concerned with relation—a proportion being a ratio of ratios—the specific relationship by which relations are themselves related in analogies or proportions seems to be one of similitude (either identity or similarity).

Finally, the idea of relation seems to be involved in the contrast between the absolute and the relative. Things are said to be considered absolutely when they are considered in themselves, and relatively when they are considered with reference to something else. By extension of these meanings, relativism tends to assert that with regard to most things, if not all, what they are depends on the point of view, *i.e.*, their relation to man, to *this* group of men, or even to *this* man. Absolutism goes to the opposite extreme of saying that things are what they are independently of man's view of them. The opposition of these two tendencies creates familiar issues concerning the true, the good, and the beautiful, which are discussed in the chapters devoted to those subjects.

OUTLINE OF TOPICS

1. The general theory of relation

 1a. The nature and being of relations: the distinction between real and logical or ideal relations

 1b. The effect of relations on the nature and being of things: internal and external relations

 1c. The coexistence of correlatives

 1d. Relational unity or identity of relation: the notion and use of analogy or proportionality

2. Order and relation in God: the divine processions and the relations constituting the Trinity of persons

3. The relation of God to the world: divine immanence and transcendence

4. Relation in the order of thought or knowledge

 4a. The definability or indefinability of relative terms

 4b. The proposition or judgment as a statement of relation: relation in reasoning

 4c. The transcendental categories of relation

 4d. Relations as objects of knowledge: ideas of relation

 4e. The relations between ideas

 4f. The types of relationship underlying the association of ideas in thought, memory, and dreams

5. Order as a system of relationships or related things

 5a. The nature and types of order: inclusion and exclusion; succession and coexistence; priority, posteriority, and simultaneity

  (1) The order of the causes or of cause and effect

  (2) The order of goods or of means and ends: the order of loves

  (3) The order of quantities: the types of proportion

  (4) The order of kinds: hierarchy; species and genus

 5b. The order of the universe or of nature: the hierarchy of beings

 5c. Order as a principle of beauty

6. The absolute and the relative modes of consideration

 6a. Absolute and relative with respect to space, time, motion

 6b. Absolute and relative with respect to truth

 6c. Absolute and relative with respect to goodness or beauty

REFERENCES

References are listed by volume number (in bold type), author's name, and page number. Bible references are to book, chapter, and verse of the Authorized King James version of the Bible. The abbreviation "esp" calls the reader's attention to one or more especially relevant parts of a whole reference; "passim" signifies that the topic is discussed intermittently rather than continuously in the work or passage cited. Where the work as a whole is relevant to the topic, the page numbers refer to the entire work. For general guidance in the use of *The Great Ideas*, consult the Preface.

1. The general theory of relation

1*a*. The nature and being of relations: the distinction between real and logical or ideal relations

7 PLATO, 8–9, 372–373, 448–449, 489, 570–574
8 ARISTOTLE, 11–13, 542–543
17 PLOTINUS, 254–257
19 AQUINAS, 68–70, 224–225
31 DESCARTES, 8
35 LOCKE, 214–217
42 KANT, 99–108
53 JAMES, 157–159, 458–459, 549–550, 865–866, 879–886

1*b*. The effect of relations on the nature and being of things: internal and external relations

7 PLATO, 521–522
8 ARISTOTLE, 13, 596–597, 620
19 AQUINAS, 167–168
20 AQUINAS, 718
31 SPINOZA, 355–356
35 LOCKE, 334–335
42 KANT, 99–101
53 JAMES, 142, 450–459, 550–551, 644–645, 660, 669

1*c*. The coexistence of correlatives

7 PLATO, 8–9, 267–268, 351–352, 520
8 ARISTOTLE, 11–13, 17, 187
10 GALEN, 169
17 PLOTINUS, 255–256
19 AQUINAS, 68–70
35 LOCKE, 215
42 KANT, 83–84

1*d*. Relational unity or identity of relation: the notion and use of analogy or proportionality

7 PLATO, 448
8 ARISTOTLE, 135, 172, 189, 537, 573–574, 599–601 passim, 664
9 ARISTOTLE, 7, 114, 167–168, 169, 378–381 passim, 640–641, 657, 662–663, 665, 693
11 EUCLID, 81–98
11 NICOMACHUS, 841
16 KEPLER, 1078–1080
19 AQUINAS, 22–23, 50–51, 66–68, 72–73, 98, 182–183, 240–241, 713–714
20 AQUINAS, 885–886, 1025–1032
24 RABELAIS, 12–13
28 HARVEY, 336
30 BACON, 157–158
35 LOCKE, 228
35 HUME, 487
42 KANT, 72–74, 601–603
49 DARWIN, 212–213
53 JAMES, 688–689 passim

2. Order and relation in God: the divine processions and the relations constituting the Trinity of persons

18 AUGUSTINE, 312–313, 327–328
19 AQUINAS, 14–20, 49–50, 157–161, 165–217 passim, 222–223, 224–230
21 DANTE, 144
22 CHAUCER, 467
23 HOBBES, 207–208, 259
31 DESCARTES, 93–96, 131, 159–161, 217–218, 232
31 SPINOZA, 355–356, 358–359, 362–365, 366, 367–369
32 MILTON, 136–144
40 GIBBON, 307, 310–313
41 GIBBON, 422
46 HEGEL, 306

3. The relation of God to the world: divine immanence and transcendence

18 AUGUSTINE, 1–2, 26–27, 43–44, 45, 73–74, 100–101, 261, 353–354, 358–359, 519–520, 627
19 AQUINAS, 19–20, 28–29, 34–38, 107–108, 238–239, 244, 277–278, 279–280, 529–530, 534–537
20 AQUINAS, 511
21 DANTE, 135, 148–150
28 HARVEY, 428
31 DESCARTES, 52, 158–159, 214
31 SPINOZA, 355–372, 373–377
32 MILTON, 306
34 NEWTON, 370–371
35 LOCKE, 165
35 BERKELEY, 442–443

NEW TESTAMENT: *Philippians*, 3:7-16
6 HERODOTUS, 6-8
7 PLATO, 23, 69-71, 165-167, 183-184, 262-264, 310, 421-427, 635-639, 643-644, 656-658, 687-688, 689-690
8 ARISTOTLE, 89-90, 162-166
9 ARISTOTLE, 339-343, 354, 403-406, 430-432, 480-481, 527, 536, 538
12 AURELIUS, 271
14 PLUTARCH, 74-75
17 PLOTINUS, 12-19, 74-75
18 AUGUSTINE, 11-12, 270-271, 331, 346-347, 416, 507-511, 516-524, 625-626, 629-630, 633-634
19 AQUINAS, 27-29, 609-643, 712-715
21 DANTE, 79-80, 145-146
22 CHAUCER, 401-432
23 HOBBES, 155
30 BACON, 91-92
31 SPINOZA, 369-372, 422-424
33 PASCAL, 326-327
35 LOCKE, 191-192, 198
42 KANT, 238-239, 256, 266-267, 271-279, 316-317, 327-329, 478-479, 584-587, 588, 594-595
43 MILL, 445-447, 448-450, 461-463
46 HEGEL, 44, 98, 267, 348
52 DOSTOEVSKY, 164-165
53 JAMES, 199-204

5*a*(3) The order of quantities: the types of proportion

8 ARISTOTLE, 330-333, 541, 542-543, 579-580, 583, 584, 611-618 passim
9 ARISTOTLE, 378-381 passim
11 EUCLID, 81-98, 117
11 NICOMACHUS, 821-831, 841-848
19 AQUINAS, 68-70
31 DESCARTES, 295-353 esp 295-298
34 NEWTON, 31-32
38 ROUSSEAU, 407-408 passim
42 KANT, 497-498
50 MARX, 19-25
53 JAMES, 551

5*a*(4) The order of kinds: hierarchy; species and genus

7 PLATO, 582-583
8 ARISTOTLE, 6-7, 20, 196, 545, 558-561, 569-570, 585-586
9 ARISTOTLE, 165-168
17 PLOTINUS, 142-143
19 AQUINAS, 17-18, 93-94, 170-171, 257-258, 270-272, 384-385, 457, 471-472, 698-699, 774-775
20 AQUINAS, 22-23, 54-55, 117-118, 710-711
35 LOCKE, 255-256, 277-278, 279-280
38 ROUSSEAU, 341-342
42 KANT, 193-200
49 DARWIN, 30-31, 64, 207-208, 210-211, 241-242
53 JAMES, 870-871

5*b*. The order of the universe or of nature: the hierarchy of beings

5 ARISTOPHANES, 551
7 PLATO, 155-157, 446-477, 618-619
8 ARISTOTLE, 275-278, 359-360, 382-384, 392, 430-433, 436-441, 505-506, 508-511, 605-606
9 ARISTOTLE, 114-115, 164, 211, 218, 272
12 LUCRETIUS, 6, 18-19, 26, 28-30, 71-72
12 EPICTETUS, 146
12 AURELIUS, 263-264, 267, 269-270, 271, 273, 277-278, 292, 297
16 KEPLER, 1023-1080
17 PLOTINUS, 44-45, 46-47, 49-50, 163, 214-215, 251
18 AUGUSTINE, 48-50, 333-334, 343-345, 516-523
19 AQUINAS, 12-14, 26-27, 124-125, 256-259, 260-261, 269-270, 295, 316-317, 339-377, 385-388, 396, 528-608
20 AQUINAS, 15-18, 1016-1025
21 DANTE, 107, 120, 126, 150
22 CHAUCER, 54-55, 87, 209
27 SHAKESPEARE, 108-109
28 HARVEY, 426-429
30 BACON, 149, 159, 179-188
31 DESCARTES, 54-56
31 SPINOZA, 369-372, 374-375, 395, 425
32 MILTON, 184-186, 232-236, 239-240
34 NEWTON, 269-372
35 LOCKE, 271-272, 321-322, 370-371
35 BERKELEY, 418-419 passim
35 HUME, 486
38 MONTESQUIEU, 1-2
42 KANT, 93-99, 133, 187-189, 199-200, 220, 307-314, 467-470, 578-580
46 HEGEL, 160-162
49 DARWIN, 55-62, 63-64, 96-98, 179-180, 228-229, 238-239, 241
53 JAMES, 95-98, 641-643, 873, 882-886

5*c*. Order as a principle of beauty

7 PLATO, 333-334, 342, 474-475
8 ARISTOTLE, 329-330
9 ARISTOTLE, 512, 685
11 NICOMACHUS, 814
17 PLOTINUS, 21, 332-333
18 AUGUSTINE, 24
19 AQUINAS, 25-26
35 LOCKE, 148
42 KANT, 488-489, 544-545, 557-558
49 DARWIN, 301-302
53 JAMES, 865

6. The absolute and the relative modes of consideration

7 PLATO, 242-244
8 ARISTOTLE, 10, 161-162, 178-179, 194-195, 200-201, 229-230, 248-249, 394-395
19 AQUINAS, 31-32, 46-47, 63-64, 167-168, 493-494, 618-619, 649-650, 688-689
20 AQUINAS, 6-7, 808-809

31 Spinoza, 358
42 Kant, 130–133, 202–203

6a. Absolute and relative with respect to space, time, motion

7 Plato, 350–351
8 Aristotle, 402–403
16 Copernicus, 514–515
16 Kepler, 1015
18 Augustine, 93–95
30 Bacon, 165–166
34 Newton, 8–13, 19, 111–114
35 Locke, 149–150, 154, 163–164, 217–218
35 Berkeley, 431–432, 434–436
53 James, 408–411, 511–512, 565, 612–624, 783–785

6b. Absolute and relative with respect to truth

7 Plato, 86, 517–532
8 Aristotle, 528–531, 580, 590–592
9 Aristotle, 651
12 Lucretius, 50–51
12 Epictetus, 164–166
18 Augustine, 523
19 Aquinas, 10–11, 453–455
23 Hobbes, 56, 65
25 Montaigne, 209–212, 240–246, 259–261, 271–272, 318–319
30 Bacon, 13, 57–58
31 Descartes, 1–3, 8–10, 46
33 Pascal, 238–239
42 Kant, 194, 218–222, 224–227, 240–243
43 Mill, 275–283 passim
50 Marx–Engels, 427, 428
53 James, 639–646
54 Freud, 880, 881–882

6c. Absolute and relative with respect to goodness or beauty

7 Plato, 86, 383–386, 531–532, 630–631, 636–639
8 Aristotle, 162–166
9 Aristotle, 339, 340, 341–342, 359, 378–381, 382–383, 430, 449, 527, 536–537, 604–607
12 Aurelius, 265
17 Plotinus, 287
18 Augustine, 16, 661–662, 663
19 Aquinas, 23–24, 47–48, 151, 339–340, 615–636 passim, 652–653, 694–696
20 Aquinas, 213–214, 223–224, 377–378, 531, 620–621
23 Hobbes, 61–62, 65, 272
25 Montaigne, 115–119, 124–125, 230
26 Shakespeare, 431
30 Bacon, 70–74
31 Spinoza, 371–372, 423–424
33 Pascal, 29–44
35 Locke, 90, 105–107, 111, 192–193, 230–231
38 Rousseau, 362
42 Kant, 377, 387–388, 397–398, 471–473, 476–495, 513–517, 525, 540–542
43 Mill, 471–476
46 Hegel, 280–281
48 Melville, 302–304
49 Darwin, 95, 302, 314–315, 577
51 Tolstoy, 611, 645–646
54 Freud, 757–759, 792

CROSS-REFERENCES

For: The conception of identity as a logical rather than a real relation, *see* Same and Other 1, 2d; and for the conception of the relation between creatures and God as partly real and partly logical, *see* God 5e; One and Many 1b; World 3b.

Another consideration of correlative terms, *see* Opposition 1a.

The theory of proportionality or analogical similitude, *see* Same and Other 3b; and for the applications of analogy and proportion in metaphysics and mathematics, *see* Idea 4b(4); Mathematics 4c; Quantity 1b; Sign and Symbol 3d, 5f.

Other discussions of indefinable terms, *see* Definition 1c; Principle 2a(3).

The issues raised by a relational theory of judgment and reasoning, *see* Idea 5b; Judgment 5c, 6d, 7c; Reasoning 2.

Discussions relevant to the conception of the categories as the transcendental concepts of the understanding, *see* Form 1c; Judgment 8c–8d; Memory and Imagination 6c(2); Mind 4d(3); Principle 2b(3).

The consideration of the relations between ideas as objects of knowledge, *see* Idea 1a; Knowledge 6a(3).

Other discussions of the association of ideas, *see* Idea 5e; Memory and Imagination 2c.

Another discussion of the prior, the posterior, and the simultaneous, *see* Time 5d.

The order of causes, *see* Cause 1b.

The order of goods, or of means and ends, *see* Good and Evil 5b–5c.

The relation of quantities and the relation of qualities, *see* QUALITY 4c; QUANTITY 1b; SAME AND OTHER 3c–3d.

The order of kinds, *see* ANIMAL 2a; EVOLUTION 1b; IDEA 4b(3); OPPOSITION 1c(2); SAME AND OTHER 3a(1)–3a(3); UNIVERSAL AND PARTICULAR 5b.

Order in the soul, in the state, and in the universe or nature, *see* MAN 5–5a; NATURE 3a–3b; ONE AND MANY 3b(5); SOUL 2b; STATE 5a–5c, 6a–6b; WORLD 1a–1c, 6a–6c.

For: The doctrine of the Trinity as concerned with order and relation in God, *see* GOD 9a.

The absolute and the relative in space, time, and motion, *see* CHANGE 7c(3); SPACE 2a; TIME 1.

The absolute and the relative in truth, goodness, and beauty, *see* BEAUTY 5; CUSTOM AND CONVENTION 9a–9b; GOOD AND EVIL 6d; OPINION 3c, 6a; PRINCIPLE 5; TRUTH 7–7b; UNIVERSAL AND PARTICULAR 7a–7c.

ADDITIONAL READINGS

Listed below are works not included in *Great Books of the Western World*, but relevant to the idea and topics with which this chapter deals. These works are divided into two groups:

I. Works by authors represented in this collection.
II. Works by authors not represented in this collection.

For the date, place, and other facts concerning the publication of the works cited, consult the Bibliography of Additional Readings which follows the last chapter of *The Great Ideas.*

I.

HUME. *A Treatise of Human Nature*, BK I, PART I, SECT V

KANT. *Metaphysical Foundations of Natural Science*, DIV III

HEGEL. *Science of Logic*, VOL I, BK II, SECT II, CH 3; SECT III, CH 1, 3

J. S. MILL. *An Examination of Sir William Hamilton's Philosophy*, CH 4–7

W. JAMES. *Essays in Radical Empiricism*

——. *The Meaning of Truth*, CH 11, 13

——. *Some Problems of Philosophy*, CH 9

II.

PETRUS HISPANICUS. *Summulae Logicales* (*Logical Treatises*)

DUNS SCOTUS. *Tractatus de Primo Principio* (*A Tract Concerning the First Principle*), CH 1–2

SUÁREZ. *Disputationes Metaphysicae*, X (1), XXVIII (3), XXXII (2), XXXIX, XLVII, XLVIII (1–4), L (4), LIII–LIV

JOHN OF SAINT THOMAS. *Cursus Philosophicus Thomisticus, Ars Logica*, PART II, Q 17

LEIBNITZ. *Philosophical Works*, CH 12 (*A New System of the Interaction of Substances*), 13 (*Reply of M. Foucher Concerning the Interaction of Substances*)

——. *New Essays Concerning Human Understanding*, BK II, CH 25, 28, 30

DE MORGAN. *Formal Logic*, CH 3–5

BOOLE. *An Investigation of the Laws of Thought*

JEVONS. *Pure Logic*, CH 1–2, 4

LOTZE. *Metaphysics*, BK III, CH 3

C. S. PEIRCE. *Collected Papers*, VOL III, par 45–149, 214–251; VOL VI, par 318–324, 386–392

BRADLEY. *Appearance and Reality*, BK I, CH 3; BK II, CH 26

——. *Collected Essays*, VOL II (31)

COUTURAT. *The Algebra of Logic*

WOODWORTH. *Psychological Issues*, CH 5–6

CASSIRER. *Substance and Function*, PART I; PART II, CH 7–8; SUP II–III

WHITEHEAD and RUSSELL. *Principia Mathematica*, PART I, SECT C, D; PART II, SECT B, C, D, E; PART IV–V

ROYCE. *The Principles of Logic*

B. RUSSELL. *Principles of Mathematics*, CH 9, 24–31

——. *The Problems of Philosophy*, CH 9

——. *Our Knowledge of the External World*, V

——. *Introduction to Mathematical Philosophy*, CH 4–6

W. E. JOHNSON. *Logic*, PART I, CH 12–13

MOORE. *Philosophical Studies*, CH 9

WHITEHEAD. *Science and the Modern World*, CH 10

TARSKI. *Introduction to Logic*, V

BLANSHARD. *The Nature of Thought*, CH 31–32

Chapter 79: RELIGION

INTRODUCTION

ARGUMENT is unprofitable—worse than that, unintelligible—when opponents do not share some common ground. Between the complete skeptic who denies reason's competence and the philosopher or scientist who appeals to it, no common ground exists. Between the man who obeys the rule not to contradict himself and the man who finds nothing repugnant in answering Yes and No to the same question, there can be no argument. There is an issue between them, but the position each takes reduces the other to silence.

Lack of a common measure for judging opposed views tends to render them incommunicable to one another. For men to be in this plight is the exception in science and philosophy, but it seems to be the typical situation where the basic issues of religion are concerned. Of all subjects the most controversial, religious issues seem to be the least capable of being settled by controversy. No divisions among men—certainly not those which separate philosophers or scientists—are as unbridgeable as the chasm between the faithful and those they call infidels, between Jew and gentile, or Christian and pagan. Faith and lack of faith, or the diversity of faiths, seem to render certain questions as imponderable as they are weighty.

On the definition of religion itself, the deepest issue lies between those who conceive it as having a supernatural foundation in God's revelation and authority, and those who think of religion as having a purely natural origin in certain human tendencies, which makes it no different from philosophy and science as an element of culture. But religion can be supernatural only for those whose faith declares it to be so. Those who deny that it is supernatural may offer many reasons for thinking so, and try in many ways to explain away faith. What they all come to is that it is an illusion to suppose faith is God's gift rather than man's own will to believe. To the man of faith this only means that his critic lacks the gift of faith or even the wish to have it.

Many consequences follow from this unarguable difference concerning the meaning of religion. Religion to the man of faith usually means much more than the acceptance of a creed. It means acts of piety and worship, recourse to prayer, the partaking of sacraments, the observance of certain rituals, the performance of sacrifices and purifications. It means rendering to God what is His due, obeying His commandments, beseeching and gaining the help of His grace, whereby to lead a life which shall seem worthy to Him. When religion is conceived as nothing more than a set of beliefs which men have adopted, it is restricted to one part of life. It may or may not involve action as well as thought, but it is not the fabric of a whole life. It does not qualify every other part of it. It does not demand that inner devotion and external conduct constitute the practice of a man's belief if he is to avoid hypocrisy.

ACCORDING TO THIS difference in the conception of religion as supernatural or natural, men seem to hold incommunicably different views of religious belief, of revelation, miracles, and prophecies. But those who agree that religion is not man-made, that it requires, in some form, divine authority and inspiration, do not all have the same faith, worship in the same way, or conform to the same rites. The issue, therefore, between men of different faiths—men who live according to the rules of different religious communities—is almost as difficult as that between the religious and the irreligious.

In the western tradition, the plurality of religions necessarily raises a question of truth and falsity for any religionist whose faith excludes the possibility of several equally true religions. "Idolatrous" and "superstitious," "heretical" and "schismatic," are epithets which draw their special significance from controversies about religion and religions. The word "pagan," as Gibbon points out, comes to mean idolatry or the worship of false gods. "The Latin Christians," he says, "bestowed it on their mortal enemies, the Mahometans." The Mohammedans, in turn, held the view, according to Gibbon, that "all except themselves deserved the reproach of idolatry and polytheism." The charges of idolatry and superstition occur also in the conflict between Jew and Christian, between Protestant and Catholic, countered often by charges of infidelity or heresy and schism.

Quite apart from the general problem of church and state, with its issues of political toleration and freedom of worship, the very meaning of religion raises the question of tolerance in its most acute form. It is not a question of political rights and liberties, but of being right or wrong in one's religious beliefs and acts. To the extent that the communicants of one religion regard themselves as believing what God has revealed to them, and to the extent that they hold their religious practices to be prescribed by divine law, they are not free in conscience, it seems, to entertain contrary beliefs and practices as conceivably true alternatives.

The conflict between men of diverse faiths, alike in their understanding of faith as divinely inspired, somehow appeals beyond any human decision to God himself for judgment. The controversy between men of any religious faith and those who treat such faith as a purely human prejudice seems to be even less susceptible of resolution by the ordinary processes of discourse.

IF THESE OBSERVATIONS are accurate and just, the materials of this chapter cannot be assembled dialectically—either as opposed views or as belonging together—simply by reference to the content of the various opinions which can be found in the great books. In this chapter, as in no others except, perhaps, those which treat of matters connected with religion—such as GOD, IMMORTALITY, SIN, and THEOLOGY—it seems necessary to pay some attention to the opinion's author as well as to the opinion, and even in some cases to the community or culture in which the opinion arises. It is not as necessary, for example, to know whether the man who writes about virtue is himself virtuous as it is to know whether the man who writes about religion is religious and to know furthermore in what sense he conceives himself as being religious and what religion he espouses.

The distinction between sacred and profane, and between religious and secular, applies to books as well as to other things. In the tradition of the great books, only one book is set apart as sacred. None of the writers included in this set regard the Koran as sacred scripture, though Gibbon as an historian reports the Mohammedan belief in the Koran. Mohammedans believe that the Koran is the word of God revealed to His one and only prophet, as Jews believe that the Old Testament is divinely inspired writing, and Christians believe in both Testaments as Holy Writ.

But though the Bible is *the* traditionally sacred book of the west, it is not read as such by all who write about it. The historian or the philosopher who is not himself a religious Jew or Christian may acknowledge the belief of others without sharing it. He reads the Bible as a collection of human writings which have exercised an unparalleled influence upon western culture. Whatever the merit of these writings as wisdom, history, preachment, or poetry, they do not command a special kind of reading unless they are distinguished from all others by being the word of God, not man. Controversies over interpretations of the Bible may thus begin with each side begging the main question in issue. Is the Bible sacred scripture, or is it no different in kind from the poetry of Homer and the sayings of the Greek wise men?

The two ways of reading the Bible are incommensurable. If the Bible is not sacred, a critical reading may be expected to disclose inconsistencies in it, and many of the things it says may be questioned in fact or in principle. But if, though humanly recorded, it is the repository of divine revelation, then it has an authority which puts it above questioning, though not beyond the need for interpretation.

There is one sort of proposition, says Locke, which challenges "the highest degree of our assent upon bare testimony, whether the thing proposed agree or disagree with common experience, and the ordinary course of things, or no. The reason whereof is, because the testimony is of such a one as cannot deceive, nor be deceived, and that is of God himself. This carries with it an assurance beyond doubt, evidence beyond exception. This is called by a peculiar name, revelation; and our assent to it, faith: which as absolutely determines our minds, and as perfectly excludes all wavering, as our knowledge itself; and we may as well doubt of our own being, as we can whether any revelation from God be true. So that faith is a settled and sure principle of assent and assurance, and leaves no manner of room for doubt or hesitation. Only we must be sure that it be a divine revelation, and that we understand it right."

Locke seems to be putting two qualifications upon his remark that "the bare testimony of revelation is the highest certainty." The first concerns our assurance that we are not mistaken in accepting something as revealed. The second concerns the correctness of our understanding of that which we take to be God's word.

On the first point, Hobbes, though he says that "faith is a gift of God, which man can neither give nor take away by promises of rewards or menaces of torture," also says that faith depends "only upon certainty or probability of arguments drawn from reason or from something men believe already." Faith does not come "by supernatural inspiration or infusion" but, according to Hobbes, "by education, discipline, correction, and other natural ways, by which God worketh them in his elect, at such time as he thinketh fit." The object of faith is not God, but the men whom God has appointed to instruct us; belief, which Hobbes distinguishes from faith, goes beyond faith to the acceptance as true of what they say. "Consequently," Hobbes writes, "when we believe that the Scriptures are the word of God, having no immediate revelation from God himself, our belief, faith, and trust is in the Church, whose word we take, and acquiesce therein."

On this same point, Aquinas gives a different answer. He distinguishes between the material and the formal aspects of the object of faith. As in the object of science, so in the object of faith there is "that which is known . . . and is the material object, so to speak," and "that whereby it is known, which is the formal aspect of the object. Thus, in the science of geometry, the conclusions are what is known materially, while the formal aspect of the science consists in the means of demonstration, through which the conclusions are known. Accordingly, if in faith we consider the formal aspect of the object, it is nothing else than the First Truth. For the faith of which we are speaking does not assent to anything, except because it is revealed by God." The articles of religious faith may be drawn from the content of Holy Writ, but that Holy Writ is the revealed truth of God must first be accepted by an act of faith. Aquinas seems to be meeting Locke's point by saying that it is faith itself which makes us sure that the propositions to which we assent by faith are the matter of divine revelation.

On Locke's other point concerning the rightness of our interpretation of Scripture, Locke himself remarks that "though everything said in the text be infallibly true, yet the reader may be, nay, cannot choose but be, very fallible in the understanding of it. Nor is to be wondered that the will of God, when clothed in words, should be liable to that doubt and uncertainty, which unavoidably attends that sort of conveyance." From which he concludes that since "the precepts of natural religion are plain, and very intelligible to all mankind, and seldom come to be controverted; and other revealed truths, which are conveyed to us by books and languages are liable to the common and natural obscurities incident to words, methinks it would become us to be more careful and diligent in observing the former, and less magisterial, positive, and imperious, in imposing our own ideas and interpretations of the latter."

That Scripture is difficult to interpret and subject to various interpretations Augustine also acknowledges, but he differs somewhat from Locke concerning the task or duty which that fact imposes upon the religious man. "Let no one then go on bothering me," Augustine writes, "with such words as 'Moses did not mean what you say, he meant what I say.' If he said to me: 'How do you know that Moses meant by these words what you say?'—I should take the question with complete calmness. . . . But when he says: 'He did not mean what you say, he meant what I say,' yet does not deny that what each of us says is true, then, O Life of the poor, O my God, in whose bosom is no contradiction, rain down the gift of moderation upon my heart, that I may hear such talk with patience. For what they say, they say not because they are godly men and have seen it in the mind of Your servant Moses, but because they are proud men: it is not that they know the opinion of Moses, but that they love their own opinion, and this not because it is true but because it is their own."

Confronted by a variety of interpretations, each of which may be true, Augustine remarks "how foolish it is, in such a flood of true meanings . . . rashly to assert that Moses intended one or the other of them. . . . If I had been Moses . . . if I had been the same as he and You had given me the book of Genesis to write, I should have wished that You would grant me such skill in writing, such an art for the construction of what I had to say, that not even those who cannot yet grasp how God creates would reject my words as too much for their strength; and again that those who can grasp so much, would find fully contained in the few words of Your servant whatever truths they had arrived at in their own thinking." Those "who thirst for truth and not for vanity" honor the human dispensers of God's revelation, Augustine thinks, by believing that, when under God's inspiration they wrote these words, they "had in mind whatever is most excellent in them by the illumination of truth and their fruitfulness for our profit.

"Thus when one man says to me: 'Moses meant what I think,' and another 'Not at all, he meant what I think,' it seems to me," Augustine declares, "that the truly religious thing is to say: Why should he not have meant both, if both are true; and if in the same words some should see a third and a fourth meaning and any other number of true meanings, why should we not believe that Moses saw them all, since by him one God tempered Sacred Scripture to the minds of many who should see truths in it, yet not all the same truths."

Augustine's position combines belief in the truth of Scripture, which is a consequence of the faith that it is God's word, with latitude of interpretation in determining what that truth is, appealing here to the ordinary standards of what seems to be true to the thinking mind. In the course of commenting on Augustine's own interpretation of certain passages in Genesis, Aquinas summarizes what he takes to be Augustine's two rules. "The first is, to hold the truth of Scripture without wavering. The second is that since Holy Scripture can be explained in a multiplicity of senses, one should adhere to a particular explanation only in such measure as to be ready to abandon it, if it be proved with certainty to be false; lest Holy Scripture be exposed to the ridicule of unbelievers, and obstacles be placed to their believing."

AS THE QUESTION whether the Bible is sacred writing affects the way it is to be read, so the distinction between religious and secular writing seems relevant to what the great books have to say about religion.

In the pagan tradition, for example, Herodotus in his *History* reports and discusses a great variety of religious doctrines and practices as characteristic of the peoples he visits or inquires about. There seems to be no indication that Herodotus is judging the truth or falsity of these various religions, either by reference to their reasonableness or from convictions born of his own adherence to one of these religions as against all the rest. For the most part, he is writing *about* religion rather than *religiously*, with the possible exception of those passages in which he expresses his own views, discussed in the chapter on PROPHECY, on the oracles, omens, and portents which reveal the will of the gods.

In contrast, the tragedies of Aeschylus, especially the Oresteian trilogy, are religious poetry, comparable to Dante's *Divine Comedy* and Milton's *Paradise Lost*. These are not books *about* religion, as, in a sense, the great poem of Lucretius *On the Nature of Things* is about religion—a passionate attack on religion by a man who is not religious. It may be thought that the aim of Lucretius is to purify religion when he wishes to banish "all belief in things degrading to the gods and inconsistent with their peace," so that men can "approach the sanctuaries of the gods with a calm breast," and "with tranquil peace of mind." But even a person who thinks this will still find a marked contrast between Lucretius and poets like Aeschylus or Dante who are writing from religious convictions to which they adhere as members of a religious community.

Both kinds of writing may be found in the same author. Hobbes, for example, in examining the phenomena of religious belief, seems to make public acceptance the criterion of the distinction between religion and superstition. "Fear of a power invisible, feigned by the mind," he says, "or imagined from tales publicly allowed," is religion; when they are "not allowed, superstition." Still writing as an observer, he says that "this fear of things invisible is the natural seed of that which everyone in himself calls religion; and in them that worship or fear that power otherwise than they do, superstition." Originating from "natural seeds" which he enumerates, "religion," he says, "by reason of the different fancies, judgments, and passions of several men, has grown up into ceremonies so different, that those which are used by one man are for the most part ridiculous to another."

Yet Hobbes also writes religiously, when he treats all other religions from the standpoint of the special truth of his own. "These natural seeds of religion," he points out, "have received culture from two sorts of men. One sort have been they that have nourished and ordered them, according to their own invention. The other have done it by God's commandment and direction. . . . Of the former sort were all the founders of commonwealths and the law-givers of the Gentiles. Of the latter sort were Abraham, Moses, and our Blessed Saviour, by whom have been derived unto us the laws of the Kingdom of God."

It is as a Christian that Hobbes compares the state religion of the Romans with the divine religion of the Jews. The Romans, he writes, "made no scruple of tolerating any religion whatsoever in the city of Rome itself, unless it had something in it that could not consist with their civil government; nor do we read that any religion was there forbidden, but that of the Jews, who (being the peculiar Kingdom of God) thought it unlawful to acknowledge subjection to any mortal King or State whatsoever. And thus you see how the religion of the Gentiles was a part of their policy.

"But where God himself," Hobbes continues, "by supernatural revelation, planted religion; there he also made to himself a peculiar kingdom, and gave laws, not only of behavior toward himself, but also toward one another; and thereby in the Kingdom of God, the policy, and laws civil, are a part of religion; and therefore, the distinction of temporal and spiritual domination has there no place."

Again it is as a man of Christian faith that Hobbes ascribes belief in Christian teachings to that faith. "The causes why men believe any Christian doctrine are various," he writes. "For faith is the gift of God, and he worketh it in each man by such ways as it seemeth good to him. The most ordinary immediate cause of our belief, concerning any point of Christian faith, is that we believe the Bible to be the Word of God." But when Hobbes goes on to say that the "only article of faith, which the Scripture makes necessary to salvation, is this, that Jesus is The Christ," he becomes the theologian with whom other theologians within the Christian community may disagree, on this or other points of dogma.

The disagreements we find between Augustine or Aquinas and Hobbes or Locke, or the differences in dogma which appear in a comparison of the *Divine Comedy* and *Paradise Lost*, represent the division between Catholic and Protestant Christians. But such theological disagreements do not obliterate certain common tenets of religious belief among all who profess Christianity. Above all, they leave untouched the belief in religion itself as transcending all merely human teaching and as providing the precepts of life through which God himself directs and helps man to his salvation.

This belief—even if no other except the belief in one God Who created the universe and made man in His image—seems to be shared by Jews and Christians. It marks the difference between the religious writings of ancient polytheism and of those which draw their inspiration from the Pentateuch and the Gospels. It makes the issue, as Pascal suggests, between those who write about a religion which they themselves either have or seek, and those who, neither having nor seeking, oppose all religions equally or treat all with the same secular detachment.

WRITING AS A CHRISTIAN apologist, Pascal says that "it is the glory of religion to have for enemies men so unreasonable; and their opposition to it is so little dangerous that it serves on the contrary to establish its truths. For the Christian faith goes mainly to establish these two facts, the corruption of nature, and redemption by Christ. Now I contend that if these men do not serve to prove the truth of the redemption by the holiness of their behavior, they at least serve admirably to show the corruption of nature by sentiments so unnatural.

"Let them at least be honest men," he adds, "if they cannot be Christians. . . . Let them recognize that there are two kinds of people one can call reasonable: those who serve God with all their heart because they know Him, and those who seek Him with all their heart because they do not know Him. But as for those who live without knowing Him and without seeking Him, they judge themselves so little worthy of their own care, that they are not worthy of the care of others; and it needs all the charity of the religion which they despise, not to despise them even to the point of leaving them to their folly."

The very existence of other religions, according to Pascal, helps to prove the truth of the Christian religion. "I should equally have rejected the religion of Mahomet and of China, of the ancient Romans and of the Egyptians, for the sole reason, that none having more marks of truth than another, nor anything which should necessarily persuade me, reason cannot incline to one rather than the other." As for Judaism, it seems to Pascal to be divinely intended as the historic foundation and the prophetic forerunner of Christianity.

Apart from these comparative judgments, Pascal attributes certain unique signs of truth to the Christian religion. "Every religion is false," he writes, "which as to its faith does not worship one God as the origin of everything, and which as to its morality does not love only God as the object of everything. . . . The true religion must have as a characteristic the obligation to love God. This is very just, and yet no other religion has commanded this; ours has done so. It must also be aware of human lust and weakness; ours is so. It must have adduced remedies for this; one is prayer. No other religion has asked of God [the power] to love and follow him. . . . That we must love one God only is a thing so evident, that it does not require miracles to prove it." Yet Pascal also interprets Christ's saying, "Though you believe not Me, believe at least the works," as meaning that miracles are the strongest proof of a religion. "Miracles," he writes, "furnish the test in matters of doubt, between Jews and heathens, Jews and Christians, Catholics and heretics, the slandered and slanderers, between the two crosses."

After criticizing the evidence for miracles on rational grounds, Hume appears to agree that "the *Christian religion* not only was at first attended with miracles, but even at this day cannot be believed by any reasonable person without one." But his meaning seems to be that belief in miracles is itself the miracle of faith. "Mere reason," he says, "is insufficient to convince us" of the veracity of the Christian religion; "and whoever is moved by *Faith* to assent to it, is conscious of a continued miracle in his own person, which subverts all the principles of his understanding, and gives him a determination to believe what is most contrary to custom and experience."

HERE IS ANOTHER ISSUE on which philosophers and theologians disagree. Where Hume says that "our most holy religion is founded on *Faith*, not on reason"—with the further implication that to adhere to it with faith requires the abandonment of reason—Augustine and Aquinas think that there can be no conflict between faith and reason, though faith declares the truth of more than reason can prove; and that the support which reason can give to faith in no way lessens the merit of believing.

With this Hobbes seems to agree, at least to the extent of holding that it discredits supernatural religion to make it consist in believing impossibilities or contradictions. Revelation, he says, can consist "of nothing against natural reason." But for Hume the difference between supernatural and natural religion turns on what one must believe both without and against reason as contrasted to what one believes as the result of a reasonable interpretation of the evidence. Like philosophy, natural religion, "which is nothing but a species of philosophy, will never be able to carry us beyond the usual course of experience, or give us measures of conduct and behavior different from those which are furnished by reflections on common life."

Those who, like Marx and Freud, regard religion as a social imposture or the response to a neurotic need, not only impute falsity or worse to the traditional religions of the west; they also tend to reject natural religion. Science is enough—for truth's sake, for the conduct of life, for society's welfare. Yet in commenting on the following lines from Goethe,

> He who has Science and has Art,
> Religion, too, has he;
> Who has not Science, has no Art,
> Let him religious be!

Freud says that "on the one hand, these words contrast religion with the two highest achievements of man, and on the other, they declare that in respect of their value in life, they can represent or replace each other." In these terms Freud thinks the religion of the ordinary man is justified—"the only religion that ought to bear the name." If a man does not have science or art to live by, he must have religion, for "life as we find it is too hard for us" and "we cannot do without palliative remedies."

It is the religion of the philosophers and the theologians which Freud questions. He criticizes the philosophers for trying "to preserve the God of religion by substituting for him an impersonal, shadowy, abstract principle"; and he challenges the grounds on which he thinks the theologians hold it to be "an impertinence on the part of science to take religion as a subject for its investigations." They deny that science has any competence whatsoever "to sit in judgment on religion. . . . If we are not deterred by this brusque dismissal," Freud declares, "but inquire on what grounds religion bases its claim to an exceptional position among human concerns, the answer we receive, if indeed we are honored with an answer at all, is that religion cannot be measured by human standards, since it is of divine origin, and has been revealed to us by a spirit which the human mind cannot grasp. It might surely be thought," he continues, "that nothing could be more easily refuted than this argument; it is an obvious *petitio principii*, a 'begging of the question.' The point which is being called in question is whether there is a divine spirit and a revelation; and it surely cannot be a conclusive reply to say that the question cannot be asked because the Deity cannot be called in question."

Marx takes a similar view of the theologians. According to him, the theologians beg the question in much the same way as do the classical economists for whom there are "only two kinds of institutions, those of art and those of nature. Feudal institutions are artificial institutions, those of the bourgeoisie are natural institutions. In this," Marx says, "they resemble the theologians who establish two kinds of religion. Every religion but their own is an invention of men, while their own religion is an emanation from God."

Plato, on the other hand, excoriates those who think that "all religion is a cooking up of words and a make-believe." It is almost as if he had Marx and Freud in mind when, in the *Laws*, the Athenian Stranger carries on the discussion of religion in terms of the distinction between nature and art, and refers to those who "would say that the Gods exist not by nature, but by art, and by the laws of states, which are different in different places, according to the agreement of those who make them." They are the very same people who hold that "the honorable is one thing by nature and another by law, and that the principles of justice have no existence at all by nature."

IN PLATO'S VIEW, the justice of the state and its laws must be founded not only on nature rather than art, but also upon religion and a right belief in the gods. The Athenian Stranger answers those who think it is "dreadful that [we] should legislate on the supposition that there are Gods," by saying why "it is a matter of no small consequence . . . to prove that there are Gods, and that they are good and regard justice more than men do." The reason he gives is that "no one who in obedience to the laws believed that there were Gods, ever intentionally did any unholy act, or uttered an unlawful word, but those who did must have supposed one of three things—either that [the Gods] did not exist, which is the first possibility, or secondly, that if they did, they took no care of man, or thirdly, that they were easily appeased and turned aside from their purpose by sacrifices and prayers." That is why the demonstration of the existence of the gods "would be the best and noblest prelude of all our laws."

Rousseau's legislator, like Plato's, is also concerned with the role which religion plays in the foundation and life of the state. But the question "Which religion?" arises at once for Rousseau, as it does not for Plato, who can treat the nature of the gods and the nature of the state as equally within the province of the political philosopher. But for Rousseau, living in a Christian civilization, the political philosopher cannot approach the subject of religion without being confronted by the theologian. He finds it necessary, therefore, to distinguish between a revealed religion like Christianity and the natural or civil religion of the citizen.

Christianity, says Rousseau, "not the Christianity of today, but that of the Gospel, which is entirely different," is the religion of man, not of the citizen. "So far from binding the hearts of the citizens to the State, it has the effect of taking them away from all earthly things. I know of nothing more contrary to the social spirit. We are told that a people of true Christians would form the most perfect society imaginable. I see in this supposition only one great difficulty: that a society of true Christians would not be a society of men. . . . The country of the Christian is not of this world."

What the state needs, Rousseau goes on to say, is "a purely civil profession of faith, of which the Sovereign should fix the articles, not exactly as religious dogmas, but as social sentiments without which a man cannot be a good citizen or a faithful subject." He then enumerates what he calls "the dogmas of civil religion" which "ought to be few, simple, exactly worded, without explanation or commentary," such as "the existence of a mighty, intelligent, and beneficent Divinity, possessed of foresight and providence, the life to come, the happiness of the just, the punishment of the wicked, the sanctity of the social contract and the laws."

Montesquieu takes the diametrically opposite view. "With regard to the true religion," he writes, "I have never pretended to make its interests submit to those of a political nature, but rather to unite them. . . . The Christian religion, which ordains that men should love each other, would, without doubt, have every nation blessed with the best civil, the best political laws; because these, next to this religion, are the greatest good that men can give and receive." Montesquieu meets the argument that "true Christians cannot form a government of any duration," by saying that the more men "believe themselves indebted to religion, the more they would think due to their country. The principles of Christianity, deeply engraved on the heart, would be infinitely more powerful than the false honor of monarchies, than the human virtues of republics, or the servile fear of despotic states."

ANY CONSIDERATION OF the political significance of religion tends to lead into the controversy over the relation between church and state. Three main positions seem to be taken: one which calls for the integration of church and state, one which calls for a subordination of either state to church or church to state, and one which insists upon the autonomy of each as a basis for their relation to one another, or carries separation even further, to the point of complete divorce.

The theocratic state of the Old Testament represents the Jewish version of the first position, distinguished by the fact that the priesthood was in the service of the king. Hobbes defines a Christian commonwealth in almost parallel terms. It is indifferent whether it is called a "church" or a "state," because it is "a company of men professing Christian religion, united in the person of one sovereign." It follows, Hobbes argues, that "there is on earth, no such universal church as all Christians are bound to obey; because there is no power on earth, to which all other commonwealths are subject. There are Christians in the dominions of several princes and states; but every one of them is subject to that commonwealth, whereof he is himself a member; and consequently, cannot be subject to the commands of any other person. And therefore a church, such a one as is able to command, to judge, absolve, condemn, or do any other act, is the same thing with a civil commonwealth, consisting of Christian men; and is called a *civil state*, for that the subjects of it are *men*; and a *church* for that the subjects thereof are *Christians*."

According to Hobbes, "*temporal* and *spiritual* government are but two words brought into the world, to make men see double, and mistake their lawful *Sovereign*. . . . There is therefore no other government in this life, neither of state, nor religion, but temporal." Agreeing with Hobbes on the unity of government and the integration of church and state, writers like Augustine and Roger Bacon place kings in the service of the priesthood, and make the supreme pontiff, who governs both spiritually and temporally, the only earthly sovereign. Gilson summarizes their view by saying that for them "the definition of the Church includes the State," and that the church has a universality which embraces "the temporal and the spiritual domains alike."

The position of Aquinas is indicated in the Treatise on Law, in the passage in which he declares that no civil law can be valid or binding if what it commands is contrary to divine law. It is more explicitly developed in his little tract *On the Governance of Rulers*. "It is not the ultimate end," he writes, "of an assembled multitude to live virtuously, but through virtuous living to attain to the possession of God. Furthermore, if it could attain this end by the power of human nature, then the duty of a king would have to include the direction of men to this end." But, Aquinas holds, men attain this end by divine, not human, power and therefore divine, not human, government is needed to direct men to their end. "Consequently," he maintains, "in order that spiritual things might be distinguished from earthly things, the ministry of this kingdom has been entrusted not to earthly kings, but to priests, and in the highest degree to the chief priest, the successor of St. Peter, the Vicar of Christ, the Roman Pontiff, to whom all the kings of Christian peoples are to be subject as to our Lord Jesus Christ Himself. For those to whom pertains the care of intermediate ends should be subject to him to whom pertains the care of the ultimate end, and be directed by his rule."

This last statement indicates that Aquinas, unlike Augustine and Roger Bacon, assigns to the state a subsidiary dominion and to the king a subordinate jurisdiction. The opponent of Aquinas is usually thought to be Marsilius of Padua, whose *Defensor Pacis* separates church and state, but subordinates priest to king, in a manner which corresponds to the Averroistic subordination of theology to philosophy. Agreeing with both that church and state are distinct, Dante agrees with neither on the relation which should obtain between the temporal and the spiritual domains, or between civil and ecclesiastical government.

Whereas Aquinas holds that only man's spiritual end is ultimate and that all temporal ends are intermediate, Dante insists that man has two ultimate goals. "Man exists for a double purpose," he says in *De Monarchia*. "Since he alone among beings partakes of both corruptibility and incorruptibility, he alone among beings belongs in two final orders—one of which is his goal as a corruptible being, the other as incorruptible." Man has two beatitudes, or two forms of happiness—an earthly perfection which consists in the complete realization throughout time of the intellectual powers of mankind, and a heavenly perfection which consists in the vision of God. "These two states of bliss," Dante argues, "like two different goals, man must reach by different ways. For we come to the first as we follow the philosophical teachings, applying them to our moral and intellectual capacities; and we come to the second as we follow the spiritual teachings, which transcend human reason according to our theological capacities, faith, hope, and charity."

In terms of this theory of man's two ends, and of the distinct spheres of reason and faith, or philosophy and civil law on the one hand, and religion and divine law on the other, Dante formulates his doctrine of the autonomy of state and church. "The reins of man," he writes, "are held by a double driver according to man's two-fold end: one is the supreme pontiff, who guides mankind with revelations to life eternal, and the other is the emperor, who guides mankind with philosophical instructions to temporal happiness." Church and state may be related as sun and moon in the sense that the state receives some illumination from the church even about matters within its own jurisdiction; but, according to Dante, the state has its own source of light in reason. "Temporal power," he maintains, "receives from spiritual power neither its being, nor its power or authority, nor even its functioning, strictly speaking; but what it receives is the light of grace, which God in heaven and the pope's blessing on earth cause to shine on it in order that it may work more effectively."

All these mediaeval theories of what should be the relation between church and state—with the exception, perhaps, of the doctrine of Marsilius of Padua—conceive religion as having a supernatural source and the church as having a supernatural foundation, both being instituted for the sake of guiding man to his supernatural end. They differ from one another according to the view they take of man's earthly or temporal goods, the power of his reason, and the jurisdiction of his laws. Their difference, according to Gilson, verifies the principle that "the manner in which one conceives the relationship of the State to the Church, that in which one conceives the relationship of philosophy to theology, and in which one conceives the relationship of nature to grace, are necessarily correlated."

These mediaeval theories of church and state persist, with certain modifications, in modern times. But the characteristically modern view of the matter begins with a different view of religion itself. Its mediaeval prototype is to be found in the rationalism of Marsilius. Within the secular state, the church is a purely human institution, religion is defended by philosophy for the contribution it makes to the peace of the civil community—or, perhaps, condemned by the apostles of earthly progress as "the opiate of the masses." The principle of religious tolerance involves not merely tolerance of religion, but tolerance for a diversity of religions and often the complete rejection of all religion.

"I esteem it above all things necessary," writes Locke in his *Letter Concerning Toleration*, "to distinguish exactly the business of civil government from that of religion, and to settle the just bounds that lie between the one and the other. . . . The commonwealth," Locke continues, "seems to me to be a society of men constituted only for the procuring, preserving, and advancing their own civil interests." A church is "a voluntary society of men, joining themselves together of their own accord in order to the public worshipping of God in such manner as they judge acceptable to Him, and effectual to the salvation of their souls."

Locke's doctrine of the separation of church and state is reflected in the Constitution of the United States. In the form which Jefferson gives it, it appears in the declaration that "Congress shall make no law respecting an establishment of religion, or prohibiting the free exercise thereof." Mill carries out the same principles in his attack on "Sabbatarian legislation." Such laws, he thinks, exceed the power of civil government. They represent an "illegitimate interference with the rightful liberty of the individual. . . . The notion that it is one's duty that another should be religious" is, in Mill's opinion, "the foundation of all the religious persecutions ever perpetrated." Hegel, on the other hand, holds that "the state should require all citizens to belong to a church," but he points out that "*a* church is all that can be said, because since the content of a man's faith depends on his private ideas, the state cannot interfere with it."

The positions men take on the great issues of church and state thus seem to be determined in part by the diverse conceptions men have of religion. This is no less true of opposing views on religious liberty, on the treatment of heresy and schism, on religious education, the missionary calling, and the conversion of infidels. In the discussion of religion, perhaps more than anywhere else, the first Yea or Nay seems to determine all other affirmations or denials.

OUTLINE OF TOPICS

1. Faith as the foundation of religion
   - 1*a*. The nature, cause, and conditions of faith: its specific objects
   - 1*b*. The sources of religious belief
     - (1) Revelation: the word of God and divine authority
     - (2) Miracles and signs as divine confirmation
     - (3) The testimony of prophets: the anointed of God

2. The virtue and practice of religion: piety as justice to God

   2*a*. Prayer and supplication: their efficacy

   2*b*. Worship and adoration: the rituals and ceremonials of religion

   2*c*. The nature, institution, and uses of the sacraments

   2*d*. Sacrifices and propitiations

   2*e*. Fasting and almsgiving

   2*f*. Purificatory rites: the remission of sin by baptism and penance

   2*g*. Profanations and sacrileges

3. The religious life: religious offices and the religious community

   3*a*. The Jewish conception of the religious community: the Torah and the Temple

   3*b*. The Christian conception of the church: the doctrine of the mystical body of Christ

   3*c*. The nature and organization of the religious community

      (1) The institution of the priesthood and other ecclesiastical offices

      (2) Ecclesiastical government and hierarchy

      (3) The support of ecclesiastical institutions: tithes, contributions, state subsidy

   3*d*. The monastic life: the disciplines of asceticism

4. Church and state: the issue concerning temporal and spiritual power

   4*a*. Religion in relation to forms of government: the theocratic state

   4*b*. The service of religion to the state and the political support of religion by the state

5. The dissemination of religion

   5*a*. The function of preaching

   5*b*. Religious conversion

   5*c*. Religious education

6. Truth and falsity in religion

   6*a*. The religious condemnation of idolatry, superstition, and other perversions of worship

   6*b*. Religious apologetics: the defense of faith

   6*c*. The unity and tradition of a religion

      (1) Orthodoxy and heresy: the role of dogma in religion; the treatment of heretics

      (2) Sects and schisms arising from divergences of belief and practice

   6*d*. The relation of men of diverse faiths: the attitude of the faithful toward infidels

   6*e*. Religious liberty: freedom of conscience; religious toleration

   6*f*. The rejection of supernatural foundations for religion: the criticism of particular beliefs and practices; the psychogenesis of religion

   6*g*. The relation between sacred doctrine and secular learning: the conflict of science and religion

7. Historical observations concerning religious beliefs, institutions, and controversies

REFERENCES

References are listed by volume number (in bold type), author's name, and page number. Bible references are to book, chapter, and verse of the Authorized King James version of the Bible. The abbreviation "esp" calls the reader's attention to one or more especially relevant parts of a whole reference; "passim" signifies that the topic is discussed intermittently rather than continuously in the work or passage cited. Where the work as a whole is relevant to the topic, the page numbers refer to the entire work. For general guidance in the use of *The Great Ideas,* consult the Preface.

1. Faith as the foundation of religion

OLD TESTAMENT: *Genesis,* 15:1–6
NEW TESTAMENT: *Mark,* 16:16–18 / *John,* 3:14–18; 5:24; 11:25–26; 14:1–14 / *Acts,* 16:25–33 / *Romans* / *II Corinthians,* 4:13–18; 5:6–8 / *Galatians* / *Philippians,* 3:8–9 / *Colossians,* 1:21–23; 2:5–7,12 / *Hebrews* / *James* / *I Peter,* 1:7–9; 2:6–7 / *I John,* 3:23; 5
18 AUGUSTINE, 323
20 AQUINAS, 62–63, 73–75, 380–416
21 DANTE, 143
25 MONTAIGNE, 209–215, 293–294
30 BACON, 95–96
33 PASCAL, 219–220, 224
42 KANT, 344–349
44 BOSWELL, 395
46 HEGEL, 349–350
52 DOSTOEVSKY, 127–137 passim

1*a*. The nature, cause, and conditions of faith: its specific objects

NEW TESTAMENT: *Mark,* 9:13–29; 11:20–24 / *Luke,* 8:4–15 / *John,* 1:6–18; 6:28–29; 12:44–46; 14:1,7–11; 20:24–31 / *Romans* / *I Corinthians,* 2:4–10 / *II Corinthians,* 4:1–6 / *Galatians,* 3 / *Hebrews* / *James,* 2 esp 2:17–26 / *I John,* 2:23–24; 4:1–3
18 AUGUSTINE, 14–15, 18–19, 33–34, 52–61, 68, 564
19 AQUINAS, 3–10, 11–12
20 AQUINAS, 61–62, 83–84, 332–333, 359–360, 380–426
21 DANTE, 142–144
23 HOBBES, 66, 78–80, 83–84, 149, 240–246
25 MONTAIGNE, 98–99, 209, 267–268
30 BACON, 95–97
31 DESCARTES, 125–126, 284
33 PASCAL, 217–218, 221–225, 243–244, 277, 284–286, 327
37 FIELDING, 379–380
38 MONTESQUIEU, 208–209
42 KANT, 179, 242–243, 320–321, 344–348, 353–354, 604–606, 607–609
44 BOSWELL, 394–395
46 HEGEL, 236, 268–271, 307–308
47 GOETHE, 83–84
49 DARWIN, 302–303, 593
51 TOLSTOY, 196–198
52 DOSTOEVSKY, 11–15, 21–24, 26–27, 64–67, 146–170, 172–177, 313–314, 337–346
53 JAMES, 652–659 passim, 661

1*b*. The sources of religious belief

1*b*(1) Revelation: the word of God and divine authority

OLD TESTAMENT: *Genesis,* 12:1–9; 13:14–17; 15; 17–18; 22:1–18; 26:1–6,23–24; 32:23–32; 35:1–15; 46:1–4 / *Exodus,* 3–4; 6:1–8; 7:1–5; 19–20; 24; 33–34 / *Numbers,* 12; 14:20–25 / *Deuteronomy,* 4:10–15; 5; 29:29; 31:14–21 / *Joshua,* 1:1–9 / *I Samuel,* 3 / *I Kings,* 3:5–15; 9:1–9; 19:9–18 / *Job,* 33:14–17; 38:1–42:5 / *Psalms,* 119:103–105,130–133 / *Isaiah,* 6; 48:3–8 / *Jeremiah,* 1; 26:1–6 / *Ezekiel,* 1–3; 8–12 / *Amos,* 7 / *Zechariah,* 1–6
APOCRYPHA: *Ecclesiasticus,* 17:6–14
NEW TESTAMENT: *Matthew,* 3:16–17; 7:28–29; 10:1–20; 11:25–27; 13:10–23; 21:23–27; 28:18–20 / *Mark,* 9:3–7 / *Luke,* 2:25–26; 10:21–22; 12:1–3 / *John,* 3:2,9–12; 4:41–42; 5:31–47; 9:35–38; 10:26–27; 12:28–30; 17:6–8 / *Acts,* 22:6–16 / *Romans,* 1:16–20; 15:4 / *I Corinthians,* 2:9–10; 12:1–7; 15:1–2 / *Galatians,* 1:11–17 / *Ephesians,* 1:3–9 / *II Timothy,* 3:14–16 / *I Peter,* 1:10–12 / *II Peter,* 1:16–25
18 AUGUSTINE, 36–37, 63–65, 114–115, 307, 323–324, 643–644
19 AQUINAS, 61–62, 175–178, 253–255
20 AQUINAS, 210–212, 240–245, 267–268, 385–387, 399–400
21 DANTE, 99–105 passim, 145–146
23 HOBBES, 165–167, 181–188, 241–242
25 MONTAIGNE, 238–239, 273
30 BACON, 2–4, 19, 38, 98–100
31 DESCARTES, 69, 168–169
32 MILTON, 238–239
33 PASCAL, 147, 163–166, 272–273, 355, 440
35 LOCKE, 291, 340, 371, 384–388
40 GIBBON, 179, 186–187, 307–308
41 GIBBON, 227–228, 231
44 BOSWELL, 394
46 HEGEL, 159–160
51 TOLSTOY, 50
52 DOSTOEVSKY, 127–137, 150–153

1*b*(2) Miracles and signs as divine confirmation

Old Testament: *Genesis*, 15 / *Exodus*, 4:1–9; 7–12; 14; 16:1–17:7; 19:1–20:22; 33:8–10; 34:10,29–35 / *Numbers*, 11:24–25; 12; 16–17 / *Deuteronomy*, 4:10–15,36; 5 / *Joshua*, 3:7–4:24 / *Judges*, 6:11–24,36–40 / *I Samuel*, 12:15–19 / *I Kings*, 17:18 / *II Kings*, 1–2; 5; 6:25–7:20; 20:1–11 / *Isaiah*, 38 / *Daniel*, 2:1–5:31; 6:18–28

Apocrypha: *Wisdom of Solomon* / *Bel and Dragon*, 31–42 / *II Maccabees*, 9

New Testament: *Matthew*, 8:1–17,23–34; 9:1–8,18–34; 12:22–29; 14:13–33; 15:22–39; 17:1–8,14–20; 21:17–22 / *Mark*, 1:23–2:12; 5; 7:24–8:26; 10:46–52; 16:16–18 / *Luke*, 1:5–66; 4:31–5:26; 7:1–23; 17:11–19 / *John*, 2:1–11,22; 4:46–54; 5:1–9; 9; 11:1–48; 20:1 / *Acts*, 2:1–22; 3:2–16; 5:1–24; 12:5–11; 14:7–10; 19:11–20 / *Hebrews*, 2:3–4

18 Augustine, 303–304, 306–307, 309–310, 589–599
20 Aquinas, 398–399
22 Chaucer, 242–243, 392–395
23 Hobbes, 166–167, 188–191
30 Bacon, 19, 33, 201–203
32 Milton, 323–324
33 Pascal, 221, 277, 328–341
35 Locke, 388
35 Berkeley, 425
35 Hume, 488–489, 495–497
40 Gibbon, 189–190, 294–296, 445–446, 465–467
41 Gibbon, 232, 398–399
44 Boswell, 126
51 Tolstoy, 219–220
52 Dostoevsky, 11, 171–180, 189–191

1*b*(3) The testimony of prophets: the anointed of God

Old Testament: *Exodus*, 4:10–16; 6:28–7:2 / *Leviticus* passim / *Numbers* passim / *Deuteronomy* passim / *Joshua*, 1; 3:7–4:14; 23–24 / *Judges*, 6:7–10 / *I Samuel*, 2:27–36; 7–13 passim; 15–16; 28:7–20 / *II Samuel*, 7:4–17; 12:1–14 / *I Kings*, 14:1–18; 18; 20; 21:17–22:38 / *II Kings*, 1–2; 3:10–27; 6–9; 19:1–7,20–34; 20; 21:10–16; 22:8–20 / *I Chronicles*, 17:3–15; 21:9–26 / *II Chronicles*, 15:1–15; 18; 20:14–27; 21:12–19; 25:5–16; 28:1–15; 34:14–33; 36:14–21 / *Isaiah* passim / *Jeremiah* passim / *Ezekiel* passim / *Daniel*, 5; 6:18–28; 7–12 passim / *Hosea* passim / *Joel* passim / *Amos* passim / *Obadiah* / *Jonah* / *Micah* passim / *Nahum* / *Habakkuk* / *Zephaniah* / *Haggai* / *Zechariah* passim

New Testament: *Matthew* / *Mark*, 1:1–8; 6:4–6; 16:15–16 / *Luke*, 1:67–79; 4:16–21; 4:24; 11:48–50 / *John*, 1:6–8; 1:45; 4:43–44; 5:39; 7:37–52; 12:37–41 / *Acts* passim / *Romans*, 10:12–11:36 / *I Corinthians*, 3–5; 14 / *Hebrews*, 1:1–2; 5:5–10; 8:4–12 / *I John*, 5:9–13

18 Augustine, 262, 419–420, 422–423, 444–448, 449–472, 483–485, 486–487, 490–491, 500, 557–560
23 Hobbes, 137–138, 160, 176–177, 182–188
32 Milton, 313–315, 324, 326
33 Pascal, 273–276, 283–284, 290–301 passim, 301–319, 320–321, 333–334
40 Gibbon, 187–188
48 Melville, 30–36

2. The virtue and practice of religion: piety as justice to God

Old Testament: *Genesis*, 28:18–22 / *Exodus* passim / *Leviticus*, 18:1–5; 26 / *Numbers* passim / *Deuteronomy*, 4:1–40; 5–6; 8–11; 28–32 / *Joshua*, 22:1–6; 24:14–28 / *I Kings*, 8:57–61 / *I Chronicles*, 22:12–13 / *Psalms* passim / *Ecclesiastes*, 12:13 / *Isaiah*, 1–3; 9–10; 29–30; 37:21–36; 42; 44; 48; 58; 64:1–7 / *Jeremiah*, 1–44 passim / *Ezekiel*, 5–8; 11–16 passim; 20; 23–24 / *Hosea* passim / *Amos* passim / *Micah*, 6:8 / *Zephaniah* / *Zechariah* passim / *Malachi*

Apocrypha: *Wisdom of Solomon* passim / *Ecclesiasticus*, 2:15–18; 35 / *Baruch*, 4:1–3

New Testament: *Matthew*, 22:21,34–40 / *Luke*, 4:6–8; 10:25–27; 17:7–10 / *John*, 4:21–24 / *Romans*, 3:19–28; 4:1–8; 8:1–17 / *Galatians*, 5:1–5

4 Homer, 3–9, 193
5 Aeschylus, 1–14, 55–56, 59–61
5 Sophocles, 131–142, 195
5 Euripides, 225–236, 282–297, 306–308 passim, 340–352
6 Herodotus, 201–202
7 Plato, 191–199, 200–212 passim / 682–683, 769–771
12 Epictetus, 122, 158, 208–210
12 Aurelius, 291, 295
18 Augustine, 138–139, 298–322, 524–525, 528, 629–630, 632–633, 638–639
20 Aquinas, 51–52, 245–337, 650–700
21 Dante, 109–110, 112–113
22 Chaucer, 463–471
23 Hobbes, 161–163
25 Montaigne, 209–213
32 Milton, 33–56, 66, 368–370, 402
33 Pascal, 256–257, 258–259
35 Locke, 1–22 passim
35 Berkeley, 444
36 Sterne, 255–268
37 Fielding, 187–188
40 Gibbon, 81–82, 180–182, 291–292
41 Gibbon, 232–233, 259–260
42 Kant, 325–327, 368, 504–505, 611
43 Mill, 290–292
46 Hegel, 175–176, 234–235, 290–292, 311
48 Melville, 30–36
51 Tolstoy, 122, 218–220, 271–274
52 Dostoevsky, 24, 37–38, 146–170
53 James, 203–204

2*a*. Prayer and supplication: their efficacy

Old Testament: *Genesis*, 18:20–33;

24:10–27; 32:9–12 / *Exodus,* 2:23–25; 3:7–10; 32:30–33; 33:12–23 / *Numbers,* 11:1–2,10–34; 14:11–20 / *Deuteronomy,* 9:18–20,25–29 / *Joshua,* 10:12–14 / *Judges,* 15:18–19; 16:27–30 / *I Samuel,* 1; 12:19–25 / *II Samuel,* 7:18–29; 22:4–20; 24:10–25 / *I Kings,* 3:5–15; 8; 18:36–39 / *II Kings,* 4:32–35; 19:14–20:11 / *I Chronicles,* 17:16–27; 21:8–27 / *II Chronicles,* 6:14–42; 7:12–22; 14:10–13; 16:12; 20:1–25; 32:19–24; 33:11–13,18–19 / *Ezra,* 9:5–15 / *Nehemiah,* 1:4–11 / *Job,* 8:5–6; 9:13–16; 10; 16:17–22; 33:26–28 / *Psalms* passim / *Isaiah,* 1:15; 37:14–38; 55:6–7 / *Jeremiah,* 14:11–15:1; 32:16–44; 42:1–6,20 / *Lamentations,* 3:8,44,55–57 / *Daniel,* 9 / *Joel,* 2:32 / *Jonah,* 2; 4:1–4 / *Micah,* 3:1–4 / *Zechariah,* 7; 8:20–23; 10:1–2

APOCRYPHA: *Tobit,* 3; 12:8; 13 / *Judith,* 4:9–15; 8:14–17,31; 9 / *Rest of Esther,* 13:8–14:19 / *Wisdom of Solomon,* 9 / *Ecclesiasticus,* 34:24–26; 35:13–17; 38:9–14; 39:5–6; 51 / *Baruch,* 2:14–19; 3:1–8 / *Song of Three Children,* 10–27 / *Susanna,* 42–44 / *I Maccabees,* 4:8–11 / *II Maccabees,* 23–30; 3:14–36; 12:39–45; 15:21–29

NEW TESTAMENT: *Matthew,* 6:5–15; 7:7–11; 18:19–20; 21:17–22; 26:36–45 / *Luke,* 11:1–13; 18:1–14 / *John,* 14:13–16; 16:23–26; 17 / *Acts,* 4:23–33; 9:36–41; 10:1–4 / *Romans,* 8:26–27; 10:12–13 / *I Corinthians,* 14:13–16 / *Colossians,* 4:2–3 / *I Timothy,* 2:1–8 / *James,* 4:3; 5:13–18 / *I John,* 3:22; 5:13–16

4 HOMER, 3–4, 62, 114, 212, 297
5 AESCHYLUS, 1–14, 17, 20–22, 28–30
5 SOPHOCLES, 100–101
5 ARISTOPHANES, 603–604
6 HERODOTUS, 20–21, 226, 239–240
7 PLATO, 447, 759
12 AURELIUS, 295
13 VIRGIL, 149–150, 172–173, 260–261, 274, 295–296, 349–350
14 PLUTARCH, 104, 107
17 PLOTINUS, 74, 174, 180
18 AUGUSTINE, 34–35, 70–73, 82, 89–90
20 AQUINAS, 823–827, 901–902, 917–922
21 DANTE, 59–61, 68–69, 73, 154, 156
22 CHAUCER, 196–199
23 HOBBES, 163
25 MONTAIGNE, 152–153, 155–156
27 SHAKESPEARE, 53–54
32 MILTON, 298–300
40 GIBBON, 82, 466–467
44 BOSWELL, 52–53, 224
47 GOETHE, 87–88
51 TOLSTOY, 281–282, 435–436, 553–554
52 DOSTOEVSKY, 167

2*b*. Worship and adoration: the rituals and ceremonials of religion

OLD TESTAMENT: *Genesis,* 12:7–8; 17:9–14,23–27; 28:18–22 / *Exodus* 15:1–21; 23:10–19; 24–31; 35–40 / *Leviticus* / *Numbers,* 5:5–9:14; 15; 18–19; 28–29 / *Deuteronomy,* 5:6–15; 12; 14; 15:19–17:1; 26; 32 passim / *Joshua,* 5:2–9; 22:9–34 / *Judges,* 11:30–40 / *I Samuel,* 2:1–10 / *II Samuel,* 6:1–15; 22 / *I Kings,* 8 / *II Kings,* 17:36 / *I Chronicles,* 15:25–16:36; 17:16–27; 29:10–22 / *II Chronicles,* 5:1–7:9; 15:1–15; 30; 35:1–19 / *Ezra,* 1–8 passim / *Nehemiah,* 9 / *Esther,* 9:20–32 / *Psalms* passim / *Song of Solomon* / *Isaiah,* 1:10–18; 2:2–3; 25–26; 29:18–19; 40:9–31; 56:1–7; 58 / *Jeremiah,* 17:21–27 / *Amos,* 5:21–24 / *Micah,* 6:6–8 / *Zechariah,* 14:16–21

APOCRYPHA: *Judith,* 16 / *Rest of Esther,* 13:14; 16:20–22 / *Ecclesiasticus,* 35:1–7; 39:15–35; 47:8–10; 50–51 / *Song of Three Children,* 28–68 / *I Maccabees,* 2:14–48; 4:52–59 / *II Maccabees,* 15:1–5

NEW TESTAMENT: *Matthew,* 12:1–12 / *John,* 4:19–26; 7:22–23 / *Acts,* 15:1–29 / *Romans,* 2:25–29; 4:8–12; 14 / *Galatians,* 5:1–11

4 HOMER, 14, 171–172, 253–254
5 SOPHOCLES, 118, 152–155
5 EURIPIDES, 279–280, 282–283, 334, 340–352
5 ARISTOPHANES, 458, 567–569
6 HERODOTUS, 31, 40–41, 45, 56–64, 95, 129–130, 138, 142, 155–156
7 PLATO, 345–346, 718–719, 731–732
12 LUCRETIUS, 22–23, 76
13 VIRGIL, 188–190
14 PLUTARCH, 49–61 passim, 214, 424
15 TACITUS, 282–283
18 AUGUSTINE, 35, 65–66, 259–262, 298–299, 300–301
20 AQUINAS, 247–248, 253–255, 265–304, 839–854, 900–917
23 HOBBES, 161–163, 180, 226–227, 261–262
25 MONTAIGNE, 300
30 BACON, 55, 101
32 MILTON, 178–179, 229–231
33 PASCAL, 62–64
35 LOCKE, 10–15
35 HUME, 468
38 MONTESQUIEU, 211
40 GIBBON, 59–60, 180–182, 184–185, 208–211 passim, 349–350, 353, 356–357, 457–467, 547, 583–584
41 GIBBON, 195–198, 207–208, 226–227
42 KANT, 504–505, 509–510
46 HEGEL, 225, 227–228, 239, 244–245, 253–254, 290–292
48 MELVILLE, 39
51 TOLSTOY, 373–377
52 DOSTOEVSKY, 131, 171

2*c*. The nature, institution, and uses of the sacraments

NEW TESTAMENT: *Matthew,* 3; 26:26–29; 28:19 / *Mark,* 14:22–24; 16:16 / *Luke,* 22:14–20 / *John,* 1:25–27,33; 3:3–7; 6 / *Acts,* 2:37–42; 8:12–17,26–40; 19:1–7 / *Romans,* 6:3–4 / *I Corinthians,* 1:12–17; 11:23–30 / *Ephesians,*

4:5; 5:21–33 / *James,* 5:14–16 / *I Peter,* 3:18–22
18 Augustine, 117–118, 362–363, 438–439, 575, 579–581, 661, 690–691
20 Aquinas, 283–292, 298–299; 332–333, 387–388, 400–401, 847–884, 978–980
21 Dante, 66–67, 94–105
22 Chaucer, 256–258, 381–382, 495–550
23 Hobbes, 206–207, 211–212, 249–250, 263–264
31 Descartes, 162–165
33 Pascal, 71–80, 128–137, 343, 344, 348–349
35 Locke, 391–392
36 Sterne, 373–376
40 Gibbon, 297
41 Gibbon, 334
44 Boswell, 481
46 Hegel, 331–332, 338
51 Tolstoy, 43–44, 476–478
52 Dostoevsky, 21–22, 80–81

2*d*. Sacrifices and propitiations

Old Testament: *Genesis,* 4:1–16; 15:6–17; 22 / *Exodus,* 8:1,25–29; 10:3–11,24–26; 12:1–13:16; 20:24–26; 22:29–30; 24:5–8; 29–30 / *Leviticus,* 1–10; 12; 14:1–32; 16–17; 19:5–7; 21–23; 27 / *Numbers,* 3:12–13; 5–9; 15–16; 18:1–19:6; 28–29; 31:25–54 / *Deuteronomy,* 12; 14:22–29; 15:19–21; 16:1–17; 21:1–9; 26:10–15 / *Joshua,* 8:30–31; 22:9–12,21–29 / *Judges,* 6:19–21,25–28; 11:28–40; 13:15–23 / *I Samuel,* 1:11,19–28; 2:12–17,27–29; 6:13–15; 7:8–10; 13:5–14; 15:1–23 / *I Kings,* 8:62–64; 18:16–39 / *II Kings,* 16:12–16 / *I Chronicles,* 29:1–9,14,20–21 / *II Chronicles,* 7:1–7; 29:20–35; 35:1–19 / *Nehemiah,* 10:29–39 / *Psalms,* 50; 51:16–19 / *Proverbs,* 3:9–10 / *Isaiah,* 1:11–17; 43:23–24 / *Jeremiah,* 7:21–23 / *Ezekiel,* 43:18–27; 44:7,30; 45:13–46:24 / *Hosea,* 8:11–9:4 / *Joel,* 2:12–14 / *Amos,* 4:4–5; 5:21–27 / *Micah,* 6:6–8 / *Malachi,* 1:7–14; 3:3–10
Apocrypha: *Judith,* 16:16–19 / *Ecclesiasticus,* 34:18–20; 35:1–12 / *Song of Three Children,* 14–17 / *Daniel,* 3:37–40 / *Bel and Dragon,* 1–22 / *I Maccabees,* 4:49–56 / *II Maccabees,* 1:18–36; 2:9–11; 3:31–35
New Testament: *Matthew,* 12:7 / *Mark,* 12:32–33,41–44 / *Romans,* 5:7–11; 12:1 / *II Corinthians,* 5:14–21 / *Hebrews,* 5:1–3; 7:26–27; 8:3–4; 9:1–10:22; 13:9–16
4 Homer, 6–8, 42–43, 49, 161–163, 193, 234–235, 253–254
5 Aeschylus, 20–22, 52–54
5 Sophocles, 159
5 Euripides, 251–253, 357, 386–387, 411–424, 425–439
5 Aristophanes, 536–537, 641–642
6 Herodotus, 57–58, 134, 142, 157, 235, 282
7 Plato, 198, 484–485, 683, 712, 768–769, 770–771, 791–792
12 Lucretius, 2
13 Virgil, 127, 157–160, 168–169, 207, 358–360
14 Plutarch, 1–15 passim, 94, 142–143, 239–240, 273
15 Tacitus, 168
18 Augustine, 300–303, 308–312, 313
20 Aquinas, 269–270, 272–276, 283–292, 299–300, 396–397, 862–863, 900–917 passim
21 Dante, 112–113
23 Hobbes, 197–198, 204
25 Montaigne, 250–251
35 Locke, 12–13
40 Gibbon, 121, 349–350, 463
41 Gibbon, 226–227
44 Boswell, 482
47 Goethe, 208–209

2*e*. Fasting and almsgiving

Old Testament: *Leviticus,* 25:35–37 / *Deuteronomy,* 15:7–11; 24:17–22; 26:12–13 / *II Samuel,* 12:15–23 / *Ezra,* 8:21–23 / *Esther,* 4:1–3,15–17 / *Job,* 29:11–16; 31:16–22 / *Psalms,* 41:1–3; 69:10–11 / *Proverbs,* 14:21,31; 21:13; 29:7 / *Isaiah,* 58:3–12 / *Ezekiel,* 18:4–21 / *Daniel,* 10:2–3 / *Zechariah,* 7
Apocrypha: *Tobit,* 1:16–17; 2; 4:7–11,16–17; 12:8–10 / *Ecclesiasticus,* 4:1–8; 7:10,32–33; 12:1–7; 29:1–2,8–13,20
New Testament: *Matthew,* 5:42; 6:1–4,16–18; 9:14–15; 19:16–22 / *Luke,* 3:11; 14:12–14; 18:11–12,18–23; 21:1–4 / *Acts,* 10:1–4 / *II Corinthians,* 8–9 / *I Timothy,* 6:17–19
6 Herodotus, 156–157
18 Augustine, 576, 583–584
20 Aquinas, 540–550, 665–673, 910–912
33 Pascal, 91–94
40 Gibbon, 197, 198, 596–597
41 Gibbon, 233
48 Melville, 60–65

2*f*. Purificatory rites: the remission of sin by baptism and penance

Old Testament: *Exodus,* 30:17–21 / *Leviticus,* 4–6; 7:1–7; 9; 11–17 / *Numbers,* 5:5–31; 6:9–12; 8:5–7; 19; 31:19–24 / *Deuteronomy,* 21:1–9; 23:9–11 / *II Chronicles,* 29–30 / *Psalms,* 51:1–2,7–10
Apocrypha: *I Maccabees,* 4:38–61 / *II Maccabees,* 1:18–36
New Testament: *Matthew,* 3; 15:1–20; 23:25–26 / *John,* 1:25–33; 3:5,22–27; 13:1–15 / *Acts,* 2:37–41; 8:12–17,20–22,35–38; 13:23–24; 19:1–5 / *Romans,* 6
4 Homer, 42–43, 174, 197, 310–311
5 Aeschylus, 84, 86
5 Sophocles, 148–149
6 Herodotus, 8, 56–57
6 Thucydides, 442–443
10 Hippocrates, 154–155
13 Virgil, 216–217
18 Augustine, 5, 314–316
20 Aquinas, 283–292, 362–363, 436–437
22 Chaucer, 495–510, 543–550

2g. Profanations and sacrileges

3. The religious life: religious offices and the religious community

3a. The Jewish conception of the religious community: the Torah and the Temple

3b. The Christian conception of the church: the doctrine of the mystical body of Christ

3c. The nature and organization of the religious community

3c(1) The institution of the priesthood and other ecclesiastical offices

28–29; 30:17–21,30; 39; 40:12–15 / *Leviticus* passim / *Numbers,* 1:49–54; 3–5; 6:10–11,16–27; 8; 10:1–10; 15:24–28; 16:1–19:7; 20:23–29; 25:6–13; 27:18–23; 35:24–28,32 / *Deuteronomy,* 10:8–9; 12:18–19; 17:8–13; 18:5–7; 20:1–4; 26:1–4; 33:8–11 / *Joshua,* 3:3,6–17; 4:1–18; 6:1–20 / *I Samuel,* 2:12–17,27–36; 4:10–18; 21:1–9; 22:9–21 / *II Samuel,* 15:24–29 / *I Kings,* 8:1–11; 12:30–32; 13:33–34 / *II Kings,* 12:4–10; 16:10–16; 17:26–28,32; 22:3–14; 23:4–9,20 / *I Chronicles,* 15:11–27; 16:4–6,37–42; 23–26 / *II Chronicles,* 5; 8:14–15; 11:13–15; 13:9–12; 19:8–11; 23:1–24:16; 29–31; 34:8–15; 35:1–9 / *Ezra,* 1:1–5; 2; 6–12 passim / *Nehemiah,* 8; 10:37–39; 12:26–47; 13:4–11,28–31 / *Isaiah,* 61:6 / *Jeremiah,* 2:8; 6:13; 23:1–4,11; 33:18–22 / *Ezekiel,* 34; 44:9–31; 45:4–5; 48:10–11 / *Hosea,* 4:4–10 / *Zechariah,* 3; 6:9–13 / *Malachi,* 1:6–2:9

APOCRYPHA: *Ecclesiasticus,* 45; 50 / *I Maccabees,* 4:42–53 / *II Maccabees,* 1:19–32; 3 passim; 4:7–29

NEW TESTAMENT: *Matthew,* 12:3–5; 26:57–65 / *John,* 18:19–24 / *Acts,* 1:15–26; 6:1–8; 14:22–23; 23:1–5 / *I Timothy,* 3; 5:17–22 / *II Timothy,* 1–3 / *Titus,* 1 / *Hebrews,* 2:17–3:2; 4:14–5:10; 6:18–9:28; 10:11–12,19–22 / *I Peter,* 5

6 HERODOTUS, 60–61, 135–136, 211, 295–296; 308
7 PLATO, 597–598, 700–701, 787
9 ARISTOTLE, 526, 533
13 VIRGIL, 128–130, 212–213, 266–267
14 PLUTARCH, 53–56
15 TACITUS, 67–68
18 AUGUSTINE, 451, 455–458
20 AQUINAS, 299–300, 389–390, 633–650, 663–665, 695–696, 827–833, 870–879
22 CHAUCER, 372–374
23 HOBBES, 177–180, 207–240, 272–274
24 RABELAIS, 119–122 passim, 186–188, 195–196
38 MONTESQUIEU, 209–210
40 GIBBON, 82, 300–301, 457–458
44 BOSWELL, 196, 218–220, 313–316, 466–467
46 HEGEL, 224–227
52 DOSTOEVSKY, 127–137, 171–180 passim

3*c*(2) Ecclesiastical government and hierarchy

OLD TESTAMENT: *Leviticus,* 21:10–15 / *Numbers,* 3:5–10 / *I Chronicles,* 23–24

NEW TESTAMENT: *Matthew,* 16:18–19; 20:25–28 / *Mark,* 10:42–44 / *Luke,* 22:24–30 / *Acts,* 1:21–26; 6:1–6; 13:1–3; 15:1–30 / *I Timothy,* 3 / *Titus* / *Hebrews,* 1:1–8; 4:14–5:10; 6:19–10:21

20 AQUINAS, 389–390
21 DANTE, 40–41
23 MACHIAVELLI, 16–17
23 HOBBES, 178–180, 207–240, 248–249, 266, 273, 275–278
24 RABELAIS, 288–297
33 PASCAL, 344–345
35 LOCKE, 4–6, 7–8
38 ROUSSEAU, 436
40 GIBBON, 194–197, 299–300, 302–303, 304, 642–643
41 GIBBON, 214–215, 517, 567–569, 582–586 passim, 589
44 BOSWELL, 173
46 HEGEL, 224–227, 310

3*c*(3) The support of ecclesiastical institutions: tithes, contributions, state subsidy

OLD TESTAMENT: *Exodus,* 22:29–30; 25:1–9; 29:27–34; 30:11–16; 35:4–36:7 / *Leviticus,* 7:6–15,30–36; 10:12–20; 23 passim; 24:5–9; 27 / *Numbers,* 5:9–10; 7 passim; 18:8–32; 31:25–54; 35:1–8 / *Deuteronomy,* 14:22–29; 18:1–8; 26:1–16 / *Joshua,* 21 / *I Samuel,* 2:13–17 / *II Kings,* 12; 22:3–7 / *II Chronicles,* 24:4–14; 31:3–12; 34:8–13 / *Ezra,* 8:24–30 / *Nehemiah,* 10:32–39 / *Proverbs,* 3:9–10 / *Ezekiel,* 44:27–31; 45:1–6; 48:8–21

APOCRYPHA: *Tobit,* 1:6–8 / *Ecclesiasticus,* 35:8–11; 45:20–22

NEW TESTAMENT: *I Corinthians,* 9:13–14; 16:1–2 / *II Corinthians,* 8:1–9:15 / *Philippians,* 4:10–19 / *Hebrews,* 7:1–10

9 ARISTOTLE, 534
20 AQUINAS, 647–649, 669–673
22 CHAUCER, 285–295, 372–374
23 HOBBES, 223–224
24 RABELAIS, 99–100
26 SHAKESPEARE, 533
38 MONTESQUIEU, 210–211, 298–302
39 SMITH, 56–57, 343–356
40 GIBBON, 82, 197–198, 301–302, 392–393, 597
41 GIBBON, 417
44 BOSWELL, 219, 342

3*d*. The monastic life: the disciplines of asceticism

OLD TESTAMENT: *Numbers,* 6:1–21 / *Judges,* 13:2–25 / *I Samuel,* 1:9–12,19–28

NEW TESTAMENT: *Matthew,* 3:1–4; 19:10–12,21 / *Luke,* 1:13–15, 12:22–36 / *I Corinthians,* 7:25–40

18 AUGUSTINE, 139–140
20 AQUINAS, 66–67, 633–634, 636–639, 646–647, 649–700, 1006–1007
21 DANTE, 109–110, 122–123, 124–125
22 CHAUCER, 162, 277, 278–295
24 RABELAIS, 32–35, 46–54, 60–67, 156–158, 168–173, 191, 253–355
26 SHAKESPEARE, 353
32 MILTON, 24–25
33 PASCAL, 265
38 MONTESQUIEU, 105
40 GIBBON, 191–193, 533, 593–599
44 BOSWELL, 283
46 HEGEL, 224, 234–235; 333, 340–341
51 TOLSTOY, 273–274

22 Chaucer, 461–471
30 Bacon, 41
33 Pascal, 205–209
35 Locke, 1–2, 3–4, 7–8, 13–16
40 Gibbon, 200–206, 296–299, 599–602
41 Gibbon, 152–161 passim, 234–245, 285–287, 345–347
44 Boswell, 174, 372, 394–395, 536
51 Tolstoy, 194–203, 216–218, 476–480
52 Dostoevsky, 153–164

5*c*. Religious education

Old Testament: *Exodus,* 12:24–27 / *Deuteronomy,* 4:1–5,9–10,14; 6:1,6–9,20–25; 17:9–10; 31:9–13 / *Joshua,* 8:30–35 / *II Chronicles,* 17:7–9; 34:29–30 / *Nehemiah,* 8 / *Psalms,* 78:1–4 / *Ezekiel,* 44:21–23
Apocrypha: *Ecclesiasticus*
New Testament: *Matthew,* 5–7; 10:1–31; 13:1–23 / *Mark,* 4:1–25 / *Luke,* 6:12–49 / *Ephesians,* 4:11–15 / *I Timothy,* 4:6–13 / *Titus,* 1:7–3:11
7 Plato, 757–771, 797–798
18 Augustine, 621–698
19 Aquinas, 1
20 Aquinas, 455–456, 618–619
23 Hobbes, 123, 154–156, 211, 269, 278
24 Rabelais, 82–83
35 Locke, 7–8, 18
39 Smith, 343–356, 357
40 Gibbon, 355, 601
43 Mill, 437–438
44 Boswell, 151
52 Dostoevsky, 150–153

6. Truth and falsity in religion

6*a*. The religious condemnation of idolatry, superstition, and other perversions of worship

Old Testament: *Exodus,* 20:1–5,22–23; 32; 34:11–17 / *Leviticus,* 20:1–6,27; 26:1,28–30 / *Numbers,* 25:1–5,16–18 / *Deuteronomy,* 4:14–28; 5:6–9; 8:19–20; 9:15–21; 12:2–3; 12:29–13:18; 16:21–17:7; 18:9–14,20; 28:14–68; 29:16–29; 30:15–20; 31:16–21 / *Joshua,* 22–23; 24:14–25 / *Judges,* 2:10–23; 6:24–32 / *I Samuel,* 7:3–4 / *I Kings,* 3:1–4; 11–16; 18:16–40; 20:22–28; 21:25–29 / *II Kings* passim / *II Chronicles,* 15:8–16; 21:5–20; 28:1–5,22–25; 33:1–13; 36:11–21 / *Psalms,* 106; 115:1–8; 135:15–18 / *Isaiah,* 2:5–21; 10:10–11; 30–31; 40:18–20; 44:9–20; 57:3–8 / *Jeremiah* passim / *Ezekiel* passim / *Daniel,* 3; 6 / *Hosea* passim / *Amos,* 2:4–16; 4:1–5; 5 / *Nahum* passim / *Habakkuk,* 2:18–19 / *Zephaniah* passim
Apocrypha: *Judith,* 5:23–6:4; 8:16–18 / *Rest of Esther,* 14:6–10 / *Wisdom of Solomon,* 12–15 / *Ecclesiasticus,* 34:1–7 / *Baruch,* 6 / *Bel and Dragon* / *I Maccabees,* 1:41–2:28 / *II Maccabees,* 6–7
New Testament: *Matthew,* 23:1–33 / *Acts,* 7:39–44; 8:9–24; 12:21–23; 14:7–18; 15:20,28–29; 17:16–31 / *Romans,* 1:18–32 / *I Corinthians,* 8 / *II Corinthians,* 6:14–17 / *Philippians,* 3:18–19 / *I John,* 5:20–21
6 Herodotus, 95
7 Plato, 769–771
14 Plutarch, 104–105, 123–124, 575–576
18 Augustine, 129–322, 474–476, 477–478, 480–482, 647–649
21 Dante, 1–2, 9–10, 26–29, 40–41, 57, 77–78, 119–120, 123, 139, 147–148
22 Chaucer, 530–531
23 Hobbes, 51–52, 78–83 passim, 247–267
25 Montaigne, 18–20, 91, 152–156, 246–258 passim, 497–501
30 Bacon, 110
32 Milton, 1–7, 100–107, 349–350, 358–359, 364–366
33 Pascal, 71–80, 87–88, 94–97
35 Locke, 13–15
35 Berkeley, 431
40 Gibbon, 184–185, 457, 458–459, 460–463, 600–601
41 Gibbon, 195–202 passim, 207–208, 229–230, 328–334 passim
44 Boswell, 173–174, 301
46 Hegel, 196–197

6*b*. Religious apologetics: the defense of faith

14 Plutarch, 191–192
18 Augustine, 35–37, 129–618, 675–677
19 Aquinas, 7–8, 175–178
20 Aquinas, 399–400
25 Montaigne, 208–294
29 Cervantes, 122
30 Bacon, 41
31 Descartes, 69–71
33 Pascal, 212–217, 245–280, 328–342
35 Hume, 499–500
38 Montesquieu, 200–201
40 Gibbon, 206, 348
46 Hegel, 309

6*c*. The unity and tradition of a religion

6*c*(1) Orthodoxy and heresy: the role of dogma in religion; the treatment of heretics

New Testament: *Acts,* 4:1–22; 5:14–42; 6:7–8:3; 9:1–25; 13:43–50; 15:1–31; 17:5–14; 18:12–16; 21–26 passim / *Galatians,* 1:6–9; 5:19–20 / *Titus,* 3:10–11 / *I John,* 3:18–19; 4:1–6
18 Augustine, 15–18, 27–34 passim, 51, 422, 502–503
19 Aquinas, 172–173
20 Aquinas, 388–389, 395–396, 412, 429–431, 432–434, 438–442
21 Dante, 12–15, 102–104
23 Hobbes, 212–215, 238–240, 248, 273
25 Montaigne, 82, 208, 250
30 Bacon, 27
32 Milton, 386

33 PASCAL, 1–7, 117–166, 323–324, 342–343, 347
35 LOCKE, 1–2, 6, 21–22
40 GIBBON, 182–184, 198–200, 305–313, 438–443, 541, 601–605
41 GIBBON, 134–151, 198–202, 328–335, 421–423
44 BOSWELL, 221–224 passim
46 HEGEL, 313
47 GOETHE, 121–122
52 DOSTOEVSKY, 128–135

6c(2) Sects and schisms arising from divergences of belief and practice

6 HERODOTUS, 52
18 AUGUSTINE, 27–34 passim
20 AQUINAS, 574–577
21 DANTE, 41–43
23 HOBBES, 229
27 SHAKESPEARE, 581
32 MILTON, 404–405, 406, 409–410
33 PASCAL, 7–13
35 LOCKE, 251, 386–387
36 STERNE, 332–334
39 SMITH, 345–346
40 GIBBON, 181–184, 305–328, 391–392, 438–441, 541, 601–608
41 GIBBON, 134–161, 195–202, 306–307, 328–335, 421–424, 462–464, 510–522, 529–534, 544–545, 583–586
44 BOSWELL, 114, 536–537
46 HEGEL, 193, 348–355

6d. The relation of men of diverse faiths: the attitude of the faithful toward infidels

APOCRYPHA: *I Maccabees*, 1–2 / *II Maccabees*, 6–7
NEW TESTAMENT: *Acts* / *Romans*, 8:35–36 / *I Corinthians*, 4:9–13 / *II Corinthians*, 1:5–8; 12:9–10 / *Galatians*, 1:13–24; 2:1–5 / *I Thessalonians*, 2:14–16
6 HERODOTUS, 97–98, 137, 138
15 TACITUS, 168
18 AUGUSTINE, 129–322, 525–528, 655–656
20 AQUINAS, 401, 426–437, 443–444
21 DANTE, 5–7, 135–138
22 CHAUCER, 236–255, 392–395
23 HOBBES, 246
25 MONTAIGNE, 116–117
26 SHAKESPEARE, 406–433
30 BACON, 96, 209
32 MILTON, 368–369
33 PASCAL, 277–301 passim
35 LOCKE, 6, 13
36 STERNE, 257–268 passim
38 MONTESQUIEU, 169, 212–214
39 SMITH, 344, 345–346
40 GIBBON, 12, 206–234, 290–291, 328–330, 348–361 passim, 457–464 passim
41 GIBBON, 148–149, 237–243, 285–288, 323, 377–380, 383–384, 386–387, 401
43 FEDERALIST, 50
43 MILL, 270–271, 307–309, 311–312
44 BOSWELL, 173–174, 285, 299, 347, 431, 436–438, 512
46 HEGEL, 322–323
48 MELVILLE, 39, 60–66
54 FREUD, 676, 788

6e. Religious liberty: freedom of conscience; religious toleration

OLD TESTAMENT: *Daniel*, 6
APOCRYPHA: *Rest of Esther*, 16
20 AQUINAS, 433–434, 435–437, 440–441
23 HOBBES, 102–103, 149, 163, 209–211
25 MONTAIGNE, 153–155, 324–326
32 MILTON, 68
35 LOCKE, 1–22
36 STERNE, 257–258
38 MONTESQUIEU, 144–145, 211–213, 218–219
38 ROUSSEAU, 439
40 GIBBON, 12–14, 231, 290–291, 383, 390–391, 464, 642, 643
41 GIBBON, 333–335
42 KANT, 444
43 CONSTITUTION OF THE U.S., 16, 17
43 MILL, 270–271, 274–293 passim, 307–309, 310–312
44 BOSWELL, 221–224, 421, 445
46 HEGEL, 353
52 DOSTOEVSKY, 127–137 passim

6f. The rejection of supernatural foundations for religion: the criticism of particular beliefs and practices; the psychogenesis of religion

12 LUCRETIUS, 17, 35–44, 63–64, 76–77, 80–81, 85
23 HOBBES, 69–71, 78–80, 165–166, 172, 188–198, 236–238, 247–278 passim
25 MONTAIGNE, 256
35 HUME, 488–497
40 GIBBON, 189–190, 200–201, 294–297, 345–347 passim, 465–467, 599
41 GIBBON, 334, 476–477
46 HEGEL, 220–221, 244–245, 253–254, 348–349, 354–355
49 DARWIN, 302–303
50 MARX, 31, 35
52 DOSTOEVSKY, 21–22, 123–125, 129–130, 337–346 passim
54 FREUD, 138, 692–693, 707, 763, 767–772, 774, 793, 875–879

6g. The relation between sacred doctrine and secular learning: the conflict of science and religion

7 PLATO, 729–730
12 LUCRETIUS, 1–3, 30–31, 61–62
14 PLUTARCH, 435
18 AUGUSTINE, 264–273, 495–496, 523, 646–656
19 AQUINAS, 60–62, 253–255, 446–447
20 AQUINAS, 338–339, 380–384, 393–394, 409
23 HOBBES, 165, 274
25 MONTAIGNE, 80–82, 155, 208–209, 212

30 BACON, 2–4, 17–20, 33, 39–42, 114, 119–120, 124
31 DESCARTES, 69, 125–126, 162–165, 283–284
33 PASCAL, 163–166, 212–213, 218–220, 221–225, 248–250, 272–273, 355–356, 365–366
35 LOCKE, 380–384, 385, 387–388
35 HUME, 497, 498, 499–500
39 SMITH, 334–335, 336–337
40 GIBBON, 159, 204–206, 307–309, 670
41 GIBBON, 335
42 KANT, 346–347
43 MILL, 455
44 BOSWELL, 102
46 HEGEL, 158–160, 361
49 DARWIN, 239, 593
50 MARX, 305–306
51 TOLSTOY, 248–249, 675–677, 684, 696
52 DOSTOEVSKY, 87
54 FREUD, 874–881

7. Historical observations concerning religious beliefs, institutions, and controversies

6 HERODOTUS, 5–6, 8, 39, 49–50, 52, 56–64, 66, 75, 76, 77, 80–85, 97–98, 99–100, 126–127, 136, 137, 140–141, 156–157, 183–184, 242–243, 308
6 THUCYDIDES, 471–472
7 PLATO, 204–205
14 PLUTARCH, 1–15 passim, 25–26, 49–61 passim, 68, 110, 114–116, 247–249, 271–273, 365–366, 541
15 TACITUS, 59, 62, 140–141, 148–149, 168, 214–215, 293–294, 295–296
18 AUGUSTINE, 129–322, 502
20 AQUINAS, 244–245, 292–298 passim, 298–304
23 HOBBES, 79–84, 207–240, 258–267
25 MONTAIGNE, 246–258
27 SHAKESPEARE, 549–585
33 PASCAL, 1–167
35 LOCKE, 114
38 MONTESQUIEU, 196–197, 208–211 passim
38 ROUSSEAU, 435–439
39 SMITH, 343–356
40 GIBBON, 12–14, 80–83, 98, 179–234, 289–330, 344–361, 382–383, 387–388, 390–393, 438–453, 457–467, 529–532, 541–542, 582–584, 593–608, 611–615, 622–624, 642–644
41 GIBBON, 9–10, 49–50, 109–11, 124–133, 134–161, 195–220, 226–310, 320–321, 323–324, 328–335, 345–347, 351–367, 371–372, 377–441, 451–453 passim, 460–464, 476–477, 480–481, 510–522, 529–537, 538–556, 557–572, 582–589
43 MILL, 278–281, 285–286, 307–309
44 BOSWELL, 314–315, 436–438
46 HEGEL, 216–217, 227–228, 233–235, 237–239, 246–247, 252, 268–271, 289–293, 303–317, 321–323, 330–335, 337–342, 348–355, 358–360
50 MARX, 358

CROSS-REFERENCES

For: Other discussions of the nature and causes of faith, *see* GOD 6c(2); KNOWLEDGE 6c(5); OPINION 4a; TRUTH 4a; WILL 3b(3); and for the relation of religious faith to theology, *see* THEOLOGY 2, 4b, 5.

Other considerations of divine revelation and the problem of interpreting the Word of God, *see* GOD 2a, 6c(1); LANGUAGE 12; RHETORIC 2d; SIGN AND SYMBOL 5e; THEOLOGY 4b.

Matters bearing on the religious significance of miracles, omens, portents, and prophecies, *see* GOD 7e; NATURE 3c(4); PROPHECY 1d, 3a–3b; SIGN AND SYMBOL 5b.

Other discussions of religion as a virtue and of the virtues of the religious life, *see* GOD 3c–3e; JUSTICE 11b; TEMPERANCE 6a; VIRTUE AND VICE 8b, 8f–8g; and for the related doctrines of grace and the theological virtues, *see* GOD 7d; HABIT 5e(1)–5e(3); LIBERTY 5c; LOVE 5b–5b(2); NATURE 6b; SIN 7; VIRTUE AND VICE 8b, 8d–8e; WILL 7e(2).

The theory of religious sacraments, *see* GOD 9e; SIGN AND SYMBOL 5c.

The comparison of ecclesiastical and civil government, and of the religious with other communities, *see* GOVERNMENT 1b; STATE 1d.

Other discussions of the Jewish and Christian conceptions of the religious community, *see* GOD 8a–8d, 9d.

The problem of church and state, *see* HISTORY 5b; STATE 2g.

Another consideration of religious education, *see* EDUCATION 7–7b; GOD 6c(1).

The general issue concerning truth and falsity in religion, and concerning orthodoxy and heresy in religion, *see* GOD 10, 12–14; LIBERTY 2b; OPINION 4b; PROPHECY 5; THEOLOGY 4c, 4e.

The relation of religion to science and philosophy, *see* PHILOSOPHY 1a; SCIENCE 2a; TRUTH 4a.

ADDITIONAL READINGS

Listed below are works not included in *Great Books of the Western World*, but relevant to the idea and topics with which this chapter deals. These works are divided into two groups:

I. Works by authors represented in this collection.
II. Works by authors not represented in this collection.

For the date, place, and other facts concerning the publication of the works cited, consult the Bibliography of Additional Readings which follows the last chapter of *The Great Ideas*.

I.

PLUTARCH. "Of Superstition, or Indiscreet Devotion," "Of Isis and Osiris, or the Ancient Religion and Philosophy of Egypt," in *Moralia*

AUGUSTINE. *De Vera Religione*

——. *De Fide et Symbolo*

——. *The Harmony of the Gospels*

AQUINAS. *Contra Impugnantes Dei Cultum et Religionem*

——. *On the Trinity of Boethius*, Q 3

——. *Summa Contra Gentiles*, BK III, CH 99–103; BK IV, CH 56–95

——. *De Perfectione Vitae Spiritualis*

——. *Contra Pestiferam Doctrinam Retrahentium Homines a Religionis Ingressu*

——. *Summa Theologica*, PART II–II, QQ 81–105, 178; PART III, QQ 66–90; SUPPL, QQ 1–68

DANTE. *On World-Government or De Monarchia*, esp BK III

F. BACON. "Of Unity in Religion," "Of Superstition," in *Essays*

MILTON. *The Reason of Church-Government Urg'd Against Prelaty*

SPINOZA. *Tractatus Theologico-Politicus* (*Theological-Political Treatise*), CH 5–10

LOCKE. *The Reasonableness of Christianity*

——. *A Second Vindication of the Reasonableness of Christianity*

——. *A Discourse of Miracles*

SWIFT. *A Tale of a Tub*

——. *An Argument to Prove That the Abolishing of Christianity in England May . . . Be Attended with Some Inconveniences*

HUME. *Dialogues Concerning Natural Religion*

——. *The Natural History of Religion*

GIBBON. *An Essay on the Study of Literature*, LVI–LXXVII

KANT. *Lectures on Ethics*, pp 71–116

——. *Religion Within the Limits of Reason Alone*

HEGEL. *The Positivity of the Christian Religion*

——. *The Spirit of Christianity*

——. *The Phenomenology of Mind*, VII

——. *The Philosophy of Mind*, SECT III, SUB-SECT B

——. *Lectures on the Philosophy of Religion*

J. S. MILL. "The Utility of Religion," "Theism," in *Three Essays on Religion*

TOLSTOY. *What Men Live By*

——. *The Gospel in Brief*

W. JAMES. *The Varieties of Religious Experience*

——. *Pragmatism*, LECT VIII

FREUD. *Totem and Taboo*

——. *The Future of an Illusion*

——. *Moses and Monotheism*

II.

HESIOD. *Works and Days*

——. *Theogony*

CICERO. *De Natura Deorum* (*On the Nature of the Gods*)

LUCIAN. *The Fisher*

——. *The Gods in Council*

——. *Icaromenippus: An Aerial Expedition*

——. *Of Sacrifice*

——. *Sale of Creeds*

——. *Alexander the Oracle-Monger*

TERTULLIAN. *Apology*, CH 7–50

——. *The Prescription Against Heretics*

LACTANTIUS. *The Divine Institutes*

EUSEBIUS PAMPHILI. *Ecclesiastical History*

ATHANASIUS. *Treatises in Controversy with the Arians*

JOHN CHRYSOSTOM. *On the Priesthood*

BOETHIUS. *De Fide Catholica* (*On the Catholic Faith*)

GREGORY OF TOURS. *History of the Franks*

——. *Libri Septem Miraculorum*

THE VENERABLE BEDE. *The Ecclesiastical History of the English Nation*

HUGH OF SAINT VICTOR. *De Sacramentis*

MAIMONIDES. *Mishneh Torah*

BONAVENTURA. *Breviloquium*, PART V–VI
R. BACON. *Opus Majus*, PART VII
ECKHART. *Tractates*, VII
The Cloud of Unknowing
Theologia Germanica
LANGLAND. *Piers Plowman*
ALBO. *The Book of Principles* (*Sefer ha-Ikkarim*), BK I, CH 1–26
THOMAS À KEMPIS. *The Imitation of Christ*, BK I, CH 15–25; BK IV
ARIOSTO. *Orlando Furioso*
MELANCHTHON. *Loci Communes*
IGNATIUS OF LOYOLA. *Spiritual Exercises*
ZWINGLI. *Commentary on True and False Religion*
CALVIN. *Institutes of the Christian Religion*, BK III, CH 1–13; BK IV
LUTHER. *A Treatise on Christian Liberty*
——. *The Babylonian Captivity of the Church*
LUTHER. *Table Talk*
TERESA OF JESUS. *The Way of Perfection*
——. *Book of the Foundations*
——. *Interior Castle*
JOHN OF THE CROSS. *Spiritual Canticle*
——. *Ascent of Mount Carmel*
TASSO. *Jerusalem Delivered*
SUÁREZ. *De Religione*
FRANCIS OF SALES. *Introduction to the Devout Life*
——. *Treatise on the Love of God*
BOEHME. *Of the Supersensual Life*
——. *The Way from Darkness to True Illumination*
——. *De Electione Gratiae* (*On the Election of Grace*)
——. *The Way to Christ*
CALDERÓN. *The Mighty Magician*
CORNEILLE. *Polyeucte*
BROWNE. *Religio Medici*
HERBERT OF CHERBURY. *De Religione Laici* (*Of a Layman's Religion*)
DRYDEN. *Absalom and Achitophel*
PENN. *Primitive Christianity Revived*
DEFOE. *The Shortest Way with the Dissenters*
J. BUTLER. *The Analogy of Religion*
DODDRIDGE. *Rise and Progress of Religion in the Soul*
J. EDWARDS. *A Treatise Concerning Religious Affections*
VOLTAIRE. *Letters on the English*, I–VII
——. "Baptism," "Blasphemy," "Christianity," "Church," "Clerk-Clergy," "Confession," "Dogmas," "Eucharist," "Expiation," "Heresy," "Jews," "Martyrs," "Mass," "Messiah," "Miracles," "Religion," "Superstition," in *A Philosophical Dictionary*
HOLBACH. *The System of Nature*
WOOLMAN. *Journal*
LESSING. *Nathan the Wise*
PALEY. *A View of the Evidences of Christianity*
JEFFERSON. *Democracy*, CH 6
BLAKE. *The Book of Thel*
——. *The Marriage of Heaven and Hell*
——. *The Everlasting Gospel*
SHELLEY. *Preface to Alastor*
SCHLEIERMACHER. *On Religion*
——. *Soliloquies*
——. *The Christian Faith*, par 1–31, 113–163
HEINE. *Religion and Philosophy in Germany*
S. R. HIRSCH. *The Nineteen Letters of Ben Uziel*
FEUERBACH. *The Essence of Christianity*
TENNYSON. *Locksley Hall*
WHEWELL. *The Elements of Morality*, BK III; BK V, CH 16–17
COMTE. *The Catechism of Positive Religion*
——. *System of Positive Polity*, VOL I, *General View of Positivism*, CH 6; VOL II, *Social Statics*, CH I
KINGSLEY. *Westward Ho!*
FECHNER. *Religion of a Scientist*
READE. *The Cloister and the Hearth*
GEORGE ELIOT. *Romola*
J. H. NEWMAN. *An Essay on the Development of Christian Doctrine*
——. *Callista*
——. *Apologia Pro Vita Sua*
J. H. NEWMAN. "An Internal Argument for Christianity," in VOL III, *Essays and Sketches*
——. *An Essay in Aid of a Grammar of Assent*
ARNOLD. *Empedocles on Etna*
——. *Literature and Dogma*
FLAUBERT. *The Temptation of Saint Anthony*
RENAN. *The Life of Jesus*
——. *Caliban*
CLIFFORD. "The Ethics of Religion," "The Influence upon Morality of a Decline in Religious Belief," in VOL II, *Lectures and Essays*
CAIRD. *An Introduction to the Philosophy of Religion*
LOTZE. *Microcosmos*, BK VIII, CH 4
——. *Outlines of a Philosophy of Religion*
——. *Outlines of Encyclopedia of Philosophy*, SECT III
PATER. *Marius the Epicurean*
MARTINEAU. *A Study of Religion, Its Sources and Contents*
C. S. PEIRCE. *Collected Papers*, VOL VI, par 428–451
NIETZSCHE. *The Will to Power*, BK II (1)
FRAZER. *The Golden Bough*
BILLOT. *De Ecclesia Sacramentis*
T. HARDY. *Jude the Obscure*
PÉGUY. *Basic Verities* (Abandonment; Sleep; A Vision of Prayer)
——. *Men and Saints* (Hope)
CHESTERTON. *Orthodoxy*
WEBER. *The Protestant Ethic and the Spirit of Capitalism*, CH I
——. *Essays in Sociology*, PART III
CLAUDEL. *The Tidings Brought to Mary*
HARRISON. *Ancient Art and Ritual*

HÜGEL. *Essays and Addresses on the Philosophy of Religion*
JOYCE. *A Portrait of the Artist as a Young Man*
BOSANQUET. *What Religion Is*
BUBER. *Jewish Mysticism and the Legends of Baalshem*
——. *Hasidism*
——. *Tales of the Hasidim*
KAFKA. *The Castle*
TAWNEY. *Religion and the Rise of Capitalism*
WHITEHEAD. *Science and the Modern World*, CH 12
——. *Religion in the Making*
J. S. HUXLEY. *Religion Without Revelation*
A. E. TAYLOR. *The Faith of a Moralist*, SERIES II
EDDINGTON. *Science and the Unseen World*
J. S. HALDANE. *The Sciences and Philosophy*, LECT XVII, XIX
BERGSON. *Two Sources of Morality and Religion*
DEWEY. *A Common Faith*
DAWSON. *Enquiries into Religion and Culture*
——. *Religion and the Modern State*
B. RUSSELL. *Philosophical Essays*, CH 2
——. *Mysticism and Logic*, CH 3
——. *Religion and Science*
BLONDEL. *L'action*
T. S. ELIOT. *After Strange Gods*
——. *Murder in the Cathedral*
——. "Religion and Literature," in *Essays, Ancient and Modern*
DE BURGH. *Towards a Religious Philosophy*
STURZO. *The Inner Laws of Society*, CH 4–5
——. *Church and State*
GILSON. *Reason and Revelation in the Middle Ages*
JUNG. *Psychology and Religion*
MARITAIN. *The Things That Are Not Caesar's*, I–III
——. *Religion and Culture*
——. *Scholasticism and Politics*, CH VIII–IX
——. *Ransoming the Time*, CH 4–6, 8
E. FRANK. *Philosophical Understanding and Religious Truth*
SANTAYANA. *Interpretations of Poetry and Religion*, CH 3–4, 9
——. *Reason in Religion*
——. *The Idea of Christ in the Gospels*
HENDEL. *Civilization and Religion*
A. J. TOYNBEE. *Civilization on Trial*, CH 12
BARTH. *Epistle to the Romans*
——. *Dogmatics in Outline*

Chapter 80: REVOLUTION

INTRODUCTION

MOST of the words commonly used as synonyms for "revolution," such as "insurrection," "uprising," "rebellion," or "civil war," carry the connotation of violence and the use of armed force. Most of the great revolutions in western history which come readily to mind—those in the city-states and empires of the ancient world, the Peasants' Revolt in Germany in the 15th century, the rebellion led by Cromwell in 17th century England, the American and French Revolutions in the 18th century, the Russian and the Spanish Revolutions in our own time—have been affairs of bloodshed. Yet neither in political theory nor in historic fact does revolution always involve the use of force or the resort to violence.

Thucydides describes both violent and nonviolent revolutions in the alternations of democracy and oligarchy in the constitution of the Greek city-states. In England, the Great Rebellion which, by civil war, succeeds in beheading one Stuart king, is followed by the Bloodless Revolution of 1688 which, without any war at all, unseats another. Some of the revolutions in the European states in the middle years of the 19th century are accompanied by barricades and fighting. Some, however, like the revolutions accomplished by the Reform Bills in England or by constitutional amendments in the United States, are fundamental changes in government effected by due process of law, by peaceful shifts in the distribution of political power.

A revolution may involve action in defiance of the law and yet be prosecuted without violence on the part of the revolutionists, as in the case of the rebellion which Gandhi led against British rule in India by the method of civil disobedience. The use of armed force may not, however, be the only technique of revolutionary violence. "Revolutions are effected in two ways," according to Aristotle, "by force and by fraud." Though fraud does no physical violence, it does violence to the will of those who are deceived. In some cases when fraud is used, "the citizens are deceived into acquiescing in a change of government, and afterwards," Aristotle observes, "they are held in subjection against their will." In other cases, they may subsequently be persuaded and their allegiance and good will won. But as Machiavelli's later consideration of these two techniques of seizing power indicates, the choice between force and fraud is one of expediency rather than of principle. He recommends guile as an alternative to force, with force held in reserve should cunning fail. Both methods, however, employ the strategy of warfare.

As opposed to both force and fraud, and even to the method of civil disobedience, which acts outside the law or in violation of it, the writers of *The Federalist* conceive the possibility of a revolutionary process which is at once peaceful and legal. It is precisely because they think that the Constitution of the United States affords the opportunity for achieving political change by constitutional amendment that they defend the clause which guarantees "to every State in this Union a republican form of government," and promises to protect each of them, upon application to the federal government, "against domestic violence." To the objection that such a guaranty may involve "an officious interference in the domestic concerns of the members," Hamilton replies: "It could be no impediment to reforms of the State constitutions by a majority of the people in a legal and peaceable mode. This right would remain undiminished. The guaranty could only operate against changes to be effected by violence. Towards the prevention of calamities of this kind, too many checks cannot be provided."

In another of the Federalist papers, Madison

considers the possibility of "an insurrection pervading all the States, and comprising a superiority of the entire force, though not a constitutional right." He thinks such a case beyond "the compass of human remedies." It is enough if the Constitution "diminishes the risk of a calamity for which no possible constitution can provide a cure." Nor does "a conflagration through a whole nation, or through a very large proportion of it, proceeding either from weighty causes of discontent given by the government or from the contagion of some violent popular paroxysm" seem to Hamilton to "fall within any ordinary rules of calculation." In his estimation, "no form of government can always either avoid or control" such revolutions. But, he adds, "where the whole power of the government is in the hands of the people, there is the less pretence for the use of violent remedies in partial or occasional distempers of the State."

WHEN ARISTOTLE THINKS of revolutions as taking place without violence, he does not have in mind the strictly modern device of constitutional amendment. Political change, he suggests, may be the result of accidents rather than of planned actions. "Political revolutions," he writes, sometimes "spring from a disproportionate increase in any part of the state. . . . And this disproportion may sometimes happen by accident, as at Terentum, from a defeat in which many of the notables were slain in a battle with the Iapygians just after the Persian War, the constitutional government in consequence becoming a democracy." Or "when the rich grow numerous or properties increase, the form of government changes into an oligarchy or a government of familes."

On the other hand, to writers like Hobbes and Locke, revolution means war and is inseparable from violence. Those who "deny the authority of the Commonwealth"—apart from which, according to Hobbes, men live in a state of war—by renouncing their subjection to the Sovereign, "relapse into the condition of war commonly called Rebellion. . . . For *rebellion* is but war renewed." Unlike bees and ants, the peace of whose societies is never threatened by rebellion, there are "amongst men . . . very many that think themselves wiser, and abler to govern the public, better than the rest; and these strive to reform and innovate, one this way, another that way; and thereby bring it into distraction and civil war."

Locke's principle seems to be that "whoever uses force without right—as everyone does in society who does it without law—puts himself into a state of war with those against whom he so uses it." Having entered into society "and introduced laws for the preservation of property, peace and unity amongst themselves," men who "set up force again in opposition to the laws, do *rebellare*—that is, bring back again the state of war—and are properly rebels."

Aquinas also seems to align revolution (which he calls "sedition") with war and strife, though he thinks it differs from them in two respects: "First, because war and strife denote actual aggression on either side, whereas sedition may be said to denote either actual aggression or the preparation for such aggression. . . . Secondly, they differ in that war is, properly speaking, carried on against external foes, being as it were between one people and another, whereas strife is between one individual and another, while sedition, in its proper sense, is between the mutually dissentient parts of one people, as when one part of the state rises in tumult against another part."

THOUGH THE WORD "revolution" may be used in both senses, it nevertheless seems to be the case that traditional discussions of the causes and prevention of revolution, theories of revolutionary strategy and tactics, and the great issue of the right of rebellion all seem to contemplate the resort to, or at least the threat of, force to gain an end. This also seems to be implied in the popular conception of the difference between revolution and evolution.

The contrast between revolution and evolution may explain why the note of violence, disorder, or disruption colors the idea of revolution. The word "evolution" usually signifies change which is gradual and which tends in one direction rather than another, that direction being for the most part toward a progressive development of changes already accomplished. Revolution is abrupt. Revolutions can occur in either direction, against the tide as well as with it. As action and reaction can be equal and opposite in physical motion, so in social change revolution and counter-revolution can aim in opposite directions. In either case, whether revolution reverses the direction of change or precipitates a radical transformation toward which things are moving too slowly, revolution seems to involve *overthrowing* the established order rather than *developing* its latent tendencies.

It is in this sense that the revolutionist is a radical. He may also be a reactionary in the sense that the radical change he is willing to use force to achieve, is a return to some earlier condition rather than one which, in the judgment of his opponents, is in the line of progress or evolution. But whether reactionary or progressive the revolutionist is never conservative. If the established order does not submit readily to the radical change which a revolutionary person or party seeks, or if it resists, it must be forced to yield. The revolutionist can be reluctant to use force, but he can never forswear it entirely.

This seems to be the sense in which Marx and Engels conceive the program of the *Communist Manifesto* as a revolutionary program. Their conception of a revolutionary class or party is not, however, limited to the proletariat in their struggle against the bourgeoisie. They apply it to the bourgeoisie, not in the contemporary world when the established order of capitalism makes the bourgeoisie conservative or reactionary, but in the 18th century when the bourgeoisie overthrew the landed aristocracy.

"The bourgeoisie," they write, "historically has played a most revolutionary part. . . . The French revolution, for example, abolished feudal property in favor of bourgeois property." And again: "When Christian ideas succumbed in the 18th century to the rationalist ideas, feudal society fought its death-battle with the then revolutionary bourgeoisie." That the French Revolution represents the struggle not between the propertied and the propertyless classes, but between two propertied classes—the bourgeoisie and the aristocrats—seems evident to Marx in the fact that "during the very first storms of the revolution, the French Bourgeoisie dared to take away from the workers the right of association just acquired."

No less than the *Communist Manifesto*, the American Declaration of Independence is a revolutionary document. Its signers are prepared to use force to overthrow the established order which, in their view, has worked grievous iniquities and injustices upon the colonies. But in the Marxist view the rebellion of the colonists, unlike the French Revolution, is political rather than economic, even if it has economic as well as political motivations. This distinction between economic and political revolution seems to be peculiarly modern.

It is not that the ancients—Thucydides, Plato, and Aristotle, for example—fail to recognize the "class war," which is paramount for Marx. They observe (as is indicated in the chapter on Oligarchy) the struggle between the rich and the poor for control of the state. They know that the opponents, in the frequent and violent revolutions which disturbed the Greek city-states, are the oligarchs and the democrats—the men of great property and the men of little or none.

The revolt of the Helots in Sparta is the exceptional case of a rebellion of slaves against their masters. For the most part, the struggle is between free men belonging to different economic classes. The oligarchical and democratic revolutions which these classes in society foment are political in the sense of seeking to change the constitution rather than the economic system itself, even though the constitutional changes may have economic as well as political effects. "In the opinion of some," Aristotle reports, "the regulation of property is the chief point of all, that being the question upon which all revolutions turn."

Aristotle is willing to admit that "the equalization of property" may "prevent the citizens from quarrelling," but he does not think that economic injustice is the only cause of revolution, or economic justice its absolute cure. "The avarice of mankind," he writes, "is insatiable; at one time two obols was pay enough; but now, when this sum has become customary, men always want more and more without end; for it is of the nature of desire not to be satisfied, and most men live only for the gratification of it. The beginning of reform," in his opinion, "is not so much to equalize property as to train the nobler sorts of natures not to desire more, and to prevent the lower from getting more; that is to say, they must be kept down, but not ill-treated." Such a reform would hardly cure the evil of chattel slavery. That requires a revolution which effects the equalization of political status, not the equalization of property.

If a rebellion of slaves in the ancient world had succeeded in abolishing the institution of slavery, it would have been, in the modern view, an economic as well as a political revolution, for it would have radically altered the mode of production. It is in this sense that what Adam Smith describes as the change from an agrarian to a manufacturing economy, is strictly an economic revolution, though it is Marx, not Smith, who gives currency to the word "revolution" as used in this sense. It is exemplified in our common understanding of the phrase "the industrial revolution" which refers to the radical change in an economy based on manufactures, when mass production by machines in factories replaces the system of production by workers using their own tools in their own homes.

"In manufacture," writes Marx, "the revolution in the mode of production begins with labor-power; in modern industry it begins with the instruments of labor. Our first inquiry then is, how the instruments of labor are converted from tools into machines, or what is the difference between a machine and the implements of a handicraft?" But for Marx the meaning of economic revolution is not limited to radical changes in the physical conditions of production. Such changes necessarily involve equally radical changes in the social relationships of economic classes, and in their possession of political power. In the *Manifesto*, "the modern bourgeoisie" is said to be "itself the product of a long course of development, of a series of revolutions in the modes of production and exchange." The bourgeoisie, in turn, "cannot exist without constantly revolutionizing the instruments of production, and thereby the relations of production, and with them the whole relations of society."

According to Marx and Engels, "each step in the development of the bourgeoisie was accompanied by a corresponding political advance of that class. An oppressed class under the sway of the feudal nobility, an armed and self-governing association in the mediaeval commune . . . afterwards in the period of manufacture proper, serving either the semi-feudal or the absolute monarchy as a counterpoise against the nobility . . . the bourgeoisie has at last, since the establishment of Modern Industry and of the world-market, conquered for itself in the modern representative State, exclusive political sway."

ON THE QUESTION whether economic revolutions, in their social and political aspects, require violence, the writers of the *Manifesto* seem to be unambiguous—at least so far as the communist program is concerned. Since "the Communist revolution is the most radical rupture with traditional property-relations," and "involves the most radical rupture with traditional ideas," it can hardly be expected to occur without open warfare, no less violent than the earlier struggle of the bourgeoisie against the aristocrats. Standing "face to face with the bourgeoisie today, the proletariat alone is a really revolutionary class," in whose development Marx and Engels see the transition from a "more or less veiled civil war, raging within existing society, up to the point where that war breaks out into open revolution, and where the violent overthrow of the bourgeoisie lays the foundation for the sway of the proletariat."

It is precisely on the use of force that the *Manifesto* distinguishes between communism and socialism, especially the "utopian" variety of the latter. The Socialists "reject all political, and especially all revolutionary action; they wish to attain their ends by peaceful means, and endeavor by small experiments, necessarily doomed to failure, and by the force of example, to pave the way for the new social Gospel. . . . They, therefore, endeavor, and that consistently, to deaden the class struggle and to reconcile the class antagonisms." Communist strategy, on the contrary, everywhere supports "every revolutionary movement against the existing social and political order of things. . . . The Communists disdain to conceal their views and aims. They openly declare that their ends can be attained only by the forcible overthrow of all existing social conditions."

Though fundamentally economic, the communist revolution cannot help having political effects. "Political power," according to Marx and Engels, "is merely the organized power of one class for oppressing another." This applies to the proletariat's conquest of power. Yet they also seem to think that the dictatorship of the proletariat is only a temporary phase in the communist revolution. "If the proletariat during its contest with the bourgeoisie is compelled, by the force of circumstances, to organize itself as a class; if, by means of a revolution, it makes itself the ruling class, and, as such, sweeps away by force the old conditions of production, then it will, along with these conditions, have swept away the conditions for the existence of class antagonisms, and of classes generally, and will thereby have abolished its own supremacy as a class." In aiming at the economically classless society, with the consequent transformation of the state, the communist program seems to conceive its revolution as abolishing the possibility of or need for any further revolutions, peaceful or violent, economic or political.

In addition to the issues raised by the economic theory and history which underlie revolutionary communism, there is the debatable question whether an economically classless society means the withering away of the state, or at least such changes in political institutions that revolution would cease to be possible or necessary. Even a hypothetical consideration of this question seems to call for attention to the various ways in which political revolutions take place. With the advent of the "classless society," no opportunity would remain, at least in theory, for the type of revolution in which one ruling class replaces another. But in such a society it is still conceivable that the equivalent of a palace revolution might substitute one ruling individual for another—by the old-fashioned methods of assassination or usurpation.

For Aristotle, however, all revolutions which produce a change from one form of government to another also involve the replacement of one ruling class by another. He distinguishes between such revolutions as affect the constitution, "when men seek to change from an existing form into some other, for example, from democracy into oligarchy, or from oligarchy into democracy," and those revolutions which do not affect the constitution, when men, "without disturbing the form of government, whether oligarchy or monarchy or any other, try to get the administration into their own hands." To these two types of revolution Aristotle adds a third, which "may be directed against only a portion of the constitution, *e.g.*, the establishment or overthrow of a particular office; as at Sparta, it is said that Lysander attempted to overthrow the monarchy, and king Pausanias, the ephoralty."

Conceivably, any of these political changes might be accomplished without violence. In modern constitutional states, the basic principle of constitutions can be changed from oligarchy to democracy by amendments or legal reforms which extend the franchise. The structure of the government, as to its offices or their organization, can be changed by some form of peaceful plebiscite. As the Federalists point out, the polls provide a "natural cure for an ill-administration in a popular or representative constitution," namely, a change of men. But such changes of government in the ancient city-states, even when constitutional, appear to Aristotle to be revolutionary in the double sense of involving violence, or the threat of it, and of being radical transformations of the polity. What is true of constitutional changes in ancient republics is also true of monarchies and tyrannies, both ancient and modern.

When absolute power is concentrated in the hands of one man, his subjects are necessarily without juridical means for redressing their grievances by changing the occupant of the throne, much less for abolishing the monarchy entirely in favor of self-government. Machiavelli's advice to the prince on safeguarding his power against usurping rivals or rebellious subjects, seems to be written against the background of force and fraud as the normal methods of changing rulers or modes of rule. They are the very same methods which the prince in power must employ to maintain his position.

"There are two ways of contesting," Machiavelli writes, "the one by law, the other by force; the first method is proper to men, the second to beasts; but because the first is frequently not sufficient, it is necessary to have recourse to the second. Therefore it is necessary for a prince to understand how to avail himself of the beast and the man. . . . Being compelled knowingly to adopt the beast, [a prince] ought to choose the fox and the lion; because the lion cannot defend himself against snares and the fox cannot defend himself against wolves." It follows, according to Machiavelli, that the prince seldom can be, though he should always try to *appear* to be, "merciful, faithful, humane, religious, upright. . . . A prince, especially a new one, cannot observe all those things for which men are esteemed, being often forced, in order to maintain the state, to act contrary to fidelity, friendship, humanity, and religion."

The stories of oriental despotism told by Herodotus, the account of the Caesars given by Tacitus and Gibbon, the chronicle of the English monarchy in the historical plays of Shakespeare, all seem to indicate that crowns seldom change heads without bloodshed. Machiavelli's rules for the prince do not greatly enlarge upon Aristotle's description of "the arts by which the tyrant preserves his power." Even when Aristotle proposes, as an alternative method, that the tyrant can try to be benevolent, he adds the Machiavellian suggestion that the tyrant should at least "appear to act" like a good king.

The tyrant, Aristotle writes, "should lop off those who are too high. He must put to death men of spirit. . . . He must be on his guard against anything which is likely to inspire either courage or confidence among his subjects. He must prohibit literary assemblies or other meetings for discussion, and he must take every means to prevent people from knowing one another." After enumerating many similar practices which he calls "Persian and barbaric arts," Aristotle concludes that "there is no wickedness too great for the tyrant" if he is to maintain himself in power.

These matters are more fully discussed in the chapter on TYRANNY. In our present consideration of the types of revolution, we must note one other political change which usually involves the widespread turbulence of civil war. That is the rebellion of subject peoples against their imperial masters. Unlike civil uprisings, which seek to overthrow governments or effect a change in the ruling classes or persons, these wars of rebellion seek to liberate one people from another or to establish the independence of colonies at the expense of empire.

Still another type of insurrection aims at the dissolution of the state itself. What Rousseau deals with in theory as the degeneration of the state into anarchy by the repudiation of the social contract, calls to mind no historic examples; but the few historic instances of "wars of secession" certainly illustrate the point. They aim to dissolve a federal state by severing ties of union which have something like a contractual character.

The distinction between these types of civil war may be clear in theory, yet difficult to apply to historic cases. Which sort of insurrection—a rebellion of colonies or a secession of states—does the Declaration of Independence announce? A theory current among American political writers in 1775 suggests that the thirteen colonies claimed the status of self-governing dominions in a confederacy united under the British crown. On this theory, does the principle stated in the Declaration—that it is sometimes "necessary for one people to dissolve the political bands which have connected them with another, and to assume among the powers of the earth the separate and equal station to which the laws of nature and of nature's God entitle them"—cover the secession of the Southern states from the American union, as well as the revolt of the American states from Great Britain, or the British Commonwealth of nations? Questions of fact are involved, of course, in any comparison of the Revolutionary War of 1776 and the war between the states in 1861; but the question of principle turns on the whole issue of whether revolution is a matter of might or right.

THE RIGHT OF REVOLUTION does not seem to be a central consideration in ancient political theory. The ancient discussion of revolutions appears to be more concerned with their causes, their methods, and their prevention. This does not mean that the ancients treat revolutions entirely as contests for power. On the contrary, Aristotle declares that "the universal and chief cause of the revolutionary impulse" is "the desire of equality, when men think that they are equal to others who have more than themselves; or, again, the desire of inequality and superiority, when conceiving themselves to be superior they think that they have not more but the same or less than their inferiors—pretensions which may or may not be just."

Nevertheless, Aristotle's elaborate treatise on revolution in the fifth book of his *Politics* deals alike with revolutions that spring from real and from fancied injustices. The object of his inquiry seems to be "what modes of destruction apply to particular states, and out of what and into what they mostly change; also what are the modes of preservation in states generally, or in a particular state, and by what means each state may be best preserved"—*not* how revolution can be justified or why rebellion is the crime of treason or the folly of anarchy. Such questions seem to come to the foreground in modern political theory, though they also have a certain prominence in mediaeval teaching.

Aquinas, for example, holds that sedition is "a special kind of sin" because it is "opposed to a special kind of good, namely, the unity and peace of a people." He qualifies this, however, in the case of an uprising against tyranny, even if it involves civil strife. Since in his view "a tyrannical government is not just, because it is directed, not to the common good but to the private good of the ruler . . . there is no sedition in disturbing a government of this kind, unless indeed the tyrant's rule be disturbed so inordinately that his subjects suffer greater harm from the consequent disturbance than from the tyrant's government. Indeed," Aquinas writes, "it is the tyrant rather who is guilty of sedition, since he encourages discord and sedition among his subjects, that he may lord over them more securely."

Holding that "the end of government is the good of mankind," Locke asks, in a similar vein, which is better: "that the people should be always exposed to the boundless will of tyranny, or that the rulers should be sometimes liable to be opposed when they grow exorbitant in the use of their power, and employ it for the destruction and not the preservation of the property of their people"? Since "force is to be opposed to nothing but unjust and unlawful force," Locke argues that a king may be resisted when he exceeds his authority or prerogative and uses his power unlawfully. Since such a king "has dethroned himself, and put himself in a state of war with his people, what shall hinder them from prosecuting him who is no king, as they would any other man who has put himself into a state of war with them?"

The right to resist a tyrant, or a king turned despot, may lead to regicide, but this seems no different to Locke from the punishment of any other criminal. "He who may resist must be allowed to strike"; and furthermore, Locke continues, "he has a right, when he prevails, to punish the offender, both for the breach of the peace, and all the evils that followed upon it." Rousseau is even less hesitant to condone tyrannicide. "The contract of government is so completely dissolved by despotism," writes Rousseau, "that the despot is master only so long as he remains the strongest; as soon as he can be expelled, he has no right to complain of violence. The popular insurrection that ends in the death or deposition of a Sultan is as lawful an act as those by which he disposed, the day before, of the life and fortunes of his subjects. As he was maintained by force alone, it is force alone that overthrows him."

Those who say that "it may occasion civil wars or intestine broils, to tell the people they are absolved from obedience when illegal attempts are made upon their liberties or properties . . . may as well say upon the same ground," in Locke's opinion, "that honest men may not oppose robbers and pirates because this may occasion disorder or bloodshed." Nor does Locke think that the right to resist injustice means that governments will be overthrown "upon every little mismanagement in public affairs. Great mistakes in the ruling part," he writes, "many wrong and inconvenient laws, and all the slips of human frailty will be borne by the people without mutiny or murmur. But if a long train of abuses, prevarications, and artifices, all tending the same way, make the design visible to the people . . . it is not to be wondered that they should then rouse themselves and endeavor to put the rule into such hands which may secure to them the ends for which government was at first erected."

Hence, to those who say that his revolutionary principle "lays a perpetual foundation for disorder," Locke replies that it will never operate until "the inconvenience is so great that the majority feel it, and are weary of it, and find it necessary to have it amended." Rebellions will occur only when the majority feel that "their laws, and with them their estates, liberties, and lives are in danger, and perhaps their religion too," and so will exercise their natural right to resist, with force if necessary, the illegal force used against them. But strictly, it is not the people who rebel; rather it is they who put down the sedition of the tyrant.

What Locke states as a right of resistance, the Declaration of Independence seems to put more positively as a right of rebellion, apparently deducing it from other natural rights—of life, liberty, and the pursuit of happiness. It is to secure these rights that "governments are instituted among men," so that "whenever any form of government becomes destructive of these ends, it is the right of the people to alter or to abolish it and to institute a new government." The Declaration admits that "governments long established should not be changed for light and transient causes"; but when a people suffer "a long train of abuses and usurpations . . . it is their right, it is their duty, to throw off such government, and to provide new guards for their security."

AGAINST SUCH REVOLUTIONARY sentiments or principles Hobbes, Kant, and Hegel seem to take a stand, though in each case they place some qualification on their denial of a right of resistance or rebellion. Hobbes, for example, denies the right of men to change their form of government, or of subjects to resist their Sovereign, *except for the sake of self-preservation*. When men covenant to form a commonwealth, they are bound, Hobbes says, to uphold the actions and judgments of the Sovereign they have created; they "cannot lawfully make a new covenant amongst themselves, to be obedient to any other . . . without his permission. . . . They that are subjects to a monarch, cannot without his leave cast off monarchy, and return to the confusion of a disunited multitude."

Furthermore, "because every subject is by this institution, author of all the actions and judgments of the Sovereign instituted, it follows," according to Hobbes," that whatsoever he doeth, it can be no injury to any of his subjects; nor ought he to be by any of them accused of injustice." Yet "every subject has liberty in all those things, the right whereof cannot by covenant be transferred," such as the right of a man to defend his own body, "to resist those that assault him," or to have access to "food, air, medicine, or any other thing without which he cannot live."

Kant disallows rebellion as a matter of right, unless resistance is required to fulfill a moral duty outside the sphere of public right. " 'Obey the authority which has power over you' (in everything which is not opposed to morality) is a Categorical Imperative." Hence, though a juridical constitution "may be vitiated by great defects and coarse errors, it is nevertheless absolutely unallowable and punishable to resist it."

Since, in his view, public right is founded on the institution of "a *sovereign* will, uniting all particular wills by one law," Kant argues that "to allow a right of resistance to this sovereignty, and to limit its power, is a contradiction." It should be remembered also that for Kant the only legitimate form of government is a republic, resting on the foundation of popular sovereignty. Kant is not considering resistance to tyrannical or despotic power which lacks all juridical authority.

A similar qualification appears in Hegel's distinction between the rebellion of a conquered people and revolution in a well-organized state. Only the latter action is a crime, for only the latter situation corresponds to the Idea of the state—fully realized, for Hegel, only in a constitutional monarchy, never in a despotism or tyranny. "A rebellion in a province conquered by war," he says, "is a different thing from a rising in a well-organized state. It is not against their prince that the conquered are in rebellion, and they are committing no crime against the state, because their connexion with their master is not a connexion within the Idea, or one within the inner necessity of the constitution. In such a case, there is only a contract, no political tie."

With such qualifications on their position, those who disfavor revolution or deny its basis in right may not be completely opposed to those who apparently think rebellions can be justified. There may be qualifications on the other side too. Aquinas, for example, justifies sedition, not against any government or ruler, but only against tyranny. The signers of the Declaration of Independence speak of a right to alter or abolish "any form of government," but the writers of the Federalist papers do not seem equally willing to acknowledge a right to overthrow the Constitution of the United States.

OUTLINE OF TOPICS

1. The nature of revolution

   1*a*. The issue concerning violent and peaceful means for accomplishing social, political, or economic change

   1*b*. The definition of treason or sedition: the revolutionist as a treasonable conspirator

   1*c*. Revolution and counter-revolution: civil strife distinguished from war between states

2. The nature of political revolutions

   2*a*. Change in the form of government or constitution

   2*b*. Change in the persons holding power: deposition, assassination, usurpation

   2*c*. Change in the extent of the state or empire: dissolution, secession, liberation, federation

3. The process of political revolution

   3*a*. The aims of political revolution: the seizure of power; the attainment of liberty, justice, equality

   3*b*. Ways of retaining power and combatting revolution

   3*c*. The causes and effects of revolution under different forms of government

      (1) Revolution in monarchies

      (2) Revolutions in republics: aristocracies, oligarchies, and democracies

      (3) Rebellion against tyranny and despotism

4. The nature of economic revolutions

   4*a*. Change in the condition of the oppressed or exploited: the emancipation of slaves, serfs, proletariat

   4*b*. Change in the economic order: modification or overthrow of a system of production and distribution

5. The strategy of economic revolution

   5*a*. Revolution as an expression of the class struggle: rich and poor, nobles and commons, owners and workers

   5*b*. The organization of a revolutionary class: the bourgeoisie and the proletariat as revolutionary classes in relation to different economic systems

   5*c*. The classless society as the goal of economic revolution: the transformation of the state

6. The justice of revolution

   6*a*. The right of rebellion: the circumstances justifying civil disobedience or violent insurrection

   6*b*. The right to abrogate the social contract or to secede from a federation

7. Empire and revolution: the justification of colonial rebellion and the defense of imperialism

REFERENCES

References are listed by volume number (in bold type), author's name, and page number. Bible references are to book, chapter, and verse of the Authorized King James version of the Bible. The abbreviation "esp" calls the reader's attention to one or more especially relevant parts of a whole reference; "passim" signifies that the topic is discussed intermittently rather than continuously in the work or passage cited. Where the work as a whole is relevant to the topic, the page numbers refer to the entire work. For general guidance in the use of *The Great Ideas,* consult the Preface.

1. The nature of revolution

1*a*. The issue concerning violent and peaceful means for accomplishing social, political, or economic change

6 THUCYDIDES, 436–438
7 PLATO, 200–212
9 ARISTOTLE, 504, 506
14 PLUTARCH, 387–388, 660–661
20 AQUINAS, 236–237
21 DANTE, 41–43
23 MACHIAVELLI, 9
23 HOBBES, 154
25 MONTAIGNE, 318–319, 462–465
31 DESCARTES, 45–46
35 LOCKE, 72–73
38 ROUSSEAU, 361–362
40 GIBBON, 292
42 KANT, 439–441
43 DECLARATION OF INDEPENDENCE, 3
43 FEDERALIST, 29, 78–79
43 MILL, 344
46 HEGEL, 147, 364
50 MARX-ENGELS, 432–434
51 TOLSTOY, 244–245

1*b*. The definition of treason or sedition: the revolutionist as a treasonable conspirator

6 HERODOTUS, 186
6 THUCYDIDES, 381–384, 532–534, 574–576, 579–581
14 PLUTARCH, 155–174, 193–195, 708–713, 802–824
20 AQUINAS, 583–584
23 HOBBES, 121–122
26 SHAKESPEARE, 39–40, 59, 342–343, 466, 470, 537, 540–541, 568–596
35 LOCKE, 77–78
36 SWIFT, 33–38, 114–115
38 MONTAIGNE, 88–90
38 ROUSSEAU, 398
40 GIBBON, 251, 525–526
41 GIBBON, 587–588
42 KANT, 439–441
43 CONSTITUTION OF THE U.S., 15–16
43 FEDERALIST, 208
47 GOETHE, 119–120, 249–250
51 TOLSTOY, 338, 505–511, 668–669

1*c*. Revolution and counter-revolution: civil strife distinguished from war between states

6 HERODOTUS, 102–107, 172–174
6 THUCYDIDES, 434–438, 577, 579–583
7 PLATO, 641–643
9 ARISTOTLE, 505–506, 558–561, 566–572
14 PLUTARCH, 875
18 AUGUSTINE, 515
23 MACHIAVELLI, 26
24 RABELAIS, 54
25 MONTAIGNE, 504–506
26 SHAKESPEARE, 11–16, 33–68, 69–104, 105–148, 434–435
35 LOCKE, 76–81
41 GIBBON, 594–585
43 DECLARATION OF INDEPENDENCE, 1–3
43 FEDERALIST, 66–68, 96–98, 99–101
46 HEGEL, 297
50 MARX-ENGELS, 424

2. The nature of political revolutions

2*a*. Change in the form of government or constitution

OLD TESTAMENT: *I Samuel*, 8
6 HERODOTUS, 14, 107–108
6 THUCYDIDES, 391, 579–583, 585–586, 587–589, 590
7 PLATO, 403–404, 408–409
9 ARISTOTLE, 470, 502–503, 504, 506, 518–519, 553–572
14 PLUTARCH, 32–35, 68–71, 195–213, 354–368, 499–538, 577–604, 620–648, 657–663, 781–802
23 MACHIAVELLI, 36–37
23 HOBBES, 150–151
25 MONTAIGNE, 462–465
35 LOCKE, 59, 73–81
38 MONTESQUIEU, 51–53, 76–78
38 ROUSSEAU, 418–420
40 GIBBON, 24–28, 50–51, 153–156, 622–623
41 GIBBON, 73–74, 202, 217–219, 561–565, 574–582
42 KANT, 438–441, 450–452
43 DECLARATION OF INDEPENDENCE, 1
43 FEDERALIST, 62, 143–144, 159–162
43 MILL, 327–332, 350–353

46 Hegel, 145, 203–206, 294–295, 300–301, 355–357
51 Tolstoy, 238–243

2*b*. Change in the persons holding power: deposition, assassination, usurpation

Old Testament: *Judges,* 9 / *II Samuel,* 15–18 / *I Kings,* 16:8–20 / *II Kings,* 8:7–15; 9:1–10:11; 11:1–16 / *II Chronicles,* 23
5 Aeschylus, 42
5 Aristophanes, 615–628
6 Herodotus, 2–3, 12–13, 84–86, 120, 171–172, 182
6 Thucydides, 523–524
9 Aristotle, 513–514
14 Plutarch, 77–81, 344–354, 369–374, 382–387, 440–445, 460–470, 499–538, 577–604, 708–713, 749–755, 802–824, 859–876
15 Tacitus, 102–103, 112–113, 169–176, 189–266
18 Augustine, 176–178
23 Machiavelli, 12–14
23 Hobbes, 152
26 Shakespeare, 13–14, 35–36, 43–44, 47–51, 69–104, 105–148, 320–351, 434–466, 467–502, 568–596
27 Shakespeare, 284–310, 534
35 Locke, 70–71
38 Rousseau, 419, 424, 432–433, 438
40 Gibbon, 33–49, 56–61, 69–79, 111–113, 114–115, 159–178, 386–387, 436–438, 515–518
41 Gibbon, 113–117, 161–194 passim, esp 166–167, 472–476
42 Kant, 440–441
43 Federalist, 78–79, 93–94, 96–98, 108–109, 146, 157

2*c*. Change in the extent of the state or empire: dissolution, secession, liberation, federation

Old Testament: *Judges,* 3:14–4:24; 6; 10:1–11:33; 13:1–5,24–25; 14–16 / *II Chronicles,* 10–11 / *Jeremiah,* 41
Apocrypha: *I Maccabees,* 1–9 passim / *II Maccabees,* 6–13 passim
6 Herodotus, 121–123, 160–185 passim, 186–191
6 Thucydides, 349–593
14 Plutarch, 20–28, 480–499
15 Tacitus, 18–20, 54–56, 76–77, 116–117, 149–151, 269–277, 283–292, 297–302
23 Hobbes, 152–153
35 Locke, 51–52, 73–74
38 Rousseau, 403–404
40 Gibbon, 144–146, 521
41 Gibbon, 218–219, 439–451, 577
43 Declaration of Independence, 1–3
43 Articles of Confederation, 5–9
43 Federalist, 62–68
43 Mill, 428–430

3. The process of political revolution

3*a*. The aims of political revolution: the seizure of power; the attainment of liberty, justice, equality

5 Aristophanes, 588–591, 617
6 Herodotus, 29–30
7 Plato, 813–814
9 Aristotle, 461–463, 468–469, 502–506, 518–519
14 Plutarch, 195–213, 233–237, 648–656, 657–663, 671–689, 781–824
15 Tacitus, 6–7, 10–11, 82–83, 89, 104, 149, 191, 195, 198–199, 215–216, 233–235, 269–270, 290
23 Hobbes, 114–115
23 Machiavelli, 36–37
26 Shakespeare, 568–596
35 Locke, 18–21, 63–64
38 Rousseau, 402
40 Gibbon, 29, 35, 44–47, 48–49, 73
41 Gibbon, 574–575
43 Declaration of Independence, 1–3
43 Federalist, 147–148
43 Mill, 267–268
46 Hegel, 299–301
51 Tolstoy, 9–10, 680–684
52 Dostoevsky, 131, 133–134

3*b*. Ways of retaining power and combatting revolution

Old Testament: *Exodus,* 1:7–22
Apocrypha: *I Maccabees,* 1:41–64; 10:22–46
5 Aristophanes, 515–516
6 Herodotus, 21, 35–36, 123, 243
6 Thucydides, 425–428
7 Plato, 806–807, 811–813
9 Aristotle, 461–463, 482–483, 509–512, 515–518, 523–524
14 Plutarch, 27–28, 119–121, 124–130, 176–184, 482–484, 648–656, 681–689, 708–713, 809–811
15 Tacitus, 6–15, 21–22, 32–33, 68–69, 155–156, 170–176, 196–198, 200–201, 209–210, 280–281
23 Machiavelli, 3–5, 8, 9–10, 14–16, 22–31
24 Rabelais, 131–133
25 Montaigne, 51–55, 324–326
26 Shakespeare, 96–97, 340
29 Cervantes, 40
30 Bacon, 78
35 Locke, 19, 75
36 Swift, 102–103
38 Rousseau, 372–377, 432–433
40 Gibbon, 14–18, 42–43, 501–503, 522–523, 525–526
43 Constitution of the U.S., 16
43 Federalist, 49–51 passim, 90–91, 141–142, 152–153, 174
43 Mill, 366, 425–426
46 Hegel, 263, 276–277
51 Tolstoy, 668–669

3c. The causes and effects of revolution under different forms of government

6 THUCYDIDES, 427–428
7 PLATO, 401–416, 801
9 ARISTOTLE, 462, 502–519
15 TACITUS, 224–225, 261–262
23 HOBBES, 102–104, 116, 121–122, 148–153, 240
27 SHAKESPEARE, 109
30 BACON, 78
38 MONTESQUIEU, 51–54
38 ROUSSEAU, 404, 418–420
39 SMITH, 269–271, 308
40 GIBBON, 436
41 GIBBON, 559–560
43 DECLARATION OF INDEPENDENCE, 1–3
43 MILL, 321
46 HEGEL, 364
50 MARX-ENGELS, 423–425

3c(1) Revolution in monarchies

6 HERODOTUS, 84, 107–108, 138
7 PLATO, 667–672
9 ARISTOTLE, 512–516
14 PLUTARCH, 482–485
15 TACITUS, 190–191, 193–194, 195–198, 209–212
23 MACHIAVELLI, 7–8, 14–16
23 HOBBES, 150–151, 153–156
26 SHAKESPEARE, 1–32, 33–68, 69–104, 105–148, 459–460, 461–462, 487–489
35 LOCKE, 71–81
38 MONTESQUIEU, 53–54, 56–57, 212
40 GIBBON, 68–69
44 BOSWELL, 120
51 TOLSTOY, 238–243, 260–262

3c(2) Revolutions in republics: aristocracies, oligarchies, and democracies

6 THUCYDIDES, 434–438, 459, 463–465, 466–469, 482–483, 502–504, 519–520, 533, 574–590
7 PLATO, 402–413, 744
9 ARISTOTLE, 470, 482–483, 492, 504, 505–512, 523–524, 553–572
14 PLUTARCH, 13–14, 35, 47–48, 61–64, 68–70, 75–76, 117–121, 176–184, 361–368, 444–445, 588–589, 648–656, 657–663, 671–689
15 TACITUS, 1–2
38 MONTESQUIEU, 6–7, 10–11, 21–22, 23–25, 51–53, 64, 91–92, 114–115
38 ROUSSEAU, 411
43 FEDERALIST, 47–53, 70–78, 90–91, 95, 99–101, 141–142, 181–182, 184, 194–195
43 MILL, 329–330, 366–367
46 HEGEL, 278–279, 355–357
50 MARX-ENGELS, 429–430, 432

3c(3) Rebellion against tyranny and despotism

OLD TESTAMENT: *I Kings,* 12:1–25 / *II Chronicles,* 10
APOCRYPHA: *I Maccabees,* 1:1–2:44 / *II Maccabees,* 6:1–11; 8:1–4
6 HERODOTUS, 170–172, 178–180
6 THUCYDIDES, 523–524
7 PLATO, 411–420
9 ARISTOTLE, 512–518, 558–561
15 TACITUS, 1–4, 169–176, 202–205, 234–235
23 HOBBES, 273
26 SHAKESPEARE, 146, 568–596
27 SHAKESPEARE, 303–304
38 MONTESQUIEU, 25–26, 28–29, 54
38 ROUSSEAU, 361–362
40 GIBBON, 29–31, 42–44, 56–59, 63–54, 68, 71–76, 126–127, 652–655
41 GIBBON, 113–115, 166–167, 464–466
43 DECLARATION OF INDEPENDENCE, 1–3
43 MILL, 274, 343–344

4. The nature of economic revolutions

4a. Change in the condition of the oppressed or exploited: the emancipation of slaves, serfs, proletariat

OLD TESTAMENT: *Exodus,* 1–14 / *Jeremiah,* 34:8–17
6 THUCYDIDES, 467
9 ARISTOTLE, 465
14 PLUTARCH, 68–70, 657–689
15 TACITUS, 70, 132
27 SHAKESPEARE, 351–353
38 MONTESQUIEU, 112–113
39 SMITH, 165–175
40 GIBBON, 16–17, 144
41 GIBBON, 82
43 CONSTITUTION OF THE U.S., 18
43 FEDERALIST, 137
43 MILL, 332, 339–340
46 HEGEL, 295–296
50 MARX, 7, 131–146, 231–248, 364–368
50 MARX-ENGELS, 415–417, 422–425
51 TOLSTOY, 211–213, 216
52 DOSTOEVSKY, 165
54 FREUD, 883–884

4b. Change in the economic order: modification or overthrow of a system of production and distribution

5 ARISTOPHANES, 615–628, 629–642
6 THUCYDIDES, 350–351
7 PLATO, 316–319, 405–408
9 ARISTOTLE, 458–463
14 PLUTARCH, 36
36 SWIFT, 104–106
39 SMITH, 27–37, 165–175
41 GIBBON, 452–453
43 FEDERALIST, 135
46 HEGEL, 335–336
50 MARX, 80–81, 153, 157–188, 205–250, 290, 308–311, 351, 354–378
50 MARX-ENGELS, 416, 419–422, 425–427, 428–429
54 FREUD, 787–788

5. The strategy of economic revolution

50 Marx-Engels, 415–416, 417, 425, 428–429, 434

5*a*. Revolution as an expression of the class struggle: rich and poor, nobles and commons, owners and workers

6 Herodotus, 202–203, 243
6 Thucydides, 434–438, 463–465, 482–483, 524–525, 564–593
7 Plato, 343
9 Aristotle, 461–463, 505–506, 508, 519, 553, 554–555
14 Plutarch, 68–70, 124–130, 176–184, 648–656, 657–663, 671–689, 708–713
26 Shakespeare, 57–59
27 Shakespeare, 351
41 Gibbon, 574–582
46 Hegel, 275–276
50 Marx, 8–9, 131–146, 209–210, 294–295
50 Marx-Engels, 415–434
51 Tolstoy, 410–421

5*b*. The organization of a revolutionary class: the bourgeoisie and the proletariat as revolutionary classes in relation to different economic systems

50 Marx, 9, 354–378
50 Marx-Engels, 416, 419–425

5*c*. The classless society as the goal of economic revolution: the transformation of the state

50 Marx, 9
50 Marx-Engels, 416, 429

6. The justice of revolution

6*a*. The right of rebellion: the circumstances justifying civil disobedience or violent insurrection

5 Sophocles, 131–142
5 Aristophanes, 583–599
6 Herodotus, 103–107
7 Plato, 216–219
14 Plutarch, 678
15 Tacitus, 6–7, 10–11, 174, 198–199, 234, 290
20 Aquinas, 584
23 Hobbes, 101–102, 104, 115–116
25 Montaigne, 47–51,
26 Shakespeare, 459–460, 487–489, 574–576, 581
27 Shakespeare, 303–306
35 Locke, 16–17, 60–61, 64, 71–81
38 Rousseau, 361–362
40 Gibbon, 71–74
41 Gibbon, 166–167
43 Declaration of Independence, 1–3
43 Federalist, 47, 62, 92–94
44 Boswell, 120, 195
46 Hegel, 342
51 Tolstoy, 680–684

6*b*. The right to abrogate the social contract or to secede from a federation

6 Thucydides, 358–360, 418–419
7 Plato, 216–219
23 Hobbes, 91–92
35 Locke, 46–47 passim, 51–53 passim, 73–74, 81
38 Rousseau, 358–359, 374
43 Declaration of Independence, 1–3
43 Articles of Confederation, 9
43 Constitution of the U.S., 18–19
43 Federalist, 84–85, 143–144
46 Hegel, 146

7. Empire and revolution: the justification of colonial rebellion and the defense of imperialism

6 Herodotus, 23–31, 160–213 esp 191, 308–310
6 Thucydides, 358–360, 368, 402–404, 418–419, 425–428, 468–469, 504–507, 530–531, 564–593 passim
9 Aristotle, 504–506, 528–529, 538
14 Plutarch, 302–313 passim
15 Tacitus, 17, 149, 269–270, 290, 301
18 Augustine, 175–176, 190, 196–197
23 Hobbes, 110–111, 279–281
26 Shakespeare, 1–32, 33–68, 69–104, 532–567 esp 534–537, 567
27 Shakespeare, 463–464
35 Locke, 66, 69, 70
36 Swift, 182–183
38 Montesquieu, 62–63
38 Rousseau, 355
39 Smith, 255–279
40 Gibbon, 21–23, 144–146, 255, 420–422, 449–451, 477–491, 521–523
41 Gibbon, 51–54, 216–217, 285, 464–466
42 Kant, 413, 454–455, 456–457
43 Declaration of Independence, 1–3
43 Mill, 339–340,, 433–442
44 Boswell, 179
46 Hegel, 241–242, 324–326
50 Marx, 379–383 passim
51 Tolstoy, 466, 498–499

CROSS-REFERENCES

For: The consideration of revolution as civil war, *see* OPPOSITION 5c; WAR AND PEACE 2a–2c.

Other discussions relevant to the process of political change by violent or peaceful means, *see* CONSTITUTION 7–7a, 8–8b; GOVERNMENT 6; LAW 7d; LIBERTY 6b–6c; MONARCHY 5a–5b; PROGRESS 4a; SLAVERY 6c–6d; STATE 3g; TYRANNY 1c, 6–8.

The cause and prevention of revolution under different forms of government, *see* ARISTOCRACY 3; CONSTITUTION 7, 7b; DEMOCRACY 7a; OLIGARCHY 3a–3b; TYRANNY 8.

For: Other discussions relevant to economic change and to the strategy of economic revolution, *see* HISTORY 4a(2); LABOR 7c(3); LIBERTY 6b; OPPOSITION 5b; PROGRESS 3b; SLAVERY 3c; STATE 5d(2)–5e; WAR AND PEACE 2c; WEALTH 9h.

The general problem of the right of rebellion or the right of secession, *see* JUSTICE 10b; LAW 6c; LIBERTY 6b; TYRANNY 3; and for the issue concerning anarchy and the condemnation of the rebel as an anarchist, *see* GOVERNMENT 1a; LIBERTY 1b; TYRANNY 3.

ADDITIONAL READINGS

Listed below are works not included in *Great Books of the Western World*, but relevant to the idea and topics with which this chapter deals. These works are divided into two groups:

I. Works by authors represented in this collection.
II. Works by authors not represented in this collection.

For the date, place, and other facts concerning the publication of the works cited, consult the Bibliography of Additional Readings which follows the last chapter of *The Great Ideas*.

I.

MACHIAVELLI. *The Discourses*, BK III, CH 1–8
——. *Florentine History*
F. BACON. "Of Seditions and Troubles," "Of Factions," in *Essays*
HOBBES. *Philosophical Rudiments Concerning Government and Society*, CH 12
——. *The Elements of Law, Natural and Politic*, PART II, CH 8
HUME. *Of Passive Obedience*
ENGELS. *The Peasant War in Germany*
——. *Germany: Revolution and Counter-Revolution*
J. S. MILL. "A Few Observations on the French Revolution" in VOL I, "Vindication of the French Revolution of February 1848" in VOL II, *Dissertations and Discussions*
——. *Thoughts on Parliamentary Reform*
DOSTOEVSKY. *The House of the Dead*
——. *The Possessed*
MARX and ENGELS. *The German Ideology*, PART I
MARX. *The Eighteenth Brumaire of Louis Bonaparte*
——. *The Civil War in France*

II.

POLYBIUS. *Histories*, VOL I, BK VI
SALLUST. *The War with Catiline*
APPIAN. *The Civil Wars*
LUTHER. *Address to the German Nobility*
——. *Against the Robbing and Murdering Hordes of Peasants*
——. *Whether Soldiers, Too, Can Be Saved*
BODIN. *The Six Bookes of a Commonweale*, BK IV
SPENSER. *The Faerie Queene*, BK I
HOOKER. *Of the Laws of Ecclesiastical Polity*
DIGGES. *Unlawfulness of Subjects Taking up Arms Against Their Soveraigne*
BENTHAM. *A Fragment on Government*, CH I (22–29)
PAINE. *Common Sense*
GODWIN. *An Enquiry Concerning Political Justice*, BK IV, CH 2
BURKE. *Reflections on the Revolution in France*
——. *Letter to a Noble Lord*
BURKE. *Thoughts on the Prospect of a Regicide Peace*
BYRON. *Prometheus*
SHELLEY. *Prometheus Unbound*
T. CARLYLE. *The French Revolution*
THOREAU. *Civil Disobedience*
TOCQEVILLE. *L'ancien régime (Ancient Regime)*
PROUDHON. *General Idea of the Revolution in the Nineteenth Century*
——. *De la justice dans la révolution et dans l'église*
DICKENS. *A Tale of Two Cities*
COSTER. *The Glorious Adventures of Tyl Ulenspiegl*
BAKUNIN. *God and the State*
HUGO. *Ninety-Three*
A. TOYNBEE. *Lectures on the Industrial Revolution*
RITCHIE. *Natural Rights*, PART II, CH 11
SHAW. *The Revolutionist's Handbook*
ANDREYEV. *The Seven Who Were Hanged*
SOREL. *Reflexions on Violence*
LENIN. *Collected Works*, VOL XXI, *Toward the Seizure of Power*
——. *The State and Revolution*

T. E. LAWRENCE. *Seven Pillars of Wisdom*
L. P. EDWARDS. *The Natural History of Revolution*
BERDYAYEV. *Christianity and the Class War*
TROTSKY. *Literature and Revolution*
——. *The History of the Russian Revolution*
MARITAIN. *Theonas, Conversations of a Sage*, IX
——. "On the Purification of Means," in *Freedom in the Modern World*
GORKY. *Mother*
——. *Forty Years—the Life of Clim Samghin*, VOL II, *The Magnet*; VOL III, *Other Fires*; VOL IV, *The Specter*
MALRAUX. *Man's Fate*
——. *Man's Hope*
BRINTON. *The Anatomy of Revolution*
B. RUSSELL. *Power*, CH 7
E. WILSON. *To the Finland Station*
ORTEGA Y GASSET. *The Revolt of the Masses*
——. *Toward a Philosophy of History*
LASKI. *Reflections on the Revolution of Our Time*
DIWAKAR. *Satyagraha: The Power of Truth*

Chapter 81: RHETORIC

INTRODUCTION

RHETORIC is traditionally regarded as one of the liberal arts. When the liberal arts are counted as seven, and divided into the three and the four—the *trivium* and the *quadrivium*—rhetoric is grouped with grammar and logic, not with the mathematical arts of arithmetic and geometry, astronomy and music. The implication of this grouping seems to be that rhetoric, like grammar, has something to do with language or discourse; and that, like logic, it is concerned with thought, with reasoning or argument. But if grammar is the art of writing or speaking correctly, and if logic is the art of thinking correctly, it may be wondered what rhetoric can add to these other arts, either on the side of language or of thought.

Logic by itself does not suffice to ensure that words are properly used to express thought; nor does grammar guarantee that discourse which is flawless in syntax also complies with the demands of rationality. Hence neither grammar nor logic seems to challenge the function of the other, as together they challenge the function of rhetoric.

Upon the way this challenge is met depends not only the definition of rhetoric, but also the value put upon it. In the tradition of the great books, rhetoric is both praised as a useful discipline which liberally educated men should possess, and condemned as a dishonest craft to which decent men would not stoop. Like the words "sophistical" and "dialectical," the epithet "rhetorical" carries, traditionally as well as currently, a derogatory implication. The three words sometimes even tend to merge in meaning, expressing the same reproach against trickery. Yet of the three, "sophistical" alone implies an unqualified rebuke.

We do not speak of good and bad sophistry. But dialectic has its defenders as well as its detractors; and even those who, like Plato, charge rhetoric with being an art of enchantment or a form of flattery also distinguish between a true and a false rhetoric, the one associated with dialectic as a wholly admirable pursuit, the other classed with sophistry as a vocation divorced from virtue. According to Bacon, the aim of rhetoric is to support reason, "not to oppress it." Rhetoric may be misused, but logic also has its abuses. "Rhetoric can be no more charged," in Bacon's opinion, "with the coloring of the worse part, than logic with sophistry, or morality with vice."

THE PURPOSE AND scope of rhetoric are capable of broad and narrow definitions. The broader view, which we shall consider subsequently, tends to merge rhetoric with poetics as together the art of eloquence in any sort of discourse. The narrower view tends to restrict rhetoric to the art of persuasion in the sphere of practical affairs. Rhetorical skill consists in getting others to embrace certain beliefs, to form the opinions or make the judgments which the speaker or writer wishes them to adopt. Usually action, not persuasion, is the ultimate goal. The rules of rhetoric are supposed to give one power not merely to move the minds of men to certain conclusions but, through persuasion of their minds, to move men to act or not act in a certain way.

The sphere of rhetoric, so conceived, is limited to moral and political problems. The things about which men deliberate before acting, the things on which they pass moral judgments or make political decisions, constitute the subject matter of oratory, or what Hobbes calls "exhortation and dehortation," that is, "counsel accompanied with signs in him that giveth it, of vehement desire to have it followed."

In the narrower conception, rhetoric seems to be confined to *oratory*. It is with oratory and orators that Socrates seems to be concerned when he discusses rhetoric with Phaedrus or with Gorgias. Gorgias, who was a teacher of rhetoric, praises the power of the orator to persuade "the judges in the courts, or the senators in the council, or the citizens in the assembly, or at any other public meeting." In view of this Socrates asks him whether he will accept the definition of rhetoric as "the artificer of persuasion." When Gorgias admits that "persuasion is the chief end of rhetoric," Socrates goes on to ask whether rhetoric is "the only art which brings persuasion, or do other arts have the same effect? Does he who teaches anything persuade men of that which he teaches or not?" If so, "then arithmetic as well as rhetoric is an artificer of persuasion."

Gorgias reminds Socrates of his initial point about the orator, that "rhetoric is the art of persuasion in courts of law and other assemblies . . . about the just and unjust." But Socrates is still not satisfied that rhetoric has been sharply defined. He introduces the distinction between knowledge and belief or opinion, and gets Gorgias to agree that, whereas there cannot be false knowledge as well as true, beliefs and opinions may be either true or false. Persuasion can, therefore, be of two sorts—"one which is the source of belief without knowledge, as the other is of knowledge."

Gorgias is willing to limit rhetoric to that form of persuasion "which only gives belief," to which Socrates adds the emphatic negative that "the rhetorician does not instruct the courts of law or other assemblies about things just and unjust, but creates beliefs about them." If an assembly wishes to learn about matters connected with medicine or shipbuilding, it consults the physician or shipwright, not the orator. But, says Gorgias, "when a decision has to be given in such matters, the rhetoricians are the advisers; they are the men who win their point." He confirms this by reminding Socrates that the speeches of Themistocles and Pericles, not the suggestions of the builders, determined the Athenian assembly in the construction of the harbor, the docks and walls.

By way of further illustration, Gorgias tells of occasions when he has succeeded in getting patients to do what they would not do on the advice of their physicians. "I have persuaded the patient," he says, "to do for me what he would not do for the physician, just by the use of rhetoric." Similarly, in a contest for public office between a rhetorician and a man of any other profession, "the rhetorician more than any other would have the power of getting himself chosen, for he can speak more persuasively to the multitude than any of them, and on any subject. Such is the nature and power of the art of rhetoric!"

In comparing it with dialectic, Aristotle seems to have a different conception of the function of rhetoric. "Neither rhetoric nor dialectic," he says, "is the scientific study of any one separate subject; both are faculties for providing arguments." Both also are concerned with arguments which fall short of scientific demonstration, that is, with matters of opinion concerning which something probable can be said on either side of the issue.

Though for Aristotle rhetoric is the counterpart of dialectic, in that both deal with arguments on any subject, his differentiation between the two disciplines seems to indicate that rhetoric is limited to the consideration of oratory in the familiar sense of public speaking. The rhetorician is concerned with persuading an audience, not, as the dialectician is, with carrying on a dispute in which two individuals may be privately engaged. The persuasion, furthermore, is directed to obtaining a certain response from that audience—not merely agreement, but either action, or a decision to act, or approval which, charged with emotional force or enthusiasm, has practical significance.

The divisions of rhetoric, according to Aristotle, are determined by the kinds of oratory, as these, in turn, are determined by the types of audience to be addressed. "Of the three elements in speech-making—speaker, subject, and person addressed," Aristotle writes, "it is the last one, the hearer, that determines the speech's end and object. The hearer must be either a judge with a decision to make about things past or future, or an observer. A member of the assembly decides about future events, a juryman about past events; while those who merely decide on the orator's skill are observers.

"From this it follows that there are three divisions of oratory: (1) political, (2) forensic, and (3) the ceremonial oratory of display"—or, as these three are sometimes named, deliberative, legal, and epideictic. "Political speaking urges us either to do or not do something. . . . Forensic speaking either attacks or defends somebody. . . . The ceremonial oratory of display either praises or censures somebody. These three kinds of rhetoric refer to three different kinds of time. The political orator is concerned with the future; he tries to persuade men about things to be done or not done hereafter. The party in a case at law is concerned with the past; one man accuses the other, and the other defends himself, with reference to things already done. The ceremonial orator is, properly speaking, concerned with the present, since all men praise or blame in view of the state of things existing at the time, though they often find it useful also to recall the past and to make guesses about the future.

"Rhetoric has three distinct ends in view, one for each of its three kinds. The political orator aims at establishing the expediency or the harmfulness of a proposed course of action. . . . Parties in a lawsuit aim at establishing the justice or injustice of some action. . . . Those who praise or attack a man aim at proving him worthy of honor or the reverse."

THIS CONCEPTION OF rhetoric as concerned with oratory or public speaking gives one answer to the question of what rhetoric adds to grammar and logic as arts of discourse. In oratory more is involved than the communication of ideas, the marshalling of arguments, the making of proofs. Discourse, whether written or spoken, has an effect upon the emotions as well as upon the mind, and disposes a man to act as well as the mind to assent.

"The communicating of ideas by words," Berkeley observes, "is not the chief and only end of language, as is commonly supposed. There are other ends, as the raising of some passion, the exciting to or deterring from an action, the putting the mind in some particular disposition—to which the former is in many cases barely subservient, and sometimes entirely omitted. . . . I entreat the reader to reflect with himself, and see if it doth not often happen, either in hearing or reading a discourse, that the passions of fear, love, hatred, admiration, disdain and the like, arise immediately in his mind upon the perception of certain words, without any ideas coming between."

Engaged in the oratorical task of persuading the people of New York to ratify the federal constitution, the writers of the Federalist papers are aware that "a torrent of angry and malignant passions will be let loose" in the debate of that issue. They realize that arguing for the adoption of certain political principles or conclusions is not like teaching geometry, the objects of which are "entirely abstracted from those pursuits which stir up and put in motion the unruly passions of the human heart."

Hamilton admits at once, in the opening paper, that "the plan offered to our deliberations affects too many particular interests, innovates upon too many local institutions, not to involve in its discussion, a variety of objects foreign to its merits, and of views, passions, and prejudices little favorable to the discovery of truth." Nevertheless, he tries to persuade his audience to judge the issue on the merits of the argument alone.

The opponents of the Constitution, he says, "may be actuated by upright intentions." The opposition may "spring from sources, blameless at least, if not respectable—the honest errors of minds led astray by preconceived jealousies and fears. So numerous indeed and so powerful are the causes which serve to give a false bias to the judgment, that we, upon many occasions, see wise and good men on the wrong as well as on the right side of questions of the first magnitude to society."

To recognize this, Hamilton tells his audience, is to be on guard "against all attempts, from whatever quarter, to influence your decision . . . by any impressions other than those which may result from the evidence of truth." He wishes them to consider him as relying upon nothing but the merits of his case. "I frankly acknowledge to you my convictions," he writes, "and I will freely lay before you the reasons on which they are founded. . . . My motives must remain in the depository of my own breast. My arguments will be open to all, and may be judged by all. They shall at least be offered in a spirit which will not disgrace the cause of truth."

We can detect here another element in the art of rhetoric. The orator seems to be concerned, not only with the strength of his arguments and with the passions of the audience which he hopes to move by these arguments, but also with the impression he makes upon that audience as a person of good character and honest intentions, devoted to the truth and, above all, to the best interests of those whom he addresses.

The great speeches reported—or perhaps polished, if not invented—by Thucydides exemplify this effort on the part of the orator, as do also the orations written by Shakespeare for his characters, of which the speeches of Brutus and Antony in *Julius Caesar* are among the most notable as well as the most familiar. The point is also illustrated by the *Communist Manifesto*, which is denounced as "propaganda" by those who mistrust the writers, but to those who trust them is powerful and persuasive oratory.

Separating the use of witnesses and documents by the forensic orator from what he calls the strictly artistic means of persuasion—*i.e.*, the means intrinsic to the art of rhetoric—Aristotle divides the latter into the three elements already noted. Persuasion, he says, depends "on the personal character of the speaker . . . on putting the audience into a certain frame of mind . . . [and] on the proof, or apparent proof, provided by the words of the speech itself. Persuasion is achieved by the speaker's personal character when the speech is so spoken as to make us think him credible. . . . Secondly, persuasion may come through the hearers when the speech stirs their emotions. . . . Thirdly, persuasion is effected through the speech itself when we have proved a truth or an apparent truth by means of the persuasive arguments suitable to the case in question."

These being the three technical means of effecting persuasion, Aristotle concludes that rhetorical skill must consist in the ability "(1) to reason logically, (2) to understand human character and goodness in their various forms, and (3) to understand the emotions . . . to know their causes and the way in which they are excited." The art of rhetoric, therefore, involves more than training in grammar and logic. It requires the study of ethics and psychology—particularly knowledge of the types of human character and knowledge of the passions.

The same consideration of the conditions of oratory seems to lead Socrates to tell Phaedrus that Thrasymachus or anyone else who teaches rhetoric ought "to give an exact description of the nature of the soul," to explain "the mode in which it acts or is acted upon." The rhetorician, he goes on, "having classified men and speeches, and their kinds and affections, and adapted them one to another," will be able to "tell the reasons of his arrangement, and show why one soul is persuaded by a particular form of argument, and another not."

THIS FACT ABOUT rhetoric—that it must adapt speech to persons as well as to subject matters—seems to occasion Socrates' definition of oratory as "the art of enchanting the soul." It is not, he tells Phaedrus, confined to courts and public assemblies. Whether this art is a good or evil thing depends on whether it requires the speaker to know—more than the nature of the person he is addressing—the truth about the matters spoken of. To engender probabilities in the minds of the many by the likeness of the truth, it is necessary, says Socrates, to know the truth. "He who knew the truth would always know best how to discover the resemblances of the truth." Such a man might be able, not only to please and so to persuade his audience, but also, perhaps, he might "be able to say what is acceptable to God."

The issue about rhetoric then—at least so far as that issue concerns its being an art consistent with virtue—seems to turn on the admixture of pleasure and truth. The question is whether, given a particular sort of audience to persuade, the orator does not have to choose between pleasing them and telling them the truth. Does the art of rhetoric extend to the persuasion of bad men as well as good? Is the skill of the orator to be measured by his success in persuading, without regard to the character of the audience he has persuaded and the means he has been forced to use? Does the goodness of the orator—and of his speech—depend upon his being morally virtuous as well as rhetorically skillful?

One view of rhetoric seems to identify persuasion with pleasure and to divorce it from truth. Pascal, for example, in his essay *On Geometrical Demonstration*, speaks of "two methods, the one of convincing, the other of pleasing" In order to persuade, he writes, "one must consider the person with whom one has to deal, whose spirit and heart one must know, the principles he accepts, the things he loves." In view of such considerations, Pascal holds that "the art of persuasion consists more in pleasing than in convincing, to such an extent is it true that men are controlled more by whim than by reason." He does not doubt that "there are rules which are as reliable with respect to pleasing as there are for demonstrating"; nor does he seem to condemn rhetoric for being such an art, unless he writes with irony when he says that "pleasing is incomparably more difficult, more subtle, more useful, and more admirable."

Rhetoric so conceived appears to Locke to be a "powerful instrument of error and deceit"; and to Plato to be no art at all, but a form of flattery. As cookery tries to please the palate without caring what is good for the health of the body, so rhetoric, according to Plato, aims to delight without caring what is good for the soul or the state. Cookery and rhetoric are shams or simulations of the genuine arts of medicine and politics, which aim at the good, not at pleasure. "This is the sort of thing," Socrates tells Callicles, "which I term flattery, whether concerned with the body or the soul, or whenever employed with a view to pleasure and without any consideration of good and evil."

Socrates then asks Callicles whether he knows rhetoricians who "aim at what is best . . . and seek to improve the citizens by their speeches," or whether all "are bent upon giving them pleasure, forgetting the public good in the thought of their own interest, playing with the people as with children, and trying to amuse them, but never considering whether they are better or worse for this."

When Callicles replies that he thinks "there are some who have a real care for the public in what they say," Socrates says that he is "contented with the admission that rhetoric is of two sorts: one, which is mere flattery and disgraceful declamation; the other, which is noble and aims at the training and improvement of the souls of the citizens, and strives to say what is best, whether welcome or unwelcome, to the audience." But, he asks Callicles, "have you ever known such a rhetoric; or if you have, and can point out any rhetorician of this stamp, who is he?"

SOCRATES MAY NOT be asking a rhetorical question. He may be presenting the defenders of rhetoric with this critical dilemma: *either* the orator adheres to the truth and aims at the good, even if such highmindedness defeats his efforts at persuasion with an audience whom he thus displeases; *or* the orator takes persuasion as his end and subordinates everything else to the rhetorical means for succeeding with any sort of audience.

Bacon rises to the defense by rejecting the dilemma as ungenuine. "The duty and office of rhetoric," he writes, "is to apply reason to the imagination for the better moving of the will." He admits that rhetoric is controlled by other considerations than the truth. Though "logic handleth reason exact and in truth," and though "the proofs and demonstrations of logic are toward all men indifferent and the same . . . the proofs and persuasions of rhetoric ought to differ according to the auditors."

Nevertheless, Bacon thinks "it was great injustice in Plato, though springing out of a just hatred for the rhetoricians of his time, to regard rhetoric as a voluptuary art, resembling it to cookery that did mar wholesome meats, and help unwholesome by a variety of sauces to please the taste. For we see that speech is much more conversant in adorning that which is good than in coloring that which is evil; for there is no man but speaketh more honestly than he can do or think; and it was excellently noted by Thucydides in Cleon, that because he used to hold on the bad side in causes of state, therefore he was ever inveighing against eloquence and good speech knowing that no man can speak fair of courses sordid and base."

Aristotle's defense of rhetoric seems to be implied in the remark that "its function is not simply to succeed in persuading, but rather to discover the means of coming as near such success as the circumstances of each case allow." Just as, for him, the sophist differs from the dialectician not in the skills of argument or dispute, but in moral purpose or respect for truth, so the name "rhetorician" may be applied to two sorts of men. Rhetoric may signify "either the speaker's knowledge of his art, or his moral purpose." For want of separate names, both the honest and the sophistical orator are called and can claim to be "rhetoricians," and it is this which confuses the issue.

IN THE TRADITION of the great books, Aristotle's *Rhetoric* occupies a place comparable to that which, as noted in the chapter on POETRY, his *Poetics* unquestionably fills. It seems to be not merely the first but the standard treatise on oratory. It divides rhetoric into three parts—the first concerned with invention, the second with the disposition or order of a speech, the third with problems of expression. To the last of these belongs the analysis of the orator's use of language and his style in speaking; to the second, the analysis of the structure of an oration into such parts as proem, statement, argument, and epilogue; and to the first, under the head of invention, belongs the consideration of the means of persuasion.

As we have already noted, the artistic means of persuasion are, according to Aristotle, threefold—emotions, character, and argument. The orator must consider how to arouse and use the passions of his audience, as well as calculate how far to go in displaying his own emotions. He must consider the moral character of the audience to which he is appealing, and in this connection he must try to exhibit his own moral character in a favorable light. Finally, he must know the various types and sources of rhetorical argument—not only what sorts of argument are available for a particular purpose, but also how to employ each argument most persuasively. In this last respect, Aristotle distinguishes rhetorical proof from rhetorical induction—the use of what he calls the "enthymeme" as opposed to the use of examples—and he relates this distinction to the difference between dialectical proof and induction which he treats in the *Topics*.

Cicero and Quintilian may extend Aristotle's analysis in certain directions, but neither they nor modern writers like Campbell and Whately depart far from the framework Aristotle sets up for the discussion of oratory. Even those who reject Aristotle's authority in logic, natural philosophy, and metaphysics pay him the tribute of following (as does Hobbes) his treatment of oratory, or of approving (as does Bacon) his contribution to rhetoric. In the case of this science, as with few others, Bacon finds no serious deficiencies in the accepted tradition. He calls rhetoric "a science excellent and excellently well labored," and places "the emulation of Aristotle" first among the causes why later writers "in their works of rhetorics exceed themselves."

Yet by another standard Aristotle's *Rhetoric* may be judged deficient. Because he confines his attention almost exclusively to oratory, Aristotle's discussion leaves rhetoric in a larger sense almost untouched. This limitation of rhetoric to the subject matter of oratory does not go unexplained. "Every other art," Aristotle writes, "can instruct or persuade about its own particular subject matter; for instance, medicine about what is healthy and unhealthy, geometry about the properties of magnitudes, arithmetic about numbers, and the same is true of the other arts and sciences. But rhetoric," he says, "we look upon as the power of observing the means of persuasion on almost any subject presented to us."

This last statement would seem to give rhetoric complete generality. Aristotle qualifies it, however. "People fail to notice," he says, "that the more correctly they handle their particular subject the further they are getting away from pure rhetoric." So far as knowing good arguments and knowing how to use them are concerned, the physicist and the mathematician need no help from rhetoric. The art of rhetoric is necessary only in dealing with such topics as do not fall within the subject matters or systems of the established arts and sciences. Such topics are precisely those with which the orator must deal. "The duty of rhetoric," Aristotle writes in summary, "is to deal with such matters as we deliberate upon without arts or systems to guide us, in the hearing of persons who cannot take in at a glance a complicated argument, or follow a long chain of reasoning." This is his answer to those who have given rhetoric "a far wider subject matter than strictly belongs to it."

But Aristotle's explanation of his limitation of rhetoric is itself limited to only one of its major parts, namely, the construction of arguments. As contrasted with the mathematician, the physician, and the philosopher, whose mastery of the subject matter of their arts or sciences gives them a command of the relevant principles and methods of argument, only the orator needs the special art of rhetoric to provide him with the topics from which examples and enthymemes can be drawn and to give him skill in the use of such arguments. But it is not only the orator who must consider the character and emotions of his audience. It is not only the orator who must consider the best way in which to order the parts of an elaborate discourse. Above all, it is not only the orator who is faced with the problem of using language more or less effectively in the expression of thought, and especially in its communication to others. All these considerations and problems are common to the orator and the teacher. They are considerations and problems which must be faced not merely by the public speaker who tries to move an audience to action, but by anyone—poet, philosopher, or scientist—who tries to write whatever he has to say as effectively as possible.

Competence in a particular art or science may give a man competence with respect to arguments in the field of his particular subject matter, but it does not seem to give him competence with respect to these other considerations and problems, which he faces when he tries to communicate his knowledge or thought. Here, then, is the possibility of a broader conception of the art of rhetoric—an art concerned not merely with being persuasive in the sphere of action, but with eloquence or effectiveness in the expression of thought.

We find this view of rhetoric reflected in Chaucer's *Canterbury Tales*. In his Prologue, the Franklin asks his companions "to forgive his crude speech"; for, he explains, "I never learned rhetoric, to tell you the truth; whatever I say must be blunt and plain. I never slept on Mount Parnassus or studied Marcus Tullius Cicero." And the Squire apologizes for the inadequacy of his English to describe the beauty of Canace. "It would take an excellent rhetorician," he says, "who knew his colorful figures of speech, to describe her adequately." Though Aristotle's *Rhetoric* for the most part neglects this broader conception of rhetoric in order to expound the rules of oratory, the third book of his treatise, which deals with the use of language, indicates that problems of style are common to oratory and poetry and to other types of discourse as well.

Kant seems to hold this broader conception of rhetoric when he says that "the arts of speech are *rhetoric* and *poetry*." In the tradition of western thought, the two arts tend to become identified when each is separated from any particular subject matter. As appears in the chapter on POETRY, poetry like rhetoric has a broader and a narrower meaning. In the narrower meaning, it is the art of the narrative, just as in its narrower meaning, rhetoric is the art of oratory. The other sense in which poetics as an art can be understood is, according to Bacon, with respect to words, not matter. "In this sense," he writes, "it is but a character of style, and belongeth to arts of speech."

In this sense the poetic art is hardly distinguishable from the rhetorical art. The problems involved in composing a good speech are not the same as those involved in writing a good poem (or what Bacon calls a "feigned history"). But when poetics and rhetoric are each separated from such problems to become the arts of writing or speaking well about anything, then, in becoming as general as discourse itself, they tend to become one and the same art—an art of style or expression, an art of preaching or teaching the truth about any matter on which one mind seeks to communicate with another.

IN THE TRADITION of the great books, no book does for the art of rhetoric in general what Aristotle's *Rhetoric* does for that art in the limited sphere of oratory. But Augustine's treatise *On Christian Doctrine* engages in a general rhetorical analysis that is in a way comparable to Aristotle's analysis of oratory. In this work Augustine brings his own professional training as an orator to bear on the problems of reading, interpreting, and expounding Sacred Scripture. The fact that he is dealing with Sacred Scripture and hence, in his view, with the teaching of the most fundamental truths, lifts him above the limited concerns of the orator; but the fact that he limits himself to Sacred Scripture also prevents him from formulating his rules of interpretation and exposition with the complete generality they would have to possess in order to be the rules of a general art of rhetoric.

At the opening of the fourth book of *Chris-*

tian Doctrine, Augustine declares that, having considered in the preceding books "the mode of ascertaining the proper meaning" of Scripture, he will now treat "the mode of making known the meaning when it is ascertained." He disclaims any intention "to lay down rules of rhetoric"; he wishes merely "to engage it on the side of truth." To this end he tries to show how Scripture itself, and such holy men as St. Cyprian and St. Ambrose in commenting on Scripture, have employed the art of rhetoric.

"It is the duty," Augustine writes, "of the interpreter and teacher of Holy Scripture . . . both to teach what is right and refute what is wrong; and in the performance of this task to conciliate the hostile, to rouse the careless, and to tell the ignorant both what is occurring at present and what is probable in the future. But once his hearers are friendly, attentive, and ready to learn, whether he has found them so, or has himself made them so, the remaining objects are to be carried out in whatever way the case requires." The first rule of a general rhetoric would thus seem to be one of creating a receptive frame of mind in the persons being addressed. This accomplished, the teacher must proceed with various alternatives in mind.

"If the hearers need teaching," Augustine writes, "the matter treated of must be made fully known by means of narrative. On the other hand, to clear up points that are doubtful requires reasoning and the exhibition of proofs. If, however, the hearers require to be roused rather than instructed, in order that they may be diligent to do what they already know, greater vigor of speech is needed. Here entreaties and reproaches, exhortations and upbraidings, and all the other means of rousing the emotions, are necessary."

In Scripture and its great commentators, Augustine finds "wisdom not aiming at eloquence, yet eloquence not shrinking from wisdom." He also finds examples of the three kinds of style which Cicero had distinguished—the eloquence of those "who can say little things in a subdued style, moderate things in a temperate style, and great things in a majestic style." These three styles Augustine connects with the three ends which Cicero had assigned to eloquence—teaching, giving pleasure, and moving. The subdued style, he says, should be used "in order to give instruction," the temperate style "in order to give pleasure," and the majestic style "in order to sway the mind."

The great books of history, science, and philosophy provide additional materials for general rhetorical analysis. They offer us the light of examples at least, even if they do not, like Augustine's commentary on Scripture, give us the guidance of rules. Such historians as Herodotus, Thucydides, Tacitus, and Gibbon exhibit a diversity of styles in the writing of history. The diversity is not only on the grammatical level of the use of language, but also on the logical level of order and argument. Rhetorical principles control the way in which the language and the organization of the parts are suited to each other and to the historian's purpose—to the effect he wishes to produce upon his reader.

The way in which Euclid writes the *Elements* is a style of exposition, having rhetorical as well as logical features. In its rhetorical (if not its strictly logical) form it is applicable to other subject matters. This may be seen in Spinoza's adoption of it in his *Ethics* and in Newton's adaptation of it in his *Mathematical Principles of Natural Philosophy*. The dialogue form which Plato seems to have invented for writing philosophy appears to recommend itself rhetorically not only to other philosophers, but also to a scientist like Galileo in the composition of his *Two New Sciences*. If the doctrines of the *Summa Theologica* or of the *Critique of Pure Reason* were separated from the very special styles of these two works, they would probably not have the same effect upon the reader; and as they are written, they affect different readers differently, as differently as do the styles of Dante, Milton, Melville, Dostoevsky, Adam Smith, and Karl Marx.

Some methods of exposition may be more appropriate than others to certain subject matters. "There is a great difference in the delivery of mathematics," says Bacon, "and of politics." But in every subject matter or field of learning, there is the common problem of how to make language serve most effectively to enlighten or convince in the communication of thought. The problem arises in the writing of a single sentence as well as in the organization of a whole discourse.

THE CHOICE OF WORDS and the formation of new words, the invention and employment of figures of speech, by which abbreviation or amplification of discourse may be achieved and the imagination freshened—these are some of the considerations of style which Aristotle discusses (both in his *Rhetoric* and in his *Poetics*) and which Augustine illustrates in his analysis of Scripture. They suggest the rules of a general rhetoric, founded on principles as universal as Pascal's insight that "words differently arranged have a different meaning, and meanings differently arranged have a different effect."

This observation indicates a further answer to the question raised much earlier, namely, why the art of rhetoric is needed over and above the skills of grammar and logic. For oratory the question has been answered by reference to those rules of rhetoric which deal with the passions and with moral character. But for a more general rhetoric, concerned with all discourse, the answer must be in terms of rules of style of the sort Pascal's observation suggests.

If there were never more than one grammatically and logically correct way of saying anything, then grammatical and logical standards would suffice for the regulation of sound discourse. But if there are always several ways of stating something and if each of them satisfies the rules of grammar and logic, but differs in the impression it makes on the mind, then criteria other than those of grammar and logic will be needed to determine our choice of which to use.

Such criteria may take the passions and the imagination into account, but they may also look primarily to the manner in which the mind itself naturally works. The fact that there are several ways of presenting the same truth to the mind—and usually several ways in which the mind can interpret the same statement—defines the scope of a general rhetoric and the relation of its rules to those of grammar and logic.

Nevertheless, some of the great authors seem to doubt the worth of rhetoric in science or philosophy. Locke, for example, admits that "in discourses where we seek pleasure and delight rather than information and improvement, such ornaments"—as "figurative speeches and allusion in language"—"can scarce pass for faults. But," he adds, "if we would speak of things as they are, we must allow that all the art of rhetoric, besides order and clearness, all the artificial and figurative application of words eloquence hath invented, are for nothing else but to insinuate wrong ideas, move the passions, and so, indeed, are perfect cheats . . . and where truth and knowledge are concerned, cannot but be thought a great fault, either of the language or person that makes use of them."

Descartes also declares that "those who have the strongest power of reasoning, and who most skilfully arrange their thoughts in order to render them clear and intelligible, have the best power of persuasion even if they can but speak the language of Lower Britanny and have never learned rhetoric." Yet he qualifies this severity somewhat by identifying dialectic with rhetoric and granting its "possible use . . . to serve to explain at times more easily to others the truths we have already ascertained."

Plato for the most part tends in the opposite direction, keeping dialectic and rhetoric poles apart. But if there were a true as opposed to a false rhetoric, a rhetoric concerned with knowledge and truth, not merely opinion and pleasure, he would be willing, it seems, to admit it to the company of dialectic, and regard it as an aid in the teaching, if not the discovery, of the truth. The pedagogical utility of rhetoric as well as dialectic appears in the summary which Socrates gives to Phaedrus, after they have finished examining the speeches about love.

"Until a man knows the truth of the several particulars of which he is writing or speaking," Socrates says, "and is able to define them as they are, and having defined them again to divide them until they can no longer be divided, and until in like manner he is able to discern the nature of the soul, and discover the different modes of discourse which are adapted to different natures, and to arrange and dispose them in such a way that the simple form of speech may be addressed to the simpler nature, and the complex and the composite to the more complex nature—until he has accomplished all this, he will be unable to handle arguments according to rules of art . . . either for the purpose of teaching or persuading."

OUTLINE OF TOPICS

1. The nature and scope of rhetoric
   - 1a. The distinction of rhetoric from dialectic and sophistry: the rhetorician and the philosopher
   - 1b. The relation of rhetoric to grammar, logic, and psychology
   - 1c. The relation of rhetoric to the arts of government: the orator and the statesman
2. The function of rhetoric in expository, speculative, and poetic discourse
   - 2a. The devices of rhetoric: figures of speech; the extension and contraction of discourse
   - 2b. The canon of excellence in style
   - 2c. Methods of exposition in history, science, philosophy, and theology
   - 2d. Principles of interpretation: the modes of meaning
3. The role of rhetoric as concerned with persuasion in the sphere of action: the analysis of oratory
   - 3a. The kinds of oratory: deliberative, forensic, epideictic
   - 3b. The structure of an oration: the order of its parts
   - 3c. The use of language for persuasion: oratorical style
4. The means of persuasion: the distinction between artistic and inartistic means
   - 4a. The orator's consideration of character and of the types of audience: the significance of his own character
   - 4b. The orator's treatment of emotion: his display of emotion; the arousal of his audience
   - 4c. Rhetorical argument: the distinction between persuasion and demonstration
     - (1) Rhetorical induction: the use of examples
     - (2) Rhetorical proof: the use of enthymemes
     - (3) The topics or commonplaces which are the source of premises: the orator's knowledge of various subject matters
5. The evaluation of oratory and the orator: the justification of rhetorical means by the end of success in persuasion
   - 5a. The purpose of oratory and the exigencies of truth
   - 5b. The orator's concern with justice, law, and the good: the moral virtue of the orator
6. The education of the orator: the schools of rhetoric
7. The history of oratory: its importance under various social conditions and in different forms of government
8. Examples of excellence in oratory

REFERENCES

References are listed by volume number (in bold type), author's name, and page number. Bible references are to book, chapter, and verse of the Authorized King James version of the Bible. The abbreviation "esp" calls the reader's attention to one or more especially relevant parts of a whole reference; "passim" signifies that the topic is discussed intermittently rather than continuously in the work or passage cited. Where the work as a whole is relevant to the topic, the page numbers refer to the entire work. For general guidance in the use of *The Great Ideas,* consult the Preface.

1. The nature and scope of rhetoric

7 PLATO, 136–141, 260–262
9 ARISTOTLE, 593–675
12 EPICTETUS, 170–172
18 AUGUSTINE, 675–677
23 HOBBES, 72
25 MONTAIGNE, 147
30 BACON, 66–67
33 PASCAL, 439–446
35 LOCKE, 299–300
42 KANT, 532
27 SHAKESPEARE, 374
30 BACON, 25, 78
38 ROUSSEAU, 369
40 GIBBON, 384–385
43 FEDERALIST, 29–30
43 MILL, 361–362
46 HEGEL, 153–154

1*a*. The distinction of rhetoric from dialectic and sophistry: the rhetorician and the philosopher

7 PLATO, 39–42, 65–84, 131–141, 200–201, 203–205, 252–294, 528–530, 555–556, 634–635
9 ARISTOTLE, 593–598
12 AURELIUS, 253
18 AUGUSTINE, 14–15, 29, 677, 683–684
24 RABELAIS, 101–106
25 MONTAIGNE, 446–450
31 DESCARTES, 16–17
43 MILL, 292–293

1*b*. The relation of rhetoric to grammar, logic, and psychology

7 PLATO, 131–141
9 ARISTOTLE, 653–667
18 AUGUSTINE, 653–654
23 HOBBES, 55, 67
25 MONTAIGNE, 75–77
30 BACON, 31, 56–67 passim
31 DESCARTES, 43

1*c*. The relation of rhetoric to the arts of government: the orator and the statesman

5 EURIPIDES, 402–403
6 THUCYDIDES, 425, 427
7 PLATO, 200–212, 254–256, 604–605, 684–686
9 ARISTOTLE, 435–436, 491 passim, 506, 593–594, 598–608, 622–623
14 PLUTARCH, 129–130, 604–605, 691–723, 724–725
15 TACITUS, 126, 290
19 AQUINAS, 652–653
23 HOBBES, 127–128, 129

2. The function of rhetoric in expository, speculative, and poetic discourse

7 PLATO, 129–141
9 ARISTOTLE, 597–598, 599, 653–667, 684–685, 691–692
18 AUGUSTINE, 638, 675–698
22 CHAUCER, 295–296
30 BACON, 11–12, 38–39, 62–69, 114
35 LOCKE, 299–300
42 KANT, 524, 532
44 BOSWELL, 180

2*a*. The devices of rhetoric: figures of speech; the extension and contraction of discourse

8 ARISTOTLE, 213
9 ARISTOTLE, 653–667, 693
14 PLUTARCH, 42–43, 803
18 AUGUSTINE, 331–332, 668, 674, 678–682
22 CHAUCER, 396–401, 494
23 HOBBES, 282
24 RABELAIS, 77–78
25 MONTAIGNE, 113–114, 196–197
27 SHAKESPEARE, 598
29 CERVANTES, xi–xvi passim
30 BACON, 24, 39, 68
35 LOCKE, 299–300
36 STERNE, 228–229, 243–244
37 FIELDING, 49–50
44 BOSWELL, 353–354
49 DARWIN, 40
51 TOLSTOY, 534
53 JAMES, 687–688

2*b*. The canon of excellence in style

5 ARISTOPHANES, 491–492, 494–495, 534–535, 573–582, 601–602
7 PLATO, 52–57, 328–331
9 ARISTOTLE, 653–667, 694–695
14 PLUTARCH, 279, 606

18 Augustine, 97–98, 653, 684–685
22 Chaucer, 40–41, 295–296, 351, 491
23 Hobbes, 67
25 Montaigne, 104–105, 148–149, 194–200 passim, 309–310, 422–423, 455, 482–483, 502–504
27 Shakespeare, 589, 597–598
29 Cervantes, 185, 251–252
30 Bacon, 11–12, 63, 64–66
32 Milton, 59–61
33 Pascal, 174, 175–177
36 Sterne, 209–210, 230–231, 287–289, 344–345
37 Fielding, 1–2, 223–225, 246–247
40 Gibbon, 494–495
41 Gibbon, 300, 327, 522–523 passim
42 Kant, 513–514, 524
44 Boswell, 59–61, 167–168, 381–382, 454

2*c*. Methods of exposition in history, science, philosophy, and theology

6 Thucydides, 354
7 Plato, 50–52, 132–140, 590–591
9 Aristotle, 161–165 passim, 599
12 Epictetus, 203
18 Augustine, 644–645, 659–660, 661–663, 675–698 passim
19 Aquinas, 1
23 Hobbes, 57–58
25 Montaigne, 197–200, 448–449, 455–456
28 Gilbert, 2
28 Harvey, 336–337
30 Bacon, 12, 65
33 Pascal, 327–328
37 Fielding, 19–20
38 Montesquieu, 266
38 Rousseau, 401–402
40 Gibbon, 213
41 Gibbon, 40, 186, 526
42 Kant, 2–4, 294, 376
44 Boswell, 217
45 Lavoisier, 2
53 James, 121–122
54 Freud, 662

2*d*. Principles of interpretation: the modes of meaning

7 Plato, 52–57
9 Aristotle, 696–698
12 Epictetus, 122–124
18 Augustine, 34, 36, 107–108, 110, 120–121, 371, 419–421, 422–423, 426–427, 450–451, 496–498, 549, 624–674
19 Aquinas, 8–10
21 Dante, 13, 64
24 Rabelais, 1–3
30 Bacon, 39, 99
33 Pascal, 163–164, 273–276, 290–301
40 Gibbon, 346
42 Kant, 339
43 Mill, 290
54 Freud, 816

3. The role of rhetoric as concerned with persuasion in the sphere of action: the analysis of oratory

7 Plato, 131–138, 252–294
9 Aristotle, 565–566, 593–675
14 Plutarch, 129–130
18 Augustine, 683–685
25 Montaigne, 147–148
32 Milton, 261–262
42 Kant, 535
43 Declaration of Independence, 1, 3
43 Federalist, 181
46 Hegel, 153–154
50 Marx-Engels, 429–433 passim
51 Tolstoy, 482–484, 572–573
52 Dostoevsky, 369–398

3*a*. The kinds of oratory: deliberative, forensic, epideictic

9 Aristotle, 593–594, 598–622, 639, 667–669 passim, 670–673 passim
12 Epictetus, 201–203
18 Augustine, 686–687
23 Hobbes, 67
30 Bacon, 38
40 Gibbon, 343

3*b*. The structure of an oration: the order of its parts

7 Plato, 132–135
9 Aristotle, 653, 667–675
25 Montaigne, 466
30 Bacon, 58–59

3*c*. The use of language for persuasion: oratorical style

7 Plato, 50–52, 57, 200
9 Aristotle, 653–667
12 Lucretius, 12, 44
12 Epictetus, 201–203
14 Plutarch, 42–43, 279–281, 692–695, 706, 713–715
18 Augustine, 682–684, 686–696
23 Hobbes, 282
26 Shakespeare, 384
35 Berkeley, 410–411
40 Gibbon, 206, 343, 529
43 Federalist, 29–30
44 Boswell, 130–131, 475
51 Tolstoy, 65–66, 194–198 passim, 302, 347–348, 402–403
52 Dostoevsky, 369–370, 386–387

4. The means of persuasion: the distinction between artistic and inartistic means

7 Plato, 131–138
9 Aristotle, 595, 619–623, 659–660
18 Augustine, 676–677
47 Goethe, 15

4a. The orator's consideration of character and of the types of audience: the significance of his own character

4 HOMER, 21
6 THUCYDIDES, 358–360, 370, 478–479, 484, 504–507, 512–513
7 PLATO, 136–137
9 ARISTOTLE, 608–611, 636–639, 643, 668–669, 671, 673
14 PLUTARCH, 129–130
15 TACITUS, 11, 12–13
18 AUGUSTINE, 678, 696–697
25 MONTAIGNE, 345
27 SHAKESPEARE, 351–353, 366–367
32 MILTON, 381–383
33 PASCAL, 441–442
43 MILL, 349
44 BOSWELL, 374
48 MELVILLE, 30–36, 117–122
51 TOLSTOY, 536–537, 622

4b. The orator's treatment of emotion: his display of emotion; the arousal of his audience

5 ARISTOPHANES, 459–461
6 THUCYDIDES, 557, 584–585
7 PLATO, 145, 169–170, 208–209
9 ARISTOTLE, 622–636, 659–660, 671, 674
12 EPICTETUS, 201–203
13 VIRGIL, 107
14 PLUTARCH, 427, 672, 682–684, 692–695, 719–720
15 TACITUS, 198–199
18 AUGUSTINE, 653, 675–676, 694
23 HOBBES, 127–128, 129
25 MONTAIGNE, 405
26 SHAKESPEARE, 580–587
30 BACON, 66–67
33 PASCAL, 174
35 HUME, 492
43 FEDERALIST, 29–30
43 MILL, 292–293
51 TOLSTOY, 497–499, 622

4c. Rhetorical argument: the distinction between persuasion and demonstration

7 PLATO, 137–138, 254–256, 558–561
8 ARISTOTLE, 97, 528
9 ARISTOTLE, 593–622, 639–653, 669–670, 672–675
10 GALEN, 180–181
12 EPICTETUS, 110
19 AQUINAS, 651–652
23 HOBBES, 127, 128
25 MONTAIGNE, 446–450, 453–454
30 BACON, 66–67
33 PASCAL, 440–442
37 FIELDING, 261
43 FEDERALIST, 62
43 MILL, 284
51 TOLSTOY, 243

4c(1) Rhetorical induction: the use of examples

8 ARISTOTLE, 90–91, 212
9 ARISTOTLE, 596–597, 640–641, 646–647
12 EPICTETUS, 113–114
42 KANT, 376

4c(2) Rhetorical proof: the use of enthymemes

8 ARISTOTLE, 92–93
9 ARISTOTLE, 594, 596–598, 641–653
12 EPICTETUS, 113–114
42 KANT, 376

4c(3) The topics or commonplaces which are the source of premises: the orator's knowledge of various subject matters

7 PLATO, 131–141, 253–262
9 ARISTOTLE, 597–662, 639–640, 643–653
30 BACON, 58–59, 83–85

5. The evaluation of oratory and the orator: the justification of rhetorical means by the end of success in persuasion

5 EURIPIDES, 261–262, 402–403
5 ARISTOPHANES, 470–487, 488–506
6 THUCYDIDES, 395–396, 425–427
7 PLATO, 74–75, 136–141, 252–294
9 ARISTOTLE, 593–595
12 EPICTETUS, 170–172
18 AUGUSTINE, 19, 675–678, 683–684, 693–696
25 MONTAIGNE, 75–76, 147–149
33 PASCAL, 439–446
42 KANT, 535
44 BOSWELL, 475
46 HEGEL, 280

5a. The purpose of oratory and the exigencies of truth

6 THUCYDIDES, 584–585
7 PLATO, 131–138, 161, 200, 252–294, 634–635
9 ARISTOTLE, 594
12 EPICTETUS, 172–174
18 AUGUSTINE, 7–8, 29, 676–678, 682–684, 696–697
23 HOBBES, 282
30 BACON, 12
32 MILTON, 113–116
43 FEDERALIST, 100

5b. The orator's concern with justice, law, and the good: the moral virtue of the orator

6 THUCYDIDES, 395–399, 424–428, 429–434, 468–469
7 PLATO, 208–209, 252–294
9 ARISTOTLE, 593–594, 598–623
14 PLUTARCH, 129–130, 604–605, 628, 643–644, 696–697, 724–725
15 TACITUS, 101–102
18 AUGUSTINE, 686–687, 694
23 HOBBES, 77, 106
26 SHAKESPEARE, 583–586
30 BACON, 66–69

32 Milton, 382–383
43 Federalist, 29–30
43 Mill, 292–293, 361–362

6. The education of the orator: the schools of rhetoric

8 Aristotle, 253
9 Aristotle, 593–675
14 Plutarch, 124–125, 692–696
18 Augustine, 14, 33–34, 676, 677
30 Bacon, 11–12, 31
39 Smith, 338–339
40 Gibbon, 389–390, 669–670

7. The history of oratory: its importance under various social conditions and in different forms of government

5 Aristophanes, 480–481
7 Plato, 200–212, 285–294, 413–416
8 Aristotle, 253
9 Aristotle, 491, 653–654
14 Plutarch, 13–14, 287–288, 628, 671–685, 691–723, 724–725
15 Tacitus, 126
25 Montaigne, 147–148
30 Bacon, 11–12
36 Sterne, 290
38 Montesquieu, 89–90
40 Gibbon, 23–24, 303–304, 364
41 Gibbon, 327
43 Federalist, 181
43 Mill, 284, 375–377

8. Examples of excellence in oratory

4 Homer, 3–6, 10–13, 59–63, 79–80, 85, 137–139
5 Aristophanes, 459–462
6 Herodotus, 214–220, 269–270, 286–287
6 Thucydides, 357–360, 365–371, 378–380, 384–386, 389–390, 402–404, 411–412, 418–420, 424–429, 449, 451–452, 461–463, 469–470, 478–479, 511–516, 518–520, 529–534, 555–557, 559–560
7 Plato, 115–141, 169–172, 200–212
13 Virgil, 334–340
14 Plutarch, 179–184, 226–227, 643–644
15 Tacitus, 26–27, 56, 198–199, 211–212, 241–242
18 Augustine, 678–682, 688–693
26 Shakespeare, 146, 555–556, 583–586
30 Bacon, 23–26, 69
32 Milton, 111–121, 189–195, 205–207, 381–412
36 Sterne, 255–256
40 Gibbon, 64, 269–270, 384–385, 427
41 Gibbon, 381, 574–575
48 Melville, 30–36
51 Tolstoy, 149–150, 380–381, 466–467, 497–499, 566
52 Dostoevsky, 148–170, 369–398

CROSS-REFERENCES

For: The general consideration of the liberal arts, *see* Art 4; Education 5b; and for the relation of rhetoric to such liberal arts as grammar and logic, *see* Language 1a–1b, 8; Logic 3b.

The role of rhetoric in the sphere of philosophy, and its relation to or distinction from dialectic and sophistry, *see* Dialectic 5; Philosophy 6b; Truth 4d.

The function of oratory in the sphere of politics, *see* Democracy 7a; Emotion 5d; State 8d(2).

Discussions relevant to the broad conception of rhetoric as the art of achieving eloquence and effectiveness in any sort of discourse, and as concerned with problems of style and principles of interpretation, *see* Language 3a, 6, 12; Poetry 8b–8c; Sign and Symbol 4c–4d.

Discussions relevant to the narrow conception of rhetoric as the art of oratory, and as concerned with the means of persuasion in the sphere of action, *see* Emotion 5d; Honor 3a–3b; Induction 4b; Reasoning 5d; Truth 4d.

ADDITIONAL READINGS

Listed below are works not included in *Great Books of the Western World*, but relevant to the idea and topics with which this chapter deals. These works are divided into two groups:

I. Works by authors represented in this collection.
II. Works by authors not represented in this collection.

For the date, place, and other facts concerning the publication of the works cited, consult the Bibliography of Additional Readings which follows the last chapter of *The Great Ideas*.

I.

TACITUS. *A Dialogue on Oratory*
PLUTARCH. "Lives of the Ten Orators," in *Moralia*
AUGUSTINE. *Divine Providence and the Problem of Evil*
——. *The Harmony of the Gospels*
HOBBES. *The Whole Art of Rhetoric*

II.

ISOCRATES. *Aegineticus*
——. *Against the Sophists*
——. *Panegyricus*
——. *Antidosis*
DEMOSTHENES. *Philippics*
CICERO. *Orations*
CICERO. *De Oratore* (*On Oratory*)
——. *Brutus*
——. *Orator*
LONGINUS. *On the Sublime*
QUINTILIAN. *Institutio Oratoria* (*Institutes of Oratory*), BK II–VI, VIII, X–XII
DEMETRIUS. *On Style*
ALCUIN. *Rhetoric*
T. WILSON. *Arte of Rhetorique*
FÉNELON. *Dialogues on Eloquence*
LA BRUYÈRE. "Of the Works of the Mind," in *Characters*
J. HARRIS. *Hermes, or A Philosophical Inquiry Concerning Universal Grammar*
BUFFON. *Discours sur le style*
VOLTAIRE. "Style," in *A Philosophical Dictionary*
W. G. HAMILTON. *Parliamentary Logic*
G. CAMPBELL. *Philosophy of Rhetoric*
BLAIR. *Lectures on Rhetoric and Belles Lettres*
BENTHAM. *The Book of Fallacies*
DE QUINCEY. *Rhetoric*
WHATELY. *Elements of Rhetoric*
T. CARLYLE. "Stump-Orator," in *Latter-Day Pamphlets*
SCHOPENHAUER. *The World as Will and Idea*, VOL II, SUP, CH 11
——. "The Art of Controversy," in *Complete Essays*
LEWES. *The Principles of Success in Literature*
EMERSON. "Eloquence," in *Society and Solitude*
VERLAINE. *Art poétique*
PATER. *An Essay on Style*
BRUNETIÈRE. *An Apology for Rhetoric*
CROCE. *Aesthetic as Science of Expression*
——. "On Telling the Truth," in *The Conduct of Life*
BUCHANAN. *Symbolic Distance*
——. *The Doctrine of Signatures*
RICHARDS. *The Philosophy of Rhetoric*
——. *Interpretation in Teaching*

Chapter 82: SAME AND OTHER

INTRODUCTION

THE problems of identity and diversity—of sameness and otherness, similarity and difference—occur at that level of philosophical thought which deals with being and with unity. Plotinus, for example, says that in addition to Being, Motion, and Rest, "we are obliged to posit the further two, Identity and Difference, so that we have in all five genera."

In Aristotle's conception, terms like 'being,' 'one,' and 'same' have a greater universality than the terms he calls the highest genera, *e.g.*, 'substance,' 'quantity,' 'quality,' 'relation,' and so forth. These latter represent categories or classes under which certain things fall and others do not. Not everything is a substance or a quantity, but in Aristotle's opinion there is nothing of which it cannot be said that it is a being in some sense, that it has some kind of unity, that it is identical with itself, and that, compared with anything else in the whole universe, it is in certain respects the same, in others different.

The fundamental relation of quantities with one another, namely, equality, consists in their being the same. The fundamental relation of qualities consists in their being alike, or the same in spite of some difference in degree or intensity, *e.g.*, a brighter and a darker red of the same hue. The notion of relation itself seems to be as fundamental as that of sameness, since in comparisons one thing is said to be the same or different only in relation to something else; yet it also seems to be true that relations can be the same or similar, for the essence of proportion or analogy lies in one thing's being related to a second as a third is to a fourth. The sameness of two relationships is the object of the comparison.

Such considerations are sometimes called "metaphysical" with an invidious tone. But no one, not even those who would eliminate metaphysical discussion as indulging in "vicious abstractions" or as verging on the meaningless, can easily avoid such notions as identity and diversity. It is not merely that ordinary speech, as well as scientific discourse, must use such words as "same" and "other" almost as frequently as the words "is" and "not" or "one" and "many." Those who are critical of theorizing and who want to save discourse itself from becoming "too metaphysical" are still obliged to give some account of what it means for things to be the same or different and of how we know when they are.

Semantics currently has vogue as a critical instrument for safeguarding discourse from ambiguity and nonsense and perhaps also for spotting metaphysical legerdemain. But semantics itself cannot go far in its own analysis of words and meanings without having to explain how the *same* word can have *different* meanings or how the *same* meaning can be expressed by *different* words. It does not seem likely that an adequate explanation could be developed without some theory of sameness and otherness.

THE "SENSE OF SAMENESS," says William James, "is the very keel and backbone of our thinking." He is here speaking "of the sense of sameness from the point of view of the mind's structure alone, and not from the point of view of the universe. . . . Whether there be any *real* sameness in *things* or not, or whether the mind be true or false in its assumptions of it," he goes on, the point remains that "the mind makes continual use of the *notion* of sameness, and if deprived of it, would have a different structure from what it has. . . . Without the psychological sense of identity, sameness might rain down upon us from the outer world forever and we be none the wiser. With the psychological sense, on the other hand, the outer world might be an unbroken flux, and yet we should perceive a repeated experience."

James distinguishes three principles of identity. In addition to the *psychological* law according to which we feel a later experience to be the same as an earlier one, he refers to the *ontological* principle which "asserts that every real thing is what it is, that *a* is *a*, and *b*, *b*"; and the *logical* principle which declares that "what is once true of the subject of a judgment is always true of that subject." James seems to think that "the ontological law is a tautological truism," whereas the logical and the psychological principles have further implications not immediately obvious. Locke appears to take a contrary view. He finds the identity of all *ideas* self-evident, while to him the real identity of *things* is much more difficult to grasp.

The principle of identity and its companion principle of contradiction are, according to Locke, expressed in the propositions 'Whatsoever is, is' and 'It is impossible for the same thing to be and not to be'—"these two general propositions amounting to no more, in short, but this, that the same is the same, and the same is not different." But, Locke adds, "the mind, without the help of any proof or reflection on either of these general propositions, perceives so clearly, and knows so certainly, that 'the idea of white is the idea of white, and not the idea of blue,' and that 'the idea of white, when it is in the mind, is there and is not absent,' that the consideration of these axioms can add nothing to the evidence or certainty of its knowledge. . . . I appeal to every-one's own mind, whether this proposition 'A circle is a circle' be not as self-evident a proposition as that consisting of more general terms 'Whatsoever is, is.'"

But unlike the comparing of an idea with itself, real identity, according to Locke, requires us to consider a thing "as existing at any determined time and place" and to "compare it with itself existing at another time. . . . When, therefore, we demand whether anything be the same or no? it refers always to something that existed at such a time in such a place, which, it was certain, at that instant, was the same with itself and no other; from whence it follows that one thing cannot have two beginnings of existence, nor two things one beginning, it being impossible for two things of the same kind to be or exist in the same instant in the very same place, or one and the same thing, in different places. That, therefore, that had one beginning is the same thing; and that which had a different beginning in time and place from that, is not the same, but diverse." In short, across a lapse of time a thing remains identical, in Locke's view, or maintains its identity, if existence having made it "one particular thing under any denomination, the same existence continued preserves it the same individual under the same denomination."

THIS UNDERSTANDING OF real identity Locke applies without difficulty to an atom of matter which, being at a given instant "what it is and nothing else . . . is the same and so must continue as long as its existence is continued; for so long it will be the same, and no other. In like manner, if two or more atoms be joined together into the same mass, every one of those atoms will be the same by the foregoing rule; and whilst they exist united together, the mass consisting of the same atoms, must be the same mass or the same body, let the parts be ever so differently jumbled. But," Locke continues, "if one of these atoms be taken away, or one new one added, it is no longer the same mass or the same body."

The problem of identity in living organisms Locke does not find so easy to solve. "In the state of living creatures," he says, "their identity depends not on a mass of the same particles, but on something else. For in them the variation of great parcels of matter alters not the identity; an oak growing from a plant to a great tree, and then lopped, is still the same oak; and a colt grown up to a horse, sometimes fat, sometimes lean, is all the while the same horse, though in both these cases there may be a manifest change of the parts, so that truly they are not, either of them, the same masses of matter."

The problem of the real identity or continuity of living things through time and change is, as we shall see presently, only a special case of the larger problem of whether anything at all remains identical for more than an instant in the universal flux of things. But supposing that problem solved in favor of enduring substances, or things which somehow remain continuously the same while changing in this or that respect, the point of Locke's observation about living things still holds, for their identity does not seem to lie in the continuity or permanence of the matter—the particles—of which they are composed.

The familiar riddle about the pipe—whether it is in any respect the same after it has its broken bowl replaced by a new one, and then has a new stem added to the new bowl—may be propounded for living organisms. But in their case, Locke argues, a principle of identity can be found. A plant, he says, "continues to be the same plant as long as it partakes of the same life, though that life be communicated to new particles of matter vitally united to the living plant, in a like continued organization conformable to that sort of plant."

The principle, he thinks, applies to animals and men. "The case is not so much different in brutes but that anyone may hence see what makes an animal and continues it the same. Something we have like this in machines, and may serve to illustrate it. For example, what is a watch? It is plain it is nothing but a fit organization or construction of parts to a certain end, which, when a sufficient force is added to it, it is capable to attain. If we would suppose this machine one continued body, all whose organized parts were repaired, increased, or diminished by a constant addition or separation of insensible parts, with one common life, we should have something very much like the body of an animal. . . . This also shows wherein the identity of the same man consists; *viz.*, in nothing but a participation of the same continued life by constantly fleeing particles of matter, in succession, vitally united to the same organized body."

In the case of man, however, Locke thinks we must face the additional problem of personal identity. What makes a man the same person from moment to moment, sleeping and waking, remembering or not remembering his past? In what does the continuity of the self consist, on the identity of which, Locke insists, "is founded all the right and justice of reward and punishment"? His answer seems to be that, as a living organism is identical throughout one and the same life, it is the continuity of the same consciousness which "makes a man be himself to himself" and establishes his personal identity.

"Whatever has the consciousness of present and past actions," Locke writes, "is the same person to whom they both belong. . . . That with which the consciousness of this present thinking thing *can* join itself, makes the same person, and is one self with it, and with nothing else. . . . If the same Socrates, waking and sleeping, do not partake of the same consciousness, Socrates, waking and sleeping, is not the same person. And to punish Socrates waking for what sleeping Socrates thought, and waking Socrates was never conscious of, would be no more right than to punish one twin for what his brother twin did, whereof he knew nothing, because their outsides were so like that they could not be distinguished."

William James also attributes the sense of personal identity to continuity of consciousness, but for him there still remains a problem of explaining that continuity. In the flow of consciousness from moment to moment, "continuity," he thinks, "makes us unite what dissimilarity might otherwise separate; similarity makes us unite what discontinuity might hold apart. . . . The sense of our personal identity, then, is exactly like any one of our other perceptions of sameness among phenomena. It is a conclusion grounded either on the resemblance in a fundamental respect, or on the continuity before the mind, of the phenomena compared."

In his opinion, "*resemblance among the parts of a continuum* of feelings (especially bodily feelings) experienced along with things widely different in all other regards, *thus constitutes the real and verifiable 'personal identity' which we feel.* There is no other identity than this in the 'stream' of subjective consciousness. . . . Its parts differ, but under all their differences they are knit in these two ways; and if either way of knitting disappears, the sense of unity departs. If a man wakes up some fine day unable to recall any of his past experiences, so that he has to learn his biography afresh . . . he *feels* and he *says* that he is a changed person. He disowns his former me, gives himself a new name, identifies his present life with nothing from out of the older time. Such cases are not rare in mental pathology."

In the tradition of the great books, other solutions are offered to the problem of personal identity. Kant thinks, for example, that a "transcendental unity of apperception" is necessary to constitute "in all possible phenomena which may come together in our experience, a connection of all these representations according to laws. Unity of consciousness," he writes, "would be impossible if the mind, in the knowledge of the manifold, could not become conscious of the identity of function by which it unites the manifold synthetically in one knowledge. Therefore, the original and necessary consciousness of the identity of one's self is at the same time a consciousness of the equally necessary unity of the synthesis of all phenomena according to concepts."

Where Kant posits a transcendental ego to account for the experienced identity of the self, other philosophers who hold one or another theory of the soul as an imperishable substance or an unchanging principle seem to find no special subtleties in the problem of the identity of living organisms or persons. So far as such theories bear upon that problem, the consideration of them belongs to the chapter on SOUL. Here we are concerned with the notions of same and other as they apply to everything in the universe. Hence we must face all the problems of how two things can be the same, not merely the problem of self-sameness or the identity of a thing with itself.

THE WORD "IDENTICAL" is sometimes used as a synonym for "same," as when we say that two things are identical in a certain respect. But without the qualification expressed by "in a certain respect," it is seldom if ever said that two things are identical, for if they can be discriminated from one another in any respect at all, they are two, not one, and therefore not identical. This seems to be the sense of Leibnitz's principle of the identity of indiscernibles, concurred in by all who understand identity as the self-sameness of that which is one in number and existence. A plurality of things involves a numerical diversity—each of the many being an *other*. To this extent at least, the traditional discussion of same and other tends to merge with matters discussed in the chapter on ONE AND MANY.

For both Plato and Aristotle, the relation between these two pairs—*one and many* and *same and other*—seems to be much closer. In the comparison of two things, Aristotle appears to treat sameness as a kind of oneness, referring to the various ways in which two things can be "one and the same." Of sameness, he says that "it is a unity of the being, either of more than one thing or of one thing when it is treated as more than one"; and of the one he says that to it "belong . . . the same and the like and the equal, and to plurality belong the other and the unlike and the unequal."

The enumeration he gives of kinds of unity seems to be paralleled by his enumeration of kinds of similitude. As a thing may be one essentially or one by accident, so two things may be the same essentially or by accident. Aristotle's statement that "some things are one in number, others in species, others in genus, others by analogy," finds its counterpart in his statement that "'different' is applied to those which, though other, are the same in some respect, only not in number, but either in species or in genus or by analogy."

As indicated in the chapter on RELATION, a distinction is traditionally made between relationships which really exist among things apart from the mind, and logical relationships which occur in thought alone. This distinction seems to separate self-sameness or identity from all relations of similitude which obtain between two things. "The relation signified by the term *the same*," Aquinas says, "is a logical relation only if it is taken in regard to absolutely the same thing, because such a relation can exist only in a certain order observed by reason as regards the order of anything to itself. The case is otherwise, however, when things are called the same, not numerically, but generically or specifically."

Nevertheless, identity seems to underlie all other relations of sameness, for among things or ideas lacking identity no comparisons can be made. Those who deny identity on the ground that everything is in flux, nullify all further discussion of sameness. The theory of a universal flux, which Plato attributes to Heraclitus, permits nothing ever to remain stationary or the same for an instant; and "the professed Heraclitean," Cratylus, went even further, according to Aristotle: he "criticized Heraclitus for saying that it is impossible to step twice into the same river; for *he* thought one could not do it even once."

In saying of men that "they are *nothing but a bundle or collection of different perceptions*, which succeed each other with an inconceivable rapidity, and are in a perpetual flux and movement," Hume does more than deny personal identity. He affirms an utter diversity—"as if there were no manner of relation" at all—between distinct perceptions, each of which is for him a distinct existence. The opposite point of view affirms things which have an enduring existence and which can, as Aristotle says of substances, undergo change in many respects "while remaining numerically one and the same."

Time and change raise the question of how any one thing can be the same from moment to moment. The question of how two things can be one and the same in any respect arises from the simple fact that, at the instant of comparison, they are two. If they were the same only for the comparing mind, then their sameness would be a logical and not a real relationship. For two things to be the same in reality seems to imply that, although two in number, they are one in some respect. To use Hegel's language, there is identity in diversity; or, in the language of Aquinas, a real community exists, according to which some one thing is common to two.

The problem of the sameness of two things can be stated in terms of the significance of what Hobbes, Berkeley, and Hume call common or general names. Denying that such words as "man" or "tree" or "stone" express abstract or general ideas, they seem to say that common names like these signify what is common to two or more individuals—whether things, perceptions, or ideas. Those who, like Aristotle, Aquinas, and Locke, take general or common names to signify abstract ideas, seem to say such ideas themselves signify that in reality two or more things have something in common. Still another view is that, apart from all individual things, real universals exist as the objects of the mind's conceptions.

If the latter alternative is chosen, then two individuals—two men, for example—may be thought alike only because both somehow resemble, as Plotinus suggests, the separate archetype Man. What is common to the two men lies in a third and separate reality, of which Plotinus says that it is "present in multiplicity," as if "in multi-impression . . . from one seal." But as Parmenides observes, in Plato's dialogue of that name, if a separate idea of Man is required to explain how two individuals are alike in being men, then still another idea is needed to account for the likeness between each individual man and the idea Man.

On the other hand, the view that the real sameness of two individuals, or the reality of the one kind to which both belong, resides in them—in their common possession of the same nature, quality, or other attribute—seems to lead to the difficulty already intimated, namely, the difficulty of understanding how distinct existences can have anything in common—how they can be two in number and yet also one in nature. If John and James are alike as men because they share a common humanity, then can it be said that each has *his own* human nature? If their natures and properties are as individual as their existences, how can two things be *really the same* in any respect? Must not kinds or universals—or whatever is supposed to be common to many and the source of their sameness—exist only in the general meaning of words, or in the mind's abstract concepts, or as separate archetypes? But, then, what truth is there in the familiar statement that two individual things are in some respect *really* alike or the same?

These questions indicate that the traditional discussion of the same and the other tends to involve not merely the theory of the one and the many, but also, in certain issues at least, the problem of the individual and the universal. As the chapter on Universal and Particular shows, the several positions traditionally taken with regard to universals afford different answers to the problem of how any sameness between two or more things exists. The factor of similitude in knowledge (the nature of the likeness between image or idea and its object) and the function of similitude in love (the attraction, or repulsion, of like by like) also extend the consideration of sameness and diversity into the field of problems dealt with in other chapters. Here attention must be given to the meaning of sameness itself, as that is affected by the distinction between the same and the similar, by the enumeration of various kinds or degrees of likeness, and by the range of opposite meanings in the notions of diversity and difference.

Discussing discrimination and comparison, William James, for example, draws a sharp line between the simple and complex components of our experience. Simple impressions, he seems to think, are either absolutely alike or absolutely unlike. Here there can be no degrees of resemblance or similarity. "Two resembling things," he writes, "owe their resemblance to their absolute identity in respect to some attribute or attributes, combined with the absolute non-identity of the rest of their being. This, which may be true of compound things, breaks down when we come to simple impressions." The latter, apart from their numerical non-identity or otherness, are either the same in quality or diverse. But compound things may be more or less alike, varying in degree of similarity or difference according to the number of simple respects in which they are or are not the same.

"Similarity, in compounds," says James, "is partial identity," and he gives the following illustrations. "The moon is similar to a gas-jet, it is also similar to a foot-ball; but a gas-jet and a foot-ball are not similar to each other.... Moon and gas-jet are similar in respect of luminosity and nothing else; moon and foot-ball in respect of rotundity, and nothing else. Football and gas-jet are in no respect similar—that is, they possess no common point, no identical attribute."

Other writers seem to agree on this distinction between the same and the similar, the diverse and the different. The latter in both cases combine elements of sameness and diversity to give degrees of likeness. Aquinas, for example, says that "we seek for difference where we also find resemblance. For this reason, things which differ must in some way be composite, since they differ in some respect and in some respect they resemble each other. In this sense, although all things that differ are diverse, yet all things that are diverse do not differ.... For simple things are diverse through themselves, and do not differ from one another by differences as their components. For instance, a man and an ass differ by the difference of rational and irrational, but we cannot say that these again differ by some further difference."

The specific difference between man and ass with respect to rationality, accompanied by their generic sameness with respect to animality, makes them similar. If they were utterly diverse, *i.e.*, the same in no respect, they would not be said to differ; just as if they were identical in all respects except number, they would not be called similar. "The other and the same," writes Aristotle, "are thus opposed. But difference is not the same as otherness. For the other and that which it is other than need not be other in some definite respect . . . but that which is different is different from some particular thing in some particular respect, so that there must be something identical by which they differ."

But within the area of this agreement on fundamental terms, there seems to be some disagreement about whether two things can be utterly diverse. Since they are two, they cannot be the same in *all* respects—certainly not in number—but can they be totally incomparable? James appears to say Yes in his remark about the football and the gas jet having "no common point, no identical attribute." Yet he also seems to hold that no two things are ever absolutely incomparable. They may not differ or be similar as the diverse species of the same genus, *e.g.*, man and ass; but regarding them as "'thinkables' or 'existents,'" he writes, "even the smoke of a cigarette and the worth of a dollar bill are comparable—still more so as 'perishables' or as 'enjoyables.'" The gas jet and the football would appear to be comparable also as 'existents' or 'usables'—or even, perhaps, as 'bodies.'

The question thus arises whether—all things being somehow comparable—they are all the same in genus, as, for example, all three-dimensional material things may be said to belong to the genus 'body' no matter how much else they differ as species or subordinate kinds within this genus. Kant answers this question by affirming a principle of ultimate homogeneousness. According to this principle, "there are no different original and first *genera*, as it were isolated and separated from each other, but all diverse *genera* are divisions only of one supreme and general *genus*." Kant states a correlative principle of variety or specification, according to which "every *genus* requires *species*, and these again *sub-species*, and as none even of these *sub-species* is without a sphere . . . reason in its utmost extension requires that no species or sub-species should in itself be considered as the lowest."

Aristotle's theory of species and genera appears to be exactly opposite to Kant's on both points. For Aristotle, there is no single all-embracing genus, but rather a number of diverse yet supreme genera, such as substance, quantity, quality, etc. There is a finite, not an infinite variety of species. The lowest species is further divisible only into kinds which differ, as individuals of the same species do, in accidental, not essential respects, *e.g.*, white man and red man differ in the same way as John and James do within the species 'man,' not as the species 'man' and 'ass' differ within the genus 'animal.' Furthermore, where Kant insists upon a third principle of continuity, according to which between any two species "there always remain possible intermediate species, differing from the first and the second by smaller degrees than those by which these differ from each other," Aristotle seems to find no intermediates possible between the contrary species of a single genus. The order of species is for him a discontinuous series like the order of the whole numbers, between proximate members of which no fractions are admitted.

Does Aristotle's position with respect to the *heterogeneity* of an animal and the color blue—the one in the genus 'substance,' the other in the genus 'quality'—mean that such things, *absolutely diverse in genus*, are absolutely incomparable? His answer seems to be twofold. In one place he says that things which are diverse in genus may still be the same by analogy: "things that are one by analogy are not all one in genus." In another, he gives us an example of analogical resemblance (between the soul and the hand): "As the hand is a tool of tools, so the mind is the form of forms and sense the form of sensible things."

If the example seems inappropriate on the ground that the soul and the hand are of the same genus, *i.e.*, both substances or parts of the same substance *man*, it may be necessary to introduce the distinction between natural and logical genera. According to this distinction, a material and a spiritual substance can both be called "substances" as a matter of logical classification, but they are not in the same genus by their own natures. In this sense, Aquinas assigns a geometrical solid and a physical body to the same logical genus 'body' but regards them as of heterogeneous natures; and Descartes, calling an extended and a thinking substance both "substances," insists upon the utter diversity of their natures.

An easier example, however, may not be too difficult to find. A man and a number belong to different genera, according to Aristotle—one a substance, the other a quantity. But the man can be related to his sons as the number *one* is related to any other whole number. The relation which is the same in both cases is that of priority, according to which the man and unity are the principles or generators respectively of his sons and other numbers. Here, then, we see two heterogeneous things—a substance and a quantity—which are, nevertheless, the same by analogy, *each standing to another in the same relationship*; both, therefore, can be called "principle" or "generator" analogically.

Aristotle's other indication that a special mode of similitude obtains between heterogeneous things, occurs in all those passages in which he says that terms like 'being' can be predicated of things in every category or genus. Just as James seems to think that any two things may be comparable as 'thinkables' or 'existents,' so Aristotle seems to hold that all things, though otherwise heterogeneous, are at least alike in *being*, *i.e.*, in having some mode of existence. Yet the term 'being' cannot be equated with Kant's single supreme genus. Though Aristotle agrees with Kant that every genus must be capable of division into species, he does not think that 'being' can be so divided by specific differences.

Two points must be observed concerning Aristotle's theory of the predication of a term like 'being' of everything in the universe.

First, he repeatedly asserts that 'being' is not said *in the same sense* of substances, quantities, qualities, and so forth. Hence when such heterogeneous things are all called 'beings,' the implication cannot be that, as beings, they are all the *same*. The point seems to be that they are somehow *at once both the same and diverse*. As, to use an example from Aristotle's *Physics*, a tone and a taste can both be sharp, though the sharpness of a tone is as diverse from the sharpness of a taste as tone and taste are qualitatively diverse from each other; so a man and a number can both have being, though their modes of being are as diverse as substance is from quantity. If the word "similarity" were to be used to signify not the combination of separable elements of sameness and diversity, but rather the inseparable fusion of the two to constitute a *diversified sameness*, then heterogeneous things should be called *similar*, not the same, in being.

Second, Aristotle does not identify such similarity of heterogeneous things with the sameness by analogy which heterogeneous things can have. 'Being' is not a relative term and therefore it cannot be predicated analogically, as 'principle' or 'generator' can be. Terms which are predicated analogically, as 'principle' can be predicated of a father and the number one, may signify *similarity* (in the sense of *diversified sameness*) rather than simple sameness in a single respect. The relation of generation which creates the analogical similitude between a father and the number one seems to be the same relation in the two cases (between a father and his sons, and between one and other numbers); it is not, however, simply the same, for that relation is diversified according as the things related—substances in the one case, quantities in the other—are absolutely diverse in genus. But in Aristotle's analysis it does not follow that because some analogical predicates signify *diversified* rather than *simple* sameness, all do; or that because some instances of *diversified sameness* happen to be analogical (*i.e.*, sameness in a relation), all are.

The interest in Aristotle's separation of these two points lies in the fact that Aquinas combines them in a theory which states that, when being and other terms (which are not genera and yet are above all genera) are predicated of heterogeneous things, they must be predicated analogically of them. The existence which is found in all things, he says, "is common to all only according to some sort of analogy," not "according to the same specific or generic formality." This is most easily seen in the "likeness of creatures to God," which is "solely according to analogy, inasmuch as God is essential being, whereas other things are beings by participation."

Aristotle's statement that "things which are one by analogy are not all one in genus," seems to be converted by Aquinas into the proposition that *things which are not one in genus, and yet are alike in some way, are all one by analogy*. For Aristotle, sameness by analogy may be either simple sameness or diversified sameness (*i.e.*, similarity); and diversified sameness may or may not be analogical, that is, it may be the kind of similarity which two heterogeneous things have in respect to being or in respect to some relation in which they stand to other things. For Aquinas, on the other hand, whenever heterogeneous things are the same in any single respect, their diversified sameness is *always analogical*; and whenever the similitude between two things is truly analogical, then it is *always similarity*, that is, a diversified, not a simple sameness. Likeness in being, according to Aquinas, affords us the prime example of a similitude which is at once an analogical and a diversified sameness.

Aquinas applies his theory of the analogy of being to the great traditional issue, which puts all theories of similitude to the test—the question of the resemblance between God and creatures, or between infinite and finite being. Against the answer first given by Maimonides, and later expressed by Spinoza when, of all comparisons between God and man, he says that "His essence . . . could resemble ours in nothing except in name"; and against those, on the other hand, who think that whatever names apply to both God and creatures (such as "being" or "good" or "one"), apply simply in the *same* sense, Aquinas seems to take the middle ground. The names which are properly applicable to both God and creatures, according to him, are said of them, not equivocally and not univocally, but analogically.

This threefold distinction of univocal, equivocal, and analogical names, especially as it concerns the names of God, is discussed in the chapter on SIGN AND SYMBOL. The theological problem of the similitude between God and creatures confronts us with three basic alternatives in man's speculation about the sameness and diversity which exists among all things. We can say, (1) that infinite and finite being are utterly diverse, and have no similarity *even* in being. We can say, (2) that they are homogeneous—that, with respect to being, for example, they have the kind of sameness which things have when they belong to the same genus. Or we can say, (3) that they are only similar in the sense of a diversified sameness, whether such similarity is or is not always analogical in character.

OUTLINE OF TOPICS

1. The principle of identity: the relation of a thing to itself

   1*a*. Oneness in number or being: numerical diversity or otherness

   1*b*. The identity of the changing yet enduring individual: personal identity, the continuity of self; the denial of identity in the realm of change

2. The sameness of things numerically diverse

   2*a*. The being of sameness or similitude: the reality of kinds or universals

   2*b*. The relation between sameness and unity: sameness as a participation in the one

   2*c*. The distinction between sameness and similarity and their opposites, diversity and difference: the composition of sameness and diversity; degrees of likeness and difference

   2*d*. The distinction of things in terms of their diversities and differences: real and logical distinctions

   2*e*. The limits of otherness: the impossibility of utter diversity

3. The modes of sameness and otherness or diversity

   3*a*. Essential sameness or difference and accidental sameness or difference

   (1) Specific and generic sameness: natural and logical genera

   (2) The otherness of species in a genus: the diversity of contraries

   (3) Generic otherness or heterogeneity

   3*b*. Relational sameness: sameness by analogy or proportional similitude

   3*c*. Sameness in quality, or likeness: variations in degree of the same quality

   3*d*. Sameness in quantity, or equality: kinds of equality

4. Sameness and diversity in the order of knowledge

   4*a*. Likeness or sameness between knower and known: knowledge as involving imitation, intentionality, or representation

   4*b*. The role of differentiation in definition: the diversity of differences

   4*c*. Sameness and diversity in the meaning of words or the significance of terms: the univocal and the equivocal

5. The principle of likeness in love and friendship

6. Similitude between God and creatures: the degree and character of the similitude; traces or images of God in creatures

REFERENCES

References are listed by volume number (in bold type), author's name, and page number. Bible references are to book, chapter, and verse of the Authorized King James version of the Bible. The abbreviation "esp" calls the reader's attention to one or more especially relevant parts of a whole reference; "passim" signifies that the topic is discussed intermittently rather than continuously in the work or passage cited. Where the work as a whole is relevant to the topic, the page numbers refer to the entire work. For general guidance in the use of *The Great Ideas,* consult the Preface.

1. The principle of identity: the relation of a thing to itself

7 PLATO, 571–574
8 ARISTOTLE, 146, 206–208, 528–530
19 AQUINAS, 157–158, 160, 213–214
35 LOCKE, 113, 218–219, 307, 337–338, 345–346
53 JAMES, 299–301

1*a*. Oneness in number or being: numerical diversity or otherness

7 PLATO, 561–574
8 ARISTOTLE, 440–441, 519–520, 569–570, 604
11 NICOMACHUS, 838
17 PLOTINUS, 205–206, 273–275, 312–313, 315–319, 353–355
19 AQUINAS, 29–30, 46–47, 530, 688–689
42 KANT, 100, 102, 105–106

1*b*. The identity of the changing yet enduring individual: personal identity, the continuity of self; the denial of identity in the realm of change

7 PLATO, 113–114, 517–534
8 ARISTOTLE, 6–9, 259–268, 299, 529–530, 591
11 NICOMACHUS, 811
12 AURELIUS, 275
20 AQUINAS, 951–956 passim
25 MONTAIGNE, 388
35 LOCKE, 123–124, 218–228
42 KANT, 49–51, 74–76, 120–129, 200–204
46 HEGEL, 24
49 DARWIN, 297
53 JAMES, 147–149, 154–157, 191–192, 194–196, 213–259

2. The sameness of things numerically diverse

2*a*. The being of sameness or similitude: the reality of kinds or universals

7 PLATO, 87–89, 240–246, 427–429, 457, 486–511, 535–536
8 ARISTOTLE, 116, 505–506, 508–511, 516, 521, 556–557, 562–563, 564, 586, 610–611, 618–619
19 AQUINAS, 99, 440–443, 446–447, 451–453, 455–457, 748–749
23 HOBBES, 55–56, 59
31 SPINOZA, 387–388
35 LOCKE, 274–283, 323
35 BERKELEY, 405–410 passim
35 HUME, 507
53 JAMES, 305–314

2*b*. The relation between sameness and unity: sameness as a participation in the one

7 PLATO, 493, 498–499
8 ARISTOTLE, 536–537, 538–539
11 NICOMACHUS, 838, 839–840

2*c*. The distinction between sameness and similarity and their opposites, diversity and difference: the composition of sameness and diversity; degrees of likeness and difference

7 PLATO, 49
8 ARISTOTLE, 330–333, 581
19 AQUINAS, 19–20, 22–23, 46–47, 66–67, 295–297
20 AQUINAS, 885–886
53 JAMES, 319–322, 344–348

2*d*. The distinction of things in terms of their diversities and differences: real and logical distinctions

7 PLATO, 595
8 ARISTOTLE, 152, 581
9 ARISTOTLE, 165–168
19 AQUINAS, 68–70, 80–81, 167–168, 171–175, 214–215, 256–258, 270–272, 391–393, 401–403
31 DESCARTES, 114–115, 119–120, 152–156, 224–225
35 LOCKE, 270–274, 279–280
42 KANT, 99–108
49 DARWIN, 25–29
53 JAMES, 315–336, 550–551, 867–874, 878, 880

2*e*. The limits of otherness: the impossibility of utter diversity

8 ARISTOTLE, 517–518
19 AQUINAS, 17–18, 480–481
25 MONTAIGNE, 518–519
31 SPINOZA, 355–356, 398
42 KANT, 107, 197–198
53 JAMES, 320–322, 344–345

3. The modes of sameness and otherness or diversity

3*a*. Essential sameness or difference and accidental sameness or difference

7 PLATO, 358–360
8 ARISTOTLE, 192, 194–196, 198–200, 208, 538–539, 561–562
9 ARISTOTLE, 7, 320–321
19 AQUINAS, 16, 162–163, 399–401, 688–689, 779–780
20 AQUINAS, 713–714, 807–808
31 DESCARTES, 136, 152–156, 231–232
31 SPINOZA, 356
35 LOCKE, 257–258, 268–283 passim, 296–297, 331–332
42 KANT, 193–200

3*a*(1) Specific and generic sameness: natural and logical genera

8 ARISTOTLE, 308, 330–333, 517–518, 536–537, 539
9 ARISTOTLE, 161, 165–168
12 LUCRETIUS, 28
19 AQUINAS, 93–94, 163–164, 170–171, 270–272, 345–347, 403, 418–419, 457–458, 493
20 AQUINAS, 54–55, 1025–1032
30 BACON, 158–159
35 LOCKE, 255–260, 263
38 ROUSSEAU, 341–342
49 DARWIN, 28–29, 207–208, 332, 347
53 JAMES, 870–871

3*a*(2) The otherness of species in a genus: the diversity of contraries

8 ARISTOTLE, 303–304, 539, 581–582, 585–586
9 ARISTOTLE, 165–168
17 PLOTINUS, 291–293
19 AQUINAS, 273–274, 723–724
20 AQUINAS, 22–23, 117–118
49 DARWIN, 30–31, 241–242

3*a*(3) Generic otherness or heterogeneity

8 ARISTOTLE, 149–152 passim, 330–333, 517–518
19 AQUINAS, 17–18, 471–472
42 KANT, 197–198

3*b*. Relational sameness: sameness by analogy or proportional similitude

7 PLATO, 448
8 ARISTOTLE, 189, 573–574, 599–601 passim
9 ARISTOTLE, 114, 169, 378–379, 640–641, 657, 662–666
11 EUCLID, 81–98
11 NICOMACHUS, 841
16 KEPLER, 1078–1080 passim
19 AQUINAS, 77–78, 492, 713–714
24 RABELAIS, 12–13
28 HARVEY, 336, 469–470
30 BACON, 157–158
31 DESCARTES, 158–161
35 LOCKE, 228
35 HUME, 487
42 KANT, 72–74, 601–603
49 DARWIN, 212–213
53 JAMES, 549–550

3*c*. Sameness in quality, or likeness: variations in degree of the same quality

8 ARISTOTLE, 8, 15–16, 166, 297
9 ARISTOTLE, 173–174
17 PLOTINUS, 7
18 AUGUSTINE, 328
20 AQUINAS, 15–19
30 BACON, 145–148
31 SPINOZA, 415
35 LOCKE, 311–312
42 KANT, 602
53 JAMES, 319–322, 346–348

3*d*. Sameness in quantity, or equality: kinds of equality

7 PLATO, 228–229, 494, 500–502, 508, 510–511
8 ARISTOTLE, 583
9 ARISTOTLE, 378–381
11 EUCLID, 2, 4, 6–7, 16–17
11 NICOMACHUS, 821–822
16 KEPLER, 1012–1014
17 PLOTINUS, 289
19 AQUINAS, 224–225
20 AQUINAS, 368–369
50 MARX, 19–25
53 JAMES, 874–875

4. Sameness and diversity in the order of knowledge

4*a*. Likeness or sameness between knower and known: knowledge as involving imitation, intentionality, or representation

7 PLATO, 124–126, 231–232, 383–398, 427–431, 538–541
8 ARISTOTLE, 605, 639–641, 659, 661–662, 663, 664, 691–692
12 LUCRETIUS, 44–45, 53–54
17 PLOTINUS, 132–133, 217–218, 221–224, 228–229, 249, 339–342
18 AUGUSTINE, 75, 76–77, 269
19 AQUINAS, 51–52, 58–59, 76–77, 79–80, 91–94 passim, 185–187, 289–290, 291, 301, 460–461, 465–466, 740–741
31 DESCARTES, 84–85, 99, 108–109, 131–132
31 SPINOZA, 375, 377–378
35 LOCKE, 238, 239, 245–246, 323–326
35 BERKELEY, 413–431, 440–441
35 HUME, 504
42 KANT, 12, 15–16, 23–24, 34–35, 55–56, 88–91, 115, 550–551
46 HEGEL, 55–56
53 JAMES, 126–129, 142–143, 307–311 esp 307, 309, 325–327

4*b*. The role of differentiation in definition: the diversity of differences

7 PLATO, 134, 548–549, 551–579, 580–608, 610–613
8 ARISTOTLE, 144–145, 196–199, 208–209, 558–562
17 PLOTINUS, 285–286, 289–291
19 AQUINAS, 401–403
20 AQUINAS, 2–4
35 LOCKE, 256–257, 268–283 passim
42 KANT, 193–200, 215–216
49 DARWIN, 30–31
53 JAMES, 669–671

4*c*. Sameness and diversity in the meaning of words or the significance of terms: the univocal and the equivocal

7 PLATO, 65–84, 809–810
8 ARISTOTLE, 5, 152, 202, 215, 227, 251, 260–262, 331–332, 508–509, 522, 553, 567, 589, 599–601, 658
9 ARISTOTLE, 172–174
19 AQUINAS, 62–75, 98, 165–167
20 AQUINAS, 54–55
23 HOBBES, 57–58
30 BACON, 60, 112–113
31 SPINOZA, 387–388
35 LOCKE, 152, 234–236, 276, 285–291, 292–293, 300–301
35 HUME, 478
42 KANT, 315–316, 547–548
53 JAMES, 332–334, 689, 875–876
54 FREUD, 517–518

5. The principle of likeness in love and friendship

7 PLATO, 19–21, 167, 285–286
9 ARISTOTLE, 406–407, 408, 410–412, 418–419, 615
12 EPICTETUS, 167–170
19 AQUINAS, 156, 731–732, 738–739, 740–741
20 AQUINAS, 511
25 MONTAIGNE, 83
31 SPINOZA, 405–406, 410, 413–414, 431–437
49 DARWIN, 317
51 TOLSTOY, 242–243, 311–313, 314–316, 631–633, 669–672
54 FREUD, 404–406, 677–684, 685–686

6. Similitude between God and creatures: the degree and character of the similitude; traces or images of God in creatures

OLD TESTAMENT: *Genesis*, 1:26–27 / *Job*, 12:7–9
APOCRYPHA: *Wisdom of Solomon*, 2:23; 13:1–5 / *Ecclesiasticus*, 42:15–43:33
NEW TESTAMENT: *I Corinthians*, 11:7; 15:49 / *II Corinthians*, 3:18 / *Colossians*, 3:9–10 / *I John* passim, / *II John*
16 KEPLER, 853–854, 1080–1085 passim
18 AUGUSTINE, 25, 119, 336–338, 357–358
19 AQUINAS, 14–16, 22–23, 28–29, 34–35, 63–68, 151–152, 153–154, 240–241, 306–307, 401, 487–488, 492–501, 530–531
20 AQUINAS, 730–731, 1025–1032
21 DANTE, 107, 109, 126
27 SHAKESPEARE, 43
30 BACON, 41
31 DESCARTES, 88, 90–91, 214, 228
31 SPINOZA, 363–363
32 MILTON, 220–221
33 PASCAL, 246–247, 249–251
46 HEGEL, 270–271, 306, 310
48 MELVILLE, 84–85
52 DOSTOEVSKY, 153

CROSS-REFERENCES

For: Other discussions of the principle of identity and of its significance for being, change, and thought, *see* BEING 2b, 7b(5); CHANGE 2; LOGIC 1a; ONE AND MANY 2a; PRINCIPLE 1c, 3a(3); RELATION 1a; and for the problems of personal identity and the identity of a state, *see* SOUL 1d; STATE 3g.

For: Other considerations of sameness or similarity, and of the problem of the reality of kinds or universals, *see* FORM 2a; IDEA 1a, 6b; ONE AND MANY 1c; UNIVERSAL AND PARTICULAR 2a–2c.

Matters relevant to the analysis of essential and accidental sameness, specific and generic sameness, and otherness in species or in genus, *see* EVOLUTION 1b; IDEA 4b(3); NATURE 1a(1); ONE AND MANY 3b(1); OPPOSITION 1c(2); RELATION 5a(4); UNIVERSAL AND PARTICULAR 5b.

The nature of the similitude between heterogeneous things, and for the problem of signifying such similitude, *see* BEING 1; SIGN AND SYMBOL 3d; and for the related distinction between univocal, equivocal, and analogical terms, *see* IDEA 4b(4); SIGN AND SYMBOL 3b–3d.

Another discussion of sameness by analogy or relational sameness, *see* RELATION 1d, 5a(3); and for sameness in quality and quantity, *see* QUALITY 3c, 4c; QUANTITY 1b.

Similitude in the relation of knower and known, of lover and loved, and in imitation, *see* Art 3; Form 1d(1); Knowledge 1, 4d; Love 4a; Nature 2a; One and Many 4f.

The principle of similarity in the association of ideas, *see* Idea 5e; Memory and Imagination 2c; Relation 4f; Sense 3d(1).

The theory of definition as constituted by the statement of genus and difference, *see* Definition 2b; Nature 4a; Opposition 1c(2).

The problem of the similitude between God and creatures, and for its bearing on the significance of the names we apply to God, *see* God 3f, 6a–6b; Man 11a; Nature 1b; One and Many 1b; Sign and Symbol 5f; World 3a–3b.

ADDITIONAL READINGS

Listed below are works not included in *Great Books of the Western World*, but relevant to the idea and topics with which this chapter deals. These works are divided into two groups:

I. Works by authors represented in this collection.

II. Works by authors not represented in this collection.

For the date, place, and other facts concerning the publication of the works cited, consult the Bibliography of Additional Readings which follows the last chapter of *The Great Ideas.*

I.

Aquinas. *On Being and Essence*, ch 2

Descartes. *The Principles of Philosophy*, part i, 60–65

Hobbes. *Concerning Body*, part ii, ch 11, 13

Hume. *A Treatise of Human Nature*, bk i, part iv, sect vi

J. S. Mill. *A System of Logic*, bk iii, ch 20

II.

Cajetan. *De Nominum Analogia*

Suárez. *Disputationes Metaphysicae*, iv–vi, xv (10), xxviii (3), xxx (10), xxxii (2), xxxiii (2), xxxiv, xxxix (3), xliv (11), xlvi (1), xlvii (11, 14–15, 17)

——. *On the Various Kinds of Distinctions* (*Disputationes Metaphysicae*, vii)

John of Saint Thomas. *Cursus Philosophicus Thomisticus, Ars Logica*, part ii, q 2 (3); q 13 (2–5); q 14 (2–3)

Leibnitz. *New Essays Concerning Human Understanding*, bk ii, ch 27

Voltaire. "Identity," in *A Philosophical Dictionary*

Whewell. *The Philosophy of the Inductive Sciences*, vol i, bk viii

Jevons. *The Substitution of Similars*

Lotze. *Logic*, bk i, ch 2 (a)

Bradley. *The Principles of Logic*, bk ii, part i, ch 6; Terminal Essays, iv

Bosanquet. *Logic*, vol ii, ch 3

——. *Science and Philosophy*, 2

Garrigou-Lagrange. *God, His Existence and Nature*, part ii, appendix 2

Whitehead. *The Concept of Nature*, ch 6

McTaggart. *The Nature of Existence*, ch 7–10

Santayana. *The Realm of Matter*, ch 8–9

Penido. *Le rôle de l'analogie en théologie dogmatique*

Maritain. *The Degrees of Knowledge*, ch 4

——. *A Preface to Metaphysics*, lect v

B. Russell. *Human Knowledge, Its Scope and Limits*, part vi, ch 3

Chapter 83: SCIENCE

INTRODUCTION

IN our time, science, philosophy, and religion have come to represent three quite distinct intellectual enterprises. Each appeals for allegiance not merely on the ground that it can answer fundamental questions, but also because of its contribution to human life and culture. In other periods, philosophy and religion competed for supremacy, though, as appears in the chapter on PHILOSOPHY, some philosophers and theologians tried to remove this conflict by arguing for the complete compatibility of reason and faith. Nevertheless, before the 19th century, the issue, if one existed, was between philosophy and religion. Science had not yet become sufficiently distinct from philosophy to complicate the picture.

When science and philosophy are not themselves sharply distinguished, men are not confronted with three separate claims upon their intellectual allegiance. Modern science as something quite distinct in method and subject matter from traditional philosophy may actually make its appearance as early as the 17th century. But not until Kant are two kinds of science plainly set apart. Not until then are they so defined that one becomes identified with what men have always called "philosophy" and the other gradually appropriates the name of "science" and regards itself as a quite separate enterprise.

Kant differentiates between the empirical and the rational sciences. This differentiation tends to correspond with the distinction by others before him of experimental and abstract philosophy. It also corresponds with a later division into the experimental or inductive and the philosophical or deductive sciences. But Kant does not seem to contemplate the possibility of conflict between science and philosophy—between the experimental study of nature and metaphysics or, what is for him the same, between empirical and rational physics.

Hume is willing to admit only mathematics to the status of a rational science, capable of demonstrating its conclusions with certainty. He insists upon experimental reasoning in the study of nature, wherein only probable conclusions can be attained. But he does not make these critical points in terms of science versus philosophy. If the traditional metaphysics is to be rejected, it is not because it is philosophy rather than science, but because it represents a failure in philosophy *or* science, resulting from the wrong method of dealing with matters of fact.

In the 19th century, however, Auguste Comte formulates a doctrine which, under the title of *Positive Philosophy*, explicitly declares that only the positive sciences—the study of natural, mental, and social phenomena by empirical methods—deserve to be called "sciences" in the eulogistic sense of that term. In contrast, philosophy is mere speculation, and religion is superstition. The word "speculation" is for the positivist only slightly less invidious than "superstition." Whereas superstition implies irrational belief, speculation represents a futile attempt by reason to go behind the phenomena in order to discover ultimate causes or substances. This cannot result in anything but guesswork or conjecture—never in knowledge or science, which are the same for the positivist. For all its show of logic and system, philosophy cannot produce conclusions which have the validity or objectivity of science, because it tries to do more than explore and describe the phenomena and because it tries to do whatever it does without investigation or experiment.

From many sources in addition to Comte similar views converge to form an attitude generally prevalent in the world today under the name of positivism. All its current varieties seem to have this much in common: the identification of science with knowledge of fact, and further, the restriction of such knowledge to conclusions obtained and verified empirically. Whatever does not accord with this conception of science is either, like mathematics or logic, a purely formal discipline or, like philosophy and religion, it is conjecture, opinion, or belief—personal, subjective, even wishful.

It seems appropriate that the most recent author in the set of great books should provide us with a declaration of positivism and that he should set science against philosophy and religion. It is also fitting that he should be a scientist in the field of psychology, since psychology is a late-comer among the disciplines which, once branches of philosophy, now claim to be positive sciences. Not only late, but last, according to Freud, for "sociology, which deals with the behavior of man in society, can be nothing other than applied psychology. Strictly speaking, indeed, there are only two sciences—psychology, pure and applied, and natural science."

In his *New Introductory Lectures on Psycho-Analysis*, Freud concludes with a statement of what he calls the "scientific *Weltanschauung*." In essence, he thinks, "it asserts that there is no other source of knowledge of the universe, but the intellectual manipulation of carefully verified observations, in fact, what is called research, and that no knowledge can be obtained from revelation, intuition, or inspiration." Freud makes the drastic implications of this statement quite explicit. "It is inadmissible to declare," he writes, "that science is one field of human intellectual activity, and that religion and philosophy are others, at least as valuable, and that science has no business to interfere with the other two, that they all have an equal claim to truth, and that everyone is free to choose whence he shall draw his convictions and in which he shall place his belief.

"Such an attitude," he goes on, "is considered particularly respectable, tolerant, broad-minded, and free from narrow prejudices. Unfortunately, it is not tenable; it shares all the pernicious qualities of an entirely unscientific *Weltanschauung*, and in practice comes to much the same thing. The bare fact is that truth cannot be tolerant and cannot admit compromise or limitations, that scientific research looks on the whole field of human activity as its own, and must adopt an uncompromisingly critical attitude towards any other power that seeks to usurp any part of its province."

As a threat to the dominion of science over man and society, "religion alone is a really serious enemy." Philosophy, Freud thinks, "has no immediate influence on the great majority of mankind"; whereas "religion is a tremendous force which exerts its power over the strongest emotions of human beings." Religion and science might be compatible if religion, offering men something "incomparably more beautiful, more comforting, and more ennobling than anything they could ever get from science," would only say: 'It is a fact that I cannot give you what men commonly call truth; to obtain that, you must go to science.' "

But religion cannot say that, Freud thinks, without losing "all influence over the mass of mankind," and science cannot, on its side, yield at all in its claim to being the *only* avenue to truth. Employing a method which "carefully examines the trustworthiness of the sense perceptions on which it bases its conclusions," which "provides itself with new perceptions . . . not obtainable by everyday means," and which "isolates the determinants of these new experiences by purposely varied experimentation," science alone can "arrive at correspondence with reality." It is "this correspondence with the real external world we call truth"; and thus when "religion claims that it can take the place of science and that, because it is beneficent and ennobling, it must therefore be true, that claim is, in fact, an encroachment, which, in the interests of everyone, should be resisted."

Philosophy does not seem to Freud to offer men a genuine alternative to scientific truth. Unlike religion, it is not in his view necessarily opposed to science; at times it even behaves "as if it were a science," and to some extent makes "use of the same methods." But insofar as it parts company with science by clinging "to the illusion that it can produce a complete and coherent picture of the universe," philosophy must be regarded as an impostor in the halls of knowledge.

The picture philosophy tries to construct, Freud says, "must needs fall to pieces with every new advance in our knowledge." Not itself knowledge, but mere opinion or speculation, philosophy does not, any more than religion, offer a substitute for science. Both together fall under Freud's interdict. Both together would be outcasts from human culture if what he calls "our best hope for the future," that is, "the intellect—the scientific spirit, reason—should in time establish a dictatorship over the human mind."

WILLIAM JAMES, ALMOST contemporary with Freud, also draws a sharp line between science and philosophy. Writing his *Principles of Psychology* at a time when the experimental methods of the natural sciences, especially physiology, have just been introduced into the study of mental phenomena, he is at pains to define the scope of psychology as a natural science, and to separate the questions which can be properly considered by a scientist from those which belong to the philosopher. But, unlike Freud, James does not seem to regard the philosopher as engaged in a futile effort to solve problems which are either insoluble or better left until science finds means for solving them.

For James the distinction between science and philosophy does not seem to lie only in the methods they employ, though the empirical or experimental approach does have a bearing on the kind of problems scientists can undertake to solve and the conclusions they can reach. The problems and the conclusions are themselves characteristically different from those of the philosopher.

The scientist *describes* the phenomena, according to James, as precisely as possible and as comprehensively, but without any implication of finality or totality. He recognizes that his descriptive formulations are tentative and incomplete, always subject to the discovery of new data or a more refined presentation of the evidence. Above all, he admits that he is only describing, not *explaining*—not laying bare the ultimate reality which gives the phenomena their deepest intelligibility, or ascertaining the causes which show why, not merely how, things happen as they do.

In the Preface to his *Principles*, James says that he has "kept close to the point of view of natural science throughout the book . . . This book, assuming that thoughts and feelings exist and are vehicles of knowledge, thereupon contends that psychology, when she has ascertained the empirical correlation of the various sorts of thought or feeling with definite conditions of the brain, can go no farther—can go no farther, that is, as a natural science. If she goes farther, she becomes metaphysical. All attempts to *explain* our phenomenally given thoughts as products of deeper-lying entities . . . are metaphysical."

This scientific point of view, James admits, "is anything but ultimate. . . . The data assumed by psychology, just like those assumed by physics, must sometime be overhauled. The effort to overhaul them clearly and thoroughly is metaphysics." James does not imply that metaphysics cannot "perform her task well," but he does think that "she . . . spoils two good things when she injects herself into a natural science."

Science and metaphysics should be kept quite separate, even though the sciences, in accumulating "a mass of descriptive details," run "into queries which only a metaphysics alive to the weight of her task can hope successfully to deal with. That will perhaps be centuries hence; and meanwhile the best mark of health that a science can show is this unfinished-seeming front."

The variance of James' conception of metaphysics and its future from other traditional views on that subject is discussed in the chapter on METAPHYSICS. Here it is relevant to observe that James has a conception of science broad enough to include both the empirical natural sciences and what he calls the "pure or *a priori* sciences of Classification, Logic, and Mathematics." Yet in his view metaphysics does represent philosophy as opposed to science, because it aims at ultimate reality or underlying causes. For example, he rejects the theory of a soul, not because he knows it to be false, but because he thinks it has no place in "a psychology which contents itself with verifiable laws" and which is to "remain positivistic and non-metaphysical."

James seems to embrace the positivist view, prevalent in the 19th century and our own day. He limits science to, as well as excludes philosophy from, the domain of empirical knowledge. In discussing the possibility of free will, he says that "Psychology will be Psychology and Science, Science, as much as ever (as much and no more) in this world, whether free-will be true in it or not. Science, however, must be constantly reminded that her purposes are not the only purposes, and that the order of uniform causation which she has use for, and is therefore right in postulating, may be enveloped in a wider order, in which she has no claims at all."

THOSE MODERN SCIENTISTS and philosophers who do not make a sharp distinction between science and philosophy and who antedate any explicit formulation of the positivist doctrine, nevertheless do for the most part conceive natural science as experimental in its method and as having for its goal the formulation of general laws describing and correlating the phenomena. They do not all exclude causes from the consideration of the natural scientist; nor do they all, as stringently as James, rule out explanation in favor of description or correlation. Furthermore, the almost universal emphasis by modern writers upon the experimental character of the natural sciences does not mean a universal identification of science with the experimental disciplines.

Mathematics, for example, is usually regarded as a science in spite of its being nonexperimental. For Locke and Hume, as well as for Descartes, it exhibits certain characteristics —the self-evidence of principles, the certainty of demonstrations—which make it more genuinely worthy of the high name of science than are the tentative hypotheses and probable conclusions of experimental physics. Other disciplines are called "sciences" by comparison with mathematics rather than physics. Descartes, for instance, seems to think that metaphysics can as surely be made a science as mathematics can be. Locke argues that demonstration from axioms is not limited to the science of quantity. As much clarity and certainty is attainable in reasoning about moral matters. Ethics is no less a science than mathematics.

Hobbes appears to take a similar view of politics, though it must be noted in his case that he differs from Descartes and Locke, from Bacon, Hume, and others in not distinguishing mathematics from physics with respect to the latter's need for experimental evidence. All the sciences are for him alike in being "the demonstrations of consequences of one affirmation to another," regardless of "the diversity of the matter." The "certain and infallible" sign that a man is a scientist in any field of subject matter is that he can "demonstrate the truth thereof perspicuously to another."

Hobbes, furthermore, seems to think that what is true of geometry is true of every science, namely, that it must begin with definitions. "In geometry," he says, "men begin at settling the signification of their words; which settling of significations, they call *definitions*." Without definitions, science is impossible. "In the right definition of names," Hobbes maintains, "lies the first use of speech, which is the acquisition of science; and in the wrong, or no definitions, lies the first abuse, from which proceed all false or senseless tenets."

Freud expresses the opposite view, which is generally more characteristic of the attitude of the modern scientist, especially the experimentalist or empiricist in method. "The view is often defended," he writes, "that sciences should be built on clear and sharply defined basal concepts." But "in actual fact, no science, not even the most exact, begins with such definitions. The true beginning of scientific activity," Freud holds, "consists rather in describing phenomena and then proceeding to group, classify and correlate them. Even at the stage of description, it is not possible to avoid applying certain abstract ideas to the material in hand, ideas derived from various sources and certainly not the fruit of new experience only. . . . They must at first necessarily possess some measure of uncertainty; there can be no question of any clear limitation of their content. So long as they remain in this condition, we come to an understanding about their meaning by repeated references to the material of observation, from which we seem to have deduced our abstract ideas, but which is in point of fact subject to them."

The basic concepts or definitions of a science are, according to Freud, "in the nature of conventions; although," he adds, "everything depends on their being chosen in no arbitrary manner, but determined by the important relations they have to the empirical material. . . . It is only after more searching investigation of the field in question that we are able to formulate with increased clarity the scientific concepts underlying it. . . . Then indeed, it may be time to immure them in definitions. The progress of science, however, demands a certain elasticity even in these definitions." This may not be true of mathematical concepts or definitions, but, Freud points out, the science of physics illustrates "the way in which even those 'basal concepts' that are firmly established in the form of definitions are constantly being altered in their content."

WITH THE EXCEPTION OF HOBBES, the notion that scientific conclusions can be drawn from definitions or can be established without recourse to experiment, is not usually extended by modern writers from mathematics and metaphysics to physics. As the chapter on PHYSICS shows, the basic division of the study of nature into philosophical and scientific physics becomes equivalent, in modern times, to a separation of the philosophy of nature from the experimental natural sciences. We shall return presently to that sense of "science" in which physics is associated with mathematics and metaphysics as a branch of theoretic philosophy or as one of the speculative sciences. All three disciplines are thought of as proceeding in the same way: by the demonstration of conclusions from principles obtained by induction from experience—ordinary sense-experience, that is, not the special experiences artificially contrived in a laboratory under experimental conditions. But it should be observed that, in the modern period, even those authors who use "science" in the foregoing sense when they discuss mathematics and metaphysics, treat physics differently. They hold that physics must be experimental if it is to be scientific.

In proportion as modern physics becomes more and more the model of science, the meaning of the word "science" tends to become reserved for experimental study, or at least for empirical investigation, so that non-experimental disciplines, like metaphysics or ethics, are questioned when they call themselves "sciences." Other disciplines try to establish themselves as sciences by imitating physics. Marx, for example, in presenting his own work as economic *science*, seeks to explain how it can be scientific even if it is not experimental.

"The physicist," he writes, "either observes physical phenomena where they occur in their most typical form and most free from disturbing influence, or, wherever possible, he makes experiments under conditions that assure the occurrence of the phenomenon in its normality." If experiment, in the strict sense, is impossible in economics, at least the student of economics can be scientific in his effort to observe the phenomena "in their most typical form." England, Marx thinks, offers the most typical example of "the capitalist mode of production, and the conditions of production and exchange corresponding to that mode." Hence, for scientific purposes, he has used England "as the chief illustration in the development of [his] theoretical ideas."

THE EXPERIMENTAL CHARACTER of modern physics, whether it is called natural science or natural philosophy, is discussed in the chapter on PHYSICS. The distinction between the construction or use of experiments and the appeal to experience—apart from experiment—either as a source or as a test of scientific formulations, is discussed in the chapter on EXPERIENCE, as well as in the chapters on HYPOTHESIS and INDUCTION. Here it seems pertinent to note that neither the distinction between induction and deduction, nor the distinction between hypotheses and axioms, unequivocally marks the line which separates science from philosophy.

Aristotle and Bacon, for example, regard induction as the source of axioms in metaphysics or *philosophia prima* as well as in physics or the philosophy of nature. They may have different theories of induction, but only insofar as one conceives induction as an intuitive generalization from *ordinary sense-experience*, and the other makes induction an inference from *experiments*, does the difference between them seem to have a bearing on the distinction between philosophy and science.

Similarly, the difference between the scientist's and the philosopher's consideration of hypotheses seems to lie not in the role they play in reasoning or argument, but rather in their having or not having a special relation to experimentation, either to guide it or to submit to its test.

Experiment, then, seems to be the distinguishing mark of science on the side of method; and, by an extension of meaning, even in those subject matters where experiments in the strict sense—in laboratories, with apparatus, under controlled conditions—are impossible, the scientist differs from the philosopher in an analogous point of method. The scientist investigates, does research, makes observations which go beyond the experiences which ordinary men have in the course of daily life.

It seems to be in this spirit that Newton opens the *Optics* with the statement that "my design in this book is not to explain the properties of light by hypotheses, but to propose and prove them by reason and experiments." In the same spirit Faraday says of himself: "As an experimentalist, I feel bound to let experiment guide me into any train of thought which it may justify; being satisfied that experiment, like analysis, must lead to strict truth if rightly interpreted; and believing also that it is in its nature far more suggestive of new trains of thought and new conditions of natural power."

Lavoisier imposes upon himself the rule "never to form any conclusion which is not an immediate consequence necessarily flowing from observation and experiment." Gilbert criticizes those who write about magnetism without recourse to experiments—philosophers who are not themselves investigators and have no first-hand acquaintance with things. Referring to "what has been held by the vulgar and by tradition" concerning the motion of the heart and arteries, Harvey proposes to separate true from false opinions "by dissection, multiplied experience and accurate observation."

Even a scientist like Fourier, who conceives physical theory as a kind of applied mathematics, says that "no considerable progress can hereafter be made which is not founded on experiments . . . for mathematical analysis can deduce from general and simple phenomena the expression of the laws of nature; but the special application of these laws to very complex effects demands a long series of exact observations." Like Fourier, Galileo also combines mathematics and experiment in the study of nature. But though he is willing to introduce experiments where they are necessary in order to test rival hypotheses or alternative mathematical formulations of the laws of motion, he seems to express a preference for the rigor of purely mathematical physics.

In the Fourth Day of the *Two New Sciences*, discussing the parabolic path of projectiles, one person in the dialogue, Sagredo, says that "the force of rigid demonstrations such as occur only in mathematics fills me with wonder and delight." The understanding thus derived, he adds, "far outweighs the mere information obtained by the testimony of others or even by repeated experiment." Agreeing with this, Salviati, another person in the dialogue, claims that "the knowledge of a single fact acquired through a discovery of its causes prepares the mind to understand and ascertain other facts without need of recourse to experiment, precisely as in the present case, where by argumentation alone the Author proves with certainty that the maximum range occurs when the elevation is 45°. He thus demonstrates what has perhaps never been observed in experience, namely, that of other shots those which exceed or fall short of 45° by equal amounts have equal ranges."

THE CONCEPTION OF SCIENCE as consisting in a rigorous demonstration of conclusions from axioms—whether in mathematics or other subject matters—seems to be modern as well as ancient. It is found in Descartes and Spinoza, in Hobbes and Locke, as well as in Plato and Aristotle. Holding that "science in its entirety is true and evident cognition," Descartes may add that "it has been mathematicians alone who have been able to succeed in making any demonstrations, that is to say, producing reasons which are evident and certain"; yet he also hopes to make metaphysics a science after the model of mathematics.

This conception of science is somewhat qualified by Descartes when he discusses the study of nature. Here he tends toward experimentalism. Here he says that "experiments . . . become so much the more necessary the more one is advanced in knowledge." Referring to particular effects which "might be deduced from the principles in many different ways," he thinks that the only way to overcome the difficulty of discovering the principles on which the effects do depend is "to try to find experiments of such a nature that their result is not the same if it has to be explained by one of the methods, as it would be if explained by the other."

On the other hand, the conception of science as knowledge founded upon experiment, or at least upon extended observation, seems to be ancient as well as modern. Aristotle criticizes those of his predecessors in physics whose "explanation of the observations is not consistent with the observations." The test of principles "in the knowledge of nature," he says, "is the unimpeachable evidence of the senses as to each fact." It is for this reason that he praises the method of Democritus as scientific.

"Lack of experience," Aristotle writes, "diminishes our power of taking a comprehensive view of the admitted facts. Hence those who dwell in intimate association with nature and its phenomena grow more and more able to formulate, as the foundations of their theories, principles such as to admit of a wide and coherent development; while those whom devotion to abstract discussions has rendered unobservant of the facts are too ready to dogmatize on the basis of a few observations. The rival treatments of the subject now before us will serve to illustrate how great is the difference between a 'scientific' and a 'dialectical' method of inquiry. For whereas the Platonists argue that there must be atomic magnitudes 'because otherwise "The Triangle" will be more than one,' Democritus would appear to have been convinced by arguments appropriate to the subject, *i.e.*, drawn from the science of nature."

There are many passages in which Aristotle rejects an astronomical hypothesis because it does not account for the observations, or favors one theory against all others because it alone seems to fit the sensible phenomena. So, too, in his biological works, he makes experience the test of theories. Speaking of the generation of bees, for example, he says that if we ever learn the truth about this matter, "credit must be given to observation rather than to theories, and to theories only if what they affirm agrees with the observed facts." And in his treatise *On the Motion of Animals*, he calls for "reference to particulars in the world of sense, for with these in view we seek general theories, and with these we believe that general theories ought to harmonize."

But Aristotle also defines science as the certain demonstration of universal and necessary conclusions from self-evident principles. "Scientific knowledge," he writes, "is judgment about things that are universal and necessary; and the conclusions of demonstration . . . follow from first principles (for scientific knowledge involves apprehension of a rational ground)." The emphasis here is on knowledge of causes, and on the certainty and necessity of conclusions which can be demonstrated from axiomatic truths.

By these criteria, metaphysics and mathematics are, in Aristotle's conception of the three philosophical sciences, perfect examples of scientific knowledge; physics as a general philosophy of nature is also scientific knowledge in this sense; but the particular natural sciences, such as astronomy or zoology, are more empirical than philosophical in character. At least they involve admixtures of demonstration from principles with the verification of hypotheses by observation. To the extent that they are empirical, they are qualified by an uncertainty and a tentativeness in formulation which do not seem to be present in Aristotle's conception of the purely philosophical sciences.

It might even be said that the knowledge of nature which depends on empirical research is not strictly scientific at all. Locke appears to say just that. "How far soever human industry may advance useful and experimental philosophy in physical things," he writes, "scientifical will still be out of our reach." Holding that "our knowledge of bodies is to be improved only by experience," Locke adds: "I deny not but a man accustomed to rational and regular experiments, shall be able to see farther into the nature of bodies, and guess righter at their yet unknown properties, than one that is a stranger to them; but yet, as I have said, this is but judgment and opinion, not knowledge and certainty. This way of getting and improving our knowledge in substances only by experience and history . . . makes me suspect that natural philosophy is not capable of being made a science."

WHETHER THE EXPERIMENTAL study of nature is the type of all scientific knowledge (in its object, its method, and the character of its conclusions) or whether, according to another conception, the philosophical disciplines are the more perfect, perhaps even the only examples of science, there seems to be no question that different values attach to these two meanings of science—or, as it is currently expressed, to science and philosophy.

The philosophical sciences may be either theoretic or practical according as they aim at wisdom or at action, but they are seldom praised as being useful productively. The practical sciences which are also traditionally regarded as branches of moral philosophy—such as ethics, politics, and economics—may be knowledge put to use in the guidance of individual conduct or the affairs of society, but apart from poetics, which may direct production in the sphere of the fine arts, there does not seem to be any philosophical science, or branch of philosophy, that provides a mastery of matter or some control over nature. None has applications in the sphere of the useful arts.

As indicated in the chapters on ART, KNOWLEDGE, and PHILOSOPHY, Bacon appears to take a contrary view. Using the word "practical" to mean productive rather than moral or civil, he divides the philosophy of nature into speculative and practical branches. He regards mechanics as the application of physics to useful purposes, and finds a productive counterpart to metaphysics in what he calls "magic."

Nor is Bacon's point merely that "the real and legitimate goal of the sciences is the endowment of human life with new inventions and riches," in opposition to those whom he criticizes for thinking that "the contemplation of truth is more dignified and exalted than any utility or extent of effects." In addition he thinks that the truth of science can be tested by its productive utility. "That which is most useful in practice," he writes, "is most correct in theory."

Bacon's position with regard to the productive utility of science would not be contrary to the traditional view if by "the philosophy of nature" he meant science in the experimental rather than the philosophical sense. His emphasis upon experimentation in all parts of the study of nature suggests that that is the case. The fact that he places equal emphasis upon machinery and inventions and power over nature also suggests that technology is the other face of any science which is experimental in method.

Bacon and Descartes seem to be the first to perceive that knowledge which is experimental in origin must be by its very nature capable of technological applications. The instruments and apparatus which Bacon regards as necessary implements of science, no less than the machinery and inventions which science can be expected to produce, represent the very same techniques of operating upon nature. Experimental science is thus seen to be at once the creature and creator of technology. As Plato's *Republic* projects a society which cannot be realized unless it is ruled by the science of the philosopher, so Bacon's *New Atlantis* prophesies a civilization which the dominance of experimentalism and technology have brought to present reality.

OUTLINE OF TOPICS

1. Conceptions of science

  1*a*. Science as a philosophical discipline: certain or perfect knowledge

    (1) The intellectual virtue of science: its relation to understanding and wisdom

    (2) The division and hierarchy of the philosophical sciences

  1*b*. Science as the discipline of experimental inquiry and the organization of experimental knowledge: the scientific spirit

    (1) The utility of science: the applications of experimental knowledge in the mastery of nature; machinery and inventions

    (2) The effects of science on human life: the economic and social implications of technology

  1*c*. The issue concerning science and philosophy: the distinction and relation between experimental and philosophical science, or between empirical and rational science

2. The relation of science to other kinds of knowledge

  2a. The relation between science and religion: the conception of sacred theology as a science

  2b. The comparison of science with poetry and history

3. The relation of science to action and production

  3a. The distinction between theoretic and practical science: the character of ethics, politics, economics, and jurisprudence as sciences

  3b. The distinction between pure and applied science: the relation of science to the useful arts

4. The nature of scientific knowledge

  4a. The principles of science: facts, definitions, axioms, hypotheses

  4b. The objects of science: the essential and necessary; the sensible and measurable

  4c. The role of cause in science: explanation and description as aims of scientific inquiry

  4d. The generality of scientific formulations: universal laws of nature

  4e. The certitude and probability or the finality and tentativeness of scientific conclusions: the adequacy of scientific theories

5. Scientific method

  5a. The role of experience: observation and experiment

  5b. Techniques of exploration and discovery: the ascertainment of fact

  5c. The use of mathematics in science: calculation and measurement

  5d. Induction and deduction in the philosophy of nature and natural science

  5e. The use of hypotheses: prediction and verification

6. The development of the sciences

  6a. The technical conditions of scientific progress: the invention of scientific instruments or apparatus

  6b. The place of science in society: the social conditions favorable to the advancement of science

7. The evaluation of science

  7a. The praise of science by comparison with opinion, superstition, magic

  7b. The satirization of science and scientists: the foibles of science

REFERENCES

References are listed by volume number (in bold type), author's name, and page number. Bible references are to book, chapter, and verse of the Authorized King James version of the Bible. The abbreviation "esp" calls the reader's attention to one or more especially relevant parts of a whole reference; "passim" signifies that the topic is discussed intermittently rather than continuously in the work or passage cited. Where the work as a whole is relevant to the topic, the page numbers refer to the entire work. For general guidance in the use of *The Great Ideas,* consult the Preface.

1. Conceptions of science

1*a*. Science as a philosophical discipline: certain or perfect knowledge

7 Plato, 391–398, 570–574
8 Aristotle, 97–99, 275, 500–502, 511–512
9 Aristotle, 388, 389
20 Aquinas, 36–37
23 Hobbes, 60, 71
31 Descartes, 2–5, 75–77
31 Spinoza, 458–460
35 Locke, 321, 322–323
35 Hume, 458
42 Kant, 1–13, 211–218, 243–250, 365–366

1*a*(1) The intellectual virtue of science: its relation to understanding and wisdom

9 Aristotle, 387–393
20 Aquinas, 36–37, 68–69, 79–80
31 Descartes, 1–2
31 Spinoza, 387–389

1*a*(2) The division and hierarchy of the philosophical sciences

7 Plato, 391–398, 634–635
8 Aristotle, 119, 270–271, 513–516, 522–525, 547–548, 587–588, 589–590, 592–593, 632
11 Nicomachus, 812–813
17 Plotinus, 10–12
18 Augustine, 336
19 Aquinas, 451–453
20 Aquinas, 23–24, 40–41
23 Hobbes, 71, 72, 268
29 Cervantes, 258
30 Bacon, 40–48, 120, 140
31 Descartes, 1–3, 5–7, 43–44, 46–48
34 Newton, 1
35 Locke, 394–395
39 Smith, 335–337
45 Kant, 15–16, 17–19, 253, 351–352

1*b*. Science as the discipline of experimental inquiry and the organization of experimental knowledge: the scientific spirit

16 Ptolemy, 5–6
28 Gilbert, 1–2
28 Galileo, 207–208
28 Harvey, 267–268, 331–337
30 Bacon, 13, 42, 57–58, 105–195 passim
31 Descartes, 60–67 passim
33 Pascal, 356–357, 361
34 Newton, 371–372, 379, 542, 543
34 Huygens, 553
35 Hume, 465, 466, 503–509 passim
42 Kant, 5–6, 146–149, 248–250, 567–568
45 Lavoisier, 1–2, 6–7
45 Faraday, 440, 659, 851
46 Hegel, 361
53 James, 89–90, 882–884
54 Freud, 818–819, 874, 879–882

1*b*(1) The utility of science: the applications of experimental knowledge in the mastery of nature; machinery and inventions

11 Nicomachus, 812–813
13 Virgil, 40–41
14 Plutarch, 252–255
28 Gilbert, 75, 85–89, 100–101
28 Galileo, 154–155, 191–193
28 Harvey, 305
30 Bacon, 14–15, 34, 56, 120, 169–170, 175–194 passim, 210–214
31 Descartes, 61
34 Newton, 412–423
39 Smith, 5–6, 308–309
40 Gibbon, 661–663
41 Gibbon, 291–292
45 Lavoisier, 41–44
45 Fourier, 183–184
45 Faraday, 433–440
46 Hegel, 267
49 Darwin, 19
50 Marx, 170, 180–188
54 Freud, 802

1*b*(2) The effects of science on human life: the economic and social implications of technology

5 Aeschylus, 44–45
30 Bacon, 120, 133, 134–135, 188–194
31 Descartes, 66–67
35 Hume, 452–453
36 Swift, 106–107
38 Rousseau, 363–366
41 Gibbon, 509–510

1c. The issue concerning science and philosophy: the distinction and relation between experimental and philosophical science, or between empirical and rational science

2. The relation of science to other kinds of knowledge

2a. The relation between science and religion: the conception of sacred theology as a science

2b. The comparison of science with poetry and history

3. The relation of science to action and production

3a. The distinction between theoretic and practical science: the character of ethics, politics, economics, and jurisprudence as sciences

3*b*. The distinction between pure and applied science: the relation of science to the useful arts

7 Plato, 261–262, 581–582
8 Aristotle, 499–500, 555–556, 571–572, 573, 605
9 Aristotle, 388–389
10 Hippocrates, 1–9, 144
10 Galen, 195–196
13 Virgil, 37–99 passim
14 Plutarch, 252–255
20 Aquinas, 37–38
28 Harvey, 305
30 Bacon, 5–6, 48–49, 50–51, 121–122, 137–140, 175–195 passim, 210–214
31 Descartes, 66–67
34 Huygens, 551–552
35 Locke, 361–362
35 Hume, 452–453
36 Swift, 106–112
39 Smith, 5–6
42 Kant, 60, 266–267, 551–556
43 Mill, 369
45 Fourier, 181
54 Freud, 123–125

4. The nature of scientific knowledge

4*a*. The principles of science: facts, definitions, axioms, hypotheses

7 Plato, 383–388, 391–398
8 Aristotle, 63–64, 97–122, 136–137, 194–195, 335–336, 397, 411, 500, 513–515, 524–532, 547–548, 589–592, 610, 631–632, 673
9 Aristotle, 389
11 Euclid, 1–2
18 Augustine, 265–271 passim
19 Aquinas, 102–103, 175–178
20 Aquinas, 221–223, 383–384
23 Hobbes, 56, 58–61
28 Galileo, 197, 200
28 Harvey, 334
30 Bacon, 56–59, 113–114, 120–121, 127–128, 137–139
31 Descartes, 4–5, 13, 15, 51–54, 75–77, 82, 83, 89, 95–96, 125, 130–131
31 Spinoza, 387–388
33 Pascal, 171–172, 430–434 passim
34 Newton, 1–2, 5–24
34 Huygens, 553, 600–601
35 Locke, 337–344, 358–360, 362
42 Kant, 68–69, 179–182, 215–216, 293–294, 302–303, 457
43 Mill, 461–464 passim
45 Fourier, 169–170, 172
53 James, 862–864 passim
54 Freud, 412

4*b*. The objects of science: the essential and necessary; the sensible and measurable

7 Plato, 383–398, 633–635
8 Aristotle, 100–104, 119–120, 121–123, 499–501, 514–516, 547–549, 593
9 Aristotle, 161–169
11 Nicomachus, 811–812
30 Bacon, 137–153
31 Descartes, 2–3, 30–32, 47
34 Newton, 1–2, 270–271
35 Locke, 268–283 passim, 311–312
35 Berkeley, 433
35 Hume, 458, 508–509
42 Kant, 46–47, 550–551, 603–604
45 Fourier, 177
53 James, 647–648, 876, 882–884
54 Freud, 879

4*c*. The role of cause in science: explanation and description as aims of scientific inquiry

7 Plato, 240–246, 455
8 Aristotle, 97–137 passim, 271, 499–500, 565–566, 568–569
9 Aristotle, 161–165, 255
10 Galen, 169
12 Lucretius, 67–68, 89
16 Kepler, 958–960
19 Aquinas, 112–113
20 Aquinas, 424–425
28 Gilbert, 5–7 passim
28 Galileo, 202–203
28 Harvey, 319, 335–336, 393
30 Bacon, 43, 45–47, 110–111, 127, 132, 137
31 Descartes, 15, 61–62, 66, 84–87, 158–162
31 Spinoza, 355, 356–357, 422–424
34 Newton, 7–8, 270, 541–542, 543–544
34 Huygens, 553
35 Locke, 315–317, 322–323
35 Berkeley, 418–419, 422–423 passim, 424–426
35 Hume, 458–459, 460, 475–476, 477, 480–482, 487, 509
42 Kant, 46–47, 285–286, 311–314, 557–558
45 Lavoisier, 9–10
49 Darwin, 239–240
51 Tolstoy, 344, 470, 650, 694–696
53 James, 745, 885–886

4*d*. The generality of scientific formulations: universal laws of nature

7 Plato, 391–398
8 Aristotle, 100–102, 107–109, 116–118, 120, 563–564
19 Aquinas, 440–442
28 Galileo, 197
28 Harvey, 332–334
30 Bacon, 108, 127–128, 138–139, 161
31 Descartes, 167
31 Spinoza, 395
33 Pascal, 358
34 Newton, 270–271, 281–282, 371–372
34 Huygens, 551–552
35 Locke, 308–309, 316, 323, 331–336 passim, 360–362 passim
35 Berkeley, 408, 409, 433–434 passim, 438
35 Hume, 454–455, 460

42 Kant, 195–200, 211–218, 562–563, 564, 581–582
45 Fourier, 169
45 Faraday, 391, 398, 595, 655, 670, 855
49 Darwin, 98
51 Tolstoy, 469–470, 693–696
53 James, 861–886 passim

4*e*. The certitude and probability or the finality and tentativeness of scientific conclusions: the adequacy of scientific theories

7 Plato, 397–398, 447
8 Aristotle, 48, 97–99, 102–103, 121–122, 384
9 Aristotle, 339–340, 349
16 Ptolemy, 83, 429
16 Copernicus, 505–506
16 Kepler, 888–890, 929
19 Aquinas, 297–298, 458–459, 463–464
20 Aquinas, 409
23 Hobbes, 65
28 Galileo, 202–203
30 Bacon, 14–15, 47–48, 150–153
31 Descartes, 1–25 passim, 47–48, 51–54, 130–131
31 Spinoza, 386–391
32 Milton, 233–234
33 Pascal, 357–358, 365–366, 430–434
34 Newton, 543
35 Locke, 309–312 passim, 316, 332–336 passim, 360–363 passim
35 Berkeley, 424
35 Hume, 454, 487, 508–509
42 Kant, 129–130, 133–134, 218–222, 227–230, 248–250, 603
43 Mill, 277, 283–284
45 Lavoisier, 32–33
45 Faraday, 774–775, 850–851
49 Darwin, 590
53 James, 647–648, 655–659 passim, 863–866
54 Freud, 463, 484–485, 546, 661–662, 818–819

5. Scientific method

5*a*. The role of experience: observation and experiment

7 Plato, 386–388, 391–398
8 Aristotle, 63–64, 111, 120, 136–137, 259, 361–362, 499–500
9 Aristotle, 35, 435–436
10 Galen, 173–177
19 Aquinas, 444–446
21 Dante, 108
23 Hobbes, 267
25 Montaigne, 285–286, 377
28 Gilbert, 6–7
28 Galileo, 203–205, 207–208
28 Harvey, 267–274, 285, 286–304, 320, 322–323, 331–335, 411
30 Bacon, 43–44, 105–195
31 Descartes, 12–13, 22–23, 28, 44, 56–59, 60–67, 75–77
33 Pascal, 355–358
34 Newton, 270–271
35 Locke, 317, 360–363
35 Berkeley, 418, 433
35 Hume, 459–460, 479
42 Kant, 227, 562–563
43 Mill, 463
45 Faraday, 385, 467, 542
49 Darwin, 14–18 passim, 136–139 passim
53 James, 56–66, 122–127, 265–268, 341–344, 352–355 passim
54 Freud, 488, 545, 815

5*b*. Techniques of exploration and discovery: the ascertainment of fact

10 Galen, 173–177
28 Galileo, 131–138, 148–149, 157–177
28 Harvey, 273, 280, 331–333, 335–336
30 Bacon, 13–14, 30–31, 56–60, 114, 116–117, 120–121, 126–129, 137–138, 140, 176–177
33 Pascal, 356–365, 382–389, 390–403 passim
34 Newton, 386–455, 457–470, 496–516
35 Locke, 281–282
42 Kant, 387
45 Lavoisier, 10–12, 17–20, 22–24, 29–33
45 Faraday, 607, 659
49 Darwin, 136–139 passim
53 James, 385, 677

5*c*. The use of mathematics in science: calculation and measurement

7 Plato, 391–398, 453–454
8 Aristotle, 477–478, 480–481
18 Augustine, 27–28
20 Aquinas, 424–425
23 Hobbes, 58
28 Galileo, 136–137, 164–166, 178–260
30 Bacon, 46, 175–188
34 Newton, 1–372
35 Hume, 460
45 Lavoisier, 33–36, 41–44, 96–103
45 Fourier, 172–173, 182–185, 196–251 passim
45 Faraday, 366–371, 444–451, 768–773, 778–793
51 Tolstoy, 469, 589–590
53 James, 348–359

5*d*. Induction and deduction in the philosophy of nature and natural science

8 Aristotle, 90, 97, 99, 111, 148, 211–212, 259, 335–336, 610
9 Aristotle, 596–598, 640–645
10 Hippocrates, 1–3
19 Aquinas, 175–178
28 Galileo, 207–208
28 Harvey, 332–334
30 Bacon, 57–58, 96–97, 105–195
31 Descartes, 10–12, 17–18, 23
33 Pascal, 365–371
34 Newton, 271, 543
34 Huygens, 551–552
35 Berkeley, 434

35 Hume, 458, 479, 487
42 Kant, 195–197
43 Mill, 475
53 James, 674–675

5e. The use of hypotheses: prediction and verification

7 Plato, 242–243, 386–388, 397–398
8 Aristotle, 379, 601–602, 603–605
10 Hippocrates, 1
16 Ptolemy, 429
16 Copernicus, 505–506, 507–508
16 Kepler, 852–853, 888–890, 911, 929, 964
28 Gilbert, 119
28 Harvey, 285, 286–304
31 Descartes, 61–62, 65–66
34 Newton, 371–372, 543
34 Huygens, 551–553
35 Locke, 362
35 Berkeley, 433
42 Kant, 457
45 Faraday, 758–759, 777–778, 850–855 esp 850–851
49 Darwin, 239
51 Tolstoy, 694–696
53 James, 647–648, 863–865
54 Freud, 400–401, 483–485 passim, 502–503, 840

6. The development of the sciences

11 Archimedes, 520, 527
16 Ptolemy, 77–83, 109–112, 223–232, 272–273
16 Copernicus, 505–509, 515, 517–520
16 Kepler, 845–850, 857–863, 907–910, 1009–1010
25 Montaigne, 276–278
30 Bacon, 14–15, 29–32, 48–49, 51–53, 116–130
31 Descartes, 41–67
34 Newton, 1–2, 266–267
34 Huygens, 552–553
39 Smith, 335–337
40 Gibbon, 148
41 Gibbon, 298–300, 325–328
45 Lavoisier, 3–4
45 Fourier, 169
45 Faraday, 824
46 Hegel, 217–219
53 James, 125–127
54 Freud, 137–139, 550–551, 880–881

6a. The technical conditions of scientific progress: the invention of scientific instruments or apparatus

16 Ptolemy, 24–26, 143–144, 166–167
16 Copernicus, 558–559, 586–589, 705–706
16 Kepler, 908
30 Bacon, 169–170, 176, 210–214
34 Newton, 412–423
34 Huygens, 599–600
45 Lavoisier, 87–133 passim
45 Faraday, 277–279, 316–318, 465–467, 768–773, 778–793
50 Marx, 170, 187–188

6b. The place of science in society: the social conditions favorable to the advancement of science

7 Plato, 395, 601–602
8 Aristotle, 500
23 Hobbes, 267
30 Bacon, 7, 14–15, 29–32, 54, 117
35 Hume, 497
40 Gibbon, 158–159, 669–671
41 Gibbon, 327–328 passim, 522–523
43 Mill, 274–293 passim
46 Hegel, 88–89, 106
53 James, 866
54 Freud, 581

7. The evaluation of science

7a. The praise of science by comparison with opinion, superstition, magic

7 Plato, 370–373
8 Aristotle, 121–122
12 Lucretius, 15, 44, 61, 80–81
16 Copernicus, 510
16 Kepler, 847
19 Aquinas, 422–423
20 Aquinas, 382–384
23 Hobbes, 56
30 Bacon, 14–15, 110–111, 113–116, 124, 133, 199–214
31 Descartes, 60–67
33 Pascal, 380–381
35 Locke, 89
35 Hume, 453–454
40 Gibbon, 159
42 Kant, 146–149, 218–227
45 Faraday, 534
46 Hegel, 361
49 Darwin, 85
53 James, 865–866, 882–883
54 Freud, 873–884 passim

7b. The satirization of science and scientists: the foibles of science

5 Aristophanes, 489–493
22 Chaucer, 471–487
25 Montaigne, 257–261
35 Berkeley, 409–410
36 Swift, 103–115, 118–119
36 Sterne, 224–225
47 Goethe, 17–18
48 Melville, 95–105, 365–367
51 Tolstoy, 689–690
53 James, 358–359, 866

CROSS-REFERENCES

For: The treatment of the philosophical sciences, *see* DEFINITION 6a; MATHEMATICS 1–1b; METAPHYSICS 1, 3b; PHILOSOPHY 1, 2b; PHYSICS 1–1a; THEOLOGY 3a; and for the consideration of science as one of the intellectual virtues, *see* VIRTUE AND VICE 2a(2); WISDOM 2a.

Matters relevant to the conception and spirit of science as experimental inquiry, *see* EXPERIENCE 3b; KNOWLEDGE 5c; OPINION 4a; PHYSICS 2; and for the discussion of particular experimental or empirical sciences, *see* ASTRONOMY 1; MAN 2b; MECHANICS 4–4a, 7–7e(5); MEDICINE 2a; PHYSICS 2; SOUL 5b.

Other considerations of the differences and relations between philosophy and science, *see* DEFINITION 6b; METAPHYSICS 3b; NATURE 4b; PHILOSOPHY 1c; PHYSICS 2, 2b; PROGRESS 6b; TRUTH 4c.

The relation of science to religion, *see* PHILOSOPHY 1a; RELIGION 6g; TRUTH 4a; and for the conception of sacred theology as a science, *see* THEOLOGY 4a–4d.

The comparison of science or philosophy with poetry and history, *see* HISTORY 1; PHILOSOPHY 1d; POETRY 5, 5b.

Other discussions relevant to the distinction between theoretic and practical science, *see* JUDGMENT 2; KNOWLEDGE 6e(1); MIND 9a; PHILOSOPHY 2a; PRUDENCE 2a; THEOLOGY 3b, 4d; TRUTH 2c; WISDOM 1b; and for the consideration of the practical or moral sciences, *see* KNOWLEDGE 6e(2), 8b–8c; LOGIC 4e; PHILOSOPHY 2c; STATE 8d; WEALTH 9.

The relation of science to art, and for the technological applications of scientific knowledge, *see* ART 6a, 6c; EXPERIENCE 3; KNOWLEDGE 6e(2), 8a; LABOR 1e; PHYSICS 5; PROGRESS 3c.

Other discussions bearing on the nature and objects of scientific knowledge, *see* ASTRONOMY 1, 3a–3b; CAUSE 5a–5b; HYPOTHESIS 4a–4b; KNOWLEDGE 5c; MECHANICS 4; PHYSICS 2a–2b; PRINCIPLE 3c(1)–3c(3); TRUTH 4c; UNIVERSAL AND PARTICULAR 4f.

Other discussions of scientific method, *see* ART 6b; ASTRONOMY 2a–2c; DEFINITION 4; EXPERIENCE 5–5c; HYPOTHESIS 4d; INDUCTION 1b; LOGIC 4b; MATHEMATICS 5–5b; MECHANICS 2–3; PHYSICS 3, 4a–4d; REASONING 4c, 5b–5b(4).

The effects of science on human life, *see* STATE 7b; WEALTH 3a; and for the social conditions favorable to the advancement of science, *see* KNOWLEDGE 10; OPINION 5b; PROGRESS 6d–6e; TRUTH 8d.

ADDITIONAL READINGS

Listed below are works not included in *Great Books of the Western World*, but relevant to the idea and topics with which this chapter deals. These works are divided into two groups:

I. Works by authors represented in this collection.
II. Works by authors not represented in this collection.

For the date, place, and other facts concerning the publication of the works cited, consult the Bibliography of Additional Readings which follows the last chapter of *The Great Ideas*.

I.

AQUINAS. *On the Trinity of Boethius*, QQ 5–6
HUME. *Of the Rise and Progress of the Arts and Sciences*
KANT. *Metaphysical Foundations of Natural Science*
GOETHE. *Zur Natur- und Wissenschaftslehre*
J. S. MILL. *A System of Logic*, BK III, CH I
FARADAY. *Observations on the Education of the Judgment*
ENGELS. *Herr Eugen Dühring's Revolution in Science*, PART I

II.

SEXTUS EMPIRICUS. *Against the Ethicists*
——. *Against the Logicians*
——. *Against the Physicists*
R. BACON. *Opus Majus*, PART VI
SUÁREZ. *Disputationes Metaphysicae*, I, XXX (15), XLIV (13)

CAMPANELLA. *The Defense of Galileo*
GLANVILL. *The Vanity of Dogmatizing*
COWLEY. *To the Royal Society*
SCHOPENHAUER. *The World as Will and Idea*, VOL II, SUP, CH 12
AMPÈRE. *Essai sur la philosophie des sciences*
COMTE. *The Positive Philosophy*, INTRO
RENAN. *The Future of Science*
COURNOT. *Essai sur les fondements de nos connaissances et sur les charactères de la critique philosophique*
WHEWELL. *The Philosophy of the Inductive Sciences*, VOL II, BK XI, CH 8
——. *On the Philosophy of Discovery*, CH 1–18
HELMHOLTZ. *Popular Lectures on Scientific Subjects*, I, VIII
JEVONS. *The Principles of Science*, BK III–IV, VI
CLIFFORD. *The Common Sense of the Exact Sciences*
——. "On the Aims and Instruments of Scientific Thought," "The Philosophy of the Pure Sciences," in VOL I, *Lectures and Essays*
T. H. HUXLEY. *Methods and Results*, I–II
MACH. *The Analysis of Sensations*
C. S. PEIRCE. *Collected Papers*, VOL I, par 43–283
NIETZSCHE. *The Will to Power*, BK III (1)
FRAZER. *The Golden Bough*, PART I, CH 4; PART VII, CH 13
PEARSON. *The Grammar of Science*
BOSANQUET. *Science and Philosophy*, I
T. VEBLEN. *The Place of Science in Modern Civilization*, pp 1–55
POINCARÉ. *The Value of Science*, PART III
SANTAYANA. *Reason in Science*, CH I, II
CASSIRER. *Substance and Function*
GREGORY. *Discovery*
WEBER. *Science as a Vocation*
N. R. CAMPBELL. *What Is Science?*
EINSTEIN. *Relativity: The Special and the General Theory*
EINSTEIN. *Sidelights on Relativity*
MEYERSON. *De l'explication dans les sciences*
G. N. LEWIS. *The Anatomy of Science*, ESSAY I, VII
BRIDGMAN. *The Logic of Modern Physics*, CH 1–2
J. S. HALDANE. *The Sciences and Philosophy*, LECT I–XIV
M. R. COHEN. *Reason and Nature*, BK I, CH 3 (1–2)
JEFFREYS. *Scientific Inference*
NORTHROP. *Science and First Principles*
TENNANT. *Philosophy of the Sciences*
WHITEHEAD. *The Organization of Thought*, CH 6–7
——. *An Enquiry Concerning the Principles of Natural Knowledge*, CH 3
——. *Science and the Modern World*, CH 1, 9, 12
——. *Adventures of Ideas*, CH 9–10
CARNAP. *The Unity of Science*
——. *Philosophy and Logical Syntax*, III (5–9)
J. S. HUXLEY. *Science and Social Needs*
W. R. THOMPSON. *Science and Common Sense*
BERNAL. *The Social Function of Science*
DEWEY. *Reconstruction in Philosophy*, CH 3
——. *Logic, the Theory of Inquiry*, CH 19, 21, 23–24
——. *Freedom and Culture*, CH 6
MARITAIN. *The Degrees of Knowledge*, CH 1
——. *Science and Wisdom*, pp 3–33
——. *Scholasticism and Politics*, CH 2
CONANT. *On Understanding Science*
B. RUSSELL. *The Analysis of Matter*, CH 15–26
——. *Skeptical Essays*, III
——. *The Scientific Outlook*, CH 1–3, 6–11
——. *Religion and Science*, CH 9
——. *Human Knowledge, Its Scope and Limits*, PART I, III–IV, VI
SARTON. *The Study of the History of Science*
——. *The Life of Science*
PLANCK. *The Philosophy of Physics*, CH 3
——. *Scientific Autobiography*
DEWEY and BENTLEY. *Knowing and the Known*

Chapter 84: SENSE

INTRODUCTION

THE nature of sensation seems at first to be as obvious as its existence. In the tradition of the great books there may be controversy concerning the existence of sense in plants as well as in animals, and there may be controversy over the existence in man of faculties higher than sense. But no one disputes that men and other animals are endowed with a power of sense.

The extent of this power may be questioned, but not the fact that animals and men, when awake, experience sensations or perceive through their senses. Sleep, according to Aristotle, can occur only in those living things which have the power of sense-perception. "If there be an animal not endowed with sense-perception, it is impossible that this should either sleep or wake, since both these are affections of the activity of the primary faculty of sense-perception."

The existence of the sensible—of an external something which causes sensation and can be sensed—also seems to escape denial or dispute. The existence of a purely intelligible reality—of a world of immaterial things incapable of being sensed—is subject to debate in all periods of western thought. The sensible world is sometimes regarded as the only reality; sometimes it is regarded as mere seeming, or appearance, in comparison with the reality of purely intelligible being. Men may also differ on the question whether things possess sensible qualities when they are not being sensed. But with few exceptions, notably Berkeley and Hume, the existence of a sensible world of material things is not denied or seriously doubted.

The controversies and issues indicated above are, for the most part, discussed elsewhere. The chapter on ANIMAL considers the sensitivity of plants. There also, as well as in the chapters on MAN, IDEA, and MIND, is considered the distinction between the senses and the higher faculties of reason or intellect. The chapter on MEMORY AND IMAGINATION deals with these two functions in their relation to sense and sense-perception; and the contrast between sensible and intelligible reality is discussed in the chapters on BEING, FORM, IDEA, and MATTER. Some of these topics necessarily recur here, especially as they bear on what for this chapter are the primary problems—the nature of sensation, the analysis of the power of sense, and the character of the knowledge which is afforded by the senses.

AS WE HAVE ALREADY observed, no difficulty seems to arise at first concerning the nature of sensation. It is supposed by many inquirers, early and late in the tradition, that matter is sensitive as well as sensible. Animals have sense-organs which react to physical stimulation. Bodies either act directly upon the sense-organs, as in the case of touch and taste; or, as in the case of vision, hearing, and smell, they exert their influence through an intervening medium, yet in a manner which seems to be no less the action and reaction of bodies.

Those who distinguish between living organisms and inanimate bodies tend to regard sensitivity as a property of living matter, but it does not follow for all who make this distinction that other than material factors are needed to explain sensation. On the contrary, some writers seem to think that the motions of matter account for sensation as readily as the laws of mechanics account for all the sensible changes we are able to perceive.

Lucretius, for example, holds that living things consist of body and soul, and that the soul (or mind) differs from the body only in the size, the fineness of texture, and the mobility of the material particles which compose it. It is, he says, "by the common motions of the two"—body and soul—that "sensation is kindled and fanned throughout our flesh." Sensation occurs when the particles of body and soul together are set in motion by the impact of external bodies upon the organs of sense. "When the pupil of the eye receives in itself a certain kind of blow, it is said to perceive white color, and another again when it perceives black." Similarly, "every kind of sound and voice is heard when they have found their way into the ears and struck upon the sense with their body; for that voice, too, and sound are bodily you must grant, since they can strike on the senses."

Either the external body itself, as in touch, strikes the sense and sets up those bodily motions in the animal which are sensation; or, according to Lucretius, minute replicas or images—composed of atoms, as all things are—fly off from the surface of distant bodies and enter through the pores of our sense-organs to awaken in us vision, hearing, or smell. In either case, sensation is a bodily reaction; and, for Lucretius, imagination and memory, even thought, are consequent motions in the atoms of the mind—further bodily reverberations, as it were, of sensation.

"The cause of sense," writes Hobbes, "is the external body or object, which presses the organ proper to each sense, either immediately, as in taste and touch, or mediately, as in seeing, hearing, and smelling; which pressure, by the mediation of nerves, and other strings and membranes of the body, continues inwards to the brain and heart, causes there a resistance or counter-pressure, or endeavor of the heart, to deliver itself; which endeavor, because outward, seems to be some matter without. And this *seeming* or *fancy* is that which men call *sense*."

The object seems to be colored or hot or sweet when it causes certain sensations in us which are projected outward upon it, in response or counter-action to the inward motions it sets up. But, says Hobbes, these sensible qualities are, in the object, nothing but "so many several motions of the matter by which it presses our organs diversely. Neither in us that are pressed, are they anything else but diverse motions (for motion produces nothing but motion)."

The foregoing theory, reducing sensation to bodily motion, seems to draw its cogency from the fact that only bodies are sensible, that sense-organs are bodily parts, and that sense-organs must be activated by some sort of physical contact for sensations to occur. Some writers, like Descartes, accept the theory for animals, but reject it for men; or they distinguish, in the case of men, between thought and sensation. They regard sensation, with its subsidiary functions of memory and imagination, as reducible to corporeal motions, but refuse to grant that external sense-impressions or interior fancy can produce knowledge without the activity of an immaterial soul.

To animals, Descartes declares, "we can ascribe . . . no knowledge at all, but only fancy of a purely corporeal kind." In contrast, "that power by which we are said to know things is purely spiritual, and not less distinct from every part of the body than blood from bone, or hand from eye." In men as well as animals, the external senses, "in so far as they are part of the body . . . perceive in virtue of passivity alone, just in the way that wax receives an impression from a seal." Fancy or imagination is also "a genuine part of the body"; and "memory, at least that which is corporeal and similar to that of the brutes, is in no respect distinct from imagination."

These corporeal faculties are, according to Descartes, of use to the understanding or the mind only when it "proposes to examine something that can be referred to the body"; but if it "deal with matters in which there is nothing corporeal or similar to the corporeal, it cannot be helped by those faculties." Hence, for Descartes, the "mind can act independently of the brain; for certainly the brain can be of no use in pure thought; its only use is for imagining and perceiving."

For others, like William James, the distinction between sensation and thought, so far as their relation to matter is concerned, seems quite untenable. He objects to those who look upon sensational consciousness as "something *quasi*-material, hardly cognitive, which one need not much wonder about," while they regard rational consciousness as "quite the reverse, and the mystery of it [as] unspeakable." We can correlate consciousness with the brain's workings only in an empirical fashion, James thinks, and we ought to confess that "no glimmer of explanation of it is yet in sight. That brains should give rise to a knowing consciousness at all, this is the one mystery which returns, no matter of what sort the consciousness or of what sort the knowledge may be. Sensations, aware of mere qualities, involve the mystery as much as thoughts, aware of complex systems, involve it."

Still others, like Plotinus and Aristotle, think that the mystery of conscious matter is not essentially different from the mystery of living matter, for if there is anything mysterious about nutrition and growth, or sensation and imagination, it consists in the same thing—the union of material and immaterial principles, of body and soul.

"If the soul were a corporeal entity," Plotinus writes, "there could be no sense-perception, no mental act, no knowledge. . . . If the sentient be a material entity (as we are invited to believe), sensation could only be of the order of seal-impressions struck by a ring on wax." Perception is not a passively received impression. It is, according to Plotinus, an act of awareness "determined by the nature and character of the living being in which it occurs. . . . In any perception we attain by sight, the object is grasped there where it lies in the direct line of vision. . . . The mind looks outward; this is ample proof that it has taken and takes no inner imprint, and does not see in virtue of some mark made upon it, like that of the ring on the wax; it need not look outward at all if, even as it looked, it already held the image of the object, seeing by virtue of an impression made upon itself."

According to Aristotle, "two characteristic marks have above all others been recognized as distinguishing that which has soul in it from that which has not—self-movement and sensation." By self-movement he appears to mean such things as the nutrition and growth which is found in plants, as well as the additional animal faculty of local motion. Both self-movement and sensation require soul as well as body. "Nothing grows or decays naturally," he writes, "except what feeds itself, and nothing feeds itself except what has a share of soul in it." So, too, "nothing except what has soul in it is capable of sensation." But "the exercise of sense-perception does not belong to soul or body exclusively." Sensation "is not an affection of the soul" by itself, nor has a soulless body "the potentiality of perception."

BUT, ARISTOTLE ASKS, are all affections of the soul "affections of the complex of body and soul, or is there any one among them peculiar to the soul by itself? . . . If we consider the majority of them, there seems to be no case in which the soul can act or be acted upon without involving the body; *e.g.*, anger, courage, appetite, and sensation generally. Thinking seems to be the most probable exception; but if this too proves to be a form of imagination, or to be impossible without imagination, it too requires a body as a condition of its existence."

Aquinas tries to answer the question Aristotle asks, with a threefold distinction which places sensation and imagination midway between the vegetative functions and rational thought. The power of thought, or "the intellectual power," Aquinas says, "does not belong to a corporeal organ, as the power of seeing is the act of the eye; for understanding is an act which cannot be performed by a corporeal organ, like the act of seeing."

At the other extreme from this "operation of the soul which so far exceeds the corporeal nature that it is not even performed by any corporeal organ," are those "operations of the soul ... performed by a corporeal organ and by virtue of a corporeal quality." Because it is a kind of self-movement, digestion requires soul as well as body, but it is a corporeal action in the way in which, according to Aquinas, it involves "the action of heat." Between these extremes, Aquinas places sensation and imagination, operations "performed through a corporeal organ, but not through a corporeal quality."

He explains this further by means of a distinction between natural and spiritual immutation—physical and psychic change. "Natural immutation takes place by the form of the thing which causes the immutation being received, according to its natural existence, into the thing in which the immutation is effected, as heat is received into the heated thing." Vegetative activities, while remaining psychic in the sense of occurring only in living or besouled matter, involve only natural immutations in the vital organs involved.

In contrast, "spiritual immutation takes place by the form of the thing causing the immutation being received, according to a spiritual mode of existence, into the thing in which the immutation is effected, as the form of color is received into the eye, which does not thereby become colored." Though some sensations may require a natural immutation of the sense-organ, as hot and cold do, all sensations necessarily involve a spiritual immutation, which enables the sense-organ to perform its proper act of knowing, as the eye knows color without becoming colored. "Otherwise," Aquinas says, "if a natural immutation alone sufficed for the sense's action, all natural bodies would feel when they undergo alteration."

These diverse views of the nature of sensation seem to be paralleled by diverse views of the sensitive faculty. That the function of the senses is somehow to apprehend or know does not seem to be disputed. But whether the senses—including memory and imagination—are the only faculty of knowing is an issue to which the great books seem to give a variety of answers.

The opposite answers appear to be correlated, not only with conflicting positions in respect to body and soul, but also with opposing theories of the distinction between men and other animals. Those who hold that the motions of matter are adequate to explain the phenomena of knowing and thinking, tend to make sense-perception the primary function of the mind and to treat not only memory and imagination, but also reasoning or thought as subsequent activities of the same general faculty which receives impressions from external sources in the first instance. Since other animals possess senses and give evidence that perception in them has consequences for memory and imagination, those who hold this view also tend to attribute thought to animals and to regard man as differing from them only in degree.

Those who take the contrary view that knowing involves an immaterial principle or cause—a soul as well as a body—tend to distinguish the various functions of sense from the activities of thought—such as conception, judgment, and reasoning. They also take the position that man, while sharing sense-perception, memory, and imagination with other animals, alone possesses the higher faculty. The difference between men and brutes is thus conceived as one of kind, not of degree, when the difference between the senses and the reason in man is also conceived as a difference in kind. A functional relationship between sensation and thought is not thereby denied, but a distinct faculty is affirmed to be necessary for going beyond the apprehension of particulars to knowledge of the universal, or for rising above the imagination to abstract thought.

The distinction between sense and reason as faculties of knowing is sometimes stated in terms of a difference in their objects—the particular versus the universal, becoming versus being, the material versus the immaterial. Sometimes it is stated in terms of the difference between a corporeal power requiring a bodily organ and a spiritual power which belongs exclusively to the soul. Sometimes it is stated in terms of the contrast between sense as intuitive and reason as discursive, the one beholding its objects immediately, the other forming concepts, judgments, or conclusions about objects which are either beheld by the senses or cannot be intuitively apprehended at all.

The exceptions to the foregoing summary are almost as numerous as the exemplifications of the points mentioned. Nothing less than this intricate pattern of agreements and differences will serve, however, to represent the complexity of the discussion and the way in which diverse theories of sense imply different views of nature and man, of mind and knowledge. The situation can be illustrated by taking certain doctrines which seem to be opposite on most points, and then considering other theories which seem to agree, on this point or that, with both extremes.

We have already observed the opposition between Hobbes and Aquinas with regard to matter and spirit in relation to the activity of the senses. Hobbes, like Lucretius, not only treats all mental phenomena as manifestations of bodily motion, but also reduces thought to the train or sequence of images. Images are in turn reducible to the sensations from which they derive.

"As we have no imagination," Hobbes writes, "whereof we have not formerly had sense, in whole or in parts; so we have no transition from one imagination to another, whereof we never had the like before in our senses." Using the word "thoughts" to stand for the images derived from sense, Hobbes goes on to say that "besides sense, and thoughts, and the train of thoughts, the mind of man has no other motion; though by the help of speech and method, the same faculties may be improved to such a height as to distinguish men from all other living creatures."

Only man's use of words makes the difference in the exercise of the imagination "that we generally call understanding," and which, according to Hobbes, "is common to man and beast." Similarly, it is only the fact that common names have general significance which gives human discourse the appearance of abstract thought, for Hobbes denies abstract ideas. Thoughts or images are no less particular than sensations, "there being nothing in the world universal but names."

Berkeley and Hume seem to agree with Hobbes that man has no abstract ideas or universal concepts; that all the operations of thought are merely elaborations of the original impressions of sense; and that no special power, but only the use of language, distinguishes men from other animals.

Berkeley uses the word "idea" to stand for sense-impressions—"ideas actually imprinted on the senses"—and for whatever is "perceived by attending to the passions and operations of the mind." To these two he adds a third: "ideas formed by the help of memory and imagination, either compounding or dividing, or barely representing those originally perceived in the aforesaid ways." The only difference between the first and the third is that "the ideas of sense are more strong, lively, and distinct than those of the imagination." But our ideas of sense and imagination do not cover all the objects of which we can think. He admits, therefore, the possibility of our having *notions*, whereby we understand the meaning of a word like "spirit" or "soul" which refers to a substance of which we can form no idea.

Hume divides "all the perceptions of the mind into two classes or species, which are distinguished by their different degrees of force and vivacity. The less forcible and lively are commonly denominated *thoughts* or *ideas*." The other he calls "impressions," meaning thereby "all our more lively perceptions." Impressions are the source of all other ideas, the creative power of the mind consisting in "no more than the faculty of compounding, transposing, augmenting, or diminishing the materials afforded us by the senses" and every simple idea being "copied from a similar impression."

Yet, though Berkeley and Hume seem to agree with Hobbes in reducing all thought to primary sense-perceptions and derived memories or imaginations, Hume does not attempt to explain thought by the motions of matter. Berkeley differs even more radically. He denies that matter or bodies exist, and so he regards sense-perception, like all the rest of thought, as purely spiritual. The soul passively receives its original impressions directly from God and actively forms the ideas it is able to derive from these impressions.

NOR DO ALL THOSE who somehow conceive man as composed of both body and soul agree upon the function of sense in relation to the rest of thought. Locke, for example, uses "understanding" to cover all sorts of mental activity. Mental activity begins with the passive reception of the simple ideas of sense—the impressions produced in us when "the bodies that surround us do diversely affect our organs"—and the simple ideas of reflection which arise from an awareness of our own mental operations. But mental activity also includes the formation of complex ideas by the compounding of simple ones, and even the act whereby we form abstract ideas, in doing which man, in Locke's opinion, is distinguished from brutes.

All these activities require soul as well as body. All are somehow nothing more than a reworking of the original sensations passively received. In this last respect, Locke's view accords with that of Hobbes, Berkeley, and Hume, though he differs from them with respect to abstract ideas and in his theory of body and soul. On the very point which he holds in common with Hobbes, Berkeley, and Hume, Locke seems to disagree with Descartes.

Thinking, for Descartes, is the activity of a

purely spiritual substance—the rational soul—peculiar to the dual nature of man; whereas sensation and imagination, common to men and brutes, are purely corporeal functions. In man, the soul or thinking substance may form certain of its ideas, those relative to bodies, under the influence of sense or fancy; but with regard to other ideas, such as those we have of geometrical figures, Descartes says he cannot admit that they "have at any time entered our minds through the senses." He objects to the use of the word "idea" for images, or what he calls "pictures in the corporeal imagination, *i.e.*, in some part of the brain." He criticizes those who "never raise their minds above the things of sense," so accustomed are they "to consider nothing except by imagining it," with the result that whatever "is not capable of being imagined appears to them not to be intelligible at all."

Against the maxim which Locke, no less than Hobbes or Berkeley, would approve—that "there is nothing in the understanding which has not first of all been in the senses"—Descartes offers the ideas of God and of the soul as plainly contrary examples, ideas clearly in the mind which have no origin in sensation or fancy. "Those who desire to make use of their imagination to understand these ideas," he adds, "act in the same way as if, to hear sounds or smell odours, they should wish to make use of their eyes."

In making a sharp distinction between the faculties of sense and understanding or reason, Descartes seems to share the position of Plato, Aristotle, Aquinas, Spinoza, and Kant. Yet for Descartes as for Plato, the intellect in its own sphere of objects is like the senses in theirs, since each is able to behold its proper objects intuitively; whereas for Kant as for Aristotle, sense alone is a faculty of intuition. The ideas by which we apprehend intelligible objects, according to Plato, Descartes, and Spinoza, are not derived from sensations or images. According to Aristotle and Aquinas, on the other hand, the intellect abstracts all its ideas, or universal concepts, from the particulars of sense.

In this respect Aristotle and Aquinas seem to be in agreement with Locke, even though that agreement must be qualified by the observation that Locke sees no need for a special faculty to obtain abstract ideas. On the other hand, Plato, Aristotle, Aquinas, and Descartes all seem to agree in holding that understanding is as immaterial as its objects. Unlike sense, which requires bodily organs, rational thought is, according to them, an activity peculiar either to the soul itself or to a power of the soul which is not embodied in an organ, as the power of vision is embodied in the eye or the powers of memory and imagination are embodied in the brain.

William James denies this. He holds the view that all forms of consciousness are somehow functions of the brain. Yet he also insists that percept and concept are radically distinct forms of consciousness. To this extent, James makes as sharp a separation as the authors above mentioned between the sensory and the rational phases of thought. He places sensation, perception, memory and imagination on one side, and conception, judgment, and reasoning on the other. But this is for him not a distinction of faculties or powers, but only of different functions which one and the same mind is able to perform.

Certain points or problems in the traditional discussion of sense are unaffected by the basic issues just considered. For example, most writers tend to make some distinction between the special exterior senses, such as vision and hearing, touch and taste, and the several interior senses, which Aquinas enumerates as the common sense, memory, imagination, and the estimative or cogitative powers. Yet not all who consider memory and imagination as activities consequent upon sense-perception call them "interior senses." Not all recognize a distinct estimative or cogitative power even when they recognize a kind of thinking about particulars done by animals and men with sensory materials. Nor do all who discuss discrimination or comparison, and the collation or combining of the impressions received from the special senses, attribute these functions to the special faculty which Aristotle first calls "the common sense."

Frequently the same analytical point is made in different ways. As indicated in the chapter on Quality, the distinction which Aristotle and Aquinas make between proper and common sensibles, according as the quality, such as color and odor, belongs to a single sense, or, like shape and motion, can be perceived by two or more senses, seems to parallel the distinction between what Locke calls "secondary" and "primary" qualities. But where Locke and others treat the so-called "secondary qualities" as entirely subjective, occurring only in the experience of the sentient organism and having no reality in the sensible thing, Aristotle takes a contrary view.

When it is not actually seen or smelled, the sensible thing, according to Aristotle, is potentially colorful or odoriferous; just as when it is not actually seeing or smelling, the sense of vision or smell is also in a state of potentiality with respect to these qualities. But when the sensible thing is actually sensed, then, Aristotle says, "the actuality of the sensible object and of the sensitive faculty is *one* actuality." The thing is actually colored when it is actually seen, though it is only potentially colored when it is merely able to be so seen. "Earlier students of nature," he writes, "were mistaken in their view that without sight there was no white or black, without taste no savor. This statement of theirs is partly true, partly false: 'sense' and 'the sensible object' are ambiguous terms, *i.e.*, they may denote either potentialities or actualities. The statement is true of the latter, false of the former."

Another example of the same analytical point (which is made differently by different writers) concerns the distinction between sensation and perception. According to William James, "perception involves sensation as a portion of itself, and sensation in turn never takes place in adult life without perception also being there." The difference between them is that the function of sensation is "that of mere acquaintance with a fact," whereas "perception's function . . . is knowledge *about* a fact, and this knowledge admits of numberless degrees of complication." Hearing a sound is having a sensation, but perception occurs when, as James points out, we "hear a sound, and say 'a horse-car.'"

But James does not agree that, when perception is so described, it is, as other psychologists have suggested, a species of reasoning. "If, every time a present sign suggests an absent reality to our mind, we make an inference, and if every time we make an inference we reason; then," James admits, "perception is indubitably reasoning. Only one sees no room in it for any unconscious part." No inference is consciously made in perception; and James thinks that "to call perception unconscious reasoning is either a useless metaphor, or a positively misleading confusion between two different things." In his opinion, "perception differs from sensation [simply] by the consciousness of further facts associated with the object of sensation." For him, "perception and reasoning are coordinate varieties of that deeper sort of process known psychologically as the association of ideas."

What James treats as the object of sensation, Aristotle refers to as a quality sensed by one or more of the special senses, either a proper or a common sensible. What James treats as the object of perception, Aristotle calls an "accidental object of sense," because it is strictly not sensible at all by any of the exterior senses, singly or in combination. When we call "the white object we see" the son of Diares or a man, we have an example of an accidental sensible or an object incidentally perceived, because "'being the son of Diares' is incidental to the directly visible white patch" we see with our eyes.

This distinction between sensation and perception seems to have a bearing on the problem of the fallibility of the senses. Again the same point seems to be differently made. Aristotle, for example, holds that whereas each of the senses is normally infallible in the apprehension of its proper object or appropriate quality, error is possible in the perception of the complex thing which is not strictly an object of the special senses. "While the perception that there is white before us cannot be false," he writes, "the perception that what is white is this or that may be false."

Lucretius likewise insists that the senses themselves are never deceived, but that all the errors attributed to the senses are the result of a false inference or judgment which reason makes on the basis of the evidence presented by the senses. That also seems to be the opinion of Descartes, who thinks that "no direct experience can ever deceive the understanding if it restricts its attention accurately to the object presented to it. . . . Thus if a man suffering from jaundice persuades himself that the things he sees are yellow, this thought of his will be composite, consisting partly of what his imagination presents to him, and partly of what he assumes on his own account, namely, that the color looks yellow, not owing to the defect in his eye, but because the things he sees really are yellow. . . . We can go wrong only when the things we believe are in some way compounded by ourselves." Descartes holds that "no falsity can reside" in sensations themselves, but only in those judgments which, on the basis of sensations, we are "accustomed to pass about things external to us."

THE MOST FUNDAMENTAL judgment which men make on the basis of sensation is that an external world exists—a reality not of our own making. Descartes argues from the evidence of the senses to the independent existence of a world of bodies. Though Berkeley argues, on the contrary, that bodies do not exist except as objects of perception, he attributes the sense-impressions, over which we seem to have no control, to the action of an external cause—to God, who uses them as signs for instructing us.

Locke defines sensitive knowledge as that which informs us of "the existence of things actually present to our senses." We may know our own existence intuitively, and God's existence demonstratively, but "the knowledge of the existence of any other thing we can have only by sensation." And though, he adds, "the notice we have by our senses of the existing of things without us . . . be not altogether so certain as our intuitive knowledge or the deductions of our reason . . . yet it is an assurance that deserves the name of knowledge."

Against such views, the most fundamental skepticism goes further than doubting the veracity of the senses because of the illusions and hallucinations they cause us to suffer. "By what arguments," Hume asks, "can it be proved that the perceptions of the mind must be caused by external objects . . . and could not arise either from the energy of the mind itself or from the suggestion of some visible or unknown spirit?"

"It is a question of fact," he adds, "whether the perception of the senses be produced by external objects, resembling them. How shall this question be determined? By experience surely; as all other questions of a like nature. But here experience is, and must be, entirely silent. The mind has never anything present to it but the perceptions, and cannot possibly reach any experience of their connexion with objects. The supposition of such a connexion is, therefore, without any foundation in reasoning."

OUTLINE OF TOPICS

1. The nature of sense

   1*a*. The power of sense as distinct from the power of understanding or reason

   1*b*. Sense and intellect in relation to becoming and being, particulars and universals

   1*c*. The distinction between perception or intuition and judgment or reasoning: the transcendental forms of intuition

   1*d*. Sense-perception as a primary function of the mind or understanding: sensations as received impressions; the distinction between sensation and reflection, ideas and notions, percepts and concepts

2. Sensitivity in relation to the grades of life

   2*a*. The differentiation of animals from plants in terms of sensitivity

   2*b*. The degrees of sensitivity in the animal kingdom: the genetic order of the several senses

   2*c*. Comparisons of human and animal sensitivity

3. The analysis of the power of sense: its organs and activities

3*a*. The anatomy and physiology of the senses: the special sense-organs, nerves, brain

3*b*. The distinction between the exterior and interior senses

(1) Enumeration of the exterior senses: their relation and order

(2) Enumeration of the interior senses: their dependence on the exterior senses

3*c*. The activity of the exterior senses

(1) The functions of the exterior senses: the nature and origin of sensations

(2) The attributes of sensation: intensity, extensity, affective tone; the psychophysical law

(3) The classification of sensations or sense-qualities: proper and common sensibles; primary and secondary qualities

(4) The distinction between sensation and perception: the accidental sensible; complex ideas of substance

(5) Sensation and attention: pre-perception and apperception; the transcendental unity of apperception

3*d*. The activity of the interior senses

(1) The functions of the common sense: discrimination, comparison, association, collation or perception

(2) Memory and imagination as interior powers of sense

(3) The estimative or cogitative power: instinctive recognition of the harmful and beneficial

3*e*. The relation of sense to emotion, will, and movement: the conception of a sensitive appetite

4. The character of sensitive knowledge

4*a*. Comparison of sensitive with other forms of knowledge

4*b*. The object of sense-perception: the evident particular fact; judgments of perception and judgments of experience

4*c*. The relation of sense and the sensible: the subjectivity or objectivity of sense-qualities

4*d*. The limit, accuracy, and reliability of sensitive knowledge: the fallibility of the senses

(1) The erroneous interpretation of sense-data: the problem of judgments based on sensation

(2) Error in sense-perception: illusions and hallucinations

5. The contribution of the senses to scientific or philosophical knowledge

5*a*. Sensation as the source or occasion of ideas: the role of memory or reminiscence; the construction of complex ideas; the abstraction of universal concepts

5*b*. Sense-experience as the origin of inductions

5*c*. The dependence of understanding or reason upon sense for knowledge of particulars: verification by appeal to the senses

6. The role of sense in the perception of beauty: the beautiful and the pleasing to sense; sensible and intelligible beauty

REFERENCES

References are listed by volume number (in bold type), author's name, and page number. Bible references are to book, chapter, and verse of the Authorized King James version of the Bible. The abbreviation "esp" calls the reader's attention to one or more especially relevant parts of a whole reference; "passim" signifies that the topic is discussed intermittently rather than continuously in the work or passage cited. Where the work as a whole is relevant to the topic, the page numbers refer to the entire work. For general guidance in the use of *The Great Ideas,* consult the Preface.

1. The nature of sense

1*a*. The power of sense as distinct from the power of understanding or reason

7 Plato, 224–225, 231–232, 386–388, 392–393, 534–536
8 Aristotle, 647–648
17 Plotinus, 189–190, 216–217
18 Augustine, 74–76, 337–338
19 Aquinas, 380–381, 407–409
20 Aquinas, 8–9
31 Descartes, 18–25, 98–99
42 Kant, 14, 23–24, 37–39, 385
53 James, 450–451, 469

1*b*. Sense and intellect in relation to becoming and being, particulars and universals

7 Plato, 126, 231–232, 383–398, 447, 457–458, 565–569
8 Aristotle, 98, 111, 120, 194–195, 505, 518, 559
9 Aristotle, 391, 397
17 Plotinus, 248–249, 266–267
18 Augustine, 50
19 Aquinas, 105–106, 288, 295–297, 382–383, 388–391, 461–462, 748–749
28 Harvey, 332–333
31 Descartes, 28–33 passim, 53, 79–81, 96, 136–137, 219
38 Rousseau, 341–342
53 James, 307–311

1*c*. The distinction between perception or intuition and judgment or reasoning: the transcendental forms of intuition

42 Kant, 23–41, 45–46, 47–48, 53–54, 58–64, 66, 112–113, 199, 282, 307–308, 461–475, 482–483, 570–572
53 James, 629–631

1*d*. Sense-perception as a primary function of the mind or understanding: sensations as received impressions; the distinction between sensation and reflection, ideas and notions, percepts and concepts

12 Lucretius, 33, 53–54
23 Hobbes, 52, 258
35 Locke, 98–99, 121–128, 133, 134, 138–141 passim, 175, 201, 204, 205, 208, 212, 261–262, 311–312, 324
35 Berkeley, 413, 417–419 passim, 440–441 passim
35 Hume, 455–457 passim
42 Kant, 115
53 James, 144–145, 313–314, 452–457

2. Sensitivity in relation to the grades of life

2*a*. The differentiation of animals from plants in terms of sensitivity

8 Aristotle, 640–641, 697
9 Aristotle, 271, 272, 281–282, 321
10 Galen, 167
12 Aurelius, 292
18 Augustine, 256
28 Harvey, 369–370
49 Darwin, 114–115
54 Freud, 429

2*b*. The degrees of sensitivity in the animal kingdom: the genetic order of the several senses

8 Aristotle, 666, 667–668, 673–674
9 Aristotle, 115, 181–188 passim, 222–223, 321–324
12 Lucretius, 52–53
19 Aquinas, 106–107
31 Descartes, 59
49 Darwin, 261–262, 432–434 passim, 447–448 passim, 456, 480–482 passim, 553–554, 595–596
53 James, 27–42 passim

2*c*. Comparisons of human and animal sensitivity

8 Aristotle, 652, 653, 681–683
9 Aristotle, 323–324, 364–365
19 Aquinas, 430–431, 486–487
25 Montaigne, 286–287, 290–291
30 Bacon, 173
31 Descartes, 156
35 Locke, 140–141
38 Rousseau, 337–338
48 Melville, 244–245
49 Darwin, 301–302, 568–570
53 James, 19–42 passim

3. The analysis of the power of sense: its organs and activities

3*a*. The anatomy and physiology of the senses: the special sense-organs, nerves, brain

7 PLATO, 454–455
8 ARISTOTLE, 651, 656–657, 658, 674–683 passim, 715–716
9 ARISTOTLE, 25, 50, 59–62, 171, 179, 182–183, 185–188, 193–194, 212, 285
10 HIPPOCRATES, 159–160
12 LUCRETIUS, 34, 47
17 PLOTINUS, 153–154
19 AQUINAS, 394–396
23 HOBBES, 49, 50–51
28 HARVEY, 456–458
30 BACON, 157
31 DESCARTES, 19–20, 209
34 NEWTON, 384–385
35 LOCKE, 135
36 STERNE, 270–271
48 MELVILLE, 244–245
49 DARWIN, 85–87, 259–261, 397–398
53 JAMES, 8–52, 151, 497–501, 533–538 passim, 546–547, 562–563, 575–584
54 FREUD, 351–352, 367, 647–648

3*b*. The distinction between the exterior and interior senses

8 ARISTOTLE, 136, 657–659, 660, 663–664, 697–698
17 PLOTINUS, 157
19 AQUINAS, 411–413, 430–431, 773
23 HOBBES, 258
28 HARVEY, 457
42 KANT, 24, 26–29
54 FREUD, 367, 384–385

3*b*(1) Enumeration of the exterior senses: their relation and order

8 ARISTOTLE, 649–659, 673–689
9 ARISTOTLE, 59–62
10 HIPPOCRATES, 159
12 LUCRETIUS, 23
19 AQUINAS, 410–411, 486–487
20 AQUINAS, 972–974
35 LOCKE, 128–129, 139–140
35 BERKELEY, 420–421
53 JAMES, 62–63, 650–651

3*b*(2) Enumeration of the interior senses: their dependence on the exterior senses

8 ARISTOTLE, 136, 449, 660–661, 666, 690–692
17 PLOTINUS, 161–162, 189–191
18 AUGUSTINE, 74–75
19 AQUINAS, 411–413
23 HOBBES, 54
28 HARVEY, 334
31 SPINOZA, 380–382
35 LOCKE, 118–119, 141–145
42 KANT, 41–42, 54–55

3*c*. The activity of the exterior senses

3*c*(1) The functions of the exterior senses: the nature and origin of sensations

7 PLATO, 453–454, 463–465, 518–522
8 ARISTOTLE, 14, 149, 423, 647–648, 673–689 passim
9 ARISTOTLE, 183, 222–223, 322–324
12 LUCRETIUS, 26–27, 44–47, 51–54
17 PLOTINUS, 3–4, 155, 169–171, 183–190
19 AQUINAS, 403–404, 410–411
20 AQUINAS, 893–897
23 HOBBES, 62
28 HARVEY, 456–457 passim
31 DESCARTES, 163, 228–229
31 SPINOZA, 377–380
34 NEWTON, 428, 434–435, 442–443, 518–519, 522
35 LOCKE, 121, 127, 134–138 passim, 239, 261, 263–264, 322
35 BERKELEY, 416–417, 423–424
38 MONTESQUIEU, 102–103
42 KANT, 518
45 LAVOISIER, 14
53 JAMES, 98–103, 108, 149–151, 184–185, 193–194, 422, 452–457, 470–471, 472–479, 520–521, 547–627
54 FREUD, 412–413, 701

3*c*(2) The attributes of sensation: intensity, extensity, affective tone; the psychophysical law

8 ARISTOTLE, 330, 651, 652, 658, 668
9 ARISTOTLE, 429
12 LUCRETIUS, 20–21, 52–53
17 PLOTINUS, 245
19 AQUINAS, 755–757
23 HOBBES, 62
35 LOCKE, 311–312
35 BERKELEY, 419
35 HUME, 455
38 MONTESQUIEU, 103
42 KANT, 69–72, 477–478
43 MILL, 450
49 DARWIN, 569
53 JAMES, 275–276, 319–321, 348–359, 498–501 passim; 526–527, 540–547, 552–554, 563–566, 651, 829–830
54 FREUD, 403–404, 701

3*c*(3) The classification of sensations or sense-qualities: proper and common sensibles; primary and secondary qualities

7 PLATO, 462–463, 464–465
8 ARISTOTLE, 428–431, 654, 676–683
10 GALEN, 169
12 LUCRETIUS, 20–21, 24–26
19 AQUINAS, 410–411
23 HOBBES, 49
31 DESCARTES, 231
34 NEWTON, 270–271, 428

35 Locke, 131, 134–138, 200, 205–208, 238, 263, 315–316
35 Berkeley, 414–416, 417–418
35 Hume, 505
42 Kant, 29–33
53 James, 185, 502–503, 569–570, 572, 627, 650–651

3c(4) The distinction between sensation and perception: the accidental sensible; complex ideas of substance

8 Aristotle, 673–674, 685
20 Aquinas, 1032–1034
35 Locke, 139–140
35 Berkeley, 420–421, 442
53 James, 452–453, 502–505, 526–527

3c(5) Sensation and attention: pre-perception and apperception; the transcendental unity of apperception

8 Aristotle, 685–689
21 Dante, 57
42 Kant, 14–108
48 Melville, 244–245
51 Tolstoy, 605
53 James, 184–185, 232–235, 262–291 esp 262–268, 295–297, 328–329, 469, 522–525, 562, 620–621

3d. The activity of the interior senses

3d(1) The functions of the common sense: discrimination, comparison, association, collation or perception

8 Aristotle, 657, 658–659, 697–698
17 Plotinus, 143, 194–195
19 Aquinas, 467–468
23 Hobbes, 52
28 Harvey, 457–458
35 Locke, 143–145
42 Kant, 14, 51, 54–64, 528–529
53 James, 313–341, 344–346, 360–399, 411–420, 506–507, 525–526, 547–552, 561–575, 584–589, 867–868

3d(2) Memory and imagination as interior powers of sense

7 Plato, 523–524
8 Aristotle, 499, 690–695
9 Aristotle, 237
17 Plotinus, 156–159
18 Augustine, 74–75
20 Aquinas, 8–9
23 Hobbes, 50–52, 262
30 Bacon, 55
31 Descartes, 20
31 Spinoza, 380–382
35 Locke, 141, 142
42 Kant, 41–42, 493
53 James, 13–15, 145, 421–431 passim, 480–501 esp 497–501
54 Freud, 352

3d(3) The estimative or cogitative power: instinctive recognition of the harmful and beneficial

9 Aristotle, 136–138 passim
19 Aquinas, 394–396, 429–431, 436–438
25 Montaigne, 286–287
31 Descartes, 100
35 Locke, 104, 141, 145–146
48 Melville, 144
49 Darwin, 121, 122, 290–291, 292
53 James, 708–709, 720–725 passim
54 Freud, 607–609, 612–614, 640–641, 720–721, 737, 751–752, 845–846

3e. The relation of sense to emotion, will, and movement: the conception of a sensitive appetite

7 Plato, 128–129, 350–353 esp 352, 466–467, 712
8 Aristotle, 330, 644, 704
9 Aristotle, 235–237, 364–365, 398, 399–400
12 Epictetus, 170–171
17 Plotinus, 156–157, 167–168
18 Augustine, 9
19 Aquinas, 428–431, 432–433, 619–620, 690–692, 720–826 passim
20 Aquinas, 32–34
23 Hobbes, 61, 62, 64
25 Montaigne, 288–290
27 Shakespeare, 55
31 Spinoza, 399
42 Kant, 259, 265, 270, 284–285, 298–300, 341–342, 385–386
53 James, 13–15, 521–522, 694–699, 738–759, 767–794, 808–810, 812–813, 827–835
54 Freud, 351–352, 363–364, 412–413, 419–420, 648

4. The character of sensitive knowledge

7 Plato, 383–398, 517–536
8 Aristotle, 528–529, 530, 591
17 Plotinus, 1–4, 169–171, 183–189
18 Augustine, 650
19 Aquinas, 53–54, 80–81
31 Descartes, 19–20, 96–103
31 Spinoza, 377–380
35 Locke, 312, 313, 354–358
35 Berkeley, 440–442 passim
42 Kant, 30–31, 58–59
53 James, 157–168, 453–479

4a. Comparison of sensitive with other forms of knowledge

7 Plato, 383–398
8 Aristotle, 647–648
9 Aristotle, 340
17 Plotinus, 228–230, 291
18 Augustine, 15
19 Aquinas, 68–70, 453–455
28 Harvey, 332–333
31 Descartes, 83–84, 96–103, 136–137, 229–230

35 LOCKE, 252, 357–358
35 BERKELEY, 416, 418
42 KANT, 34, 199, 542–543, 570–572
53 JAMES, 144–145, 311–312, 450–451, 453–459

4*b*. The object of sense-perception: the evident particular fact; judgments of perception and judgments of experience

7 PLATO, 383–388, 517–536
8 ARISTOTLE, 264, 397, 530, 648
9 ARISTOTLE, 391
17 PLOTINUS, 189–190
18 AUGUSTINE, 23
19 AQUINAS, 84–86, 306–307, 458–459
23 HOBBES, 49
38 HARVEY, 332–333
31 DESCARTES, 80–81, 229–230
35 LOCKE, 312, 316, 354–358
42 KANT, 16–17, 108
53 JAMES, 150–151, 453–457, 472–479, 569–570, 606–610, 867–868
54 FREUD, 430

4*c*. The relation of sense and the sensible: the subjectivity or objectivity of sense-qualities

7 PLATO, 517–520
8 ARISTOTLE, 12–13, 328, 329–330, 647–648, 655–656, 657–659, 661, 664, 673–689
9 ARISTOTLE, 429
10 GALEN, 167
12 LUCRETIUS, 24–26
20 AQUINAS, 971–972
23 HOBBES, 57
31 DESCARTES, 162–165, 228–229, 231
35 LOCKE, 133–138 passim, 200, 205–208, 214, 239, 245–246
35 BERKELEY, 413–431, 432–433
35 HUME, 504–506
42 KANT, 29–33, 88–89, 101–102, 115
53 JAMES, 98–105, 150–151, 176–177, 459–479

4*d*. The limit, accuracy, and reliability of sensitive knowledge: the fallibility of the senses

7 PLATO, 224–225, 386–398
8 ARISTOTLE, 182, 530, 648–649, 680
12 LUCRETIUS, 48–51
17 PLOTINUS, 64–65, 228–229
19 AQUINAS, 102
25 MONTAIGNE, 285–292
28 HARVEY, 322–323
30 BACON, 107, 109, 111, 169–173
31 DESCARTES, 13, 75–77, 83–84, 96–103, 206–207
31 SPINOZA, 383–385, 388
32 MILTON, 187
33 PASCAL, 188–189
35 LOCKE, 206–208, 238, 245–246, 312, 355–357
35 BERKELEY, 405, 415–416, 420, 429–430, 432
35 HUME, 461
42 KANT, 27–33, 337
49 DARWIN, 96
53 JAMES, 125–126, 400–405, 460–471, 544–545, 589–625

4*d*(1) The erroneous interpretation of sense-data: the problem of judgments based on sensation

7 PLATO, 431, 538–541
8 ARISTOTLE, 415, 528–529, 591, 680
12 LUCRETIUS, 48–50
19 AQUINAS, 102
30 BACON, 58
31 DESCARTES, 22–23
35 LOCKE, 247–248
42 KANT, 108
44 BOSWELL, 13
53 JAMES, 460–469, 568–570, 589–595, 617–625

4*d*(2) Error in sense-perception: illusions and hallucinations

7 PLATO, 520–522
8 ARISTOTLE, 702–706
12 LUCRETIUS, 53–54
14 PLUTARCH, 816–817
19 AQUINAS, 571
23 HOBBES, 50–52, 172, 258
29 CERVANTES, 50–52
30 BACON, 213
31 DESCARTES, 75, 101–102
36 STERNE, 234–236
53 JAMES, 132–139, 248–249, 462–469, 475–477, 508–520, 521–522, 527–538, 601–606, 610–625, 780–785, 786–787, 842–847
54 FREUD, 3, 31–38 passim, 102–106, 148–150, 337, 354–355

5. The contribution of the senses to scientific or philosophical knowledge

7 PLATO, 383–398
8 ARISTOTLE, 108, 259, 397, 673–674
10 HIPPOCRATES, 1–3
19 AQUINAS, 447–451, 465–466, 477–478
20 AQUINAS, 778–779
23 HOBBES, 60
25 MONTAIGNE, 260–261
28 GILBERT, 6–7
28 GALILEO, 131-138 passim
28 HARVEY, 267–268, 322–323, 331–335, 411
30 BACON, 16, 50–51, 57, 114, 126–128, 169–175
31 DESCARTES, 10–12, 28–33, 61–62, 75–76, 97–103
34 NEWTON, 543
35 LOCKE, 127, 204, 211–214, 304–305, 317, 321–323 passim, 360–362, 370–371
35 BERKELEY, 424, 433
35 HUME, 458–466 passim, 477, 479, 501–502
42 KANT, 5–13, 15–16, 46, 66–67, 68–69, 86–87, 94–95, 211–218, 253, 254, 295, 312, 329–330, 331–332
43 MILL, 445–447 passim
45 LAVOISIER, 1–2, 6–7

46 Hegel, 156–190
53 James, 647–648, 851–884
54 Freud, 400–401, 412, 815, 879

5*a*. Sensation as the source or occasion of ideas: the role of memory or reminiscence; the construction of complex ideas; the abstraction of universal concepts

7 Plato, 228–230, 392–393, 455
8 Aristotle, 120, 136–137, 632, 663–664, 690–691
19 Aquinas, 380–381, 416–419, 442–443, 447–449, 451–453
23 Hobbes, 52, 54, 262
28 Harvey, 332–335
31 Descartes, 53
35 Locke, 93–395 passim
35 Berkeley, 405–409 passim
35 Hume, 455–457, 471
42 Kant, 45–46, 281–282
53 James, 171–175, 327–331, 405–407, 480–484, 540–635
54 Freud, 442–443, 700–701

5*b*. Sense-experience as the origin of inductions

8 Aristotle, 64, 111, 136–137, 499–500, 631–632
9 Aristotle, 343–344, 392–393
28 Harvey, 322–323, 324
30 Bacon, 43–44, 108, 169–175
31 Descartes, 10–12, 28, 167
31 Spinoza, 387–388
35 Berkeley, 433–434
38 Rousseau, 341–342
45 Faraday, 659
53 James, 862–865

5*c*. The dependence of understanding or reason upon sense for knowledge of particulars: verification by appeal to the senses

8 Aristotle, 267, 361, 397, 411
9 Aristotle, 355, 426
12 Lucretius, 6, 50–51
18 Augustine, 269
19 Aquinas, 84–85, 175–178, 295–297, 449–451, 461–462
23 Hobbes, 249–250
25 Montaigne, 260–261
28 Harvey, 331–335
30 Bacon, 57–58, 111, 116–117, 137–195 passim
31 Descartes, 75–77, 229–230
35 Locke, 362
35 Hume, 488–489, 509
42 Kant, 85–93, 114–115, 146–149, 153, 231, 337
43 Mill, 461
44 Boswell, 129
45 Faraday, 774–775
53 James, 647–648, 863–865, 881

6. The role of sense in the perception of beauty: the beautiful and the pleasing to sense; sensible and intelligible beauty

7 Plato, 167, 370–373, 385–386
9 Aristotle, 429–430, 685
12 Epictetus, 240–242
17 Plotinus, 21–26, 239–246, 336–338
18 Augustine, 625
19 Aquinas, 25–26, 737
20 Aquinas, 608–609, 1020–1023
27 Shakespeare, 594
28 Galileo, 175–176
29 Cervantes, 381–382
42 Kant, 476–479, 482–483, 492–495, 501–502, 506–511, 537–539
46 Hegel, 220, 266–267
47 Goethe, 274–275
48 Melville, 307–308
49 Darwin, 95, 301–302
53 James, 755–758
54 Freud, 775

CROSS-REFERENCES

For: Discussions relevant to the controversy over the distinction between sense and reason or intellect, and the distinction between the sensible and the intelligible, *see* Being 7e, 8a–8b; Experience 4a; Idea 1b–1c, 2c–2g; Knowledge 6a(1), 6a(4); Memory and Imagination 1a, 5b, 6c(1), 6d; Mind 1a, 1d, 1g; Universal and Particular 4d; and for the related issue concerning the difference between animal and human faculties, *see* Animal 1c(2); Evolution 7b(3); Man 1a–1c; Soul 2c(2)–2c(3).

The intuitive character of sense-perception as contrasted with the discursive nature of judgment and reasoning, *see* Induction 1a; Knowledge 6b(4), 6c(1); Principle 2b(1); Reasoning 1b; and for the theory of space and time as transcendental forms of intuition, *see* Form 1c; Mathematics 1c; Memory and Imagination 6c(2); Mind 1e(1), 4d(3); Space 4a; Time 6c.

The differentiation of plant, animal, and human life with respect to sensitivity, *see* ANIMAL 1a(1), 1b, 1c(1); LIFE AND DEATH 3a–3b; MAN 4b; SOUL 2c(1)–2c(2).

The discussion of the nervous system, *see* ANIMAL 5g.

The theory of memory and imagination as interior powers of sense and as dependent on the exterior senses, *see* MEMORY AND IMAGINATION 1a, 1c; and for another consideration of the estimative power, *see* HABIT 3b.

The pleasantness and unpleasantness of sensations, *see* PLEASURE AND PAIN 4b, 4e; and for the variation of sense-qualities in degree or intensity, *see* QUALITY 3c; SAME AND OTHER 3c.

The distinction between proper and common sensibles, or between primary and secondary qualities, *see* QUALITY 2b; and for the issue concerning the objectivity or subjectivity of these qualities, *see* QUALITY 6c.

The distinction between sensation and perception, and the problem of our sensitive knowledge of substances as opposed to qualities, *see* BEING 8c; IDEA 2f; KNOWLEDGE 6b(1); MEMORY AND IMAGINATION 1a; PRINCIPLE 2a(1); and for the doctrine of the transcendental unity of apperception, *see* MEMORY AND IMAGINATION 6c(2); ONE AND MANY 4b.

For: The relation of sense to emotion and will, and for the distinction between the sensitive and the rational appetite, *see* DESIRE 3b(1); EMOTION 1; GOOD AND EVIL 4a; MEMORY AND IMAGINATION 1d; WILL 2b(2).

The comparison of sensitive with other forms of knowledge, *see* KNOWLEDGE 6b(1)–6b(3); and for the problem of truth and falsity in sensation and sense-perception, *see* MEMORY AND IMAGINATION 2e(4), 5c; PRINCIPLE 2b(1); TRUTH 3a(1)–3a(2).

The contribution of sense to thought, and for the role of sense in theories of reminiscence, induction, and abstraction, *see* EXPERIENCE 3b, 4b; IDEA 2b, 2f–2g; INDUCTION 2; MEMORY AND IMAGINATION 3a, 3c, 6c–6d; MIND 1a(2); REASONING 1c; UNIVERSAL AND PARTICULAR 4c.

The role of sense in the perception of beauty, *see* BEAUTY 4–5; PLEASURE AND PAIN 4c(1).

ADDITIONAL READINGS

Listed below are works not included in *Great Books of the Western World*, but relevant to the idea and topics with which this chapter deals. These works are divided into two groups:

I. Works by authors represented in this collection.
II. Works by authors not represented in this collection.

For the date, place, and other facts concerning the publication of the works cited, consult the Bibliography of Additional Readings which follows the last chapter of *The Great Ideas.*

I.

AUGUSTINE. *Answer to Skeptics*
AQUINAS. *Quaestiones Disputatae, De Anima*, A 13
DESCARTES. *The Principles of Philosophy*, PART I, 45–46, 48, 66–70; PART II, 3; PART IV, 189–198
HOBBES. *Concerning Body*, PART IV, CH 25, 29
BERKELEY. *An Essay Towards a New Theory of Vision*
——. *Three Dialogues Between Hylas and Philonous*
HUME. *A Treatise of Human Nature*, BK I, PART III, SECT V–VII
KANT. *De Mundi Sensibilis (Inaugural Dissertation)*
HEGEL. *The Phenomenology of Mind*, I–III
W. JAMES. *Some Problems of Philosophy*, CH 4–6

II.

THEOPHRASTUS. *On the Senses*
EPICURUS. *Letter to Herodotus*
CICERO. *Academics*
SEXTUS EMPIRICUS. *Outlines of Pyrrhonism*
ALBERTUS MAGNUS. *De Sensu et Sensato*
R. BACON. *Opus Majus*, PART V
JOHN OF SAINT THOMAS. *Cursus Philosophicus Thomisticus, Philosophia Naturalis*, PART IV, QQ 4–8
MALEBRANCHE. *De la recherche de la vérité*, BK I, CH 5–9, 10 (2, 4–6), 12–15, 17–20
——. *Dialogues on Metaphysics and Religion*, IV–V

LEIBNITZ. *New Essays Concerning Human Understanding*, BK II, CH 2-9
——. *Monadology*, par 10–18
CONDILLAC. *Treatise on the Sensations*
VOLTAIRE. "Sensation," in *A Philosophical Dictionary*
T. REID. *An Inquiry into the Human Mind*
T. REID. *Essays on the Intellectual Powers of Man*, II
SCHOPENHAUER. *The World as Will and Idea*, VOL II, SUP, CH 1–4
BROWN. *Lectures on the Philosophy of the Human Mind*, VOL I, pp 417–548; VOL II, pp 90–152
J. MILL. *Analysis of the Phenomena of the Human Mind*, CH I
W. HAMILTON. *Lectures on Metaphysics and Logic*, VOL I (21–28)
BAIN. *The Senses and the Intellect*
FECHNER. *Elemente der Psychophysik*
WHEWELL. *On the Philosophy of Discovery*, CH 19–21
HELMHOLTZ. *Treatise on Physiological Optics*
——. *On the Sensation of Tone as a Physiological Basis for the Theory of Music*
——. *Popular Lectures on Scientific Subjects*, VI
HERSCHEL. *Familiar Lectures on Scientific Subjects*, IX
E. HARTMANN. *Philosophy of the Unconscious*, (B) VIII
LOTZE. *Metaphysics*, BK III, CH 2
GALTON. *Inquiries into Human Faculty and Its Development* (Sensitivity, Sequence of Test Weights, Whistles for Audibility of Shrill Notes, Appendices C, D, E)
MACH. *The Analysis of Sensations*
BRADLEY. *Appearance and Reality*, BK I, CH I, 5
BERGSON. *Matter and Memory*, CH 4
WUNDT. *Principles of Physiological Psychology*, PART I
——. *Outlines of Psychology*, (6, 8–11)
WOODWORTH. *Psychological Issues*, CH 5
MCTAGGART. *The Nature of Existence*, CH 35
MOORE. *Philosophical Studies*, CH 2, 5, 7
BROAD. *Perception, Physics, and Reality*, CH 4
——. *The Mind and Its Place in Nature*, CH 4
BROAD. *Scientific Thought*, PART II
PARSONS. *An Introduction to the Theory of Perception*
B. RUSSELL. *Our Knowledge of the External World*, III–IV
——. *Mysticism and Logic*, CH 8
——. *The Analysis of Mind*, LECT 7–8
——. *The Analysis of Matter*, CH 15–26
ADRIAN. *The Basis of Sensation*
KOEHLER. *Gestalt Psychology*, CH 5
WHITEHEAD. *Process and Reality*, PART III
LOVEJOY. *The Revolt Against Dualism*
POWYS. *In Defence of Sensuality*
DEWEY. "Appearing and Appearance," "A Naturalistic Theory of Sense Perception," "Perception and Organic Action," in *Philosophy and Civilization*
PRICE. *Perception*
BORING. *The Physical Dimensions of Consciousness*, CH 2–8
HARTSHORNE. *The Philosophy and Psychology of Sensation*
KOFFKA. *Principles of Gestalt-Psychology*
STRAUS. *Vom Sinn der Sinne*
BLANSHARD. *The Nature of Thought*, CH 1–6

Chapter 85: SIGN AND SYMBOL

INTRODUCTION

A SIGN points to something. A symbol stands for or takes the place of another thing. Sign and symbol are sometimes differentiated according to whether emphasis is placed on that which is signified or pointed out, or on that which functions as a surrogate or substitute.

Yet "sign" and "symbol" are often used interchangeably. We call the notations of music or mathematics either "signs" or "symbols." Words, too, are traditionally spoken of as signs or symbols. Words and other conventional notations for expressing meaning both point to and stand for something else. It is only in certain cases that one of these two functions seems to predominate, as the road marker points out the direction to take, and paper money takes the place of the precious metal whose value it represents.

On what is common to signs and symbols of all sorts there seems to be no disagreement throughout the tradition of western thought. From Augustine's statement that "a sign is a thing which, over and above the impression it makes on the senses, causes something else to come into mind as a consequence of itself," to Freud's analysis of the symbolism of dreams, of symptoms, and symptomatic acts, the great books consider sign or symbol as one term in a relation, the relation being one of meaning or, as Freud says, of "significance, intention, tendency." The fundamental problems traditionally discussed concern the nature of meaning itself, and the modes of signification which vary with the kinds of things that function as signs and the kinds of things they signify.

WITH RESPECT TO THINGS which function symbolically, the primary distinction seems to be that between natural and conventional signs. Augustine at first suggests a threefold division. Some things are simply things, and not signs at all. Some (for example, "the ram which Abraham offered up instead of his son") are not only things, but "also signs of other things." And some things, such as words, "are never employed except as signs." Augustine adds that words are not merely signs. "Every sign," he writes, "is also a thing, for what is not a thing is nothing at all."

The distinction between natural and conventional signs falls within this threefold division. "Natural signs," Augustine says, "are those which, apart from any intention or desire of using them as signs, do yet lead to the knowledge of something else, as, for example, smoke when it indicates fire. For it is not from any intention of making it a sign that it is so, but through attention to experience we come to know that fire is beneath, even when nothing but smoke can be seen. And the footprint of an animal passing by belongs to this class of signs."

Augustine seems to find natural signs in things that are related as cause and effect. Berkeley, on the other hand, tends to substitute the relation of sign and thing signified for the relation of cause and effect. "The fire which I see," he writes, "is not the cause of the pain I suffer upon my approaching, but the mark that forewarns me. In like manner the noise that I hear is not the effect of this or that motion or collision of the ambient bodies, but the sign thereof."

Every natural thing or event thus tends to become the sign of something else, so that the whole of nature constitutes a vast symbolism or language by which God informs us of his plan. Aristotle tends, in the opposite direction, to limit natural signs to those things which, according to our knowledge and experience, permit a necessary or probable inference to something else. The fact that a woman is giving milk he regards as an infallible sign that she has lately borne a child; the fact that a man is breathing fast is merely a probable and refutable sign that he has a fever.

In any case, signs are generally acknowledged to be natural if they satisfy Augustine's criterion that they were not intentionally devised by men for the purpose of signifying. "Conventional signs, on the other hand," he writes, "are those which living beings mutually exchange for the purpose of showing, as well as they can, the feelings of their minds, or their perceptions, or their thoughts." Of conventional signs, Augustine goes on to say, words hold the chief place, because everything which can be expressed by gestures, or by such non-verbal symbols as flags or bugle calls, can also be expressed in words, whereas many thoughts which words readily express do not lend themselves easily to other modes of expression.

Except for the hypothesis (discussed in the chapter on LANGUAGE) of a natural form of speech common to all men and consisting of words perfectly adapted to the objects they name, it is never proposed that words are anything but conventional signs. As Aristotle says, "nothing is by nature a noun or a name—it is only so when it becomes a symbol." The audible sound or the visible mark becomes a symbol only by human institution or convention.

Yet not all the audible sounds which men and other animals make to express their feelings or desires are, in Aristotle's opinion, to be regarded as words. "Inarticulate sounds, such as those which brutes produce, are significant, yet none of these constitutes a noun." Nor are such cries, whereby one animal calls another or communicates fear or anger, strictly conventional signs; for, as Augustine points out, they are instinctive modes of expression, and so are natural rather than conventional. They are not voluntarily instituted.

IN TERMS OF THE ancient distinction between the conventional and the natural—that which changes from time to time and place to place and that which is everywhere and always the same—no one would question the conventionality of words and of all other non-verbal symbols which are peculiar to one people, one culture, or one epoch. That words are conventional signs raises the central problem concerning their meaning or significance. Utterly dissimilar words in different languages can have the same meaning, and identical sounds or marks in different languages can mean quite different things. Since the sounds or marks which constitute spoken and written words do not possess meaning naturally, from what source do such conventional signs get the meanings they have?

The usual answer, given by Aristotle, Locke, and others, is that words get their meanings from the ideas, thoughts, or feelings which men use them to express. "Spoken words," writes Aristotle, "are the symbols of mental experience and written words are the symbols of spoken words. Just as all men do not have the same writing, so all men do not have the same speech sounds, but the mental experiences, which these directly symbolize, are the same for all, as also are those things of which our experiences are the images."

In addition to being able to make articulate sounds, it was necessary for man, Locke says, to "be able to use these sounds as signs of internal conceptions, and to make them stand as marks for the ideas within his own mind, whereby they might be made known to others." Thus words came to be used by men "as the signs of their ideas; not by any natural connexion that there is between particular articulate sounds and certain ideas, for then there would be but one language amongst all men; but by a voluntary imposition, whereby such a word is made arbitrarily the mark of such an idea. The use then of words is to be sensible marks of ideas, and the ideas they stand for are their proper and immediate signification."

Locke goes further. Not only does the immediate signification of words lie in the ideas they stand for, but in his view words "can be signs of nothing else." Yet he also considers the fact that men, because they "would not be thought to talk barely of their own imaginations, but of things as they really are . . . often suppose their words to stand also for the reality of things." Locke thinks, nevertheless, that "obscurity and confusion" enter into the signification of words "whenever we make them stand for anything but those ideas we have in our own minds."

But though the meaning of a word may come from the idea it signifies, the word which is thus made meaningful seems, in the common usage of mankind, to serve as the name or designation of some real thing. It refers to something other than ideas or concepts in the human mind. Locke himself talks of "the application of names to things," and in his consideration of the distinction between proper and common names is concerned to point out that, though they differ in meaning (*i.e.*, differ in the type of idea they signify), both refer to the same sort of reality—individual existences. Aristotle and other writers who distinguish between things in the order of nature and the concepts we form of them, tend to take both views of the significance of words. Words signify the real things which they name as well as the ideas whose meanings they express. If we waive for the moment the possibility that some words may signify *only* ideas, whereas others signify both ideas and things, two questions may be asked. Are there any words which signify things alone? What is the relation between the idea and the thing a word signifies, when a word signifies them both; that is, when a word has both sorts of significance, how are they related to one another?

Aquinas answers the second question by saying that since "words are the signs of ideas, and ideas the similitudes of things, it is evident that words function in the signification of things through the conceptions of the intellect." Ideas may be the immediate or proximate object which words signify, but through them words ultimately signify the real things which are themselves the objects of ideas. According to this theory, an idea may be both the *object signified* by a word and the *medium through which* that word also signifies the thing of which we have the idea. Aquinas seems to think that ideas are always required as the medium whereby words signify things. "We can give a name to anything," he says, "only insofar as we can understand it." Accordingly, it is impossible for words to signify things directly, *i.e.*, without the mediation of ideas.

THIS POSITION HAS A number of consequences for the theory of signs and raises a number of issues. Augustine's statement that "every sign is also a thing" has a different meaning when it is said of the sensible things which also happen to be signs and of the things of the mind—concepts or ideas—which cannot *be* without *being signs*. The understanding of this difference helps to explain the relation between verbal signs and the mental signs through which they signify or from which they get their meanings.

Whereas words are in the first instance meaningless marks and sounds which get meaning when men use them to express their thoughts or feelings, ideas and images are at once meaningful, however they arise in the mind. They are natural signs in the sense that it seems to be their very nature to signify. They do not get meaning. They do not even have meaning, in the way in which smoke as a natural sign of fire has a meaning which is distinct from, though a consequence of, its nature as smoke. An idea *is* a meaning, an intention of the mind, as it is sometimes called, a reference to an object thought about. The idea of fire is the meaning the word "fire" has when it designates the natural phenomenon which that word is conventionally used to name; and as Aristotle suggests, the conventional signs of different languages [*e.g.*, "fire" and "*feuer*"]—have the same meaning because the idea of fire is the same, and the natural phenomenon experienced and thought about is the same, for men of diverse tongues.

That ideas or mental images are themselves meanings or intentions—the symbols of things thought about—seems to be recognized in different ways by many writers in the tradition of the great books. In the *Cratylus*, Socrates suggests that signs should be like the things they signify. Some conventional signs, he thinks, are better than others in this respect. He implies that all words are inferior to mental images, which, by their very nature, imitate or resemble their objects.

The act of memory, according to Aristotle, requires a memory image which is "something like an impression or picture" of the thing remembered. If the memory image, through its resemblance to something once experienced, did not function as the sign of that absent thing, memory would not be memory, for, Aristotle argues, it would consist in beholding the memory image itself, which is present, rather than the absent thing it stands for.

Aquinas, perhaps, is the writer most explicit in his treatment of images and ideas as in their very nature meanings or intentions of the mind. His calling them "mental words" seems to indicate that in his view they, like physical and sensible words, are signs; but the added qualification of "mental" also implies their difference. "The vocal sound which has no signification," he writes, "cannot be called a word; wherefore the exterior vocal sound is called a word from the fact that it signifies the interior concept of the mind. It follows that, first and chiefly, the interior concept of the mind is called a word." The mental word or concept suffices "when the mind turns to the actual consideration of what it knows habitually," for then, he adds, "a person speaks to himself." But unlike angels, who can make their concepts known to one another immediately, men require the medium of external speech. They must use sensible physical signs to communicate their thoughts.

Without referring to ideas as mental words, Locke does appear to identify ideas with meanings and to regard them as signs. The definition of a word, he says, is an attempt to make known "the meaning or idea it stands for." Denying that the general and the universal belong to the real existence of things, he holds that they "concern only signs, whether words or ideas. Words are general . . . when used for signs of general ideas . . . and ideas are general when they set up as the representatives of many particular things; but universality belongs not to things themselves, which are all of them particular in their existence, even those words and ideas which, in their signification, are general."

The basic issue to which Locke is addressing himself is discussed in the chapter on Universal and Particular. Locke's solution seems to involve the affirmation of abstract ideas, which are general or universal in their significance and through which common names come to have a different sort of meaning from the meaning of proper names. "Ideas become general by separating them from the circumstances of time and place, and any other ideas that may determine them to this or that particular existence." Common nouns like "man" or "cat" become general in their significance, according to Locke, "by being made the signs of general ideas."

To the question of what kind of signification it is that general words have, Locke replies: "As it is evident, that they do not signify barely one particular thing; for then they would not be general terms, but proper names; so, on the other side, it is as evident, they do not signify a plurality; for man and men would then signify the same. . . . That, then, which general words signify," Locke declares, "is a sort of things, and each of them does that by being a sign of an abstract idea in the mind."

It seems to follow, therefore, that those who, like Hobbes and Berkeley, deny the existence of abstract ideas or universal concepts, must offer a different explanation of the meaning of common nouns or general names. "There being nothing in the world universal but names," Hobbes writes, a name is universal when it "is imposed on many things for their similitude in some quality or other accident; and whereas a proper name bringeth to mind one thing only, a universal recalls any one of those many."

On similar grounds, Berkeley criticizes Locke's theory of how words acquire general significance. His own theory is that words become general "by being made the sign, not of an abstract general idea, but of several particular ideas, any one of which it indifferently suggests to the mind." And, in another place, he says that "an idea which, considered in itself, is particular becomes general by being made to represent or stand for all other particular ideas of the same sort." He does not himself explain how we come by the notion of "the same sort," or how one particular idea can represent the sort to which other particular ideas belong. But he rejects Locke's explanation because it involves ideas which are not only general, but also abstract.

The attempt to account for the meaning of general names is, in Berkeley's view, the cause of Locke's acceptance of abstract ideas. "If there had been no such thing as speech or universal signs," he writes, "there never [would have] been any thought of abstraction." Not only do men mistakenly suppose that "every name has, or ought to have, one only precise and settled signification, which inclines [them] to think there are certain abstract, determinate ideas that constitute the true and only immediate signification of each general name"; but they also suppose that "it is by the mediation of these abstract ideas that a general name comes to signify any particular thing. Whereas, in truth," Berkeley concludes, "there is no such thing as one precise and definite signification annexed to any general name." Where Locke would say that a common name gets its general meaning by signifying one idea which itself has general significance, Berkeley reiterates that a general name gets its meaning from "a great number of particular ideas," all of which it signifies indifferently.

THE RELATION OF WORDS to ideas raises still other problems in the theory of signs, problems which have peculiar interest in the tradition of the liberal arts. One of these problems has already been mentioned. It is the question whether some words signify ideas alone, in contrast to words which signify ideas and, through them, things. This suggests the parallel problem of words which signify words, in contrast to words which are the names of things.

In his little tract *Concerning the Teacher*, Augustine points out that some words, such as "noun" and "adjective," signify kinds of words, just as other words, such as "man" and "stone," signify kinds of things. Furthermore, in the sentence "man is a noun," the word "man" signifies itself as the object referred to; whereas in the sentence "man is an animal," the word "man" signifies a living organism of a certain sort. The same word, therefore, may signify both itself and some thing other than itself.

These differences which Augustine observes in the signification of words come to be formulated in the traditional distinction between the first and second imposition of words. A word is used in the first imposition when it is used to signify things which are not words, as, for example, the word "man" when it refers to a human being. A word is used in the second imposition when it is applied to words rather than things, as, for example, the word "noun" said of "man," or the word "man" when it is used to refer to itself in the sentence "man is a noun."

A parallel distinction is that between words used in the first and the second intention. When the word "man" is used to signify a living organism of a certain sort, it is used in the first intention because it signifies a reality, not an idea. A word is said to be used in the second intention when it signifies an idea rather than a thing. For example, in the sentence, "man is a species," the word "species" signifies a logical classification and so is in the second intention; and the word "man" is also in the second intention because it refers to the idea which is denominated a species.

In some cases, an idea may not signify things at all, but only other ideas, such as the logical notions of *genus* and *species*. Words like "genus" and "species," unlike the words "man" and "stone," can therefore be used only in the second intention. The idea *man* is called a "first intention of the mind" because its primary function is to signify the living thing. Only secondarily does it signify itself as an object able to be considered. The idea *species*, on the other hand, is called a "second intention" because its sole function is to signify ideas which stand to other ideas in a certain relation.

Hobbes concisely summarizes most of these points when he points out that some words "are the names of the things conceived," whereas "others are the names of the imaginations themselves, that is to say, of those ideas or mental images we have of all the things we see and remember. And others again are names of names . . . . as 'universal,' 'plural,' 'singular,' are the names of names." The names which we apply to particular species and genera, such as "man" and "animal," Aquinas says, "signify the common natures themselves, but not the intentions of these common natures, which are signified by the terms *genus* or *species*."

ANOTHER TRADITIONAL distinction in the modes of signification is that between intrinsic and extrinsic denomination. A name is said to be an intrinsic denomination when it is applied to a thing in order to signify its nature or its inherent properties and attributes, as, for example, when we call a thing "animal" or "rational," "white" or "square." A name is said to be an extrinsic denomination when it is applied to a thing only in order to signify some relation in which that thing stands to something else, as, for example, when we call sunshine "healthy" because it helps to produce healthy organisms or when we apply the names of animals, such as "pig" or "fox," to men because we think the men bear certain resemblances to these animals. The same word can be used in different connections both as an intrinsic and as an extrinsic denomination. "Healthy" means an inherent quality when it is applied to living organisms, and a causal relation to organic health when it is applied to sunshine; "pig" means a certain kind of animal when it is applied to the four-footed mammal, and only a resemblance to this animal in certain characteristics when it is applied to men.

This double use of the same word exemplifies what is traditionally called "equivocal speech" or the equivocal use of a name. Some writers tend to identify equivocation with ambiguity, on the ground that both involve a multiplicity of meanings for the same word. Others seem to think that a word is used ambiguously only if its user is indefinite as to which of its several meanings he intends to express; but they hold that a word can be used equivocally without ambiguity if its user makes plain that he is employing it now in this sense, now in that.

Aristotle says that two things are named equivocally "when though they have the same name, the definition corresponding with the name differs for each"; and "on the other hand, things are said to be named univocally which have both the name and the definition answering to the name in common." When we call a man and a pig an "animal," we are using that word univocally because we are using it with the same definition or meaning in both cases; but when we call a pig and a man a "pig," we are using that word equivocally because we are using it with different meanings, signifying *having the nature of a pig* in one instance and *being like a pig in certain respects* in the other.

Aristotle distinguishes several types of equivocation, of which we have already noted two. The use of the word "healthy" to describe an animal and sunshine is that type of equivocation in which the same word is used to name an inherent attribute and also a cause of that attribute; in other instances of the same type, it might be used to name the nature or attribute and the effect rather than the cause. Speaking of a man and a pig as a "pig" represents the metaphorical type of equivocation, in which the same word is used to name the nature of a thing and something else of a different nature which has only a likeness to that nature.

Metaphors, in turn, can be divided into types. Some are based on a direct similitude between two things in some accidental respect, *e.g.*, the man who is like a pig in manner of eating. Some, Aristotle says, are based on analogies or proportions, as, for example, when we call a king the "father of his people." Here the metaphor is based on the similarity of the relationship of a king to his subjects and of a father to his children. The name "father" is used metaphorically when it is transferred from one term in this proportion to the term which stands in an analogous position.

A third kind of metaphor, according to Aristotle, consists in the use of the same word now in a more generic, now in a more specific sense, or with broader and narrower meanings. Of this he gives an example in the *Ethics* when he discusses general and special justice, using the word "justice" narrowly to signify one of the special virtues and broadly to mean all the virtues considered in their social aspect. There is a sense of the word "justice," he writes, in which it signifies "not part of virtue but virtue entire"; "this form of justice is complete virtue, though not absolutely, but only in relation to our neighbor." The word "injustice" is also used in a correspondingly wide sense. But there is "another kind of injustice which is a part of injustice in the wide sense." This "particular injustice," Aristotle says, "shares the name and nature of the first, because its definition falls within the same genus." As Aristotle treats this type of equivocation in the *Rhetoric* and the *Poetics*, it includes three possibilities: the transfer of the name of a genus to one of its species, the transfer of the name of a species to its genus, and the transfer of the name of one species to another in the same genus.

It may be questioned whether this type of equivocation is properly classified as metaphorical, on Aristotle's own definition of metaphor as "giving a thing a name that belongs to something else." In the type of equivocation exemplified by the use of the word "justice," now with a generic and now a specific meaning, the name does not seem to belong to the genus any more than it does to the species, or conversely. In contrast, when the name "father" is given to a king in relation to his people, the usage is metaphorical, because the name "father" belongs to something else, *i.e.*, the man who is a progenitor.

The same point can be made in terms of intrinsic and extrinsic denomination. When "justice" is used as the name for the whole of virtue (regarded socially) and also for one particular virtue, the word is an intrinsic denomination in both instances. In all other types of equivocation, the equivocal word is used once as an intrinsic and once as an extrinsic denomination; for example, as applied to the animal, the word "pig" is an intrinsic denomination, but it is an extrinsic denomination when it is applied to a man in order to signify a certain resemblance to the animal to which the name belongs. The same is true in the case of the word "healthy" as said of an animal and of sunshine.

In all these cases of equivocation, the two meanings of the same word are not totally distinct. On the contrary, the two senses have something in common. One of the meanings seems to be derived from the other; one appears to be secondary (usually the one involved in the extrinsic denomination) and the other primary. What is traditionally called "equivocation by chance," in contrast to equivocation by intention, is the extreme case in which the same word is used in two utterly distinct senses, having no common element of meaning at all; *e.g.*, the word "pen" used for a writing instrument and an enclosure for animals. Equivocation by intention, in which the different meanings of a word have something in common, thus appears to be intermediate between equivocation by chance (in which the meanings share no common element) and univocal usage (in which the meaning is exactly the same each time the word is used).

In the *Physics*, Aristotle seems to discover still another type of equivocation. "A pen, a wine, and the highest note in a scale are not commensurable," he writes. "We cannot say whether any one of them is sharper than any other . . . because it is only equivocally that the same term 'sharp' is applied to them." This does not seem to be equivocation by chance, for the word "sharp" seems to have some common meaning as applied to the three objects which affect the diverse senses of touch, taste, and hearing; nor is it like all other cases of equivocation by intention, in that no one of these three meanings of "sharp" seems to be primary and the others derived from it. Furthermore, in all three meanings, the word "sharp" is used as an intrinsic denomination.

In the *Metaphysics*, Aristotle also considers the special pattern of meaning which words like "being" or "one" have when they are applied to such heterogeneous things as substances, quantities, qualities, etc. He refers to these words as ambiguous or equivocal, comparing them with the word "healthy" as said of an animal, and of other things which either cause health or are effects of health. It may be questioned, however, whether "being" is equivocal in the same way that "healthy" is, since it always carries the significance of an intrinsic, never of an extrinsic denomination. "Being" as said of heterogeneous things seems to be more like "sharp" said of diverse sensible qualities—having a meaning which remains somehow the same while it is diversified in each case according to the diversity of the objects to which it applies.

THESE CONSIDERATIONS of the univocal and the equivocal sign, along with the treatment of ambiguity and intrinsic and extrinsic denomination, indicate the extent and manner in which the great books anticipate the kind of analysis which in our time has come to be called "semantics." The chapter on LANGUAGE gives further evidence of the fact that many of the points and distinctions made in contemporary semantics have a long history in the tradition of the liberal arts. Furthermore, as the chapter on LANGUAGE indicates, contemporary semantics cannot even claim novelty for its great interest in freeing men from the tyranny of words or in serving as a critical instrument to cut through the "vicious abstractions" of metaphysics. Hobbes and Locke frequently dismiss theories not on the ground that they are false, but rather because they think that the statement of them consists in so many meaningless words.

In the tradition of the great books, the analysis of words and their modes of signification seems to be motivated by other interests as well as these. The distinction between the univocal and the equivocal sign, for example, is considered in its bearing on the logical problems of definition and demonstration as well as for the sake of proposing remedies to safeguard discourse against ambiguity. It is also brought to bear upon the theological problem of the meaning of the names men apply to God and on the way in which they interpret the words of Sacred Scripture.

The problem of the names of God is discussed in the chapter on SAME AND OTHER in terms of the kind of likeness which can obtain between an infinite being and finite creatures. As there appears, Aquinas takes the position that God and creatures are neither the same in any respect, nor are they in all respects so diverse as to be utterly incomparable. Though an infinite and a finite being are in his view incommensurable, yet they can also have some sort of similitude—not an unqualified sameness, but the kind of similarity which can be described as an intrinsically diversified sameness.

Aquinas holds, therefore, that no names can be applied to God and creatures univocally, for "no name belongs to God in the same sense that it belongs to creatures." Nor, he goes on, "are names applied to God and creatures in a purely equivocal sense," for it would follow then that "from creatures nothing at all could be known or demonstrated about God," which supposition Aquinas denies. Between these two extremes of the simply univocal and the purely equivocal, he finds a middle ground in a type of signification which he calls "analogical." The meaning of an analogical name, he says, "is not, as it is in univocals, one and the same; yet it is not totally diverse as in equivocals."

What he means by "pure equivocation" seems to be what earlier writers call "equivocation by chance," and what he means by the "analogical" seems to correspond to what they call "equivocation by intention." "Univocal names have absolutely the same meaning," he writes, "while equivocal names have absolutely diverse meanings; whereas in analogicals, a name taken in one signification must be placed in the definition of the same name taken in other significations; as, for instance, "being" which is applied to *substance* is placed in the definition of "being" as applied to *accident*; and "healthy" applied to *animal* is placed in the definition of "healthy" as applied to *urine* and *medicine*."

But, as we have seen, there are many types of equivocation by intention—the attributive, based on cause and effect, as exemplified by the word "healthy"; that involving broader and narrower meanings, exemplified by the word "justice"; metaphors, of the sort exemplified by calling a man "pig," and of the sort based on analogies, when we speak of a king as the "father" of his people; and, finally, the very special type of equivocation found in "sharp" applied to a tone, a taste, and a touch.

If Aquinas places the kind of signification he calls "analogical" in the general area of equivocation by intention, it may be asked whether the various names of God are all analogical *in the same way*. The answer seems to be negative, for he distinguishes those names which have only a metaphorical sense when said of God, such as "angry" or "jealous"; and he denies the opinion of those who say that God is called "good" only in an attributive sense, *i.e.*, signifying him to be the cause of the goodness found in creatures. On the contrary, he thinks that words like "good" and "wise," and especially the name "being," are to be interpreted as intrinsic denominations when applied to both God and creatures.

For Aquinas, as for Aristotle, that would appear to make the pattern of meaning exhibited by the word "sharp" the model for the significance of "being" rather than that found in the merely attributive equivocation of the word "healthy"—whether "being" is said of substance and accidents, or of God and creatures. The point seems to be unaffected by the fact that Aquinas calls this type of signification "analogical," whereas Aristotle always refers to "being" as equivocal. Aristotle never treats any type of equivocation as analogical except the metaphor which results from transferring the name of one term in a proportion to another term standing in the same or a similar relationship.

THE DISTINCTION BETWEEN literal and figurative or metaphorical speech seems to be of prime importance in the theologian's rules for interpreting the word of God. As indicated in the chapter on RELIGION, Augustine insists that the language of Holy Writ must be read in many senses. Aquinas distinguishes a basic literal sense from three modes of spiritual meaning. That signification "whereby words signify things belongs to the first sense, the historical or literal. That signification whereby things signified by words have themselves also a signification is called the spiritual sense, which is based on the literal and presupposes it." The spiritual sense Aquinas divides into the allegorical, the moral, and the analogical.

To grasp the various spiritual meanings, the reader must understand that in Holy Scripture "divine things are metaphorically described by means of sensible things." As in the symbolism of the sacraments, physical things serve as the outward and visible signs of an inward and spiritual grace, so also "in Holy Scripture spiritual truths are fittingly taught under the likeness of material things."

A theologian like Aquinas thus justifies metaphors not only in Scripture, but also in sacred doctrine or theology, as "both necessary and useful," whereas in his view the poet's employment of them is solely for the sake of pleasure. Philosophers and scientists, on the other hand, often take the opposite view—that metaphors have a place only in poetry and should be avoided in the exposition of knowledge.

In the writing of poetry, "the command of metaphor," says Aristotle, "is the mark of genius," but all his rules for the construction of scientific definitions and demonstrations require the avoidance of metaphors, as of all other forms of equivocation. So, too, Hobbes inveighs against metaphors and figures of speech, giving as one of the main causes of absurdity in science "the use of metaphors, tropes, and other rhetorical figures, instead of words proper; for though it be lawful to say (for example) in common speech, *the way goeth, or leadeth hither or thither, the Proverb says this or that* (whereas ways cannot go, nor Proverbs speak); yet in reckoning, and seeking of truth, such speeches are not to be admitted."

Darwin looks forward to the day when "the terms used by naturalists, of affinity, relationship, community of type, paternity, morphology, adaptive characters, rudimentary and aborted organs, and so forth, will cease to be metaphorical and will have a plain significance." Freud, on the other hand, aware of how pervasive symbolism is in all the works of man, normal and neurotic, dreaming and awake, seems to be reconciled to the inevitability of metaphors in scientific discourse. The difficulty we meet with in picturing certain psychological processes, he writes, "comes from our being obliged to operate with scientific terms, *i.e.*, with the metaphorical expressions peculiar to psychology. . . . Otherwise we should not be able to describe the corresponding processes at all, nor in fact even to have remarked them. The shortcomings of our description would disappear if for the psychological terms we could substitute physiological or chemical ones. These, too, only constitute a metaphorical language, but one familiar to us for a much longer time and perhaps also simpler."

OUTLINE OF TOPICS

1. The theory of signs

1a. The distinction between natural and conventional signs

1b. The intentions of the mind: ideas and images as natural signs

1c. The things of nature functioning symbolically: the book of nature

1d. The conventional notations of human language: man's need for words

1e. The invention of non-verbal symbols: money, titles, seals, ceremonies, courtesies

1f. Natural signs as the source of meaning in conventional signs: thought as the medium through which words signify things

2. The modes of signification

2a. The first and second imposition of words: names signifying things and names signifying names

2b. The first and second intention of names: words signifying things and words signifying ideas

2c. Intrinsic and extrinsic denominations: the naming of things according to their natures or by reference to their relations

2d. Proper and common names

2e. Abstract and concrete names

3. The patterns of meaning in human discourse

3a. Verbal ambiguity: indefiniteness or multiplicity of meaning

3b. The distinction between univocal and equivocal speech

3c. The types of equivocation

(1) The same word used literally and figuratively: metaphors derived from analogies or proportions and from other kinds of similitude

(2) The same word used with varying degrees of generality and specificity: the broad and narrow meaning of a word

(3) The same word used to signify an attribute and its cause or effect

3d. The significance of names predicated of heterogeneous things: the analogical as intermediate between the univocal and the equivocal

4. The determination of meaning in science and philosophy

4a. The relation between univocal meaning and definition

4b. The dependence of demonstration on univocal terms: formal fallacies due to equivocation

4c. The nature and utility of semantic analysis: the rectification of ambiguity; the clarification and precision of meanings

4d. The use of metaphors and myths in science and philosophy

4e. The use of signs in reasoning: necessary and probable signs; the interpretation of symptoms in medicine

5. Symbolism in theology and religion

5a. Natural things as signs of divinity

5b. Supernatural signs: omens, portents, visitations, dreams, miracles

5c. The symbolism of the sacraments and of sacramental or ritualistic acts

5d. The symbolism of numbers in theology

5e. The interpretation of the word of God

5f. The names of God: the use of words to signify the divine nature

6. Symbolism in psychological analysis

6a. The symbolism of dreams: their latent and manifest content

6b. The symbolism of apparently normal acts: forgetting, verbal slips, errors

6c. The symbolism of anxieties, obsessions, and other neurotic manifestations

REFERENCES

References are listed by volume number (in bold type), author's name, and page number. Bible references are to book, chapter, and verse of the Authorized King James version of the Bible. The abbreviation "esp" calls the reader's attention to one or more especially relevant parts of a whole reference; "passim" signifies that the topic is discussed intermittently rather than continuously in the work or passage cited. Where the work as a whole is relevant to the topic, the page numbers refer to the entire work. For general guidance in the use of *The Great Ideas,* consult the Preface.

1. The theory of signs

1*a*. The distinction between natural and conventional signs

6 HERODOTUS, 49
7 PLATO, 85–114
8 ARISTOTLE, 25
11 NICOMACHUS, 832
18 AUGUSTINE, 624–625, 636–637
20 AQUINAS, 849–850
31 DESCARTES, 59–60
38 ROUSSEAU, 341

1*b*. The intentions of the mind: ideas and images as natural signs

8 ARISTOTLE, 664, 691–692
18 AUGUSTINE, 627
19 AQUINAS, 62–63, 75–77, 185–187, 197–199, 549–550
20 AQUINAS, 215–216
31 DESCARTES, 81–89 passim, 130, 132
31 SPINOZA, 373, 374
35 LOCKE, 238, 244, 245–246, 312, 295
35 BERKELEY, 415–416, 420–421, 425–426
53 JAMES, 161–176, 478, 502–503, 553–558, 606–610, 620–621

1*c*. The things of nature functioning symbolically: the book of nature

5 AESCHYLUS, 44–45
8 ARISTOTLE, 92–93
16 KEPLER, 853–856
19 AQUINAS, 298–299
20 AQUINAS, 778–779, 848
26 SHAKESPEARE, 103–104, 450, 468–469
27 SHAKESPEARE, 249
33 PASCAL, 203–204
35 BERKELEY, 434, 442–444 passim
46 HEGEL, 203, 252, 263–265
47 GOETHE, 116–117
48 MELVILLE, 1–3, 115–122, 135–137, 138–145, 204–205, 236–238, 331–332

1*d*. The conventional notations of human language: man's need for words

OLD TESTAMENT: *Genesis,* 11:1–9
6 HERODOTUS, 171
7 PLATO, 138–139, 612–613
12 LUCRETIUS, 74–75
15 TACITUS, 103
18 AUGUSTINE, 76, 119–120, 307, 636–638, 648–649
19 AQUINAS, 549–550
23 HOBBES, 54–56
30 BACON, 62–63
31 DESCARTES, 59–60
35 LOCKE, 174–175, 201–202, 251–253, 265–266, 280–283, 298
35 BERKELEY, 436–437
36 SWIFT, 111
38 ROUSSEAU, 339–342
46 HEGEL, 218
49 DARWIN, 298–299
53 JAMES, 683–685
54 FREUD, 516

1*e*. The invention of non-verbal symbols: money, titles, seals, ceremonies, courtesies

4 HOMER, 10–11, 135–136
5 AESCHYLUS, 31–34
5 EURIPIDES, 387–388
6 HERODOTUS, 146–147, 264, 306
9 ARISTOTLE, 380–381, 601–602
17 PLOTINUS, 242
18 AUGUSTINE, 649
19 AQUINAS, 615–617
20 AQUINAS, 858–859
23 HOBBES, 73–75
24 RABELAIS, 11–14, 101–106
25 MONTAIGNE, 215–216
26 SHAKESPEARE, 394, 417–418, 420–421, 494, 554
27 SHAKESPEARE, 508–509
35 LOCKE, 35–36
37 FIELDING, 310
38 MONTESQUIEU, 174–175
39 SMITH, 10–12
40 GIBBON, 154–155, 240–244
41 GIBBON, 75, 317–319
43 MILL, 462
46 HEGEL, 28, 59, 122–123, 124
50 MARX, 40–45, 58–60
51 TOLSTOY, 232–233
52 DOSTOEVSKY, 171
54 FREUD, 4, 815

1*f*. Natural signs as the source of meaning in conventional signs: thought as the medium through which words signify things

7 Plato, 104–114, 809–810
8 Aristotle, 674
18 Augustine, 637
19 Aquinas, 65–66, 153–154, 453–455
20 Aquinas, 215–216
35 Locke, 253–254, 257–258, 266–267
35 Berkeley, 410
53 James, 18

2. The modes of signification

2*a*. The first and second imposition of words: names signifying things and names signifying names

23 Hobbes, 57, 270

2*b*. The first and second intention of names: words signifying things and words signifying ideas

19 Aquinas, 163–164, 170–171, 453–455
23 Hobbes, 57–58
35 Locke, 252–254 passim, 257, 273, 282, 305
45 Lavoisier, 4
53 James, 127–128

2*c*. Intrinsic and extrinsic denominations: the naming of things according to their natures or by reference to their relations

Old Testament: *Genesis*, 2:19–20
7 Plato, 85–114
8 Aristotle, 149, 150–151
19 Aquinas, 63–65, 68–71, 162–163, 188–189
35 Locke, 214–217, 252, 268–283 passim
35 Berkeley, 409

2*d*. Proper and common names

8 Aristotle, 246, 560
19 Aquinas, 73–74, 181–183, 185–188, 555–558
22 Chaucer, 462–463
23 Hobbes, 55
35 Locke, 145, 254–256, 257
35 Berkeley, 407–408
36 Sterne, 217–221, 351–353
38 Rousseau, 341–342
53 James, 310–311, 447–448

2*e*. Abstract and concrete names

8 Aristotle, 66
19 Aquinas, 16, 71–72, 178–179, 205–209
23 Hobbes, 57
53 James, 304–308, 689
54 Freud, 516

3. The patterns of meaning in human discourse

3*a*. Verbal ambiguity: indefiniteness or multiplicity of meaning

5 Aristophanes, 482–483, 554–555, 575
6 Herodotus, 11, 21–22
7 Plato, 65–84, 132–133, 138–141, 297–300, 478, 609–610
8 Aristotle, 149–152, 154–155, 215, 217, 251, 510, 525, 567, 658
9 Aristotle, 172–174, 456–457, 657–658
20 Aquinas, 848–849
25 Montaigne, 253–254, 517–519
26 Shakespeare, 205, 230, 297–298, 328
30 Bacon, 60, 109–110, 112–113
31 Descartes, 208
31 Spinoza, 390–391
35 Locke, 155, 234–236, 276, 282–283, 285–291, 292–293, 300–301, 348
35 Hume, 470–471, 478
36 Sterne, 234–236
38 Montesquieu, 89
42 Kant, 113
43 Federalist, 120
53 James, 549–550
54 Freud, 277–278, 540

3*b*. The distinction between univocal and equivocal speech

8 Aristotle, 5, 202, 589
19 Aquinas, 66–67, 72–73, 165–167
35 Locke, 288–289, 343–344
36 Sterne, 307–308
42 Kant, 400
53 James, 875–876

3*c*. The types of equivocation

3*c*(1) The same word used literally and figuratively: metaphors derived from analogies or proportions and from other kinds of similitude

8 Aristotle, 192–193
9 Aristotle, 655, 657, 662–666, 693
18 Augustine, 34, 450–451, 640–641, 659–674
19 Aquinas, 63–64, 67–68, 185–187, 349–350
20 Aquinas, 756–757
23 Hobbes, 176–177, 193–195
25 Montaigne, 422–423
28 Harvey, 267
30 Bacon, 65
35 Locke, 252
35 Berkeley, 441
40 Gibbon, 775
42 Kant, 547–548
53 James, 380–381

3*c*(2) The same word used with varying degrees of generality and specificity: the broad and narrow meaning of a word

9 Aristotle, 376–378
18 Augustine, 670–672
19 Aquinas, 154–155, 358–359
20 Aquinas, 1–2, 650–651
39 Smith, 123
43 Mill, 447
54 Freud, 509

3c(3) The same word used to signify an attribute and its cause or effect

8 ARISTOTLE, 149, 522, 589
19 AQUINAS, 67–68, 72–73, 98, 713–714
20 AQUINAS, 847–848

3d. The significance of names predicated of heterogeneous things: the analogical as intermediate between the univocal and the equivocal

8 ARISTOTLE, 25–26, 149–152 passim, 260–262, 522, 536–538, 550–551, 578–579, 580, 599–601
9 ARISTOTLE, 341
19 AQUINAS, 22–23, 66–68
20 AQUINAS, 54–55
35 LOCKE, 152
42 KANT, 181–182

4. The determination of meaning in science and philosophy

4a. The relation between univocal meaning and definition

7 PLATO, 552
8 ARISTOTLE, 7, 192–193, 202–203, 215
9 ARISTOTLE, 165–167
19 AQUINAS, 62–63
23 HOBBES, 56
33 PASCAL, 430–434
35 LOCKE, 302
49 DARWIN, 247

4b. The dependence of demonstration on univocal terms: formal fallacies due to equivocation

8 ARISTOTLE, 105–106, 228–229, 525
9 ARISTOTLE, 650
12 EPICTETUS, 112–113
19 AQUINAS, 66–67
35 LOCKE, 297–298, 301–306 passim
35 HUME, 478

4c. The nature and utility of semantic analysis: the rectification of ambiguity; the clarification and precision of meanings

7 PLATO, 52–57, 68, 107–114
8 ARISTOTLE, 11–12, 15, 149–152, 154–155, 184–185, 243–247, 371–372, 533–547, 574–575
9 ARISTOTLE, 376
10 GALEN, 167
12 EPICTETUS, 122–123
18 AUGUSTINE, 657–674
19 AQUINAS, 153–237 passim
23 HOBBES, 54–60, 269–272
33 PASCAL, 1–14, 430–434
35 LOCKE, 267–268, 288–289, 300–306 passim
35 HUME, 484
36 STERNE, 418–419
38 ROUSSEAU, 419
42 KANT, 546–547
43 MILL, 465–469 passim
44 BOSWELL, 81–82
45 LAVOISIER, 4–5
53 JAMES, 121–122

4d. The use of metaphors and myths in science and philosophy

7 PLATO, 44–45, 124–129, 157–159, 246–250, 292–294, 437–441, 444–446, 478, 542–544, 565, 586–589
9 ARISTOTLE, 655–656, 662–666
19 AQUINAS, 8–9, 71–72, 349–351
28 HARVEY, 336–337
45 FARADAY, 758–759
49 DARWIN, 40, 242
54 FREUD, 510 passim, 566–567

4e. The use of signs in reasoning: necessary and probable signs; the interpretation of symptoms in medicine

8 ARISTOTLE, 92–93
9 ARISTOTLE, 596–597, 652–653
10 HIPPOCRATES, 19–26, 38–40, 46, 49, 94–95, 109, 111–112, 122–126 passim, 131, 132–134 passim, 135–144 passim
23 HOBBES, 53
25 MONTAIGNE, 372–373, 531–532
30 BACON, 49–50, 77–78
36 SWIFT, 112–113, 114
37 FIELDING, 145–146
54 FREUD, 31, 38–40, 54–55, 60–62 passim, 87–90, 550–557 esp 556, 593, 605–607 passim

5. Symbolism in theology and religion

5a. Natural things as signs of divinity

OLD TESTAMENT: *Genesis*, 9:8–17 / *Job*, 37–41 / *Psalms*, 8; 19:1–4
APOCRYPHA: *Wisdom of Solomon*, 13:1–5 / *Ecclesiasticus*, 42:15–43:33
NEW TESTAMENT: *Romans*, 1:18–20
12 LUCRETIUS, 22–23, 62–63
12 EPICTETUS, 121–124, 177
16 KEPLER, 853–854, 1049–1050, 1080–1085 passim
18 AUGUSTINE, 335–338, 438–439
19 AQUINAS, 14–15, 52–53, 256–257, 339–340, 528–529
20 AQUINAS, 778–779, 1032–1034
21 DANTE, 148–149
23 HOBBES, 78–79, 81
25 MONTAIGNE, 212
28 HARVEY, 490–494
30 BACON, 2–4, 38, 41
32 MILTON, 234–235
33 PASCAL, 301–317
35 BERKELEY, 418–419, 442–444 passim
42 KANT, 187–190
46 HEGEL, 228, 235–236, 252–255, 266–267, 268–271
47 GOETHE, 84

5*b*. Supernatural signs: omens, portents, visitations, dreams, miracles

OLD TESTAMENT: *Genesis*, 4:1–16; 28:10–22; 37:1–11; 40–41 / *Exodus*, 3:1–4:9; 7–17 passim / *Numbers*, 9:15–23; 11–12; 16–17; 20:1–13; 22 / *Deuteronomy*, 4:9–14,32–39; 6:20–25; 13:1–5; 28:1–29:9 / *Joshua*, 3–4; 5:13–6:20 / *Judges*, 6:11–24,36–40; 13 / *I Samuel*, 10:1–16; 12:12–20 / *I Kings*, 13:4–6; 17; 18:16–39 / *II Kings*, 1–6 passim; 13:20–21; 20:1–11 / *Job*, 4:13–21 / *Psalms*, 105 / *Isaiah*, 6; 7:10–16; 38:1–8 / *Ezekiel* passim, / *Daniel*, 2–12 passim / *Hosea*, 1–3 / *Amos*, 7–8 / *Jonah* / *Zacharias*, 1–6

APOCRYPHA: *Rest of Esther*, 10–11 / *Bel and Dragon*, 30–42 / *II Maccabees*, 15:11–17

NEW TESTAMENT: *Matthew* passim / *Mark* passim / *Luke* passim / *John* passim / *Acts* passim / *Revelation*

4 HOMER, 3–4, 10, 13, 84, 189–190, 207, 299
5 AESCHYLUS, 45, 53, 75
5 SOPHOCLES, 127–129, 139–140, 159–160
5 EURIPIDES, 411, 422
6 HERODOTUS, 8, 12, 18, 60–61, 79, 95, 116, 135, 150, 155, 190, 200–201, 204, 238–239, 266, 267, 270–271, 283, 313–314
7 PLATO, 467
8 ARISTOTLE, 707–709
12 LUCRETIUS, 76–77, 80–81, 85
12 EPICTETUS, 123–124
13 VIRGIL, 128–130, 143–144, 149–150, 216, 259–261, 273
14 PLUTARCH, 82, 198, 239–240, 268, 371–372, 568, 698–699, 818, 822
15 TACITUS, 79, 124, 168–169, 212–213, 228, 235, 293–294
18 AUGUSTINE, 303, 306–307, 308–310, 591–599
19 AQUINAS, 538, 544, 567–568
21 DANTE, 66
23 HOBBES, 51–52, 80, 81–82, 165–167, 177, 183–187, 188–191
26 SHAKESPEARE, 572–573
27 SHAKESPEARE, 30–31, 482
29 CERVANTES, 381
30 BACON, 54, 55, 202–203
32 MILTON, 303–307
33 PASCAL, 328–341 passim
35 LOCKE, 388
35 BERKELEY, 425
35 HUME, 491–497
40 GIBBON, 180, 189–190, 206, 294–296, 445–446, 465–467, 605
41 GIBBON, 232, 398–399
44 BOSWELL, 126
47 GOETHE, 12–14
54 FREUD, 138, 477

5*c*. The symbolism of the sacraments and of sacramental or ritualistic acts

OLD TESTAMENT: *Genesis*, 17:9–14 / *Exodus*, 12:1–13:16; 24:5–8; 31:13–17 / *Leviticus* passim / *Numbers*, 15:37–41; 16:37–40 / *Deuteronomy*, 6:5–9; 16:1–17 / *Joshua*, 4:1–9 / *Esther*, 9:20–32

APOCRYPHA: *II Maccabees*, 1:18–22

NEW TESTAMENT: *Matthew*, 26:26–28 / *John*, 3:3–7; 6:30–59 / *I Corinthians*, 10:16–17; 11:23–27

18 AUGUSTINE, 301–302, 310–311, 575, 579–581, 690–691
20 AQUINAS, 265–304, 847–884
22 CHAUCER, 495–510
23 HOBBES, 180, 206–207, 211–212, 249–250
33 PASCAL, 71–80, 128–137, 343
35 HUME, 468
41 GIBBON, 334
46 HEGEL, 331–332, 338
51 TOLSTOY, 198–203, 248–249

5*d*. The symbolism of numbers in theology

NEW TESTAMENT: *Revelation*

16 KEPLER, 853–854, 1049–1050
18 AUGUSTINE, 339–340, 354, 414–415, 535–536, 618, 644–645, 672
20 AQUINAS, 1054–1055
21 DANTE, 1–163
51 TOLSTOY, 377–378

5*e*. The interpretation of the word of God

OLD TESTAMENT: *Daniel*, 5:5–28

NEW TESTAMENT: *Matthew*, 13, 18:23–35; 19:3–9; 20:1–16; 21:28–45; 22:1–14; 25:1–30 / *Mark*, 2:23–28; 12:1–12,18–27 / *Luke*, 6:39–49; 12:16–21,36–48; 14:15–33; 15–16; 18:1–8; 19:11–27; 20:9–19 / *John*, 5:38–39 / *Acts*, 7; 13:16–36 / *Romans*, 4; 9–11 passim; 15:1–4 / *Galatians*, 3–4 passim / *I Peter*, 1:10–16

5 AESCHYLUS, 46–47
5 SOPHOCLES, 103
5 ARISTOPHANES, 470–472, 537–539
6 HERODOTUS, 295–296
7 PLATO, 201–203
18 AUGUSTINE, 15, 36, 107–108, 110–125, 371, 398–399, 419–421, 422–423, 426–427, 444–445, 496–498, 530–560, 624–674
19 AQUINAS, 8–10, 14–15, 339–377 passim
23 HOBBES, 165–188, 191–199, 215–216, 247–258
27 SHAKESPEARE, 488
30 BACON, 17–20, 98–100
33 PASCAL, 163–164, 273–277, 290–301
35 LOCKE, 291, 294
36 STERNE, 256–258
43 MILL, 290
47 GOETHE, 30
52 DOSTOEVSKY, 129–135, 150–153

5*f*. The names of God: the use of words to signify the divine nature

OLD TESTAMENT: *Exodus*, 3:13–14; 6:2–3; 15:3; 20:7; 34:5–7,14 / *Isaiah*, 41:4; 47:4; 54:5 / *Jeremiah*, 50:34 / *Amos*, 4:13

NEW TESTAMENT: *Revelation*, 1:8

5 AESCHYLUS, 53–54
6 HERODOTUS, 49–50, 80, 134
7 PLATO, 91, 93–97
18 AUGUSTINE, 626
19 AQUINAS, 16, 20–21, 22–23, 24–25, 62–75, 677–678
21 DANTE, 147
23 HOBBES, 78–79, 162–163, 172–173
25 MONTAIGNE, 238–239
28 HARVEY, 443
31 SPINOZA, 362–363
34 NEWTON, 370–371
35 LOCKE, 152
38 ROUSSEAU, 435
51 TOLSTOY, 248

6. Symbolism in psychological analysis

54 FREUD, 9–14, 123–124, 279–291, 504–513, 815–816

6a. The symbolism of dreams: their latent and manifest content

4 HOMER, 294–295
5 AESCHYLUS, 17
5 EURIPIDES, 411
6 HERODOTUS, 25, 28–29, 47, 78, 218–220
7 PLATO, 221–222
8 ARISTOTLE, 707–709
14 PLUTARCH, 329, 398–399, 548–549, 702–703, 727
21 DANTE, 81–82
22 CHAUCER, 127, 143–144, 147–149, 451–455
26 SHAKESPEARE, 36–37, 114–115, 291
27 SHAKESPEARE, 481–482
32 MILTON, 176–178
51 TOLSTOY, 249–250, 561–562, 673–674
54 FREUD, 11–13, 173–174, 178–205, 230–231, 252–340, 356–373 passim, 476–478, 489–494, 504–526, 539–544, 808–817

6b. The symbolism of apparently normal acts: forgetting, verbal slips, errors

54 FREUD, 13, 453–476, 546–547, 852

6c. The symbolism of anxieties, obsessions, and other neurotic manifestations

5 EURIPIDES, 394–398
12 LUCRETIUS, 42–43
27 SHAKESPEARE, 306–307
54 FREUD, 1–5, 8–9, 25–26, 31–38, 43–49, 54–59, 83–85, 116–118, 200, 425–427, 440–442, 550–557, 558–562, 568–569, 571–572, 593–594, 596–597, 609–615, 718–747, 841–843

CROSS-REFERENCES

For: The theory of language, and for the distinction between the natural and the conventional in language, *see* LANGUAGE 1–3c.

The conception of ideas as intentions of the mind, *see* IDEA 6a.

The treatment of things or events in nature as signs or symbols, *see* LANGUAGE 10; MEDICINE 3c.

Another discussion of the distinction between first and second intentions, *see* IDEA 3a.

Other discussions bearing on the distinction between proper and common names and between abstract and concrete names, *see* IDEA 4b(1)–4b(2); UNIVERSAL AND PARTICULAR 2c, 5a.

The problems of verbal ambiguity, and for the distinction between univocal and equivocal speech, *see* IDEA 4b(4); LANGUAGE 5–5b.

Discussions relevant to the theory of analogical names, or to the problem of how names can signify what is common to heterogeneous things, *see* BEING 1; IDEA 4b(4); RELATION 1d; SAME AND OTHER 3a(3)–3b, 4c.

The relation of the univocal and the equivocal to definition and demonstration, *see* DEFINITION 3; LANGUAGE 1a, 7; REASONING 3b; and for other logical considerations in the use of language, *see* LANGUAGE 6–7; LOGIC 3a.

Other discussions of the language of poetry, and of problems of style in the exposition of knowledge, *see* LANGUAGE 9; POETRY 8b; RHETORIC 2c.

The role of signs in divination and prophecy, *see* LANGUAGE 10; PROPHECY 3b–3c.

The general theory of the sacraments, *see* GOD 9e; RELIGION 2c.

The problem of the names of God and the problem of the interpretation of Sacred Scripture, *see* GOD 6a; LANGUAGE 12; THEOLOGY 4b.

Other discussions of the symbolism of dreams, *see* LANGUAGE 10; MEMORY AND IMAGINATION 8d(1)–8e; and for the theory of the neuroses and neurotic behavior relevant to the interpretation of psychological signs, *see* DESIRE 4a–4d; EMOTION 3a–3c(4); MEMORY AND IMAGINATION 2e(2); OPPOSITION 4c.

ADDITIONAL READINGS

Listed below are works not included in *Great Books of the Western World*, but relevant to the idea and topics with which this chapter deals. These works are divided into two groups:

I. Works by authors represented in this collection.
II. Works by authors not represented in this collection.

For the date, place, and other facts concerning the publication of the works cited, consult the Bibliography of Additional Readings which follows the last chapter of *The Great Ideas*.

I.

AUGUSTINE. *Concerning the Teacher*
——. *The Harmony of the Gospels*
AQUINAS. *Summa Contra Gentiles*, BK I, CH 22–25
AQUINAS. *Quaestiones Disputatae, De Veritate*, Q 4
DANTE. *Convivio (The Banquet)*, SECOND TREATISE, CH I, 14–16
——. *Epistle to Can Grande della Scala*
HOBBES. *Concerning Body*, PART I, CH 2
J. S. MILL. *A System of Logic*, BK I
FREUD. *The Psychopathology of Everyday Life*, CH 8–12
——. *A Review of "The Antithetical Sense of Primal Words"*
——. *A Connection Between a Symbol and a Symptom*

II.

PHILODEMUS. *On Methods of Inference*
QUINTILIAN. *Institutio Oratoria (Institutes of Oratory)*, BK VII, CH 9
SEXTUS EMPIRICUS. *Against the Logicians*, BK II, CH 2
MAIMONIDES. *The Guide for the Perplexed*, PART I, CH 1–30, 37–45, 61–64
BONAVENTURA. *Breviloquium*, PROLOGUE
——. *Itinerarium Mentis in Deum (The Itinerary of the Mind to God)*
DUNS SCOTUS. *Opus Oxoniense*, BK IV
OCKHAM. *Studies and Selections, Logic*, CH 11–12
THOMAS OF ERFURT. *Grammatica Speculativa*
NICOLAS OF CUSA. *De Docta Ignorantia*, BK I, CH 12
CAJETAN. *De Nominum Analogia*
SUÁREZ. *Disputationes Metaphysicae*, XXVIII (3), XXX (13), XXXII (2), XXXIX (3)
BOEHME. *The Signature of All Things*
JOHN OF SAINT THOMAS. *Cursus Philosophicus Thomisticus, Ars Logica*, PART I, QQ 1–3; PART II, QQ 21–22
ARNAULD. *Logic or the Art of Thinking*, PART I, CH 11, 15
LEIBNITZ. *Characteristica*
——. *New Essays Concerning Human Understanding*, BK III
CONDILLAC. *Essai sur l'origine des connaissances humaines*, PART II
J. HARRIS. *Hermes, or A Philosophical Inquiry Concerning Universal Grammar*
VOLTAIRE. "Allegories," "Figure in Theology," in *A Philosophical Dictionary*
T. REID. *Essays on the Intellectual Powers of Man*, I, CH 1; VI, CH 5
CREUZER. *Symbolik und Mythologie der alten Völker*
EMERSON. *Nature*
VENN. *Symbolic Logic*
C. S. PEIRCE. *Collected Papers*, VOL II, par 219–444; VOL V, par 388–410
FRAZER. *The Golden Bough*, PART I, CH 3, 8–21; PART II, CH 5–6; PART III, CH 8; PART IV, BK I, CH 4; PART V, CH 1–9
BRÉAL. *Semantics*
ROYCE. *The World and the Individual*, SERIES I (7); Supplementary Essay (2)
J. C. WILSON. *Statement and Inference*, PART II (18)
WHITEHEAD and RUSSELL. *Principia Mathematica*, CH 3
WELBY-GREGORY. *What Is Meaning?*
——. *Significs and Language*
W. E. JOHNSON. *Logic*, PART I, CH 6–8; PART II, CH 3
WITTGENSTEIN. *Tractatus Logico-Philosophicus*
OGDEN and RICHARDS. *The Meaning of Meaning*
SANTAYANA. *Scepticism and Animal Faith*, CH 18
EATON. *Symbolism and Truth*
EDDINGTON. *The Nature of the Physical World*, CH 12
WHITEHEAD. *An Enquiry Concerning the Principles of Natural Knowledge*, CH 1
——. *Symbolism, Its Meaning and Effects*
——. *Process and Reality*, PART II, CH 8
PENIDO. *Le rôle de l'analogie en théologie dogmatique*
RICHARDS. *Mencius on the Mind*
BUCHANAN. *The Doctrine of Signatures*, CH 1–2, 5–6
DEWEY. *Essays in Experimental Logic*, IV
——. *Experience and Nature*, CH 5
——. *Logic, the Theory of Inquiry*, CH 18
B. RUSSELL. *Principles of Mathematics*, CH 4–8, 27
——. *The Analysis of Mind*, LECT 10
——. *An Inquiry into Meaning and Truth*, CH 1–6, 13–15, 22
MARITAIN. *The Degrees of Knowledge*, CH 2
——. *Ransoming the Time*, CH 9
M. R. COHEN. *A Preface to Logic*, II–IV
CASSIRER. *Language and Myth*
——. *An Essay on Man*
——. *The Myth of the State*, PART I (1–3)
AYER. *Thinking and Meaning*
CARNAP. *Foundations of Logic and Mathematics*
——. *Introduction to Semantics*
——. *Meaning and Necessity*
DEWEY and BENTLEY. *Knowing and the Known*

Chapter 86: SIN

INTRODUCTION

THE sin of Satan and the sin of Adam are among the great mysteries of the Christian religion. Satan is highest among the angels, the first of God's spiritual creatures. He is only less than God in the perfection of his nature. Adam is created with supernatural graces and gifts, his immortal body is completely responsive to his spirit, his appetite in all things is submissive to his reason, and his reason is turned toward God, according to the original justice which harmonized his faculties and the elements of his nature.

The only evil latent in either Satan or Adam would seem to reside in the privation of infinite being, power, and knowledge. But this is not a moral evil in them; it is neither a sin nor a predisposition to sin. Hence the only cause of their sinning, if God himself does not predestine them to sin, must be a free choice on their part between good and evil. If God positively predestines them to sin, then they would seem to be without responsibility, and so without sin. If they are not predetermined to evil—if, except for the weakness of being finite, they are without positive blemish—how does the conflict arise in them which opens the choice between good and evil and impels them, almost against the inclination of their natures, away from good and toward evil?

In Milton's *Paradise Lost*, God says of Adam: "I made him just and right, sufficient to have stood, though free to fall." Of Satan and fallen angels, as well as of Adam, God observes:

They therefore as to right belongd,
So were created, nor can justly accuse
Thir maker, or thir making, or thir Fate;
As if Predestination over-rul'd
Their will, dispos'd by absolute Decree
Of high foreknowledge; they themselves decreed
Thir own revolt, not I: if I foreknew,
Foreknowledge had no influence on their fault,
Which had no less prov'd certain unforeknown.

Yet there is a difference between Adam and Satan. The fallen angels "by their own suggestion fell, self-tempted, deprav'd." Satan, having sinned, becomes man's tempter. "Man falls deceiv'd by the other first: Man therefore shall find grace, the other none."

As Satan approaches the Garden of Eden to work his will on man, he contemplates his plight. He does not deny his sin, he does not repent it, he does not seem fully to understand it. Thus Milton has him speak:

O thou that with surpassing Glory crowned,
Look'st from the sole Dominion like the God
Of this new World; at whose sight all the Starrs
Hide thir diminisht heads; to thee I call,
But with no friendly voice, and add thy name
O Sun, to tell thee how I hate thy beams
That bring to my remembrance from what state
I fell, how glorious once above thy Spheare;
Till Pride and worse Ambition threw me down
Warring in Heav'n against Heav'ns matchless King;
Ah wherefore! he deserved no such return
From me, whom he created what I was
In that bright eminence, and with his good
Upbraided none; nor was his service hard.
What could be less than to afford him praise,
The easiest recompense, and pay him thanks,
How due! yet all his good prov'd ill in me,
And wrought but malice; lifted up so high
I sdeind subjection, and thought one step higher
Would set me highest, and in a moment quit
The debt immense of endless gratitude,
So burthensome, still paying, still to owe . . .
O had his powerful Destiny ordained
Me some inferior Angel, I had stood
Then happie; no unbounded hope had rais'd
Ambition. Yet why not? some other Power
As great might have aspir'd, and me through mean
Drawn to his part; but other Powers as great
Fell not, but stand unshak'n, from within
Or from without, to all temptations arm'd.
Hads't thou the same free Will and Power to stand?
Thou hads't: whom has thou then or what to accuse,
But Heav'ns free Love, dealt equally to all?
Be then his Love accurst, since love or hate
To me alike, it deals eternal woe.
Nay cursed be thou; since against his, thy will

Chose freely what it now so justly rues.
Me miserable! which way shall I flie
Infinite wrauth, and infinite despaire?
Which way I flie is Hell; my self am Hell;
And in the lowest deep a lower deep
Still threatning to devour me opens wide,
To which the Hell I suffer seems a Heav'n.
O then at last relent: is there no place
Left for Repentance, none for Pardon left?
None left but by submission; and that word
Disdain forbids me, and my dread of shame
Among the spirits beneath, whom I seduc'd
With other promises and other vaunts
Then to submit, boasting I could subdue
Th' Omnipotent.

Before Satan approaches Eve, Adam reminds her of their debt of obedience, saying that God requires

From us no other service than to keep
This one, this easie charge, of all the Trees
In Paradise that beare delicious fruit
So various, not to taste that onely Tree
Of Knowledge, planted by the Tree of Life.
So neer grows Death to Life, what ere Death is,
Some dreadful thing no doubt; for well thou knowst
God hath pronounc'd it death to taste that Tree,
The only sign of our obedience left
Among so many signes of power and rule
Conferrd upon us, and Dominion giv'n
Over all other Creatures that possesse
Earth, Aire, and Sea. Then let us not think hard
One easie prohibition, who enjoy
Free leave so large to all things else, and choice
Unlimited of manifold delights.

The temptation to disobey first moves Eve in a dream in which the apparition of an angel speaks of the forbidden fruit

. . . . as onely fit
For Gods, yet able to make Gods of Men;
And why not Gods of Men, since good, the more
Communicated, more abundant growes,
The Author not impair'd, but honourd more?

"Here, happie Creature," the vision says to her,

Happier thou mayst be, worthier canst not be:
Taste this, and be henceforth among the Gods
Thy self a Goddess, not to Earth confind,
But sometimes in the Air, as wee, sometimes
Ascend to Heav'n, by merit thine, and see
What life the Gods live there, and such live thou.

Later when Satan in the guise of the Serpent actually addresses Eve, he argues in the same vein, that as he, by tasting of this fruit, speaks as a man, so Eve and Adam, if they too partake, "shall be as Gods, knowing both Good and Evil as they know." Eve succumbs and, as Milton tells the story, Adam, knowing fully the evil of his act, joins Eve in disobedience, not from envy of the gods, but out of love for her, willing to die because unwilling to live without her.

Willing "to incurr divine displeasure for her sake, or Death. . . .

. . . . he scrupl'd not to eat
Against his better knowledge, not deceav'd,
But fondly overcome with Femal charm.
Earth trembled from her entrails, as again
In pangs, and Nature gave a second groan,
Skie lowr'd, and muttering Thunder, som sad drops
Wept at compleating of the mortal Sin
Original.

In the poet's expansion of the third chapter of Genesis, the basic elements in the Judaeo-Christian conception of sin seem to be plainly accented: the pride and envy which move Satan and Eve, the disobedience which results from the disorder of Adam's loving Eve more than he loves God. In the *Divine Comedy*, another great poem of sin and salvation, Adam speaks to Dante in Paradise and tells him that "the tasting of the tree was not by itself the cause of so great an exile, but only the overpassing of the bound." Earlier Beatrice explains why, in order to redeem man from sin, the Word of God assumed human nature—"the nature which has estranged itself from its Maker." She tells Dante that "this nature, thus united with its Maker, was pure and good such as it was created; but by itself it had been banished from Paradise, because it turned aside from the way of truth and from its own life." Man can fall from his nobility by "sin alone . . . which disfranchises him, and makes him unlike the Supreme Good, so that he is little illumined by Its light; and to his dignity he never returns, unless where fault empties, he fills up with just penalties against evil delight."

In both the pagan and the Christian conceptions of sin, man's pride and his disobedience of divine commandment are usually connected with the very notion of sin. The heroes of the Greek tragedies, exhibiting the tragic fault of pride, seem to forget that, though they strive with gods, they are only men, subject to laws they cannot disobey without catastrophe. In the *Iliad*, Phoenix cautions Achilles to "battle with your pride and beat it; cherish not your anger for ever; the might and majesty of heaven are more than ours, but even heaven may be appeased; and if a man has sinned he prays the gods, and reconciles them to himself by his piteous cries."

In pride and disobedience we find the deep disorder of love which lies at the heart of sin. Pride is self-love in excess of what the self deserves. Disobedience, as in the case of Milton's Adam, may be prompted by a love which, too, exceeds the worth of the object loved. The measure of that worth, or the bounds put upon the love of self or other, is set by the Supreme Good which, ordering all other goods, should also order our loves in proportion to their goodness.

This seems to be the central insight of the *Divine Comedy*. It is given a summary statement in Purgatory, where Virgil explains how love is the root both of virtue and of sin. "Neither Creator nor creature," he says to Dante, "was ever without love, either natural or of the mind, and this thou knowest. The natural is always without error; but the other may err either through an evil object, or through little or too much vigor. While love is directed on the primal goods, and with due measure on the secondary, it cannot be the cause of ill delight. But when it is bent to evil, or runs to good with more zeal, or with less, than it ought, against the Creator his own creature is working. Hence thou canst comprehend that love is of necessity the seed in you of every virtue, and of every action that deserves punishment."

Dostoevsky offers us further thoughts concerning the relation of love and sin. In the *Brothers Karamazov*, Father Zossima makes lack of love the punishment as well as the substance of sin. To those who ask, "What is Hell?" Father Zossima replies: "I maintain that it is the suffering of being unable to love. . . . They talk of hell fire in the material sense. I don't go into that mystery and I shun it. But I think if there were fire in the material sense, they would be glad of it, for, I imagine, that in material agony, their still greater spiritual agony would be forgotten for a moment. . . . Oh, there are some who remain proud and fierce even in hell, in spite of their certain knowledge and contemplation of the absolute truth; there are some fearful ones who have given themselves over to Satan and his proud spirit entirely. For such, hell is voluntary and ever consuming; they are tortured by their own choice. For they have cursed themselves, cursing God and life."

To avoid sin, the only positive commandment, according to Father Zossima, is to love in accordance with God's love. "Love a man even in his sin," he counsels, "for that is the semblance of Divine Love and is the highest love on earth. . . . And let not the sin of men confound you in your doings. Fear not that it will wear away your work and hinder its being accomplished. There is only one means of salvation; then take unto yourself, and make yourself responsible for, all men's sins; that is the truth, you know, friends, for as soon as you sincerely make yourself responsible for everything and for all men, you will see at once that it is really so, and you are to blame for everyone and for all things. But throwing your own indolence and impotence on others, you will end by sharing the pride of Satan and murmuring against God. Of the pride of Satan, what I think is this: it is hard for us on earth to comprehend it, and therefore it is so easy to fall into error and to share it, even imagining that we are doing something grand and fine."

In the disorder of love which leads to sin, sin is itself enjoyed for its own sake, and the disobedient act is pleasant because it is forbidden. In that also there is the pride of supposing one's self to be a law unto one's self. In his *Confessions*, concerned most immediately with his own sinfulness, Augustine reflects upon the pears he stole in his youth, not, as he says, from "any desire to enjoy the things I stole, but only the stealing of them and the sin." He asks himself: "What was it then that in my wretched folly I loved in you, O theft of mine, deed wrought in that dark night when I was sixteen?" He had no need of the pears. "Once I had gathered them," he says, "I threw them away, tasting only my own sin and savouring that with delight; for if I took so much as a bite of any one of those pears, it was the sin that sweetened it."

He keeps on asking himself what it was that attracted him in that theft, what it was that he enjoyed in that childish act of stealing. "Perhaps," he finally answers, "it was the thrill of acting against Your law—at least in appearance, since I had no power to do so in fact, the delight a prisoner might have in making some small gesture of liberty—getting a deceptive sense of omnipotence from doing something forbidden without immediate punishment. I was that slave, who fled from his Lord and pursued his Lord's shadow. O rottenness, O monstrousness of life and abyss of death! Could you find pleasure only in what was forbidden, and only because it was forbidden?"

In the pagan and Judaeo-Christian conceptions of sin, the fundamental meaning seems to depend upon the relation of man to the gods or to God, whether that itself be considered in terms of law or love. The vicious act may be conceived as one which is contrary to nature or reason. The criminal act may be conceived as a violation of the law of man, injurious to the welfare of the state or to its members. Both may involve the notions of responsibility and fault. Both may involve evil and wrongdoing. But unless the act transgresses the law of God, it is not sinful. The divine law which is transgressed may be the natural law that God instills in human reason, but the act is sinful if the person who commits the act turns away from God to the worship or love of other things.

To disbelieve in God, in divine law and divine punishment, is also to disbelieve in sin—at least in the sense in which religious men have distinguished between saints and sinners, between the righteous and the wicked in the eyes of God. "There are only two kinds of men," writes Pascal: "the righteous who believe themselves sinners; the rest, sinners, who believe themselves righteous."

Those who reject the religious meaning of sin do not deny the wide prevalence of a sense of sin, nor do they deny that many men suffer remorse for transgressions which they suppose to be evil in God's eyes; but, with Freud, they interpret these feelings of guilt in terms of natural causes. They hold that the person who is tormented by conscience suffers from an illusion concerning the true nature of his guilt. When the sense of sin is intensely active and is, in addition, apparently unexplained by the character and conduct of the person, the guilt-feelings, according to the Freudian view, take on the attributes of pathological distortion and become part of the symptomology of the neuroses. There is no question about the sincerity of the person who is thus agonized, but only about the true causes of the agony.

"When one asks how a sense of guilt arises in anyone," Freud says, "one is told something one cannot dispute: people feel guilty (pious people call it 'sinful') when they have done something they know to be 'bad.' But then one sees how little this answer tells one." What accounts for the judgment a man makes of himself as good or bad? Freud's answer is that "what is bad is, to begin with, whatever causes one to be threatened with a loss of love; because of the dread of this loss, one must desist from it. That is why it makes little difference whether one has already committed the bad deed or only intends to do so."

The external authority of the father and, through him, of society becomes, according to Freud, "internalized by the development of a super-ego. The manifestations of conscience are then raised to a new level; to be strict one should not call them conscience and sense of guilt before this. . . . At this second stage of development, conscience exhibits a peculiarity which was absent in the first. . . . That is, the more righteous a man is, the stricter and more suspicious will his conscience be, so that ultimately it is precisely those people who have carried holiness farthest who reproach themselves with the deepest sinfulness. . . . A relatively strict and vigilant conscience is the very sign of a virtuous man, and though saints may proclaim themselves sinners, they are not so wrong, in view of the temptations of instinctual gratifications to which they are peculiarly liable—since, as we know, temptations do but increase under constant privation, whereas they subside, at any rate, temporarily, if they are sometimes gratified."

Freud applies his theory of the origin of feelings of guilt (in "the dread of authority" first and later in "the dread of the super-ego,") to the religious sense of sin. "The people of Israel," he writes, "believed themselves to be God's favorite child, and when the great Father hurled visitation after visitation upon them, it still never shook them in this belief or caused them to doubt His power and His justice; they proceeded instead to bring their prophets into the world to declare their sinfulness to them, and out of their sense of guilt they constructed the stringent commandments of their priestly religion."

In general, Freud thinks, the great religions "have never overlooked the part played by the sense of guilt in civilization. What is more, they come forward with a claim . . . to save mankind from this sense of guilt which they call sin. We have drawn our conclusion from the way in which in Christianity this salvation is won—the sacrificial death of one who therewith takes the whole of the common guilt of all upon himself, about the occasion on which this primal sense of guilt was first acquired." The conclusion referred to is developed in two of Freud's works which are devoted to the consideration of religion and sin—the *Future of an Illusion* and *Totem and Taboo*. In the latter of these books, Freud tells us, he had first "expressed a suspicion that perhaps the sense of guilt in mankind as a whole, which is the ultimate source of religion and morality, was acquired in the beginning of history through the Oedipus complex."

OTHER WRITERS, who approach the problem of sin in legalistic rather than psychological terms, either make no distinction between crime and sin or make the distinction without referring to God. Spinoza, for example, prefaces his explanation of the meanings of "praise and blame, merit and crime," with a discussion of the difference between "the natural and civil state of man." In a state of nature, he says, no one is "bound by any law to obey any one but himself. Hence in a natural state sin cannot be conceived, but only in a civil state, where it is decided by universal consent what is good and what is evil, and where everyone is bound to obey the State. Sin, therefore, is nothing but disobedience, which is punished by the law of the State alone."

Though Hobbes does not identify crime and sin, his distinction between them does not seem to be based on the contrast between the civil law and the divine law, unless the latter is equated with the law of nature. "A crime is a sin," he writes, "consisting in the committing (by deed or word) of that which the law forbiddeth, or the omission of that which it hath commanded. So that every crime is a sin, but not every sin a crime. To intend to steal or kill is a sin, though it never appear in word or fact, for God that seeth the thoughts of man, can lay it to his charge; but till it appear by something done, or said, by which the intention may be argued by a human judge, it hath not the name of crime.

"From this relation of sin to the law," Hobbes continues, "and of crime to the civil law, may be inferred, first, that where law ceaseth, sin ceaseth. But because the law of nature is eternal, violation of covenants, ingratitude, arrogance, and all facts contrary to any moral virtue, can never cease to be sin. Secondly, that the civil law ceasing, crimes cease; for there being no other law remaining, but that of nature, there is no place for accusation; every man being his own judge, and accused only by his own conscience, and cleared by the uprightness of his own intention. When therefore his intention is right, his fact is no sin; if otherwise, his fact is sin, but not crime."

The more strictly religious conception of sin seems to be exemplified by Pascal's remark that "all that God does not permit is forbidden" and that "sins are forbidden by the general declaration that God has made, that He did not allow them." Whatever God does not permit, "we ought to regard as sin," for "the absence of God's will, which is all goodness and all justice, renders it unjust and wrong."

With the precision of a theologian in these matters, Aquinas defines the peculiar type of evil which is sin. "Evil," he writes, "is more comprehensive than sin, as also is good than right. . . . Now in those things that are done by the will, the proximate rule is the human reason, while the supreme rule is the eternal law. When, therefore, a human act tends to the end according to the order of reason and of the eternal law, then that act is right; but when it turns aside from that rectitude, then it is said to be a sin." Elsewhere he says that "every created will has rectitude of act only so far as it is regulated according to the divine will. . . . Thus only in the divine will can there be no sin, whereas in the will of every creature, considered according to its nature, there can be sin."

THE THEOLOGICAL DISCUSSION of sin involves a tremendous range of topics, and problems as significant as they are subtle. The dogma of original sin, for example, raises questions not only about the cause and character of Adam's transgression, but also about the punishment which is visited upon the children of Adam in perpetuity, and about the conditions under which man can be reclaimed from his bondage to sin, both original and actual or personal.

There seems to be some resemblance between the Christian doctrine that Adam's sin merits a penalty to be paid by all subsequent generations, and the Jewish doctrine of the collective responsibility of the people of Israel for the sins of their ancestors, even unto the third and fourth generation. But the points of difference appear to be more fundamental than the similarity.

In the first place, the sins of the fathers from which later generations suffer are the individual sins of men whose natures are predisposed to sin, as Adam's, before the fall, was not. In the second place, the punishment is visited not upon the whole human race, but only upon the Chosen People, and in the form of temporal scourges rather than in a corruption of human nature itself.

Furthermore, the Hebrew prophet Ezekiel questions the justice of collective responsibility. "What mean ye," he asks,

> that ye use this proverb concerning the land of Israel, saying, The fathers have eaten sour grapes, and the children's teeth are set on edge?
>
> As I live, saith the Lord God, ye shall not have occasion any more to use this proverb in Israel. . . .
>
> The soul that sinneth, it shall die. The son shall not bear the iniquity of the father, neither shall the father bear the iniquity of the son: the righteousness of the righteous shall be upon him, and the wickedness of the wicked shall be upon him.
>
> But if the wicked will turn from all his sins that he hath committed, and keep all my statutes, and do that which is lawful and right, he shall surely live, he shall not die.
>
> All his transgressions that he hath committed, they shall not be mentioned unto him: in his righteousness that he hath done he shall live.
>
> Have I any pleasure at all that the wicked should die? saith the Lord God: and not that he should return from his ways, and live?
>
> But when the righteous turneth away from his righteousness, and committeth iniquity, and doeth according to all the abominations that the wicked man doeth, shall he live? All his righteousness that he hath done shall not be mentioned: in his trespass that he hath trespassed, and in his sin that he hath sinned, in them shall he die.

According to Christian teaching, the justice of individual punishment for the sins which individuals commit in their own lifetime does not apply to the penalty which all men must pay for the sin of Adam. "Wherefore, as by one man sin entered into the world," St. Paul writes to the Romans,

> and death by sin; and so death passed upon all men, for that all have sinned:
>
> (For until the law sin was in the world: but sin is not imputed when there is no law.
>
> Nevertheless, death reigned from Adam to Moses, even over them that had not sinned after the similitude of Adam's transgression, who is the figure of him that was to come.
>
> But not as the offence, so also is the free gift. For if through the offence of one many be dead, much more the grace of God, and the gift by grace, which is by one man, Jesus Christ, hath abounded unto many.
>
> And not as it was by one that sinned, so is the gift: for the judgment was by one to condemnation, but the free gift is of many offences unto justification.
>
> For if by one man's offence death reigned by one; much more they which receive abundance of grace and of the gift of righteousness shall reign in life by one, Jesus Christ.)
>
> Therefore as by the offence of one judgment came upon all men to condemnation; even so by the righteousness of one the free gift came upon all men unto justification of life.
>
> For as by one man's disobedience many were made sinners, so by the obedience of one shall many be made righteous.

The Christian doctrine of original sin thus appears to be closely connected with the Christian doctrine of the need for a divine saviour —God Himself become man to redeem man from the taint of sin, and through the sacraments He instituted to provide the instruments of healing grace and the means of repentance for, and absolution from, both original sin and the individual's own personal sins.

The understanding of the sacraments; the theory of grace in relation to the original and fallen nature of man; the issue concerning grace and good works, or God's justification and man's merit, in the achievement of sanctity and salvation; the distinction between the everlasting perdition of Hell and the expiatory punishments of Purgatory—all these fundamental theological problems are involved in the consideration of sin and its consequences, both temporal and eternal.

Some of these problems are discussed in the chapters on MAN, ANGEL, IMMORTALITY, and PUNISHMENT. Other matters, such as the classification of sins according to the distinction between spiritual and carnal, mortal and venial, and the enumeration of the various species of both mortal and venial sin in the order of their gravity, are problems of moral theology. Though they belong primarily to this chapter, they are also related to the classification of virtues and vices, especially to the theory of the theological virtues; and among the theological virtues, especially to charity, which is the principle of sanctity, even as pride is the principle of sin.

Of all points in the consideration of sin, the distinction between original and acquired sin is perhaps the most important, not only because inherited sinfulness is conceived as the predisposing cause of all other sins, but also because the human nature corrupted by sin is conceived as fallen below the perfection of a purely natural man as well as below the state of grace in which Adam was created. As Adam had gifts which made him superior to the natural man—immortality, infused knowledge and freedom from error, immunity from concupiscence, exemption from labor and servility—so the children of Adam, cast out of Eden, have ingrained weaknesses which make them unable to achieve the goods or attain the ends proportionate to their human nature.

According to some theologians, the purely natural man, without either the gifts of grace or the wounds of sin, has never existed. It is this mystery of man, having natural aspirations which exceed the weakened powers of his fallen nature, that Pascal seems to contemplate in all his observations on "the greatness and wretchedness of man"—the "astonishing contradictions" which he thinks only the Christian religion explains. In the state in which men now are, he writes, "there remains to them some feeble instinct of the happiness of their former state; and they are plunged in the evils of their blindness and their lust, which have become their second nature."

"As the result of original justice," Aquinas writes, "the reason had perfect hold over the lower parts of the soul, while reason itself was perfected by God in being subject to Him. Now this same original justice was forfeited by the sin of our first parent . . . so that all the powers of the soul are left, as it were, destitute of their proper order, whereby they are naturally directed to virtue. This destitution is called a wounding of nature. . . . In so far as the reason is deprived of its order to the true, there is the wound of ignorance; in so far as the will is deprived of its order to the good, there is the wound of malice; in so far as the irascible is deprived of its order to the arduous, there is the wound of weakness; and in so far as the concupiscible is deprived of its order to the delectable as moderated by reason, there is the wound of concupiscence. Accordingly, these are the four wounds inflicted on the whole of human nature as a result of our first parent's sin."

Aquinas rejects the supposition that "the entire good of human nature can be destroyed by sin," arguing that what sin diminishes is "the natural inclination to virtue, which is befitting to man from the very fact that he is a rational being." But "sin cannot entirely take away from man the fact that he is a rational being, for then he would no longer be capable of sin."

Other theologians take a more extreme view than Aquinas and Augustine. They attribute depravity rather than weakness to human nature as a consequence of original sin. "On the Calvinistic theory," Mill writes, "the one great offense of man is self-will." Under the maxim that "whatever is not a duty, is a sin," men are left with no choice. "Human nature being radically corrupt," Mill continues, "there is no redemption for any one until human nature is killed within him." But, according to Augustine and Aquinas, original sin does not deprive the individual man entirely of the power to establish his worth, though it puts him in need of God's help to be worthy of salvation. Between the one extreme which holds that men can be saved by God's grace alone, and the other extreme which supposes that men can win salvation by the merit of their own good works, Augustine and Aquinas try to take the middle position, according to which neither grace without good works nor good works without grace will avail.

OUTLINE OF TOPICS

1\. The nature of sin: violation of divine law; disorder in man's relation to God

2\. The kinds and degrees of sin

- 2*a*. The distinction between original and actual sin
- 2*b*. The distinction between spiritual and carnal sin
- 2*c*. The distinction between mortal and venial sin
  - (1) The classification and order of mortal sins
  - (2) The classification and order of venial sins

3\. The doctrine of original sin

- 3*a*. The condition of Adam before sin: his supernatural state of grace; his preternatural gifts
- 3*b*. The sin of Adam
- 3*c*. The nature of fallen man in consequence of Adam's sin
- 3*d*. The need for a mediator between God and man to atone for original sin
- 3*e*. The remission of sin: baptism; the state of the unbaptized

4\. Actual or personal sin

- 4*a*. The relation of original sin to actual sin
- 4*b*. The causes and occasions of actual sin
- 4*c*. Pride as the principle of sin: the tragic fault of *hybris*
- 4*d*. The consequences of actual sin: the loss of charity and grace
- 4*e*. The prevention and purging of sin: purification by sacrifice; the sacrament of penance; contrition, confession, and absolution

5\. The remorse of conscience and feelings of guilt: the psychogenesis and pathological expression of the sense of sin

6\. Guilt and the punishment of sin

- 6*a*. Man's freedom in relation to responsibility and guilt for sin: divine predestination or election
- 6*b*. Collective responsibility for sin: the sins of the fathers
- 6*c*. The temporal punishment of sin: divine scourges
- 6*d*. The eternal punishment of sin: the everlasting perdition of the unrepentant in Hell
- 6*e*. The purifying punishments of Purgatory

7\. Grace and good works in relation to salvation from sin

REFERENCES

References are listed by volume number (in bold type), author's name, and page number. Bible references are to book, chapter, and verse of the Authorized King James version of the Bible. The abbreviation "esp" calls the reader's attention to one or more especially relevant parts of a whole reference; "passim" signifies that the topic is discussed intermittently rather than continuously in the work or passage cited. Where the work as a whole is relevant to the topic, the page numbers refer to the entire work. For general guidance in the use of *The Great Ideas,* consult the Preface.

1. The nature of sin: violation of divine law; disorder in man's relation to God

OLD TESTAMENT: *Genesis,* 2:15–17; 3 / *Psalms,* 36:1–4 / *Isaiah,* 59:2
NEW TESTAMENT: *Matthew,* 4:1–11 / *Romans,* 7:7–11 / *I John,* 3:4–8
5 AESCHYLUS, 40–51, 86–87
5 SOPHOCLES, 131–142, 143–155
5 EURIPIDES, 225, 335, 340–352 esp 351, 435–436
12 AURELIUS, 291
18 AUGUSTINE, 17–18, 50, 343–344, 378–379
19 AQUINAS, 325–333, 717
20 AQUINAS, 105–111, 128–137, 761–763
21 DANTE, 15–16, 79–80, 99–102
22 CHAUCER, 507–508, 516, 520–524 passim, 526, 530, 534, 543
30 BACON, 100
31 SPINOZA, 435–426
32 MILTON, 93–333
33 PASCAL, 24–26, 45, 294–295
35 LOCKE, 229–230
43 MILL, 296
48 MELVILLE, 30–36
52 DOSTOEVSKY, 165

2.The kinds and degrees of sin

OLD TESTAMENT: *Exodus,* 20:1–17
NEW TESTAMENT: *I Corinthians,* 8:10–12 / *Galatians,* 5:19–21
12 AURELIUS, 291
18 AUGUSTINE, 10–12, 17
20 AQUINAS, 111–128, 253–258
21 DANTE, 15–16, 53–105
22 CHAUCER, 495–550
23 HOBBES, 257–258
33 PASCAL, 27–127
44 BOSWELL, 196

2a. The distinction between original and actual sin

18 AUGUSTINE, 376–377, 378
20 AQUINAS, 163–164, 168, 706–707
22 CHAUCER, 507

2b. The distinction between spiritual and carnal sin

OLD TESTAMENT: *Deuteronomy,* 5:6–21
NEW TESTAMENT: *Luke,* 4:1–13
18 AUGUSTINE, 17, 27–28, 81–87 esp 85, 377–378, 658
19 AQUINAS, 326–327
20 AQUINAS, 112–113, 123
21 DANTE, 7
22 CHAUCER, 507

2c. The distinction between mortal and venial sin

NEW TESTAMENT: *Matthew,* 12:31–32 / *I John,* 5:16–17
18 AUGUSTINE, 577–578
20 AQUINAS, 115–116, 131, 134–137, 151–152, 192–198, 199, 661–662
21 DANTE, 12–13, 15–16, 79
22 CHAUCER, 509
33 PASCAL, 66
51 TOLSTOY, 477

2c(1) The classification and order of mortal sins

OLD TESTAMENT: *Exodus,* 20:1–17 / *Deuteronomy,* 5:6–21
20 AQUINAS, 64–65, 426–454, 474–480, 558–592, 603–605
22 CHAUCER, 290–291, 374–377, 510–542
33 PASCAL, 118–119

2c(2) The classification and order of venial sins

20 AQUINAS, 199–200
22 CHAUCER, 509–510
33 PASCAL, 67, 118–119

3. The doctrine of original sin

OLD TESTAMENT: *Genesis,* 2:16–17; 3
NEW TESTAMENT: *Romans,* 5
18 AUGUSTINE, 357, 360–366, 376–377, 385–390, 571
20 AQUINAS, 162–174
21 DANTE, 115–116
22 CHAUCER, 506–507
30 BACON, 17–18
32 MILTON, 93–333, 394–395
33 PASCAL, 248–251, 251–253
43 MILL, 296
46 HEGEL, 118, 304–306
50 MARX, 354
54 FREUD, 763

3*a*. The condition of Adam before sin: his supernatural state of grace; his preternatural gifts

OLD TESTAMENT: *Genesis,* 1:27–29; 2:7–8,15–25
APOCRYPHA: *Ecclesiasticus,* 17:1–15
18 AUGUSTINE, 329, 357–358, 360, 369–370, 385–397 passim
19 AQUINAS, 501–527
20 AQUINAS, 200–201, 339–342, 347, 704–706
21 DANTE, 96–98, 125–126
22 CHAUCER, 434, 506–507
23 HOBBES, 191, 192
32 MILTON, 136–143, 153–164, 165–169, 175–187, 218–219, 228–229, 232–246, 251–257
46 HEGEL, 179–180

3*b*. The sin of Adam

OLD TESTAMENT: *Genesis,* 3
APOCRYPHA: 2:23–24
NEW TESTAMENT: *Romans,* 5:12
18 AUGUSTINE, 365–366, 385–390
20 AQUINAS, 167
21 DANTE, 115–116
22 CHAUCER, 375, 507
23 HOBBES, 112
31 SPINOZA, 445
32 MILTON, 94–95, 163–164, 261–269
33 PASCAL, 82

3*c*. The nature of fallen man in consequence of Adam's sin

OLD TESTAMENT: *Genesis,* 3:9–24; 6:5–13 / *Job,* 15:14–16; 25:4–6 / *Psalms,* 14:1–3; 53:1–3 / *Ecclesiastes,* 7:20,27–29; 9:3
NEW TESTAMENT: *Romans,* 3:9–5:21; 7; 8:20–21 / *Galatians,* 2:16; 3; 4:1–7; 5:19–21 / *Ephesians,* 2:1–5
18 AUGUSTINE, 5, 360–366, 372–380, 388–397, 572–573, 606–608
19 AQUINAS, 692–693
20 AQUINAS, 162–174, 178–184, 212–213, 760, 784–796
21 DANTE, 56, 68
22 CHAUCER, 374–382
23 HOBBES, 112, 192
24 RABELAIS, 81
25 MONTAIGNE, 233–234, 238–239
30 BACON, 195
32 MILTON, 139–140, 141–142, 264–273, 274–298, 302–303, 304–305
33 PASCAL, 245–247, 248–253
46 HEGEL, 304–305
51 TOLSTOY, 275

3*d*. The need for a mediator between God and man to atone for original sin

NEW TESTAMENT: *Matthew,* 26:26–28 / *Mark,* 2:3–11 / *Luke,* 19:1–10; 24:44–47 / *John,* 3:16–17; 10:9–18 / *Acts,* 3:19–26; 4:10–12; 5:30–31; 10:37–43; 13:32–39 / *Romans,* 3:20–26; 5–6; 8:1–11,31–39; 9:29–10:21 / *I Corinthians,* 15:1–4,12–23 / *II Corinthians,* 5:14–21 / *Galatians,* 1:3–4; 2:16–21; 3:19–27 / *Ephesians,* 1:5–7,12–14; 2 / *Colossians,* 1:12–14,19–24; 2:11–15 / *I Timothy,* 2:5–7 / *Hebrews,* 2:9–18; 5; 7:1–10:22 / *I Peter,* 1:18–21 / *I John,* 2:1–2
18 AUGUSTINE, 50–51, 293–295, 312–314, 323, 372–376, 462–463, 627–629, 634
19 AQUINAS, 642
20 AQUINAS, 701–709, 729–730, 829–830
23 HOBBES, 197–198, 204
32 MILTON, 4–5, 10–12, 93–333
33 PASCAL, 264–267, 270–272, 300–301, 324–325
44 BOSWELL, 482
46 HEGEL, 331–333
52 DOSTOEVSKY, 127–137 passim

3*e*. The remission of sin: baptism; the state of the unbaptized

NEW TESTAMENT: *Matthew,* 3:11–17 / *John,* 3:5 / *Acts,* 2:38–41, 10:43–48; 19:1–5 / *Romans,* 5–6; 8:1–11; 9:29–10:10 / *Galatians,* 3:19–27 / *Ephesians,* 2 / *Colossians,* 2:8–15 / *Titus,* 3:5–7
18 AUGUSTINE, 5, 12, 362–363
20 AQUINAS, 360–370, 883–884, 889–893
21 DANTE, 5–7, 62, 135–136
22 CHAUCER, 496
23 HOBBES, 206–207, 211–212
36 STERNE, 221–224
40 GIBBON, 297–298

4. Actual or personal sin

4*a*. The relation of original sin to actual sin

NEW TESTAMENT: *Romans,* 5:12–21
18 AUGUSTINE, 376–377, 378
19 AQUINAS, 583
20 AQUINAS, 163–164, 203–204
22 CHAUCER, 507–508
32 MILTON, 141–143, 269–271

4*b*. The causes and occasions of actual sin

OLD TESTAMENT: *Job,* 31 / *Proverbs,* 1:10–19; 10–19 passim; 30:8–9 / *Isaiah,* 5:11–12
APOCRYPHA: *Wisdom of Solomon,* 2; 14:22–29 / *Ecclesiasticus,* 8:2; 10:9; 12:13–14; 23:1–6,13,16,18; 26:29; 31:5–11,25–31
NEW TESTAMENT: *Matthew,* 15:10–20 / *Mark,* 4:1–20; 7:14–23 / *Romans,* 1:18–32 / *I Corinthians,* 8:9–13 / *Galatians,* 5:16–21 / *Colossians,* 3:5–7 / *I Timothy,* 6:9–10 / *James,* 2; 4:1–6 / *I Peter,* 5:8–9 / *II Peter,* 2:10–22
18 AUGUSTINE, 10–13, 44, 81–88, 139–146, 378–380, 416, 514–515
19 AQUINAS, 263, 331–333, 488–489, 581–585, 614–615, 802–803
20 AQUINAS, 137–178
21 DANTE, 1–52 passim, 53–105 passim
22 CHAUCER, 278–284, 374–382, 421–425, 495–550

23 HOBBES, 138–139
26 SHAKESPEARE, 66–67
27 SHAKESPEARE, 183–184, 187–188, 421–423, 573
32 MILTON, 175–177, 356–358
33 PASCAL, 19–26, 29–61, 66–70, 91–111 passim
47 GOETHE, 7–9
52 DOSTOEVSKY, 64–67

4c. Pride as the principle of sin: the tragic fault of *hybris*

OLD TESTAMENT: *Psalms,* 10:1–6; 12:1–5 / *Proverbs,* 16:18–19; 21:4 / *Isaiah,* 2:11–17; 10:12–15; 14:4–22; 16:6–7 / *Jeremiah,* 48:26,29–31 / *Ezekiel,* 16:49–50 / *Daniel,* 5:18–20
APOCRYPHA: *Ecclesiasticus,* 10:7–18; 11:30–31; 13:1
NEW TESTAMENT: *Luke,* 18:10–14
4 HOMER, 3–9, 57–64
5 AESCHYLUS, 15–26, 31–34, 40–51, 61–62
5 SOPHOCLES, 99–113, 132, 143–155
6 HERODOTUS, 217
18 AUGUSTINE, 86–87, 345, 396–397
20 AQUINAS, 148–149, 175–176
21 DANTE, 36, 67–71
22 CHAUCER, 434–448, 510–515
27 SHAKESPEARE, 117–118, 572
32 MILTON, 93–110, 111–113, 117–119, 153–155, 188–195, 249–251
33 PASCAL, 245–247
36 SWIFT, 183–184
52 DOSTOEVSKY, 130–135, 168

4d. The consequences of actual sin: the loss of charity and grace

APOCRYPHA: *Ecclesiasticus,* 21:2–3
NEW TESTAMENT: 27:3–5 / *Romans,* 1:16–32; 7:5–13
18 AUGUSTINE, 381–385, 519–520
19 AQUINAS, 334–337
20 AQUINAS, 178–192, 225–226, 338–347 passim, 499–500
21 DANTE, 1–52, 68–70
32 MILTON, 299–333
33 PASCAL, 19–26, 28–31, 36–61

4e. The prevention and purging of sin: purification by sacrifice; the sacrament of penance; contrition, confession, and absolution

OLD TESTAMENT: *Exodus,* 29:36–37; 30:10–16 / *Leviticus* passim / *Numbers,* 5:5–9; 6:9–12; 15:22–29; 19:1–10 / *Deuteronomy,* 21:1–9 / *I Kings,* 8:31–50 / *II Chronicles,* 6:24–42; 7:12–14; 29:21 / *Psalms,* 32:1–5,10; 51; 69:5–13 / *Isaiah,* 1:16–20; 58:1–7 / *Ezekiel,* 43:18–27 / *Daniel,* 9:3–20 / *Joel,* 1:8–15; 2:12–17 / *Jonah,* 3 / *Micah,* 6:6–8
APOCRYPHA: *Ecclesiasticus,* 17:24–26; 28:2–5; 34:18–19,25–26
NEW TESTAMENT: *Matthew,* 3:1–12 / *Luke,* 7:35–50; 13:1–5; 15 / *Acts,* 8:9–24 / *Romans,* 2:4–6 / *I Corinthians,* 6:9–11 / *Hebrews,* 5:1–10; 7:20–10:18 / *James,* 4:8–10 / *Revelation,* 3:1–6,19
4 HOMER, 62
5 AESCHYLUS, 80, 81–91
5 EURIPIDES, 338–339
18 AUGUSTINE, 27, 64–65
20 AQUINAS, 191–192, 272–276, 855–884
21 DANTE, 40–41, 57, 59–60, 65–67, 86–87
22 CHAUCER, 372–374, 495–510, 543–550
25 MONTAIGNE, 388–395
27 SHAKESPEARE, 56, 503–504
29 CERVANTES, 427–429
32 MILTON, 298–300, 350–351
33 PASCAL, 28, 62–64, 132, 344, 348–349
36 STERNE, 476–477
40 GIBBON, 199, 452
41 GIBBON, 384–385
46 HEGEL, 349
48 MELVILLE, 34–36
51 TOLSTOY, 476–478
52 DOSTOEVSKY, 22–24, 64–67, 167–169

5. The remorse of conscience and feelings of guilt: the psychogenesis and pathological expression of the sense of sin

OLD TESTAMENT: *Psalms,* 37 / *Joel,* 2:12–13
APOCRYPHA, *Wisdom of Solomon,* 5:1–13; 17 / *Ecclesiasticus,* 14:1–2 / *Maccabees,* 6:1–15
NEW TESTAMENT: *Matthew,* 27:3–5 / *Luke,* 15:11–32 / *John,* 8:1–9 / *II Corinthians,* 7:8–12
5 SOPHOCLES, 140–142
5 EURIPIDES, 322, 337–338, 375–377, 394–398
6 HERODOTUS, 9–10
9 ARISTOTLE, 419–420
15 TACITUS, 87
18 AUGUSTINE, 12–13, 27, 381–383
20 AQUINAS, 997–1000
21 DANTE, 45–46, 99–102
22 CHAUCER, 370–371, 496–506
25 MONTAIGNE, 14, 174–176
26 SHAKESPEARE, 114–115, 145, 396–397, 412
27 SHAKESPEARE, 46, 53–54, 291–292, 296–297, 298–299, 306–307, 479
31 SPINOZA, 440
32 MILTON, 37–38
35 LOCKE, 106
36 STERNE, 255–268
37 FIELDING, 379–380
42 KANT, 306–307, 333–334, 374–379
43 MILL, 458–459
46 HEGEL, 304, 354
47 GOETHE, 86–88, 92–93, 108–109, 110–114
49 DARWIN, 312–314
51 TOLSTOY, 248–250, 320–323, 370–372, 406–410, 505–511 passim, 549–551
52 DOSTOEVSKY, 95–109 passim, 157–164, 217–218, 317–320, 337–346, 402–408
54 FREUD, 582, 690–691, 703, 706–707, 712–715, 792–799, 852

6. Guilt and the punishment of sin

6*a*. Man's freedom in relation to responsibility and guilt for sin: divine predestination or election

OLD TESTAMENT: *Deuteronomy,* 30:15–20 / *Psalms,* 81:11–12 / *Isaiah,* 6:8–10
APOCRYPHA: *Ecclesiasticus,* 15:11–20
NEW TESTAMENT: *Matthew,* 13:13–15 / *John,* 10:26–29; 12:37–40; 13:18–27 / *Acts,* 4:27–28 / *Romans,* 1:16–32; 9:9–24; 11 passim / *Ephesians,* 1:3–12 / *II Thessalonians,* 2:11–14
4 HOMER, 43
5 AESCHYLUS, 70–80, 81–91
5 SOPHOCLES, 99–113, 114–130
5 EURIPIDES, 327–339, 394–410
12 AURELIUS, 258
18 AUGUSTINE, 213–216, 346–347, 397–398, 586–587, 617–618
19 AQUINAS, 116–117, 128–130, 134–135, 142–143, 323–324
20 AQUINAS, 123–124, 128–137, 150–151, 152–162
21 DANTE, 77–78, 79–80, 107, 111, 137–138
31 DESCARTES, 89–93 passim
32 MILTON, 93–333, 340–341, 347–348
33 PASCAL, 155–157, 158–159
35 HUME, 485–487
42 KANT, 594
51 TOLSTOY, 689
52 DOSTOEVSKY, 121–135
54 FREUD, 581–582

6*b*. Collective responsibility for sin: the sins of the fathers

OLD TESTAMENT: 20:5–6; 34:6–7 / *II Samuel,* 21:1–9 / *II Kings,* 14:1–6 / *Psalms,* 109:1–16 / *Jeremiah,* 31:29–30 / *Ezekiel,* 18
APOCRYPHA: *Wisdom of Solomon,* 3:11–13 / *Ecclesiasticus,* 41:5–7 / *Baruch,* 3:7–8
NEW TESTAMENT: *Romans,* 5:12–19
5 AESCHYLUS, 27–39, 52–69, 70–80, 81–91
5 SOPHOCLES, 99–113, 114–130, 131–142, 156–169
5 EURIPIDES, 378–393, 394–410
6 HERODOTUS, 237–239
6 THUCYDIDES, 380
18 AUGUSTINE, 361, 376–377, 439
20 AQUINAS, 162–167, 191–192
26 SHAKESPEARE, 554
32 MILTON, 141–142
37 FIELDING, 20
51 TOLSTOY, 606–607
52 DOSTOEVSKY, 122, 149–150, 313–314

6*c*. The temporal punishment of sin: divine scourges

OLD TESTAMENT: *Genesis,* 3:9–19; 4:8–15; 6:1–7,11–13; 18:20–19:29 / *Exodus,* 7–12; 14; 22:18–20,22–24; 32 / *Leviticus,* 10:1–3; 18:24–30; 20; 24:10–23; 26 / *Numbers,* 12; 14; 15:32–36; 16; 21:5–9; 25 / *Deuteronomy,* 4:20–31; 11:16–17; 28:15–68; 29:16–29 / *Joshua,* 5:6; 7 / *Judges,* 9 / *I Samuel,* 3:11–15; 5; 15; 28:3–20 / *II Samuel,* 6:6–8; 12; 21:1; 24 / *I Kings,* 8:31–53; 9:6–9; 11; 13; 14:7–16; 16:1–13; 21:18–24 / *II Kings,* 5:20–27; 9:1–10:11; 17:6–18:12 / *I Chronicles,* 10; 13:9–11; 21 / *II Chronicles,* 6:24–42; 12; 21:12–20; 26:16–21; 36 / *Job* passim / *Psalms,* 11; 21; 37; 89:28–33; 94 / *Proverbs,* 1:20–33; 2:10–22; 3:33–35; 5:3–14,21–23; 10–30 passim / *Ecclesiastes,* 8:11–13 / *Isaiah* passim / *Jeremiah* passim / *Lamentations passim* / *Ezekiel,* 3–39 passim / *Daniel,* 4; 5:17–30; 9:3–20 / *Hosea* passim / *Joel* passim / *Amos* passim / *Obadiah* / *Jonah,* 3 / *Micah* passim / *Nahum* passim / *Habakkuk* passim / *Zephaniah* passim / *Zechariah,* 9:3–6; 11:1–9
APOCRYPHA: *Tobit,* 3:1–6 / *Judith,* 5:17–18; 8:18–25; 9; 11:9–19 / *Wisdom of Solomon,* 1:12–16; 3:9–19; 5:17–6:9; 10:1–8; 11:9–20; 12; 14:7–31; 15:18–16:19; 17; 18:10–19:22 / *Ecclesiasticus,* 10:13–16; 16:6–13; 23:18–26; 27:25–28:6; 39:27–30 / *Baruch,* 1–5 passim / *I Maccabees,* 2:62–63; 6:1–16 / *II Maccabees,* 6:12–17; 7:31–38; 9; 12:40–42
NEW TESTAMENT: *Acts,* 12:20–23; 13:4–12 / *Revelation,* 8–9; 11; 16–18
5 AESCHYLUS, 15–26, 27–39, 40–51, 52–69, 70–80, 81–91
5 SOPHOCLES, 99–113, 114–130, 131–142, 143–155
5 EURIPIDES, 327–339, 340–352, 394–410
6 HERODOTUS, 70–71, 95, 103, 159, 199, 201–202, 246–247, 283
14 PLUTARCH, 107
18 AUGUSTINE, 521, 571–572
20 AQUINAS, 188
21 DANTE, 59–60, 132–133, 134–135, 147–148
22 CHAUCER, 374–382, 437–447
23 HOBBES, 160–161, 163–164
30 BACON, 204–205
32 MILTON, 354–355, 364–365, 376
35 LOCKE, 1–2, 5–6, 14–15
38 MONTESQUIEU, 85–86
40 GIBBON, 188, 198–200, 302–303
41 GIBBON, 93–94 passim
44 BOSWELL, 314–315
48 MELVILLE, 30–36
52 DOSTOEVSKY, 30–32

6*d*. The eternal punishment of sin: the everlasting perdition of the unrepentant in Hell

OLD TESTAMENT: *Psalms,* 9:16–17 / *Proverbs,* 7:6–27 / *Isaiah,* 33:10–14
APOCRYPHA: *Judith,* 16:17 / *Wisdom of Solomon,* 4:16–20; 5:1–14 / *Ecclesiasticus,* 7:16–17
NEW TESTAMENT: *Matthew,* 5:29–30; 11:20–24; 25:31–46 / *Mark,* 9:42–49 / *Luke,* 16:19–26 / *II Thessalonians,* 1:7–9 / *Hebrews,* 10:26–31

/ *James,* 5:1–6 / *Jude,* 6–13 / *Revelation,* 2:20–23; 14:9–11; 19:17–20:15; 21:8
4 HOMER, 248–249
5 ARISTOPHANES, 565–566
12 LUCRETIUS, 42–43
18 AUGUSTINE, 360–361, 365–366, 388–390, 529–530, 543–544, 560–586
19 AQUINAS, 42–43
20 AQUINAS, 187–189, 897–900, 1066–1085
21 DANTE, 1–52
22 CHAUCER, 278–284, 497–498, 549
23 HOBBES, 193–195, 253–255
24 RABELAIS, 119–122
32 MILTON, 93–125, 152–155
44 BOSWELL, 363
52 DOSTOEVSKY, 10–11, 169–170

6*e*. The purifying punishments of Purgatory

APOCRYPHA: *II Maccabees,* 12:43–46
13 VIRGIL, 230–231
18 AUGUSTINE, 554–556, 571–572
20 AQUINAS, 886–887, 891–893
21 DANTE, 53–105
23 HOBBES, 244, 250–251, 255–258
41 GIBBON, 234, 520
44 BOSWELL, 173
52 DOSTOEVSKY, 341–342

7. Grace and good works in relation to salvation from sin

OLD TESTAMENT: *I Kings,* 8:33–39,46–50 / *II Chronicles,* 6:20–30,36–39 / *Psalms,* 32:1–5; 51; 78:38; 103:1–13; 130 / *Hosea,* 14:1–7 / *Micah,* 7:18–20
APOCRYPHA: *Ecclesiasticus,* 16:11–14; 18:11–14
NEW TESTAMENT: *Matthew,* 6:12,14–15; 9:2–6; 18:21–35 / *Luke,* 1:77–78; 6:36–37; 7:37–50 / *John,* 3:16–17 / *Acts,* 15:1–11 / *Romans,* 3–8, 9:15–18; 9:30–10:21; 11:5–32 / *II Corinthians,* 5:15–6:2 / *Galatians,* 2:16–21; 3:13–14 / *Ephesians,* 1:1–10; 2:4–9 / *Titus,* 2:11–14; 3:3–8 / *Hebrews,* 8:1–10:22 / *James,* 1:22–27; 2:14–26 / *II Peter,* 1:3–11 / *I John,* 3:1–10
18 AUGUSTINE, 12, 376–377, 388–389, 392, 396–397, 511–513, 571, 573–574, 617–618
19 AQUINAS, 318–321
20 AQUINAS, 64–65, 344–347, 352–353
21 DANTE, 1–4, 5–6, 11–13, 34–35, 53–105, 149–150, 155
22 CHAUCER, 467, 495–550
26 SHAKESPEARE, 554
32 MILTON, 66, 136–144, 274–276, 297–298, 328–332
33 PASCAL, 1–13, 15, 19–26, 29–34, 65, 78–80, 155–157, 158–159
37 FIELDING, 38
41 GIBBON, 233–234
46 HEGEL, 349
52 DOSTOEVSKY, 164–169, 180–191
53 JAMES, 200

CROSS-REFERENCES

For: The meaning of sin, and for discussions bearing on the difference of sin from crime and vice, *see* LAW 3a–3b, 6e–6e(3); PUNISHMENT 3b, 5b; RELIGION 2; VIRTUE AND VICE 1, 8a–8b.

Discussions relevant to the doctrine of original sin, *see* ANGEL 5a; GOOD AND EVIL 3f; MAN 9b–9b(2); VIRTUE AND VICE 8a; WILL 7e(1); and for the conditions of man's atonement for and remission from original sin, *see* GOD 9c, 9e; RELIGION 2c.

The causes and consequences of actual or personal sin, *see* GOOD AND EVIL 3f; VIRTUE AND VICE 8b; WILL 8b(1).

The conditions of man's salvation from sin, and the issue concerning grace and good works, *see* GOD 7d; LIBERTY 5c; NATURE 6b; PUNISHMENT 5c; VIRTUE AND VICE 8b.

The nature of sanctity and heroic virtue, *see* PLEASURE AND PAIN 7b; RELIGION 3d; TEMPERANCE 6a; VIRTUE AND VICE 8f–8g.

Other considerations of man's freedom and responsibility for sin in relation to divine predestination, *see* FATE 4; GOD 7f; LIBERTY 5a–5b; PUNISHMENT 2a; WILL 5b(4), 7e(2).

Other discussions of the divine punishment of sin, both temporal and eternal, *see* ETERNITY 4d; GOD 5i; HAPPINESS 7c(3); IMMORTALITY 5d–5e; PUNISHMENT 2, 5d–5e(2); VIRTUE AND VICE 8c.

Treatments of the sense of sin in relation to duty, honor, conscience, and abnormal feelings of guilt, *see* DUTY 4–4b; HONOR 2a; PUNISHMENT 5c, 6.

ADDITIONAL READINGS

Listed below are works not included in *Great Books of the Western World*, but relevant to the idea and topics with which this chapter deals. These works are divided into two groups:

I. Works by authors represented in this collection.

II. Works by authors not represented in this collection.

For the date, place, and other facts concerning the publication of the works cited, consult the Bibliography of Additional Readings which follows the last chapter of *The Great Ideas*.

I.

PLUTARCH. "Of the Love of Wealth," in *Moralia*

AUGUSTINE. *On Free Will*, BK III, CH 14

——. *On Baptism, Against the Donatists*

——. *Reply to Faustus*, BK XXII (27)

——. *On the Merits and Remissions of Sins*

——. *On the Grace of Christ and on Original Sin*

——. *Against Two Letters of the Pelagians*, BK IV, CH 7

——. *Of Marriage and Concupiscence*, BK II (XXIV)

AQUINAS. *Summa Contra Gentiles*, BK III, CH 139–162; BK IV, CH 50–52

——. *Quaestiones Disputatae, De Veritate*, Q 17; *De Malo*, QQ 2–5, 7–15

——. *Summa Theologica*, PART II–II, QQ 161–165

F. BACON. "Of Envy," in *Essays*

HOBBES. *Philosophical Rudiments Concerning Government and Society*, CH 14

——. *The Elements of Law, Natural and Politic*, PART I, CH 7

SPINOZA. *Correspondence*, XIX, XXI

W. JAMES. *The Varieties of Religious Experience*, LECT VI–VII

FREUD. *Totem and Taboo*

——. *The Future of an Illusion*

II.

Pirke Aboth (*Sayings of the Fathers*), CH 4 (5)

BENEDICT OF NURSIA. *The Rule*

GREGORY THE GREAT. *Morals*, BK XXXI

SAADIA GAON. *The Book of Beliefs and Opinions*, TREATISE IV–V

ANSELM OF CANTERBURY. *Cur Deus Homo?*

——. *De Conceptu Virginali et Originali Peccato*

ABAILARD. *Ethics* (*Scito Teipsum*)

MAIMONIDES. *The Guide for the Perplexed*, PART III, CH 40–41

FRANCIS OF ASSISI. *The Rules*

BONAVENTURA. *Breviloquium*, PART III, V

R. BACON. *Opus Majus*, PART VII

ALBERTUS MAGNUS. *Summa Theologiae*, PART I, Q 26, MEMB I, ART 2 (2)

LANGLAND. *Piers Plowman*

ALBO. *The Book of Principles* (*Sefer ha-Ikkarim*), BK IV, CH 5–6

THOMAS À KEMPIS. *The Imitation of Christ*, BK I

IGNATIUS OF LOYOLA. *Spiritual Exercises*

LUTHER. *A Treatise on Christian Liberty*

——. *The Schmalkald Articles*, PART III

——. *Table Talk*

CALVIN. *Institutes of the Christian Religion*, BK II, CH 1–3, 6–17

——. *Commentaries on the Epistle of Paul the Apostle to the Romans*, CH 5 (12)

SUÁREZ. *Disputationes Metaphysicae*, XI (1–3), XIX (7)

MARLOWE. *The Tragical History of Doctor Faustus*

BAXTER. *The Saints' Everlasting Rest*

J. TAYLOR. *Of Holy Living*

——. *Of Holy Dying*

RACINE. *Phèdre*

MALEBRANCHE. *De la recherche de la vérité*, BK II (1), CH 7 (5)

BUNYAN. *Pilgrim's Progress*

LEIBNITZ. *Discourse on Metaphysics*, XXX–XXXII

BOSSUET. *Traité de la concupiscence*

CLARKE. *An Inquiry into the Cause and Origin of Evil*

LAW. *A Serious Call to a Devout and Holy Life*

J. EDWARDS. *The Great Christian Doctrine of Original Sin Defended*

VOLTAIRE. "Conscience," "Original Sin," in *A Philosophical Dictionary*

COLERIDGE. *The Rime of the Ancient Mariner*

SCHOPENHAUER. *The World as Will and Idea*, VOL I, BK IV (65)

J. H. NEWMAN. *Lectures on the Doctrine of Justification*

WHEWELL. *The Elements of Morality*, BK II, CH 13–17

KIERKEGAARD. *The Concept of Dread*

——. *The Sickness Unto Death*, SECT II

HAWTHORNE. *The Scarlet Letter*

BAUDELAIRE. *Flowers of Evil*

FLAUBERT. *The Temptation of Saint Anthony*

NIETZSCHE. *The Genealogy of Morals*, II

FRAZER. *The Golden Bough*, PART II; PART VI; PART VII, CH 4–7

ROYCE. *Studies of Good and Evil*

PÉGUY. *Men and Saints* (Mortal Sin and Leprosy)

TENNANT. *The Concept of Sin*

JOYCE. *A Portrait of the Artist as a Young Man*

O'NEILL. *Mourning Becomes Electra*

TSANOFF. *The Nature of Evil*

NIEBUHR. *The Nature and Destiny of Man*, VOL I

C. S. LEWIS. *The Screwtape Letters*

——. *Perelandra*

Chapter 87: SLAVERY

INTRODUCTION

MORALISTS and political philosophers who appear to be in substantial agreement on the principles of justice differ remarkably from one another on whether slavery is just. The sharpness of this disagreement is made all the more remarkable by the almost unanimous condemnation of slavery—in two senses of that term.

As appears in the chapter on TYRANNY, the condition of those who live under tyrannical rule is generally conceived as a kind of slavery, involving not only the loss of political freedom but also the suffering of other abuses or injuries. With the possible exception of Hobbes, who says that tyranny is merely monarchy "misliked," none of the great authors from Plato and Aristotle to Rousseau, Hegel, and Mill, writes of tyranny except as a perversion of government—unjust, lawless, or illegitimate. The evil of tyranny for them lies in the enslavement of men who deserve to be free, who should govern themselves or at least should be governed for their own good, not exploited by a ruler who uses them for his own private interests.

Some writers, like Montesquieu, who tend to identify despotism and tyranny see little difference between subjection and slavery, regarding both alike as degradations. Yet Montesquieu—and with him Aristotle—also thinks that for certain races of mankind subjection or slavery may be justified. Mill later makes the comparable point that for a people at a certain stage of political development, subjection may be necessary for a time in preparation for citizenship. The two basic distinctions in political status which are here implied —between slavery and subjection and between subjection and citizenship—are developed more fully in the chapter on CITIZEN. The first of these distinctions relates to the difference in the condition of men under tyranny and under benevolent despotism; the second, to the difference in the condition of men under absolute and under constitutional government.

The other sense in which the word "slavery" seems always to be used with the connotation of evil is the sense in which Augustine speaks of man's slavery to lust as a consequence of original sin; or in which Spinoza writes of human bondage—the condition of men enslaved by the tyranny of their passions—as compared with human freedom under the rule of reason. This meaning of slavery is discussed in other chapters, such as EMOTION and LIBERTY.

The slavery which results from the tyranny of the passions is a disorder from which any man may suffer; it stems from a weakness in the human nature which is common to all. Similarly, the slavery of a whole people under tyrannical rule is a perversion of government for all the members of the community, not just for some. But whenever slavery is defended, it is justified only for *some men* within a community, not for all; or if for a whole people, not for all mankind, but only for *certain peoples* under certain conditions. With regard to slavery, the basic issue of justice is, therefore, whether *some* men should be slaves or *all* should be free, not whether *all* should be slaves or *all* free.

THE DISTINCTION BETWEEN the slavery of some men within a community and the enslavement of a whole people appears to be related to the distinction between economic and political enslavement. In the ancient meaning of the word "economic," the economic slave is the slave of the household or family. "A complete household," writes Aristotle, "consists of slaves and freemen." The elements of a family are "master and slave, husband and wife, father and children."

That the distinction between slave and free man signifies economic rather than political status for Aristotle, and for the ancients generally, seems to be indicated by the fact that, under certain types of oligarchical constitution, free men are excluded from citizenship without thereby becoming slaves. But in all ancient republics, democratic as well as oligarchical, slaves are ineligible for citizenship.

Though the relation of master and slave is essentially economic rather than political, such slavery has a political aspect in the sense that some men have no function in the state except to serve other men. Aristotle speaks of them as necessary to the state, but not, as are citizens, parts of it. "The necessary people," he says, "are either slaves who minister to the wants of individuals, or mechanics and laborers who are the servants of the community."

The mark of economic slavery seems to be the kind of work a man does and the conditions under which he labors, whereas political slavery seems to depend upon the kind of life a man leads and the conditions under which he lives in society. The economic slave serves a master by his work. The political slave lives under a tyrant. In Aristotle's view it is only the man who is economically free who has anything to lose from being enslaved by a tyrant. "No free man, if he can escape from it, will endure such government," he writes; but the barbarians, who "are by nature slaves," do not rebel against tyranny. Where some men are by nature free, there is also a natural distinction between women and slaves, "but among barbarians," according to Aristotle, "no distinction is made between women and slaves, because there is no natural ruler among them: they are a community of slaves, male and female."

The difference between economic bondage—which can include what Marx calls the wage slavery of the proletariat, as well as chattel slavery and other forms of serfdom—and the political condition of those enslaved by a tyrant does not seem to affect the issue of justice. Those, like Hobbes and Locke, who think that the vanquished in war must pay for being allowed to live by submitting to slavery, do not seem concerned whether the servitude takes the form of private possession by an individual master or the subjugation of a whole people by the conquering state. Nor do those, like Aristotle and Montesquieu, who regard some men or some races as naturally servile, seem to offer reasons for political slavery different from those which they think justify economic servitude.

What does seem to affect the issue concerning the justice of slavery is the difference between the natural slave and the slave by force or law. This is the difference between the man who is born a slave (not merely born of slaves and into slavery) and the man who, born with a nature fit for freedom, is made a slave, either because his parents before him were slaves, because he is sold into slavery, or because, for one reason or another, he forfeits his birthright to freedom.

If no men are by nature slaves, then the only questions of justice concern the conditions which justify making slaves of free men. These may remain the only questions even if there are natural slaves, since it cannot be unjust to treat as slaves those who are by nature slaves, any more than it is unjust to treat animals as brutes.

In both cases some consideration may be given to how slaves or animals should be treated. "The right treatment of slaves," Plato declares in the *Laws*, "is to behave properly to them, and to do to them, if possible, even more justice than to those who are our equals." Justice also requires, according to Plato, that if a slave or an animal do any harm, the master shall pay for the injury.

We have already observed that, with regard to natural slavery, the main issue is one of fact. The fact in question concerns human equality and inequality. Within that equality of all men which rests upon their common possession of human nature, are some men by nature inferior to others in their use of reason or their capacity for leading the life of reason? Does such inferiority prevent them from directing their own lives or even their own work to the ends which are the natural fulfillment of man's powers? And if so, do not such men profit from being directed by their superiors, as well as from serving them and, through serving them, participating in the greater good their betters are able to achieve?

These are the questions of fact which Aristotle seems to answer affirmatively as he develops his theory of natural slavery. If the facts are granted, then no issue of justice arises, for Aristotle can say that "the slave by nature and the master by nature have in reality the same interests." It is by the justice inherent in the relation of master and slave *when both are naturally so related* that Aristotle can criticize the injustice of all *conventional* forms of slavery. But the question of fact must be faced, as Aristotle himself is aware.

"Is there any one intended by nature to be a slave," he asks, "and for whom such a condition is expedient and right, or is all slavery a violation of nature?" Aristotle recognizes that "others affirm the rule of a master over slaves to be contrary to nature and that the distinction between slave and free man exists by law only, and not by nature, and being an interference with nature is therefore unjust." He himself questions the justice of making slaves of captives taken in war, for that may violate the natures of men of high rank who have had the misfortune to be captured or sold. But he thinks that the same kind of difference which exists between male and female—the male being by nature superior, the female inferior; the one ruling, the other submitting to rule—can be extended to all mankind.

"Where there is such a difference," Aristotle explains, "as that between soul and body, or between men and animals . . . the lower sort are by nature slaves, and it is better for them as for all inferiors that they should be under the rule of a master. For he who can be, and therefore is, another's and he who participates in a rational principle enough to apprehend, but not to have, such a principle, is a slave by nature; whereas the lower animals cannot even apprehend a principle; they obey their instincts. And indeed the use made of slaves and of tame animals is not very different; for both with their bodies minister to the needs of life . . . If men differed from one another in the mere forms of their bodies as much as the statues of the gods do from men, all would acknowledge that the inferior class should be slaves of the superior. And if this is true of the body, how much more just that a similar distinction should exist in the soul . . . It is clear, then, that some are by nature free, and others slaves, and that for these latter slavery is both expedient and right."

According to the theory of natural slavery, it is as good for the slave to have a master as for the master to have a slave. This reciprocity of interest does not occur in legal or conventional slavery. In both types of slavery, the slave is a piece of property, a possession. Whether by nature or by institution, a slave does not own himself; he is another's man. "He may be called another's man," Aristotle says, "who, being a human being, is also a possession." Does this mean that the slave belongs wholly to the master, in all that he is and has? He would seem to belong to his master insofar as he is a *possession*; but not wholly—in all that he is and has—insofar as he is a *human being*. Aristotle does not introduce such a qualification where he says that "the slave is a part of the master, a living but separated part of his bodily frame"; yet he adds: "where the relation of master and slave is natural they are friends and have a comon interest, but where it rests merely on law and force, the reverse is true."

Aristotle considers the difference between the natural slave and other forms of personal property, whether domestic animals, beasts of burden, or the inanimate instruments used in the household for productive purposes. Do slaves, he asks, have any excellence "beyond and higher than merely instrumental and ministerial qualities" of the sort to be found in tools and animals? Do they have virtues, and if so, then "in what way will they differ from freemen?"

Aristotle answers by saying that "since they are men and share in the rational principle, it seems absurd to say that they have no virtue." But since the rational principle in them is weak and consists only in the ability to execute decisions—not to make them or to know the end for which they are made—the slave will have a capacity for only so much virtue as he requires; enough virtue, for example, to "prevent him from failing in his duty through cowardice or lack of self-control."

It is precisely because of his limited competence and virtue that the slave needs, and profits by having, a master. Aristotle thinks that he is better off than the artisan out of bondage. "The slave shares in his master's life; the artisan is less closely connected with him, and only attains excellence in proportion as he becomes a slave. The meaner sort of mechanic has a special and separate slavery, and whereas the slave exists by nature, not so the shoemaker or other artisan."

The "separate slavery" of the artisan makes him more like an animal or an inanimate tool in the way he is used; for, according to Aristotle, he is an instrument of production, while the natural slave participates in his master's life by being an instrument not of production, but of action. The work the slave does enables the master to live well—to achieve the happiness of the political or contemplative life—and since "life is action, not production . . . the slave is a minister of action." If the slave had in his own nature the capacity for human happiness, he would not be by nature a slave, nor be limited to the good of serving another man's happiness.

"Slaves and brute animals cannot form a state," Aristotle says, because "the state exists for the sake, not of life, but the good life" and slaves "have no share in happiness or in a life of free choice. . . . No one assigns to a slave a share in happiness," he says in another place, "unless he assigns to him also a share in human life." At best, that share could come only from being a part of the master and contributing to the master's happiness. But though to this extent "the slave by nature and the master by nature have in reality the same interests," the rule under which the slave lives "is nevertheless exercised primarily with a view to the interest of the master."

ARISTOTLE'S DOCTRINE OF natural slavery is rejected by those who affirm the fundamental equality of all men in their common humanity and who, in addition, insist that their inequality as individuals in talent or capacity, should not affect their status or determine their treatment. On these grounds, Roman Stoics and Christian theologians seem to agree—and with them such modern thinkers as Rousseau, Kant, Hegel, and Mill—that all men are by nature born to be free. Freedom, writes Kant, belongs "to every man in virtue of his Humanity. There is, indeed, an innate Equality belonging to every man which consists in his right to be independent of being bound to others . . . in virtue of which he ought to be *his own master by Right.*" That "all persons are deemed to have a *right* to equality of treatment" seems to follow for Mill from the principle that "one person's happiness, supposed equal in degree (with the proper allowance made for kind), is counted for exactly as much as another's." The "equal claim of everybody to happiness" involves "an equal claim to all the means of happiness," among them freedom.

But though theologians like Augustine and Aquinas deny that slavery is instituted by nature, they do not seem to regard it as contrary to natural law or to the will of God. Something can be according to natural law in two ways, Aquinas says: "First, because nature inclines thereto. . . . Secondly, because nature does not require the contrary." Just as we can say, in the second sense, that nakedness is natural for man, "because nature did not give him clothes, but art invented them," so we can say that all men are by nature free because slavery was not instituted by nature, "but devised by human reason for the benefit of human life."

The institution of slavery, whereby one man belongs to another for his use, seems due to the fallen nature of man, as one of the penal consequences of original sin. If man had remained in a state of innocence, one man would have ruled another for the latter's good, but no man would have been the master of slaves to be used for the master's good. Since "it is a grievous matter to anyone to yield to another what ought to be one's own," it follows, says Aquinas, that "such dominion necessarily implies a pain inflicted on the subject." This painfulness of slavery in turn seems to imply a contradiction to Aristotle's view that slavery fits certain natures and is for their benefit.

"By nature, as God first created us," writes Augustine, "no one is the slave either of man or of sin." Both sorts of slavery are "introduced by sin and not by nature." Both are punishments for sin, though one seems to Augustine more grievous than the other. "It is a happier thing," he says, "to be the slave of a man than of a lust; for even this very lust of ruling . . .

lays waste men's hearts with the most ruthless dominion. Moreover, when men are subjected to one another in a peaceful order, the lowly position does as much good to the servant as the proud position does harm to the master."

Not sin, but climate, according to Montesquieu, is the cause of slavery and to some extent its excuse. Though he thinks that "the state of slavery is in its own nature bad . . . neither useful to the master nor to the slave," Montesquieu, like Hippocrates before him, regards the Asiatics as reduced to servility by the physical conditions of their life. "There reigns in Asia," he writes, "a servile spirit which they have never been able to shake off." Under Asiatic despotism, where whole peoples live in political servitude, domestic slavery is more tolerable than elsewhere. In those countries "where the excess of heat enervates the body and renders men so slothful that nothing but the fear of chastisement can oblige them to perform any laborious duty, slavery is... more reconcilable to reason."

Montesquieu seems to accept Aristotle's doctrine with some qualifications. "Aristotle endeavors to prove that there are natural slaves, but what he says is far from proving it. If there be any such, I believe they are those of whom I have been speaking." Slavery is both natural and unnatural. "As all men are born equal," Montesquieu declares, "slavery must be accounted unnatural, though in some countries it be founded on natural reason . . . Natural slavery, then, is to be limited to some particular parts of the world." But in arguing the right of Europeans "to make slaves of the negroes," he concludes with the equivocal remark that "it is impossible for us to suppose these creatures to be men, because, allowing them to be men, a suspicion would follow that we ourselves are not Christians."

Hegel's comment on the enslavement of African negroes by Europeans runs somewhat differently. "Bad as this may be," he writes, "their lot in their own land is even worse, since there a slavery quite as absolute exists." But though Hegel thinks that the negroes are naturally given to slavery, he regards "the 'natural condition' itself as one of absolute and thorough injustice." To remove this injustice, however, is not easy. "Man must be matured" for freedom, Hegel writes. "The gradual abolition of slavery is therefore wiser and more equitable than its sudden removal."

Mill also looks upon slavery as a stage in the rise of certain peoples from savagery to political life, and maintains that the transition to freedom must be gradually effected. "A slave properly so called," he says, "is a being who has not learnt to help himself. He is, no doubt, one step in advance of a savage. He has not the first lesson of political life still to acquire. He has learnt to obey. But what he obeys is only a direct command. It is the characteristic of *born* slaves to be incapable of conforming their conduct to a rule, or a law. . . . They have to be taught self-government, and this, in its initial stage, means the capacity to act on general instructions." Extenuations of the injustice of ruling men as slaves, such as those proposed by Hegel and Mill, are rejected by Rousseau.

The notion that some men are by nature slaves, whether in Asia or in Europe, seems to Rousseau to be an illusion due to the fact that those who are made slaves by force have had their natures debased to slavishness. Aristotle, he says, "took the effect for the cause. Nothing can be more certain than that every man born in slavery is born for slavery. Slaves lose everything in their chains, even the desire of escaping from them . . . If then there are slaves by nature, it is because there have been slaves against nature. Force made the first slaves, and their cowardice perpetuated the condition."

It is sophistry, he thinks, for philosophers to "attribute to man a natural propensity to servitude, because the slaves within their observation are seen to bear the yoke with patience; they fail to reflect that it is with liberty as with innocence and virtue; the value is known only to those who possess them, and the taste for them is forfeited when they are forfeited themselves."

THE ISSUE CONCERNING slavery as a social or legal institution does not seem to be resolved by the views men take of natural slavery. Aristotle, who holds that *only* natural slavery is justified, criticizes those who "affirm to be unjust and inexpedient in their own case what they are not ashamed of practising towards others; they demand just rule for themselves," he writes, "but where other men are concerned they care nothing about it. Such behavior is irrational, unless the one party is, and other is not, born to serve." This cannot be determined by conquest. Aristotle questions, therefore, the convention "by which whatever is taken in war is supposed to belong to the victors," or the principle that "because one man has the power of doing violence and is superior in brute strength, another shall be his slave and subject." Those who "assume that slavery in accordance with the custom of war is justified by law," are confronted by Aristotle with the question: "What if the cause of the war be unjust?"

Hobbes and Locke appear to take an opposite view. Men in a state of nature are free, though they can actually enjoy only as much freedom as they have power to secure. Yet the natural inequality in their powers does not establish a natural right on the part of the stronger to enslave the weaker. Hobbes makes the right of mastership or what he calls "despotical dominion" depend not merely upon victory in war, but upon a covenant into which the vanquished enter voluntarily, "when the vanquished, to avoid the present stroke of death, covenanteth . . . that so long as his life, and the liberty of his body, is allowed him, the victor shall have the use thereof at his pleasure." Only "after such covenant is made, the vanquished is a servant, and not before . . . It is not, therefore, the victory, that giveth the right of dominion over the vanquished, but his own covenant." That Hobbes means chattel slave when he says "servant," seems to be indicated by his remark that "the master of the servant is master also of all he hath, and may exact the use thereof; that is to say, of his goods, of his labour, of his servants, and of his children, as often as he shall think fit."

Locke disagrees with Hobbes that one man can give another the right to enslave him by contracting to become a slave in order to avoid death. "A man not having the power of his own life," he writes, "cannot by compact, or his own consent, enslave himself to anyone. . . . Nobody can give more power than he has himself; and he that cannot take away his own life, cannot give another power over it." As among the ancient Jews, men can sell themselves into temporary service to requite a debt. But this was a kind of drudgery, not slavery; "the person sold was not under an absolute, arbitrary, despotical power, for the master could not have the power to kill him at any time, whom at a certain time he was obliged to let go free out of his service." No Jew, Aquinas concurs, "could own a Jew as a slave absolutely, but only in a restricted sense, as a hireling for a time. And in this way the Law permitted that through stress of poverty a man might sell his son or daughter."

Absolute slavery, for Locke, "is nothing else but the state of war continued between a lawful conqueror and a captive." It is lawful, he thinks, to kill a violent aggressor, "for to that hazard does he justly expose himself whoever introduces a state of war, and is aggressor in it." But he who has forfeited his life necessarily forfeits his freedom. Slaves, then, are those "who, being captives taken in a just war, are by right of nature subjected to the absolute dominion and arbitrary power of their masters." In contrast to the limited servitude which a man can contract for wages, absolute slavery "is the effect only of forfeiture which the aggressor makes of his own life when he puts himself into the state of war with another."

Against Locke and Hobbes, as well as Aristotle, Rousseau denies that there is any justice in slavery—by nature, by covenant or compact, or by right of war. To think as Hobbes appears to, that "the child of a slave comes into the world as a slave," is, in Rousseau's opinion, to say that "a man shall come into the world not a man." Holding that slavery is "contrary to nature," Rousseau also holds that it "cannot be authorized by any right or law." A man cannot alienate his freedom by selling himself into slavery, for "to renounce liberty is to renounce being a man."

In Kant's language, "a contract by which the one party renounces his *whole* freedom for the advantage of the other, ceasing thereby to be a person and consequently having no duty even to observe a contract, is self-contradictory, and is therefore of itself null and void." Agreeing that such a contract is a nullity, Hegel holds that the "slave has an absolute right to free himself," but he adds that "if a man is a slave, his own will is responsible for his slavery. . . . Hence the wrong of slavery lies at the door not simply of enslavers or conquerors, but of the slaves and the conquered themselves."

As for Grotius and the others who "find in war another origin for the so-called right of slavery"—on the ground that "the victor having . . . the right of killing the vanquished, the latter can buy back his life at the price of his liberty"—Rousseau thinks their argument begs the question. "The right of conquest," he says, "has no foundation other than the right of the strongest. If war does not give the conqueror the right to massacre the conquered peoples, the right to enslave them cannot be based upon a right which does not exist."

Since Rousseau denies that victory gives the victors a right to kill those who have laid down their arms, he regards it unfair to make the captive "buy at the price of his liberty his life, over which the victor holds no right. . . . From whatever aspect we regard the question," he concludes, "the right of slavery is null and void, not only as being illegitimate, but also because it is absurd and meaningless. The words *slave* and *right* contradict each other and are mutually exclusive."

In modern as well as ancient times, in the European colonies in the New World if not in Europe itself, slave labor characterizes a certain type of economy and determines the mode of production, especially in agriculture and mining. The slave as chattel is bought and sold like other property. He may be a source of profit to his owner in exchange as well as in production. The traffic in slaves depends upon an original acquisition, either through the spoils of war or by the activity of slave traders who hunt men as if they were animals, to transport them in chains and sell them into slavery.

In the ancient world, individual slave owners emancipated their slaves, even as, under modern feudalism, a great landowner like Prince Andrew in *War and Peace* freed his serfs. Aristotle speaks of those in his own time who opposed the institution of slavery; and the Roman Stoics did a great deal to ameliorate the condition of the slave and to protect him legally against abuse. But there seems to have been no political party or active political movement among the ancients corresponding to the abolitionists and their struggle in the 18th and 19th centuries. Even then, however, the abolitionists were looked upon as a radical minority who had no respect for the rights of property in their overzealous sentimentality about the rights of men. Those who were willing to outlaw the African slave trade as outrageous were less outraged by the treatment of men as chattel, once they were possessed.

Madison, for example, referring to the prohibition affecting the importation of slaves into the United States, which the Constitution postponed until 1808, thinks it "a great point gained in favor of humanity, that a period of twenty years may terminate forever, within these States, a traffic which has so long and so loudly upbraided the barbarism of modern policy." But in another paper the writers of *The Federalist* present their version of the Southern argument defending the Constitution's apportionment of representation, "determined by adding to the whole number of free persons, including those bound to service for a term of years, and excluding Indians not taxed, three-fifths of all other persons." They do not object to the view of the negro slave as two-fifths property and three-fifths a person, confessing themselves reconciled to reasoning which, though "it may appear a little strained in some points," appeals to a principle they themselves approve, namely, that "government is instituted no less for the protection of property than of persons."

There are even those, in the 18th century, who defend the slave trade. Boswell reports an argument set forth by Dr. Johnson in favor of granting liberty to a negro, who claimed his freedom before a Scottish Court of Session. The sum of Dr. Johnson's argument, according to Boswell, came to this: "No man is by nature the property of another; the defendant is, therefore, by nature free. The rights of nature must be in some way forfeited before they can be justly taken away . . . and if no proof of such forfeiture can be given, we doubt not but the justice of the court will declare him free." Admitting that Johnson may have been right in the particular case at hand, Boswell protests his general attitude toward slavery and the slave trade.

"To abolish a status," Boswell writes, "which in all ages God has sanctioned, and man has continued, would not only be robbery to an innumerable class of our fellow-subjects; but it would be extreme cruelty to the African savages, a portion of whom it saves from massacre, or intolerable bondage in their own country, and introduces into a much happier state of life, especially now when their passage to the West Indies and their treatment there is humanely regulated."

Issues of justice aside, economists like Smith and Marx question the productivity of slave labor. Improvements in machinery "are least of all to be expected," writes Smith, when the proprietors "employ slaves for their workmen. The experience of all ages and nations, I believe, demonstrates that the work done by slaves, though it appears to cost only their maintenance, is in the end the dearest of any. A person who can acquire no property, can have no interest but to eat as much, and to labor as little as possible." He explains the lack of mechanical progress in Greece and Rome by the fact that "slaves . . . are very seldom inventive; and all the most important improvements in machinery, or in the arrangement and distribution of work, which facilitate and abridge labor, have been the discoveries of free men."

Marx also judges "production by slave labor" to be "a costly process . . . The principle, universally applied in this method of production," is "to employ the rudest and heaviest implements and such as are difficult to damage owing to their sheer clumsiness. In the slave-states, bordering on the Gulf of Mexico, down to the date of the civil war, ploughs constructed on old Chinese models, which turned up the soil like a hog or a mole, instead of making furrows, were alone to be found."

But Marx does not limit his judgment of slavery to criteria of efficiency, nor does he limit his consideration of servitude to its more obvious forms of chattel slavery and feudal serfdom. For him, all use of labor by those who own the instruments of production involves exploitation; it differs only in the degree to which the owner derives a surplus value from the labor power he possesses, through property rights or wage payments.

According to Marx, "the essential difference between the various economic forms of society, between, for instance, a society based on slave labor and one based on wage labor, lies only in the mode in which this surplus-labor is in each case extracted from the actual producer, the laborer." As all the value produced by a slave, in excess of the cost of keeping him alive, profits his owner, so during "the period of surplus-labor, the usufruct of the labor-power creates a value for the capitalist that costs him no equivalent . . . In this sense it is that surplus-labor can be called unpaid labor"—whether it is the labor of chattel or wage slaves.

Because a laborer is forced to sell his labor-power in the open market in order to subsist, Marx regards his so-called "freedom" as a pious fiction. "The contract by which he sold to the capitalist his labor-power proved in black and white," Marx writes, "that he disposed of himself freely. The bargain concluded, it is discovered that he was no 'free-agent,' that the time for which he is free to sell his labor-power is the time for which he is forced to sell it."

Others take the view that there is a fundamental moral difference between chattel slaves and men who work for wages. Hobbes, for example, thinks that between slaves who "are bought and sold as beasts" and servants "to whose service the masters have no further right than is contained in the covenants made betwixt them," there is only this much in common—"that their labor is appointed them by another." In slightly varying terms, Aquinas, Locke, and Kant make a similar distinction between the free servant, or paid worker, and the slave. The point is summarized by Hegel as a difference between alienating to someone else "products of my particular physical and mental skill," and alienating "the whole of my time, as crystallized in my work." In the latter case, "I would be making into another's property the substance of my being."

Debating with Douglas, Lincoln insisted that political freedom was the difference between the white slaves of the North and the black slaves of the South. The legal right, won by the proletariat, to organize and strike, seems to be a difference which Marx himself recognizes between the wage earner and the bonded slave. Until his chains are struck, the slave is not in the position of the free workingman to fight for political rights and privileges. Citizenship is not always extended to the laboring classes, but it is never conferred upon slaves.

OUTLINE OF TOPICS

1. The nature of enslavement: the relation of master and slave

2. The theory of natural slavery and the natural slave

  2*a*. Characteristics of the natural slave: individual and racial differences in relation to slavery

  2*b*. The conception of the natural slave as the property or instrument of his master

  2*c*. Slavery in relation to natural or to divine law

  2*d*. Criticisms of the doctrine of natural slavery

3. Slavery as a social institution: the conventionality of slavery

  3*a*. The acquisition of slaves: conquest, purchase, indenture, forfeiture

  3*b*. Laws regulating slavery: the rights and duties of master and slave

  3*c*. The emancipation or manumission of slaves: the rebellion of slaves

  3*d*. Criticisms of the institution of slavery: the injustice of slavery; its transgression of inalienable human rights

4. The forms of economic slavery

  4*a*. Chattel slavery: slaves of the household and slaves of the state

  4*b*. Serfdom or peonage

  4*c*. Wage slavery: the exploitation of the laborer

5. The political aspect of economic slavery

  5*a*. The disfranchisement of chattel slaves and serfs: their exclusion from the body politic or political community

  5*b*. The political deprivations of the laboring classes or wage slaves: the struggle for enfranchisement; the issue between oligarchy and democracy with respect to suffrage

6. Political enslavement or subjection

  6*a*. Slavery as the condition of men living under tyrannical government

  6*b*. Subjection as the condition of men living under benevolent despotism or paternalistic government

  6*c*. The transition from subjection to citizenship: the conditions fitting men for self-government

  6*d*. The imperialistic subjection or enslavement of conquered peoples or colonial dependencies

7. The analogy of tyranny and slavery in the relations between passions and reason or will: human bondage

REFERENCES

References are listed by volume number (in bold type), author's name, and page number. Bible references are to book, chapter, and verse of the Authorized King James version of the Bible. The abbreviation "esp" calls the reader's attention to one or more especially relevant parts of a whole reference; "passim" signifies that the topic is discussed intermittently rather than continuously in the work or passage cited. Where the work as a whole is relevant to the topic, the page numbers refer to the entire work. For general guidance in the use of *The Great Ideas,* consult the Preface.

1. The nature of enslavement: the relation of master and slave

APOCRYPHA: *Ecclesiasticus,* 33:24–31
NEW TESTAMENT: *Ephesians,* 6:5–9 / *Titus,* 2:9–10 / *I Peter,* 2:18–25
4 HOMER, 260–265, 309–310
5 AESCHYLUS, 63
5 SOPHOCLES, 153–154
5 EURIPIDES, 427
6 HERODOTUS, 223
7 PLATO, 709–710
9 ARISTOTLE, 446–449, 476
12 EPICTETUS, 126
14 PLUTARCH, 185–186, 287
15 TACITUS, 151–152
19 AQUINAS, 124–125, 488–489
20 AQUINAS, 434–435
23 HOBBES, 261–262
35 LOCKE, 29–30
38 MONTESQUIEU, 109, 111–112
38 ROUSSEAU, 389–390
42 KANT, 445–446
46 HEGEL, 198–199
50 MARX, 128–129
51 TOLSTOY, 277–287 passim

2. The theory of natural slavery and the natural slave

7 PLATO, 709–710
9 ARISTOTLE, 446–449
18 AUGUSTINE, 521
20 AQUINAS, 224–225
23 HOBBES, 94
38 MONTESQUIEU, 109–111
38 ROUSSEAU, 388
42 KANT, 445
44 BOSWELL, 363–364
46 HEGEL, 26–27

2*a*. Characteristics of the natural slave: individual and racial differences in relation to slavery

6 HERODOTUS, 124
7 PLATO, 709–710
9 ARISTOTLE, 445, 448, 454–455, 477–478, 531–532, 534
10 HIPPOCRATES, 15–16
38 MONTESQUIEU, 122, 123, 124
38 ROUSSEAU, 347
43 FEDERALIST, 170–171
43 MILL, 340
46 HEGEL, 198–199
50 MARX, 95
51 TOLSTOY, 215

2*b*. The conception of the natural slave as the property or instrument of his master

7 PLATO, 772–773
9 ARISTOTLE, 413, 447
19 AQUINAS, 512–513
42 KANT, 445–446
43 FEDERALIST, 170–171
46 HEGEL, 198–199

2*c*. Slavery in relation to natural or to divine law

OLD TESTAMENT: *Genesis,* 9:25
NEW TESTAMENT: *Colossians,* 3:22–4:1 / *I Timothy,* 6:1–3 / *Philemon*
18 AUGUSTINE, 521
19 AQUINAS, 512–513
20 AQUINAS, 224–225
22 CHAUCER, 531–532
23 HOBBES, 94
32 MILTON, 321
35 LOCKE, 65
38 MONTESQUIEU, 109–111
38 ROUSSEAU, 357–358, 368, 389
42 KANT, 401–402
44 BOSWELL, 363–364
48 MELVILLE, 3

2*d*. Criticisms of the doctrine of natural slavery

9 ARISTOTLE, 448–449
12 EPICTETUS, 120
19 AQUINAS, 512–513
22 CHAUCER, 531–532
23 HOBBES, 94
35 LOCKE, 36
38 MONTESQUIEU, 110–111
38 ROUSSEAU, 347, 356–358, 388–390
42 KANT, 401–402, 421–422
43 MILL, 316
44 BOSWELL, 363–364
46 HEGEL, 26–27, 122, 161
50 MARX, 25

3. Slavery as a social institution: the conventionality of slavery

3*a*. The acquisition of slaves: conquest, purchase, indenture, forfeiture

3*b*. Laws regulating slavery: the rights and duties of master and slave

3*c*. The emancipation or manumission of slaves: the rebellion of slaves

3*d*. Criticisms of the institution of slavery: the injustice of slavery; its transgression of inalienable human rights

4. The forms of economic slavery

4*a*. Chattel slavery: slaves of the household and slaves of the state

4*b*. Serfdom or peonage

4*c*. Wage slavery: the exploitation of the laborer

50 Marx-Engels, 422–423, 424–425, 426

5. The political aspect of economic slavery

5a. The disfranchisement of chattel slaves and serfs: their exclusion from the body politic or political community

6 Thucydides, 467
9 Aristotle, 474, 492, 533, 553–555
35 Locke, 43
38 Montesquieu, 114–115
38 Rousseau, 429
40 Gibbon, 16, 17
41 Gibbon, 82
43 Federalist, 170–171
46 Hegel, 273

5b. The political deprivations of the laboring classes or wage slaves: the struggle for enfranchisement; the issue between oligarchy and democracy with respect to suffrage

7 Plato, 740–741
9 Aristotle, 464, 469–470, 475, 477–481 passim, 495–496, 502–519, 553–555
14 Plutarch, 68–71, 674–689
39 Smith, 27–37, 168–169
43 Federalist, 178
43 Mill, 345–346, 383–384, 392–399 passim, 419
46 Hegel, 364
50 Marx, 137–141, 283–286, 364–368
50 Marx-Engels, 415, 429

6. Political enslavement or subjection

6a. Slavery as the condition of men living under tyrannical government

5 Euripides, 262
6 Herodotus, 238
7 Plato, 413–416
9 Aristotle, 483, 516–517
10 Hippocrates, 15–16
15 Tacitus, 1, 3
20 Aquinas, 307–309
23 Hobbes, 150–151
35 Locke, 28–29, 45–46
38 Montesquieu, 12–13, 15, 33–34
38 Rousseau, 356–358, 360, 361
40 Gibbon, 33–34, 51
41 Gibbon, 161–162, 320–321
43 Mill, 342–344
46 Hegel, 222, 302

6b. Subjection as the condition of men living under benevolent despotism or paternalistic government

14 Plutarch, 21–27
19 Aquinas, 488–489
30 Bacon, 27
35 Locke, 41–42
36 Sterne, 216
38 Rousseau, 357
40 Gibbon, 255
42 Kant, 439
43 Mill, 271–272, 273
46 Hegel, 134–135, 172
52 Dostoevsky, 127–137 passim

6c. The transition from subjection to citizenship: the conditions fitting men for self-government

6 Herodotus, 120, 171–175, 187
9 Aristotle, 470–471, 484–485, 496–497, 498, 505–506, 522–523, 553–558
15 Tacitus, 106–107
35 Locke, 47–51, 63–64
38 Montesquieu, 118, 122–125
38 Rousseau, 402–403, 411
40 Gibbon, 513, 521–523, 624
41 Gibbon, 562–565
42 Kant, 436–437
43 Mill, 267–268, 328–331, 339–340, 350–355
46 Hegel, 271

6d. The imperialistic subjection or enslavement of conquered peoples or colonial dependencies

Old Testament: *I Kings*, 9:20–23
Apocrypha: *I Maccabees*, 1:41–64 / *II Maccabees*, 5:21–7:42
6 Herodotus, 16–20, 30–31, 35–36, 37–40, 46–48, 139–159, 184–191
6 Thucydides, 367–369, 406–407, 424–434, 461–463, 468–469, 504–508, 529, 559
9 Aristotle, 448–449, 528–529, 538
13 Virgil, 278
15 Tacitus, 76, 117, 149, 286–287, 290
18 Augustine, 216–218, 524
23 Machiavelli, 3–8
23 Hobbes, 110–111, 280–281
26 Shakespeare, 1–32, 33–68, 532–567
35 Locke, 66
36 Swift, 182–183
38 Montesquieu, 62–63, 83–84
38 Rousseau, 389–390
39 Smith, 248, 251, 253
40 Gibbon, 14–16, 420, 550–551, 608–609
41 Gibbon, 51–53 passim, 443
42 Kant, 413, 454–455
43 Declaration of Independence, 1–3
43 Mill, 436–442 passim
46 Hegel, 299
50 Marx, 372–374, 379–383 passim

7. The analogy of tyranny and slavery in the relations between passions and reason or will: human bondage

New Testament: *John*, 8:31–36 / *Romans*, 6:16–23; 7:14–8:21 / *Galatians*, 4:1–5:1
7 Plato, 120, 275–276, 296, 347–348, 416–418, 419–421, 425–427, 528–529
9 Aristotle, 448
12 Epictetus, 137, 213–223, 225

18 AUGUSTINE, 190, 573–574
20 AQUINAS, 112–113
27 SHAKESPEARE, 49
32 MILTON, 200
36 SWIFT, 135–184
38 ROUSSEAU, 393
42 KANT, 586–587
46 HEGEL, 233
52 DOSTOEVSKY, 164
54 FREUD, 715–716, 838–839

CROSS-REFERENCES

For: Other discussions relevant to the theory of natural slavery, *see* JUSTICE 6, 6c; LAW 4h; LIBERTY 1a; WILL 7a.

Other discussions of the institution of slavery, *see* JUSTICE 6c; LABOR 1f, 5a–5c, 7c(1); PROGRESS 3b; PUNISHMENT 4b(3); STATE 5a, 5c; TYRANNY 1b; WEALTH 7b(1).

The discussion of slave rebellions and of the emancipation of slaves, *see* LIBERTY 6b; PROGRESS 3b; REVOLUTION 4a.

Other discussions of the forms of economic slavery or servitude in relation to different systems of production, *see* JUSTICE 8c(1); LABOR 1f, 5a–5c; WEALTH 6a, 7b(1); and for the political aspects of economic slavery or servitude, *see* CITIZEN 2c; CONSTITUTION 5a; DEMOCRACY 4a(1)–4a(2); LABOR 7d, 7f; LIBERTY 2d; OLIGARCHY 4, 5a.

The differentiation of citizenship, subjection, and slavery as three conditions of men under political rule, *see* CITIZEN 2b; LIBERTY 1f; TYRANNY 5a–5b; and for factors involved in the change from subjection to citizenship, *see* DEMOCRACY 4d; MONARCHY 4e(2); TYRANNY 4b.

Discussions of imperialism and of the government of colonial dependencies and conquered peoples, *see* GOVERNMENT 5b; LIBERTY 6c; MONARCHY 5–5b; STATE 10b; TYRANNY 6.

Other discussions of the slavery of men in bondage to their passions, *see* LIBERTY 3a.

ADDITIONAL READINGS

Listed below are works not included in *Great Books of the Western World*, but relevant to the idea and topics with which this chapter deals. These works are divided into two groups:

I. Works by authors represented in this collection.
II. Works by authors not represented in this collection.

For the date, place, and other facts concerning the publication of the works cited, consult the Bibliography of Additional Readings which follows the last chapter of *The Great Ideas*.

I.

HOBBES. *Philosophical Rudiments Concerning Government and Society*, CH 8
——. *The Elements of Law, Natural and Politic*, PART II, CH 3
HEGEL. *The Phenomenology of Mind*, IV (A)
DOSTOEVSKY. *Poor Folk*

II.

SENECA. *De Beneficiis (On Benefits)*, BK III, CH 18–25
LA BOÉTIE. *Anti-Dictator, the Discours de la servitude volontaire*
BODIN. *The Six Bookes of a Commonweale*, BK I, CH 5
GROTIUS. *The Rights of War and Peace*, BK II, CH 5; BK III, CH 7
VOLTAIRE. "Master," "Slaves," in *A Philosophical Dictionary*
FRANKLIN. *Essay on the African Slave Trade*
CHANNING. *Slavery*
GOGOL. *Dead Souls*
WHEWELL. *The Elements of Morality*, BK II, CH 24
THOREAU. *Civil Disobedience*
COMTE. *The Positive Philosophy*, BK VI, CH 6–12
——. *System of Positive Polity*, VOL III, *Social Dynamics*
NIEBOER. *Slavery as an Industrial System*
VINOGRADOFF. *The Growth of the Manor*
HOBHOUSE. *Morals in Evolution*, PART I, CH 7
KOHLER. *Philosophy of Law*, CH 6 (12)
MARITAIN. *Freedom in the Modern World*
MANN. *Joseph and His Brothers*
——. *Young Joseph*
——. *Joseph in Egypt*
BERDYAYEV. *Slavery and Freedom*

Chapter 88: SOUL

INTRODUCTION

IN the language of the poets as well as in the discourse of the philosophers, body and soul are correlative terms. Each affects the meaning of the other. The words are used together in daily speech. Men who are unaware of, or deny, the metaphysical and theological significance of having a soul, nevertheless use the word "soul" with a sense of contrast to body, even if only to refer to vague manifestations of spirit —feelings and sympathies which seem to be alien to the world of matter.

With few exceptions, traditional theories of the soul involve its distinction from and relation to the body. Berkeley represents one of the major exceptions. Denying the reality of matter, he conceives the soul as existing in and by itself; souls or spirits differ from God as finite from infinite spiritual beings. The something "which knows and perceives" and which "exercises divers operations, as willing, imagining, remembering," Berkeley says, "is what I call *mind, spirit, soul,* or *myself.*" Berkeley, therefore, would not speak of himself or other men as having souls, but rather as *being* souls.

The other major exception is exemplified by Lucretius. It is not that Lucretius denies soul as Berkeley denies body. Nor does he deny that soul adds something to body which differentiates living organisms from inorganic things. On the contrary, he declares the mind to be "a part of man no whit less than hand and foot and eyes are parts of the whole living being." Distinct from mind, soul is also part of a living being. "Mind and soul are held in union one with the other, and form of themselves a single nature," but whereas the mind is, as it were, the lord or head of the whole body, "the rest of the soul, spread abroad throughout the body, obeys and is moved at the will and inclination of the mind."

But when Lucretius refers to mind and soul as parts of the body, he means no more than is implied in speaking of the hand and eye as parts of the body. "The nature of mind and soul is bodily," he writes. Just as flesh and bones are composed of atomic particles, so the mind is formed of atoms "exceeding small and smooth and round," and the soul is "made of very tiny seeds linked together throughout veins, flesh, and sinews."

APART FROM THESE exceptions, the traditional discussion of soul considers it as somehow conjoined with body to constitute a whole of which it is the immaterial principle or part. Even those who, like Descartes, define the soul as an immaterial substance, capable of existing by itself, do not actually ascribe to the human soul complete independence of the human body. Nor do the theologians who think of God as a purely spiritual being and of angels as immaterial substances attribute soul to them.

Precisely because God and the angels do not have bodies, neither do they have souls. Whether everything which has a body also has a soul is another question. It is variously answered; but certainly those who, like Plato and Plotinus, speak of a world-soul or a soul of the universe, confirm the point that soul is the co-principle or complement of body. The same point appears in theories of the celestial bodies which conceive them as being alive and as therefore having souls.

Unfolding to Socrates the story of the creation, Timaeus says: "Using the language of probability, we may say that the world became a living creature endowed with soul and intelligence by the providence of God." To the world, Timaeus explains, God "gave a body, smooth and even, having a surface in every direction equidistant from the center, a body entire and perfect, and formed out of perfect bodies. And in the center, he put the soul which he diffused throughout the body, making it also to be the exterior environment of it."

Comparing the magnetic force of the loadstone with the animation of a soul, Gilbert says that "this one eminent property is the same which the ancients held to be a soul in the heavens, in the globes, and in the stars, in sun and moon. . . . The ancient philosophers . . . all seek in the world a certain universal soul, and declare the whole world to be endowed with a soul. Aristotle held that not the universe is animate, but the heavens only. . . . As for us," Gilbert writes, "we deem the whole world animate, and all globes, stars, and this glorious earth, too, we hold to be from the beginning by their own destinate souls governed . . . Pitiable is the state of the stars, abject the lot of earth, if this high dignity of soul is denied them, while it is granted to the worm, the ant, the roach, to plants and morels; for in that case, worms, roaches, moths, were more beauteous objects in nature and more perfect, inasmuch as nothing is excellent, nor precious, nor eminent, that hath not a soul."

On the question whether the earth, each heavenly body, or the whole world is endowed with life, intelligence, and soul, Kepler differs from Gilbert, Augustine from Plato and Plotinus, Aquinas from Aristotle. Nevertheless, the many-sided controversy indicates the traditional connection of soul with life and mind on the one hand, and with animate or organic bodies on the other—bodies which manifest certain properties and tendencies to motion.

THE MAJOR ISSUES CONCERNING soul seem to follow from these traditional associations. Does the soul which is somehow conjoined with a body exist as an immaterial substance or principle, in such a way that the being composed of body and soul consists of two distinct substances or entities, united as related parts of a whole? Or is the soul the substantial form of an organic body, with the consequence that the form and matter together constitute a single composite substance, which is the living thing? In the latter alternative the unity of soul and body, according to Aristotle, is like that of "the wax and the shape given to it by the die."

On either conception of soul and its relation to body or matter, further questions arise concerning the soul's existence apart from the body. Does it exist before being united to the body? Does it exist after the union is dissolved? How does it exist when it exists separately or apart from matter? For those, like Lucretius, who conceive the soul as itself composed of material particles within the framework of the body, such questions can have little meaning. For those, like Plato and Descartes, who conceive the soul as an immaterial entity having being in its own right, these questions can be immediately answered in favor of the soul's capacity for separate existence. Only when the soul is conceived as a form which, together with matter, constitutes the substance of a living body, does there seem to be both meaning and difficulty to the question whether the soul continues to endure separately when a plant, an animal, or a man dies, *i.e.*, when such composite substances decompose.

If the individual soul ceases to be when the body with which it is somehow united perishes, it is as mortal as the body. The traditional theories of personal immortality—such as the Platonic myths concerning the transmigration or reincarnation of souls, and the Christian doctrine of man's immortal soul, specially created for union with the body, but destined to survive its separation from the body—are theories which involve conceptions of the soul as capable of self-subsistence. The controversy over these doctrines is dealt with in the chapter on IMMORTALITY. Here are we concerned to see how different implications for immortality necessarily follow from various theories of the soul.

Still other issues concerning soul arise in connection with other chapters. For example, the question whether soul is to be found only in living things, or only in animals but not in plants, or in man alone, is discussed in the chapters on LIFE AND DEATH and on MIND. If soul, on any conception, is the principle or cause of life, then the distinction between animate and inanimate bodies is identical with the distinction between things which have and things which do not have a soul. If, furthermore, the kind of life possessed by a vegetable or plant is radically different from animal life, and that in turn from human life, then souls, too, may have to be differentiated in kind according to the mode of life or the range of vital powers of which each type is the principle.

Some writers, however, tend to equate "soul" with "mind" or "understanding." When, as by Descartes, soul is identified with rational soul or thinking substance, it is usually attributed to man alone. Soul is then not thought necessary to explain the phenomena of life in plants and animals, at least in no sense of soul which implies either an incorporeal or a formal principle; that is, anything beyond the complex interaction of organic parts. Other authors, like Locke, who conceive soul or understanding not merely in terms of rational thought, but also in terms of sensation, imagination, and memory, may exclude plants, but not animals, from the possession of soul or mind.

Descartes takes notice of these ambiguities in the traditional use of the word "soul." Probably because "men in the earliest times," he writes, "did not distinguish in us that principle in virtue of which we are nourished, grow, and perform all those operations which are common to us with the brutes . . . from that by which we think, they called both by the single name *soul*; then, perceiving the distinction between nutrition and thinking, they called that which thinks *mind*, believing also that this was the chief part of the soul. But I, perceiving that the principle by which we are nourished is wholly distinct from that by means of which we think have declared that the name *soul* when used for both is equivocal; and I say that, when soul is taken to mean the *primary actuality* or *chief essence of man*, it must be understood to apply only to the principle by which we think, and I have called it by the name *mind* as often as possible to avoid ambiguity; for I consider the mind not as part of the soul, but as the whole of that soul which thinks."

In another place, he uses the word "soul" to stand for "that subtle fluid styled the animal spirits" which, pervading the organs of brute animals, accounts for their peculiar type of animation. "We can recognize no principle of motion in them beyond the disposition of their organs and the continual discharge of the animal spirits that are produced by the beat of the heart as it rarefies the blood." Soul in this sense is not to be confused with "the incorporeal and spiritual nature of man's soul." It is "something corporeal, of a fine structure and subtle, spread throughout the external body, and the principle of all sensation, imagination, and thought. Thus there are three grades of being, Body, the Corporeal or soul, and Mind or spirit."

In the opening pages of his treatise *On the Soul*, Aristotle says that "to attain any assured knowledge about the soul is one of the most difficult things in the world." The difficulty seems to apply both to *what the soul is* and to *whether it exists*. The questions are connected. Even Lucretius, who regards the soul as material in nature, does not claim to know its existence by direct observation. It is not, like the body itself or like other parts of the body, a sensible object. It must be inferred to exist. Just as the existence of unobservable atoms is inferred in order to explain the constitution and change of all natural objects, so the existence of soul is inferred in order to explain the constitution and motion of living things. Those who conceive the soul as immaterial—whether as substance, principle, or form—would seem to face an even greater difficulty in establishing its existence and in describing its nature. Admittedly, the soul as some sort of immaterial being cannot be discovered by observation and experiment. The alternatives, which represent traditional solutions of the problem, seem to include the soul's reflexive knowledge of its own existence, inferential knowledge about the soul based on observed facts, various religious beliefs concerning the nature and destiny of the soul, and the postulation of the soul's existence on practical, not theoretic, grounds.

Not all writers agree with Aristotle that the soul is an object difficult to know, or with Kant that it is absolutely impossible for us to reach any sound theoretic conclusions about the soul's existence. Descartes, for example, says that if there are "any persons who are not sufficiently persuaded of the existence of God and of the soul by the reasons which I have brought forward, I wish them to know that all other things of which they perhaps think themselves more assured (such as possessing a body, and that there are stars and an earth and so on) are less certain."

The argument for the soul's existence which

precedes this remark is the famous *Cogito, ergo sum*—"I think; therefore, I am." From the fact that, in the very act of doubting the existence of everything else, he could not doubt that he was doubting, and hence thinking, Descartes assures himself of his own existence, or, more precisely, of the existence of himself as a thinking being. "I knew," he writes, "that I was a substance the whole essence or nature of which is to think, and that for its existence there is no need of any place, nor does it depend on any material thing; so that this 'me,' that is to say, the soul by which I am what I am, is entirely distinct from body, and is even more easy to know than is the latter; and even if the body were not, the soul would not cease to be what it is."

Locke appears to agree that "if I doubt of all other things, that very doubt makes me perceive my own existence, and will not suffer me to doubt of that.... I have as certain perception of the existence of the thing doubting," he goes on, "as of that thought which I call doubt. Experience then convinces us that we have an intuitive knowledge of our own existence, and an internal infallible perception that we are."

But Locke does not turn the proposition that a thinking being exists into the assertion that a spiritual being, the soul as an immaterial substance, exists. "We have the idea of matter and thinking," he writes, "but possibly shall never be able to know whether any mere material being thinks or no; it being impossible for us, by the contemplation of our own ideas, without revelation, to discover whether Omnipotency has not given to some systems of matter fitly disposed, a power to perceive and think, or else joined and fixed to matter so disposed, a thinking immaterial substance: it being, in respect of our notions, not much more remote from our comprehension to conceive that God can, if he pleases, superadd to matter a faculty of thinking, than that he should superadd to it another substance with a faculty of thinking."

For Locke, however, our idea of soul is as clear as our idea of body. "Our idea of body," he says, "is an extended, solid substance capable of communicating motion by impulse; and our idea of soul, as an immaterial spirit, is of a substance that thinks, and has a power of exciting motion in body, by willing or thought . . . I know that people whose thoughts are immersed in matter, and have so subjected their minds to their senses, that they seldom reflect on anything beyond them, are apt to say, that they cannot comprehend a thinking thing; which, perhaps, is true: but I affirm, when they consider it well, they can no more comprehend an extended thing." And in another place, he adds: "If this notion of immaterial spirit may have, perhaps, some difficulties in it, not easy to be explained, we have, therefore, no more reason to deny or doubt the existence of such spirits, than we have to deny or doubt the existence of body, because the notion of body is cumbered with some difficulties, very hard, and, perhaps, impossible to be explained or understood by us."

Berkeley differs from Locke not only in maintaining that we have no idea of matter at all, but also in holding that, if we use the word "idea" for sense-impressions or the images derived from them, we can have no idea of soul or spiritual substance. But we can, he thinks, form what he calls a "notion" of the soul, which grasps the meaning of the word "spirit" as signifying "that which thinks, wills, or perceives." He differs from Locke further in proportion as he tends to agree with Descartes, asserting that the existence of a spiritual substance, a thinking being, necessarily follows from the undeniable existence of thinking itself.

For both Descartes and Berkeley, the immortality of the soul can be directly concluded from our knowledge of the soul's existence and nature. "The soul," writes Berkeley, "is indivisible, incorporeal, unextended, and it is consequently incorruptible. Nothing can be plainer than that the motions, changes, decays and dissolutions which we hourly see befall natural bodies . . . cannot possibly affect an active, simple, uncompounded substance; such a being therefore is indissoluble by the force of nature; that is to say, 'the soul of man is naturally immortal.'"

The arguments in Plato's *Phaedo* for the proper existence of the soul before it joins a particular body, and for its existence after it leaves the body to dwell apart before entering another body—arguments, in short, for the soul's immortality—seem to stem from a slightly different principle. It is not merely that the soul is simple or uncompounded and hence indissoluble, or that the knowledge we have of the absolute ideas requires us to posit a principle of knowledge other than the bodily senses which can apprehend only changing things. In addition, Socrates argues that the knower must be like the known. If it is the soul which knows the unchangeable and eternal essences, it must be as unchangeable and eternal as they are. When the soul uses "the body as instrument of perception," Socrates says, it is "then dragged by the body into the region of the changeable . . . But when returning into herself she reflects, then she passes into the other world, the region of purity, and eternity, and immortality, and unchangeableness, which are her kindred."

Against any form of argument for the existence and immortality of the human soul which proceeds from the nature of our thought or knowledge, Kant takes the position that the premises do not warrant the conclusion. He claims to expose the fallacies in what he calls the "paralogism of a rational psychology." The "I" of the *Cogito, ergo sum* may be the necessary logical subject of all our judgments, but this does not give us intuitive knowledge of a really existing substance which has the attributes of simplicity, spirituality, and permanence or immortality.

"In all our thinking," Kant writes, "the I is the subject in which our thoughts are inherent; nor can that I ever be used as a determination of any other thing. Thus everybody is constrained to look upon himself as the substance, and on thinking as the accident of his being." But, he goes on, "though the I exists in all thoughts, not the slightest intuition is connected with that representation by which it might be distinguished from other objects of intuition. . . . Hence it follows that in the first syllogism of transcendental psychology reason imposes upon us an apparent knowledge only, by representing the constant logical subject as the knowledge of the real subject in which that knowledge inheres. Of that subject, however, we have not and cannot have the slightest knowledge. . . . In spite of this, the proposition that the soul is a substance may well be allowed to stand, if only we see that this concept cannot help us on in the least or teach us any of the ordinary conclusions of rational psychology, as, for instance, the everlasting continuance of the soul amid all changes and even in death; and that it therefore signifies a substance in idea only, and not in reality."

Similarly with respect to the simplicity of the soul, Kant contends that the absolute, but merely logical, unity of apperception or thought is illegitimately converted into the absolute unity of a real substance. The proposition, *I am a simple substance*, he declares, "teaches us nothing at all with reference to myself as an object of experience." Its only value is to enable us "to distinguish the soul from all matter, and thus to exempt it from that decay to which matter is at all times subject."

To this extent, rational psychology may "guard our thinking self against the danger of materialism." The concept of the soul as an immaterial and simple substance may thus function regulatively, but we deceive ourselves with the illusion of knowledge when we treat that concept as if it had intuitive content—when, as he says, we change "thoughts into things." Kant does not deny that the "I" is substantial in concept or simple in concept. Though these propositions are "incontestably true," he says, "nevertheless, what we really wish to know of the soul, becomes by no means known to us in that way, because all these predicates are with regard to intuition non-valid, entailing no consequences with regard to objects of experience, and therefore entirely empty."

The existence and immortality of the soul is, for Kant, a postulate or demand of the practical reason. "Of the psychic substance, regarded as an immortal soul, it is absolutely impossible to obtain any proof from a theoretical point of view," but if such an object must be thought *a priori* in order for "pure practical reason to be used as duty commands," it becomes what Kant calls "matter of faith." Immortality seems to him rationally required as the practically necessary condition for the fulfillment of the moral law and the endless progress of the soul toward holiness of will.

William James questions even such practical arguments for the soul. The imperishability of a simple substance does not, he thinks, guarantee "immortality of a sort *we care for*." Nor, following Locke, does it seem to him that a substantial soul is required for personal identity and moral responsibility. Writing as an empirical or scientific psychologist, who feels "entirely free to discard the word Soul" because he finds the concept useless "so far as accounting for the actually verified facts of conscious experience goes," James tells those who may find "any comfort in the idea" that they are "perfectly free to continue to believe in it; for our reasonings have not established the non-existence of the Soul; they have only proved its superfluity for scientific purposes."

JAMES' CONCLUSION THAT "the substantial Soul . . . explains nothing and guarantees nothing," along with the arguments of Kant and Locke, may not apply to the soul conceived as the principle of life rather than as the agent of thought, or to the soul conceived as the form of an organic body rather than as a spiritual being associated with or somehow imprisoned in the body. Precisely because this other conception affirms reality of soul as something other than a complete substance, precisely because it applies to plants and animals as well as men, this other conception of soul would seem to require a different sort of criticism.

The Greek and Latin words—*psyche* and *anima*—which we translate by "soul" seem to have life as their primary connotation. In the *Cratylus*, Socrates suggests that "those who first used the name *psyche* meant to express that the soul when in the body is the source of life, and gives the power of breath and revival." Other dialogues express the Greek conception of the living thing as that which has the power of self-motion, and ascribe this power to the soul as source. In the *Phaedo*, for example, Socrates asks, "What is that the inherence of which will render the body alive?" to which Cebes answers, "Soul," and agrees with Socrates' further statement that "whatever the soul takes possession of, to that she comes bearing life." In the *Laws*, Cleinias having identified the power of self-motion with life, the Athenian Stranger gains his assent to the proposition that whatever has life or self-motion also has soul.

To this much Aristotle also agrees. "What has soul in it," he says, "differs from what has not, in that the former displays life"; to which he adds that "living may mean thinking or perception or local movement, or movement in the sense of nutrition and growth," so that we must "think of plants also as living," and as having souls. But Aristotle goes further. In defining soul as the cause of life, and in differentiating three kinds of souls—vegetative, sensitive, and rational—according to the vital powers manifested by the activities of plants, animals, and men, he uses his general theory of corporeal substances to state precisely what the soul is and how it is related to the body.

Corporeal substances are, according to him, all composite of two principles, form and matter. "What is called matter is potentiality, what is called form, actuality." As exemplified in works of art, wood is the matter which has the potentiality for a certain shape and a certain function that is the actuality or form of a chair. In the case of natural things, that which determines "the essential whatness" of a body is its form or, as Aristotle sometimes says, "its formulable essence."

If living things are essentially distinct from inert bodies, as Aristotle supposes them to be, then the forms which determine their essences must be different from the forms of inanimate substances. It is this difference in forms which Aristotle appropriates the word "soul" to signify. In each kind of living thing, the soul is the substantial form or "the first grade of actuality of a natural body having life potentially in it."

He speaks of the first grade of actuality here to distinguish merely being alive or besouled from the various acts which, as operations of the vital powers, constitute living. If an axe or an eye had a soul, it would consist of its power to cut or to see, not in its actually cutting or seeing. While nourishing or thinking "is actuality corresponding to the cutting and the seeing, the soul is actuality in the sense corresponding to the power of sight and the power in the tool . . . As the pupil *plus* the power of sight constitutes the eye, so the soul *plus* the body constitutes the animal."

From this conception of soul as the form or actuality of a living substance, "it indubitably follows," Aristotle says, "that the soul is inseparable from its body, or at any rate certain parts of it are—for the actuality of some of them is nothing but the actualities of their bodily parts." Where Plato holds that the soul is prior in existence to the body, Aristotle holds that soul and body come into existence together when the organism is generated. Where Plato attributes an independent mode of being to the soul, distinct in character from that of bodies, Aristotle says that "the soul cannot be without a body. Yet it cannot *be* a body; it is not a body, but something relative to a body. That is why it is *in* a body and a body of a definite kind," being nothing more than "the actuality or formulable essence of something that possesses the potentiality of being besouled."

FURTHER CONSEQUENCES follow from these conflicting conceptions of soul. In the *Timaeus*, Plato advances the view that only the lowest grade of soul—the plant soul—is mortal, in contrast to the souls of animals and men. Aristotle would seem to attribute mortality to every grade of soul. If any exception is to be made, it is only for the human soul because it involves the power of rational thought. Mind or the power to think, he writes, "seems to be a widely different kind of soul, differing as what is eternal from what is perishable."

The critical point is whether thinking, unlike all other psychic powers, is an activity of the soul alone. For the most part, "there seems to be no case in which the soul can act or be acted upon without involving the body.... Thinking seems the most probable exception; but," Aristotle adds, "if this too proves to be a form of imagination or to be impossible without imagination, it too requires a body as the condition of its existence. If there is any way of acting or being acted upon proper to soul, soul will be capable of separate existence; if there is none, its separate existence is impossible."

Is there any way of acting or being acted upon proper to soul? Aristotle seems to answer this question affirmatively when he says that "insofar as the realities it knows are capable of being separated from their matter, so is it also with the powers of mind." On one interpretation this means that the mind or intellect is as immaterial in its mode of operation as some of its objects are in their mode of being; with the further consequence that what is capable of acting apart from body is also able to exist apart from body. But whether Aristotle's further statement that "mind set free from its present conditions . . . is immortal and eternal" applies to the intellect alone or to the rational soul as a whole, has been disputed by various interpreters. Adopting Aristotle's conception of soul as the form which is the actuality of life in an organic body, Aquinas for one seems to think that the immortality of a rational soul can be demonstrated from the special character of its intellectual powers.

A theory of the soul which regarded it as a simple and incorporeal substance, or as having a being independent of the body, would seem to harmonize more readily with the Christian belief in the human soul's special creation and its individual survival after death. But Aquinas rejects such a theory on the ground that then man would be two substances or two beings, not one; or else if the human person is identified with the soul, man would be a soul using a body rather than a single substance of composite nature. The doctrine of body and soul which holds them to be related as matter and form, preserves the unity of man and, in the opinion of Aquinas, fits the way in which man learns through his senses, experiences passions, and, in thinking, depends upon imagination.

But though he admits that men cannot think without images, Aquinas also insists, contrary to Locke, that thinking, insofar as it involves abstract concepts, cannot be performed by matter. To make matter think is beyond even the power of God. Unlike nourishing or sensing, *understanding* is not and cannot be "the act of a body, nor of any corporeal power."

This theory—that the acts of understanding by which the intellect abstracts and receives universal concepts cannot be accounted for by the motions of the brain—is further discussed in the chapter on UNIVERSAL AND PARTICULAR. Here we are concerned simply to note that, for Aquinas, the fact that the concepts with which men think are universal, means that they are abstracted from matter; and the fact that they are abstracted from matter means that the various acts of understanding must also be immaterial—that is, not acts of bodily organs like the brain. To these premises Aquinas adds one further principle, namely, that a thing's mode of being is indicated by its mode of operation. In these terms he concludes that, since the intellect has "an operation *per se* apart from the body," the human soul, which is called rational because of its power of understanding, can have a being *per se* apart from the body. Hence it is "something incorporeal and subsistent."

Nevertheless, according to Aquinas, though the human soul can subsist separately, it belongs to its nature to be embodied, that is, to be the form of a material substance. "The soul, as part of human nature," he writes, "has its natural perfection only as united to the body. Therefore it would have been unfitting for the soul to be created without the body." Furthermore, if the entire nature of man were to be a soul—the soul making "use of the body as an instrument, or as a sailor uses a ship"—there would be no need for the resurrection of the body after the Last Judgment. The Christian dogma of the resurrected body more properly accords, in Aquinas' view, with a conception of soul "united to the body as form to matter"; for, as he says in another place, "if it is natural to the soul to be united to the body, it is unnatural for it to be without a body, and as long as it is without a body it is deprived of its natural perfection."

In the consideration of the relation of body and soul, an opposite estimation of the body's role goes with an opposite theory of the soul's nature. Socrates, in the *Phaedo*, describes the body as the soul's prison-house, or worse, the source of the soul's contamination by the impurities of sense and passion. "In this life," he says, "we make the nearest approach to knowledge when we have the least possible intercourse or communion with the body, and are not surfeited with the bodily nature." But complete purification requires "the separation of the soul from the body .. the release of the soul from the chains of the body." That is why, Socrates tells his friends gathered in the cell where he is to drink the hemlock, "true philosophers are ever seeking to release the soul" and "are always occupied in the practice of dying."

It is also the opinion of Plotinus that it is evil for the soul to be in the body. But Christian theologians, for the most part, take a contrary view. Aquinas, for example, criticizes Origen for holding that "souls were embodied in punishment of sin." To him there is nothing "of a penal and afflicting nature" in the soul's union with the body. Though Scripture says that "the corruptible body weigheth down the soul, and the earthly tabernacle presseth down the mind," Augustine interprets this to mean, not that the flesh is evil in itself, but that man is beset by sin when "the flesh lusteth against the spirit."

"There is no need, therefore," according to Augustine, "that in our sins and vices we accuse the nature of the flesh to the injury of the Creator, for in its own kind and degree the flesh is good." Man is both body and soul, human nature is a thing of both flesh and spirit, and "he who extols the nature of the soul as the chief good," Augustine continues, "and condemns the nature of the flesh as if it were evil, assuredly is fleshly both in his love of the soul and his hatred of the flesh."

OUTLINE OF TOPICS

1. Conceptions of soul
   - 1*a*. Soul as the ordering principle of the universe: the world soul and its relation to the intellectual principle; the souls of the heavenly bodies
   - 1*b*. Soul as the principle of self-motion or life in living things: soul as the form of an organic body
   - 1*c*. Soul as the principle of distinction between thinking and non-thinking beings: the identity or distinction between soul and mind or intellect
   - 1*d*. Soul as the principle of personal identity: the doctrine of the self; the empirical and the transcendental ego

2. The analysis of the powers of the soul

  2a. The distinction between the soul and its powers or acts

  2b. The order, connection, and interdependence of the parts of the soul: the id, ego, and super-ego in the structure of the psyche

  2c. The kinds of soul and the modes of life: vegetative, sensitive, and rational souls and their special powers

    (1) The vegetative powers: the powers proper to the plant soul

    (2) The sensitive powers: the powers proper to the animal soul

    (3) The rational powers: the powers proper to the human soul

3. The immateriality of the soul

  3a. The soul as an immaterial principle, form, or substance

  3b. The immateriality of the human soul in comparison with the materiality of the plant and animal soul: the intellect as an incorporeal power

  3c. The relation of soul and body: the relation of formal and material principles, or of spiritual and corporeal substances

  3d. The denial of soul as an immaterial principle, form, or substance: the atomic theory of the soul

  3e. The corporeal or phenomenal manifestation of disembodied souls as ghosts, wraiths, or spirits

4. The being of the soul

  4a. The unity of the human soul: the human mode of the vegetative and sensitive powers

  4b. The issue concerning the self-subsistence or immortality of the human soul: its existence or capacity for existence in separation from the human body

  4c. The origin of the human soul: its separate creation; its emanation or derivation from the world soul

  4d. The life of the soul apart from the body

    (1) The doctrine of transmigration or perpetual reincarnation

    (2) Comparison of separated souls with men and angels

    (3) The need of the soul for its body: the dogma of the body's resurrection for the soul's perfection

    (4) The contamination of the soul by the body: the purification of the soul by release from the body

5. Our knowledge of the soul and its powers

  5a. The soul's knowledge of itself by reflection on its acts: the soul as a transcendental or noumenal object; the paralogisms of rational psychology

  5b. The concept of the soul in empirical psychology: experimental knowledge of the soul

REFERENCES

References are listed by volume number (in bold type), author's name, and page number. Bible references are to book, chapter, and verse of the Authorized King James version of the Bible. The abbreviation "esp" calls the reader's attention to one or more especially relevant parts of a whole reference; "passim" signifies that the topic is discussed intermittently rather than continuously in the work or passage cited. Where the work as a whole is relevant to the topic, the page numbers refer to the entire work. For general guidance in the use of *The Great Ideas,* consult the Preface.

1. Conceptions of soul

1*a*. Soul as the ordering principle of the universe: the world soul and its relation to the intellectual principle; the souls of the heavenly bodies

7 PLATO, 204–205, 447–455, 618–619, 757–765, 797–798
8 ARISTOTLE, 383–384, 641
12 AURELIUS, 267, 280, 286, 297, 310
16 KEPLER, 890–895, 896–897, 932–933, 959–960, 1080–1085
17 PLOTINUS, 36–37, 40–42, 48–50, 79–80, 103–104, 130–131, 211–213, 247, 251
18 AUGUSTINE, 194–196, 249–250, 367
19 AQUINAS, 19–20, 104–105
28 GILBERT, 104–105
28 HARVEY, 426–429
34 NEWTON, 542–543
51 TOLSTOY, 216–218, 608
53 JAMES, 658–659

1*b*. Soul as the principle of self-motion or life in living things: soul as the form of an organic body

7 PLATO, 93, 763–764
8 ARISTOTLE, 559, 631–668
9 ARISTOTLE, 163–164, 274–276, 278, 279, 281–282
10 GALEN, 167
12 AURELIUS, 292
17 PLOTINUS, 1–6 passim, 46–47, 146, 173–174, 208–209
18 AUGUSTINE, 561
19 AQUINAS, 106–107, 365–367, 368–369, 378–399
20 AQUINAS, 483–484, 737–739
21 DANTE, 109
23 HOBBES, 47, 251
28 HARVEY, 384–390 passim, 488–496 passim

1*c*. Soul as the principle of distinction between thinking and non-thinking beings: the identity or distinction between soul and mind or intellect

8 ARISTOTLE, 636–637
12 LUCRETIUS, 31–35
31 DESCARTES, 51–52, 71, 77–81, 119–120, 135–136, 152–156 passim, 219–220, 224–226, 249–250
35 LOCKE, 208, 211–212
35 BERKELEY, 418, 430, 440–441 passim
53 JAMES, 139–140

1*d*. Soul as the principle of personal identity: the doctrine of the self; the empirical and the transcendental ego

35 LOCKE, 113, 220–221, 222–228
35 BERKELEY, 440
42 KANT, 49–51, 200–204
46 HEGEL, 24
53 JAMES, 188–197, 213–240

2. The analysis of the powers of the soul

2*a*. The distinction between the soul and its powers or acts

8 ARISTOTLE, 642, 643–644, 664–665
17 PLOTINUS, 107–108, 169–171
19 AQUINAS, 399–401
20 AQUINAS, 7–8, 172–173, 741–742, 893–895
21 DANTE, 57
31 DESCARTES, 20, 208–209
35 LOCKE, 123–127, 176, 179–180
53 JAMES, 130–131

2*b*. The order, connection, and interdependence of the parts of the soul: the id, ego, and super-ego in the structure of the psyche

7 PLATO, 128–129, 316–356
8 ARISTOTLE, 641, 662–668
9 ARISTOTLE, 239, 347–348, 387–388
17 PLOTINUS, 166
19 AQUINAS, 403–406, 657–659, 783–784
20 AQUINAS, 794–795
23 HOBBES, 151
28 HARVEY, 444–445
54 FREUD, 701–708, 712–717, 721–722, 830–840

2*c*. The kinds of soul and the modes of life: vegetative, sensitive, and rational souls and their special powers

7 PLATO, 350–353, 421–427
8 ARISTOTLE, 631–632, 640–641, 643–645
9 ARISTOTLE, 164

12 Lucretius, 33–34
12 Aurelius, 262–263
17 Plotinus, 41–42, 151–152, 164–165, 172–173, 215, 220–221
18 Augustine, 256, 261
19 Aquinas, 361–362, 365–367, 399–440, 692–693
20 Aquinas, 350–351
21 Dante, 91–92
28 Harvey, 369–370, 386–388, 397–398, 445, 447
31 Descartes, 207
32 Milton, 185–186
35 Locke, 140–141, 220
42 Kant, 465–467

2c(1) The vegetative powers: the powers proper to the plant soul

7 Plato, 469–470
8 Aristotle, 417–420, 643, 645–647
10 Galen, 167–215
17 Plotinus, 97–98, 168–169, 171–172
19 Aquinas, 407–410, 604–607
20 Aquinas, 959–963
28 Harvey, 418–419, 427–428
31 Descartes, 78–79

2c(2) The sensitive powers: the powers proper to the animal soul

7 Plato, 466–467
8 Aristotle, 641, 644, 647–661, 664–668, 687–688
9 Aristotle, 196, 238–239
17 Plotinus, 153–154, 167–168
19 Aquinas, 380–381, 410–413, 427–431
31 Descartes, 19–20, 56, 59–60, 156, 226
35 Locke, 138–143 passim, 220

2c(3) The rational powers: the powers proper to the human soul

7 Plato, 386–388, 389–390, 535–536
8 Aristotle, 571–572, 573, 659–664
9 Aristotle, 347–348, 387–388
10 Galen, 173
12 Epictetus, 170–171
12 Aurelius, 271, 302
17 Plotinus, 202, 213–214
18 Augustine, 357–358
19 Aquinas, 394–396, 413–428, 431–440
20 Aquinas, 9–10
21 Dante, 79–80
28 Harvey, 427–428
30 Bacon, 55
31 Descartes, 71, 82–83, 89–93
32 Milton, 177
35 Locke, 131, 143–147, 178–183 passim, 211–212, 364–365, 371–372
36 Sterne, 270–271
42 Kant, 41–42, 474–475, 522, 568–575
46 Hegel, 168
49 Darwin, 278
54 Freud, 384–385

3. The immateriality of the soul

3a. The soul as an immaterial principle, form, or substance

7 Plato, 124–126, 223–225, 231–234, 435–436, 761–765
8 Aristotle, 632, 642–644
17 Plotinus, 139–141, 146, 206, 297, 299–300, 303–305
19 Aquinas, 378–379, 381–383
31 Descartes, 78–80, 86–103 passim, 170, 209, 261, 276
35 Locke, 205, 208, 313–315
35 Berkeley, 442
40 Gibbon, 186
42 Kant, 120–129
53 James, 220–223

3b. The immateriality of the human soul in comparison with the materiality of the plant and animal soul: the intellect as an incorporeal power

8 Aristotle, 638, 662
9 Aristotle, 277
17 Plotinus, 195–196
19 Aquinas, 14–15, 436–438, 440–443, 444–446, 447–449
28 Harvey, 494
31 Descartes, 60

3c. The relation of soul and body: the relation of formal and material principles, or of spiritual and corporeal substances

7 Plato, 2–3, 93, 220–251, 474–475, 761–765
8 Aristotle, 569–570, 632, 642–644, 645–646, 714–716 passim, 720–721
9 Aristotle, 163–164, 195–196, 238–239, 448
12 Lucretius, 31–40
12 Aurelius, 260
13 Virgil, 230–231
16 Kepler, 893
17 Plotinus, 1–6, 108–109, 139–207, 297–300, 303–305, 323–324
18 Augustine, 510, 561–562, 588
19 Aquinas, 275–276, 385–399, 430–431, 444–446, 565–566, 632–634
20 Aquinas, 710–711, 715–716, 740–741, 742–743, 808–809, 935–937, 1025–1032
21 Dante, 91–92
25 Montaigne, 264
28 Harvey, 431–434
30 Bacon, 49–50
31 Descartes, 72–73, 96–103, 119–120, 130, 133, 152–156, 207–208, 219–220, 224–226, 231–232, 248, 276
31 Spinoza, 377–378, 451–452
35 Locke, 123–124, 178–179, 208–212
35 Berkeley, 416–417
35 Hume, 472–473, 476
36 Sterne, 270–271
42 Kant, 557–558
46 Hegel, 24, 115

48 MELVILLE, 27–28
53 JAMES, 1–4, 118–119

3*d*. The denial of soul as an immaterial principle, form, or substance: the atomic theory of the soul

7 PLATO, 235–236, 238–240
8 ARISTOTLE, 633–641
12 LUCRETIUS, 55–56
17 PLOTINUS, 79, 191–200
18 AUGUSTINE, 268
19 AQUINAS, 378–379, 442–443
23 HOBBES, 176, 250–251, 269–271
25 MONTAIGNE, 264–267
31 DESCARTES, 226
35 LOCKE, 313–315, 351–352, 353
35 BERKELEY, 431, 440
42 KANT, 600
51 TOLSTOY, 689–690
53 JAMES, 95–119

3*e*. The corporeal or phenomenal manifestation of disembodied souls as ghosts, wraiths, or spirits

OLD TESTAMENT: *I Samuel*, 28:8–19
4 HOMER, 161–162, 243–249, 317–319
5 AESCHYLUS, 21–24, 82
6 HERODOTUS, 126–127
12 LUCRETIUS, 2
13 VIRGIL, 146, 206, 211–235
14 PLUTARCH, 781–782, 816–817
17 PLOTINUS, 200
19 AQUINAS, 479–480
20 AQUINAS, 887–889
21 DANTE, 109
23 HOBBES, 51–52, 80, 258, 274
26 SHAKESPEARE, 144–145, 591
27 SHAKESPEARE, 30–31, 36–37, 55–56, 298, 481–482
44 BOSWELL, 95, 114–115, 193, 394, 412, 472
54 FREUD, 763–764

4. The being of the soul

4*a*. The unity of the human soul: the human mode of the vegetative and sensitive powers

8 ARISTOTLE, 641, 643–644
17 PLOTINUS, 143, 151–152, 200, 205–206
19 AQUINAS, 385–393
20 AQUINAS, 953–955
21 DANTE, 109

4*b*. The issue concerning the self-subsistence or immortality of the human soul: its existence or capacity for existence in separation from the human body

7 PLATO, 124, 179–183, 211–212, 220–251, 793
8 ARISTOTLE, 632, 662
9 ARISTOTLE, 277
12 LUCRETIUS, 34, 35–44
12 AURELIUS, 258, 259, 271
14 PLUTARCH, 29
17 PLOTINUS, 165, 191–200
18 AUGUSTINE, 243, 319, 360–361
19 AQUINAS, 379–380, 383–384
20 AQUINAS, 182–184
21 DANTE, 91–92
23 HOBBES, 192–193, 253–255
25 MONTAIGNE, 264–269
31 DESCARTES, 69–71 passim, 72–73, 127
31 SPINOZA, 458, 459–460
32 MILTON, 290–292
33 PASCAL, 206–210, 271
35 BERKELEY, 441
40 GIBBON, 186–187
42 KANT, 120–129, 218–223, 234–240, 344, 348–351, 606–607
46 HEGEL, 255–256
48 MELVILLE, 25–28
49 DARWIN, 593
53 JAMES, 224–225

4*c*. The origin of the human soul: its separate creation; its emanation or derivation from the world soul

OLD TESTAMENT: *Isaiah*, 42:5 / *Zechariah*, 12:1
APOCRYPHA: *Wisdom of Solomon*, 15:11
NEW TESTAMENT: *I Corinthians*, 15:45
7 PLATO, 452–454, 618–619
12 LUCRETIUS, 38–39
12 AURELIUS, 310
17 PLOTINUS, 67–68, 69–70, 97–99, 139–145, 146–151, 202–207, 299, 303–305
18 AUGUSTINE, 357–358
19 AQUINAS, 383–384, 480–484, 600–604
20 AQUINAS, 742–743
21 DANTE, 77
23 HOBBES, 176, 251
30 BACON, 54
31 DESCARTES, 56
31 SPINOZA, 366–367
40 GIBBON, 186
41 GIBBON, 640

4*d*. The life of the soul apart from the body

4*d*(1) The doctrine of transmigration or perpetual reincarnation

6 HERODOTUS, 75
7 PLATO, 179–183, 226–234, 246–250, 437–441, 767–768
8 ARISTOTLE, 635
12 LUCRETIUS, 38–40
12 AURELIUS, 265
13 VIRGIL, 229–231
17 PLOTINUS, 5, 88–89, 91–92, 97–98, 149–150, 161, 304–305, 324–325
18 AUGUSTINE, 318–319, 355–357, 613–614
20 AQUINAS, 943–944, 951–953
21 DANTE, 111
25 MONTAIGNE, 249–250, 268–269
35 LOCKE, 220, 223–224, 227–228
46 HEGEL, 187

51 Tolstoy, 295

4*d*(2) Comparison of separated souls with men and angels

New Testament: *Luke*, 20:34–36
17 Plotinus, 151
18 Augustine, 569–570, 614
19 Aquinas, 406–407, 473–480
20 Aquinas, 81–87, 887–889, 893–900
44 Boswell, 192–193, 363
52 Dostoevsky, 22–23

4*d*(3) The need of the soul for its body: the dogma of the body's resurrection for the soul's perfection

18 Augustine, 317–318, 367–371, 378, 612–613, 630–631
19 Aquinas, 162–163, 473–475, 632–635
20 Aquinas, 935–939, 956–957, 966–967, 1037–1039
21 Dante, 9, 126–127
25 Montaigne, 311

4*d*(4) The contamination of the soul by the body: the purification of the soul by release from the body

7 Plato, 223–226, 230–234, 350–355, 434–441, 474–476, 805–806
12 Epictetus, 115
17 Plotinus, 5–10, 14–19, 24, 26–27, 28–29, 30–31, 33, 76–77, 81–82, 108–109, 158–159, 200–201, 208–209, 213–214, 338–339, 358–360
18 Augustine, 378, 379–380, 512–513
19 Aquinas, 473–475

5. Our knowledge of the soul and its powers

5*a*. The soul's knowledge of itself by reflection on its acts: the soul as a transcendental or noumenal object; the paralogisms of rational psychology

7 Plato, 220–251
8 Aristotle, 631–632
12 Epictetus, 105
18 Augustine, 336–338
19 Aquinas, 464–468
25 Montaigne, 261–269 passim
31 Descartes, 51–54 passim, 69–71, 77–81, 96–103, 207
31 Spinoza, 382–383
35 Locke, 121–123, 175, 185, 208–212
35 Hume, 453–455
42 Kant, 32, 55–56, 99–101, 120–129, 200–209 passim, 218–223, 234–240, 271, 281–282, 291–293, 307–310, 311–314, 337
46 Hegel, 14, 21, 120, 121, 257–258
53 James, 122–126, 177–178, 191–197, 232–238
54 Freud, 429–430

5*b*. The concept of the soul in empirical psychology: experimental knowledge of the soul

53 James, 1–4, 126–127, 221–226
53 Freud, 428–429, 431, 434, 549–550, 830–831 passim

CROSS-REFERENCES

For: Other discussions of the notion of a world soul and of the theory that the heavenly bodies have souls, *see* Astronomy 8b; World 1a.

Another consideration of the soul as the principle of life, *see* Animal 1a; Life and Death 1–2; and for other considerations of the soul as identical with mind or intellect and as the principle of thought, *see* Mind 1b–1d, 1f.

The problem of personal identity, *see* One and Many 3b(5); Same and Other 1b.

Other discussions of the parts or powers of the soul, and for discussions relevant to the distinction of several kinds of soul, *see* Animal 1–1c(2); Life and Death 3–3b; Man 1–1c, 4–5a; Sense 1a, 2a–2c.

The treatment of specific powers of the soul and of their relation to one another, *see* Desire 3–3d, 5–6c; Emotion 1–1a; 2–2c, 4a; Memory and Imagination 1–1d; Mind 1a–1a(4), 1e–1f, 1g(2); One and Many 3b(5), 4a; Opposition 4a; Sense 1a–1d, 3–3e; Will 1–3b.

The controversy over the immateriality of the soul and its relation to the body, *see* Animal 1e; Being 7b(2), 7b(4); Element 5e–5f; Form 2c–2c(1), 2d; Life and Death 2; Man 3a–3c; Matter 2d, 3a, 4c–4d; Mechanics 4c; Mind 2a–2e; One and Many 3b(4); and for the related controversy over the immortality of the soul, *see* Immortality 2–3b; Metaphysics 2d.

Other discussions of the transmigration of souls, *see* Immortality 5a.

Theories about the state and operations of the soul in separation from the body, *see* ANGEL 4; IMMORTALITY 5b; MAN 3b; MIND 4e; and for the doctrine of the resurrection of the body, *see* GOD 7g; IMMORTALITY 5g.

Other discussions relevant to the spiritual dignity of human nature which requires all men to be treated as ends, *see* JUSTICE 6, 6c; LIBERTY 1a; SLAVERY 2d, 3d; WILL 7a.

The nature and problems of psychology as the science of the soul or of man, *see* KNOWLEDGE 5a(6); MAN 2a–2b(4); MIND 6; and for discussions relevant to the distinction between rational and empirical, or philosophical and scientific psychology, *see* PHYSICS 2; SCIENCE 1c.

ADDITIONAL READINGS

Listed below are works not included in *Great Books of the Western World*, but relevant to the idea and topics with which this chapter deals. These works are divided into two groups:

I. Works by authors represented in this collection.
II. Works by authors not represented in this collection.

For the date, place, and other facts concerning the publication of the works cited, consult the Bibliography of Additional Readings which follows the last chapter of *The Great Ideas*.

I.

PLUTARCH. "Concerning the Procreation of the Soul, as Discoursed in Timaeus," in *Moralia*

AUGUSTINE. *On the Immortality of the Soul*

——. *The Magnitude of the Soul*

——. *The Soul and Its Origin*

AQUINAS. *On Being and Essence*, CH IV

——. *Summa Contra Gentiles*, BK II, CH 56–90; BK IV, CH 79–95

——. *On Spiritual Creatures*, A II

——. *Quaestiones Disputatae, De Veritate*, Q 19; *De Anima*, AA 1–2, 6–15, 17–21

——. *The Unicity of the Intellect*, II

DANTE. *Convivio (The Banquet)*, THIRD TREATISE, CH 5–8

DESCARTES. *The Principles of Philosophy*, PART I, 7–8, 11–12, 52–53, 62–65; PART IV, 196–197

HOBBES. *Concerning Body*, PART II, CH II

BERKELEY. *Three Dialogues Between Hylas and Philonous*

HUME. *A Treatise of Human Nature*, BK I, PART IV, SECT V–VI

——. *Of the Immortality of the Soul*

——. *Of Suicide*

KANT. *Prolegomena to Any Future Metaphysic*, par 46–49

II.

EPICURUS. *Letter to Herodotus*

TERTULLIAN. *A Treatise on the Soul*

GREGORY OF NYSSA. *On the Soul and the Resurrection*

PROCLUS. *The Elements of Theology*, (N)

SAADIA GAON. *The Book of Beliefs and Opinions*, TREATISE VI–VII

ALBERTUS MAGNUS. *De Natura et Origine Animae*

——. *On the Intellect and the Intelligible*, TREATISE I–II

MELANCHTHON. *Commentarius de Anima*

JOHN OF THE CROSS. *Spiritual Canticle*

——. *Dark Night of the Soul*

——. *The Living Flame of Love*

SUÁREZ. *Disputationes Metaphysicae*, XIII (14), XXXIV (5)

BURTON. *The Anatomy of Melancholy*, PART I, SECT I, MEMB II, SUB-SECT 5–11

JOHN OF SAINT THOMAS. *Cursus Philosophicus Thomisticus, Philosophia Naturalis*, PART IV, QQ 1–12

MARVELL. *Dialogue Between the Soul and the Body*

MALEBRANCHE. *De la recherche de la vérité*, BK I, CH 10 (1, 3)

——. *Dialogues on Metaphysics and Religion*, I

LEIBNITZ. *Discourse on Metaphysics*, XXXIII–XXXIV

——. *Philosophical Works*, CH 12 (*A New System of the Interaction of Substances*), 13 (*The Reply of M. Foucher Concerning the Interaction of Substances*), 23 (*Considerations on the Doctrines of a Universal Spirit*), 34 (*The Principles of Nature and of Grace*)

——. *New Essays Concerning Human Understanding*, BK IV, CH 9

——. *Monadology*, par 19–28

LAMETTRIE. *Histoire naturelle de l'âme*

LAMETTRIE. *Man a Machine*

VOLTAIRE. "Soul," in *A Philosophical Dictionary*

HELVÉTIUS. *Traité de l'esprit*

——. *A Treatise on Man*

SCHELLING. *Von der Weltseele*

EMERSON. "The Over-Soul," in *Essays*, I

GRATRY. *Philosophie. De la connaissance de l'âme*

BAIN. *Mind and Body*

CLIFFORD. "Body and Mind," in VOL II, *Lectures and Essays*

LOTZE. *Microcosmos*, BK II–III

——. *Metaphysics*, BK III, CH I

——. *Outlines of Psychology*

FRAZER. *The Golden Bough*, PART II; PART III, CH 7; PART V, CH 16; PART VII, CH 10–11

BRADLEY. *Appearance and Reality*, BK I, CH 9–10; BK II, CH 23

——. *Collected Essays*, VOL I (20)
VONIER. *The Human Soul and Its Relations with Other Spirits*
DRIESCH. *Mind and Body*
BERGSON. *Matter and Memory*, CH 4
——. *Mind-Energy*, CH 2
WHITEHEAD. *Religion in the Making*, CH 3
——. *Adventures of Ideas*, CH 2
B. RUSSELL. *Religion and Science*, CH 5
JUNG. *Modern Man in Search of a Soul*
——. *Psychology and Religion*
SANTAYANA. *Scepticism and Animal Faith*, CH 24, 26
——. *The Realm of Matter*, CH 8–9
——. *The Realm of Spirit*, CH 1–3

Chapter 89: SPACE

INTRODUCTION

ON the level of our everyday observations, space and time seem to be the obvious, the common, and the connected properties of physical things. We distinguish things from one another by their position in space, as we mark happenings by the date of their occurrence. The where and when of a thing is often used to identify it, for it is generally agreed that two bodies cannot occupy the same place at the same time, and that at the same time two distinct places cannot be occupied by the same body. According to a theologian like Aquinas, these limitations of space and time apply even to bodiless things, *i.e.*, to angels.

"An angel and a body are said to be in a place," he writes, "in quite a different sense." Whereas a body is in the place which contains it, "an angel is said to be in a corporeal place by application of the angelic power . . . not as being contained, but as somehow containing it." It follows, nevertheless, that at a given time an angel "is not everywhere, nor in several places, but in only one place." Nor does the incorporeality of angels permit more than one angel to be at the same time in the same place. According to the manner in which an angel is at a place—by the action of his power—"there can be only one angel in one place," Aquinas declares, even as there can be only one body in one place at a time.

Location or position in space, and spatial relationships such as higher and lower, nearer and farther, are so familiar and intelligible that they provide terms of reference whereby men speak metaphorically of the moral hierarchy and spiritual distances. The whole of Dante's *Divine Comedy*, for example, involves a spatial metaphor which sets forth the gradations of sin and the degrees of blessedness in terms of places beneath the earth and in the heavens above.

As he mounts from sphere to sphere in Paradise, Dante meets Piccarda Donati in the Heaven of the Moon. She explains to him that this place "which appears so far down," is assigned to those who have violated their vows in some particular. Dante wonders why she and the others do not "desire a more exalted place, in order to see more." Piccarda replies: "Brother, virtue of charity quiets our will, and makes us wish only for that which we have, and quickens not our thirst for aught else. . . . So that as we are, from seat to seat throughout this realm, to all the realm is pleasing, as to the King who inwills us with His will; and His will is our peace."

This speech of Piccarda's makes it clear to Dante "how everywhere in Heaven is Paradise, even if the grace of the Supreme Good does not there rain down in one measure." These different measures of beatitude in the diffusion of God's love and light are represented by the celestial spheres from the earth-adjacent moon to the Crystalline Heaven, the outermost bound of the physical universe, of which Dante says that it "has no other Where than in the Divine Mind."

WHEN THE WHOLE EXPANSE of physical space or the boundary of the universe is considered, Newton no less than Dante conceives the omnipresence and eternity of God as that which somehow encompasses all space and time. God "is not duration or space," Newton writes at the end of the *Principles*, "but He endures and is present . . . and by existing always and everywhere, He constitutes duration and space." In the concluding queries of the *Optics*, Newton appears to think of infinite space as the Divine Sensorium in which all things are at once present to God, who "being in all places is more able by His will to move the bodies within His boundless uniform sensorium, and thereby to form and reform the parts of the Universe, than we are by our will to move the parts of our own bodies."

The physicist does not have to turn theologian, however, to be confronted with the mysteries of space. Even without the modern complication of the relation of its three dimensions to time as a fourth dimension, the physical concept of space raises difficulties for analysis.

In the tradition of western thought conflicting definitions of space seem to result from a fundamental difference in the object being defined—whether it is an inseparable property of bodies, perhaps even identical with unformed matter, or a reality apart from the bodies which move and have their being in it. Sometimes this difference is signified by a difference between the meaning of the word "place" or "extension" and the meaning of "space." It appears also to be involved in the contrast between filled space and empty space (*i.e.*, the void or vacuum); and it bears some relation to Aristotle's distinction between space and place, and to Newton's distinction between absolute and relative space.

The controversial character of space in physical theory may be appreciated in terms of these oppositions in meaning, and the issues which they raise. In addition, physical theory is confronted with the problem of action-at-a-distance (*i.e.*, action through a void or through an ethereal medium), the problem of the infinity of space (or the question of a bounded or unbounded universe), and the distinction between one physical space and the variety of geometrical spaces.

Space, which at first seems easily apprehended by sense and susceptible to measurement, becomes upon examination so subtle as to be almost a vanishing object. Reason finds it difficult to say precisely *what* space is in itself, and how it is related to matter and motion. Even the familiar space of ordinary sense-perception seems to have its puzzles. A psychologist like James is concerned with how the different fields of touch, vision, and hearing coalesce to form the single space of our experience; and in dealing with the process by which we learn to perceive the spatial manifold of positions and directions, he cannot avoid the issue of innate as opposed to acquired space-perception.

Plato's theory of space is set forth in the *Timaeus* as part of "the likely story" which Timaeus tells about the production and constitution of the universe. The sensible things which come into being and pass away are, according to him, patterned after the eternal forms. To the eternal patterns and their copies in the world of change, Timaeus finds it necessary to add a third factor in order to account for the physical elements and their generation. This factor, he says, is "difficult to explain and dimly seen. . . . It is the receptacle, and in a manner the nurse, of all generation." In contrast to the elements which are perpetually changing into and out of one another, the receptacle "never departs from her own nature, and never in any way assumes a form like that of any of the things which enter into her. . . . The forms which enter into and go out of her are the likenesses of real existences modelled after their patterns in a wonderful and inexplicable manner."

Timaeus distinguishes the three principles as that which comes to be and passes away in the process of generation, that in which the generation takes place, and that which the generated thing resembles and which is its source. He likens the receptacle or "receiving principle to a mother, the source to a father, and the intermediate nature to a child," and adds that "if the model is to take every variety of form, then the matter in which the model is fashioned will not be duly prepared, unless it is formless and free from the impress of any of those shapes which it is hereafter to receive from without. . . . Wherefore, that which is to receive all forms should have no form. . . . The mother and receptacle of all created, visible, and in any way sensible things, is not to be termed earth, or air, or fire, or water, or any of their compounds, or any of the elements from which these are derived, but is an invisible and formless being which receives all things, and in some mysterious way partakes of the intelligible, and is most incomprehensible."

This third factor which Timaeus sometimes calls "matter" as well as "receptacle," he also sometimes calls "space." When matter and space are identified with each other under the conception of a receptacle for the forms, they have the characteristics of being absolutely formless and imperceptible to the senses. Nor are they, as are the forms, genuinely intelligible to reason. "The third nature, which is space, and is eternal," Timaeus says, "admits not of destruction and provides a home for all created things, and is apprehended without the help of sense, by a kind of spurious reason, and is hardly real; which we beholding as in a dream, say of all existence that it must of necessity be in some place and occupy a space, but that which is neither in heaven nor on earth has no existence."

The precise meaning of this conception of space is difficult to determine. Does it, for example, find an echo in Plotinus' statement that "space is a container, a container of body; it is the home of such things as consist of isolated parts"? But he also says that space "in a strict sense is unembodied and is not, itself, body," and that "body is not a void," but rather that "the void must be that in which body is placed," seeming thereby to imply that space is essentially the void. The statement in the *Timaeus* that "there can be no such thing as a vacuum," may apply only to the filled space of the created heaven and earth. May it not also be said that space is a void when it is identified with the formless matter of the receptacle prior to creation?

This raises further questions. Is the receptacle space or matter? And is the conception of space in the *Timaeus* rightly interpreted by Aquinas, in commenting on Augustine's reading of "the earth was void and empty" in Genesis 1:2? Augustine holds that by the word "earth" in this passage formless matter is to be understood. Because of its formlessness, Aquinas writes, "the earth is said to be *void and empty*, or *invisible and shapeless*," and, he adds, "that is why Plato says matter is place."

HOWEVER THESE QUESTIONS are answered, one thing seems to be clear. Space, functioning as receptacle, can be identified only with matter devoid of form, not with the matter of three-dimensional bodies. The relation of space to matter seems to be differently conceived by Descartes. Space is for him not an antecedent principle involved in the original production of sensible things, but rather—as the extension of bodies—it is inseparable in existence from them. It is a property which signifies the essence of material substances, as thinking signifies the essence of mind or soul. "By extension," Descartes writes, "we understand whatever has length, breadth, and depth, not inquiring whether it be a real body or merely space." Nevertheless, he goes on to say that "by extension we do not here mean anything distinct and separate from the extended object itself."

Descartes considers the significance of three statements: "*extension occupies place*, *body possesses extension*, and *extension is not body*." The first statement, he thinks, means no more than "*that which is extended occupies place*." The second statement seems to imply that "the meaning of *extension* is not identical with that of *body*; yet," Descartes insists, "we do not construct two distinct ideas in our imagination, one of body, the other of extension, but merely a single image of extended body; and from the point of the view of the thing it is exactly as if I had said: *body is extended*, or better, *the extended is extended*." Finally, in the statement that *extension is not body*, the word "extension," according to Descartes, expresses a purely abstract conception—nothing which in itself has any sensible reality. So far as its existence is concerned, the thing conceived as extension cannot be separated from body. Those who think otherwise, Descartes asserts, are involved in "the contradiction of saying that *the same thing is at the same time body and not body*."

The point is summarized in his *Principles of Philosophy* by the statement that "the nature of matter or of body in its universal aspect, does not consist in being hard, or heavy, or colored . . . but solely in the fact that it is a substance extended in length, breadth, and depth." But, it may be asked, are the dimensions of a body the same as space? Descartes replies that "the same extension which constitutes the nature of a body constitutes the nature of space . . . not only that which is full of body, but also of that which is called a vacuum."

If there were a vacuum, or empty space, extension might be separated from body. This Descartes flatly denies. "As regards a vacuum in the philosophic sense of the word, *i.e.*, a space in which there is no substance, it is evident that such cannot exist, because the extension of space or internal place is not different from that of body." And even "when we take this word vacuum in its ordinary sense," Descartes goes on, "we do not mean a place or space in which there is absolutely nothing, but only a place in which there are none of those things which we expected to find there."

These points made in the *Principles* confirm the identification of three-dimensional space or extension with body which appears in the *Rules*. They seem to be further confirmed in the *Discourse* by the reference to "a continuous body, or a space indefinitely extended in length, height or depth" which is "the object of the geometricians." Descartes does not, however, neglect the distinction between space as the extension of body, and place as the position one body occupies in relation to another. According to common usage, he says, the word "place" signifies that "in virtue of which a body is said to be here or there." He objects to those who, like Aristotle, mean by "place" the surrounding surface of a body. Local motion or change of place is not, he argues, a change in the body's surrounding surface, but a change in its relative position.

IT IS PLACE RATHER THAN space which Aristotle seeks to define, and place in the sense of the circumference of a body rather than its position in space. He rejects the notion that place is the extension of a magnitude, for that would, he thinks, identify it with matter. Place belongs to body, not as matter or a property of matter, but as its boundary. It is, Aristotle writes, "the innermost motionless boundary . . . a kind of surface and, as it were, a vessel, *i.e.*, a container of the thing." This boundary is itself made at the surface of a body by a surrounding body or bodies. "If a body has another body outside it and containing it," Aristotle writes, "it is in place, and if not, not."

The consequences of this conception of place are, first, a denial of space in the sense of void or empty place, since place is always "coincident with the thing" contained or bounded; second, a denial of any infinite place, since that would presuppose an actually infinite body—to Aristotle, an impossibility; and third, the conclusion that the whole universe itself does not have a place, for outside the outermost heaven which bounds the world, there can be no containing body by which the universe is bounded.

Aristotle explains that by "heaven" he means "the extreme circumference of the whole"—a whole "composed of all natural perceptible body." The two words which Einstein uses when he discusses "the possibility of a 'finite' and yet 'unbounded' universe" seem to apply to Aristotle's conception of the world—finite in body or matter, yet unbounded, *i.e.*, without anything outside itself to determine or define its boundary.

Aristotle's view of the world seems to be directly opposed to that of the ancient atomists. For them, the whole of matter is discontinuous, existing in indivisible units or atoms, each of which is a plenum—that is, a unit of matter absolutely continuous without void in it—but between which there is void or empty space. For Aristotle, the material world as a whole is a plenum, *i.e.*, continuous body without void. Hence if by "space" is meant not place but void—a bodyless interval between or within bodies—there is no space. Aristotle considers the arguments of Democritus that without void local motion would be impossible, but he thinks "there is no necessity for there being a void if there is movement."

Following Democritus, Lucretius gives another reason for positing void or empty space. As the indivisibility of the simple bodies or atoms consists in their absolute solidity—their lack of void—so the divisibility of composite bodies derives from their being constituted by both atoms and void. "Wherever space lies empty, which we call the void," Lucretius writes, "body is not there; moreover wherever body has its station, there is by no means empty void. Therefore the first bodies are solid and free from void. . . . If there were nothing which was empty and void, the whole would be solid; unless . . . there were bodies determined, to fill all the places that they held, the whole universe would be but empty void space."

For Aristotle, in contrast, the divisibility of matter seems to depend upon its being continuous. On his view, the composite body, constituted by atoms separated from one another by void, is not divisible, but is already actually divided; whereas the very thing which Lucretius regards as indivisible because it is continuous—the voidless atom—is for Aristotle divisible. To call an atom divisible is, of course, to deny that it is atomic or, in the language of Lucretius, an uncuttable bit of "solid singleness."

Thus diametrically opposite theories of space and place seem to be connected with opposite theories of matter or body. Space as the empty interval or void *between* solid bodies goes along with atomism, whereas place as "the boundary of the containing body at which it is in contact with the contained body" goes along with the theory of the world as a material plenum.

The atomic theory and the plenum theory are opposed in one other fundamental respect concerning space. According to Aristotle, the impossibility of an actually infinite body makes the largest place finite. According to Lucretius, the infinite number of atoms requires an infinite space. Asking whether "the void that we have discovered, or room or space . . . is altogether bounded or spreads out limitless and immeasurably deep," Lucretius answers that "the whole universe is bounded in no direction." His argument seems to be like Aristotle's for an "unbounded universe." Since there can be "nothing outside the whole sum," he writes, "it lacks therefore bound or limit." But where Aristotle's meaning seems to be that the universe has no place, since all places are inside it, Lucretius appears to mean that empty space extends infinitely in all directions.

MODERN ATOMISTS like Newton and Locke hold a theory of space which accords with the view of matter existing in discontinuous units, separated by intervals of emptiness. Newton's distinction, for example, between absolute and relative space acknowledges a space that is relative to bodies, but also affirms an absolutely independent space, which has being in separation from matter or bodies. "Absolute space, in its own nature, without relation to anything external," he writes, "remains always similar and immovable. Relative space is some movable dimension or measure of the absolute spaces, which our senses determine by its position to bodies and which is commonly taken for immovable space." As for place in distinction from space, Newton holds that it is "a part of space which a body takes up, and is according to the space, either absolute or relative." In opposing Aristotle's view, he adds that place is "not the situation, nor the external surface of the body. For the places of equal solids are always equal; but their surfaces, by reason of their dissimilar figures, are often unequal."

Locke also distinguishes between space and place, the one consisting in "the relation of distance between any two bodies or points," the other in "the relation of distance betwixt any thing and any two or more points which are considered as keeping the same distance one with another and, so considered, as at rest." With this conception of place, he holds in apparent agreement with Aristotle that "we can have no idea of the place of the universe, though we can of all the parts of it." Yet he goes on to say that what lies beyond the universe is "one uniform space or expansion, wherein the mind finds no variety or marks."

This seems to indicate that Locke's idea of space, like that of Lucretius, conceives an infinite void. "Those who assert the impossibility of space existing without matter must," he writes, "make body infinite." Furthermore, "those who dispute for or against a vacuum, do thereby confess that they have distinct ideas of vacuum and plenum, *i.e.*, that they have an idea of extension void of solidity, though they deny its existence, or else they dispute about nothing at all. For they who so much alter the signification of words, as to call extension, body, and consequently make the whole essence of body to be nothing but pure extension, must talk absurdly whenever they speak of vacuum, since it is impossible for extension to be without extension: for vacuum, whether we affirm or deny it, signifies space without body, whose very existence no one can deny to be possible who will not make matter infinite, and take from God a power to annihilate any particle of it."

Precisely because he thinks no one can affirm an infinite body, and because he conceives space to be a void, distinct from bodies, Locke finds it necessary to affirm the infinity of space. "I would ask," he says, "whether if God placed a man at the extremity of corporeal beings, he could not stretch his hand beyond his body. If he could, then he would put his arm where there was before space without body." Furthermore, if "it be impossible for any particle of matter to move but into empty space, the same possibility of a body's moving into a void space, beyond the utmost bounds of body, as well as into a void space interspersed amongst bodies, will always remain clear and evident. . . . So that, wherever the mind places itself by any thought, either amongst or remote from all bodies, it can, in this uniform idea of space, no where find any bounds, any end; and so must necessarily conclude it . . . to be actually infinite."

It may seem paradoxical that pure space—space existing without matter—is denied by one who also denies the existence of matter. "When I speak of pure or empty space," Berkeley writes, "it is not to be supposed that the word 'space' stands for an idea distinct from or conceivable without body or motion." What is meant, he suggests, is merely that the resistance one body gives to another in motion is absent when space is relatively empty. But this is always relative. "In proportion as the resistance is lesser or greater," Berkeley says, "the space is more or less *pure*." There would be absolutely pure space only if all bodies other than his own were annihilated. "If that, too, were annihilated," Berkeley concludes, "then there could be no motion, and consequently no Space."

All these contradictions concerning space enter into Kant's statement of the first cosmological antinomy, in which the thesis that the world is limited with regard to space and the antithesis that the world is infinite in space seem to be equally susceptible to proof—and so to disproof! Both alternatives violate our empirical concepts.

If space "is *infinite* and unlimited," Kant writes, "it is *too large* for every possible empirical concept. If it is *finite* and limited, you have a perfect right to ask what determines that limit. Empty space is not an independent correlate of things, and cannot be a final condition, still less an empirical condition forming part of possible experience—for how can there be experience of what is absolutely void? But in order to produce an absolute totality in an empirical synthesis, it is always requisite that the unconditioned should be an empirical concept. Thus it follows that a *limited world* would be *too small* for your concept."

Space itself, however, is for Kant "not an empirical concept which has been derived from external experience." Rather it "is a necessary representation *a priori* forming the very foundation of all external intuitions" and, as Kant explains in his *Prolegomena*, it establishes geometry as an *a priori* science. "Space is nothing but the form of all phenomena of the external senses; it is the subjective condition of our sensibility, without which no external intuition is possible for us. . . . Nothing which is seen in space is a thing by itself," nor is "space a form of things supposed to belong to them by themselves." The external objects which we perceive in space "are nothing but representations of our senses, the form of which is space."

So far as the experience of space is concerned, William James seems to take an opposite view. Time and space relations, he says, "are impressed from without" and "*stamp copies of themselves within*." To the Kantian theory that space is "a *quality produced* out of the inward resources of the mind, to envelope sensations which, as given originally, are not spatial," James replies that he can find "no introspective experience of mentally producing or creating space."

He proposes two other alternatives: "either (1) there is no spatial *quality* of sensation at all, and space is a mere symbol of succession; or (2) there is an *extensive quality given immediately* in certain particular sensations." The second seems to James best suited to explain the development of our perceptions of space, and he does not think it inconsistent with the *a priori* or non-empirical character of geometry, whose necessary truths refer to ideal objects, not to experienced things in physical space.

The chapter on Mathematics considers the relation of the postulates of diverse geometries to the diversity of Euclidean and non-Euclidean spaces, such as that of the flat plane, the surface of a sphere, and the surface of a pseudosphere. Just as different parallel postulates select different spaces for geometrical construction, so a postulate like Euclid's concerning the equality of all right angles seems to assume a uniformity of space which permits geometrical figures to be transposed without alteration. "If translation through space warped or magnified forms," James remarks, "then the relations of equality, etc., would always have to be expressed with a position-qualification added."

Confronted with a variety of purely mathematical spaces, the physicist is concerned with the problem of which geometry is, as Einstein says, in "correspondence with a 'real' object," or true of the real world. "According to the general theory of relativity, the geometrical properties of space are not independent," Einstein writes, "but are determined by matter." It follows that our assumptions about the distribution of matter determine the character of the world's space.

On the assumption of a world "not inhabited by matter everywhere," in whose infinite space "the average density of matter would necessarily be *nil*," Einstein says we can imagine "a quasi-Euclidean universe" analogous to "a surface which is irregularly curved in its individual parts, but which nowhere departs appreciably from a plane: something like the rippled surface of a lake." But if the "average density of matter . . . differs from zero, however small may be that difference, then the universe cannot be quasi-Euclidean." It would be spherical (or elliptical) if the matter were uniformly distributed; but "since in reality the detailed distribution of matter is not uniform," Einstein concludes that "the real universe will deviate in individual parts from the spherical, *i.e.*, the universe will be quasi-spherical. But it will be necessarily finite."

The nature of the actual space of the universe thus seems to be related to the issue whether physical as opposed to mathematical space is a void or filled with matter. Defining a vacuum as "a space empty of all bodies known to the senses," Pascal insists that "there is as much difference between nothingness and space, as there is between empty space and a material body," so that "empty space occupies the mean between matter and nothingness." Torricelli's experiments seem to him complete proof against the disciples of Aristotle, for they upset the belief that "nature abhors a vacuum."

Gilbert's observations on magnetic influences, Newton's observations on the transmission of light and heat as well as gravitational pull, and Faraday's on electrical phenomena, all seem to admit the possibility of action at a distance, or through a vacuum. But the question remains whether the so-called physical vacuum is an absolute void or merely empty of "all bodies known to the senses."

"Is not the heat of the warm room conveyed through the *vacuum*," Newton asks, "by the vibrations of a much subtiler medium than air which after the air was drawn out remained in the *vacuum*? And is not this medium the same with that medium by which light is refracted and reflected, and by whose vibrations light communicates heat to bodies? . . . And is not this medium exceedingly more rare and subtile than the air, and exceedingly more elastic and active? And does it not readily pervade all bodies? And is it not (by its elastic force) expanded through all the heavens?"

Huygens also refers to an ethereal matter as the medium for the propagation of light. "One will see," he writes, "that it is not the same that serves for the propagation of sound . . . It is not the same air, but another kind of matter in which light spreads; since if the air is removed from the vessel, the light does not cease to traverse it as before." But this ethereal medium, without which bodies would act at a distance upon one another—gravitationally, magnetically, electrically—through an absolute void, seems to have contrary properties. It is not only "subtiler" than air, but, as Newton suggests, it may be "denser than quick-silver or gold," since "planets and comets, and all gross bodies perform their motions more freely, and with less resistance in this aethereal medium than in any fluid, which fills all space adequately without leaving any pores." And, in still another place, he asks: "What is there in places almost empty of matter, and whence is it that the Sun and Planets gravitate towards one another, without dense matter between them?"

Whatever may be thought of the ether as a physical hypothesis, the problem still remains whether action can take place at a distance through a void or must employ what Faraday calls "*physical* lines of force" through filled space. Faraday thinks the evidences support the latter alternative for both electricity and magnetism. He quotes a letter from Newton to Bentley to show that Newton was "an unhesitating believer in physical lines of gravitating force."

In that letter, posthumously discovered, Newton says: "That gravity should be innate, inherent and essential to matter, so that one body may act upon another at a distance through a *vacuum*, without the mediation of anything else, by and through which their action and force may be conveyed from one to another, is to me so great an absurdity, that I believe no man who has in philosophical matters a competent faculty of thinking, can ever fall into it."

OUTLINE OF TOPICS

1. Space, place, and matter

 1*a*. Space or extension as the essence or property of bodies: space, the receptacle, and becoming

 1*b*. Place as the envelope or container of bodies: place as a part of space or as relative position in space

 1*c*. The tridimensionality of bodies: the indeterminate dimensions of pure space or prime matter

 1*d*. The exclusiveness of bodily occupation of space: impenetrability

2. Space, void, and motion

 2*a*. The role of space or place in local motion: the theory of proper places; absolute and relative space

 2*b*. The issue of the void or vacuum

  (1) The distinction between empty and filled space

  (2) The indispensability of void or vacuum for motion and division: the absence of void in atoms

  (3) The denial of void or vacuum in favor of a plenum

 2*c*. Space as a medium of physical action: the ether and action-at-a-distance; the phenomena of gravitation, radiation, and electricity

3. Space, quantity, and relation

 3*a*. The finitude or infinity of space: the continuity and divisibility of space

 3*b*. The relation of physical and mathematical space: sensible and ideal space

 3*c*. Geometrical space, its kinds and properties: spatial relationships and configurations

 3*d*. The measurement of spaces, distances, and sizes: trigonometry; the use of parallax

4. The knowledge of space and figures

 4*a*. Space as the divine sensorium and space as a transcendental form of intuition: the *a priori* foundations of geometry

 4*b*. The controversy concerning innate and acquired space-perception

 4*c*. The perception of space: differences between visual, auditory, and tactual space; perspective and spatial illusions

5. The mode of existence of geometrical objects: their character as abstractions; their relation to intelligible matter

6. The spiritual significance of place, position, and space

REFERENCES

References are listed by volume number (in bold type), author's name, and page number. Bible references are to book, chapter, and verse of the Authorized King James version of the Bible. The abbreviation "esp" calls the reader's attention to one or more especially relevant parts of a whole reference; "passim" signifies that the topic is discussed intermittently rather than continuously in the work or passage cited. Where the work as a whole is relevant to the topic, the page numbers refer to the entire work. For general guidance in the use of *The Great Ideas,* consult the Preface.

1. Space, place, and matter

1*a*. Space or extension as the essence or property of bodies: space, the receptacle, and becoming

7 PLATO, 455–458
8 ARISTOTLE, 288, 290–291
17 PLOTINUS, 114–115
23 HOBBES, 270–271
31 DESCARTES, 29–32, 130, 154
35 LOCKE, 150–154, 269
42 KANT, 28–33

1*b*. Place as the envelope or container of bodies: place as a part of space or as relative position in space

8 ARISTOTLE, 287–292, 366
17 PLOTINUS, 152, 260
19 AQUINAS, 35–36, 269–270, 278–280, 348–349
20 AQUINAS, 984–985
23 HOBBES, 172, 270–271
31 DESCARTES, 26
33 PASCAL, 375–376
34 NEWTON, 9, 10–11
35 LOCKE, 149–150, 163–164
53 JAMES, 139–140, 626

1*c*. The tridimensionality of bodies: the indeterminate dimensions of pure space or prime matter

7 PLATO, 455–458
8 ARISTOTLE, 359, 551
11 NICOMACHUS, 832
17 PLOTINUS, 50–57
18 AUGUSTINE, 99–100
19 AQUINAS, 343–345
20 AQUINAS, 951–953, 963–964
23 HOBBES, 269
31 DESCARTES, 93
35 LOCKE, 162–164 passim

1*d*. The exclusiveness of bodily occupation of space: impenetrability

8 ARISTOTLE, 293
20 AQUINAS, 976–983
28 GALILEO, 156–157
30 BACON, 179–180
31 DESCARTES, 78
33 PASCAL, 370
34 NEWTON, 270
35 LOCKE, 129–131, 338
45 FARADAY, 854–855

2. Space, void, and motion

2*a*. The role of space or place in local motion: the theory of proper places; absolute and relative space

7 PLATO, 460, 762
8 ARISTOTLE, 283–284, 287, 288, 290, 292, 294, 312–325 passim, 359–361, 367–369, 370, 376–377, 395–396, 399, 401–404, 541, 595–596, 635
11 NICOMACHUS, 832
12 LUCRETIUS, 17–18
16 PTOLEMY, 10–11
16 COPERNICUS, 517–518, 519–520
16 KEPLER, 931–932
17 PLOTINUS, 123–124
19 AQUINAS, 280–284
20 AQUINAS, 984–989
21 DANTE, 107
23 HOBBES, 50, 61
28 GILBERT, 110
28 GALILEO, 162, 164, 197–260
30 BACON, 163, 166, 179–180, 181
34 NEWTON, 5–24, 25–267 passim
35 LOCKE, 163–164
35 BERKELEY, 434–436
42 KANT, 29
51 TOLSTOY, 469

2*b*. The issue of the void or vacuum

2*b*(1) The distinction between empty and filled space

8 ARISTOTLE, 292–297
12 LUCRETIUS, 7
17 PLOTINUS, 152
19 AQUINAS, 250–252
20 AQUINAS, 976–978
31 SPINOZA, 361
33 PASCAL, 359–361, 363–365, 370, 373–376
35 LOCKE, 129–131, 152–154, 168
35 BERKELEY, 435–436
42 KANT, 71–72, 84

2*b*(2) The indispensability of void or vacuum for motion and division: the absence of void in atoms

8 ARISTOTLE, 292–295, 400–401, 423–424
12 LUCRETIUS, 5–6, 14
28 GALILEO, 138–141, 151–153, 156–160
31 SPINOZA, 361
33 PASCAL, 359–381, 405–415
34 NEWTON, 281, 541
35 LOCKE, 153
45 FARADAY, 850–855

2*b*(3) The denial of void or vacuum in favor of a plenum

7 PLATO, 470–471
8 ARISTOTLE, 292–297, 370, 393, 396
10 GALEN, 188–189
19 AQUINAS, 250–252
30 BACON, 187
31 SPINOZA, 361
33 PASCAL, 376, 379–380
42 KANT, 71–72
45 FARADAY, 854–855

2*c*. Space as a medium of physical action: the ether and action-at-a-distance; the phenomena of gravitation, radiation, and electricity

8 ARISTOTLE, 354, 393, 649–651
12 LUCRETIUS, 92–94
16 KEPLER, 897–905, 922
19 AQUINAS, 34–35
28 GILBERT, 26–40, 43, 45–47, 51, 54–55, 102–104
30 BACON, 167, 168–169, 176–177, 183
31 DESCARTES, 15
33 PASCAL, 366–367
34 NEWTON, 6–8, 130–131, 371–372, 516, 520–522, 525–529, 531–542 passim
34 HUYGENS, 553–560
35 BERKELEY, 432–434 passim
35 HUME, 475
42 KANT, 8, 227
45 LAVOISIER, 9
45 FARADAY, 441–442, 451–454, 463–465, 513–514, 521–524, 528–532, 648, 685–686, 816–819, 824, 840–842

3. Space, quantity, and relation

3*a*. The finitude or infinity of space: the continuity and divisibility of space

8 ARISTOTLE, 9, 370, 595–596
11 ARCHIMEDES, 520–526 passim
12 LUCRETIUS, 12–13, 16, 28
16 COPERNICUS, 516–517
16 KEPLER, 882–886
18 AUGUSTINE, 324–325
19 AQUINAS, 37–38, 250–252
20 AQUINAS, 985–989
23 HOBBES, 54
30 BACON, 110–111
31 DESCARTES, 112
33 PASCAL, 434–439
34 NEWTON, 8–11
35 LOCKE, 152–153, 160, 162–164 passim, 167–174 passim
35 BERKELEY, 436
42 KANT, 135–137, 152, 160–163
51 TOLSTOY, 693–694 passim
53 JAMES, 631

3*b*. The relation of physical and mathematical space: sensible and ideal space

8 ARISTOTLE, 296
20 AQUINAS, 978–980
31 DESCARTES, 28–33, 169–170
33 PASCAL, 373–374
34 NEWTON, 8–13
35 LOCKE, 160
35 BERKELEY, 437–438
42 KANT, 161–163, 574–575

3*c*. Geometrical space, its kinds and properties: spatial relationships and configurations

8 ARISTOTLE, 359
11 EUCLID, 1, 4, 6–7, 16–17, 18–19, 191–192
11 ARCHIMEDES, 527
11 NICOMACHUS, 832
16 KEPLER, 865
17 PLOTINUS, 287–289
19 AQUINAS, 460–461
31 DESCARTES, 28–33, 52–53, 228–229
35 LOCKE, 149
35 BERKELEY, 437–439
42 KANT, 24–26
52 DOSTOEVSKY, 121
53 JAMES, 550–551, 876–878

3*d*. The measurement of spaces, distances, and sizes: trigonometry; the use of parallax

16 PTOLEMY, 165–176, 270
16 COPERNICUS, 521–529, 705–714
16 KEPLER, 861–863, 868–887, 1016–1018
30 BACON, 170
31 DESCARTES, 31–33
34 NEWTON, 333–337
53 JAMES, 551–673

4. The knowledge of space and figures

4*a*. Space as the divine sensorium and space as a transcendental form of intuition: the *a priori* foundations of geometry

34 NEWTON, 370–371, 529, 542–543
42 KANT, 23–26, 31, 55–56, 68–69, 86, 87, 94–95, 99–101, 110, 131, 135, 153–155, 211–218, 312–313, 551–553
53 JAMES, 629–631, 876–878

4*b*. The controversy concerning innate and acquired space-perception

42 KANT, 23–24, 25–26, 307–308
53 JAMES, 474–475, 627–635, 860–861

4c. The perception of space: differences between visual, auditory, and tactual space; perspective and spatial illusions

8 ARISTOTLE, 683, 694
12 LUCRETIUS, 19, 47–50
17 PLOTINUS, 64–65
35 LOCKE, 149
35 BERKELEY, 420–421
53 JAMES, 318, 400, 406, 410, 471–479 esp 474–477, 540–635

5. The mode of existence of geometrical objects: their character as abstractions; their relation to intelligible matter

7 PLATO, 387, 394, 809–810
8 ARISTOTLE, 111, 197, 270, 390, 516, 520–521, 559, 560, 589, 607–610, 616–618, 622–623 passim
11 NICOMACHUS, 811–812
19 AQUINAS, 25, 49, 238–239
20 AQUINAS, 978–980
31 DESCARTES, 28–33, 76, 93, 96, 169–170, 217–218
35 LOCKE, 324–325
35 BERKELEY, 408–409, 415–416, 438
35 HUME, 458, 505, 506–507
42 KANT, 16, 17–18, 35–36, 46, 62, 87, 91
53 JAMES, 876–878, 880–881

6. The spiritual significance of place, position, and space

8 ARISTOTLE, 361, 375–376, 384–385
16 COPERNICUS, 526–528
16 KEPLER, 853–854, 857–860, 1080–1085
18 AUGUSTINE, 49–50
19 AQUINAS, 14–15, 316–317, 523–527
21 DANTE, 12, 57–58, 84–85, 111, 148–150, 151–156
32 MILTON, 129–133, 234–235
33 PASCAL, 211
42 KANT, 360–361
54 FREUD, 562

CROSS-REFERENCES

For: Other discussions of the theory of the receptacle, *see* FORM 1d(1); MATTER 1; WORLD 4b.

Other discussions of extension as a property of bodies, *see* BEING 7b(4); FORM 2d; MATTER 2a.

Other discussions of the doctrine of prime matter, *see* BEING 7c(3); CHANGE 2a; FORM 2c(3); INFINITY 4c; MATTER 1a.

The role of space or place in local motion, *see* CHANGE 7a; RELATION 6a.

Discussions bearing on the measurement of space, *see* MATHEMATICS 5a; MECHANICS 3a; QUANTITY 6b–6c.

Matters relevant to space as a transcendental form of intuition and to the related problem of the foundations of geometry, *see* FORM 1c; MATHEMATICS 1c; MEMORY AND IMAGINATION 6c(2); MIND 1e(1), 4d(3); TIME 6c; and for other discussions bearing on space-perception, *see* QUALITY 2b; SENSE 3c(3).

The problem of the mode of being which is possessed by the objects of geometry, *see* BEING 7d(3); IDEA 2g; MATHEMATICS 2a–2b; MATTER 1c.

The issue concerning a void or vacuum, and for the related problem of action-at-a-distance, *see* ASTRONOMY 3b; CHANGE 7a; ELEMENT 5c; MECHANICS 5d, 6d(2).

Other considerations of the infinity or continuity of space, *see* INFINITY 3d; MATHEMATICS 2c; ONE AND MANY 3a(4); QUANTITY 2, 5a; and for discussions of astronomical space and the size of the universe, *see* ASTRONOMY 5, 9e; WORLD 6a, 7.

The analysis of geometrical space, spatial relationships and configurations, *see* QUALITY 3b; QUANTITY 3–3e(2).

The relation of spiritual being or action to place or space, *see* ANGEL 3f; ASTRONOMY 6; GOD 7g; IMMORTALITY 5g; SOUL 3e, 4d(3).

ADDITIONAL READINGS

Listed below are works not included in *Great Books of the Western World*, but relevant to the idea and topics with which this chapter deals. These works are divided into two groups:

I. Works by authors represented in this collection.
II. Works by authors not represented in this collection.

For the date, place, and other facts concerning the publication of the works cited, consult the Bibliography of Additional Readings which follows the last chapter of *The Great Ideas*.

I.

DESCARTES. *The Principles of Philosophy*, PART II, 4–19, 21
HOBBES. *Concerning Body*, PART II, CH 7
HUME. *A Treatise of Human Nature*, BK I, PART II
BERKELEY. *An Essay Towards a New Theory of Vision*
——. *Siris*
KANT. *On the First Grounds of the Distinction of Regions in Space*
——. *De Mundi Sensibilis* (*Inaugural Dissertation*)
——. *Metaphysical Foundations of Natural Science*
W. JAMES. *Collected Essays and Reviews*, XXI

II.

SEXTUS EMPIRICUS. *Against the Physicists*, BK II, CH I
——. *Outlines of Pyrrhonism*, BK III, CH 1–20
SUÁREZ. *Disputationes Metaphysicae*, XXX (7), XXXIX, XL (7), LI–LIII
LEIBNITZ. *New Essays Concerning Human Understanding*, BK II, CH 13
——. *Correspondence with Clarke*
D'ALEMBERT. *Traité de dynamique*
VOLTAIRE. "Space," in *A Philosophical Dictionary*
WHEWELL. *The Philosophy of the Inductive Sciences*, VOL I, BK II, CH 2–6
RIEMANN. *Über die Hypothesen welche der Geometrie zu Grunde liegen* (*The Hypotheses of Geometry*)
HODGSON. *Time and Space*
HELMHOLTZ. *Popular Lectures on Scientific Subjects*, II
CLIFFORD. *The Common Sense of the Exact Sciences*, CH 2, 4
LOTZE. *Metaphysics*, BK II, CH 1–2; BK III, CH 4
STALLO. *Concepts and Theories of Modern Physics*, CH 13–15
BRADLEY. *Appearance and Reality*, BK I, CH 4; BK II, CH 18
HILBERT. *The Foundations of Geometry*
MACH. *Space and Geometry in the Light of Physiological, Psychological and Physical Inquiry*
POINCARÉ. *Science and Hypothesis*, PART II
——. *The Value of Science*, PART I, CH 3–4
——. *Science and Method*, BK II, CH I
CASSIRER. *Substance and Function*, PART I, CH 3; SUP IV–V
J. W. YOUNG. *Lectures on Fundamental Concepts of Algebra and Geometry*, LECT XVI–XVII
ROBB. *A Theory of Time and Space*
WEYL. *Space—Time—Matter*
S. ALEXANDER. *Space, Time, and Deity*
EDDINGTON. *Space, Time, and Gravitation*
WHITEHEAD. *The Organization of Thought*, CH 8
——. *An Enquiry Concerning the Principles of Natural Knowledge*, CH 14
——. *The Concept of Nature*, CH 5–6
BERGSON. *Time and Free Will*
——. *Durée et simultanéité, à propos de la théorie d'Einstein*, CH 6
EINSTEIN. *Relativity: The Special and the General Theory*
——. *Sidelights on Relativity*
——. *The Meaning of Relativity*
G. N. LEWIS. *The Anatomy of Science*, ESSAY II
SANTAYANA. *The Realm of Matter*, CH 4
LENZEN. *The Nature of Physical Theory*, PART II, CH 11
BORING. *The Physical Dimensions of Consciousness*, CH 4
B. RUSSELL. *An Essay on the Foundations of Geometry*
——. *Principles of Mathematics*, CH 44–52
——. *The Analysis of Matter*, CH 28–29, 32, 36
——. *Human Knowledge, Its Scope and Limits*, PART III, CH 6; PART IV, CH 6–7

Chapter 90: STATE

INTRODUCTION

IS man gregarious in the same sense as other animals are? Is he, unlike other social animals, the only political animal? Does man pattern the state after his own nature, or does he, in imitation of the angels, try to live up to a "city in the skies"—a model of rationality or a utopian illusion? According to the way such questions are answered, different theories of the state develop in the tradition of western thought.

But it is not only the view man takes of his social nature which affects his view of society or the state. His conception of the state is also colored by his understanding of man's place in nature and by his understanding of man's relation to God. On one view the state is ordered to the service of man; on another, man is thought to be a creature of the state, and the state is made God; on still another, man—like Antigone in Sophocles' play—seems to be torn between serving the state and serving God.

If man admits anything to be his superior, he acknowledges his inferiority only to God or to the state. That the idea of God and the idea of the state compete for maximum attention in the tradition of western thought is a significant and readily intelligible fact. That the word "sovereign," which connotes *absolute supremacy*, has both political and religious significance throws further light on this rivalry. It immediately suggests all the issues of church and state, of the spiritual and the temporal power, of the city of God and the city of man.

Even without the aura of divinity, the state, in the conception of many writers, assumes by comparison with the individual man the proportions of the greatest living thing on earth. For Plato it is the counterpart of the human soul, many times magnified. For Aristotle it is like an organic whole to which the individual belongs, just as his own arm or leg belongs to him as an organic part. For Hobbes it is the body politic—that Leviathan which dwarfs its members. For Rousseau it is the corporate person, having a general will more perfect than the individual will—infallible, or almost infallible. When to these images of the state is added the highest transfiguration—that by which the state becomes, according to Hegel, the image of God on earth or the embodiment of Absolute Spirit—the greatness of the state cannot be magnified further.

THE PASSAGES IN WHICH these conceptions first appear are among the most famous in the literature of the theory of the state. In the *Republic*, Socrates proposes that "we inquire into the nature of justice and injustice, first as they appear in the State and secondly in the individual, proceeding from the greater to the lesser and comparing them." After the structure of the state has been examined in terms of its constituent classes and their functions or relations to one another, Socrates returns to the individual. We may assume, he says, that "he has the same three principles in his own soul which are found in the state"; and in another place he adds that "there appear to be as many forms of the soul as there are distinct forms of the State."

Whereas Plato analogizes the social classes in the state with the parts of the soul, Aristotle compares the state in relation to the individual with the body in relation to its members. "The state is by nature clearly prior to the family and to the individual," Aristotle writes, "since the whole is of necessity prior to the part; for example, if the whole body be destroyed, there will be no foot or hand, except in an equivocal sense. . . . The proof that the state is a creation of nature and prior to the individual is that the individual, when isolated, is not self-sufficing;

and therefore he is like a part in relation to the whole."

The analogical conception of the state takes a different turn with Hobbes. The state is a work of art, not a creation of nature. "Nature (the Art whereby God hath made and governs the world)," says Hobbes, "is by the Art of man, as in many other things, so in this also, imitated that it can make an Artificial Animal." The machines men make—"engines that move themselves by springs and wheels as doth a watch"—seem to Hobbes to "have an artificial life." But "Art goes yet further, imitating that Rational and most excellent work of Nature, Man. For by Art is created that great Leviathan called a Commonwealth or State (in Latin *Civitas*) which is but an Artificial Man; though of greater stature and strength than the Natural, for whose protection and defense it was intended; and in which the Sovereignty is an Artificial Soul, as giving life and motion to the whole body."

Hobbes also speaks of the multitude being "united in one Person" as the "generation of that great Leviathan, or rather (to speak more reverently) of that Mortal God, to which we owe under the Immortal God, our peace and defence." It is both divine and human, for "that which is compounded of the powers of most men, united by consent in one person, natural or civil" is, according to Hobbes, "the greatest of human powers."

Rousseau has a number of different names for the "moral and collective body" formed by the association of individuals. "This public person," he says, "formerly took the name *city*, and now takes that of *Republic* or *body politic*; it is called by its members *State* when passive, *Sovereign* when active, and *Power* when compared with others like itself." But Rousseau's primary emphasis seems to be upon the personality of the State; it is a corporate person, with moral qualities and intellectual faculties. He refers repeatedly to the State "as a *persona ficta*" and as "a moral person whose life is in the union of its members."

Many of these comparisons or analogies recur in Hegel's theory of the state. But for Hegel they are no longer metaphors, they are the elements of a literal definition. "The state is an organism," says Hegel. It is the organic whole no part of which can have a separate life. As "occurs with life in the physical organism," he writes, "life is present in every cell" and "separated from that life, every cell dies. This is the same as the ideality of every single class, power, and Corporation as soon as they have the impulse to subsist and be independent. It is with them as with the belly in the organism. It, too, asserts its independence, but at the same time its independence is set aside and it is sacrificed and absorbed into the whole."

But the state is not merely a living organism. "To the mature state," says Hegel, "thought and consciousness essentially belong. . . . As high as mind stands above nature, so high does the state stand above physical life. Man must therefore venerate the state as the divine on earth, and observe that if it is difficult to comprehend nature, it is infinitely harder to understand the state." In saying this Hegel seems to go beyond analogy to the assertion of a definition. "The march of God in the world, that is what the state is," he declares. "The basis of the state is the power of the reason actualizing itself as will. In considering the Idea of the state, we must not have our eyes on particular states or on particular institutions. Instead we must consider the Idea, this actual God, by itself."

To those who object that the state is finite, Hegel replies that "to hold that mind on earth, *i.e.*, the state, is only a finite mind, is a one-sided view, since there is nothing irrational about actuality. Of course, a bad state is worldly and finite and nothing else. But the rational state is inherently infinite." As simply stated by Hegel in the Introduction to his *Philosophy of History*, "the State is the Divine idea as it exists on Earth."

The diverse conceptions of the state raise major issues in political theory concerning the origin of the state and the ends it serves, in both of which is involved the problem of the individual's relation to the state. That problem is touched on in the chapter on Citizen, and wherever the problem of the common good or the general welfare is discussed. Here the question whether the state is made for man or man for the state, whether the state subordinates the individual in every phase of his life or only in those matters wherein the public welfare takes precedence over private interests, serves critically to test the practical significance of different theories of the state. Here also questions concerning the relation of the family to the state—discussed from the point of view of the domestic community in the chapter on FAMILY—throw light on the nature and origin of the political community.

The word "community" and its synonym "society" seem to be more inclusive in meaning than "state." The family and the state are both communities—associations of individuals for a common purpose and sharing in a common life. The word "state" is customarily used only for the developed political society—whether a city-state, a feudal state, or a nation-state; the word "society" usually covers the tribal community, the village, or any community which is politically primitive and has some of the characteristics of a large family. In addition there are within the state, at least in its modern formation, many organized groups which deserve the name "society"—economic corporations and other associations, religious, educational, professional, recreational; and more comprehensive than any particular political community are the cities of God and man which, in Augustine's conception of them, are not to be identified with either the Church or the State.

With the rise of the science of sociology in our time, the idea of society has come to be regarded as more general than that of state. But in the tradition of the great books, particularly those of political theory, the state seems to be considered the epitome of human society. All other forms of association are, for the most part, discussed only in their relation to the state, either as the antecedents from which the state develops, or as the subordinate organizations which it includes, or sometimes, as in the case of the church, a distinct but coordinate community.

The nature of society in general and the problem of different types of social organization and development are not treated in the great books except in their bearing on the family, the church, or the state—the three communities which seem to be taken as representative or basic. Hence there is no chapter on society or community as such. What for modern sociology is a unified subject matter here divides into a number of related yet distinct ideas—the domestic community being treated in the chapter on FAMILY, the religious community in the chapter on RELIGION, the various forms of economic organization in the chapters on LABOR and WEALTH. In this chapter, therefore, we shall confine our attention to the specifically political community, both in itself and in relation to these other communities or social groups.

CONCEIVED IN POLITICAL terms, the problems of the state would seem to be inseparable from the problems of government. Yet the ideas of state and government may be separated to the extent that one signifies the political community as a whole and the other the organization of its members according to relationships of ruler and ruled. Furthermore, the state may in one sense remain the same while in another it changes with changes in its form of government.

Some writers, like Aristotle and Hegel, tend to identify state and government. Aristotle, for example, says that "the sameness of the state consists chiefly in the sameness of its constitution." Others, like Locke and Rousseau, seem to regard government as part of the state, the chief institution of a civil society or political community, but definitely a means for securing the ends for which the state is formed. For Locke government is primarily the legislative power, for Rousseau it is "the supreme administration, the legitimate exercise of the executive power," but for both it is a representative body—an organ of the whole body politic.

Insofar as the great political theorists distinguish problems of the external relation of states with one another from those which concern the internal organization of the state, and the relation of the state to its own members, they also tend to distinguish state from government. Hegel's distinction between external and internal sovereignty, for example, conceives the whole community as a sovereign state in relation to other communities and the state as a sovereign government in relation to its own members.

Such questions of sovereignty, or more generally of the relation of states to one another, belong to this chapter as well as to the chapter on WAR AND PEACE; but the theory of government is for the most part treated elsewhere—in the chapters on GOVERNMENT and CONSTITUTION, and in all the chapters dealing with the special forms of government. Still other problems of government, which have a bearing on the nature of the state, its powers, and its limits, are dealt with in the chapters on JUSTICE and LAW.

THAT IT IS SOMEHOW natural for men to associate politically is generally affirmed, even by those who also think the state is artificial or conventional. No one takes either of the possible extreme positions: that the state as a purely voluntary association is without any basis at all in man's nature and needs; or that the state, like the bee hive and the ant mound, is purely a production of instinct.

Saying that "man is by nature a political animal," Aristotle goes on to remark that "man is more of a political animal than bees or other gregarious animals." But the difference Aristotle points out between man and other social animals may make man the *only* political animal. It consists in the fact that man, being "the only animal . . . endowed with the gift of speech," can communicate with his fellows concerning "the expedient and inexpedient, and therefore likewise the just and the unjust." What characterizes human associations, according to Aristotle, is that they are built upon a shared sense of the expedient and the just. "Justice," he writes, "is the bond of men in states."

Hobbes also distinguishes between human and animal societies, but seems to interpret the distinction differently "Bees and ants live sociably one with another," he says, "and yet have no other direction than their particular judgments and appetites; nor speech, whereby one of them can signify to another what he thinks expedient for the common benefit." Inquiring "why mankind cannot do the same"—that is, live sociably without government and law—Hobbes offers a number of explanations, of which the last is that "the agreement of these creatures is natural; that of men is by covenant only, which is artificial; and therefore it is no wonder if there be somewhat else required (besides covenant) to make their agreement constant and lasting, which is common power to keep them in awe and to direct their actions to the common benefit."

But though Hobbes calls the state artificial because he holds it to be the product of a contract, he does not deny the natural necessity which drives men to the creation of a commonwealth. Man quits the state of nature, which is a "war of every man against every man," to achieve self-preservation, or at least to enjoy the security of civil peace and the freedom from fear of violence.

As natural as it may be for men to be "in that condition which is called war" when "they live without a common power to keep them all in awe," it is equally natural, according to Hobbes, for men to seek peace. "The passions that incline men to peace are fear of death, desire of such things as are necessary to commodious living; and a hope by their industry to obtain them. And reason suggesteth convenient articles of peace, upon which men may be drawn to agreement." The commonwealth is therefore natural, to the extent that man's needs and passions require it and man's reason recognizes certain natural laws for constructing it.

The state is naturally necessary, not as the effect of instinctive determinations, but as the rationally determined means to an end. If the end the state serves were not naturally sought, or if there were any other means which reason could devise for accomplishing that end, the state would be purely conventional—and dispensable. "The final cause, end, or design of men in the introduction of that restraint upon themselves (in which we see them live in commonwealths) is," according to Hobbes, "the sight of their own preservation and of a more contented life thereby."

In this main particular Aristotle's account of the origin of the state seems to be the same. Though he does not attribute its formation to a contract, and does not make fear the predominant motive, he does regard the state as natural *only because* of its indispensability as a means for achieving the ends men naturally seek. The family is natural, Aristotle suggests, because it is necessary for the perpetuation of the race and "for the supply of men's everyday wants." When men aim "at something more than the supply of daily needs, the first society to be formed is the village"—normally, an association of families. And "when several villages are united in a single complete community, large enough to be nearly or quite self-sufficing, the state comes into existence, originating in the bare needs of life, and continuing in existence for the sake of a good life. Therefore, if the earlier forms of society are natural, so is the state."

The implication seems to be that if men were not naturally impelled to seek a better life than the family or the tribal community can provide —in other words, if the family or village satisfied all of man's natural needs for society—the larger community, the state, would be neither natural nor necessary. That man is by nature a political animal does not, therefore, mean that men have always and everywhere lived in states.

Aristotle refers to the man who lives apart from society, describing the natural outcast— "the 'tribeless, lawless, heartless one' whom Homer denounces"—as "a lover of war." He conceives the state as coming into being subsequent to more primitive forms of social life, each type of community being successively "established with a view to some good, for mankind always act in order to obtain that which they think good." Since he thinks that the state "aims at good in a greater degree than any other, and at the highest good," he praises the man "who first founded the state" as "the greatest of benefactors."

FOR ARISTOTLE, THEN, there seems to be no inconsistency in saying that the state is as natural as the family and also that it is the result of a convention, *i.e.*, a voluntary association of men. Nor does there seem to be any inconsistency between Hobbes' view that the state is produced by a "covenant of every man with every man" and his understanding of the naturalness of the state in terms of the impulses which lead men to enter into this contract. The same double note appears in the account of the state's origin which Locke, Rousseau, and Kant give. The issue raised by the contract theory thus seems to turn on the interpretation of the original convention—whether or not it has legal significance and what obligations or limitations it imposes.

Where Hobbes, for example, interprets the contract as creating, along with the commonwealth, a sovereign person having absolute power, Locke seems to make majority rule the legal consequence of the original compact. God "designed man for a sociable creature," according to Locke, "with an inclination and under a necessity to have fellowship with those of his own kind." Yet even what he calls "the first society . . . between man and wife," Locke says, "is made by a voluntary compact." It makes no difference to Locke's theory whether political societies develop by expansion from the family (which he takes to be the normal course of events) or result from a voluntary association of independent men.

In either case, political as distinguished from domestic society does not begin until "every man, by consenting with others to make one body politic under one government, puts himself under an obligation to every one of that society, to submit to the determination of the majority. . . . This is done by barely agreeing to unite into one political society, which is all the compact that is, or needs be, between the individuals that enter into or make up a commonwealth. And thus that which begins and actually constitutes any political society is nothing but the consent of any number of free men capable of a majority to unite and incorporate into such a society."

If it is "that, and that only, which did or could give beginning to any lawful government in the world," it seems to be equally evident to Locke that "absolute monarchy, which by some men is counted the only government in the world, is indeed inconsistent with civil society, and so can be no form of civil government at all."

Though Rousseau says that the most ancient of all societies, the family, is "the only one that is natural," he qualifies this by adding that it remains natural only so long as the children need the family for their preservation. If the members of the family remain united thereafter, "they continue so no longer naturally, but voluntarily; and the family itself is then maintained only by convention." By the same criterion, civil society would seem to be natural, at least on Rousseau's own supposition that "the obstacles in the way of their preservation in the state of nature" are greater than the power of isolated individuals or families to maintain themselves, and so "the human race would perish unless it changed its manner of existence."

Rousseau, furthermore, explicitly denies that the transition from a state of nature to a state of civil society can be treated as an historical fact. It is an hypothesis "calculated to explain the nature of things, [rather] than to ascertain their actual origin." The social contract, which Rousseau sometimes calls the "first convention," is, therefore, the legal, not the historical, origin of the state. As he formulates the compact, "each of us puts his person and all his power in common under the supreme direction of the general will, and, in our corporate capacity, we receive each member as an indivisible part of the whole."

Though "all the qualities of the general will" may "reside in the majority," so that the general will can be discovered by a majority vote, unanimity is required to create the sovereign body politic, with the right as well as the power to compel "whoever refuses to obey the general will." Rousseau points out that "the law of majority voting is itself something established by convention, and presupposes unanimity, on one occasion at least." To this extent Rousseau agrees with Locke about the juridical significance of the original convention or the universal consent which establishes a civil society; and just as Locke calls absolute monarchy inconsistent with the very nature of the state, so Rousseau uses the words "republic" and "body politic" interchangeably. "To be legitimate," he writes, "the government must be, not one with the sovereign, but its minister."

But Rousseau identifies government with the executive, rather than primarily with the legislative as Locke does. He therefore denies that the original convention institutes government as well as the body politic itself—"the Sovereign having no force other than the legislative power." In consequence, Rousseau and Locke differ somewhat in their discussion of the dissolution of government as distinguished from the dissolution of society, or the death of the body politic. Rousseau regards no law as irrevocable, "not excluding the social compact itself; for if all the citizens assembled of one accord to break the compact, it is impossible to doubt that it would be very legitimately broken."

According to Kant, "a state is the union of a number of men under juridical laws"—the opposite of the state of nature, "in which there is no distributive justice." It is incumbent on men, says Kant, "to accept the principle that it is necessary to leave the state of nature, in which every one follows his own inclinations, and to form a union of all those who cannot avoid coming into reciprocal communication, and thus subject themselves in common to the external restraint of public compulsory laws."

Kant refers to this principle as the "postulate of public right" which obliges "all men to enter into the relations of a civil state of society." The state thus seems to be both necessary and voluntary; for though he says that "the act by which a people is represented as constituting itself into a state is termed *the original contract*," yet he also adds that "this is properly only an outward mode of representing the idea by which the rightfulness of the process of organizing the constitution may be made conceivable."

Against all these notions of the original contract, Hegel, criticizing Kant's treatment of marriage under the concept of contract, says that "it is equally far from the truth to ground the nature of the state on the contractual relation, whether the state is supposed to be a contract of all with all, or of all with the monarch and the government." Contract, according to Hegel, belongs to the sphere of "relationships concerning private property generally." Hence "the intrusion of this contractual relation . . . into the relation between the individual and the state has been productive of the greatest confusion in both constitutional law and public life."

A contract, Hegel explains, "springs from a person's arbitrary will, an origin which marriage too has in common with contract. But the case is quite different with the state; it does not lie with an individual's arbitrary will to separate himself from the state, because we are already citizens of the state by birth. The rational end of man is life in the state, and if there is no state there, reason at once demands that one be founded. Permission to enter a state or leave it must be given by the state; this then is not a matter which depends on an individual's arbitrary will and therefore the state does not rest on contract, for contract presupposes arbitrariness. It is false to maintain that the foundation of the state is something at the option of all its members. It is nearer the truth to say that it is absolutely necessary for every individual to be a citizen."

Hegel dismisses all questions concerning historical origins in general or particular as "no concern of the Idea of the state." In the Idea itself, its antecedents are to be found. The family and civil society are the earlier—logical—moments in the development of the Idea of the State. "Civil society," Hegel writes, "is the [state of] difference which intervenes between the family and the state, even if its formation follows later in time than that of the state." The social contract theory applies only to what he calls "civil society," by which he means the modern conception of the state "as a unity which is only a partnership. . . . Many modern constitutional lawyers," Hegel goes on, "have been able to bring within their purview no theory of the state but this. In civil society each member is his own end" and, "except by contract with others, he cannot attain the whole compass of his ends, and therefore these others are means to the end of the particular members."

In another place, Hegel describes civil society as a system of complete interdependence for the attainment of selfish ends, "wherein the livelihood, happiness, and legal status of one man is interwoven with the livelihood, happiness, and rights of all." In still another, he observes that only when the state is confused with civil society, only when "its specific end is laid down as the security and protection of property and personal freedom," does "the interest of the individuals as such become the ultimate end of their association." Whence "it follows that membership in the state is something optional. But the state's relation to the individual is quite different from this. Since the state is mind objectified, it is only as one of its members that the individual himself has objectivity, genuine individuality, and an ethical life."

The unity of the state, unlike that of civil society, is, according to Hegel, "an absolute unmoved end in itself, in which freedom comes into its supreme right. . . . This final end has supreme right against the individual, whose supreme duty is to be a member of the state."

IT DOES NOT SEEM to be an inevitable corollary of the social contract theory that the state be conceived as serving the private interests of individuals. "The welfare of the state," Kant declares, "is its own highest good." It is not to be understood merely as "the individual *well-being* and *happiness* of the citizens of the state; for—as Rousseau asserts—this end may perhaps be more agreeably and more desirably attained in the state of nature." Kant and Locke both affirm a social contract, but where Kant makes the safety of the republic itself the highest law (*salus reipublicae suprema lex*), Locke makes it the security of the people (*salus populi*).

"The reason why men enter into society is the preservation of their property," writes Locke. The property of the individual is insecure in a state of nature; to avoid this insecurity "men unite into societies that they may have the united strength of the whole society to secure and defend their properties." When Locke says that the chief end of civil society is "the preservation of property," he does not refer solely to economic goods, but to all the goods to which he thinks man has a natural right—"his life, liberty, and estate." Men would not quit the state of nature, he writes, "were it not to preserve their lives, liberties and fortunes, and by stated rules of right and property to secure their peace and quiet."

In the light of Locke's conception of "property," his position resembles Hobbes' statement of the end which men seek in forming a commonwealth: "to live peaceably amongst themselves and be protected against other men" and to get "themselves out from that miserable condition of war" in which life is "solitary, poor, nasty, brutish, and short."

It seems to be in a different sense of property that Rousseau holds that "the foundation of the social compact is property; and its first condition, that everyone should be maintained in the peaceful possession of what belongs to him." Restricting "property" to economic possessions, Rousseau asks, "Are not all the advantages of society for the rich and powerful?" Society, he observes, "provides a powerful protection for the immense possessions of the rich, and hardly leaves the poor man in quiet possession of the cottage he builds with his own hands."

This and Adam Smith's statement that "civil government, so far as it is instituted for the security of property, is in reality instituted for the defence of the rich against the poor, or of those who have some property against those who have none at all," seem to anticipate the Marxist view of the state as the bulwark of property rights and an instrument of class oppression. If the protection of property and the maintenance of economic inequalities is the sole purpose of the state, then the ultimate resolution of the class war in favor of a classless society will, in the opinion of Marx and Engels, be accompanied by what they call "the withering away of the state"—an atrophy from loss of function.

But even in a classless society, the state would not cease to function if its end were to secure not merely the individual's wealth, but his whole well-being. Then, however, we must face another question—whether the happiness of the individual is the end of the state. Plato, for example, seems to answer this question in opposite ways.

In the *Protagoras*, it is said that "the desire for self-preservation gathered men into cities." This is part of the Promethean legend of the origin of civilization. As told by Aeschylus—and in a similar account of early history by Lucretius—the story intimates that men contract to live together for protection against violence and to enjoy a better life—the fruits of civil society or civilization.

But in the *Republic*, Socrates says that, in constructing the ideal state, the aim is "not the disproportionate happiness of any one class, but the greatest happiness of the whole." To the objection of Adeimantus that the citizens may be miserable in such a state, Socrates replies that we must consider whether "we would look to their greatest happiness individually, or whether this principle of happiness does not rather reside in the State as a whole." Later Socrates reminds Glaucon, who wonders whether the members of the guardian (or ruling) class will not be unhappy, that we are "fashioning the State with a view to the greatest happiness, not of any particular class, but of the whole."

Aristotle criticizes Socrates for depriving even the guardians of happiness and for saying that "the legislator ought to make the whole state happy." In his own view, "the whole cannot be happy unless most, or all, or some of its parts enjoy happiness. In this respect, happiness is not like the even principle in numbers, which may exist only in the whole, but in neither of the parts." When Aristotle asserts that "the state exists for the sake of a good life," he seems to have the happiness of individuals in mind, for he excludes slaves and brute animals from membership in the state on the ground that they can have "no share in happiness or in a life of free choice."

But Aristotle also seems to give the state preeminence over the individual. "Even if the end is the same for a single man and for a state," he writes, "that of the state seems at all events something greater and more complete, whether to attain or to preserve." This does not seem to him inconsistent with thinking that that "form of government is best in which every man, whoever he is, can act best and live happily."

Nor is Hegel reluctant to embrace both horns of the dilemma. Civil society rather than the state in its perfect realization seems to be devoted to the "attainment of selfish ends," such as individual happiness. But Hegel also says it is "perfectly true" that "the end of the state is the happiness of the citizens. . . . If all is not well with them, if their subjective aims are not satisfied, if they do not find that the state as such is the means to their satisfaction, then the footing of the state is itself insecure."

THE FOREGOING CONSIDERATIONS of the nature, origin, and end of political society enter into the various conceptions of the ideal state which appear in the tradition of western thought. They also have a bearing on the division of social classes in the state, on the duties of the statesman or prince, and the principles of statecraft—the art or science of the ruler. Finally, they have implications for the relation of states to one another and for the different historic formations of the state.

All the modern writers who make some distinction between the state of nature and the state of civil society seem to agree that independent or sovereign states in their relation to one another are in a state of nature. Identifying the state of nature with the state of war, Hobbes remarks that "though there had never been any time, wherein particular men were in a condition of war one against another, yet in all times, kings and persons of sovereign authority" are "in the state and posture of gladiators . . . which is the posture of war."

Similarly, to the question, "Where are or ever were there any men in a state of nature?" Locke replies, "all princes and rulers of independent governments all through the world are in a state of nature." Because "bodies politic" remain "in a state of nature among themselves," they experience, according to Rousseau, "all the inconveniences which had obliged individuals to forsake it." With the same intent, Montesquieu observes that "princes who live not among themselves under civil law are not free; they are governed by force; they may continually force or be forced."

In Kant's opinion, "states, viewed as nations in their external relations to one another—like lawless savages—are naturally in a non-juridical condition," and he adds that "this natural condition is a state of war." Similarly, Hegel writes that "since the sovereignty of a state is the principle of its relations to others, states are to that extent in a state of nature in relation to each other."

On any of the theories concerning the origin of the state, it may be asked why political society cannot be enlarged to include all mankind. If, for example, in Aristotle's view, the state is a union of villages, as the village is a union of families, why may not a further expansion of political society be brought about by a union of states?

The question is not simply one of geographical limits or extent of population. The modern national state, though normally larger than the ancient city-state, remains an individual state and in the same external relationship to other states. Even the expansion of a city-state like Rome, at the greatest extent of its imperial domain, does not exemplify the principle of the world-state unless it is proposed that the political unification of mankind be brought about by conquest and maintained by despotism.

Though Aristotle describes the state as formed by a combination of villages, he does not propose a combination of states to form a larger community. His reason may be that the essence of the state lies in its self-sufficiency. Consequently, "the best limit of the population of a state is the largest number which suffices for the purposes of life, and can be taken in at a single view"; and the territory need be no larger than one which enables the population to be "most entirely self-sufficing."

The moderns, in contrast, propose the expansion of the political community by the amalgamation of separate political units. Montesquieu, for example, suggests that by entering into a "confederate republic," a number of small states can obtain the security which none of them has by itself. "If a republic be small," he writes, "it is destroyed by a foreign force; if it be large, it is ruined by an internal imperfection." A confederate republic, he thinks, "has all the internal advantages of a republican, together with the external force of a monarchical, government. . . . This form of government," Montesquieu continues, "is a convention by which several petty states agree to become members of a larger one, which they intend to establish. It is a kind of assemblage of societies, that constitute a new one, capable of increasing by means of further associations, till they arrive at such a degree of power as to be able to provide for the security of the whole body."

It is not security against external aggression, but internal peace, which leads Rousseau to propose an association more extensive than anything Montesquieu seems to have in mind—a confederation of *all* the states of Europe. But he does not see beyond Europe to all the states of the world. He regards "the great city of the world" as something less than a political society with civil laws, for he speaks of it as "the body politic whose general will is always the law of nature."

Nor are the American Federalists, Hamilton, Madison, and Jay, able, at the end of the 18th century, to envisage the unlimited extension of the principle of federal union. They content themselves with arguing for the possibility of so extensive a union as the projected United States of America, against those who quoted "the observations of Montesquieu on the necessity of a contracted territory for a Republican Government."

Before our own day Kant alone seems to contemplate the possibility of a world state *through federal union*. The "cosmopolitical ideal," he says, is "a universal union of states analogous to that by which a nation becomes a state." The postulate of reason which obliges men to quit the state of nature and form a civil union applies to states as well. "The natural state of nations, as well as of individual men," Kant writes, "is a state which it is a duty to pass out of, in order to enter into a legal state." But the ideal is impracticable in Kant's opinion—again because of the supposed limits of government with respect to extended territories and populations.

"With the too great extension of such a union of states over vast regions, any government of it, and consequently the protection of its individual members, must at last become impossible." Kant therefore proposes as an alternative a "permanent congress of nations," but one which, being "a voluntary combination of states . . . would be dissolvable at any time"—a mere league or confederacy, and not such a federal union "as is embodied in the United States of America, founded upon a political constitution, and therefore indissoluble."

The further implications of Kant's proposal, the alternative it replaces, and Hegel's objections to either, are discussed in the chapter on WAR AND PEACE. Here it seems appropriate to conclude with that vision of the world state which appears early in the tradition of the great books. It is conceived not as a world-wide federal union, but as a universal or unlimited community in which all men are citizens together even as they belong to one human brotherhood.

"If our intellectual part is common," argues the philosophical Roman Emperor, Marcus Aurelius, "the reason also, in respect of which we are rational beings, is common; if this is so, common also is the reason which commands us what to do, and what not to do; if this is so, there is a common law also; if this is so, we are fellow-citizens; if this is so, we are members of some political community; if this is so, the world is in a manner a state."

Centuries later Dante, in the first book of his *De Monarchia*, recaptures this ancient vision of the world state. Because "a plurality of authorities is disorder," authority must be single; and therefore, Dante argues, "world government is necessary . . . for the well-being of the world." It must be conceived as governing "mankind on the basis of what all have in common." By that "common law, it leads all toward peace."

OUTLINE OF TOPICS

1. The nature of human society

   1*a*. Comparison of human and animal gregariousness: human and animal societies

   1*b*. Comparison of the family and the state in origin, structure, and government

   1*c*. Associations intermediate between the family and the state: the village or tribal community; civil society as the stage between family and state

   1*d*. Social groups other than the family or the state: religious, charitable, educational, and economic organizations; the corporation

2. The general theory of the state

   2*a*. Definitions of the state or political community: its form and purpose

   (1) Comparison of the state and the soul: the conception of the state as a living organism; the body politic

   (2) The state as a corporate person

   (3) The progressive realization of the state as the process of history: the state as the divine idea as it exists on earth; the national spirit

2b. The state as a part or the whole of society

2c. The source or principle of the state's sovereignty: the sovereignty of the prince; the sovereignty of the people

2d. The economic aspect of the state: differentiation of states according to their economic systems

2e. The political structure of the state: its determination by the form of government

2f. The primacy of the state or the human person: the welfare of the state and the happiness of its members

2g. Church and state: the relation of the city of God to the city of man

3. The origin, preservation, and dissolution of the state

3a. The development of the state from other communities

3b. The state as natural or conventional or both

(1) Man as by nature a political animal: the human need for civil society

(2) Natural law and the formation of the state

3c. The condition of man in the state of nature and in the state of civil society: the state of war in relation to the state of nature

3d. The social contract as the origin of civil society or the state: universal consent as the basis of the constitution or government of the state

3e. Love and justice as the bond of men in states: friendship and patriotism

3f. Fear and dependence as the cause of social cohesion: protection and security

3g. The identity and continuity of a state: the dissolution of the body politic or civil society

4. The physical foundations of society: the geographical and biological conditions of the state

4a. The territorial extent of the state: its importance relative to different forms of government

4b. The influence of climate and geography on political institutions and political economy

4c. The size, diversity, and distribution of populations: the causes and effects of their increase or decrease

5. The social structure or stratification of the state

5a. The political distinction between ruling and subject classes, and between citizens and denizens

5b. The family as a member of the state: its autonomy and its subordination

5c. The classes or sub-groups arising from the division of labor or distinctions of birth: the social hierarchy

5d. The conflict of classes within the state

(1) The opposition of social groups: the treatment of national, racial, and religious minorities

(2) The clash of economic interests and political factions: the class war

5e. The classless society

6. The ideal or best state: the contrast between the ideal state and the best that is historically real or practicable
   - 6*a*. The political institutions of the ideal state
   - 6*b*. The social and economic arrangements of the ideal state

7. Factors affecting the quality of states
   - 7*a*. Wealth and political welfare
   - 7*b*. The importance of the arts and sciences in political life
   - 7*c*. The state's concern with religion and morals: the cultivation of the virtues
   - 7*d*. The educational task of the state: the trained intelligence of the citizens

8. The offices of state: the statesman, king, or prince
   - 8*a*. The duties of public office and the responsibilities of office holders: the relation of the statesman or king to the people he represents or rules
   - 8*b*. The qualities or virtues necessary for the good statesman or king
   - 8*c*. The education or training of the statesman or prince
   - 8*d*. Statecraft: the art or science of governing; political prudence
     - (1) The employment of the military arts
     - (2) The occasions and uses of rhetoric
     - (3) The role or function of experts in the service of the state
   - 8*e*. The advantages and disadvantages of participation in political life

9. The relation of states to one another
   - 9*a*. Commerce and trade between states: commercial rivalries and trade agreements; free trade and tariffs
   - 9*b*. Social and cultural barriers between states: the antagonism of diverse customs and ideas
   - 9*c*. Honor and justice among states
   - 9*d*. The sovereignty of independent states: the distinction between the sovereignty of the state at home and abroad; internal and external sovereignty
   - 9*e*. War and peace between states
     - (1) The military problem of the state: preparation for conquest or defense
     - (2) Treaties between states: alliances, leagues, confederacies, or hegemonies
   - 9*f*. Colonization and imperialism: the economic and political factors in empire

10. Historic formations of the state: the rise and decline of different types of states
    - 10*a*. The city-state
    - 10*b*. The imperial state
    - 10*c*. The feudal state
    - 10*d*. The national state
    - 10*e*. The federal state: confederacies and federal unions
    - 10*f*. The ideal of a world state

REFERENCES

References are listed by volume number (in bold type), author's name, and page number. Bible references are to book, chapter, and verse of the Authorized King James version of the Bible. The abbreviation "esp" calls the reader's attention to one or more especially relevant parts of a whole reference; "passim" signifies that the topic is discussed intermittently rather than continuously in the work or passage cited. Where the work as a whole is relevant to the topic, the page numbers refer to the entire work. For general guidance in the use of *The Great Ideas,* consult the Preface.

1. The nature of human society

7 PLATO, 664–666
9 ARISTOTLE, 473, 475–476
12 AURELIUS, 256, 271, 288, 293
18 AUGUSTINE, 161–162, 359–360, 513–514, 519–523
20 AQUINAS, 233
23 HOBBES, 99–101
31 SPINOZA, 433–436
35 LOCKE, 42–46
38 ROUSSEAU, 369–370
42 KANT, 433–434
43 MILL, 460
54 FREUD, 664–696

1*a*. Comparison of human and animal gregariousness: human and animal societies

9 ARISTOTLE, 8–9, 136, 149–153, 446
12 AURELIUS, 292
13 VIRGIL, 87–89
23 HOBBES, 100
25 MONTAIGNE, 228–229
35 LOCKE, 42–43
36 SWIFT, 135–184
38 MONTESQUIEU, 1–2
43 MILL, 469
48 MELVILLE, 282–284
49 DARWIN, 304–310
51 TOLSTOY, 499–500, 683–684
54 FREUD, 684–686, 791–792

1*b*. Comparison of the family and the state in origin, structure, and government

7 PLATO, 360–365, 666
9 ARISTOTLE, 382, 413, 453–454, 455–456, 476, 484
18 AUGUSTINE, 517
20 AQUINAS, 207
23 HOBBES, 67–68, 86, 109–111, 121
35 LOCKE, 36–46, 63, 64–65 passim
36 STERNE, 216, 410–411
38 MONTESQUIEU, 118, 140
38 ROUSSEAU, 357, 367–368, 387–388
41 GIBBON, 82–83
46 HEGEL, 101–102, 135, 172, 211–212, 246–247, 288–289
54 FREUD, 686–689, 781–782

1*c*. Associations intermediate between the family and the state: the village or tribal community; civil society as the stage between family and state

6 HERODOTUS, 154–158
6 THUCYDIDES, 391
7 PLATO, 664–666
9 ARISTOTLE, 445–446
35 LOCKE, 48–51
37 FIELDING, 267
38 ROUSSEAU, 411
39 SMITH, 309–311
40 GIBBON, 91, 412–413
41 GIBBON, 33–34
42 KANT, 452
43 MILL, 352–353
46 HEGEL, 63–80, 134, 140, 194–195, 237, 260–261, 287
49 DARWIN, 581
50 MARX, 174–175
54 FREUD, 686–687

1*d*. Social groups other than the family or the state: religious, charitable, educational, and economic organizations; the corporation

6 HERODOTUS, 56–57
14 PLUTARCH, 58
21 DANTE, 122–125
23 HOBBES, 117–122, 198
36 SWIFT, 106
38 MONTESQUIEU, 149, 199–200
38 ROUSSEAU, 369–370
39 SMITH, 28, 51–56, 343–346
40 GIBBON, 191–200, 299–304, 668–670
42 KANT, 442
46 HEGEL, 78–80, 97, 101–103, 141, 146–147, 335–336, 340–341
51 TOLSTOY, 198–203
54 FREUD, 674–676

2. The general theory of the state

2*a*. Definitions of the state or political community: its form and purpose

7 PLATO, 301–319, 363–365
9 ARISTOTLE, 445, 446, 459, 473, 475–476, 477–478

18 Augustine, 190, 524–528
20 Aquinas, 206–207, 230–231, 252–253
23 Hobbes, 99–104
27 Shakespeare, 108–109
35 Locke, 46–47, 53–54, 55–58 passim, 75–76
38 Montesquieu, 69
38 Rousseau, 370, 380–382, 395, 396–398
42 Kant, 408–409
43 Federalist, 132
46 Hegel, 79–81, 82–83, 84–89, 143–144, 170–178, 230

2a(1) Comparison of the state and the soul: the conception of the state as a living organism; the body politic

7 Plato, 316–356, 401–416
9 Aristotle, 447–448, 454, 474
14 Plutarch, 177, 605, 648–649
23 Hobbes, 47, 116, 117, 122–124, 148–153
25 Montaigne, 504–505
27 Shakespeare, 352–353
35 Locke, 74
36 Swift, 112–115
36 Sterne, 215–216
38 Rousseau, 419–420
46 Hegel, 142, 143, 145, 188, 222, 302–303

2a(2) The state as a corporate person

23 Hobbes, 97, 101–102, 104, 117–120, 122
35 Locke, 46–47
38 Rousseau, 392–393, 406–409 passim
46 Hegel, 55–114, 150

2a(3) The progressive realization of the state as the process of history: the state as the divine idea as it exists on earth; the national spirit

46 Hegel, 79–82, 84–89, 110–114, 119–120, 141, 144–145, 170–178, 180–182, 203–206, 230–231, 257–258, 266–267, 271, 287–288, 351–354

2b. The state as a part or the whole of society

9 Aristotle, 412, 532–533
18 Augustine, 522–523
19 Aquinas, 719–720
20 Aquinas, 434–435
35 Locke, 57–58
40 Gibbon, 299
43 Mill, 272–273, 302–312
46 Hegel, 143–144, 174, 175–176, 177–178

2c. The source or principle of the state's sovereignty: the sovereignty of the prince; the sovereignty of the people

Old Testament: *I Samuel*, 8
9 Aristotle, 472
14 Plutarch, 678
15 Tacitus, 197
20 Aquinas, 207, 235
23 Hobbes, 100–105, 109, 117, 149–150
35 Locke, 55–56, 59, 63, 66–67, 70–71
38 Rousseau, 392–393, 399–400
42 Kant, 436, 439–441, 448, 450, 451
43 Constitution of the U.S., 11
43 Federalist, 84–85, 126–128, 252
43 Mill, 267–269, 355
46 Hegel, 92, 93–94, 106, 145, 355, 365–366
51 Tolstoy, 680–684 passim

2d. The economic aspect of the state: differentiation of states according to their economic systems

6 Thucydides, 352
7 Plato, 316–319, 341, 692–697
9 Aristotle, 458–463, 466, 511–512, 522–523, 532–534
14 Plutarch, 32–48, 64–77, 671–689
23 Hobbes, 124–126, 156–157
35 Locke, 33, 34–35, 52–53
38 Montesquieu, 29–30, 109, 110–112, 151–153, 174, 183–184
38 Rousseau, 377–385
39 Smith, 163–181, 182–300
40 Gibbon, 21–22
43 Federalist, 53–60 passim, 79–80, 112–114
50 Marx, 163, 171–176, 275–278 passim
54 Freud, 882–884

2e. The political structure of the state: its determination by the form of government

7 Plato, 401–416, 598–604
9 Aristotle, 445, 473, 475, 486–487, 488–491, 495–497, 600, 608
15 Tacitus, 72
23 Hobbes, 101, 104–105, 117–124, 228
35 Locke, 55
38 Montesquieu, 2–4
38 Rousseau, 359, 406–409, 423–424
42 Kant, 436, 450–452
43 Mill, 327–332
46 Hegel, 90–92, 145–146, 173–175, 364–365

2f. The primacy of the state or the human person: the welfare of the state and the happiness of its members

5 Aeschylus, 27–39
5 Sophocles, 131–142, 182–195
5 Euripides, 385–387, 425–439
6 Thucydides, 397–398, 402–404
7 Plato, 213–219, 342, 600–601, 754
9 Aristotle, 446, 473–476, 527–530, 536–537
12 Epictetus, 148–150
12 Aurelius, 272, 293
14 Plutarch, 44–45, 51–52, 699–700
18 Augustine, 162, 524–525
19 Aquinas, 313–314, 718–719
20 Aquinas, 213–214, 221–223, 239–240
23 Hobbes, 113–115
25 Montaigne, 48–51 passim, 381–388, 486–489
30 Bacon, 71–76 passim
35 Locke, 46–47

38 MONTESQUIEU, 69, 221–222
38 ROUSSEAU, 392–394, 396–399
42 KANT, 272–273
43 DECLARATION OF INDEPENDENCE, 1
43 FEDERALIST, 147–148
43 MILL, 267–274, 293–323, 453–454, 460–461, 464–476 passim
46 HEGEL, 65, 80, 82–83, 84–89, 98, 109–110, 124, 135–136, 139–140, 142, 164, 166, 170–172, 298–299
51 TOLSTOY, 238–243, 260–262, 505–511, 513–521, 527–532, 537–538
54 FREUD, 757

2*g*. Church and state: the relation of the city of God to the city of man

OLD TESTAMENT: *I Samuel*, 8; 10:18–19; 12:12–14,17–19; 13 / *Psalms*, 2; 48:1–8 / *Daniel*, 2:44; 4
APOCRYPHA: *Wisdom of Solomon*, 6:1–4
NEW TESTAMENT: *Matthew*, 17:24–27; 22:15–22 / *Romans*, 13:1–8 / *I Peter*, 2:13–17
7 PLATO, 757–761, 769–771
9 ARISTOTLE, 412, 517, 525, 526, 533
12 EPICTETUS, 138, 143–144
13 VIRGIL, 376
14 PLUTARCH, 114–116, 142–143
15 TACITUS, 59–60
18 AUGUSTINE, 17, 129–618 passim
20 AQUINAS, 434–436, 440–441, 443–444
21 DANTE, 51–52, 61–62, 77–78, 103–105, 113–114
23 MACHIAVELLI, 16–17
23 HOBBES, 80–81, 111–112, 155–156, 163, 165–246, 248–249, 251–252, 266, 273–274, 275–278
26 SHAKESPEARE, 376–405, 487–488, 489–490
27 SHAKESPEARE, 568–573
32 MILTON, 68, 69, 329–331, 386–388
35 LOCKE, 2–21
38 MONTESQUIEU, 85–86, 134, 144–145, 196–197, 200–215, 218–219, 284–285, 298–308
38 ROUSSEAU, 327, 435–439
39 SMITH, 56–57, 343–356, 357
40 GIBBON, 13, 197, 229–230, 289–294, 299–304, 328–330, 349–351, 382–383, 390–393 passim, 443–446, 451–453, 457–460 passim, 623–624, 642–643
41 GIBBON, 147–148, 199–202, 204–207, 212–213, 214–215, 352–353, 360–361, 381–383, 417–418, 557–562, 567–569, 582–589
42 KANT, 442, 444
43 MILL, 279, 290–291, 341
44 BOSWELL, 314–315, 445
46 HEGEL, 84–89, 143–144, 175–177, 205–206, 216–217, 245–247, 309–310, 311, 316, 321–322, 325–326, 331, 336–337, 345–346, 351–354
47 GOETHE, 267–268
51 TOLSTOY, 374–377, 435–436
52 DOSTOEVSKY, 28–32, 127–137 passim

3. The origin, preservation, and dissolution of the state

3*a*. The development of the state from other communities

6 THUCYDIDES, 391
7 PLATO, 666
9 ARISTOTLE, 445–446
35 LOCKE, 46–53
36 STERNE, 410
46 HEGEL, 63, 111–112

3*b*. The state as natural or conventional or both

7 PLATO, 663–666
9 ARISTOTLE, 445–446
12 AURELIUS, 264, 297
20 AQUINAS, 229–230
23 HOBBES, 47
25 MONTAIGNE, 462–463
31 SPINOZA, 435–436
33 PASCAL, 227–228
35 LOCKE, 28, 44, 46–53
38 ROUSSEAU, 387–392, 399, 423
42 KANT, 412–413, 435–436
46 HEGEL, 68, 164
54 FREUD, 780

3*b*(1) Man as by nature a political animal: the human need for civil society

7 PLATO, 316
9 ARISTOTLE, 446, 475–476
12 EPICTETUS, 128
12 AURELIUS, 266, 280, 290, 292, 303, 310
18 AUGUSTINE, 513–514
19 AQUINAS, 512–513
20 AQUINAS, 221–223
23 HOBBES, 84–86, 279
28 HARVEY, 454
31 SPINOZA, 429
35 LOCKE, 28, 42
36 SWIFT, 159–163
38 ROUSSEAU, 330–331, 362, 387–388
43 FEDERALIST, 65
46 HEGEL, 65–67
49 DARWIN, 310, 321
54 FREUD, 684, 787

3*b*(2) Natural law and the formation of the state

23 HOBBES, 86–87, 91–96
31 SPINOZA, 435–436
35 LOCKE, 25–54 passim, 56
38 MONTESQUIEU, 1–2
38 ROUSSEAU, 329–334
43 DECLARATION OF INDEPENDENCE, 1
43 FEDERALIST, 143

3*c*. The condition of man in the state of nature and in the state of civil society: the state of war in relation to the state of nature

7 PLATO, 44–45
9 ARISTOTLE, 446
15 TACITUS, 51

18 AUGUSTINE, 517–518
23 HOBBES, 84–87, 90, 94, 96
25 MONTAIGNE, 93–94
30 BACON, 20
35 LOCKE, 25–29, 53–54, 56–57
38 ROUSSEAU, 329–334, 342–345, 362–366
41 GIBBON, 86–87, 237
42 KANT, 405–406, 435–436
44 BOSWELL, 204–205
46 HEGEL, 65, 66, 171–172

3*d*. The social contract as the origin of civil society or the state: universal consent as the basis of the constitution or government of the state

7 PLATO, 216–219, 311
12 LUCRETIUS, 74
18 AUGUSTINE, 528
20 AQUINAS, 309–316
23 HOBBES, 100–102, 113
31 SPINOZA, 435–436
35 LOCKE, 44–53, 65, 69, 73–81 passim
38 MONTESQUIEU, 58–60
38 ROUSSEAU, 353–355, 358, 387–394, 423–424
42 KANT, 435–436, 437, 450–452
43 FEDERALIST, 84–85
43 MILL, 302–303
46 HEGEL, 31–32, 80–81, 124

3*e*. Love and justice as the bond of men in states: friendship and patriotism

5 EURIPIDES, 382, 387
6 THUCYDIDES, 397–398, 534
7 PLATO, 308–309, 346–356, 360–365
9 ARISTOTLE, 411–414 passim, 420–421, 446, 457
14 PLUTARCH, 20–21, 238–239
15 TACITUS, 284–285
18 AUGUSTINE, 528
21 DANTE, 47–52, 75–76
31 SPINOZA, 448
35 LOCKE, 49, 104
36 SWIFT, 165–166
38 MONTESQUIEU, 18–19
38 ROUSSEAU, 373–374
43 FEDERALIST, 62, 69–70
43 MILL, 424–425, 428, 464–476 passim
46 HEGEL, 84, 300–301
49 DARWIN, 310
51 TOLSTOY, 384–388, 475–476
54 FREUD, 672–678, 685–686, 707

3*f*. Fear and dependence as the cause of social cohesion: protection and security

5 AESCHYLUS, 88
5 SOPHOCLES, 132
6 THUCYDIDES, 402–404
7 PLATO, 44–45
9 ARISTOTLE, 477–478, 510
23 MACHIAVELLI, 15, 24
23 HOBBES, 84–87, 90, 99–101, 109, 116
35 LOCKE, 53–54
38 ROUSSEAU, 374–375, 381–382, 398
39 SMITH, 309–311
43 FEDERALIST, 65
43 MILL, 422
46 HEGEL, 283, 287–288, 289, 328–330, 342
49 DARWIN, 321
52 DOSTOEVSKY, 127–137 passim

3*g*. The identity and continuity of a state: the dissolution of the body politic or civil society

9 ARISTOTLE, 473
15 TACITUS, 212
23 HOBBES, 148–153, 154, 280–281
25 MONTAIGNE, 464–465
35 LOCKE, 65, 73–81 passim
38 ROUSSEAU, 418–420
42 KANT, 450–451
43 FEDERALIST, 142–143
46 HEGEL, 90, 111

4. The physical foundations of society: the geographical and biological conditions of the state

4*a*. The territorial extent of the state: its importance relative to different forms of government

7 PLATO, 343–344
9 ARISTOTLE, 500, 522–523, 530–531
14 PLUTARCH, 58
18 AUGUSTINE, 172–173
35 LOCKE, 33
38 MONTESQUIEU, 56–57, 58–59
38 ROUSSEAU, 323, 403–404, 412, 413
40 GIBBON, 1, 8–11, 33–34
43 FEDERALIST, 31, 41–42, 47–48, 51–53, 59–62 passim, 192–193, 253–254
43 MILL, 330, 432
46 HEGEL, 243, 273–274

4*b*. The influence of climate and geography on political institutions and political economy

6 THUCYDIDES, 349
7 PLATO, 677
9 ARISTOTLE, 468, 505, 530–532, 535
10 HIPPOCRATES, 15–16
14 PLUTARCH, 96
36 STERNE, 224, 295–296
38 MONTESQUIEU, 102–108, 116–120, 122–134
38 ROUSSEAU, 415–417
39 SMITH, 8–10
40 GIBBON, 87–91, 236–237, 567, 655–657
41 GIBBON, 220–225 passim, 341–343 passim, 427–428
43 FEDERALIST, 46–47, 55–56, 88–89
43 MILL, 424–428 passim
46 HEGEL, 78, 190–201, 243–244, 248–249, 251–252
49 DARWIN, 323
50 MARX, 253–255

4c. The size, diversity, and distribution of populations: the causes and effects of their increase or decrease

6 THUCYDIDES, 391–392, 399–401
7 PLATO, 663–667, 693
9 ARISTOTLE, 460–461, 466, 504–505, 530, 531
25 MONTAIGNE, 330
35 LOCKE, 61–62
38 MONTESQUIEU, 187–200
38 ROUSSEAU, 404, 407–408, 417–418
39 SMITH, 33–34, 71, 163–165
40 GIBBON, 17–18, 88, 90, 239, 486
41 GIBBON, 108–109, 221
43 FEDERALIST, 52–53, 170–172 passim
43 MILL, 424–428 passim
44 BOSWELL, 172, 373–374
49 DARWIN, 275–277, 323–327, 383–384, 391–394
50 MARX, 249–250, 317–319, 348–350, 360–364

5. The social structure or stratification of the state

5a. The political distinction between ruling and subject classes, and between citizens and denizens

5 SOPHOCLES, 153–154
5 ARISTOPHANES, 572
7 PLATO, 339–350
9 ARISTOTLE, 454, 459–460, 471–475 passim, 489–491, 532–533
14 PLUTARCH, 46–47, 62
15 TACITUS, 106–107
20 AQUINAS, 306–307, 316–318
23 HOBBES, 108–109
35 LOCKE, 53
38 MONTESQUIEU, 112, 114–115
38 ROUSSEAU, 392, 427, 428–430
40 GIBBON, 16–17
41 GIBBON, 81–82
42 KANT, 436–437
43 FEDERALIST, 138–139
43 MILL, 345–346, 366–370, 380–389 passim

5b. The family as a member of the state: its autonomy and its subordination

5 SOPHOCLES, 131–142
5 EURIPIDES, 436
5 ARISTOPHANES, 622
6 HERODOTUS, 223
7 PLATO, 360–365, 707–708, 775–781
9 ARISTOTLE, 455–457, 465–466
14 PLUTARCH, 21–26, 39–41, 62–64
15 TACITUS, 32, 51–52, 162
18 AUGUSTINE, 521–522
20 AQUINAS, 306–307, 318–321
23 HOBBES, 121, 155
35 LOCKE, 43, 67–68, 69
36 SWIFT, 29–31
38 MONTESQUIEU, 22–23, 140, 189, 192–199
38 ROUSSEAU, 376–377
42 KANT, 420–421
44 BOSWELL, 280–281, 304
46 HEGEL, 59–60, 61, 62–63, 76, 140
50 MARX, 241
50 MARX-ENGELS, 427–428

5c. The classes or sub-groups arising from the division of labor or distinctions of birth: the social hierarchy

6 HERODOTUS, 84–85
7 PLATO, 316–350, 358–360, 413, 480–481, 740–741, 774–775
9 ARISTOTLE, 459–460, 463, 464, 473–475, 488–491, 496–497, 532–534, 555–556
14 PLUTARCH, 9, 20–21
21 DANTE, 130–132
22 CHAUCER, 159–174, 530–532
25 MONTAIGNE, 131–132, 411
26 SHAKESPEARE, 56–64
29 CERVANTES, 221–222
36 SWIFT, 158
38 MONTESQUIEU, 11–12, 151–152, 184
38 ROUSSEAU, 381–382
39 SMITH, 6–8, 51–62 passim, 169–170, 301–309 passim
40 GIBBON, 242, 497–501 passim
41 GIBBON, 81, 317–318, 452–456, 571–572
42 KANT, 444–445
43 FEDERALIST, 113–114, 114–115
43 MILL, 270, 385, 392–399 passim
44 BOSWELL, 124–126, 127, 140–141, 247
46 HEGEL, 68–69, 101–103, 137, 222–223, 250
50 MARX, 95–96, 164–180, 218–219, 239–240, 317–321, 355–364, 366, 368–369
50 MARX-ENGELS, 419–420, 422–424, 430
51 TOLSTOY, 1–11, 204–206, 281–284, 384–388, 403–405, 503–505

5d. The conflict of classes within the state

5d(1) The opposition of social groups: the treatment of national, racial, and religious minorities

7 PLATO, 678–679, 742, 790
9 ARISTOTLE, 475, 504–505
14 PLUTARCH, 21–27, 49–61
22 CHAUCER, 392–395, 463–471
26 SHAKESPEARE, 410–411
35 LOCKE, 1–22
38 ROUSSEAU, 428
40 GIBBON, 83, 206–234, 348–361, 390–391, 607–608
41 GIBBON, 285–288
43 FEDERALIST, 170–172
43 MILL, 270–271, 278–282, 307–312 passim, 424–428
46 HEGEL, 86–87, 287–288

5d(2) The clash of economic interests and political factions: the class war

5 EURIPIDES, 260
6 HERODOTUS, 202–203

6 Thucydides, 434–438, 463–469, 564–593
7 Plato, 343, 695
9 Aristotle, 461–463 passim, 488–491, 495–497, 503–511, 524–525, 553–572 passim
14 Plutarch, 68–71, 75–76, 176–177, 179–184, 648–656, 657–663, 671–689, 708–713
15 Tacitus, 224–225
21 Dante, 41–43
23 Machiavelli, 14
23 Hobbes, 121–122
26 Shakespeare, 56–64
27 Shakespeare, 351–354
36 Swift, 21–23, 80, 154–155
38 Rousseau, 375, 381–382, 429–431
39 Smith, 28, 109–110, 170–173, 175–179, 269–271, 309–311, 420–421
40 Gibbon, 144
41 Gibbon, 574–582, 588–589, 594
43 Federalist, 49–53, 164–165, 185–186
43 Mill, 289–290, 345–346, 366–370, 387
46 Hegel, 76, 275–276, 294–297, 335–336, 356–357
50 Marx, 6–7, 9, 63, 113, 127–146, 275, 295, 317, 355–368 passim, 377–378
50 Marx-Engels, 415–434
51 Tolstoy, 410–421
54 Freud, 787, 882, 884

5*e*. The classless society

50 Marx, 9
50 Marx-Engels, 416, 429

6. The ideal or best state: the contrast between the ideal state and the best that is historically real or practicable

6 Thucydides, 395–399
7 Plato, 295–441, 442–443, 598–604, 640–799
9 Aristotle, 455–465, 487–488, 493, 527–548
14 Plutarch, 48, 49–64
23 Hobbes, 164
25 Montaigne, 462–465
30 Bacon, 94–95, 199–214
38 Rousseau, 402–403
42 Kant, 114, 455–458
43 Federalist, 117–125 passim, 132, 257
43 Mill, 327–355, 368
46 Hegel, 173–175
50 Marx-Engels, 432–433

6*a*. The political institutions of the ideal state

5 Aristophanes, 615–628
7 Plato, 316–350, 598–604, 640–799
9 Aristotle, 456, 459–460, 461, 463–465, 495–496
14 Plutarch, 34–35, 45–46
20 Aquinas, 307–309
37 Fielding, 268–269
38 Rousseau, 323–325, 410–411
42 Kant, 450–451
43 Mill, 338, 341–350, 369–389
46 Hegel, 64, 251, 300

6*b*. The social and economic arrangements of the ideal state

5 Aristophanes, 542–563, 629–642
7 Plato, 339–344, 356–365, 401, 481–485, 640–799
9 Aristotle, 455–465, 532–536
14 Plutarch, 36–47
27 Shakespeare, 533
50 Marx, 377–378
50 Marx-Engels, 425–429
54 Freud, 787–788, 883–884

7. Factors affecting the quality of states

7*a*. Wealth and political welfare

5 Aristophanes, 629–642
6 Thucydides, 350–352, 397
7 Plato, 339–344, 405–408, 687–688, 694–695, 733
9 Aristotle, 462–463, 532–533
14 Plutarch, 36–37, 180, 291–292
15 Tacitus, 31, 57–58
18 Augustine, 147–149
36 Swift, 73–76
38 Montesquieu, 23–25, 44–48, 146–147
38 Rousseau, 327–328, 365–366, 377–385, 415–417
39 Smith, 27–31, 33–35
40 Gibbon, 22–23, 88–89, 456–457, 498–501
43 Federalist, 79–80
44 Boswell, 210–211
49 Darwin, 324
50 Marx, 319–321

7*b*. The importance of the arts and sciences in political life

5 Aristophanes, 462, 554–555, 564–582
7 Plato, 320–339, 344–345, 388–401, 427–441, 604–608, 653–663, 675–676, 713–730
9 Aristotle, 542–548
14 Plutarch, 43–44
18 Augustine, 153–157, 202–203, 649
30 Bacon, 210–214
36 Swift, 104–107
38 Montesquieu, 17–18, 191
39 Smith, 337–339
40 Gibbon, 23–24
41 Gibbon, 298–300, 326–328, 527–528
42 Kant, 586–587
46 Hegel, 185–186, 217–218, 346–348
54 Freud, 778–779

7*c*. The state's concern with religion and morals: the cultivation of the virtues

6 Herodotus, 294
6 Thucydides, 370
7 Plato, 206–207, 287–290, 316–356, 669–670, 682–683, 731–732, 735–738, 757–771, 794–799
9 Aristotle, 378, 434, 462, 512, 527–530, 536–548

14 PLUTARCH, 32–48, 49–77, 247–248
18 AUGUSTINE, 129–230
20 AQUINAS, 213–215, 226–227, 231–233
21 DANTE, 129–132
35 LOCKE, 15, 105
38 MONTESQUIEU, 9–11, 21–23, 135–142, 200–208
38 ROUSSEAU, 372–377, 435–439
39 SMITH, 337–338, 346–347
40 GIBBON, 100–101, 291–292, 601
43 MILL, 302–323 passim, 332–341 passim
46 HEGEL, 228–229, 346
49 DARWIN, 325–327
52 DOSTOEVSKY, 28–32, 127–137 passim, 164–170 passim

7*d*. The educational task of the state: the trained intelligence of the citizens

5 ARISTOPHANES, 576–577
7 PLATO, 43–47, 213–219, 316–356, 380–381, 640–663, 675–676, 713–731, 732–735
9 ARISTOTLE, 339, 434–436, 462, 474–475, 536–548, 572
14 PLUTARCH, 39–45, 64–77 passim
23 HOBBES, 150–151, 153–155
24 RABELAIS, 81–83
25 MONTAIGNE, 60–62
30 BACON, 23
32 MILTON, 384–385
35 HUME, 453
36 SWIFT, 76–80
38 MONTESQUIEU, 13–18
38 ROUSSEAU, 372–377
39 SMITH, 303–305, 340–343
40 GIBBON, 6, 669–670
43 MILL, 283, 317–323, 332–341 passim, 349–350, 381–387 passim, 418, 424
46 HEGEL, 65, 133, 140, 148–149, 271–272
50 MARX, 237–240

8. The offices of state: the statesman, king, or prince

8*a*. The duties of public office and the responsibilities of office holders: the relation of the statesman or king to the people he represents or rules

OLD TESTAMENT: *Deuteronomy,* 17:14–20 / *I Samuel,* 8:11–18 / *I Kings,* 3:7–9 / *Psalms,* 72 / *Proverbs,* 16:12–15 / *Isaiah,* 22:20–22 / *Jeremiah* 23:3–6
5 AESCHYLUS, 5–7
5 SOPHOCLES, 104–105, 132
5 EURIPIDES, 260–261
5 ARISTOPHANES, 470–487
6 THUCYDIDES, 402–404, 427
7 PLATO, 301–306, 339–341, 390–391, 697–705 passim, 794–799, 806–807, 814
9 ARISTOTLE, 474–475, 476, 525–526, 528–529, 537–538
14 PLUTARCH, 51–52, 276–290, 455–456, 620–648
15 TACITUS, 61–62
18 AUGUSTINE, 514–515, 521–522
21 DANTE, 77–78
23 MACHIAVELLI, 21–30
23 HOBBES, 153–159
25 MONTAIGNE, 24–25, 315
26 SHAKESPEARE, 494–496, 552–553
27 SHAKESPEARE, 366–369
29 CERVANTES, 340–348, 352–356, 360–364
30 BACON, 74–75
35 LOCKE, 44–46, 62–64
38 MONTESQUIEU, 94–95
38 ROUSSEAU, 372–373, 412–414
40 GIBBON, 243–245, 288–289, 437–438, 577–578, 639–644 passim
41 GIBBON, 95, 320–321, 563–564, 586–587
42 KANT, 444–445
43 CONSTITUTION OF THE U.S., 11–16 passim
43 FEDERALIST, 76, 113–114, 168–169 passim, 174–179, 212–215
43 MILL, 341–344, 398–399, 401–406 passim, 410–411
46 HEGEL, 98–99, 102–104, 147
51 TOLSTOY, 465–467

8*b*. The qualities or virtues necessary for the good statesman or king

OLD TESTAMENT: *Genesis,* 41:33,39–40 / *Exodus,* 18:21–26 / *I Samuel,* 15:10–35 / *I Kings,* 3:5–28; 4:29–34 / *Psalms,* 72 / *Proverbs,* 8:15–16; 20:26–28; 25:2–5; 28:15–16; 31:4–5 / *Ecclesiastes,* 10:16–17
APOCRYPHA: *Wisdom of Solomon,* 1:1; 6; 9 / *Ecclesiasticus,* 10:1–3 / *I Maccabees,* 14
5 AESCHYLUS, 21–22, 24
5 SOPHOCLES, 136–137
5 ARISTOPHANES, 470–487, 532–534, 617
6 HERODOTUS, 164–165
6 THUCYDIDES, 383–384, 513–514
7 PLATO, 285–292, 319–320, 368–383, 442, 604–608, 679–682, 796, 801–802, 804–805
9 ARISTOTLE, 454–455, 466–467, 469–470, 473–475, 480–483, 486–487, 511, 528–529
12 AURELIUS, 253–256, 261, 276–277
14 PLUTARCH, 49–61, 121–141, 193–195, 262–292, 423–430, 604–619, 620–648, 661, 781–802
15 TACITUS, 215
21 DANTE, 40–41, 63–64, 126, 134–137
23 MACHIAVELLI, 22–26
24 RABELAIS, 132–133
25 MONTAIGNE, 381–388, 436–438, 451–453
26 SHAKESPEARE, 327–331, 453–454, 533
27 SHAKESPEARE, 174–177, 303–306, 351–392
29 CERVANTES, 331–336
30 BACON, 1–2, 20–25
32 MILTON, 69
35 LOCKE, 48–51
36 SWIFT, 28–29
38 MONTESQUIEU, 262
40 GIBBON, 61–64 passim, 74, 142, 255–257 passim, 338–344, 430, 448–449

9. The relation of states to one another

9*a*. Commerce and trade between states: commercial rivalries and trade agreements; free trade and tariffs

5 ARISTOPHANES, 463–466
6 HERODOTUS, 158
7 PLATO, 788–789
9 ARISTOTLE, 451, 531
23 HOBBES, 119–120, 124
38 MONTESQUIEU, 98–99, 146–150, 152–173, 177–181
39 SMITH, 173–175, 182–192, 197–200, 201–204, 209–213, 233–236, 256–266
40 GIBBON, 656–658
41 GIBBON, 314–315, 355, 427
43 FEDERALIST, 35–36, 42–43, 53–56 passim, 80–81
46 HEGEL, 243–244
50 MARX, 66–68, 221–223, 372–375 passim
50 MARX-ENGELS, 420

9*b*. Social and cultural barriers between states: the antagonism of diverse customs and ideas

5 EURIPIDES, 261–263
6 HERODOTUS, 2, 12–13, 137–138, 216, 232–233, 253–254, 298–302, 308–310
6 THUCYDIDES, 350, 366, 589–590
7 PLATO, 582–583
9 ARISTOTLE, 531–532
10 HIPPOCRATES, 18
14 PLUTARCH, 99, 254–256, 287–288, 303–310
18 AUGUSTINE, 515
25 MONTAIGNE, 91–98
38 ROUSSEAU, 355
43 FEDERALIST, 55–56
43 MILL, 436–439
46 HEGEL, 277–279
50 MARX-ENGELS, 428
51 TOLSTOY, 170–171, 362–363
54 FREUD, 755–757, 761, 788

9*c*. Honor and justice among states

OLD TESTAMENT: *II Samuel*, 10
5 AESCHYLUS, 12–13
6 HERODOTUS, 1–2, 177–180, 237–239
6 THUCYDIDES, 355, 378–380, 386, 426–428, 429–434, 468–469, 504–508
7 PLATO, 367–368
9 ARISTOTLE, 432, 528–529
23 HOBBES, 159
24 RABELAIS, 54–56
25 MONTAIGNE, 387–388
27 SHAKESPEARE, 114–115
36 SWIFT, 76–78
38 MONTESQUIEU, 61–65
38 ROUSSEAU, 369
40 GIBBON, 535–536
42 KANT, 452–455
43 FEDERALIST, 63, 190–191, 235
43 MILL, 434–435 passim
46 HEGEL, 109, 110
48 MELVILLE, 292–295
51 TOLSTOY, 232–233

9*d*. The sovereignty of independent states: the distinction between the sovereignty of the state at home and abroad; internal and external sovereignty

27 SHAKESPEARE, 463–464
35 LOCKE, 58–59
38 MONTESQUIEU, 223–224
38 ROUSSEAU, 392–393, 406–409
42 KANT, 452–458
43 DECLARATION OF INDEPENDENCE, 3
43 FEDERALIST, 105–107, 126–128
43 MILL, 428–433
46 HEGEL, 92–94, 106–107, 108–109

9*e*. War and peace between states

9*e*(1) The military problem of the state: preparation for conquest or defense

6 HERODOTUS, 144–148, 158–159, 206–208, 214–314 passim
6 THUCYDIDES, 349–386 passim, 389, 402–404, 469–471, 529–534
7 PLATO, 366–368, 677–678, 732–735, 784–786
9 ARISTOTLE, 432, 462–463, 490, 524–525, 531, 535, 600
14 PLUTARCH, 41–45, 59–60, 88–102
15 TACITUS, 253–254, 269–278, 283–292, 297–302
23 MACHIAVELLI, 17–22, 30–31, 34–35
24 RABELAIS, 127–130
25 MONTAIGNE, 299–300
26 SHAKESPEARE, 532–567
38 MONTESQUIEU, 58–62, 100–101
38 ROUSSEAU, 389–390
39 SMITH, 187–190, 301–309, 342–343
40 GIBBON, 4–8, 245–248, 495–497, 558–560
41 GIBBON, 321–325
42 KANT, 452–458 passim
43 FEDERALIST, 35–37, 44–47, 53–56 passim, 85–101, 110–111, 132–136 passim
43 MILL, 425–426, 435
46 HEGEL, 107–108, 109, 144, 242–243, 297–300
51 TOLSTOY, 308–309, 344–355, 588–589

9*e*(2) Treaties between states: alliances, leagues, confederacies, or hegemonies

OLD TESTAMENT: *Joshua*, 9
APOCRYPHA: *I Maccabees*, 8
5 ARISTOPHANES, 455–457, 595–599
6 HERODOTUS, 6, 144–146, 239–242, 243–245, 286–287, 289–290
6 THUCYDIDES, 353, 356–360, 366–371, 373–374, 394–395, 418–420, 461–462, 468–469, 476–477, 486–496, 502–504, 529–534, 568, 572, 578–579
9 ARISTOTLE, 478
14 PLUTARCH, 21–24, 427–428
23 MACHIAVELLI, 32

CROSS-REFERENCES

For: Other discussions bearing on the comparison of human and animal societies, *see* ANIMAL 1d; LANGUAGE 1; MIND 9e.

Other treatments of the differences and relations between family and state, *see* EDUCATION 8a; FAMILY 2a–2c; GOVERNMENT 1b; MONARCHY 4a; ONE AND MANY 5d; TYRANNY 4b.

Discussions relevant to the analogy of state and soul, to the conception of the state as a corporate person, and to the conception of the state as the historical embodiment of the divine idea, *see* HISTORY 4a(3); LAW 7f; PROGRESS 4b.

The consideration of the various economic systems which are involved in the organization of states, *see* LABOR 5–5d; WEALTH 6a.

The consideration of the political institutions of the state, the nature of government, the branches of government, and the forms of government, *see* ARISTOCRACY 1–2e; CONSTITUTION 1–3b, 5–5b; DEMOCRACY 1–4d; GOVERNMENT 1–1a, 2–2d, 3–3e(2); JUSTICE 9c; LAW 7a; MONARCHY 1–1b(2), 4–4e(4); OLIGARCHY 1–2, 4–5; TYRANNY 1–5.

The consideration of the relation between church and state, and the relation between the city of God and the city of man, *see* CITIZEN 7; HISTORY 5b; RELIGION 4–4b.

The problem of the natural and the conventional in the formation of the political community, and for the contrast between the state of nature and the state of civil society, *see* CUSTOM AND CONVENTION 1; GOVERNMENT 1a, 5; LAW 4b; LIBERTY 1b; NATURE 2b, 5c; WAR AND PEACE 1.

The theory of the social contract in relation to the idea of a constitution, *see* CONSTITUTION 6.

The problem of the identity and continuity of the state, *see* REVOLUTION 2a, 2c, 6b.

Other discussions of the physical foundations of society, and of its geographical or territorial conditions, *see* DEMOCRACY 5a; HISTORY 4a(2); MAN 7b; MONARCHY 4c.

The motives or impulses underlying political association, *see* EMOTION 5a; GOVERNMENT 1c; JUSTICE 9b; LOVE 4–4b; WEALTH 7a.

The problem of the individual and the common good in the relation of man to the state, *see* CITIZEN 1; DUTY 10; GOOD AND EVIL 5d; HAPPINESS 5–5b; LAW 1a; LIBERTY 1e.

The political classification of men as citizens, subjects, and slaves, *see* CITIZEN 2b; DEMOCRACY 4a–4a(1); JUSTICE 9d; LABOR 7d; LIBERTY 1f; SLAVERY 5a–6c; TYRANNY 5–5b; and for discussions relevant to the formation of economic or social classes within the state, *see* ARISTOCRACY 1; DEMOCRACY 2b, 5b(4); LABOR 4b; OLIGARCHY 1, 4; OPPOSITION 4e, 5a; SLAVERY 3–3b, 4a–4c.

The conflict of classes within the state, and especially for other discussions of the class war and the classless society, *see* DEMOCRACY 5b(4); LABOR 7c–7c(3); OLIGARCHY 5c; OPPOSITION 5b; REVOLUTION 5a–5c; WAR AND PEACE 2c; WEALTH 9h.

Other discussions relevant to the ideal state or concerned with the factors which affect the excellence of states, *see* ARISTOCRACY 6; CITIZEN 5–6; DEMOCRACY 4, 6; GOVERNMENT 2e; LIBERTY 1h; MONARCHY 4d(2)–4d(3); PROGRESS 4a; RELIGION 4b; SCIENCE 1b(2); VIRTUE AND VICE 7a–7c; WEALTH 9f.

The consideration of the duties or responsibilities, the qualities and virtues, of the statesman or prince, *see* ARISTOCRACY 5; CITIZEN 3–6; CONSTITUTION 9a; DEMOCRACY 5b; DUTY 10; EDUCATION 8d; MONARCHY 3a; VIRTUE AND VICE 7d; and for the art or science of politics and the elements of statecraft, *see* ART 9c–9d; EMOTION 5d; KNOWLEDGE 8c; OPINION 7a; PHILOSOPHY 2c; RHETORIC 1c; SCIENCE 3a; WAR AND PEACE 10a.

The relation of states to one another, politically and economically, in war and peace, *see* CUSTOM AND CONVENTION 7b; GOVERNMENT 5–5a; JUSTICE 9f; WAR AND PEACE 3a, 10g, 11c; WEALTH 4g.

For: The special relation of an imperial state to colonies or subject peoples, *see* DEMOCRACY 7b; GOVERNMENT 5b; LIBERTY 6c; MONARCHY 5–5b; SLAVERY 6d; TYRANNY 6.

The general theory of sovereignty as it applies to the state in its external relations with other states, and as it applies to a state, or its government, in relation to its own people, *see* DEMOCRACY 4b; GOVERNMENT 1d, 1g–1g(3), 5; LAW 6b; LIBERTY 1b; MONARCHY 1a(2), 4e(3); ONE AND MANY 5e; TYRANNY 5c.

Other discussions of confederacies and federal unions, *see* GOVERNMENT 5d; ONE AND MANY 5d–5e; REVOLUTION 6b; and for discussions bearing on the possibility of a world state, *see* CITIZEN 8; LOVE 4c; WAR AND PEACE 11d.

ADDITIONAL READINGS

Listed below are works not included in *Great Books of the Western World*, but relevant to the idea and topics with which this chapter deals. These works are divided into two groups:

I. Works by authors represented in this collection.
II. Works by authors not represented in this collection.

For the date, place, and other facts concerning the publication of the works cited, consult the Bibliography of Additional Readings which follows the last chapter of *The Great Ideas*.

I.

TACITUS. *Germania*
DANTE. *Convivio* (*The Banquet*), FOURTH TREATISE, CH 4–10
——. *On World-Government or De Monarchia*
F. BACON. "Of Faction," in *Essays*
HOBBES. *Philosophical Rudiments Concerning Government and Society*, CH 1, 5
——. *The Elements of Law, Natural and Politic*
SPINOZA. *Tractatus Theologico-Politicus* (*Theological-Political Treatise*), CH 16–19
MONTESQUIEU. *Considerations on the Causes of the Grandeur and Decadence of the Romans*
ENGELS. *The Origin of the Family, Private Property and the State*

II.

JOHN OF SALISBURY. *The Statesman's Book*
Völsung Saga
Njalssaga
MARSILIUS OF PADUA. *Defensor Pacis*
T. MORE. *Utopia*
LUTHER. *Secular Authority*
BODIN. *The Six Bookes of a Commonweale*
HOOKER. *Of the Laws of Ecclesiastical Polity*
ALTHUSIUS. *Politica Methodice Digesta Atque Exemplis Sacris et Profanis Illustrata*
CAMPANELLA. *The City of the Sun*
PENN. *An Essay Towards the Present and Future Peace of Europe*
DEFOE. *Robinson Crusoe*
BURLAMAQUI. *Principles of Natural and Politic Law*
VATTEL. *The Law of Nations*
VOLTAIRE. "States-Governments," in *A Philosophical Dictionary*
GODWIN. *An Enquiry Concerning Political Justice*
BENTHAM. *A Fragment on Government*, CH 1 (1–21, 36–48)
——. *The Theory of Legislation*
J. G. FICHTE. *Addresses to the German Nation*, IV–VIII
——. *The Science of Rights*
FOURIER. *Traité de l'association domestique-agricole*
LIEBER. *Manual of Political Ethics*
WHEWELL. *The Elements of Morality*, BK II, CH 20; BK V, CH 1–6, 10–17
CALHOUN. *A Disquisition on Government*
——. *A Discourse on the Constitution and Government of the United States*
THOREAU. *Civil Disobedience*
HAWTHORNE. *The Blithedale Romance*
COMTE. *System of Positive Polity*, VOL II, *Social Statics*, CH 5
LOTZE. *Microcosmos*, BK VIII, CH 5
FREEMAN. *History of Federal Government in Greece and Italy*
BAGEHOT. *Physics and Politics*
BURCKHARDT. *Force and Freedom*, CH 2–3
S. BUTLER. *Erewhon*
RUSKIN. *Munera Pulveris*
J. H. NEWMAN. *A Letter to the Duke of Norfolk*
L. H. MORGAN. *Ancient Society*
T. H. GREEN. *The Principles of Political Obligation*, (G)
SPENCER. *The Man Versus the State*
TÖNNIES. *Fundamental Concepts of Sociology*
NIETZSCHE. *The Will to Power*, BK III (3)
W. WILSON. *The State*
FRAZER. *The Golden Bough*, PART I, CH 6
TREITSCHKE. *Politics*
BOSANQUET. *The Philosophical Theory of the State*
KROPOTKIN. *Mutual Aid, a Factor of Evolution*
——. *The State, Its Historic Role*

SANTAYANA. *Reason in Society*, CH 8
OPPENHEIMER. *The State, Its History and Development Viewed Sociologically*
DEWEY and TUFTS. *Ethics*, PART III, CH 20–21
SOREL. *Reflexions on Violence*
PIRANDELLO. *The Old and the Young*
BELLOC. *The Servile State*
DUGUIT. *Law in the Modern State*
WALLAS. *The Great Society*
PARETO. *The Mind and Society*, VOL IV
HOBHOUSE. *The Metaphysical Theory of the State*
LENIN. *The State and Revolution*
T. VEBLEN. *The Vested Interests and the State of the Industrial Arts*, CH 6
WEBER. *Essays in Sociology*, PART II
——. *Politics as a Vocation*
HAUPTMANN. *The Island of the Great Mother*
HOCKING. *Man and the State*
CROCE. *Politics and Morals*
DEWEY. *Reconstruction in Philosophy*, CH 8
——. *The Public and Its Problems*
HSIAO. *Political Pluralism*
M. R. COHEN. *Reason and Nature*, BK III, CH 3
A. HUXLEY. *Brave New World*
LASKI. *The State in Theory and Practice*
STURZO. *The Inner Laws of Society*
——. *Church and State*
MARITAIN. *The Things That Are Not Caesar's*, I–III
——. *Ransoming the Time*, CH 2
BORGESE. *Common Cause*
KOHN. *The Idea of Nationalism*
CASSIRER. *The Myth of the State*, PART II
KELSEN. *Der soziologische und der juristische Staatsbegriff*
——. *General Theory of Law and State*
MERRIAM. *Systematic Politics*
EWING. *The Individual, the State and World Government*
A. J. TOYNBEE. *Civilization on Trial*, CH 5, 7
BORGESE *et al. Preliminary Draft of a World Constitution*

Chapter 91: TEMPERANCE

INTRODUCTION

MOST outstanding figures in history, most heroes of legend or fiction, are men of strong passions, of ambition, and of pride. They are driven by desires which tend to be limitless. Few exemplify moderation. Few stop short of excess in anger or love, or in their striving for power and pleasure. They may curb their appetites in one direction, only to indulge them without rein in another. They do not follow in all things the counsels of temperance, expressed by the ancient maxim "Nothing overmuch."

Achilles is not temperate in his wrath, nor does Odysseus, for all his craft and cunning, exhibit self-control when his vanity or curiosity is at stake. The tragedies of Euripides, more perhaps than those of Sophocles and Aeschylus, embody the hubris, or pride, which is common to all tragic figures in some particular form of intemperance, such as the boundless hate of Medea or the abstemiousness of Hippolytus. One play especially, *Bacchantes*, takes intemperance for its central theme and sets the disciples of the dionysiac spirit in mortal conflict with the puritans and their prohibitions. Comedy as well as tragedy flows from intemperance, as when we smile at the exaggerated sentimentality of the romantic lovers described by Cervantes and Fielding, Chaucer and Shakespeare, or find merriment in the indulgences of Sir John Falstaff, Pantagruel and Panurge, or Tristram Shandy.

The great books of history add their evidence. They make fiction seem pale by comparison with the excesses of cruelty and sensuality which, if they were not presented as fact, might be dismissed as unimaginable. Page after page of Tacitus and Gibbon often describe, in an unrelieved sequence, human debauchery, brutalities and revelries ingeniously designed to reach some new extreme in order to procure, through novelty, satisfaction for appetites already over-indulged and weary of familiar pleasures.

Nor is the historian's panorama of intemperance limited to the uncontrolled indulgences of the few—the oriental despots described by Herodotus, or the Caesars and their retinues in the imperial court of Rome. Armies in the field and the mob-formations of civilian life are depicted in wanton and riotous behavior. Whole peoples are described as being given to luxurious living or as wanting in standards of public decency. The few exceptions in antiquity, such as Spartan rigor or the chastity, if not the sobriety, of the primitive Germans, only accentuate by contrast the immoderate tenor of life in most ancient societies.

DARWIN SEEMS TO think that a much greater degree of self-control characterizes modern life, both public and private, though his opinion on this score may give undue weight to the conventions so much insisted upon in England under Queen Victoria. Temperance, according to him, is a virtue peculiar to civilized life. "The greatest intemperance," he writes, "is no reproach with savages."

Darwin places temperance along with prudence among the "so-called self-regarding virtues, which do not obviously, though they may really, affect the welfare of the tribe" and which "have never been esteemed by savages, though now highly appreciated by civilized nations." That Darwin has modern society in mind when he speaks of "civilized nations," may be inferred from his remarks about the sensuality of the Greeks and Romans. This seems to be confirmed by his statement that "the hatred of indecency . . . which is so valuable an aid to chastity, is a modern virtue, appertaining exclusively . . . to civilized life."

What may be noted here and questioned—

in addition to the validity of Darwin's comparison of modern and ancient culture—is the tendency to identify temperance with chastity, or at least with restraint, if not abstinence, in the sphere of the sexual impulses. In our day, the general notion of virtue is often restricted to the virtue of chastity, as when we use the words "virtuous woman" to signify one who is chaste, or "woman of easy virtue" to signify one who is not. But spectacles of gluttony and drunkenness, of avarice or greed, are ever present to remind us that man can be intemperate in more ways than one. Darwin's implication of progress from licentious to moderate living may have less justification when we consider all the forms which intemperance can take.

Darwin, furthermore, seems to distinguish between courage and temperance in relation to the level or degree of civilization. Unlike temperance, courage, he thinks, is demanded by primitive as well as civilized life because it concerns the welfare of society as much as the well-being of the individual. Since "no man can be useful or faithful to his tribe without courage, this quality," he says, "has universally been placed in the highest rank." On the point of this comparison between the two virtues, Freud appears to disagree. Though he too considers temperance or self-control largely in the sphere of the sexual instincts, he seems to think that any form of organized social life, whether regarded as primitive or civilized, exacts certain restraints from the individual for the sake of the common good. Temperance no less than courage serves the tribe or the state.

"Civilization has been built up," Freud writes, "under the pressure of the struggle for existence, by sacrifices in gratification of the primitive impulses, and that is to a great extent forever being re-created as each individual, successively joining the community, repeats the sacrifice of his instinctive pleasures for the common good. The sexual are amongst the most important of the instinctive forces thus utilized; they are in this way sublimated, that is to say, their energy is turned aside from its sexual goal and diverted towards other ends, no longer sexual, and socially more valuable."

Society may depend on the temperance of its members without being able to exact temperance from them. Writers like J. S. Mill, for example, question the right of society to enforce temperance upon its members by the enactment of sumptuary laws, especially with regard to food and drink. The supposition seems to be that the intemperate man injures only himself—to do which is the prerogative of his personal liberty—whereas the unjust man injures others. We shall return to the consideration of this issue later, after we have examined the nature of temperance and its relation to other virtues, such as justice, courage, and wisdom or prudence.

IF THE POETS AND the historians describe the prevalence and the range of man's intemperance, the moralists tend to be unanimous in recommending self-control or moderation. There is hardly any variety of moral theory—whether developed in terms of law and duty or in terms of happiness and virtue, whether appealing to *a priori* principles or to criteria of utility empirically applied—which does not recommend the discipline of desire by reason and which does not condemn sensuality, self-indulgence, unchecked appetites, or passions run wild.

The word "temperance" itself is not always used, nor is the technical notion of virtue always implied, by those who advocate what Milton calls "the rule of not too much, by temperance taught." For some writers, on the other hand, temperance and virtue are almost identical. They think the essence of temperance is moderation and the virtuous life is the reasonable one. It is one in which reason moderates the passions and limits the pursuit of pleasure.

For example, Freud's theory of the reality-principle seems to reflect traditional notions of temperance. A person dominated by the pleasure-principle is infantile in character. "The transition from the pleasure-principle to the reality-principle," he points out, "is one of the most important advances in the development of the ego." When "the ego learns that it must inevitably go without immediate satisfaction, postpone gratification, learn to endure a degree of pain, and altogether renounce certain sources of pleasure," it "becomes 'reasonable,' is no longer controlled by the pleasure-principle, but follows the reality-principle," which seeks "a delayed and diminished pleasure, one which is assured by its realization of fact, its relation to reality."

So, too, Spinoza's doctrine that human bondage consists in being subject to the tyranny of the passions, whereas human freedom stems from the rule of reason, can be read as an apostrophe to temperance. Descartes' maxim, "to try always to conquer myself rather than fortune, and to alter my desires rather than change the order of the world," is still another expression of the insight that peace of mind comes from self-control. Though Kant does not think temperance deserves "to be called good without qualification," he does affirm that "moderation in the affections and passions, self-control and calm deliberation, are not only good in many respects, but even seem to constitute part of the intrinsic worth of the person."

It is Montaigne who magnifies temperance beyond virtue, and makes it the measure of the sound pursuit of every sort of good, even virtue itself. Without temperance, he writes in his essay "Of Moderation," we can "corrupt things that in themselves are laudable and good; we may grasp virtue so that it becomes vicious, if we embrace it too stringently and with too violent a desire." Montaigne opposes "those who say there is never any excess in virtue." On the contrary, he thinks that "a man may both be too much in love with virtue, and be excessive in a just action . . . I love temperate and moderate natures. An immoderate zeal, even to that which is good, though it does not offend, astonishes me, and puts me to study what name to give it."

As with virtue, so with wisdom or philosophy. He quotes Holy Writ to the effect that we should be soberly wise, not try to be wiser than befits our natures. We should not "dive into philosophy beyond the limits of profit; taken moderately, it is pleasant and useful." There is, in short, "no pleasure so just and lawful, where intemperance and excess are not to be condemned."

Montaigne sees temperance as augmenting the pleasure of life rather than diminishing it. He subscribes to Plato's statement in the *Laws* that "the temperate life is in all things gentle, having gentle pains and gentle pleasures; whereas the intemperate life . . . has violent pains and pleasures, and vehement and stinging desires, and loves utterly insane; and in the temperate life the pleasures exceed the pains, but in the intemperate life the pains exceed the pleasures in greatness and number and frequency." To overlook this, Montaigne elsewhere suggests, is to suppose that "the regimen which stops the toper before he has drunk himself drunk, the glutton before he has eaten to a surfeit, and the lecher before he has got the pox, is an enemy to pleasure." Yet, in his love of "temperate and moderate natures," Montaigne repeatedly counsels us to avoid being overzealous even about temperance itself. The maxim "Nothing overmuch" applies to virtue as well as to the pleasure-seeking that virtue tries to control.

Considered in terms of Aristotle's theory that all the moral virtues consist in a mean between excess and defect, Montaigne seems to be identifying moderation with the observance of the mean, so that moderation becomes an aspect of every virtue, including temperance itself as one virtue among others. Thus the courageous man is one who fears neither too much nor too little, but is moderate with respect to peril and pain. Accordingly, a man cannot be too courageous, but only too fearless, and so rash or foolhardy.

But it may be supposed that if moderation enters into all the virtues, such virtues as temperance and courage are not distinct. Holding them to be distinct in regard to the objects with which they deal, Aquinas admits that each of the major virtues can be "taken to denote certain general conditions of virtue," so that in a sense "they overflow into one another." He defines temperance as "a disposition of the soul, moderating any passions or acts, so as to keep them within bounds," and fortitude as "a disposition whereby the soul is strengthened for that which is in accord with reason, against any assaults of the passions or the toil involved in any work to be done." So conceived, Aquinas thinks it is possible to see how temperance and fortitude are in some sense one.

The man who can curb his desires for the pleasures of touch is more able to check his daring in the face of danger, "and in this sense fortitude is said to be temperate." The man who is able to stand firm against the dangers of death is more able to remain firm against the onslaught of pleasures, and so "temperance can be said to be brave." Thus temperance enters into other virtues, insofar as it leads men to "observe the mean in all things," just as fortitude enters into temperance because it strengthens men against "the enticements of pleasure" as well as against the fear of pain.

The general theory of virtue, in terms of which the several virtues are distinguished and their connections traced, is discussed in the chapter on VIRTUE AND VICE; and the special virtues to which temperance is related are considered in the chapters on COURAGE, JUSTICE, and PRUDENCE. Here we must be concerned to observe how the general conception of virtue is exemplified in the definitions of temperance given by those who, like Plato, Aristotle, and Aquinas, consider it to be, not the whole of virtue, but one of the major virtues and distinct from the others.

THOUGH PLATO AND Aristotle do not conceive virtue in the same way, and though they diverge in analyzing particular virtues, such as justice or wisdom, and in describing how particular virtues are related to one another, they nevertheless seem to concur on a number of points in their treatment of temperance.

In the *Gorgias*, Callicles asserts that only those who are unable to satisfy their desire for pleasures praise temperance, and call intemperance base. But, he asks, "what could be more truly base or evil than temperance to a man . . . who might freely be enjoying every good and has no one to stand in his way?" And he concludes by saying that "luxury and intemperance and license, if they be provided with means, are virtue and happiness."

In reply, Socrates tries to persuade Callicles that "instead of the intemperate and insatiate life," one should "choose that which is orderly and sufficient and has a due provision for daily needs." He compares the intemperate man "to a vessel full of holes, because it can never be satisfied." By analogy with the sound and the leaky vessel, Socrates describes the temperate man as able to satisfy his limited desires, whereas the intemperate man, of boundless desire, can never pause in his search for pleasure. "If he pauses for a moment, he is in an agony of pain. Such are their respective lives," he adds, "and now would you say that the life of the intemperate is happier than that of the temperate?"

Callicles claims to be unconvinced, but later Socrates gets him to admit that in all things—in a house or a ship, in the body or the soul—order is good, and disorder evil. He then proceeds to point out that order is the principle of health in the body and of temperance in the soul. It is in these terms that Socrates defines temperance in the *Republic* as "the ordering or controlling of certain pleasures and desires." In the human soul, he explains, "there is a better and also a worse principle; and when the better has the worse under control, then a man is said to be master of himself."

The words "temperance" and "self-mastery" are almost interchangeable; both signify "the rule of the better part over the worse." Just as the courageous man is one "whose spirit retains in pleasure and in pain the commands of reason about what he ought or ought not to fear," so the temperate man is one in whom the "ruling principle of reason and the two subject ones of spirit and desire are equally agreed that reason ought to rule."

In somewhat similar terms, Aristotle defines temperance and courage by reference to pleasure and pain. "The man who abstains from bodily pleasures and delights in this very fact is temperate, while the man who is annoyed at it is self-indulgent; and he who stands his ground against things that are terrible and delights in this or at least is not pained is brave, while the man who is pained is a coward." Like Plato, Aristotle makes the rational principle the source of these virtues. It is reason, or more precisely one of reason's virtues, prudence, which determines the mean between excess and defect with regard to pleasure and pain, or fear, anger, and the other passions.

Like Freud, Aristotle regards self-indulgence as infantile or childish. Children "live at the beck and call of appetite, and it is in them that the desire for what is pleasant is strongest." When such desire is not regulated by reason, "it will go to great lengths; for in an irrational being the desire for pleasure is insatiable even if it tries every source of gratification." Where Freud speaks of the pleasure-principle submitting to the reality-principle, Aristotle says, "as the child should live according to the direction of his tutor, so the appetitive element should live according to the rational principle. The appetitive element in a temperate man should harmonize with the rational principle."

According to Aristotle, temperance is concerned not with all pleasures, but "with the kind of pleasures that other animals share in, which therefore appear slavish and brutish; these are touch and taste." Self-indulgence is a matter of reproach "because it attaches to us not as men but as animals. To delight in such things and to love them above all others is brutish."

The endurance of pain, which is central to the nature of courage, enters into temperance incidentally. The self-indulgent man "is pained more than he ought at not getting pleasant things," whereas the temperate man "is not pained at the absence of what is pleasant or at his abstinence from it." But total abstinence is not temperance, any more than over-indulgence is. "The temperate man occupies a middle position" between those who have an insatiable craving for pleasure and those "who fall short with regard to pleasures and delight in them less than they should." Such insensibility, Aristotle declares, is not human either.

When reason curbs the desire for bodily pleasures, "it is not to lessen sensual pleasure," in the opinion of Aquinas, "but to prevent the force of concupiscence from cleaving to it immoderately. By *immoderately*," he explains, "I mean going beyond the bounds of reason, as a sober person does not take less pleasure in food eaten in moderation than the glutton, but his concupiscence lingers less in such pleasures." Though Aquinas agrees with Aristotle in defining temperance strictly as moderation with respect to the pleasures of taste and touch, "such as the pleasures of the table or of sex," he associates with temperance those virtues which involve moderation with respect to other pleasures.

For example, there is liberality with respect to money as an object of love or pleasure. Neither the spendthrift nor the miser is temperate. Friendliness or affability and gentleness represent temperance in the relation of a man to the pleasures of fellowship; and the virtue which Aristotle calls *eutrapelia* is similarly classified by Aquinas, as being a moderate indulgence in the pleasures of recreation, of sport and games, the opposites of which, in excess and defect, can be called "buffoonery" and "boorishness." Even the pleasures of learning can be pursued intemperately, so that an undue craving for knowledge—beyond the proper limits and for the wrong reasons—is, according to Aquinas, the vice of curiosity.

The notions of abstinence and continence seem to be closely related to the idea of temperance. The words are often used interchangeably. But as we have seen, according to the theory of virtue as a mean between extremes of excess and defect, temperance calls for a moderate indulgence in pleasures, not abstinence from them entirely. This raises the question whether the asceticism of the religious life violates the rule of reason by a kind of immoderate withdrawal from ordinary pleasures. What to the psychoanalyst may look like pathological self-denial, or to the philosopher like a violation of nature, takes, in the eyes of the Christian theologian, the form of heroic temperance, a supernatural perfection of the virtue.

When in the religious life a man does "his utmost to strive onward to divine things," then, according to Aquinas, in those who are "tending towards the divine similitude," temperance is a *perfecting* virtue. "So far as nature allows," it "neglects the needs of the body." In those "who have already attained to the divine likeness, the *perfect* virture of temperance" is one which "knows no earthly desires."

Since "use of sexual union hinders the mind from giving itself wholly to the service of God," and since "the use of venery withdraws the mind from that perfect intentness on tending to God," the perpetual continence of the celibate life, as well as the voluntary poverty of the monastic life, seem to Aquinas "requisite for religious perfection."

Augustine, in his *Confessions*, tells of the time when "I thought I should be impossibly miserable if I had to forego the embraces of a woman; and I did not think of Your mercy as a healing medicine for that weakness, because I had never tried it. I thought that continency was a matter of our own strength, and I knew that I had not the strength; for in my utter foolishness I did not know the word of Your Scripture that none can be continent unless you give it."

Though he separated from his mistress in order to prepare for marriage, he discovered that "it was not really marriage that I wanted. I was simply a slave to lust." He recounts the struggles which finally enabled him to turn in the other direction and to "see the austere beauty of Continence, serene and indeed joyous"; and with her, he adds, "I saw such hosts of young men and women . . . gray widows and women grown old in virginity, and in them all Continence herself, not barren but the fruitful mother of children, her joys, by You, Lord, her Spouse."

But there is another meaning of continence according to which it is condemned by the philosopher who conceives temperance as a natural virtue. The reason for Aristotle's condemnation of continence differs from the reason he gives for his disapproval of abstinence. Abstinence—at least on the natural plane—is an immoderate denial of pleasure. Continence is opposed to temperance because it merely represents reason's inhibition of the act prompted by a licentious desire for pleasure. It is not an habitual moderation of desire itself. Aristotle's emphasis on habit, therefore, leads him to insist upon the distinction between temperance and continence.

"We group together the incontinent and the self-indulgent, the continent and the temperate man," Aristotle writes, "because they are concerned somehow with the same pleasures and pain; but though they are concerned with the same objects, they are not similarly related to them." The difference lies in the fact that a man acts continently in a particular situation when his reason is able to overcome an immoderate desire for pleasure, and incontinently when the force of his desire brushes reason aside; whereas a man not only acts temperately, but is temperate in character, when his desires are themselves habitually moderated to be in accord with reason.

The temperate man, therefore, has no need for continence. Nor is the incontinent man to be confused with the intemperate, for the latter is not convinced that his desires are inordinate. The continent man is one who, when acting against reason, knows that he is doing so. Though both the continent and the temperate man do nothing contrary to the rule of reason for the sake of bodily pleasures, the one, according to Aristotle, has bad appetites, the other is free from them.

THE CONTINENT MAN is not the only one who gives the appearance of temperance without being really temperate in character. Some men, says Aristotle, are moderate by nature—"from the very moment of birth fitted for self-control." What appears to be temperance in them, therefore, is not, in his opinion, a virtuous habit acquired by good acts, but simply a natural capacity to control their desires or a temperamental constitution which happens not to be ridden by very strong desires. They do not deserve to be praised for their apparent self-control; neither do those who manage to be moderate about certain pleasures but give themselves free rein with respect to other desires. The miser who limits his bodily comforts in order to amass a pile of gold is hardly temperate.

Gibbon writes of the Emperor Julian that he "seldom recollected the fundamental maxim of Aristotle, that true virtue is placed at an equal distance between the opposite vices." Julian's lack of temperance appears, however, not merely in the opposite extreme to which he went to express his contempt for luxury, sleeping on the ground and renouncing the decencies of dress and cleanliness. Though genuinely moderate in some things, such as his diet, he went to excess in others, overdoing his preoccupation with affairs of state and working incessantly for long hours day after day. He "considered every moment as lost that was not devoted to the advantage of the public or the improvement of his own mind. By this avarice of time," Gibbon observes, "he seemed to protract the short duration of his reign."

Temperance in a particular respect is sometimes praised as a virtue relative to a specific and limited goal. Considering the wealth of nations, Adam Smith looks upon prodigality as a major vice, and regards parsimony as an indispensable virtue. "Capitals are increased by parsimony," he writes, "and diminished by prodigality and misconduct . . . Parsimony, and not industry, is the immediate cause of the increase of capital . . . By what a frugal man annually saves, he not only affords maintenance to an additional number of productive hands, for that or the ensuing year, but, like the founder of a public workhouse, he establishes as it were a perpetual fund for the maintenance of an equal number in all times to come."

Capital funds are perverted by the prodigal. "By not confining his expenses within his income," Smith declares, "he encroaches upon his capital . . . By diminishing the funds designed for the employment of productive labor, he necessarily diminishes . . . the quantity of that labor which adds a value to the subject upon which it is bestowed, and, consequently, the value of the annual produce of the land and labour of the whole country. . . . If the prodigality of some was not compensated by the frugality of others, the conduct of every prodigal, by feeding the idle with the bread of the industrious, tends not only to beggar himself, but to impoverish his country."

From the point of view of augmenting wealth, Smith may be right in calling every prodigal "a public enemy and every frugal man a public benefactor." Marx, however, raises the question whether thrift or parsimony represents moral virtue in the capitalist himself. He mocks the classical, or what he calls the "vulgar," economic theory which tends to identify capital with abstinence, and, taking Adam Smith's statement that "industry furnishes the material which saving accumulates," he interprets *saving* to mean the *reconversion of the greatest possible portion of surplus-value or surplus-product into capital.*

For Marx the question is, in addition to being economic, a moral and psychological one. He describes the capitalist as suffering from "a Faustian conflict between the passion for accumulation and the desire for enjoyment." His parsimony, or abstinence from certain pleasures, hardly signifies genuine temperance; for, according to Marx, the capitalist is like the hoarder who "makes a sacrifice of the lusts of the flesh to his gold fetish." Elsewhere he says that the "boundless greed after riches . . . . is common to the capitalist and the miser; but while the miser is merely a capitalist gone mad, the capitalist is a rational miser."

In Marx's opinion the capitalist cannot even boast of personal thrift to any great extent. "The capitalist gets rich, not like the miser, in proportion to his personal labor and restricted consumption, but at the same rate as he squeezes out the labor-power of others, and enforces on the laborer abstinence from all life's enjoyments."

THESE CONSIDERATIONS OF political economy lead us naturally back to the issue raised earlier, concerning the significance of temperance for society, or the effect of private intemperance on the public welfare.

What is the relation between temperance and justice? Aristotle answers this question in terms of his conception of general justice as including the social aspect of all the other moral virtues. To the extent that his courage or temperance can affect others or the common good, a man is required by justice to be temperate and brave. It is proper for the law, he says, to bid us do "both the acts of a brave man (*e.g.*, not to desert our post nor take flight nor throw away our arms) and those of a temperate man (*e.g.*, not to commit adultery nor to gratify one's lust)."

Though he accepts Aristotle's notion of general justice, Aquinas puts a limitation on the extent to which the positive law of the state can regulate or enforce the acts of a virtue like temperance. Because it is "framed for a multitude of human beings, the majority of whom are not perfect in virtue . . . human laws do not forbid all vices, from which the virtuous abstain, but only the more grievous vices, from which it is possible for the majority to abstain; and chiefly those that are injurious to others, without the prohibition of which human society could not be maintained." The point is not that some acts of temperance cannot be prescribed by law, but rather that the human law does not command every act of temperance, but only those "which are ordainable to the common good."

The principle being clear, the problem remains extremely difficult when the question is one of regulating certain types of behavior, such as insobriety, extravagance, or adultery.

Montesquieu discusses the difficulties of administering, under the Julian law, the "punishments decreed by the Roman emperors against the incontinence of women." He considers the advantages and disadvantages, relative to different forms of government, of sumptuary laws directed at maintaining frugality and avoiding luxury; as, for example, in Venice, where the rich were "compelled by laws to moderation" and were thus so "habituated to parsimony that none but courtesans could make them part with their money." As for sobriety, he seems to think that the problem varies with the climate, the Mohammedan law against the drinking of wine being "improper for cold countries where the climate seems to force them to a kind of national intemperance, very different from personal inebriety. . . . A German drinks through custom, and a Spaniard by choice."

The reasons which have been offered against the legal prohibition of intoxicants are many and various. To those who hold that temperance consists in moderation, not abstinence, "temperance laws" are misguided as well as misnamed. To others, like William James, "drunkenness . . . as teetotalers use the word, is one of the deepest functions of human nature. Half of both the poetry and tragedy of human life would vanish if alcohol were taken away." To still others, like Mill, such sumptuary laws are wrong in principle because consumption, which they try to regulate, is a private matter.

If an individual's intemperance injures only himself, he may be morally reprobated, but, Mill holds, he ought not to be prosecuted by law. A man who, "through intemperance or extravagance, becomes unable to pay his debts," or becomes incapable of supporting his family, "might be justly punished; but it is for the breach of duty to his family or creditors, not for the extravagance." Again Mill writes: "No person ought to be punished simply for being drunk; but a soldier or a policeman should be punished for being drunk on duty. Whenever, in short, there is a definite damage, or a definite risk of damage, either to another individual or to the public, the case is taken out of the province of liberty, and placed in that of morality or law."

OUTLINE OF TOPICS

1. The nature of temperance
    - 1*a*. The relation of temperance to virtue generally, and to the virtues of courage and justice
    - 1*b*. The relation of temperance to knowledge and prudence: the determination of the mean of temperance
    - 1*c*. Temperance and continence: the counterfeits of temperance
2. The varieties of intemperance: the related vices of sensuality, abstemiousness, cruelty, curiosity, inordinate desire
3. Temperance in relation to duty or happiness
4. The cultivation of temperance: the training of a temperate character
5. The social aspects of temperance
    - 5*a*. The temperance of rulers and citizens: intemperate conduct as inimical to the common good
    - 5*b*. The temperance of a people: luxurious indulgences; the intemperance of the mob
    - 5*c*. Laws concerning temperance: the extent to which the sphere of temperance can be regulated by law
6. The extremes of temperance and intemperance
    - 6*a*. Asceticism: heroic temperance
    - 6*b*. The dionysiac spirit: the cult of pleasure

REFERENCES

References are listed by volume number (in bold type), author's name, and page number. Bible references are to book, chapter, and verse of the Authorized King James version of the Bible. The abbreviation "esp" calls the reader's attention to one or more especially relevant parts of a whole reference; "passim" signifies that the topic is discussed intermittently rather than continuously in the work or passage cited. Where the work as a whole is relevant to the topic, the page numbers refer to the entire work. For general guidance in the use of *The Great Ideas,* consult the Preface.

1. The nature of temperance

7 Plato, 1–13, 275–284, 627–628
9 Aristotle, 364–366, 404
12 Epictetus, 158–161, 225–228
12 Aurelius, 283
18 Augustine, 511–512
19 Aquinas, 768–769
20 Aquinas, 650–651
22 Chaucer, 535
25 Montaigne, 489–490
32 Milton, 310–311
42 Kant, 256
49 Darwin, 313–314

1*a*. The relation of temperance to virtue generally, and to the virtues of courage and justice

5 Euripides, 429–430
6 Thucydides, 370
7 Plato, 1–13, 284–285, 346–355, 407–408, 673–674, 689–690
8 Aristotle, 164, 204
9 Aristotle, 348, 349–350, 351–352, 354, 365–366, 422, 608–609
12 Aurelius, 261, 271
17 Plotinus, 7
19 Aquinas, 309–310, 777–778
20 Aquinas, 49–59, 70–73, 75–76, 78–79, 1058–1061
27 Shakespeare, 183–184
30 Bacon, 72, 80–81
32 Milton, 40–44, 351–352, 390
42 Kant, 378–379
49 Darwin, 315–316

1*b*. The relation of temperance to knowledge and prudence: the determination of the mean of temperance

Apocrypha, *Wisdom of Solomon,* 8:5–7
7 Plato, 1–13 esp 7, 61–62, 183–184, 338–339, 557
9 Aristotle, 349, 351–355, 385, 387, 394, 401–403, 434
17 Plotinus, 9–10
20 Aquinas, 39–40, 42–43, 65–66, 67–68
33 Pascal, 238
39 Smith, 346–347
42 Kant, 376–377
44 Boswell, 309, 404–405

1*c*. Temperance and continence: the counterfeits of temperance

7 Plato, 59–60, 225–226
9 Aristotle, 348, 391–392, 395–399, 400–403
18 Augustine, 41, 60
19 Aquinas, 517–519
20 Aquinas, 43–44, 63–64, 145–148, 746–747, 1053–1055
22 Chaucer, 540–542
23 Hobbes, 272
25 Montaigne, 89–91, 394–395

2. The varieties of intemperance: the related vices of sensuality, abstemiousness, cruelty, curiosity, inordinate desire

Old Testament: *Ecclesiastes,* 5:10–6:12 / *Isaiah,* 3:16–17; 5:11–14,22–23; 28:7–8 / *Habakkuk,* 2:4–5,15–17
Apocrypha: *Ecclesiasticus,* 14:5–10; 26:8; 31:25–31
New Testament: *Romans,* 1:18–32 / *Galatians,* 5:16–21 / *Colossians,* 3:5,8 / *James,* 4:1–6 / *I Peter,* 4:1–5 / *II Peter,* 2:9–22
4 Homer, 188, 231–233
5 Aeschylus, 1–14, 34–35
5 Euripides, 212–224, 225–236, 336–337, 340–352
5 Aristophanes, 499–502
6 Herodotus, 2–3, 95–98
7 Plato, 120, 153–155, 276–277, 474, 751
9 Aristotle, 352–354, 398–399, 401–402, 452
12 Lucretius, 57–58
12 Epictetus, 161–162, 228–230
12 Aurelius, 257–258
14 Plutarch, 419–420, 783–784
15 Tacitus, 86
18 Augustine, 17, 40–43, 81–86, 664–666
20 Aquinas, 123, 143–144, 149–150, 603–605
21 Dante, 7–10, 81–96
22 Chaucer, 374–382, 401–402, 512–514
24 Rabelais, 186–193
25 Montaigne, 162–167, 244–246, 270–271, 350–354, 538
26 Shakespeare, 385–386, 448–449, 456
27 Shakespeare, 37, 238–243, 311–350
29 Cervantes, 120–137

32 MILTON, 125–130, 243–245, 269–272
36 STERNE, 521
38 MONTESQUIEU, 117
39 SMITH, 346–347
40 GIBBON, 70–71, 90, 389
41 GIBBON, 169
43 MILL, 303–307 passim
46 HEGEL, 323
47 GOETHE, 49–56, 63–114, 245–276
49 DARWIN, 315–316
50 MARX, 72, 293–294
51 TOLSTOY, 248–250, 321–322
52 DOSTOEVSKY, 4, 50–62, 122–125, 191–235, 370
53 JAMES, 800–805

3. Temperance in relation to duty or happiness

OLD TESTAMENT: *Proverbs,* 5; 6:23–35; 7; 23:20–21,27–35 / *Jeremiah,* 35
APOCRYPHA: *Ecclesiasticus,* 18:30–32; 19:1–3; 31:12–31; 37:26–31
NEW TESTAMENT: *I Corinthians,* 6:9–10 / *Titus,* 1:5–9; 2 passim / *James,* 1:12–15; 4:1–10 / *II Peter,* 2:9–22
5 EURIPIDES, 225–236
7 PLATO, 156–157, 275–284, 416–427 passim, 689–690
9 ARISTOTLE, 432–434 passim, 460
12 LUCRETIUS, 15, 79
18 AUGUSTINE, 40–41, 81–86, 511–513
20 AQUINAS, 253–255
23 HOBBES, 163–164
25 MONTAIGNE, 71–72, 382–383
40 GIBBON, 192
42 KANT, 366–367
51 TOLSTOY, 605
54 FREUD, 599, 772–773, 793–794, 800–801

4. The cultivation of temperance: the training of a temperate character

APOCRYPHA: *Ecclesiasticus* passim
NEW TESTAMENT: *Romans,* 6:12–13; 13:13–14 / *I Corinthians,* 5:9–13; 7:1–9; 9:24–27 / *Colossians,* 3:2–8 / *I Thessalonians,* 4:3–5; 5:5–8 / *I Timothy,* 6:8–11 / *II Timothy,* 2:22 / *Titus,* 2 / *James,* 4:5–10 / *I John,* 2:15–17
5 ARISTOPHANES, 576–577
7 PLATO, 326–339 passim, 605–608, 645–663 passim, 672–674, 712
9 ARISTOTLE, 107, 348–351, 434–435, 465–466, 541, 545–546
12 EPICTETUS, 175–177, 178–180, 187–188, 208–210
14 PLUTARCH, 38–45
18 AUGUSTINE, 60
20 AQUINAS, 226–227
21 DANTE, 77–78
25 MONTAIGNE, 69–75 passim, 534
30 BACON, 69–70, 78, 79–80
32 MILTON, 385
40 GIBBON, 32, 338–339
42 KANT, 356–360
43 MILL, 305–307
51 TOLSTOY, 248–250, 577–578
54 FREUD, 407, 573, 592–593, 870

5. The social aspects of temperance

5*a*. The temperance of rulers and citizens: intemperate conduct as inimical to the common good

OLD TESTAMENT: *Leviticus,* 10:8–11 / *Deuteronomy,* 21:18–21 / *Proverbs,* 31: 4–5 / *Ecclesiastes,* 10:16–17 / *Isaiah,* 28:1–9; 56:9–12
APOCRYPHA: *Ecclesiasticus,* 47:19–21
NEW TESTAMENT: *I Timothy,* 3:1–13
5 SOPHOCLES, 152
5 EURIPIDES, 265–266, 382–383
5 ARISTOPHANES, 499–502, 588
6 HERODOTUS, 95–98, 222, 311–312
6 THUCYDIDES, 513
7 PLATO, 326–339, 346–355, 416–418, 605–608, 669–671, 672–676, 679, 733, 806–807
9 ARISTOTLE, 454–455, 474–475, 539
12 EPICTETUS, 184
12 AURELIUS, 254–255
14 PLUTARCH, 32–48, 549–551, 621–622, 661, 699–700
15 TACITUS, 166, 230–231
21 DANTE, 26–28, 81–85
24 RABELAIS, 133–140
25 MONTAIGNE, 436–438
26 SHAKESPEARE, 129–130, 453–454, 495–496, 499
27 SHAKESPEARE, 133–134, 178, 184, 192, 303–304, 421–425
38 MONTESQUIEU, 8–9, 10–11, 37–38, 51–53, 94–95
39 SMITH, 146–148, 346–347
40 GIBBON, 35–39 passim, 55–56, 138–140 passim, 256–257, 338–340, 448–449
43 FEDERALIST, 29–30, 190, 192
43 MILL, 302–312 passim
44 BOSWELL, 393
49 DARWIN, 325–327 passim

5*b*. The temperance of a people: luxurious indulgences; the intemperance of the mob

OLD TESTAMENT: *Numbers,* 11 / *Isaiah,* 3:16–26 / *Ezekiel,* 7:17–27 / *Amos,* 6
5 EURIPIDES, 400–401, 402–403
6 THUCYDIDES, 400–401, 436–438
7 PLATO, 318–319, 342, 408–411
9 ARISTOTLE, 465–466
14 PLUTARCH, 61–64, 648–649
15 TACITUS, 197–199, 204, 210–212, 213–214, 222, 238–239, 264–265, 277
18 AUGUSTINE, 147–149
25 MONTAIGNE, 54
26 SHAKESPEARE, 56–64, 473–474
27 SHAKESPEARE, 351–353

38 Montesquieu, 10, 118
40 Gibbon, 92, 216, 509–510
41 Gibbon, 397–398, 551–552
43 Mill, 329
46 Hegel, 198–199
52 Dostoevsky, 164–165
53 James, 719–720
54 Freud, 666–668 passim, 670–671

5c. Laws concerning temperance: the extent to which the sphere of temperance can be regulated by law

Old Testament: *Leviticus,* 18:22–23 / *Deuteronomy,* 21:18–21
7 Plato, 348, 643–663, 675–676, 708–709, 712, 713–716, 718–720
9 Aristotle, 348–349 passim, 377, 434–435
14 Plutarch, 32–48, 361
15 Tacitus, 31, 57–58
20 Aquinas, 231–233, 252–259, 263–264
25 Montaigne, 131–132
27 Shakespeare, 190
32 Milton, 393–395
38 Montesquieu, 44–48, 49–50, 87–88, 105–106
38 Rousseau, 434–435
39 Smith, 150, 211
40 Gibbon, 100–101
41 Gibbon, 93–94
42 Kant, 389
43 Constitution of the U.S., 19, 20
43 Mill, 309–310, 314–316
44 Boswell, 301

6. The extremes of temperance and intemperance

6a. Asceticism: heroic temperance

Old Testament: *Genesis,* 39:7–21 / *Numbers,* 6:1–21 / *Judges,* 13: 1–7 / *I Kings,* 19:4–8
New Testament: *Matthew,* 4:1–11 / *Luke,* 1:5–17 / *I Corinthians,* 7:36–38; 9:24–27 / *I Timothy,* 4:1–10
5 Euripides, 225–236
7 Plato, 737–738
12 Epictetus, 190–191
17 Plotinus, 8–9, 18, 24
18 Augustine, 139–140, 630–631
20 Aquinas, 66–67, 630–632, 650–656, 658–660, 1055–1058
22 Chaucer, 463–471
24 Rabelais, 152
25 Montaigne, 111, 120–121, 165–167, 350–351, 353–354
26 Shakespeare, 254–256, 353
29 Cervantes, 81–91
32 Milton, 35–56
33 Pascal, 64–65
38 Montesquieu, 210
40 Gibbon, 191–193, 338–340 passim, 593–599
42 Kant, 327
44 Boswell, 283
46 Hegel, 224, 340–34
52 Dostoevsky, 85–87

6b. The dionysiac spirit: the cult of pleasure

Old Testament: *Ecclesiastes,* 8:15
Apocrypha: *Wisdom of Solomon,* 2
4 Homer, 238–240
5 Euripides, 244, 340–352, 441, 444–445
5 Aristophanes, 458
6 Herodotus, 77
7 Plato, 801
9 Aristotle, 340, 366
14 Plutarch, 161–162, 572, 748–779
15 Tacitus, 103, 107, 108, 145, 166
24 Rabelais, 7–8, 60–66
26 Shakespeare, 435–436, 448–449, 486–487
40 Gibbon, 60, 649–650
41 Gibbon, 174–175
42 Kant, 387–388
43 Mill, 447–449
47 Goethe, 93–103
51 Tolstoy, 321–322
52 Dostoevsky, 46–82 passim

CROSS-REFERENCES

For: The general theory of virtue in its bearing on temperance, and for discussions bearing on the nature of temperance, *see* Desire 6a; Emotion 4b(1); Mind 9b–9c; Pleasure and Pain 8a; Virtue and Vice 1, 1c, 5a–5c.

Temperance in relation to knowledge and to other virtues, *see* Courage 4; Prudence 3b, 3d; Virtue and Vice 1b–1c, 2a(1), 3a–3b.

Other discussions of continence, *see* Prudence 3d; Virtue and Vice 1e.

The consideration of extreme forms of intemperance, *see* Desire 7a–7a(3); Infinity 6a; Sin 4c; Wealth 10e(3).

Other discussions which show the relation of temperance to duty and happiness, *see* Happiness 2b(3); Virtue and Vice 1d, 6a.

The problems involved in training a temperate character, *see* EDUCATION 4a–4d; PUNISHMENT 3a; VIRTUE AND VICE 4a–4d(4); and for the extent to which temperance can be regulated by law, *see* LAW 6d; PLEASURE AND PAIN 9; VIRTUE AND VICE 4d(3).
The issue concerning asceticism and self-denial, *see* DESIRE 6b; PLEASURE AND PAIN 7b; RELIGION 3d; VIRTUE AND VICE 8f–8g; WEALTH 10e(2).
Another consideration of the dionysiac or bacchic spirit, *see* PLEASURE AND PAIN 4d, 7b.

ADDITIONAL READINGS

Listed below are works not included in *Great Books of the Western World*, but relevant to the idea and topics with which this chapter deals. These works are divided into two groups:

I. Works by authors represented in this collection.
II. Works by authors not represented in this collection.

For the date, place, and other facts concerning the publication of the works cited, consult the Bibliography of Additional Readings which follows the last chapter of *The Great Ideas.*

I.

PLUTARCH. "Of Curiosity, or an Over-Busy Inquisitiveness into Things Impertinent," in *Moralia*
AUGUSTINE. *Of Continence*
AQUINAS. *Summa Theologica*, PART II–II, QQ 141–170
A. SMITH. *The Theory of Moral Sentiments*, PART VI, SECT III

II.

CICERO. *De Officiis (On Duties)*
HORACE. *Satires*, BK II (2)
BERNARD OF CLAIRVAUX. *On Consideration*
CALVIN. *Institutes of the Christian Religion*, BK III, CH 10
SPENSER. *The Faerie Queene*, BK II
H. MORE. *An Account of Virtue (Enchiridion Ethicum)*, BK II, CH 7, 9; BK III, CH 8
BOSSUET. *Traité de la concupiscence*
MANDEVILLE. *The Fable of the Bees*
J. BUTLER. *Fifteen Sermons upon Human Nature*
FRANKLIN. *Poor Richard's Almanack*
SCHOPENHAUER. *The World as Will and Idea*, VOL I, BK IV
T. H. GREEN. *Prolegomena to Ethics*, BK III, CH 5
NIETZSCHE. *Thus Spake Zarathustra*
——. *The Genealogy of Morals*, III
WEBER. *The Protestant Ethic and the Spirit of Capitalism*, CH 4–5
HILDEBRAND. *In Defense of Purity*
MERSCH. *Love, Marriage and Chastity*
VANN. *On Being Human*
HUIZINGA. *In the Shadow of Tomorrow*

Chapter 92: THEOLOGY

INTRODUCTION

IT has seldom been disputed that the questions with which theology deals are of critical significance for all the rest of human knowledge. Even those who deny that theology is or can be a science might be willing to concede that, if it were, it would deserve its traditional title, "queen of the sciences."

It has been said that the great questions of theology are unanswerable. It has been said that theological dispute or controversy is futile because the issues are not resolvable by argument. But it has rarely been asserted, or even implied, that our outlook would be unaltered and our actions unaffected if we could know, in any degree, the answers to questions concerning the existence of the supernatural and its relation to the visible world of nature. To Plato it is of such importance that he asks: "Who can be calm when he is called upon to prove the existence of the gods?"

The main controversy, not in, but about, theology turns on the use of such words as "knowledge" and "science" for a discipline which, both in method and conclusion, seems compelled to go beyond experience and to push reason to (or even beyond) the limit of its powers. In the minds of many, especially in our day, theology is associated with religion and is opposed to science or, if not opposed, at least it is set apart from science as entirely different. Those who conceive science as limited by its empirical methods to the investigation of observable phenomena might not quarrel with the allocation of theology to philosophy, but whether or not they did would in turn depend on their conception of philosophy.

As the chapters on SCIENCE and PHILOSOPHY indicate, these two terms are identified through a large part of the western tradition. The various sciences are regarded as branches of philosophy. But we also find a distinction being made in the 18th century between the empirical and rational or philosophical sciences; and in our day those who regard philosophy as mere speculation or opinion contrast it to the experimental disciplines which are thought to be the *only* established bodies of knowledge, that is, sciences.

The question whether theology is a science may, therefore, embrace a number of alternatives. That it is an empirical or experimental science has seldom been proposed. It may be treated as a science, however, by those who consider it as a part of philosophy; or it may be denied that honor precisely because it belongs to philosophy. A third alternative remains—that theology is separate from philosophy, that it is a science as distinct in character from the philosophical sciences as they are from the experimental disciplines. In this third alternative, the association of theology with religion or religious faith seems to determine the character of theology.

It is this third alternative which Hume seems to have in mind at the conclusion of his *Enquiry.* "Divinity or Theology, as it proves the existence of a Deity and the immortality of souls . . . has," he writes, "a foundation in *reason*, so far as it is supported by experience. But its best and most solid foundation is *faith* or divine revelation." To the extent that its principles come from religious faith, theology does not seem to fit perfectly into Hume's twofold division of the sciences into those which involve "abstract reasoning concerning quantity or number" and those which involve "experimental reasoning concerning matter of fact and existence."

When he says that he would commit to the flames "any volume of divinity or school metaphysics which does not contain either of these two kinds of reasoning"—for then "it can contain nothing but sophistry and illusion"—he can hardly be condemning the theology he has himself described as resting primarily on faith or divine revelation, though it may also have some foundation in reasoning from experience.

THE DISCUSSION OF THE nature and scope of theology, its principles and methods, may refer either to the theology which is a part of philosophy or to the theology which is sometimes called "dogmatic" because it expounds and explains the dogmas of a religious faith. Furthermore, those who make the distinction between the two kinds of theology raise questions concerning their relation to one another. In so doing they enter into the larger problem of the relation of faith and reason, and the limited part which reason can play in the development of a theology which rests on faith.

The distinction itself is made by many writers and in diverse ways. The theology which is entirely philosophical and independent of any religious faith is usually called "natural theology." The name "sacred theology" is given to a body of doctrine which finds its fundamental principles in the articles of a religious faith. The ultimate source of these articles of faith in Jewish, Christian, and Mohammedan theology is the truth revealed in a sacred scripture—the Old and New Testament or the Koran—from which, by interpretation, the articles of faith are drawn.

Bacon, for example, defines "divine philosophy or natural theology" as "that knowledge or rudiment of knowledge concerning God, which may be obtained by the contemplation of his creatures; which knowledge may be truly termed divine in respect of the object, and natural in respect of the light. The bounds of this knowledge are that it suffices to convince atheism, but not to inform religion." In contrast, "inspired theology" or "sacred theology (which in our idiom we call divinity) is grounded only upon the word and oracle of God, and not upon the light of nature."

Kant makes a similar distinction when he says that theology is based either "on reason alone (*theologia rationalis*) or upon revelation (*theologia revelata*)." But for Kant "natural theology" designates only one kind of rational theology. Another kind is "transcendental theology," which differs from the first in the method which reason employs. He also differentiates between speculative and moral theology. Though both fall within the sphere of reason, one is the work of the pure theoretic reason, the other of the pure practical reason.

In the opening question of the *Summa Theologica*, Aquinas tries to explain why, in addition to the "philosophical science built up by reason, there should be a sacred science learned through revelation." To an objection which claims that "there is no need of any further knowledge," because philosophical science can attain to knowledge even of God Himself, he replies that "there is no reason why those things which may be learnt from philosophical science, so far as they can be known by natural reason, may not also be taught us by another science so far as they fall within revelation." Though they may deal with the same object, "sciences are differentiated according to the various means through which knowledge is obtained. . . . Hence the theology included in sacred doctrine differs in kind from that theology which is part of philosophy."

In another place, Aquinas refers to the theological conclusions which the philosopher thinks he can demonstrate—"the existence of God and other like truths about God which can be known by natural reason." Of these he says that they "are not articles of faith, but are preambles to the articles. . . . Nevertheless," he adds, "there is nothing to prevent a man, who cannot grasp a proof, accepting as a matter of faith, something which in itself is capable of being scientifically known and demonstrated." But such propositions, which belong to both reason and faith, are only part of sacred doctrine. In addition, there are the propositions which belong to faith alone.

"It is impossible," Aquinas writes, "to attain to the knowledge of the Trinity by natural reason." The triune nature of the Godhead cannot be demonstrated philosophically; nor can the dogma be fully comprehended by human understanding. In Purgatory, Dante learns that "Mad is he who hopes that our reason can traverse the infinite way which One Substance in Three Persons holds."

Though it is not a theological mystery in the same sense, another example of a dogma not demonstrable by reason is the proposition that the world began to be. "That the world did not always exist," Aquinas declares, "we hold by faith alone; it cannot be proved demonstratively; which is what was said above of the mystery of the Trinity." We find in Sacred Scripture the words *In the beginning God created heaven and earth*, "in which words the newness of the world is stated" and so "the newness of the world is known only by revelation."

With respect to such matters as belong to faith alone, a theologian like Aquinas cautions against the misuse of reason. "When anyone in the endeavor to prove what belongs to faith, brings forward arguments which are not cogent, he falls under the ridicule of the unbelievers; since they suppose that we base ourselves upon such arguments, and that we believe on their account. Therefore, we must not attempt to establish what is of faith, except by authority alone" and only "to those who accept the authority." For those who do not accept the authority of Scripture, the most that reason can do concerning propositions peculiar to faith is "to prove that what faith teaches is not impossible." Elsewhere Aquinas points out that "although the argument from authority based on human reason is the weakest, yet the argument from authority based on divine revelation is the strongest."

The foregoing throws some light on Montaigne's defense of a book by Raimond de Sebonde, bearing the title *La theologie naturelle*. Though he calls his work "natural theology," de Sebonde, according to Montaigne, "undertakes by human and natural reasons to establish and make good against the atheists all the articles of the Christian religion." What his opponents "reprehend in his work is that Christians are to blame to repose upon human reasons their belief, which is only conceived by faith and the particular inspiration of divine grace."

Montaigne agrees that it is "faith alone that vividly and certainly comprehends the deep mysteries of our religion." But he also thinks that it is "a brave and very laudable attempt to accommodate the natural and human capabilities that God has endowed us with to the service of our faith. It is not to be doubted," he says, "that it is the most noble use we can put them to, and that there is no design or occupation more worthy of a Christian man than to make it the aim and end of all of his thoughts and studies to embellish, extend, and amplify the truth of his belief."

The conception of natural theology which Montaigne appears to entertain in his "Apology for Raimond de Sebonde" does not seem to differentiate it from sacred theology, insofar as all its principles are articles of faith. Quite apart from de Sebonde, Montaigne himself does not think that the existence of God or the immortality of the soul can be demonstrated by reason. Montaigne observes "how short the most constant and firm maintainers of this just and clear persuasion of the immortality of the soul fall, and how weak their arguments are, when they go about to prove it by human reason. . . . Let us ingenuously confess that God alone has dictated it to us, and faith; 'tis no lesson of nature and our own reason."

Though the denial of God's existence is, according to Montaigne, "a proposition unnatural and monstrous, difficult also and hard to establish in the human understanding," he thinks the affirmation to be no less beyond reason's power to establish with certitude, for "all things produced by our own reasoning and understanding, whether true or false, are subject to incertitude and controversy."

In this, Montaigne differs not only from a theologian like Aquinas, who assigns certain truths to natural theology as capable of being demonstrated by reason without the aid of faith, but also from such philosophers as Descartes, Spinoza, and Locke, who hold that we can know God by reason with more certainty, and even (according to Spinoza) more adequately, than we can know most other things. "I have always considered," Descartes writes, "that the two questions respecting God and the Soul were the chief of those that ought to be demonstrated by philosophical rather than theological argument. For although it is quite enough for us faithful ones to accept by means of faith the fact that the human soul does not perish with the body, and that God exists, it certainly does not seem possible ever to persuade infidels of any religion . . . unless, to begin with, we prove these two facts by means of the natural reason."

Descartes, it appears, reserves the use of the

word "theology" for sacred doctrine. What others, like Bacon, call "natural theology," he treats simply as philosophy, or that branch of it which he calls "metaphysics." Dedicating his *Meditations* to "the dean and doctors of the sacred faculty of theology in Paris," he says: "I have noticed that you, along with all the theologians, did not only affirm that the existence of God may be proved by the natural reason, but also that it may be inferred from the Holy Scriptures, that knowledge of Him is much clearer than that which we have of many created things, and, as a matter of fact, is so easy to acquire that those who have it not are culpable in their ignorance."

But Descartes wishes to confess the limitations of the mere philosopher's knowledge of God. When he came to inquire "how God may be more easily and certainly known than the things of this world," no matter how much "certainty and evidence I find in my reasons," he could not persuade himself, he says, that "all the world is capable of understanding them. . . . There are not so many in the world who are fitted for metaphysical speculations as there are for those of geometry."

Answering a critic who quotes Aquinas against him, he later writes: "I admit along with all theologians that God cannot be comprehended by the human mind, and also that He cannot be distinctly known by those who try mentally to grasp Him at once in His entirety. . . . Wherever I have said that God can be clearly and distinctly known, I have understood this to apply only to this finite cognition of ours, which is proportionate to the diminutive capacity of our minds."

SO FAR WE HAVE considered the distinction between natural and sacred theology—or between philosophy and theology—as it is made in the Christian tradition by writers conscious of the difference between faith and reason, or revelation and demonstration. In pagan antiquity, there seems to be no equivalent of sacred theology. "The various modes of worship, which prevailed in the Roman world," Gibbon tells us, "were all considered by the people as equally true; by the philosopher as equally false; and by the magistrate as equally useful. . . . The superstition of the people was not embittered by theological rancour; nor was it confined by the chains of any speculative system." It was "the elegant mythology of Homer," he says, not reasoning, which "gave a beautiful, and almost a regular form to the polytheism of the ancient world."

Of the Greek philosophers, Gibbon remarks that "they meditated on the Divine Nature as a very curious and important speculation," but only the Stoics and the Platonists "endeavored to reconcile the jarring interests of reason and piety." Plato's criticism of the poets in the *Republic* for their impiety, and his rational defense of piety in the *Laws*, accompanied by a demonstration of the existence of the gods, may be taken as examples of ancient theological discourse within a religious context. Another example, and from quite another point of view, is Cicero's *De Natura Deorum*, which Gibbon praises as the best guide to the opinions of the philosophers concerning the tenets of polytheism.

But neither Cicero nor Plato treats theology as a science. The ancient philosopher who does and who, moreover, regards theology as the highest of the speculative sciences, seems to proceed without reference to or benefit of prevailing religious beliefs. Aristotle dismisses "the school of Hesiod and all the theologians [who] thought only of what was plausible to themselves." He refers to the legends of the gods which "our forefathers in the most remote ages have handed down to their posterity . . . in the form of a myth . . . with a view to the persuasion of the multitude and to its legal and utilitarian expediency." But the highest science, which Aristotle sometimes calls "first philosophy," he also calls "theology." It deals with the immaterial and the insensible, the immovable and eternal. We may call it "theology," he writes, "since it is obvious that if the divine is present anywhere, it is present in things of this sort." In another place he says, "there are three kinds of theoretical sciences—physics, mathematics, theology . . . and of these the last named is best, for it deals with the highest of existing things."

At the beginning of the *Metaphysics*, Aristotle gives another reason for thinking that theology is a divine science: not that it is divinely inspired, but that, having the divine for its object, it is the science "most meet for God to have. . . . Such a science either God alone can have, or God above all others." The title given the book in which Aristotle attempts to develop this science comes in the later tradition to be the name given to speculation concerning immaterial and insensible substances. What Aristotle calls "theology," Descartes, as we have seen, calls "metaphysics" in order to distinguish it from the theology based on revelation.

Whether the theology of a pagan philosopher is commensurable with the theology of Jewish or Christian thinkers, even when the latter attempt to be purely philosophical or natural theologians, is a question which deeply probes the relation of reason to faith. For even when reason tries to proceed independently of faith, the religious faith of a community may tinge the concepts the philosopher uses and define the problems he undertakes to solve. It may be one thing to prove the existence of a Prime Mover, and another to know by reason the nature and existence of the God who in the beginning created heaven and earth—the God of Abraham, Isaac, and Jacob, the God of the Christians, whom Pascal distinguishes from the God of the philosophers.

Augustine explains his attitude as a theologian toward the theories of the philosophers touching divine matters. "I have not undertaken," he says, "to refute all the vain theological opinions of all the philosophers, but only of such of them as, agreeing in the belief that there is a divine nature, and that this divine nature is concerned about human affairs, do nevertheless deny that the worship of the one unchangeable God is sufficient for the obtaining of a blessed life after death, as well as at the present time." Since "Plato defined the wise man as one who imitates, knows, and loves this God, and who is rendered blessed through fellowship with Him in His own blessedness, why discuss with the other philosophers? It is evident that none come nearer to us than the Platonists."

Plato, according to Augustine, "is justly preferred to all the other philosophers of the Gentiles"; those among his followers who show "the greatest acuteness in understanding him . . . entertain such an idea of God as to admit that in Him are to be found the cause of existence, the ultimate reason for the understanding, and the end in reference to which the whole life is to be regulated." So amazing, to his mind, are the parallels between certain insights expressed by Plato and the wisdom of Sacred Scripture, that Augustine is almost inclined to believe that "Plato was not ignorant of those writings." But he does not think it necessary to determine whether Plato had acquaintance with the writings of Moses and the prophets, because certain basic truths, which were revealed to the Hebrews, were made known to the gentiles through the light of nature and reason. "That which is known of God," the apostle had said, "has been manifested among them, for God hath manifested it to them."

Therefore Augustine feels justified in taking any truth from Plato which is consistent with Christian faith. Aquinas, borrowing much from Aristotle, explains that "sacred doctrine makes use of the authority of philosophers in those questions in which they were able to know the truth by natural reason." Sacred theology uses the doctrines of the philosophers, he adds, "not as though it stood in need of them, but only in order to make its teaching clearer." It is in this sense that Aquinas calls philosophy the handmaiden of theology.

Others seem to take a different view of this relationship. Montaigne wonders whether it would not be better if "the divine doctrine, as queen and regent of the rest," kept herself apart, and he quotes St. Chrysostom to the effect that philosophy has "long been banished from the holy schools as a handmaid altogether useless." Hobbes goes further. He describes the traditional theology as a mingling of Aristotle's metaphysics with Scripture, and claims that the "bringing of the philosophy and doctrine of Aristotle into religion by the Schoolmen" caused the "many contradictions and absurdities" which "brought the clergy into a reputation both of ignorance and of fraudulent intention, and inclined people to revolt from them."

Hegel, however, dismisses the criticism that is often made concerning the dependence of Christian theology, at least in its formative period, on pagan philosophy. "The Fathers of the Church and the Councils," he writes, "constituted the dogma; but a chief element in this constitution was supplied by the previous development of *philosophy*." That certain dogmas were introduced into the Christian religion through "the instrumentality of philosophy . . . is not sufficient ground for asserting that they were foreign to Christianity and had nothing to do with it. It is a matter of perfect indifference where a thing originated; the only question," Hegel insists, "is, 'Is it true in and for itself?' Many think that by pronouncing the doctrine to be Neo-Platonic, they have *ipso facto* banished it from Christianity. Whether a Christian doctrine stands exactly thus and thus in the Bible . . . is not the only question. The Letter kills, the Spirit makes alive."

COMPARED WITH SACRED theology, the subject matter of natural theology and the scope of its problems seem to be extremely narrow. At most, it is only a part of philosophy, and some writers treat it as no more than one part of metaphysics.

Kant, for example, divides metaphysics into three parts—theology, cosmology, and psychology—according to his conception of metaphysics as having "for the proper object of its inquiries only three grand ideas: God, Freedom, and Immortality." As a branch of transcendental speculation, theology is concerned primarily with the problem of God's existence. Similarly, Aristotle's metaphysical inquiries include more than his theology. His theology begins only after he has discussed the nature and being of sensible substances. It is stated mainly in Book XII of the *Metaphysics* where he considers the existence and character of immaterial substances, and of the one purely actual being which is God.

Descartes' conception seems to be broader, for he regards the immortality of the soul as well as the existence and nature of God as being characteristically theological problems even when they are treated in metaphysics and by the methods of the philosopher. Because these two problems concern spiritual beings, Adam Smith also groups them together under the name "pneumatics" or "pneumatology," which he identifies with metaphysics—that part of philosophy most emphasized "in the universities of Europe where philosophy was taught only as subservient to theology." Bacon alone seems to separate natural theology entirely from metaphysics, which, along with physics, is for him a part of natural rather than divine philosophy. But though he would limit natural theology to that knowledge of God which can be drawn from nature, and excludes attempts to induce from nature "any verity or persuasion concerning the points of faith," he grants that natural as well as divine theology may treat of "the nature of angels and spirits," as "neither inscrutable nor interdicted."

The subject matter of sacred theology, or what he calls "divinity," is, according to Bacon's account, much more extensive. He first divides it into "matter of belief" and "matter of service and adoration"; and from these two derives the "four main branches of divinity: faith, manners, liturgy, and government." The matter of faith contains "the doctrine of the nature of God, of the attributes of God, and of the works of God." Under manners, Bacon lists the consideration of divine law and the breach of it by sin: liturgy concerns the sacraments and rituals of religion; government, the organization, offices, and jurisdictions of the church.

As its title indicates, the *Summa Theologica* of Aquinas endeavors to set forth the sum of theological knowledge. In addition to the topics and problems peculiar to sacred doctrine, the subject matters treated in the *Summa* seem to represent the whole range of human inquiry—almost co-extensive with the scope of the natural sciences and philosophy, both speculative and moral.

Aquinas explains the encyclopedic character of the *Summa* by pointing out that to have God as the subject matter of theology means that sacred doctrine treats "all things under the aspect of God, either because they are God Himself, or because they refer to God as their beginning and end." The unity of theology in covering so wide a diversity of matters consists in the single formality under which they are considered—the formality of being divinely revealed. That is why "objects which are the subject matter of different philosophical sciences can yet be treated by this one single sacred science under one aspect, namely, insofar as they can be included in revelation."

Thus, for example, in the preamble to his Treatise on Man, Aquinas writes: "The theologian considers the nature of man in relation to the soul; but not in relation to the body, except insofar as the body has relation to the soul." This emphasis is dictated by the articles of Christian faith which concern man, in both body and soul. Similarly, with respect to moral matters, Aquinas explains that the theologian "considers human acts inasmuch as man is thereby directed to happiness," and he takes account of the circumstances of human acts because they may excuse from sin, "the consideration of which belongs to the theologian." It belongs to the theologian only when sin is conceived "as an offense against God," but to the moral philosophers when it is conceived "as something contrary to reason."

It appears from the foregoing that sacred theology is both speculative and practical (or moral). It deals with the nature of divine things and with human acts, but with the latter only so far as they have God for their rule or end. "Although among the philosophical sciences," Aquinas writes, "some are speculative and others practical, sacred doctrine includes both."

Even though it is made on the level of the philosophical sciences, Kant's distinction between speculative and moral theology seems to be based on a different principle. For Aquinas the speculative and the practical parts of theology deal with different problems, such as God, the Trinity, creation, and the angels on the one hand, and beatitude, the virtues, divine law, sin, grace, and sacraments on the other. But for Kant both speculative and moral theology deal with the problem of God's existence. They differ only according to the manner in which the theoretic and the practical reason undertake to solve this problem.

"All attempts of reason to establish a theology by the aid of speculation alone are fruitless," writes Kant. Consequently, "a rational theology can have no existence unless it is founded upon the laws of morality." The postulates of pure practical reason—of immortality, free will, and the existence of God—"all proceed from the principle of morality, which is not a postulate but a law by which reason determines the will directly." The moral law involves, as a necessary condition, "the existence of the *summum bonum*," and that in turn involves "the supposition of the supreme independent good, that is, the existence of God."

According to Kant, a Supreme Being is "for the speculative reason, a mere ideal, though a faultless one—a conception which perfects and crowns the system of human cognition, but the objective reality of which can neither be proved nor disproved by pure reason." It is this defect which moral theology remedies. "We must assume," he says, "a moral world-cause, that is, an Author of the world, if we are to set before ourselves a final end in conformity to the moral law." But, he adds, "this moral argument is not intended to supply an objectively valid proof of the existence of God. It is not meant to demonstrate to the skeptic that there is a God, but that he *must adopt* the assumption of this proposition as a maxim of his practical reason, if he wishes to think in a manner consistent with morality."

The problem of the proof of God's existence, though central in theology, is more fully discussed in the chapter on God. Here we are concerned with the nature of theology itself as a branch of learning or inquiry. Since the chapter on Metaphysics necessarily touches on theology as a philosophical discipline, it seems advisable to devote attention here to some of the things which are peculiarly the concern of sacred theology.

Heresy is one of these. A scientist or philosopher may be criticized for his errors, but only a theologian, only the man who tries to explain some article of faith, can be called a heretic in the strict sense of that word. According to his view of the relation between church and state, Hobbes defines heresy in political terms. "Heresy," he writes, "is nothing else but a private opinion, obstinately maintained, contrary to the opinion which the Public Person"—*i.e.*, the Sovereign—"has commanded to be taught." But, according to Pascal, "none but God was able to instruct the Church in the faith," and so "it is heresy to resist the decisions of the faith, because this amounts to an opposing of our own spirit to the Spirit of God." But, he adds, "it is no heresy, though it may be an act of presumption, to disbelieve certain particular facts, because this is no more than opposing reason—it may be enlightened reason—

to an authority which is great indeed, but in this matter is not infallible."

The aspect of choice, of obstinately preferring one's own opinion against a superior authority, is emphasized by Aquinas, but he adds the specification that heresy is a corruption of Christian faith, a species of unbelief in which the heretic defies the authority of the Church, choosing "not what Christ really taught, but the suggestions of his own mind." He quotes a statement by Augustine that we should not accuse of heresy "those who, however false and perverse their opinion may be, defend it without obstinate fervor" and are "ready to mend their opinion when they have found the truth because they do not make a choice in contradiction to the doctrine of the Church." It is not the falsity of the opinion which makes it heresy, for until the point of faith has been defined by the authority of the Church, theologians may differ, and even be in error, without being heretical.

The inference may be drawn that progress is made in the refinement and precision of theological doctrine as the dogmas of a religion are more fully stated and the line between orthodoxy and heresy becomes more clearly defined. Augustine, who is one of the great formative theologians for the Protestant as well as the Catholic tradition, devotes a large part of his writing to the criticism of heresies—the great Arian heresy concerning the Trinity, the Nestorian or Monophysite heresy concerning the Incarnation, the Manichean heresy concerning the existence of evil, and the Pelagian heresy concerning grace and good works.

"While the hot restlessness of heretics," Augustine writes, "stirs questions about many articles of the catholic faith, the necessity of defending them forces us . . . to investigate them more accurately, to understand them more clearly, and to proclaim them more earnestly"; and the question mooted by an adversary becomes the occasion of instruction. According to Aquinas, "the profit that ensues from heresy is beside the intention of heretics, for it consists in the constancy of the faithful being put to the test and makes us shake off our sluggishness and search the Scriptures more carefully."

To Augustine and Aquinas, theological argument and controversy seem to be serviceable in the propagation and defense of the faith. Aquinas, for example, distinguishes the various types of dispute in which a Christian theologian can engage—with heretics, with Jews, with infidels. "We can argue with heretics from texts in Holy Scripture," he writes, "and against those who deny one article of faith we can argue from another. If our opponent believes nothing of divine revelation, there is no longer any means of proving the articles of faith by argument, but only of answering his objections—if he has any—against faith."

But it is necessary to add the qualification that the reasons employed "to prove things that are of faith are not demonstrations; they are either persuasive arguments showing that what is proposed by faith is not impossible; or else they are proofs drawn from the principles of faith, *i.e.*, from the authority of Holy Writ. . . . Whatever is based on these principles is as well-proved in the eyes of the faithful, as a conclusion drawn from self-evident principles is in the eyes of all."

Furthermore, Aquinas points out, "since faith rests upon infallible truth, and since the contrary of a truth can never be demonstrated, it is clear that the proofs brought against faith are not demonstrations, but arguments that can be answered." Descartes seems to hold a similar view. Defending his opinions in a letter to Father Dinet, he declares: "As to theology, as one truth can never be contrary to another, it would be a kind of impiety to fear that the truths discovered in philosophy were contrary to those of the true Faith."

A SOMEWHAT CONTRARY view of the relation of faith and reason seems to be taken by Locke. "Whatever God hath revealed," he says, "is certainly true; no doubt can be made of it. This is the proper object of faith; but whether it be a divine revelation, or no, reason must judge." Reason, not faith, is the ultimate test of truth, in theology as in philosophy. "Reason must be our last judge and guide in everything." If reason finds something "to be revealed from God, reason then declares for it, as much as for any other truth, and makes it one of her dictates."

In many of the great books we find a less

favorable view of the merit or profit in theological controversy. Its excesses and mumbo-jumbo are travestied and caricatured by Rabelais and Sterne; its futility and folly are the subject of bitter complaint by Hobbes and Bacon; its intolerance is condemned by Locke and Mill. Gibbon, who reports the disputes which raged through ten centuries of Christendom, seldom speaks kindly of the disputants. He refers to "the exquisite rancor of theological hatred"; and in describing the fury of the conflict between the Arians and the defenders of the Nicene creed, he says that, "in the midsts of their fierce contentions, they easily forgot the doubt which is recommended by philosophy, and the submission which is enjoined by religion."

In the Middle Ages, mystical theologians, like Peter Damiani or Bernard of Clairvaux, attack as impious or irreligious the kind of theology which borrows from the philosophers and makes use of the liberal arts, especially the techniques of the dialectician. In similar vein Protestant reformers, like Luther, later attack theology itself as detrimental to the purity of Christian faith and the spirit of religion. It is in this vein also that Bacon deplores the "unprofitable subtility or curiosity" and the "fruitless speculation or controversy" in divinity, and speaks of the "extreme prejudice which both religion and philosophy have received and may receive by being commixed together."

When the Student in *Faust* says, "I'm now almost inclined to try Theology," Mephistopheles replies:

> I would not wish to lead you so astray.
> In what this science touches, it would be
> So hard to shun the false, misleading way;
> So much of hidden poison lies therein,
> You scarce can tell it from its medicine.

That, however, is the voice of the devil; and from the point of view of those who see no conflict between faith and reason or between piety and inquiry, the attempt to separate religion from theology often looks diabolical.

OUTLINE OF TOPICS

1. The subject matter of theology: the scope of its inquiry; the range of its problems

2. The distinction between natural and sacred theology: its relation to the distinction between reason and faith

3. Theology as a philosophical discipline

   3*a*. Natural theology in relation to other parts of philosophy: *philosophia prima*, metaphysics, natural philosophy

   3*b*. The distinction between speculative and moral theology: theology as a work of the practical reason

   3*c*. The limitations of speculative theology: the insoluble mysteries or antinomies

4. Sacred theology: faith seeking understanding

   4*a*. The relation of sacred theology to philosophy: theology as the queen of the sciences

   4*b*. The principles of sacred theology: revealed truth; articles of faith; interpretation of Scripture

   4*c*. The roles of reason and authority in the development of sacred doctrine: theological argument and proof

   4*d*. Sacred theology as a speculative and practical science

   4*e*. The nature and forms of theological heresy

5. Criticisms of theology: the dogmatic, sophistical, or over-dialectical character of theological controversy

REFERENCES

References are listed by volume number (in bold type), author's name, and page number. Bible references are to book, chapter, and verse of the Authorized King James version of the Bible. The abbreviation "esp" calls the reader's attention to one or more especially relevant parts of a whole reference; "passim" signifies that the topic is discussed intermittently rather than continuously in the work or passage cited. Where the work as a whole is relevant to the topic, the page numbers refer to the entire work. For general guidance in the use of *The Great Ideas,* consult the Preface.

1. The subject matter of theology: the scope of its inquiry; the range of its problems

7 PLATO, 389–391, 397–398, 757–771
8 ARISTOTLE, 501, 547–548
18 AUGUSTINE, 323
19 AQUINAS, 3–10, 378, 440
20 AQUINAS, 354–355
30 BACON, 95–101
33 PASCAL, 355–356
35 HUME, 509
39 SMITH, 336–337
42 KANT, 176, 190, 236–240

2. The distinction between natural and sacred theology: its relation to the distinction between reason and faith

18 AUGUSTINE, 47–52, 264–273
19 AQUINAS, 3–4, 11–12, 60–62, 175–178, 253–255
20 AQUINAS, 383–384, 392–394, 399–400
23 HOBBES, 66
25 MONTAIGNE, 208–209, 212, 238–239
30 BACON, 41–42, 96–97
31 DESCARTES, 4–5, 43, 69–71, 125–126, 168–169
32 MILTON, 331–332
33 PASCAL, 221–225, 266
35 LOCKE, 291, 380
40 GIBBON, 307–309, 346
43 MILL, 455
51 TOLSTOY, 196–197

3. Theology as a philosophical discipline

3*a*. Natural theology in relation to other parts of philosophy: *philosophia prima*, metaphysics, natural philosophy

7 PLATO, 388–398, 442–477
8 ARISTOTLE, 268, 271, 275, 390, 499–501, 592–593
16 PTOLEMY, 5–6
19 AQUINAS, 7–8
23 HOBBES, 269
30 BACON, 2–4, 15–16, 43–46
31 DESCARTES, 283–284
42 KANT, 33, 239–240, 350–352, 603–613 esp 606–607
46 HEGEL, 368–369

3*b*. The distinction between speculative and moral theology: theology as a work of the practical reason

42 KANT, 236–240, 291–296, 588–613

3*c*. The limitations of speculative theology: the insoluble mysteries or antinomies

18 AUGUSTINE, 36–37, 264–273
19 AQUINAS, 10–12, 62–75, 175–178, 472–473, 501–503
21 DANTE, 56
23 HOBBES, 163
30 BACON, 41
31 DESCARTES, 112–114, 127
33 PASCAL, 205–210, 212–217
35 HUME, 487
40 GIBBON, 12–13, 186
42 KANT, 143–145, 174–177, 187–192, 200–209, 218–223, 234–240, 291–292, 344–349, 588–607

4. Sacred theology: faith seeking understanding

4*a*. The relation of sacred theology to philosophy: theology as the queen of the sciences

18 AUGUSTINE, 47–52, 264–273, 323
19 AQUINAS, 5–7, 446–447
23 HOBBES, 247, 260, 269
25 MONTAIGNE, 155
30 BACON, 17–20, 39–40, 41, 114, 124
31 DESCARTES, 69–71, 162–165
39 SMITH, 336–337
40 GIBBON, 307–309
46 HEGEL, 308–309

4*b*. The principles of sacred theology: revealed truth; articles of faith; interpretation of Scripture

18 AUGUSTINE, 621–698
19 AQUINAS, 3–10, 164–165, 354–355
20 AQUINAS, 271–272, 383–390
23 HOBBES, 137–138, 160, 167, 181–182, 241–244
30 BACON, 95–96
33 PASCAL, 78–80, 163–164, 273–276, 290–301, 440
40 GIBBON, 307–308, 346

41 Gibbon, 230
46 Hegel, 308–309

4*c*. The roles of reason and authority in the development of sacred doctrine: theological argument and proof

18 Augustine, 36–37, 47–52, 107–108, 110, 120, 530, 621–698 passim
19 Aquinas, 3–10, 11–12, 17–18, 175–178
21 Dante, 142–144
23 Hobbes, 149, 165, 167, 241–242
25 Montaigne, 208–294 passim
30 Bacon, 41, 95–96
31 Descartes, 162–165
33 Pascal, 163–166, 217–220, 221–225, 272–273, 348, 355–356
35 Locke, 5, 380–384 passim, 387–388
35 Hume, 497–503 passim
40 Gibbon, 206, 307–314, 348, 438–442, 670
41 Gibbon, 134–151, 462–463, 520–521
44 Boswell, 173–174
46 Hegel, 158–160

4*d*. Sacred theology as a speculative and practical science

19 Aquinas, 5
20 Aquinas, 600–601

4*e*. The nature and forms of theological heresy

18 Augustine, 15–16, 51, 422, 502–503
19 Aquinas, 172–173, 180
20 Aquinas, 163–164, 438–442
21 Dante, 13–15, 126
23 Hobbes, 213–214, 238–239, 248
25 Montaigne, 154
33 Pascal, 128–137, 141–166, 342–343
35 Locke, 1–2, 21–22
38 Rousseau, 438–439
40 Gibbon, 182–184, 310–313 passim
41 Gibbon, 134–138, 143–145, 149–152 passim, 198, 422
52 Dostoevsky, 127–137

5. Criticisms of theology: the dogmatic, sophistical, or over-dialectical character of theological controversy

23 Hobbes, 51–52, 54, 71, 247–248, 269–271, 274
24 Rabelais, 21–24, 101–106, 186–188
35 Hume, 499–500
36 Sterne, 222–224, 366–376
40 Gibbon, 312–313, 345–346, 439, 441
41 Gibbon, 476–477
46 Hegel, 313, 360
47 Goethe, 47

CROSS-REFERENCES

For: The consideration of topics or problems which fall within the scope of theology, *see* Astronomy 6; Beauty 7a; Cause 7–7d; Desire 7b; Eternity 3, 4d; God 2b, 2d, 4–5i; Good and Evil 2–2b; Happiness 7–7d; History 5a–5b; Honor 6–6b; Immortality 2, 3a; Infinity 7a–7d; Justice 11–11b; Liberty 5a–5d; Love 5a–5c; Matter 3d; Mind 10g; One and Many 1b, 6a–6c; Opposition 2d–2e; Punishment 5e(1)–5e(2); Relation 2–3; Religion 2c; Same and Other 6; Sin 3–3e, 6a–6e; Soul 4b–4c; Time 2b–2c; Virtue and Vice 8d–8d(3); Will 4a–4b, 7e–7e(2); Wisdom 1d; World 3a–4e(3), 8.

Other discussions of the relation of reason and faith, or of the relation of theology to religion, *see* Knowledge 6c(5); Logic 4f; Opinion 4a; Philosophy 6c; Religion 1a, 1b(1), 6b, 6g; Truth 4a; Wisdom 1c.

The relation of philosophy to theology, and for the conception of natural theology as a part of philosophy, *see* Metaphysics 3a; Philosophy 1a; Religion 6f–6g.

Discussions bearing on sacred theology as a science, and on its principles and methods, *see* Logic 4f; Reasoning 6a; Religion 6b, 6c(1); Science 2a.

Discussions bearing on the nature and extent of revealed truth and on the articles of religious faith, *see* Angel 3–4; Evolution 7a; God 2a, 7–9f; Immortality 3b; Man 9b(1)–9b(3), 11a–11c; Prophecy 4a–4d; Sin 3–3e; Soul 4d(3); Virtue and Vice 8e; World 4e(3).

The problems of interpreting the Word of God or Sacred Scripture, *see* Language 12; Sign and Symbol 5e.

Considerations relevant to the relation of theology to jurisprudence, *see* Law 3a–3b(2).

Various attacks on theological doctrines, and for criticisms directed against the kind of speculation which is theological, *see* Dialectic 3c; God 10–13; Immortality 2; Knowledge 5c; Metaphysics 2d, 4a; Opinion 4b; Philosophy 6b; Religion 6f–6g; Soul 3d; Will 5c; World 4a.

ADDITIONAL READINGS

Listed below are works not included in *Great Books of the Western World*, but relevant to the idea and topics with which this chapter deals. These works are divided into two groups:

I. Works by authors represented in this collection.
II. Works by authors not represented in this collection.

For the date, place, and other facts concerning the publication of the works cited, consult the Bibliography of Additional Readings which follows the last chapter of *The Great Ideas*.

I.

AUGUSTINE. *On the Profit of Believing*
——. *On Faith in Things Unseen*
AQUINAS. *On the Trinity of Boethius*, QQ 1–3
——. *Summa Contra Gentiles*, BK I, CH 1–9
——. *Compendium of Theology*
SPINOZA. *Tractatus Theologico-Politicus* (*Theological-Political Treatise*), CH 14–15
KANT. *Untersuchung über die Deutlichkeit der Grundsätze der natürlichen Theologie und der Moral*
J. S. MILL. "Theism," in *Three Essays on Religion*

II.

CICERO. *De Natura Deorum* (*On the Nature of the Gods*), II
PROCLUS. *The Elements of Theology*
SAADIA GAON. *The Book of Beliefs and Opinions*, INTRODUCTORY TREATISE
ABAILARD. *Introductio ad Theologiam*
MAIMONIDES. *The Guide for the Perplexed*, INTRO
BONAVENTURA. *On the Reduction of the Arts to Theology*
——. *Breviloquium*, PART I (1)
——. *Itinerarium Mentis in Deum* (*The Itinerary of the Mind to God*)
R. BACON. *Opus Majus*, PART II
ALBERTUS MAGNUS. *Summa Theologiae*, PART I
DUNS SCOTUS. *Opus Oxoniense*, PROLOGIUM
ALBO. *The Book of Principles* (*Sefer ha-Ikkarim*)
CALVIN. *Institutes of the Christian Religion*
BOEHME. *The Way from Darkness to True Illumination*
H. MORE. *The Antidote Against Atheism*, BK I, CH 1–10
R. BARCLAY. *An Apology for the True Christian Divinity*
CUDWORTH. *The True Intellectual System of the Universe*
MALEBRANCHE. *Dialogues on Metaphysics and Religion*, II, VIII
LEIBNITZ. *Theodicy*
J. BUTLER. *The Analogy of Religion*
VOLTAIRE. "Figure in Theology," "Theologian," in *A Philosophical Dictionary*
PALEY. *Natural Theology*
COMTE. *The Catechism of Positive Religion*
J. H. NEWMAN. *An Essay on the Development of Christian Doctrine*
——. *The Idea of a University*, DISCOURSE II–IV
——. *An Essay in Aid of a Grammar of Assent*
L. STEPHEN. *An Agnostic's Apology*
HARNACK. *History of Dogma*
STIRLING. *Philosophy and Theology*
WARD. *Naturalism and Agnosticism*
A. E. TAYLOR. *The Faith of a Moralist.* SERIES I (1)
J. S. HALDANE. *The Sciences and Philosophy*, LECT XVII
PENIDO. *Le rôle de l'analogie en théologie dogmatique*
WHITEHEAD. *Adventures of Ideas*, CH 10
MARITAIN. *Science and Wisdom*, pp 70-136
GILSON. *The Unity of Philosophical Experience*, CH 2
——. *Reason and Revelation in the Middle Ages*
FENTON. *The Concept of Sacred Theology*
JAEGER. *Humanism and Theology*
BARTH. *Dogmatics in Outline*

Chapter 93: TIME

INTRODUCTION

"DEVOURING Time," "wasteful Time," "this bloody tyrant, Time"—Time is the predatory villain with whom not only the lover, but all men must contend. The sonnets of Shakespeare make war upon Time's tyranny—to stay "Time's scythe," to preserve whatever of value can be kept from "the wastes of time," and to prove that "Love's not Time's fool" entirely.

Yet, viewing the almost universal depredations of Time, the poet fears that love may not escape Time's ruin.

When I have seen by Time's fell hand defaced
The rich-proud cost of outworn buried age;
When sometime lofty towers I see down-razed,
And brass eternal slave to mortal rage;
When I have seen the hungry ocean gain
Advantage on the kingdom of the shore,
And the firm soil win of the watery main,
Increasing store with loss and loss with store;
When I have seen such interchange of state,
Or state itself confounded to decay;
Ruin hath taught me thus to ruminate,
That Time will come and take my love away.
This thought is as a death, which cannot choose
But weep to have that which it fears to lose.

The lover knows that he cannot save his love from change and her beauty from decay. Time is too much for him. But when the lover is also a poet he may hope to defeat Time, not by making his love last forever, but by making the memory of it immortal. "Do thy worst, old Time," he can say, "despite thy wrong, My love shall in my verse ever live young." Or again:

Since brass, nor stone, nor earth, nor boundless sea,
But sad mortality o'er-sways their power,
How with this rage shall beauty hold a plea,
Whose action is no stronger than a flower?
O, how shall summer's honey breath hold out
Against the wreckful siege of battering days,
When rocks impregnable are not so stout,
Nor gates of steel so strong, but Time decays?
O fearful meditation! where, alack,
Shall Time's best jewel from Time's chest lie hid?
Or what strong hand can hold his swift foot back?
Or who his spoil of beauty can forbid?
O, none, unless this miracle have might,
That in black ink my love may still shine bright.

But the poet may have the cast of a theologian rather than a lover. He may, as Milton does, stand not in awe or fear but in contempt of Time, willing to wait while Time runs out its race. Milton bids Time

. . . glut thyself with what thy womb devours,
Which is no more than what is false and vain,
And merely mortal dross;
So little is our loss,
So little is thy gain.
For when as each thing bad thou hast entomb'd,
And last of all thy greedy self consum'd,
Then long Eternity shall greet our bliss
With an individual kiss . . .
Then all this Earthly grossness quit,
Attir'd with Stars, we shall forever sit,
Triumphing over Death, and Chance, and thee
O Time.

A philosopher like Marcus Aurelius neither defies nor despises time. He enjoins himself to accept the mutability of all things as fitting and "suitable to universal nature. . . . Dost thou not see," he asks himself, "that for thyself also to change is just the same, and equally necessary for the universal nature?" To him it seems "no evil for things to undergo change"; nor is he oppressed by the image of Time as "a river made up of the events which happen, and a violent stream; for as soon as a thing has been seen, it is carried away, and another comes in its place, and this will be carried away too."

For man to resign himself to time's passage, Pascal thinks, requires no special effort. "Our nature consists in motion," he says; "complete rest is death." Time fits our nature, not only because it "heals griefs and quarrels," but because time's perpetual flow washes away the desperate ennui men suffer when they feel themselves imprisoned in the present.

Just as we seek and multiply diversions as means to escape from ourselves, so, according to Pascal, when we are dissatisfied with the present, "we anticipate the future as too slow in coming . . . or we recall the past, to stop its too rapid flight. . . . For the present is generally painful to us. . . . Let each one examine his thoughts, and he will find them all occupied with the past and the future. . . . The past and present are our means; the future alone is our end. So we never live, but we hope to live; and, as we are always preparing to be happy, it is inevitable we should never be so."

THESE ARE ONLY SOME of the conflicting attitudes toward time and mutability which express man's desire for permanence, for the eternity of a now that stands still, or his restless weariness, his avidity for the novelties time holds in store. Wherever in the great books of poetry, philosophy, or history men reflect upon their loves and aspirations, their knowledge and their institutions, they face man's temporality. It is not that man alone of earthly things has a time-ridden existence, but that his memory and imagination enable him to encompass time, and so save him from being merely rooted in it. Man not only reaches out to the past and future, but he also sometimes lifts himself above the whole of time by conceiving the eternal and the immutable.

Man's apprehension of the past and future is discussed in the chapter on MEMORY AND IMAGINATION. The bent of his mind or his striving toward the unchanging, the everlasting, the eternal, is considered in the chapter on CHANGE. Here we are concerned with his examination of time itself.

Though the idea of time is traditionally linked with that of space, it seems to be much more difficult to grasp. In addition to provoking opposite emotions from the poets, it seems to engage the philosophers in a dispute about its intelligibility. This goes deeper than conflicting definitions or analyses, such as occur in the discussion of both space and time. Whereas time seems no less clear than space to some thinkers, to others it is irremediably obscure. Struggling to say what it is and how it exists, they are exasperated by its evanescence as an object of thought.

Aristotle indicates some initial difficulties in the consideration of time. It is not itself a movement, yet "neither does time exist without change. . . . Time is neither movement nor independent of movement." Furthermore, according to Aristotle, time is a continuous quantity. "Time, past, present, and future, forms a continuous whole." But the very nature of a continuous quantity is to be divisible. The present moment, however—the 'now' which is "the link of time" and the dividing line between past and future—seems to be an indivisible instant.

If the present had an extended duration, Aristotle points out, it would have to include parts, some of which would be past and some future. Hence though the present seems to be a part of time, it is, unlike the rest of time, indivisible; and though it separates past and future, yet it must also somehow belong to both, for otherwise time would not be continuous. "The 'now' is an end and a beginning of time, not of the same time however, but the end of that which is past and the beginning of that which is to come."

"If we conceive of some point of time which cannot be divided into even the minutest parts of moments," Augustine writes, "that is the only point that can be called the present; and that point flees at such lightning speed from being future to being past, that it has no extent of duration at all." Only past time and future time can be called long or short. Only they have duration. "But in what sense," Augustine asks, "can that which does not exist be long or short? The past no longer is; the future is not yet."

The past and future, it seems, have duration, or at least extent, but no existence. The present exists but does not endure. "What then *is* time? If no one asks me," Augustine says, "I know; if I want to explain it to a questioner, I do not know." All the words with which we speak of time and times "are the plainest and commonest of words, yet again they are profoundly obscure and their meaning remains to be discovered."

Augustine returns again and again to the point that "we measure time *in its passing*." But, he says, "if you ask me how I know this, my answer is that I know it because we measure time, and we cannot measure what does not exist, and the past and future do not exist. But how do we measure time present, since it has no extent"; and "where does time come from, and by what way does it pass, and where does it go to, while we are measuring it? Where is it from?—obviously from the future. By what way does it pass?—by the present. Where does it go?—into the past. In other words, it passes from that which does not exist, by way of that which lacks extension, into that which is no longer."

The more he reflects on time and its measurement, the more Augustine is perplexed, the more he is forced to say, "I still do not know what time is." He realizes that he has been "talking of time for a long time, and this long time would not be a long time unless time has passed. But how do I know this, since I do not know what time is?" It seems to him true that we measure time, and yet he must say, "I do not know what I am measuring." It seems to him that "time is certainly extendedness—but," he must add, "I do not know what it is extendedness of."

Berkeley suggests that the difficulties in understanding time may be of our own making. "Bid your servant meet you at such a *time* in such a place, and he shall never stay to deliberate on the meaning of those words. . . . But if *time* be taken exclusive of all those particular actions and ideas that diversify the day, merely for the continuation of existence or duration in the abstract, then it will perhaps gravel even a philosopher to comprehend it.

"For my own part," Berkeley goes on to say, "whenever I attempt to frame a simple idea of *time*, abstracted from the succession of ideas in my own mind, which flows uniformly and is participated by all beings, I am lost and embrangled in inextricable difficulties. I have no notion of it at all."

To THOSE WHO conceive time as a mathematical magnitude or as a physical dimension, there seems to be no difficulty about its definition or a precise statement of its properties. So considered, time appears to be no less intelligible than space, for when it is so considered it is being treated exactly like space—not as a property of things, not as relative to bodies or their motions, but as an extensive manifold capable of being occupied by things, and in which they exist and move.

As in what Einstein calls "the four-dimensional space-time continuum" (which comprises three space coordinates and one time coordinate) time is merely one dimension among others, so in Newton's theory time and space are also given parallel treatment. "Times and spaces," Newton writes, "are as it were, the places as well of themselves as of all other things. All things are placed in time as to order of succession; and in space as to order of situation." Einstein criticizes Newtonian mechanics for its "habit of treating time as an independent continuum," yet Newton no less than Einstein appears to conceive time and space alike as dimensions, even if he conceives them in separation from one another.

But if time and space are something to be occupied or filled, they can also be thought of as unoccupied or empty. The opposition, discussed in the chapter on SPACE, between those who think of space in itself as empty, and those who deny a void or vacuum, seems to be paralleled here by the issue concerning empty time—time apart from all change or motion, time in itself. Waiving for the moment the question whether such time exists or is only a mathematical abstraction, we can see that this time may be more susceptible to analysis than the time of ordinary experience, the time which, according to Lucretius, no one feels "by itself abstracted from the motion and calm rest of things."

Newton explains that he does not define time, space, place, and motion, because they are "well known to all." But he observes that men commonly "conceive these quantities under no other notions but from the relation they bear to sensible objects." He finds it necessary, therefore, to distinguish each of them "into absolute and relative, true and apparent, mathematical and common."

By "absolute, true, and mathematical time," Newton means that which "of itself, and from its own nature, flows equably without relation to anything external, and by another name is called duration." In contrast, "relative, apparent, and common time, is some sensible and external (whether accurate or unequable) measure of duration by the means of motion, which is commonly used instead of true time, such as an hour, a day, a month, a year." In astronomy, Newton points out, absolute time "is distinguished from relative, by the equation or correction of the apparent time. For the natural days are truly unequal, though they are commonly considered as equal, and used for measures of time; astronomers correct this inequality that they may measure the celestial motions by a more accurate time."

Newton seems to be saying that time measures motion and also that it is measured by it. If his distinction between absolute and relative time is ignored, his theory of time does not appear to be very different from that of Aristotle, who says, "not only do we measure the movement by the time, but also the time by the movement." Insofar as movement or change involves a sequence in which one part comes after another, time measures it by numbering the *befores* and *afters*. But we also judge the length of the time according to the duration of the movement, and in this sense the movement measures time.

As both Aristotle and Augustine point out, time measures rest as well as motion, for, in Aristotle's words, "all rest is in time. . . . Time is not motion, but the 'number of motion' and what is at rest can be in the number of motion. Not everything that is not in motion can be said to be 'at rest'—but only that which can be moved, though it actually is not moved."

But where Aristotle, in defining time as the measure of motion or rest, makes time an attribute of movement, Newton regards absolute time as the perfect measure of motion precisely because its nature is independent of all physical change. Only relative time depends on motion, and that is the time which is measured by motion, not the measure of it. Those "who confound real quantities with their relations and sensible measures," Newton declares, "defile the purity of mathematical and philosophical truths."

Distinguishing between duration and time, Locke expresses in another way the difference between Newton and Aristotle. Time for Locke is that portion of duration which consists of definite periods and is measured by the motion of bodies. "We must, therefore, carefully distinguish betwixt duration itself, and the measures we make use of to judge its length. Duration in itself is to be considered as going on in one constant, equal uniform course; but none of the measures which we make use of, can be known to do so." It seems wrong to Locke to define time as the measure of motion when, on the contrary, it is motion—"the motion of the great and visible bodies of the world"—which measures time.

What Locke calls "duration" seems to be the same as Newton's absolute time. It is in no way relative to the existence of bodies or motion. Just as space or, as he calls it, "expansion," is not limited by matter, so duration is not limited by motion. As place is that portion of infinite space "which is possessed by and comprehended within the material world, and is thereby distinguished from the rest of expansion," so time is "so much of infinite duration, as is measured by, and coexistent with, the existence and motions of the great bodies of the universe."

MANY ISSUES ARE RAISED by absolute time or infinite duration conceived as independent of all bodily motions. Einstein, for example, challenges the classical notion of simultaneity, according to which two events taking place a great distance from one another are said to occur *at the same time*, that is, at the same moment in the absolute flow of time.

"Before the advent of the theory of relativity," he writes, "it had always been tacitly assumed in physics that the statement of time had an absolute significance, *i.e.*, that it is independent of the state of motion of the body of reference." But if the world of physical events is a four-dimensional manifold in which the time coordinate is always associated with the space coordinates for any reference-body under observation, then "every reference-body (coordinate system) has its own particular time"; and, Einstein adds, "unless we are told the reference-body to which the statement of time refers, there is no meaning in a statement of the time of an event."

There is also the issue of the emptiness of that part of absolute time or infinite duration which comes before or after the existence of the world, comparable to the issue concerning the void or empty space beyond the borders of the material universe. Those who regard time as relative to and inseparable from motion deny the possibility of such empty time.

For Plato, as for Christian theologians like Augustine and Aquinas, time itself is created with the creation of the heavenly bodies and their motions. As the story of the world's becoming is told in the *Timaeus*, the maker "resolved to have a moving image of eternity, and when he set in order the heaven, he made this image eternal but moving according to number, while eternity itself rests in unity; and this image we call time. . . . Time, then, and the heaven came into being at the same instant."

Augustine undertakes to answer "those who agree that God is the Creator of the world, but have difficulties about the time of its creation." He asserts that "there is no time before the world. For if eternity and time are rightly distinguished by this, that time does not exist without some movement and transition, while in eternity there is no change, who does not see that there could have been no time had not some creature been made, which by some motion could give birth to change. . . . I do not see," Augustine continues, "how God can be said to have created the world after spaces of time had elapsed, unless it be said that prior to the world there was some creature by whose movement time could pass." But the existence of a creature prior to creation is impossible. Hence Augustine concludes that "if in the world's creation change and motion were created," then "the world and time were simultaneously created."

Though the existence of a creature prior to creation is impossible, it is not impossible, according to Aquinas, for the created world to be coeval with its Creator. While he rejects the opinion of those who assert that the world now exists without any dependence on God, and who deny that it was ever made by God, he entertains, as possible, the view that "the world has a beginning, not of time, but of creation." Those who hold this view, he explains, mean that "it was always made. . . . For just as, if a foot were always in the dust from eternity, there would always be a footprint which without doubt was caused by him who trod on it, so also the world always was, because its Maker always existed."

It does not necessarily follow, Aquinas admits, that "if God is the active cause of the world, He must be prior to the world in duration, because creation, by which He produced the world, is not a successive change." But Aquinas does not think that the question whether the world and time began with creation or has always co-existed with its Creator, can be resolved by reason. "The newness of the world," he says, "is known only by revelation. . . . That the world did not always exist we hold by faith alone; it cannot be proved demonstratively." In saying this, he is not unmindful of the fact that Aristotle advances arguments to show that there can be no beginning to either time or motion. "Since time cannot exist and is unthinkable apart from the moment, and the moment is a kind of middle point, uniting as it does in itself both . . . a beginning of future time and an end of past time, it follows that there must always be time. . . . But if this is true of time, it is evident that it must also be true of motion, time being an attribute of motion."

With one exception, all his predecessors, according to Aristotle, are in agreement that time is uncreated. "In fact," he says, "it is just this that enables Democritus to show that all things cannot have had a becoming. . . . Plato alone asserts the creation of time, saying that it had a becoming together with the universe." But Aristotle's own arguments for the eternity of time and motion do not seem to Aquinas to be "absolutely demonstrative, but only relatively so—*viz.*, as against the arguments of some of the ancients who asserted that the world began to be in some actually impossible ways." As for the present moment, or the *now* of time, always requiring something which comes *before* as well as *after*, Aquinas admits that "time cannot be made except according to some *now*," yet "not because there is time in the first *now*, but because from it time begins."

The position of Aquinas, that arguments for the initiation or the endlessness of time are only dialectical, seems to be confirmed by Kant. In the Transcendental Dialectic of the *Critique of Pure Reason*, Kant sets forth as one of the cosmological antinomies the opposed arguments for the beginning of the world and for a world without beginning. The reasoning on either side being equal in its *appearance* of cogency, neither conclusion, according to Kant, is genuinely demonstrated.

But those who, like Newton and Locke, separate absolute time or infinite duration from the existence of a world in motion, seem to be unaffected by arguments which concern only the time of the material world, the time that is relative to motion. For them, absolute or infinite time is eternity. It may be empty of motion, but it is filled with God's everlasting being. "Though we make duration boundless, as certainly it is," Locke writes, "we cannot yet extend it beyond all being. God, every one easily allows, fills eternity." God is not eternity, says Newton, but He is eternal. "His duration reaches from eternity to eternity. . . . He endures forever, and is everywhere present; and, by existing always and everywhere, He constitutes duration and space."

The issue is again brought into focus by the denial that God's eternity can be identified with infinite or absolute time. "Even supposing that the world always was," Aquinas writes, it would not be eternal in the sense in which God is, "for the divine being is all being simultaneously without succession." He distinguishes "the *now* that stands still" as the eternal present from the continually shifting *now* in the flow of time's passing moments. For him God's everlasting being does not endure through endless time, but rather exists unchanging in the eternal present. "As eternity is the proper measure of being, so time is the proper measure of movement; and hence," Aquinas writes, "according as any being recedes from permanence in being, and is subject to change, it recedes from eternity and is subject to time."

THE TWO MEANINGS OF eternity—infinite time and utter timelessness—are discussed in the chapter on ETERNITY. The distinction between time and eternity, which is considered both there and here, seems to be understood differently by those who contrast timelessness with temporality and by those who equate eternity with endless time. For the latter, the point of difference between eternity and time seems to be only one of infinite as opposed to limited duration. Yet, as we have just observed, writers like Newton and Locke also distinguish absolute or infinite time (which they tend to identify with eternity) from definite periods or limited spans of time, by making the one independent of, the other relative to and measured by, motion.

The question remains whether absolute time is real time or only a mathematical abstraction, whether it exists apart from perceived time—the experienced duration of observable motions or the elapsed time of events in succession.

Considering this question, Kant says that "those who maintain the absolute reality of time and space, whether as essentially subsisting, or only inhering, as modifications in things, must find themselves at utter variance with the principles of experience itself. For, if they decide for the first view, and make space and time into substances, this being the side taken by mathematical natural philosophers, they must admit two self-subsisting nonentities, infinite and eternal, which exist (yet without their being anything real) for the purpose of containing in themselves everything that is real. If they adopt the second view of inherence, which is preferred by some metaphysical natural philosophers, and regard space and time as relations . . . abstracted from experience . . . they find themselves in that case necessitated to deny the validity of mathematical doctrine *a priori* in reference to real things."

On Kant's own view, the synthetic judgments of mathematics can have the apodictic certainty of *a priori* propositions only if space and time are themselves *a priori* forms of intuition. As the *a priori* form of space makes possible the pure science of geometry, according to Kant, so the *a priori* form of time makes possible the pure science of numbers, *i.e.*, arithmetic. But whereas "space, as the pure form of external intuition is limited . . . to external phenomena alone," time, as "the form of the internal sense," is for Kant "the formal condition *a priori* of all phenomena whatsoever."

Without sharing Kant's theory of *a priori* forms of intuition, or of the foundations of pure mathematics, other writers appear to agree to some extent with his denial of independent reality to time. Aristotle raises the question "whether if soul did not exist, time would exist or not." He thinks the question may be fairly asked because "if there cannot be someone to count, there cannot be anything that can be counted, so that evidently there cannot be number"—for number is the counted or the countable. "But if nothing but soul, or in soul reason, is qualified to count, there would not be time unless there were soul." Yet Aristotle qualifies this somewhat by adding that "if *movement* can exist without soul, and the before and after are attributes of movement," time may exist as "these *qua* numerable."

Augustine takes a less qualified position. Asking what it is that time is the "extendedness of," he answers: "Probably of the mind itself." Insisting that neither future nor past time can be measured because neither exists, Augustine concludes that it is only passing time we can measure, and that we can measure it only in the mind. "It is in you, O my mind," he says, "that I measure time. . . . What I measure is the impress produced in you by things as they pass and abiding in you when they have passed . . . I do not measure the things themselves whose passage produced the impress; it is the impress that I measure when I measure time."

Yet William James, while giving a similar analysis of our experience of time, insists that time is objective as well as subjective. Time and space relations, he writes, "*are* impressed from without." The time and space in which the objects of our thought exist, exist as independently of the mind as do those objects themselves. "*The time- and space-relations between things do stamp copies within*"; as, for example, when "things sequent in time impress their sequence on our memory."

William James proposes a solution of the mystery of how time exists—at least how it exists in experience. So far as our experience goes, past and future can exist only in the present. But how can these extended parts of time exist in the present if the present is but a fleeting moment, without any extent of duration, "gone," as James says, "in the instant of becoming"? His answer is in terms of something he calls "the specious present."

Unlike the real present, the specious present is "no knife-edge but a saddle-back, with a certain breadth of its own on which we sit perched, and from which we look in two directions into time. The unit of composition of our perception of time is a *duration*, with a bow and a stern, as it were—a rearward- and a forward-looking end. It is only as parts of this *duration-block* that the relation of *succession* of one end to the other is perceived."

On the basis of some experimental evidence, James estimates that the specious present may vary in length "from a few seconds to probably not more than a minute." It has "a vaguely vanishing backward and forward fringe; but its nucleus is probably the dozen seconds or less that have just elapsed."

The irreversible flow of time—the succession of moments which constitute the motion of the future through the present into the past—occurs in the specious present, though not, according to James, without the accompaniment of observed or experienced change. "Awareness of *change* is . . . the condition on which our perception of time's flow depends." But that awareness must take place in the specious present "with its content perceived as having one part earlier and the other part later." In consequence, James considers the specious present to be, not only "the original intuition of time," but also "*the original paragon prototype of all conceived times*."

The problems of time, its own process and being as well as its relation to all other existence and change, its character as an aspect of experience and as an object of thought, seem to belong to many subject matters—to psychology and to experimental or mathematical physics, to the philosophy of nature, metaphysics, and theology.

For some thinkers—in our own time notably Bergson, Whitehead, and Dewey—the concept of time, of the burgeoning future, of the continuum of events, seems to determine a whole philosophical outlook. If it is not equally decisive throughout the tradition of the great books, it is at least of critical significance in speculations about the origin and end of the world, in the contrast between physical and spiritual modes of being, in the consideration of the processes of life, thought, and feeling, and in the analysis of more inclusive concepts, such as that of order.

The temporal relationships of succession and simultaneity, for example, may be the source from which we derive the notions of prior, posterior, and simultaneous, but they are traditionally viewed as exemplifying rather than exhausting these types of order. When Augustine deals with the perplexing theological question of the priority of eternity to time, he finds it necessary to distinguish "priority in eternity, priority in time, priority in choice, priority in origin."

When Aristotle deals with metaphysical questions concerning the order of cause and effect, of potentiality and actuality, of essence and accident, he differentiates between temporal and logical priority, and between priority in thought and priority in nature. When Harvey tries to solve the familiar biological riddle (which came first, the chicken or the egg?), he also finds his solution in a distinction. "The fowl is prior by nature," he writes, "but the egg is prior in time."

Space and spatial relationships, no less than time and the temporal, figure in the general analysis of order or relatedness and have a bearing on other problems in physics and philosophy. But in addition to time's having more significance than space for the theologian, time also has peculiar importance for one subject matter in which space is of much less concern, namely, history and the philosophy of history.

Besides the general view which the historian takes of time as the locus of history, or the medium in which the pattern of history unfolds, the writer of history usually employs certain conventional time divisions to mark the major phases or epochs of the story he has to tell. Clocks and calendars record or represent the passage of time in conventional units, but these conventions have some natural basis in astronomical time, solar or sidereal. In contrast, the distinction between historic and prehistoric time, or the division of history into such periods as ancient, mediaeval, and modern, seems to be purely a matter of social or cultural convention.

With Hegel, however, the division of the whole of history into three epochs, and of each epoch again into three periods, follows from the dialectical triad of thesis, antithesis, and synthesis which is the indwelling form of history's development. The division of each of the three phases of world-history—the Oriental, the Graeco-Roman, and the German worlds—into a first, second, and third period produces in each case the same pattern of origin, conflict, and resolution. For the most part, Hegel does not identify these three periods with ancient, mediaeval, and modern times; yet in one case, that of the German world, he does refer to the second period as "the middle ages" and the third as "the modern time."

Such words as "ancient" and "modern" have conventional significance for most historians. Furthermore, the meanings of modernity and antiquity are themselves subject to historical relativity. In the tradition of the great books, this appears most plainly in the references made to ancients and moderns by writers whom we today classify as ancient and mediaeval.

Thucydides, for example, begins his history with a description of what is for him the antiquity of Greece. Nicomachus opens his *Introduction to Arithmetic* with a remark about "the ancients, who under the leadership of Pythagoras first made science systematic, defined philosophy as the love of wisdom." Mathematics, Aristotle says, "has come to be identical with philosophy for modern thinkers."

In another place, Aristotle contrasts "the thinkers of the present day" with "the thinkers of old"; and in still another he speaks of "ancient and truly traditional theories." Like Aristotle in the sphere of thought, so Tacitus in the sphere of politics frequently compares ancient and modern institutions or practices.

In the Middle Ages, Aquinas speaks of the "teachings of the early philosophers" and, as frequently as Aristotle, he refers to ancient and modern doctrines. In the Renaissance, Kepler treats as ancient a scientist who, in point of time, comes much later than those whom Aristotle and Aquinas call modern. Classifying three schools of astronomical thought, he distinguishes an ancient one, which had "Ptolemy as its coryphaeus," from two modern ones, respectively headed by Copernicus and Tycho Brahe.

Such references, which have occurred in all three periods of the western tradition, suggest the probability that at some future date the whole tradition with which we are now acquainted will be referred to as the thought and culture of ancient times.

OUTLINE OF TOPICS

1. The nature of time: time as duration or as the measure of motion; time as a continuous quantity; absolute and relative time

2. The distinction between time and eternity: the eternity of endless time distinguished from the eternity of timelessness and immutability

    2*a*. Aeviternity as intermediate between time and eternity

    2*b*. Arguments concerning the infinity of time and the eternity of motion or the world

    2*c*. The creation of time: the priority of eternity to time; the immutability of the world after the end of time

3. The mode of existence of time

    3*a*. The parts of time: its division into past, present, and future

    3*b*. The reality of the past and the future in relation to the existence of the present

    3*c*. The extent of the present moment: instantaneity

4. The measurement of time: sun, stars, and clocks

5. Temporal relationships: time as a means of ordering

    5*a*. Simultaneity or coexistence: the simultaneity of cause and effect, action and passion, knowledge and object known

    5*b*. Succession or priority and posteriority: the temporal order of cause and effect, potentiality and actuality

    5*c*. Succession and simultaneity in relation to the association of ideas

    5*d*. Comparison of temporal with non-temporal simultaneity and succession: the prior in thought, by nature, or in origin

6. The knowledge of time and the experience of duration

    6*a*. The perception of time by the interior senses: the difference between the experience and memory of time intervals

    6*b*. Factors influencing the estimate of time elapsed: empty and filled time; illusions of time perception; the variability of experienced durations

    6*c*. Time as a transcendental form of intuition: the *a priori* foundations of arithmetic; the issue concerning innate and acquired time perception

    6*d*. The signifying of time: the distinction between noun and verb; the tenses of the verb

    6*e*. Knowledge of the past: the storehouse of memory; the evidences of the past in physical traces or remnants

    6*f*. Knowledge of the future: the truth of propositions about future contingents; the probability of predictions

7. The temporal course of the passions: emotional attitudes toward time and mutability

8. Historical time

    8*a*. Prehistoric and historic time: the antiquity of man

    8*b*. The epochs of history: myths of a golden age; the relativity of modernity

REFERENCES

References are listed by volume number (in bold type), author's name, and page number. Bible references are to book, chapter, and verse of the Authorized King James version of the Bible. The abbreviation "esp" calls the reader's attention to one or more especially relevant parts of a whole reference; "passim" signifies that the topic is discussed intermittently rather than continuously in the work or passage cited. Where the work as a whole is relevant to the topic, the page numbers refer to the entire work. For general guidance in the use of *The Great Ideas,* consult the Preface.

1. The nature of time: time as duration or as the measure of motion; time as a continuous quantity; absolute and relative time

7 PLATO, 450–451
8 ARISTOTLE, 297–304, 312–325 passim, 439, 541, 601
17 PLOTINUS, 123–129, 254
18 AUGUSTINE, 93–99
19 AQUINAS, 32–33, 40–41, 283–284, 330–331, 753–754
20 AQUINAS, 366–367
28 GALILEO, 201–202
31 SPINOZA, 373, 399
33 PASCAL, 432–435
34 NEWTON, 9–10, 31–32
35 LOCKE, 155–162
35 HUME, 506–507
36 STERNE, 292–293
42 KANT, 26–33
46 HEGEL, 206

2. The distinction between time and eternity: the eternity of endless time distinguished from the eternity of timelessness and immutability

APOCRYPHA: *Ecclesiasticus,* 18:10
8 ARISTOTLE, 301–302, 315, 321, 372–375, 576, 620–621
12 AURELIUS, 275
17 PLOTINUS, 20, 119–129
18 AUGUSTINE, 89–99, 102–103, 324–325, 333, 349–355
19 AQUINAS, 40–45
23 HOBBES, 271
29 CERVANTES, 366–367
31 DESCARTES, 216–217
31 SPINOZA, 355, 364, 390, 458, 459
32 MILTON, 12
33 PASCAL, 211
35 LOCKE, 161–162, 162–164, 165, 167–174 passim, 237
42 KANT, 185
51 TOLSTOY, 295

2*a*. Aeviternity as intermediate between time and eternity

18 AUGUSTINE, 101–102, 103–104, 351–352
19 AQUINAS, 44–46

2*b*. Arguments concerning the infinity of time and the eternity of motion or the world

OLD TESTAMENT: *Job,* 38:1–13 / *Psalms,* 90:2; 102:25–26; 148:1–6 / *Proverbs,* 8:22–29 / *Isaiah,* 45:12,18
APOCRYPHA: *II Maccabees,* 7:23
NEW TESTAMENT: *Matthew,* 24:3–35 / *Luke,* 21:5–33 / *John,* 1:1–3 / *Colossians,* 1:16–17 / *Hebrews,* 1:10–12 / *II Peter,* 3:3–13
7 PLATO, 124, 447
8 ARISTOTLE, 302, 325, 334–337, 344–346, 348–352, 361–362, 370–375, 437–441, 458–459, 462, 601–605
9 ARISTOTLE, 234–235, 236
12 LUCRETIUS, 2–4, 7–8, 12–14, 16, 18–19, 28, 61–66
12 AURELIUS, 271, 293–294, 297
16 KEPLER, 888–891
17 PLOTINUS, 35–39, 69–70
18 AUGUSTINE, 49–50, 89–99, 348–357
19 AQUINAS, 85–86, 250–255, 315–316, 348–349
20 AQUINAS, 945–946
23 HOBBES, 50
30 BACON, 163, 186
31 DESCARTES, 228
33 PASCAL, 195
34 NEWTON, 8, 14, 540–541
35 LOCKE, 160
42 KANT, 130–133, 135–137, 152, 160–161, 334–335
51 TOLSTOY, 693–694 passim

2*c*. The creation of time: the priority of eternity to time; the immutability of the world after the end of time

7 PLATO, 450–451
17 PLOTINUS, 165–166
18 AUGUSTINE, 109–110, 324–325, 349–350, 351–354
19 AQUINAS, 250–255, 348–349
20 AQUINAS, 1017–1020
21 DANTE, 150
32 MILTON, 187–188, 218–219

3. The mode of existence of time

8 ARISTOTLE, 297, 303
12 LUCRETIUS, 6–7
17 PLOTINUS, 126–129

18 Augustine, 92–99
19 Aquinas, 40–41
35 Locke, 155–156
35 Berkeley, 432
42 Kant, 28
46 Hegel, 186–190
53 James, 398–399

3*a*. The parts of time: its division into past, present, and future

7 Plato, 494–495, 502
8 Aristotle, 298–299, 302–303
17 Plotinus, 259–260
31 Descartes, 131, 213
35 Locke, 164
46 Hegel, 153–156

3*b*. The reality of the past and the future in relation to the existence of the present

8 Aristotle, 301
12 Aurelius, 258
18 Augustine, 93–98
19 Aquinas, 147
25 Montaigne, 293–294
46 Hegel, 190
53 James, 398, 421

3*c*. The extent of the present moment: instantaneity

7 Plato, 505
8 Aristotle, 297–298, 299–300, 301–302, 315–316, 335, 350
18 Augustine, 93–94
19 Aquinas, 35–36, 225–227
35 Locke, 157
53 James, 398–399, 420

4. The measurement of time: sun, stars, and clocks

Old Testament: *Genesis,* 1:3–5,14–18 / *Psalms,* 104:19–20
Apocrypha: *Ecclesiasticus,* 43:1–10
6 Herodotus, 49–50
6 Thucydides, 487
7 Plato, 450–451
8 Aristotle, 300
14 Plutarch, 58–59, 599–600
16 Ptolemy, 34–38, 77–86, 104–107
16 Copernicus, 568–576, 646–652, 672–674
17 Plotinus, 122–124
18 Augustine, 95–98, 351–352
19 Aquinas, 352–354, 364–365
24 Rabelais, 69–70
25 Montaigne, 497
28 Galileo, 167–168
30 Bacon, 177–179
32 Milton, 147–148
34 Newton, 291–294
34 Huygens, 554–557
35 Locke, 158–162 passim
36 Sterne, 229
41 Gibbon, 376
53 James, 407–408

5. Temporal relationships: time as a means of ordering

5*a*. Simultaneity or coexistence: the simultaneity of cause and effect, action and passion, knowledge and object known

7 Plato, 519–520, 533
8 Aristotle, 12–13, 20, 129–130, 134
19 Aquinas, 59
42 Kant, 83–84, 312
53 James, 862–863

5*b*. Succession or priority and posteriority: the temporal order of cause and effect, potentiality and actuality

8 Aristotle, 19–20, 134, 275, 575, 576
9 Aristotle, 283
19 Aquinas, 253–255, 455–457
20 Aquinas, 7–8
28 Galileo, 135–136
28 Harvey, 445, 447
31 Descartes, 87, 159
34 Newton, 379
35 Hume, 470–478
42 Kant, 76–83, 95, 311–314, 331–333

5*c*. Succession and simultaneity in relation to the association of ideas

31 Spinoza, 382
35 Locke, 139–140
35 Hume, 457
53 James, 361–364, 367–370, 559–561
54 Freud, 74

5*d*. Comparison of temporal with non-temporal simultaneity and succession: the prior in thought, by nature, or in origin

8 Aristotle, 19–20, 119, 194–196, 539–540, 575–577, 608–609
9 Aristotle, 170
11 Nicomachus, 813
18 Augustine, 92, 109–110, 319
19 Aquinas, 18–19, 97, 455–457, 504–505
31 Descartes, 228
46 Hegel, 20

6. The knowledge of time and the experience of duration

6*a*. The perception of time by the interior senses: the difference between the experience and memory of time intervals

8 Aristotle, 298, 687, 694–695
17 Plotinus, 161–162
18 Augustine, 92–99
19 Aquinas, 41–42
31 Spinoza, 443
35 Locke, 133, 155–158
35 Berkeley, 431–432

42 KANT, 26–29, 74–76
53 JAMES, 130, 131, 396–420

6b. Factors influencing the estimate of time elapsed: empty and filled time; illusions of time perception; the variability of experienced durations

6 HERODOTUS, 77
8 ARISTOTLE, 298
21 DANTE, 57
26 SHAKESPEARE, 612
35 LOCKE, 156–157
36 STERNE, 292–293
53 JAMES, 264–268 esp 268–269, 400–411, 417–420
54 FREUD, 335–336

6c. Time as a transcendental form of intuition: the *a priori* foundations of arithmetic; the issue concerning innate and acquired time perception

35 LOCKE, 155–156, 161–162
42 KANT, 61–62, 68–69, 94–95, 100–101, 213–215, 307–308
53 JAMES, 420, 852–853, 860–861
54 FREUD, 648

6d. The signifying of time: the distinction between noun and verb; the tenses of the verb

7 PLATO, 450–451, 495, 575–576
8 ARISTOTLE, 25
19 AQUINAS, 89–90
25 MONTAIGNE, 293–294

6e. Knowledge of the past: the storehouse of memory; the evidences of the past in physical traces or remnants

6 HERODOTUS, 1–2
6 THUCYDIDES, 349–355 passim
7 PLATO, 538–544
8 ARISTOTLE, 690–695
9 ARISTOTLE, 640
12 LUCRETIUS, 6–7
15 TACITUS, 38–39
17 PLOTINUS, 190–191
18 AUGUSTINE, 74–80
19 AQUINAS, 411–413, 419–420
30 BACON, 61–62
31 SPINOZA, 424
35 LOCKE, 357
36 SWIFT, 79–80
38 ROUSSEAU, 428
40 GIBBON, 88, 96, 413
42 KANT, 579–580, 583–584
46 HEGEL, 153–156, 181–182, 190, 237, 239–241, 247
49 DARWIN, 152–180 passim, 217–229 passim, 231–233, 238–239, 242–243, 255–265, 332–335, 336–337, 348–349
53 JAMES, 396–397, 421–427
54 FREUD, 4, 526–527

6f. Knowledge of the future: the truth of propositions about future contingents; the probability of predictions

5 EURIPIDES, 314
7 PLATO, 531–532
8 ARISTOTLE, 28–29
9 ARISTOTLE, 640
10 HIPPOCRATES, 19
18 AUGUSTINE, 94–95
19 AQUINAS, 86–88, 297–298, 463–464, 475–476, 478–479
21 DANTE, 132
23 HOBBES, 53, 65
31 SPINOZA, 385, 444
34 NEWTON, 371–372
34 HUYGENS, 551–552
35 BERKELEY, 420–421, 433
35 HUME, 458, 469–470
47 GOETHE, 209
49 DARWIN, 59–60, 243
51 TOLSTOY, 685
53 JAMES, 883–884
54 FREUD, 387

7. The temporal course of the passions: emotional attitudes toward time and mutability

5 SOPHOCLES, 120, 125
6 HERODOTUS, 7–8, 224–225
7 PLATO, 154–155, 165–166, 295–296, 717–718
9 ARISTOTLE, 340, 345, 391, 393, 407–408, 636–638
12 LUCRETIUS, 29–30, 41–42, 43–44
12 AURELIUS, 258, 262, 263–264, 266, 267, 281, 282, 293, 299
14 PLUTARCH, 225
18 AUGUSTINE, 22
19 AQUINAS, 796–797
21 DANTE, 39, 69–70, 74–75, 128–132
22 CHAUCER, 70, 256–269
23 HOBBES, 63, 79
25 MONTAIGNE, 6–7, 33–36, 292–294, 394–395, 540–541
26 SHAKESPEARE, 350, 465, 483, 533
27 SHAKESPEARE, 63, 66, 124, 128, 132, 220, 308–309, 505, 590, 593, 594, 595–596, 603–604, 605
30 BACON, 15
31 SPINOZA, 426–428
32 MILTON, 12, 63
33 PASCAL, 195, 196–200, 202–203, 211
35 LOCKE, 250
37 FIELDING, 35
43 MILL, 449–450
44 BOSWELL, 350–351
46 HEGEL, 178
47 GOETHE, 115–116
51 TOLSTOY, 305, 356
53 JAMES, 759–760
54 FREUD, 17–18, 579–581, 704–706, 758, 760, 768–770

8. Historical time

8*a*. Prehistoric and historic time: the antiquity of man

5 Aristophanes, 548
6 Herodotus, 49–52, 124–132, 161
7 Plato, 480
12 Lucretius, 71–76
40 Gibbon, 88, 413
46 Hegel, 179–182, 209, 235–236, 260–262
49 Darwin, 153–155, 336–337

8*b*. The epochs of history: myths of a golden age; the relativity of modernity

7 Plato, 92, 444–446, 478–485 passim, 586–589, 681
8 Aristotle, 361–362, 370, 375–376
10 Hippocrates, 4
10 Galen, 207
12 Lucretius, 65
13 Virgil, 14–15, 40–41, 110–111, 267–268
15 Tacitus, 51, 72, 106, 255
18 Augustine, 124, 307–308, 313–314, 397–507, 618
21 Dante, 97
23 Hobbes, 267
24 Rabelais, 143
29 Cervantes, 27–28, 208
30 Bacon, 119
32 Milton, 306–332
33 Pascal, 357–358
35 Hume, 499–500
36 Swift, 118–119
40 Gibbon, 79, 900
46 Hegel, 188, 231–232, 241, 259, 282–284, 286–287, 315–317, 348

CROSS-REFERENCES

For: Other discussions of time as a quantity and its relation to motion, *see* Change 5a; Mechanics 1c; Quantity 5b; Relation 6a; and for the measurement of time, *see* Astronomy 7; Quantity 6c.

Discussions relevant to the distinction between time and eternity, and to the problem of the infinity of time and the eternity of the world, *see* Astronomy 8c(1); Change 13; Eternity 1–2; Infinity 3e; World 4a, 8.

Time in relation to theories of creation, *see* Eternity 1a; World 4e(2).

Another treatment of the relations of succession and simultaneity, *see* Relation 5a; and for the temporal aspects of such relations as that between cause and effect, potentiality and actuality, and the various acts of the mind, *see* Being 7c(1); Cause 1b; Education 5d; Idea 5d–5e; Relation 4f.

The analysis of memory and imagination as interior senses, *see* Memory and Imagination 1; Sense 3b, 3d(2).

Considerations relevant to the conception of time as a transcendental form of intuition and to the related problem of the foundations of arithmetic, *see* Form 1c; Mathematics 1c; Memory and Imagination 6c(2); Mind 1e(1), 4d(3); Space 4a.

The general theory of the parts of speech which involves the distinction between noun and verb, *see* Language 4a.

Other considerations of our knowledge of the past and the future, *see* History 3a; Knowledge 5a(5); Memory and Imagination 3b; Necessity and Contingency 4c; Prophecy 1a–1b; Truth 3b(2).

The influence of time on human development, *see* Experience 6a; Life and Death 6b–6c; Man 6c; and for man's attitude toward time and change, *see* Change 12b; Progress 5.

Other treatments of the problem of time and free will in relation to God's foreknowledge and foreordination, *see* God 7b, 7f; History 5a; Liberty 5a–5b; Will 7c.

Other discussions of historical time and the antiquity of man, *see* Evolution 7c; History 4a(3), 4c; Man 9c.

ADDITIONAL READINGS

Listed below are works not included in *Great Books of the Western World*, but relevant to the idea and topics with which this chapter deals. These works are divided into two groups:

I. Works by authors represented in this collection.
II. Works by authors not represented in this collection.

For the date, place, and other facts concerning the publication of the works cited, consult the Bibliography of Additional Readings which follows the last chapter of *The Great Ideas*.

I.

AUGUSTINE. *On Music*
AQUINAS. *De Aeternitate Mundi*
HOBBES. *Concerning Body*, PART II, CH 7
SPINOZA. *Cogita Metaphysica*, PART I, CH 4; PART II, CH I
HUME. *A Treatise of Human Nature*, BK I, PART II
KANT. *De Mundi Sensibilis* (*Inaugural Dissertation*)
——. *Metaphysical Foundations of Natural Science*, DIV I

II.

SEXTUS EMPIRICUS. *Against the Physicists*, BK II, CH 3
——. *Outlines of Pyrrhonism*, BK III, CH 1–20
PROCLUS. *The Elements of Theology*, (F)
MAIMONIDES. *The Guide for the Perplexed*, PART II, CH 13
CRESCAS. *Or Adonai*, PROPOSITION 15
JOHN OF SAINT THOMAS. *Cursus Philosophicus Thomisticus, Philosophia Naturalis*, PART I, Q 18
LEIBNITZ. *New Essays Concerning Human Understanding* BK II, CH 14–15
WHEWELL. *The Philosophy of the Inductive Sciences*, VOL I, BK II, CH 7–10
HODGSON. *Time and Space*
LOTZE. *Metaphysics*, BK II, CH 3
FRAZER. *The Golden Bough*, PART IV, BK III, CH 2
BRADLEY. *Appearance and Reality*, BK I, CH 4; BK II, CH 18
BOSANQUET. *Science and Philosophy*, 7
ROYCE. *The World and the Individual*, SERIES II (3)
POINCARÉ. *The Value of Science*, PART I, CH 2
MEYERSON. *Identity and Reality*, CH 6
CASSIRER. *Substance and Function*, SUP V
ROBB. *A Theory of Time and Space*
WEYL. *Space—Time—Matter*
S. ALEXANDER. *Space, Time, and Deity*
PROUST. *Remembrance of Things Past*
WHITEHEAD. *An Enquiry Concerning the Principles of Natural Knowledge*, CH 6
——. *The Concept of Nature*, CH 3
EINSTEIN. *Relativity: The Special and the General Theory*
——. *Sidelights on Relativity*
MARITAIN. *Theonas, Conversations of a Sage*, VI
MCTAGGART. *The Nature of Existence*, CH 33
BERGSON. *Time and Free Will*
——. *Creative Evolution*
——. *Durée et simultanéité, à propos de la théorie d'Einstein*, CH 1–5
MANN. *The Magic Mountain*
DEWEY. *Experience and Nature*, CH 1–3, 7, 9
G. N. LEWIS. *The Anatomy of Science*, ESSAY III
HEIDEGGER. *Sein und Zeit*
EDDINGTON. *Space, Time, and Gravitation*
——. *The Nature of the Physical World*, CH 3
MEAD. *Philosophy of the Present*
SANTAYANA. *The Realm of Matter*, CH 4
BORING. *The Physical Dimensions of Consciousness*, CH 5
WEISS, *Reality*, BK II, CH 6
B. RUSSELL. *The Analysis of Matter*, CH 28–29, 32, 36
——. *Human Knowledge, Its Scope and Limits*, PART III, CH 5; PART IV, CH 5, 7

Chapter 94: TRUTH

INTRODUCTION

NOT everyone knows Josiah Royce's definition of a liar as a man who willfully misplaces his ontological predicates, but everyone who has ever told a lie will recognize its accuracy. To restate the definition less elegantly, lying consists in saying the contrary of what one thinks or believes. To speak truthfully we must make our speech conform to our thought, we must say that something is the case if we think it is, or that it is not, if we think it is not. If we deliberately say "is" when we think *is not*, or say "is not" when we think *is*, we lie.

Of course, the man who speaks truthfully may in fact say what is false, just as the man whose intent is to falsify may inadvertently speak the truth. The intention to speak one's mind does not guarantee that one's mind is free from error or in possession of the truth. Herein lies the traditional distinction between truth as a social and as an intellectual matter. What Dr. Johnson calls *moral* truth consists in the obligation to say what we mean. In contrast what he calls *physical* truth depends not on the veracity of what we say but on the validity of what we mean.

The theory of truth in the tradition of the great books deals largely with the latter kind of truth. The great issues concern whether we can know the truth and how we can ever tell whether something is true or false. Though the philosophers and scientists, from Plato to Freud, seem to stand together against the extreme sophistry or skepticism which denies the distinction between true and false or puts truth utterly beyond the reach of man, they do not all agree on the extent to which truth is attainable by men, on its immutability or variability, on the signs by which men tell whether they have the truth or not, or on the causes of error and the means for avoiding falsity.

Much that Plato thinks is true Freud rejects as false. Freud searches for truth in other quarters and by other methods. But the ancient controversy in which Socrates engages with the sophists of his day, who were willing to regard as true whatever anyone wished to think, seems to differ not at all from Freud's quarrel with those whom he calls "intellectual nihilists." They are the persons who say there is no such thing as truth or that it is only the product of our own needs and desires. They make it "absolutely immaterial," Freud writes, "what views we accept. All of them are equally true and false. And no one has a right to accuse anyone else of error."

Across the centuries the arguments against the skeptic seem to be the same. If the skeptic does not mind contradicting himself when he tries to defend the truth of the proposition that all propositions are equally true or false, he can perhaps be challenged by the fact that he does not act according to his view. If all opinions are equally true or false, then why, Aristotle asks, does not the denier of truth walk "into a well or over a precipice" instead of avoiding such things. "If it were really a matter of indifference what we believed," Freud similarly argues, "then we might just as well build our bridges of cardboard as of stone, or inject a tenth of a gramme of morphia into a patient instead of a hundredth, or take tear-gas as a narcotic instead of ether. But," he adds, "the intellectual anarchists themselves would strongly repudiate such practical applications of their theory."

Whether the skeptic can be refuted or merely silenced may depend on a further step in the argument, in which the skeptic substitutes probability for truth, both as a basis for action and as the quality of all our opinions about the real world. The argument takes different forms according to the different ways in which probability is distinguished from truth or according to the distinction between a complete and limited skepticism. Montaigne, for example, seems to think that the complete skeptic cannot even acknowledge degrees of probability to be objectively ascertainable without admitting the criterion of truth, whereas Hume, defending a mitigated skepticism, offers criteria for measuring the probability of judgments about matters of fact.

THE POSITION OF THE skeptic, in its bearing on truth and probability, is discussed in the chapters on KNOWLEDGE and OPINION. Here we shall proceed to other controversial questions concerning truth. But we must first observe that there is one major question which does not seem to cause much dispute. Not only do the great authors (with the possible exception of Montaigne and Hume) seem to be unanimous in their conviction that men can attain and share the truth—at least some truths—but they also appear to give the same answer to the question, What is truth?

The apparently unanimous agreement on the nature of truth may seem remarkable in the context of the manifold disagreements in the great books concerning what is true. As already indicated, some of these disagreements occur in the theory of truth itself—in divergent analyses of the sources of error, or in conflicting formulations of the signs of truth. But even these differences do not affect the agreement on the nature of truth. Just as everyone knows what a liar is, but not as readily whether someone is telling a lie, so the great philosophers seem able to agree on what truth is, but not as readily on what is true. That the definitions—of lying and of truth—are intimately connected will be seen from Plato's conception of the nature of truth as a correspondence between thought and reality. If truthfulness, viewed socially, requires a man's words to be a faithful representation of his mind, truth in the mind itself (or in the statements which express thought) depends on their conformity to reality.

A false proposition, according to Plato, is "one which asserts the non-existence of things which are, and the existence of things which are not." Since "false opinion is that form of opinion which thinks the opposite of the truth," it necessarily follows, as Aristotle points out, that "to say of what is that it is, and of what is not that it is not, is true," just as it is false "to say of what is that it is not, or of what is not that it is."

In one sense, the relation between a true statement and the fact it states is reciprocal. "If a man is," Aristotle declares, then "the proposition in which we allege that he is, is true; and conversely, if the proposition wherein we allege that he is, is true, then he is." But the true proposition "is in no way the cause of the being of the man," whereas "the fact of the man's being does seem somehow to be the cause of the truth of the proposition, for the truth or falsity of the proposition depends on the fact of the man's being or not being."

THIS SIMPLE STATEMENT about the nature of truth is repeated again and again in the subsequent tradition of western thought. What variation there is from writer to writer seems to be in phrasing alone, though the common insight concerning truth as an agreement or correspondence between the mind and reality may occur in the context of widely varying conceptions concerning the nature of the mind and of reality or being.

Plotinus may be an exception, insofar as his theory of knowledge involves a relation of identity rather than of mere correspondence. "The object known," he writes, "must be identical with the knowing act . . . If this identity does not exist, neither does truth . . . Truth cannot apply to something conflicting with itself; what it affirms it must also be."

But others, like Augustine, Aquinas, Descartes, and Spinoza, adopt the conception of truth as an agreement between the mind and reality. Falsehood occurs, says Augustine, when "something is thought to be which is not." According to Aquinas, "any intellect which understands a thing to be otherwise than it is, is false." Truth in the human intellect consists "in the conformity of the intellect with the thing." The same point is implied, at least, in Descartes' remark that if we do not relate our ideas "to anything beyond themselves, they cannot properly speaking be false." Error or, for that matter, truth can only arise in "my judging that the ideas which are in me are similar or conformable to the things which are outside me." Spinoza states it as an axiom rather than a definition that "a true idea must agree with that of which it is the idea."

Making a distinction between verbal and real truth, Locke writes: "Though our words signify nothing but our ideas, yet being designed by them to signify things, the truth they contain, when put into propositions, will be only verbal, when they stand for ideas in the mind that have not an agreement with the reality of things." Precisely because he considers truth to consist "in the accordance of a cognition with its object," Kant holds that, so far as the content (as opposed to the form) of a cognition is concerned, it is impossible to discover a universal criterion of truth.

We shall return to Kant's point in a subsequent discussion of the signs of truth, as also we shall have occasion to return to Locke's distinction between real and verbal truth. Neither affects the insight that truth consists in the agreement of our propositions or judgments with the facts they attempt to state, unless it is the qualification that truth so defined is real, not verbal.

In his Preface to *The Meaning of Truth*, James comments on the excitement caused by his earlier lectures on pragmatism, in which, offering the pragmatist's conception of truth, he had spoken of an idea's "working successfully" as the sign of its truth. He warns his critics that this is not a new definition of the nature of truth, but only a new interpretation of what it means to say that the truth of our ideas consists in "their agreement, as falsity means their disagreement, with reality. Pragmatists and intellectualists," he adds, "both accept this definition as a matter of course.

"To agree in the widest sense with reality," James then explains, "can only mean to be guided either straight up to it or into its surroundings, or to be put into such working touch with it as to handle either it or something connected with it better than if we disagreed. Better either intellectually or practically . . . Any idea that helps us to deal, whether practically or intellectually, with either the reality or its belongings . . . that *fits*, in fact, and adapts our life to the reality's whole setting, will agree sufficiently to meet the requirement. It will be true of that reality."

Without enlarging on its meaning as James does, Freud affirms that the ordinary man's conception of truth is that of the scientist also. Science, he says, aims "to arrive at correspondence with reality, that is to say with what exists outside of us and independently of us. . . . This correspondence with the real external world we call truth. It is the aim of scientific work, even when the practical value of that work does not interest us."

The definition of truth as the agreement of the mind with reality leaves many problems to be solved and further explanations to be given by those who accept it. As James indicates, the theory of truth begins rather than ends with its definition. How do we know when our ideas—our statements or judgments—correspond with reality? By what signs or criteria shall we discover their truth or falsity? To this question the great books give various answers which we shall presently consider. There are other problems about the nature of truth which deserve attention first.

For example, one consequence of the definition seems to be that truth is a property of ideas rather than of things. Aristotle says that "it is not as if the good were true and the bad were in itself false"; hence "falsity and truth are not in things . . . but in thought." Yet he also applies the word "false" to non-existent things or to things whose appearance somehow belies their nature. Aquinas goes further. He distinguishes between the sense in which truth and falsity are primarily in the intellect and secondarily in things.

The equation between intellect and thing, he points out, can be looked at in two ways, depending on whether the intellect is the cause of the thing's nature, or the nature of the thing is the cause of knowledge in the intellect. When "things are the measure and rule of the intellect, truth consists in the equation of the intellect to the thing. . . . But when the intellect is the rule or measure of things, truth consists in the equation of things to the intellect"—as the product of human art may be said to be true when it accords with the artist's plan or intention. Thus "a house is said to be true that fulfills the likeness of the form in the architect's mind."

But, according to Aquinas, not only artificial things, but natural things as well, can have truth when they are viewed in relation to the intellect on which they depend. The divine intellect which is the creative cause of natural things measures their truth, as the human intellect measures the truth of artificial things. "Natural things are said to be true," Aquinas writes, "in so far as they express the likeness of the ideas that are in the divine mind; for a stone is called true, which possesses the nature proper to a stone, according to the preconception in the divine intellect."

Aquinas' conclusion—that "truth resides primarily in the intellect and secondarily in things according as they are related to the intellect as their source"—at once suggests the profound difference between truth in the divine and in the human intellect. The difference is more than that between infinite and finite truth. The distinction between uncreated and created truth affects the definition of truth itself.

The definition of truth as an equation of thought to thing, or thing to thought, does not seem to hold for the divine intellect. The notion of "conformity with its source," Aquinas acknowledges, "cannot be said, properly speaking, of divine truth." Divine truth has no source. It is not truth by correspondence with anything else. Rather it is, in the language of the theologian, the "primal truth." "God Himself, Who is the primal truth . . . is the rule of all truth," and "the principle and source of all truth."

IN THE HUMAN SPHERE, the definition of truth seems to be differently interpreted according as truth is made a property of words or of ideas. "To form a clear notion of truth," Locke writes, "it is very necessary to consider truth of thought and truth of words distinctly from one another." The truth of signs, or what is sometimes called "truth of signification," is "nothing but the joining or separating of words in propositions as the ideas they stand for agree or disagree in men's minds." In contrast to such verbal truth, what Locke calls mental truth consists in the joining or separating of our ideas themselves in a manner to accord with the realities they represent.

For Locke, verbal truth is "chimerical" or "barely nominal" because it can exist without any regard to "whether our ideas are such as really have, or are capable of having, an existence in nature." The signs we use may truly represent our thought even though what we think or state in words is false in fact. Hobbes takes a somewhat contrary view. "*True* and *false*," he writes, "are attributes of speech, not of things. And where speech is not, there is neither truth nor falsehood."

What is the cause of truth in speech? Hobbes replies that, since it consists "in the right ordering of names in our affirmations," a man needs only "to remember what every name he uses stands for." If men begin with definitions or "the settling of significations," and then abide by their definitions in subsequent discourse, their discourse will have truth. From want of definitions or from wrong definitions arise "all false and senseless tenets."

Agreement with reality would seem to be the measure of truth for Hobbes only to the extent that definitions can be right or wrong by reference to the objects defined. If definitions themselves are merely nominal and have rightness so far as they may be free from contradiction, then truth tends to become, more than a property of speech, almost purely logistical—a matter of playing the game of words according to the rules. Reasoning is reckoning with words. It begins with definitions and if it proceeds rightly, it produces "general, eternal and immutable truth. . . . For he that reasoneth aright in words he understandeth, can never conclude in error."

Hobbes' position seems to have a bearing not only on the issue concerning verbal and real truth, but also on the question whether the logical validity of reasoning makes the conclusion it reaches true as a matter of fact. Some writers, like Kant, distinguish between the truth which a proposition has when it conforms to the rules of thought and the truth it has when it represents nature. Valid reasoning alone cannot guarantee that a conclusion is true in fact. That depends on the truth of the premises—upon their being true of the nature of things. Aristotle criticizes those who, accepting certain principles as true, "are ready to accept any consequence of their application.

As though some principles," he continues, "did not require to be judged from their results, and particularly from their final issue. And that issue . . . in the knowledge of nature is the unimpeachable evidence of the senses as to each fact."

BUT NOT ALL TRUTH may require or admit of such certification. The truths of mathematics may be different from those of physics or metaphysics, and those of philosophy or religion from those of the empirical natural sciences. It is sometimes supposed, for example, that the truths of mathematics are purely formal or without reference to real existence. That seems to be the position of Hobbes and Hume, both of whom take geometry as the model of truth. For them statements of fact about real existence are at best probable opinions. For others, like James, there can be truth in the natural sciences, but such empirical truth is distinct in type from what he calls the "necessary" or "*a priori*" truths of mathematics and logic.

Does the definition of truth as agreement with reality apply to all kinds of truth, or only to truths about the realm of nature? The question has in mind more than the distinction between mathematics and physics. It is concerned with the difference between the study of nature and the moral sciences, or between the theoretic and the practical disciplines. "As regards nature," writes Kant, "experience presents us with rules and is the source of truth," but not so in ethical matters or morality. A theoretic proposition asserts that something exists or has a certain property, and so its truth depends on the existence of the thing or its real possession of an attribute; but a practical or moral judgment states, not what is, but what should occur or ought to be. Such a judgment cannot be true by correspondence with the way things are. Its truth, according to Aristotle, must consist rather "in agreement with right desire."

On this theory, all that remains common to speculative and practical truth is the conformity of the intellect to something outside itself—to an existing thing or to desire, will, or appetite. Stressing the difference, Aquinas declares that "truth is not the same for the practical as for the speculative intellect." The "conformity with right appetite" upon which practical truth depends, he goes on to say, "has no place in necessary matters, which are not effected by the human will, but only in contingent matters which can be effected by us, whether they be matters of interior action or the products of external work." In consequence, "in matters of action, truth or practical rectitude is not the same for all as to what is particular, but only as to the common principles"; whereas in speculative matters, concerned chiefly with necessary things, "truth is the same for all men, both as to principles and as to conclusions."

THE PROBLEM OF THE criteria or signs of truth does not seem to be of equal concern to all who discuss the nature of truth. For the ancients, at one extreme, it seems to be hardly a problem at all. For William James, at the other extreme, it seems to be the central problem. In the controversy over the pragmatic theory of truth, in which James engages with Bradley and Russell, some confusion tends to result from the fact that James seldom discusses what truth is except in terms of how we know what is true, while his opponents often ignore the signs of truth in discussing its nature. The important point for James is not that truth consists in agreement with reality, but that "true ideas are those we can assimilate, validate, corroborate, and verify." Whether we can assimilate or validate or verify an idea in turn depends upon its consequences, either for thought or action, or what James calls "truth's cash-value in experiential terms."

In his *Psychology*, James suggests another aspect of his theory of the expediency of a true idea, which he later developed in *Pragmatism*. Not only must our conceptions or theories be "able to account satisfactorily for our sensible experience," but they are also to be weighed for their appeal "to our aesthetic, emotional, and active needs." Apart from this added criterion, which became the subject of much dispute, the pragmatic theory of truth represents one of the traditional solutions of the problem of how to tell whether something is true or false. It looks mainly to extrinsic signs—not to some feature of the idea or thought itself, but to its consequences.

"The test of real and vigorous thinking,"

writes J. S. Mill, "the thinking which ascertains truths instead of dreaming, is successful application to practice." In similar vein, Bacon says that "of all the signs there is none more certain or worthy than that of the fruits produced, for the fruits and effects are the sureties and vouchers, as it were, for the truth of philosophy." The man who supposes that the end of learning lies in contemplation of the truth will "propose to himself as the test of truth, the satisfaction of his mind and understanding, as to the causes of things long since known." Only those who recognize that "the real and legitimate goal of the sciences is the endowment of human life with new inventions and riches," will submit truth to the test of its leading "to some new earnest of effects." To take effects as "pledges of truth" is, for Bacon, equivalent to declaring that truth and utility are "perfectly identical."

Verification by appeal to observation or sensible evidences may be regarded as one way of testing the truth of thought in terms of its consequences, but it also involves the principle of contradiction as a criterion of truth. When Aristotle recommends, for example, that we should accept theories as true "only if what they affirm agrees with the observed facts," he is saying that when the truth of a particular perception is indisputable, because the observed fact is evident, the general or theoretical statement which it contradicts must be false.

But the principle of contradiction as a criterion of truth goes further than testing theories by their consistency with observation. One of two contradictory statements must be false and the other must be true "if that which it is true to affirm is nothing other than that which it is false to deny." Even a single statement may show itself false by being self-contradictory, and in consequence its opposite can be seen to be true. What Aristotle calls axioms, or self-evident and indisputable truths, are those propositions immediately known to be true, and necessarily true, because their contradictories, being self-contradicatory, are impossible statements, or necessarily false. The truth of any proposition which is neither a self-evident axiom nor the statement of an evident, perceived fact, is tested, according to the principle of contradiction, by its consistency with axioms or perceptions.

As opposed to consequences or effects, contradiction or consistency as a sign of truth seems to be an intrinsic criterion. But this criterion is not universally accepted. "Contradiction," writes Pascal, "is not a sign of falsity, nor the want of contradiction a sign of truth." Nor, even when accepted, is it always judged adequate to solve the problem. It is, for Kant, a "merely logical criterion of truth . . . the *conditio sine qua non*, or negative condition of all truth. Farther than this logic cannot go, and the error which depends not on the form, but on the content of the cognition, it has no test to discover."

Some thinkers seem to rely upon an intrinsic mark by which each idea reveals its own truth or falsity. Augustine, for example, considers by what criterion he would know whether what Moses said was true. "And if I did know it," he asks, "would it be from him that I knew it? No," he replies, "but within me, in the inner retreat of my mind, the Truth, which is neither Hebrew nor Greek, nor Latin nor Barbarian, would tell me, without lips or tongue or sounded syllables: 'He speaks truth.' "

For Augustine, God is the warranty of the inner voice which plainly signifies the truth. For Spinoza, the truth of an idea depends upon its relation to God. Because "a true idea in us is that which in God is adequate, in so far as He is manifested by the nature of the human mind," it follows, according to Spinoza, that "he who has a true idea knows at the same time that he has a true idea, nor can he doubt the truth of the thing"; for "he who knows a thing truly must at the same time have an adequate idea or a true knowledge of his knowledge, that is to say (as is self-evident) he must be certain."

It is impossible, Spinoza maintains, to have a true idea without at the same time knowing that it is true. To the question, "How can a man know that he has an idea which agrees with that of which it is the idea?" he replies that "he knows it simply because he has an idea which agrees with that of which it is the idea, that is to say, because truth is its own standard." For what can be clearer, Spinoza asks, "or more certain than a true idea as the standard of truth? Just as light reveals both itself and the darkness, so truth is the standard of itself and of the false."

Spinoza defines an adequate idea as one which, "in so far as it is considered in itself, without reference to the object, has all the properties or internal signs of a true idea." He explains, moreover, that by "internal" he means to exclude even "the agreement of the idea with its object." This, he thinks, meets the objection that "if a true idea is distinguished from a false idea only in so far as it is said to agree with that of which it is the idea, the true idea [would have] no reality or perfection above the false idea (since they are distinguished by an external sign alone), and consequently the man who has true ideas will have no greater reality or perfection than he who has false ideas only."

Although Descartes and Locke also employ an intrinsic criterion of truth—not the adequacy, but the clarity and distinctness, of ideas—they do not seem to mean, as Spinoza does, that a single idea, in and of itself, can be true or false. Like Aristotle before them or Kant later, they regard a simple idea or concept as, strictly speaking, incapable of being either true or false.

"Truth and falsity," writes Locke, "belong . . . only to propositions"—to affirmations or denials which involve at least two ideas; or, as Kant says, "truth and error . . . are only to be found in a judgement," which explains why "the senses do not err, not because they always judge correctly, but because *they do not judge at all.*"

Nevertheless, for Locke the clarity and distinctness of the ideas which enter into the formation of propositions enable the mind to judge intuitively and certainly of their truth. When ideas are clear and distinct, "the mind perceives the agreement or disagreement of two ideas immediately by themselves. . . . Such kind of truths the mind perceives at the first sight of the ideas together by bare intuition . . . and this kind of knowledge is the clearest and most certain that human frailty is capable of."

The problem of the criterion of truth is sometimes closely connected with the problem of the causes of error. Descartes seems to pass by natural steps from one to the other. Having decided that "the things which we conceive very clearly and distinctly are all true," he reminds himself that there may be "some difficulty in ascertaining which are those that we distinctly conceive." The mystery of error looms large for Descartes because it seems to him that the human intellect, being created by God, must have a kind of natural infallibility, the infallibility of an instrument designed by God for knowing the truth, not for ignorance or error.

"If we did not know," Descartes reflects, "that all that is in us of reality and truth proceeds from a perfect and infinite being, however clear and distinct were our ideas, we should not have any reason to assure ourselves that they had the perfection of being true." But once we have "recognized that there is a God . . . and also recognized that all things depend upon Him, and that He is not a deceiver," we can infer that whatever we "perceive clearly and distinctly cannot fail to be true."

What, then, is the source of our errors? "I answer," writes Descartes, "that they depend on a combination of two causes, to wit, on the faculty of knowledge that rests in me, and on the power of choice or free will." Each perfect in its own sphere, neither the will nor the understanding by itself causes us to fall into error. "Since I understand nothing but by the power which God has given me for understanding, there is no doubt," Descartes declares, "that all that I understand, I understand as I ought, and it is not possible that I err in this."

The trouble lies in the relation of the will to the intellect. "Since the will is much wider in its range and compass than the understanding, I do not restrain it within the same bounds, but extend it also to things which I do not understand." It is not God's fault, says Descartes, if, in the exercise of my freedom, I do not "withold my assent from certain things as to which He has not placed a clear and distinct knowledge in my understanding." But as long as "I so restrain my will within the limits of knowledge that it forms no judgment except on matters which are clearly and distinctly represented to it by the understanding, I can never be deceived."

There are other accounts of error, less elaborate than Descartes', which are similar to the extent that they place the cause in some combination of human faculties rather than in their simple and separate operation. Socrates explains to Theaetetus that false opinions arise when the senses and the mind do not cooperate properly. Aristotle suggests that it is the imagination which frequently misleads the mind. Looking at the problem from the point of view of the theologian, Aquinas holds that Adam, in his state of innocence before the fall, could not be deceived. "While the soul remained subject to God," he writes, "the lower powers in man were subject to the higher, and were no impediment to their action." But man born in sin can be deceived, not because the intellect itself ever fails, but as a result of the wayward influence "of some lower power, such as the imagination or the like."

Lucretius, for whom sense, not mind, is infallible, attributes error to the fault of reason, which misinterprets the veridical impressions of the senses. "What surer test can we have than the senses," he asks, "whereby to note truth and falsehood?" He explains that the mind, not the senses, is responsible for illusions and hallucinations. "Do not then fasten upon the eyes this frailty of the mind."

Other writers, like Descartes, take the opposite view, that the senses are much less trustworthy than the intellect. Still others, like Montaigne, seem to find that error and fallacy, rather than any sort of infallibility, are quite natural to all human faculties, and beset sense and reason alike. "Man," says Pascal, is "full of error, natural and ineffaceable, without grace. Nothing shows him the truth. Everything deceives him. Those two sources of truth, reason and the senses, besides being both wanting in sincerity, deceive each other in turn."

Considering the extremes to which men have gone in their appraisal of human prowess or frailty, Locke's moderate statement of the matter is worth pondering. "Notwithstanding the great noise made in the world about errors and opinions," he writes, "I must do mankind that right, as to say, there are not so many men in errors and wrong opinions as is commonly supposed. Not that I think they embrace the truth; but, indeed, because concerning these doctrines they keep such a stir about, they have no thought, no opinion at all. . . . And though one cannot say that there are fewer improbable or erroneous opinions in the world than there are, yet this is certain, there are fewer that actually assent to them, and mistake them for truths, than is imagined."

OUTLINE OF TOPICS

1. The nature of truth
    - *1a.* The signs or criteria of truth: methods of verification
    - *1b.* The relation between truth and being or reality
    - *1c.* The relation of truth, goodness, and beauty

2. The modes of truth and falsity
    - *2a.* The distinction between truth and falsity in the mind and in things: logical and ontological truth
    - *2b.* The distinction between truth of statement and truth of signification: the distinction between real and verbal truth
    - *2c.* The distinction between theoretical and practical truth: conformity to existence and conformity to right desire
    - *2d.* The comparison of human and divine truth: finite truths and the infinite truth
    - *2e.* The distinction between truth and probability: its relation to the distinction between knowledge and opinion

3. Truth and error in relation to human knowing and learning
    - *3a.* Truth in the apprehensions of the sensitive faculty
        - (1) The truth of sensations: judgments of perception
        - (2) Truth in the memory and imagination

3*b*. Truth in the acts of the mind

(1) The truth of ideas: concepts and definitions

(2) The truth of propositions: the special problem of judgments about future contingencies

(3) Truth in reasoning: the truth of premises in relation to the truth of conclusions; logical validity and truth about reality

3*c*. The principle of contradiction as the foundation of truth in judgment and in reasoning

3*d*. The nature and causes of error

(1) The infallibility of the senses and the mind: the respects in which they are incapable of error

(2) The nature and sources of error in human perception and thought: the distinction between error and ignorance

(3) Rules for the correction or prevention of error in thought

4. Comparison of the various disciplines with respect to truth

4*a*. Truth in science and religion: the truth of reason and the truth of faith

4*b*. Truth in science and poetry: the truth of fact and the truth of fiction

4*c*. Truth in metaphysics, mathematics, and the empirical sciences: the truth of principles, hypotheses, and conclusions in the several speculative disciplines

4*d*. Truth and probability in rhetoric and dialectic

5. The eternal verities and the mutability of truth

6. The accumulation or accretion of truth, and the correction of error, in the progress of human learning

7. The skeptical denial of truth

7*a*. The impossibility of knowing the truth: the restriction of all human judgments to degrees of probability; the denial of axioms and of the possibility of demonstration

7*b*. The defense of truth against the skeptic

8. The moral and political aspect of truth

8*a*. Prevarication and perjury: the injustice of lying or bearing false witness

8*b*. The expediency of the political lie

8*c*. Truth in relation to love and friendship: the pleasant and the unpleasant truth

8*d*. Civil liberty as a condition for discovering the truth: freedom of thought and discussion

8*e*. The love of truth and the duty to seek it: the moral distinction between the sophist and the philosopher; martyrdom to the truth

REFERENCES

References are listed by volume number (in bold type), author's name, and page number. Bible references are to book, chapter, and verse of the Authorized King James version of the Bible. The abbreviation "esp" calls the reader's attention to one or more especially relevant parts of a whole reference; "passim" signifies that the topic is discussed intermittently rather than continuously in the work or passage cited. Where the work as a whole is relevant to the topic, the page numbers refer to the entire work. For general guidance in the use of *The Great Ideas,* consult the Preface.

1. The nature of truth

7 PLATO, 85–89
8 ARISTOTLE, 531
19 AQUINAS, 74–75, 94–100, 103–104
23 HOBBES, 56
31 DESCARTES, 83, 89–93 passim
31 SPINOZA, 355, 388–389
35 LOCKE, 329–331
42 KANT, 36–37

1*a*. The signs or criteria of truth: methods of verification

7 PLATO, 421–422
8 ARISTOTLE, 361, 397
9 ARISTOTLE, 343–344, 433–434
10 GALEN, 173
12 LUCRETIUS, 50
18 AUGUSTINE, 75–76
19 AQUINAS, 175–178
23 HOBBES, 165
25 MONTAIGNE, 260–261
28 HARVEY, 322–323
30 BACON, 57–58, 107–108, 116–117, 128, 137–195 passim
31 DESCARTES, 2–3, 123–125, 153, 157–158, 168, 206–207, 210, 237–238
31 SPINOZA, 386–389, 453
33 PASCAL, 356–366, 435–436
34 NEWTON, 271
35 LOCKE, 93–94, 305, 323–326, 362
35 HUME, 487, 488–491
38 ROUSSEAU, 348
42 KANT, 77, 85–87, 146–149, 153
43 MILL, 446–447, 461, 463
45 LAVOISIER, 1
46 HEGEL, 2, 74
53 JAMES, 141–142, 636–660

1*b*. The relation between truth and being or reality

7 PLATO, 71–74, 368–373, 423–424, 447, 507–509, 534–536, 537, 561–577
8 ARISTOTLE, 20, 72–73, 550, 577–578
17 PLOTINUS, 218
18 AUGUSTINE, 48–50, 328
19 AQUINAS, 96, 99–100, 107–108, 238–239, 467–468, 604–607
31 DESCARTES, 226–227, 261
31 SPINOZA, 375, 383–385
35 LOCKE, 330
42 KANT, 36–37, 91–93, 102–103
46 HEGEL, 113–114, 156–157
53 JAMES, 638–643

1*c*. The relation of truth, goodness, and beauty

7 PLATO, 124–129, 167, 383–388, 556–559, 561, 630–631, 637–638, 654–662
8 ARISTOTLE, 663–664
12 EPICTETUS, 141, 241
12 AURELIUS, 265
17 PLOTINUS, 10, 22–26, 336–338
19 AQUINAS, 25–26, 94–95, 97, 424–425, 434–435, 626–627, 657–658, 737, 747–748
20 AQUINAS, 608–609
30 BACON, 26–27
35 LOCKE, 319
46 HEGEL, 46, 278
52 DOSTOEVSKY, 153

2. The modes of truth and falsity

2*a*. The distinction between truth and falsity in the mind and in things: logical and ontological truth

8 ARISTOTLE, 546
19 AQUINAS, 99, 100–101, 125
31 DESCARTES, 126–127
35 LOCKE, 243

2*b*. The distinction between truth of statement and truth of signification: the distinction between real and verbal truth

8 ARISTOTLE, 525
19 AQUINAS, 99–100
23 HOBBES, 56
31 SPINOZA, 390–391
35 LOCKE, 244–248 passim, 323–326 passim, 330
53 JAMES, 880–882

2*c*. The distinction between theoretical and practical truth: conformity to existence and conformity to right desire

8 ARISTOTLE, 512
9 ARISTOTLE, 339–340, 387–388
20 AQUINAS, 39–40, 223–224

23 Hobbes, 78
31 Descartes, 126, 206–207
35 Locke, 331
42 Kant, 190–191, 253, 264, 271, 283–287, 291–297, 310, 319–321, 329–337, 388, 596–598
46 Hegel, 2–3
53 James, 643–645, 655–659, 886–888

2*d*. The comparison of human and divine truth: finite truths and the infinite truth

Old Testament: *Psalms,* 119:142,160 / *Proverbs,* 30:5–6
New Testament: *John,* 7:14–18; 8:12–59; 14:6,16–17; 18:37–38 / *Romans,* 1:18–25 / *I Corinthians,* 1:17–2:16 / *Ephesians,* 4:21–24 / *II Thessalonians,* 2:10–14 / *I Timothy,* 2:3–4; 3:15 / *James,* 5:19–20 / *I John,* 3:18–19; 5:5–12
18 Augustine, 15, 28, 90, 627, 634
19 Aquinas, 97–100, 550–551, 628
20 Aquinas, 216–217
21 Dante, 111–112, 135, 139
25 Montaigne, 80–82, 208–209, 267–268
31 Spinoza, 385
32 Milton, 219–220
46 Hegel, 349–350
51 Tolstoy, 216–218
53 James, 671

2*e*. The distinction between truth and probability: its relation to the distinction between knowledge and opinion

7 Plato, 370–373, 517, 527, 531–532, 633–635
8 Aristotle, 97–99, 102–103, 104, 119, 121–122, 563–564
9 Aristotle, 391, 596–597, 652–653
16 Copernicus, 505–506
19 Aquinas, 56–57, 422–423
20 Aquinas, 36–37
25 Montaigne, 271–273
31 Descartes, 2–4, 75–78, 95–96
31 Spinoza, 388–390
33 Pascal, 205–217 passim
35 Locke, 316, 322–323, 331–336, 365–366, 371–372, 378–379
42 Kant, 1–4, 228, 240–243, 600–604
45 Faraday, 391
46 Hegel, 49–54, 131

3. Truth and error in relation to human knowing and learning

3*a*. Truth in the apprehensions of the sensitive faculty

3*a*(1) The truth of sensations: judgments of perception

7 Plato, 392–393, 431, 622–626
8 Aristotle, 530, 591, 649, 659–660, 680
12 Lucretius, 49–51
19 Aquinas, 102, 458–459
25 Montaigne, 285–286
28 Harvey, 333
30 Bacon, 109, 111
31 Descartes, 13, 53, 75–77, 101–103, 206–207
31 Spinoza, 383–384, 388
35 Locke, 324, 355
35 Berkeley, 415–416, 429–430
35 Hume, 504–506
42 Kant, 108–109
53 James, 460–471, 475–478, 508–520, 521–522, 565, 593–626, 648, 780–785
54 Freud, 430

3*a*(2) Truth in the memory and imagination

7 Plato, 538–541
8 Aristotle, 660
19 Aquinas, 288
29 Cervantes, 1–429 passim
31 Descartes, 75–77
31 Spinoza, 381, 389–390
33 Pascal, 186–189
35 Locke, 357
40 Gibbon, 88
51 Tolstoy, 294–295
53 James, 240–241, 480–484, 498–499, 527–538, 662–663
54 Freud, 341–343, 597–599

3*b*. Truth in the acts of the mind

7 Plato, 386–388, 536–544
8 Aristotle, 662–663
18 Augustine, 269
19 Aquinas, 94–96, 458–459, 505–506, 690
31 Descartes, 82–86, 89–93, 123–125, 229–230
31 Spinoza, 389, 391–394
42 Kant, 110–112, 115–119, 233–234
53 James, 867–868

3*b*(1) The truth of ideas: concepts and definitions

7 Plato, 85–114 passim, 323–324, 809–810
8 Aristotle, 25, 192, 194–211 passim, 546–547, 577–578
18 Augustine, 76, 653
19 Aquinas, 303–304, 451–453
23 Hobbes, 56
28 Galileo, 200
31 Descartes, 82–86, 130, 131–132, 156–158
31 Spinoza, 357, 373
33 Pascal, 373, 430–431
35 Locke, 238–248 passim
42 Kant, 85–87, 179–182, 215–217, 570–572
46 Hegel, 9–10
53 James, 299–302, 305–312, 669–671

3*b*(2) The truth of propositions: the special problem of judgments about future contingencies

7 Plato, 561–577
8 Aristotle, 6, 8–9, 25, 26–36 passim, 531–532, 550, 660
9 Aristotle, 387–388

19 AQUINAS, 74–75, 86–88, 89–90, 95–96, 102–104, 297–298, 457–458, 463–464, 505–506
20 AQUINAS, 39–40
22 CHAUCER, 107–108
23 HOBBES, 56, 57
30 BACON, 54–55, 57–58
31 DESCARTES, 90–91, 123–125, 156–157, 215–216
31 SPINOZA, 392–394
35 LOCKE, 243–244, 247–248, 331, 336
35 HUME, 458
42 KANT, 99–100, 193
53 JAMES, 671–672, 889–890

3b(3) Truth in reasoning: the truth of premises in relation to the truth of conclusions; logical validity and truth about reality

7 PLATO, 65–84, 236–238
8 ARISTOTLE, 72–77, 104–105, 106–107, 335–336
9 ARISTOTLE, 339–340, 696
10 GALEN, 178
12 EPICTETUS, 112–113
18 AUGUSTINE, 651–653
19 AQUINAS, 443–444
23 HOBBES, 58–59, 65
30 BACON, 57–58, 59–60
31 DESCARTES, 4, 126–127
42 KANT, 36–37, 64–65, 110–111, 180–182, 211–218
44 BOSWELL, 134
53 JAMES, 867–882

3c. The principle of contradiction as the foundation of truth in judgment and in reasoning

7 PLATO, 72–73, 350–351, 527–528
8 ARISTOTLE, 19, 86–87, 105–106, 524–531, 590–592
19 AQUINAS, 302–303
30 BACON, 59–60
31 DESCARTES, 82
35 LOCKE, 99, 100, 113, 337–338
42 KANT, 64–65, 174
53 JAMES, 639–641

3d. The nature and causes of error

3d(1) The infallibility of the senses and the mind: the respects in which they are incapable of error

7 PLATO, 224, 539–540
8 ARISTOTLE, 530, 578, 648–649, 659–661, 665–666
12 LUCRETIUS, 9
19 AQUINAS, 102–103, 458–459
31 DESCARTES, 22–23, 77–78, 83, 89–93, 124, 215–216, 229–230
31 SPINOZA, 388–394 passim
35 LOCKE, 239, 245–246
35 BERKELEY, 420
42 KANT, 108, 233–234
53 JAMES, 125–126, 361

3d(2) The nature and sources of error in human perception and thought: the distinction between error and ignorance

7 PLATO, 224–225, 520–522, 536–544, 557–558, 622–626
8 ARISTOTLE, 66, 85–89, 101–102, 106–107, 109–111, 182, 220–221, 227–253, 528–529, 577–578, 659, 702–706
9 ARISTOTLE, 356–357, 359, 391–392
12 LUCRETIUS, 49–51
14 PLUTARCH, 816–817
18 AUGUSTINE, 514–515, 627
19 AQUINAS, 100–104, 450–453, 477–478, 505–506
20 AQUINAS, 19–21
21 DANTE, 126
23 HOBBES, 51–52, 57, 78–79, 139, 258
25 MONTAIGNE, 269–294, 517–518
27 SHAKESPEARE, 608–609
28 GILBERT, 105
28 HARVEY, 333, 335, 411
30 BACON, 13–15, 16, 43–44, 51, 60–61, 66, 98, 107, 109–117, 119–125, 128
31 DESCARTES, 75–81 passim, 89–93, 100–103, 123–126, 215–216, 229–230
31 SPINOZA, 381, 385–386, 387–388, 390–394 passim, 424–425
33 PASCAL, 186–189
35 LOCKE, 193–197, 248–251, 290–300 passim, 342–344 passim, 378, 388–394
35 BERKELEY, 405–412 passim, 429–430
35 HUME, 469
36 STERNE, 234–236
42 KANT, 133–134, 200–209, 219–220, 224–227, 260–261, 294–295, 302
43 FEDERALIST, 29–30, 103–104, 122
48 MELVILLE, 313
53 JAMES, 240–241, 264–268, 460–469, 506–520 passim, 533–538, 610–625
54 FREUD, 148–149, 210, 337, 354–355, 379, 472, 760–761, 819

3d(3) Rules for the correction or prevention of error in thought

7 PLATO, 582–584, 610–613
8 ARISTOTLE, 143–223, 227–253
12 EPICTETUS, 112–113
23 HOBBES, 58–60
28 HARVEY, 268, 331–332
30 BACON, 11–17, 33–34, 47–49, 51, 60–61, 64–66, 105–195
31 DESCARTES, 2–25, 41–67, 75–77, 103, 206
33 PASCAL, 430–434
35 LOCKE, 300–306
35 BERKELEY, 405–412 passim
35 HUME, 453–454
42 KANT, 5–13, 101, 129–130, 209–211, 218–227, 248–250, 293–294
43 MILL, 276–277, 283–288 passim

4. Comparison of the various disciplines with respect to truth

4*a*. Truth in science and religion: the truth of reason and the truth of faith

18 Augustine, 323, 523
19 Aquinas, 3–4
20 Aquinas, 338–339, 380–384, 392–394, 399–400, 409
21 Dante, 108–109 passim
23 Hobbes, 274
25 Montaigne, 208–209, 212–215, 238–239, 291–294
30 Bacon, 33, 55, 95–101
31 Descartes, 125–126, 284
33 Pascal, 147–148, 163–166, 248–250, 339, 342–343
35 Locke, 340, 380, 383
35 Hume, 497
40 Gibbon, 190
42 Kant, 601–607
43 Mill, 455
46 Hegel, 158–160, 349–350
51 Tolstoy, 196–197, 695–696
53 James, 864
54 Freud, 874–881

4*b*. Truth in science and poetry: the truth of fact and the truth of fiction

6 Herodotus, 71–73
6 Thucydides, 354
7 Plato, 52–57, 320–324, 427–431, 561, 577–579, 660–662
9 Aristotle, 696–698
14 Plutarch, 390
21 Dante, 23
22 Chaucer, 171–172, 212, 400–401
23 Hobbes, 67
25 Montaigne, 41–42, 199–200, 258–259
26 Shakespeare, 370–371
29 Cervantes, 183–193, 212–215
30 Bacon, 38–39
31 Descartes, 43
37 Fielding, 49–50
40 Gibbon, 88, 186
44 Boswell, 282
46 Hegel, 285–286
51 Tolstoy, 405–406
53 James, 641–643
54 Freud, 692–693

4*c*. Truth in metaphysics, mathematics, and the empirical sciences: the truth of principles, hypotheses, and conclusions in the several speculative disciplines

7 Plato, 383–388, 391–398, 633–635
8 Aristotle, 120–121, 609
9 Aristotle, 283–284
16 Ptolemy, 429
16 Copernicus, 505–506
16 Kepler, 888–890
23 Hobbes, 59, 269
30 Bacon, 48–49
31 Descartes, 47–48, 66
35 Locke, 315–323 passim
42 Kant, 15–16, 17–19, 217, 245–248, 311–313, 351–352, 388
43 Federalist, 103–104
43 Mill, 283–284, 445
49 Darwin, 590
53 James, 862–866, 870–878, 882–886
54 Freud, 661–662, 873–875

4*d*. Truth and probability in rhetoric and dialectic

5 Euripides, 382
6 Thucydides, 425
7 Plato, 39–42, 65–84, 131–141, 200, 252–294, 386–388
8 Aristotle, 143, 523
9 Aristotle, 594, 596–597, 652–653
18 Augustine, 19, 653, 677, 683–684
30 Bacon, 12
31 Descartes, 16–17
35 Locke, 299–300
43 Mill, 292–293

5. The eternal verities and the mutability of truth

Old Testament: *Psalms,* 119:160 / *Proverbs,* 8:22–30
Apocrypha: *Wisdom of Solomon,* 7:24–26 / *Ecclesiasticus,* 24:9
New Testament: *II John,* 2
7 Plato, 113–114, 125, 528
8 Aristotle, 8–9, 104, 512
18 Augustine, 3, 91–92, 626–627, 654
19 Aquinas, 99–100
20 Aquinas, 216–217
30 Bacon, 27–28
31 Descartes, 93–94, 216–217, 229
31 Spinoza, 356–357, 363
35 Locke, 308–309, 358
46 Hegel, 1–2, 6–7, 115, 176
50 Marx-Engels, 428
51 Tolstoy, 216–218
53 James, 879–882, 889–890

6. The accumulation or accretion of truth, and the correction of error, in the progress of human learning

8 Aristotle, 253, 506, 511–512, 513, 606
9 Aristotle, 165
10 Galen, 180–182, 199, 207
16 Kepler, 846–850
18 Augustine, 267–268, 271–272, 655–656
20 Aquinas, 236, 385–387
23 Hobbes, 114–115, 164, 267–269 passim, 282
25 Montaigne, 271, 276–278
28 Gilbert, 2
28 Harvey, 267–269, 279–280, 293, 306, 331–332, 364–365, 377, 433, 457
30 Bacon, 14–15, 47–48, 64, 121, 125–130 passim

31 DESCARTES, 41–67
32 MILTON, 381–412
33 PASCAL, 357–358
35 LOCKE, 85, 89
36 SWIFT, 118–119
36 STERNE, 224–225
38 ROUSSEAU, 330
40 GIBBON, 23–24
41 GIBBON, 274, 298–300
42 KANT, 5–6, 248–250, 513–514
43 MILL, 274–293 passim
44 BOSWELL, 129
45 FARADAY, 332
51 TOLSTOY, 342–343
54 FREUD, 550–551, 880–881

7. The skeptical denial of truth

7*a*. The impossibility of knowing the truth: the restriction of all human judgments to degrees of probability; the denial of axioms and of the possibility of demonstration

7 PLATO, 86, 107–109, 236–238, 517–532 passim
8 ARISTOTLE, 99, 524–532, 590–592
12 LUCRETIUS, 50
12 EPICTETUS, 164–166
18 AUGUSTINE, 32
19 AQUINAS, 440–442
25 MONTAIGNE, 208–294, 318–319, 497–502, 517–519
30 BACON, 57–58
31 DESCARTES, 272–273
33 PASCAL, 181–184, 238–239
35 BERKELEY, 432–433
35 HUME, 460–466, 477
42 KANT, 129–130, 294–295
46 HEGEL, 2, 23, 86, 159
47 GOETHE, 11–12, 17–18, 45–46
50 MARX-ENGELS, 428
51 TOLSTOY, 194–195
53 JAMES, 884–886
54 FREUD, 881–882

7*b*. The defense of truth against the skeptic

7 PLATO, 179–183, 517–532
8 ARISTOTLE, 525–532, 590–592
12 LUCRETIUS, 50–51
12 EPICTETUS, 164–166
18 AUGUSTINE, 523
19 AQUINAS, 94–95, 453–455
30 BACON, 13, 115–116
31 DESCARTES, 95–96, 206–207, 272–273
33 PASCAL, 238, 349–351
35 LOCKE, 94–95
35 BERKELEY, 404, 405, 429–431, 432–433
35 HUME, 454–455, 507–508
42 KANT, 218–222, 224–227, 311–313
44 BOSWELL, 126
46 HEGEL, 3–5
54 FREUD, 881–882

8. The moral and political aspect of truth

8*a*. Prevarication and perjury: the injustice of lying or bearing false witness

OLD TESTAMENT: *Genesis,* 4:8–10; 27; 39:7–20 / *Leviticus,* 6:2–7 / *Deuteronomy,* 5:20; 19:15–21 / *II Chronicles,* 18 / *Psalms,* 50:16–21; 52:1–5; 120:1–3/ *Proverbs,* 12:17–22; 26:18–28 / *Isaiah,* 59 passim / *Jeremiah,* 9:1–9; 23:16–40 / *Zechariah,* 8:16–19 / *Malachi,* 3:5–18
APOCRYPHA: *Ecclesiasticus,* 7:12–13; 20:18,24–26 / *Susanna*
NEW TESTAMENT: *Matthew,* 5:33–37; 26:55–75 / *Mark,* 14:48–72 / *Acts,* 5:1–10; 6:11–15 / *I Timothy,* 4:1–3
5 SOPHOCLES, 101–103, 182–195
6 HERODOTUS, 201–202, 217
7 PLATO, 208–210, 783–784
9 ARISTOTLE, 374–375, 621–622
12 AURELIUS, 291
18 AUGUSTINE, 634–635
21 DANTE, 15, 33–34, 151
25 MONTAIGNE, 16–17, 314–316, 323–324
33 PASCAL, 67–69, 117–127
36 SWIFT, 146
37 FIELDING, 40–41, 66, 318–319, 382
40 GIBBON, 215–216
42 KANT, 260, 267–268, 269, 272
43 MILL, 455–456
44 BOSWELL, 124, 157, 372–373
46 HEGEL, 49–54
51 TOLSTOY, 134, 304–305, 366–367

8*b*. The expediency of the political lie

4 HOMER, 101, 257–258
5 SOPHOCLES, 173–174, 182–183
6 HERODOTUS, 105, 186
6 THUCYDIDES, 427
7 PLATO, 323–324, 326, 340–341
13 VIRGIL, 124–131
14 PLUTARCH, 160–161, 357, 365–366
15 TACITUS, 256
21 DANTE, 38–41
23 MACHIAVELLI, 25–26
25 MONTAIGNE, 11–13, 306, 381–388
43 MILL, 277–278
44 BOSWELL, 212
54 FREUD, 197

8*c*. Truth in relation to love and friendship: the pleasant and the unpleasant truth

OLD TESTAMENT: *Proverbs,* 11:9–13
NEW TESTAMENT: *I John,* 3:18–19
5 SOPHOCLES, 99–113, 173–174, 190
5 EURIPIDES, 385–386
7 PLATO, 201–203, 234–235, 356–357, 622–631
12 EPICTETUS, 213–223 passim
19 AQUINAS, 788–789
20 AQUINAS, 255–257
21 DANTE, 25–26, 38–41, 43–46
22 CHAUCER, 457–460

25 Montaigne, 320–321, 323–324
26 Shakespeare, 468–469
27 Shakespeare, 121–122, 313, 393–420, 607–609
33 Pascal, 191–192
44 Boswell, 94, 106, 299, 393, 402, 542
49 Darwin, 315
51 Tolstoy, 310, 333–334
52 Dostoevsky, 20

8*d*. Civil liberty as a condition for discovering the truth: freedom of thought and discussion

5 Sophocles, 135, 137
6 Herodotus, 216–217
7 Plato, 200–210 passim, 601–602
15 Tacitus, 189
23 Hobbes, 102–103
31 Descartes, 283
32 Milton, 381–412
35 Locke, 1–22
35 Hume, 497, 503
40 Gibbon, 669–671 passim
41 Gibbon, 300
42 Kant, 220–221
43 Mill, 274–293 passim, 297–298
44 Boswell, 221–224, 300–301, 512
46 Hegel, 104

8*e*. The love of truth and the duty to seek it: the moral distinction between the sophist and the philosopher; martyrdom to the truth

Old Testament: *Psalms,* 25:4–5; 43:3; 51:6; 119:30
Apocrypha: *II Maccabees,* 6:18–7:42
New Testament: *John,* 8:31–32 / *Acts,* 6:8–7:60 / *II Corinthians,* 13:7–8
6 Thucydides, 397
7 Plato, 54–55, 124–127, 179–180, 182–183, 200–212, 223–225, 234–235, 251, 370–373, 377–379, 518–519, 528–531, 551–579, 808–809
8 Aristotle, 523
9 Aristotle, 168–169
12 Epictetus, 115–116, 144–145, 160–161, 177–178, 186–187, 190, 193–198, 207–210, 213–223 passim, 235–237
12 Aurelius, 261, 262, 270
16 Kepler, 1009–1010
18 Augustine, 14–15, 30, 33–34, 60–61, 79–80, 284–285
19 Aquinas, 747–748
20 Aquinas, 1058–1061
22 Chaucer, 164, 463–471
25 Montaigne, 446–450
28 Harvey, 268, 331–332
30 Bacon, 117
31 Descartes, 13–14
32 Milton, 197, 331
33 Pascal, 276
35 Locke, 87, 384
40 Gibbon, 217–220, 327–328
42 Kant, 187–188, 221–222
43 Mill, 278–283
44 Boswell, 151, 221–224
46 Hegel, 276, 279–281
47 Goethe, 16
48 Melville, 35–36
54 Freud, 125–127, 874–875

CROSS-REFERENCES

For: Other discussions bearing on the nature of truth and its relation to being, goodness, and beauty, *see* Beauty 1b; Being 4–4b; Good and Evil 1c; Knowledge 1, 4a; Opinion 3a.

Other discussions of the signs or criteria of truth and of methods of verification, *see* Experience 4b; Hypothesis 4d; Idea 6c–6e; Sense 5c.

The significance of the distinction between theoretic and practical truth, *see* Judgment 2; Knowledge 6e(1); Philosophy 2a; Prudence 2a; Science 3a; Wisdom 1b.

Discussions of what is involved in the comparison of human and divine truth, *see* God 5f; Infinity 7d; Knowledge 7a; Wisdom 1d.

Matters surrounding the distinction between truth and probability, and the related distinction between knowledge and opinion, *see* Judgment 9; Knowledge 6d(1)–6d(3); Necessity and Contingency 4a; Opinion 3–3b.

The consideration of truth and falsity in the apprehensions of the sensitive faculty, *see* Memory and Imagination 2e(4), 5c; Principle 2b(1); Sense 4d–4d(2).

The consideration of truth and falsity in the acts of the mind, *see* Definition 1e; Idea 6f; Judgment 10; Necessity and Contingency 4c; Principle 2b(2); Reasoning 3a–3c; Time 6f.

Other discussions of the principle of contradiction as the principle of truth in judgment and reasoning, *see* Logic 1a; Opposition 1d(1); Principle 3a(3).

The theory of error, its nature and causes, and the respects in which the human mind is fallible or infallible, *see* KNOWLEDGE 4a; MIND 5a; SENSE 4d, 4d(2); and for the suggestion of various methods of saving the mind from error, *see* KNOWLEDGE 5d–5e; LANGUAGE 6; LOGIC 4; MIND 5b; REASONING 3b–3c; SIGN AND SYMBOL 4c.

Discussions relevant to the contrast between truth in one discipline and truth in another, *see* DIALECTIC 5; HISTORY 3a; MATHEMATICS 1c; OPINION 4a; POETRY 8a(2); RHETORIC 5a; THEOLOGY 4b.

The eternity or immutability of truth, and for the change or growth of truth in the tradition of human learning, *see* CHANGE 15a; ETERNITY 4c; KNOWLEDGE 10; PROGRESS 6c.

Various expressions of skepticism and of the answers to the skeptic, *see* CUSTOM AND CONVENTION 9b; KNOWLEDGE 5c–5d; OPINION 3c; PRINCIPLE 5; RELATION 6b; UNIVERSAL AND PARTICULAR 7a.

For: Another consideration of truth as a source of moral or spiritual freedom, *see* LIBERTY 3b; and for freedom of thought and discussion as a condition of discovering the truth, *see* KNOWLEDGE 9b; LIBERTY 2a–2b; OPINION 5b; PROGRESS 6e.

The love of truth and its pursuit as the distinguishing marks of the philosopher, *see* LOVE 1d; PHILOSOPHY 6a; WISDOM 3.

ADDITIONAL READINGS

Listed below are works not included in *Great Books of the Western World*, but relevant to the idea and topics with which this chapter deals. These works are divided into two groups:

I. Works by authors represented in this collection.
II. Works by authors not represented in this collection.

For the date, place, and other facts concerning the publication of the works cited, consult the Bibliography of Additional Readings which follows the last chapter of *The Great Ideas*.

I.

AUGUSTINE. *Concerning the Teacher*
——. *On Free Will*, BK II
AQUINAS. *Quaestiones Disputatae, De Veritate*, Q I
F. BACON. "Of Truth," in *Essays*
DESCARTES. *The Principles of Philosophy*, PART I, 1–5, 29–38, 42–44, 48–50, 70–76
HOBBES. *Concerning Body*, PART I, CH 5
SPINOZA. *Correspondence*, II
——. *Of the Improvement of the Understanding*
KANT. *Introduction to Logic*, VII
HEGEL. *Science of Logic*, VOL II, SECT III, CH 2 (A)
W. JAMES. *Pragmatism*, LECT VI–VII
——. *The Meaning of Truth*

II.

CICERO. *Academics*
SEXTUS EMPIRICUS. *Against the Logicians*, BK I (Does a Criterion of Truth Exist?, Concerning the Criterion, Concerning Truth); BK II, CH I
ANSELM OF CANTERBURY. *Dialogue on Truth*
GROSSETESTE. *On Truth*
R. BACON. *Opus Majus*, PART I
DUNS SCOTUS. *Oxford Commentary*, BK I, DIST 3, Q 4
ALBO. *The Book of Principles (Sefer ha-Ikkarim)*, BK II, CH 27
NICOLAS OF CUSA. *De Docta Ignorantia*, BK I, CH 3
SUÁREZ. *Disputationes Metaphysicae*, III, VIII–IX, X (1), XXXI (12)
CAMPANELLA. *The Defense of Galileo*
HERBERT OF CHERBURY. *De Veritate (Of Truth)*
CORNEILLE. *Polyeucte*
MOLIÈRE. *Tartuffe*
MALEBRANCHE. *De la recherche de la vérité*, BK I, CH 3–9, 11, 15–17; BK III (II), CH 9–11
——. *Dialogues on Metaphysics and Religion*, I–II
LEIBNITZ. *Philosophical Works*, CH 3 (*Thoughts on Knowledge, Truth and Ideas*)
——. *New Essays Concerning Human Understanding*, BK II, CH 29, 32; BK IV, CH 5, 20
——. *Monadology*, par 33–37
VOLTAIRE. "Falsity," "Truth," in *A Philosophical Dictionary*
VOLTAIRE. *The Ignorant Philosopher*, CH 33
T. REID. *Essays on the Intellectual Powers of Man*, VI, CH 5–6, 8
W. HAMILTON. *Lectures on Metaphysics and Logic*, VOL II (27–31)
EMERSON. "Truth," in *English Traits*
WHEWELL. *On the Philosophy of Discovery*, CH 29
LOTZE. *Microcosmos*, BK VIII, CH I
——. *Logic*, BK III, CH 5
CLIFFORD. "The Ethics of Belief," in VOL II, *Lectures and Essays*
BOSANQUET. *Logic*, VOL II, CH 9–10

C. S. PEIRCE. *Collected Papers*, VOL V, par 358–410, 464–496, 538–604
FRAZER. *The Golden Bough*, PART VII, CH 13
ROYCE. *The World and the Individual*, SERIES I (6)
DEWEY. "The Intellectual Criterion for Truth," "A Short Catechism Concerning Truth," in *The Influence of Darwin on Philosophy*
JOACHIM. *The Nature of Truth*
BRADLEY. *The Principles of Logic*, BK III, PART II, CH 3–4; Terminal Essays, VIII
——. *Appearance and Reality*, BK II, CH 16, 24
——. *Essays on Truth and Reality*, CH 4–5, 7–9, 11
PÉGUY. *Basic Verities* (The Search for Truth)
BERGSON. *The Creative Mind*, CH 1, 8
MCTAGGART. *The Nature of Existence*, CH 44–45
WITTGENSTEIN. *Tractatus Logico-Philosophicus*
CROCE. "On Telling the Truth," in *The Conduct of Life*
WHITEHEAD. *Religion in the Making*, CH 4
——. *Adventures of Ideas*, CH 16, 18
SANTAYANA. *Scepticism and Animal Faith*, CH 25
——. *The Realm of Truth*
BLANSHARD. *The Nature of Thought*, CH 25–27
CASSIRER. *The Myth of the State*, PART I (4), III (18)
B. RUSSELL. *Philosophical Essays*, CH 5–7
——. *The Problems of Philosophy*, CH 12–13
——. *The Analysis of Mind*, LECT 13
——. *An Inquiry into Meaning and Truth*, CH 16–17, 21–23
——. *Human Knowledge, Its Scope and Limits*, PART II, CH 8–11

Chapter 95: TYRANNY

INTRODUCTION

IF any point in political theory is indisputable, it would seem to be that tyranny is the worst corruption of government—a vicious misuse of power and a violent abuse of the human beings who are subject to it. Aristotle's remark that "no freeman, if he can escape from it, will endure such government," would seem to express the sentiments of all who, loving liberty and abhoring slavery, look upon tyranny as destroying the one and establishing the other.

Certainly the word "tyranny" is seldom if ever used eulogistically. Such phrases as "a just tyranny" or "a good tyrant" are at once seen to be as self-contradictory as "a round square." The great books of history give the impression that tyrants and despots, who vastly outnumber good rulers, are always objects of hate and fear, never of love and admiration. If there are exceptions, if there are peoples who willingly submit to or even deserve the yoke of despotism and tyranny, they are, in the judgment of ancients and moderns alike, politically primitive.

The traditional association of the word "despotism" with "tyranny" requires us to consider whether our understanding of these terms is as uniformly clear as the denunciation of what they denote seems to be universal. Are despotism and tyranny the same? It may be thought that the tyrant must always have despotic power at his disposal, power unlimited by law, so that the lawless ruler is at once both despot and tyrant. But need the despot, the absolute ruler, always rule tyrannically?

The familiar phrase, "benevolent despotism," at once suggests the negative answer, and also some line of distinction between despotism and tyranny. Tyranny can never be benevolent. But despotism may be no worse than paternalism. While its injustice may consist in treating adults, able to govern themselves, as if they were children, it may also derive an air of justice from the fact that the despot, like the father, rules his subjects for their own good. If he treats them like slaves rather than children, exploiting them to serve his own interests, then he is not a benevolent but a tyrannical despot.

This understanding of the meaning of "despotism" and "tyranny" seems to be only partly supported by their etymology. The Greek word from which "despot" comes signifies the head of a household, the *paterfamilias* (as he is called by the Romans) who exercises the absolute authority of a master over chattel slaves, and of a parent over his children. In contrast, the Greek word *týrannos* refers to the ruler of a state rather than a family, and is sometimes used as if it were equivalent in meaning to "king." Yet both words carry the connotation of absolute power, and when, in addition, the subjects of a tyrant are considered to be no better off than slaves, the difference in the meaning of the two words almost disappears.

The difficulty of grasping what is essential to the nature of tyranny and despotism seems to be complicated by certain criteria, originally proposed by the Greeks, for distinguishing between king and tyrant, or between royal and despotic rule. Both Plato and Aristotle speak of the king as a good monarch and the tyrant as a bad one. Both say that monarchy, or rule by a single man, is royal when it is for the welfare of the ruled and tyrannical when it serves only the interests of the ruler. Both make lawlessness—either a violation of existing laws or government by personal fiat without settled laws—a mark of tyranny.

Yet, for Aristotle at least, some of these criteria also apply to despotism, and even to royal government, insofar as these are distinguished from political or constitutional government—government by law rather than by men. Furthermore, the association of either tyranny or despotism with monarchy—rule by *one* man, whether just or unjust—seems to be counterbalanced by Aristotle's discussion of the tyranny of the *few* and of the *many*. In a monarchy, the king can turn tyrant; but so can the wealthy become despotic in an oligarchy, or the poor in a lawless democracy.

The nature of tyranny thus seems to be more difficult to define precisely than would at first appear from the almost universal condemnation of it as the worst perversion of government.

To some extent, the difficulties may be verbal. The word "tyranny" is used with many meanings, not only by the Greeks, but throughout the tradition of the great books. Some writers identify tyranny and despotism; some distinguish the two sharply. Some writers consider tyranny and despotism only in connection with monarchy; some extend the consideration to other forms of government. The words are sometimes used descriptively, without the connotation of good or evil; and sometimes they are more derogatory than descriptive.

Even when the necessary verbal clarifications are achieved, genuine issues still remain. Conflicting accounts are given of the causes of tyranny or the circumstances from which it develops. Concerning despotism, some writers take the position that it may be justified by conquest, or by the need of a people for absolute government, or, in the form of a temporary dictatorship, by emergency conditions. Not even the condemnation of tyranny seems to be unanimous, if the views of Hobbes are to be reckoned with; nor, among those who condemn tyranny, is the fairly general approval of tyrannicide free from the strong dissenting voice of Kant.

THE FOREGOING INDICATES how the notions of tyranny and despotism are involved in other chapters dealing with the various forms of government and, in addition, such chapters as JUSTICE, LIBERTY, and SLAVERY. The distinction, for example, between domestic and political slavery bears on one of the ways in which despotism and tyranny are distinguished; and the discussion in the chapters on MONARCHY and CONSTITUTION concerning absolute and limited government raises a question which must also be considered here, namely, whether absolute monarchy can be distinguished from despotism and whether it has an inveterate tendency to become tyrannical.

That question deserves immediate attention, because its answers are connected with opposed views of the justice or defensibility of tyranny and despotism. Plato and Aristotle, for example, treat tyranny as the prototype of political injustice, and the tyrant as the extreme case of the vicious man; yet there are passages which appear to have a contrary tenor. In the *Laws*, the Athenian Stranger proposes a good tyrant as the best means for establishing the laws. To the question, "What are the conditions which you require in a state before you can organize it?" he thinks the legislator's answer should be: "Give me a state which is governed by a tyrant, and let the tyrant be young and have a good memory; let him be quick at learning and of a courageous and noble nature"—in short, let him have temperance and every other virtue.

More readily than monarchy, democracy, or oligarchy, tyranny is the stepping stone to the best state, according to the Athenian Stranger, because it involves the greatest power concentrated in a single man. The combination of virtue and power may rarely be found, but, he says, "when the supreme power in man coincides with the greatest wisdom and temperance, then the best laws and the best constitution come into being, and in no other way."

Aristotle's classification of the types of kingship, or the forms of royal government, seems to include tyranny among them. He refers to the kind of monarchy which prevails among the barbarians who, "being more servile in character than Hellenes . . . do not rebel against a despotic government. Such royalties," he goes on, "have the nature of tyrannies because the people are by nature slaves, but there is no danger of their being overthrown, for they are hereditary and legal." Even among the Hellenes in ancient times, Aristotle points out, there was a form of monarchy or "dictatorship" that may be defined "as an elective tyranny, which like the barbarian monarchy, is legal, but differs from it in not being hereditary."

These two forms of tyranny, Aristotle says elsewhere, "are both according to law, and therefore easily pass into royalty." The line between king and tyrant is not, however, as shadowy as might first appear. "Kings rule according to law over voluntary subjects, but tyrants over involuntary; and the one are guarded by their fellow citizens, the others are guarded against them." The forms of monarchy which Aristotle also calls "tyrannies" seem to him to have a mixed character. "They are royal," he says, "in so far as the monarch rules according to law over willing subjects; but they are tyrannical in so far as he is despotic and rules according to his own fancy." But there is also a kind of tyranny which, being unmixed, is "the counterpart of perfect monarchy. This tyranny is just that arbitrary power of an individual which is responsible to no one, and governs all alike, whether equals or better, with a view to its own advantage, not to that of its subjects, and therefore against their will."

Aristotle explains his association of tyranny with monarchy on the ground that "both are forms of one-man rule, but," he adds, "there is the greatest difference between them; the tyrant looks to his own advantage, the king to that of his subjects." Tyrannical government is "monarchy exercising the rule of a master over political society," and therefore deserves to be called "despotic" as well as tyrannical. When it has no admixture of royalty, tyranny is not only self-serving but lawless rule. It is "the very reverse of a constitution," or rule by law. Except for the hypothetical case in which the truly superior, the almost god-like man is king, Aristotle seems to identify absolute or unconstitutional monarchy with tyranny and despotism, and he condemns both for violating the very nature of the state conceived as "a community of free men."

THE LINE BETWEEN KING and tyrant is similarly drawn by Plato. Monarchy for him "divides into royalty and tyranny" according as one man rules by law or lawlessly, over voluntary or involuntary subjects. If the one man were like a god in relation to other men, it would be fitting for him to rule the state by his wisdom or science and without recourse to laws. "If there could be such a despot," the Eleatic Stranger says in the *Statesman*, "he alone would be the happy ruler of a true and perfect state," but men "can never be made to believe that any one can be worthy of such authority." (History suggests the contrary in such cases as Caesar, Napoleon, and Hitler.)

Giving the name of "king" to the monarch who abides by and maintains established laws, the Stranger gets Socrates to agree that the ruler should be called a "tyrant" when he "governs neither by law nor by custom, but, imitating the true man of science, pretends that he can only act for the best by violating the laws, while in reality appetite and ignorance are the motives of the imitation."

In the *Republic*, Socrates refers to Euripides' praise of "tyranny as god-like," and gives, as another reason for excluding the poets from the state, the fact that "they are the eulogists of tyranny." Far from being god-like, the tyrannical man is described by Socrates as "drunken, lustful, passionate." Tyrants "are always either the masters or servants and never the friends of anybody; the tyrant never tastes of true freedom or friendship." Oriental despotism, Hegel later writes, appears to give freedom to one man, but "the freedom of that one is only caprice, ferocity—brutal recklessness of passion. ... That *one* is therefore only a despot; not a *free man*."

According to Plato, tyranny is not only the greatest evil a state can suffer, but the tyrant is also the unhappiest of men. "Will not he who has been shown to be the wickedest," Socrates asks, "be also the most miserable?" Polus, in the *Gorgias*, tries to prove that, like the successful criminal who goes unpunished, the tyrant who does injustice to everybody, but suffers none, achieves more happiness than other men. But Socrates, taking the position that it is better to suffer than to do injustice, argues to the contrary that the tyrant is more miserable than those whom he oppresses.

If this is true, the confirmed tyrant is probably the man least able to perceive or acknowledge it. Plutarch reports the story of Plato's first meeting with Dionysius, the tyrant of Syracuse. When Plato tried to prove to him that "tyrants, of all men, had the least pretence to virtue," and that, since they lacked justice, they suffered "the miserable condition of the unjust," Dionysius would not hear the argument out. "He asked the philosopher in a rage," Plutarch relates, "what business he had in Sicily. To which Plato answered, 'I come to seek a virtuous man.' 'It seems, then,' replied Dionysius, 'you have lost your labor.'" According to Plutarch, Dionysius tried to have Plato killed on his return voyage to Greece; or failing that, to have him sold into slavery. He would not be harmed by that, Dionysius reasoned, because, "being the same just man as before, he would enjoy his happiness, though he lost his liberty."

On the whole, then, Aristotle's and Plato's disapproval of tyrants and tyranny seems to be unequivocal. The passages which might cause this to be questioned can perhaps be accounted for by the ancient tendency to use the word "tyrant" descriptively to denote the possessor of absolute power. Yet even in the *Laws*, where such usage occurs, Plato observes that kings, unable "to sustain the temptation of arbitrary power," tend to overthrow the laws and so become tyrannical in the invidious sense of the word.

With the exception of Hobbes, mediaeval and modern writers are no less disapproving than the ancients. "Tyrannical government," according to Aquinas, "is altogether corrupt" and completely lawless. It is the tyrant himself, rather than those who may rebel against a government so lacking in justice, who is "guilty of sedition, since he encourages discord and sedition among his subjects, that he may lord over them more securely." When a king, by becoming a tyrant, "has dethroned himself and put himself in a state of war with his people, what shall hinder them" asks Locke, "from prosecuting him who is no king, as they would any other man who has put himself in a state of war with them?"

In Locke's view, it is a mistake to think that the fault of tyranny "is proper only to monarchies. For wherever the power that is put in any hands for the government of the people and the preservation of their properties is applied to other ends, and made use of to impoverish, harass, or subdue them to the arbitrary irregular commands of those that have it, there it presently becomes tyranny, whether those that thus use it are one or many. . . . Wherever law ends, tyranny begins, if the law be transgressed to another's harm."

Tyranny is thus defined by Locke as "the exercise of power beyond right, which nobody can have a right to." Such "absolute arbitrary power, or governing without settled standing laws, can neither of them consist with the ends of society and government." Tyranny so defined may not be limited to monarchies; but, according to Locke, absolute monarchy is always tyrannical. For that very reason it is, he writes, "inconsistent with civil society, and so can be no form of civil government at all."

What Locke calls "tyranny" or, without change of meaning, "absolute monarchy," Kant calls "autocracy." But Kant distinguishes the monarch "who has the *highest* power" from the autocrat "who has *all* power." Hegel calls "despotism" that "state of affairs where law has disappeared and where the particular will as such, whether of a monarch or a mob, counts as law or rather takes the place of law." The writers of the *Federalist* use the words "tyranny" and "despotism" interchangeably, but do not vary from the definition which Montesquieu gives of despotic government as "that in which a single person directs everything by his own will and caprice." In all other governments, even in monarchy when it is constitutional, the separation of powers puts some limitation on the power entrusted to the offices of state.

Following Montesquieu's doctrine, Madison declares: "The accumulation of all powers, legislative, executive, and judiciary, in the same hands, whether of one, a few, or many, and whether hereditary, self-appointed, or elective, may justly be pronounced the very definition of tyranny." He reinforces his point by quoting Jefferson's dictum that concentrating "all the powers of government . . . in the same hands, is precisely the definition of despotic government."

Hobbes seems to be the one exception in the great books to this variously expressed opinion of the evil of absolute power. Locke may have him in mind when he says that absolute monarchy is "by some men . . . counted the only government in the world." Certainly Hobbes would not repudiate the charge that he thinks none but absolute government feasible; nor is he dismayed by the tendency of other writers to call absolute government "tyrannical" or "despotic." On the contrary, he dismisses this as so much empty name-calling.

In every form of government, according to Hobbes, the sovereign power must be absolute to be effective. "Though of so unlimited a power, men may fancy many evil consequences, yet the consequences of the want of it, which is perpetual war of every man against his neighbor, are much worse." Describing the absolute dominion of the father over his children, and the equally absolute dominion of the master over his slaves, Hobbes says that "the rights and consequences of both paternal and despotical dominion are the very same with those of a sovereign by institution," for unless the sovereign is also absolute, "there is no sovereignty at all."

To the cry "Tyranny," Hobbes replies that just as men who "find themselves grieved under a *Democracy*, call it *Anarchy*," or those who "are displeased with *Aristocracy*, call it *Oligarchy*," so "they that are discontented under *Monarchy*, call it *Tyranny*." He holds Aristotle's *Politics* responsible for spreading the fallacy of regarding anything except popular government as tyrannical; and in general he blames the Greek and Roman writers for fomenting sedition against kings by treating tyrannicide as lawful.

Hobbes offers an historical explanation of the origin of these confusions. "A *Tyrant*," he writes, "originally signified no more simply, but a *Monarch*. But when afterwards in most parts of Greece that kind of government was abolished, the name began to signify, not only the thing it did before, but with it the hatred which the popular states bore towards it; as also the name of King became odious after the deposing of the Kings of Rome."

A word like "tyranny" carries only emotional force. Used descriptively, Hobbes declares, "it signifies nothing more nor less than the name of Sovereignty, saving that they that use the former word are understood to be angry with them they call Tyrants." He is willing to make himself the object of that anger by identifying "a professed hatred of Tyranny" with "hatred to Commonwealth in general," and by regarding the toleration of both hatreds alike as evil seeds of sedition.

IN ONE NEGATIVE RESPECT, Rousseau seems to agree with Hobbes. Not that the man who holds that only republican institutions are legitimate, in any way accepts the identification of either prince or popular government with sovereign power. But he, like Hobbes, rejects Aristotle's distinction between the king and the tyrant as good and bad monarchs, the one governing for the good of his subjects, the other in his own interest. Rousseau contends not only that most Greek authors used "the word *tyrant* in a different sense . . . but also," he adds, "it would follow from Aristotle's distinction that, from the very beginning of the world, there has not yet been a single king."

It is only according to a vulgar usage that a tyrant is conceived as "a king who governs violently and without regard for justice or law." The more precise conception, Rousseau insists, defines the tyrant as "an individual who arrogates to himself the royal authority without having a right to it. This is how the Greeks understood the word 'tyrant'; they applied it indifferently to good and bad princes whose authority was not legitimate. *Tyrant* and *usurper* are thus perfectly synonymous terms."

The usurpation of power is, according to Rousseau, the root of both tyranny and despotism, but they are not for that reason to be confused. "I call him who usurps the royal authority a tyrant," Rousseau writes, "and him who usurps the sovereign power a *despot*. The tyrant is he who thrusts himself in contrary to the laws to govern in accordance with the laws; the despot is he who sets himself above the laws themselves. Thus the tyrant cannot be a despot, but the despot is always a tyrant."

Other writers distinguish between tyranny and despotism on different principles. They accept, where Rousseau rejects, the notion that tyranny is not merely a usurpation of power, but always a self-serving or unjust use of that power. They reject Rousseau's conception of despotism as inseparable from usurpation. Absolute power can be gained and held in other ways.

Locke, for example, conceives despotical dominion as the rule of a master over slaves, or the government of a vanquished people by their conquerors in a just war. "Despotical power," in his opinion, "is an absolute arbitrary power one man has over another to take away his life whenever he pleases." Unlike tyranny, it is not "power beyond right," for "the conqueror, if he have a just cause, has a despotical right over the persons of all that actually aided and concurred in the war against him." Since, in Locke's view, "a usurper can never have right on his side," despotic dominion, when justified, is not achieved by usurpation.

For Montesquieu, despotisms constitute one of the three major forms of government, the other two being republics (aristocratic or democratic) and monarchies. Though he regards despotism as an intrinsically corrupt form of government, in which the rulers wield personal power without the restraint of law, he also judges it to be appropriate to the servile natures or temperaments of certain peoples. Like Aristotle and Hippocrates before him, he attributes to the climate and disposition of the Asiatic peoples their submissiveness to the worst excesses of despotism.

Montesquieu does not so much condemn despotism as he deplores the conditions which seem to render it necessary or natural for a large part of mankind. He does not suggest, as Mill does, that despotic government can and should serve to civilize those who are as yet unprepared for self-government. Despotism is benevolent, according to Mill, only if it prepares a people for freedom; if it tries to perpetuate itself, it is tyrannical or enslaving.

Though Mill holds the view that, relative to a free society, there cannot be a "good despot" no matter how benevolent his intentions, he also thinks that, in dealing with barbarians, "despotism is a legitimate mode of government . . . provided the end be their improvement, and the means justified by actually effecting that end. Liberty, as a principle, has no application to any state of things anterior to the time when mankind has become capable of being improved by free and equal discussion. Until then, there is nothing for them but implicit obedience to an Akbar or a Charlemagne, if they are so fortunate as to find one."

Under certain "conditions of society . . . a vigorous despotism," according to Mill, "is in itself the best mode of government for training the people in what is specifically wanting to render them capable of a higher civilization." In his opinion, still other conditions justify despotism. "I am far from condemning," he writes, "in cases of extreme exigency, the assumption of absolute power in the form of a temporary dictatorship." In another place, he says that "the establishment of the despotism of the Caesars was a great benefit to the entire generation in which it took place" because "it put a stop to civil war, and abated a vast amount of malversation and tyranny by praetors and proconsuls."

But in all these cases the essential point is that the despotic rule should be temporary. Mill applies the same criterion to the despotism which occurs in the government of colonial dependencies. It should aim to benefit a subject people by training them in the arts of government, and it should not seek to outlast the conferring of this benefit. "The ruling country," he thinks, "ought to be able to do for its subjects all that could be done by a succession of absolute monarchs, guaranteed by irresistible force against the precariousness of tenure of barbarian despotisms. . . . Such is the ideal rule of a free people over a barbarous or semi-barbarous one."

This may be the ideal, but critics of imperialism, like Swift or Marx, think that colonial policies are in fact otherwise motivated—by land-grabbing, by the desire for national aggrandizement, and by the profits to be made from the economic exploitation of colonies or subject peoples. Throughout the pages of Thucydides and Tacitus, the spokesmen for empire dwell upon the blessings which Athenian or Roman rule bestows, only to be answered by the protests of the colonists or the conquered, who seem to prefer the insecurities and uncertainties of liberty to the mixed motives of even the best despot.

As ALREADY INDICATED, the political significance of tyranny and despotism is broader than the conception of the tyrant as an unjust king or of the despot as an absolute monarch. The reign of the Thirty Tyrants at Athens and of the Decemviri at Rome are classical examples of oligarchical tyranny. Advocates of republican or democratic institutions, like the writers of the *Federalist* or J. S. Mill, are as much concerned to safeguard constitutional or representative government from the tyranny of special interests—whether of a dominant majority or of concentrated wealth—as they are to protect the rule of law from the encroachments of despotism which begin with usurpations of power by elected officials.

Moderns and ancients alike fear the susceptibility of the mob to the wiles of the demagogue, who encourages their lawlessness in order to take the law into his own hands. Both Hegel and Plato see in the alliance between a scheming demagogue and an unruly populace the step by which a corrupt democracy turns into a tyranny. Though Aristotle disagrees with what he takes to be the theory of Socrates in the *Republic*, that tyranny normally arises from democracy in the progressive degeneration of the state, his own opinion seems to be that "tyranny is a compound of oligarchy and democracy in their most extreme forms" and that "almost all tyrants have been demagogues who gained the favor of the people by their accusation of the notables."

These aspects of tyranny are discussed in the chapters on DEMOCRACY and OLIGARCHY. The traditional emphasis, however, is on the individual tyrant, whether he is an hereditary prince who misuses his autocratic power, the usurper of an established throne, or the demagogue who makes himself dictator. However tyranny arises, monarchy is the form it usually takes in the pages of history or poetry—the domination of the state by one man. But while the great political philosophers offer conflicting theories of the origin of tyranny, there seems to be remarkable agreement concerning the methods the tyrant uses to maintain himself in power.

Other political practices may vary greatly from one historical epoch to another, but the devices of tyranny seem to have a certain timelessness. When they are describing the actions of the tyrant, Herodotus, Plutarch, Tacitus, and Gibbon tell stories of iniquity, of cruelty, of cowardly and unscrupulous stratagems, so alike in detail that the reader loses all sense of time and place. Nor need he exert any effort of imagination to place the figure of the tyrant thus delineated in the setting of contemporary events.

The past also speaks with contemporary relevance in Plato's enumeration of the tyrant's desperate measures, his stirring up of foreign wars to smother domestic discord, his assassination of enemies, his purging of friends or followers, and his confiscation of property as well as his generally indiscriminate blood-letting. The resort to unwarranted searches and seizures, the creation of *ex post facto* crimes, the arrest and punishment of men without trial "have been," writes Hamilton, "in all ages the favorite and most formidable instruments of tyranny." So, too, in all ages, the tyrant, fearing reprisal and revenge, lives in a state of war, turns his palace into an armed camp, and goes nowhere without a numerous bodyguard which, as both Aristotle and Machiavelli suggest, functions most efficiently when composed of hirelings or mercenaries.

The great books contain not only the record of tyrannical perfidy and violence, but also recommendations to the would-be tyrant of the best means to use for his nefarious purposes. Though Rousseau refers to Machiavelli's *Prince* as "the book of Republicans," and thinks that "the choice of his detestable hero, Caesar Borgia, clearly enough shows his hidden aim," the rules which Machiavelli formulates for the prince seem, on the surface at least, to be essentially similar to the advice Aristotle gives the tyrant.

The end in both cases is the same—success in the effort to gain and keep power. The means, in general, are force and fraud or, as Machiavelli phrases it, the methods of the lion and the fox. Machiavelli counsels the prince "to inspire fear in such a way that, if he does not win love, he avoids hatred." He tells him that he should appear to keep faith without hesitating to break his promises, that he should avoid flatterers and sycophants, and that he should acquire a reputation for liberality without cost to himself. Not very different is Aristotle's advice to the tyrant—to lop off the heads of those who are too high and to humble all the rest, to sow discord among his subjects, to impoverish the people by multiplying taxes, to employ informers, and to encourage the betrayal of one faction by another.

But in his suggestion of another course for the tyrant to take—the policy of not merely pretending, but of actually trying, to conduct himself like a just king—Aristotle seems to deviate from the spirit of Machiavelli's maxim that the appearance of virtue is profitable so long as it does not interfere with doing whatever is expedient, however vicious. Yet even here Aristotle says that "the tyrant must be careful ... to keep power enough to rule over his subjects, whether they like him or not, for if he once gives this up he gives up his tyranny."

The best commentary on these recommendations seems to be indirectly expressed by their authors. Both Aristotle and Machiavelli draw one striking conclusion from the history of those—call them princes or tyrants—who have tried to put such rules into practice. Whether its collapse is due to the inherent weakness of might without right, as Aristotle suggests, or, in Machiavelli's terms, to the unforeseeable mishaps of fortune, tyranny, of all forms of government, seems to be the shortest-lived.

OUTLINE OF TOPICS

1. The nature and origin of tyranny

   1*a*. The lawlessness of tyrannical rule: might without right

   1*b*. The injustice of tyrannical government: rule for self-interest

   1*c*. Usurpation: the unauthorized seizure of power

   1*d*. The character of the tyrannical man: the friends of the tyrant

2. Tyranny as the corruption of other forms of government

   2*a*. The perversion of monarchy: the tyrannical king

   2*b*. The degeneration of oligarchy: the tyranny of the wealthy

   2*c*. The corruption of democracy: the tyranny of the masses or of the majority; the rise of the demagogue

3. The choice between tyranny or despotism and anarchy

4. The nature and effects of despotism

   4*a*. The relation of despotism to tyranny and monarchy: the benevolence of despots

   4*b*. The comparison of paternal and despotic dominion: the justification of absolute rule by the incapacity of the ruled for self-government

5. The contrast between despotic and constitutional government: government by men and government by laws

   5*a*. Despotic and constitutional government with respect to political liberty and equality: the rights of the governed

   5*b*. Despotic and constitutional government with respect to juridical defenses against misgovernment, or redress for grievances through due process of law

   5*c*. The location of sovereignty in despotic and constitutional government: the sovereign person, the sovereign office, the sovereign people

   5*d*. The analogues of despotic and constitutional rule in the relation of the powers of the soul: the tyranny of the passions

6. Imperial rule as despotic, and as tyrannical or benevolent: the government of conquered peoples or colonies

7. The ways of tyrants or despots to attain and maintain power

8. The fate of tyrants: revolutions for liberty and justice against tyranny and despotism; tyrannicide

REFERENCES

References are listed by volume number (in bold type), author's name, and page number. Bible references are to book, chapter, and verse of the Authorized King James version of the Bible. The abbreviation "esp" calls the reader's attention to one or more especially relevant parts of a whole reference; "passim" signifies that the topic is discussed intermittently rather than continuously in the work or passage cited. Where the work as a whole is relevant to the topic, the page numbers refer to the entire work. For general guidance in the use of *The Great Ideas,* consult the Preface.

1. The nature and origin of tyranny

5 SOPHOCLES, 107
5 EURIPIDES, 262
6 HERODOTUS, 12–14, 178–180
6 THUCYDIDES, 352
7 PLATO, 301–309, 411–420
9 ARISTOTLE, 412–413
14 PLUTARCH, 196–197
15 TACITUS, 72
23 HOBBES, 273
32 MILTON, 319–321
33 PASCAL, 232
35 LOCKE, 65–81 passim
38 MONTESQUIEU, 70
38 ROUSSEAU, 356–358, 388
40 GIBBON, 32–34
42 KANT, 450
43 DECLARATION OF INDEPENDENCE, 1–3

1*a*. The lawlessness of tyrannical rule: might without right

5 EURIPIDES, 262
5 ARISTOPHANES, 512–513
6 THUCYDIDES, 504–508
7 PLATO, 411–416
9 ARISTOTLE, 478–479
14 PLUTARCH, 344–354, 382–387, 591
20 AQUINAS, 213–214, 233
35 LOCKE, 44–46, 56–57, 71–73, 75–76, 78–79
38 ROUSSEAU, 361–362, 388–389, 419
43 DECLARATION OF INDEPENDENCE, 1–3
51 TOLSTOY, 8–10

1*b*. The injustice of tyrannical government: rule for self-interest

OLD TESTAMENT: *I Kings,* 12:1–15 / *Isaiah,* 1:23; 3:14–15; 10:1–3; 14 / *Ezekiel,* 45:8–9 / *Micah,* 3:1–3
5 SOPHOCLES, 104–105, 131–142
6 THUCYDIDES, 353
7 PLATO, 262–270, 304, 413–416
9 ARISTOTLE, 486, 528–529
14 PLUTARCH, 742–743
15 TACITUS, 90–91
20 AQUINAS, 584
21 DANTE, 17
27 SHAKESPEARE, 186, 303–304
35 LOCKE, 28, 58, 63
38 ROUSSEAU, 368, 419
40 GIBBON, 35–39 passim, 55, 59–61 passim
41 GIBBON, 39
43 FEDERALIST, 251–252
43 MILL, 366–370

1*c*. Usurpation: the unauthorized seizure of power

OLD TESTAMENT: *II Samuel,* 15–18 / *I Kings,* 16:8–20 / *II Kings,* 12:19–21; 14:17–21; 15:13–14,23–25,30; 21:18–26
5 AESCHYLUS, 44, 69
6 HERODOTUS, 102–106, 243
7 PLATO, 263–265
9 ARISTOTLE, 513
14 PLUTARCH, 369–374, 382–387, 469–470, 499–538, 577–604
15 TACITUS, 1–2, 32–33, 195–201
26 SHAKESPEARE, 87–88, 105–148
35 LOCKE, 66, 70–71, 74–75 passim
38 MONTESQUIEU, 78–79
38 ROUSSEAU, 424, 432–433
40 GIBBON, 24–28, 43–44, 69–71, 111–113, 386–387, 436–438, 489–491, 515–518 passim
43 FEDERALIST, 78–79, 94, 104–105, 108–109, 133, 230–232
51 TOLSTOY, 647–649, 381

1*d*. The character of the tyrannical man: the friends of the tyrant

OLD TESTAMENT: *I Kings,* 21 / *Proverbs,* 28:15–16
5 SOPHOCLES, 107
6 HERODOTUS, 107
7 PLATO, 285–287, 311–312, 416–427
9 ARISTOTLE, 413, 462, 516
12 EPICTETUS, 125–126, 215
14 PLUTARCH, 201–202, 362–365, 387–388, 409–410, 726–747, 780–781, 782–788, 835–836, 846–858
15 TACITUS, 63–64, 65–67, 145, 153–154, 172–173, 195, 224, 238–240
22 CHAUCER, 366–371
23 MACHIAVELLI, 13, 22–30, 33–34
25 MONTAIGNE, 3–5, 126–131 passim, 337, 351–353
26 SHAKESPEARE, 105–148, 570–571, 580–581
27 SHAKESPEARE, 184–186, 304, 501–504

40 GIBBON, 34–39, 53–56, 59–61, 70–71, 167, 388–389
41 GIBBON, 113–114, 166–167, 173–174, 189–193
48 MELVILLE, 107
51 TOLSTOY, 465–467

2. Tyranny as the corruption of other forms of government

2*a*. The perversion of monarchy: the tyrannical king

5 SOPHOCLES, 136–137
5 EURIPIDES, 366–367
6 HERODOTUS, 107–108
7 PLATO, 590, 598–604, 672–674
9 ARISTOTLE, 412, 483, 486, 495, 512–513, 514–515, 517–518
14 PLUTARCH, 30
20 AQUINAS, 307–309
23 HOBBES, 273
26 SHAKESPEARE, 146
27 SHAKESPEARE, 303–304
30 BACON, 27
35 LOCKE, 44–46, 49–51 passim, 62–64 passim, 71–73
38 MONTESQUIEU, 53
38 ROUSSEAU, 412–413, 414
40 GIBBON, 255–257
43 MILL, 366
44 BOSWELL, 195
46 HEGEL, 173

2*b*. The degeneration of oligarchy: the tyranny of the wealthy

7 PLATO, 681–682
9 ARISTOTLE, 492–493, 496, 510, 511–512
14 PLUTARCH, 180
27 SHAKESPEARE, 351–354
35 LOCKE, 71
38 MONTESQUIEU, 23–25 passim
38 ROUSSEAU, 359
42 KANT, 450
43 FEDERALIST, 176–179 passim
43 MILL, 393–394
50 MARX-ENGELS, 420

2*c*. The corruption of democracy: the tyranny of the masses or of the majority; the rise of the demagogue

5 ARISTOPHANES, 470–487, 515–516, 591
6 THUCYDIDES, 516–517, 524–525, 533
7 PLATO, 411–413, 416–417
9 ARISTOTLE, 470, 478–479, 491, 506–507, 512, 514–515
14 PLUTARCH, 648–649
18 AUGUSTINE, 162
27 SHAKESPEARE, 361–362, 370–371, 383–384
38 MONTESQUIEU, 10, 51–52
38 ROUSSEAU, 411
41 GIBBON, 73
43 FEDERALIST, 45–47 passim, 49–53 passim, 141–142, 156–159 passim, 164–165, 192–193
43 MILL, 268–274, 298–299, 366–389 passim
46 HEGEL, 148, 273–274, 365–366

3. The choice between tyranny or despotism and anarchy

6 HERODOTUS, 23–24
14 PLUTARCH, 68–70, 525–526, 588–591
15 TACITUS, 51–52
23 HOBBES, 104, 112
35 LOCKE, 44–46, 56–57, 76–78
38 ROUSSEAU, 356, 389, 433–434
43 FEDERALIST, 45–47 passim, 66–78 passim
43 MILL, 344, 350–355 passim

4. The nature and effects of despotism

7 PLATO, 590, 598–604
9 ARISTOTLE, 447–448, 482–484
35 LOCKE, 28–30, 43
38 MONTESQUIEU, 4, 8–9, 12–13, 15, 26–30, 33–35, 39–40, 54, 57–58, 68, 137–140
38 ROUSSEAU, 387–391
40 GIBBON, 50, 91, 154
41 GIBBON, 320–321
43 MILL, 297, 341–344
46 HEGEL, 161, 213–214, 230, 302

4*a*. The relation of despotism to tyranny and monarchy: the benevolence of despots

6 THUCYDIDES, 523–524
7 PLATO, 598–604, 672–674
9 ARISTOTLE, 413, 486, 495, 513, 559
14 PLUTARCH, 9, 75–76, 80–82, 540–576 passim
24 RABELAIS, 131–133
35 LOCKE, 44–46, 49
36 SWIFT, 74–76
38 MONTESQUIEU, 32–35, 36, 37–38, 56–57, 60–61, 75, 97
38 ROUSSEAU, 357
40 GIBBON, 24, 40–41, 338–344 passim, 389–390
41 GIBBON, 39–40
43 MILL, 341–344, 348–349, 351–354 passim
46 HEGEL, 96–97

4*b*. The comparison of paternal and despotic dominion: the justification of absolute rule by the incapacity of the ruled for self-government

5 EURIPIDES, 261–262
6 HERODOTUS, 120
7 PLATO, 670–671, 679–680
9 ARISTOTLE, 413, 453–455, 528–529
15 TACITUS, 193–194
18 AUGUSTINE, 161–162, 524–525
23 HOBBES, 104, 109–112
35 LOCKE, 36–42 passim, 48–50, 64–65
37 FIELDING, 359–362
38 MONTESQUIEU, 22–23, 110–11, 116–120, 122–123
38 ROUSSEAU, 324, 357, 367–368 passim, 402–403

5. The contrast between despotic and constitutional government: government by men and government by laws

5*a*. Despotic and constitutional government with respect to political liberty and equality: the rights of the governed

5*b*. Despotic and constitutional government with respect to juridical defenses against misgovernment, or redress for grievances through due process of law

5*c*. The location of sovereignty in despotic and constitutional government: the sovereign person, the sovereign office, the sovereign people

5*d*. The analogues of despotic and constitutional rule in the relation of the powers of the soul: the tyranny of the passions

6. Imperial rule as despotic, and as tyrannical or benevolent: the government of conquered peoples or colonies

40 Gibbon, 14–15, 23, 147, 420, 550–551, 608–609
41 Gibbon, 51–53 passim, 216–217, 307, 505
42 Kant, 413, 454–455
43 Declaration of Independence, 1–3
44 Boswell, 179
46 Hegel, 298–299, 301–302
50 Marx, 372–374

7. The ways of tyrants or despots to attain and maintain power

Old Testament: *Daniel*, 3:1–12
Apocrypha: *I Maccabees*, 1:41–64; 10:22–46
5 Aeschylus, 42
5 Aristophanes, 515–516
6 Herodotus, 23–24, 25–29, 102–106, 114–115, 172–174, 187, 243
6 Thucydides, 380–382, 425–426
7 Plato, 411–415, 803, 811–813
9 Aristotle, 512–513, 516–518
14 Plutarch, 27–28, 77–86 passim, 117–121, 176–184, 344–354, 382–387, 482–484, 521, 648–656, 671–681, 809–811
15 Tacitus, 2–4, 21–22, 29–30, 40, 68–69, 82, 155–156, 168, 198–199, 208, 209–210
23 Machiavelli, 1–37
25 Montaigne, 51–55
26 Shakespeare, 105–148, 376–405
35 Locke, 45–46
36 Swift, 37, 102–103
38 Montesquieu, 68, 95–96, 140, 212
38 Rousseau, 361–362, 380, 412–413
40 Gibbon, 24–30, 42–43, 50–51, 53–59, 153–155, 171, 525–526
43 Federalist, 66–67, 100–101
43 Mill, 366

8. The fate of tyrants: revolutions for liberty and justice against tyranny and despotism; tyrannicide

Old Testament: *Judges*, 3:14–4:24; 6–7; 9:1–11:33 / *I Kings*, 12:1–25 / *II Kings*, 9:1–10:11; 11; 21:18–26 / *II Chronicles*, 10; 23 / *Jeremiah*, 41
Apocrypha: *I Maccabees*, 1–9 passim / *II Maccabees*, 1–13
6 Herodotus, 84, 85, 160–185 passim
6 Thucydides, 387–389, 523–524, 579–590
7 Plato, 285–286, 438
9 Aristotle, 506, 513–515, 518, 558–561
13 Virgil, 272
14 Plutarch, 77–86 passim, 195–213 passim, 232–246 passim, 598–604, 620–656 passim, 671–689, 781–824, 826–846 passim
15 Tacitus, 9–15, 17, 18–20, 76–77, 82–83, 112–114, 169–176, 234–265, 269–277, 283–292, 298–302
23 Machiavelli, 8
23 Hobbes, 150–151
26 Shakespeare, 105–148, 573, 574, 575–576, 583–584
27 Shakespeare, 305–306
35 Locke, 63–64, 66, 71–72, 73–81
38 Montesquieu, 25–26
40 Gibbon, 29, 37–38, 39–40, 44, 56, 71–76, 144, 420, 521
41 Gibbon, 51–54, 114–116, 166–167, 574–577, 587–588
42 Kant, 441
43 Declaration of Independence, 1, 3
43 Federalist, 68, 97–98
46 Hegel, 295–296, 345, 363–367

CROSS-REFERENCES

For: Other discussions bearing on the nature and injustice of tyranny, *see* Government 1d–1f; Justice 9c; Law 7d; Slavery 6a.

The relation of tyranny to other forms of government, *see* Aristocracy 2e; Democracy 2a; Monarchy 4b; Oligarchy 3a.

For: The distinction between tyranny and despotism in terms of the distinction between slavery and subjection, *see* Slavery 6a–6b; and for the relation of despotism to absolute monarchy, *see* Monarchy 4a–4b, 4e(1).

Other statements of the justification of benevolent despotism or of absolute monarchy relative to certain conditions, *see* Democracy 4d; Government 2c; Monarchy 4e(2); Slavery 6c; and for comparisons of domestic and political government which are relevant to this justification of despotism, *see* Family 2a; Monarchy 4a, 4e(1); State 1b.

The distinction between despotism and constitutional government in terms of the distinction between subjection and citizenship, *see* Citizen 2b; Justice 9d; Law 7b; Liberty 1d; Slavery 6b.

The distinction between government by men and government by law, *see* Constitution 1; Law 7a; Monarchy 1a(1); and for the political significance of this distinction, *see* Con-

STITUTION 7b; DEMOCRACY 4b; GOVERNMENT 1g(1)–1g(3); LAW 7b; LIBERTY 1d; MONARCHY 4e(3).

The analogies of despotic and constitutional rule in the relations of reason and the passions, *see* LIBERTY 3a–3b; SLAVERY 7.

The analogies in the economic order of political tyranny and despotism, *see* JUSTICE 8c–8c(1); LABOR 5a–5d, 7f; SLAVERY 4a–4c.

Other discussions of imperialism, *see* DEMOCRACY 7b; GOVERNMENT 5b; MONARCHY 5–5b; REVOLUTION 7; SLAVERY 6d; STATE 10b; WAR AND PEACE 6a.

The struggle for power and for liberty as between tyrants or despots and the people they oppress, *see* LABOR 7c–7c(3); LIBERTY 6b–6c; OLIGARCHY 5c; PROGRESS 3b; REVOLUTION 3a–3b, 3c(3), 4a, 5b; SLAVERY 3c.

ADDITIONAL READINGS

Listed below are works not included in *Great Books of the Western World*, but relevant to the idea and topics with which this chapter deals. These works are divided into two groups:

I. Works by authors represented in this collection.
II. Works by authors not represented in this collection.

For the date, place, and other facts concerning the publication of the works cited, consult the Bibliography of Additional Readings which follows the last chapter of *The Great Ideas.*

I.

MACHIAVELLI. *The Discourses*
——. *Castruccio Castracani*
MILTON. *The Readie and Easie Way to Establish a Free Commonwealth*
DOSTOEVSKY. *The Possessed*

II.

MARSILIUS OF PADUA. *Defensor Pacis*
LUTHER. *Whether Soldiers, Too, Can Be Saved*
LA BOÉTIE. *Anti-Dictator, the Discours de la servitude volontaire*
MARLOWE. *Tamburlaine the Great*
BEN JONSON. *Sejanus*
RACINE. *Britannicus*
VOLTAIRE. "Tyranny," "Tyrant," in *A Philosophical Dictionary*
GODWIN. *An Enquiry Concerning Political Justice*, BK IV, CH 3
SCHILLER. *William Tell*
SHELLEY. *Prometheus Unbound*
PUSHKIN. *Boris Godunov*
DICKENS. *A Tale of Two Cities*
MAZZINI. *From the Council to God*
IBSEN. *An Enemy of the People*
BRYCE. *Address on Colonial Policy*
T. HARDY. *The Dynasts*
LENIN. *Imperialism, the Highest Stage of Capitalism*
KELSEN. *Sozialismus und Staat*
TROTSKY. *The Defense of Terrorism*
URE. *The Origin of Tyranny*
SHOLOKHOV. *The Silent Don*
MARRIOTT. *Dictatorship and Democracy*
KOHN. *Revolutions and Dictatorships*
MERRIAM. *The New Democracy and the New Despotism*
STRAUSS. *On Tyranny*

Chapter 96: UNIVERSAL AND PARTICULAR

INTRODUCTION

ON such speculative problems as the existence of God, the immortality of the soul, the infinity of time and space, or the limits of human knowledge, the conversation of philosophers seems to make contact with the discourse of scientists, the language of poets, and the speech of ordinary men. The philosophers usually begin at least by propounding questions which correspond to those asked by men who do not profess to be philosophers. But throughout the tradition of western thought, the problem of the universal, unlike these others, seems to have the character of a professional secret.

The various solutions of the problem of the universal are so many esoteric doctrines, each with its own sectarian name. The initiated can distinguish themselves from the novices by their proficiency in this area; and the outsider who overhears the discussion of professionals may be completely left behind, wondering as much about how the question arose as about the meaning of the conflicting answers.

No genuine philosophical problem, it seems reasonable to suppose, can be so remote from questions intelligible to common sense. If it is not just a specious riddle to amuse the experts, the problem of the universal, despite its technical appearance, should raise issues from which, in some form or other, no one can escape. Whether or not this is so can be tested by considering the various ways in which the problem occurs in other chapters under different guises and in different contexts.

In the chapter on SAME AND OTHER, we find the question how two individuals can be the same in some particular respect—how in spite of their separate existence they can share in the possession of a common nature or attribute. Anyone who classifies things or tries to make definitions may be led to wonder whether classifications are entirely verbal and definitions fictions of the mind, or whether things themselves belong together in some real community based upon an inherent sameness or similarity.

In the chapter on ONE AND MANY, the question takes the form of asking how two or more things can be one in any way. Again, both science and common sense seem able to deal with an infinite number of individuals by applying a single name to them or apprehending them all under a single concept or notion. But it may be asked what justifies the denomination of many things by one name. What unity in the things verifies the tendency of thought to unify them conceptually? Does a real unity exist in things, by virtue of their being somehow one as well as many, or as a result of the many somehow participating in a one which exists separately from them?

In the chapters on DEFINITION and SIGN AND SYMBOL the same questions are at least implicit. In connection with the object of definition, one issue is whether what Aristotle calls "the formulable essence" exists as the common nature of many individuals, or whether, as Locke suggests, definitions formulate only the nominal, not the real, essences of things. As that and related issues are faced, anyone who acknowledges the familiar distinction between proper and common names may become involved in questioning what common or general names signify and how they get the meanings with which they are used in everyday discourse.

The problem of the sameness of things distinct from one another, the problem of the one *in* the many or the one *and* the many, the problem of essences and common names, are other statements of the problem of the universal and the particular. Attention to the words themselves confirms this. The word "*uni*versal" connotes a unity—the one as opposed to the many, the common as opposed to the unique or special. The word "*part*icular" connotes participation—the part as opposed to the whole, the member as opposed to the class. As the reference already made to essence and individual indicates, these are not the only pairs of terms which somehow correspond in significance to universal and particular, but others, like model and imitation, form and matter, abstract and concrete, are more obscure in meaning. The discussion of universal and particular throws light on them rather than gains clarity from them.

THE READER OF THE great books can witness the origin of the problem of the universal and particular as it occurs in a conversation, not between technical philosophers, but between Socrates and his friends. In the *Meno*, Socrates and Meno get into a discussion of how virtue is acquired. Socrates thinks it is necessary to inquire first what virtue is. Meno responds by enumerating different virtues, but Socrates is not satisfied. He wants a definition which will cover all the virtues. Even if Meno could say what justice or temperance is, that would not do, for each of these is, as Socrates says, *a* virtue, not *virtue*—a particular virtue or a part of virtue, not the whole of it.

"In searching after one virtue," Socrates tells Meno, "we have found many . . . but we have been unable to find the common virtue which runs through them all." To help Meno, who claims he is not able to follow Socrates in his "attempt to get at one common notion of virtue," Socrates shifts the discussion to colors and figures. He warns Meno that color cannot be defined by naming colors, and that, even if he could define a square, a circle, and all other figures, he would not be saying what *figure* is. To proceed in this way is to be "landed in particulars."

"Tell me then," Socrates says, "since you call them by a common name, and say that they are all figures, even when opposed to one another, what is that common nature which you designate as figure?"

If Meno were to reply, "I do not know what you want," not much further explanation could be given. To someone who remained perplexed at this point, we could only say, Socrates suggests, "Do you not understand that we are looking for the same in the many?" Or, put in another form, we might ask, he says, "What is that [one in many] which you call figure, and which includes not only the round and straight figures, but all?"

Thus stated, the problem of the universal seems inescapable—a problem for everyone, not just for philosophers. But the philosophers complicate the problem almost as soon as it is stated. Giving his version of the history of philosophy, Aristotle offers an explanation of how the problem shifted to another level. Socrates, he writes, "was busying himself about ethical matters" and, "seeking the universal in these ethical matters, [he] fixed thought for the first time on definitions. Plato accepted his teaching, but held that the problem applied not to sensible things, but to entities of another kind—for this reason, that the common definition could not be a definition of any sensible thing, as they were always changing. Things of this other sort he called Ideas, and sensible things, he said, were all named after these, and in virtue of a relation to these; for the many existed by participation in the Ideas that have the same name as they."

It is at this point, according to Aristotle, that the great philosophical controversy begins. Whereas "the thinkers of old ranked particular things as substances, *e.g.*, fire and earth, not what is common to both, body," the Platonists or idealists—"the thinkers of the present day"—"tend to rank universal as substances, for genera are universal." Aristotle repeatedly tries to distinguish between the Socratic inquiry and what he regards as the Platonic doctrine—the theory of Ideas. "The first to raise the problem of universal definition . . . Socrates," he writes, "did not make the universals or the definitions exist apart; they, however,"—the Platonists—"gave them separate existence, and this was the kind of thing they called Ideas."

As between Socrates and his disciple, Aristotle does not hesitate to take sides. "Socrates gave the impulse to this theory of ideas . . . but he did not *separate* universals from individuals; and in not separating them," Aristotle adds, "he thought rightly." The issue between Aristotle and his own teacher, Plato, cannot, however, be stated by so simple an affirmation and denial.

On Aristotle's side, it involves the fundamental principles of his metaphysics, especially his doctrine of substance, as well as his theory of what and how the intellect knows, as contrasted with the perceptions of the senses. On Plato's side, it involves many questions concerning the intelligible and the sensible, being and becoming, the one and the many—questions the Aristotelian answers to which would not satisfy Plato.

Wherever the truth lies, Aristotle recognizes that on this issue, perhaps more than on any other, he is most sharply opposed to Plato. It is the one matter wherein he feels a conflict between devotion to his teacher and to the truth as he sees it. The consideration of the universal good, he declares in the *Ethics*, is made difficult "by the fact that the Forms have been introduced by friends of our own," but "while both are dear, piety requires us to honor truth above our friends."

THE HISTORIANS OF PHILOSOPHY, beginning with Aristotle, attribute one solution of the problem of universals to Plato. That solution comes to be called "realism" because it affirms the independent reality of universals as separately existing Ideas or Forms. But all the commentators do not, like Aristotle, dissent from Plato's solution. In our own time, for example, Bertrand Russell, treating of "the world of universals" in the *Problems of Philosophy*, says, "the problem with which we are now concerned is a very old one, since it was brought into philosophy by Plato. Plato's 'theory of ideas' is an attempt to solve this very problem, and in my opinion it is one of the most successful attempts hitherto made. The theory to be advocated in what follows is largely Plato's, with merely such modifications as time has shown to be necessary."

For one thing, Russell thinks "the word 'idea' has acquired in the course of time many associations which are quite misleading when applied to Plato's 'ideas.' We shall, therefore," he writes, "use the word 'universal' instead of the word 'idea' to describe what Plato meant. ... We speak of whatever is given in sensation ... as a *particular*; by opposition to this, a *universal* will be anything which may be shared by many particulars. ... Broadly speaking, proper names stand for particulars, while other substantives, adjectives, prepositions, and verbs stand for universals."

Russell here calls attention to another point which he thinks has too seldom been observed, namely, that universals are not exclusively signified by common nouns and adjectives, but that, in addition, there are relational universals signified by prepositions and verbs. This sort of universal, according to him, most readily shows that universals have being apart from particulars. It can also be shown, he argues, "that their being is not merely mental ... that whatever being belongs to them is independent of their being thought of or in any way apprehended by minds."

If the word "existence" implies definite location in time and space, then, Russell concludes, in the sense in which "thoughts and feelings, minds and physical objects *exist*... universals do not exist." We must say instead that "they *subsist* or *have being*, where 'being' is opposed to 'existence' as being timeless. The world of universals, therefore, may also be described as the world of being. The world of being is unchangeable. ... The world of existence is fleeting. ... According to our temperaments, we shall prefer the contemplation of the one or the other. The one we do not prefer will probably seem to us a pale shadow of the one we prefer, and hardly worthy to be regarded as in any sense real. But the truth is that both have the same claim on our impartial attention, both are real, and both are important to the metaphysician. Indeed no sooner have we distinguished the two worlds than it becomes necessary to consider their relations."

IT IS THIS CONSIDERATION which seems to be for Plato *the* problem of the universal—the central difficulty in the theory of Ideas or separate Forms. As indicated in the chapters on FORM and IDEA, the separation of the two worlds—the sensible world of becoming and the intelligible world of being—always calls for some explanation of their resemblance.

Socrates sometimes refers to the doctrine of Ideas as if its truth could be assumed, and sometimes argues the necessity of a realm of immutable and intelligible being as the object of thought, comparable to sensible, changing things as the object of perception. In the *Phaedo*, for example, he gets Cebes to admit that the ideas, "which in the dialectical process we define as essences or true existences," are not subject to change, but that they are "always what they are, having the same simple self-existent and unchanging forms." In contrast to absolute beauty or goodness, the many beautiful or good things "are always in a state of change." These, Socrates says, "you can touch and see and perceive with the senses, but the unchanging things you can only perceive with the mind. Let us suppose then," he adds, "that there are two sorts of existences—one seen, the other unseen."

Later in the same dialogue, Socrates repeats the assumption that "there is an absolute beauty and goodness and greatness and the like." No other assumption seems to him to provide as satisfactory an explanation of how particular things can be beautiful or good or have any other characteristics. "Nothing makes a thing beautiful," he declares, "but the presence and participation of beauty in whatever way or manner obtained; for as to the manner I am uncertain, but I stoutly contend that by beauty all beautiful things become beautiful."

In later Platonic dialogues, the question of the manner comes to the fore. Though the Eleatic Stranger in the *Sophist* refers to the "endless conflict raging" between the materialists and the idealists concerning the existence of the unseen world of ideas, he himself seems to be doubtful only on the point of how the changing things of sense participate in the immutable forms. One answer is suggested in the *Timaeus*. According to the story of creation which Timaeus tells, the artificer of the world made its sensible particulars copy an eternal pattern. When many things seem to be of one nature or to share the same quality, they are so by virtue of imitating the eternal forms, which are not only absolute essences in themselves, but are also the models for created or generated things.

But in the *Parmenides* Socrates seems unable to defend the view that "the ideas are, as it were, patterns fixed in nature, and other things are like them, and resemblances of them—for what is meant by the participation of other things in the ideas, is really assimilation to them." Nor can he meet other objections which Parmenides raises, such as the difficulty of two or more individuals participating in one idea; for if the idea is wholly in one individual, it cannot be in another, and if each of the many partake of the idea only in part, then the idea cannot be one and indivisible. "In what way, Socrates," Parmenides asks, "will all things participate in ideas, if they are unable to participate in them as parts or wholes?"

In the course of the discussion Parmenides rebukes Socrates for being squeamish about positing absolute essences for "such things as hair, mud, dirt, or anything else which is vile and paltry," as well as for things which are beautiful and good. But his main intention seems to be to leave Socrates with an unresolved dilemma. On the one hand, the difficulties with the theory of Ideas make the denial of their separate existence reasonable; on the other, the denial of their existence seems to make thought and reasoning impossible, because it deprives the mind of its proper objects.

SOME OF ARISTOTLE'S arguments against the separate existence of universals repeat the objections raised by Parmenides, to which no answer is given in the dialogues of Plato. If it were not for the fact that Aristotle attributes to Plato himself the theory he criticizes, the dialogues would leave us in some doubt as to whether it is Plato or his followers, the Platonists, who hold that theory. But whether or not Aristotle's criticisms apply to Plato—and even if they involve some misunderstanding of his doctrine—the objections Aristotle raises help define his own position.

To say that the Forms "are patterns and that other things share in them," Aristotle writes, "is to use empty words and poetical metaphors." In his view, "the most paradoxical thing of all is the statement that there are certain things besides those in the material universe, and that these are the same as sensible things except that they are eternal while the latter are perishable." To posit the separate being of the forms of things seems to him a useless multiplication of existences. To say that "there must be Ideas of all things that are spoken of universally" is to make substances of ideas.

Those who say the Forms exist would be right, Aristotle concedes, "*if* they are substances." He does not think it is impossible to establish the existence of imperishable and insensible substances, but such substances, if they exist, would not stand in relation to sensible substances as universal to particular, or as one to many. His objection to the theory of Ideas is that, in speaking of absolute beauty or beauty-itself, of the idea Man or man-itself, the Platonists do no more than add words like "absolute" or "itself" to the names of sensible things, and posit the existence of these absolutes or universals over and above the existence of the sensible particulars having the same name.

Aristotle's own position seems to be that only individual substances exist, whether they are sensible or intelligible, perishable or eternal, and that "no universal can be a substance" or exist separately in and of itself. He does not thereby deny the reality of the universal. On the contrary, he holds that "without the universal it is not possible to get knowledge," *i.e.*, scientific knowledge in distinction from mere sense-perception. "All knowledge is of the universal and of the 'such,'" he writes; yet in adding that "substance is not a universal, but is rather a 'this,'" Aristotle indicates what is for him the central problem of the universal.

Aristotle's theory that the mind abstracts universal concepts from the particulars of sense-experience, and that such concepts are the terms of the universal propositions constituting scientific knowledge, leaves a question concerning the object of science. If science is knowledge of real existence, not of our own concepts, and if only individual things really exist, then how can the object of science be the universal, not the individual? What is the object apprehended by the universal concept 'man' or 'horse'?

Aristotle's answer seems to be that if the universal term 'man' can be truly predicated of an indefinite number of individuals, it must signify something common to them all. The common nature or properties shared by a number of individuals cannot be actually universal, however, since, in Aristotle's opinion, whatever exists in the individual—the form as well as the matter of the concrete substance—is itself individual. He finds it necessary to say, therefore, that the universal exists potentially, not actually, whenever a number of individuals have something in common.

The form which constitutes human nature, for example, is an individual form in Socrates and Callias; but it has the potentiality of being universal insofar as it is capable of being separated from the individual matter of these two men by the abstractive power of the mind. When the abstraction takes place and results in the universal concept 'man,' the form thus received in the mind becomes actually universal and enables the mind to apprehend the nature common to all individual men.

Aristotle's doctrine that the universal exists potentially in individual things and actually in the abstract concepts of the mind, later comes to be called "moderate realism," in contrast to the extreme realism of the position which asserts the actual subsistence of universals, outside of minds as well as apart from individual things. It affirms that the universal has what Russell calls "extra-mental reality," even though it severely qualifies the real being of the universal by saying it is neither actual nor subsistent.

As Aristotle denies unqualified reality to universals, later philosophers deny that they have any reality at all. Those who are sometimes called "conceptualists" admit the existence of universals only as abstract ideas in the mind. The "nominalist" position, taken by Hobbes and Berkeley, goes further and even denies abstract ideas or universal notions in the mind. It holds that universality is a property of words alone, which manifests itself in the meaning of general or common names.

In the progressive complication of the controversy, each of the theories which has acquired a traditional title undergoes modification as it is reformulated in different contexts. This is especially true of the two middle positions which tend to lean toward one or the other of the extremes.

Locke, for example, may be called a conceptualist because he thinks that general names derive their universal significance from the abstract ideas they signify. But though he denies that by means of our universal notions or abstract ideas we can know the real essences of things, he does not deny real essences. To this extent, he may lean toward moderate realism more than a philosopher like William of Ockham, or a psychologist like William James who says, "*We must decide in favor of the conceptualists*, and affirm that the power to think things, qualities, relations . . . isolated and abstracted from the total experience in which they appear, is the most indisputable function of our thought." Similarly, the development which Aquinas gives to Aristotle's views, especially in the point he adds concerning ideas in the mind of God—the "eternal exemplars"—may be a form of moderate realism which, more than Aristotle's, has some affinity with the theory of self-subsistent ideas as the eternal archetypes for sensible particulars.

Aquinas presents his own theory in the context of stating his understanding of the issue between Plato and Aristotle. "Plato supposed," he declares, "that the forms of natural things subsisted apart from matter, and consequently that they are intelligible, for a thing is actually intelligible from the very fact that it is immaterial. And he called such forms *species* or *ideas*. From a participation in these, he said that even corporeal matter was formed, in order that individuals might be naturally established in their proper genera and species. . . . But since Aristotle did not allow that the forms of natural things exist apart from matter, and since forms existing in matter are not actually intelligible, it follows that the natures or forms of the sensible things which we understand are not actually intelligible."

Aquinas speaks of the forms (which exist only in union with matter in individual things) as "universal forms," even though they are not actually intelligible. "We abstract universal forms from their particular conditions," he says, and by doing so we "make them actually intelligible." The Platonic error, in his opinion, consists in thinking that "the form of the thing known must be in the knower in the same manner as in the thing known." From the fact that "the form of the thing understood is in the intellect under conditions of universality, immateriality, and immobility," Plato concluded, erroneously, according to Aquinas, "that the things which we understand must subsist in themselves under the same conditions of immateriality and immobility."

As Aquinas states what he takes to be Aristotle's correction of this error, it consists in distinguishing two ways in which the universal can be considered. "First, the universal nature may be considered together with the intention of universality. And since the intention of universality—*viz.*, the relation of one and the same to many—is due to intellectual abstraction, the universal thus considered is subsequent, in our knowledge. . . . Secondly, the universal can be considered according to the nature itself (for instance, *animality* or *humanity*) as existing in the individual." In the order of generation and time, the potential universal precedes the actual universal; that is, the universal form or common nature exists in individual things under conditions of particularity before it exists in the human mind under conditions of abstraction.

Even as forms exist in things (though they are not actually universal prior to their existence as universal concepts of the mind), so they have a mode of being prior to their existence in things. Here Aquinas attributes to Augustine the correction of a pagan error and the substitution for it of a Christian truth. "Whenever Augustine, who was imbued with the doctrines of the Platonists," he writes, "found in their teaching anything consistent with the faith, he adopted it; and those things which he found contrary to faith, he amended."

Plato, positing "the forms of things subsisting of themselves apart from matter," had supposed that, "just as corporeal matter, by participating in the Idea of stone, becomes a stone, so our intellect, by participating in the same Idea, has knowledge of the stone." But, according to Aquinas, "it seems contrary to faith that the forms of things should subsist of themselves without matter outside the things themselves. . . . Therefore, in place of the Ideas defended by Plato, Augustine said that the exemplars of all creatures existed in the divine mind. It is according to these that all things are formed, as well as that the human soul knows all things."

THE SOLUTION TO THE problem of universals which Aquinas proposes seems to involve a threefold distinction with respect to the being of forms: they are (1) in the human mind by abstraction from our experience of sensible particulars; (2) in individual things; and (3), prior to their existence in things, in the divine mind.

But Aquinas himself says that in God there is no distinction between universal and particular; nor does knowledge "exist in God after the mode of created knowledge, so as to be universal or particular." The divine ideas, whether considered as the exemplars by which God creates things or as the types and likeness by which God knows them, are not abstractions and so do not have the universality characteristic of human concepts. Whereas our abstract universals do not give us knowledge of individual things in their singularity, the divine ideas, according to Aquinas, are the principles whereby God at once knows the singular and the universal.

If the universal *as such* is not in the divine mind, neither, in Ockham's opinion, is it really in things—not even potentially. Everything that exists in an individual—its form and matter, all its parts and properties—is the unique and singular possession of that individual. If there were something common to two things, it would have to be one and two at the same time. As common to both, it would have to be somehow one and the same in both, yet as existing in each, it would have to be distinct in each; it would have to be as singular in each as each individual thing in which it existed. But since Ockham regards this as impossible, he concludes that "no universal really exists outside the soul in an individual substance; nor is it of the substance or the being of things, but is only in the soul."

The old riddle thus returns in another form. If abstract concepts are in the mind—or if, as Ockham suggests, the logical "terms 'animal' and 'man' are universals because predicable of many, not through themselves, but for the things they signify"—then what in reality is the object signified by the universal term or concept? It cannot be the many unless the numerically distinct individuals are also alike as men or animals; and how can they be really alike, as opposed to being merely conceived as such, unless they have a common nature or attribute and to that extent are one and the same?

Locke puts the question another way. "Since all things are only particulars," he asks, "how come we by general terms, or where find we those general natures they are supposed to stand for?" He answers that "words become general, by being made the signs of general ideas; and ideas become general by separating from them the circumstances of time and place, and other ideas that may determine them to this or that particular existence. By this way of abstraction, they are made capable of representing more individuals than one; each of which having in it a conformity to that abstract idea is (as we call it) of that sort."

But if, as Locke goes on to say, general natures (or genera and species) are "nothing else but abstract ideas, more or less comprehensive, with names annexed to them," then in what way do the many individuals represented by one abstract idea have in them "a conformity to that abstract idea"? Locke's position seems to avoid this problem. "Abstract ideas," he writes, give us "no knowledge of existence at all." Only particular propositions are about real existences. "Universal propositions, of whose truth or falsehood we can have certain knowledge, concern not existence." Such propositions express nothing but "the agreement or disagreement of our abstract ideas."

In addition to denying their reference to reality, Locke regards abstract ideas as "fictions or contrivances of the mind," which are imperfect precisely to the extent that they succeed in being universal. The general idea of triangle, he observes, must be neither equilateral, isosceles, nor scalene, "but all and none of these at once. In effect, it is something imperfect, that cannot exist." Where Locke seems to mean only that there can be no counterpart in reality to our general ideas, Berkeley, observing the same "imperfection" in what are supposed to be abstract ideas, denies that they can exist even in the mind. "I deny," he writes, "that I can abstract from one another, or conceive separately, those qualities which it is impossible should exist so separated, or that I can frame a general notion by abstracting from particulars."

Berkeley admits that "a man may consider a figure merely as triangular, without attending to the particular qualities of the angles or relations of the sides. So far he may abstract; but this will never prove that he can frame an abstract, general, inconsistent idea of a triangle." He recognizes also that all our common names have general significance, but he rejects Locke's explanation of their general meaning. "A word becomes general," he says, "by being made the sign, not of an abstract general idea, but of several particular ideas, any one of which it indifferently suggests to the mind."

Does a nominalist like Berkeley escape the persistent riddle? Does it not reappear in the question which must be asked: what is there in this set of particular ideas, as opposed to some other set, which makes it possible for a general name to signify any one of them indifferently? If each particular idea were absolutely unique and had nothing in common with any other, would the universal have any truth even on the level of names?

James thinks the nominalists are somehow forced to "admit a *quasi*-universal, something which we think *as if it were* universal, though it is not; and in all that they say about this something which they explain to be 'an indefinite number of particular ideas,' the same vacillation between the subjective and objective points of view appears. The reader never can tell," James continues, "whether an 'idea' spoken of is supposed to be a knower or a known. The authors themselves do not distinguish. They want to get something in the mind which shall *resemble* what is out of the mind, however vaguely, and they think that when that fact is accomplished, no farther questions will be asked."

SOME PHILOSOPHERS DEAL with the universal and particular in a manner which leads away from rather than into the traditional problem.

To Spinoza, for example, universal terms, such as *man*, *horse*, *dog*, represent confused images drawn from sense-experience. They provide us with an inadequate knowledge of things. To know things adequately we must proceed "from an adequate idea of the formal essence of certain attributes of God to the adequate knowledge of the essence of things." Quite opposite to the abstract universal (or indeterminate image from experience), the adequate idea is universal in the totally different sense of comprehending an infinite whole.

Hegel also distinguishes between abstract universality and "true infinity or concrete universality." The former is "something determinate; *i.e.*, being abstraction from all determinacy, it is itself not without determinacy; to be something abstract and one-sided constitutes its determinacy, its defectiveness, its finitude." The antithesis of the abstract universal is the particular, the determinate content implicitly contained in an abstract universal. The synthesis is the individual; not the particular individual, but the infinite individual which is the concrete universal.

The concrete universal is neither "the universal as a common characteristic, nor the abstract universality which stands outside and over against the individual, the abstract identity of the Understanding." It is "the universality which has the particular as its opposite, but the particular which by its reflection into itself has been equalized with the universal. This unity is individuality, not individuality in its immediacy as a unit . . . but individuality in accordance with its concept." For Hegel, the concrete universal is the immanent Idea itself. It is the manifestation of the Absolute Spirit or God.

HOWEVER IT IS formulated and whether or not it is or can be solved, the problem of the universal seems to have a critical bearing on the discussion of many other great ideas. In addition to the chapters enumerated at the beginning, we can now see that the universal, the particular, and the individual are implicated in the consideration of BEING and INFINITY, FORM and IDEA, MATTER and MIND, EXPERIENCE, INDUCTION, JUDGMENT, and SCIENCE. These chapters, in turn, do more than throw light on the various solutions proposed to the problem of the universal. They help us understand the importance of the problem—certainly to the philosophers of the western tradition. If in the broader context of connected issues, it is discovered that the proof of man's distinctive rationality, or even the possibility of an immortal soul, may depend on the affirmation or denial of universals, at least as concepts in the mind, then, perhaps, some tolerance and patience may be won for the burdensome technicalities of the problem.

OUTLINE OF TOPICS

1. The distinction and relation between universal and particular: essence and individual, whole and part, class and member, one and many, same and other, the common and the unique

2. The problem of the universal

   2*a*. The reality of universals: their actual existence as separate forms, or their potential existence in the forms of things

   2*b*. Universals as abstractions or concepts in the human mind

   2*c*. The reduction of universals or abstractions to the meaning of general or common names

3. The problem of the individual: the principle of individuality; the concrete universal

4. Universals and particulars in the order of knowledge

   4*a*. Universals as objects of knowledge: the intuitive or reflexive apprehension of universals

   4*b*. Universals in relation to the angelic intellect and the divine mind

   4*c*. The abstraction of universal concepts from the particulars of sense

   4*d*. The distinction between particular and universal in relation to the distinction between percept and concept, or between image and idea

   4*e*. The inadequacy of our knowledge of individuals: their indefinability

   4*f*. The generality of science: the universality of its principles

5. Universal and particular in relation to grammar and logic

   5*a*. The distinction between proper and common names

   5*b*. The classification of universals: their intension and extension; their degrees of generality

   5*c*. Particulars and universals in predications or judgments: the quantity of propositions; the universal, the particular, and the singular judgment

   5*d*. Rules concerning the universality and particularity of premises in reasoning: the quantity of the conclusion in relation to the quantity of the premises

6. Applications of the distinction between universal and particular

   6*a*. Particular and universal in the analysis of matter and form

   6*b*. Universal and particular causes

   6*c*. The universality of law and particular dispensations of equity

7. Universality and particularity in relation to the distinction between the objective and the subjective, the absolute and the relative

   7*a*. The issue concerning the universality of truth

   7*b*. The issue concerning the universality of moral principles

   7*c*. The issue concerning the universality of aesthetic standards: the subjective universal

REFERENCES

References are listed by volume number (in bold type), author's name, and page number. Bible references are to book, chapter, and verse of the Authorized King James version of the Bible. The abbreviation "esp" calls the reader's attention to one or more especially relevant parts of a whole reference; "passim" signifies that the topic is discussed intermittently rather than continuously in the work or passage cited. Where the work as a whole is relevant to the topic, the page numbers refer to the entire work. For general guidance in the use of *The Great Ideas,* consult the Preface.

1. The distinction and relation between universal and particular: essence and individual, whole and part, class and member, one and many, same and other, the common and the unique

7 PLATO, 32–33, 174–179, 392–394, 514–515, 534–536, 610–613
8 ARISTOTLE, 116, 117, 369, 505–506, 517–518, 537, 545, 558–559, 578–580, 598, 599–601
17 PLOTINUS, 142–143, 205–207
18 AUGUSTINE, 670
19 AQUINAS, 16–18, 20–21, 49, 80–81, 169–170, 227–228, 399–401, 662–663
20 AQUINAS, 710–711, 755–756
28 HARVEY, 332–333
31 DESCARTES, 8–10
31 SPINOZA, 386–388
35 LOCKE, 268–283 passim
35 BERKELEY, 408–409
42 KANT, 193–200
46 HEGEL, 64
53 JAMES, 308–312

2. The problem of the universal

2*a*. The reality of universals: their actual existence as separate forms, or their potential existence in the forms of things

7 PLATO, 87–89, 228–230, 231–232, 426–429, 447, 457, 487–491, 561–574
8 ARISTOTLE, 105–106, 505–506, 508–511, 514, 516, 518, 519–520, 521, 556–557, 562–563, 564–565, 569–570, 586, 598, 599, 607, 610–611
17 PLOTINUS, 307–308
18 AUGUSTINE, 76
19 AQUINAS, 93–94, 99, 163–164, 418–419, 444–447, 455–457
20 AQUINAS, 715–716
30 BACON, 43–44
35 LOCKE, 257, 274–276, 277
42 KANT, 551–552
53 JAMES, 309–311 passim

2*b*. Universals as abstractions or concepts in the human mind

7 PLATO, 489
8 ARISTOTLE, 116–118, 330, 648, 661
18 AUGUSTINE, 269, 337–338
19 AQUINAS, 71–72, 382–383, 388–391, 416–417, 440–444, 453–455
20 AQUINAS, 1025–1032
28 HARVEY, 332–333
31 DESCARTES, 216–217
35 LOCKE, 145, 244, 255–260, 263–283 passim, 331–332, 338–339, 349
35 BERKELEY, 405–410 passim
35 HUME, 505
46 HEGEL, 17–18
53 JAMES, 305–311

2*c*. The reduction of universals or abstractions to the meaning of general or common names

23 HOBBES, 55–56
31 SPINOZA, 387–388
35 LOCKE, 278
35 BERKELEY, 407–408
35 HUME, 507

3. The problem of the individual: the principle of individuality; the concrete universal

8 ARISTOTLE, 518, 521–522, 536–537 passim, 618–619
17 PLOTINUS, 238–239
19 AQUINAS, 84–85, 162–163, 257–258, 381–382, 384–385, 388–391
20 AQUINAS, 713–714
31 SPINOZA, 373
35 LOCKE, 218–228 passim
46 HEGEL, 13–14, 17, 69, 112, 115, 117, 119, 156–157, 158–159, 160–178, 285

4. Universals and particulars in the order of knowledge

4*a*. Universals as objects of knowledge: the intuitive or reflexive apprehension of universals

7 PLATO, 113–114, 179–183, 228–230, 370–373, 383–388, 489–491, 535–536, 570–574, 809–810
8 ARISTOTLE, 508–509, 648
18 AUGUSTINE, 654
19 AQUINAS, 440–442, 444–446, 447–450, 451–453, 461–462, 748–749

20 AQUINAS, 1025–1032
35 LOCKE, 323
53 JAMES, 308–314 passim

4*b*. Universals in relation to the angelic intellect and the divine mind

19 AQUINAS, 128–130, 289–291, 295–297, 545–546

4*c*. The abstraction of universal concepts from the particulars of sense

8 ARISTOTLE, 87–89, 97, 136, 663–664, 690
19 AQUINAS, 71–72, 84–85, 215–216, 291, 295–297, 382–383, 416–419, 440–457, 462–463, 476–477
20 AQUINAS, 1025–1032
31 DESCARTES, 53
31 SPINOZA, 387–388
35 LOCKE, 145, 147, 263, 277–278, 338–339
35 BERKELEY, 405–409 passim, 414, 431–432
35 HUME, 505
38 ROUSSEAU, 341–342
42 KANT, 45–46
53 JAMES, 308–311

4*d*. The distinction between particular and universal in relation to the distinction between percept and concept, or between image and idea

7 PLATO, 126, 386–388, 534–536
8 ARISTOTLE, 111, 120, 264, 499–500
18 AUGUSTINE, 75–76
19 AQUINAS, 295–297, 455–457, 461–462, 690–692
31 DESCARTES, 96–97, 136–137, 218
31 SPINOZA, 389–390
35 BERKELEY, 408–409
42 KANT, 23–24, 115
53 JAMES, 480–484

4*e*. The inadequacy of our knowledge of individuals: their indefinability

8 ARISTOTLE, 6–7, 518, 521–522, 563–564, 618–619
19 AQUINAS, 292, 295–297, 476–477
20 AQUINAS, 772–773
53 JAMES, 312

4*f*. The generality of science: the universality of its principles

7 PLATO, 383–388, 391–398
8 ARISTOTLE, 100–102, 107–109, 116–118, 120, 135–137, 259, 499–500, 548
9 ARISTOTLE, 435, 596
19 AQUINAS, 440–442
28 HARVEY, 332–334
30 BACON, 108, 127–128, 138–139, 161
31 DESCARTES, 167
33 PASCAL, 358
34 NEWTON, 1–2, 270–271, 543
35 LOCKE, 308–309, 316, 322–323, 331–336 passim
35 BERKELEY, 408, 409, 425–426, 433–434 passim, 438
35 HUME, 454–455, 460
42 KANT, 195–198, 211–218, 562–563
45 FOURIER, 169
46 HEGEL, 182–183, 361
53 JAMES, 671–672, 861–886 passim

5. Universal and particular in relation to grammar and logic

5*a*. The distinction between proper and common names

8 ARISTOTLE, 246
19 AQUINAS, 71–72, 73–74, 170–171, 181–183
23 HOBBES, 55
35 LOCKE, 98–99, 251–252, 254–256, 257, 280
35 BERKELEY, 410
38 ROUSSEAU, 341–342
45 LAVOISIER, 4
53 JAMES, 310–311, 447–448

5*b*. The classification of universals: their intension and extension; their degrees of generality

7 PLATO, 569–574
8 ARISTOTLE, 5–8, 60, 100–101, 111–115, 131–133, 144–147, 534, 561–563, 587–588
19 AQUINAS, 270–272, 391–393, 471–472, 697–703 passim
20 AQUINAS, 54–55
35 LOCKE, 256

5*c*. Particulars and universals in predications or judgments: the quantity of propositions; the universal, the particular, and the singular judgment

8 ARISTOTLE, 5, 6–8, 26–27
9 ARISTOTLE, 356, 397–398
19 AQUINAS, 170–171, 457–458
20 AQUINAS, 145–147
35 LOCKE, 331–336
42 KANT, 14–15, 39–41, 51–52

5*d*. Rules concerning the universality and particularity of premises in reasoning: the quantity of the conclusion in relation to the quantity of the premises

8 ARISTOTLE, 40–45, 58, 108–109, 116–118
9 ARISTOTLE, 397–398, 596–597
20 AQUINAS, 141
35 LOCKE, 377
42 KANT, 110–112, 118

6. Applications of the distinction between universal and particular

6*a*. Particular and universal in the analysis of matter and form

8 ARISTOTLE, 546, 599–601, 618–619
17 PLOTINUS, 50–57, 282
19 AQUINAS, 15–16, 31, 113–114, 162–164,

257–258, 341–342, 381–382, 391–393, 451–453, 585–587, 604–607
20 AQUINAS, 711–712

6*b*. Universal and particular causes

8 ARISTOTLE, 534, 599–601
19 AQUINAS, 128–130, 291, 587–588, 610–611, 662, 813–814
20 AQUINAS, 733–734
31 SPINOZA, 365–366

6*c*. The universality of law and particular dispensations of equity

7 PLATO, 699–700, 754
9 ARISTOTLE, 382–383, 385–386, 485–486, 593, 617, 618–619
20 AQUINAS, 205–206, 235, 238–239, 259–261
23 HOBBES, 94, 133–135
35 LOCKE, 55–58
36 SWIFT, 152–154
38 MONTESQUIEU, 3
38 ROUSSEAU, 397, 399–400
41 GIBBON, 88–89
42 KANT, 399–400
43 FEDERALIST, 237, 244–245 passim
46 HEGEL, 71–75, 137–138, 139

7. Universality and particularity in relation to the distinction between the objective and the subjective, the absolute and the relative

7*a*. The issue concerning the universality of truth

7 PLATO, 86, 517–532
8 ARISTOTLE, 528–531, 590–592
12 LUCRETIUS, 50–51
12 EPICTETUS, 164–166
19 AQUINAS, 453–455
23 HOBBES, 65
25 MONTAIGNE, 240–246, 259–261, 267, 271–272
30 BACON, 57–58, 115–116
31 DESCARTES, 1–3, 95–96, 272–273
33 PASCAL, 181–184, 238–239
35 LOCKE, 94–95, 357–358
35 BERKELEY, 404, 405
35 HUME, 454–455, 507–508
42 KANT, 36–37, 202–203, 218–222, 224–227, 240–243
43 MILL, 274–293 passim
46 HEGEL, 160–178
53 JAMES, 639–646

7*b*. The issue concerning the universality of moral principles

6 HERODOTUS, 97–98
7 PLATO, 58–62, 183–184, 187–190, 271–277 passim, 528–532
9 ARISTOTLE, 339–340, 349, 359, 430
12 AURELIUS, 264
18 AUGUSTINE, 16, 663
20 AQUINAS, 223–224
23 HOBBES, 91–92, 95–96, 140, 272
25 MONTAIGNE, 46–47, 93, 115–119, 209–212, 281–284
31 DESCARTES, 46
31 SPINOZA, 422–424, 426
33 PASCAL, 29–44, 230–231
35 LOCKE, 103–111 passim, 192–193
38 ROUSSEAU, 330–331, 343–345, 369–370
42 KANT, 173–174, 253–254, 260–261, 264, 265–266, 270–271, 273–287, 294–295, 297–314, 317, 372, 390–391, 392–393, 397–398, 478–479
43 MILL, 269–270, 274–293 passim, 445–446, 461–464, 471–476
46 HEGEL, 40, 47, 129, 137, 280–281
49 DARWIN, 314–316
50 MARX-ENGELS, 428
51 TOLSTOY, 213–216, 645–646
53 JAMES, 886–888

7*c*. The issue concerning the universality of aesthetic standards: the subjective universal

7 PLATO, 142–148, 167, 593–595, 653–656, 660–662
12 AURELIUS, 265
17 PLOTINUS, 21–23, 287
18 AUGUSTINE, 24
19 AQUINAS, 25–26, 737
20 AQUINAS, 608–609
25 MONTAIGNE, 230–231
31 SPINOZA, 371–372
42 KANT, 480–482, 488–492, 513–517, 540–542
46 HEGEL, 185
49 DARWIN, 95, 301–302, 571–577
53 JAMES, 755–757

CROSS-REFERENCES

For: Other general discussions of the distinction between the universal and the particular, *see* IDEA 4b(2); ONE AND MANY 1c.

The problem of the reality or existence of universals, *see* BEING 7d(2); FORM 2a, 3b; SAME AND OTHER 2a.

The character and conditions of individual existence, *see* IDEA 1f; MATTER 1c; and for the problem of our knowledge of individuals, *see* FORM 3b; KNOWLEDGE 5a(4)

Discussions relevant to the consideration of universals as objects of knowledge, *see* FORM 1a; IDEA 1a; KNOWLEDGE 6a(3).

Various statements of the theory of abstraction and of the distinction between sensory images and abstract ideas, *see* IDEA 2g; MEMORY AND IMAGINATION 5b, 6c(1); SENSE 5a; and for the abstraction of universal concepts in relation to inductive generalization, *see* EXPERIENCE 2b; INDUCTION 1a.

The universality of scientific laws, *see* SCIENCE 4d.

Another discussion of proper and common names, *see* SIGN AND SYMBOL 2d.

The ordering of universal concepts according to their degrees of generality, *see* IDEA 4b(3), 5d; RELATION 5a(4); SAME AND OTHER 3a(1).

Universal and particular in the logical theory of judgment and reasoning, *see* JUDGMENT 6a; REASONING 2a(2).

Other discussions of the good in general and the order of goods, *see* BEING 3–3b; GOOD AND EVIL 5a–5d; HAPPINESS 2b–2b(7).

The conception of equity as rectifying the imperfection of laws which results from their universality, *see* JUSTICE 10d; LAW 5h.

Other comparisons of history, poetry, and philosophy, *see* HISTORY 1; PHILOSOPHY 1d; POETRY 5b; TRUTH 4b.

Other discussions of the true, the good, and the beautiful as objective or subjective, absolute or relative, *see* BEAUTY 5; CUSTOM AND CONVENTION 5a, 9a–9b; GOOD AND EVIL 6d; RELATION 6b–6c; TRUTH 7b.

ADDITIONAL READINGS

Listed below are works not included in *Great Books of the Western World*, but relevant to the idea and topics with which this chapter deals. These works are divided into two groups:

I. Works by authors represented in this collection.
II. Works by authors not represented in this collection.

For the date, place, and other facts concerning the publication of the works cited, consult the Bibliography of Additional Readings which follows the last chapter of *The Great Ideas*.

I.

AQUINAS. *On Being and Essence*, CH III–IV
——. *Quaestiones Disputatae, De Anima*, A 4
DESCARTES. *The Principles of Philosophy*, PART I, 58–59
HEGEL. *Science of Logic*, VOL II, SECT I, CH I
J. S. MILL. *A System of Logic*, BK I, CH 2; BK II, CH 3

II.

PORPHYRY. *Introduction to Aristotle's Predicaments*
BOETHIUS. *In Isagogem Porphyri Commenta*
ABAILARD. *Glosses on Porphyry*
JOHN OF SALISBURY. *Metalogicon*, BK II, CH 17
ALBERTUS MAGNUS. *On the Intellect and the Intelligible*, TREATISE I–II
DUNS SCOTUS. *Reportata Parisiensia*, BK I–II
OCKHAM. *Summa Totius Logicae*
——. *Expositio Aurea et Admodum Utilis Super Artem Veterem*, PART I–II
CAJETAN. *In De Ente et Essentia D. Thomae Aquinatis Commentaria*
SUÁREZ. *Disputationes Metaphysicae*, IV (4–8), V–VI, XXV
JOHN OF SAINT THOMAS. *Cursus Philosophicus Thomisticus, Ars Logica*, PART II, QQ 3–12
T. REID. *Essays on the Intellectual Powers of Man*, V
BROWN. *Lectures on the Philosophy of the Human Mind*, VOL II, pp 458–497
W. HAMILTON. *Lectures on Metaphysics and Logic*, VOL I (34–36)
ROYCE. *The World and the Individual*, SERIES I (9–10)
WHITEHEAD and RUSSELL. *Principia Mathematica*, PART I, SECT C, D, E; PART II, SECT A
BRADLEY. *The Principles of Logic*, Terminal Essays, V
——. *Essays on Truth and Reality*, CH 3
W. E. JOHNSON. *Logic*, PART I, CH 8, 11
MCTAGGART. *The Nature of Existence*, BK III
WHITEHEAD. *An Introduction to Mathematics*, CH 2
——. *Science and the Modern World*, CH 10
SANTAYANA. *The Realm of Essence*, CH 1–11
DEWEY. *Logic, the Theory of Inquiry*, CH 13–14
BLANSHARD. *The Nature of Thought*, CH 16–17
B. RUSSELL. *Principles of Mathematics*, CH 4–8
——. *The Problems of Philosophy*, CH 9–10
——. *Introduction to Mathematical Philosophy*, CH 13, 15–17
——. *The Analysis of Mind*, LECT 11
——. *The Analysis of Matter*, CH 27
——. *Human Knowledge, Its Scope and Limits*, PART II, CH 3, 10; PART IV, CH 8

Chapter 97: VIRTUE AND VICE

INTRODUCTION

IN their currently popular connotations, the words "virtue" and "vice" have extremely limited significance. Virtue tends to be identified with chastity or at least with conformity to the prevailing standards of sexual behavior. The popular notion of vice retains a little more of the traditional meaning, insofar as it implies injury to a person's character or health as the result of strong *habitual* addictions. But, as in the case of virtue, the things which are popularly called "vices" are largely concerned with pleasures or sensual indulgences.

In the tradition of the great books, however, the scope of these terms and the range of the problems in which they are involved seem to be co-extensive with morality; or, in other words, with the broadest consideration of good and evil in human life, with what is right and wrong for man not only to do, but also to wish or desire, and even to think. For some of the great moral philosophers, other terms—such as duty for Marcus Aurelius and Kant, or pleasure and utility for Mill—seem to be more central. But for Plato, Aristotle, and Aquinas virtue is a basic moral principle. By reference to it they define the good man, the good life, and the good society. Yet even for them it is not the first principle of ethics. They define virtue itself by reference to a more ultimate good—happiness. For them the virtues are ordered to happiness as means to an end.

THE ANCIENT ENUMERATION of particular virtues may show the range of things comprehended under the notion of virtue generally. It may also further sharpen the contrast with the contemporary tendency to use the words "virtue" and "vice" as if they applied only to matters which fall within the sphere of one of the virtues. That one is the virtue which both Plato and Aristotle call "temperance," and which they conceive as concerned chiefly with the bodily appetites and pleasures. Plato and Aristotle give somewhat different enumerations, but courage and justice are as fundamental for them as temperance; and when certain virtues come later to be classified as the cardinal or principal virtues, these three are always named together. In that classification, there is a fourth—prudence or, as it is sometimes called, "practical wisdom."

Plato's enumeration of the virtues in the *Republic* also adds wisdom to temperance, courage, and justice. This indicates at once that the ancient conception of virtue as the quality which makes a man good, extends to his mind as well as to his character—to the sphere of thinking and knowing as well as to desire, emotion, and action. Aristotle makes this explicit by dividing all the virtues into moral and intellectual, or excellences of character and of mind. He names five intellectual virtues: in addition to wisdom and prudence (which he distinguishes as speculative and practical wisdom), he lists art, science, and what he calls "intuitive reason," which Aquinas later calls "understanding."

The division of the virtues into moral and intellectual leads, in Aristotle's analysis, to the further distinction between those intellectual virtues—understanding, science, wisdom—which represent the possession of speculative insight or theoretic knowledge, and those—art and prudence—which represent skill in practical thinking or in the application of knowledge to production and action respectively. Because it is concerned with action, or moral conduct, the virtue of prudence is most closely associated with the moral virtues of justice, courage, and temperance. The grouping together by Aquinas of these four as the cardinal virtues carries the implication that the remaining four (*i.e.*, art and the three virtues of the speculative reason) play a secondary role. The implication is simply that a man may be made good as a scientist or good as an artist by the acquisition of these virtues, but he is not made good as a man by these virtues, nor do they enable him to lead a good life and achieve happiness, as do the moral virtues accompanied by prudence.

In line with the principle by which he regards certain virtues as cardinal or indispensable for human rectitude and welfare, the Christian moralist goes further than the moral philosopher in developing the theory of virtue. Considering man's limitations and his fallen nature, he holds that more than all the natural virtues (*i.e.*, the virtues which men can attain by their own effort) is required for salvation—for the supernatural end of eternal happiness. Faith, hope, and charity, according to St. Paul, are indispensable to lift man's life to a plane, and direct it to a goal, which exceed his nature. These gifts of God's grace are subsequently treated by Augustine and Aquinas as virtues—supernatural, not natural virtues. Aquinas specifically calls them "theological virtues" to distinguish them from other supernatural endowments, such as the infused moral virtues and the gifts of the Holy Ghost.

THE READER MAY OBSERVE that of all the virtues so far named, only the three theological virtues are not the subject of separate chapters in this collection of great ideas. The chapters on COURAGE, JUSTICE, TEMPERANCE, PRUDENCE, WISDOM may include discussions of these qualities which do not specifically treat them as virtues. Certainly that is true of the chapters on ART and SCIENCE, and the chapter on PRINCIPLE, wherein the virtue of intuitive reason or the understanding of first principles is considered. Nevertheless, that all but one of these chapters bear the name of the traditionally recognized virtues indicates how widely and variously they make their appearance throughout the great books—by example and comment in poetry and history as well as by definition and analysis in the ethical and political treatises. In contrast, the theological virtues appear only in Christian, not pagan literature, and then mainly in religious rather than secular writing.

It is also of interest to note the relation which this chapter bears to those dealing with other fundamental concepts of moral philosophy or theology. Some of the terms mentioned in the foregoing paragraphs—duty, pleasure, happiness, good—name chapters which are co-implicated with this one in the problem of how men should live and what they should seek. The Outline of Topics will reveal still others—knowledge, desire, emotion, reason, will, wealth, honor, friendship, teaching, family, state, citizen, law, sin, and grace—each of which is (or indicates) the title of a chapter that treats of matters related to virtue as cause or consequence, as psychological factor or external condition.

One chapter not yet mentioned has maximum relevance for most of the authors who offer some analysis of virtue. The chapter on HABIT treats an idea that is crucial to the definition of virtue. Aquinas, for example, allocates the discussion of virtue and vice to his Treatise on Habit in the *Summa Theologica*. He divides this treatise into questions concerning habits in general and questions concerning good and evil habits—or virtues and vices—in particular. But the notion that virtue combines the elements of habit and goodness is not peculiarly his. With varying degrees of emphasis and explicitness, it appears in Plato and Aristotle, in Augustine, Bacon, Hegel, and James. Kant alone expressly dissents, declaring that virtue "is not to be defined and esteemed merely as *habit*, and . . . as a long *custom* acquired by the practice of morally good actions."

THE DISCUSSION OF VIRTUE originates in the dialogues of Plato and the *Ethics* of Aristotle with a number of related questions. Meno's opening question—"Can you tell me, Socrates, whether virtue is acquired by teaching or by practice; or if by neither teaching nor practice, then whether it comes to man by nature, or in some other way?"—requires, in the opinion of Socrates, other questions to be faced: what virtue is, how virtue is related to knowledge, whether virtue is one or many, and if many, how the several particular virtues are related to one another.

In the course of the dialogue, each of the alternatives is considered. If virtue were identical with knowledge, it could be taught and learned just as geometry is. If virtue were simply a habit, it could be acquired by practice, that is, by the repetition of similar acts. But neither practice nor teaching seems by itself to explain how men come by virtue, and even less why virtuous fathers should so often fail to produce virtue in their sons. Yet Socrates does not completely dismiss these possibilities or the possibility considered at the end, that "virtue comes to the virtuous by the gift of God." What truth there is in each of them, he concludes, cannot be determined until we know precisely what virtue is.

Another dialogue, the *Protagoras*, pursues a similar inquiry and seems to reach a similarly indeterminate conclusion. The relation of virtue to knowledge here leads to the question whether "wisdom and temperance and courage and justice and holiness" are "five names of the same thing." To the extent that each depends on knowledge of what is good and evil, they would seem to be, if not identical, at least inseparable aspects of the same thing. Protagoras objects on the score that a man may be courageous and at the same time "utterly unrighteous, unholy, intemperate, ignorant." But Socrates finally gets him to admit reluctantly that courage consists in knowledge, and cowardice in ignorance, of what is and is not dangerous.

It was Protagoras, however, who originally contended against Socrates that virtue can be taught. The reduction of all the virtues to some form of knowledge would therefore seem to confirm his opinion. Socrates, in winning the argument about virtue and knowledge, seems to overthrow his own view that virtue cannot be taught. "The result of our discussion," Socrates says at the end, "appears to me to be singular. For if the argument had a human voice, that voice would be heard laughing at us and saying: 'Protagoras and Socrates, you are strange beings; there are you, Socrates, who were saying that virtue cannot be taught, contradicting yourself now by your attempt to prove that all things are knowledge, including justice and temperance and courage—which tends to show that virtue can certainly be taught. . . . Protagoras, on the other hand, who started by saying that it might be taught, is now eager to prove it to be anything rather than knowledge.' "

The only way "this terrible confusion of our ideas" might be cleared up, Socrates suggests, is for the conversation to go on "until we ascertain what virtue is." But that particular conversation does not go on; nor do the definitions of virtue which are proposed in other Platonic dialogues seem to be decisive on the point whether virtue is knowledge or whether it can be taught. In the *Laws*, for example, the Athenian Stranger, saying that "harmony of the soul, taken as a whole, is virtue," proposes that education should consist in training "the first instincts of virtue in children" by producing suitable habits in them. But his training does not seem to be, like ordinary teaching, the inculcation of knowledge. It is "training in respect of pleasure and pain," whereby we are led to hate what we ought to hate and love what we ought to love.

In the *Republic*, Socrates compares the harmony produced by virtue in the soul with the harmony of the parts in a healthy body. "Virtue is the health and beauty and well-being of the soul," he declares, "and vice the disease and weakness and deformity of the same." Though wisdom consists in the rule of the other parts of the soul by reason in the light of "knowledge of what is for the interest of each of the parts and of the whole," it does not seem to be the whole of virtue, nor does Socrates suggest that men become virtuous simply by becoming wise. On the contrary, he intimates that "good practices lead to virtue, and evil practices to vice," and that, like certain bodily qualities, the "virtues of the soul . . . can be implanted by habit and exercise."

It is sometimes supposed that Aristotle differs from Plato on fundamental points in the theory of virtue. The fact that Aristotle criticizes Socrates for "thinking that all the virtues are forms of practical wisdom," seems to imply a basic disagreement on the relation of virtue to knowledge. But Aristotle also remarks that Socrates was right "in saying they implied practical wisdom." His own view that the moral virtues of courage, temperance, and justice are inseparable from the intellectual virtue of prudence does not seem to differ substantially from the statements of Socrates that "virtue must be a sort of wisdom or prudence" and that "virtue is either wholly or partly wisdom." Such difference as there is appears to be not so much in what is being affirmed or denied as in the manner of statement or analysis, and beyond that, perhaps, in a method of exposition which permits Aristotle to give definite answers to questions Plato's dialogues often leave unanswered.

Aristotle's analysis, of course, sometimes changes the questions themselves to make them answerable, but this is not always so. His summary of existing opinions concerning the acquisition of virtue—that "some think we are made good by nature, others by habituation, others by teaching"—is nearly equivalent, as an enumeration of the possibilities, to Meno's opening question. But where Socrates in answering Meno contents himself with suggesting that there may be some truth in each possibility as against the others, Aristotle definitely affirms that the whole truth about the matter combines all three factors. "There are three things," he writes, "which make men good and virtuous: these are nature, habit, rational principle." Even Socrates' final point, that virtue may be a gift of God, seems to be affirmed by Aristotle's comment that, in effecting virtue, "nature's part evidently does not depend on us, but as a result of some divine causes is present in those who are truly fortunate."

But in the case of two Platonic questions—the one about the relation of virtue to knowledge and the other about the unity of virtue—Aristotle's analysis transforms the problem. His basic distinction between moral and intellectual virtue turns the question about virtue and knowledge into one concerning the role which one very special kind of knowledge, represented by the virtue of prudence, plays in the formation and operation of good moral habits— habits in the sphere of action and passion, or of the will and the emotions. By substituting a number of distinct intellectual virtues for the single term 'knowledge,' Aristotle can definitely answer both Yes and No to the question. Not all the intellectual virtues, not art and science, or even speculative wisdom, are needed for courage, temperance, and justice; but if by "knowledge" is meant nothing more than prudence, then Aristotle affirms these moral virtues to involve knowledge of a sort.

The distinction between moral and intellectual virtue also enables Aristotle to reformulate the problem of the unity of virtue. Instead of asking whether there is only one virtue, having many aspects, or many distinct virtues, he considers which virtues are interdependent and which can exist separately from one another. Virtue has unity in the inseparability of the moral virtues from one another and from prudence. The sailor who appears to be courageous without being temperate, or the thief who appears to be prudent without being just, has only the appearance of these virtues. But though Aristotle uses the phrase "perfect virtue" to signify both the integration of these virtues and the perfection of each when it is integrated with the others, he does not include all the particular virtues in the unity of virtue. Some, like art and science, can exist apart from prudence or the moral virtues, and they from it.

By showing how all of the moral virtues depend upon prudence or practical wisdom, Aristotle thinks he is able to "refute the argument . . . that the virtues exist in separation from each other." But he does not find any greater unity of the virtues than is involved in their inseparability as a result of their common dependence on prudence. Following Aristotle, Aquinas criticizes those who assert a more profound unity by claiming that prudence, temperance, fortitude, and justice signify "only certain general conditions . . . to be found in all the virtues." This, according to Aquinas, is tantamount to denying that they are distinct habits.

Insisting that they are really distinct as habits, Aquinas nevertheless suggests that "these four virtues qualify one another by a kind of overflow. For," he explains, "the qualities of prudence overflow into the other virtues in so far as they are directed by prudence. And each of the others overflows into the rest, for the reason that whoever can do what is more difficult, can do what is less difficult." The man who "can curb his desires for the pleasures of touch, which is a very hard thing to do . . . is more able to check his daring in dangers of death . . . which is much easier"; the man who can withstand the "dangers of death, which is a matter of great difficulty, is more able to remain firm against the onslaught of pleasures."

As for justice, Aquinas holds that legal justice, "by commanding the other virtues . . . draws them all into the service of the commonweal." Aristotle also sees a certain unification of the virtues, at least all the moral virtues, in terms of justice—the kind of justice he calls "general" to distinguish it from the special virtue of justice. He conceives general justice as comprising all the moral virtues, including special justice, insofar as all these virtues are directed toward the welfare of society and the good of other men. "Justice in this sense," he writes, "is not a part of virtue, but virtue entire." Holding that it "is complete virtue, not absolutely, but in relation to our neighbor," he also adds that "it is complete because he who possesses it can exercise his virtue not only in himself, but towards his neighbor as well."

Some writers tend in the opposite direction toward a greater separation of the virtues. Justice, according to Marcus Aurelius, is prior to the other virtues, for "in justice the other virtues have their foundation." In suggesting that a man can secure "a favorable and commodious interpretation of his vices" by coloring them in the light of his virtues, Bacon seems to accept the conjunction of virtue with vice which is expressed in the familiar phrase "the defects of one's virtues." That a gentleman may with honor be permitted certain failings is similarly implied by Dr. Johnson's reference to "the genteel vices."

This comfortable doctrine that a man can be truly virtuous in some aspects of character while vicious in others seems, however, to be rejected by Montaigne and Kant, as well as by Plato and Aristotle. The standard of Christian virtue is even more stringent. What may appear to be virtues are, according to Augustine, "rather vices than virtues so long as there is no reference to God in the matter. For although some suppose that virtues which have a reference only to themselves, and are desired only on their own account, are yet true and genuine virtues, the fact is that even they are inflated with pride, and are therefore to be reckoned vices."

The theological virtue of charity—the love of God—is held by the theologians to be indispensable to the perfection of all the other virtues in a Christian life. Not only, according to Aquinas, do faith and hope lack "the perfect character of virtue without charity," but all the other virtues are imperfect in its absence.

"It is possible by means of human works," he writes, "to acquire the moral virtues in so far as they produce good works that are directed to an end not surpassing the natural ability of man. And when they are acquired thus, they can be without charity, even as they were in many of the pagans. But in so far as they produce good works in relation to a supernatural last end, thus they have the character of virtue truly and perfectly, and cannot be acquired by human acts, but are infused by God. Such moral virtues cannot be without charity. . . . Only the infused virtues are perfect, and deserve to be called virtues absolutely. . . . The other virtues, those, namely, that are acquired, are virtues in a restricted sense."

THAT VIRTUE IS GOOD and vice evil seems to go undisputed in the tradition of the great books, even by Machiavelli who bemoans the "necessity" of vice in a successful prince. But unanimity on this point does not preclude a variety of answers to the question, What is the good of virtue?

Is it an end in itself, or a means, and if a means, what end does it serve? Moreover, what is the principle of goodness in the virtues? Does it lie in the rule of reason, in conformity to nature, in obedience to the moral law and the imperative of duty, in submission to God's will? Or are the virtues good only to the extent that they are useful and profitable? To the individual alone or to society as well? As these questions are differently answered, different conceptions of virtue appear.

Marcus Aurelius gives the simplest and most familiar answer. Virtue is its own reward. "What more dost thou want," the Stoic asks, "when thou hast done a man a service? Art thou not content that thou hast done something conformable to thy nature, and dost thou seek to be paid for it?" The virtues are not only self-rewarding but they are the only things in which a good man can take delight. "When thou wishest to delight thyself," Aurelius says, "think of the virtues of those who live with thee . . . For nothing delights so much as the examples of the virtues."

Locke seems to make profit or utility the source of goodness in the virtues. "God, having, by an inseparable connexion, joined virtue and public happiness together," Locke writes, "and made the practice thereof necessary to the preservation of society, and visibly beneficial to all with whom the virtuous man has to do, it is no wonder that everyone should not only allow, but recommend and magnify those rules to others, from whose observance of them he is sure to reap advantage to himself."

The virtues seem to become conventional in Locke's view. They are whatever the members of a particular society deem advantageous. "Virtue and vice are names pretended, and supposed, everywhere to stand for actions in their nature, right and wrong; and as far as they are really so applied, they are so far coincident with the divine law . . . But yet, whatever is pretended," Locke adds, "this is visible, that these names, virtue and vice, in the particular instances of their application, through the several nations and societies of men in the world, are constantly attributed only to such actions as, in each country and society, are in reputation or discredit. . . . Thus, the measure of what is everywhere called and esteemed virtue and vice, is the approbation or dislike, praise or blame," which establishes itself in a society "according to the judgment, maxims, or fashion of that place. . . . That this is the common measure of virtue and vice, will appear," Locke thinks, "to anyone who considers, that though that passes for vice in one country, which is counted a virtue, or at least not a vice, in another; yet everywhere, virtue and praise, vice and blame, go together."

Hobbes also regards the names of the virtues as "inconstant names" varying according to "the nature, disposition and interest of the speaker . . . for one man calleth *wisdom*, what another calleth *fear*; and one *cruelty*, what another *justice*; one *prodigality*, what another *magnanimity*." Yet this does not prevent Hobbes from proposing a list of virtues which derive their goodness from the natural law. "All men agree on this," he writes, "that peace is good; and therefore also the ways or means of peace, which . . . are *justice*, *gratitude*, *modesty*, *equity*, *mercy*, and the rest of the Laws of Nature, are good; that is to say, *Moral Virtues*; and their contrary *Vices*, evil."

Moral philosophy, according to Hobbes, is "the science of Virtue and Vice" and "therefore the true doctrine of the Laws of Nature is the true moral philosophy." Though other writers of moral philosophy "acknowledge the same virtues and vices," Hobbes thinks they do not see "wherein consisted their goodness; nor that they come to be praised as the means of peaceable, sociable, and comfortable living."

Like Kant, he criticizes Aristotle's doctrine of the mean; or, as Hobbes refers to it, the notion that virtue consists in "a mediocrity of the passions; as if not the cause, but the degree of daring, made *fortitude*; or not the cause, but the quantity of a gift, made *liberality*." The cause of virtue, according to Hobbes, is the natural law, commanding men to do whatever is required for peace and self-preservation. In terms of a quite different conception of law and duty, Kant also says that "the difference between virtue and vice cannot be sought in the degree in which certain maxims are followed, but only in the specific *quality* of the maxims. In other words, the vaunted principle of Aristotle, that virtue is the *mean* between two vices, is false."

It is not Kant but Spinoza who seems to bear an affinity to Hobbes in the theory of virtue. Both make self-preservation the end which determines the direction of virtuous conduct. Both consider civil peace or the good of others in relation to self. Both draw up lists of moral virtues from their enumeration of the passions, Hobbes by reference to natural law, Spinoza in terms of adequate ideas of God's nature. Spinoza identifies virtue with power and holds that "the more each person strives and is able to seek his own profit, that is to say, to preserve his own being, the more virtue does he possess." But though he makes "the endeavor after self-preservation . . . the primary and only foundation of virtue," he conceives self-preservation itself to have its foundation in knowledge of God.

"To act in conformity with virtue," Spinoza maintains, "is to act according to the guidance of reason, and every effort which we make through reason is an effort to understand, and therefore the highest good of those who follow after virtue is to know God, that is to say, it is a good which is common to all men, and can be equally possessed by all in so far as they are of the same nature." In direct consequence, he declares that "the good which everyone who follows after virtue seeks for himself, he will desire for other men; and his desire on their behalf will be greater in proportion as he has greater knowledge of God."

ALL THOSE WHO RELATE virtue to happiness do not do so in the same way. "The multiplication of happiness," writes Mill, "is, according to the utilitarian ethics, the object of virtue." He attributes to "a very imperfect state of the world's arrangements" the fact that "anyone can best serve the happiness of others by the absolute sacrifice of his own; yet so long as the world is in that imperfect state," he goes on to say, "the readiness to make such a sacrifice is the highest virtue which can be found in man."

But Mill repeatedly insists that only an increase of happiness justifies sacrifice, and only its contribution to happiness makes virtue good. He criticizes the Stoics for striving "to raise themselves above all concern about anything but virtue" and for supposing that "he who has that has everything. . . . No claim of this description is made for the virtuous man by the utilitarian doctrine."

While admitting that virtue may come to be desired disinterestedly, as an ingredient of happiness rather than as a means to it, Mill does not regard virtue as a natural and necessary condition of happiness. "Virtue, according to the utilitarian doctrine, is not naturally and originally part of the end, but it is capable of becoming so." If there are some who do not desire virtue, either because it gives them no pleasure or because the lack of it causes them no pain, they can be happy without it.

The view taken by Plato and Aristotle seems to be directly contrary. All things which have ends appointed by their nature, Socrates argues at the beginning of the *Republic*, must also be capable of virtues or excellences whereby to achieve their ends. If happiness is the end of the soul or of human life, then we must look to such excellences as the virtue of justice and temperance to provide the means. When Glaucon and Adeimantus ask Socrates to prove that only the virtuous man can be happy, he undertakes the long analysis of the parts of the soul and the parts of the state to discover the virtues appropriate to each and to the whole. When the virtues are defined, Glaucon admits that the question he originally asked "has now become ridiculous."

The answer to the question is evident as soon as virtue and happiness are seen to be reciprocal notions, like cause and effect. Yet Aristotle's definition of moral virtue as a habit of choice, consisting in a mean—a mean relative to ourselves, determined by reason or as the prudent man would determine it—does not immediately explain why happiness is defined as "the realization and perfect exercise of virtue." The connection between virtue as means and happiness as end becomes apparent only in terms of the conception that happiness is the ultimate end *because* it includes all good things and leaves nothing to be desired.

As an object of desire, as something worth having in itself, virtue is only one type of good. It does not constitute happiness. Happiness, according to Aristotle, includes as well such bodily and external goods as health and pleasure, friendship and wealth. But unlike these other goods, the virtues alone are capable of producing happiness because, in Aristotle's view, they are the causes of our thinking and acting well with respect to all other goods.

"We do not acquire or preserve virtue by the help of external goods," Aristotle says, "but external goods by the help of virtue." This applies to health and pleasures, no less than to wealth and friends. Because the moral virtues, together with prudence, direct our desires, determine our choices, and govern our actions in accordance with reason's discrimination between real and apparent goods, the exercise of these habits results in happiness or living well. But since external goods are goods of fortune and not entirely within our control, Aristotle finds it necessary to qualify the definition of happiness. To the statement that the happy man is one "who is active in accordance with complete virtue," he adds that he is one "who is sufficiently equipped with external goods, not for some chance period, but throughout a complete life."

According to Kant, "the connexion of virtue and happiness may be understood in two ways: either the endeavor to be virtuous and the rational pursuit of happiness are not two distinct actions, but absolutely identical . . . or the connexion consists in this, that virtue produces happiness as something distinct from the consciousness of virtue, as a cause produces an effect." Kant thinks that both the Stoic and Epicurean doctrines choose the first of these alternatives. They differ from each other, in his opinion, only in the way they conceive the identity of virtue and happiness. "The Epicurean notion of virtue," he writes, "was already involved in the maxim: to promote one's own happiness. According to the Stoics, on the other hand, the feeling of happiness was already contained in the consciousness of virtue."

Kant's own resolution of what he calls "the antinomy of practical reason" seems to depend on his conception of the *summum bonum*. For him it is not happiness; it consists rather in being worthy of happiness through doing one's duty. "Morality," he says, "is not properly the doctrine how we should *make* ourselves happy, but how we should become *worthy* of happiness." Under the moral law, to be happy is not a duty, but to be worthy of happiness is. In Kant's view, therefore, virtue is related to happiness through the medium of duty. Virtue, he declares, is "a coincidence of the rational will with every duty firmly settled in the character." It is "the moral strength of a man's will in his obedience to duty."

But in addition to being the will's strength in overcoming obstacles—"the natural inclinations which may come into conflict with the moral purpose"—virtue, or rather "the imperative, which commands the duty of virtue," includes "besides the notion of constraint, that of an end." Not an end that we have, Kant explains, but one that "we ought to have," an end "which, therefore, pure practical reason has in itself, whose highest, unconditional end (which, however, continues to be a duty) consists in this: that virtue is its own end, and by deserving well of men is also its own reward."

THE ISSUE BETWEEN KANT and Aristotle concerning the good of virtue, as a means or an end, involves the whole of their moral philosophy. It goes to the central conflict between their fundamental principles, which is discussed in the chapters on DUTY and HAPPINESS. Fundamental differences in political philosophy also arise from different views of virtue in relation to the forms of government and the ends of the state.

The ancients, for example, define aristocracy in terms of virtue. The point is not only that aristocracy is a form of government in which the few who are most virtuous rule; it is also that form of government the principle of which is virtue, as liberty is the principle of democracy, and wealth of oligarchy. Montesquieu makes virtue the principle in republican government, in contrast to honor as the principle in monarchies and fear in despotism. "What I distinguish by the name of virtue, in a republic," he explains, "is the love of one's country—that is, the love of equality. It is not a moral, nor a Christian, but a political virtue; and it is the spring which sets republican government in motion, as honor is the spring which gives motion to monarchy." Since for Montesquieu both democracy and aristocracy are forms of republican government, the former rests on virtue as much as the latter.

Agreeing that the conditions Montesquieu sets for republican government "could not exist without virtue," Rousseau criticizes him for failing to see that, "the sovereign authority being everywhere the same, the same principle should be found in every well-constituted state, in a greater or less degree, it is true, according to the form of government." So for Mill, virtue defines the aim of good government itself, without respect to particular forms. "The most important point of excellence which any form of government can possess," he writes, "is to promote the virtue and intelligence of the people themselves."

The virtues which a government promotes, however, may be those of the good citizen rather than the good man. This distinction between civic and moral virtue occupies the ancients, related as it is to the problem of the virtuous man living in a bad society—a problem which Socrates actually faces, as well as discusses, in the *Apology* and the *Crito*.

"The virtue of the citizen," Aristotle writes, "must be relative to the constitution of the state of which he is a member. . . . Hence it is evident that the good citizen need not of necessity possess the virtue which makes a good man." Yet "in some states, the good man and the good citizen are the same."

In this vein Aquinas, considering whether the laws should try to make men good, says of a tyrannical or unjust law that "in so far as it has something of the nature of law, its aim is that the citizens be good." At least "it aims at being obeyed by them; and this," he adds, "is to make them good, not absolutely, but with respect to that particular government." But Aquinas also contemplates the need for disobeying a civil ordinance if it demands too great a sacrifice of virtue by requiring the citizen to violate the natural or the divine law. As Rousseau later says, "a man's duty" takes precedence over "that of a citizen."

OUTLINE OF TOPICS

REFERENCES

References are listed by volume number (in bold type), author's name, and page number. Bible references are to book, chapter, and verse of the Authorized King James version of the Bible. The abbreviation "esp" calls the reader's attention to one or more especially relevant parts of a whole reference; "passim" signifies that the topic is discussed intermittently rather than continuously in the work or passage cited. Where the work as a whole is relevant to the topic, the page numbers refer to the entire work. For general guidance in the use of *The Great Ideas,* consult the Preface.

1. Diverse conceptions of virtue

5 EURIPIDES, 330, 382–383, 429–430
7 PLATO, 101, 174–190, 257–276, 530, 557, 650, 686–690
8 ARISTOTLE, 329–330
9 ARISTOTLE, 347–349, 351–352, 387–394, 608–609
12 EPICTETUS, 144–145
12 AURELIUS, 259, 275, 277–278, 285
14 PLUTARCH, 265
17 PLOTINUS, 6–10, 24, 32–33, 107–108, 344–345
18 AUGUSTINE, 380–385, 517–519
19 AQUINAS, 508–509
20 AQUINAS, 24–25, 64–65, 105–108
23 HOBBES, 66–68 passim, 92
25 MONTAIGNE, 389–390, 391
31 SPINOZA, 395, 422–450
32 MILTON, 46–47
35 LOCKE, 109, 230–231
37 FIELDING, 38–39, 316
42 KANT, 173–174, 273–277, 366–369, 371–372, 376–379
43 MILL, 303–305
46 HEGEL, 56–57
51 TOLSTOY, 198–203

1*a*. The relation between knowledge and virtue

OLD TESTAMENT: *Genesis,* 3 / *Proverbs,* 1:20–2:22; 8:1–15,20
APOCRYPHA: *Wisdom of Solomon,* 1:1–7; 6; 8; 9:9–10:14; 14:22–27
NEW TESTAMENT: *Romans,* 2:17–23; 7:15–25
7 PLATO, 7, 12–13, 33–37, 38–64, 69–71, 74–76, 174–190, 306–308, 337, 388–401, 439–441, 530–531, 669–670
8 ARISTOTLE, 160
9 ARISTOTLE, 355–361 passim, 393–394, 395–398
12 EPICTETUS, 131
12 AURELIUS, 283–284
18 AUGUSTINE, 55–56, 266, 271
19 AQUINAS, 6–7
20 AQUINAS, 30–31, 39–40, 608–609
25 MONTAIGNE, 208
26 SHAKESPEARE, 408
30 BACON, 26–27
31 DESCARTES, 49–50
31 SPINOZA, 428, 454–456
32 MILTON, 41–42, 163–164, 262–264
35 LOCKE, 186
35 BERKELEY, 432
35 HUME, 451, 452
36 SWIFT, 165–166
42 KANT, 260–261, 282–283
46 HEGEL, 48–54 passim, 280–281
51 TOLSTOY, 195–201, 244–245

1*b*. The unity of virtue and the plurality of virtues

7 PLATO, 48–50, 58–64, 175, 346–355, 605–607, 795–797
9 ARISTOTLE, 347–348, 377–378
12 AURELIUS, 303
17 PLOTINUS, 9–10
20 AQUINAS, 49–50, 70–72, 119–120, 488–489
25 MONTAIGNE, 204
33 PASCAL, 175
42 KANT, 373

1*c*. The doctrine of virtue as a mean between the extremes of vice

7 PLATO, 338–339
9 ARISTOTLE, 349, 351–355, 361–387
11 NICOMACHUS, 820
17 PLOTINUS, 7
20 AQUINAS, 66–70
22 CHAUCER, 424
25 MONTAIGNE, 89
29 CERVANTES, 256, 291, 362
30 BACON, 79–81
31 DESCARTES, 48–49
31 SPINOZA, 437–438
33 PASCAL, 234–235, 238
42 KANT, 376–377

1*d*. Virtue as an intrinsic good: its relation to happiness

7 PLATO, 275–284, 309–310, 418–421
9 ARISTOTLE, 342–345, 423–424, 430–434, 527–530, 536–537, 600–601
12 EPICTETUS, 108–110, 206–210, 233
12 AURELIUS, 262, 273
17 PLOTINUS, 7–8, 74–75
18 AUGUSTINE, 270–271, 507–513
19 AQUINAS, 618

14 PLUTARCH, 156, 174–175
17 PLOTINUS, 10–11
20 AQUINAS, 12–13, 63–65, 223
22 CHAUCER, 274–276
23 HOBBES, 86, 96
25 MONTAIGNE, 43, 307–308
27 SHAKESPEARE, 36
28 HARVEY, 455–456
30 BACON, 76–78
31 SPINOZA, 453
38 ROUSSEAU, 337–338, 343–345
40 GIBBON, 192
42 KANT, 263–264, 303–304
43 MILL, 367–368, 459–460, 469–470
44 BOSWELL, 413
44 HEGEL, 132
49 DARWIN, 310, 318
52 DOSTOEVSKY, 19–20, 38–40
53 JAMES, 886–888
54 FREUD, 758–759

4*b*. The role of teaching in the spheres of moral and intellectual virtue

OLD TESTAMENT: *Proverbs,* 5:7–13
APOCRYPHA: *Ecclesiasticus,* 7:23; 30:3
NEW TESTAMENT: *Titus,* 2:1–3:2
7 PLATO, 26–37, 38–64, 65–84, 183–190, 258–259, 320–355, 389–398, 556–558, 796–799, 801–802, 809–810
9 ARISTOTLE, 345, 348, 350–351, 434–435, 542–548
12 EPICTETUS, 108–110, 175–177
14 PLUTARCH, 121–122, 156–158, 726, 782–788
18 AUGUSTINE, 696–697
20 AQUINAS, 226–227
25 MONTAIGNE, 55–62, 69–72, 321
40 GIBBON, 34, 435
42 KANT, 264, 327, 356–360
46 HEGEL, 65
51 TOLSTOY, 47–48
52 DOSTOEVSKY, 83–88 passim
54 FREUD, 122, 573–574, 592, 870

4*c*. Training or practice as cause of virtue or vice: the process of habit formation

OLD TESTAMENT: *Jeremiah,* 13:23
5 EURIPIDES, 265–266
7 PLATO, 174–190, 329–331, 389–390, 474–475, 649, 653
9 ARISTOTLE, 345, 348–349, 350–351, 389, 434–435
12 EPICTETUS, 106–108, 187–188
12 AURELIUS, 271
20 AQUINAS, 13–15, 108–109
25 MONTAIGNE, 176–177, 200–205, 390–393
30 BACON, 69–70, 78–81
35 LOCKE, 197–198
42 KANT, 327
43 MILL, 449–450
46 HEGEL, 132–133
49 DARWIN, 311, 313–314
53 JAMES, 78–83, 711–712

4*d*. The role of the family and the state in the development of moral virtue

4*d*(1) The influence of parental authority on the formation of character

OLD TESTAMENT: *Deuteronomy,* 6:6–7 / *Proverbs,* 1:8–9; 4:1–13; 6:20–24; 23:13–24:34; 29:15,17
APOCRYPHA: *Tobit,* 4:1–19 / *Ecclesiasticus,* 7:23–24; 30:1–13
7 PLATO, 26–30, 45–47, 186–187, 687–688, 745–746
9 ARISTOTLE, 434–435, 454–455, 541
12 AURELIUS, 253–256
14 PLUTARCH, 286–287
18 AUGUSTINE, 9–10, 18–19, 67
20 AQUINAS, 318–321
22 CHAUCER, 367–368
25 MONTAIGNE, 63–64, 184–187, 414
31 SPINOZA, 419
35 LOCKE, 36–40 passim
36 SWIFT, 29–31, 166
38 MONTESQUIEU, 15, 22–23
42 KANT, 420–421
44 BOSWELL, 199–200
46 HEGEL, 61, 134–135
52 DOSTOEVSKY, 369–373 passim, 395–398 passim
54 FREUD, 704–707, 794–795

4*d*(2) The moral use of rewards and punishments: the role of precept and counsel, praise and blame

OLD TESTAMENT: *Psalms,* 94:10–13 / *Proverbs,* 1:8–9,20–33
APOCRYPHA: *Wisdom of Solomon,* 12:25–26 / *Ecclesiasticus,* 30:1–13
NEW TESTAMENT: *I Thessalonians,* 2:11–13 / *Titus,* 2 / *Hebrews,* 12:5–11
5 AESCHYLUS, 86–87, 88
5 ARISTOPHANES, 504–506
7 PLATO, 45, 283–285, 313, 426–427, 643, 745–746, 760–761
9 ARISTOTLE, 359–360, 434–435
14 PLUTARCH, 41–42, 45
18 AUGUSTINE, 4–7
20 AQUINAS, 186–187
22 CHAUCER, 401–432
23 HOBBES, 141
25 MONTAIGNE, 73–74, 181–183, 184–185, 300–306
35 LOCKE, 229–231 passim
37 FIELDING, 41
38 MONTESQUIEU, 37–38, 39–40, 86
40 GIBBON, 92
42 KANT, 325–327
43 FEDERALIST, 217
43 MILL, 302–312 passim, 457–461 passim, esp 458, 464
44 BOSWELL, 199–200, 314
49 DARWIN, 322
54 FREUD, 757, 758–759, 792–795, 876

4d(3) The guidance of laws and customs: the limits of positive law with respect to commanding virtue and prohibiting vice

5 EURIPIDES, 399
7 PLATO, 271–272, 377–379, 607–608, 642–648, 650, 735–738
9 ARISTOTLE, 378, 458–460 passim, 462, 465–466, 536–542
14 PLUTARCH, 32–48, 61–64, 70–74
15 TACITUS, 57–58
18 AUGUSTINE, 662–663
20 AQUINAS, 213–214, 231–233, 244–245, 246–247, 250–251, 261–262
21 DANTE, 77–78, 129–132
23 HOBBES, 131
25 MONTAIGNE, 131–132
27 SHAKESPEARE, 177, 190
30 BACON, 78–81
32 MILTON, 325–326, 381–412
35 LOCKE, 105–106, 110–111
35 HUME, 485
38 MONTESQUIEU, 13–17, 18–19, 21–25, 44–45, 47–50, 87–88, 119, 137–142
38 ROUSSEAU, 434–435
40 GIBBON, 92, 291–292
41 GIBBON, 93–94
42 KANT, 367, 373
43 MILL, 269–271, 272–273, 278–281 passim, 286–287, 295–296, 300–301, 301–323, 335, 456, 457–458
44 BOSWELL 222–223
46 HEGEL, 56–57
49 DARWIN, 317
52 DOSTOEVSKY, 28–32
54 FREUD, 758

4d(4) The influence on moral character of poetry, music, and other arts: the guidance of history and example

APOCRYPHA: *Wisdom of Solomon*, 4:1–2
NEW TESTAMENT: *I Corinthians*, 10:5–11/ *II Thessalonians*, 3:7–9 / *I Peter*, 2:21–23
5 ARISTOPHANES, 488–506, 576–577, 600–614
7 PLATO, 320–355, 388–401, 427–434, 653–662, 675–676, 724–730
9 ARISTOTLE, 542–548
14 PLUTARCH, 43, 195
15 TACITUS, 146
18 AUGUSTINE, 6–7, 13–14, 83–85, 147–149, 153–157, 202–203
22 CHAUCER, 550
25 MONTAIGNE, 197–199, 455–456
26 SHAKESPEARE, 431
29 CERVANTES, xiii, 1–3, 13–16, 183–187, 189–191, 252
30 BACON, 38–39, 85
32 MILTON, 385–386
33 PASCAL, 173–174
38 MONTESQUIEU, 17–18
39 SMITH, 337–338
40 GIBBON, 94, 449
41 GIBBON, 225, 311
42 KANT, 513–514, 523
44 BOSWELL, 259, 308
46 HEGEL, 155

4e. The moral quality of human acts

4e(1) The distinction between human and moral acts and the nonvoluntary or reflex acts of a man

7 PLATO, 45, 474
9 ARISTOTLE, 355–357, 359–361
12 AURELIUS, 304–305
19 AQUINAS, 609–612, 644–651, 697–698, 718
21 DANTE, 77
27 SHAKESPEARE, 70
31 SPINOZA, 424–429
42 KANT, 164, 235, 282–283
49 DARWIN, 311
51 TOLSTOY, 688–690
53 JAMES, 186–187, 807–808, 814–819 passim

4e(2) The criteria of goodness and evil in human acts

7 PLATO, 439, 747
9 ARISTOTLE, 350–352 passim
12 EPICTETUS, 110–112, 116–118, 178–180, 192–193, 228–232
12 AURELIUS, 258, 265, 267, 271, 283, 291
18 AUGUSTINE, 17–18
19 AQUINAS, 693–720
21 DANTE, 15–16, 79
23 HOBBES, 91–92, 149
25 MONTAIGNE, 159–162
30 BACON, 70–71
31 SPINOZA, 422–431, 438, 439–440, 441–442
35 LOCKE, 188, 192–193
36 STERNE, 257–268
37 FIELDING, 38–40
38 ROUSSEAU, 343–345
39 SMITH, 346–347
42 KANT, 253–254, 262, 270, 317–318, 321–329, 341–342, 389–390, 595
43 MILL, 270–271, 286–287, 307, 445–476
46 HEGEL, 41–42, 49–54, 131
53 JAMES, 796–798 passim
54 FREUD, 792

4e(3) Circumstances as affecting the morality of human acts

9 ARISTOTLE, 356–357, 372–373
19 AQUINAS, 651–655, 701–703
20 AQUINAS, 124–125
23 HOBBES, 91
25 MONTAIGNE, 103–104
30 BACON, 76–78
33 PASCAL, 19–62 passim
35 LOCKE, 192
35 HUME, 485
37 FIELDING, 271–273
38 ROUSSEAU, 343, 363–366
42 KANT, 169–170
44 BOSWELL, 429–430

46 HEGEL, 42, 127–128, 140
51 TOLSTOY, 9–10, 303–305, 645–646, 686–687

5*a*. The emotions and pleasure and pain as the matter of virtue: the role of desire or appetite

7 PLATO, 59–62, 120–122, 275–285, 644–653, 714–716
9 ARISTOTLE, 349–350, 357, 363–366, 372–373, 375, 426–430 passim, 544–546 passim
12 EPICTETUS, 161–162, 208–210
14 PLUTARCH, 753–754
18 AUGUSTINE, 379–385
19 AQUINAS, 727–730, 771–772, 790–791
20 AQUINAS, 32–33, 45–54, 453–454
21 DANTE, 1–4, 53–105
23 HOBBES, 61–63, 272
25 MONTAIGNE, 89–91, 118–119, 124–125, 159–162 passim, 350–354
27 SHAKESPEARE, 212
31 SPINOZA, 424–429, 442–447
33 PASCAL, 64–67, 202, 242, 243, 260–261
35 LOCKE, 191–193, 197–198
42 KANT, 258–259, 286, 385
43 MILL, 295
49 DARWIN, 311–314 passim
51 TOLSTOY, 248–250
53 JAMES, 808–814 passim
54 FREUD, 501–504, 837–838

5*b*. Deliberation and judgment in the formation of virtue: the role of reason

5 EURIPIDES, 228
6 THUCYDIDES, 370
7 PLATO, 350–355
9 ARISTOTLE, 355–361, 387–388, 389, 400–403 passim, 422
12 AURELIUS, 257
18 AUGUSTINE, 512
19 AQUINAS, 812–813
20 AQUINAS, 31–32
23 HOBBES, 64
25 MONTAIGNE, 115–119, 124–125, 162, 200–205, 353–354
30 BACON, 66–67
31 SPINOZA, 430, 442, 452–458
32 MILTON, 254–255
33 PASCAL, 238
35 LOCKE, 189–192, 196–197
38 ROUSSEAU, 344–345
42 KANT, 256–257, 321–325, 357–360
46 HEGEL, 165–166
49 DARWIN, 312–313, 593
53 JAMES, 886–888

5*c*. Intention and choice as conditions of virtue: the role of will

APOCRYPHA: *Ecclesiasticus*, 15:11–20
9 ARISTOTLE, 348, 351–352, 355–361, 387–388, 400–403, 421–422, 433
18 AUGUSTINE, 387–388
20 AQUINAS, 10, 26–27, 34–35
21 DANTE, 80
24 RABELAIS, 65–66
25 MONTAIGNE, 13–14
35 LOCKE, 191–192
38 ROUSSEAU, 337–338
42 KANT, 304, 378
43 MILL, 295–297
46 HEGEL, 126
52 DOSTOEVSKY, 20, 129–132
53 JAMES, 186–187, 271–275 passim, 806–808, 814–819 passim, 825–827

6. Virtue in relation to other moral goods or principles

6*a*. Duty and virtue

12 AURELIUS, 287–288
18 AUGUSTINE, 523
21 DANTE, 79–80
25 MONTAIGNE, 300–307
30 BACON, 74
38 ROUSSEAU, 369–370, 372–373
42 KANT, 262–263, 267, 305–307, 325–329, 366–368, 373, 383–390
43 MILL, 290–291, 453–454
46 HEGEL, 47, 129
49 DARWIN, 592–593 passim

6*b*. The relation of virtue to pleasure

7 PLATO, 59–62, 275–285, 421–425, 656–658, 689–690
8 ARISTOTLE, 165–166
9 ARISTOTLE, 344, 375, 395–406 passim, 423–424
12 EPICTETUS, 151
12 AURELIUS, 257–258, 286–287
18 AUGUSTINE, 81–85
19 AQUINAS, 762–763, 768–769, 771–772
20 AQUINAS, 52–54
21 DANTE, 99–102
25 MONTAIGNE, 28, 162–167, 200–205, 540
30 BACON, 71–72
35 LOCKE, 186
42 KANT, 298–300, 304–307, 338–355 passim, 387–388
43 MILL, 447–450, 463–464

6*c*. The relation of virtue to wealth

OLD TESTAMENT: *Leviticus*, 19:9–11,13,35–36; 25 / *Deuteronomy*, 15:7–15; 22:1–3; 24:10–22 / *Nehemiah*, 5 / *Job*, 29:12–17; 31:16–23 / *Proverbs*, 1:10–19; 11:1,24–28; 23:4–5 / *Ecclesiastes*, 5:10–20 / *Isaiah*, 10:1–3 / *Jeremiah*, 22:13–17
NEW TESTAMENT: *Matthew*, 6:1–4,19–21,24–34; 19:16–30 / *Luke*, 12:13–34 / *Acts*, 20:33–34 / *II Corinthians*, 8–9 / *I Timothy*, 6:6–11,17–19 / *James*, 5:1–6
5 AESCHYLUS, 60
5 EURIPIDES, 330
5 ARISTOPHANES, 629–642
6 HERODOTUS, 201–202

6*d*. Virtue and honor

6*e*. Virtue in relation to friendship and love

7. The role of virtue in political theory

7*a*. The cultivation of virtue as an end of government and the state

7*b*. Civic virtue: the virtue of the good citizen compared with the virtue of the good man

7*c*. The aristocratic principle: virtue as a condition of citizenship or public office

7*d*. The virtues which constitute the good or successful ruler: the vices associated with the possession of power

8. The religious aspects of virtue and vice

8*a*. The moral consequences of original sin

8*b*. The influence of religion on moral character: the indispensability of divine grace for the acquisition of natural virtue by fallen man

Corinthians, 12:7–9 / *Galatians*, 5:16–26 / *Ephesians*, 2:1–9; 4:17–5:21; 6:10–17 / *Colossians*, 1:9–11 / *Titus*, 2–3 / *James*, 1:22–27; 2:14–26; 4:1–10 / *I Peter*, 1:13–16; 4:1–6 / *II Peter*, 1:2–10 / *I John*, 2:3–6; 3:23–24

18 AUGUSTINE, 12, 300, 511–513, 524–525, 528, 572–574
20 AQUINAS, 338–347, 855–858
21 DANTE, 1–4, 53–54, 65–67, 99–102
22 CHAUCER, 493–550
25 MONTAIGNE, 209–212
32 MILTON, 66, 133, 136–144, 299, 304–305, 353–354
33 PASCAL, 243–244, 267, 294–295
35 LOCKE, 105
35 HUME, 503
36 STERNE, 255–268
37 FIELDING, 38
38 MONTESQUIEU, 200–208
38 ROUSSEAU, 366
40 GIBBON, 191–194, 297–298, 631–632
42 KANT, 238, 595–596
43 MILL, 290–291, 296
44 BOSWELL, 151, 482
46 HEGEL, 228–229, 346, 349, 353–354
51 TOLSTOY, 271–274, 524–527, 606–607
52 DOSTOEVSKY, 33–34, 127–137, 310–317 passim, 335–336
53 JAMES, 203–204

8*c*. The divine reward of virtue and punishment of vice: here and hereafter

OLD TESTAMENT: *Genesis*, 6–8; 18:20–19:25 / *Exodus*, 22:22–24 / *II Samuel*, 22 / *I Kings*, 21:19–24 / *II Kings*, 9:7–10,30–37 / *Job* / *Psalms*, 1; 7:8–17; 9; 11–12; 15; 18; 21; 34; 37; 58; 73; 89:23–33; 94; 107:10–20; 112; 125; 140 / *Proverbs*, 1:29–31; 3:9–10,31–35; 5:21–23; 10:2–6,24–30; 11; 14:11–12,19,32; 15:29; 16:17; 17:5,13; 19:16; 21:12–13,15–16,18,21,28; 22:8–9; 25:21–22 / *Ecclesiastes*, 2:26; 8:12–14; 9:1–2 / *Isaiah*, 1:4–24; 2:10–4:1; 5; 9:13–10:6; 28; 32; 33:15–16; 47; 58:3–12; 59 / *Jeremiah*, 4:13–22; 5:7–9,25–29; 7:1–16; 9:1–9; 18:1–12; 22:3–5,13–19; 23:9–20; 25:12–14 / *Lamentations* / *Ezekiel*, 3:17–21; 16; 18; 22–25; 28:1–19; 33:7–19 / *Daniel*, 4:4–5:31 / *Joel* / *Amos* / *Jonah* / *Micah* / *Nahum* passim / *Habakkuk*, 2:4–17 / *Zephaniah*, 3:1–8 / *Zechariah* passim / *Malachi*, 3:5; 4:1–3

APOCRYPHA: *Wisdom of Solomon*, 3–5; 6:1–7; 11–12; 14:10–11,27–31; 16–17; 18:10–19:22 / *Ecclesiasticus*, 5:1–8; 7:1–3,16–17; 11:16–17,26; 12:6; 16:4–14; 17:23–24; 21:2–3,9–10; 35:12–20; 39:25–30; 40:9–15; 41:8–10 / *Baruch*, 1:22–2:9 / *I Maccabees*, 2:49–63 / *II Maccabees*, 6:13–15

NEW TESTAMENT: *Matthew*, 5:1–30; 11:20–24; 13:41–43,49–50; 18:7–9; 23:14–39; 25:31–46 / *Mark*, 9:43–50 / *Luke*, 16:19–26 / *Acts*, 12:20–23 / *Romans*, 2:1–10 / *I Corinthians*, 3:8–17; 6:9–10 / *Galatians*, 6:7–10 / *II Thessalonians*, 1:7–9; 2:1–15 / *Hebrews*, 2:2–3; 10:26–31 / *I Peter*, 3:10–12 / *II Peter*, 2 / *Jude* passim / *Revelation*, 2–3; 18; 20:12–15; 21:8

4 HOMER, 248–249
5 AESCHYLUS, 9–10, 15–26, 55–56, 81–91
5 SOPHOCLES, 136, 186
5 EURIPIDES, 306–308
6 HERODOTUS, 7, 76–77, 237–239
7 PLATO, 313–314, 321–322, 436–441
12 LUCRETIUS, 42–43
13 VIRGIL, 225–227, 230–231
18 AUGUSTINE, 220–221, 519–520, 529–530, 560–586 passim, 629
20 AQUINAS, 158–159, 187–189, 1025–1085
21 DANTE, passim
22 CHAUCER, 370–371, 374–382, 434–448, 498–502
23 HOBBES, 160–161, 163–164, 193–195, 250–251, 253–255
24 RABELAIS, 119–122
26 SHAKESPEARE, 115
32 MILTON, 93–125, 152–155, 354–355, 376
35 LOCKE, 107–108, 194, 198
35 HUME, 500
37 FIELDING, 20–21
40 GIBBON, 198–199
41 GIBBON, 233–234
42 KANT, 594
43 MILL, 458
44 BOSWELL, 363, 482
48 MELVILLE, 30–36
51 TOLSTOY, 272
52 DOSTOEVSKY, 33–34, 127–137
54 FREUD, 878

8*d*. The theory of the theological virtues

NEW TESTAMENT: *I Corinthians*, 13:13

18 AUGUSTINE, 635–636
20 AQUINAS, 59–63, 65, 69–70, 80–81, 83–87
21 DANTE, 142–146
23 HOBBES, 240
32 MILTON, 331–332

8*d*(1) Faith and disbelief

OLD TESTAMENT: *Habakkuk*, 2:4

APOCRYPHA: *Wisdom of Solomon*, 3:9

NEW TESTAMENT: *Matthew*, 17:14–21; 21:17–22,31–32 / *Mark*, 9:17–30 / *Luke*, 8:4–15 / *John*, 3:9–18; 5:31–47; 10:24–28,37–38; 12:36–46; 14:1–14; 20:24–29,31 / *Romans* passim / *II Corinthians*, 4:13–5:9 / *Galatians* passim / *Colossians*, 1:21–23 / *I Thessalonians*, 3 / *Hebrews*, 4:2–3; 11:1–12:3 / *James*, 1:3–7 / *I Peter*, 1:7–9; 2:6–7 / *I John*, 4:1–3,14–16

18 AUGUSTINE, 36–37, 323, 436
20 AQUINAS, 73–75, 380–456
21 DANTE, 142–144
23 HOBBES, 241–242
25 MONTAIGNE, 209–215 passim, 293–294

30 BACON, 95–96
32 MILTON, 66
33 PASCAL, 219–220, 224, 261, 319
35 LOCKE, 3–4, 10
35 HUME, 496–497
46 HEGEL, 349–350
48 MELVILLE, 30–36
51 TOLSTOY, 196–197
52 DOSTOEVSKY, 64–70, 127–137 passim, 337–346 passim

8*d*(2) Hope and despair

OLD TESTAMENT: *Numbers*, 13:16–14:10 / *Psalms*, 22; 33:18–22; 42:5–11; 130:5–7; 146:5–10
APOCRYPHA: *II Maccabees*, 15:7–9
NEW TESTAMENT: *Romans*, 5:1–5; 8:19–39 / *Hebrews*, 6:9–20 / *I John*, 3:1–3
18 AUGUSTINE, 114
20 AQUINAS, 456–482
21 DANTE, 11–13, 57, 144–145
22 CHAUCER, 529–530, 549–550

8*d*(3) Charity and the disorder of love

OLD TESTAMENT: *Leviticus*, 19:18,33–34 / *Deuteronomy*, 6:5; 10:12,18–19; 11:1,13,22; 13:3; 19:9; 30:6,15–20 / *Psalms* passim / *Proverbs*, 25:21–22 / *Song of Solomon*
APOCRYPHA: *Ecclesiasticus*
NEW TESTAMENT: *Matthew*, 5:21–26,38–46; 19:16–21; 22:35–40 / *Luke*, 6:27–36; 10:25–37 / *John*, 13:31–17:26 / *Romans*, 12:9–21 / *I Corinthians*, 8:1–3; 13:1–14:1 / *Ephesians*, 5:1–2,25–33 / *Philippians* / *I Peter*, 1:7–8,22; 4:8–10 / *I John* / *II John*, 5–6
18 AUGUSTINE, 50–51, 380–381, 629–630, 631–632, 635–636
19 AQUINAS, 309–310, 735–736
20 AQUINAS, 61–63, 72–73, 80–81, 87, 373, 376, 404–407, 469, 472, 482–605, 629, 1039–1040
21 DANTE, 1–157 passim
22 CHAUCER, 168
30 BACON, 2–4, 80–81
33 PASCAL, 78–80, 293–295 passim
37 FIELDING, 26–27
51 TOLSTOY, 127–128, 213–216, 525–526, 560–562
52 DOSTOEVSKY, 26–27, 117–137 passim

8*e*. The infused virtues and the moral and intellectual gifts

OLD TESTAMENT: *I Kings*, 3:5–15; 4:29–34 / *Psalms*, 119:34–40 / *Proverbs*, 2 / *Daniel*, 1; 2:20–23
APOCRYPHA: *Wisdom of Solomon* / *Ecclesiasticus*
NEW TESTAMENT: *Ephesians*, 1:16–18
7 PLATO, 189–190
18 AUGUSTINE, 300–301
19 AQUINAS, 576
20 AQUINAS, 15, 28–29, 65–66, 87–96, 416–426, 598–603
21 DANTE, 100, 124, 138, 145
23 HOBBES, 149, 176–177, 270

8*f*. The qualities which flow from charity: humility, mercy, chastity, obedience

OLD TESTAMENT: *Genesis*, 22:1–18 / *Deuteronomy*, 8:11–17 / *I Samuel*, 12:14–15; 15:22–23 / *II Samuel*, 15 / *Psalms*, 37:21,25–26; 131 / *Proverbs*, 16:5–6,18–19
APOCRYPHA: *Ecclesiasticus*, 3:17–20; 10:13–14,28–29
NEW TESTAMENT: *Matthew*, 5:1–12,27–32; 10:35–39; 12:46–50; 16:24–26; 18; 19:10–12,18; 20:20–28 / *Luke*, 14:7–14; 18:1–14,20; 22:40–45 / *John*, 13:1–17 / *Romans*, 12:1–15:13 / *I Corinthians*, 3:18–21; 7:7–11,37–40; 13 / *II Corinthians*, 6:1–10; 10–12 / *Galatians*, 5:22–23; 6:1–10 / *Ephesians*, 5:1–6:9 / *Philippians*, 1:9–11; 2:1–16 / *Colossians*, 3:5–25 / *I Thessalonians*, 5:12–28 / *Titus*, 2–3 / *Hebrews*, 10:19–39 / *James* passim / *I Peter* passim
18 AUGUSTINE, 66–67, 227–230
20 AQUINAS, 527–558
21 DANTE, 67–68, 75–76
22 CHAUCER, 236–255, 401–432, 463–471, 533–534
26 SHAKESPEARE, 427
32 MILTON, 33–56
33 PASCAL, 91–94
35 LOCKE, 1–2
42 KANT, 325–327
48 MELVILLE, 30–36
52 DOSTOEVSKY, 26–27, 145–170 passim, 269, 411–412

8*g*. The vows and practices of the monastic life in relation to virtue

NEW TESTAMENT: *Matthew*, 19:10–12 / *I Corinthians*, 7:25–40
20 AQUINAS, 66–67, 637–639, 649–663
21 DANTE, 109–113, 122–125
22 CHAUCER, 161–163, 167–168, 170–171
23 HOBBES, 272–273
25 MONTAIGNE, 111
40 GIBBON, 191–194, 533, 593–599 passim
41 GIBBON, 232–233
44 BOSWELL, 283
46 HEGEL, 333, 340–341
51 TOLSTOY, 273–274
52 DOSTOEVSKY, 11–15, 83–88 passim, 146–170 passim, 189–191

9. The advance or decline of human morality

13 VIRGIL, 110–111
15 TACITUS, 51
29 CERVANTES, 27–28
30 BACON, 15, 54
32 MILTON, 306–332
35 LOCKE, 50–51
36 SWIFT, 121
38 ROUSSEAU, 338
40 GIBBON, 633–634
43 MILL, 335–336
46 HEGEL, 182–184
49 DARWIN, 321–323, 596–597

CROSS-REFERENCES

For: The issue concerning the relation between knowledge and virtue, *see* EDUCATION 4a; GOOD AND EVIL 6a; KNOWLEDGE 8b(1); WISDOM 2b.

Another discussion of the unity of virtue, *see* ONE AND MANY 5a.

Discussions relevant to the doctrine of the mean, *see* COURAGE 2; PRUDENCE 3b, 3e; TEMPERANCE 1b.

Virtue in relation to happiness, *see* HAPPINESS 2b(3); PUNISHMENT 3b.

The role of habit in the conception of virtue, *see* HABIT 6b; and for the distinction between virtuous and continent acts by reference to habit, *see* PRUDENCE 3d; TEMPERANCE 1c.

Other treatments of the distinction between the moral and the intellectual virtues, *see* HABIT 2b, 5b, 5d; and for the analysis of particular moral or intellectual virtues, and their relation to one another, *see* ART 1; COURAGE 1, 4; JUSTICE 1c–1d; PRUDENCE 2a–2c, 3a; SCIENCE 1a(1); TEMPERANCE 1a–1b; WISDOM 2a.

Other treatments of the theological virtues, the infused virtues, and the supernatural gifts, *see* GOD 6c(2); HABIT 5e(2)–5e(3); KNOWLEDGE 6c(5); LOVE 5b(2); OPINION 4a; RELIGION 1a; WISDOM 1c.

The moral significance of temperamental dispositions, *see* EMOTION 4c; MAN 6a.

Discussions relevant to the independence or interdependence of particular virtues, *see* JUSTICE 1d; PRUDENCE 3–3a.

For: Discussions bearing on the acquisition of virtue, *see* ART 10a; CUSTOM AND CONVENTION 5b; EDUCATION 4, 4b–4d; FAMILY 6d; GOVERNMENT 2d; HABIT 4a–4b; HISTORY 2; LAW 6d; NATURE 6b; NECESSITY AND CONTINGENCY 5a; PLEASURE AND PAIN 10a; POETRY 9a; PUNISHMENT 3a; SIN 7; WILL 3a–3a(2).

The role of the various faculties in the formation of virtue, *see* DESIRE 6a; EMOTION 4b(1); MIND 9c; PLEASURE AND PAIN 8a; PRUDENCE 3; REASONING 5e–5e(3); WILL 5b(4), 8c.

The relation of virtue to other moral goods or principles, *see* DUTY 4, 5; GOOD AND EVIL 3b–3b(2); HONOR 2b; LAW 4d; LOVE 2b(3), 3a; PLEASURE AND PAIN 8a; TEMPERANCE 3; WEALTH 10a, 10c; and for the issue in moral philosophy between the ethics of duty and the ethics of virtue and happiness, *see* DUTY 2; HAPPINESS 3.

The political consideration of virtue, *see* ARISTOCRACY 6; CITIZEN 5; MONARCHY 3a; STATE 7c, 8b.

The relation of virtue to sin and sanctity, *see* RELIGION 3d; SIN 3c, 4d, 7; TEMPERANCE 6a.

The doctrine of divine law and divine rewards and punishments, *see* HAPPINESS 7c–7c(3); IMMORTALITY 5e–5f; LAW 3a–3b(2); PUNISHMENT 5d–5e(2); SIN 6c–6e.

The influence of religion on the moral life, and for the moral virtues or qualities peculiar to the religious life, *see* RELIGION 3d; SIN 7; TEMPERANCE 6a; WEALTH 10e(2).

ADDITIONAL READINGS

Listed below are works not included in *Great Books of the Western World*, but relevant to the idea and topics with which this chapter deals. These works are divided into two groups:

I. Works by authors represented in this collection.
II. Works by authors not represented in this collection.

For the date, place, and other facts concerning the publication of the works cited, consult the Bibliography of Additional Readings which follows the last chapter of *The Great Ideas*.

I.

PLUTARCH. "That Virtue May be Taught," "Of Moral Virtue," "Of Virtue and Vice," in *Moralia*
EPICTETUS. *The Manual*
AUGUSTINE. *On the Morals of the Catholic Church*, CH XV
——. *Of Continence*
——. *The Enchiridion on Faith, Hope and Love*
——. *Admonition and Grace*
AQUINAS. *Quaestiones Disputatae, De Virtutibus in Communi; De Caritate*, AA 2–5; *De Spe; De Virtutibus Cardinalibus*
——. *Summa Theologica*, PART II–II, QQ 155–156
DANTE. *Convivio (The Banquet)*, FOURTH TREATISE, CH 17–21
SPINOZA. *Correspondence*, XLIII
HUME. *A Treatise of Human Nature*, BK II, PART I, SECT VII; BK III, PART I, III
FIELDING. *Joseph Andrews*
A. SMITH. *The Theory of Moral Sentiments*, PART VI
KANT. *Lectures on Ethics*, pp 116–247
HEGEL. *The Phenomenology of Mind*, V, B (2, c); VI, C
J. S. MILL. *A System of Logic*, BK VI, CH 5
DOSTOEVSKY. *The Idiot*

II.

THEOPHRASTUS. *The Characters*
CICERO. *De Finibus (On the Supreme Good)*
——. *Tusculan Disputations*, V
——. *De Officiis (On Duties)*
HORACE. *Satires*
Pirke Aboth (Sayings of the Fathers)
SAADIA GAON. *The Book of Beliefs and Opinions*, TREATISE V, X
IBN GABIROL. *The Improvement of the Moral Qualities*
BERNARD OF CLAIRVAUX. *On Consideration*, BK I, CH 7–8
MAIMONIDES. *Eight Chapters on Ethics*, CH 2–4
——. *The Guide for the Perplexed*, PART III, CH 38–39, 42
BONAVENTURA. *Breviloquium*, PART V
R. BACON. *Opus Majus*, PART VII
LANGLAND. *Piers Plowman*
THOMAS À KEMPIS. *The Imitation of Christ*, BK I
SPENSER. *The Faerie Queene*
SUÁREZ. *Disputationes Metaphysicae*, XXX (16), XLIV
BEN JONSON. *Volpone*
BURTON. *The Anatomy of Melancholy*, PART I, SECT I, MEMB II, SUB-SECT II
CORNEILLE. *Cinna*
J. TAYLOR. *Ductor Dubitantium*, BK IV
MOLIÈRE. *L'école des maris (The School for Husbands)*
——. *L'école des femmes (The School for Wives)*
——. *Le misanthrope (The Man-Hater)*
BAXTER. *Chapters from A Christian Directory*
BUNYAN. *Pilgrim's Progress*
MANDEVILLE. *The Fable of the Bees*
SHAFTESBURY. *Characteristics of Men, Manners, Opinions, Times*
DEFOE. *Moll Flanders*
J. BUTLER. *Fifteen Sermons upon Human Nature*, PREFACE; III, X, XIII
LAW. *A Practical Treatise upon Christian Perfection*
VAUVENARGUES. *Introduction à la connaissance de l'esprit humain*
RICHARDSON. *Pamela*
——. *Clarissa*
J. EDWARDS. *Charity and Its Fruits*
——. *A Dissertation on the Nature of True Virtue*
GOLDSMITH. *The Vicar of Wakefield*
VOLTAIRE. "Virtue," in *A Philosophical Dictionary*
——. *The Ignorant Philosopher*, CH 46
R. BURNS. *Address to the Unco Guid*
AUSTEN. *Pride and Prejudice*
BROWN. *Lectures on the Philosophy of the Human Mind*, VOL III, pp 473–563
LEOPARDI. *Essays, Dialogues, and Thoughts*
KIERKEGAARD. *Either/Or*
WHEWELL. *The Elements of Morality*, BK II, CH 1–4
THACKERAY. *Vanity Fair*
LOTZE. *Microcosmos*, BK V, CH 5
FLAUBERT. *Madame Bovary*
MEREDITH. *The Ordeal of Richard Feverel*
H. SIDGWICK. *The Methods of Ethics*, BK III, CH 2–3
T. H. GREEN. *The Principles of Political Obligation*, (O)
——. *Prolegomena to Ethics*, BK III, CH 4 (b), 5
NIETZSCHE. *Beyond Good and Evil*, CH V, VII
——. *The Genealogy of Morals*
FRAZER. *The Golden Bough*, PART II, CH 3
BONAR. *The Intellectual Virtues*
L. STEPHEN. *Social Rights and Duties*
BILLOT. *De Virtutibus Infusis*
A. E. TAYLOR. *The Problem of Conduct*
BUBER. *Jewish Mysticism and the Legends of Baalshem*
GIDE. *Strait Is the Gate*
DEWEY. *Human Nature and Conduct*
N. HARTMANN. *Ethics*, VOL II, *Moral Values*

Chapter 98: WAR AND PEACE

INTRODUCTION

THE twentieth century may go down in history as the century of war and peace—the first in which world wars were fought, the first in which men established world peace, and so, perhaps, the last in which peace among nations was merely an armed truce, a breathing spell between wars. Even if world peace is not actually begun in our time, we may prove to be the first generation of men on earth who, under the impact of world wars, have made a firm attempt to draw a decisive conclusion from all the accumulated wisdom concerning war and peace.

It may be thought that antiquity anticipates, and that at all times the tradition contains, the fundamental notions which have recently gained so wide a currency. Socrates and Epictetus, for example, speak of world citizenship. Marcus Aurelius and Zeno the Stoic even more explicitly envision a world community. Alexander tries to conquer the world to make it one; Virgil proclaims a peace which will be as universal as the Roman empire; and Dante, recasting Virgil's vision, advocates the re-enactment of that empire and with it monarchy—by which he means *one* government—to give all Christendom political as well as spiritual unity.

To neglect these anticipations would be to overlook wisdom's perennial aspirations for unity. But if, because of their significance for peace, they should not be neglected here, neither should their importance be exaggerated. For one thing, man has always acted at variance with his wisdom, nullifying the hope of peace by preparing always for the next war. For another thing, it is doubtful that peace by conquest or by empire—the only ways in which the past could conceive the world's coming to the unity of peace—would be a peace perpetual as well as universal. The latter without the former is but a fraction of the ideal.

Even when in modern times the ideal is at last stated in terms of peaceful methods for achieving peace—by law, not by force; by consent, not by imposition—something less than the whole world in its global reality is the object of consideration. William Penn and Rousseau, for example, state the indispensable legal conditions for turning Europe from a continent perpetually wracked by wars into a society able to perpetuate peace, but their historical location causes them to limit their proposals to Europe.

Kant alone first makes the generalization which lies dormant in their reasoning, and which almost begs to be inductively drawn from the conceptions of war and peace so plainly stated by Hobbes and Locke. He conceives the possibility of a peace not only perpetual but truly world-wide. Yet for all the rightness he perceives in what he calls "the cosmopolitical ideal," it seems to remain for him an ideal—not attainable except by approximation. Yet because it is right, he holds that it must be pursued even though it is impossible. We are the first generation to argue for world peace as a conclusion on the level of reality and to conclude that it is possible because it is necessary.

The argument is not yet won, nor the conclusion enacted, but henceforth the problem of war and peace can hardly be discussed without stating the issue as a choice of world government and peace, or of world anarchy and war. If it does no more than seriously face that choice for the first time, the twentieth century makes a signal advance in understanding one of the great ideas—an advance which can change the course of history and the life of man more than the discovery of atomic fission, which is only an instrument of war or a tool of peace. But just as the release of heat and energy from nuclear combustion has its prototype in ordinary fire, which the ancients associate with the beginning of civilization, so the insight which may exert a new civilizing force has its origin in the fundamental thinking man does about war and peace as soon as he begins to think about society.

In the tradition of the great books, war and peace are usually discussed in political terms, or at least in terms of the relation of men to one another, individually or in groups. But the psychologist, the moralist, and the theologian sometimes use the word "peace" in another sense to signify the absence of conflict within the individual or to signify an inner harmony—peace of mind on earth or the heavenly rest of the blessed in the presence of God.

In their spiritual meanings, war and peace are considered in other chapters; *e.g.*, interior conflict is a topic in the chapter on Opposition and interior peace is discussed in the chapter on Happiness. We shall not treat these matters here except in their bearing on the social or political discussion; nor shall we consider civil war except for the light it throws on the nature of war and peace in general. The special problem of discord and strife within a single community belongs to the chapter on Revolution.

Certain attitudes toward war between states seem to recur in every century. In the face of the ever-present fact of war, men deplore its folly or find some benefit to compensate for its devastation. But throughout most of the tradition, those who see only suffering, no less than those who celebrate the martial spirit, seem to accept the necessity of war. Good or bad, or a mixture of the glorious and the horrible, war seems, to most of those who write about it, an inevitable thing—as ineradicable as disease and death for the living body, as inescapable as tragedy. Only in recent times has the inevitability of war been questioned, and the possibility of lasting peace proposed.

The two books which look most steadily and searchingly on the face of war—Homer's *Iliad* and Tolstoy's *War and Peace*—seem to behold it as a mixed thing. Battle with sword and javelin on the plains of Troy or with musket and howitzer on the Russian steppes lets loose a fury which sweeps human nature to extremes of nobility and baseness, to actions of heroic strength and cringing weakness. To both Homer and Tolstoy, war is the realm of force and chance, and though both see in it occasions for courage and magnanimity and even for a kind of charity or at least compassion, the whole spectacle is one of agony, pervaded by darkness and dismay, torn bodies and ruined minds. "Grievous war" is Homer's repeated epithet. "Pale fear" and "black death" are the colors of battle. They are everywhere that Ares reigns, "Ares, blood stained bane of mortals," "stubborn god of war."

To the poet of any century, Homer or Tolstoy, Virgil or Shakespeare, war's human features appear to be unchanged even if its mechanical dress and physical lineaments are altered—its weapons and armor, its organization of men and materials, its scope of operations in space and time. The historian who measures the contestants and keeps the score of victories and defeats takes a different view. He dwells on all the differences which mark progress in the art of war, or which enable wealthier and more advanced societies to wage wars of greater magnitude. To Herodotus, no military undertaking ever assumed the proportions of Xerxes' army on the march, raising a cloud of dust from horizon to horizon. Yet Thucydides says that before the Peloponnesian War "there was nothing on a great scale either in war or in other matters."

The historian is attentive not only to weights and numbers, to the changing accoutrement of war and its mechanical elaboration, but also to inventions in the sphere of strategy and tactics. The Alexandrian phalanx, the patience of Fabius, the forced marches of Caesar, Hannibal's outflanking and enveloping movements at the battle of Cannae, the deployment in depth of the Roman legions on the Rhine—these are but a few of the inventions of military genius which, as Plutarch, Tacitus, and Gibbon recognize, have an effect far beyond the advantage that novelty initially gives them. They become the classical models of war's art and the principles of its science.

Tolstoy may scoff at the historians who stand in awe of military genius. He may be right that Kutuzov's lack of plans rather than Napoleon's air of outwitting all contingencies is the essence of great generalship. Nevertheless Tolstoy magnifies the campaign of 1812 as beyond comparison the greatest mass movement of humanity, from west to east and then from east to west, just as Herodotus apotheosizes the movement of the Persian horde from east to west and Thucydides the rise of Athenian naval power.

Writing from the center of a whole continent in arms a century later, Freud in 1915 gives his impression of what was yet to become the first world war. A war of such proportions and ferocity was almost incredible before it happened. "Then the war in which we had refused to believe broke out," and, Freud writes, "not only is it more sanguinary and more destructive than any war of other days, because of the enormously increased perfection of weapons of attack and defense; but it is at least as cruel, as embittered, as implacable as any that preceded it. . . . It tramples in blind fury on all that comes in its way, as though there were to be no future and no goodwill among men after it has passed. It rends all bonds of fellowship between the contending peoples, and threatens to leave such a legacy of embitterment as will make any renewal of such bonds impossible for a long time to come."

THE ENEMIES OF WAR use a variety of weapons in their attack. The *Trojan Women* of Euripides cries out with the bitterness of Andromache and Hecuba against the misery of war's innocent victims—the women and children who are left to mourn the vanquished or to become the victors' spoils. Aristophanes turns laughter rather than pity and fear against the waste of war. Such comedies as the *Peace*, the *Acharnians*, the *Lysistrata* make light of the issues over which men fight, and give war the aspect of a wearisome business, preposterous in its motives and hollow in its victories.

The genial satire of Rabelais exposes the impostures of war, but beneath the horseplay which deflates by its exaggerations, there is the earnest, serious note of Grangousier's resolution not to "undertake war until I have first tried all the ways and means of peace." Swift's satire is not so amiable. In the eyes of the truly rational Houyhnhnms, war appears to be as senseless and despicable as the Yahoos who wage it. Gulliver tries to tell the Houyhnhnm who is his master about the wars of Europe, their causes and their cost. "I was going on to more particulars," he relates, "when my master commanded me silence. He said whoever understood the nature of the Yahoos might easily believe it possible for so vile an animal to be capable of every action I had named, if their strength and cunning equalled their malice. . . . When a creature pretending to reason could be capable of such enormities, he dreaded lest the corruption of that faculty might be worse than brutality itself. He seemed therefore confident that, instead of reason, we were only possessed of some quality fitted to increase our natural vices."

According to Augustine, it is not man's nature but his sinfulness which degrades him below the beasts "devoid of rational will," who "live more securely and peaceably with their own kind than men. . . . For not even lions or dragons have ever waged with their kind such wars as men have waged with one another." Calling it "the greatest and most pompous of human actions," Montaigne asks whether war is not "the testimony of our weakness and imperfection; for, in truth the science of undoing and killing one another, and of ruining and destroying our own kind, has nothing in it so tempting as to make it coveted by beasts who have it not."

But in his essay *Of Ill Means Employed to a Good End*, Montaigne also quotes Juvenal's remark that "we suffer the ills of a long peace; luxury is more pernicious than war." He seems to approve the Roman policy of maintaining wars "not only to keep their own men in action, for fear lest idleness, the mother of corruption, should bring upon them some worse inconvenience; but also to serve for a bloodletting to their Republic, and a little to evaporate the too vehement heat of their youth." War as a purgative is a familiar theme. Hobbes, like Malthus later, suggests that "when all the world is overcharged with inhabitants, then the last remedy of all is war; which provideth for every man, by victory or death."

Many writers seem to be ambivalent about war. Plato, for example, seems to see both sides of the question though he does not give them equal weight. In the *Republic*, Socrates proclaims the discovery that war is "derived from causes which are also the causes of almost all the evils in states, private as well as public." In the *Laws*, the Athenian Stranger admits to Cleinias the Cretan that the laws of his city, devised primarily with a view to war, can be justified insofar as they aim at courage; but he reminds him later that insofar as such laws "regarded a part only, and not the whole of virtue, I disapproved of them."

That he regards permanent peace as the ideal toward which the moral law commands us to strive, does not prevent Kant from saying that "a prolonged peace favours the predominance of a mere commercial spirit, and with it a debasing self-interest, cowardice, and effeminacy, and tends to degrade the character of the nation." Nor is war to be absolutely condemned. "Provided it is conducted with order and a sacred respect for the rights of civilians," war itself, says Kant, "has something sublime about it, and gives nations that carry it on in such a manner a stamp of mind only the more sublime the more numerous the dangers to which they are exposed, and which they are able to meet with fortitude." Yet even while thinking that war can be a "spur for developing to the highest pitch all talents that minister to culture," Kant reflects that the underlying purpose of war may be "to prepare the way for a rule of law governing the freedom of states, and thus bring about their unity in a system established on a moral basis."

Hegel alone is not ambivalent. Not only is war not "to be regarded as an absolute evil," but it is, according to Hegel, a necessary corrective for the corrosive influence of peace. "War is a state of affairs," he writes, "which deals in earnest with the vanity of temporal goods and concerns—a vanity at other times the common theme of edifying sermonizing. . . . War has the higher significance that by its agency, as I have remarked elsewhere, 'the ethical health of peoples is preserved in their indifference to the stabilization of finite institutions; just as the blowing of the winds preserves the sea from foulness which would be the result of a prolonged calm, so also the corruption in nations would be the product of prolonged, let alone "perpetual," peace.'"

Far from agreeing with those who advocate "perpetual peace . . . as an ideal towards which humanity should strive," Hegel points out that "in peace civil life continually expands; all its departments wall themselves in, and in the long run men stagnate. . . . As a result of war, nations are strengthened, and people involved in civil strife also acquire peace at home through making wars abroad."

To Prince Andrew in *War and Peace* who says that "the aim of war is murder; the methods of war are spying, treachery, and their encouragement"; or to Freud who says that "the warring state permits itself every such misdeed, every such act of violence, as would disgrace the individual man," Hegel has an answer. "States are not private persons," he says, "but completely autonomous totalities in themselves, and so the relation between them differs from a moral relation and a relation involving private rights. . . . The relation between states is a relation between autonomous entities which make mutual stipulations, but which at the same time are superior to these stipulations."

Self-interest, or "a will for its own welfare pure and simple," is, according to Hegel, "the highest law governing the relation of one state to another." Therefore, "when politics is alleged to clash with morals . . . the doctrine propounded rests on superficial ideas about morality, the nature of the state, and the state's relation to the moral point of view."

IN HEGEL'S VIEW, "wars occur when the necessity of the case requires." He is not alone in thinking war inevitable, but others who think the same do not do so in the same mood, or with the same opinion of the reason for its inevitability. "Drain the blood from men's veins," declares Prince Andrew's father, "and put in water instead, then there will be no more war!" It is an illusion, Freud thinks, to suppose that civilization so transforms human nature as to lift it above the impulses of war. In war, he says, "our fellow-citizens have not sunk so low as we feared, because they have never risen so high as we believed." The sad fact, he concludes, is that "war is not to be abolished; so long as the conditions of existence among the nations are so varied, and the repulsions between peoples so intense, there will be, there must be, wars."

William James finds the human race as bellicose as its individual members are instinctively pugnacious; and Alexander Hamilton says that if we "judge from the history of mankind, we shall be compelled to conclude that the fiery and destructive passions of war reign in the human breast with much more powerful sway than the mild and beneficent sentiments of peace; and that to model our political systems upon speculations of lasting tranquility, is to calculate on the weaker springs of human character."

To the extent that even those who deplore war despair of lasting peace, Machiavelli may not be too cynical a realist when he advises the prince that he "ought to have no other aim or thought, nor select anything else for his study, than war and its rules and discipline. . . . When princes have thought more of ease than of arms, they have lost their states." The prince "ought never, therefore, to have out of his thoughts this subject of war, and in peace he should addict himself more to its exercise than in war." The prince who delays in order to save himself from war makes a serious mistake. War, Machiavelli tells him, "is not to be avoided, but is only deferred to your disadvantage."

Like Machiavelli, Cleinias the Cretan in Plato's *Laws* justifies his city's constant preoccupation with war or preparation for war. The world is foolish, he thinks, "in not understanding that all men are always at war with one another. . . . For what men in general term peace [is] only a name; in reality every city is in a natural state of war with every other, not indeed proclaimed by heralds, but everlasting."

Both Plato and Aristotle seem to agree that war is somehow rooted in the nature of things —in the nature of men and the nature of cities. Yet both also look upon war as transitory, even if recurrent. "No one can be a true statesman," the Athenian Stranger tells Cleinias, "who looks only, or first of all, to external warfare; nor will he ever be a sound legislator who orders peace for the sake of war, and not war for the sake of peace." The whole of life, according to Aristotle, is "divided into two parts, business and leisure, war and peace. . . . There must be war for the sake of peace, business for the sake of leisure, things useful and necessary for the sake of things honorable. . . . Men must be able to engage in business and go to war, but leisure and peace are better; they must do what is necessary and indeed what is useful, but what is honorable is better."

But how does war produce peace? One answer may be Tristram Shandy's, that "as war begets poverty, poverty peace." Another may be Virgil's. In the opening book of his *Aeneid*, Jove predicts the coming of a Caesar "destined to bound with ocean his domain, as with the stars his glory." When at last Rome has conquered the world, the golden age of peace—or at least the *pax Romana*—will supplant war's age of iron. "Then war shall be laid aside, and the harsh world soften to peace . . . the accursed gates of Battle shall be shut with iron bar and clenching bolt; and godless Frenzy shall sit within upon the weapons of savagery."

In accordance with this heaven-laid destiny, Anchises bids his son Aeneas to make war for the sake of peace. "Roman, be this thy care—these thine arts—to bear dominion over the nations and to impose the law of peace, to spare the humbled and to war down the proud!" But some of the proud who are subjugated by Rome's legions take a different view of the peace that is imposed by force of arms. Tacitus reports the speech of the British chieftain Galgacus, in which he refers to those "terrible Romans, from whose oppression escape is vainly sought by obedience and submission. . . .To robbery, slaughter, plunder, they give the lying name of empire; they create a wilderness and call it peace."

Augustine more soberly reflects on the inevitable frustration of the Roman kind of peace. "The imperial city," he writes, "has endeavored to impose on subject nations not only her yoke, but her language, as a bond of peace. . . . How many great wars, how much slaughter and bloodshed, have provided this unity. And though these are past, the end of these miseries has not yet come. For though there have never been wanting, nor are yet wanting, hostile nations beyond the empire, against whom wars have been and are waged, yet supposing there were no such nations, the very extent of the empire itself has produced wars of a more obnoxious description—social and civil wars—and with these the whole race has been agitated, either by the actual conflict or the fear of a renewed outbreak."

DESPITE HIS PERCEPTION of war's failures, despite his enjoining the wise men, not merely to wage, but "to lament the necessity of just wars," Augustine holds that it is "with the desire for peace that wars are waged. . . . Every man seeks peace by waging war, but no man seeks war by making peace. For even they who intentionally interrupt the peace in which they are living have no hatred of peace, but only wish it changed into a peace that suits them better. . . . Even those whom they make war against they wish to make their own, and impose on them the laws of their own peace."

Peace, according to Augustine, consists in harmony and concord. "Peace between man and man is well-ordered concord. Domestic peace is the well-ordered concord between those of the family who rule and those who obey. Civil peace is a similar concord among the citizens. . . . The peace of all things is the tranquillity of order." Without disagreeing essentially, Aquinas explains that peace involves more than concord. "Wherever peace is," he says, "there is concord, but there is not peace wherever there is concord, if we give peace its proper meaning." The peace between men may consist in concord, "not indeed any kind of concord, but that which is well-ordered, through one man agreeing with another in respect of something befitting to them both. For if one man agree with another, not of his own accord, but through being forced . . . such concord is not really peace."

For men to be at peace with one another, Aquinas believes, each must be at peace with himself, but "man's heart is not at peace, so long as he has not what he wants, or if, having what he wants, there still remains something for him to want." This, according to Aquinas, explains why Augustine defined peace not simply as concord, but as *the tranquillity of order*, for by "tranquillity" is meant all the desires of each individual man "being set at rest together." It also explains why "those who seek war and dissension, desire nothing but peace, which they deem themselves not to have. For," Aquinas reminds us, "there is no peace when a man enters into concord with another counter to what he would prefer. Consequently men seek by means of war to break this concord, because it is a defective peace, in order that they may obtain peace, where nothing is contrary to their will. Hence all wars are waged that men may find a more perfect peace than that which they had heretofore."

The fundamental insight here seems to be that, though charity or love produces the unity of peace, peace is also "the work of justice"—indirectly, as Aquinas says, "insofar as justice removes the obstacles to peace." Thucydides gives us an historian's confirmation of the theologian's point. He tells us why he considers the long truce or armistice—a period of no actual fighting—to be a part of the war. "Only a mistaken judgment," he writes, "can object to including the interval of treaty in the war. Looked at by the light of facts it cannot, it will be found, be rationally considered a state of peace, where neither party either gave or got back all that they had agreed upon."

To the same effect is the speech of Hermocrates the Syracusan, which Thucydides reports. "That war is an evil is a proposition so familiar to everyone that it would be tedious to develop it. No one," he declares, "is forced to engage in it by ignorance, or kept out of it by fear, if he fancies there is anything to be gained by it. . . . I suppose that no one will dispute that we went to war at first, in order to serve our several interests; that we are now, in view of the same interests, debating how we can make peace; and that if we separate without having as we think our rights, we shall go to war again."

THUCYDIDES' OBSERVATION THAT periods of armistice or truce are part of war, and the remark of Cleinias in Plato's *Laws* that "every city is in a natural state of war with every other," may anticipate Hobbes, but full clarity on the point is not reached until Hobbes explicitly distinguishes between war as battle and the state of war which always prevails between men or nations when they do not live together under a common government.

"War consisteth not in battle only," Hobbes explains, "or in the act of fighting; but in a tract of time, wherein the will to contend by battle is sufficiently known; and therefore the notion of time is to be considered in the nature of war, as it is in the nature of weather. For as the nature of foul weather lyeth not in a shower or two of rain, but in an inclination thereto of many days together, so the nature of War consisteth not in actual fighting but in the known disposition thereto, during all the time there is no assurance to the contrary. All other time is Peace."

Hobbes does not exclude from the condition of peace differences between men or even discord, but only fighting or the need to resort to fighting as a way of settling differences or resolving conflicts. He is cognizant of the distinction which Machiavelli paraphrases from Cicero. "There are two ways of contesting," Machiavelli writes, "the one by law, the other by force; the first method is proper to men, the second to beasts." Here Machiavelli adds the comment that "because the first is frequently not sufficient, it is necessary to have recourse to the second." But Hobbes does not think it is always necessary. At least there is a cure for "the war of every man against every man." That cure is the formation of a commonwealth and the institution of government with sufficient coercive force to maintain law and secure peace. "Anarchy and the condition of war," according to Hobbes, are one and the same, a condition in which each man, being a law unto himself and judge in his own case, must of necessity resort to force if he would impose his will upon, or resist the will of, another.

Since men are everywhere found in societies, living under law and government, it might seem that the universal state of war to which Hobbes refers is now abolished. Not so, according to Hobbes, for "though there had never been a time wherein particular men were in a condition of war one against another; yet," in his opinion, "in all times, kings and persons of sovereign authority, because of their independency, are in continual jealousies, and in the state and posture of gladiators; having their weapons pointing, and their eyes fixed on one another; that is, their forts, garrisons, and guns upon the frontiers of their kingdoms, and continual spies upon their neighbors; which is a posture of War."

This notion that sovereigns are always in a state of war with one another—because being sovereigns they are autonomous, *i.e.*, not subject to any superior government—seems to be accepted by most of the great political writers who come after Hobbes. The point is sometimes differently formulated, but the basic insight remains essentially the same.

Locke, for example, makes a threefold distinction between the state of nature, which is anarchy or complete independence; the state of war, in which force without authority is resorted to by men to settle their differences; and the state of civil society which provides law and government for the arbitration of disputes. "Civil society," he writes, is "a state of peace amongst those who are of it, from whom the state of war is excluded by the umpirage which they have provided in their legislative for the ending all differences that may rise amongst any of them."

Since Locke holds that "want of a common judge with authority puts all men in a state of nature," it follows for him that, though the state of nature and the state of war may not be identical, the state of nature, unlike that of civil society, inevitably lapses into the state of war. If in a state of nature men fail to settle their differences by reason, they enter into the state of war which is the realm of force "or a declared design of force . . . where there is no common superior on earth to appeal to for relief."

With these qualifications, Locke not only agrees with Hobbes that "all princes and rulers of independent governments all through the world are in a state of nature," but also draws from this the same implication for war and peace. Since "the whole community is one body in the state of nature in respect of all other states or persons out of its community," Locke argues that the government of each state must have "the power of war and peace, leagues and alliances," in relation to everything external to itself.

Montesquieu and Rousseau slightly alter Hobbes' point by attributing the origin of war itself to the existence of separate societies. War, writes Rousseau, "is a relation, not between man and man, but between State and State." Because they are "in a state of nature among themselves," bodies politic experience, in his opinion, "the inconveniences which had obliged individuals to forsake it. . . . Hence arose national wars, battles, murders and reprisals, which shock nature and outrage reason."

Hegel's ultimate reason for thinking that war is ineradicable seems to be not merely that sovereign states are "in a state of nature in relation to each other," but that they must always remain so. "There is no Praetor to judge between states," he writes; "at best there may be an arbitrator or a mediator, and even he exercises his functions contingently only, *i.e.*, in dependence on the particular wills of the disputants."

That is why Hegel dismisses Kant's idea "for securing 'perpetual peace' by a League of Nations to adjust every dispute. . . . This idea," Hegel writes, "presupposes an accord between states; this would rest on moral and religious or other grounds and considerations, but in any case would always depend ultimately on a particular sovereign will and for that reason would remain infected with contingency." Hence, he concludes, "if states disagree and their particular wills cannot be harmonized, the matter can only be settled by war."

KANT AGREES THAT, in the absence of what he calls a "cosmo-political constitution" or world state, "*war* is inevitable." In their external relations to one another, states, "like lawless savages, are naturally in a non-juridical condition," and this, according to Kant, "is a state of war, in which the right of the stronger prevails; and although it may not in fact be always found as a state of actual war and incessant hostility . . . yet the condition is wrong in itself in the highest degree, and the nations which form States contiguous to each other are bound mutually to pass out of it."

How shall this be accomplished? Is Kant's idea the one Hegel attributes to him? Is the "alliance of nations," of which he speaks, to be a "league of nations" or does he have something more than that in mind when he says that "this mutual connection by alliance" must "take the form of a Federation"?

On the one hand, he calls for "a universal Union of States analogous to that by which a Nation becomes a State," and argues that "it is only thus that a real *state of Peace* could be established." But on the other, he explains that he means "only a voluntary combination of different States that would be *dissoluble* at any time, and not such a union as is embodied in the United States of America, founded upon a political constitution, and therefore indissoluble."

The arguments for the federal constitution of the United States help to make this issue clear. The authors of the Constitution regard it as providing "a more perfect union" than the Articles of Confederation under which the thirteen separate colonies are banded together by little more than treaties or alliances. To the writers of *The Federalist*, who advocate the adoption of a federal union to replace the loose confederacy or league of states, there is no middle ground between the establishment of peace through federal union and the continuation of the state of war between separate states.

"A man must be far gone in Utopian speculations," Hamilton declares, "who can seriously doubt that, if these States should either be wholly disunited, or only united in partial confederacies, the subdivisions into which they might be thrown would have frequent and violent contests with each other. . . . To look for a continuation of harmony between a number of independent, unconnected sovereignties in the same neighborhood, would be to disregard the uniform course of events, and to set at defiance the accumulated experience of ages." In another paper, Hamilton admits that "there is nothing absurd or impracticable in the idea of a league or alliance between independent nations for certain defined purposes precisely stated in a treaty," but he thinks that Europe has taught "an instructive but afflicting lesson to mankind, how little dependence is to be placed on treaties which have no other sanction than the obligations of good faith."

He returns therefore to attack the "visionary or designing men, who stand ready to advocate the paradox of perpetual peace between the States, though dismembered and alienated from each other." What reason have we to expect, he asks, "peace and cordiality between the members of the present confederation, in a state of separation"? It seems to him "an established truth that the several states, in the case of disunion . . . would be subject to those vicissitudes of peace and war, of friendship and enmity with each other, which have fallen to the lot of all neighboring nations not united under one government."

The Federalists do not seriously recommend their prescription for peace as a plan for the whole world. Yet they see the generalization that is implicit in all their reasoning. "Happy would it be," Madison says, "if such a remedy for its infirmities could be enjoyed by all free governments; if a project equally effectual could be established for the universal peace of mankind!"

John Stuart Mill, writing somewhat later and in the light of the experience of American federation as a peace plan, seems to be even less ready to propose world federal government as the indispensable condition of world peace. He has no doubt that federal union "puts an end to war and diplomatic quarrels." But he does not think that abrogating the distinction between fellow countrymen and foreigners by making them all fellow citizens of an encompassing state—an object which is "one of the worthiest to which human endeavor can be directed"—can, "in the present state of civilization, be promoted by keeping different nationalities of anything like equivalent strength under the same government."

Not only does Kant definitely dismiss the notion of a world union formed along American lines, but even that less perfect union of states which would have the form of a "*Permanent Congress of Nations*," seems to him an impracticable idea in the world as it is at the end of the eighteenth century. "With the too great extension of such a Union of States over vast regions," he writes, "any government of it, and consequently the protection of its individual members, must at last become impossible; and thus a multitude of such corporations would again bring round a state of war."

Nevertheless, Kant refuses to yield completely to this conclusion. "The morally practical reason," he affirms, "utters within us its irrevocable *Veto*: '*There shall be no War*.' . . . Hence the question no longer is as to whether Perpetual Peace is a real thing or not a real thing, or as to whether we may not be deceiving ourselves when we adopt the former alternative, but we must *act* on the supposition of its being real. We must work for what may perhaps not be realized . . . and thus we may put an end to the evil of wars, which have been the chief interest of the internal arrangements of all States without exception."

And in his *Idea of a Universal History on a Cosmo-Political Plan*, Kant does more than urge upon us our moral duty to work for perpetual peace as prerequisite to "the highest political good." He engages in prophecy. He pictures the nations of the world "after many devastations, overthrows, and even complete internal exhaustion of their powers" as "driven forward to the goal which Reason might well have impressed upon them, even without so much sad experience. This is none other than the advance out of the lawless state of savages and the entering into a Federation of Nations. . . . However visionary this idea may appear to be . . . it is nevertheless the inevitable issue of the necessity in which men involve one another."

THE ARGUMENT FOR WORLD GOVERNMENT as the means to world peace is nowhere made in the great books as explicitly as in Dante's *De Monarchia*. "Wherever there can be contention," Dante writes, "there judgment should exist; otherwise things should exist imperfectly, without their own means of adjustment or correction. . . . Between any two governments, neither of which is in any way subordinate to the other, contention can arise either through their own fault or that of their subjects. This is evident. Therefore there should be judication between them. And since neither can know the affairs of the other, not being subordinate (for among equals there is no authority), there must be a third and wider power which rules both within its own jurisdiction.

"This third power," Dante continues, "is either the world-government, or it is not. If it is, we have reached our conclusion; if it is not, it must in turn have its equal outside its jurisdiction, and then it will need a third party as a judge, and so *ad infinitum*, which is impossible. So we must arrive at a first and supreme judge for whom all contentions are judicable either directly or indirectly. . . . Therefore, world-government is necessary for the world." Aristotle, according to Dante, "saw this argument when he said, 'Things hate to be in disorder, but a plurality of authorities is disorder; therefore authority is single." But Aristotle certainly did not draw the conclusion that a single government embracing all mankind should be instituted so that "by common law it might lead all toward peace." Nor, with the exception of Kant, does any other great author argue to this conclusion. But, as we have seen, Kant, unlike

Dante, reaches this conclusion only to qualify his acceptance of it and his advocacy of world government.

Nevertheless, several of the great books do contain the nerve of the argument. It is contained in one fundamental proposition that is variously enunciated by Hobbes and Locke, Rousseau and the Federalists. That proposition is: *As anarchy leads to war, government establishes peace, and just laws preserve it.* By inductive generalization, it seems to follow that, if local peace depends on local government, world peace depends on world government.

But if, except for Dante and Kant, no one until the present made this inference, the tradition of western thought does include, not only the essential premise for making the inference, but also the controlling vision of a politically united humanity—all men as fellow citizens in a single political society embracing the earth.

Kant speaks of "the right of man as a citizen of the world to *attempt* to enter into communion with all others." Epictetus says, "there is but one course open to men, to do as Socrates did: never to reply to one who asks his country, 'I am an Athenian,' or 'I am a Corinthian,' but 'I am a citizen of the universe.'"

Reflecting on the fact that man's "nature is rational and social," Marcus Aurelius declares: "My city and my country, so far as I am Antoninus, is Rome, but so far as I am a man, it is the world." If we look at "what value everything has with reference to the whole," we will perceive that man "is a citizen of the highest city, of which all other cities are like families." The reason which is common to all men dictates a common law of human life. "If this is so," Aurelius argues, "we are fellow citizens; if this is so, we are members of one political community; if this is so, the world is in a manner a state."

Aristotle describes how the family is formed by the union of man and wife, parents and children; and from this first of all social units, the tribe or village is formed by a union of families, and the city or state by a union of villages. He does not carry this series on to its natural terminus, but Augustine does. "After the state or city," Augustine says, "comes the world, the third circle of human society—the first being the family, the second the city."

Yet Augustine, who orders earthly peace to the peace of heaven, does not prophesy a single political community of all men living together under one government. The heavenly city, he says, "while it sojourns on earth, calls citizens out of all nations, and gathers together a society of pilgrims of all languages, not scrupling about diversities in the manners, laws, and institutions whereby earthly peace is secured and maintained, but recognizing that, however various these are, they all tend to one and the same end of earthly peace."

One and the same end of earthly peace may require one city of man as well as one city of God. That, according to Dostoevsky, seems to be implied in the fact that "the craving for universal unity is the third and last anguish of men. Mankind as a whole," he writes, "has always striven to organize a universal state. There have been many great nations with great histories, but the more highly developed the more unhappy they were, for they felt more acutely than other people the craving for world-wide union."

OUTLINE OF TOPICS

1. War as the reign of force: the state of war and the state of nature

2. The kinds of war

2a. Civil war and war between states or international war

2b. Religious wars: the defense and propagation of the faith

2c. The class war: the conflict of economic groups

3. The rights of war

  3*a*. The distinction between just and unjust warfare: wars of defense and wars of conquest

  3*b*. Justice and expediency in relation to the initiation and prosecution of a war: laws governing the conduct of warfare

4. The causes or occasions of war

  4*a*. The precipitation of war between states: remote and proximate causes; real and apparent causes

  4*b*. The factors responsible for civil strife

5. The effects of war

  5*a*. The moral consequences of war: its effects on the happiness and virtue of men and on the welfare of women and children

  5*b*. The political consequences of war: its effects on different forms of government

  5*c*. The economic consequences of war: the cost of war and the by-products of war

6. The conception of war as a political means or instrument

  6*a*. Conquest, empire, political expansion as ends of war

  6*b*. Liberty, justice, honor, peace as ends of war

7. The inevitability of war: the political necessity of military preparations

8. The desirability of war: its moral and political benefits

9. The folly and futility of war

10. The military arts and the military profession: their role in the state

  10*a*. The formation of military policy: the relation between the military and the statesman or prince

  10*b*. Different types of soldiery: mercenaries, volunteers, conscripts, militia

  10*c*. The military virtues: the qualities of the professional soldier; education for war

  10*d*. The principles of strategy and tactics: the military genius

  10*e*. The rise of naval power and its role in war

  10*f*. The development of weapons: their kinds and uses

  10*g*. The making of truces or alliances as a military device

11. The nature, causes, and conditions of peace

  11*a*. Law and government as indispensable conditions of civil peace: the political community as the unit of peace

  11*b*. Justice and fraternity as principles of peace among men

  11*c*. International law and international peace: treaties, alliances, and leagues as instrumentalities of international peace

  11*d*. World government and world peace

REFERENCES

References are listed by volume number (in bold type), author's name, and page number. Bible references are to book, chapter, and verse of the Authorized King James version of the Bible. The abbreviation "esp" calls the reader's attention to one or more especially relevant parts of a whole reference; "passim" signifies that the topic is discussed intermittently rather than continuously in the work or passage cited. Where the work as a whole is relevant to the topic, the page numbers refer to the entire work. For general guidance in the use of *The Great Ideas,* consult the Preface.

1. War as the reign of force: the state of war and the state of nature

4 Homer, 3–179
5 Aeschylus, 56
5 Euripides, 385
7 Plato, 44, 640–641
13 Virgil, 124–146, 236–379
18 Augustine, 517–518
22 Chaucer, 192–193
23 Hobbes, 76–77, 84–86
27 Shakespeare, 108–109
30 Bacon, 20
32 Milton, 313–314
35 Locke, 25–30, 65
38 Montesquieu, 2–3
38 Rousseau, 335–336, 343–345, 346, 351–352, 364
42 Kant, 434, 435–436
46 Hegel, 36, 171–172
51 Tolstoy, 1–696
53 James, 717

2. The kinds of war

2*a*. Civil war and war between states or international war

6 Herodotus, 102–107, 172–174
6 Thucydides, 434–438, 459, 463–465, 575–576, 577, 579–583, 595–586, 587–589, 590
7 Plato, 806–807
9 Aristotle, 558–561, 566–572
14 Plutarch, 533, 875
15 Tacitus, 12–13, 248, 261–262
20 Aquinas, 583–584
23 Machiavelli, 31
23 Hobbes, 68–69, 99–100, 114, 121–122, 147, 150–151
25 Montaigne, 504–506
26 Shakespeare, 11–16, 33–68, 69–104, 105–148, 342–343, 434–435, 583
35 Locke, 60–61, 76–81
40 Gibbon, 35, 48–49, 71–74, 111–113, 652–655
41 Gibbon, 570–571, 572, 594–595
43 Declaration of Independence, 1–3
43 Federalist, 141–142
46 Hegel, 297

2*b*. Religious wars: the defense and propagation of the faith

Apocrypha: *Judith,* 1–9; 14:29–37 / *II Maccabees,* 6–10
20 Aquinas, 432–433, 579–580, 677–678, 1058–1061
24 Rabelais, 117
26 Shakespeare, 434
32 Milton, 329–331
35 Locke, 1–2, 13, 20–21
38 Rousseau, 435–436
40 Gibbon, 233–234, 310–328 passim, 382, 391
41 Gibbon, 128–129, 134–161 passim, 199–202, 237–243, 253–310, 323, 331–333, 378–453, 531–551, 583–586, 588–589
46 Hegel, 313, 322–323, 337–339, 358–360

2*c*. The class war: the conflict of economic groups

5 Euripides, 260
6 Thucydides, 466–469, 482–483, 524–525, 564–593
7 Plato, 342–344, 405–406, 412–415
9 Aristotle, 461–463 passim, 495–496, 502–519 passim, 553–555
14 Plutarch, 68–70, 671–689, 708–713
23 Machiavelli, 14
23 Hobbes, 156
27 Shakespeare, 351–392
38 Montesquieu, 78–80
38 Rousseau, 353–356, 375
39 Smith, 28, 309–311
40 Gibbon, 127, 144
41 Gibbon, 574–582 passim
46 Hegel, 193, 275–276, 287–288, 295–296, 356–357
50 Marx, 7, 8–9, 134–146, 209–215
50 Marx-Engels, 415–434
51 Tolstoy, 410–421
52 Dostoevsky, 165–166
54 Freud, 882–884

3. The rights of war

3*a*. The distinction between just and unjust warfare: wars of defense and wars of conquest

5 Aeschylus, 11–13, 23–24

3b. Justice and expediency in relation to the initiation and prosecution of a war: laws governing the conduct of warfare

4. The causes or occasions of war

4a. The precipitation of war between states: remote and proximate causes; real and apparent causes

4b. The factors responsible for civil strife

40 GIBBON, 35, 48–49, 69–76, 111–112 passim, 127, 159–178 passim, 267–272 passim, 324–326, 330–335, 420–422, 446–447, 449–450, 453–454, 652–654
41 GIBBON, 113–115, 466
43 DECLARATION OF INDEPENDENCE, 1–3
43 FEDERALIST, 47–53, 66–68, 95
43 MILL, 428–431 passim
50 MARX, 377–378
51 TOLSTOY, 680–683

5. The effects of war

5*a*. The moral consequences of war: its effects on the happiness and virtue of men and on the welfare of women and children

OLD TESTAMENT: *II Kings*, 25 / *Jeremiah*, 39–40; 52
APOCRYPHA: *I Maccabees*, 1:20–64
4 HOMER, 43–45, 130–131, 171–179
5 AESCHYLUS, 16, 20–21, 28–31, 55, 56–57, 61
5 SOPHOCLES, 153
5 EURIPIDES, 258–269, 270–281, 316, 353–364
5 ARISTOPHANES, 532–533, 583–599
6 THUCYDIDES, 398, 436–438, 545–546, 559, 562–563
13 VIRGIL, 131–146
14 PLUTARCH, 590–591
15 TACITUS, 12–13, 202, 217–218, 229, 250–251, 255, 265, 266
18 AUGUSTINE, 174–175
21 DANTE, 61–62
22 CHAUCER, 174–176, 404
24 RABELAIS, 143–144
25 MONTAIGNE, 95–97, 504–509
26 SHAKESPEARE, 23–26, 67–68, 74–76, 81–83, 148, 545–546, 552–554, 583
35 LOCKE, 67–69 passim
36 STERNE, 448–451
38 ROUSSEAU, 380
40 GIBBON, 509–510, 511–512, 573–574, 627–628
41 GIBBON, 397–398, 437–440 passim, 551–553
46 HEGEL, 107
51 TOLSTOY, 12–14, 55–59, 90–91, 102–104, 109–110, 128–131, 179–180, 221–222, 225–228, 232–234, 275–276, 410–421, 442–443, 467–468, 475–476, 485–496, 497–513, 527–532, 537–562
54 FREUD, 756–761

5*b*. The political consequences of war: its effects on different forms of government

5 ARISTOPHANES, 479–480
6 THUCYDIDES, 564–593
9 ARISTOTLE, 566
14 PLUTARCH, 119–120, 332–354, 368–387
15 TACITUS, 1
35 LOCKE, 65–70
38 MONTESQUIEU, 60–61
41 GIBBON, 452–453
43 FEDERALIST, 45–47

5*c*. The economic consequences of war: the cost of war and the by-products of war

5 ARISTOPHANES, 532–533
6 HERODOTUS, 235–236
6 THUCYDIDES, 354–355, 390–391, 399–401, 551, 564
14 PLUTARCH, 179–180
15 TACITUS, 213–214, 229, 236–237
26 SHAKESPEARE, 563–564
38 MONTESQUIEU, 100–101
38 ROUSSEAU, 380
39 SMITH, 181
40 GIBBON, 503–504, 510–511 passim
41 GIBBON, 437–438
43 ARTICLES OF CONFEDERATION, 6–7
43 FEDERALIST, 102–103, 110–111
51 TOLSTOY, 500–502, 634–635

6. The conception of war as a political means or instrument

6*a*. Conquest, empire, political expansion as ends of war

OLD TESTAMENT: *Joshua*, 6–12 / *Judges*, 18
APOCRYPHA: *Judith*, 1–2 / *I Maccabees*, 1:16–24
5 AESCHYLUS, 15–26
6 HERODOTUS, 138–159 passim, 161–162, 165–166, 169, 211
6 THUCYDIDES, 368–371, 384–386, 396, 402–404, 461–462, 504–508, 510–516, 529, 530–532, 533
7 PLATO, 318–319
13 VIRGIL, 275–278
14 PLUTARCH, 599
15 TACITUS, 290
18 AUGUSTINE, 196–197, 216–218
23 MACHIAVELLI, 31–32
25 MONTAIGNE, 440–442
26 SHAKESPEARE, 1–32, 33–68, 69–104, 532–567 esp 533–537
27 SHAKESPEARE, 463–464
35 LOCKE, 65–70
36 SWIFT, 23–26
38 MONTESQUIEU, 61–68
38 ROUSSEAU, 389–390, 403–404
39 SMITH, 245
40 GIBBON, 2–3, 84–86, 98–99, 109–110, 121–125 passim, 264–265, 398, 414–418, 446, 540, 558, 571–572
41 GIBBON, 212, 255–288 passim, 347–451 passim, 494–505 passim, 539–540
43 FEDERALIST, 35–41 passim
46 HEGEL, 242–243, 275, 281–282, 297, 299, 357–358
48 MELVILLE, 292–295

6*b*. Liberty, justice, honor, peace as ends of war

OLD TESTAMENT: *Judges*, 3–7; 14–16; 19–20 / *II Samuel*, 10 / *II Chronicles*, 32:1–22
APOCRYPHA: *Judith* / *I Maccabees*, 1–9; 14:29–37 / *II Maccabees*, 6–10
4 HOMER, 3–179 passim

10*b*. Different types of soldiery: mercenaries, volunteers, conscripts, militia

10*c*. The military virtues: the qualities of the professional soldier; education for war

10*d*. The principles of strategy and tactics: the military genius

10*e*. The rise of naval power and its role in war

11*d*. World government and world peace

CROSS-REFERENCES

For: The psychological meanings of war and peace as conflict and harmony in the individual life, *see* Emotion 4a; Justice 1b; Man 5–5a; Medicine 4, 5e; Opposition 4–4a; and for the theological meaning of peace as heavenly rest, *see* Happiness 7c(1); Immortality 5f; Love 5a(2); Will 7d.

Other discussions of the state of nature and the state of war, *see* Government 5; Law 4g; Liberty 1b; Nature 2b; State 3c.

The general theory of revolution or civil war, *see* Revolution 1–1b; and for the distinction between civil and international war, *see* Revolution 1c.

Various considerations of the class war, *see* Labor 7c–7c(3); Oligarchy 5c; Opposition 5b; Revolution 5a; State 5d(2); Wealth 9h.

The issue concerning the justice of making war, *see* Justice 9f.

Another discussion of the effect of war upon women and children, *see* Family 5c.

The weakness or strength of democracy in the sphere of war, *see* Democracy 7c.

The costs of war, *see* Wealth 9g.

Other discussions of imperialism which have a bearing on wars of conquest and rebellions against the conquerors, *see* Liberty 6c; Monarchy 5–5b; Slavery 6d; State 9f.

Other discussions of the inevitability of war and the necessity of military preparedness, *see* Necessity and Contingency 5d; Opposition 5c; State 9e(1).

Another treatment of the role of the military in the life of the state, *see* State 8d(1), 9e(1); and for another discussion of the military arts, *see* Art 9c.

The consideration of treaties, alliances, and international law in relation to war and peace, *see* Government 5a; Law 4g; State 9e(2).

The conception of law and government as indispensable to civil peace, *see* Government 1a; Law 1a; and for the conception of lawlessness or crime as breaching the peace of a society, *see* Law 6e–6e(1).

The consideration of justice and law as principles of civil peace, *see* Justice 9b; Love 4a–4b; State 3e.

Discussions bearing on the idea of world government and its relation to world peace, *see* Citizen 8; Love 4c; State 10f.

ADDITIONAL READINGS

Listed below are works not included in *Great Books of the Western World*, but relevant to the idea and topics with which this chapter deals. These works are divided into two groups:

I. Works by authors represented in this collection.
II. Works by authors not represented in this collection.

For the date, place, and other facts concerning the publication of the works cited, consult the Bibliography of Additional Readings which follows the last chapter of *The Great Ideas.*

I.

AUGUSTINE. *Reply to Faustus*
DANTE. *Convivio (The Banquet)*, FOURTH TREATISE, CH 4
——. *On World-Government or De Monarchia*
MACHIAVELLI. *The Discourses*, BK II; BK III, CH 10–18, 30–33, 37–41, 45, 48
——. *The Art of War*
F. BACON. "Of Empire," in *Essays*
ROUSSEAU. *A Lasting Peace*
A. SMITH. *Lectures on Justice, Police, Revenue and Arms*
KANT. *The Idea of a Universal History on a Cosmo-Political Plan*
——. *Perpetual Peace*
HEGEL. *The Phenomenology of Mind*, VI, A (2, a)
TOLSTOY. *The Law of Love and the Law of Violence*
——. *The Kingdom of God*
——. *Christianity and Patriotism*
——. *Notes for Soldiers*
W. JAMES. *Memories and Studies*, CH 4
FREUD. *Why War?*

II.

CAESAR. *The Gallic War*
MAIMONIDES. *Mishneh Torah*, BK XIV, CH 5
DUBOIS. *De Recuperatione Terre Sancte*
T. MORE. *Utopia*, BK II
ERASMUS. *The Complaint of Peace*
——. *Antipolemus*
LUTHER. *Whether Soldiers, Too, Can Be Saved*
VITORIA. *De Indis et De Jure Belli*
GENTILI. *De Jure Belli (On the Laws of War)*
SUÁREZ. *On War*
CRUCÉ. *The New Cyneas*
GROTIUS. *The Rights of War and Peace*
PENN. *An Essay Towards the Present and Future Peace of Europe*
SAINT-PIERRE. *Scheme for Lasting Peace*
VATTEL. *The Law of Nations*, BK III–IV
VOLTAIRE. "War," in *A Philosophical Dictionary*
——. *The Ignorant Philosopher*, CH 48
BURKE. *Resolutions for Conciliation with America*
FRANKLIN. *On War and Peace*
BENTHAM. *A Plan for a Universal and Perpetual Peace*
——. *Principles of International Law*
GODWIN. *An Enquiry Concerning Political Justice*, BK V, CH 16–19
SCHILLER. *Wallenstein*
CHANNING. *Discourses on War*
CLAUSEWITZ. *On War*
GOGOL. *Taras Bulba*
PUSHKIN. *The Captain's Daughter*
STENDHAL. *The Charterhouse of Parma*
WHEWELL. *The Elements of Morality*, SUP, CH 4
PROUDHON. *La guerre et la paix*
T. H. GREEN. *The Principles of Political Obligation*, (J)
MAHAN. *The Influence of Sea Power upon History*
H. SIDGWICK. *Practical Ethics*, IV
SHAW. *Arms and the Man*
CRANE. *The Red Badge of Courage*
BLOCH. *The Future of War in Its Technical, Economic, and Political Relations*
FOCH. *The Principles of War*
SUMNER. "War," in *War and Other Essays*
SANTAYANA. *Reason in Society*, CH 3
LIEBKNECHT. *Militarism*
PÉGUY. *Basic Verities* (War and Peace)
VANDERPOL. *Le droit de guerre*, CH 4
J. A. HOBSON. *Towards International Government*
LENIN. *Collected Works*, VOL XVIII, *The Imperialist War*
T. VEBLEN. *An Inquiry into the Nature of Peace and the Terms of Its Perpetuation*
DELBRÜCK. *Geschichte der Kriegskunst im Rahmen der politischen Geschichte*
BALFOUR. *Essays Speculative and Political*, CH 9
BERNHARDI. *The War of the Future in the Light of the Lessons of the World War*
DOUHET. *The Command of the Air*
DEWEY. *Characters and Events*, VOL II, BK IV (1, 6, 20–23)
——. *The Public and Its Problems*, CH 5
STURZO. *The International Community and the Right of War*
FERRERO. *Peace and War*
SHOLOKHOV. *The Silent Don*
ROMAINS. *Verdun*
FOERTSCH. *The Art of Modern Warfare*
VANN. *Morality and War*
WELLS. *The New World Order*
KELSEN. *Law and Peace in International Relations*
WRIGHT. *A Study of War*
BORGESE. *Common Cause*
ADLER. *How to Think About War and Peace*
DIWAKAR. *Satyagraha: The Power of Truth*

Chapter 99: WEALTH

INTRODUCTION

IF the only questions about wealth concerned the means of getting and keeping it, the causes of its increase and decrease, the idea of wealth would be confined to economics. "The end of the medical art is health," writes Aristotle in the *Ethics*, and "that of economics, wealth." But as the *Ethics* indicates, the moralist and the statesman are also concerned with health and wealth—not simply as things to get and keep, but in relation to all other goods and as constituents of the good life and the good society. What is regarded as the end in economics may be only a means in ethics and politics; in which case, Aristotle suggests, the latter sciences subordinate economics, even as politics subordinates military strategy, and military strategy the making and use of armaments.

The discussion of riches in the tradition of the great books exhibits these two ways of considering wealth. The Bible, the poets, historians, and philosophers deal with wealth as a factor in the life of men and societies. They scrutinize the desire for wealth or the love of money in relation to sin and virtue. They raise questions of justice concerning the distribution of wealth, the rights of property, and fairness in exchange —in buying and selling, borrowing and lending, and in compensating the laborer. They describe the effect of poverty and prosperity or opulence upon states, and prescribe the attitude which individual men as well as societies should take toward wealth and poverty.

Throughout it seems to be assumed that wealth is merely a means, however important or indispensable. Though wealth may also be viewed as an end when the problem is one of how to acquire, produce, or increase it, the fact that, when possessed, it should be treated as a means, leads the moralist to condemn not only the miser, the hoarder, or the man who devotes his whole life to making money, but also those who elevate wealth into the sort of end which justifies any means that can advance its pursuit.

The other approach is that of the economist. Two of the great books—Smith's *Wealth of Nations* and Marx's *Capital*—deal not with wealth as a means, but with the means to wealth. A third, though by title *A Discourse on Political Economy*, is concerned with the principles of government, and with wealth only insofar as, in Rousseau's conception, government includes "the administration of property" as well as the protection of persons. "Provision for the public wants," he writes, is "the third essential duty of government."

Rousseau explains the title of his treatise by reference to the etymology of the word "economy," which "meant originally only the wise and legitimate government of the household for the common good of the whole family." It is in this sense that Aristotle employs the word and that a work sometimes attributed to him bears it as the title. "The meaning of the term," Rousseau goes on, "was then extended to the government of that great family, the State. To distinguish these two senses of the word, the latter is called *general* or *political* economy, the former domestic or particular economy."

Adam Smith uses the term more narrowly. Not only does he limit his inquiry to the nature and causes of wealth, but by specifying "the wealth of nations," he restricts himself to political economy which, he says, has "two distinct objects: first, to provide a plentiful revenue or subsistence for the people, or more properly to enable them to provide such a revenue or subsistence for themselves; and secondly, to supply the state or commonwealth with a revenue sufficient for the public services." In saying that the political economist aims "to enrich both the people and the sovereign," and that "the great object of the political economy of every country is to increase the riches and power of that country," Smith takes wealth as an end (though it may also be a means, "so far as power depends upon riches") and tries to formulate the natural laws of wealth-making.

Nowhere does he define the quantity of wealth which should satisfy a nation. The natural resources of a country, the size and industry of its population, and various unfavorable contingencies, may set certain bounds to the maximization of wealth. Within these bounds the country which adopts and follows a sound system of political economy—one which accords with the right conception of wealth and its causes—can (and deserves to) become as wealthy as possible.

Yet Smith, in treating wealth as an end and its increase without limit as a good, does not make economics absolutely autonomous. He regards political economy as a part of politics—"a branch of the science of a statesman or legislator"—and to that extent implies that other considerations than wealth may control the policies of a nation in its regulation of agriculture, industry, domestic commerce, and foreign trade.

Furthermore, the larger moral questions which accompany Smith's economic speculations in his *Lectures on Jurisprudence* and his earlier treatise *Of the Moral Sentiments* are not entirely absent from the *Wealth of Nations*. But to the extent that he writes purely as an economist concerned with securing "cheapness or plenty" or, what for him is the same, "wealth and abundance," he adheres to considerations of expediency and only infrequently permits himself *obiter dicta* on justice or questions of right and wrong.

Karl Marx also writes as an economist. He details the factors which govern the production and distribution of wealth as these manifest themselves in the great historic systems of production—the slave economy, the feudal economy, and the bourgeois or capitalist economy. So far he is a scientist and, even more than Adam Smith, an historian who describes how wealth is acquired and how it multiplies by reproducing itself. But Marx is much less content than Smith to stop there. Smith tries to describe the economic process scientifically in order to prescribe the means a nation should use to become increasingly prosperous, but Marx undertakes to describe it in order to criticize the way in which some men get richer than they need be while others become poorer than they should be.

His critical purpose makes inevitable the expression of moral judgments concerning such inequities; and by implication they are everywhere present. For example, a descriptive phrase like "surplus value" connotes "unearned increment"; an apparently neutral economic term like "profit" is given the invidious moral significance traditionally attached to "usury." Nor does Marx rest with criticism. He has an economic program to propose, a program he reveals more clearly in the *Communist Manifesto* than in *Capital*. The aim is not primarily to increase the production of wealth, but to remedy its inequitable distribution under all past economic systems. This program looks forward to the final revolution which will bring the necessary historic motion of progress to its culmination when socialism replaces capitalism.

SMITH AND MARX, IT APPEARS, are not economists in the same sense. But it may be supposed that, in spite of their different purposes, they would as scientists agree in their description of economic phenomena. To some extent they do, yet the difference in their point of view and aim leads to a quarrel about facts, or at least about their interpretation.

Classical economists in the tradition of Adam Smith dispute the consequences which Marx draws from the labor theory of value, especially with regard to the origin of profit from the surplus product of unpaid labor time. Profit seems to them as much a part of the natural price of commodities as the wages paid to labor and the rent paid to the landlord.

"In exchanging the complete manufacture either for money, for labor, or for other goods, over and above what may be sufficient to pay the price of the materials, and the wages of the workmen, something," writes Smith, "must be given for the profits of the undertaker of the work who hazards his stock in this adventure. The value which the workmen add to the materials, therefore, resolves itself in this case into two parts, of which the one pays their wages, the other the profits of their employer upon the whole stock of materials and wages which he advanced. He could have no interest to employ them, unless he expected from the sale of their work something more than what was sufficient to replace his stock to him; and he could have no interest to employ a great stock rather than a small one, unless his profits were to bear some proportion to the extent of his stock."

It is precisely on this point of profit as a return for risking one's capital stock that Marx charges Smith, and after him, Ricardo and J. S. Mill, with being apologists for the capitalistic system. He quotes Mill's statement that "the cause of profit is that labor produces more than is required for its support." The fact that Mill does not question the validity of this surplus value, which accrues as profit to the *entrepreneur*; the fact that Ricardo treats surplus value, according to Marx, "as a thing inherent in the capitalist mode of production, which mode, in his eyes, is the natural form of social production," is explicable, in Marx's view, only if we recognize that their economic theories mix special pleading with science. "These bourgeois economists instinctively saw, and rightly so," he says, "that it is very dangerous to stir too deeply the burning question of the origin of surplus value."

Though he distinguishes between its classical and vulgar forms, political economy for Marx is a bourgeois science, which "first sprang into being during the period of manufacture." Political economy "has generally been content to take, just as they were, the terms of commercial and industrial life," Engels remarks in a prefatory note to *Capital*, and so it "never went beyond the received notions of profit and rent, never examined this unpaid part of the product (called by Marx surplus-product) in its integrity as a whole, and therefore never arrived at a clear comprehension, either of its origin and nature, or of the laws that regulate the subsequent distribution of its value."

Marx's work is, in his own conception of it, at one and the same time a criticism of the capitalist economy and of the science of economics which accepts and defends that economic system. In his own preface to *Capital*, Marx tells the reader that the "volume which I now submit to the public forms the continuation" of an earlier work—*A Contribution to the Critique of Political Economy*. Within the sphere of political economy as defined by the problem of augmenting a nation's wealth, the author of the *Wealth of Nations* similarly finds a critique of prevalent economic fallacies—those of the physiocrats and the mercantilists—inseparable from the constructive statement of his own theory.

Economists engage in controversy over technical points in the analysis of production, exchange, and distribution, or in the development of theories of value and price, money and capital, property and poverty. Such controversy tends to become complicated both by the larger questions in which the economic issues are imbedded, and also by the different points of departure and the different objectives of the economists. What at first may look like a simple issue of fact often fails on closer examination to be capable of resolution by scientific inquiry, or simply by an accurate description of the phenomena.

Even when all relevant matters of fact are determined, conflicting interpretations of their significance remain. Behind these lie divergent presuppositions, often unexpressed. Those who start with different conceptions of the problem, and from different principles assumed rather than argued, tend to reach conclusions which may appear to be opposed but which do not really exclude one another—at least not totally. Each from its own point of view may be true, and from that point of view the other is not so much false as irrelevant.

Smith may be right, for example, when he says that "the consideration of his own private profit is the sole motive which determines the owner of any capital to employ it either in agriculture, in manufactures, or in some particular branch of the wholesale or retail trade. The different quantities of productive labor which it may put into motion, and the different values which it may add to the annual produce of the land and labor of the society, according as it is employed in one or other of those different ways, never enter his thoughts." Smith may be right, not only as to the fact asserted, but also with regard to its implication for the increase of the nation's wealth: that the wealth of a society increases as owners of capital act from self-interest in a system of free enterprise which permits the possibility of profits to indemnify them against the risk of losses and to reward them for the thrift whereby they accumulated capital to invest productively.

But Marx may also be right when he says that the system of free enterprise and capitalistic production could not have started simply through the thrift of individuals, but required a primitive accumulation of capital. "The accumulation of capital," he says, "presupposes surplus-value; surplus-value presupposes capitalistic production; capitalistic production presupposes the existence of considerable masses of capital and labor-power in the hands of producers of commodities. The whole movement, therefore, seems to turn in a vicious circle, out of which we can only get by supposing a primitive accumulation (previous accumulation of Adam Smith) preceding capitalistic accumulation," a primitive accumulation which is "nothing else than the historical process of divorcing the producer from the means of production." He may be right, furthermore, when he goes on to say that "the economic structure of capitalistic society has grown out of the economic structure of feudal society. . . . The historical movement which changes the producers into wage-workers appears, on the one hand, as their emancipation from serfdom and from the fetters of the guilds . . . but, on the other hand, these new freedmen became sellers of themselves only after they had been robbed of all their own means of production, and of all the guarantees of existence afforded by the old feudal arrangements."

It may be true that a capitalist who privately owns means of production would not invest them without the possibility of gaining a profit. It may be true, as Smith would insist, that he would not be justified in doing so. This, however, does not invalidate—as it is not invalidated by—Marx's theory of the "original expropriation" which, in his opinion, initiated capitalistic enterprise; nor does it conflict with Marx's insistence that the capitalist must exploit labor in order to make profits, since he can derive them only from the surplus value created by wage-laborers who produce more than is returned to them for their own needs or subsistence.

THE FOREGOING POINT AND counter-point in economic theory must serve as one example of the way in which Smith and Marx pass each other, rather than meet, on many of the basic economic issues. It would be impossible, within the compass of this Introduction, to chart the intricate relationship of their thought, including their agreements and clear oppositions as well as the matters on which they simply diverge because they are discussing the same problem from different viewpoints. The reader can discover for himself in greater detail the pattern of conversation between these two great economists by studying the passages from their works which are cited in the References.

As a glance at the Outline of Topics will show, many of the headings represent technical problems or issues in economic theory, as that is narrowly conceived in modern times. Some, however, are more general. They state themes which place the discussion of wealth in the larger context of moral and political questions and which, throughout the whole tradition, engage poets, historians, and philosophers—not merely the economists of the eighteenth and nineteenth centuries.

To some extent the more general themes are treated in other chapters, such as LABOR, JUSTICE, OLIGARCHY, VIRTUE and HAPPINESS, FAMILY and STATE. Here we shall consider them for their bearing on the nature and kinds, the sources and uses, of wealth, and also its goodness and evil.

THE ANCIENTS CONCEIVE WEALTH as consisting in the variety of external goods which sustain life—food, clothing, and shelter. But wealth may include more than the bare necessities. When Socrates in the *Republic* outlines a simple economy which aims to satisfy only basic needs, Glaucon tells him that he is "providing for a city of pigs." More is required, he says, for "the ordinary conveniences of life. People who are to be comfortable are accustomed to lie on sofas, and dine off tables, and they should have sauces and sweets in the modern style." Socrates replies by projecting "a luxurious State"—"a State at fever heat"—which goes beyond the necessaries, "such as houses and clothes and shoes. The arts of the painter and the embroiderer," he says, "will have to be set in motion, and gold and ivory and all sorts of materials procured"; and the city will "have to fill and swell with a multitude of callings which are not required by any natural want."

This distinction between necessities and luxuries, which has many implications for ethics and economics as well as for politics, does not draw the line between natural and artificial wealth. Nor is natural wealth identified exclusively with natural resources in their pure state, unconverted by labor for use or consumption. Wealth is generally thought to comprise all consumable goods, whether necessities or luxuries, whether products of hunting, agriculture, or manufacture, and all the means of producing them. Only money is excluded. Only money is declared to be either not wealth at all or artificial wealth.

Yet the confusion of money with wealth seems to be prevalent at all times, as repeated attempts to correct the fallacy indicate. The use of money originates, according to Aristotle, with retail trade, which is "not a natural part of the art of getting wealth"; for, he goes on, "had it been so, men would have ceased to exchange when they had enough." What Aristotle calls retail trade replaces "the barter of necessary articles." Made possible by the use of coin, retail trade, he says, comes to be thought of as "the art which produces riches and wealth.

"Indeed," Aristotle continues, "riches is assumed by many to be only a quantity of coin." But he agrees with those who maintain, to the contrary, that "coined money is a mere sham, a thing not natural, but conventional only . . . because it is not useful as a means to any of the necessities of life, and he who is rich in coin may often be in want of necessary food. But how can that be wealth of which a man may have a great abundance and yet perish with hunger, like Midas in the fable, whose insatiable prayer turned everything that was set before him into gold?"

To say that money in itself cannot satisfy any natural need does not imply that it serves no economic purpose. Plato and Aristotle, Hobbes, Locke, and Kant, as well as Smith and Marx, understand the utility of money as a medium of exchange, indispensable for "the circulation of commodities"—to use Marx's phrase—beyond the stage of barter. Money is not only a medium of exchange, according to Plato; it "reduces the inequalities and incommensurabilities of goods to equality and common measure"; and Aristotle seems to anticipate Marx's conception of money as the universal form in which all economic values can be expressed when he defines "wealth" to mean "all things whose value is measured by money."

The economic utility of money in exchange and as a measure of value, or even the fact that gold and silver coin may have some intrinsic value because of the labor involved in mining and minting the metals, does not alter the distinction between natural and artificial wealth. "Natural wealth," Aquinas explains, "is that which serves man as a remedy for his natural wants, such as food, drink, clothing, cars, dwellings, and such like; while artificial wealth, such as money, is that which is not a direct help to nature, but is invented by man for the convenience of exchange and as a measure of all things saleable."

The same point is restated by Locke in the seventeenth century, but it is still necessary for Smith a century later to argue against the mercantilist theory of national prosperity, on the ground that it confuses wealth with money. "It would be too ridiculous to go about seriously to prove," Smith writes, "that wealth does not consist in money, or in gold or silver; but what money purchases, and is valuable only for purchasing. . . . Goods can serve many other purposes besides purchasing money, but money can serve no other purpose besides purchasing goods. Money, therefore, necessarily runs after goods, but goods do not always or necessarily run after money. The man who buys, does not always mean to sell again, but frequently to use or consume; whereas he who sells, always means to buy again."

Nevertheless, that "wealth consists in money, or in gold and silver, is a popular notion which naturally arises from the double function of money, as the instrument of commerce, and as the measure of value." The notion is so familiar that, Smith observes, "even they, who are convinced of its absurdity, are very apt to forget their own principles, and in the course of their reasonings to take it for granted as a certain and undeniable truth. Some of the best English writers on commerce set out with observing that the wealth of a country consists, not in its gold and silver only, but in its lands, houses, and consumable goods of all different kinds. In the course of their reasonings, however, the land, houses, and consumable goods seem to slip out of their memory, and the strain of their argument frequently supposes that all wealth consists in gold and silver, and to multiply these metals is the great object of national industry and commerce."

The two principles of the mercantilist policy are, according to Smith, that "wealth consisted in gold and silver, and that those metals could be brought into a country which had no mines only by the balance of trade, or by exporting to a greater value than it imported." A favorable balance of trade thus necessarily became the sole object of the mercantilists; and, Smith adds, "its two great engines for enriching the country, therefore, were restraints upon importation, and encouragements to exportation."

Since in his opinion the wealth of a nation consists in "the whole annual produce of its land and labor," Smith opposes all such restraints, and with them the protection of monopolies. He advocates free trade and the free competition of producers, within a country as well as between domestic and foreign producers, on the ground that "consumption is the sole end and purpose of all production; and the interest of the producer ought to be attended to, only so far as it may be necessary for promoting that of the consumer. But in the mercantile system," Smith claims, "the interest of the consumer is almost constantly sacrificed to that of the producer." A *laissez-faire* economy, he thinks, not only reverses this situation, but also, by preferring more consumable commodities to more gold and silver, tends to increase the real, not the artificial wealth of a nation.

Marx also criticizes the mercantilist error, but in terms of his theory that "since the production of surplus-value is the chief end and aim of capitalist production . . . the greatness of a man's or a nation's wealth should be measured, not by the absolute quantity produced, but by the relative magnitude of the surplus-value."

Surplus value cannot be produced by exchange. Against the mercantilists who "derived the excess of the price over the cost of production of the product, from the act of exchange, from the product being sold above its value," Marx quotes Mill's statement that "profit arises, not from the incident of exchange, but from the productive power of labor; and the general profit of the country is always what the productive power of labor makes it, whether any exchange takes place or not."

But this is not the whole picture, according to Marx. Although it is impossible for capital or surplus value "to be produced by circulation," or the exchange of commodities, he also thinks it is "impossible that outside the sphere of circulation, a producer of commodities can, without coming into contact with other commodity owners, expand value, and consequently convert money or commodities into capital." The two sides of the picture are brought together, in Marx's view, by the treatment of labor itself as a commodity, and the buying and selling of labor power in the open market.

THE DISTINCTION BETWEEN REAL wealth and money and the distinction between necessities and luxuries have more than economic significance. They are basic to the moralist's strictures concerning the desire for wealth, its place in the order of goods, and the way it can be put to good use.

It is not only St. Paul who says that "the love of money is the root of all evil." It is not only Christian theologians like Augustine and Aquinas who explain how "lust of the eyes" or covetousness is a capital sin and as such the principle of many other transgressions. As Marx points out, the Greeks also "denounced money as subversive of the economical and moral order of things." In the passage in Sophocles' *Antigone* which he quotes, Creon declares: "Nothing so evil as money ever grew to be current among men. This lays cities low, this drives men from their homes, this trains and warps honest souls till they set themselves to works of shame; this still teaches folk to practice villainies, and to know every godless deed."

Plato condemns the oligarchical state by

comparing it to the miser and money-maker among men. "Such a State," he says, "aims to become as rich as possible, a desire which is insatiable." In the *Laws*, the Athenian Stranger explains why the reasonable statesman should not aim to make "the state for the true interests of which he is advising . . . as great and as rich as possible," if he also "desires to have the city the best and happiest possible"; for though each may be possible alone, they are not possible together. It is impossible, he holds, to be "good in a high degree and rich in a high degree at the same time."

What Plato says of the oligarch, Marx says of the capitalist: "He shares with the miser the passion for wealth as wealth." But, Marx adds, "that which in the miser is a mere idiosyncrasy is, in the capitalist, the effect of the social mechanism, of which he is but one of the wheels." Involved as he is by the system in "the restless never-ending process of profit-making," the individual capitalist, like the miser, exhibits "this boundless greed after riches, this passionate chase after exchange-value."

The root of the evil in the love of money—of "gold, yellow, glittering, precious gold," which Shakespeare calls the "common whore of mankind"—is the boundlessness of the lust. The hoarding of anything springs from an insatiable desire, but because money can be converted into every sort of commodity, it is, according to Marx, the ideal object of hoarding. "The antagonism between the quantitative limits of money and its qualitative boundlessness," he writes, "continually acts as a spur to the hoarder in his Sisyphus-like labor of accumulating."

In the light of such observations, Marx cites with approval Aristotle's distinction between "economic" and "chrematistic" or what Aristotle differentiates as the two arts of wealth-getting. Considering economics as the management of a household, Aristotle says that the art of acquisition which is a natural part of it "must either find ready to hand, or itself provide, such things necessary to life, and useful for the community of the family or state, as can be stored. They are the elements of true riches; for the amount of property which is needed for a good life is not unlimited." But "there is another variety of the art of acquisition which is commonly and rightly called an art of wealth-getting, and has in fact suggested that riches and property have no limit."

The two arts tend to become confused in men's minds. "Some persons are led to believe," Aristotle observes, "that getting wealth is the object of household management, and the whole idea of their lives is that they ought either to increase their money without limit, or at any rate not to lose it. The origin of this disposition in men is that they are intent upon living only, and not upon living well; and as their desires are unlimited, they also desire that the means of gratifying them should be without limit." Even "those who do aim at a good life seek the means of obtaining bodily pleasures; and, since the enjoyment of these appears to depend upon property, they are absorbed in getting wealth; and thus there arises the second kind of wealth-getting."

Plato, like Aristotle, while admitting the service of retail trade in effecting the exchange of commodities, condemns the tendency of its practitioners to make "gains without limit." In the *Laws*, furthermore, he prohibits interest on loans; and in the *Republic*, he describes this form of money-making as a process in which "men of business . . . insert their sting—that is, their money—into someone else who is not on his guard against them, and recover the parent sum many times over multiplied into a family of children." This biological metaphor for making money out of money appears also in Aristotle. The term "interest," he says, "means the birth of money from money." Of all forms of money-making, this "breeding of money" is, in his opinion, the most unnatural. "Usury, which makes a gain out of money itself," Aristotle writes, violates the natural object of money—"intended to be used in exchange, but not to increase at interest."

Interest and usury are not distinguished in the Old Testament. "Take thou no usury of him, or increase," is the command in Leviticus. But this rule does not apply to the stranger. "Unto a stranger thou mayst lend upon usury," Deuteronomy says, "but unto thy brother thou shalt not lend upon usury."

A theologian like Aquinas, following both Scripture and Aristotle, condemns, for Christians, all interest as usury; and Luther also appeals to pagan precept as well as to Scriptural warrant. "The heathen were able, by the light of reason, to conclude that a usurer is a double-dyed thief and murderer," Luther says in a passage which Marx quotes under the comment that the usurer is "that old-fashioned but ever renewed specimen of the capitalist." Castigating his fellow-Christians for holding usurers "in such honor that we fairly worship them for the sake of their money," Luther declares that "whoever eats up, robs, and steals the nourishment of another, that man commits as great a murder (so far as in him lies) as he who starves a man or utterly undoes him. Such does a usurer."

It seems to be a later consequence of the Protestant reformation, as Weber and Tawney point out, that the exaction of interest for the loan of money or goods is defended, and only exorbitant rates of interest are denounced as usurious. The signs of the change may be seen in Pascal's diatribe against the specious casuistry which tries to exempt some forms of interest-taking from the charge of usury; and also in the fact that Montesquieu attributes to the schoolmen, "who adopted from Aristotle, a great many notions on lending upon interest," the mistake of condemning it "absolutely and in all cases." In his own opinion, "to lend money without interest is certainly an action laudable and extremely good; but is is obvious that it is only a counsel of religion, and not a civil law."

Montesquieu thinks a price for the use of money is necessary for the carrying on of trade. If a fair rate of interest is not allowed, nobody will lend money; or rather, Montesquieu says, because "the affairs of society will ever make it necessary," moneylending will inevitably take the form of usury. "Usury increases in Mohammedan countries," he points out, "in proportion to the severity of the prohibition. The lender indemnifies himself for the danger he undergoes of suffering the penalty."

Smith agrees that prohibition, "instead of preventing, has been found from experience to increase the evil of usury." A fair rate of interest is justified, he thinks, because "as something can everywhere be made by the use of money, something ought everywhere to be paid for the use of it. . . . In countries where interest is permitted, the law, in order to prevent the extortion of usury, generally fixes the highest rate which can be taken without incurring a penalty. This rate ought always to be somewhat above the lowest market price, or the price which is commonly paid for the use of money by those who can give the most undoubted security." Smith offers the British practice as a good example. "Where money is lent to government at three per cent, and to private people upon good security at four, and four and a half, the present legal rate, five per cent, is perhaps as proper as any."

Interest and profit, while not the same in Smith's view, are closely connected. As the revenue from land is rent, from labor wages, and "that derived from stock, by the person who manages or employs it, is called profit," interest is "the compensation which the borrower pays to the lender, for the profit which he has an opportunity of making by the use of the money. Part of that profit naturally belongs to the borrower, who runs the risk and takes the trouble of employing it; and part to the lender, who affords him an opportunity of making this profit." Conceiving interest as a derivative revenue, Smith holds it to be a maxim that "wherever a great deal can be made by the use of money, a great deal will be commonly given for the use of it," so that we may expect to find "the usual market rate of interest" to vary with "the ordinary profits of stock."

THE THEORY WHICH PLACES wealth lowest in the order of goods determines its contribution to human happiness accordingly, and leads to a disapproval of luxuries, on the part of both the individual and society.

"Riches are for the sake of the body, as the body is for the sake of the soul. The latter are good," writes Plato, "and wealth is intended by nature to be for the sake of them, and is therefore inferior to them both, and third in the order of excellence." Aristotle similarly orders wealth, or external goods, to health and other goods of the body, as these in turn are subordinate to the virtues, or goods of the soul; and Hobbes, in somewhat different terms, holds that, of all goods, "those that are dearest to a man are his own life and limbs; and in the next degree (in most men), those that concern conjugal affection; and after them riches and means of living."

While Aristotle admits that happiness requires some external prosperity, he always adds that only a moderate amount of external goods is needed. "Happiness, whether consisting in pleasure or virtue, or both," he writes, "is more often found with those who are most highly cultivated in their mind and in their character, and have only a moderate share of external goods, than among those who possess external goods to a useless extent, but are deficient in higher qualities." Aristotle praises Solon for telling Croesus, one of the world's wealthiest men, that happiness requires more than riches. The conversation is narrated by Herodotus.

"What, stranger of Athens," Herodotus reports Croesus as saying, "is my happiness, then, valued so little by you, that you do not even put me on a level with private men?" To which, Solon replies: "Croesus, I see that you are wonderfully rich, and the lord of many nations," but "he who possesses a great store of riches is no nearer happiness than he who has what suffices for his daily needs, unless luck attends him, and so he continue in the enjoyment of all his good things to the end of his life." Aristotle adds the further observation that "one can with but moderate possessions do what one ought" and that "a good life requires a supply of external goods in a less degree when men are in a good state and in a greater degree when they are in a lower state."

Aquinas agrees with Aristotle so far as the happiness of the active life is concerned, but he holds that wealth "does not conduce to the happiness of the contemplative life; rather is it an obstacle thereto." With regard to achieving "the happiness of heaven" in the life hereafter, Aquinas not only thinks wealth an obstacle, but he also explains why the religious orders take the vow of voluntary poverty. "Man is directed to future happiness by charity," he writes; and "in the attainment of the perfection of charity the first foundation is voluntary poverty, whereby a man lives without property of his own."

The opinion that wealth is an obstacle or that it should be sought in moderation does not seem to be universally shared. As Herodotus, Plato, and Aristotle report the prevalence in the ancient world of the notion that "external goods are the cause of happiness," so Melville reflects that in modern society "the urbane activity with which a man receives money is really marvellous, considering that we so earnestly believe money to be the root of all earthly ills, and that on no account can a monied man enter heaven. Ah! how cheerfully we consign ourselves to perdition!" Marx quotes a still more extravagant claim. In a letter from Jamaica in 1503, Christopher Columbus exclaims: "Gold is a wonderful thing! Whoever possesses it is lord of all he wants. By means of gold one can even get souls into Paradise."

Against Rousseau's attack upon opulence as the cause of civilization with all its miseries, Dr. Johnson rises in the defense of luxuries and the advantages of wealth. "Rousseau's treatise on the inequality of mankind," Boswell writes, "was at this time a fashionable topick. It gave rise to an observation by Mr. Dempster that the advantages of fortune and rank were nothing to a wise man." To this, Dr. Johnson replies: "If a man were a savage, living in the woods by himself, this might be true," but "in civilized society, external advantages make us more respected. . . . Sir, you may make the experiment. Go into the street, and give one man a lecture on morality, and another a shilling, and see which will respect you the most . . .

"And, Sir," he continues, "if six hundred pounds a year procure a man more consequence, and, of course, more happiness than six pounds, the same proportion will hold as to six thousand, and so on as far as opulence can be carried. Perhaps he who has a large fortune may not be so happy as he who has a small one; but that must proceed from other causes than from his having the large fortune; for, *ceteris paribus*, he who is rich in a civilized society, must be happier than he who is poor."

On one occasion, Dr. Johnson seems to share Solon's view. When Boswell suggests that the proprietor of a great estate "must be happy," he exclaims: "Nay, Sir, all this excludes but one evil—poverty." But for the most part, his opinion is that "it is in refinement and elegance that the civilized man differs from the savage," and that it is right for every society to be as luxurious as it can be.

"Many things which are false are transmitted from book to book," he says to General Oglethorpe, "and gain credit in the world. One of these is the cry against the evil of luxury. Now the truth is that luxury produces much good. You will hear it said, very gravely, Why was not the half-guinea, thus spent in luxury, given to the poor? To how many might it have afforded a good meal. Alas! has it not gone to the *industrious* poor, whom it is better to support than the *idle* poor? You are much surer that you are doing good when you *pay* money to those who work as the recompense of their labor, than when you *give* money in charity. . . . And as to the rout that is made about people who are ruined by extravagance, it is no matter to the nation that some individuals suffer. When so much general productive exertion is the consequence of luxury, the nation does not care though there are debtors in gaol."

Dr. Johnson's pronouncements may silence Mr. Dempster and General Oglethorpe, but not Smith or Marx. To Smith, spendthrift extravagance squanders wealth which might have been capitalized for productive purposes; to Marx, the multiplication of luxury products diverts labor power that is socially necessary for producing the means of subsistence into what Veblen later calls forms of "conspicuous waste." Not only, in Marx's view, can the capitalistic system be charged with indifference as to whether its profits are made out of the production of luxuries or necessities; but the workers on starvation wages engaged in the luxury trades constitute a signal indictment of the inequitable distribution of wealth.

AS THE NEEDS OF THE individual are thought to set a natural limit to his acquisition of wealth, or at least to provide him with a rational standard for stopping short of wanton luxuries when he seeks the decencies or amenities of life, so the needs of society as a whole are thought to establish a criterion of justice in the distribution of wealth.

"God gave the world to men in common," says Locke, and "the measure of property nature has well set by the extent of man's labor and the convenience of life. . . . No man's labor could subdue or appropriate all; nor could his enjoyment consume more than a small part; so that it was impossible for any man, this way, to intrench upon the right of another, who would still have room for as good and as large a possession (after the other had taken out his) as before it was appropriated. Which measure did confine every man's possession to a very moderate proportion, and such as he might appropriate to himself without injury to anybody, in the first age of the world."

This rule of property—"that every man should have as much as he could make use of" without prejudice or injury to others—worked well in the beginning when, as Locke puts it, "all the world was America." It "would still hold in the world without straitening anybody," Locke thinks, "since there is land enough in the world to suffice double the inhabitants, had not the invention of money . . . introduced (by consent) larger possessions and a right to them"; for gold and silver being relatively imperishable, men can hoard excesses of them without appearing to waste them, as they would if they amassed perishable commodities which they could not consume or use.

It is not money but property itself which Rousseau claims to be the origin of inequality among men and of the inequitable distribution of wealth. "The first man who, having enclosed a piece of ground, bethought himself of saying *This is mine*, and found people simple enough to believe him, was the real founder of civil society." Once established as a right, property tends to expand. The larger proprietors avoid the question, "Do you not know that numbers of your fellow-creatures are starving, for want of what you have too much of?" Instead, according to Rousseau, they conceive "the profoundest plan that ever entered the mind of man" to protect their possessions against invasion or plunder. They institute civil government, ostensibly for the security of all, but really to secure for themselves their property and power.

"Such was, or may well have been," Rousseau writes, "the origin of society and law, which bound new fetters on the poor, and gave new powers to the rich; which irretrievably destroyed natural liberty, eternally fixed the law of property and inequality, converted clever usurpation into unalterable right, and, for the advantage of a few ambitious individuals, subjected all mankind to perpetual labor, slavery, and wretchedness." Adam Smith seems to agree. "Where there is no property," he says, "or at least none that exceeds the value of two or three days labor, civil government is not so necessary. . . . Civil government, so far as it is instituted for the security of property, is in reality for the defense of the rich against the poor, or of those who have some property against those who have none at all."

But, unlike Smith, Rousseau has an alternative to propose. "Since it is plainly contrary to the law of nature . . . that the privileged few should gorge themselves with superfluities while the starving multitude are in want of the bare necessities of life," he thinks it is "one of the most important functions of government to prevent extreme inequalities of fortunes; not by taking away wealth from its possessors, but by depriving all men of means to accumulate it; not by building asylums for the poor, but by securing the citizens from becoming poor."

THIS STATES AN END, but not the means for achieving it. The problem of poverty is not so easily solved, if it can be solved at all, once the right of property is admitted. Rousseau, for example, no less than Locke and others before him, affirms this right which, for Kant and Hegel later, is almost the whole substance of private or abstract right. "The right of property," says Rousseau, "is the most sacred of all the rights of citizenship, and even more important in some respects than liberty itself." Yet it is difficult, he admits, "to secure the property of individuals on one side, without attacking it on another; and it is impossible that all the regulations which govern the order of succession, wills, contracts, etc., should not lay individuals under some constraint as to the disposition of their goods, and should not consequently restrict the right of property."

To Hegel, poverty seems to be an inevitable consequence of property, as war is an inevitable consequence of sovereignty, and in neither case can the cause be abolished. "When the masses begin to decline into poverty," as they must, they can be supported from public funds and private charities, thus receiving "subsistence directly, not by means of their work," or as an alternative, "they might be given subsistence indirectly through being given work." But, Hegel adds, "in this event the volume of production would be increased, but the evil consists precisely in an excess of production and in the lack of a proportionate number of consumers who are themselves also producers, and thus it is simply intensified by both of the methods by which it is sought to alleviate it." Hence, Hegel concludes, it "becomes apparent that despite an excess of wealth civil society is not rich enough . . . to check excessive poverty and the creation of a penurious rabble. This inner dialectic of civil society thus drives it—or at any rate a specific civil society—to push beyond its own limits and seek markets, and . . . its necessary means of subsistence, in other lands which are either deficient in the goods it has over-produced, or else generally backward in industry."

Imperialism, according to Marx, will not long work as a cure for what Tawney later calls "the sickness of an acquisitive society"—the inner frustration which Marx sees manifested in recurring economic crises and depressions of greater and greater magnitude. Nor does he propose the abolition of all private property as the remedy for poverty, when he calls for "the expropriation of the expropriators." On the contrary, only the possession by each individual of an adequate supply of consumer's goods can abolish poverty. Differentiating between individual and capitalist property, according as its owners are or are not laborers, and according as it consists in consumable goods or the means of production, Marx would transfer the latter from private property to public ownership.

The socialist economy he outlines also includes "abolition of property in land, and application of all rents of land to public purposes; a heavy progressive or graduated income tax; abolition of all right of inheritance." It includes "centralization of credit in the hands of the state, by means of a national bank with State capital and an exclusive monopoly," and also "centralization of the means of communication and transport." Last but not least, it includes "equal liability of all to labor."

More radical than Marx's socialism is the communism Plato proposes in the *Republic*. Plato's aim is not to solve the problem of poverty or economic injustice. By abolishing for his guardian class *all* private property, he hopes that his guardians through sharing common possessions (including wives and children) will have no cause for rivalry, dissension, or personal ambition. Common possessions should mould them into a fraternity and free them from private interests to work for the common good. In this matter of property, the condition of Plato's imagined guardians was not so different from that of Jesus' disciples as recounted in the Book of Acts, or of the monastic orders whose vows include that of voluntary poverty.

Aristotle's criticisms of the arrangements for the guardian class in the *Republic* are largely directed against the community of women and children and the elimination of private property. "Property," he says, "should be in a certain sense common, but as a general rule private; for, when everyone has a distinct interest, men will not complain of one another, and they will make more progress, because everyone will be attending to his own business." He thinks "it is clearly better that property should be private, but the use of it common," in the sense that its use have the common welfare in mind.

Not only does Aristotle defend private property on many counts, but he objects to schemes for equalizing it, such as Plato sets forth in the *Laws*. For one thing, "the legislator ought not only to aim at the equalization of properties, but at moderation in their amount." Yet if the legislator "prescribe this moderate amount equally to all, he will be no nearer the mark; for it is not the possessions but the desires of mankind which need to be equalized, and this is impossible unless a sufficient education is provided by the laws."

Whether or not communism is desirable, there are those who think it is impossible, not so much on the level of the economic, as on the level of the moral, revolution for which Aristotle looks to education. The skeptic thinks human nature cannot be so transformed. It may be only in the twentieth century that the world is divided into two camps on this subject, but the issue is as old as the western tradition. At its beginning Aristophanes expresses the skeptical position in a form that is still current. His *Ecclesiazusae* simply laughs at the idea that inequalities of property can ever be done away with—by law or by education.

OUTLINE OF TOPICS

4*d*. The source of value: the labor theory of value

4*e*. Causes of the fluctuation of market price: supply and demand

4*f*. The consequences of monopoly and competition

4*g*. Commerce between states: tariffs and bounties; free trade

5. Money

5*a*. The nature of money as a medium or instrument of exchange, and as a measure of equivalents in exchange

5*b*. Monetary standards: the coining or minting of money; good and bad money

5*c*. The price of money: the exchange rate of money as measured in terms of other commodities

5*d*. The institution and function of banks: monetary loans, credit, the financing of capitalistic enterprise

5*e*. The rate of interest on money: the condemnation of usury

6. Capital

6*a*. Comparison of capitalist production with other systems of production: the social utility of capital

6*b*. Theories of the nature, origin, and growth of capital stock: thrift, savings, excesses beyond the needs of consumption, expropriation

6*c*. Types of capital: fixed and circulating, or constant and variable capital

6*d*. Capital profits

(1) The distinction of profit from rent, interest, and wages

(2) The source of profit: marginal or surplus value; unearned increment and the exploitation of labor

(3) Factors determining the variable rate of capital profit

(4) The justification of profit: the reward of enterprise and indemnification for risk of losses

6*e*. The recurrence of crises in the capitalist economy: depressions, unemployment, the diminishing rate of profit

7. Property

7*a*. The right of property: the protection of property as the function of government

7*b*. Kinds of economic property

(1) Chattel slaves as property

(2) Property in land

(3) Property in capital goods and in monetary wealth

7*c*. The uses of property: for production, consumption, or exchange

7*d*. The ownership of property: possession or title; the legal regulation of property

(1) Private ownership: partnerships, joint-stock companies

(2) Government ownership: eminent domain

7*e*. The inheritance of property: laws regulating inheritance

8. The distribution of wealth: the problem of poverty

8*a*. The sharing of wealth: goods and lands held in common; public ownership of the means of production

8*b*. The division of common goods into private property: factors influencing the increase and decrease of private property

8*c*. The causes of poverty: competition, incompetence, indigence, expropriation, unemployment; the poverty of the proletariat as dispossessed of the instruments of production

8*d*. Laws concerning poverty: the poor laws, the dole

9. Political economy: the nature of the science of economics

9*a*. Wealth as an element in the political common good

9*b*. Factors determining the prosperity or opulence of states: fluctuations in national prosperity

9*c*. Diverse economic programs for securing the wealth of nations: the physiocratic, the mercantilist, and the laissez-faire systems

9*d*. Governmental regulation of production, trade, or other aspects of economic life

9*e*. The economic support of government and the services of government

(1) The charges of government: the cost of maintaining its services; elements in the national budget

(2) Methods of defraying the expenses of government: taxation and other forms of levy or impost; confiscations, seizures, and other abuses of taxation

9*f*. Wealth or property in relation to different forms of government

9*g*. Wealth and poverty in relation to crime and to war between states

9*h*. The struggle of economic classes for political power

10. The moral aspects of wealth and poverty

10*a*. The nature of wealth as a good: its place in the order of goods and its relation to happiness

10*b*. Natural limits to the acquisition of wealth by individuals: the distinction between necessities and luxuries

10*c*. Temperance and intemperance with respect to wealth: liberality, magnificence, miserliness, avarice

10*d*. The principles of justice with respect to wealth and property: fair wages and prices

10*e*. The precepts of charity with respect to wealth

(1) Almsgiving to the needy and the impoverished

(2) The religious vow of poverty: voluntary poverty

(3) The choice between God and Mammon: the love of money as the root of all evil

11. Economic determinism: the economic interpretation of history

12. Economic progress: advances with respect to both efficiency and justice

REFERENCES

References are listed by volume number (in bold type), author's name, and page number. Bible references are to book, chapter, and verse of the Authorized King James version of the Bible. The abbreviation "esp" calls the reader's attention to one or more especially relevant parts of a whole reference; "passim" signifies that the topic is discussed intermittently rather than continuously in the work or passage cited. Where the work as a whole is relevant to the topic, the page numbers refer to the entire work. For general guidance in the use of *The Great Ideas,* consult the Preface.

1. The elements of wealth: the distinction between natural and artificial wealth; the distinction between the instruments of production and consumable goods

7 PLATO, 316–318
9 ARISTOTLE, 601
23 HOBBES, 124
35 LOCKE, 33–35
38 MONTESQUIEU, 152
38 ROUSSEAU, 348–355
39 SMITH, 163, 182–300
50 MARX, 13, 279–286

2. The acquisition and management of wealth in the domestic and tribal community

7 PLATO, 664–666
9 ARISTOTLE, 446–455 passim
14 PLUTARCH, 130, 286–287, 439, 455
18 AUGUSTINE, 520
25 MONTAIGNE, 458–462, 472–473
29 CERVANTES, 148–149
35 LOCKE, 67–68
36 STERNE, 376–379
38 MONTESQUIEU, 50, 129–132, 216
38 ROUSSEAU, 367–368
39 SMITH, 50, 165–167
40 GIBBON, 16–17, 66–67, 88–90 passim, 498–501 passim
41 GIBBON, 86–89
44 BOSWELL, 147–148, 274–278
46 HEGEL, 60–61, 134, 135
49 DARWIN, 324
50 MARX, 34, 163, 171–172, 174–175
51 TOLSTOY, 211–213, 275–302 passim, 650–652, 654–655

3. The production of wealth in the political community

3*a*. Factors in productivity: natural resources, raw materials, labor, tools and machines, capital investments

OLD TESTAMENT: *Proverbs,* 6:6–11; 14:23; 24:30–34
6 HERODOTUS, 51, 194
7 PLATO, 316–319, 482
9 ARISTOTLE, 447, 453
23 HOBBES, 124
38 MONTESQUIEU, 152, 191
38 ROUSSEAU, 352–353, 404
39 SMITH, 1, 3–10, 106, 142–151, 155–157, 158–159, 163–165, 173
46 HEGEL, 67, 137, 194–195
50 MARX, 85–89, 96–99, 149–150, 157–161, 170–171, 180–192, 197–198, 216–219, 239, 249–250, 251–252, 253–254, 285, 298, 299–300
50 MARX-ENGELS, 425

3*b*. The use of land: kinds of land or real estate; the general theory of rent

6 HERODOTUS, 70
35 LOCKE, 32–34
38 MONTESQUIEU, 191
39 SMITH, 15–16, 20–23, 163–181, 243–244, 246–247
41 GIBBON, 90
44 BOSWELL, 172
46 HEGEL, 34
50 MARX, 63, 65–66

3*c*. Agricultural production: the produce of land

6 HERODOTUS, 43–44, 112, 158
9 ARISTOTLE, 450
12 LUCRETIUS, 78–79
35 LOCKE, 33–35 passim
38 MONTESQUIEU, 96–97, 105, 125–126
38 ROUSSEAU, 352
39 SMITH, 62–110 passim, 157, 162, 163–170, 175–181 passim, 288–299
40 GIBBON, 21–22, 367–368
43 FEDERALIST, 56
46 HEGEL, 68, 137
50 MARX, 249–250, 318, 333–353 passim, 368–371

3*d*. Industrial production: domestic, guild, and factory systems of manufacturing

38 MONTESQUIEU, 105
38 ROUSSEAU, 365–366
39 SMITH, 3–10, 163–165 esp 163, 173–175, 189, 288–299
41 GIBBON, 314–315
46 HEGEL, 68, 77, 243–244, 335–336
50 MARX, 111–146 passim, 149, 157–250, 369–371

4. The exchange of wealth or the circulation of commodities: the processes of commerce or trade

4*a*. The forms of value: the distinction between use-value and exchange-value

4*b*. Types of exchange: barter economies and money economies

4*c*. Rent, profit, wages, interest as the elements of price: the distinction between the real and the nominal price and between the natural and the market price of commodities

4*d*. The source of value: the labor theory of value

4*e*. Causes of the fluctuation of market price: supply and demand

4*f*. The consequences of monopoly and competition

4*g*. Commerce between states: tariffs and bounties; free trade

5. Money

5*a*. The nature of money as a medium or instrument of exchange, and as a measure of equivalents in exchange

5*b*. Monetary standards: the coining or minting of money; good and bad money

5*c*. The price of money: the exchange rate of money as measured in terms of other commodities

40 Gibbon, 197
46 Hegel, 23–24
50 Marx, 163, 174–175

8*b*. The division of common goods into private property: factors influencing the increase and decrease of private property

Old Testament: *Numbers*, 26:52–56
6 Herodotus, 70
19 Aquinas, 516–517
23 Hobbes, 124–125
35 Locke, 30–36
38 Montesquieu, 19–21
38 Rousseau, 393–394
39 Smith, 27–28, 239, 311
42 Kant, 414–415, 426–428
46 Hegel, 62, 76, 121
50 Marx, 288, 358–361, 368–369, 377–378

8*c*. The causes of poverty: competition, incompetence, indigence, expropriation, unemployment; the poverty of the proletariat as dispossessed of the instruments of production

15 Tacitus, 194–195
38 Montesquieu, 147, 190
39 Smith, 28, 30–31
40 Gibbon, 501
44 Boswell, 428
46 Hegel, 76–77, 140–141
50 Marx, 150, 160–162, 209–225, 280–286, 288, 303–305, 307, 315–321, 325–327, 349–350, 354–355, 357–358, 360–361, 370–371, 375
50 Marx-Engels, 424–425

8*d*. Laws concerning poverty: the poor laws, the dole

Old Testament: *Leviticus*, 19:9–10; 25:25,35–54 / *Deuteronomy*, 15:7–11; 26:12–13
5 Aristophanes, 619
7 Plato, 342–344, 783
9 Aristotle, 523–524
14 Plutarch, 87
15 Tacitus, 32
23 Hobbes, 157
31 Spinoza, 448
38 Montesquieu, 199–200
39 Smith, 59–61, 200–201
40 Gibbon, 175, 501–502
42 Kant, 443–444
43 Mill, 322, 383–384
44 Boswell, 442–443
46 Hegel, 77
50 Marx, 358, 364–366

9. Political economy: the nature of the science of economics

9 Aristotle, 339 passim
38 Rousseau, 367–385
39 Smith, 182
46 Hegel, 65–66, 136
50 Marx, 6, 8–11 passim, 33–37, 178–179, 305

9*a*. Wealth as an element in the political common good

5 Aristophanes, 629–642
6 Thucydides, 396, 397
7 Plato, 485, 665, 694–695, 733
9 Aristotle, 452, 462–463, 465–466, 530–531, 532–533
14 Plutarch, 291–292, 361
15 Tacitus, 31, 57–58, 232–233
23 Hobbes, 124–127
38 Montesquieu, 19–21, 23–25, 44–48
38 Rousseau, 327–328, 375, 377–385 passim
40 Gibbon, 456–457, 498–501, 642
43 Federalist, 79–80
44 Boswell, 124–125, 172–173
50 Marx, 320–321
51 Tolstoy, 572–573

9*b*. Factors determining the prosperity or opulence of states: fluctuations in national prosperity

7 Plato, 677
9 Aristotle, 531
23 Hobbes, 154
38 Montesquieu, 44–47, 125, 127, 152
38 Rousseau, 352–353, 360–361, 365–366, 375, 383
39 Smith, 3–300
40 Gibbon, 236–237, 239, 501, 655–658
41 Gibbon, 221–222, 314–315, 558, 597–598
43 Federalist, 31, 53–56 passim, 79
43 Mill, 335
44 Boswell, 171
46 Hegel, 77–78, 263
50 Marx, 31–37 passim, 218–219, 253–254, 377–378

9*c*. Diverse economic programs for securing the wealth of nations: the physiocratic, the mercantilist, and the laissez-faire systems

38 Rousseau, 365–366, 377–385
39 Smith, 182–300
40 Gibbon, 66
41 Gibbon, 87
43 Federalist, 55
43 Mill, 312–313
44 Boswell, 280–281
50 Marx, 251–252
50 Marx-Engels, 426

9*d*. Governmental regulation of production, trade, or other aspects of economic life

7 Plato, 408, 742, 771–775
14 Plutarch, 36–37, 61–62, 127–128
15 Tacitus, 90
23 Hobbes, 119–120
38 Montesquieu, 148, 149–150
39 Smith, 51–62, 161, 182–300, 315–331 passim
40 Gibbon, 249–250, 392–393, 486
41 Gibbon, 87–91
43 Federalist, 80–81, 137–138

9e. The economic support of government and the services of government

9e(1) The charges of government: the cost of maintaining its services; elements in the national budget

9e(2) Methods of defraying the expenses of government: taxation and other forms of levy or impost: confiscations, seizures, and other abuses of taxation

9f. Wealth or property in relation to different forms of government

9g. Wealth and poverty in relation to crime and to war between states

9h. The struggle of economic classes for political power

10. The moral aspects of wealth and poverty

10*a*. The nature of wealth as a good: its place in the order of goods and its relation to happiness

OLD TESTAMENT: *Job*, 21:7–13; 31:24–28; 36:18–19 / *Psalms*, 49 / *Proverbs*, 10:2; 13:7; 14:20; 15:16–17; 19:4,6–7; 22:1; 23:4–5; 28:6,11,20,22 / *Ecclesiastes*, 2:3–11; 5:9–6:2
APOCRYPHA: *Wisdom of Solomon*, 7:7–11 / *Ecclesiasticus*, 10:30–31; 11:18–27; 12:8; 13; 29:22–23; 30:14–16; 31:1–11; 40:25–26
NEW TESTAMENT: *Matthew*, 6:19–34; 19:16–30 / *Mark*, 4:1–20; 10:17–31 / *Luke*, 8:5–15; 16:19–25 / *James*, 5:1–6
5 AESCHYLUS, 17
5 EURIPIDES, 330, 335, 443
5 ARISTOPHANES, 630–631, 633–636
6 HERODOTUS, 6–8, 121
7 PLATO, 177–178, 296–297, 341–343
8 ARISTOTLE, 162, 163, 165, 248
9 ARISTOTLE, 340, 342 passim, 371, 527–528, 532–533, 601, 603, 638
12 EPICTETUS, 230–232
15 TACITUS, 154
18 AUGUSTINE, 133–136
19 AQUINAS, 615–616, 635–636
22 CHAUCER, 235–236, 274–276, 422–425, 430–431
23 MACHIAVELLI, 26
23 HOBBES, 74–75
26 SHAKESPEARE, 385–386
27 SHAKESPEARE, 393–420, 425–426
29 CERVANTES, 338
30 BACON, 86, 92
35 LOCKE, 192–193
37 FIELDING, 17, 103–104, 263
38 MONTESQUIEU, 19
41 GIBBON, 297–298
42 KANT, 370
43 MILL, 462–463
44 BOSWELL, 140–141, 189–190, 210–211, 300, 492
47 GOETHE, 146–151
51 TOLSTOY, 30–31, 111–113, 311–313
52 DOSTOEVSKY, 110–111, 191–235, 308
53 JAMES, 188–189, 202–203
54 FREUD, 777–779

10*b*. Natural limits to the acquisition of wealth by individuals: the distinction between necessities and luxuries

5 EURIPIDES, 306–307, 382
7 PLATO, 316–319, 409–410
8 ARISTOTLE, 164–165
9 ARISTOTLE, 450, 451–452
12 EPICTETUS, 237–238
15 TACITUS, 57–58
22 CHAUCER, 422–424
25 MONTAIGNE, 110, 131–132, 489–490
33 PASCAL, 91–94
35 LOCKE, 31–33
38 MONTESQUIEU, 44
38 ROUSSEAU, 350, 352–353
39 SMITH, 63, 70–71, 163–164, 383
41 GIBBON, 451–452
43 FEDERALIST, 102
43 MILL, 470–471
44 BOSWELL, 313
46 HEGEL, 66–67, 136
50 MARX, 71–72, 81, 112, 147–148, 251–255, 261, 282–283, 292–296

10*c*. Temperance and intemperance with respect to wealth: liberality, magnificence, miserliness, avarice

OLD TESTAMENT: *II Samuel*, 12:1–6 / *I Kings*, 21 / *II Kings*, 5:20–27 / *Job*, 31:16–23 / *Psalms*, 62:10 / *Proverbs*, 1:10–19; 15:27; 28:22; 30:8–9 / *Ecclesiastes*, 5:10–6:12 / *Jeremiah*, 22:13–19 / *Ezekiel*, 22:12–13 / *Amos*, 2:6–7; 5:11–12 / *Micah*, 3:9–11
APOCRYPHA: *Ecclesiasticus*, 12:1–6; 14:3–10; 18:32–33; 29:1–2,7–13,20–28; 31:1–11,23–24 / *II Maccabees*, 3–4
NEW TESTAMENT: *Luke*, 12:13–21 / *I Timothy*, 6:6–12
5 ARISTOPHANES, 630–631
6 HERODOTUS, 221–222, 305–306
7 PLATO, 405–408, 733–734, 751
9 ARISTOTLE, 353, 366–370, 458, 460, 554–555, 608–609
12 LUCRETIUS, 75
14 PLUTARCH, 218, 223–224, 233, 276–290, 291–292, 361, 388, 394–395, 419–420, 755–758
15 TACITUS, 31, 35
18 AUGUSTINE, 40
20 AQUINAS, 70–72
21 DANTE, 9–10, 15–16, 26–28, 82–87
22 CHAUCER, 424–426, 512–514
23 MACHIAVELLI, 22–23
24 RABELAIS, 62, 133–140
25 MONTAIGNE, 122–124, 436–439, 462
27 SHAKESPEARE, 393–420
29 CERVANTES, 221–222
31 SPINOZA, 450
33 PASCAL, 91–94
36 SWIFT, 53–56
37 FIELDING, 87–88
38 MONTESQUIEU, 10, 19–21, 44–45, 140, 146, 152, 211
38 ROUSSEAU, 360–361, 421
39 SMITH, 142–151, 189–190, 346–347
40 GIBBON, 139–140 passim, 155–156, 339–340, 510, 660–661
44 BOSWELL, 194–195, 319, 403, 447
47 GOETHE, 139
50 MARX, 60–62, 292–295
51 TOLSTOY, 25–32 passim, 197, 275–278, 291–292, 329–332, 414–416, 490–493, 633, 664–665
52 DOSTOEVSKY, 164–165
53 JAMES, 725–726

10*d*. The principles of justice with respect to wealth and property: fair wages and prices

OLD TESTAMENT: *Deuteronomy*, 25:13–16 / *I Kings*, 21 / *II Kings*, 5:20–27 / *Nehemiah*, 5:1–12 / *Job*, 24 / *Proverbs*, 30:8–9 / *Isaiah*, 3:14–15; 10:1–2 / *Ezekiel*, 22:12–13,25–29; 45:9–12 / *Amos*, 2:6–7; 5:11–12; 8:1–7
NEW TESTAMENT: *Ephesians*, 4:28
5 EURIPIDES, 306–307
5 ARISTOPHANES, 629–642
6 HERODOTUS, 73–74, 87, 158, 201–202
7 PLATO, 340–343, 738–743, 772–775, 814
9 ARISTOTLE, 377–378, 380–381, 416–417, 458–460, 461–463, 557–558
14 PLUTARCH, 36–37, 68–70
20 AQUINAS, 309–316
22 CHAUCER, 422–424
23 HOBBES, 93, 124–126, 156–157
27 SHAKESPEARE, 351–353
33 PASCAL, 97–98
38 MONTESQUIEU, 96, 128, 199–200
38 ROUSSEAU, 375, 377–385, 415–417
39 SMITH, 13–16, 20–23, 27–37, 52–62, 106–107, 225–228, 309–311
40 GIBBON, 22
43 FEDERALIST, 218–219
43 MILL, 322, 335, 470–471 passim
44 BOSWELL, 124–125
46 HEGEL, 24–25, 76, 121, 140
48 MELVILLE, 292–297
50 MARX, 13–50 passim, 69–84, 89–102 passim, 150–151, 161–162, 171, 256–260, 264–275, 280–286, 296–298, 305–307, 324–327, 366–368, 376–378
50 MARX-ENGELS, 425–427
51 TOLSTOY, 211–213, 650–652
54 FREUD, 787–788

10*e*. The precepts of charity with respect to wealth

10*e*(1) Almsgiving to the needy and the impoverished

OLD TESTAMENT: *Leviticus*, 19:9–10; 25:35–37 / *Deuteronomy*, 15:7–11; 26:12–13 / *Ruth*, 2 / *Job*, 29:12–17; 31:16–23 / *Psalms*, 41:1–3 / *Proverbs*, 14:21,31 / *Isaiah*, 58:1–12
APOCRYPHA: *Tobit*, 1:1–8, 4:7–11; 12:8–10 / *Ecclesiasticus*, 4:1–10; 7:32–33; 12:1–6; 29:1–2,7–13
NEW TESTAMENT: *Matthew*, 6:1–4 / *Mark*, 10:17–22 / *Luke*, 6:30–38; 14:12–14; 18:18–25 / *II Corinthians*, 8–9
20 AQUINAS, 540–550
22 CHAUCER, 547
33 PASCAL, 91–94
40 GIBBON, 198, 392–393
41 GIBBON, 233
46 HEGEL, 77

10*e*(2) The religious vow of poverty: voluntary poverty

NEW TESTAMENT: *Matthew*, 19:16–30 / *Mark*, 10:17–31 / *Luke*, 9:1–5; 12:22–30,33; 18:18–30
20 AQUINAS, 652–655, 657–661, 1006–1007
21 DANTE, 122–123
40 GIBBON, 597
46 HEGEL, 307–308, 340–341
52 DOSTOEVSKY, 85–86

10*e*(3) The choice between God and Mammon: the love of money as the root of all evil

OLD TESTAMENT: *Job*, 31:24–28 / *Proverbs*, 30:8–9 / *Ezekiel*, 22:25–29
APOCRYPHA: *Ecclesiasticus*, 11:26; 14:1–10; 31:5–11
NEW TESTAMENT: *Matthew*, 6:19–24 / *Luke*, 12:13–21; 16:1–13; 18:22–30 / *I Timothy*, 6:6–19
5 SOPHOCLES, 133
7 PLATO, 733
20 AQUINAS, 174–175
21 DANTE, 26–28, 82–87
22 CHAUCER, 430–431, 530–531
32 MILTON, 108
33 PASCAL, 94–97
47 GOETHE, 135–151
50 MARX, 61
51 TOLSTOY, 50
52 DOSTOEVKSY, 130–132

11. Economic determinism: the economic interpretation of history

50 MARX, 10–11, 25, 35–36, 187, 239–241, 377–378
50 MARX-ENGELS, 416, 421–422, 427, 428
54 FREUD, 882–883

12. Economic progress: advances with respect to both efficiency and justice

14 PLUTARCH, 36–37
38 MONTESQUIEU, 111, 126, 128
38 ROUSSEAU, 352
39 SMITH, 163–181, 190–191
40 GIBBON, 633–634
41 GIBBON, 452–453
43 FEDERALIST, 56
43 MILL, 452
46 HEGEL, 323, 335–336
50 MARX, 377–378
50 MARX-ENGELS, 428–429
54 FREUD, 778–779, 883–884

CROSS-REFERENCES

For: The treatment of the domestic economy, *see* FAMILY 3a–3b.

Discussions bearing on the factors in productivity, *see* ART 6c, 9b; KNOWLEDGE 8a; SCIENCE 1b(2).

Another consideration of the concept of value, *see* GOOD AND EVIL 4d; and for another discussion of the labor theory of value, *see* LABOR 6d.

The political aspect of commerce between states, *see* STATE 9a.

The issue concerning usury, *see* JUSTICE 8d.

Other comparisons of the capitalist economy with the slave, the feudal, and the socialist economies, *see* LABOR 5a–5d.

The consideration of the nature of wages and of wages in relation to profits, *see* LABOR 6–6c; and for the theory of profit as derived from surplus value, *see* JUSTICE 8c(1)–8c(2).

The theory of property and property rights, *see* JUSTICE 6b, 8a; LABOR 7b; OLIGARCHY 4, 5a; and for the conception of slaves as chattel or property, *see* LABOR 5a; SLAVERY 4a.

The doctrine of common as opposed to individual goods, *see* GOOD AND EVIL 4e.

Another discussion of the problem of poverty, *see* LABOR 7e.

The consideration of economics as a science, *see* PHILOSOPHY 2c; SCIENCE 3a.

The problem of governmental regulation of the economic process, *see* LIBERTY 2c.

The problem of the economic support of government, *see* GOVERNMENT 4.

The issue concerning the oligarchical conception of the political significance of wealth, *see* DEMOCRACY 4a(1)–4a(2); OLIGARCHY 4–5a.

The economic causes and effects of war, *see* WAR AND PEACE 5c.

Other discussions of the conflict between economic classes, or the class war, *see* LABOR 7c–7c(3); OPPOSITION 5a; REVOLUTION 5a; STATE 5d(2); WAR AND PEACE 2c.

The general discussion of the order of goods, and for the relation of wealth to happiness and to other types of good, *see* GOOD AND EVIL 5–5d; HAPPINESS 2b(1); TEMPERANCE 2, 5b; VIRTUE AND VICE 6c.

Other discussions of the distinction between necessities and luxuries, *see* NATURE 5b; NECESSITY AND CONTINGENCY 5e.

The consideration of the problems of economic justice, *see* JUSTICE 8–8d.

The discussion of the virtue of charity and the things which flow from charity, *see* LOVE 5b–5b(2); VIRTUE AND VICE 8g.

Another statement of the economic theory of history, *see* HISTORY 4a(2); and for the examination of economic progress, *see* PROGRESS 3a–3c.

ADDITIONAL READINGS

Listed below are works not included in *Great Books of the Western World*, but relevant to the idea and topics with which this chapter deals. These works are divided into two groups:

I. Works by authors represented in this collection.
II. Works by authors not represented in this collection.

For the date, place, and other facts concerning the publication of the works cited, consult the Bibliography of Additional Readings which follows the last chapter of *The Great Ideas*.

I.

AQUINAS. *Summa Contra Gentiles*, BK III, CH 131–135

——. *Quaestiones Disputatae, De Malo*, Q 13, A 4

——. *Summa Theologica*, PART II–II, Q 66, AA 1–2; PART II–II, Q 78

F. BACON. "Of Riches," "Of Usury," in *Essays*

LOCKE. *Some Considerations of the Consequences of Lowering the Interest, and Raising the Value of Money*

FIELDING. *Amelia*

HUME. *Of the Balance of Trade*

——. *Of Commerce*

HUME. *Of Interest*
——. *Of Money*
——. *Of Refinement in the Arts*
——. *Of Taxes*
A. SMITH. *Lectures on Justice, Police, Revenue and Arms*
J. S. MILL. *Principles of Political Economy*
——. *Socialism*
DOSTOEVSKY. *A Raw Youth*
MARX. *The Poverty of Philosophy*, CH 1, 2 (3–4)
——. *A Contribution to the Critique of Political Economy*
——. *Critique of the Gotha Programme*
ENGELS. *Herr Eugen Dühring's Revolution in Science*, PART II–III
——. *The Origin of the Family, Private Property and the State*

II.

LANGLAND. *Piers Plowman*
BIEL. *Treatise on the Power and Utility of Moneys*
T. MORE. *Utopia*, BK I
LUTHER. *On Trading and Usury*
CALVIN. *Institutes of the Christian Religion*, BK III, CH 10
T. WILSON. *A Discourse upon Usury*
MUN. *A Discourse of Trade*
MOLIÈRE. *L'avare (The Miser)*
MANDEVILLE. *The Fable of the Bees*
FRANKLIN. *Poor Richard's Almanack*
VOLTAIRE. "Commerce," "Money," "Property," in *A Philosophical Dictionary*
LESSING. *Minna von Barnhelm*
TURGOT. *Reflections on the Formation and Distribution of the Riches*
CRABBE. *The Village*
BENTHAM. *Defence of Usury*
MALTHUS. *An Essay on Population*
SOUTHEY. *Essays, Moral and Political*, IV
RICARDO. *The Principles of Political Economy and Taxation*
J. MILL. *Elements of Political Economy*
BALZAC. *Eugénie Grandet*
——. *Old Goriot*
——. *The Rise and Fall of César Birotteau*
COURNOT. *Researches into the Mathematical Principles of the Theory of Wealth*
GOGOL. *Dead Souls*
PROUDHON. *What Is Property?*
——. *The Philosophy of Misery*
BASTIAT. *Economic Sophisms*
——. *Harmonies of Political Economy*
THOREAU. *Walden*
DICKENS. *Oliver Twist*
——. *Great Expectations*
LESLIE. *The Love of Money*
WHEWELL. *The Elements of Morality*, BK IV, CH 3–4; BK VI, CH 3
——. *Six Lectures on Political Economy*
LASSALLE. *What Is Capital?*
MENGER. *Grundsätze der Volkswirtschaftslehre*
RUSKIN. *Munera Pulveris*
JEVONS. *The Theory of Political Economy*
——. *Money and the Mechanism of Exchange*
BAGEHOT. *The Postulates of English Political Economy*
L. H. MORGAN. *Ancient Society*
GEORGE. *Progress and Poverty*
T. H. GREEN. *The Principles of Political Obligation*, (M)
HOWELLS. *The Rise of Silas Lapham*
S. BUTLER. *Note-Books*
FRAZER. *The Golden Bough*, PART V
A. MARSHALL. *Principles of Economics*
J. N. KEYNES. *The Scope and Method of Political Economy*
HAUPTMANN. *The Weavers*
KROPOTKIN. *Anarchism*
BERNSTEIN. *Evolutionary Socialism*
J. B. CLARK. *The Distribution of Wealth*
WEBER. *The Protestant Ethic and the Spirit of Capitalism*, CH 2, 5
SINCLAIR. *The Jungle*
PÉGUY. *Basic Verities* (Destitution and Poverty; Socialism and the Modern World)
DEWEY and TUFTS. *Ethics*, PART III, CH 22–25
W. C. MITCHELL. *Business Cycles*
T. VEBLEN. *The Theory of the Leisure Class*
——. *The Place of Science in Modern Civilization*, pp 56–456
——. *The Instinct of Workmanship, and the State of the Industrial Arts*, CH 5
HAMSUN. *Growth of the Soil*
DEWEY. *Reconstruction in Philosophy*, CH 8
UNDSET. *Kristin Lavransdatter*
TAWNEY. *The Acquisitive Society*
——. *Religion and the Rise of Capitalism*
SHAW. *Widowers' Houses*
——. *Major Barbara*
——. *The Intelligent Woman's Guide to Socialism and Capitalism*
BEVERIDGE. *Unemployment*
BERLE and MEANS. *The Modern Corporation and Private Property*
E. CHAMBERLIN. *The Theory of Monopolistic Competition*
MARITAIN. *Freedom in the Modern World*, APPENDIX I
FANFANI. *Catholicism, Protestantism and Capitalism*
BELLOC. *The Restoration of Property*
A. R. BURNS. *The Decline of Competition*
J. M. KEYNES. *A Treatise on Money*
——. *The General Theory of Employment, Interest and Money*
GILL. *Work and Property*
STEINBECK. *The Grapes of Wrath*
VON NEUMANN and MORGENSTERN. *Theory of Games and Economic Behavior*

Chapter 100: WILL

INTRODUCTION

THE great controversy over the freedom of the will tends to overshadow the theory of the will itself. For some thinkers the two notions are inseparable. As the word "choice" popularly connotes freedom in choosing between alternatives, so for them liberty belongs to the very nature of the will. But others who affirm that men can act freely or voluntarily also deny that the will itself is ever free.

Still others who distinguish between voluntary and reflex actions—on the part of brute animals as well as men—also distinguish between the voluntary and the free. They reserve freedom to men alone on the ground that men alone have wills. Far from identifying will with free will, they differentiate between those acts of the will which are necessitated and those which are free.

It would appear from this sampling of conflicting opinions that the issue concerning free will presupposes, and often conceals, diverse theories of the will—different conceptions of its nature, its various acts, and its relation to other faculties. Those who affirm and those who deny the will's freedom of action hardly meet on that issue if they proceed from different conceptions of what the will is and how it operates.

The matter is further complicated by different conceptions of freedom. Even those who define will in somewhat similar terms conceive its liberty differently. As the chapter on LIBERTY indicates, freedom has many meanings—theological, metaphysical, psychological, moral, natural, and civil. What is called free in one of these senses may not be so regarded in another. But one thing is clear. If, as Hobbes thinks, the only sense in which freedom can be affirmed is that of natural or political liberty—the sense in which a man can *do* what he *wills* without restraint or compulsion—then the will is not free, for its freedom depends on how its own acts are caused, or how it causes other acts, not on how the acts it causes are affected by outward circumstances beyond its control.

The problem of the freedom of the will seems, therefore, to be primarily psychological and metaphysical. It requires us to consider freedom in terms of *cause* and *necessity*. It appeals to such distinctions as that between the caused, the uncaused, and the self-caused, or to the difference between the predetermined, the contingent, and the spontaneous event. To this extent the problem is metaphysical. But it is psychological insofar as the kind of event with which we are concerned is an interior act of a living thing and, even more specifically, of an intelligent being, a being which has *mind* in some sense of that term. We do not ask whether stones and vegetables have free will because we do not usually suppose that they have will. Even those who, like Aristotle, attribute *desire* to all things or who, like William James, find a striving toward goals in at least all living things, do not refer to volition or the voluntary in the absence of imagination or thought.

The italicized words in the foregoing paragraph indicate ideas which have the most fundamental bearing on the discussion of will, and hence the relation of this to other chapters. The chapters on CAUSE and NECESSITY (and those on FATE and CHANCE) deal with doctrines which both affect and are affected by various theories of the will's freedom. But if we are to postpone the question of free will until the nature of will itself is considered, we must begin with definitions which employ terms discussed in the chapters on MIND and DESIRE.

THE DISTINCTION BETWEEN thought and action sets the stage for the discovery of a factor or faculty which serves to connect them. Acting may follow upon thinking, but not without the intervention of a determination or a desire to translate thought into deed. Plato, in the *Republic*, divides the soul into three parts, of which one, reason, is the faculty of thought and knowledge, and the other two, spirit and appetite, are principles of action. Both spirit and appetite need to be guided and ruled by reason but, according to Plato, reason depends also upon spirit, for without its support even wisdom must fail to influence conduct. Though he does not use the word, the role he assigns to spirit as the auxiliary of reason corresponds to the function performed by what later writers call "will."

The word "will" appears in the English translation of Aristotle. It is used less frequently than other words—such as "wish," "choice," "purpose," "impulse," "appetite," "desire"—to designate a motivating force, but along with them it signifies the factor which turns thought into action. Unlike Plato, who separates spirit and appetite, Aristotle makes appetite the generic notion, and treats will and desire as modes of appetite. But sometimes "desire" is used as a synonym for "appetite," and sometimes "wish" or "choice" is substituted for "will."

In his treatise *On the Motion of Animals*, we find Aristotle saying that "the living creature is moved by intellect, purpose, wish, and appetite. All these are reducible to mind and desire. For both imagination and sensation have this much in common with mind, that all three are faculties of judgment. However, will, impulse, and appetite are all three forms of desire, while purpose belongs both to intellect and to desire." But in the treatise *On the Soul*, we find him insisting that appetite be considered as the single "faculty of originating local movement," though if the soul were to be divided into a rational and an irrational part, he would assign wish to the calculative or deliberative reason, desire and passion to the irrational part. "Wish," he writes, "is a form of appetite, and when movement is produced according to calculation, it is also according to wish, but appetite can originate movement contrary to calculation, for desire is also a form of appetite."

What is said of purpose and wish is also said of choice. All three somehow combine reason and desire. Giving choice as the cause of specifically human action, and desire combined with deliberation as the origin of choice, Aristotle speaks of choice as "either desiderative reason or ratiocinative desire." Lacking reason, animals do not have choice, according to Aristotle, or for that matter wish or purpose either; but insofar as their appetites are stirred by sensation or imagination, and the desires aroused lead to action, animals behave voluntarily.

When the words "desire" and "appetite" are so used, not to name the generic faculty of originating movement, but to signify a motivation different in kind from wish, purpose, or choice, they correspond to what Aquinas later calls "animal appetite" or "sensitive desire." This is for him the sphere of the emotions or passions. He treats the impulses of fear and anger, for example, as acts of the sensitive appetite.

The kind of desire which, for Aristotle, depends upon practical reason, Aquinas calls "intellectual appetite" or "rational desire." Since "will" is for him just another name for the desire or appetite which is determined by reason rather than sense, he necessarily holds that irrational animals do not have will.

Aristotle says that "the apparent good is the object of appetite, and the real good is the primary object of rational wish." Aquinas distinguishes somewhat differently between the object of the passions and the object of the will. For each sort of appetite or desire, the object takes its special character from the faculty by which it is apprehended. The sensible good, perceived or imagined, stands to the sensitive appetite as the intelligible good, judged by reason, stands to the intellectual appetite or will.

In one place Aristotle differentiates between wish and choice by saying that we can wish for the impossible, whereas choice is always of things within our power. But his more usual distinction is in terms of means and ends. "The end is what we wish for," he writes, "the means what we deliberate about and choose." Aquinas also divides the acts of the will according as they concern means or ends, but where Aristotle mentions only choice and wish, Aquinas enumerates three acts of the will with respect to ends (volition, intention, and enjoyment) and three with respect to means (consent, choice, and use).

According to Aquinas, each of these acts of the

will responds to a distinct act of the practical reason and, except for the will's last acts, each may in turn be followed by further practical thought. This progressive determination of the will by reason goes on until the *use* of means leads to action, and action leads to the enjoyment of the end accomplished. As in practical reasoning ends come before means, so for the will the end comes first in the order of intention; but in the order of execution action begins with the means.

LIKE ARISTOTLE AND Aquinas, Kant and Hegel conceive will as a faculty of desire or activity founded upon reason, and so they attribute will, as they attribute reason, to man alone. But both Kant and Hegel go further and almost identify will in its pure state with reason.

"The faculty of desire," writes Kant, "in so far as its inner principle of determination as the ground of its liking or predilection lies in the reason of the subject, constitutes the will"; and he goes on to say that the will, "in so far as it may determine the voluntary act of choice . . . is the practical reason itself." Only man can claim "possession of a will which takes no account of desires and inclinations, and on the contrary conceives action as possible to him, nay, even necessary, which can only be done by disregarding all desires and sensible inclinations."

In this last statement, Kant seems to use the word "desire" in a sense which is opposed to will. The context indicates that he has in mind something like the distinction made by Aquinas between sensitive and rational desire. This indication is confirmed by his own distinction between brute and human choice. "That act which is determinable only by inclination as a sensuous impulse or stimulus would be irrational brute choice (*arbitrium brutum*). The human act of choice, however, as human, though in fact *affected* by such impulses or stimuli, is not *determined* by them; and it is, therefore, not pure in itself when taken apart from the acquired habit of determination by reason." But, according to Kant, the human act of choice can be determined solely by reason. Only then is it "determined to action by the pure will."

One point must be observed, to which we shall subsequently return. The pure will is for Kant a free will. "The act of choice that is determined by pure reason," he writes, "is the act of free will. . . . The freedom of the act of volitional choice is its independence of being determined by sensuous impulses or stimuli. This forms the negative conception of the free will. The positive conception of freedom is given by the fact that the will is the capability of pure reason to be practical of itself." Insofar as pure reason is able to become practical, that is, to determine choices and direct action, independently of all sensuous impulses or inclinations, that reason is in itself the pure will, and that will is in its very essence free.

For Hegel also, freedom is of the essence of will. "Freedom," he writes, "is just as fundamental a character of the will as weight is of bodies. Heaviness constitutes the body and is the body. The same is the case with freedom and will, since the free entity is the will. Will without freedom is an empty word, while freedom is actual only as will, as subject."

Though the passions enter into the sphere of the subjective will, according to Hegel, will transforms them. "Subjective volition—Passion—is that which sets men in activity, that which effects 'practical' realization." When it is occupied with the passions, the subjective will, Hegel writes, "is dependent and can gratify its desires only within the limits of this dependence." The passions, however, are common to both men and animals. "An animal too has impulses, desires, inclinations," Hegel says, "but it has no will and must obey its impulses if nothing external deters it." Only man, "the wholly undetermined, stands above his impulses and may make them his own, put them into himself as his own. An impulse is something natural, but to put it into my ego depends on my will."

Hegel explains this aspect of the will by reference to that "element of pure indeterminacy or that pure reflection of the ego into itself which involves the dissipation of every restriction and every content either immediately presented by nature, by needs, desires, and impulses, or given and determined by any means whatever." But indeterminacy is only one moment of the will, its negative aspect. The second moment occurs in "the transition from undifferentiated indeterminacy to the differentiation, determination, and positing of a determinacy as a content and object." Both of these moments are partial, each the negation of the other. "The indeterminate will," in Hegel's opinion, is "just as one-sided as the will rooted in sheer determinacy. What is properly called the will includes in itself both the preceding moments."

As the unity of both these moments, the will "is particularity reflected into itself and so brought back to universality, *i.e.*, it is individuality. It is," Hegel continues, "the *self*-determination of the ego, which means that at one and the same time the ego posits itself as its own negative, *i.e.*, as restricted and determinate, and yet remains by itself, *i.e.*, in its self-identity and universality." While the two previous moments of the will are "through and through abstract and one-sided," the third moment gives us the individual will and freedom in the concrete. "Freedom lies neither in indeterminacy nor in determinacy; it is both of these at once. . . . Freedom is to will something determinate, yet in this determinacy to be by oneself and to revert once more to the universal."

IN THE TRADITION OF THE great books, other writers place the essence of the will not in its freedom, but in its being the cause of the voluntary acts performed by animals and men. The students of physiology from Aristotle to William James distinguish the movements of the various bodily organs—the heart, the lungs, the organs of digestion, excretion, and reproduction—from those movements of the whole animal or of its members which are somehow based upon desire and imagination or thought.

Aristotle sometimes calls these physiological changes "non-voluntary" and sometimes "involuntary," though he has another meaning for "involuntary" when he describes the conduct of a man, compelled by fear, to do something contrary to his wishes, *e.g.*, the captain who throws his cargo overboard to save his ship. The completely non-voluntary motion is one which occurs quite apart from any *knowledge* of the end, or without conscious desire, whereas the involuntary involves some conflict of desires. When the involuntary in this special sense is not considered, only a twofold division is made, as in James' distinction between reflex and voluntary movements, Harvey's distinction between natural and animal motions, or Hobbes' distinction between vital and animal motions.

"There be in animals," Hobbes writes, "two sorts of motions peculiar to them: one called vital . . . such as are the course of the blood, the pulse, the breathing, the concoction, nutrition, excretion, etc.; to which motions there needs no help of imagination. The other is *animal motion*, otherwise called *voluntary motion*, as to go, to speak, to move any of our limbs, in such manner as is first fancied in our minds. . . . Because going, speaking, and the like voluntary motions, depend always upon a precedent thought of *whither*, *which way*, and *what*, it is evident that the imagination is the first internal beginning of all voluntary motion."

But the imagination, according to Hobbes, gives rise to voluntary motions through arousing desire or appetite. When desires and aversions, hopes and fears, alternately succeed one another, what Hobbes means by "deliberation" takes place; and, he declares, "in deliberation the last appetite or aversion, immediately adhering to the action, or to the omission thereof, is that which we call Will, the act (not the faculty) of willing. And beasts that have deliberation must necessarily also have will. The definition of the will given commonly by the Schools, that it is a *rational appetite*, is not good. For if it were, then could there be no voluntary act against reason. For a voluntary act is that which proceedeth from the will, and no other."

Locke disagrees with Hobbes' view that willing is an act of desire. "That the will is perfectly distinguished from desire," he thinks, may be seen in the fact that desire "may have a quite contrary tendency from that which our wills set us upon." Desire, according to Locke, "is an uneasiness of the mind for want of some absent good"; whereas will is the "power to begin or forbear, continue or end, the several actions of our minds, and motions of our bodies, barely by a thought or preference of the mind ordering or, as it were, commanding the doing or not doing, such or such a particular action. . . . The actual exercise of that power, by directing any particular action or its forbearance, is that which we call volition or willing."

Though volition is not an act of desire, Locke holds that it is the uneasiness of desire which "determines the will to the successive voluntary actions." And though Locke speaks of willing as if it were an act of thought, he distinguishes between the mind's power of understanding and of willing. The one is a passive, the other is an active power. Understanding or perceptivity is "a power to receive ideas or thoughts"; will or motivity is the "power to direct the operative faculties to motion or rest."

In this conception of the will as the power the mind has to control the faculties, or the motions of the body, which can be voluntarily exercised, Locke, like Hobbes before him and William James after, explains the will's action in terms of thinking of the motion to be performed or the deed to be done. Discussing the theory of what he calls "ideo-motor action," James says that "a supply of ideas of the various movements that are possible, left in the memory by experiences of their involuntary performance, is thus the first prerequisite of the voluntary life." Reflexive or other innately determined movements do not depend upon consciousness of the movement to be performed. That is why "voluntary movement must be secondary, not primary functions of our organism"; or as he says in another place, the action which is performed voluntarily "must before that, at least once, have been impulsive or reflex."

The kind of idea which initiates a voluntary movement James calls a "kinaesthetic image"—an image of the sensations which will be experienced when the movement takes place. "In perfectly simple voluntary acts," he writes, "there is nothing else in the mind but the kinaesthetic image, thus defined, of what the act is to be." In certain cases, however, there must be "an additional mental antecedent, in the shape of a fiat, decision, consent, volitional mandate . . . before the movement can follow." This becomes necessary when contrary kinaesthetic images vie with one another to initiate antagonistic movements. "The express fiat, or act of mental consent to the movement, comes in when the neutralization of the antagonistic and inhibitory idea is required.

"With the prevalence, once there as a fact, of the motive idea," James goes on, "the *psychology* of volition properly stops. The movements which ensue are exclusively physiological phenomena, following according to physiological laws upon neural events to which the idea corresponds. The *willing* terminates with the prevalence of the idea. . . . We thus find that we reach the heart of our inquiry into volition when we ask by what process it is that the thought of any given object comes to prevail stably in the mind." The answer James gives is that it is "the essential achievement of the will . . . to attend to a difficult object and hold it fast before the mind. The so-doing *is* the *fiat*. . . . Effort of attention is thus the essential phenomenon of the will."

Though Freud does not use the word "will," or analyze voluntary movements in ideo-motor terms, he does attribute to what he calls "the ego" the function which Locke and James ascribe to will. "In popular language," he writes, "we may say that the ego stands for reason and circumspection, while the id stands for the untamed passions." To the ego is given "the task of representing the external world for the id," and so of protecting it from destructive conflicts with reality.

In discharging this function, "on behalf of the id, the ego controls the path of access to motility, but," Freud continues, "it interpolates between desire and action the procrastinating factor of thought, during which it makes use of the residues of experience stored up in memory. In this way it dethrones the pleasure-principle, which exerts undisputed sway over the processes in the id, and substitutes for it the reality-principle, which promises greater security and greater success."

As THE PROBLEM OF the will's freedom involves the question of whether or how its acts are caused, so the will's action raises a problem concerning how it causes the voluntary effects it produces. In Locke's view, we are equally at a loss to explain how one body moves another and how our own bodies are moved by our will. "The passing of motion out of one body into another," he thinks, "is as obscure and inconceivable as how our minds move or stop our bodies by thought; which we every moment find that they do."

If we could "explain this and make it intelligible," Locke says in another place, "then the next step would be to understand creation."

Hume agrees that "it must forever escape our most diligent inquiry" how "the motion of our body follows upon the command of our will." That it does, he says, "is a matter of common experience, like other natural events. But the power and energy by which this is effected, like that in other natural events, is unknown and inconceivable."

No less mysterious to Hume is the coming into "existence of an idea, consequent to the command of the will," which seems to imply a "creative power, by which it raises from nothing a new idea, and with a kind of *Fiat*, imitates the omnipotence of its Maker." How "this operation is performed, the power by which it is produced," seems to him "entirely beyond our comprehension."

Spinoza and Descartes take a different view of the relation between the will and the intellect or understanding. Neither admits that the human will forms new ideas, or, as Spinoza says, that there are "mere fancies constructed by the free power of the will." Both conceive the will's activity as consisting in assent or dissent to ideas, their affirmation or negation. But beyond this point they part company.

For one thing, Descartes distinguishes between the will as a faculty of choice and the understanding as a faculty of knowledge, where Spinoza holds that "the will and the intellect are one and the same." Since Spinoza denies that will and intellect are anything except "the individual volitions and ideas themselves," it is more precise, he suggests, to say that the individual volition (*i.e.*, the affirmation or negation of *this* idea) and the individual idea affirmed or denied are one and the same.

In consequence, they differ with respect to the power of volition. Spinoza criticizes the supposition he finds in Descartes, that "the will extends itself more widely than the intellect, and is therefore different from it." Whereas Descartes thinks that "the faculty of comprehension which I possess . . . is of very small extent and extremely limited," Spinoza says, "I am conscious of a will so extended as to be subject to no limits." We can affirm or deny much more than we can know with certitude.

This difference between Spinoza and Descartes reveals itself most strikingly in their conception of God's will. According to Descartes, the omnipotence of God lies in the supremacy of his will—in its absolute independence even with respect to the divine intellect. "It is self-contradictory that the will of God should not have been from eternity indifferent to all that has come to pass or ever will occur. . . . Thus, to illustrate, God did not will . . . the three angles of a triangle to be equal to two right angles because he knew that they could not be otherwise. On the contrary . . . it is because he willed the three angles of a triangle to be necessarily equal to two right angles that this is true and cannot be otherwise." Against Descartes' voluntarism, Spinoza declares it absurd to say that "God could bring it about that it should not follow from the nature of a triangle that its three angles should be equal to two right angles."

Such different conceptions of the will or of its power necessarily lead to opposite conclusions concerning free will—in man or God. The human mind, according to Spinoza, "cannot be the free cause of its own actions." In each of its volitions, as in each of its ideas, it is determined by a cause. The supposition of an infinite will in God does not exempt that will from the need to be determined in its acts; nor can God "on this account be said to act from freedom of will." Yet Spinoza also affirms that "God alone is a free cause, for God alone exists and acts from the necessity of his own nature." Freedom does not reside in the will, nor in the absence of necessity or causal determination, but rather in self-determination. It does not consist in choice, but in the absence of compulsion by causes which lie outside one's own nature. Hence only an infinite being—a *causa sui* in Spinoza's sense—can be free.

Descartes, on the other hand, places freedom in the will and identifies it with the power of choice. "The faculty of will," he writes, "consists alone in our having the power of choosing to do a thing or choosing not to do it . . . or rather it consists alone in the fact that in order to affirm or deny, pursue or shun, those things placed before us by the understanding, we act so that we are unconscious that any outside force constrains us in so doing." Descartes seems to conceive the will as cause of itself in its acts of choice. But he does not attribute to the human will the autonomy Spinoza ascribes to God. "The knowledge of the understanding," he writes, "should always precede the determination of the will"; and in another place he says that "our will impels us neither to follow after nor to flee from anything, except as our understanding represents it as good or evil."

In order to be free, Descartes explains, "it is not necessary that I should be indifferent as to the choice of one or the other of two contraries; but contrariwise the more I lean to the one—whether I recognize clearly that the reasons of the good and the true are to be found in it, or whether God so disposes my inward thought—the more freely do I choose and embrace it." The will always retains "the power of directing itself towards one side or the other apart from any determination by the understanding." The human will is, in this sense, always undetermined from without, though it is not always indifferent to the alternatives confronting it. It is indifferent, Descartes holds, only when a man "does not know what is the more true or the better, or at least when he does not see clearly enough to prevent him from doubting about it. Thus the indifference which attaches to human liberty is very different from that which belongs to the divine."

The denial of free will in the tradition of western thought seems to follow from the principle that every happening must have a cause. In the sphere of human conduct, voluntary acts are no less determined effects of prior causes than involuntary acts. Though both are equally necessitated, the difference between the voluntary and the involuntary, according to Hobbes, Locke, and Hume, consists in the fact that when a man acts voluntarily, he does what he himself has decided to do.

The fact that his decision to act in a certain way is itself caused, does not, in the opinion of these writers, abolish the freedom of his action, but only the freedom of his will. If freedom is attributed not to a man's will, but to the man who can do what he wills, then, these writers think, there is no conflict between freedom and necessity—or between freedom and the universal reign of causality. For them freedom is abridged only by external forces which coerce a man to act contrary to his wishes or constrain him from acting as he wills. Freedom in this sense is incompatible only with exterior compulsion, not with the inner causal determination of every act of the will.

To those who deny free will, it does not seem to be an entirely satisfactory answer to say, as Descartes does, that we are immediately conscious of our freedom of choice. In the Third Set of Objections, urged by Thomas Hobbes against Descartes, Objection XII (which is directed against Meditation IV wherein Descartes discusses free will) contains this statement: "We must note here also that the freedom of the will has been assumed without proof, and in opposition to the opinion of the Calvinists." In replying, Descartes merely repeats his original statement of the evidence for free will.

"I made no assumption concerning freedom," he writes, "which is not a matter of universal experience. Though there are many who, looking to the divine foreordination, cannot conceive how that is compatible with liberty on our part, nevertheless no one, when he considers himself alone, fails to experience that to will and to be free are the same thing (or rather that there is no difference between what is voluntary and what is free)." To Gassendi who, in another set of objections, also denies "the indeterminateness of the will," Descartes replies: "These matters are such that anyone ought to experience them in himself rather than be convinced of them by ratiocination. . . . Refuse then to be free, if freedom does not please you; I at least shall rejoice in my liberty, since I experience it in myself, and you have assailed it not with proof but with bare negations merely."

The experience of free will is no proof either, the opponents reply, for the experience is open to the suspicion that it is illusory rather than real. It may be, Hume suggest, only "a false sensation or seeming experience which we have . . . of liberty or indifference in many of our actions." We suffer this illusion, even foist it upon ourselves, he further suggests, because we are motivated by "the fantastical desire of shewing liberty." In the same vein, Freud later discounts objections to the determinism of psychoanalysis on the part of those who refuse to recognize the hidden causes which control their actions. "You have an illusion of a psychic freedom within you which you do not want to give up," he says. But this "deeply rooted belief in psychic freedom and choice" must be given up because it "is quite unscientific. . . . It must give way before the claims of a determinism which governs even mental life."

THE DILEMMA OF FREE WILL or determinism does not seem to other writers to be so easily resolvable. "All theory is against the freedom of the will," says Dr. Johnson; "all experience for it." Tolstoy states the dilemma in similar terms. "Regarding man as a subject of observation" by the rational methods of the sciences, Tolstoy writes, "we find a general law of necessity to which he (like all that exists) is subject. But regarding him from within ourselves as what we are conscious of, we feel ourselves to be free. This consciousness is a source of self-cognition quite apart from and independent of reason. Through his reason man observes himself, but only through consciousness does he know himself. . . . You say: I am not free. But I have lifted my hand and let it fall. Everyone understands that this illogical reply is an irrefutable demonstration of freedom. That reply is the expression of a consciousness that is not subject to reason."

The problem cannot be solved, Tolstoy thinks, by ignoring one side of the question. To do that is to put the problem "on a level on which the question itself cannot exist. In our time," Tolstoy continues, "the majority of so-called advanced people—that is, the crowd of ignoramuses—have taken the work of the naturalists who deal with one side of the question for a solution of the whole problem." But to admit that "from the point of view of reason man is subject to the law of necessity . . . does not advance by a hair's breadth the solution of the question, which has another, opposite, side, based on the consciousness of freedom." Not only does this "unshakable, irrefutable consciousness of freedom, uncontrolled by experiment or argument" constitute for Tolstoy "the other side of the question," but it is also for him that "without which no conception of man is possible."

William James takes a somewhat different view of the dilemma of free will or determinism. Conceiving the act of free will in terms of the exertion of an effort on our part which is not determined by its object, James is willing to admit that our consciousness of freedom may be a delusion. "Even in effortless volition we have the consciousness of the alternative being also possible. This is surely a delusion here," he writes; "why is it not a delusion everywhere?" Hence it seems to him that "the question of free will is insoluble on strictly psychological grounds."

But if the existence of free will cannot be proved from experience, neither, in his opinion, can determinism be scientifically demonstrated. "The most that any argument can do for determinism," he says, "is to make it a clear and seductive conception, which a man is foolish not to espouse, so long as he stands by the great scientific postulate that the world must be one unbroken fact, and that prediction of all things without exception must be ideally, if not actually, possible." For those who accept this postulate, "a little fact like effort can form no real exception to the overwhelming reign of deterministic law."

Yet it remains a postulate, and postulation is not proof. Furthermore, there is "a *moral* postulate about the Universe . . . which would lead one to espouse the contrary view . . . the postulate that *what ought to be can be, and that bad acts cannot be fated, but that good ones must be possible in their place.*" As scientific law and prediction seem to call for the postulate of determinism, so moral responsibility and the genuineness of moral options seem to demand free will.

Hume recognizes that "it may be said . . . that, if voluntary actions be subjected to the same laws of necessity with the operations of matter, there is a continued chain of necessary causes, pre-ordained, and pre-determined, reaching from the original cause of all to every single volition of every human creature." But he does not think that the assertion of "no contingency anywhere in the universe; no indifference; no liberty," requires us to give up our notions of moral responsibility, and to abstain from making judgments of praise or blame concerning human actions. "The mind of man is so formed by nature," he writes, "that, upon the appearance of certain characters, dispositions, and actions, it immediately feels the sentiment of approbation or blame. The characters which engage our approbation are chiefly such as contribute to the peace and security of human society; as the characters which excite blame are chiefly such as tend to public detriment and disturbance."

In Hume's opinion, "remote and uncertain speculations" concerning the causation of human character or conduct, or concerning the general structure of the universe, do not affect "the sentiments which arise from the natural and immediate view of the objects. . . . Why should not the acknowledgement of a real distinction between vice and virtue," he asks, "be reconcileable to all speculative systems of philosophy, as well as that of a real distinction between personal beauty and deformity?" James takes the exactly opposite view. A doctrine of necessity or determinism is for him incompatible with moral responsibility, or with the distinction between virtue and vice. Holding that free will is indispensable to the moral life, James chooses "the alternative of freedom." In doing so he confesses that "the grounds of his opinion are ethical rather than psychological."

He does go one step further into what he calls "the logic of the question." Since postulation is not proof—since a postulate is not an undeniable axiom but an expression of what James elsewhere calls "the will to believe"—the kind of dilemma which is formed by conflicting postulates can be resolved only by the exercise of free choice. The alternatives of free will and determinism constitute that kind of dilemma for James, and so it seems to him quite proper that the first act of free will should be to believe in free will.

"When scientific and moral postulates war thus with each other," he writes, "and objective proof is not to be had, the only course is voluntary choice, for skepticism itself, if systematic, is also voluntary choice." Hence belief in free will "should be voluntarily chosen from amongst other possible beliefs. Freedom's first deed should be to affirm itself. We ought never to hope for any other method of getting at the truth if indeterminism be a fact. Doubt of this particular truth will therefore probably be open to us to the end of time, and the utmost that a believer in free will can *ever* do will be to show that the deterministic arguments are not coercive. That they are seductive," James concludes, "I am the last to deny; nor do I deny that effort may be needed to keep the faith in freedom, when they press upon it, upright in the mind."

In the tradition of the great books, not all who affirm free will think that to do so requires them to deny the universal reign of causality in nature; nor do they base their affirmation on our immediate consciousness of free choice or make it an act of faith—a pragmatic postulate. Kant, for example, explicitly disclaims that freedom is a matter of faith. "It is the only one of all the ideas of pure reason," he says, "whose object is a matter of fact." This means for him that its objective reality can be proved. In contrast, "the existence of God and the immortality of the soul are matters of faith," by which Kant means that they must be postulated by the practical reason as conditions necessary for the conceivability of the *summum bonum* which the moral law commands us to seek.

In order to understand Kant's proof of freedom, it is necessary to remember that he conceives the freedom of the will in terms of its autonomy, and its autonomy in terms of the fact that the practical reason, with which the pure will is identical, legislates for itself in proclaiming, and obeys only itself in upholding, the moral law. "Autonomy of the will," he writes, "is that property of it by which it is a law unto itself. . . . Now the idea of freedom is inseparably connected with the conception of *autonomy*, and this again with the universal principle of morality." The moral law, Kant goes on, "expresses nothing else than the *autonomy* of the pure practical reason," and "this *self-legislation* of the pure and, therefore, practical reason is freedom in the positive sense."

In saying that "a free will and a will subject to moral laws are one and the same," Kant thinks that he may be suspected of circular reasoning, in that he appears to make freedom a condition of morality and at the same time to infer freedom from the existence of the moral law. There is no question that for him freedom "must be the foundation of all moral laws and the consequent responsibility." But, he explains, no inconsistency results from calling "freedom the condition of the moral law" and also maintaining that "the moral law is the condition under which we can first *become conscious* of freedom," if it be understood that "freedom is the *ratio essendi* [ground of being] of the moral law, while the moral law is the *ratio cognoscendi* [ground of knowing] of freedom."

We know that our will is free from knowing the existence of the moral law. We know that the moral law exists, for otherwise reason could never judge, as it does, that we ought to have done what we did not do. It is not freedom but the moral law "of which we become directly conscious (as soon as we trace for ourselves maxims of the will)." This, Kant says, "first presents itself to us, and leads directly to the concept of freedom." Whenever a man judges that "he can do a certain thing because he is conscious that he ought," then, according to Kant, "he recognizes that he is free, a fact which but for the moral law he would never have known."

The freedom which Kant thinks can be directly deduced from the moral law is a very special kind of causality. In the sensible world of nature, each cause is in turn the effect of some prior cause. None is the first or unconditioned cause, an uncaused cause. But for Kant freedom is "a faculty of absolute spontaneity" and consists in "the unconditioned causality of the cause . . . a causality capable of producing effects independently of and even in opposition to the power of natural causes, and capable, consequently, of *spontaneously* originating a series of events."

How are these two modes of causality—which Kant calls "the causality of *nature* and of *freedom*"—compatible with one another? To affirm both would appear to get us into the antinomy in which the thesis that "causality according to the laws of nature is not the only causality . . . a causality of freedom is also necessary," is contradicted by the antithesis that "there is no such thing as freedom, but everything in the world happens solely according to the laws of nature." Yet Kant thinks he can show that "this antinomy is based upon a mere illusion, and that nature and freedom are at least *not opposed*."

It would be impossible, he admits, "to escape this contradiction if the thinking subject, which seems to itself free, conceived itself in *the same sense* or in *the very same relation* when it calls itself free as when in respect to the same action it assumes itself to be subject to the laws of nature." But the contradiction is only apparent or illusory if man belongs to two worlds—the sensible world of natural phenomena and the supersensible world of intelligible beings or noumena. "The notion of a being that has free will," writes Kant, "is the notion of a *causa noumenon*"—of a cause which does not operate under the temporal conditions of natural causality. "The notion of causality as *physical necessity* . . . concerns only the existence of things so far as it is determinable *in time* and, consequently, as phenomena, in opposition to their causality as things in themselves."

To remove "the apparent contradiction between freedom and the mechanism of nature in one and the same action, we must remember . . . that the necessity of nature, which cannot coexist with the freedom of the subject, appertains only to the attributes of the thing that is subject to time-conditions, consequently only to those of the acting subject as a phenomenon. . . . But the very same subject," Kant continues, "being on the other side conscious of himself as a thing in himself, considers his existence also *in so far as it is not subject to time-conditions*, and regards himself as only determinable by laws which he gives himself through reason."

In the latter mode of supersensible existence, man exercises the causality of a free will. He is not in any way subject to the natural necessity which governs all physical things. Yet the two worlds—the moral world of freedom and the physical world of necessity—meet in the same act. "The rational being," Kant explains, "can justly say of every unlawful action that he performs, that he could very well have left it undone; although as appearance it is sufficiently determined in the past, and in this respect is absolutely necessary."

THE APPARENT CONFLICT BETWEEN freedom and nature arises for Kant because he conceives the act of free will to be absolutely spontaneous. It is as uncaused as the swerve of the atoms (discussed in the chapter on CHANCE) on which Lucretius bases the existence of free will. There is another conception of freedom that does not attribute to free will any special character which brings it into conflict with ordinary causality. It does not belong to liberty, Aquinas thinks, that "what is free should be the first cause of itself." Not only is God the ultimate cause of what a man freely chooses to do, as He is the first cause of every natural event, but the will as a natural faculty of man never moves itself to operation. It is always moved by the reason, even in its acts of choice, and so these acts, wherein the will is free, are also caused.

Where Kant identifies will with free will (which implies that the will is free in all its acts), Aquinas distinguishes between those acts of the will which are necessitated and those which are free. He quotes Augustine to the effect that "natural necessity does not take away the liberty of the will," for that liberty exists only in the will's choice of means, not in its volition of the end. "Just as the intellect naturally and of necessity adheres to first principles," Aquinas explains, "so the will adheres to the last end." And just as the intellect assents of necessity to those "propositions which have a necessary connection with first principles, namely, demonstrable conclusions," so the will adheres of necessity only to those things "which have a necessary connection with happiness." With regard to all else—the whole realm of particular goods which are merely contingent means—the will is not necessitated, and so its choice among them is free.

Although Aquinas says that unless man has free choice, "counsels, exhortations, commands, prohibitions, rewards and punishments would be in vain," he does not postulate free will as an indispensable condition of moral conduct. Rather he shows how reason in causing the will's choices at the same time leaves them free. "The root of liberty," he writes, "is the will as the subject thereof, but it is the reason as its cause. For the will can tend freely towards various objects precisely because the reason can have various perceptions of good." When, for example, "the deliberating reason is indifferently disposed to opposite things, the will can be inclined to either." The freedom of the will's choice with respect to particular means thus lies in the fact that, with respect to all contingent matters, "the judgment of reason may follow opposite courses, and is not determinate to one."

"In all particular goods," Aquinas writes, "the reason can consider an aspect of some good and the lack of some good, which has the aspect of evil; and in this respect it can apprehend any single one of such goods as something to be chosen or to be avoided. The perfect good alone, which is happiness, cannot be apprehended by reason as an evil, or lacking in any way. Consequently man wills happiness of necessity, nor can he will not to be happy, or to be unhappy. Now since choice is not of the end, but of the means, it is not of the perfect good, which is happiness, but of particular goods. Therefore, man chooses not of necessity, but freely."

Like Aquinas, Locke holds that "to be determined by our own judgment is no restraint to liberty." But where Locke thinks the "constant determination to a pursuit of happiness, no abridgment of liberty," Aquinas holds that because "man wills happiness of necessity," his will is not free in the volition of its natural end. Yet Locke does mention the case "wherein a man is at liberty in respect of willing"—the case in which "a man may suspend the act of his choice from being determined for or against the thing proposed, till he has examined whether it be really of a nature in itself and consequences to make him happy or not."

In this type of case Aquinas locates what is peculiar to the causality of freedom. Sometimes the judgment of reason is determined by its object, as when it contemplates the final end of actions. But when it deliberates about alternative means (which are both particular and contingent), reason can judge either way. What determines it to judge this way rather than that? Aquinas' answer is that such judgments of the reason are voluntary, in contrast to reason's involuntary assent to self-evident truths, wherein it is determined entirely by the object being considered. But if a voluntary judgment is one in which the will determines the reason's assent, and if reason's judgments concerning means are voluntary in this sense, then the act of the reason which causes the will's act of choice is itself an act caused by the will. The will's choice is, therefore, not uncaused; but, as Aquinas conceives it, the way in which it is caused makes it self-determining, and to this extent free.

The general theory of the will figures most prominently in the theology of Aquinas and in the philosophy of Kant and Hegel. They not only present the most elaborate analyses of its nature and its relation to reason but, in the tradition of the great books, they are the most stalwart defenders of its freedom. Their differences in principle and in reasoning may, however, obscure the common ground they share.

This may be seen in their conception of freedom. Aquinas does not attribute autonomy or spontaneity to the will. Yet in his view of free choice as a self-determining act of the will, there is something analogous to Kant's autonomy; and where Kant makes the pure will essentially free and spontaneous, Aquinas holds that the will, with respect to willing or not willing, is always free and inviolable. It is absolutely within "the power of the will," he writes, "not to act and not to will." He does not try to explain such freedom of exercise in the same way as freedom of choice.

It is only with regard to the latter that Aquinas appeals to the causal reciprocity between reason and will to show how the will's act of choice can be both free and caused. The kind of causation which Aquinas thinks takes place in free choice—the will determining the reason to make the practical judgment by which it is itself determined—seems to involve a circularity, or perhaps simultaneity, in action and reaction. If this is possible only because reason and will are *spiritual* powers, then here too there is some likeness to Kant's theory of the will's action as belonging to the supersensible world rather than to the domain of physical movement.

On one other point, they tend to agree even more plainly. "Free choice," writes Aquinas, "is part of man's dignity." Man's dignity for Kant—his membership in what Kant calls "the kingdom of ends"—is "rendered possible by the freedom of the will." But though they share this opinion of the source of human dignity in rationality and freedom, they do not draw the same moral consequences from their affirmation of free will as pivotal in human life.

Aquinas, like Aristotle, does not find moral goodness only in the will. On the contrary, the rectitude of the will depends on the goodness of the end it adheres to and the means it chooses. But like the Stoics, Kant makes the will the sole repository of moral goodness.

As Epictetus says that all good and evil lie in man's will, and that the morally neutral sphere is "in the region outside the will's control," so Kant begins his moral philosophy with the statement, "Nothing can possibly be conceived in the world, or even out of it, which can be called good without qualification, except a Good Will." In his view, "a good will is good not because of what it performs or effects, not by its aptness for the attainment of some proposed end, but simply by virtue of the volition; that is, it is good in itself." In another place, he adds that "though not indeed the sole and complete good," the will, *good in itself*, "must be the supreme good and the condition of every other, even of the desire of happiness."

These fundamental issues concerning the will in moral philosophy are more fully treated in the chapter on DUTY. The problems of the will in political theory are considered in the chapters on LAW and STATE—especially those problems which involve the concept of the sovereign will and the distinction of the particular will and the general will, the majority will and the will of all. The strictly theological problems concerning God's freedom and man's freedom in relation to God's will are also reserved for treatment elsewhere.

OUTLINE OF TOPICS

1. The existence and nature of will: its relation to reason or mind and to desire or emotion

2. The analysis of the power and acts of the will

  2*a*. The objects of the will: the scope of its power

  2*b*. The motivation of the will

    (1) The rational determination of the will's acts by judgments concerning good and evil or by the moral law

    (2) The sensitive determination of the will's acts by estimations of benefit and harm, or pleasure and pain: the impulsion of the passions

6. The analysis of the will's range of freedom

6*a*. The limitations on the freedom of the will: the distinction between acts of the will which are necessitated and acts of the will which are free

6*b*. The distinction between the will's freedom of exercise and the will's freedom of choice

6*c*. The distinction between voluntary behavior and behavior resulting from free choice: comparison of men and animals with respect to freedom

7. The implications of free will

7*a*. Free will as a source of human dignity: its relation to slavery and civil liberty

7*b*. The factors of freedom and necessity in the philosophy of history

7*c*. Human freedom in relation to the will of God: fate, predestination, and providence

7*d*. God as the object of the human will: the quiescence of the will in the beatific vision

7*e*. Free will in relation to sin and salvation

(1) The freedom to sin: Adam's freedom and the freedom of fallen human nature

(2) The relation of freedom to grace

8. The will as a factor in morality and in society

8*a*. The inviolability of the will: its freedom from external compulsions or constraints

8*b*. The goodness or malice of the will

(1) The conditions of the will's rectitude or disorder

(2) A good will as the exclusive or principal human good

8*c*. The will and virtue: justice and charity as habits of the will

8*d*. The will and duty: the categorical imperative

8*e*. The will and right: the harmony of individual wills in external practical relations

9. Differences among men in the sphere of will

9*a*. The distinction between men of strong and weak will: cultivation of will power

9*b*. The pathology of the will: indecision, obsession, compulsion, inhibition

10. Will as a term in political theory

10*a*. The sovereign will: the will of the people; the will of the majority

10*b*. The relation of law to will

10*c*. The general will, particular wills, the will of each, and the will of all

REFERENCES

References are listed by volume number (in bold type), author's name, and page number. Bible references are to book, chapter, and verse of the Authorized King James version of the Bible. The abbreviation "esp" calls the reader's attention to one or more especially relevant parts of a whole reference; "passim" signifies that the topic is discussed intermittently rather than continuously in the work or passage cited. Where the work as a whole is relevant to the topic, the page numbers refer to the entire work. For general guidance in the use of *The Great Ideas,* consult the Preface.

1. The existence and nature of will: its relation to reason or mind and to desire or emotion

7 Plato, 350–353
8 Aristotle, 664
9 Aristotle, 235–236, 387–388
12 Epictetus, 149–150, 170–172
17 Plotinus, 108–109, 342–353
18 Augustine, 380–385
19 Aquinas, 108–109, 306–310, 428, 431–436, 468, 646, 650–651, 662–663, 669–670, 672–673, 675–676, 686–687
21 Dante, 79–80
23 Hobbes, 272
27 Shakespeare, 121
30 Bacon, 67
31 Descartes, 215–216
31 Spinoza, 399, 416
35 Locke, 179–180, 181, 211, 363–364
35 Berkeley, 418
42 Kant, 164–165, 256, 271, 314, 385, 386, 483–484
46 Hegel, 18, 163–164
53 James, 814–820
54 Freud, 837–838

2. The analysis of the power and acts of the will

2*a*. The objects of the will: the scope of its power

8 Aristotle, 602, 665–666
9 Aristotle, 357–359
12 Epictetus, 203–210, 213–223
17 Plotinus, 81–82, 177–178
18 Augustine, 346–347
19 Aquinas, 108–109, 120–121, 468, 541–542, 609–643, 657–658, 663–664, 673–674, 698–699, 703–705
21 Dante, 79–80
23 Hobbes, 165
27 Shakespeare, 212
31 Descartes, 89–93
31 Spinoza, 398–400, 429, 443–444
35 Locke, 354
35 Hume, 472–474, 476
42 Kant, 259, 298–300, 304–307, 327–329, 403–404
46 Hegel, 40, 41, 117, 121, 127, 319–320
53 James, 767–768, 814–819
54 Freud, 715–716, 838–839

2*b*. The motivation of the will

8 Aristotle, 665–666
9 Aristotle, 357–359, 611–613
18 Augustine, 287–289
19 Aquinas, 434–435, 657–662, 689–690
31 Descartes, 90–93
31 Spinoza, 426–429
35 Locke, 131–132, 177, 184–193 passim
42 Kant, 259, 262, 279–287, 304, 330–331, 341–342
46 Hegel, 21, 120
49 Darwin, 310, 592
53 James, 790–799, 807–814

2*b*(1) The rational determination of the will's acts by judgments concerning good and evil or by the moral law

8 Aristotle, 200–201, 665–666
9 Aristotle, 235–236, 357–358, 359, 387–388, 394
12 Lucretius, 55
14 Plutarch, 121, 197–198
17 Plotinus, 342–344
19 Aquinas, 28, 114–115, 124–125, 155–156, 438–439, 657–658, 660, 672–673, 674–675, 677–681, 683–684, 689–690
21 Dante, 1–4
27 Shakespeare, 115
31 Descartes, 50, 89–93
31 Spinoza, 443, 450
35 Locke, 186, 187, 190–191
42 Kant, 169–170, 264–265, 271, 279, 282–283, 318–321, 397–398, 477, 571–572, 605–606
46 Hegel, 48–49, 130–131
53 James, 796–798, 807–808

2*b*(2) The sensitive determination of the will's acts by estimations of benefit and harm, or pleasure and pain: the impulsion of the passions

8 Aristotle, 665–666
9 Aristotle, 357, 359
19 Aquinas, 647–648, 649–650, 658–659, 664–665

20 AQUINAS, 145
21 DANTE, 1–4
22 CHAUCER, 490
23 HOBBES, 64
31 SPINOZA, 426–429
35 LOCKE, 180–181, 185
42 KANT, 234–236, 260, 284–285, 298–300, 306–307, 385–386, 477
43 MILL, 463–464
49 DARWIN, 316–317
53 JAMES, 796–797, 808–814
54 FREUD, 363–364, 377–378, 412–414 passim, 419–420, 639–640, 838

2*c*. The acts of the will

2*c*(1) The classification and order of the will's acts: means and ends

9 ARISTOTLE, 340, 357, 358–359
19 AQUINAS, 112–113, 120–121, 614, 656, 657, 671–672, 674–675, 682–683, 685–686, 708–709
35 LOCKE, 191–192
42 KANT, 257, 274–275, 327–329

2*c*(2) The several acts of the will with respect to ends: their antecedents and consequences

8 ARISTOTLE, 665–666
9 ARISTOTLE, 357, 358–359
19 AQUINAS, 655–672
42 KANT, 265–267, 271–279, 327–329, 586, 594–595
53 JAMES, 767–798

2*c*(3) The several acts of the will with respect to means: their antecedents and consequences

8 ARISTOTLE, 665–666
9 ARISTOTLE, 357–359, 387–388
19 AQUINAS, 311–312, 672–693
42 KANT, 265–267
53 JAMES, 767–790, 827–835

3. The functioning of will in human conduct and thought

3*a*. The role of the will in behavior

8 ARISTOTLE, 695
9 ARISTOTLE, 235–239, 355–361
12 EPICTETUS, 116–118
18 AUGUSTINE, 58–60
19 AQUINAS, 609–615, 625–626, 644–651, 684–693, 697–698, 712–716, 718
30 BACON, 55
35 LOCKE, 179
35 HUME, 472–473
42 KANT, 169–170, 264–265, 279–287, 293, 296, 307–314, 331–337, 463–467, 571–572, 587–588
46 HEGEL, 165–166
53 JAMES, 291–295, 790–798
54 FREUD, 715–716

3*a*(1) The distinction between the voluntary and the involuntary: the conditions of voluntariness; comparison of men and animals with respect to voluntary behavior

7 PLATO, 746–748
8 ARISTOTLE, 535, 573, 664–667
9 ARISTOTLE, 239, 355–357, 359–361, 383–384
10 GALEN, 173
17 PLOTINUS, 342–344
19 AQUINAS, 218–219, 430–431, 541–542, 644–651, 652–653, 673–674, 682, 684–685, 707–708
20 AQUINAS, 113–114
23 HOBBES, 61
33 PASCAL, 24–26
35 LOCKE, 180
38 ROUSSEAU, 337–338
42 KANT, 164–165, 234–237, 282–283, 286–287, 386
46 HEGEL, 42, 116–118
50 MARX, 85
51 TOLSTOY, 548–549, 578–579, 689–690
53 JAMES, 4–7, 8, 9–17, 47–52, 269–274, 291–295, 704–706, 767–790, 827–835
54 FREUD, 13, 454–476 passim

3*a*(2) The range of purposive conduct: the relation of habit and instinct to the voluntary

8 ARISTOTLE, 647–648
9 ARISTOTLE, 359–361
18 AUGUSTINE, 55–56
19 AQUINAS, 106–107
20 AQUINAS, 8–9, 10, 108–109
28 HARVEY, 456–458 passim
42 KANT, 256–257, 279–287, 378
44 BOSWELL, 135–136
46 HEGEL, 16, 44, 118
49 DARWIN, 288
51 TOLSTOY, 665
53 JAMES, 8–9, 74–78, 90–93, 704–706, 788–789, 790–791

3*b*. The role of the will in thought

8 ARISTOTLE, 647–648
18 AUGUSTINE, 58–59
19 AQUINAS, 657–658, 663–664, 677–678, 686–687
31 DESCARTES, 83, 167
31 SPINOZA, 391–392
33 PASCAL, 191, 439–441
35 LOCKE, 182, 363–364, 393–394
35 HUME, 473–474
46 HEGEL, 13–14, 15
53 JAMES, 381–385, 818–820

3*b*(1) The distinction between knowledge and opinion in relation to the willful in thought: the will to believe and wishful thinking

12 LUCRETIUS, 54

19 Aquinas, 690
20 Aquinas, 391–392
24 Rabelais, 148–150, 154–156, 159–163, 166–171, 175–178
30 Bacon, 27
31 Descartes, 125–126
31 Spinoza, 369–372
35 Locke, 363–364
42 Kant, 240–243
53 James, 636, 644, 652–659 passim, 660–661
54 Freud, 819, 882

3*b*(2) The will as cause of error

31 Descartes, 89–93
31 Spinoza, 392–393

3*b*(3) Religious faith as dependent on an act of will or practical reason

18 Augustine, 36–37, 57–61
20 Aquinas, 398–400, 403–404
30 Bacon, 41
31 Descartes, 4–5
33 Pascal, 219–220, 222–223
35 Locke, 15
40 Gibbon, 296
42 Kant, 604–606, 607–610
46 Hegel, 350
51 Tolstoy, 196–198
53 James, 652–653, 826–827

4. The divine will

12 Epictetus, 218–219, 224
18 Augustine, 103, 111, 350–351, 587–588
19 Aquinas, 108–127, 325–326, 709–711
20 Aquinas, 218, 810–815, 826–827
21 Dante, 110
30 Bacon, 38
31 Spinoza, 362–363, 367–369
35 Berkeley, 418–419
42 Kant, 276–277, 325–326
51 Tolstoy, 675–677

4*a*. The relation of the divine will and intellect

18 Augustine, 115, 354
19 Aquinas, 82–83, 125, 127–144, 155–157, 538–539
31 Descartes, 228, 229
31 Spinoza, 367–369
42 Kant, 265, 321, 324–325

4*b*. The freedom of the divine will: the divine will in relation to the possible and the impossible

Old Testament: *Psalms*, 135:6 / *Isaiah*, 14:24–27; 46:9–13
New Testament: *Matthew*, 20:1–16 / *Romans*, 8:28–39; 9:15–26 / *Ephesians*, 1:3–11
17 Plotinus, 342–353
18 Augustine, 123, 215–216, 565–568
19 Aquinas, 110–112, 117–118, 145–150, 218–219, 315–316, 537–538
20 Aquinas, 1016–1017
31 Descartes, 228
31 Spinoza, 355, 362–363, 367–369, 374, 422–424
32 Milton, 220–221, 346
35 Locke, 191
42 Kant, 393
51 Tolstoy, 684

5. The freedom of the will

5*a*. Interpretations of the meaning of free will

5*a*(1) The freedom of the will as consisting in a freely determined choice or a free judgment of the reason

18 Augustine, 617–618
19 Aquinas, 117–118, 436–440, 646, 676–677, 686–687
31 Descartes, 49
33 Pascal, 154–159
35 Locke, 193, 198–199
44 Boswell, 392–393
53 James, 820–822, 825–826

5*a*(2) The freedom of the will as consisting in the freedom of a man to act or not to act: freedom from external constraints or coercions

23 Hobbes, 86, 112–113
35 Locke, 180–184
35 Hume, 483–484

5*a*(3) The freedom of the will as consisting in a totally uncaused or spontaneous act

12 Lucretius, 18
31 Spinoza, 367, 391
42 Kant, 140–143, 164–165, 167–171, 281–283, 292–293, 307–308, 311
51 Tolstoy, 692–694
53 James, 223

5*a*(4) The freedom of the will as the autonomy of the reason legislating for itself: the identity of pure will and free will

42 Kant, 279–287, 291–293, 296, 297–314, 326, 327–329, 386–387, 392–393, 463–465, 571–572, 587
46 Hegel, 12–16, 17, 40, 56, 116, 117, 118, 119, 126–127, 132

5*b*. Arguments for the freedom of the will

5*b*(1) Man's immediate consciousness of his freedom of choice: reason's reflexive knowledge of its autonomy

18 Augustine, 44
31 Descartes, 141
35 Hume, 483
38 Rousseau, 338
42 Kant, 283, 302–303, 310–311, 604, 606–607
51 Tolstoy, 688–689
53 James, 797–798, 820–823, 848–849

5b(2) The freedom of the will as deriving from the indetermination of practical reason judging particular goods

9 ARISTOTLE, 357–359
19 AQUINAS, 110–111, 308–309, 436–438, 663–666, 690
20 AQUINAS, 339–340
35 LOCKE, 191–192, 198–199

5b(3) The deduction of free will from the moral law or from the fact of pure practical reason

42 KANT, 164–171, 279–287, 291, 302–303, 304, 307–314, 331–337

5b(4) Free will as a pragmatic option: the postulation of free will as an indispensable condition of moral responsibility and action

42 KANT, 348–349
51 TOLSTOY, 688–694
53 JAMES, 294–295, 820–827

5c. Arguments against the freedom of the will: free will as a violation of the course of nature or the reign of causality; the impossibility of proving free will

17 PLOTINUS, 78–82
18 AUGUSTINE, 213–216
19 AQUINAS, 436–438
23 HOBBES, 113
31 SPINOZA, 365–372, 391–394, 395
35 LOCKE, 108–109, 183–184
35 HUME, 478–487
42 KANT, 140–143, 164–171, 279–287, 291–293, 296, 301–302, 307–314, 331–337, 340–342, 571–572
51 TOLSTOY, 692–696
53 JAMES, 291–295, 822–826
54 FREUD, 454

6. The analysis of the will's range of freedom

6a. The limitations on the freedom of the will: the distinction between acts of the will which are necessitated and acts of the will which are free

9 ARISTOTLE, 357–358, 359–361 passim, esp 360, 388
12 EPICTETUS, 105–245
12 AURELIUS, 253–310
18 AUGUSTINE, 213–216
19 AQUINAS, 311–312, 323–324, 613–615, 662–666, 675–677, 690–693
20 AQUINAS, 10
31 DESCARTES, 132
42 KANT, 164–165 esp 164, 234–236, 259–260, 325–326
46 HEGEL, 42–43, 130
48 MELVILLE, 159
51 TOLSTOY, 577–582, 688–694
53 JAMES, 291–295, 821–822

6b. The distinction between the will's freedom of exercise and the will's freedom of choice

19 AQUINAS, 646–647, 659–660, 663–664, 676–677
35 LOCKE, 180–181

6c. The distinction between voluntary behavior and behavior resulting from free choice: comparison of men and animals with respect to freedom

17 PLOTINUS, 93–94
19 AQUINAS, 117–119, 589–590, 664–665, 667, 672, 673–674, 682, 687–688
25 MONTAIGNE, 218–219
31 DESCARTES, 59–60, 156
35 LOCKE, 180
38 ROUSSEAU, 337–338
42 KANT, 372, 584–585, 587–588
46 HEGEL, 15, 116, 117–118, 121
49 DARWIN, 311

7. The implications of free will

7a. Free will as a source of human dignity: its relation to slavery and civil liberty

19 AQUINAS, 323–324, 512–513, 718–719
21 DANTE, 112–113
24 RABELAIS, 65
26 SHAKESPEARE, 570–571
31 SPINOZA, 394
32 MILTON, 394–395
38 ROUSSEAU, 389, 393
42 KANT, 271–279, 325–326, 341–342, 346–348, 355, 594–595
43 MILL, 316
46 HEGEL, 16, 17, 24, 26–27, 122, 126, 161, 230, 236, 350
51 TOLSTOY, 577–578, 688–690
52 DOSTOEVSKY, 127–137 passim

7b. The factors of freedom and necessity in the philosophy of history

15 TACITUS, 69, 91
18 AUGUSTINE, 206, 207–208
21 DANTE, 77
43 MILL, 332
46 HEGEL, 110–111, 112–114, 160–164, 168, 170–172, 175–176, 179, 186, 203–206, 368–369
50 MARX, 7, 10–11
51 TOLSTOY, 342–344, 389–391, 447–448, 469–472, 563–571, 618–621, 645–650, 675–696

7c. Human freedom in relation to the will of God: fate, predestination, and providence

OLD TESTAMENT: *Genesis*, 3 / *Exodus*, 7–14 / *Deuteronomy*, 11:26–28; 30:15–20 / *Joshua*, 24:14–24 / *Job*, 3:23; 12:14–25 / *Psalms*, 139:15–16 / *Ecclesiastes*, 1:2–4,14–15; 3:14–15; 7:13–15; 9:1–2 / *Isaiah*, 63:17; 64:8

Apocrypha: *Ecclesiasticus,* 15:11–20
New Testament: *John,* 6:22–71; 10:26–29; 12:37–40; 13:18–27 / *Acts,* 4:27–28 / *Romans,* 8:28–9:26; 11:1–10 / *I Corinthians,* 9:16–17; 12 / *Ephesians,* 2:8–10; 4:7–14 / *Philippians,* 2:12–13 / *II Thessalonians,* 2:11–14 / *James,* 4:13–15
4 Homer, 43, 137–138, 176–177
5 Aeschylus, 53–54, 70–80, 81–91
5 Sophocles, 99–113, 114–130, 183–184, 193–194
5 Euripides, 304–305, 327–339, 376, 394–410 esp 398–400
6 Herodotus, 7–8, 20–22, 98–99, 218–220, 291
7 Plato, 439–441, 650, 765–769
12 Epictetus, 106, 118–120, 123, 197–198, 208–210, 233–234
12 Aurelius, 258, 262, 278
13 Virgil, 176–177
14 Plutarch, 370–371
15 Tacitus, 91
17 Plotinus, 82–97 passim
18 Augustine, 12, 149, 206, 207–208, 213–216, 472–473
19 Aquinas, 116, 128–130, 132–141, 541–542, 592–595 passim, 662, 665–666
21 Dante, 10, 137–138
22 Chaucer, 108, 456–457
23 Machiavelli, 35
23 Hobbes, 113
25 Montaigne, 250, 342
27 Shakespeare, 249
29 Cervantes, 408
31 Spinoza, 369–372 passim
32 Milton, 137–138, 186–187, 274–275, 287–288
35 Hume, 485–487
42 Kant, 334–335
44 Boswell, 173, 392–393
46 Hegel, 158–160, 182–184
48 Melville, 409–410
51 Tolstoy, 342–344, 357–358, 630–631, 650, 675–677, 684
52 Dostoevsky, 121–137 passim
54 Freud, 246–247, 582

7*d*. God as the object of the human will: the quiescence of the will in the beatific vision

Old Testament: *Exodus,* 33:18–23 / *I Chronicles,* 28:9 / *II Chronicles,* 15:2–4,12–15 / *Psalms,* 42:1–6; 63:1–6 / *Isaiah,* 26:8–9
Apocrypha: *Wisdom of Solomon,* 1:1; 13:1–9
New Testament: *Philippians,* 3:7–10
18 Augustine, 1, 385–387, 415–416, 617–618, 625, 628
19 Aquinas, 50–51, 57–58, 541–542, 621–622, 625–626, 636–637, 639–641, 709–711
20 Aquinas, 522–527, 764–765
21 Dante, 107, 109–110
42 Kant, 325–327, 337–355

7*e*. Free will in relation to sin and salvation

7*e*(1) The freedom to sin: Adam's freedom and the freedom of fallen human nature

Old Testament: *Genesis,* 3 / *Deuteronomy,* 30:15–20 / *Isaiah,* 5:1–7
Apocrypha: *Ecclesiasticus,* 15:11–20
New Testament: *Romans,* 5:12–8:21 / *Hebrews,* 10:26–31
18 Augustine, 357, 388–390, 587
19 Aquinas, 128–130, 142–143, 323–324, 325–326, 329–332, 333, 521–522, 650–651, 718
20 Aquinas, 129–130, 339–340, 344–347
21 Dante, 111
30 Bacon, 17–18
32 Milton, 139–140, 180, 254–255, 347–348
35 Locke, 10, 15–16
46 Hegel, 304–305
52 Dostoevsky, 127–137 passim

7*e*(2) The relation of freedom to grace

Old Testament: *Proverbs,* 1:20–33 / *Isaiah,* 5:1–7
New Testament: *John,* 1:1–18; 6:37,64–66; 8:31–36 / *Acts,* 13:38–48; 15:1–11 / *Romans,* 4–8; 9:9–18; 11:5–10,26–32 / *Galatians,* 4; 5:1–4,13 / *Ephesians,* 2:4–10 / *Titus,* 3:3–7 / *James,* 1:25
18 Augustine, 319–322, 398, 587
19 Aquinas, 134–138, 506–507
20 Aquinas, 331–332, 352–353, 362–363, 364–365
21 Dante, 53–54, 62–63, 95–96, 115–116, 137–139
31 Descartes, 91
32 Milton, 136–144, 331–332
33 Pascal, 141–166
43 Mill, 296–297
52 Dostoevsky, 127–137 passim

8. The will as a factor in morality and in society

8*a*. The inviolability of the will: its freedom from external compulsions or constraints

7 Plato, 285
12 Epictetus, 105–245
12 Aurelius, 253–310
18 Augustine, 216
19 Aquinas, 436–438, 541–542, 647–648
21 Dante, 111
32 Milton, 369
35 Locke, 3–4
42 Kant, 168–170, 235, 281–283, 284–285, 301–302, 304, 307–308
46 Hegel, 35–36
51 Tolstoy, 577–582, 605, 630–631

8*b*. The goodness or malice of the will

9 Aristotle, 376
17 Plotinus, 177–178

8*b*(1) The conditions of the will's rectitude or disorder

8*b*(2) A good will as the exclusive or principal human good

8*c*. The will and virtue: justice and charity as habits of the will

8*d*. The will and duty: the categorical imperative

8*e*. The will and right: the harmony of individual wills in external practical relations

9. Differences among men in the sphere of will

9*a*. The distinction between men of strong and weak will: cultivation of will power

9*b*. The pathology of the will: indecision, obsession, compulsion, inhibition

10. Will as a term in political theory

10*a*. The sovereign will: the will of the people; the will of the majority

10*b*. The relation of law to will

42 Kant, 401–402, 435–437, 448, 450–452
43 Federalist, 230–232
43 Mill, 327–332
46 Hegel, 170–178

10c. The general will, particular wills, the will of each, and the will of all

23 Hobbes, 100–101
35 Locke, 29, 59–60, 74
38 Rousseau, 372, 395–398, 409–410, 425–427
42 Kant, 114, 437, 451–452
43 Mill, 268–271, 327–332
46 Hegel, 57, 80–81, 84–86, 124, 143–144, 170–171, 172–173, 203–206, 211, 363, 366–367
54 Freud, 686–687

CROSS-REFERENCES

For: The general consideration of the will in relation to desire, emotion, and mind or reason, *see* Desire 3b(1); Emotion 1; Mind 1b(2), 1d, 1e(3)–1g; Prudence 4a, 5b; Reasoning 5e(3); Sense 3e.

Other discussions of the voluntary, the involuntary, and the nonvoluntary, *see* Animal 1a(3), 4b; Habit 6c; Knowledge 8b(2); Man 1a; Necessity and Contingency 5a; Virtue and Vice 4e(1).

The bearing of the voluntary on the distinction between knowledge and opinion, *see* Knowledge 4b; Opinion 2b.

The discussion of rationalization or wishful thinking, *see* Desire 5b; Emotion 3b; Opinion 2a; Reasoning 5a.

The theory of error which attributes error to free will, *see* Mind 5a; Truth 3d(2).

The conception of faith as dependent on an act of the will or practical reason, *see* God 6c(2); Knowledge 6c(5); Metaphysics 2d; Opinion 4a; Religion 1a.

The understanding of the divine will and its relation to the divine intellect, and for the problem of God's freedom, *see* God 4e, 4g, 5c, 5g; Liberty 5d; Mind 10g.

Discussions relevant to the various doctrines of, and the many-sided controversy over, the freedom of the will, *see* Cause 3; Chance 1b; Fate 3, 5; Liberty 1c, 3c, 4a–4b, 5a–5c; Man 1a; Metaphysics 2d; Mind 1e(3); Nature 2f; Necessity and Contingency 5a–5a(1), 5a(3); Prudence 4a; Punishment 2a; Virtue and Vice 5c.

Other discussions which have a bearing on the implications of free will, *see* God 7d; History 4a(1); Liberty 1c, 5a, 5c; Love 5a, 5a(2); Nature 6b; Sin 3b–3c, 6a; Slavery 2d, 3d; Virtue and Vice 8b.

The ethical doctrine which makes a good will the exclusive or principal good, *see* Good and Evil 3b–3b(2); and for the relation of the will to duty, the moral law, and the categorical imperative, *see* Duty 1, 5; Justice 1e; Law 4c; Liberty 3c; Necessity and Contingency 5a(2); Principle 4b.

The moral theory which judges the rectitude of the will by the ends it adheres to and by the means it chooses, *see* Happiness 3; Liberty 3c; Prudence 3a; Virtue and Vice 4e(2)–4e(3); and for the consideration of the will in relation to virtue, especially prudence, justice, and charity, *see* Habit 5b; Justice 1c, 1e; Love 1a, 5b; Prudence 4a; Virtue and Vice 2a(1), 5c, 8d(3).

Another treatment of the pathology of the will, *see* Desire 6b; Emotion 3c(2).

The will as a concept in political theory, and especially in relation to law and sovereignty, *see* Democracy 5b; Government 1h; Law 1b; Monarchy 1a(2).

ADDITIONAL READINGS

Listed below are works not included in *Great Books of the Western World*, but relevant to the idea and topics with which this chapter deals. These works are divided into two groups:

I. Works by authors represented in this collection.
II. Works by authors not represented in this collection.

For the date, place, and other facts concerning the publication of the works cited, consult the Bibliography of Additional Readings which follows the last chapter of *The Great Ideas*.

I.

EPICTETUS. *The Manual*
AUGUSTINE. *On Free Will*
——. *On Grace and Free Will*
——. *On the Predestination of the Saints*
AQUINAS. *Summa Contra Gentiles*, BK I, CH 72–88; BK III, CH 88–98
——. *Quaestiones Disputatae, De Veritate*, QQ 22, 24; *De Malo*, Q 6
DESCARTES. *The Principles of Philosophy*, PART I, 6, 32, 34–35, 37, 39, 41–42
HUME. *A Treatise of Human Nature*, BK II, PART III
HEGEL. *Science of Logic*, VOL II, SECT II, CH 3
J. S. MILL. *A System of Logic*, BK VI, CH 2
——. *An Examination of Sir William Hamilton's Philosophy*, CH 26
W. JAMES. "The Dilemma of Determinism," in *The Will to Believe*
FREUD. *The Predisposition to Obsessional Neurosis*

II.

EPICURUS. *Letter to Menoeceus*
CICERO. *De Finibus* (*On the Supreme Good*), III–IV
ANSELM OF CANTERBURY. *De Libero Arbitrio*
BERNARD OF CLAIRVAUX. *Concerning Grace and Free Will*
DUNS SCOTUS. *Opus Oxoniense*, BK I–II, IV
——. *Reportata Parisiensia*, BK I, DIST 10, QQ 1, 3; BK IV, DIST 49, QQ 9, 17
VALLA. *Dialogue on Free Will*
LUTHER. *A Treatise on Christian Liberty*
CALVIN. *Institutes of the Christian Religion*, BK II, CH 5
SUÁREZ. *Disputationes Metaphysicae*, XI (3), XIX, XXIII–XXIV, XXX (9, 16–17), XXXV (5)
BURTON. *The Anatomy of Melancholy*, PART I, SECT I, MEMB II, SUB-SECT II
JOHN OF SAINT THOMAS. *Cursus Philosophicus Thomisticus, Philosophia Naturalis*, PART IV, Q 12
MALEBRANCHE. *De la recherche de la vérité*, BK I, CH I (2), 2
BOSSUET. *Traité du libre arbitre*
CUDWORTH. *A Treatise of Freewill*
LEIBNITZ. *New Essays Concerning Human Understanding*, BK II, CH 21
J. EDWARDS. *A Careful . . . Enquiry into the Modern . . . Notions of Freedom of Will*
VOLTAIRE. "Free-Will," "Will," in *A Philosophical Dictionary*
——. *The Ignorant Philosopher*, CH 13
T. REID. *Essays on the Active Powers of the Human Mind*, I–II
BENTHAM. *An Introduction to the Principles of Morals and Legislation*, CH 8–10
GODWIN. *An Enquiry Concerning Political Justice*, BK IV, CH 5–6
J. G. FICHTE. *The Vocation of Man*
SCHELLING. *Of Human Freedom*
SCHOPENHAUER. *The World as Will and Idea*, VOL I, BK II, IV; VOL II, SUP, CH 19–20; VOL III, SUP, CH 28
J. MILL. *Analysis of the Phenomena of the Human Mind*, CH 24–25
BALZAC. *The Wild Ass's Skin*
LOTZE. *Microcosmos*, BK II, CH 5
BAIN. *The Emotions and the Will*
EMERSON. "Power," in *The Conduct of Life*
E. HARTMANN. *Philosophy of the Unconscious*, (A) I–II, IV, VII
H. SIDGWICK. *The Methods of Ethics*, BK I, CH 5
GEORGE ELIOT. *Daniel Deronda*
T. H. GREEN. *The Principles of Political Obligation*, (F, G)
——. *Prolegomena to Ethics*, BK II
RIBOT. *The Diseases of the Will*
BERGSON. *Time and Free Will*
WUNDT. *Outlines of Psychology*, (14)
BOSANQUET. *Science and Philosophy*, 15
BRADLEY. *Ethical Studies*, I
——. *Collected Essays*, VOL I (14); VOL II (26–28)
ROYCE. *The World and the Individual*, SERIES I (10)
MANN. *Buddenbrooks*
H. COHEN. *Ethik des reinen Willens*
T. HARDY. *The Dynasts*
WOODWORTH. *Psychological Issues*, CH 2
MOORE. *Ethics*, CH 6
MCTAGGART. *The Nature of Existence*, CH 40, 57
B. RUSSELL. *Our Knowledge of the External World*, VIII
——. *The Analysis of Mind*, LECT 14
LOSSKY. *Freedom of Will*
GARRIGOU-LAGRANGE. *God, His Existence and Nature*, PART II, CH 4; APPENDIX 4
——. *The One God*, CH 19, 22–23
MARITAIN. *Scholasticism and Politics*, CH V
SANTAYANA. *The Realm of Spirit*, CH 4–5

Chapter 101: WISDOM

INTRODUCTION

THE special character of wisdom among the attainments of the mind shows itself in the things which everyone will agree can be said about wisdom—things which cannot be said about art and science, or knowledge and learning generally. We believe that, with the centuries, knowledge can be steadily increased and learning advanced, but we do not suppose that the same progress can be achieved in wisdom. The individual may grow in wisdom. The race does not seem to.

In the tradition of the great books, the moderns usually assert their superiority over the ancients in all the arts and sciences. They seldom claim superiority in wisdom. The phrase "modern science" needs no elucidation, but if anyone were to speak of modern wisdom, he would have to explain his meaning. As "modern" seems to have an immediately acceptable significance when it qualifies "science," so "ancient" seems to go with "wisdom," and to suggest that, with the centuries, far from increasing, wisdom may be lost.

Wisdom is more frequently and extensively the subject of discussion in the ancient and mediaeval than in the modern books. The ancients seem to have not only a greater yearning for wisdom, but also a greater interest in understanding what wisdom is and how it can be gained. The traditional discussion of wisdom, furthermore, has its foundations in the literature of the Old and the New Testament, as well as in the books of pagan antiquity.

This is not true of other forms of knowledge. The teachings of revealed religion open a path to the "heart of wisdom." They do not propose methods of scientific research. Again and again the Scriptures proclaim that "fear of the Lord is the beginning of wisdom"—a wisdom which develops with piety and worship, as science develops with experiment and proof.

Still another distinctive mark of wisdom is that it cannot be misused. We recognize that bad men as well as good may possess other kinds of knowledge. We have seen artistic skill and scientific truth put to evil use. But we do not ordinarily think a man wise unless he acts wisely. To act wisely is to act well, even as to have wisdom is to use it. The satirist's praise of folly condemns a useless wisdom. The theologian's condemnation of "worldly wisdom" dismisses it as the worst of folly—a counterfeit of wisdom.

Other forms of learning may separate knowledge from action; wisdom tends to unite them. Other forms of inquiry may be content with knowing and understanding the facts; the pursuit of wisdom aspires to a knowledge of good and evil. Plato, for example, makes the vision of the good the goal of a dialectic which ascends to wisdom, yet which does not rest there, but returns enlightened to the realm of action. This conception of wisdom is hinted at whenever we refrain from calling a man wise simply because he is learned—a scholar, scientist, or philosopher.

Again it is Plato who respects wisdom so highly that he will not call the philosopher wise, but only a lover of wisdom. "No god is a philosopher or seeker after wisdom, for he is wise already," Socrates says in the *Symposium*; "nor does any man who is wise seek after wisdom. Neither do the ignorant seek after wisdom." The lovers of wisdom are neither the wise nor the ignorant and foolish. As Socrates points out, they are "in a mean between the wise and the ignorant."

Aristotle would seem to disagree, not from a lower regard for wisdom, but because he identifies wisdom with philosophical knowledge, and especially with that highest branch of speculative science which is called "theology," "first philosophy," or "metaphysics." His use of the phrase "philosophical wisdom" to distinguish speculative from practical or political wisdom suggests that the philosopher may attain the wisdom he pursues. Yet Aristotle, like Plato, speaks of "philosophers or lovers of wisdom"; and Plato, like Aristotle, treats wisdom as one of the basic human virtues.

WE SHALL RETURN TO THE distinction which both Aristotle and Aquinas make between practical and speculative wisdom; they often call the latter simply "wisdom," in contrast to "prudence," which is their name for practical wisdom. Other writers, who treat wisdom as one, sometimes emphasize its speculative, and sometimes its practical, aspect. But for all of them, this double aspect remains part of wisdom's special character.

Lucretius, for example, finds nothing "more gladdening than to dwell in the calm high places, firmly embattled on the heights by the teaching of the wise, whence you can look down on others, and see them wandering hither and thither, going astray as they seek the way of life." The way of life, free from pain, the distress of fear, and futile struggle, is known only to the wise. Calm and repose are here suggested as attributes of the wise man. That also seems to be the implication of Dr. Johnson's "approbation of one who had attained to the state of the philosophical wise man, that is, to have no want of anything." When Boswell observes that then "the savage is a wise man," Johnson retorts: "Sir, I do not mean simply being without —but not having a want."

For Plotinus, wisdom seems to be purely speculative, and its repose a condition of the reasoning mind at rest. "Wisdom," he writes, "is a condition in a being that possesses repose. Think what happens when one has accomplished the reasoning process; as soon as we have discovered the right course, we cease to reason. We rest because we have come to wisdom." Still wisdom has a moral or, for Plotinus, an aesthetic aspect. "One Soul," he says, is "wise and lovely, another foolish and ugly. Soul-beauty is constituted by wisdom."

The practical or moral aspect of wisdom predominates in Milton, Rabelais, and Tolstoy. In *Paradise Lost*, Adam communicates his reflections on human knowledge to Raphael.

But apte the Mind or Fancie is to roave
Uncheckt, and of her roaving is no end;
Till warn'd, or by experience taught, she learn
That not to know at large of things remote
From use, obscure and suttle, but to know
That which before us lies in daily life,
Is the prime Wisdom; what is more, is fume,
Or emptiness, or fond impertinence,
And renders us in things that most concerne
Unpractis'd, unprepar'd, and still to seek.

Gargantua, writing a letter to his son Pantagruel while the latter is a student in Paris, admonishes him in the words of Solomon that "Wisdom entereth not into a malicious mind, and that knowledge without conscience is but the ruin of the soul." In *War and Peace*, Pierre, after reiterating that "All we can know is that we know nothing. And that's the height of human wisdom," learns from the Mason that "the highest wisdom is not founded on reason alone, nor on those worldly sciences of physics, chemistry, and the like, into which intellectual knowledge is divided." The highest wisdom, the Mason continues, is "but one science—the science of the whole—the science explaining the whole creation and man's place in it. To receive that science it is necessary to purify and renew one's inner self. . . . And to attain this end, we have the light called conscience that God has implanted in our souls."

Though Plato defines wisdom as the virtue of reason—that part of the soul which is for him the faculty of knowledge—he gives it the function of directing conduct as well as contemplating truth. "Him we call wise," Socrates declares in the *Republic*, "who has in him that little part which rules" and which has "a knowledge of what is for the interest of each of the three parts and of the whole." In the state as in the soul, "how can there be the least shadow of wisdom," the Athenian Stranger asks in the *Laws*, "where there is no harmony?"

There is no harmony or wisdom "when fair reasonings have their habitation in the soul, and yet do no good, but rather the reverse of good" because reason fails to rule or be obeyed. "When the soul is opposed to knowledge, or opinion, or reason, which are her natural lords," the Athenian Stranger goes on, "that I call folly, just as it is in the state, when the multitude refuses to obey their rulers or the laws."

The four virtues which Plato enumerates

in both the *Republic* and the *Laws* are wisdom, temperance, courage, justice. Justice is given a certain preeminence in the *Republic* as somehow embracing the other three, but in the *Laws*, the ruling virtue is wisdom. Calling the virtues "divine goods" to distinguish them from such things as health, beauty, strength, and wealth, the Athenian Stranger makes wisdom "chief and leader of the divine class of goods.... Next," he says, "follows temperance; and from the union of these two with courage springs justice, and fourth in the scale of virtue is courage." As the principle of these other virtues, wisdom like them engages in the life of action. It does not move solely in the realm of thought.

When he refers to wisdom as one of the four virtues, Aristotle uses the word "wisdom" as if it named a single virtue. In the passage in the *Politics* in which he says that "the courage, justice, and wisdom of a state have the same form and nature as the qualities which give the individual who possesses them the name of just, wise or temperate," he does not divide wisdom into the speculative and the practical. But he seldom overlooks that separation. The passage just cited, for instance, begins with the statement that "each one has just so much happiness as he has of virtue and wisdom, and of virtuous and wise action."

Here the reference to virtue *and* wisdom places wisdom outside the virtues, when the latter are conceived exclusively as *moral* virtues. Wisdom for Aristotle is a virtue only in the order of intellectual excellence, not of moral excellence or character. As an intellectual virtue, wisdom is not even involved in the growth or exercise of the moral virtues. It is as possible, Aquinas says, following Aristotle, to have the cardinal moral virtues without wisdom, as it is to have them without art or science. But for both Aquinas and Aristotle this is neither true nor intelligible unless we bear in mind the distinction between philosophical and practical wisdom, or between wisdom and prudence.

Though prudence is, no less than wisdom, an intellectual virtue—a quality of mind rather than of character—it belongs with the moral virtues. As the chapter on Virtue indicates, the cardinal virtues according to Aquinas include prudence, not wisdom. Similarly, as may be seen in the chapter on Prudence, Aristotle's theory holds it impossible to be good "without practical wisdom," just as it is impossible to be "practically wise without moral virtue."

Practical wisdom, Aristotle writes, "is concerned with things human and things about which it is possible to deliberate." Philosophic wisdom, on the other hand, "will contemplate none of the things that make a man happy." To explain the difference, Aristotle uses the example of the early Greek sages. "We say Anaxagoras, Thales, and men like them have philosophic but not practical wisdom, when we see them ignorant of what is to their own advantage.... They know things that are remarkable, admirable, difficult, and divine, but useless; *viz.*, because it is not human goods they seek."

If "wisdom" connotes the highest form of knowledge, then the name, according to Aristotle, is more properly applied to speculative than to practical wisdom. The highest form of knowledge, in his view, is concerned with the highest objects. Hence, he says, "it would be strange to think that... practical wisdom is the best knowledge, since man is not the best thing in the world.... But if the argument be that man is the best of the animals, this makes no difference; for there are other things much more divine in their nature than man," and wisdom is knowledge "of the things that are highest by nature."

When Hobbes distinguishes between prudence and sapience, he does not assign a special object to wisdom. "As much experience is *Prudence*," he writes, "so is much science, *Sapience*." It is the amount of science a man possesses, not his possession of a particular kind of knowledge, which makes him wise. Descartes seems to take a similar view when he says that "the sciences taken all together are identical with human wisdom." But for Aristotle and Aquinas, philosophical wisdom can be differentiated from the other speculative virtues, such as the understanding of first principles or the scientific knowledge of the conclusions which can be demonstrated from them. It involves them, but it is distinct from them insofar as it uses principles to demonstrate conclusions concerning the highest causes. Wisdom can be called a science if it is understood that by reason of its object it stands at the apex of the sciences, crowning and perfecting them.

In the opening pages of his *Metaphysics*, Aristotle identifies wisdom with the supreme philosophical science—the science which investigates first principles and causes. He calls it a "divine science" or "theology," for, as he says, "God is thought to be among the causes of all things and to be a first principle." It is not the most useful science, but the most "desirable on its own account and for the sake of knowing. . . . It alone exists for its own sake. . . . All the sciences, indeed, are more necessary than this, but none is better."

While adopting Aristotle's conception of wisdom, Aquinas finds it most eminently represented among the sciences, not by metaphysics or the theology of the philosophers, but by sacred doctrine or the theology based on revelation. "Since it is the part of a wise man to order and to judge," he writes, "and since lesser matters can be judged in the light of some higher cause . . . therefore, he who considers absolutely the highest cause of the whole universe, namely God, is most of all called wise. . . . But sacred doctrine essentially treats of God viewed as the highest cause, for it treats of Him not only so far as He can be known through creatures just as the philosophers know Him . . . but also so far as He is known to Himself alone and revealed to others. Hence," Aquinas concludes, "sacred doctrine is especially called wisdom."

THE CONTRAST BETWEEN THE wisdom of the philosopher and the wisdom of the theologian is more fully discussed in the chapters on METAPHYSICS and THEOLOGY. But we are concerned here with the further implications of the difference between natural and supernatural wisdom, or the wisdom of man and of God.

The Greeks insistently raise the question whether man can have wisdom. In the *Apology*, Socrates tells his accusers that his "cross-examination of the pretenders to wisdom" was a duty imposed upon him by the oracle which declared that there was no man wiser than himself. To understand the oracle's meaning, he tried to seek out wisdom in other men but, he says at his trial, "I found that the men most in repute were all but the most foolish." This gave him an insight into the kind of wisdom which he himself possessed.

"My hearers always imagine," Socrates declares, "that I myself possess the wisdom which I find wanting in others; but the truth is, O men of Athens, that God only is wise; and by his answer he intends to show that the wisdom of men is worth little or nothing; he is not speaking of Socrates, he is only using my name by way of illustration, as if he said, He, O men, is the wisest, who, like Socrates, knows that his wisdom is in truth worth nothing." Again in the *Phaedrus*, Socrates refuses to call any man wise, "for that is a great name which belongs to God alone." For men, "lovers of wisdom or philosophers is the modest and befitting title."

Aristotle also says of the science which most deserves the name of wisdom, because it is a science of divine things, that "such a science either God alone can have, or God above all others." He does not think that the divine power can be jealous, but if there were any truth in what the poets say about the jealousy of the gods, "it would probably occur in this case above all, and all who excelled in this knowledge would be unfortunate." To whatever extent the possession of wisdom "might be justly regarded as beyond human power," it would be unfitting, in Aristotle's opinion, "for man not to be content to seek the knowledge that is suited to him."

This is even more typically a Christian than a pagan sentiment. "Christians have a special knowledge," writes Montaigne, "how natural and original an evil curiosity is in man: the thirst of knowledge, and the desire to become more wise, was the first ruin of human kind, and the way by which it precipitated itself in eternal damnation." In *Paradise Lost*, as he is about to leave the Garden of Eden, Adam says to the angel Michael:

> Greatly instructed I shall hence depart.
> Greatly in peace of thought, and have my fill
> Of knowledge, what this vessel can containe;
> Beyond which was my folly to aspire.

To which the angel replies:

> This having learnt, thou hast attained the summe
> Of wisdom . . .

But Sacred Scripture does more than enjoin man to humble himself before the chasm between human wisdom at its best and the infinite wisdom of God. It does more than say in the words of Jeremiah: "Let not the wise man glory in his wisdom," for it also says that "fools despise wisdom." In the Epistle of James we find true wisdom set apart from false. If the knowledge of the wise man is not accompanied by the "meekness of wisdom," if instead there is "bitter envying and strife in your hearts," then "this wisdom descendeth not from above, but is earthly, sensual, devilish. . . . But the wisdom that is from above is first pure, then peaceable, gentle, and easy to be intreated, full of mercy and good fruits, without partiality, and without hypocrisy."

St. Paul asks: "Hath not God made foolish the wisdom of this world? When

> . . . the world by wisdom knew not God, it pleased God by the foolishness of preaching to save them that believe.
>
> For the Jews require a sign, and the Greeks seek after wisdom:
>
> But we preach Christ crucified, unto the Jews a stumbling-block, and unto the Greeks foolishness;
>
> But unto them which are called both Jews and Greeks, Christ the power of God, and the wisdom of God.
>
> Because the foolishness of God is wiser than men; and the weakness of God is stronger than men.

"My speech and my preaching," St. Paul continues to the Corinthians,

> . . . was not with enticing words of man's wisdom, but in demonstration of the Spirit and of power:
>
> That your faith should not stand in the wisdom of men, but in the power of God.
>
> Howbeit we speak wisdom among them that are perfect; yet not the wisdom of this world, nor of the princes of this world, that come to nought:
>
> But we speak the wisdom of God in a mystery, even the hidden mystery, which God ordained before the world unto our glory.

Wonder is the beginning of the kind of natural wisdom which a philosopher like Aristotle regards as the ultimate goal of human inquiry. But the supernatural wisdom of which Scripture speaks begins with the fear of God and comes to man not through his efforts at learning, but only as a divine gift. "If any of you lack wisdom," St. James declares, "let him ask God, that giveth to all men liberally and upbraideth not; and it shall be given him." It is wrong for a man to take pride in his own learning but, according to Pascal, "the proper place for pride if in wisdom, for it cannot be granted to a man that he has made himself wise. . . . God alone gives wisdom, and that is why *Qui gloriatur, in Domino glorietur*."

The theologians dwell at length on the text of the Psalmist that "the fear of the Lord is the beginning of wisdom." Enumerating seven steps to wisdom, Augustine writes: "First of all, it is necessary that we should be led by the *fear of God* to seek the knowledge of His will, what He commands us to desire and what to avoid. Now this fear will of necessity excite in us the thought of our mortality and of the death that is before us, and crucify all the motions of pride as if our flesh were nailed to the tree." Then in succession come the steps of piety, knowledge, resolution, counsel, purification of heart; and, finally, the "holy man will be so single and so pure in heart that he will not step aside from the truth, either for the sake of pleasing men or with a view to avoid any of the annoyances which beset this life. Such a man ascends to *wisdom*, which is the seventh and the last step, and which he enjoys in peace and tranquility."

Only the wisdom which begins with faith, according to Aquinas, also begins with fear. "A thing may be called the beginning of wisdom in two ways," he explains; "in one way, because it is the beginning of wisdom itself as to its essence; in another way, as to its effect. Thus the beginning of an art as to its essence consists in the principles from which that art proceeds, while the beginning of an art as to its effect is that wherefrom it begins to operate." Aquinas then points out that wisdom is considered by theologians "in one way, and in another way by philosophers." As the wisdom of the philosophers does not begin with articles of faith but with axioms of reason, so it does not begin with fear but with wonder.

The wisdom of the philosophers and the wisdom of the religious both consist in knowledge of divine things, but "wisdom, as we look at it," Aquinas writes, "is considered not only as being cognizant of God, as it is with the philosophers, but also as directing human conduct, since this is directed not only by the human law, but by the divine law. . . . Accordingly the beginning of wisdom as to its essence consists in the first principles of wisdom, *i.e.*, the articles of faith,

tradition of western thought. No one who can separate true wisdom from folly in disguise places anything but the highest value on it in the order of human goods.

The final utterance of the Chorus in *Antigone*, that "wisdom is the supreme part of happiness"; the Aristotelian doctrine that "the activity of philosophic wisdom is admittedly the pleasantest of virtuous activities" and "all the other attributes ascribed to the supremely happy man are evidently those connected with this activity"; the statement by Plato in his *Seventh Letter*, in which he demands that his myth of the philosopher-king be taken seriously, for "the human race will not see better days until either the stock of those who rightly and genuinely follow philosophy acquire political authority, or else the class who have political control be led by some dispensation of providence to become real philosophers"—all these express the tribute which pagan antiquity pays to wisdom in human life and society.

To the Christian—theologian, mystic, or poet—it is in Heaven with the saints who dwell in God's presence that wisdom, like love, reigns supreme. Nor are these two unconnected. As charity is the perfection of the will, so wisdom is the perfection of the intellect. In the *Divine Comedy*, Aquinas explains to Dante when they meet in Paradise how lack of wisdom's order in the mind goes hand in hand with love's disorder. "He is very low down among the fools," the spirit says, "who affirms or denies without distinction, alike in the one and in the other case: because it happens that oftentimes the rash judgment bends in false directions, and then self-love binds the intelligence."

With the accent on earth rather than on heaven, with reliance upon reason rather than upon faith, Spinoza voices a comparable insight that to have wisdom is to love wisely, for to know wisely is to love God. "It is therefore most profitable to us in this life," he writes, "to make perfect the intellect or reason as far as possible, and in this one thing consists the highest happiness or blessedness of man; for blessedness is nothing but the peace of mind which springs from the intuitive knowledge of God." Not only does "the highest possible peace of mind" arise from this kind of knowledge but, he adds, from it also "necessarily springs the intellectual love of God."

OUTLINE OF TOPICS

1. The nature, origins, and kinds of wisdom

   1*a*. Diverse conceptions of natural wisdom: the supreme form of human knowledge

   1*b*. The distinction between speculative and practical wisdom, or between philosophical and political wisdom

   1*c*. Theological and mystical wisdom: the supernatural wisdom of faith and vision; the gift of wisdom

   1*d*. The wisdom of God: the defect of human wisdom compared with divine wisdom; the folly or vanity of worldly wisdom

2. Wisdom, virtue, and happiness

   2*a*. Wisdom as an intellectual virtue: its relation to other intellectual virtues, especially science and understanding; the vice or sin of folly

   2*b*. Wisdom and man's knowledge of good and evil: the relation of wisdom to the moral virtues

   2*c*. Wisdom as a good: its role in the happy life; the place of the wise man in society

3. The love of wisdom and the steps to wisdom: the sophist, the philosopher, and the wise man

4. The praise of folly: the wisdom of fools and innocents

REFERENCES

References are listed by volume number (in bold type), author's name, and page number. Bible references are to book, chapter, and verse of the Authorized King James version of the Bible. The abbreviation "esp" calls the reader's attention to one or more especially relevant parts of a whole reference; "passim" signifies that the topic is discussed intermittently rather than continuously in the work or passage cited. Where the work as a whole is relevant to the topic, the page numbers refer to the entire work. For general guidance in the use of *The Great Ideas*, consult the Preface.

1. The nature, origins, and kinds of wisdom

1*a*. Diverse conceptions of natural wisdom: the supreme form of human knowledge

7 PLATO, 7–9, 11, 12–13, 476, 634–635, 809–810
8 ARISTOTLE, 499–501, 511–512, 514–516, 522–525, 587–590
9 ARISTOTLE, 390
12 LUCRETIUS, 61
12 EPICTETUS, 228–230
12 AURELIUS, 270
16 PTOLEMY, 5
17 PLOTINUS, 9–12, 216–217
18 AUGUSTINE, 264–271
19 AQUINAS, 75–76, 423–424
20 AQUINAS, 424–425
23 HOBBES, 267
25 MONTAIGNE, 520–522
30 BACON, 40–48
31 SPINOZA, 388, 458–463
35 HUME, 453–454
37 FIELDING, 182
42 KANT, 1–4, 115–117, 172–174, 243–248, 360–361
46 HEGEL, 6–7
51 TOLSTOY, 197

1*b*. The distinction between speculative and practical wisdom, or between philosophical and political wisdom

7 PLATO, 633–635
9 ARISTOTLE, 390–391, 393
18 AUGUSTINE, 266–267
19 AQUINAS, 6–7
20 AQUINAS, 79–80, 600–601
21 DANTE, 126
23 HOBBES, 60–61, 84
25 MONTAIGNE, 327
30 BACON, 4–6 passim, 16–17, 42
42 KANT, 260–261, 365

1*c*. Theological and mystical wisdom: the supernatural wisdom of faith and vision; the gift of wisdom

OLD TESTAMENT: *I Kings*, 3:5–14; 4:29 / *II Chronicles*, 1:7–12 / *Job*, 28 / *Psalms*, 119:34–40,73,97–104 / *Proverbs*, 2:1–11; 3:5–6; 8 / *Ecclesiastes*, 2:26 / *Isaiah*, 11:1–5 / *Daniel*, 1; 2; 4–5
APOCRYPHA: *Wisdom of Solomon*, 6–9 / *Ecclesiasticus*, 1; 6:18–37; 17:1,6–14; 24
NEW TESTAMENT: *Matthew*, 11:25–27 / *John*, 16:12–14 / *I Corinthians*, 1:17–2:16; 3:16–20 / *Ephesians*, 1:15–18; 3:1–12
18 AUGUSTINE, 271, 323, 638–639, 655–656
19 AQUINAS, 3–4, 5–7, 60–62, 175–178
20 AQUINAS, 416–426 passim, 469–470, 598–603, 1025–1037
25 MONTAIGNE, 208–209
30 BACON, 17, 95–96
31 DESCARTES, 43
32 MILTON, 331–332
33 PASCAL, 243–270
35 HUME, 509
37 FIELDING, 182
40 GIBBON, 308–309
42 KANT, 346–347
51 TOLSTOY, 196–198
52 DOSTOEVSKY, 146–170, 189–191, 313–314

1*d*. The wisdom of God: the defect of human wisdom compared with divine wisdom; the folly or vanity of worldly wisdom

OLD TESTAMENT: *Job* passim / *Psalms*, 139 / *Proverbs*, 3:5–8,19–20; 8:22–31 / *Ecclesiastes* passim / *Isaiah*, 40:12–31 esp 40:28; 44:24–25 / *Jeremiah*, 8:8–9; 9:23–24; 51:15–18 / *Ezekiel*, 28:1–7 / *Daniel*, 2:20–23
APOCRYPHA: *Wisdom of Solomon* / *Ecclesiasticus*, 1:1–10; 15:18–19; 24:1–9,24–29; 42:17–25
NEW TESTAMENT: *Matthew*, 11:16–19 / *John*, 1:1,4–5,9 / *Romans*, 11:33–36 / *I Corinthians*, 1:17–2:16 / *James*, 3:13–18
5 EURIPIDES, 343
7 PLATO, 203
8 ARISTOTLE, 501, 602–603, 605
12 EPICTETUS, 120–121
17 PLOTINUS, 163–165
18 AUGUSTINE, 28, 103, 296–297, 626–628
19 AQUINAS, 21–22, 75–76, 154–155, 185–187, 210–213, 240–241
20 AQUINAS, 209–210, 603–605 passim
25 MONTAIGNE, 212–215, 238–239
30 BACON, 98–99
32 MILTON, 219–220, 236

CROSS-REFERENCES

For: Other discussions of the distinction between speculative and practical wisdom, or between wisdom and prudence, *see* Philosophy 2a; Prudence 2a; Theology 3b.

The relation of wisdom to other intellectual virtues, *see* Science 1a(1); Virtue and Vice 2a(2).

Various conceptions of the supreme form of human knowledge, *see* Dialectic 2a; Metaphysics 1.

The relation of philosophical to theological wisdom, *see* Knowledge 6c(5); Philosophy 1a; Theology 2, 4a.

Comparisons of divine and human wisdom, *see* Knowledge 7a; Truth 2d.

Other discussions of the knowledge of good and evil, and of the relation of knowledge to virtue, *see* Good and Evil 6a; Knowledge 8b(1); Virtue and Vice 1a; and for the relation of wisdom to happiness, *see* Happiness 2b(7); Philosophy 4a.

The conception of the philosopher king, or of the place of the wise man in society, *see* Monarchy 2b; Philosophy 4c; State 8b.

The conception of philosophy as the love of wisdom, and for the distinction between the sophist, the philosopher, and the wise man, *see* Philosophy 6a–6b; Truth 8e.

ADDITIONAL READINGS

Listed below are works not included in *Great Books of the Western World*, but relevant to the idea and topics with which this chapter deals. These works are divided into two groups:

I. Works by authors represented in this collection.
II. Works by authors not represented in this collection.

For the date, place, and other facts concerning the publication of the works cited, consult the Bibliography of Additional Readings which follows the last chapter of *The Great Ideas*.

I.

AUGUSTINE. *Divine Providence and the Problem of Evil*
——. *On the Trinity*, BK XIII
AQUINAS. *On the Trinity of Boethius*
——. *Summa Theologica*, PART II–II, QQ 176–177
F. BACON. *The Wisdom of the Ancients*
——. "Of Wisdom for a Man's Self," "Of Seeming Wise," in *Essays*

II.

CICERO. *De Officiis* (*On Duties*), II
HORACE. *Satires*, BK II (3, 7)
Pirke Aboth (*Sayings of the Fathers*)
MAIMONIDES. *The Guide for the Perplexed*, PART III, CH 54
BONAVENTURA. *On the Reduction of the Arts to Theology*
NICOLAS OF CUSA. *De Venatione Sapientiae*
ERASMUS. *The Praise of Folly*
DONNE. *The Triple Foole*
SUÁREZ. *Disputationes Metaphysicae*, I (5)
CHARRON. *De la sagesse*
GRACIÁN Y MORALES. *The Art of Worldly Wisdom*
S. JOHNSON. *History of Rasselas*
SCHOPENHAUER. *The World as Will and Idea*, VOL I, BK IV; VOL II, SUP, CH 17
——. "The Wisdom of Life," in *Complete Essays*
R. BROWNING. *Rabbi Ben Ezra*
NIETZSCHE. *Thus Spake Zarathustra*
MANN. *The Magic Mountain*
WHITEHEAD. *Adventures of Ideas*, CH 4
MARITAIN. *The Degrees of Knowledge*, CH 6–7
——. *Science and Wisdom*, pp 3–33

Chapter 102: WORLD

INTRODUCTION

"HE who does not know what the world is," writes Marcus Aurelius, "does not know where he is. And he who does not know for what purpose the world exists, does not know who he is, nor what the world is." According to the Stoic emperor, for whom "there is one universe made up of all things, and one God who pervades all things," man has only to exercise the divine spark of reason in himself in order to be at home in a world which reason rules.

He does not hesitate long before the dilemma that "it is either a well-arranged universe or a chaos huddled together." In the belief that it is through and through an orderly world—a cosmos rather than a chaos, governed by providence rather than by chance—Aurelius is willing to assume whatever place destiny allots him in the universal scheme. "Everything harmonizes with me," he says, "which is harmonious to thee, O Universe."

With a Christian's faith in God's plan and providence, Montaigne is also willing to conceive the universe as the stage on which man acts his destined part. But suppose, Montaigne adds, that we consider "man alone, without foreign assistance, armed only with his own proper arms, and unfurnished with the divine grace and wisdom, which is all his honor, strength, and the foundation of his being." How then does the world appear? Is it, in all its vastness, the human habitat—the home of man, its lord and master?

Man deceives himself, Montaigne thinks, if he thus pictures the world in terms of his own reason and knowledge. What could lead him to believe, he asks, that "this admirable movement of the celestial arch, the eternal light of those planets and stars that roll so proudly over his head, the fearful motions of that infinite ocean, were established, and continue so many ages, for his service and convenience? Can anything be imagined so ridiculous as that this miserable and wretched creature, who is not so much as master of himself . . . should call himself master and emperor of the world?"

If, as Montaigne thinks he should, man "feels and sees himself lodged here in the dirt and filth of the world, nailed and riveted to the worst and deadest part of the universe, in the lowest story of the house, and most remote from the heavenly arch," how absurd for him to imagine himself "above the circle of the moon and bringing heaven under his feet." Except "by the vanity of the same imagination" by which "he equals himself to God," how can he regard himself as occupying an exalted position in the universe?

Deprived of the religious faith that he is made in God's image and that all the rest of the visible universe is made for him, only presumption or conceit can save man from being dwarfed by the world. But science robs man of such conceit, according to Freud. The cosmology that "is associated in our minds with the name of Copernicus" displaces man and shrinks him. Humanity cannot hold on to "its naive self-love," Freud writes, when it realizes that the earth is "not the center of the universe, but only a tiny speck in a world-system of a magnitude hardly conceivable."

NOT ONLY IN THE REFLECTIONS of Aurelius, Montaigne, and Freud, but throughout the tradition of the great books, the conception of the world or universe is inseparable from the ideas of God and man. These three ideas always interpenetrate each other, though the resulting pattern of thought varies according to the direction in which thought moves from any one of the three to the other two.

Sometimes the whole universe lies on one

side of the infinite distance between the Creator and His creation, and man has a special place of honor in the hierarchy of beings which constitutes the order of the created world. Though man is greater than the earth he treads or the skies he watches, the whole world is less than God, Who has made it out of nothing and Who, in the freedom of His act of creation, is unaffected by the world's coming to be or passing away. On this view, taken by Christian theologians, God is not part of the world, the world is not part of God, nor is there any whole which embraces both; and if "world" means the physical totality, then man belongs both to this world and to another—the realm of spiritual creatures which is also part of the created universe.

Sometimes "world" means the all-embracing universe, uncreated and co-eternal with the divinity which dwells in it, a thing of soul as well as body, including mind as well as matter. Whether God is the prime mover of the universe; the transcendent One from which emanates in all degrees of being the multiplicity of intelligible and sensible things; the infinite substance which exceeds the sum of all the finite things that exist only as its modifications; or the Absolute Spirit which manifests itself historically in both physical and psychical nature—on any of these views cosmology merges with theology, as in the theories of Aristotle, Plotinus, Spinoza, and Hegel. For Spinoza and Hegel, as for the Stoics, to know the world is to know God. Its order or structure is more than divinely instituted. It is the indwelling divinity itself.

Such views of the world tend, for the most part, to look upon the individual man as a microcosm mirroring the macrocosm. The world's body and soul, its matter and mind, are there to be seen in miniature. Considering the philosophers who assert that "mind is the king of heaven and earth," Socrates suggests in the *Philebus* that "in reality they are magnifying themselves." Nevertheless, the doctrine of a world-soul animating the body of the universe is repeatedly proposed in the dialogues of Plato as a way of understanding man; and that mad or at least cryptic Platonist, Captain Ahab, gazing on the gold doubloon he has nailed to the mast as a reward for sighting Moby Dick, observes in soliloquy that "this round gold is but the image of the rounder globe, which, like a magician's glass, to each and every man in turn but mirrors back his own mysterious self."

A third alternative remains. Sometimes, as with Lucretius and later philosophers of a materialist cast, the world is all there is and all there is of it can be reduced to atoms and the void. It is thrown together by blind chance rather than designed by a presiding intelligence. The universe obeys no laws except the laws of its own matter in motion. "Rid of its haughty lords," nature, according to Lucretius, is "seen to do all things spontaneously of herself without the meddling of the gods." For their own happiness, Lucretius exiles his papier-maché gods to the interspaces where they "lead a life without care." But man is not so fortunate.

In a world that is not made for him, and in which, godless, he must be entirely self-reliant, man is burdened with heavy cares. Since he is one of nature's progeny, he may not be wholly alien in this world of material forces; but neither is he, like a beloved son, assured of nature's hospitality. The dominant note here is that of man *against* the world; and in this unequal struggle science alone gives him the sense—or perhaps the illusion—that at least in his little corner of the world his mind may dominate. Yet from time to time defeat reminds him that the world remains unruly. Bridle its matter and harness its energies as he will, he holds no check-rein to prevent his being overthrown.

AS THE CHAPTER ON NATURE indicates, the word "nature" in one of its meanings seems to be synonymous with "world." This fact, as well as the various ways in which "world" has been used in the foregoing discussion, requires us to note a certain ambiguity. When we speak of the world, our meaning may range from the earth or globe which man inhabits to the solar system in which our planet revolves and beyond that to the whole physical universe, however far-flung. We also use "world" to signify an entire realm of things which is distinctively set apart from another order of existence, as when we speak of material and spiritual worlds, or when we refer to the world of thought or the world of sense. Such phrases as "world government" and "world peace" use "world" in a political sense which evokes the image of the whole order of human society upon this globe.

We shall restrict ourselves in this chapter to that sense of "world" in which it signifies the object of cosmological speculations and controversies. We are concerned with the idea of the universe or cosmos. As we have already observed, the universe may be quite differently conceived according to the way in which it is related to God, but it is almost always conceived as that totality in which man and his earth and solar system exist, and outside of which nothing can exist except God. According to the theologians, the angelic hierarchies are no exception, for they fall within the created universe. But philosophers like Plato and Plotinus, who identify the world with the physical universe, set apart from it the eternal ideas or the order of the pure intelligences.

The traditional issues concerning the world or universe, so understood, can be summarized by three basic questions: Are there many worlds or is there only one? What is the structure of the world? Does the world have a beginning and does it have an end?

The first of these questions seems to violate the meaning of "world" as *the* universe—the complete totality of things. How can there be more than one *all*? But that difficulty, as we shall see, may be avoided by the hypothesis of a plurality of worlds succeeding one another in infinite time. It may even be met by the supposition that the infinity of space permits the possibility of two or more coexistent but unrelated worlds. Considerations of the time and space of the world, amplified in the chapters on SPACE and TIME, have a bearing on this issue of one or many worlds.

The second question presupposes agreement that the world has a structure, for if it does not, no problem arises concerning what that structure is. Such agreement is present in the tradition, and is unaffected by the dispute over the role of chance or design in the world's production, and by the controversy concerning the world's creation. As Harvey points out, the Greek word "cosmos" connotes order and beauty. Its opposite is chaos.

Writers may disagree about an original chaos prior to the formation of the cosmos. Plato, for example, refers to a time when the elements "were all without reason and measure"—"before they were arranged so as to form a universe." Milton also writes of a time when "yet this world was not, and *Chaos* wilde reign'd where these Heav'ns now rowl." In the "dark illimitable Ocean without bound"—before "the Heav'ns and Earth rose out of *Chaos*"—"eldest Night and *Chaos*, Ancestors of Nature, held eternal *Anarchie*." In contrast, Aristotle maintains that "chaos or Night did not exist for an infinite time" prior to the world, and he argues against "the theologians who generate the world from Night."

But these differences of opinion leave the main point unaffected. The world is a cosmos, not a chaos. The universe has some order. Even those who doubt the perfection of its order, or who point out how it is marred by evil and irrationality, affirm an order or structure, according to which the universe hangs together and is in some degree intelligible to man. The disputed question of the world's structure, therefore, centers on what the structure is. What precisely is the principle or pattern of cosmic coherence? By what image or analogy shall man try to hold the world before his mind as if it were a single intelligible object?

This problem, as well as the issue concerning one or many worlds, cannot be completely discussed apart from the last of the three questions—the question of the world's beginning and end. For example, if world follows world in succession, each must have a beginning and an end. So, too, the world's structure takes on a different aspect for those who affirm and those who deny its creation by a divine intelligence; and according to at least one view of the order in the universe, men are persuaded that it must be made or ruled by reason, and argue against its being the result of chance.

But the question of the world's beginning must not be confused with the issue of creation, or the problem of the world's relation to God. Aquinas may agree with Berkeley's criticism of "the ancient philosophers who maintained the being of a God," while holding "Matter to be uncreated and co-eternal with Him"; but he does not wholly agree with Hobbes that "to say the world was not Created, but Eternal (seeing that which is Eternal has no cause), is to deny there is a God." For Aquinas, to deny creation is to deny God, but whether the created world ever began to be is a question for faith, not reason. Nor does the denial of creation necessarily imply the eternity of the world—at least not in the sense in which Lucretius imagines the world to have both a beginning and an end.

TWO GREAT EXPONENTS of atomism in the tradition of the great books—Lucretius and Newton—show us that agreement on some of the basic questions of cosmology does not preclude disagreement on others. Both conceive the world as built of indestructible atomic particles. They conceive its structure to be determined by the motions of its parts, both large and small, through the forces exerted by body upon body. Both, furthermore, favor the hypothesis of a plurality of worlds, but only Lucretius holds that this world had a chance beginning and will come to a similar end.

When Lucretius refers to the infinite universe, which, "bounded in no direction . . . spreads out free from limit," he does not mean this world in which man now lives. He means the void in which our world as well as other worlds are formed out of the infinite number of atoms which, combining and separating, cause the birth and death of worlds. "In no wise can it be deemed probable," he writes, "when space yawns illimitable towards all points, and seeds in number numberless and sum unfathomable fly about in manifold ways driven on in ceaseless motion, that this single earth and heaven have been brought into being, that those bodies of matter so many in number do nothing outside them."

The existence of other worlds than this seems probable to him, not only because of the infinity of the universe in respect to its space and matter, but also because the atoms form each world "without purpose, without foresight, without result." As chance produced this world, so it can produce others. Hence, Lucretius argues, "you must admit that there are elsewhere other combinations of matter like to this which ether holds in its greedy grasp. . . . You must admit that in other parts of space there are other earths and various races of men and kinds of wild beasts. Moreover in the sum of all there is no one thing which is begotten single in its kind." On this principle, he thinks, "you must admit that earth and sun, moon, sea, and all things else . . . are not single in their kind, but rather in number past numbering."

By calling the atoms eternal bodies and first-beginnings, Lucretius indicates that it is each particular world, not the universe of matter and the void, which has a beginning and an end. The atoms or first-beginnings "fall into arrangements such as those out of which this, our sum of things, has been formed," he explains, "not by design . . . but because many in number and shifting about in many ways throughout the universe they are driven and tormented by blows during infinite time past." Thus a world is born, and so even does it grow by the addition of bodies from without. But as a world is born and grows, it also decays and dies. "Many bodies ebb away and withdraw from things," Lucretius writes, "but still more must join them, until they have touched the utmost point of growth. Then piece by piece age breaks their powers and matured strength, and wastes away on the side of decay," until finally "in this way even the walls of the wide world all around will be stormed and fall to decay and crumbling ruin."

According to Newton, the atoms are indestructible but not eternal bodies. Upon their indestructibility or permanence depends the uniform and enduring texture of nature in all ages. "That Nature may be lasting," Newton says, "the changes of corporeal things are to be placed only in the various separations and new associations and motions of these permanent particles." But for Newton the indivisibility of the ultimate particles of matter does not preclude their being created. "It seems probable to me," he writes, "that God in the beginning formed matter in solid, massy, hard, impenetrable movable particles, of such size and figures, and with such other properties . . . as most conduced to the end for which he formed them."

Not through the chance colligation of atoms, but through their being "variously associated in the first creation by the counsel of an intelligent agent," is the world formed. "For it became him who created them to set them in order. And if he did so," Newton adds, "it's unphilosophical to seek for any other origin of the world, or to pretend that it might arise out of a chaos by the mere laws of nature; though being once formed, it may continue by those laws through many ages."

Newton differs from Lucretius in these particulars, but shares his view of the probability of many worlds. "Since space is divisible *in infinitum*, and matter is not necessarily in all places, it may also be allowed," Newton declares, "that God is able to create particles of matter of several sizes and figures, and in several proportions to space . . . and thereby to vary the laws of nature, and make worlds of several sorts in several parts of the universe. At least," he continues, "I see nothing of contradiction in all this."

OTHER WRITERS SEEM TO FIND a plurality of worlds repugnant to reason, if not flatly contradictory. Plato, for example, appears to think that the possibility of other worlds is inconsistent with the perfection of this one—certainly if this world is made in the image of the eternal ideas. Because "the original of the universe contains in itself all intelligible beings," Plato's Timaeus argues that there cannot be many worlds, but "one only, if the created copy is to accord with the original." It belongs to the world's perfection to be solitary, and for this reason, Timaeus explains, "the creator made not two worlds or an infinite number of them; but there is and ever will be one only-begotten and created heaven."

Aristotle reasons differently to the conclusion that "there cannot be more worlds than one." The conclusion follows in his view from the impossibility of an infinity of body or matter, and with it an infinity of space. "The universe is certainly a particular and a material thing," he writes. "If it is composed not of a part but of the whole of matter, then though the being of 'universe' and of 'this universe' are still distinct, yet there is no other universe, and no possibility of others being made, because all the matter is already included in this." He thinks it a tenable hypothesis that "the world as a whole includes *all* its appropriate matter"; hence, he concludes, "neither are there now, nor have there ever been, nor can there ever be formed, more heavens than one, but this heaven of ours is one and unique and complete."

On theological grounds, Augustine challenges those who suppose "either that this is not the only world, but that there are numberless worlds, or that indeed it is the only one, but that it dies, and is born again at fixed intervals, and this times without number." On theological grounds also, though with a different conception of God and the universe, Spinoza maintains that "besides God no substance can be or be conceived"; that "God is one, which is to say, in nature there is but one substance, and it is absolutely infinite"; that all finite things have their existence in the one infinite substance of God; and that God is "not only the cause of the commencement of their existence, but also of their continuance in existence." Because God's liberty consists, in Spinoza's conception, in acting according to the necessity of His own nature, not in freedom of will, he insists that "things could be produced by God in no other way and in no other order than that in which they have been produced." This is not merely the only actual but the only possible world.

Aquinas agrees that there is only one actual world. "The very order of things created by God," he writes, "shows the unity of the world." Since "whatever things come from God have relations of order to each other and to God himself . . . it is necessary that all things should belong to one world. Therefore," Aquinas continues, "only those were able to assert the existence of many worlds who do not acknowledge any ordaining wisdom, but rather believed in chance; as did Democritus, who said that this world, besides an infinite number of other worlds, was made by a coming together of atoms."

Aquinas places God's liberty in freedom of choice, and so he contemplates the possibility of other worlds than this. This is the only world God actually created, but since, in creating, "God does not act from natural necessity," and since, in the act of creation, the divine will "is not naturally and from any necessity determined to these creatures," Aquinas concludes that "in no way is the present scheme of things produced by God with such necessity that other things could not come to be."

As the chapter on WILL indicates, Spinoza holds that God does not have the power of free choice. He therefore argues that the actual world, being the only possible one, cannot be bettered. All things, he writes, have been "produced by God in the highest degree of perfection, since they have necessarily followed from the existence of a most perfect nature." Aquinas, on the other hand, denies that this is the best of all possible worlds. "Given the things which actually exist," he says, "the universe cannot be better, for the order which God has established in things, and in which the good of the universe consists, most befits things. ... Yet God could make other things, or add something to the present creation; and then there would be another and a better universe."

OTHER SPECULATIONS CONCERNING the cosmos seem to divide into three sorts, according as they consider the matter and space, the size and shape, of the universe; or they try to discover the principle by which all things are ordered together in one world; or they examine whatever order is found, and judge its perfection, its goodness, and its beauty.

The first of these three types of cosmological theory belongs primarily to the physicist and the astronomer. From Aristotle to Einstein, observation, mathematical calculation, and imaginative hypotheses have propounded the alternatives of a finite or infinite universe or, as Einstein prefers to put it, of a "finite yet unbounded universe," as opposed to one which is either simply finite or both infinite and unbounded.

Archimedes in the *Sand-Reckoner* undertakes to show that the number of the grains of sand in a universe whose outer sphere extends to the distance of the fixed stars, is, however large, a finite rather than an infinite number. Lucretius and Newton, as we have seen, embrace the opposite hypothesis, while Aristotle defends the proposition that the universe is finite, bounded and spherical in shape. Among the great astronomers, Copernicus and Kepler, no less than Ptolemy, conceive the world as bounded by an outer sphere. Copernicus opens his treatise by remarking that "the world is like a globe; whether because this form is the most perfect of all ... or because it is the figure having the greatest volume ... or because the separate parts of the world, *i.e.*, the sun, moon, and stars, are seen under such a form; or because all things seek to be delimited by such a form, as is apparent in the case of drops of water and other liquid bodies, when they become delimited through themselves."

A spherical or (if matter is not distributed uniformly) an elliptical or quasi-spherical universe, "will be necessarily finite," according to Einstein, but it will also "have no bounds." Among the conceivable "closed spaces without limits," Einstein points out that "the spherical space (and the elliptical) excels in its simplicity, since all points on it are equivalent." But "whether the universe in which we live is infinite, or whether it is finite in the manner of the spherical universe," he thinks is a question that "our experience is far from being sufficient to enable us to answer." Recent astronomical observations of the velocity of the receding nebulae have suggested the hypothesis of an infinitely expanding universe.

These cosmological theories are more fully discussed in the chapter on SPACE. Another point of physical speculation concerning the uniformity of the world's matter—not the uniformity of its distribution, but the sameness or difference in kind of terrestrial matter and the matter of the heavenly bodies—is considered in the chapters on ASTRONOMY and MATTER. We turn, therefore, to the question of the world's structure, apart from its size, its shape, and the disposition of its matter.

THREE METAPHORS SEEM to express the great traditional images of the world's structure. The world is a living organism. *It is like an animal* with a soul, even a soul endowed with reason. The world is a multitude of diverse and unequal individual things, forming a hierarchy and associated, according to their natures and functions, for the common good of the whole. *It is like a society*, a society under divine law and government. The world is a system of interdependent moving parts, linked together from the least to the greatest in an unbroken chain of causation. *It is like a machine*.

The first of these world views is proposed by Plato. It is not the earliest of the three, perhaps, if the atomistic cosmology of Democritus, which Lucretius later expounds, can be interpreted as adopting the mechanical analogy. Full-fledged mechanism may, however, be thought to await 17th century developments in the science of mechanics, when, for Descartes, Newton, and others, the laws of mechanics become the only laws of nature. The conception of the world as a divinely instituted and governed society seems to be a product of Jewish and Christian faith. Though that expression of it which includes a hierarchical ordering of all things from the elemental bodies to the angels belongs to Christian theologians and poets, there may be a pre-Christian version in the Stoic theory of the world as governed by a divine intelligence.

According to Plato, in the *Timaeus*, "God desired all things to be good and nothing bad," and he "found that no unintelligent creature taken as a whole was fairer than the intelligent taken as a whole; and that intelligence could not be present in anything which was devoid of soul. For which reason," Timaeus explains, "when he was framing the universe, he put intelligence in soul, and soul in body.... Wherefore, using the language of probability, we may say that the world became a living creature truly endowed with soul and intelligence by the providence of God." Since his intention was that "the animal should be as far as possible a perfect whole and of perfect parts," he gave it self-sufficiency, a spherical body—which figure "comprehends within itself all other figures"—and circular movement. The universe did not require, therefore, sense-organs or hands or feet.

"Such was the whole plan of the eternal God about the god that was to be, to whom for this reason he gave a body, smooth and even, having a surface in every direction equidistant from the center.... And in the center," according to Timaeus, "he put the soul, which he diffused throughout the body, making it also to be the exterior environment of it; and he made the universe a circle moving in a circle.... Having these purposes in view he created the world a blessed god."

The theory of a world soul and of an animated, organic universe appears not only in the *Timaeus*, but also in other Platonic dialogues. In the *Phaedrus*, for example, Socrates says that "the soul in her totality has the care of inanimate being everywhere"; and in the *Laws*, the Athenian Stranger, asking whether "it is the soul which controls heaven and earth, and the whole world," replies that "the best soul takes care of the world and guides it along the good path."

In somewhat different form, the theory of a world soul appears in Plotinus, according to whom the cosmic soul belongs only to the material universe and is, therefore, third and lowest in the scale of the "authentic existents." It appears in Gilbert and Kepler, though in the latter largely as the expansion of a metaphor. It is considered by William James, whose comment on the "materialistic, or so-called 'scientific,' conceptions of the universe" is that "they leave the emotional and active interests cold," whereas he thinks "the perfect object of belief would be a God or 'Soul of the World,' represented both optimistically and moralistically. ... All science and all history would thus be accounted for in the deepest and simplest fashion."

Precisely because exponents of the doctrine attribute divinity to the world soul, Augustine and Aquinas object to it. "Impious and irreligious consequences follow," in Augustine's opinion, from the notion that "God is the soul of the world, and the world is as a body to Him." To those who compare the microcosm with the macrocosm by saying that "the soul is in the body as God is in the world," Aquinas replies that "the comparison holds in a certain respect, namely, because as God moves the world, so the soul moves the body. But it does not hold in every respect, for the soul did not create the body out of nothing as God created the world."

Furthermore, according to Aquinas, "God is not a part of it, but far above the whole universe, possessing within Himself the entire perfection of the universe in a more eminent way." God in relation to the world should not be conceived by analogy with soul and body, but by comparison to a king who "is said to be in the whole kingdom by his power, although he is not everywhere present." This analogy fits better with the conception of the universe as a society under divine government.

Although Aurelius reminds himself to "regard the universe as one living being, having one substance and one soul," he also takes the view that the world is a community of things ordered to one another. "The intelligence of the universe is social," he writes. "Accordingly it has made the inferior things for the sake of the superior, and it has fitted the superior to one another. . . . It has subordinated, co-ordinated, and assigned to everything its proper portion." This view of the universe as a community is the one most fully developed in Christian thought. Augustine and Aquinas go much further than Aurelius in depicting the hierarchy of things and their ordination to one another under the eternal law. Both take as a basic text from Scripture the statement that God has "ordered all things in measure, and number, and weight." According to its dignity or worth, each thing occupies a place and plays its part in the general scheme of things.

"The parts of the universe are ordered to each other," Aquinas writes, "according as one acts on another, and according as one is the end and exemplar of the other." The government of the universe by the divine reason produces a perfection of order in the whole, which is the intrinsic common good of the universe, and directs each thing to the attainment of its end, in which consists its own perfection. "It belongs to the divine goodness," Aquinas says, "as it brought things into being, to lead them to their end. And this is to govern." But neither the perfection of each thing, nor the order of the universe itself, is the ultimate end of divine government. "Some good outside the whole universe," he says, "is the end of the government of the universe"—for the end of all things, as their beginning, lies in the goodness of God.

THE CONCEPTION OF THE WORLD as divinely governed, and cared for by divine providence, excludes chance as a factor in the formation of the world or in its structure. With Democritus and Epicurus in mind, Aquinas points out that "certain ancient philosophers denied the government of the world, saying that all things happened by chance." But the rejection of chance does not seem to be peculiar to Christian faith or theology.

Plato and Plotinus also deny that the order in the universe can be the result of chance. For Plato it is not merely that the world is animated by a rational soul, but also, as the Athenian Stranger suggests in the *Laws*, that it is a work of art rather than of nature or chance.

"'Atoms' or 'elements'—it is in either case an absurdity, an impossibility," writes Plotinus, "to hand over the universe and its contents to material entities, and out of the disorderly swirl thus occasioned to call order . . . into being." According to him, "there is nothing undesigned, nothing of chance, in all the process." Aristotle, too, speaks against the atomists who "ascribe this heavenly sphere and all the worlds to spontaneity" or chance. "When one man," he writes, referring to Anaxagoras, "said that reason was present—as in animals, so throughout nature—as the cause of order and of all arrangement, he seemed like a sober man in contrast with the random talk of his predecessors."

It might be supposed that those who view the world through the eyes of Newton or Descartes (when they say, as Fielding does, "the world may indeed be considered as a vast machine"), would be inclined to favor chance rather than reason or design. But this does not seem to be the case, at least not for Newton or Descartes. "This most beautiful system of the sun, planets, and comets," Newton declares, "could only proceed from the counsel and dominion of an intelligent and powerful Being."

Descartes asks us to consider what would happen if God were now to create a new world "somewhere in an imaginary space." Suppose that He agitated its matter in various ways "so that there resulted a chaos as confused as the poets ever feigned, and concluded His work by merely lending His concurrence to Nature in the usual way, leaving her to act in accordance with the laws which He had established." Something like this orderly universe would be the result. The laws of matter in motion, Descartes thinks, are "of such a nature that even if God had created other worlds, He could not have created any in which these laws would fail to be observed."

In the tradition of the great books, only the ancient atomists seem to take the position that the universe is a thing of chance. But this does not mean that, except for the atomists, agreement prevails concerning the manifestation of purpose or design in the world's structure. "Is the Kosmos an expression of intelligence, rational in its inward nature, or," James asks, "a brute external fact pure and simple?" James finds two answers to this question which he calls "the deepest of all philosophic problems" —one which regards the world "as a realm of final purposes, that . . . exists for the sake of something," and one which sees "the present only as so much mere mechanical sprouting from the past, occurring with no reference to the future."

As the chapter on MECHANICS indicates, Newton and Descartes are, in a sense, mechanists; yet they also affirm final causes—ends or purposes—in the plan of the universe. Newton speaks of God's "most wise and excellent contrivance of things, and final causes." It is true that Descartes, while referring to the universe as a work of divine art, says that God's purpose may not be visible to us in all its arrangements. Therefore "the species of cause termed final finds no useful employment in physical (or natural) things; for it does not appear to me," he explains, "that I can without temerity seek to investigate the (inscrutable) ends of God." But this states a rule of method in natural science, not the denial of a cosmic plan.

That denial is to be found, however, most plainly in Spinoza. "It is commonly supposed," he writes, "that all things in nature, like men, work to some end; and indeed it is thought to be certain that God Himself directs all things to some sure end, for it is said that God has made all things for man, and man that he may worship God." Against this view, which he regards as the most besetting of all human prejudices, Spinoza holds that "nature does nothing for the sake of an end, for that eternal and infinite Being whom we call God or Nature acts by the same necessity by which He exists." Since "He exists for no end, He acts for no end; and since He has no principle or end of existence, He has no principle or end of action. A final cause, as it is called," Spinoza continues, "is nothing, therefore, but human desire, in so far as this is considered as the principle or primary cause of anything."

Because man discovers things in nature which serve as means to his own ends, man is led to infer, Spinoza declares, that "some ruler or rulers of nature exist, endowed with human liberty, who have taken care of all things for him, and have made all things for his use . . . and hence he affirmed that the gods direct everything for his advantage, in order that he may be bound to them and hold them in the highest honor. . . . Thus has this prejudice been turned into a superstition, and has driven deep roots into the mind—a prejudice which was the reason why everyone has so eagerly tried to discover and explain the final causes of things." The attempt, however, to show that nature does nothing in vain (that is to say, nothing which is not profitable to man) seems, in Spinoza's opinion, "to end in showing that nature, the gods, and man are alike mad."

WHERE SPINOZA DENIES purpose or plan in the universe because everything exists or happens from the necessity of efficient, not final, causes (and ultimately from the necessity of nature or God himself), Lucretius argues against design or providence from the imperfection of the world. To those who "suppose that the gods designed all things for the sake of men," Lucretius says: "Even if I did not know what first-beginnings are, yet this, judging from the very arrangements of heaven, I would venture to affirm, and led by many other circumstances to maintain, that the nature of the world has by no means been made for us by divine power: so great are the defects with which it stands encumbered."

Spinoza would dismiss this argument. He thinks he can easily answer those who ask, "How is it that so many imperfections have arisen in nature—corruption, for instance, of things till they stink; deformity, exciting disgust; confusion, evil, crime, etc.?" He holds that "the perfection of things is to be judged by their nature and power alone; nor are they more or less perfect because they delight or offend the human senses, or because they are beneficial or prejudicial to human nature."

Others deal differently with the apparent imperfections in the world. Descartes, for example, makes the point that "the same thing which might possibly seem very imperfect . . . if regarded by itself, is found to be very perfect if regarded as part of the whole universe." Marcus Aurelius goes further. "Nothing is injurious to the part," he writes, "if it is for the advantage of the whole. . . . By remembering, then, that I am part of such a whole, I shall be content with everything that happens."

In terms of another principle, Berkeley asks

us to "consider that the very blemishes and defects of nature are not without their use, in that they make an agreeable sort of variety, and augment the beauty of the rest of creation, as shades in a picture serve to set off the brighter and more enlightened parts. . . . As for the mixture of pain or uneasiness which is in the world, pursuant to the general laws of nature," he thinks that "this, in the state we are in at present, is indispensably necessary to our well-being."

In the opinion of those "philosophers who, after an exact scrutiny of all the phenomena of nature, conclude that the *whole*, considered as one system is, in every period of its existence, ordered with perfect benevolence," Hume sees only a specious, if also sublime, consolation for all human ills. But he does not think such convictions ever really work in practice. "These enlarged views may, for a moment," he says, "please the imagination of a speculative man, who is placed in ease and security; but neither can they dwell with constancy on his mind, even though undisturbed by the emotions of pain or passion; much less can they maintain their ground when attacked by such powerful antagonists."

But according to theologians like Augustine and Aquinas, evil does not and cannot exist in the world except as a privation or corruption of some good. "Evil neither belongs to the perfection of the universe, nor comes under the order of the universe," writes Aquinas, "except accidentally, that is, by reason of some good joined to it." But how does evil enter into a world created by a supremely good deity? What "God chiefly intends in created things," Aquinas answers, "is the good of the order of the universe. Now the order of the universe requires . . . that there should be some things that can, and sometimes do, fail. And thus God, by causing in things the good order of the universe, consequently and, as it were by accident, causes the corruptions of things." Furthermore, "the order of justice belongs to the order of the universe; and this requires that penalty should be dealt out to sinners. And so God is the author of the evil which is penalty, but not of the evil which is fault."

ON THIS POINT OF THE PERFECTION of the universe, the great conversation passes from the order of the world to the problem of evil and to related issues. When Freud, for example, in commenting on what he calls "the religious Weltanschauung," says that "earthquakes, floods and fires do not differentiate between the good and devout man, and the sinner and unbeliever," he raises questions which are considered in the chapters on JUSTICE, PUNISHMENT, and GOOD AND EVIL. The perfection of the universe also leads to a discussion of the beauty of its order. The praises which are differently voiced by the astronomers, the theologians, and the poets extol not the visible beauties of nature, but the intelligible beauty of the cosmic structure—perceptible to a Kepler in his mathematical and musical formulation of the harmonies of the world.

In addition to questions of its goodness and beauty, the problem of the world's order is sometimes stated in terms of its rationality. For some writers, such as Hegel, rationality is affirmed as the very foundation of existence. "*What is rational is actual and what is actual is rational*," he writes. "On this conviction the plain man like the philosopher takes his stand, and from it philosophy starts in its study of the universe of mind as well as the universe of nature." To others, like William James, "the whole war of the philosophies is over that point of faith. Some say that they can see their way already to the rationality; others that it is hopeless in any other but the mechanical way. To some the very fact that there is a world at all seems irrational."

Against the Hegelian notion of the world as a perfectly ordered whole (to which James applies the epithet "block universe"), James proposes the conception of a "concatenated universe." "The real world as it is given at this moment," James declares, "is the sum total of all its beings and events now. But can we think of such a sum? Can we realize for an instant what a cross-section of all existence at a definite point in time would be? While I talk and the flies buzz, a sea-gull catches a fish at the mouth of the Amazon, a tree falls in the Adirondack wilderness, a man sneezes in Germany, a horse dies in Tartary, and twins are born in France.

"What does that mean?" James asks. "Does the contemporaneity of these events with each other, and with a million more as disjointed as they, form a rational bond between them, and unite them into anything that means for us a world?" It would certainly not mean a universe or cosmos for those who, like Hegel, insist upon the pervasive unity of the universe as a whole which completely and rationally relates all its parts. But for James, who conceives the universe in a pluralistic rather than in a monistic fashion, the "collateral contemporaneity" of all things, "and nothing else, is the *real* order of the world."

All of these issues carry the discussion back to what is perhaps the decisive question—the question of the world's origin. According as men believe it to be the purposeful work of a beneficent intelligence or the product of blind chance or of equally blind necessity, their other judgments about the world tend in the general directions of optimism or pessimism. Yet this is only true for the most part.

The problem of the world's origin involves some technical issues which do not seem to have such consequences for man's appraisal of the universe. One is the question whether a created world has a beginning in time or is co-eternal with its creator. As is indicated in the chapters on Eternity and Time, whichever way the disputed question concerning the eternity of the world is answered, its creation may be affirmed or denied. Those who think the world is created declare that the power needed to maintain the world in being is identical with the creative power needed to initiate it. "The divine conservation," as Berkeley points out, is conceived as "a continual creation."

The most difficult point in issue concerns the meaning of creation itself. According to Christian doctrine, the essence of creation consists in making something out of nothing. On this principle Aquinas, for example, contrasts creation with generation or procreation and with artistic production. In biological generation, the offspring is produced out of the substance of its progenitors. In artistic production, some pre-existent material is transformed by the craftsman. But according to the theologian, creation is not change, "for change means that the same thing should be different now from what it was previously."

In becoming or alteration, some being is presupposed. "Creation is more perfect and more excellent than generation and alteration," Aquinas says, "because the term *whereto* is the whole substance of the thing; whereas what is understood as the term *wherefrom* is absolutely non-being," which, as he remarks, is the same as *nothing*. Since the distance between total non-being and being is infinite, only an infinite power can create, or make something out of nothing.

Lucretius flatly denies this possibility when he asserts as a first principle that "nothing can be produced from nothing." Not even the gods can violate this principle. "Nothing," he declares, "is ever gotten out of nothing by divine power." To Locke, on the other hand, the inconceivability of creation constitutes no argument against it. Writers like Lucretius "must give up their great maxim, *Ex nihilo nihil fit*. . . . It is not reasonable to deny the power of an infinite Being because we cannot comprehend its operations. We do not deny other effects upon this ground," Locke continues, "because we cannot possibly conceive the manner of their production. . . . It is an overvaluing ourselves, to reduce all to the narrow measure of our capacities, and to conclude all things impossible to be done, whose manner of doing exceeds our comprehension."

But may not the world be related to a supreme cause or principle in some way which does not involve *exnihilation*? The great books present various alternatives. Aristotle's prime mover is the unmoved and eternal cause of the world's eternal motion, not of its coming into being or its conservation in being. Plato's demiurge is a divinity which, according to the myth of the world's origin in the *Timaeus*, fashions the universe after the model of the eternal ideas, artistically producing their sensible replicas in the matter or space which is called "the receptacle."

The emanation of the sensible as well as the intelligible world from the transcendent All-One in the cosmogony of Plotinus, or the production of finite things from the infinite substance of God in Spinoza's theory, seem to be more like generation or procreation than like creation in the meaning of the opening chapter of Genesis.

Such theories, according to theologians like Augustine and Aquinas, or philosophers like Berkeley and Locke, deny what is meant by creation in the Judaeo-Christian tradition. To Berkeley they are all equally forms of atheism. Yet it should be remarked that to Spinoza a theory like that of Plato's is also impious; for it places "something outside of God which is independent of Him, to which He looks while He is at work as to a model, or at which He aims as if at a certain mark. This is indeed nothing else than to subject God to fate, the most absurd thing which can be affirmed of Him whom we have shown to be the first and only free cause of the essence of all things as well as of their existence."

THE VARIOUS THEORIES OF the world's origin usually extend also to the problem of the world's end. Aristotle, for example, who denies a beginning to the motions of the heavens and all other cycles of natural change, affirms them to go on in everlasting perpetuity. But it is not merely those who think the world has no beginning or source who attribute endless endurance to it. If the world did not have endless duration, it would not be for Plato the moving image of eternity. And though they conceive the world as somehow a divine emanation or production, Plotinus and Spinoza, no less than Aristotle, hold it to be everlasting if not eternal. "We hold that the ordered universe, in its material mass," Plotinus writes, "has existed for ever and will for ever endure."

The proposition that nothing is ever reduced to nothing is, for Lucretius, as true as the principle that nothing ever comes from nothing. He applies these principles, however, only to the eternal atoms, uncreated and indestructible, not to the world after world which arises and perishes as the atoms come together and disperse. Just as any compound body which atoms form can be dissolved into its simple bodies, so whole worlds are subject to similar dissolution, and will suffer it in the course of long ages. Yet though world succeeds world in the ceaseless activity of the eternal atoms, Lucretius contemplates a universe without beginning or end.

Since annihilation (or reduction to nothingness) is the opposite of exnihilation (or creation out of nothing), it might be expected that the doctrine which rests on the faith that "in the beginning God created heaven and earth," would also foresee an end to all things—a return of the whole created universe to the nothingness from which it came. Sacred Scripture does contain the prophecy of a final cataclysm. "The earth shall reel to and fro like a drunkard, and shall be removed like a cottage," says Isaiah. Reciting the parable of the tares in the field, Matthew explains that as "the tares are gathered and burned in the fire, so shall it be in the end of this world." In the Gospel according to Luke, Christ foretells His second coming:

> And there shall be signs in the sun, and in the moon, and in the stars; and upon the earth distress of nations, with perplexity; the sea and the waves roaring;
>
> Men's hearts failing them for fear, and for looking after those things which are coming on the earth: for the powers of heaven shall be shaken;
>
> And then shall they see the Son of man coming in a cloud with great power and great glory . . .
>
> Heaven and earth shall pass away; but my word shall not pass away.

But there is one other text which exercises a controlling influence on the theologian's interpretation of Scripture. In the second Epistle of Peter, we find:

> . . . . . . the day of the Lord will come as a thief in the night; in the which the heavens shall pass away with a great noise, and the elements shall melt with fervent heat, the earth also and the works that are therein shall be burned up . . . . . .
>
> Nevertheless we, according to his promise, look for new heavens and a new earth, wherein dwelleth righteousness.

The final conflagration will be the end of the world as we know it, but it will bring about the re-formation, not the annihilation, of the material universe. As God has the power to create, so, according to Aquinas, He has the power to annihilate, but "since the power and goodness of God are rather manifested by the conservation of things in being . . . we must conclude by denying absolutely that anything at all will be annihilated." In the concluding treatises of the *Summa Theologica*—dealing with the end of the world, the Last Judgment, and the resurrection of the body—the final cataclysm is described as the cleansing of the world by fire to bring into being a new earth and a new heaven.

In our time, men talk of the end of the world as an event which might by chance occur if a chain reaction set up by atomic fission got out of control and exploded the whole material universe. The physicist's theory of entropy also forecasts the eventual dissipation of energy to the point at which the universe will be a frozen mass of inert matter. These are secular alternatives to the religious prophecy of the world's end. But what Jesus said of the Last Judgment —that its time is a secret hidden from men— may be applicable to any termination of the world, certainly if it lies in the hands of God, and not merely at the disposal of man or nature.

OUTLINE OF TOPICS

1. Diverse conceptions of the universe
   - 1*a*. The universe as a living organism: the doctrine of the world soul
   - 1*b*. The universe as a machine: the system of its moving parts
   - 1*c*. The universe as an ordered community of beings diverse in kind: eternal law and divine government
2. The universe and man: macrocosm and microcosm
3. The universe and God: divine immanence and transcendence
   - 3*a*. The unity of God and the world: the distinction between *natura naturans* and *natura naturata*
   - 3*b*. The duality of God and the world: the distinction between Creator and creature
4. The origin of the world: cosmos out of chaos
   - 4*a*. The denial of ultimate origins: the eternity of the world and its motions without beginning or end
   - 4*b*. Myths or hypotheses concerning the world's origin by artistic production: the demiurge, the creative ideas, the receptacle
   - 4*c*. The formation of the world by a fortuitous concourse of atoms
   - 4*d*. The emanation of the world from the One
   - 4*e*. The creation of the world *ex nihilo*
     - (1) The distinction between creation and motion, generation, and artistic production
     - (2) The problem of time and eternity in relation to creation: the conservation of creatures in time
     - (3) The revelation and dogma of creation: interpretations of Genesis 1; the work of the six days
5. The number of worlds: the uniqueness of this world; the possibility or actuality of other worlds
6. The structure of the world
   - 6*a*. The parts and places of the world: the uniformity of the matter of the world
   - 6*b*. The diversity, inequality, and hierachy of things
   - 6*c*. The rationality or intelligibility of the universe
   - 6*d*. The goodness and beauty of the universe: its evil and imperfections
7. The space of the world: astronomical theories concerning the size or extent of the universe
8. The end of the world

REFERENCES

References are listed by volume number (in bold type), author's name, and page number. Bible references are to book, chapter, and verse of the Authorized King James version of the Bible. The abbreviation "esp" calls the reader's attention to one or more especially relevant parts of a whole reference; "passim" signifies that the topic is discussed intermittently rather than continuously in the work or passage cited. Where the work as a whole is relevant to the topic, the page numbers refer to the entire work. For general guidance in the use of *The Great Ideas,* consult the Preface.

1. Diverse conceptions of the universe

1*a*. The universe as a living organism: the doctrine of the world soul

7 PLATO, 124, 447–450, 586–590, 618–619, 757–765
8 ARISTOTLE, 336, 641
12 AURELIUS, 266, 267, 269–270, 273, 277, 292, 310
13 VIRGIL, 230–231
16 KEPLER, 1083–1084
17 PLOTINUS, 36–37, 40–42, 46–47, 48–50, 79–80, 90–91, 141–149 passim, 161–166, 168–172, 201–202, 204–205, 208–209, 247, 251, 310
18 AUGUSTINE, 194–196, 247–248, 249–250, 256–257
19 AQUINAS, 19–20, 480–481
28 GILBERT, 104–105
34 NEWTON, 542–543
40 GIBBON, 307, 767
51 TOLSTOY, 608
53 JAMES, 658–659

1*b*. The universe as a machine: the system of its moving parts

12 LUCRETIUS, 6, 15–19
12 AURELIUS, 297
17 PLOTINUS, 78–79
23 HOBBES, 172, 269
30 BACON, 114–115
31 DESCARTES, 54–56
31 SPINOZA, 378–380
34 NEWTON, 269–372, 540–542
35 LOCKE, 334–335
35 HUME, 475, 485–486
42 KANT, 558–559, 561–564, 568–570
53 JAMES, 882–884

1*c*. The universe as an ordered community of beings diverse in kind: eternal law and divine government

7 PLATO, 479
8 ARISTOTLE, 445, 598–606
12 EPICTETUS, 204
12 AURELIUS, 269–270, 274
17 PLOTINUS, 44–45, 82–97 passim, 149, 163
18 AUGUSTINE, 216, 268–269, 339
19 AQUINAS, 12–14, 124–125, 127–132, 240–241, 258–259, 528–608
20 AQUINAS, 208, 215–220
21 DANTE, 107, 117–118, 148
22 CHAUCER, 87
27 SHAKESPEARE, 108–109
30 BACON, 71
31 SPINOZA, 369–372
35 BERKELEY, 433–434 passim
38 MONTESQUIEU, 1
40 GIBBON, 346–347
42 KANT, 200–209, 239–240, 578–587 passim, 594
51 TOLSTOY, 216–218

2. The universe and man: macrocosm and microcosm

7 PLATO, 124–126, 466
12 EPICTETUS, 143–144, 188–189, 232–235
12 AURELIUS, 266
16 KEPLER, 915–916
19 AQUINAS, 484–485
24 RABELAIS, 137–139
25 MONTAIGNE, 213–215, 259
26 SHAKESPEARE, 349–350, 608–609
27 SHAKESPEARE, 262–263
30 BACON, 33–34, 50
32 MILTON, 233–236
33 PASCAL, 181–184, 233–234
42 KANT, 360–361, 497–498, 591–592
46 HEGEL, 156–190
47 GOETHE, 1–294 passim
48 MELVILLE, 120–121, 168, 347, 353–354, 360–361
51 TOLSTOY, 216–218
52 DOSTOEVSKY, 168
53 JAMES, 655–659
54 FREUD, 562

3. The universe and God: divine immanence and transcendence

3*a*. The unity of God and the world: the distinction between *natura naturans* and *natura naturata*

APOCRYPHA: *Wisdom of Solomon,* 1:7
12 EPICTETUS, 120–121
12 AURELIUS, 280

17 PLOTINUS, 75–76, 129–136, 208–209, 214–215, 224–226, 242–244
18 AUGUSTINE, 15, 48–50, 195–196, 248, 358–359
19 AQUINAS, 22–23, 34–38, 480–481
28 HARVEY, 428
31 DESCARTES, 99
31 SPINOZA, 355–372, 373–377, 425
34 NEWTON, 370–371
35 LOCKE, 152, 162–163
35 BERKELEY, 442–443
42 KANT, 334–335, 566, 580
46 HEGEL, 176, 220–221, 227–228
48 MELVILLE, 115–117
51 TOLSTOY, 631

3*b*. The duality of God and the world: the distinction between Creator and creature

NEW TESTAMENT: *I John*, 2:15–17
9 ARISTOTLE, 234–235
12 LUCRETIUS, 17, 29, 63, 80–81
18 AUGUSTINE, 1–2, 36, 48–50, 73–74, 100–101, 261, 353–354
19 AQUINAS, 19–20, 34–35, 107–108, 238–240, 542–543
21 DANTE, 135, 148–150
22 CHAUCER, 209–210
23 HOBBES, 162
30 BACON, 17
31 DESCARTES, 54–56, 99, 110–112, 123, 158–159
38 MONTESQUIEU, 1
42 KANT, 190, 192
46 HEGEL, 245–246

4. The origin of the world: cosmos out of chaos

5 ARISTOPHANES, 551
7 PLATO, 458
8 ARISTOTLE, 601–602
12 LUCRETIUS, 66
31 DESCARTES, 54–56
32 MILTON, 129–133, 135–136
47 GOETHE, 191–193

4*a*. The denial of ultimate origins: the eternity of the world and its motions without beginning or end

7 PLATO, 447
8 ARISTOTLE, 334–337, 348–353, 361–362, 370–376, 379–380, 437–441, 458–459, 601–605
12 LUCRETIUS, 13, 16, 18–19, 22
12 AURELIUS, 271, 275, 297
16 KEPLER, 846–848, 890–891
17 PLOTINUS, 35–39, 67–68, 69–70
18 AUGUSTINE, 324, 348–350
19 AQUINAS, 41–42, 43–44, 250–255
20 AQUINAS, 1017–1020
31 SPINOZA, 362–363, 367–369
35 LOCKE, 160
42 KANT, 132–133, 135–137, 152, 160–161

4*b*. Myths or hypotheses concerning the world's origin by artistic production: the demiurge, the creative ideas, the receptacle

7 PLATO, 447–477
9 ARISTOTLE, 164
12 LUCRETIUS, 63
17 PLOTINUS, 58–59, 70, 72–73, 147–149, 242–243, 245–246
18 AUGUSTINE, 90–91
31 SPINOZA, 370–371
40 GIBBON, 307
42 KANT, 188–189

4*c*. The formation of the world by a fortuitous concourse of atoms

8 ARISTOTLE, 272–273
12 LUCRETIUS, 13, 17–18, 28, 66–67
12 AURELIUS, 297
17 PLOTINUS, 79
19 AQUINAS, 128–130, 256–257
34 NEWTON, 542

4*d*. The emanation of the world from the One

17 PLOTINUS, 37, 48–50, 67–68, 69–70, 90–91, 126–127, 163, 164–165, 174–180, 182–183, 209–213, 221–223, 226–228, 242–243, 279–280, 297–298, 299–300, 305–310, 321–323, 330

4*e*. The creation of the world *ex nihilo*

12 LUCRETIUS, 2–3
18 AUGUSTINE, 73, 90–93
19 AQUINAS, 126–127, 238–255, 339–349, 534–538, 692
21 DANTE, 116, 135
31 DESCARTES, 132–133, 229
31 SPINOZA, 362–363
32 MILTON, 218–231
34 NEWTON, 542–543
35 LOCKE, 352–354
35 BERKELEY, 431
35 HUME, 509
42 KANT, 135–137, 152
49 DARWIN, 239
54 FREUD, 877

4*e*(1) The distinction between creation and motion, generation, and artistic production

18 AUGUSTINE, 90–91
19 AQUINAS, 82–83, 111–112, 128–130, 154–155, 241–250, 343–345, 565–566
23 HOBBES, 47
35 LOCKE, 217
42 KANT, 188–189

4*e*(2) The problem of time and eternity in relation to creation: the conservation of creatures in time

17 PLOTINUS, 126

18 AUGUSTINE, 49–50, 91–93, 98–99, 109–110, 324–326, 351–254
19 AQUINAS, 34–35, 39–40, 250–255, 315–316, 348–349
31 DESCARTES, 87, 228
32 MILTON, 187–188
35 LOCKE, 160–161
35 BERKELEY, 421
42 KANT, 334–335

4e(3) The revelation and dogma of creation: interpretations of Genesis 1; the work of the six days

OLD TESTAMENT: *Genesis,* 1–2 / *Exodus,* 20:8–11 / *Nehemiah,* 9:6 / *Job,* 9:4–13; 12:7–10; 26:7–14; 38:4–13 / *Psalms,* 8; 33:6–9; 102:25–26; 104; 148 / *Proverbs,* 8:22–31 / *Isaiah,* 40:21–28; 42:5
APOCRYPHA: *Judith,* 16:14 / *Wisdom of Solomon,* 7:15–21 / *Ecclesiasticus,* 17:1–9; 39:16–35; 42:15–43:27 / *Song of Three Children,* 34–60
NEW TESTAMENT: *Colossians,* 1:16–17 / *Hebrews,* 1:10–11
18 AUGUSTINE, 45, 99–125, 261, 270–273, 324–342, 586–587
19 AQUINAS, 36–37, 126–127, 238–255, 339–377
21 DANTE, 126, 150
30 BACON, 17
32 MILTON, 150–151, 192–194, 218–231
52 DOSTOEVSKY, 120–121

5. The number of worlds: the uniqueness of this world; the possibility or actuality of other worlds

7 PLATO, 448, 459, 586–590
8 ARISTOTLE, 334, 367–370, 370–371
12 LUCRETIUS, 28–30
18 AUGUSTINE, 324–325, 349, 350, 353–354
25 MONTAIGNE, 252–253, 443
31 DESCARTES, 54–56
31 SPINOZA, 367–369

6. The structure of the world

6a. The parts and places of the world: the uniformity of the matter of the world

NEW TESTAMENT: *I Corinthians,* 15:40–41
7 PLATO, 247–250
8 ARISTOTLE, 359–360, 361–362, 370, 380
12 LUCRETIUS, 6, 14, 68
16 PTOLEMY, 8, 9–11
16 COPERNICUS, 517–518, 519–520
16 KEPLER, 853–857, 888–890, 929–930, 931–932
17 PLOTINUS, 35–39, 52–53
19 AQUINAS, 44–45, 289–290, 345–347, 354–355, 365–367, 443–444, 588–589
21 DANTE, 140–141
23 HOBBES, 172
28 GILBERT, 110
34 NEWTON, 270–271, 281–282

6b. The diversity, inequality, and hierarchy of things

OLD TESTAMENT: *Genesis,* 1–2
APOCRYPHA: *Ecclesiasticus,* 33:7–15
7 PLATO, 447–455
8 ARISTOTLE, 383–384, 605–606
9 ARISTOTLE, 272
17 PLOTINUS, 44–45, 46–47, 86
18 AUGUSTINE, 48–50, 216, 331–332, 333–334, 343, 344–345, 609–612
19 AQUINAS, 106–107, 116, 138–140, 256–259, 272–273, 295, 316, 343–369, 384–385, 393–394, 548–549, 552–564
20 AQUINAS, 1020–1022
21 DANTE, 115–116, 126, 148–150
22 CHAUCER, 209
32 MILTON, 185–186
35 LOCKE, 271–272, 370–371

6c. The rationality or intelligibility of the universe

7 PLATO, 447–477, 757–765
8 ARISTOTLE, 281, 502, 512–513
12 AURELIUS, 267, 273, 274, 277, 285, 286, 297
16 KEPLER, 863–872, 1023–1080
17 PLOTINUS, 129–131, 249–251
18 AUGUSTINE, 653
31 SPINOZA, 362, 375
42 KANT, 127–128, 200–209, 239–240, 550–613 passim
45 FOURIER, 173, 183
46 HEGEL, 6–7, 156–158, 160
53 JAMES, 862–863, 882–886, 889–890

6d. The goodness and beauty of the universe: its evil and imperfections

OLD TESTAMENT: *Genesis,* 1 / *Psalms,* 19:1–6; 104; 136:1–9
APOCRYPHA: *Wisdom of Solomon,* 13:1–5 / *Ecclesiasticus,* 16:26–30; 17:7–9; 39:12–35; 42:22–43:33
7 PLATO, 247–250, 447–448, 586–590
8 ARISTOTLE, 383–384, 502, 603, 605–606, 624
9 ARISTOTLE, 168–169
12 LUCRETIUS, 63–64
12 EPICTETUS, 233
12 AURELIUS, 259–260
16 COPERNICUS, 526–529
16 KEPLER, 863–872, 1023–1085
17 PLOTINUS, 57, 65–77 passim, 83–84, 88–89, 243–244, 245–246
18 AUGUSTINE, 73–74, 268–269, 307–308, 333–335, 343, 344–345, 517–520
19 AQUINAS, 25, 30, 100–101, 128–130, 149–150, 259–261, 266, 343–345, 375–377, 488–489, 529–530
20 AQUINAS, 925–926
21 DANTE, 109
22 CHAUCER, 54–55
31 DESCARTES, 214–215
31 SPINOZA, 367–369, 422–424

32 MILTON, 229
35 BERKELEY, 442, 443–444
35 HUME, 486, 499–500 passim
40 GIBBON, 81
42 KANT, 187–188, 544–546
48 MELVILLE, 144–145
52 DOSTOEVSKY, 153
54 FREUD, 878

7. The space of the world: astronomical theories concerning the size or extent of the universe

OLD TESTAMENT: *Job*, 38:18–20
8 ARISTOTLE, 362–367, 378–379
11 ARCHIMEDES, 520–526
12 LUCRETIUS, 12–14, 28–29
16 PTOLEMY, 10
16 COPERNICUS, 516–517
16 KEPLER, 882–886
19 AQUINAS, 37–38
32 MILTON, 233–236
35 LOCKE, 320
42 KANT, 135–137, 160–161, 501

8. The end of the world

OLD TESTAMENT: *Psalms*, 102:25–26 / *Isaiah*, 13:6–22; 24; 34; 51:6; 65:17–66:24 / *Daniel*, 12 / *Joel*, 2:1–11 / *Micah*, 4:1–3 / *Zechariah*, 14 / *Malachi*, 3–4
NEW TESTAMENT: *Matthew*, 11:20–24; 13:33–43,47–50; 24 / *Mark*, 13:4–37 / *Luke*, 17:20–37; 21:5–38 / *Acts*, 2:17–21 / *I Corinthians*, 7:29–31 / *I Thessalonians*, 4:15–5:4 / *II Peter*, 3:7–13 / *I John*, 2:18–19 / *Jude* / *Revelation*
9 ARISTOTLE, 234–235
12 LUCRETIUS, 62, 64–66
18 AUGUSTINE, 504–505, 530–560
20 AQUINAS, 922–935, 945–946, 1002–1004, 1016–1025
23 HOBBES, 230, 244
32 MILTON, 141–143, 220, 300–301
40 GIBBON, 187–188
41 GIBBON, 233

CROSS-REFERENCES

For: Discussions relevant to the conception of the universe as a living organism, as extension and thought, as the objectification of mind, and as an ordered community, *see* CAUSE 7c; GOD 7c; MIND 10f–10f(1); SOUL 1a.

Other considerations of the world and man, *see* MAN 10c, 10e.

The problem of the unity or duality of God and the world, *see* GOD 5d–5e, 11; NATURE 1b; ONE AND MANY 1b; RELATION 3.

The issues concerning the world's origin, its eternity, and its creation, *see* ART 2c; ASTRONOMY 8c(1); CHANGE 13; ELEMENT 5h; ETERNITY 2; GOD 7a; INFINITY 3e; ONE AND MANY 1a; TIME 2b–2c.

The issue concerning divine freedom in relation to the necessity of this world and the possibility of other worlds, *see* GOD 4e, 5g; LIBERTY 5d; WILL 4b.

Other discussions of the uniformity of the world's matter, *see* ASTRONOMY 8a; CHANGE 10c; MATTER 1b; MECHANICS 4a.

Other treatments of the space and the size of the world, *see* ASTRONOMY 5; INFINITY 3d, 4a; SPACE 3a.

The issue concerning hierarchy or continuity in the order of nature, *see* BEING 3a; GOOD AND EVIL 1b; LIFE AND DEATH 2, 3a; NATURE 3b.

The consideration of the world's rationality or intelligibility, *see* MIND 10a; NATURE 3a.

Another discussion of the beauty of the world, *see* BEAUTY 7b; and for the goodness of the universe in relation to God's goodness and the problem of evil, *see* GOD 4f, 5h–5i; GOOD AND EVIL 1d, 2b.

The atomistic theory of the world's growth and decay, *see* ELEMENT 5h; and for the religious dogma of the world's end and related theological doctrines, *see* GOD 7g–7h; IMMORTALITY 5g; PROPHECY 4d; SOUL 4d(3).

ADDITIONAL READINGS

Listed below are works not included in *Great Books of the Western World*, but relevant to the idea and topics with which this chapter deals. These works are divided into two groups:

I. Works by authors represented in this collection.
II. Works by authors not represented in this collection.

For the date, place, and other facts concerning the publication of the works cited, consult the Bibliography of Additional Readings which follows the last chapter of *The Great Ideas.*

I.

AUGUSTINE. *De Genesi ad Litteram*
AQUINAS. *Summa Contra Gentiles*, BK II, CH 32–38; BK IV, CH 96–97
——. *De Aeternitate Mundi*
GALILEO. *The Sidereal Messenger*
——. *Dialogo dei massimi sistemi*
DESCARTES. *The World*, CH I–II, VI–XIV
——. *The Principles of Philosophy*, PART II, 21–22
HOBBES. *Concerning Body*, PART IV, CH 26
KANT. *Cosmogony*
——. *De Mundi Sensibilis (Inaugural Dissertation)*
——. *Prolegomena to Any Future Metaphysic*, par 50–54
W. JAMES. *A Pluralistic Universe*

II.

ARISTARCHUS. *On the Sizes and Distances of the Sun and Moon*
EPICURUS. *Letter to Herodotus*
——. *Letter to Pythocles*
PHILO JUDAEUS. *On the Eternity of the World (De Aeternitate Mundi)*
——. *On the Creation of the World (De Opificio Mundi)*
PROCLUS. *The Elements of Theology*
SAADIA GAON. *The Book of Beliefs and Opinions*, TREATISE I
BERNARD SYLVESTRIS. *De Mundi Universitate*
MAIMONIDES. *The Guide for the Perplexed*, PART I, CH 72; PART II, CH 8–16, 22–23, 25–30
BONAVENTURA. *Breviloquium*, PART II
R. BACON. *Opus Majus*, PART IV
NICOLAS OF CUSA. *De Docta Ignorantia*, BK II, CH 4–13
BRUNO. *De Immenso et Innumerabilibus*
SUÁREZ. *Disputationes Metaphysicae*, XX–XXII, XXIX, XXXI (9, 14)
FONTENELLE. *Conversations on the Plurality of Worlds*
LEIBNITZ. *Monadology*, par 56–90
VOLTAIRE. *Micromegas*
——. *Candide*
——. "Chain of Created Beings," "End of World," in *A Philosophical Dictionary*
LAPLACE. *The System of the World*
SCHLEIERMACHER. *The Christian Faith*, par 59
A. HUMBOLDT. *Cosmos*
WHEWELL. *The Plurality of Worlds*
CLIFFORD. "The First and the Last Catastrophe," in VOL I, *Lectures and Essays*
STALLO. *Concepts and Theories of Modern Physics*, CH 13–15
C. S. PEIRCE. *Collected Papers*, VOL VI, par 185–237
HAECKEL. *The Riddle of the Universe*
ROYCE. *The World and the Individual*
DUHEM. *Le système du monde*
EINSTEIN. *Relativity: The Special and the General Theory*
——. *Sidelights on Relativity*
MCTAGGART. *The Nature of Existence*, CH 28–31
G. N. LEWIS. *The Anatomy of Science*, ESSAY VI
HEIDEGGER. *Sein und Zeit*
JEANS. *Problems of Cosmogony and Stellar Dynamics*
——. *Astronomy and Cosmogony*
——. *The Universe Around Us*, CH 4, 6
SITTER. *Kosmos*
WEYL. *The Open World*, LECT I
EDDINGTON. *Stellar Movements and the Structure of the Universe*
——. *The Nature of the Physical World*, CH 4, 11
——. *The Expanding Universe*
LOVEJOY. *The Great Chain of Being*
WHITEHEAD. *Process and Reality*
——. *Adventures of Ideas*, CH 7–8
PLANCK. "The Unity of the Physical Universe," in *A Survey of Physics*
——. *The Philosophy of Physics*, CH I
MILNE. *Kinematical Relativity*
C. S. LEWIS. *Out of the Silent Planet*
E. T. WHITTAKER. *Space and Spirit*
HARTSHORNE. *The Divine Relativity*
VON WEIZSÄCKER. *The History of Nature*

APPENDICES

Appendix I

BIBLIOGRAPHY OF ADDITIONAL READINGS

The Bibliography of Additional Readings provides information concerning the authors and works cited in the Additional Readings. In addition to the full name and dates of each author, the Bibliography gives as much of the following information as is appropriate to each work cited: the full title (and subtitle, if any); the name of the editor or translator, if these are identified in the recommended edition; the place of publication of the edition or translation recommended; the name of the publisher and the date of publication; the original title; the date and, in some cases, the place of composition or publication.

Since the Additional Readings are 102 separate lists of authors and works, and the Bibliography is a single compilation of the titles which comprise these 102 lists, each was constructed according to different principles. The following statement of these principles serves to guide the reader in using the Bibliography in relation to the Additional Readings.

Authors' Names: In the Additional Readings, surnames are used, with initials added only where necessary to distinguish identical surnames; for example, J. H. Newman. In a few exceptional cases, full names are used because this is the more recognizable form; for example, Leonardo da Vinci. The common Anglicized spelling is employed for reference to foreign names.

The alphabetical order of authors' names in the Bibliography is determined by the way in which the names appear in the Additional Readings. Initials do not affect the order; for example, J. H. Newman appears in the Bibliography as Newman, John Henry. When full names are used in the Additional Readings, the first name determines the alphabetical location of the author in the Bibliography; for example, Leonardo da Vinci is listed under "L," not under "D" or "V."

Titles of Works: In the Additional Readings, full titles are generally used. In some cases abbreviated forms are employed to avoid undue length. All subtitles are omitted.

In the Bibliography, both title and subtitle are used; and, with few exceptions, the title is given as it appears on the title page of the edition cited.

Titles are arranged in alphabetical order under the names of their authors. The alphabetization of titles disregards initial English articles (*a*, *an*, and *the*), but not prepositions (*of*, *on*, etc.).

The titles of anonymous works are placed in alphabetical order among the authors' names; for example, *Aucassin and Nicolette* appears in the Bibliography between Athanasius and Augustine.

The opening words of a shortened title in the Additional Readings sometimes differ from those of the full title. In these cases, the short title precedes the full title in the Bibliography, and is placed in brackets; for example, Faraday's *Various Forces of Matter* appears in the Bibliography as [Various Forces of Matter] *A Course of Six Lectures on the Various Forces of Matter and Their Relations to Each Other*.

The full title sometimes includes the names of a number of works, of which the Additional Readings cites only one. If the opening words of the full title differ from those of the title in the Additional Readings, the latter is placed in brackets and precedes the full title in the Bibliography; for example, Shaw's *Crude Criminology* appears in the Bibliography as [Crude Criminology] *Doctors' Delusions, Crude Criminology, and Sham Education*. The alphabetization is determined by the bracketed title, since this is the title which appears in the Additional Readings.

Translations: The manner of citing titles in the Additional Readings indicates whether a foreign work is available in English translation. If no translation exists or is available, the title is given only in its original language. If, however, the work has been translated, the English title is always used, sometimes in conjunction with its original foreign title. When two titles are thus given, which appears first depends in large part on the wording of the title page or the backbone of the volume which contains the translation.

Some translations carry the original title in the primary place, and use the translation as a secondary title. Some translations use only the English title. In these cases, where the work is well-known under its original title, this is added in parentheses after the English title. Some translations use only the foreign title. In these cases, an English version is added in parentheses after the original title.

In the Bibliography, the titles of translated works are listed alphabetically according to the way in which they are cited in the Additional Readings. If the original title is given first in the Additional Readings, then only it is used in the Bibliography. If the English title is given first in the Additional Readings, or if only it is used, then the work is listed alphabetically in the Bibliography according to the English title. In these cases the English title is always accompanied by the original title in parentheses.

COLLECTIONS: In the Additional Readings, the titles of essays or papers which are parts of a published collection are sometimes given within quotation marks, followed by the title of the collection, the latter appearing in italics; for example, J. H. NEWMAN. "Private Judgment," in VOL II, *Essays and Sketches*, or MCILWAIN. "The Fundamental Law Behind the Constitution," in *The Constitution Reconsidered*. In these cases it is the italicized title of the collection in which the essay or paper is published, rather than the quoted title of the essay or paper, which is listed in the Bibliography; for example, the essay by McIlwain in the example above is represented in the Bibliography by the following entry under MCILWAIN, CHARLES HOWARD: *The Constitution Reconsidered*.

The title of an individual essay or paper, or of a single lyric poem, is sometimes cited in the Additional Readings without reference to the collection in which it is published. In these cases, the title is italicized, not quoted. The individual work is represented in the Bibliography by this title, and the bibliographical information includes the title of the collection in which it is published.

A work listed in the Additional Readings may be available only in a collection or set of volumes with a single collective title. The collective title and the number of the volume in which the cited work appears are included in the bibliographical information; for example, what is cited in the Additional Readings as "AUGUSTINE. *On the Trinity*," is represented in the Bibliography by the following entry under AUGUSTINE, AURELIUS, SAINT, BISHOP OF HIPPO: "*On the Trinity*. In Vol. III, *Select Library*." *Select Library* is a shortened form of the collective title of a set of volumes; *i.e.*, *A Select Library of the Nicene and Post-Nicene Fathers of the Christian Church*. Ed. by P. Schaff. First Series, 8 vols.

When the full title of a collection, and bibliographical information about it, is given as part of the entry for a particular title, subsequent listings of other parts of the same collection may refer back to the collective title by using *ibid.* or *q.v.* or "see above." In other cases, only a shortened form of the collective title is given in the entry itself. Here the collective title in full, accompanied by bibliographical information, is given in a note appended to the last entry for that author.

WHOLE AND PART CITATIONS: In all cases in which parts of a work are recommended in the Additional Readings, the citation indicates these parts in a number of ways. It usually gives author's, editor's, or translator's divisions of the work, such as book, part, chapter, section, etc. In the few cases where such divisions are not citable, it gives page references to a particular edition. When page numbers are given, it is, of course, necessary to use this edition to find the pages cited.

When author's or editor's divisions are used, they are usually applicable to all standard editions of the work, especially if it was originally written in English. In the case of translations, it sometimes happens that the translator has made his own divisions of the work. Where this is so, the divisions indicated must be found in the particular translation specified in the Bibliography. The author's or translator's divisions are given in the same manner as similar divisions are given in the Reference sections of the 102 chapters; *i.e.*, BK, PART, CH, SECT, etc., followed by the number of the division in Arabic or Roman numerals according to the usage of the work cited.

Sometimes letters or numbers, without part names, signify subordinate divisions of the author's work; for example, HEGEL. *The Phenomenology of Mind*, IV, B (3). These are given precisely as they appear in the works themselves.

In a few cases, the recommended part of an author's work is titled. Such titles are placed in parentheses after the title of the work itself; for example, PÉGUY. *Basic Verities* (Freedom).

BIBLIOGRAPHY

Chronological Order: In the Additional Readings, the titles are listed in a chronological order; or, more precisely, they are divided into two groups, each in chronological order. The first of these consists of works written by the authors represented in *Great Books of the Western World*, but not published in this set; the second consists of works by other authors.

The order is determined in the same way in both groups—by the date of an author's work, not by his birth or death date. For each title listed in the Additional Readings, the determining or order date is given in the Bibliography.

For all contemporary works, and works written in English which appear in only one edition, the date which follows the place of publication and the name of the publisher is the order date.

For all translations, the order date is the date of the original writing or publication. This is given in parentheses, along with information about the original title and its place of writing or publication.

Similarly, for works which have been recently republished or which exist in several editions, the order date is the date of the original publication, or perhaps the date of composition. This date is given in parentheses. If it is the date of composition, it is given by itself. If it is the date of a first edition or an original publication of the work, it is given with other bibliographical information.

When parts of collections—poems, essays, plays—are individually cited, the order is determined by the date, in parentheses, of the individual work, not by the publication date of the collection.

When the entry for a particular title in the Bibliography includes two dates, the order date is always the one in the parentheses at the end of the entry.

A question mark in conjunction with a date signifies that it cannot be determined with certainty; the letter *c.* (for *circa*, or "about") signifies that the date is regarded as an approximation.

In a great many cases, more than one work is cited for a particular author, and often the publication date, or even the date of composition, is difficult to ascertain. This is especially true of works written in antiquity. Hence the chronological principle had to be applied with the following qualifications:

1. When two or more works by the same author are cited, they are grouped together under his name in strict chronological sequence. The chronological position of such a group of titles is determined by the date of the most recent title in the group. Hence, the whole series of individual titles in a list of Additional Readings may not be in strict chronological sequence.

2. If the work was published in the author's lifetime, the date used (if available) was that of its first publication. In the case of posthumously published works, the date of composition was used.

3. In the case of works for which no publication or composition date was available, the date of the author's death was usually substituted; or, as indicating the period in which he flourished, the median date of the author's life.

4. In the case of lectures later compiled and published as books, the date the lectures were first delivered was used.

5. In the case of a work published in several volumes over a period of years, the publication date of the first volume was used.

6. In the case of collections of papers or essays published during the author's lifetime and within a short time of the first scattered publication of the individual papers or essays, the date used was the publication date of the collection. But when the collection was published posthumously, or a long time elapsed between the first scattered publication and the publication of the collection, the median date of original publication dates was used. Whenever one set of dates could not be definitely determined, the other was used.

7. If a collection, published posthumously, represented the bulk of an author's writing, a date in the middle of his productive period was chosen.

8. When a single essay from a collection was cited, the date of the original publication of that essay was used, not the publication date of the collection.

9. In the case of single plays, the date used was that of original publication or first performance, whichever could be more definitely ascertained. If both were equally ascertainable, the earlier was used.

10. The publication date of a single lyric poem was used if it appeared separately before its appearance in a collection. Otherwise the date of the collection was used.

Because the foregoing factors affected the application of the chronological principle, the authors are frequently not listed in strict chronological order in the Additional Readings. However, the precise chronological position of each author can be determined by his life dates, which appear in the Bibliography. A question mark in conjunction with these dates signifies that they cannot be determined with certainty; the letter *c.* signifies that a date is regarded as an approximation; and *fl.* (for *floruit*) indicates that a date given is the period when the author flourished.

A

Abailard, Peter (1079–1142)
Dialectica. In *Ouvrages inédits pour servir à l'histoire de la philosophie scolastique en France.* Ed. by V. Cousin. Paris: Imprimerie Royale, 1836 (before 1125).
—*Ethics.* Ed. and trans. by J. R. McCallum. Oxford: Blackwell, 1935 (*Scito Teipsum, seu Ethica,* before 1140).
—*The Glosses of Peter Abailard on Porphyry.* In *Selections from Medieval Philosophers.* Ed. and trans. by Richard McKeon. 2 vols. New York: Scribner's, 1929–1930 (*Petri Abaelardi Glossae in Porphyrium*).
—*Introductio ad Theologiam.* Ed. by V. Cousin. Paris, 1859 (1136–1140).
—*The Letters of Abelard and Heloise.* Trans. by C. K. Scott Moncrieff. New York: A. A. Knopf, 1929 (*c.* 1130–1140).
—*Sic et Non.* In *Petri Abaelardi, Opera Omnia.* Ed. by J. P. Migne. Paris: Garnier, 1885.

Abercrombie, Lascelles (1881–1938)
An Essay Towards a Theory of Art. London: M. Secker, 1922.
—*The Theory of Poetry.* New York: Harcourt Brace, 1926 (originally pub. as *The Theory of Poetry* and *The Idea of Great Poetry,* London, 1924; 1925).

Abetti, Giorgio (1882–)
The Sun: Its Phenomena and Physical Features. Trans. by A. Zimmermann and F. Borghouts. New York: Van Nostrand, 1938 (*Il sole,* Milan, 1936).

Acton, John Emerich Edward Dalberg, Lord (1834–1902)
Essays on Freedom and Power. Boston: Beacon Press, 1948 (*The History of Freedom in Antiquity* and *The History of Freedom in Christianity,* both Bridgnorth, 1877).

Adams, Brooks (1848–1927)
The Law of Civilization and Decay: An Essay on History. New York: A. A. Knopf, 1943 (London, 1895).
—*The Theory of Social Revolutions.* New York: Macmillan, 1913.

Adams, Henry Brooks (1838–1918)
The Degradation of the Democratic Dogma. Ed. by B. Adams. New York: Macmillan, 1920 (1894–1910).
—*The Education of Henry Adams.* Modern Library, New York: Random House, 1941 (1906).
—*Mont-Saint-Michel and Chartres.* New York: Houghton Mifflin Co., 1927 (Washington, 1904).

Adams, John (1735–1826)
A Defense of the Constitutions of Government of the United States of America. In Vols. iv–vi, *Works of John Adams.* Ed. by C. F. Adams. 10 vols. Boston: Little, Brown & Co., 1850–1856 (1787).

Adler, Mortimer Jerome (1902–)
Art and Prudence, a Study in Practical Philosophy. New York: Longmans, Green & Co., 1937.
—*Dialectic.* New York: Harcourt Brace, 1927.
—*A Dialectic of Morals; Towards the Foundations of Political Philosophy.* Notre Dame, Ind.: The Review of Politics, University of Notre Dame, 1941.
—*How to Think About War and Peace.* New York: Simon & Schuster, 1944.
—*Problems for Thomists: The Problem of Species.* New York: Sheed & Ward, 1940.

Adrian, Edgar D. (1889–)
The Basis of Sensation. New York: W. W. Norton, 1928.

Aesop's Fables. Trans. by V. S. Vernon Jones. New York: Garden City Publishing Co., 1939.

Agard, Walter Raymond (1894–)
What Democracy Meant to the Greeks. Chapel Hill, N. C.: University of North Carolina Press, 1942.

Airy, Sir George Biddell (1801–1892)
Gravitation. An Elementary Explanation of the Principal Perturbations in the Solar System. London: Macmillan, 1884 (London, 1834).

Alain, pseud. for Émile Chartier (1868–1951)
Système des beaux-arts. Paris: Éditions de la Nouvelle Revue Française, 1920.

ALBERTI, LEONE BATTISTA (1404–1472)
Della Famiglia. Milan: Instituto Editoriale Italiano, 1910? (1443).

ALBERTUS MAGNUS (1193/1206–1280)
De Memoria et Reminiscentia. In Vol. IX, *Opera* (before 1256).
—*De Natura et Origine Animae. Ibid.* (before 1256).
—*De Sensu et Sensato. Ibid.* (before 1256).
—[On the Intellect and the Intelligible] *Treatises on the Intellect and the Intelligible*. In *Selections from Medieval Philosophers*. Ed. and trans. by Richard McKeon. 2 vols. New York: Scribner's, 1929–1930 (before 1256).
—*On Union with God*. Trans. by "a Benedictine of Princethorpe Priory." London: R. & T. Washbourne, 1912 (*De Adhaerendo Deo*, *c.* 1278–1280).
—*Summa Theologiae*. In Vol. XXXI, *Opera* (*c.* 1274).
NOTE:
B. Alberti Magni Opera Omnia. Ed. by A. Borgnet. 38 vols. Paris: Vivès, 1890–1899.

ALBO, JOSEPH (1380?–1444)
Sefer ha-Ikkarim (*The Book of Principles*). Ed. and trans. by I. Husik. 4 vols. Philadelphia: Jewish Publication Society of America, 1929 (*c.* 1425).

ALCUIN (FLACCUS ALBINUS) (*c.* 735–804)
The Rhetoric of Alcuin and Charlemagne. Ed. and trans. by W. S. Howell. Princeton University Press, 1941 (*Disputatio de Rhetorica et de Virtutibus*, 794).

ALEMÁN, MATEO (1547–*c.* 1614)
The Rogue; or, The Life of Guzman de Alfarache. Trans. by J. Mabbe. 4 vols. New York: A. A. Knopf, 1924 (Madrid, 1599).

ALEXANDER, FRANZ (1891–1964)
The Psychoanalysis of the Total Personality. Washington, D. C.: Nervous and Mental Disease Publishing Co., 1935 (*Die Psychoanalyse der Gesamtpersönlichkeit. Neun Vorlesungen über die Anwendung von Freuds Ichtheorie auf die Neurosenlehre*, Leipsic, 1927).

ALEXANDER, SAMUEL (1859–1938)
Space, Time, and Deity. 2 vols. London: Macmillan, 1927 (London, 1920).

AL-GHAZZALI (1058–1111)
[The Destruction of Philosophy] *Tahâfot al-Falâsifat*. Ed. by M. Bouyges. Beyrouth: Imprimerie Catholique, 1927. Also *Destructio Philosophorum*. In *Opera Omnia* of Averroës. Venice, 1527 (*c.* 1095).

ALIBERT, JEAN LOUIS MARIE (*c.* 1766–1837)
Physiologie des passions; ou, Nouvelle doctrine des sentiments moraux. 2 vols. Paris: Béchet jeune, 1825.

ALLEN, ARTHUR HENRY BURLTON (1872–)
Pleasure and Instinct: A Study in the Psychology of Human Action. New York: Harcourt Brace, 1930.

ALLEN, SIR CARLETON KEMP (1887–1966)
Law in the Making. Oxford: Clarendon Press, 1939 (Oxford, 1927).

ALLEN, EDGAR *et al.* (1892–1943)
Sex and Internal Secretions; a Survey of Recent Research. Baltimore, Md.: Williams & Wilkins, 1932.

ALTHUSIUS, JOHANNES (1557–1638)
Politica Methodice Digesta Atque Exemplis Sacris et Profanis Illustrata. Ed. by C. J. Friedrich. 2 vols. Cambridge, Mass.: Harvard University Press, 1932 (Herborn, 1603).

ALVERDES, FRIEDRICH (1889–)
Social Life in the Animal World. Trans. by K. C. Creasy. New York: Harcourt Brace, 1927 (*Tiersoziologie*, Leipsic, 1925).

Amis and Amilon. Ed. by MacEdward Leach. New York: Oxford University Press, 1937 (11th century).

AMPÈRE, ANDRÉ MARIE (1775–1836)
Essai sur la philosophie des sciences, ou Exposition analytique d'une classification naturelle de toutes les connaissances humaines. 2 vols. Paris: Bachelier, 1856 (Paris, 1834–1843).

ANDRADE, EDWARD NEVILLE DA COSTA (1887–1971)
The Atom and Its Energy. London: G. Bell & Sons, 1948.

ANDRÉ LE CHAPELAIN (b. *c.* 1170)
The Art of Courtly Love. Trans. by J. J. Parry. New York: Columbia University Press, 1941 (*Liber de Arte Honeste Amandi et de Reprobatione Inhonesti Amoris*, early 13th century).

ANDREYEV, LEONID NIKOLAEVICH (1871–1919)
Lazarus. Trans. by A. Yarmolinsky. Boston: Stratford Co., 1918 (Stuttgart, 1906).
—*The Seven Who Were Hanged. A Story*. Trans. by H. Berstein. New York: Illustrated Editions Co., 1941 (Berlin, 1908).

ANSELM OF CANTERBURY, SAINT (*c.* 1033–1109)
Cur Deus Homo? See *Proslogium* (*c.* 1098).
—*De Conceptu Virginali et Originali Peccato*. In Vol. CLVIII, *Patrologia Latina* (1099 or 1100).
—*De Libero Arbitrio. Ibid.* (1063–1078).
—*De Potestate et Impotentia; Possibilitate et Impossibilitate; Necessitate et Libertate. Ein neues unvollendetes Werk des Heiligen Anselm von Canterbury*. Ed. by F. S. Schmitt. Münster: Aschendorff, 1936 (1109?).
—*Dialogue on Truth*. In *Selections from Medieval Philosophers*. Ed. and trans. by Richard McKeon. 2 vols. New York: Scribner's, 1929–1930 (*Dialogus de Veritate*, 1063–1078).
—*Monologium*. See *Proslogium* (1063–1078).
—*Proslogium; Monologium; an Appendix, In Behalf of the Fool, by Gaunilon; and Cur Deus Homo*. Ed. and trans. by S. M. Deane. Chicago: Open Court, 1903 (1063–1078).

APPELL, PAUL ÉMILE (1855–1930)
Traité de mécanique rationnelle. 5 vols. Paris: Gauthier-Villars, 1893–1926.

APPIAN OF ALEXANDRIA (*c.* 95–*c.* 165 A.D.)
The Civil Wars. Vols. III–IV, *Appian's Roman History.* Trans. by H. White. 4 vols. New York: Macmillan, 1913.

AQUINAS, SAINT THOMAS (*c.* 1225–1274)
Compendium of Theology. Trans. by C. Vollert. St. Louis, Mo.: Herder Book Co., 1949 (*Compendium Theologiae,* 1273).
—*Concerning the Teacher.* In M. H. Mayer, *The Philosophy of Teaching of St. Thomas Aquinas.* Milwaukee, Wis.: Bruce Publishing Co., 1929 (*Quaestiones Disputatae de Veritate,* Q XI, 1256–1259).
—*Contra Impugnantes Dei Cultum et Religionem.* In Vol. IV, *Opuscula* (1257).
—*Contra Pestiferam Doctrinam Retrahentium Homines a Religionis Ingressu. Ibid.* (1270).
—*De Aeternitate Mundi Contra Murmurantes.* In Vol. I, *ibid.* (1270).
—*De Fallaciis.* In Vol. IV, *ibid.* (1244).
—*De Mixtione Elementorum ad Magistrum Philippe.* In Vol. I, *ibid.* (1273).
—*De Natura Materiae et Dimensionibus Interminalis.* In Vol. V, *ibid.*
—*De Natura Verbi Intellectus. Ibid.*
—*De Perfectione Vitae Spiritualis.* In Vol. IV, *ibid.* (1269).
—*De Principiis Naturae.* In Vol. I, *ibid.* (1255).
—*De Propositionibus Modalibus.* In Vol. IV, *ibid.* (1244–1245).
—*De Substantiis Separatis.* In Vol. I, *ibid.* (1272–1273).
—*On Being and Essence.* Ed. and trans. by A. Maurer. Toronto: Pontifical Institute of Mediaeval Studies, 1948 (*De Ente et Essentia,* 1254–1256).
—*On Spiritual Creatures.* Trans. by M.C. Fitzpatrick and J. J. Wellmuth. Milwaukee, Wis.: Marquette University Press, 1949 (*De Spiritualibus Creaturis,* 1266–1269).
—*On the Governance of Rulers.* Trans. by G. P. Phelan. Toronto: St. Michael's College, 1949 (*De Regimine Principum,* 1265–1266).
—*On the Power of God.* Trans. by Fathers of the English Dominican Province. 3 vols. London: Burns, Oates, & Washbourne, 1932–1934 (*Quaestiones Disputatae de Potentia Dei,* 1265–1267).
—[On the Trinity of Boethius] '*The Trinity*' and '*The Unicity of the Intellect.*' Trans. by Sister R. E. Brennan. London: Herder Book Co., 1946 (*Expositio Super Librum Boethii de Trinitate,* 1257–1258).
—*Quaestiones Disputatae* [... *de Veritate* (1256–1259) ... *de Malo* (1268–1269) ... *de Anima* (1269–1270) ... *de Unione Verbi Incarnati* (1268–1272) ... *de Virtutibus Cardinalibus* (1269–1272) ... *de Virtutibus in Communi* (1269–1272) ... *de Caritate* (1269–1272) ... *de Spe* (1269–1272)]. Ed. by P. Mandonnet. 3 vols. Paris: Lethielleux, 1925.
—*Summa Contra Gentiles.* Trans. by Fathers of the English Dominican Province. 5 vols. New York: Benziger Bros., 1924–1929 (1258–1264).
—*Summa Theologica.* Trans. by Fathers of the English Dominican Province. 22 vols. New York: Benziger Bros., 1911–1920 (1265–1272).
—*Super Boethium de Hebdomadibus.* In Vol. I, *Opuscula* (1258).
—[Two Precepts of Charity] *The Commandments of God; Conferences on the Two Precepts of Charity and the Ten Commandments.* London: Burns, Oates, & Washbourne, 1937 (*De Duobus Praeceptis Caritatis et Decem Legis Praeceptis,* 1273).
—*The Unicity of the Intellect.* See *On the Trinity* (*c.* 1270).
NOTE:
S. Thomae Aquinatis Opuscula Omnia. Ed. by P. Mandonnet. 5 vols. Paris: Lethielleux, 1927.

ARIOSTO, LUDOVICO (1474–1533)
Orlando Furioso. Trans. by W. S. Rose. 2 vols. New York: G. Bell & Sons, 1892 (Ferrara, 1516).

ARISTARCHUS (*fl. c.* 280 B.C.)
On the Sizes and Distances of the Sun and Moon. In Sir Thomas Heath, *Aristarchus of Samos: A History of Greek Astronomy.* Oxford: Clarendon Press, 1913.

ARNAULD, ANTOINE (1612–1694)
Logic or the Art of Thinking: Being the Port Royal Logic. Ed. and trans. by T. S. Baynes. London: W. Blackwood, 1850 (*La logique ou l'art de penser; contenant outre les règles communes, plusieurs observations nouvelles, propres à former le jugement,* Paris, 1662).

ARNAULD, ANTOINE and LANCELOT, CLAUDE (1615–1695)
A General and Rational Grammar Containing the Principles of the Art of Speaking. London, 1753 (*Grammaire générale et raisonnée contenant les fondemens de l'art de parler,* Paris, 1660).

ARNOLD, MATTHEW (1822–1888)
Culture and Anarchy; an Essay in Political and Social Criticism. Ed. by J. D. Wilson. 5 vols. Cambridge University Press, 1932 (London, 1869).
—*Empedocles on Etna.* In *The Poems of Matthew Arnold, 1849–1867.* World's Classics, New York: Oxford University Press, 1940 (London, 1852).
—*Essays in Criticism* (First and Second Series). 2 vols. London: Macmillan, 1935–1937 (London, 1865; 1888).
—*Literature and Dogma; an Essay Towards a Better Apprehension of the Bible.* New York: Macmillan, 1903 (London, 1873).
—*Mixed Essays, Irish Essays and Others.* New York: Macmillan, 1904 (London, 1879).

ARRHENIUS, SVANTE AUGUST (1859–1927)
The Destinies of the Stars. Trans. by J. E. Fries. New York: Putnam's, 1918 (Stockholm, 1915).

ASCH, SHOLEM (1880–1957)
The Apostle. Trans. by M. Samuel. New York: Putnam's, 1943.

—*The Nazarene*. Trans. by M. Samuel. New York: Putnam's, 1939.

ATHANASIUS, SAINT (*c.* 293–373)
Select Treatises of St. Athanasius in Controversy with the Arians. Trans. by J. H. Newman. London: Longmans, Green & Co., 1903 (*c.* 348–359).

Aucassin and Nicolette, and other Medieval Romances and Legends. Everyman's Library, New York: E. P. Dutton, 1910 (12th century).

AUGUSTINE, AURELIUS, SAINT, BISHOP OF HIPPO (354–430)
Admonition and Grace. Trans. by J. C. Murray. In Vol. IV, *Fathers* (*De Correptione et Gratia*, 427).
—*Against Two Letters of the Pelagians*. In Vol. XV, *Works* (*Contra Duas Epistolas Pelagianorum*, 420).
—*Answer to Skeptics*. Trans. by D. J. Kavanagh. In Vol. I, *Fathers* (*Contra Academicos*, 386).
—*Concerning the Nature of Good*. In Vol. I, *Basic Writings* (*De Natura Boni, Contra Manichaeos*, 404?).
—*Concerning the Teacher*. *Ibid.* (*De Magistro*, 389).
—*De Fide et Symbolo*. In Vol. XL, *Patrologia Latina* (393).
—*De Genesi ad Litteram Libri XII*. In Vol. XXXIV, *ibid.* (401?–415?).
—*De Vera Religione*. *Ibid.* (390).
—*Divine Providence and the Problem of Evil*. Trans. by R. P. Russell. In Vol. I, *Fathers* (*De Ordine*, 386).
—*The Enchiridion on Faith, Hope and Love*. In Vol. I, *Basic Writings* (*Enchiridion ad Laurentium, seu de Fide, Spe, et Caritate Liber*, 421).
—*The Happy Life*. Trans. by L. Schopp. In Vol. I, *Fathers* (*De Beata Vita*, 386).
—*The Harmony of the Gospels*. In Vol. VI, *Select Library* (*De Consensu Evangelistarum*, 400).
—*The Magnitude of the Soul*. Trans. by J. J. McMahon. In Vol. II, *Fathers* (*De Quantitate Animae*, 388).
—*Of Continence*. In Vol. III, *Select Library* (*De Continentia*, 395).
—*Of Marriage and Concupiscence*. In Vol. V, *ibid.* (*De Nuptiis et Concupiscentia*, 419–420).
—*Of the Work of Monks*. In Vol. III, *ibid.* (*De Opere Monachorum*, 401?).
—*On Baptism, Against the Donatists*. In Vol. IV, *ibid.* (*De Baptismo, Contra Donatistas*, 400).
—*On Faith in Things Unseen*. Trans. by R. J. Defferari and M. F. McDonald. In Vol. II, *Fathers* (*De Fide Rerum Quae Non Videntur*, 400).
—*On Free Will*. Trans. by C. M. Sparrow. Charlottesville, Va.: University of Virginia Press, 1947 (*De Libero Arbitrio*, 395).
—*On Grace and Free Will*. In Vol. I, *Basic Writings* (*De Gratia et Libero Arbitrio*, 426?).
—*On Music*. Trans. by R. C. Taliaferro. In Vol. II, *Fathers* (*De Musica*, 386).
—*On Nature and Grace*. In Vol. I, *Basic Writings* (*De Natura et Gratia, Contra Pelagium*, 415).
—*On the Good of Marriage*. In Vol. III, *Select Library* (*De Bono Conjugali*, 400).
—*On the Good of Widowhood*. *Ibid.* (*De Bono Viduitatis*, 414?).
—*On the Grace of Christ and on Original Sin*. In Vol. I, *Basic Writings* (*De Gratia Christi et Peccato Originali, Contra Pelagium*, 418).
—*On the Immortality of the Soul*. *Ibid.* (*De Immortalitate Animae*, 387).
—*On the Merits and Remissions of Sins*. In Vol. V, *Select Library* (*De Peccatorum Meritis et Remissione, et De Baptismo Parvulorum*, 412).
—*On the Morals of the Catholic Church*. In Vol. I, *Basic Writings* (*De Moribus Ecclesiae Catholicae*, 368).
—*On the Predestination of the Saints*. *Ibid.* (*De Praedestinatione Sanctorum*, 428?).
—*On the Profit of Believing*. *Ibid.* (*De Utilitate Credendi*, 391–392).
—*On the Spirit and the Letter*. *Ibid.* (*De Spiritu et Littera*, 412).
—*On the Trinity*. In Vol. III, *Select Library* (*De Trinitate*, 400–416).
—*Reply to Faustus*. In Vol. IV, *ibid.* (*Contra Faustum Manichaeum*, 400–404).
—*The Soliloquies of Saint Augustine*. In Vol. I, *Basic Writings* (*Soliloquia*, 387).
—*The Soul and Its Origin*. Trans. by A. C. Pegis. In Vol. III, *Fathers* (*De Anima et Eius Origine*, 419).
NOTE:
Basic Writings of Saint Augustine. Ed. by W. J. Oates. 2 vols. New York: Random House, 1948.
—[Fathers] *Writings of St. Augustine*, in *The Fathers of the Church*. Ed. by L. Schopp. New York: Cima, 1947.
—*A Select Library of the Nicene and Post-Nicene Fathers of the Christian Church*. Ed. by P. Schaff. First Series, 8 vols. Buffalo, N. Y.: Christian Literature Co., 1886–1888.
—*Works of Aurelius Augustine*. Ed. by M. Dods, trans. by P. Holmes and R. E. Wallis. 15 vols. Edinburgh: T. & T. Clark, 1876.

AUSTEN, JANE (1775–1817)
Pride and Prejudice. Garden City, N. Y.: Doubleday Doran, 1945 (London, 1813).

AUSTIN, JOHN (1790–1859)
Lectures on Jurisprudence; or, The Philosophy of Positive Law. Ed. by R. Campbell. 2 vols. London: J. Murray, 1911 (London, 1832).
—*The Province of Jurisprudence Determined*. 3 vols. London: J. Murray, 1861–1863 (London, 1832).

AVEBURY, SIR JOHN LUBBOCK (1834–1913)
The Pleasures of Life. 2 vols. London: Macmillan, 1887.

AVENARIUS, RICHARD (1843–1896)
Kritik der reinen Erfahrung. Ed. by J. Petzold. 2 vols. Leipsic: R. Reisland, 1907 (Leipsic, 1888–1890).

AVERROËS (1126–1198)
[The Destruction of the "Destruction"] *Tahâfot at-Tahâfot*. Ed. by M. Bouyges. Beyrouth: Imprimerie Catholique, 1930. Also *Destructio Destructionum*. In *Opera Omnia* of Averroës. Venice, 1527 (*c.* 1180).

AVICENNA (*c.* 980–1037)
A Treatise on the Canon of Medicine of Avicenna, Incorporating a Translation of the First Book. Trans. by O. C. Gruner. London: Luzac & Co, 1930.

AYER, ALFRED JULES (1910–)
Thinking and Meaning. London: H. K. Lewis, 1947.

B

BABBITT, IRVING (1865–1933)
The New Laokoön; an Essay on the Confusion of the Arts. New York: Houghton Mifflin Co., 1910.

BACHOFEN, JOHANN JAKOB (1815–1887)
Das Mutterrecht. Eine Untersuchung über die Gynäkokratie der alten Welt nach ihrer religiösen und rechtlichen Natur. Basle: B. Schwabe, 1897 (Stuttgart, 1861).

BACON, FRANCIS (LORD VERULAM) (1561–1626)
The Essayes; or Counsels Civill and Morall. Everyman's Library, New York: E. P. Dutton, 1932 (London, 1625).
—*The Maxims of the Law*. In Vol. XIV, *The Works of Francis Bacon*. Ed. by J. Spedding, R. L. Ellis and D. D. Heath. 15 vols. Boston: Brown & Taggard, 1861 (London, 1630).
—*Of the Colours of Good and Evil*. In Vol. I, *ibid*. (first pub. with *Essays*, London, 1597).
—*The Wisdom of the Ancients*. *Ibid*. (*De Sapientia Veterum*, London, 1609).

BACON, ROGER (*c.* 1214–1294)
On the Errors of Physicians. In *Essays on the History of Medicine*. Ed. by C. Singer and H. E. Sigerist, trans. by E. T. Withington. New York: Oxford University Press, 1924 (*De Erroribus Medicorum*, 1250?–1260?).
—*Opus Majus*. Trans. by R. B. Burke. 2 vols. Philadelphia: University of Pennsylvania Press, 1928 (1268).

BAGEHOT, WALTER (1826–1877)
The English Constitution. New York: Oxford University Press, 1933 (London, 1867).
—*Physics and Politics; or Thoughts on the Application of the Principle of "Natural Selection" and "Inheritance" to Political Society*. New York: D. Appleton, 1906 (1867–1869).
—*The Postulates of English Political Economy*. New York: Putnam's, 1894 (London, 1876).

BAIN, ALEXANDER (1818–1903)
Education as a Science. New York: D. Appleton, 1897 (London, 1879).
—*The Emotions and the Will*. New York: D. Appleton, 1888 (London, 1859).
—*Mind and Body: The Theories of Their Relation*. London: K. Paul, Trench, Trübner, 1910 (London, 1872).
—*The Senses and the Intellect*. New York: D. Appleton, 1894 (London, 1855).

BAKUNIN, MIKHAIL ALEKSANDROVICH (1814–1876)
God and the State. New York: Mother Earth Publishing Association, 1916? (*Dieu et l'Etat*, 1871–1872).

BALFOUR, ARTHUR JAMES (1848–1930)
Essays Speculative and Political. London: Hodder & Stoughton, 1920.
—*The Foundations of Belief; Being Notes Introductory to the Study of Theology*. New York: Longmans, Green & Co., 1902 (London, 1895).

BALL, SIR ROBERT STAWELL (1840–1913)
A Treatise on the Theory of Screws. Cambridge University Press, 1900 (1887).

BALZAC, HONORÉ DE (1799–1850)
At the Sign of the Cat and Racket. Everyman's Library, New York: E. P. Dutton, 1930 (*Gloire et malheur*, Paris, 1830).
—*Cousin Bette*. Trans. by K. P. Wormeley. Boston: Little, Brown & Co., 1928 (*La cousine Bette*, Paris, 1846).
—*Eugénie Grandet*. Ed. by G. Saintsbury, trans. by E. Marriage. Everyman's Library, New York: E. P. Dutton, 1907 (Paris, 1834).
—[Gobseck] *Father Goriot and M. Gobseck*. Trans. by E. Marriage. Philadelphia: Gebbie Publishing Co., 1900 (*Les dangers de l'inconduite*, Paris, 1830).
—*Old Goriot*. Trans. by E. Marriage. Everyman's Library, New York: E. P. Dutton, 1935 (*Le père Goriot*, Paris, 1835).
—*A Passion in the Desert*. In *Short Stories by Honoré de Balzac*. Modern Library, New York: Random House, 1920 (1830).
—*The Petty Annoyances of Married Life*. Trans. by O. W. Wight and F. B. Goodrich. New York: Rudd & Carleton, 1861 (*Petites misères de la vie conjugale*, Paris, 1845).
—*The Physiology of Marriage*. New York: Liveright, 1932 (*Physiologie du marriage; ou, Méditations de philosophie éclectique sur le bonheur et le malheur conjugal*, Paris, 1829).
—*The Rise and Fall of César Birotteau*. Trans. by E. Marriage. Everyman's Library, New York: E. P. Dutton, 1925 (*Grandeur et décadence de César Birotteau*, Paris, 1837).
—*The Wild Ass's Skin*. Trans. by E. Marriage. Everyman's Library, New York: E. P. Dutton, 1933 (*La peau de chagrin*, Paris, 1831).

BARCLAY, ROBERT (1648–1690)
An Apology for the True Christian Divinity, Being an Explanation and Vindication of the Principles and Doctrines of the People Called Quakers. Philadelphia: Friends Book-Store, 1869 (Amsterdam, 1676).

BARCLAY, WILLIAM (1546–1608)
De Regno et Regali Potestate, Adversus Buchana-

num, Brutum, Boucherium, et Reliquos Monarchomachos. Paris: G. Chaudière, 1600.

Barker, Sir Ernest (1874–1960)
Reflections on Government. New York: Oxford University Press, 1942.

Barrow, Isaac (1630–1677)
Lectiones Mathematicae. In *The Mathematical Works of Isaac Barrow.* Ed. by William Whewell. Cambridge University Press, 1860 (London, 1664).
—*Thirteen Geometrical Lectures.* Ed. and trans. by J. M. Child. Chicago: Open Court, 1916 (*Lectiones Geometricae*, London, 1670).
—*A Treatise of the Pope's Supremacy. To Which Is Added a Discourse Concerning the Unity of the Church.* In Vol. viii, *The Theological Works of Isaac Barrow.* Ed. by A. Napier. 8 vols. Cambridge University Press, 1859.

Barth, Karl (1886–1968)
Dogmatics in Outline. New York: Philosophical Library, 1949.
—*Epistle to the Romans.* Trans. by E. C. Hoskyns. New York: Oxford University Press, 1933 (*Der Römerbrief*, Bern, 1919).

Bartholomaeus Anglicus (*fl.* 1230–1260)
[On Medicine] *De Proprietatibus Rerum* (*Bk. VII, On Medicine*). Trans. by J. Walsh. New York: Froben Press, 1933.

Barzun, Jacques Martin (1907–)
Teacher in America. Boston: Little, Brown & Co., 1945.

Bastiat, Claude Frédéric (1801–1850)
Economic Sophisms. Trans. by P. J. Stirling. New York: Putnam's, 1922 (1845–1848).
—*Harmonies of Political Economy.* Trans. by P. J. Stirling. Edinburgh: Oliver & Boyd, 1880 (*Harmonies économiques*, Paris, 1850).

Bateson, William (1861–1926)
Problems of Genetics. New Haven, Conn.: Yale University Press, 1913.

Baudelaire, Charles Pierre (1821–1867)
Curiosités esthétiques. Paris: L. Conard, 1923 (1845–1859).
—*Flowers of Evil.* Trans. by G. Dillon and E. St. Vincent Millay. New York: Harper, 1936 (*Les fleurs du mal*, Paris, 1857).

Baxter, Richard (1615–1691)
Chapters from A Christian Directory; or, A Summ of Practical Theology and Cases of Conscience. Ed. by J. Tawney. London: G. Bell & Sons, 1925 (London, 1673).
—*The Saints' Everlasting Rest.* Abr. ed. by B. Fawcett. New York: American Tract Society, 1851 (London, 1650).

Beard, Charles Austin (1874–1948)
The Economic Basis of Politics. New York: A. A. Knopf, 1945 (New York, 1922).
—*An Economic Interpretation of the Constitution of the United States.* New York: Macmillan, 1944 (New York, 1913).
—*Economic Origins of Jeffersonian Democracy.* New York: Macmillan, 1949 (1915).
—*The Supreme Court and the Constitution.* New York: Paisley Press, 1938 (New York, 1912).

Beattie, James (1735–1803)
An Essay on Poetry and Music, as They Affect the Mind. In Vols. ii–iii, *Essays by James Beattie.* 3 vols. Philadelphia: Hopkins & Earle, 1809 (Edinburgh, 1776).
—*An Essay on the Nature and Immutability of Truth, in Opposition to Sophistry and Scepticism.* In Vols. i–ii, *ibid.* (Edinburgh, 1770).

Beaumont, Francis (1584–1616) and Fletcher, John (1579–1625)
The Maid's Tragedy. In *Beaumont and Fletcher.* Ed. by F. E. Schelling. New York: American Book Co., 1912 (1610–1611).

Beccaria, Cesare Bonesana (*c.* 1738–1794)
Crimes and Punishments; Including a New Translation of Beccaria's 'Dei delitti e delle pene.' Trans. by J. A. Farrer. London: Chatto & Windus, 1880 (*Dei delitti e delle pene*, Leghorn, 1764).

Becker, Carl Lotus (1873–1945)
Everyman His Own Historian: Essays on History and Politics. New York: Crofts, 1935.
—*Modern Democracy.* New Haven, Conn.: Yale University Press, 1941.
—*New Liberties for Old.* New Haven, Conn.: Yale University Press, 1941.

Bede, The Venerable (*c.* 673–735)
The Ecclesiastical History of the English Nation. Everyman's Library, New York: E. P. Dutton, 1930 (*Historia Ecclesiastica Gentis Anglorum*, 731?).

Beebe-Center, John Gilbert (1897–1958)
The Psychology of Pleasantness and Unpleasantness. New York: Van Nostrand, 1932.

Bell, Eric Temple (1883–1960)
The Development of Mathematics. New York: McGraw-Hill, 1945 (1940).

Bellamy, Edward (1850–1898)
Looking Backward, 2000–1887. Modern Library, New York: Random House, 1942 (Boston, 1888).

Bellarmine, Saint Robert (1542–1621)
De Laicis; or, The Treatise on Civil Government. Trans. by K. E. Murphy. New York: Fordham University Press, 1928 (from *Disputationes de Controversiis Christianae Fidei Adversus Hujus Temporis Haereticos*, Ingolstadt, 1586–1592).

Belloc, Joseph Hilaire Pierre (1870–1953)
The Restoration of Property. New York: Sheed & Ward, 1936.
—*The Servile State.* New York: Henry Holt, 1946 (London, 1912).

Ben Jonson (*c.* 1573–1637)
Every Man in His Humour. In Vol. i, *The Complete Plays of Ben Jonson.* 2 vols. Everyman's Library, New York: E. P. Dutton, 1934 (1598).

—*Sejanus: His Fall. Ibid.* (1603).
—*Volpone: or, The Fox. Ibid.* (1605 or 1606).

Benedict of Nursia, Saint (*c.* 480–*c.* 544)
The Rule of St. Benedict. Ed. and trans. by F. A. Gasquet. London: Chatto & Windus, 1925 (*Regula Monachorum, c.* 516).

Benes, Eduard (1884–1948)
Democracy Today and Tomorrow. New York: Macmillan, 1939.

Bentham, Jeremy (1748–1832)
The Book of Fallacies. In Vol. ii, *Works* (London, 1824).
—*A Comment on the Commentaries. A Criticism of Wm. Blackstone's Commentaries on the Laws of England.* Ed. by C. W. Everett. Oxford: Clarendon Press, 1928 (1775).
—*Defence of Usury.* Washington, D.C.: Hayworth Publishing House, 1916 (London, 1787).
—*Deontology; or, The Science of Morality.* Ed. by J. Bowring. 2 vols. London: Longmans, 1834 (1832).
—*A Fragment on Government.* Ed. by F. C. Montague. New York: Oxford University Press, 1931 (London, 1776).
—*An Introduction to the Principles of Morals and Legislation.* Oxford: Clarendon Press, 1907 (London, 1789).
—*On the Liberty of the Press.* In Vol. ii, *Works* (1821).
—*A Plan for a Universal and Perpetual Peace.* Ed. by C. J. Colombos. London: Peace Book Co., 1939 (1789).
—*Principles of International Law.* In Vol. ii, *Works* (1789).
—*Rationale of Judicial Evidence.* In Vols. vi–vii, *ibid.* (*Traité des preuves judiciaires*, Paris, 1823).
—*The Rationale of Punishment.* In Vol. i, *ibid.* (in *Théorie des peines et des récompenses*, Paris, 1811).
—*The Rationale of Reward.* In Vol. ii, *ibid.* (in *Théorie des peines et des récompenses*, Paris, 1811).
—*The Theory of Legislation.* Ed. by C. K. Ogden, trans. by R. Hildreth. New York: Harcourt Brace, 1931 (*Traités de législation civile et pénale*, Paris, 1802).
note:
The Works of Jeremy Bentham. Ed. by J. Bowring. 11 vols. Edinburgh: W. Tait, 1838–1843.

Beowulf, the Oldest English Epic. Trans. by C. W. Kennedy. New York: Oxford University Press, 1940 (7th to 8th century).

Berdyayev, Nikolai Alexandrovitch (1874–1948)
Christianity and the Class War. Trans. by Donald Attwater. New York: Sheed & Ward, 1933 (Paris, 1931).
—*Freedom and the Spirit.* Trans. by O. F. Clarke. New York: Scribner's, 1935 (Paris. 1927).
—*The Meaning of History.* New York: Scribner's, 1936 (Berlin, 1923).
—*Slavery and Freedom.* New York: Scribner's, 1944.

Bergson, Henri (1859–1941)
Creative Evolution. Trans. by A. Mitchell. Modern Library, New York: Random House, 1944 (*L'évolution créatrice*, Paris, 1907).
—*The Creative Mind.* Trans. by M. L. Andison. New York: Philosophical Library, 1946 (*La pensée et le mouvant; essais et conférences*, Paris, 1934 [1903–1934]).
—*Dreams.* Trans. by E. E. Slosson. New York: B. W. Huebsch, 1914 (1901).
—*Durée et simultanéité, à propos de la théorie d'Einstein.* Paris: F. Alcan, 1929 (Paris, 1922).
—*An Introduction to Metaphysics.* Trans. by T. E. Hulme. New York: Putnam's, 1912 (1903).
—*Laughter; an Essay on the Meaning of the Comic.* Trans. by C. Brereton *et al.* New York: Macmillan, 1911 (*Le rire. Essai sur la signification du comique*, Paris, 1900).
—*Matter and Memory.* Trans. by N. M. Paul and W. Scott Palmer. New York: Macmillan, 1929 (*Matière et mémoire; essai sur la relation du corps à l'esprit*, Paris, 1896).
—*Mind-Energy. Lectures and Essays.* Trans. by H. W. Carr. New York: Henry Holt, 1920 (*L'énergie spirituelle, essais et conférences*, Paris, 1919).
—*Time and Free Will, an Essay on the Immediate Data of Consciousness.* Trans. by F. L. Pogson. London: Swan Sonnenschein, 1910 (*Essai sur les données immédiates de la conscience*, Paris, 1889).
—*Two Sources of Morality and Religion.* Trans. by R. A. Audra and C. Brereton. New York: Henry Holt, 1935 (*Les deux sources de la morale et de la religion*, Paris, 1932).

Berkeley, George, Bishop of Cloyne (1685–1753)
Alciphron, or The Minute Philosopher, in Seven Dialogues. In Vol. ii, *The Works of George Berkeley.* Ed. by A. C. Fraser. 4 vols. Oxford: Clarendon Press, 1901 (London, 1732).
—*The Analyst; or, A Discourse Addressed to an Infidel Mathematician.* In Vol. iii, *ibid.* (London, 1734).
—*De Motu. Ibid.* (1721).
—*A Defence of Free Thinking in Mathematics. Ibid.* (London, 1735).
—*An Essay Towards a New Theory of Vision.* In Vol. i, *ibid.* (Dublin, 1709).
—*Passive Obedience, or, The Christian Doctrine of Not Resisting the Supreme Power Proved and Vindicated upon the Principle of the Law of Nature.* In Vol. iii, *ibid.* (London, 1712).
—*Siris: A Chain of Philosophical Reflexions and Inquiries Concerning the Virtues of Tar-Water, and Divers Other Subjects, etc. Ibid.* (London, 1744).
—*Three Dialogues Between Hylas and Philonous.* In Vol. i, *ibid.* (London, 1713).

Berle, Adolph A., Jr. (1895–1971) and Means, Gardiner C. (1896–)
The Modern Corporation and Private Property. New York: Macmillan, 1934 (1932).

Bernal, John Desmond (1901–1971)
The Social Function of Science. London: G. Routledge, 1939.

Bernard, Claude (1813–1878)
An Introduction to the Study of Experimental Medicine. Trans. by H. C. Greene. New York: Macmillan, 1927 (*Introduction à l'étude de la médecine expérimentale*, Paris, 1865).

Bernard of Clairvaux, Saint (*c*. 1090–1153)
Concerning Grace and Free Will. Ed. and trans. by W. W. Williams. New York: Macmillan, 1920 (*De Gratia et Libero Arbitrio*, 1127?).
—*On Consideration*. Trans. by G. Lewis. Oxford: Clarendon Press, 1908 (*De Consideratione Libri V*, 1149–1152).
—*On the Love of God*. Ed. and trans. by E. G. Gardner. New York: E. P. Dutton, 1915 (*De Diligendo Deo*, 1126–1141).

Bernard Sylvestris (12th century)
De Mundi Universitate Libri Duo; sive, Megacosmus et Microcosmus. Ed. by C. S. Barach and J. Wrobel. Innsbruck: Wagner, 1876 (1145–1153).

Bernhardi, Friedrich Adam Julius von (1849–1930)
The War of the Future in the Light of the Lessons of the World War. Trans. by F. A. Holt. New York: D. Appleton, 1921 (*Vom Kriege der Zukunft, nach den Erfahrungen des Weltkrieges*, Berlin, 1920).

Bernheim, Ernst (1850–1942)
Lehrbuch der historischen Methode und der Geschichtsphilosophie. Munich: Duncker & Humblot, 1914 (Munich, 1889).

Bernstein, Eduard (1850–1932)
Evolutionary Socialism; a Criticism and Affirmation. Trans. by E. C. Harvey. New York: B. W. Huebsch, 1911 (*Die Voraussetzungen des Socialismus und die Aufgaben der Sozialdemokratie*, Stuttgart, 1899).

Bertrand, Louis Marie Émile (1866–1941)
The Art of Suffering. Abr. trans. by E. F. Peeler. New York: Sheed & Ward, 1937 (*Le livre de consolation*, Paris, 1933).

Best, Charles Herbert (1899–) and Taylor, Norman Burke (1885–)
The Physiological Basis of Medical Practice, a University of Toronto Text in Applied Physiology. Baltimore, Md.: Williams & Wilkins, 1945 (Baltimore, Md., 1937).

Beveridge, William Henry, Lord (1879–1963)
Unemployment: A Problem of Industry. New York: Longmans, Green & Co., 1930.

Bichat, Marie François Xavier (1771–1802)
General Anatomy, Applied to Physiology and Medicine. Trans. by G. Hayward. 3 vols. Boston: Richardson & Lord, 1822 (*Anatomie générale appliquée à la physiologie et à la médecine*, Paris, 1801).

Biel, Gabriel (*c*. 1430–1495)
Treatise on the Power and Utility of Moneys. Trans. by R. B. Burke. Philadelphia: University of Pennsylvania Press, 1930 (*De Monetarum Potestate Simul et Utilitate*).

Billot, Louis (1846–1932)
De Ecclesia Sacramentis. Commentarius in Tertiam Partem S. Thomae. 2 vols. Rome: Sacra Congregatio de Propaganda Fide, 1893–1897.
—*De Virtutibus Infusis*. Rome: Sacra Congregatio de Propaganda Fide, 1901.

Birkhoff, George David (1884–1944)
Aesthetic Measure. Cambridge, Mass.: Harvard University Press, 1933.

Black, Joseph (1728–1799)
Experiments upon Magnesia Alba, Quicklime, and Some Other Alcaline Substances. University of Chicago Press, 1902 (from Vol. II, *Essays and Observations*, Edinburgh, 1756).

Blackstone, Sir William (1723–1780)
Commentaries on the Laws of England. Ed. by W. D. Lewis. 2 vols. Philadelphia: G. T. Bisel, 1922 (1758).

Blair, Hugh (1718–1800)
Lectures on Rhetoric and Belles Lettres. Philadelphia: Porter & Coates, 1886 (London, 1783).

Blake, William (1757–1827)
The Book of Thel. In *Poetry and Prose of William Blake*. Ed. by G. Keynes. New York: Random House, 1927 (London, 1789).
—*The Everlasting Gospel*. *Ibid*. (*c*. 1810).
—*The Marriage of Heaven and Hell*. *Ibid*. (London, 1790).
—*Songs of Experience*. *Ibid*. (London, 1794).
—*Songs of Innocence*. *Ibid*. (London, 1789).

Blanshard, Brand (1892–)
The Nature of Thought. 2 vols. London: Allen & Unwin, 1939.

Bloch, Jan Gotlib (1836–1902)
The Future of War in Its Technical, Economic, and Political Relations. Trans. by R. C. Long. Boston: Ginn & Co., 1903 (St. Petersburg, 1898).

Blondel, Maurice (1861–1949)
La pensée. 2 vols. Paris: F. Alcan, 1934.
—*L'action*. 2 vols. Paris: F. Alcan, 1936–1937.
—*L'être et les êtres; essai d'ontologie concrète et intégrale*. Paris: F. Alcan, 1935.

Blood, Benjamin Paul (1832–1919)
Pluriverse; an Essay in the Philosophy of Pluralism. Boston: Marshall Jones, 1920.

Boccaccio, Giovanni (1313–1375)
The Decameron. Trans. by John Payne. Modern Library, New York: Random House, 1930 (1353).
—*Il Filocolo*. Ed. by S. Battaglia. Bari: G. Laterza, 1938 (1341–1346).
—*On Poetry; Being the Preface and the Fourteenth and Fifteenth Books of Boccaccio's Genealogia Deorum Gentilium*. Ed. and trans. by C. G. Osgood. Princeton University Press, 1930 (*c*. 1363).
—*Patient Griselda*. Tenth Day, Story x, in the *Decameron, q.v.*

Bodin, Jean (1530–1596)
Method for the Easy Comprehension of History. Trans. by B. Reynolds. New York: Columbia University Press, 1945 (*Methodus ad Facilem Historiarum Cognitionem*, Paris, 1566).
—*The Six Bookes of a Commonweale.* Trans. by R. Knolles. London: G. Bishop, 1606 (*Six livres de la République*, Paris, 1576).

Boehme, Jakob (1575–1624)
The Aurora. Ed. by C. J. Barker and D. S. Hehner, trans. by J. Sparrow. London: J. M. Watkins, 1914 (1612).
—*De Electione Gratiae* [with *Quaestiones Theosophicae*]. Trans. by J. R. Earle. London: Constable & Co., 1919 (1623).
—*Of the Supersensual Life.* In *The Signature of All Things, with Other Writings.* Ed. by C. Bax, trans. by J. Ellistone. Everyman's Library, New York: E. P. Dutton, 1926 (1618?–1624).
—*The Signature of All Things. Ibid.* (1618?–1624).
—*The Way from Darkness to True Illumination. Ibid.* (1618?–1624).
—*The Way to Christ.* Trans. by J. J. Stoudt. New York: Harper, 1947 (1623).

Boethius, Anicius Manlius Severinus (*c.* 480–524)
The Consolation of Philosophy. In *The Theological Tractates* and *The Consolation of Philosophy.* Trans. by H. F. Stewart and E. K. Rand. Loeb Library, Cambridge, Mass.: Harvard University Press, 1936 (510–524).
—*Contra Eutychen.* In *Theological Tractates.* See above (512).
—*De Fide Catholica. Ibid.*
—*De Trinitate. Ibid.*
—*In Isagogem Porphyri Commenta.* Ed. by S. Brandt. Vienna: F. Tempsky, 1906 (before 505).
—*Quomodo Substantiae in eo quod Sint cum Non Sint Substantialia Bona.* In *Theological Tractates.* See above.

Bohr, Niels Henrik David (1885–1962)
Atomic Theory and the Description of Nature. Cambridge University Press, 1934 (1925–1929).
—*On the Application of the Quantum Theory to Atomic Structure.* Trans. by L. F. Curtiss. Cambridge University Press, 1924 (1923).
—*The Theory of Spectra and Atomic Constitution, Three Essays.* Trans. by A. D. Udden. Cambridge University Press, 1922 (1914–1921).

Boileau-Despréaux, Nicolas (1636–1711)
The Art of Poetry. Ed. by A. S. Cook, trans. by W. Soames. New York: G. E. Stechert, 1926 (*L'art poétique*, Paris, 1674).

Bolingbroke, Henry Saint-John (1678–1751)
A Dissertation upon Parties. In Vol. II, *The Works of Lord Bolingbroke.* 4 vols. Philadelphia: Carey & Hart, 1841 (London, 1734).

Boltzmann, Ludwig (1844–1906)
Vorlesungen über die Principe der Mechanik. 3 vols. Leipsic: Barth, 1897–1920.

Bolzano, Bernhard (1781–1848)
Paradoxien des Unendlichen. Ed. by A. Höfler and H. Hahn. Leipsic: Philosophische Bibliothek, 1920 (1847–1848).

Bonar, James (1852–1941)
The Intellectual Virtues. New York: Macmillan, 1894.

Bonaventura, Saint (1221–1274)
Breviloquium. Trans. by E. E. Nemmers. St. Louis, Mo.: Herder Book Co., 1946 (before 1257).
—*Itinerarium Mentis in Deum.* Trans. by J. and J. R. Cresswell. London: Burns, Oates, & Washbourne, 1937 (1259?).
—*On the Reduction of the Arts to Theology.* Trans. by C. G. Wallis. Annapolis, Md.: St. John's Press, 1938 (*De Reductione Artium ad Theologiam*, 1250?).

Bonola, Roberto (1874–1911)
Non-Euclidean Geometry. Trans. by H. S. Carslaw. Chicago: Open Court, 1912 (1906).

Boole, George (1815–1864)
An Investigation of the Laws of Thought on Which are Founded the Mathematical Theories of Logic and Probabilities. Chicago: Open Court, 1940 (London, 1854).
—*Mathematical Analysis of Logic.* New York: Philosophical Library, 1949 (1847).
—*A Treatise on Differential Equations.* New York: G. E. Stechert, 1931 (London, 1859).
—*A Treatise on the Calculus of Finite Differences.* New York: G. E. Stechert, 1926 (London, 1860).

Borgese, G. A. (1882–1952)
Common Cause. New York: Duell, Sloan and Pearce, 1943.

Borgese, G. A. *et al.*
Preliminary Draft of a World Constitution. University of Chicago Press, 1948.

Boring, Edwin Garrigues (1886–1968)
The Physical Dimensions of Consciousness. New York: Century Co., 1933.

Borne, Étienne and Henry, François
A Philosophy of Work. Trans. by F. Jackson. New York: Sheed & Ward, 1938 (*Le travail et l'homme*, Paris, 1937).

Bosanquet, Bernard (1848–1923)
Implication and Linear Inference. London: Macmillan, 1920.
—*Knowledge and Reality.* London: Swan Sonnenschein, 1892 (London, 1885).
—*Logic; or, The Morphology of Knowledge.* 2 vols. Oxford: Clarendon Press, 1911 (Oxford, 1888).
—*The Philosophical Theory of the State.* London: Macmillan, 1920 (London, 1899).
—*Science and Philosophy, and Other Essays.* Ed. by J. H. Muirhead and R. C. Bosanquet. New York: Macmillan, 1927 (1886–1919).
—*Three Chapters on the Nature of Mind.* Ed. by H. Bosanquet. London: Macmillan, 1923.

—*Three Lectures on Aesthetic*. London: Macmillan, 1915.

—*The Value and Destiny of the Individual*. London: Macmillan, 1913.

—*What Religion Is*. London: Macmillan, 1920.

Bose, Sir Jagadis Chunder (1858–1937)
Growth and Tropic Movements of Plants. New York: Longmans, Green & Co., 1929.

—*Life Movements in Plants*. 4 vols. Calcutta: Bose Research Institute, 1918–1921.

Bossuet, Jacques Bénigne (1627–1704)
De la connaissance de Dieu et de soi-même. Paris: Garnier, 1937 (1677).

—*Discours sur l'histoire universelle*. Ed. by A. Gasté. Paris: E. Flammarion, 1928 (Paris, 1681).

—*Politique tirée des propres paroles de l'Écriture Sainte*. Turin: A. Alliana, 1824–1825 (1677–1701).

—*Traité de la concupiscence*. Paris: F. Roches, 1930 (1694).

—*Traité du libre arbitre*. In Vol. iv, *Oeuvres choisies de Bossuet*. 5 vols. Paris: Hachette, 1887–1901 (1670–1681).

Bouglé, Célestin C. (1870–1940)
Essais sur le régime des castes. Paris: F. Alcan, 1935 (Paris, 1908).

Boutroux, Étienne Émile Marie (1845–1921)
The Contingency of the Laws of Nature. Trans. by F. Rothwell. Chicago: Open Court, 1916 (*De la contingence des lois de la nature*, Paris, 1874).

Boyle, Robert (1627–1691)
A Defence of the Doctrine Touching the Spring and Weight of the Air ... Against the Objections of Franciscus Linus, Wherewith the Objector's Funicular Hypothesis Is also Examined. In Vol. i, *The Works of the Honourable Robert Boyle*. 6 vols. London, 1772 (originally pub. in 2nd ed. of *New Experiments Physical-Mechanical, Touching the Air*, Oxford, 1662).

—*A Disquisition About the Final Causes of Natural Things, Wherein Is Inquired Whether, and (if at All) with What Caution a Naturalist Should Admit Them?* In Vol. v, *ibid*. (London, 1688).

—*Experiments, Notes, etc., About the Mechanical Origine or Production of Divers Particular Qualities*. In Vol. iv, *ibid*. (London, 1675–1676).

—*A Free Inquiry into the Vulgarly Received Notion of Nature*. In Vol. v, *ibid*. (London, 1686).

—*New Experiments Physico-Mechanical, Touching the Spring of the Air, and Its Effects*. In Vol. i, *ibid*. (Oxford, 1660).

—*The Origin of Forms and Qualities, According to the Corpuscular Philosophy*. In Vol. iii, *ibid*. (Oxford, 1666).

—*Reflections upon the Hypothesis of Alkali and Acidum*. In Vol. iv, *ibid*. (London, 1675).

—*The Sceptical Chymist*. Everyman's Library, New York: E. P. Dutton, 1911 (London, 1661).

Bracton, Henry de (d. 1268)
De Legibus et Consuetudinibus Angliae. Ed. and trans. by T. Twiss. 6 vols. London: Longman & Co., 1878–1883 (1232–1259).

Bradley, Francis Herbert (1846–1924)
Aphorisms. Oxford: Clarendon Press, 1930.

—*Appearance and Reality; a Metaphysical Essay*. London: Allen & Unwin, 1925 (London, 1893).

—*Collected Essays*. Ed. by M. de Glehn and H. J. Joachim. 2 vols. Oxford: Clarendon Press, 1935 (1874–1924).

—*Essays on Truth and Reality*. Oxford: Clarendon Press, 1914 (1893–1914).

—*Ethical Studies*. Oxford: Clarendon Press, 1927 (London, 1876).

—*The Principles of Logic*. 2 vols. New York: Oxford University Press, 1928 (London, 1883).

Bréal, Michel Jules Alfred (1832–1915)
Semantics: Studies in the Science of Meaning. Trans. by Mrs. Henry Cust. New York: Henry Holt, 1900 (*Essai de sémantique, science des significations*, Paris, 1897).

Brentano, Franz (1838–1917)
The Origin of the Knowledge of Right and Wrong. Trans. by C. Hague. New York: E. P. Dutton, 1902 (*Vom Ursprung der sittlichen Erkenntnis*, Leipsic, 1889).

Bridgman, Percy Williams (1882–1961)
The Logic of Modern Physics. New York: Macmillan, 1927.

Briefs, Goetz (1889–)
The Proletariat, a Challenge to Western Civilization. Trans. by R. A. Eckhardt. New York: McGraw-Hill, 1937 (*Das gewerbliche Proletariat*, Vol. i of *Grundriss der Sozialökonomik*, Tübingen, 1926).

Briffault, Robert Stephen (1876–1948)
The Mothers: A Study of the Origins of Sentiments and Institutions. 3 vols. New York: Macmillan 1927.

Brinton, Clarence Crane (1898–)
The Anatomy of Revolution. New York: W. W. Norton, 1938.

Broad, Charlie Dunbar (1887–)
The Mind and Its Place in Nature. New York: Harcourt Brace, 1925.

—*Perception, Physics, and Reality*. Cambridge University Press, 1914.

—*Scientific Thought*. New York: Harcourt Brace, 1927 (London, 1923).

Broglie, Louis Victor de (1892–)
An Introduction to the Study of Wave Mechanics. Trans. by H. T. Flint. London: Methuen, 1930 (*Introduction à l'étude de la mécanique ondulatoire*, Paris, 1930).

Brontë, Charlotte (1816–1855)
Jane Eyre. Everyman's Library, New York: E. P. Dutton, 1946 (London, 1847).

Brontë, Emily Jane (1818–1848)
Wuthering Heights. Everyman's Library, New York: E. P. Dutton, 1943 (London, 1847).

Brooke, Fulke Greville, Lord (1554–1628)
An Inquisition upon Fame and Honour. In Vol. i,

Poems and Dramas of Fulke Greville First Lord Brooke. Ed. by G. Bullough. 2 vols. Edinburgh: Oliver & Boyd, 1939.

BROWN, THOMAS (1778–1820)
An Inquiry into the Relation of Cause and Effect. London: H. G. Bohn, 1835 (Edinburgh, 1818).
—*Lectures on the Philosophy of the Human Mind*. 4 vols. London: W. Tegg, 1860 (Edinburgh, 1820).

BROWNE, SIR THOMAS (1605–1682)
Hydriotaphia. Urne Buriall; or, A Discourse of the Sepulchrall Urnes Lately Found in Norfolk. In *The Religio Medici and Other Writings*. Everyman's Library, New York: E. P. Dutton, 1934 (London, 1658).
—*Pseudodoxia Epidemica*. In Vols. II–III, *The Works of Sir Thomas Browne*. Ed. by G. Keynes. 6 vols. New York: W. E. Rudge, 1928–1931 (London, 1646).
—*Religio Medici*. Everyman's Library. See above (London, 1643).

BROWNING, ELIZABETH BARRETT (1806–1861)
Sonnets from the Portuguese. New York: Thomas Y. Crowell, 1945 (London, 1850).

BROWNING, ROBERT (1812–1889)
The Bishop Orders His Tomb at Saint Praxed's Church. In *The Shorter Poems of Robert Browning*. Ed. by W. C. De Vane. New York: Crofts, 1945 (London, 1845).
—*Rabbi Ben Ezra*. *Ibid*. (London, 1864).
—*The Ring and the Book*. Ed. by A. K. Cook. New York: Oxford University Press, 1940 (London, 1868–1869).
—*Why I Am a Liberal*. In *Shorter Poems*. See above (London, 1885).

BRUNETIÈRE, FERDINAND (1849–1906)
An Apology for Rhetoric. In *Brunetière's Essays in French Literature*. Trans. by D. N. Smith. London: T. F. Unwin, 1898 (1890).

BRUNO, GIORDANO (*c*. 1548–1600)
De Immenso et Innumerabilibus. In Vols. I–II, *Jordani Bruni . . . Opera Latina*. 3 vols. Naples: D. Morano, 1879–1891 (Frankfort, 1591).
—*De la causa, principio, e uno*. In Vol. I, *Opere Italiane*. Ed. by G. Gentile. 2 vols. Bari: Laterza, 1925–1927 (Venice, 1584).
—*De l'infinito, universo e mondi*. *Ibid*. (Venice, 1583).

BRYANT, WILLIAM CULLEN (1794–1878)
Thanatopsis. In *Poetical Works of William Cullen Bryant*. New York: D. Appleton, 1906 (1817).

BRYCE, JAMES (1838–1922)
Address on Colonial Policy. London, 1892.
—*The American Commonwealth*. 2 vols. New York: Macmillan, 1931–1933 (London, 1888).
—*The Functions of a University*. Adelaide, Australia: W. K. Thomas, 1912.
—*The Hindrances to Good Citizenship*. New Haven, Conn.: Yale University Press, 1909.
—*Marriage and Divorce*. New York: Oxford University Press, 1905 (from *Studies in History and Jurisprudence*, New York, 1901).
—*Modern Democracies*. 2 vols. New York: Macmillan, 1931 (New York, 1921).
—*Studies in History and Jurisprudence*. New York: Oxford University Press, 1901.

BUBER, MARTIN (1878–1965)
Hasidism. Trans. by G. Hort *et al*. New York: Philosophical Library, 1948 (1920).
—*I and Thou*. Trans. by R. G. Smith. Edinburgh: T. & T. Clark, 1937 (1923).
—*Jewish Mysticism and the Legends of Baalshem*. Ed. by Martin Buber, trans. by L. Cohen. London: J. M. Dent, 1931 (late 18th century).
—*Tales of the Hasidim*. Ed. by Martin Buber, trans. by O. Marx. New York: Schocken Books, 1947 (late 18th century).

BUCHANAN, SCOTT (1895–1968)
The Doctrine of Signatures; a Defence of Theory in Medicine. New York: Harcourt Brace, 1938.
—*Poetry and Mathematics*. New York: John Day, 1929.
—*Possibility*. New York: Harcourt Brace, 1927.
—*Symbolic Distance in Relation to Analogy and Fiction*. London: K. Paul, Trench, Trübner, 1932.

BUCHEZ, PHILIP JOSEPH BENJAMIN (1796–1865)
Introduction à la science de l'histoire. Paris: Paulin, 1833.

BUCKLE, HENRY THOMAS (1821–1862)
History of Civilization in England. 3 vols. New York: Oxford University Press, 1925–1931 (London, 1857–1861).

BÜCHER, KARL (1847–1930)
Arbeit und Rhythmus. Leipsic: E. Reinicke, 1924 (Leipsic, 1896).

BÜCHNER, LUDWIG (1824–1899)
Force and Matter, Empirico-philosophical Studies. Ed. and trans. by J. F. Collingwood. London: Trübner & Co., 1870 (*Kraft und Stoff. Empirisch-naturphilosophische Studien*, Frankfort, 1855).

BÜHLER, KARL (1879–1963)
Sprachtheorie: die Darstellungsfunktion der Sprache. Jena: G. Fischer, 1934.

BUFFON, GEORGES LOUIS LECLERC (1707–1788)
Discours sur le style. Paris: C. Delagrave, 1903 (1753).
—*Natural History, General and Particular*. Trans. by W. Smellie. 9 vols. London: A. Strahan, 1791 (*Histoire naturelle, générale et particulière*, Paris, 1749–1788).

BUKHARIN, NIKOLAI IVANOVICH (1888–1938)
Historical Materialism: A System of Sociology. New York: International Publishers, 1929 (Moscow, 1921).

BUNYAN, JOHN (1628–1688)
The Pilgrim's Progress. Everyman's Library, New York: E. P. Dutton, 1932 (London, 1678).

BURCKHARDT, JAKOB (1818–1897)
The Civilization of the Renaissance in Italy. Trans. by S. G. C. Middlemore. New York: Oxford

University Press, 1944 (*Die Kultur der Renaissance in Italien*, Basle, 1860).
—*Force and Freedom, Reflections on History*. Ed. by J. H. Nichols. New York: Pantheon Books, 1943 (*Welthistorische Betrachtungen*, Leipsic, 1905 [1868–1871]).

BURGESS, JOHN WILLIAM (1844–1931)
The Reconciliation of Government with Liberty. New York: Scribner's, 1915.

BURKE, EDMUND (1729–1797)
An Appeal from the New to the Old Whigs in Consequence of Some Late Discussions in Parliament Relative to the Reflections on the Revolution in France. In Vol. III, *The Works of the Right Honourable Edmund Burke*. 8 vols. New York: G. Bell & Sons, 1890–1894 (1791).
—*Hints for an Essay on the Drama*. In Vol. VI, *ibid*. (1756).
—*A Letter to a Noble Lord on the Attacks Made upon Him and His Pension*. In Vol. V, *ibid*. (London, 1796).
—*Letter to Sir Hercules Langrishe, Bart. M.P., on the Subject of the Roman Catholics of Ireland, and the Propriety of Admitting Them to the Elective Franchise*. In Vol. III, *ibid*. (1792).
—*Letter to the Sheriffs of Bristol, on the Affairs of America, April 3, 1777*. In Vol. II, *ibid*. (1777).
—*On the Reform of the Representation in the House of Commons*. In Vol. VI, *ibid*. (1782).
—*A Philosophical Enquiry into the Origin of Our Ideas of the Sublime and Beautiful with an Introductory Discourse Concerning Taste*. In Vol. I, *ibid*. (London, 1756).
—*Reflections on the Revolution in France, and on Proceedings in Certain Societies in London Relative to That Event*. In Vol. II, *ibid*. (London, 1790).
—[Resolutions] *Speech on Moving His Resolutions for Conciliation with America*. In Vol. I, *ibid*. (London, 1775).
—*Thoughts on the Cause of the Present Discontents*. *Ibid*. (London, 1770).
—[Thoughts on the Prospect of a Regicide Peace] *Three Letters Addressed to a Member of the Present Parliament, on the Proposals for Peace with the Regicide Directory of France*. In Vol. V, *ibid*. (London, 1796–1797).

BURLAMAQUI, JEAN JACQUES (1694–1748)
The Principles of Natural and Politic Law. Trans. by Nugent. Philadelphia: Lippincott, 1859 (*Principes du droit naturel*, Geneva, 1747, and *Principes du droit politique*, Geneva, 1751).

BURNHAM, JAMES (1905–)
The Machiavellians, Defenders of Freedom. New York: John Day, 1943.

BURNS, ARTHUR ROBERT (1895–)
The Decline of Competition: A Study of the Evolution of American Industry. New York: McGraw-Hill, 1936.

BURNS, ROBERT (1759–1796)
Address to the Unco Guid, or the Rigidly Righteous. In *The Poetical Works of Robert Burns*. Ed. by J. L. Robertson. New York: Oxford University Press, 1916 (Edinburgh, 1787).
—*The Cotter's Saturday Night*. *Ibid*. (Kilmarnock, 1786).

BURNSIDE, WILLIAM (1852–1927)
Theory of Groups of Finite Order. Cambridge University Press, 1911 (1897).

BURTON, ROBERT (1577–1640)
The Anatomy of Melancholy. Everyman's Library, New York: E. P. Dutton, 1932 (Oxford, 1621).

BURY, JOHN BAGNELL (1861–1927)
A History of Freedom of Thought. New York: Henry Holt, 1913.
—*The Idea of Progress; an Inquiry into its Origin and Growth*. New York: Macmillan, 1932 (London, 1920).
—*The Science of History, an Inaugural Lecture*. Cambridge University Press, 1903.

BUTLER, JOSEPH (1692–1752)
The Analogy of Religion, Natural and Revealed. Everyman's Library, New York: E. P. Dutton, 1927 (London, 1736).
—*Fifteen Sermons upon Human Nature*. In Vol. II, *The Works of Bishop Butler*. Ed. by J. H. Bernard. 2 vols. London: Macmillan, 1900 (London, 1726).

BUTLER, SAMUEL (1835–1902)
Darwin Among the Machines. In *Note-Books*, *q.v.* (essay cited, 1863).
—*Erewhon, or Over the Range*. Modern Library, New York: Random House, 1927 (London, 1872).
—*Evolution, Old and New; or, The Theories of Buffon, Dr. Erasmus Darwin and Lamarck, as Compared with That of Charles Darwin*. New York: E. P. Dutton, 1914 (London, 1879).
—*Life and Habit*. London: J. Cape, 1924 (London, 1877).
—*The Note-Books of Samuel Butler*. Ed. by H. F. Jones. London: A. C. Fifield, 1912.
—*Unconscious Memory*. New York: E. P. Dutton, 1911 (London, 1880).
—*The Way of All Flesh*. Ed. by W. L. Phelps. Everyman's Library, New York: E. P. Dutton, 1934 (1872–1884).

BYRON, GEORGE GORDON (LORD BYRON) (1788–1824)
Don Juan. In *The Complete Poetical Works of Lord Byron*. New York: Macmillan, 1927 (London, 1819–1824).
—[The Isles of Greece] Canto III (LXXXVI) of *Don Juan*. *Ibid*. (London, 1821).
—*Prometheus*. *Ibid*. (London, 1816).
—*Sonnet on Chillon*. *Ibid*. (London, 1816).

C

CAESAR, GAIUS JULIUS (100–44 B.C.)
The Gallic War. Trans. by H. J. Edwards. Loeb Library, Cambridge, Mass.: Harvard University Press, 1919 (*Commentarii de Bello Gallico*, 51 B.C.).

CAIRD, JOHN (1820–1898)
An Introduction to the Philosophy of Religion. Glasgow: J. MacLehose, 1901 (Glasgow, 1880).

CAJETAN, THOMAS DE VIO (1468–1534)
De Conceptu Entis. Ed. by P. M. Zammit. Rome: Institutum Angelicum, 1934 (Rome, 1519).
—*De Nominum Analogia.* Ed. by P. M. Zammit. Rome: Institutum Angelicum, 1934 (Pavia, 1498).
—*In De Ente et Essentia D. Thomae Aquinatis Commentaria.* Ed. by P. M. H. Laurent. Turin: Marietti, 1934 (Venice, 1496).

CALDERÓN DE LA BARCA, PEDRO (1600–1681)
Life Is a Dream. In *Continental Drama.* Trans. by W. F. Stirling. "The Harvard Classics." New York: P. F. Collier, 1910 (*La vida es sueño,* Madrid, 1636).
—*The Mighty Magician.* In *Eight Dramas of Calderón.* Freely trans. by E. Fitzgerald. New York: Macmillan, 1906 (*El mágico prodigioso.* 1637).
—*The Physician of His Own Honour.* In Vol. I, *Dramas of Calderón, Tragic, Comic, and Legendary.* Trans. by D. F. McCarthy. 2 vols. London: C. Dolman, 1853 (*El médico de su honra,* Madrid, 1637).

CALHOUN, JOHN CALDWELL (1782–1850)
A Discourse on the Constitution and Government of the United States. In Vol. I, *The Works of John Calhoun.* Ed. by R. K. Crallé. 6 vols. New York: D. Appleton, 1861–1864 (1850).
—*A Disquisition on Government.* New York: Political Science Classics, 1947 (1849).

CALVIN, JOHN (1509–1564)
Commentaries on the Epistle of Paul the Apostle to the Romans. In Vol. XXXVIII, *Works of John Calvin.* Ed. and trans. by John Owen. 51 vols. Edinburgh: Calvin Translation Society, 1849 (*Commentarius in Epistolam ad Romanos,* Strasbourg, 1540).
—*Institutes of the Christian Religion.* Ed. and trans. by John Allen. 2 vols. Philadelphia: Presbyterian Board of Christian Education (*Christianae Religionis Institutio,* Basle, 1536).

CAMFIELD, BENJAMIN (1638–1693)
A Theological Discourse of Angels and Their Ministries. London: H. Brome, 1678.

CAMPANELLA, TOMMASO (1568–1639)
The City of the Sun. In *Ideal Commonwealths.* Ed. and trans. by H. Morley. New York: Colonial Press, 1901 (*Civitas Solis,* Frankfort, 1623).
—*The Defense of Galileo of Thomas Campanella.* Ed. and trans. by G. McColley. In Vol. XXII, *Smith College Studies in History.* Northampton, Mass.: Smith College, 1937 (*Apologia pro Galileo,* Frankfort, 1622).
—*A Discourse Touching the Spanish Monarchy.* Trans. by E. Chilmead. London: P. Stevens, 1654 (*De Monarchia Hispanica Discursus,* Amsterdam, 1640).

CAMPBELL, GEORGE (1719–1796)
Philosophy of Rhetoric. Ed. by G. S. Keith. London: Harper, 1868 (London, 1776).

CAMPBELL, NORMAN ROBERT (1880–1949)
Physics; the Elements. Cambridge University Press, 1920.
—*What Is Science?* London: Methuen, 1921.

CANNON, WALTER BRADFORD (1871–1945)
Bodily Changes in Pain, Hunger, Fear and Rage; an Account of Recent Researches into the Function of Emotional Excitement. New York: D. Appleton, 1929 (New York, 1915).
—*The Wisdom of the Body.* New York: W. W. Norton, 1932.

CANTOR, GEORG (1845–1918)
Contributions to the Founding of the Theory of Transfinite Numbers. Trans. by P. E. B. Jourdain. Chicago: Open Court, 1915 (1895; 1897).

CARDOZO, BENJAMIN NATHAN (1870–1938)
The Growth of the Law. New Haven, Conn.: Yale University Press, 1944 (New Haven, Conn., 1924).
—*The Nature of the Judicial Process.* New Haven, Conn.: Yale University Press, 1941 (New Haven, Conn., 1921).

CAREW, THOMAS (*c.* 1595–*c.* 1639)
A Rapture. In *Poems of Thomas Carew.* Ed. by A. Vincent. New York: E. P. Dutton, 190–.

CARLSON, ANTON JULIUS (1875–1956)
The Control of Hunger in Health and Disease. University of Chicago Press, 1916.

CARLYLE, ALEXANDER JAMES (1861–1943)
Political Liberty, a History of the Conception in the Middle Ages and Modern Times. Oxford: Clarendon Press, 1941.

CARLYLE, THOMAS (1795–1881)
Chartism. In *English and Other Critical Essays.* Everyman's Library, New York: E. P. Dutton, 1925 (London, 1839).
—*The French Revolution: A History.* Modern Library, New York: Random House, 1934 (London, 1837).
—*Latter-Day Pamphlets.* New York: Scribner's, 1901 (London, 1850).
—[On Heroes, Hero-Worship] *Sartor Resartus, On Heroes, Hero-Worship and the Heroic in History.* Everyman's Library, New York: E. P. Dutton, 1934 (London, 1841).
—*On History.* In *English and Other Critical Essays.* Everyman's Library. See *Chartism* (1830).
—*Sartor Resartus.* See *On Heroes, Hero-Worship* (1833–1834).

CARNAP, RUDOLF (1891–1970)
Foundations of Logic and Mathematics (International Encyclopedia of Unified Science). University of Chicago Press, 1939.
—*Introduction to Semantics.* Cambridge, Mass.: Harvard University Press, 1942.
—*The Logical Syntax of Language.* Trans. by A.

Smeaton. New York: Harcourt Brace, 1937 (*Die Logische Syntax der Sprache*, Vienna, 1934).
—*Meaning and Necessity: A Study in Semantics; Modal Logic*. University of Chicago Press, 1947.
—*Philosophy and Logical Syntax*. London: K. Paul, Trench, Trübner, 1935.
—*The Unity of Science*. Trans. by M. Black. London: K. Paul, Trench, Trübner, 1934 (1932).

Carnot, Lazare Nicolas Marguerite (1753–1823)
Principes fondamentaux de l'équilibre et du mouvement. Paris: Deterville, 1803 (1782).
—*Réflexions sur la métaphysique du calcul infinitésimal*. Paris: Gauthier-Villars, 1921 (1797).

Carritt, Edgar Frederick (1876–)
The Theory of Beauty. New York: Macmillan, 1914.

Cartwright, John (1740–1824)
Take Your Choice! Representation and Respect: Imposition and Contempt. Annual Parliaments and Liberty: Long Parliaments and Slavery. London: J. Almon, 1776.

Cassiodorus Senator, Flavius Magnus Aurelius (*c.* 490–*c.* 583)
[Institutiones] *An Introduction to Divine and Human Readings*. Trans. by L. W. Jones. New York: Columbia University Press, 1947 (543–545).

Cassirer, Ernst (1874–1945)
An Essay on Man; an Introduction to a Philosophy of Human Culture. New Haven, Conn.: Yale University Press, 1944.
—*Language and Myth*. Trans. by S. K. Langer. New York: Harper, 1946 (1925).
—*The Myth of the State*. New Haven, Conn.: Yale University Press, 1946 (1944–1945).
—*Philosophie der symbolischen Formen*. Vol. 1, *Die Sprache*. Berlin: B. Cassirer, 1923.
—*Substance and Function, and Einstein's Theory of Relativity*. Trans. by W. C. Swabey. Chicago: Open Court, 1923 (*Substanzbegriff und Funktionsbegriff*, Berlin, 1910, and *Zur Einstein'schen Relativitätstheorie*, Berlin, 1921).

Castiglione, Baldassare (1478–1529)
The Book of the Courtier. Trans. by T. Hoby. Everyman's Library, New York: E. P. Dutton, 1928 (*Il Libro del Cortegiano*, Venice, 1528).

Catullus, Gaius Valerius (*c.* 84–54 b.c.)
The Poems. In *Catullus, Tibullus, and Pervigilium Veneris*. Trans. by F. W. Cornish. Loeb Library, Cambridge, Mass.: Harvard University Press, 1935.

Cavendish, Henry (1731–1810)
Electrical Researches. In Vol. 1, *The Scientific Papers of the Honourable Henry Cavendish, F.R.S.* Ed. by J. C. Maxwell and E. Thorpe. 2 vols. Cambridge University Press, 1921 (1771–1781).
—[Experiments of Factitious Air] *Three Papers, Containing Experiments of Factitious Air*. In Vol. II. *ibid.* (1766).
—*Experiments on Air. Ibid.* (1784–1785).

Cellini, Benvenuto (1500–1571)
Autobiography of Benvenuto Cellini. Everyman's Library, New York: E. P. Dutton, 1942 (1558–1564).

Celsus, Aulus Cornelius (*fl.* 14–37 a.d.)
De Medicina. Trans. by W. G. Spencer. 3 vols. Loeb Library, Cambridge, Mass.: Harvard University Press, 1935–1938.

Chalmers, Thomas (1780–1847)
On the Power, Wisdom, and Goodness of God, as Manifested in the Adaptation of External Nature to the Moral and Intellectual Constitution of Man. London: G. Bell & Sons, 1884 (*Bridgewater Treatise on the Power, etc.*, London, 1833).

Chamberlin, Edward Hastings (1899–1967)
The Theory of Monopolistic Competition: A Reorientation of the Theory of Value. Cambridge, Mass.: Harvard University Press, 1933.

Chamberlin, Thomas Chrowder (1843–1928)
The Origin of the Earth. University of Chicago Press, 1916.

Chambers, Robert (1802–1871)
Vestiges of the Natural History of Creation. New York: G. Routledge, 1890 (London, 1844).

Channing, William Ellery (1780–1842)
[Discourses on War] *War. Discourse Before the Congregational Ministers of Massachusetts, Boston, 1816; War. Discourse Delivered January 25, 1835; Lecture on War (1838)*. In *The Works of William E. Channing*. Boston: American Unitarian Association, 1903.
—*Slavery. Ibid.* (Boston, 1835).

Charron, Pierre (1541–1603)
De la sagesse, trois livres. Paris: Lefèvre, 1836 (Bordeaux, 1601).

Chateaubriand, François Auguste René (1768–1848)
René. London: T. Hamilton, 1813 (Paris, 1802).

Chaucer, Geoffrey (*c.* 1340–1400)
The House of Fame. In *The Complete Works of Geoffrey Chaucer (Student's Cambridge Edition)*. Ed. by F. N. Robinson. New York: Houghton Mifflin Co., 1933 (1385).
—*The Legend of Good Women. Ibid.* (1385).
—*A Treatise on the Astrolabe. Ibid.* (1391).

Chekhov, Anton Pavlovich (1860–1904)
Letters on the Short Story, the Drama and Other Literary Topics. Ed. by L. S. Friedland. New York: Minton Balch, 1924.
—*The Sea-Gull*. In *The Plays of Anton Tchekov*. Trans. by C. Garnett. Modern Library, New York: Random House, 1930 (first performed, 1896).
—*Three Sisters. Ibid.* (first performed, 1901).
—*Ward No. 6*. In *The Horse-Stealers and Other Stories*. Trans. by C. Garnett. New York: Macmillan, 1921 (1892).

CHESTERFIELD, FOURTH EARL OF (1694–1773)
Letters to His Son and Others. Everyman's Library, New York: E. P. Dutton, 1946 (1738–1768).

CHESTERTON, GILBERT KEITH (1874–1936)
The Everlasting Man. London: Hodder & Stoughton, 1927 (1925).
—*The Man Who Was Thursday; a Nightmare*. Modern Library, New York: Random House, 1917 (London, 1908).
—*The Napoleon of Notting Hill*. London: J. Lane, 1937 (London, 1904).
—*Orthodoxy*. New York: Dodd, Mead & Co., 1936 (London, 1908).
—*What's Wrong with the World*. London: Cassell, 1910.

CHRÉTIEN DE TROYES (12th century)
Arthurian Romances by Chrétien de Troyes. Trans. by W. W. Comfort. Everyman's Library, New York: E. P. Dutton, 1935.

CICERO, MARCUS TULLIUS (106–43 B.C.)
[Academics] *De Natura Deorum, Academica*. Trans. by H. Rackham. Loeb Library, Cambridge, Mass.: Harvard University Press, 1933 (45 B.C.).
—*Brutus, Orator*. Trans. by G. L. Hendrickson. Loeb Library, Cambridge, Mass.: Harvard University Press, 1939 (46 B.C.).
—[De Divinatione] *De Senectute, De Amicitia, De Divinatione*. Trans. by W. A. Falconer. Loeb Library, Cambridge, Mass.: Harvard University Press, 1923 (44 B.C.).
—*De Domo Sua*. In *Pro Archia Poeta, etc*. Trans. by N. H. Watts. Loeb Library, Cambridge, Mass.: Harvard University Press, 1923 (57 B.C.).
—*De Fato*. Trans. by C. D. Yonge. London: G. Bell, 1907 (44 B.C.).
—*De Finibus Bonorum et Malorum*. Trans. by H. Rackham. Loeb Library, Cambridge, Mass.: Harvard University Press, 1914 (45 B.C.).
—*De Legibus, De Republica*. Trans. by C. W. Keyes. Loeb Library, Cambridge, Mass.: Harvard University Press, 1928 (50 B.C.?).
—*De Natura Deorum*. See *Academics* (45 B.C.).
—*De Officiis*. Trans. by W. Miller. Loeb Library, Cambridge, Mass.: Harvard University Press, 1913 (44 B.C.).
—*De Oratore*. Trans. by E. W. Sutton and H. Rackham. 2 vols. Loeb Library, Cambridge, Mass.: Harvard University Press, 1942 (55 B.C.?).
—*De Republica*. See *De Legibus* (51 B.C.?).
—*De Senectute*. See *De Divinatione* (44 B.C.).
—*Laelius de Amicitia*. See *De Divinatione* (44 B.C.).
—*The Orations of Marcus Tullius Cicero*. Trans. by C. D. Yonge. 4 vols. London: G. Bell, 1913–1921.
—*Orator*. See *Brutus* (46 B.C.).
—*Tusculan Disputations*. Trans. by J. E. King. Loeb Library, Cambridge, Mass.: Harvard University Press, 1927 (*Tusculanae Disputationes*, 45 B.C.).

CLARK, JOHN BATES (1847–1938)
The Distribution of Wealth; a Theory of Wages, Interest, and Profits. New York: Macmillan, 1899.

CLARK, JOHN MAURICE (1884–)
Alternative to Serfdom. New York: A. A. Knopf, 1948 (1947).

CLARKE, JOHN (1682–1757)
An Inquiry into the Cause and Origin of Evil. London, 1720.

[Clarke Papers] *Puritanism and Liberty, Being the Army Debates (1647–1649) from the Clarke Manuscripts with Supplementary Documents*. Ed. by A. S. P. Woodhouse. London: J. M. Dent, 1938.

CLAUDEL, PAUL (1868–1955)
Poetic Art. Trans. by Renee Spodheim. New York: Philosophical Library, 1948 (*Art Poétique*, 1904).
—*The Tidings Brought to Mary: A Mystery*. Trans. by L. M. Sill. New Haven, Conn.: Yale University Press, 1927 (*L'Annonce faite à Marie*, Paris, 1912).

CLAUSEWITZ, KARL VON (1780–1831)
On War. Ed. by J. Greene, trans. by O. J. Matthijs Jolles. Modern Library, New York: Random House, 1943 (*Vom Kriege*, Berlin, 1832–1834 [1816–1831]).

CLEANTHES OF ASSOS (*c*. 331–*c*. 232 B.C.)
Hymn to Zeus. Trans. by J. Adam. In *Greek Literature in Translation*. Ed. by W. J. Oates and C. T. Murphy. New York: Longmans, Green & Co., 1945.

CLIFFORD, WILLIAM KINGDOM (1845–1879)
The Common Sense of the Exact Sciences. Ed. by K. Pearson and J. Newman. New York: A. A. Knopf, 1946 (1875–1879).
—*Lectures and Essays*. Ed. by L. Stephen and F. Pollock. 2 vols. London: Macmillan, 1901 (London, 1879).
—*On the Canonical Form and Dissection of a Riemann's Surface*. In *Mathematical Papers*. Ed. by R. Tucker. London: Macmillan, 1882 (1877).
—*Preliminary Sketch of Biquaternions*. *Ibid*. (1873).
—*Seeing and Thinking*. London: Macmillan, 1890 (London, 1879).

The Cloud of Unknowing, and Other Treatises by an English Mystic of the Fourteenth Century, with a Commentary on the Cloud by Father Augustine Baker. Ed. by J. McCann. London: Burns, Oates, & Washbourne, 1924.

COHEN, FELIX S. (1907–1953)
Ethical Systems and Legal Ideals; an Essay on the Foundations of Legal Criticism. New York: Falcon Press, 1933.

COHEN, HERMANN (1842–1918)
Ethik des reinen Willens. Berlin: B. Cassirer, 1921 (Berlin, 1904).

COHEN, MORRIS RAPHAEL (1880–1947)
Law and the Social Order; Essays in Legal Philosophy. New York: Harcourt Brace, 1933.

—*The Meaning of Human History*. La Salle, Ill.: Open Court, 1947 (1944).
—*A Preface to Logic*. New York: Henry Holt, 1944.
—*Reason and Nature, an Essay on the Meaning of Scientific Method*. New York: Harcourt Brace, 1931.

COKE, SIR EDWARD (1552–1634)
Institutes of the Laws of England. 4 parts, 7 vols. London: E. & R. Brooke, 1809 (1614–1634).

COLERIDGE, SAMUEL TAYLOR (1772–1834)
Biographia Literaria; or, Biographical Sketches of My Literary Life and Opinions. Everyman's Library, New York: E. P. Dutton, 1934 (London, 1817).
—*The Pains of Sleep*. In *The Poems of Samuel Taylor Coleridge*. World's Classics, New York: Oxford University Press, 1930 (London, 1828).
—*The Rime of the Ancient Mariner*. *Ibid*. (London, 1798).
—*Treatise on Method, as Published in the Encyclopaedia Metropolitana*. Ed. by A. D. Snyder. London: Constable & Co., 1934 (from *Encyclopaedia Metropolitana*, 1818).

COLLINGWOOD, ROBIN GEORGE (1889–1943)
The Idea of History. Ed. by T. M. Knox. Oxford: Clarendon Press, 1946 (1936).
—*The Idea of Nature*. Oxford: Clarendon Press, 1945 (1933–1943).

COLLINS, WILLIAM (1721–1759)
The Passions, An Ode for Music. In *The Poetical Works of Gray and Collins*. Ed. by A. L. Poole. New York: Oxford University Press, 1926 (London, 1747).

COMENIUS, JOANNES AMOS (1592–1670)
The Great Didactic. Ed. and trans. by M. W. Keatinge. London: A. & C. Black, 1923 (*Didactica Magna*, in *Opera Didactica Omnia*, Amsterdam, 1657).
—*School of Infancy*. Ed. and trans. by W. S. Monroe. London: D. C. Heath, 1865 (*Schola Infantiae*, in *Opera Didactica Omnia*, Amsterdam, 1657).

COMTE, AUGUSTE (1798–1857)
The Catechism of Positive Religion. Trans. by R. Congreve. London: J. Chapman, 1858 (*Catéchisme positiviste*, Paris, 1852).
—*The Philosophy of Mathematics*. Trans. by W. M. Gillespie. New York: Harper, 1851 (from *Cours de philosophie positive*, Vol. I, Paris, 1830).
—*The Positive Philosophy of Auguste Comte*. Abr. trans. by H. Martineau. London: G. Bell & Sons, 1896 (*Cours de philosophie positive*, Paris, 1830–1842).
—*System of Positive Polity*. Vol. I, *General View of Positivism;* Vol. II, *Social Statics;* Vol. III, *Social Dynamics;* Vol. IV, *Theory of the Future of Man*. Trans. by J. H. Bridget *et al*. London: Longmans, Green & Co., 1875–1877 (*Système de politique positive; ou, Traité de sociologie instituant la religion de l'humanité*, Paris, 1851–1854).

CONANT, JAMES BRYANT (1893–)
Education in a Divided World. Cambridge, Mass.: Harvard University Press, 1948.
—*On Understanding Science*. New Haven, Conn.: Yale University Press, 1947.

CONDILLAC, ÉTIENNE BONNOT DE (1715–1780)
Essai sur l'origine des connaissances humaines: ouvrage où l'on réduit à un seul principe tout ce qui concerne l'entendement. Paris: A. Colin, 1924 (Amsterdam, 1746).
—*La langue des calculs*. In Vol. XXIII, *Oeuvres de Condillac*. 23 vols. Paris: Houel, 1798.
—*Logique*. In Vol. XXII, *ibid*. (Paris, 1780).
—*Traité des animaux*. In Vol. III, *ibid*. (Amsterdam, 1755).
—*Treatise on the Sensations*. Ed. and trans. by G. Carr. London: Favil Press, 1930 (*Traité des sensations*, Paris, 1754).

CONDORCET, MARIE JEAN ANTOINE NICOLAS CARITAT (1743–1794)
Outlines of an Historical View of the Progress of the Human Mind. Baltimore, 1802 (*Esquisse d'un tableau historique des progrès de l'esprit humain*, Paris, 1795).

CONGREVE, WILLIAM (1670–1729)
The Way of the World: A Comedy. London: J. M. Dent, 1933 (London, 1700).

COOK, ARTHUR BERNARD (1868–1952)
Zeus: A Study in Ancient Religion. 3 vols. Cambridge University Press, 1914–1940.

COOMARASWAMY, ANANDA KENTISH (1877–1947)
The Transformation of Nature in Art. Cambridge, Mass.: Harvard University Press, 1934.

COPE, EDWARD DRINKER (1840–1897)
The Primary Factors of Organic Evolution. Chicago: Open Court, 1896.

COPERNICUS, NICOLAUS (1473–1543)
Commentariolus. In *Three Copernican Treatises*. Trans. by E. Rosen. New York: Columbia University Press, 1939 (1508).
—*Letter Against Werner*. *Ibid*. (1524).

CORNEILLE, PIERRE (1606–1684)
Cinna. In *Six Plays of Corneille and Racine*. Ed. and trans. by P. Landis. Modern Library, New York: Random House, 1931 (1640).
—*Examens*. Prefixed to each play in *Oeuvres de Pierre Corneille*. Ed. by C. Marty-Laveaux. 10 vols. Paris: Hachette, 1862–1868 (appeared first in *Le théâtre de Corneille*, Paris, 1660).
—*Horace*. Ed. by F. L. Marcou. Paris: Garnier frères, 1920 (1640).
—*La Place Royale*. In Vol. II, *Oeuvres*. See *Examens* (1634).
—*Le Cid*. In *Six Plays*. See *Cinna* (1636).
—*Polyeucte*. Trans. by T. Constable. In *Continental Drama*. "Harvard Classics," New York: P. F. Collier, 1910 (1640).
—*Trois discours sur l'art dramatique*. In Vol. X, *Oeuvres*. See *Examens* (*Discours de l'utilité et des parties de la tragédie*, *Discours de la tragédie*, *Dis-*

cours des trois unités, in *Le théâtre de Corneille*, Paris, 1660).

COSTER, CHARLES THÉODORE HENRI DE (1827–1879)
The Glorious Adventures of Tyl Ulenspiegl. Trans. by A. R. Macdougall. New York: Pantheon Books, 1943 (*La légende d'Ulenspiegel*, Paris, 1868).

COURANT, RICHARD (1888–1972) and ROBBINS, HERBERT (1915–)
What Is Mathematics? An Elementary Approach to Ideas and Methods. New York: Oxford University Press, 1941.

COURNOT, ANTOINE AUGUSTIN (1801–1877)
Essai sur les fondements de nos connaissances et sur les charactères de la critique philosophique. Paris: Hachette, 1912 (Paris, 1851).
—*Exposition de la théorie des chances et des probabilités*. Paris: Hachette, 1843.
—*Researches into the Mathematical Principles of the Theory of Wealth*. Trans. by N. T. Bacon. New York: Macmillan, 1927 (*Recherches sur les principes mathématiques de la théorie des richesses*, Paris, 1838).

COUSIN, VICTOR (1792–1867)
Lectures on the True, the Beautiful and the Good. Trans. by O. W. Wight. New York: D. Appleton, 1875 (*Du vrai, du beau et du bien*, Paris, 1853 [1818]).

COUTURAT, LOUIS (1868–1914)
The Algebra of Logic. Trans. by L. G. Robinson. Chicago: Open Court, 1914 (*L'algèbre de la logique*, Paris, 1905).
—*De l'infini mathématique*. Paris: F. Alcan, 1896.

COUTURAT, LOUIS and LEAU, LÉOPOLD
Histoire de la langue universelle. Paris: Hachette, 1903.

COWLEY, ABRAHAM (1618–1667)
To the Royal Society. In *Poems: Miscellanies, etc*. Ed. by A. R. Waller. Cambridge University Press, 1905 (1667).

CRABBE, GEORGE (1754–1832)
The Village. In *The Poetical Works of George Crabbe*. Ed. by A. J. and R. M. Carlyle. New York: Oxford University Press, 1932 (London, 1783).

CRANE, STEPHEN (1871–1900)
The Red Badge of Courage. Modern Library, New York: Random House, 1942 (New York, 1895).

CRASHAW, RICHARD (*c*. 1613–1649)
The Flaming Heart. In *The Poems, English, Latin and Greek of Richard Crashaw*. Ed. by L. C. Martin. Oxford: Clarendon Press, 1927 (from *Steps to the Temple*, 2nd ed., London, 1648, and *Carmen Deo Nostro*, Paris, 1652).

CRESCAS, CHASDAI BEN ABRAHAM (1340–1410)
Or Adonai. Bk. 1, ed. and trans. by H. A. Wolfson. Cambridge, Mass.: Harvard University Press, 1929.

CREUZER, GEORG FRIEDRICH (1771–1858)
Symbolik und Mythologie der alten Völker, besonders der Griechen. 4 vols. Leipsic: Leske, 1836–1843 (Leipsic, 1810–1812).

CRILE, GEORGE WASHINGTON (1864–1943)
The Origin and Nature of the Emotions; Miscellaneous Papers. Ed. by A. F. Rowland. Philadelphia: W. B. Saunders, 1915.

CROCE, BENEDETTO (1866–1952)
Aesthetic as Science of Expression and General Linguistic. Trans. by D. Ainslie. New York: Macmillan, 1929 (*Estetica come scienza dell'espressione e linguistica generale*, Milan, 1902).
—*The Conduct of Life*. Trans. by A. Livingston. New York: Harcourt Brace, 1924 (1922).
—*The Defense of Poetry, Variations on the Theme of Shelley*. Trans. by E. F. Carritt. Oxford: Clarendon Press, 1933.
—*The Essence of Esthetics*. Trans. by D. Ainslie. London: W. Heinemann, 1921 (1912).
—*Freedom, Its Meaning*. Ed. by R. N. Anshen, trans. by A. Livingston. London: Allen & Unwin, 1942.
—*History as the Story of Liberty*. Trans. by S. Sprigge. New York: W. W. Norton, 1941 (*La storia come pensiero e come azione*, Bari, 1938).
—*History, Its Theory and Practice*. Trans. by D. Ainslie. New York: Harcourt Brace, 1923 (*Teoria e storia della storiografia*, 1911–1913).
—*Logic as the Science of Pure Concept*. Trans. by D. Ainslie. New York: Macmillan, 1917 (*Logica come scienza del concetto puro*, Bari, 1909).
—*The Philosophy of the Practical: Economic and Ethic*. Trans. by D. Ainslie. New York: Macmillan, 1913 (*Filosofia della practica economia ed etica*, Bari, 1908).
—*Politics and Morals*. Trans. by S. J. Castiglione. New York: Philosophical Library, 1945 (sel. from *Elementi di politica*, Bari, 1925, and *Aspetti morali della vita politica*, Bari, 1928).

CROLY, HERBERT DAVID (1869–1930)
Progressive Democracy. New York: Macmillan, 1915.

CROOKSHANK, FRANCIS GRAHAM (1873–1933)
Individual Diagnosis. London: K. Paul, Trench, Trübner, 1930.

CRUCÉ, ÉMERIC (*c*. 1590–1648)
The New Cyneas of Émeric Crucé. Ed. and trans. by T. W. Balch. Philadelphia: Allen, Lane & Scott, 1909 (*Le Nouveau Cynée, ou, Discours d'estat représentant les occasions et moyens d'establir une paix généralle et la liberté du commerce par tout le monde*, Paris, 1623).

CUDWORTH, RALPH (1617–1688)
A Treatise of Freewill. Ed. by J. Allen. London: J. W. Parker, 1838.
—*The True Intellectual System of the Universe: Wherein All the Reason and Philosophy of Atheism is Confuted, and Its Impossibility Demonstrated*. 2

vols. New York: Andover, Gould & Newman, 1837–1838 (London, 1678).

Curie, Marie (1867–1934)
Traité de radioactivité. Paris: Gauthier-Villars, 1910.

Cuvier, Georges Léopold Chrétien Frédéric Dagobert (1769–1832)
The Animal Kingdom, Arranged After Its Organization, Forming a Natural History of Animals, and an Introduction to a Comparative Anatomy. With Considerable Additions by W. B. Carpenter and J. O. Westwood. London: W. H. Allen, 1890 (*Le règne animal distribué d'après son organization*, Paris, 1817).

D

D'Abro, A.
The Decline of Mechanism in Modern Physics. New York: Van Nostrand, 1939.

D'Alembert, Jean Le Rond (1717–1783)
Traité de dynamique. 2 vols. Paris: Gauthier-Villars, 1921 (Paris, 1743).

Dalton, John (1766–1844)
A New System of Chemical Philosophy. 2 vols. Manchester: R. Bickerstaff, 1808–1827.

Dante Alighieri (1265–1321)
The Convivio of Dante Alighieri. Trans. by P. H. Wicksteed. Temple Classics, London: J. M. Dent, 1912 (*c.* 1304–1307).
—*De Vulgari Eloquentia*. In *A Translation of the Latin Works of Dante Alighieri* by A. G. F. Howell and P. H. Wicksteed. Temple Classics, London: J. M. Dent, 1904 (*c.* 1303–1304).
—*Epistle to Can Grande della Scala* (Letter x). *Ibid.* (1318?).
—*La Vita Nuova*. Trans. by T. Okey and P. H. Wicksteed. Temple Classics, London: J. M. Dent, 1911 (1293?).
—*On World-Government or De Monarchia*. Trans. by H. W. Schneider. New York: Liberal Arts Press, 1949 (*c.* 1310–1313).

D'Arcy, Martin Cyril (1888–)
The Mind and Heart of Love, Lion and Unicorn; a Study in Eros and Agape. New York: Henry Holt, 1947 (London, 1945).

Darwin, Charles Galton (1887–1962)
The New Conceptions of Matter. New York: Macmillan, 1931.

Darwin, Charles Robert (1809–1882)
The Different Forms of Flowers on Plants of the Same Species. New York: D. Appleton, 1903 (London, 1877).
—*The Expression of Emotions in Man and Animals*. Ed. by F. Darwin. New York: D. Appleton, 1929 (London, 1872).
—*Foundations of the Origin of Species*. Ed. by F. Darwin. Cambridge University Press, 1909 (1842–1843).
—*A Posthumous Essay on Instinct*. In G. J. Romanes, *Mental Evolution in Animals*. London: K. Paul & Co., 1883 (before 1859).
—*The Variation of Animals and Plants Under Domestication*. 2 vols. New York: D. Appleton, 1900 (London, 1868).

Darwin, Erasmus (1731–1802)
The Loves of the Plants. In *The Botanic Garden*. London: J. Johnson, 1799 (Lichfield, 1789).
—*Zoonomia; or, The Laws of Organic Life*. 2 vols. Philadelphia: E. Earle, 1818 (London, 1794–1796).

Darwin, George Howard (1845–1912)
The Evolution of the Satellites. Smithsonian Institution, Annual Report. Washington, D.C., 1898.
—*The Tides and Kindred Phenomena in the Solar System*. London: J. Murray, 1911 (New York, 1898).

Daudet, Alphonse (1840–1897)
Letters from My Mill. Trans. by F. H. Potter. New York: Dodd, Mead & Co., 1893 (*Lettres de mon moulin*, 1866–1869).

Davy, Sir Humphrey (1778–1829)
Elements of Chemical Philosophy: As Regards Laws of Chemical Changes: Undecomposed Bodies and Their Primary Combinations. London: Smith, Elder & Co., 1840 (London, 1812).

Dawson, Christopher Henry (1889–1970)
Enquiries into Religion and Culture. New York: Sheed & Ward, 1933.
—*Progress and Religion: An Historical Enquiry*. New York: Sheed & Ward, 1938 (London, 1929).
—*Religion and the Modern State*. New York: Sheed & Ward, 1935.

De Burgh, William George (1866–1943)
Towards a Religious Philosophy. London: Macdonald & Evans, 1937.

Dedekind, Julius Wilhelm Richard (1831–1916)
Essays on the Theory of Numbers. Trans. by W. W. Beman. Chicago: Open Court, 1924 (*Stetigkeit und irrationale Zahlen*, Brunswick, 1872, and *Was sind und sollen die Zahlen*, Brunswick, 1888).

Defoe, Daniel (*c.* 1661–1731)
[Moll Flanders] *The Fortunes and Misfortunes of the Famous Moll Flanders*. Everyman's Library, New York: E. P. Dutton, 1945 (London, 1721).
—*Robinson Crusoe*. Everyman's Library, New York: E. P. Dutton, 1947 (1719).
—*The Shortest Way with the Dissenters and Other Pamphlets*. Oxford: Blackwell, 1927 (London, 1702).

Dekker, Thomas (*c.* 1570–*c.* 1641)
The Shoemaker's Holiday. In *Thomas Dekker*. Ed. by E. Rhys. Mermaid Series, London: T. F. Unwin, 1904 (London, 1599).

Delacroix, (Ferdinand Victor) Eugène (1799–1863)
The Journal of Eugène Delacroix. Trans. by W. Pach. New York: Covici-Friede, 1937 (1822–1824; 1847–1863).

Delacroix, Henri Joachim (1873–1937)
Le langage et la pensée. Paris: F. Alcan, 1924.
—*Psychologie de l'art, essai sur l'activité artistique*. Paris: F. Alcan, 1927.

Delbrück, Hans (1848–1929)
Geschichte der Kriegskunst im Rahmen der politischen Geschichte. 7 vols. Berlin: G. Stilke, 1900–1936.

De Man, Henri (1885–)
Joy in Work. Trans. by E. and C. Paul. New York: Henry Holt, 1929 (*Der Kampf um die Arbeitsfreude*, 1927).

Demetrius (1st century A.D.)
On Style. Trans. by W. R. Roberts. Loeb Library, Cambridge, Mass.: Harvard University Press, 1932.

De Morgan, Augustus (1806–1871)
A Budget of Paradoxes. Ed. by S. De Morgan. 2 vols. Chicago: Open Court, 1915 (1863–1867).
—*An Essay on Probabilities, and on Their Application to Life Contingencies and Insurance Offices*. London: Longmans, Orme & Co., 1849 (London, 1838).
—*Formal Logic*. Ed. by A. E. Taylor. Chicago: Open Court, 1926 (London, 1847).
—*On the Study and Difficulties of Mathematics*. Chicago: Open Court, 1910 (London, 1831).

Demosthenes (384–322 B.C.)
De Corona and De Falsa Legatione. Trans. by C. A. and J. H. Vince. Loeb Library, Cambridge, Mass.: Harvard University Press, 1926 (330 B.C.).
—[Philippics] *Olynthiacs, Philippics, Minor Public Speeches*. Trans. by J. H. Vince. Loeb Library, Cambridge, Mass.: Harvard University Press, 1930.

De Quincey, Thomas (1785–1859)
Confessions of an English Opium-Eater. World's Classics, New York: Oxford University Press, 1934 (1821).
—*Letters to a Young Man Whose Education Has Been Neglected*. In *Essays*. New York: Ward, Lock & Co., 1886 (1823).
—*The Literature of Knowledge and the Literature of Power*. In *Masters of Literature: De Quincey*. Ed. by Sidney Low. London: G. Bell & Sons, 1911 (1823; 1848).
—*On the Knocking at the Gate in Macbeth*. In *De Quincey's Literary Criticism*. Ed. by H. Darbishire. London: H. Frowde, 1904 (1823).
—*Rhetoric*. In *Masters of Literature: De Quincey*. See above (1828).

Descartes, René (1596–1650)
The Passions of the Soul. In Vol. 1, *Philosophical Works*. Trans. by E. S. Haldane and G. R. T. Ross. 2 vols. Cambridge University Press, 1931 (*Les passions de l'âme*, Paris, 1649).
—*The Principles of Philosophy*. *Ibid.* (*Principia Philosophiae*, Amsterdam, 1644).
—*The World; or Essay on Light*. In *Descartes. Selections*. Ed. by R. M. Eaton. New York: Scribner's, 1927 (*Traité de la lumière*, 1630–1633).

Descoqs, Pedro (1877–1946)
Essai critique sur l'hylémorphisme. Paris: G. Beauchesne, 1924.

Dewey, John (1859–1952)
Art as Experience. New York: Minton Balch, 1934.
—*Characters and Events; Popular Essays in Social and Political Philosophy*. Ed. by J. Ratner. 2 vols. New York: Henry Holt, 1929 (1891–1928).
—*A Common Faith*. New Haven, Conn.: Yale University Press, 1934.
—*Democracy and Education; an Introduction to the Philosophy of Education*. New York: Macmillan, 1931 (New York, 1916).
—*Essays in Experimental Logic*. University of Chicago Press, 1916 (1903–1916).
—*Experience and Education*. New York: Macmillan, 1938.
—*Experience and Nature*. New York: W. W. Norton, 1929 (Chicago, 1925).
—*Freedom and Culture*. New York: Putnam's, 1939.
—*How We Think; a Restatement of the Relation of Reflective Thinking to the Educative Process*. Boston: D. C. Heath, 1933 (Boston, 1910).
—*Human Nature and Conduct; an Introduction to Social Psychology*. Modern Library, New York: Random House, 1930 (New York, 1922).
—*The Influence of Darwin on Philosophy, and Other Essays in Contemporary Thought*. New York: Henry Holt, 1910 (1897–1909).
—*Interest and Effort in Education*. Boston: Houghton Mifflin Co., 1913.
—*Logic, the Theory of Inquiry*. New York: Henry Holt, 1938.
—*Outlines of a Critical Theory of Ethics*. Ann Arbor, Mich.: Register Publishing Co., 1891.
—*Philosophy and Civilization*. New York: Minton Balch, 1931 (1902–1931).
—*The Public and Its Problems*. New York: Henry Holt, 1927.
—*The Quest for Certainty: A Study of the Relation of Knowledge and Action*. New York: Minton Balch, 1929.
—*Reconstruction in Philosophy*. New York: Henry Holt, 1920.
—*The School and Society*. University of Chicago Press, 1926 (Chicago, 1899).
—*The Study of Ethics: A Syllabus*. Ann Arbor, Mich: Register Publishing Co., 1894.

Dewey, John *et al.*
Creative Intelligence; Essays in the Pragmatic Attitude. New York: Henry Holt, 1917.
—*Studies in Logical Theory*. University of Chicago Press, 1903.

Dewey, John and Bentley, Arthur F. (1870–1957)
Knowing and the Known. Boston: Beacon Press, 1949.

DEWEY, JOHN and TUFTS, JAMES H. (1862–1942)
Ethics. New York: Henry Holt, 1938 (New York, 1908).

DIAMOND, ARTHUR SIGISMUND (1897–)
Primitive Law. New York: Longmans, Green & Co., 1935.

DIAZ DE GAMEZ (*c.* 1379–*c.* 1450)
The Unconquered Knight; a Chronicle of the Deeds of Don Pedro Niño, Count of Buelno, by His Standard Bearer Gutierre Diaz de Gamez. Trans. by Joan Evans. London: G. Routledge, 1928 (1431–1449).

DICEY, ALBERT VENN (1835–1922)
Introduction to the Study of the Law of the Constitution. London: Macmillan, 1939 (London, 1885).
—*Lectures on the Relation Between Law and Public Opinion in England During the Nineteenth Century*. London: Macmillan, 1924 (London, 1905).

DICKENS, CHARLES (1812–1870)
Bleak House. Everyman's Library, New York: E. P. Dutton, 1948 (London, 1852–1853).
—*Great Expectations*. Everyman's Library, New York: E. P. Dutton, 1932 (1860–1861).
—*Little Dorritt*. Everyman's Library, New York: E. P. Dutton, 1907 (1856).
—[Nicholas Nickleby] *The Life and Adventures of Nicholas Nickleby*. Everyman's Library, New York: E. P. Dutton, 1930 (1838–1839).
—*Oliver Twist*. Everyman's Library, New York: E. P. Dutton, 1946 (1837–1839).
—*Our Mutual Friend*. Everyman's Library, New York: E. P. Dutton, 1929 (London, 1864–1865).
—[Pickwick Papers] *The Posthumous Papers of the Pickwick Club*. Everyman's Library, New York: E. P. Dutton, 1934 (London, 1836–1837).
—*A Tale of Two Cities*. Everyman's Library, New York: E. P. Dutton, 1948 (1859).

DICKINSON, GOLDSWORTHY LOWES (1862–1932)
Justice and Liberty; A Political Dialogue. New York: McClure, 1908.

DICKINSON, JOHN (1894–)
Administrative Justice and the Supremacy of Law in the United States. Cambridge, Mass.: Harvard University Press, 1927.

DICKSON, LEONARD EUGENE (1874–1954)
Introduction to the Theory of Numbers. University of Chicago Press, 1929.

DIDEROT, DENIS (1713–1784)
Citoyen. Article from the *Encyclopédie*, reprinted in Vol. XIV, *Oeuvres complètes de Diderot*. Ed. by J. Assézat and M. Tourneux. 20 vols. Paris: Garnier, 1875–1877 (1753).
—[Le rêve de d'Alembert] *Entretien entre d'Alembert et Diderot; Rêve de d'Alembert; Suite de l'entretien*. Ed. by G. Maire. Paris: Éditions Bossard, 1921 (1769).

DIGBY, SIR KENELM (1603–1665)
[The Nature of Bodies] *Two Treatises: In the One of Which, the Nature of Bodies; in the Other, the Nature of Man's Soul, Is Looked into: In Way of Discovery of the Immortality of Reasonable Souls*. 2 vols. London: J. Williams, 1658 (Paris, 1644).

DIGGES, DUDLEY (1613–1643)
Unlawfulness of Subjects Taking up Arms Against Their Soveraigne, in What Case Soever. London: P. Parker, 1679 (London, 1643).

DILTHEY, WILHELM (1833–1911)
Das Erlebnis und die Dichtung: Lessing, Goethe, Novalis, Hölderlin. Leipsic: B. G. Teubner, 1922 (Leipsic, 1905).

DINGLE, HERBERT (1890–)
Modern Astrophysics. New York: Macmillan, 1924 (London, 1921).

DIOGENES LAËRTIUS (3rd century)
Lives of Eminent Philosophers. Trans. by R. D. Hicks. 2 vols. Loeb Library, Cambridge, Mass.: Harvard University Press, 1925.

DIONYSIUS (THE PSEUDO-AREOPAGITE)(*fl. c.* 500)
On Mystical Theology. In Vol. I, *The Works of Dionysius the Areopagite*. Ed. and trans. by J. Parker. 2 vols. London: J. Parker, 1897–1899 (*De Mystica Theologica*).
—*On the Celestial Hierarchy*. In Vol. II, *ibid*. (*De Celesti Hierarchia*).
—*On the Divine Names*. In Vol. I, *ibid*. (*De Divinis Nominibus*).

DIRAC, PAUL ADRIEN MAURICE (1902–)
The Principles of Quantum Mechanics. Oxford: Clarendon Press, 1930.

DIWAKAR, RANGANATH RAMACHANDRA (1894–)
Satyagraha: The Power of Truth. Hinsdale, Ill.: H. Regnery, 1948.

DOBZHANSKY, THEODOSIUS GRIGORIEVICH (1900–)
Genetics and the Origin of Species. New York: Columbia University Press, 1937.

DODDRIDGE, PHILIP (1702–1751)
Rise and Progress of Religion in the Soul; Illustrated in a Course of Serious and Practical Addresses, Suited to Persons of Every Character, etc. New York: American Tract Society, 1849? (London, 1745).

DOMET DE VORGES, EDMOND CHARLES EUGÈNE (1829–?)
Cause efficiente et cause finale. Paris: Bureau des "Annales de Philosophie Chrétienne," 1888.

DONNE, JOHN (1573–1631)
Songs and Sonnets [includes *Aire and Angells*, *Lovers Infinitenesse*, and *The Triple Foole*]. In *The Complete Poetry and Selected Prose of John Donne*. Ed. by John Hayward, New York: Random House, 1941 (*c.* 1590–*c.* 1601).

DOSTOEVSKY, FYODOR MIKHAILOVICH (1821–1881)
Crime and Punishment. Everyman's Library, New York: E. P. Dutton, 1933 (1866).
—*The House of the Dead*. Everyman's Library, New York: E. P. Dutton, 1933 (1861–1862).
—*The Idiot*. Trans. by C. Garnett. Modern Library, New York: Random House, 1942 (1868–1869).

—*Notes from Underground*. In *The Short Novels of Dostoevsky*. Trans. by C. Garnett. New York: Dial Press, 1945 (1864).
—*Poor Folk*. Trans. by C. J. Hogarth. Everyman's Library, New York: E. P. Dutton, 1935 (1846).
—*The Possessed*. Trans. by C. Garnett. Modern Library, New York: Random House, 1936 (1871).
—*A Raw Youth: A Novel in Three Parts*. Trans. by C. Garnett. New York: Macmillan, 1923 (1875).

DOUHET, GIULIO (1869–1930)
The Command of the Air. Trans. by D. Ferrari. New York: Coward-McCann, 1942 (1921–1930).

DREYER, JOHN LOUIS EMIL (1852–1926)
History of the Planetary Systems from Thales to Kepler. Cambridge University Press, 1906.

DRIESCH, HANS ADOLF EDUARD (1867–1941)
Mind and Body. Trans. by T. Besterman. New York: Dial Press, 1927 (*Leib und Seele*, Leipsic 1916).
—*The Science and Philosophy of the Organism*. London: A. & C. Black, 1929 (London, 1908).

DRYDEN, JOHN (1631–1700)
Absalom and Achitophel. In *Poems of John Dryden*. Everyman's Library, New York: E. P. Dutton, 1934 (London, 1681).
—*All for Love; or, The World Well Lost*. Ed. by W. Strunk. Boston: D. C. Heath, 1911 (London, 1678).
—*A Discourse Concerning the Original and Progress of Satire*. In Vol. II, *Essays of John Dryden*. Ed. by W. P. Ker. 2 vols. Oxford: Clarendon Press, 1900 (prefixed to his translation of Juvenal and Persius, London, 1693).
—*An Essay of Dramatic Poesy*. In *Dramatic Poesy and Other Essays*. Everyman's Library, New York: E. P. Dutton, 1939 (London, 1668).
—*Of Heroic Plays*. *Ibid*. (prefixed to *The Conquest of Granada*, London, 1672).

DUBISLAV, WALTER (1895–)
Die Definition. Leipsic: F. Meiner, 1930.

DUBOIS, PIERRE (*c*.1250–*c*.1322)
De Recuperatione Terre Sancte. Traité de politique générale. Ed. by C. V. Langlois. Paris: A. Picard, 1891 (1305–1307).

DUCASSE, CURT JOHN (1881–1969)
Causation and the Types of Necessity. Seattle, Wash.: University of Washington Press, 1924.

DUGUIT, LÉON (1859–1928)
Law in the Modern State. Trans. by F. and H. Laski. New York: B. W. Huebsch, 1919 (*Les transformations du droit public*, Paris, 1913).
—*L'état, le droit objectif et la loi positive*. Paris: A. Fontemoing, 1901.
—*Souveraineté et liberté, leçons faites à l'Université Columbia*. Paris: F. Alcan, 1922.

DUHEM, PIERRE MAURICE MARIE (1861–1916)
Études sur Léonard de Vinci. 3 vols. Paris: A. Hermann, 1906–1913.
—*La théorie physique, son objet—sa structure*. Paris: M. Rivière, 1914 (Paris, 1906).
—*Le système du monde. Histoire des théories cosmologiques de Plato à Copernic*. 5 vols. Paris: Hermann & fils, 1913–1917.
—*Les origines de la statique*. Paris: A. Hermann, 1905–1906.
—*L'évolution de la mécanique*. Paris: A. Hermann, 1903.

DUNKMANN, KARL (1868–1933)
Soziologie der Arbeit. Halle: C. Marhold, 1933.

DUNS SCOTUS, JOANNES (*c*.1266–1308)
Opus Oxoniense (*Commentaria in Libros Sententiarum*). Vols. VIII–XXI, *Ioannis Duns Scoti Opera Omnia*. 26 vols. Paris: L. Vivès, 1891–1895 (1300?).
—*Oxford Commentary*. In Vol. II, *Selections from Medieval Philosophers*. Ed. and trans. by Richard McKeon. 2 vols. New York: Scribner's, 1929–1930 (1300?).
—*Reportata Parisiensia* (*Opus Parisiensis*). Vols. XXII–XXIV, *Opera*. See above (1304?).
—*Tractatus de Primo Principio*. Ed. and trans. by E. Roche. St. Bonaventure, N.Y.: The Franciscan Institute, 1949 (before 1302?).

DURKHEIM, ÉMILE (1858–1917)
The Division of Labor in Society. Trans. by G. Simpson. New York: Macmillan, 1933 (*De la division du travail social; étude sur l'organisation des sociétés supérieures*, Paris, 1893).

E

EATON, RALPH MONROE (1892–1932)
Symbolism and Truth; an Introduction to the Theory of Knowledge. Cambridge, Mass.: Harvard University Press, 1925.

EBBINGHAUS, HERMANN (1850–1909)
Memory. A Contribution to Experimental Psychology. Trans. by H. A. Ruger. New York: Columbia University Press, 1913 (*Über das Gedächtnis*, Leipsic, 1885).

EBREO, LEONE (LEO HEBRAEUS) (*c*.1460–*c*.1525)
The Philosophy of Love. Trans. by F. Friedeberg-Seeley. London: Soncino Press, 1937 (*Dialoghi d'amore*, *c*.1502).

ECKHART, JOHANNES (*c*.1260–*c*.1327)
Meister Eckhart [Sermons and Collations; Tractates; Sayings and *Liber Positionum*]. Abr. trans. of Franz Pfeiffer's *Eckhart* by C. de B. Evans. London: M. Watkins, 1924.

EDDINGTON, SIR ARTHUR STANLEY (1882–1944)
The Expanding Universe. New York: Macmillan, 1933.
—*The Internal Constitution of the Stars*. Cambridge University Press, 1926.
—*The Mathematical Theory of Relativity*. Cambridge University Press, 1930 (Cambridge, 1923).
—*The Nature of the Physical World*. London: J. M. Dent, 1942 (Cambridge, 1928).
—*The Philosophy of Physical Science*. New York: Macmillan, 1939.

—*Science and the Unseen World*. London: Allen & Unwin, 1929.
—*Space, Time, and Gravitation; an Outline of the General Relativity Theory*. Cambridge University Press, 1920.
—*Stars and Atoms*. New Haven, Conn.: Yale University Press, 1927.
—*Stellar Movements and the Structure of the Universe*. London: Macmillan, 1914.

EDWARDS, JONATHAN (1703–1758)
A Careful and Strict Enquiry into the Modern Prevailing Notions of That Freedom of Will, Which Is Supposed to Be Essential to Moral Agency, Virtue and Vice, Reward and Punishment, Praise and Blame. New York: Carter & Bros., 1869 (Boston, 1754).
—*Charity and Its Fruits*. Ed. by T. Edwards. New York: Carter & Bros., 1852 (1738).
—*A Dissertation on the Nature of True Virtue*. In Vol. I, *The Works of Jonathan Edwards*. 2 vols. London: H. G. Bohn, 1865 (1755).
—*The Great Christian Doctrine of Original Sin Defended; Evidences of Its Truth Produced, and Arguments to the Contrary Answered*. Edinburgh: J. Murray, 1798 (Boston, 1758).
—*A Treatise Concerning Religious Affections, in Three Parts*. Philadelphia: J. Crissy, 1821 (Boston, 1746).

EDWARDS, LYFORD PATERSON (1882–)
The Natural History of Revolution. University of Chicago Press, 1927.

EDWARDS, RICHARD (*c.*1523–1566)
Damon and Pithias. In Vol. IV, *A Select Collection of Old English Plays*. Ed. by R. Dodsley. 15 vols. London: Reeves & Turner, 1874–1876 (1564).

EINSTEIN, ALBERT (1879–1955)
The Meaning of Relativity. Trans. by E. P. Adams. Princeton University Press, 1950 (*Vier Vorlesungen über Relativitätstheorie*, Brunswick, 1922).
—*On the Method of Theoretical Physics*. New York: Oxford University Press, 1933.
—*Relativity: The Special and the General Theory. A Popular Exposition*. Trans. by R. W. Lawson. London: Methuen, 1931 (*Über die spezielle und die allgemeine Relativitätstheorie*, Brunswick, 1917).
—*Sidelights on Relativity*. Trans. by G. B. Jeffery and W. Perrett. London: Methuen, 1922 (*Äther und Relativitätstheorie*, Berlin, 1920, and *Geometrie und Erfahrung*, Berlin, 1921).

EINSTEIN, ALBERT and INFELD, LEOPOLD (1898–)
The Evolution of Physics; the Growth of Ideas from Early Concepts to Relativity and Quanta. New York: Simon & Schuster, 1938.

ELIOT, THOMAS STEARNS (1888–1965)
After Strange Gods; a Primer of Modern Heresy. New York: Harcourt Brace, 1934.
—*Essays, Ancient and Modern*. New York: Harcourt Brace, 1936.
—*The Family Reunion: A Play*. New York: Harcourt Brace, 1939.
—*Four Quartets*. New York: Harcourt Brace, 1943.
—*Murder in the Cathedral*. New York: Harcourt Brace, 1935.
—*Notes Towards the Definition of Culture*. New York: Harcourt Brace, 1949.
—*The Sacred Wood; Essays in Poetry and Criticism*. London: Methuen, 1934 (London, 1920).
—*Selected Essays, 1917–1932*. New York: Harcourt Brace, 1932.
—*The Use of Poetry and the Use of Criticism, Studies in the Relation of Criticism to Poetry in England*. Cambridge, Mass.: Harvard University Press, 1933.

ELLIS, HENRY HAVELOCK (1859–1939)
Man and Woman: A Study of Human Secondary Sexual Characters. New York: Scribner's, 1926 (New York, 1894).
Studies in the Psychology of Sex. 4 vols. New York: Random House, 1936 (New York, 1897–1928).

ELYOT, SIR THOMAS (*c.* 1490–1546)
The Governour. Everyman's Library, New York: E. P. Dutton, 1937 (London, 1531).

EMERSON, RALPH WALDO (1803–1882)
The American Scholar. An Oration Delivered Before the Phi Beta Kappa Society, August 31, 1837. In *Complete Essays* (Boston, 1837).
—*The Conduct of Life, Nature, and Other Essays*. Everyman's Library, New York: E. P. Dutton, 1927 (Boston, 1860).
—*English Traits, Representative Men and Other Essays*. Everyman's Library, New York: E. P. Dutton, 1932 (Boston, 1856).
—*Essays*. In *Complete Essays* (First Series, Boston, 1841; Second Series, Boston, 1844).
—*Natural History of Intellect and Other Papers*. New York: Houghton Mifflin, 1899 (1870).
—*Nature*. See *Conduct of Life* (Boston, 1836).
—*Representative Men*. See *English Traits* (Boston, 1850).
—*Society and Solitude and Other Essays*. Everyman's Library, New York: E. P. Dutton, 1922 (Boston, 1870).
—*Threnody*. In *Complete Essays* (London, 1847).
NOTE:
The Complete Essays and Other Writings of Ralph Waldo Emerson. Ed. by B. Atkinson. Modern Library, New York: Random House, 1940.

ENGELS, FRIEDRICH (1820–1895)
The Condition of the Working Classes in England. Trans. by F. Kelly-Wischnewetzky. London: Swan Sonnenschein, 1892 (Leipsic, 1845).
—*Dialectics of Nature*. Ed. by J. B. S. Haldane, trans. by C. P. Dutt. New York: International Publishers, 1940 (*c.* 1872–1882).
—*Germany: Revolution and Counter-Revolution*. New York: International Publishers, 1933 (1851–1852).
—*Herr Eugen Dühring's Revolution in Science*.

Trans. by E. Burns. New York: International Publishers, 1935 (1877–1878).

—*Ludwig Feuerbach and the Outline of Classical German Philosophy*. Ed. by C. P. Dutt. New York: International Publishers, 1934 (1886).

—*The Origin of the Family, Private Property and the State*. New York: International Publishers, 1940 (Zürich, 1884).

—*The Peasant War in Germany*. Trans. by M. J. Olgin. New York: International Publishers, 1926 (1850).

ENRIQUES, FEDERIGO (1871–1946)
Problems of Science. Trans. by K. Royce. Chicago: Open Court, 1914 (*Problemi della scienza*, Bologna, 1906).

EPICTETUS (b. *c.* 60 A.D.)
The Manual. In *The Stoic and Epicurean Philosophers*. Ed. by W. J. Oates. New York: Random House, 1940.

EPICURUS (341–270 B.C.)
Epicurus to Herodotus; . . . . to Menoeceus; . . . . to Pythocles. In *The Stoic and Epicurean Philosophers*. Ed. by W. J. Oates. New York: Random House, 1940.

ERASMUS, DESIDERIUS (*c.* 1467–1536)
Antipolemus: Erasmus Against War. Ed. by J. W. Mackail. Boston: Merrymount Press, 1907 (*Bellum*, Basle, 1517).

—*The Complaint of Peace*. Trans. attributed to T. Paynell. Chicago: Open Court, 1917 (*Querela Pacis Undique Gentium Ejectae Profligataeque*, Basle, 1516).

—*De Pueris Statim ac Liberaliter Instituendis*. Trans. in W. H. Woodward, *Desiderius Erasmus Concerning the Aim and Method of Education*. Cambridge University Press, 1904 (1529).

—*The Education of a Christian Prince*. Trans. by L. K. Born. New York: Columbia University Press, 1936 (*Institutum Principis Christiani*, 1516).

—*The Praise of Folly*. Trans. by H. H. Hudson. Princeton University Press, 1941 (*Encomium Moriae, Id Est Stultitiae Laus*, Paris, 1509?).

ERIGENA, JOANNES SCOTUS (d. *c.* 877)
De Divisione Naturae. Vol. CXXII, *Patrologia Latina* (862–866).

EULER, LEONHARD (1707–1783)
Elements of Algebra. Trans. by J. Hewlett. London: Longmans, Orme & Co., 1840 (*Anleitung zur Algebra*, St. Petersburg, 1770).

—*Letters of Euler on Different Subjects in Natural Philosophy, Addressed to a German Princess*. 2 vols. New York: Harper, 1842 (*Lettres à une princesse d'Allemagne sur divers sujets de physique et de philosophie*, St. Petersburg, 1768–1772).

—*Mechanik oder analytische Darstellung der Wissenschaft von der Bewegung*. Ed. by J. P. Wohlfers. 3 vols. Greifswald: C. A. Koch, 1848–1853 (*Mechanica, sive Motus Scientia*, St. Petersburg, 1736).

EUSEBIUS PAMPHILI, BISHOP OF CAESAREA (*c.* 260–*c.* 340)
The Ecclesiastical History of Eusebius Pamphilius. Ed. and trans. by C. F. Crusé. London: G. Bell & Sons, 1892 (*Historia Ecclesiastica*, 323–340).

EWING, ALFRED CYRIL (1899–1973)
The Definition of Good. New York: Macmillan, 1947.

—*The Individual, the State and World Government*. New York: Macmillan, 1947.

—*The Morality of Punishment, with Some Suggestions for a General Theory of Ethics*. London: K. Paul, Trench, Trübner, 1929.

F

FANFANI, AMINTORE (1908–)
Catholicism, Protestantism and Capitalism. New York: Sheed & Ward, 1935 (*Cattolicesimo e protestantesimo nella formazione storica del capitalismo*, Milan, 1934).

FARADAY, MICHAEL (1791–1867)
Lectures on Education. London: J. W. Parker, 1855.

—*Observations on the Education of the Judgment*. In *The Culture Demanded by Modern Life; a Series of Addresses and Arguments on the Claims of Scientific Education*. Ed. by E. L. Youmans. New York: D. Appleton, 1871 (1854).

—[Various Forces of Matter] *A Course of Six Lectures on the Various Forces of Matter and Their Relations to Each Other*. Ed. by W. Crookes. New York: Harper, 1868 (London, 1860).

FARNELL, LEWIS RICHARD (1856–1934)
Greek Hero Cults and Ideas of Immortality. Oxford: Clarendon Press, 1921.

FARRAND, MAX (1869–1945)
The Framing of the Constitution of the United States. New Haven, Conn.: Yale University Press, 1936 (New Haven, 1913).

FARRAR, FREDERIC WILLIAM (1831–1903)
Chapters on Language. London: Longmans, Green & Co., 1865.

FAUCONNET, PAUL (1874–)
La responsabilité; étude de sociologie. Paris: F. Alcan, 1920.

FEARING, KENNETH (1902–1961)
The Hospital. New York: Random House, 1939.

FECHNER, GUSTAV THEODOR (1801–1887)
Elemente der Psychophysik. 2 vols. Leipsic: Breitkopf & Härtel, 1907 (Leipsic, 1860).

—*Life After Death*. Trans. by M. C. Wadsworth *et al.* New York: Pantheon Books, 1943 (principally from *Das Büchlein vom Leben nach dem Tode*, Leipsic, 1836).

—*Religion of a Scientist*. Sel. and trans. by W. Lowrie. New York: Pantheon Books, 1946.

—*Über die physikalische und philosophische Atomenlehre*. Leipsic: H. Mendelssohn, 1855.

FÉNELON, FRANÇOIS DE SALIGNAC DE LA MOTHE (1651–1715)
Adventures of Telemachus. Ed. by O. W. Wight, trans. by Dr. Hawkesworth. Boston: Houghton Mifflin, 1887 (*Suite du quatrième livre de "l'Odyssée" d'Homère, ou les Avantures de Télémaque, fils d'Ulysse*, Paris, 1699).

—*A Demonstration of the Existence and Attributes of God.* Harrisburg, Pa.: W. Gillmor, 1811 (*Démonstration de l'existence de Dieu, tirée de la connaissance de la nature*, Paris, 1712).
—*Dialogues on Eloquence in General, Particularly That Kind Which Is Fitted for the Pulpit.* Ed. by J. Creighton, trans. by W. Stevenson. Boston: Farrand, Mallory & Co., 1810 (*Dialogues sur l'éloquence en général et sur celle de la chaire en particulier*, Paris, 1718 [1681–1686]).
—*A Treatise on the Education of Daughters.* Ed. and trans. by T. F. Dibdin. Boston: C. Ewer, 1821 (*Éducation des filles*, Paris, 1687).

FENTON, JOSEPH CLIFFORD (1906–)
The Concept of Sacred Theology. Milwaukee, Wis.: Bruce Publishing Co., 1941.

FERGUSON, ADAM (1723–1816)
An Essay on the History of Civil Society. Philadelphia: A. Finley, 1819 (Edinburgh, 1767).

FERRERO, GUGLIELMO (1871–1942)
Peace and War. Trans. by B. Pritchard. New York: Macmillan, 1933 (*La fin des aventures; guerre et paix*, Paris, 1931).
—*The Principles of Power: The Great Political Crises of History.* Trans. by T. R. Jaeckel. New York: Putnam's, 1942.

FEUERBACH, LUDWIG ANDREAS (1804–1872)
The Essence of Christianity. Trans. by M. Evans. London: K. Paul, Trench, Trübner, 1893 (*Das Wesen des Christentums*, Leipsic, 1841).
—*Gedanken über Tod und Unsterblichkeit.* In Vol. I, *Sämtliche Werke.* Ed. by W. Bolin and F. Jodl. 10 vols. Stuttgart: F. Frommann, 1903–1911 (first pub. anon., 1830).

FICHTE, IMMANUEL HERMANN VON (1796–1879)
Die Idee der Persönlichkeit und der individuellen Fortdauer. Elberfelde: Büschler, 1834.
—*Ontologie.* Vol. III, *Grundzüge zum System der Philosophie.* 3 vols. Heidelberg: C. B. Mohr, 1836.

FICHTE, JOHANN GOTTLIEB (1762–1814)
Addresses to the German Nation. Trans. by R. F. Jones and G. H. Turnbull. Chicago: Open Court, 1922 (*Reden an die Deutsche Nation*, Berlin, 1808).
—*The Dignity of Man.* In *The Science of Knowledge*, *q.v.* (*Über die Würde des Menschen*, 1794).
—*The Science of Knowledge.* Trans. by A. E. Kroeger. London: Trübner & Co., 1889 (*Über den Begriff der Wissenschaftslehre oder der sogenannten Philosophie*, Weimar, 1794; *Grundlage der gesammten Wissenschaftslehre*, Leipsic, 1794; *Grundriss des Eigenthümlichen der Wissenschaftslehre in Rücksicht auf das theoretische Vermögen*, Jena, 1795).
—*The Science of Rights.* Trans. by A. E. Kroeger. London: Trübner & Co., 1889 (*Rechtslehre*, Berlin, 1812).
—*The Vocation of Man.* Trans. by W. Smith. Chicago: Open Court, 1940 (*Die Bestimmung des Menschen*, Berlin, 1800).

FICINO, MARSILIO (1433–1499)
Five Questions Concerning the Mind. Trans. by J. L. Burroughs. In *The Renaissance Philosophy of Man.* Ed. by E. Cassirer *et al.* University of Chicago Press, 1948 (1476).

FIELDING, HENRY (1707–1754)
Amelia. 2 vols. Everyman's Library, New York: E. P. Dutton, 1930 (London, 1752).
—*Jonathan Wild.* Everyman's Library, New York: E. P. Dutton, 1932 (London, 1743).
—*Joseph Andrews.* Everyman's Library, New York: E. P. Dutton, 1935 (London, 1742).

FIGGIS, JOHN NEVILLE (1866–1919)
Theory of the Divine Right of Kings. Cambridge University Press, 1914 (Cambridge, 1896).

FILMER, SIR ROBERT (d. 1653)
The Anarchy of a Limited or Mixed Monarchy; or, A Succinct Examination of the Fundamentals of Monarchy. In *Patriarcha, and Other Political Works.* Ed. by P. Laslett. New York: Macmillan, 1949 (London, 1648).
—*Patriarcha. Ibid.* (London, 1680).

FISHER, RONALD AYLMER (1890–1962)
The Design of Experiments. London: Oliver & Boyd, 1942 (London, 1935).

FISKE, JOHN (1842–1901)
Essays: Historical and Literary. 2 vols. New York: Macmillan, 1907 (1895–1900).
—*Life Everlasting.* New York: Houghton Mifflin Co., 1901.

FITZGERALD, FRANCIS SCOTT KEY (1896–1940)
The Great Gatsby. Modern Library, New York: Random House, 1934 (New York, 1925).

FLAUBERT, GUSTAVE (1821–1880)
Madame Bovary. Trans. by E. M. Aveling. Modern Library, New York: Random House, 1940 (Paris, 1857).
—*The Temptation of Saint Anthony.* Trans. by L. Hearn. New York: Harper, 1932 (*La tentation de Saint Antoine*, Paris, 1874).

FLUGEL, JOHN CARL (1884–1955)
The Psycho-Analytic Study of the Family. London: Hogarth Press, 1939 (London, 1921).

FOCH, FERDINAND (1851–1929)
The Principles of War. Trans. by J. de Morinni. New York: H. K. Fly, 1918 (*Des principes de la guerre, conférences faites à l'École supérieure de guerre*, Paris, 1903).

FOERTSCH, HERMANN (d. 1961)
The Art of Modern Warfare. Ed. by G. F. Eliot, trans. by T. W. Knauth. New York: O. Piest, 1940 (*Kriegskunst heute und morgen*, Berlin, 1939).

FONTENELLE, BERNARD LE BOVIER DE (1657–1757)
Conversations on the Plurality of Worlds. Trans. by E. Gunning. London: T. Hurst, 1803 (*Entretiens sur la pluralité des mondes*, Paris, 1686).
—*Histoire des oracles.* Paris: E. Droz, 1934 (Paris, 1686).

FOREST, AIMÉ
La structure métaphysique du concret selon Saint Thomas d'Aquin. Paris: J. Vrin, 1931.

FORSTER, EDWARD MORGAN (1879–1970)
Aspects of the Novel. New York: Harcourt Brace, 1927.

FORTESCUE, SIR JOHN (*c.* 1389–*c.* 1476)
De Laudibus Legum Angliae. Ed. and trans. by S. B. Chrimes. Cambridge University Press, 1942 (*c.* 1470).
—*Governance of England: Otherwise Called the Difference Between an Absolute and a Limited Monarchy*. Ed. by C. Plummer. Oxford: Clarendon Press, 1885 (after 1471).

FOURIER, FRANÇOIS MARIE CHARLES (1772–1837)
Social Destinies. In *General Introduction to Social Sciences*. Ed. by A. Brisbane. New York: C. P. Somerby, 1876 (*Théorie des quatre mouvements et des destinées générales*, Leipsic, 1808).
—*Traité de l'association domestique-agricole*. 2 vols. Paris: Bossange, 1822.

FRANCE, ANATOLE (1844–1924)
The Crime of Sylvestre Bonnard. Trans. by Lafcadio Hearn. New York: Dodd, Mead & Co., 1931 (*Le crime de Sylvestre Bonnard, membre de l'Institut*, Paris, 1881).
—*Penguin Island*. Trans. by A. W. Evans. New York: Dodd, Mead & Co., 1924 (*L'île des pingouins*, Paris, 1908).
—*The Revolt of the Angels*. Trans. by W. Jackson. New York: Dodd, Mead & Co., 1927 (*La révolte des anges*, Paris, 1914).

FRANCIS OF ASSISI, SAINT (*c.* 1182–1226)
The Little Flowers of St. Francis of Assisi with the "Mirror of Perfection" (attributed to St. Francis). Trans. by T. Okey *et al.* Everyman's Library, New York: E. P. Dutton, 1944 (*I fioretti di San Francesco*, *c.* 1322).
—[The Rules] *The Rule of the Friars Minor from the Text of 1210–1221 and The Rule of the Friars Minor from the Text of 1223*. In *The Writings of St. Francis of Assisi*. Ed. and trans. by C. de la Warr. London: Burns, Oates, & Washbourne, 1905.

FRANCIS OF SALES, SAINT (1567–1622)
Introduction to the Devout Life. Trans. by A. Ross. London: Burns, Oates, & Washbourne, 1937 (*Introduction à la vie dévote*, Lyons, 1609).
—*Treatise on the Love of God*. Trans. by H. B. Mackay. Westminster, Md.: Newman Bookshop, 1942 (*Traité de l'amour de Dieu*, Lyons, 1616).

FRANK, ERICH (1883–1949)
Philosophical Understanding and Religious Truth. New York: Oxford University Press, 1945.

FRANK, PHILIPP (1884–1966)
Between Physics and Philosophy. Cambridge, Mass.: Harvard University Press, 1941.

FRANKLIN, BENJAMIN (1706–1790)
The Autobiography of Benjamin Franklin, the Unmutilated and Correct Version. Ed. by J. Bigelow. New York: Putnam's, 1927 (1771–1790).
—*A Dissertation on Liberty and Necessity, Pleasure and Pain*. Ed. by L. C. Worth. New York: Facsimile Text Society, 1930 (London, 1725).
—*Essay on the African Slave Trade*. Philadelphia: D. Humphreys, 1790.
—*Experiments*. Ed. by J. B. Cohen. Cambridge, Mass.: Harvard University Press, 1941 (originally pub. as *Experiments and Observations on Electricity*, London, 1751–1753).
—*On Marriage*. Larchmont, N.Y.: Peter Pauper Press, 1929.
—*On War and Peace*. Boston: Directors of the Old South Work, 1902 (1776–1789).
—*Poor Richard's Almanack and Other Papers*. East Aurora, N.Y.: Roycrofters, 1924 (1728–1780).

FRAZER, SIR JAMES GEORGE (1854–1941)
The Golden Bough; a Study in Comparative Religion. 12 vols. London: Macmillan, 1911–1915 (London, 1890).
—*Man, God, and Immortality; Thoughts on Human Progress*. New York: Macmillan, 1927.
—*Psyche's Task, a Discourse Concerning the Influence of Superstition on the Growth of Institutions*. London: Macmillan, 1909.

FREEMAN, EDWARD AUGUSTUS (1823–1892)
History of Federal Government in Greece and Italy. Augmented ed. by J. B. Bury. New York: Macmillan, 1893 (originally pub. as *History of Federal Government, from the Foundation of the Achaian League to the Disruption of the United States*, London, 1863).

FREGE, FRIEDRICH LUDWIG GOTTLOB (1848–1925)
Grundgesetze der Arithmetik, begriffschriftlich abgeleitet. 2 vols. Jena: H. Pohle, 1893–1903.

FRESNEL, AUGUSTIN JEAN (1788–1827)
Théorie de la lumière. In Vols. I–II, *Oeuvres Complètes*. 3 vols. Paris: Imprimerie Impériale, 1866–1870 (1820).

FREUD, SIGMUND (1856–1939)
A Childhood Memory from "Dichtung und Wahrheit." Collected Papers, XXI (1917).
—*"Civilized" Sexual Morality and Modern Nervousness*. *Ibid.*, VII (1908).
—*A Connection Between a Symbol and a Symptom*. *Ibid.*, XV (1916).
—*Contributions to the Psychology of Love*. *Ibid.*, XI–XIII (1910–1918).
—*The Dynamics of the Transference*. *Ibid.*, XXVIII (1912).
—*The Employment of Dream-Interpretation in Psycho-Analysis*. *Ibid.*, XXVII (1912).
—*The Future of an Illusion*. Trans. by E. Jones. New York: Liveright, 1928 (Vienna, 1927).
—*Leonardo da Vinci: A Psycho-Sexual Study of an Infantile Reminiscence*. Trans. by A. A. Brill. New York: Dodd, Mead & Co., 1932 (Vienna, 1910).
—*Moses and Monotheism*. Trans. by K. Jones. New York: A. A. Knopf, 1939.
—*The Moses of Michelangelo*. *Collected Papers*, XVI (1914).
—*Mourning and Melancholia*. *Ibid.*, VIII (1916).

—*An Outline of Psychoanalysis*. Trans. by J. Strachey. New York: W. W. Norton, 1949 (1939).
—*The Predisposition to Obsessional Neurosis. Collected Papers*, XI (1913).
—*The Psychopathology of Everyday Life*. Trans. by A. A. Brill. New York: Macmillan, 1930 (Berlin, 1904).
—*Recommendations for Physicians on the Psycho-Analytic Method of Treatment. Collected Papers*, XXIX (1912).
—*A Review of "The Antithetical Sense of Primal Words." Ibid.*, X (1910).
—*The Theme of the Three Caskets. Ibid.*, XV (1913).
—*Three Contributions to the Theory of Sex*. Trans. by A. A. Brill. New York: Nervous & Mental Diseases Publishing Co., 1925 (Vienna, 1905).
—*Totem and Taboo; Resemblances Between the Psychic Lives of Savages and Neurotics*. Trans. by A. A. Brill. New York: Dodd, Mead & Co., 1930? (Vienna, 1913).
—*Why War?* In *Civilization, War and Death*. Ed. by John Rickman. New York: Hogarth Press, 1939 (1933).
—*Wit and Its Relation to the Unconscious*. Trans. by A. A. Brill. New York: Moffat, Yard & Co., 1916 (Vienna, 1905).
NOTE:
Collected Papers. Ed. and trans. by J. Riviere. 4 vols. New York: The International Psychoanalytical Press, 1924–1925. (The Roman numerals indicate the number of the paper in that edition.)

FRIEDRICH, CARL JOACHIM (1901–)
Constitutional Government and Democracy; Theory and Practice in Europe and America. Boston: Little, Brown & Co., 1941 (rev. ed. of *Constitutional Government and Politics*, New York, 1937).

FROEBEL, FRIEDRICH WILHELM AUGUST (1782–1852)
The Education of Man. Trans. by W. N. Hailmann. New York: D. Appleton, 1887 (*Menschenerziehung*, Keilhau, 1826).

FROISSART, SIR JOHN (*c*.1338–*c*.1410)
The Chronicles of Froissart. Abr. ed. by G. C. Macaulay, trans. by J. Bourchier. New York: Macmillan, 1904.

FROUDE, JAMES ANTHONY (1818–1894)
The Science of History. A Lecture Delivered at the Royal Institution, 1864. In *Short Stories on Great Subjects*, First Series. New York: Oxford University Press, 1924.

FULLERTON, GEORGE STUART (1859–1925)
The Conception of the Infinite, and the Solution of the Mathematical Antinomies: A Study in Psychological Analysis. Philadelphia: Lippincott, 1887.

FUSTEL DE COULANGES, NUMA DENIS (1830–1889)
The Ancient City: A Study on the Religion, Laws, and Institutions of Greece and Rome. Trans. by W. Small. Boston: Lothrop, Lee & Shepard, 192– (*La cité antique*, Paris, 1864).

G

GAIUS (d. *c*. 180 A.D.)
The Commentaries of Gaius. Ed. and trans. by J. T. Abdy and B. Walker. Cambridge University Press, 1885.

GALEN (*fl*. 2nd century A.D.)
Claudii Galeni Opera Omnia. Ed. by C. G. Kühn. 20 vols. Leipsic: C. Cnobloch, 1821–1833.
—*On Medical Experience*. Trans. by R. Walzer. New York: Oxford University Press, 1944.
—*On the Utility of Parts*. Trans. by R. McCoy. New York: Pantheon Press, 1951.

GALILEO GALILEI (1564–1642)
Dialogo dei massimi sistemi. In Vol. 1, *Galileo Galilei Opera*. Ed. by S. Timpanaro. 2 vols. Milan: Rizzoli & Co., 1936–1938 (Florence, 1632).
—*The Sidereal Messenger of Galileo Galilei and a Part of the Preface to Kepler's Dioptrics*. Ed. and trans. by E. S. Carlos. London: Rivington's, 1880 (*Nuncius Sidereus*, Venice, 1610).

GALSWORTHY, JOHN (1867–1933)
The Forsyte Saga. 3 vols. New York: Scribner's, 1934 (New York, 1922).

GALTON, SIR FRANCIS (1822–1911)
Essays in Eugenics. London: Eugenics Education Society, 1909.
—*Hereditary Genius: An Inquiry into Its Laws and Consequences*. London: Macmillan, 1914 (London, 1869).
—*Inquiries into Human Faculty and Its Development*. Everyman's Library, New York: E. P. Dutton, 1928 (London, 1883).
—*Natural Inheritance*. London: Macmillan, 1889.

GALVANI, LUIGI (1737–1798)
De Viribus Electricitatis in Motu Musculari Commentarius. In *Opere*. Bologna: E. Dall'Olmo, 1841 (1791).

GAMOW, GEORGE (1904–1968)
Atomic Energy in Cosmic and Human Life. New York: Macmillan, 1946.
—*The Birth and Death of the Sun; Stellar Evolution and Sub-Atomic Energy*. New York: Viking Press, 1940.

GARRIGOU-LAGRANGE, RÉGINALD (1877–1964)
God, His Existence and Nature; a Thomistic Solution of Certain Agnostic Antinomies. Trans. by B. Rose. 2 vols. St. Louis, Mo.: Herder Book Co., 1939–1941 (*Dieu, son existence et sa nature*, Paris, 1915).
—*The One God: A Commentary on the First Part of St. Thomas' Theological Summa*. Trans. by B. Rose. St. Louis, Mo.: Herder Book Co., 1943 (*De Deo Uno: Commentarium in Primam Partem S. Thomae*, Paris, 1938).

GAUNILON (11th century)
In Behalf of the Fool. See ANSELM OF CANTERBURY, *Proslogium* (*Liber pro Insipiente Adversus Anselmi in Proslogio Ratiocinationem*, *c*. 1070).

GAUSS, KARL FRIEDRICH (1777–1855)
General Investigations of Curved Surfaces of 1827 and 1825. Trans. by J. C. Morehead and A. M. Hiltebeitel. Princeton University Library, 1902 (*Disquisitiones Generales Circa Superficies Curvas*. In Vol. VI, *Commentationes Societatis Regiae Scientiarum Gottingensis Recentiores*, Göttingen, 1828).
—*Inaugural Lecture on Astronomy and Papers on the Foundations of Mathematics*. Trans. by G. W. Dunnington. Baton Rouge, La.: Louisiana State University Press, 1937 (1808).
—*Untersuchungen über höhere Arithmetik*. Ed. and trans. by H. Maser. Berlin: J. Springer, 1889 (*Disquisitiones Arithmeticae*, Leipsic, 1801).

GENTILI, ALBERICO (1552–1608)
De Jure Belli Libri Tres. Trans. by J. C. Rolfe. 2 vols. Oxford: Clarendon Press, 1933 (Hanau, 1598).

GEORGE ELIOT, pseud. for MARY ANN EVANS (1819–1880)
Daniel Deronda. New York: T. Y. Crowell, 1917 (Edinburgh, 1876).
—*Romola*. Everyman's Library, New York: E. P. Dutton, 1931 (London, 1863).

GEORGE, HENRY (1839–1897)
Progress and Poverty. Modern Library, New York: Random House, 1948 (San Francisco, 1879).

GERSONIDES (LEVI BEN-GERSON) (1288–1344)
The Commentary of Levi ben-Gerson (Gersonides) on the Book of Job. Ed. and trans. by A. L. Lassen. New York: Bloch Publishing Company, 1946.

GIBBON, EDWARD (1737–1794)
An Essay on the Study of Literature. London: T. Becket, 1764 (*Essai sur l'étude de la littérature*, London, 1761).

GIBBS, JOSIAH WILLARD (1839–1903)
Collected Works. 2 vols. New Haven, Conn.: Yale University Press, 1949.

GIBSON, ALEXANDER GEORGE (1875–1950)
The Physician's Art; an Attempt to Expand John Locke's Fragment, De Arte Medica. Oxford: Clarendon Press, 1933.

GIDDINGS, FRANKLIN HENRY (1855–1931)
Democracy and Empire; with Studies of Their Psychological, Economic, and Moral Foundations. New York: Macmillan, 1900.

GIDE, ANDRÉ PAUL GUILLAUME (1869–1951)
The Counterfeiters. Trans. by D. Bussy. Modern Library, New York: Random House, 1931 (*Les faux-monnayeurs*, Paris, 1925).
—*The Immoralist*. Trans. by D. Bussy. New York: A. A. Knopf, 1930 (*L'Immoraliste*, Paris, 1902).
—*Strait Is the Gate*. Trans. by D. Bussy. New York: A. A. Knopf, 1943 (*La porte étroite*, Paris, 1909).

GILBERT DE LA PORRÉE (1076–1154)
Liber de Sex Principiis. In Vol. CLXXXVIII, *Patrologia Latina*.

GILBY, THOMAS (1902–)
Poetic Experience; an Introduction to Thomist Aesthetic. New York: Sheed & Ward, 1934.

GILL, (ARTHUR) ERIC ROWTON PETER JOSEPH (1882–1940)
Art-Nonsense and Other Essays. London: Cassell, 1929.
—*Beauty Looks After Herself*. New York: Sheed & Ward, 1933.
—*The Necessity of Belief: an Enquiry into the Nature of Human Certainty, the Causes of Scepticism and the Grounds of Morality, and a Justification of the Doctrine that the End Is the Beginning*. London: Faber & Faber, 1936.
—*Work and Leisure*. London: Faber & Faber, 1935.
—*Work and Property*. London: J. M. Dent, 1937.

GILSON, ÉTIENNE HENRY (1884–)
Being and Some Philosophers. Toronto: Pontifical Institute of Mediaeval Studies, 1949.
—*Christianisme et philosophie*. Paris: J. Vrin, 1936.
—*God and Philosophy*. New Haven, Conn.: Yale University Press, 1941.
—*History of Philosophy and Philosophical Education*. Milwaukee, Wis.: Marquette University Press, 1948 (1947).
—*L'être et l'essence*. Paris: J. Vrin, 1948.
—*Réalisme thomiste et critique de la connaissance*. Paris: J. Vrin, 1939.
—*Reason and Revelation in the Middle Ages*. New York: Scribner's, 1938.
—*The Unity of Philosophical Experience*. New York: Scribner's, 1937.

GLANVILL, JOSEPH (1636–1680)
The Vanity of Dogmatizing. New York: Columbia University Press, Facsimile Text Society, 1931 (London, 1661).

GLOVER, TERROT REAVELEY (1869–1943)
Greek Byways. New York: Macmillan, 1932.

GOBINEAU, JOSEPH ARTHUR, COMTE DE (1816–1882)
The Inequality of Human Races. Trans. by A. Collins. New York: Putnam's, 1915 (Vol. I, *Essai sur l'inégalité des races humaines*, Paris, 1853).

GODWIN, WILLIAM (1756–1836)
An Enquiry Concerning Political Justice, and Its Influence on General Virtue and Happiness. 2 vols. London: J. Watson, 1842 (London, 1793).

GOETHE, JOHANN WOLFGANG VON (1749–1832)
Beiträge zur Optik. In Vol. XXVII, *Goethes Sämmtliche Werke*. 30 vols. Stuttgart and Tübingen: Cotta, 1850–1851.
—*Conversations of Goethe with Eckermann and Soret*. Trans. by J. Oxenford. New York: G. Bell & Sons, 1892 (*Gespräche mit Goethe in den letzten Jahren seines Lebens*, Leipsic and Magdeburg, 1836–1848 [1822–1832]).
—*The Elective Affinities*. In *Novels and Tales by*

Goethe. London: G. Bohn, 1854 (*Die Wahlverwandtschaften*, Tübingen, 1809).

—*The Maxims and Reflections of Goethe*. Trans. by B. Saunders. New York: Macmillan, 1893.

—[Metamorphose] *Versuch, die Metamorphose der Pflanzen zu erklären*. In Vol. XXXIX, *Goethes Sämtliche Werke* ("Jubiläumsausgabe"). 40 vols. Berlin: J. G. Cotta, 1902–1907 (1790).

—*Poetry and Truth from My Own Life*. Trans. by J. Oxenford and A. J. W. Morrison. 2 vols. New York: Harcourt Brace, 1925 (*Aus meinem Leben: Dichtung und Wahrheit*, Tübingen, 1811–1814).

—*The Sorrows of Young Werther*. Trans. by R. D. Boylan. In *Novels and Tales*. See *Elective Affinities* (*Die Leiden des jungen Werther*, Leipsic, 1774).

—*Theory of Colours*. Trans. by C. L. Eastlake. London: J. Murray, 1840 (*Zur Farbenlehre*, Tübingen, 1810).

—*Travels in Italy: Together with His Second Residence in Rome and Fragments on Italy*. Trans. by A. J. W. Morrison and C. Nisbet. London: G. Bell, 1885 (*Die italienische Reise*, Tübingen, 1816–1817).

—*William Meister's Apprenticeship and Travels*. Trans. by Thomas Carlyle. Everyman's Library, New York: E. P. Dutton, 1903 (*Wilhelm Meisters Lehrjahre*, Berlin, 1795–1796; *Wilhelm Meisters Wanderjahre, oder die Entsagenden*, Stuttgart, 1821).

—*Zur Natur- und Wissenschaftslehre*. In Vol. XXXIX, *Goethes Sämtliche Werke* ("Jubiläumsausgabe") See *Metamorphose*.

GOGOL, NIKOLAI VASILIEVICH (1809–1852)
Dead Souls. Trans. by C. Garnett. Modern Library, New York: Random House, 1936 (first pub., 1842).

—*The Government Inspector and Other Plays*. Trans. by C. Garnett. New York: A. A. Knopf, 1927 (first performed, 1836).

—*The Nose*. In *The Overcoat, q.v.* (1836).

—*The Overcoat and Other Stories*. Trans. by C. Garnett. New York: A. A. Knopf, 1923 (first pub., 1842).

—*Taras Bulba, a Tale of the Cossacks*. Trans. by I. Hapgood. New York: A. A. Knopf, 1931 (first pub., 1835).

GOLDSMITH, OLIVER (1728–1774)
The Citizen of the World and *The Bee*. Ed. by A. Dobson. Everyman's Library, New York: E. P. Dutton, 1934 (London, 1760–1761).

—*The Deserted Village*. In *Poems and Plays*. Ed. by A. Dobson. Everyman's Library, New York: E. P. Dutton, 1930 (London, 1770).

—*She Stoops to Conquer*. *Ibid*. (London, 1773).

—*The Vicar of Wakefield*. Everyman's Library, New York: E. P. Dutton, 1934 (London, 1766).

GOLDSTEIN, KURT (1878–1965)
The Organism: A Holistic Approach to Biology Derived from Pathological Data in Man. New York: American Book Co., 1939 (*Der Aufbau des Organismus*, The Hague, 1934).

GORKY, MAXIM, pseud. for ALEXEY MAXIMOVICH PESHKOV (1868–1936)
Decadence. Trans. by V. Dewey. New York: R. M. McBride, 1927 (Berlin, 1925).

—*Forty Years—the Life of Clim Samghin* [tetralogy comprising: Vol. I, *Bystander*, trans. by B. G. Guerney; Vol. II, *The Magnet*, trans. by A. Bakshy. Both New York: Cape & Smith, 1930; 1931. Vol. III, *Other Fires*, trans. by A. Bakshy. New York: D. Appleton, 1933. Vol. IV, *The Specter*, trans. by A. Bakshy. New York: D. Appleton-Century Co., 1938]. (Moscow, 1927; 1928; 1931; 1937).

—*Mother*. New York: D. Appleton, 1919 (first pub., 1907).

GOSSE, SIR EDMUND WILLIAM (1849–1928)
Father and Son; a Study of Two Temperaments. New York: Oxford University Press, 1934 (London, 1907).

GOURMONT, RÉMY DE (1858–1915)
The Natural Philosophy of Love. Trans. by Ezra Pound. New York: Liveright, 1932 (*Physique de l'amour: essai sur l'instinct sexuel*, Paris, 1903).

GOWER, JOHN (*c.*1325–1408)
Confessio Amantis. In *The English Works of John Gower*. Ed. by G. C. Macaulay. 2 vols. London: K. Paul, Trench, Trübner, 1900–1901 (1390).

GRACIÁN Y MORALES, BALTASAR (1601–1658)
The Art of Worldly Wisdom. Trans. by J. Jacobs. New York: Macmillan, 1945 (*Oráculo manual y arte*, Aragon, *c.*1647).

GRATRY, AUGUSTE JOSEPH ALPHONSE (1805–1872)
Logic. Trans. by H. and M. Singer. La Salle, Ill.: Open Court, 1944 (*Philosophie. Logique*, Paris, 1855).

—*Philosophie. De la connaissance de l'âme*. Paris: C. Douniol, 1857.

GRAY, THOMAS (1716–1771)
Elegy Written in a Country Church-Yard. In *The Poetical Works of Gray and Collins*. Ed. by A. L. Poole. New York: Oxford University Press, 1926 (London, 1751).

—*The Progress of Poesy. A Pindaric Ode*. *Ibid*. (London, 1757).

GREEN, SANFORD MOON (1807–1901)
Crime: Its Nature, Causes, Treatment and Prevention. Philadelphia: Lippincott, 1889.

GREEN, THOMAS HILL (1836–1882)
Lectures on the Principles of Political Obligation. Ed. by B. Bosanquet. New York: Longmans, Green & Co., 1941 (1879–1880).

—*Prolegomena to Ethics*. Ed. by A. C. Bradley. Oxford: Clarendon Press, 1883 (1878–1882).

GREGORY, SIR RICHARD ARMAN (1864–1952)
Discovery; or, The Spirit and Service of Science. New York: Macmillan, 1923 (London, 1916).

GREGORY OF NYSSA, SAINT (*c.* 335-*c.* 395)
On the Soul and the Resurrection. In Vol. V, *A Select Library of Nicene and Post-Nicene Fathers of the Christian Church*, Second Series. Ed. by P.

Schaff and H. Wace. 14 vols. New York: Christian Literature Co., 1890–1900 (380).

GREGORY OF TOURS, SAINT (*c.* 538–*c.* 594)
History of the Franks. Trans. by E. Brehaut. In *Records of Civilization: Sources and Studies*. New York: Columbia University Press, 1926 (*Gregori Turonensis Episcopi Historiarum Precipue Gallicarum Libri X*, 576?–591).
—[Libri Septem Miraculorum] *De Gloria Beatorum Martyrum; De Passione, Virtutibus, et Gloria Sancti Juliani Martyris; Liber de Gloria Beatorum Confessorum; De Miraculis Sancti Martini Episcopi, Libri Quatuor*. In Vol. LXXI, *Patrologia Latina* (573–594).

GREGORY THE GREAT, POPE (SAINT GREGORIUS I) (*c.* 540–604)
Morals on the Book of Job, by S. Gregory the Great, the First Pope of That Name. Trans. by J. Bliss. 3 vols. Oxford: J. H. Parker, 1844–1850 (*Magna Moralia*, 578?–600?).

GRIMM, JAKOB LUDWIG KARL (1785–1863)
Über den Ursprung der Sprache. Berlin: F. Dümmler, 1851.

GROOS, KARL (1861–1946)
The Play of Animals. Trans. by E. L. Baldwin. New York: D. Appleton, 1898.
—*The Play of Men*. Trans. by E. L. Baldwin. New York: D. Appleton, 1899 (*Die Spiele der Menschen*, Jena, 1896).

GROSSE, ERNST (1862–1927)
The Beginnings of Art. New York: D. Appleton, 1914 (*Die Anfänge der Kunst*, Leipsic, 1894).

GROSSETESTE, ROBERT (*c.* 1175–1253)
On Truth. In Vol. I, *Selections from Medieval Philosophers*. Ed. and trans. by Richard McKeon. 2 vols. New York: Scribner's, 1929–1930 (*De Veritate*, *c.* 1239).

GROTIUS, HUGO (1583–1645)
The Rights of War and Peace, Including the Law of Nature and of Nations. Trans. by A. C. Campbell. London: M. W. Dunne, 1901 (*De Jure Belli et Pacis*, Paris, 1625).

GUERICKE, OTTO VON (1602–1686)
Experimenta Nova. Leipsic: W. Drugulin, 1881 (1672).

GUICCIARDINI, FRANCESCO (1483–1540)
Dialogo e discorsi del reggimento di Firenze. Ed. by R. Palmarocchi. Bari: Laterza, 1932 (1521–1526).

GUIZOT, FRANÇOIS PIERRE GUILLAUME (1787–1874)
General History of Civilization in Europe. Ed. by G. W. Knight. New York: D. Appleton, 1907 (*Histoire générale de la civilisation en Europe*, Paris, 1828).

GUYAU, JEAN MARIE (1854–1888)
Esquisse d'une morale sans obligation ni sanction. Paris: F. Alcan, 1935 (Paris, 1885).
—*L'art au point de vue sociologique*. Paris: F. Alcan, 1909 (Paris, 1889).

H

HAECKEL, ERNST HEINRICH (1834–1919)
The Riddle of the Universe at the Close of the Nineteenth Century. Trans. by J. McCabe. New York: Harper, 1900 (*Die Welträthsel. Gemeinverständliche Studien über monistische Philosophie*, Bonn, 1899).

HAHNEMANN, SAMUEL (1755–1843)
Organon of the Rational Art of Healing. Trans. by C. E. Wheeler. Everyman's Library, New York: E. P. Dutton, 1913 (*Organon der rationellen Heilkunde*, Dresden, 1810).

HALDANE, JOHN BURDON SANDERSON (1892–1964)
Daedalus; or, Science and the Future. New York: E. P. Dutton, 1924.
—*The Inequality of Man, and Other Essays*. London: Chatto & Windus, 1932.
—*Possible Worlds and Other Essays*. London: Chatto & Windus, 1927.

HALDANE, JOHN SCOTT (1860–1936)
Mechanism, Life and Personality; an Examination of the Mechanistic Theory of Life and Mind. New York: E. P. Dutton, 1923 (London, 1913).
—*The Sciences and Philosophy*. Garden City, N.Y.: Doubleday Doran, 1929.

HALDANE, JOHN SCOTT and PRIESTLEY, JOHN GILLIES (1880–1941)
Respiration. New Haven, Conn.: Yale University Press, 1935 (New Haven, Conn., 1922).

HAMILTON, SIR WILLIAM (1788–1856)
Discussions on Philosophy and Literature, Education and University Reform. New York: Harper, 1856 (1829–1839).
—*Lectures on Metaphysics and Logic*. Ed. by H. L. Mansel and J. Veitch. 4 vols. Edinburgh: W. Blackwood, 1877 (Edinburgh, 1859–1860 [1836–1838]).

HAMILTON, WILLIAM GERARD (1729–1796)
Parliamentary Logic. Ed. by C. S. Kenny. Cambridge: W. Heffer & Sons, 1927 (1754–1796).

HAMILTON, SIR WILLIAM ROWAN (1805–1865)
Dynamics. In Vol. II, *Mathematical Papers*. Ed. by A. W. Conway and J. L. Synge. Cambridge University Press, 1931 (1834).
—*Lectures on Quaternions*. Dublin: Hodge & Smith, 1853.

HAMSUN, KNUT, pseud. for KNUT PEDERSEN (1859–1952)
Growth of the Soil. Trans. by W. W. Worster. Modern Library, New York: Random House, 1935 (Christiania, 1917).

HARDY, GODFREY HAROLD (1877–1947)
A Course of Pure Mathematics. Cambridge University Press, 1938 (Cambridge, 1908).
—*A Mathematician's Apology*. Cambridge University Press, 1940.

HARDY, THOMAS (1840–1928)
The Dynasts: A Drama of the Napoleonic Wars, in Three Parts, Nineteen Acts, and One Hundred and

Thirty Scenes. New York: Macmillan, 1936 (London, 1903–1908).
—*Jude the Obscure*. Modern Library, New York: Random House, 1927 (1894–1895).
—*Life's Little Ironies; a Set of Tales, with Some Colloquial Sketches*. London: Macmillan, 1928 (London, 1894).
—*The Return of the Native*. Modern Library, New York: Random House, 1949 (London, 1878).
—*Tess of the D'Urbervilles*. Modern Library, New York: Random House, 1932 (London, 1891).

HARNACK, ADOLF VON (1851–1930)
History of Dogma. Trans. by N. Buchanan. 7 vols. London: Williams & Norgate, 1894–1903 (*Lehrbuch der Dogmengeschichte*, Tübingen, 1885).

HARRINGTON, JAMES (1611–1677)
The Commonwealth of Oceana. London: G. Routledge, 1887 (London, 1656).

HARRIS, JAMES (1709–1780)
Hermes, or A Philosophical Inquiry Concerning Universal Grammar. London: J. Collingwood, 1825 (London, 1751).
—*Three Treatises. The First Concerning Art. The Second Concerning Music, Painting, and Poetry. The Third Concerning Happiness*. London: F. Wingrave, 1792 (London, 1744).
—*Upon the Rise and Progress of Criticism*. London, 1752.

HARRIS, JAMES RENDEL (1852–1941)
Boanerges. Cambridge University Press, 1913.

HARRISON, JANE ELLEN (1850–1928)
Ancient Art and Ritual. New York: Henry Holt, 1913.

HARTLAND, EDWIN SIDNEY (1848–1927)
Primitive Society, the Beginnings of the Family and the Reckoning of Descent. London: Methuen, 1921.

HARTLEY, DAVID (1705–1757)
Observations on Man, His Frame, His Duty and His Expectations. London: T. Tegg, 1834 (London, 1749).

HARTMANN, EDUARD VON (1842–1906)
Kategorienlehre. Leipsic: H. Haacke, 1896.
—*Philosophy of the Unconscious*. Trans. by W. C. Coupland. London: Trübner & Co., 1884 (*Die Philosophie des Unbewussten*, Berlin, 1869).

HARTMANN, NICOLAI (1882–1950)
Ethics. Vol. I, *Moral Phenomena;* Vol. II, *Moral Values;* Vol. III, *Moral Freedom*. Trans. by S. Coit. New York: Macmillan, 1932 (*Ethik*, Berlin, 1926).

HARTSHORNE, CHARLES (1897–)
The Divine Relativity. New Haven, Conn.: Yale University Press, 1948.
—*Man's Vision of God, and the Logic of Theism*. Chicago: Clark & Co., 1941.
—*The Philosophy and Psychology of Sensation*. University of Chicago Press, 1934.

HAUPTMANN, GERHART JOHANN ROBERT (1862–1946)
The Island of the Great Mother, or, The Miracle of Île des Dames: A Story from the Utopian Archipelago. Trans. by W. and E. Muir. New York: Viking Press, 1925 (*Die Insel der grossen Mutter*, Berlin, 1924).
—*The Weavers. A Drama of the Forties*. Trans. by M. Morison. New York: B. W. Huebsch, 1911 (*Die Weber*, Berlin, 1892).

HAWTHORNE, NATHANIEL (1804–1864)
The Blithedale Romance. Everyman's Library, New York: E. P. Dutton, 1926 (Boston, 1852).
—*The Scarlet Letter*. Everyman's Library, New York: E. P. Dutton, 1947 (Boston, 1850).

HAZLITT, WILLIAM (1778–1830)
Lectures on the English Poets. New York: Oxford University Press, 1924 (London, 1818).
—*My First Acquaintance with Poets*. In *Selections from William Hazlitt*. Ed. by W. D. Howe. New York: Ginn & Co., 1913 (1823).
—*On Taste*. In *Sketches and Essays*. New York: Oxford University Press, 1936 (1818–1819).
—*On the Feeling of Immortality in Youth*. In *Selections*. See above (1827).
—*Table Talk*. Everyman's Library, New York: E. P. Dutton, 1930 (London, 1821–1822).

HEAD, HENRY (1861–1940)
Aphasia and Kindred Disorders of Speech. 2 vols. New York: Macmillan, 1926.

HEAVISIDE, OLIVER (1850–1925)
Electromagnetic Theory. 3 vols. New York: Van Nostrand, 1894–1912.

HECHT, SELIG (1892–1947)
Explaining the Atom. New York: Viking Press, 1947.

HEGEL, GEORG WILHELM FRIEDRICH (1770–1831)
Lectures on the History of Philosophy. Trans. by E. S. Haldane and F. H. Simson. London: K. Paul, Trench, Trübner, 1894 (1822–1831).
—*Lectures on the Philosophy of Religion Together with a Work on the Proofs of the Existence of God*. Trans. by E. B. Speirs and J. B. Sanderson. 3 vols. London: K. Paul, Trench, Trübner, 19—? (1821–1831).
—*The Logic of Hegel*. Trans. by W. Wallace. Oxford: Clarendon Press, 1892 (*Enzyklopädie der philosophischen Wissenschaften, I. Teil: Die Wissenschaft der Logik*, Heidelberg, 1817).
—*On the Proofs of the Existence of God*. See *Lectures on the Philosophy of Religion* (Berlin, 1832 [1831]).
—*The Phenomenology of Mind*. Trans. by J. B. Baille. 2 vols. New York: Macmillan, 1910 (*System der Wissenschaft, I: Die Phänomenologie des Geistes*, Bamberg, 1807).
—*The Philosophy of Fine Art*. Trans. by F. P. B. Omaston. 4 vols. London: G. Bell & Sons, 1920 (1817–1829).
—*The Philosophy of Mind*. Trans. by W. Wallace. Oxford: Clarendon Press, 1894 (*Enzyklopädie der philosophischen Wissenschaften, 3. Teil: Die Philosophie des Geistes*, Heidelberg, 1817).
—*The Positivity of the Christian Religion*. In *Early*

Theological Writings. Trans. by T. M. Knox. University of Chicago Press, 1948.
—*Science of Logic*. Trans. by W. H. Johnston and L. G. Struther. 2 vols. London: Allen & Unwin, 1929 (*Wissenschaft der Logik*, Nürnberg, 1812–1816).
—*The Spirit of Christianity*. In *Early Theological Writings*. See *Positivity*.

HEIDEGGER, MARTIN (1889–)
Sein und Zeit. Halle: M. Niemeyer, 1935 (1927).
—*Was ist Metaphysik?* Frankfort: V. Klostermann, 1943 (Bonn, 1929).

HEINE, HEINRICH (1797–1856)
Gods in Exile. In *The Prose Writings of Heinrich Heine*. Ed. by H. Ellis. London: W. Scott, 1887 (1853).
—*Religion and Philosophy in Germany: A Fragment*. Trans. by J. Snodgrass. London: K. Paul, Trench, Trübner, 1891 (1834).

HEISENBERG, WERNER (1901–)
The Physical Principles of the Quantum Theory. Trans. by C. Eckart and F. C. Hoyt. University of Chicago Press, 1930.

HELMHOLTZ, HERMANN LUDWIG FERDINAND VON (1821–1894)
Counting and Measuring. Trans. by C. L. Bryan. New York: Van Nostrand, 1930 (1887).
—*On the Sensation of Tone as a Physiological Basis for the Theory of Music*. Trans. by A. J. Ellis. London: Longmans, Green & Co., 1930 (*Die Lehre von den Tonempfindungen als physiologische Grundlage für die Theorie der Musik*, Brunswick, 1863).
—*Popular Lectures on Scientific Subjects*. Trans. by E. Atkinson *et al.* First and second series, New York: D. Appleton & Co., 1900; 1901 (*Populäre wissenschaftliche Vorträge*, Brunswick, 1865; 1876).
—*Treatise on Physiological Optics*. Ed. and trans. by J. P. Southall. 3 vols. Rochester, N.Y.: Optical Society of America, 1924–1925 (*Handbuch der physiologischen Optik*, Leipsic, 1856).

HELVÉTIUS, CLAUDE ADRIEN (1715–1771)
Traité de l'esprit. 4 vols. Paris: Bibliothèque Nationale, 1880 (Paris, 1758).
—*A Treatise on Man; His Intellectual Faculties and His Education*. Trans. by W. Hooper. 2 vols. London: Vernor, Hood, & Sharpe, 1810 (1771).

HENDEL, CHARLES WILLIAM (1890–)
Civilization and Religion. New Haven, Conn.: Yale University Press, 1948 (1947).

HENDERSON, LAWRENCE JOSEPH (1878–1942)
Blood; A Study in General Physiology. New Haven, Conn.: Yale University Press, 1928.
—*The Fitness of the Environment; an Inquiry into the Biological Significance of the Properties of Matter*. New York: Macmillan, 1927 (New York, 1913).
—*The Order of Nature; an Essay*. Cambridge, Mass.: Harvard University Press, 1917.

HERBART, JOHANN FRIEDRICH (1776–1841)
The Science of Education, Its General Principles Deduced from Its Aim [with *The Aesthetic Revelation of the World*]. Trans. by H. M. and E. Felkin. Boston: D. C. Heath, 1902 (*Allgemeine Pädagogik aus dem Zweck der Erziehung abgeleitet*, Göttingen, 1806).

HERBERT, GEORGE (1593–1633)
The Temple and A Priest to the Temple. Everyman's Library, New York: E. P. Dutton, 1927.

HERBERT OF CHERBURY (BARON EDWARD HERBERT) (1583–1648)
De Religione Laici. Ed. and trans. by H. R. Hutcheson. New Haven, Conn.: Yale University Press, 1944 (originally pub. with *De Causis Errorum*, London, 1645).
—*De Veritate*. Trans. by M. H. Carré. Bristol: J. W. Arrowsmith, 1937 (Paris, 1624).

HERDER, JOHANN GOTTFRIED VON (1744–1803)
God, Some Conversations. Trans. by F. H. Burkhardt. New York: Veritas Press, 1940 (*Gott. Einige Gespräche*, Gotha, 1787).
—*Outlines of a Philosophy of the History of Man*. Trans. by T. O. Churchill. London: Hansard, 1803 (*Ideen zu einer Philosophie der Geschichte der Menschheit*, Riga, 1784–1791).
—*Plastik: Einige Wahrnehmungen über Form und Gestalt aus Pygmalion's bildendem Traume*. In Vol. VIII, *Herder's Sämtliche Werke*. Ed. by B. Suphan. 33 vols. Berlin: Weidmann, 1877–1913 (Riga, 1778).

HERING, EWALD (1834–1918)
Memory; Lectures on the Specific Energies of the Nervous System. Chicago: Open Court, 1913 (*Über das Gedächtnis als eine allgemeine Function der organisierten Materie*, Vienna, 1870).

HERSCHEL, SIR JOHN FREDERICK WILLIAM (1792–1871)
Familiar Lectures on Scientific Subjects. New York: G. Routledge, 1869 (London, 1866).
—*A Preliminary Discourse on the Study of Natural Philosophy*. London: Longman, Brown, Green & Longman, 1851 (from *Cabinet Cyclopaedia*, 1830).

HERTWIG, OSCAR (1849–1922)
The Cell; Outlines of General Anatomy and Physiology. Ed. by H. Johnstone-Campbell, trans. by M. Campbell. New York: Macmillan, 1909 (*Die Zelle und die Gewebe*, Jena, 1893–1898).

HERTZ, HEINRICH RUDOLPH (1857–1894)
The Principles of Mechanics Presented in a New Form. Trans. by D. E. Jones and J. T. Walley. New York: Macmillan, 1899 (*Die Prinzipien der Mechanik in neuem Zusammenhange dargestellt*, Leipsic, 1895 [1891–1894]).

HESIOD (8th century? B.C.)
Theogony. In *Hesiod, the Homeric Hymns and Homerica*. Trans. by H. Evelyn-White. Loeb Library, Cambridge, Mass.: Harvard University Press, 1936.
—*Works and Days*. *Ibid.*

Hess, Moses (1812–1875)
Sozialistische Aufsätze, 1841–1847. Ed. by T. Zlocisti. Berlin: Welt Verlag, 1921.

Heywood, Thomas (*c*.1574–1641)
The Hierarchie of the Blessed Angells. Their Names, Orders and Offices. The Fall of Lucifer with His Angells. London: A. Islip, 1635.
—*A Woman Killed with Kindness*. In *Thomas Heywood*. Mermaid Series, London: T. F. Unwin, 1903 (1602?).

Hilbert, David (1862–1943)
The Foundations of Geometry. Trans. by E. Y. Townsend. Chicago: Open Court, 1902 (1899).

Hilbert, David and Ackermann, W. (1896–)
Grundzüge der theoretischen Logik. New York: Dover Publications, 1946 (Berlin, 1928).

Hildebrand, Dietrich von (1889–)
In Defense of Purity: An Analysis of the Catholic Ideal of Purity and Virginity. New York: Sheed & Ward, 1938 (*Reinheit und Jungfräulichkeit*, Cologne, 1927).

Hinton, James (1822–1875)
The Mystery of Pain: A Book for the Sorrowful. London: C. K. Paul & Co., 1866.

Hirn, Yrjö (1870–1952)
The Origins of Art. New York: Macmillan, 1900.

Hirsch, Max (1853–1909)
Democracy Versus Socialism, a Critical Examination of Socialism as a Remedy for Social Injustice and an Exposition of the Single-Tax Doctrine. New York: Macmillan, 1901.

Hirsch, Samson Raphael (1808–1888)
The Nineteen Letters of Ben Uziel, Being a Spiritual Presentation of the Principles of Judaism. Trans. by B. Drachman. New York: Bloch Publishing Co., 1942 (*Neunzehn Briefe über Judenthum*, Altona, 1836).

Hobbes, Thomas (1588–1679)
The Art of Sophistry. In Vol. vi, *English Works*.
—*Behemoth*. Ed. by F. Tönnies. London: Simpkin, 1889 (1668).
—*Concerning Body*. In Vol. i, *English Works* (*Elementa Philosophiae Sectio Prima: de Corpore*, London, 1655).
—*A Dialogue Between a Philosopher and a Student of the Common Laws of England*. In Vol. vi, *ibid*. (1667?).
—*Dialogus Physicus de Natura Aeris*. In Vol. iv, *Opera Philosophica quae Latine Scripsit Omnia*. Ed. by Sir William Molesworth. 5 vols. London: Longman, Brown, Green, & Longman, 1839–1845 (1661).
—*The Elements of Law, Natural and Politic* and *Human Nature, or The Fundamental Elements of Policy*. Ed. by F. Tönnies. Cambridge University Press, 1928 (London, 1650).
—*Examinatio et Emendatio Mathematicae Hodiernae*. In Vol. v, *Opera*. See above (1660).
—*Philosophical Rudiments Concerning Government and Society*. In Vol. ii, *English Works* (Amsterdam, 1647).
—*Six Lessons to the Savilian Professors of Mathematics*. In Vol. vii, *ibid*. (London, 1656).
—*A Treatise of Liberty and Necessity*. In Vol. iv, *ibid*. (London, 1654).
—*The Whole Art of Rhetoric*. In Vol. vi, *ibid*. (1679).
note:
The English Works of Thomas Hobbes. Ed. by Sir William Molesworth. 11 vols. London: J. Bohn, 1839–1845.

Hobhouse, Leonard Trelawney (1864–1929)
The Elements of Social Justice. New York: Henry Holt, 1922.
—*The Metaphysical Theory of the State; a Criticism*. New York: Macmillan, 1926 (New York, 1918).
—*Mind in Evolution*. London: Macmillan, 1926 (New York, 1901).
—*Morals in Evolution: A Study in Comparative Ethics*. New York: Henry Holt, 1915 (New York, 1906).

Hobson, Ernest William (1856–1933)
The Theory of Functions of a Real Variable and the Theory of Fourier's Series. 2 vols. Cambridge University Press, 1926–1927 (Cambridge, 1907).

Hobson, John Atkinson (1858–1940)
Democracy and a Changing Civilisation. London: J. Lane, 1934.
—*The Evolution of Modern Capitalism*. New York: Scribner's, 1917 (New York, 1894).
—*Towards International Government*. New York: Macmillan, 1915.
—*Work and Wealth: A Human Valuation*. London: Allen & Unwin, 1933 (New York, 1914).

Hocart, Arthur Maurice (1884–1939)
Kingship. New York: Oxford University Press, 1927.

Hocking, William Ernest (1873–1966)
Freedom of the Press. University of Chicago Press, 1947.
—*Man and the State*. New Haven, Conn.: Yale University Press, 1926.
—*Present Status of the Philosophy of Law and of Rights*. New Haven, Conn.: Yale University Press, 1926.
—*Thoughts on Death and Life*. New York: Harper, 1937.

Hodder, Alfred (1866–1907)
The Adversaries of the Sceptic; or, The Specious Present, A New Inquiry into Human Knowledge. New York: Macmillan, 1901.

Hodgson, Shadworth Hollway (1832–1912)
The Metaphysic of Experience. 4 vols. New York: Longmans, Green & Co., 1898.
—*The Theory of Practice, an Ethical Enquiry*. 2 vols. London: Longman, Green, Reader, & Dyer, 1870.
—*Time and Space; a Metaphysical Essay*. London: Longman, Green, Reader, & Dyer, 1865.

HOLBACH, PAUL HENRI THIRY, BARON D' (1723–1789)
The System of Nature; or, Laws of the Moral and Physical World. Trans. by H. D. Robinson. Boston: J. P. Mendum, 1889 (*Système de la nature, ou Des lois du monde physique et moral,* London, 1770).

HOLMES, OLIVER WENDELL (1809–1894)
Currents and Counter-Currents in Medical Science. In *Medical Essays, 1842–1882.* Boston: Houghton Mifflin Co., 1911 (Boston, 1860).

HOLMES, OLIVER WENDELL, JR. (1841–1935)
The Common Law. Boston: Little, Brown & Co., 1938 (Boston, 1881).

HOLT, EDWIN BISSELL (1873–1946)
The Concept of Consciousness. New York: Macmillan, 1914.

HOOK, SIDNEY (1902–)
Education for Modern Man. New York: Dial Press, 1946.
—*The Metaphysics of Pragmatism.* Chicago: Open Court, 1927.
—*Reason, Social Myths and Democracy.* New York: John Day Co., 1940.

HOOKER, RICHARD (1553–1600)
Of the Laws of Ecclesiastical Polity. Everyman's Library, New York: E. P. Dutton, 1907 (London, 1594?–1597).

HORACE (QUINTUS HORATIUS FLACCUS) (65–8 B.C.)
The Art of Poetry. In *The Complete Works of Horace.* Trans. by E. H. Blakeney. Modern Library, New York: Random House, 1936 (13–8 B.C.).
—[Epistles] *Letters in Verse. Ibid.* (19–8 B.C.).
—[Satires] *Conversation Pieces. Ibid.* (35 B.C.; 29 B.C.).

HOUSMAN, ALFRED ERNEST (1859–1936)
The Name and Nature of Poetry. New York: Macmillan, 1933.

HOWARD, JOHN (*c.* 1726–1790)
The State of the Prisons. Everyman's Library, New York: E. P. Dutton, 1929 (Warrington, 1777–1780).

HOWELLS, WILLIAM DEAN (1837–1920)
The Rise of Silas Lapham. Boston: Houghton Mifflin Co., 1937 (Boston, 1885).

HSIAO, KUNG-CHUAN
Political Pluralism; a Study in Contemporary Political Theory. New York: Harcourt Brace, 1927.

HUBBLE, EDWIN POWELL (1889–1953)
The Realm of the Nebulae. New Haven, Conn.: Yale University Press, 1936.

HUDSON, MICHAEL (1605–1648)
The Divine Right of Government, Naturall, and Politique. London, 1647.

HÜGEL, FRIEDRICH VON (1852–1925)
Essays and Addresses on the Philosophy of Religion. First and Second Series. New York: E. P. Dutton, 1921; 1926 (1904–1922).
—*Eternal Life: A Study of Its Implications and Applications.* Edinburgh: T. & T. Clark, 1912.
—*The Mystical Element of Religion as Studied in Saint Catherine of Genoa and Her Friends.* 2 vols. New York: E. P. Dutton, 1923 (New York, 1908).

HUGH OF SAINT VICTOR (1096–1141)
De Sacramentis. In Vol. CLXXVI, *Patrologia Latina* (1134).
—*Didascalicon: De Studio Legendi.* Ed. by C. H. Buttimer. Washington: Catholic University Press, 1937.

HUGO, VICTOR MARIE (1802–1885)
Les Misérables. Trans. by C. E. Wilbour. Modern Library, New York: Random House, 1931 (Paris, 1862).
—*Ninety-Three.* Trans. by F. L. Benedict. 2 vols. New York: G. Routledge, 1889 (*Quatre-vingt-treize,* Paris, 1874).
—*Préface de 'Cromwell.'* Ed. by E. Wahl. Oxford: Clarendon Press, 1909 (Paris, 1827).

HUIZINGA, JOHAN (1872–1945)
In the Shadow of Tomorrow. Trans. by J. H. Huizinga. New York: W. W. Norton, 1936 (Haarlem, 1936).

HUMBOLDT, ALEXANDER VON (1769–1859)
Cosmos, a Sketch of a Physical Description of the Universe. Trans. by E. C. Otté. 5 vols. London: G. Bell & Sons, 1899–1901 (*Kosmos: Entwurf einer physischen Weltbeschreibung,* Stuttgart, 1845–1862).

HUMBOLDT, WILHELM VON (1767–1835)
The Sphere and Duties of Government. Trans. by J. Coulthart. London: J. Chapman, 1854 (*Ideen zu einem Versuch, die Grenzen der Wirksamkeit des Staates zu bestimmen,* 1792).

HUME, DAVID (1711–1776)
Dialogues Concerning Natural Religion. Ed. by N. K. Smith. Oxford: Clarendon Press, 1935 (1751–1755).
—*A Dissertation on the Passions.* In Vol. II, *Essays* (in *Four Dissertations,* London, 1757).
—*Idea of a Perfect Commonwealth.* In Vol. I, *ibid.* (in *Political Discourses,* Edinburgh, 1752).
—*An Inquiry Concerning the Principles of Morals.* Chicago: Open Court, 1930 (London, 1751).
—*The Natural History of Religion.* In Vol. II, *Essays* (in *Four Dissertations,* London, 1757).
—*Of Commerce.* In Vol. I, *ibid.* (in *Political Discourses,* Edinburgh, 1752).
—*Of Interest. Ibid.* (in *Political Discourses,* Edinburgh, 1752).
—*Of Money. Ibid.* (in *Political Discourses,* Edinburgh, 1752).
—*Of Passive Obedience. Ibid.* (in *Three Essays, Moral and Political,* London, 1748).

—*Of Refinement in the Arts*. *Ibid*. ("Of Luxury," in *Political Discourses*, Edinburgh, 1752).
—*Of Some Remarkable Customs*. *Ibid*. (in *Political Discourses*, Edinburgh, 1752).
—*Of Suicide*. In Vol. II, *ibid*. (*c*. 1750).
—*Of Taxes*. In Vol. I, *ibid*. (in *Political Discourses*, Edinburgh, 1752).
—*Of the Balance of Trade*. *Ibid*. (in *Political Discourses*, Edinburgh, 1752).
—*Of the Immortality of the Soul*. In Vol. II, *ibid*. (*c*. 1750).
—*Of the Original Contract*. In Vol. I, *ibid*. (in *Three Essays, Moral and Political*, London, 1748).
—*Of the Rise and Progress of the Arts and Sciences*. *Ibid*. (Edinburgh, 1742).
—*Of the Standard of Taste*. *Ibid*. (in *Four Dissertations*, London, 1757).
—*Of Tragedy*. *Ibid*. (in *Four Dissertations*, London, 1757).
—*A Treatise of Human Nature*. 2 vols. Everyman's Library, New York: E. P. Dutton, 1940 (London, 1739).
NOTE:
Essays, Moral, Political and Literary. Ed. by T. H. Green and T. H. Grose. 2 vols. London: Longmans, Green & Co., 1912.

Hunt, (James Henry) Leigh (1784–1859)
Imagination and Fancy . . . and an Essay in Answer to the Question "What Is Poetry?" London: Smith, Elder & Co., 1891 (London, 1844).

Huntington, Edward Vermilye (1874–1952)
The Continuum, and Other Types of Serial Order, with an Introduction to Cantor's Transfinite Numbers. Cambridge, Mass.: Harvard University Press, 1917 (1905).
—*The Fundamental Propositions of Algebra*. In *Monographs on Topics of Modern Mathematics, Relevant to the Elementary Field*. Ed. by J. W. Young. New York: Longmans, Green & Co., 1932 (New York, 1911).

Huntington, Ellsworth (1876–1947)
Earth and Sun; an Hypothesis of Weather and Sunspots. New Haven, Conn.: Yale University Press, 1923.

Hurd, Richard (1720–1808)
Hurd's Letters on Chivalry and Romance, with the Third Elizabethan Dialogue. Ed. by E. J. Morley. London: H. Frowde, 1911 (London, 1762).

Husserl, Edmund (1859–1938)
Ideas: General Introduction to Pure Phenomenology. Trans. by W. R. B. Gibson. New York: Macmillan, 1931 (1913).
—*Logische Untersuchungen*. 2 vols. Halle: M. Niemeyer, 1913–1922 (Halle, 1900–1901).
—*Méditations Cartésiennes; Introduction à la phénoménologie*. Trans. by G. Peiffer and M. E. Levinas. Paris: A. Colin, 1931.

Hutcheson, Francis (1694–1746)
An Essay on the Nature and Conduct of the Passions and Affections. Glasgow: R. & A. Foulis, 1769 (London, 1728).
—*An Inquiry into the Original of Our Ideas of Beauty and Virtue*. London: R. Ware, 1753 (London, 1725).
—*A System of Moral Philosophy*. Ed. by F. Hutcheson. 2 vols. London: A. Millar, 1755 (1734–1737).

Hutchins, Robert Maynard (1899–)
Education for Freedom. Baton Rouge, La.: Louisiana State University Press, 1943.
—*The Higher Learning in America*. New Haven, Conn.: Yale University Press, 1936.

Huxley, Aldous Leonard (1894–1963)
Brave New World: A Novel. New York: Harper, 1944 (London, 1932).
—*The Perennial Philosophy*. New York: Harper, 1945.

Huxley, Julian Sorell (1887-)
Evolution, the Modern Synthesis. London: Allen & Unwin, 1942.
—*Evolutionary Ethics*. In *Touchstone for Ethics*. New York: Harper, 1947 (1943).
—*Religion Without Revelation*. London: Watts & Co., 1941 (London, 1927).
—*Science and Social Needs*. New York: Harper, 1935 (originally pub. as *Scientific Research and Social Needs*, London, 1934).

Huxley, Thomas Henry (1825–1895)
Darwiniana. Essays. New York: D. Appleton, 1893 (1859–1888).
—*Evolution and Ethics*. In *Touchstone for Ethics*. New York: Harper, 1947 (1893).
—*Man's Place in Nature, and Other Essays*. Everyman's Library, New York: E. P. Dutton, 1911 (title essay, London, 1863).
—*Methods and Results. Essays*. New York: D. Appleton, 1911 (1868–1890).

Huygens, Christiaan (1629–1695)
Force centrifuge. In Vol. XVI, *Oeuvres complètes de Christiaan Huygens*. 17 vols. The Hague: M. Nijhoff, 1888.
—*L'horloge à pendule*. In Vol. XVII, *ibid*. (Paris, 1673).
—*Percussion*. In Vol. XVI, *ibid*. (*Tractatus de motu corporum ex percussione*, 1668).
—*Question de l'existence et de la perceptibilité du mouvement absolu*. *Ibid*.
—[Sur la cause de la pesanteur] *Traité de la lumière . . . Avec un discours de la cause de la pesanteur*. Leipsic: Gressner & Schramm, 1885 (Leyden, 1666).
—*Travaux divers de statique et de dynamique de 1659 à 1666*. In Vol. XVI, *Oeuvres complètes*.

I

Ibn Ezra, Abraham (*c*. 1092–1167)
The Beginning of Wisdom: An Astrological Treatise. Ed. and trans. by R. Levy and F. Cantero. Baltimore, Md.: Johns Hopkins University Press, 1939 (1148).

IBN GABIROL (AVICEBRON) (*c.* 1021–*c.* 1058)
The Improvement of the Moral Qualities. Trans. by S. S. Wise. New York: Macmillan, 1901 (*Sefer Tikkun Hamiddoth*, 1045).

IBSEN, HENRIK (1828–1906)
A Doll's House. In *Eleven Plays of Henrik Ibsen.* Modern Library, New York: Random House, 1935 (Copenhagen, 1879).
—*An Enemy of the People. Ibid.* (Copenhagen. 1882).
—*Ghosts. Ibid.* (Copenhagen, 1881).
—*Hedda Gabler. Ibid.* (Copenhagen, 1890).
—*The Master Builder. Ibid.* (Copenhagen, 1892).
—*The Pillars of Society. Ibid.* (Copenhagen, 1877).

IGNATIUS OF LOYOLA, SAINT (1491–1556)
The Constitutions. In *St. Ignatius and the Ratio Studiorum.* Ed. by E. A. Fitzpatrick, trans. by M. H. Mayer. New York: McGraw-Hill, 1933 (*Constitutiones Societatis Jesu*, 1541–1550).
—*The Spiritual Exercises of Ignatius Loyola.* Trans. by C. Seager. London: Webb, M'Gill & Co., 1849 (1522).

IHERING, RUDOLPH VON (1818–1892)
Law as a Means to an End. Trans. by I. Husik. Boston: Boston Book Co., 1913 (Vol. I of *Der Zweck im Recht*, Leipsic, 1877).
—*The Struggle for Law.* Trans. by J. J. Lalor. Chicago: Callaghan & Co., 1915 (*Der Kampf um's Recht*, Vienna, 1872).

ISOCRATES (436–338 B.C.)
Aegineticus. In Vol. III, *Isocrates.* Vols. I and II trans. by George Norlin, Vol. III by L. Van Hook. 3 vols. Loeb Library, Cambridge, Mass.: Harvard University Press, 1928–1945 (*c.* 393 B.C.).
—*Against the Sophists.* In Vol. II, *ibid.* (*c.* 391 B.C.).
—*Antidosis. Ibid.* (353 B.C.).
—*Panegyricus. Ibid.* (380 B.C.).

J

JACKSON, THOMAS ALFRED (1879–)
Dialectics; the Logic of Marxism, and Its Critics—an Essay in Exploration. London: Lawrence & Wishart, 1936.

JACOBUS DE VORAGINE (*c.*1228–1298)
The Golden Legend. Trans. by G. Ryan and H. Ripperger. London: Longmans, Green & Co., 1941 (*Legenda Aurea*, before 1273?).

JAEGER, WERNER WILHELM (1888–1961)
Humanism and Theology. Milwaukee, Wis.: Marquette University Press, 1943.
—*Paideia: The Ideals of Greek Culture.* Trans. by G. Highet. 3 vols. Oxford: Blackwell, 1939 (*Paideia: Die Formung des Griechischen Menschen.* Vol. I only, Berlin, 1934).

JAENSCH, ERICH (1883–1940)
Eidetic Imagery and Typological Methods of Investigation; Their Importance for the Psychology of Childhood, the Theory of Education, General Psychology, and the Psychophysiology of Human Personality. Trans. by Oscar Oeser. New York: Harcourt Brace, 1930 (*Die Eidetik und die typologische Forschungsmethode*, Leipsic, 1925).

JAMES I, KING OF ENGLAND (1566–1625)
An Apologie for the Oath of Allegiance. In *The Political Works of James I.* Reprinted from the ed. of 1616. Cambridge, Mass.: Harvard University Press, 1918 (London, 1609).
—*A Defence of the Right of Kings, Against Cardinall Perron. Ibid.* (1615).
—*A Premonition to all Christian Monarches, Free Princes and States. Ibid.* (1609).
—*The Trew Law of Free Monarchies. Ibid.* (1603).

JAMES, HENRY (1843–1916)
The American. Boston: Houghton Mifflin Co., 1907 (New York, 1877).
—*The Art of the Novel; Critical Prefaces.* Ed. by R. P. Blackmur. New York: Scribner's, 1934 (1907–1909).
—*The Beast in the Jungle.* London: M. Secker, 1915 (in *The Better Sort*, New York, 1903).
—*Daisy Miller.* New York: Harper, 1916 (1878).
—*Notes of a Son and Brother.* New York: Scribner's, 1914.
—*A Small Boy and Others.* New York: Scribner's, 1914.
—*The Turn of the Screw.* Modern Library, New York: Random House, 1930 (in *The Two Magics*, New York, 1898).

JAMES, WILLIAM (1842–1910)
Collected Essays and Reviews. New York: Longmans, Green & Co., 1920 (1869–1910).
—*Essays in Radical Empiricism.* Ed. by R. B. Perry. New York: Longmans, Green & Co., 1943 (1884–1907).
—*Human Immortality; Two Supposed Objections to the Doctrine.* Boston: Houghton Mifflin Co., 1898.
—*The Meaning of Truth, a Sequel to 'Pragmatism.'* New York: Longmans, Green & Co., 1909 (New York, 1909).
—*Memories and Studies.* New York: Longmans, Green & Co., 1917 (1897–1910).
—*A Pluralistic Universe; Hibbert Lectures at Manchester College on the Present Situation in Philosophy.* New York: Longmans, Green & Co., 1909.
—*Pragmatism, a New Name for Some Old Ways of Thinking.* Ed. by R. B. Perry. New York: Longmans, Green & Co., 1943 (New York, 1907).
—*Some Problems of Philosophy; a Beginning of an Introduction to Philosophy.* New York: Longmans, Green & Co., 1928 (1909–1910).
—*The Varieties of Religious Experience; a Study in Human Nature.* Modern Library, New York: Random House, 1936 (New York, 1902).
—*The Will to Believe, and Other Essays in Popular Philosophy.* New York: Longmans, Green & Co., 1937 (1879–1896).

JANET, PAUL ALEXANDRE RENÉ (1823–1899)
Final Causes. Trans. by W. Affleck. New York: Scribner's, 1892 (*Les causes finales*, Paris, 1876).

—*The Theory of Morals*. Trans. by M. Chapman. New York: Scribner's, 1900 (*Éléments de morale*, Paris, 1870).

JANET, PIERRE MARIE FÉLIX (1859–1947)
The Major Symptoms of Hysteria. New York: Macmillan, 1929 (New York, 1907).

JASPERS, KARL (1883–)
Man in the Modern Age. Trans. by E. and C. Paul. London: G. Routledge, 1933 (*Die geistige Situation der Zeit*, Leipsic, 1931).
—*The Perennial Scope of Philosophy*. New York: Philosophical Library, 1949.

JEAN PAUL, pseud. for JOHANN PAUL FRIEDRICH RICHTER (1763–1825)
Levana; or, The Doctrine of Education. Boston: D. C. Heath, 1886 (Brunswick, 1807).
—*Vorschule der Ästhetik*. In Vol. IX, *Jean Pauls Sämtliche Werke*. Preussische Akademie der Wissenschaften, 36 vols. Weimar: H. Böhlau, 1927 (Hamburg, 1804).

JEANS, SIR JAMES HOPWOOD (1877–1946)
Astronomy and Cosmogony. Cambridge University Press, 1928.
—*Problems of Cosmogony and Stellar Dynamics*. Cambridge University Press, 1919.
—*The Universe Around Us*. New York: Macmillan, 1944 (New York, 1929).

JEFFERSON, THOMAS (1743–1826)
The Commonplace Book of Thomas Jefferson. A Repertory of His Ideas on Government. Ed. by G. Chinard. Baltimore, Md.: Johns Hopkins University Press, 1926 (*c*.1775).
—*Democracy*. Sel. and ed. by S. K. Padover. New York: D. Appleton-Century Co., 1939.
—*Notes on the State of Virginia*. Richmond, Va.: J. W. Randolph, 1853 (Philadelphia, 1788).

JEFFREYS, HAROLD (1891–)
Scientific Inference. Cambridge University Press, 1937 (Cambridge, 1931).
—*Theory of Probability*. Oxford: Clarendon Press, 1939.

JELLINEK, GEORG (1851–1911)
Allgemeine Staatslehre. Berlin: O. Häring, 1914 (Berlin, 1900).
—*The Declaration of the Rights of Man and Citizens: A Contribution to Modern Constitutional History*. Trans. by M. Farrand. New York: Henry Holt, 1901 (*Die Erklärung der Menschen- und Bürgerrechte*, Leipsic, 1895).

JENNER, EDWARD (1749–1823)
An Inquiry into the Causes and Effects of the Variolae Vaccinae, a Disease Discovered in Some of the Western Counties of England . . . and Known by the Name of Cow-Pox. Springfield, Mass.: Ashley & Brewer, 1802 (London, 1798).

JENNINGS, HERBERT SPENCER (1868–1947)
Behavior of the Lower Organisms. New York: Columbia University Press, 1931 (New York, 1906).

JENSEN, JOHANNES VILHELM (1873–1950)
The Long Journey. Trans. by A. G. Chater. New York: A. A. Knopf, 1945 (Christiania, 1908–1921).

JESPERSEN, JENS OTTO HARRY (1860–1943)
Language: Its Nature, Development and Origin. New York: Henry Holt, 1934 (London, 1922).
—*The Philosophy of Grammar*. New York: Henry Holt, 1924.

JEVONS, WILLIAM STANLEY (1835–1882)
Money and the Mechanism of Exchange. New York: D. Appleton, 1919 (London, 1875).
—*On a General System of Numerically Definite Reasoning*. In *Pure Logic and Other Minor Works*. Ed. by R. Adamson and H. Jevons. New York: Macmillan, 1890 (1870).
—*On Geometrical Reasoning*. *Ibid*. (1877).
—*On the Mechanical Performance of Logical Inference*. *Ibid*. (1870).
—*The Principles of Science: A Treatise on Logic and Scientific Method*. London: Macmillan, 1924 (London, 1874).
—*Pure Logic, or the Logic of Quality Apart from Quantity: With Remarks on Boole's System and on the Relation of Logic and Mathematics*. New York: Macmillan, 1890 (London, 1864).
—*The State in Relation to Labour*. Ed. by F. W. Hirst. London: Macmillan, 1910 (London, 1882).
—*Studies in Deductive Logic. A Manual for Students*. New York; Macmillan, 1896 (London, 1880).
—*The Substitution of Similars*. In *Pure Logic, q.v.* (London, 1869).
—*The Theory of Political Economy*. Ed. by H. S. Jevons. London: Macmillan, 1931 (London, 1871).

JOACHIM, HAROLD HENRY (1868–1938)
The Nature of Truth, an Essay. New York: Oxford University Press, 1939 (Oxford, 1906).

JOHN CHRYSOSTOM, SAINT (*c*. 345–407)
On the Priesthood. Ed. and trans. by B. H. Cowper. London, 1866 (381–385).

JOHN OF SAINT THOMAS (JOANNIS A SANCTO THOMA) (1589–1644)
Cursus Philosophicus Thomisticus. Vol. I, *Ars Logica;* Vols. II–III, *Philosophia Naturalis*. Ed. by B. Reiser. Rome: Marietti, 1930–1937 (Madrid, 1637).

JOHN OF SALISBURY (*c*. 1115–1180)
Metalogicon. Ed. by C. Webb. Oxford: Clarendon Press, 1929 (*c*. 1159).
—*The Statesman's Book*. Bks. IV–VIII, *Polycraticus*. Ed. and trans. by J. Dickinson. New York: A. A. Knopf, 1927 (before 1159).

JOHN OF THE CROSS, SAINT (1542–1591)
Ascent of Mount Carmel. In Vol. I, *The Complete Works of Saint John of the Cross*. Ed. and trans. by E. A. Peers. 3 vols. London: Burns, Oates, & Washbourne, 1934–1935 (*Subida del Monte Carmelo*, 1578–1584).
—*Dark Night of the Soul*. *Ibid*. (*Noche Oscura del Sentido*, 1582–1584).

—*The Living Flame of Love*. In Vol. III, *ibid.* (*Llamo de amor viva*, 1585–1587).
—*Spiritual Canticle*. In Vol. II, *ibid.* (*Cántico Espiritual*, 1577–1584).

JOHNSON, ALEXANDER BRYAN (1786–1867)
A Treatise on Language: or, The Relation Which Words Bear to Things. New York: Harper, 1836 (New York, 1828).

JOHNSON, SAMUEL (1709–1784)
History of Rasselas, Prince of Abyssinia. Oxford: Clarendon Press, 1931 (London, 1759).
—*Lives of the English Poets*. 2 vols. Everyman's Library, New York: E. P. Dutton, 1925 (1779–1781).

JOHNSON, WILLIAM ERNEST (1858–1931)
Logic. 3 vols. Cambridge University Press, 1921.

JONES, ERNEST (1879–1958)
Nightmare, Witches, and Devils. New York: W. W. Norton, 1931.

JOULE, JAMES PRESCOTT (1818–1889)
The Scientific Papers of James Prescott Joule. 2 vols. London: Taylor & Francis, 1884–1887 (1840–1878).

JOURDAIN, PHILIP EDWARD BERTRAND (1879–1919)
The Nature of Mathematics. London: T. C. & E. C. Jack, 1919 (London, 1913).

JOYCE, JAMES (1882–1941)
Dubliners. Modern Library, New York: Random House, 1926 (London, 1914).
—*Finnegans Wake*. New York: Viking Press, 1939.
—*A Portrait of the Artist as a Young Man*. Modern Library, New York: Random House, 1928 (New York, 1916).
—*Ulysses*. Modern Library, New York: Random House, 1942 (Paris, 1922).

JUDAH HA-LEVI (*c.* 1085–*c.* 1142)
Kitab al Khazari (*Al Chusari*). Trans. by H. Hirschfeld. New York: B. G. Richards, 1927 (1140).

JUNG, CARL GUSTAV (1875–1961)
Instinct and the Unconscious. In *Contributions* (1919).
—*Marriage as a Psychological Relationship*. *Ibid.* (1925).
—*Mind and the Earth*. *Ibid.* (1927).
—*Modern Man in Search of a Soul*. Trans. by W. S. Dell and C. F. Baynes. New York: Harcourt Brace, 1933 (1929–1932).
—*On the Relations of Analytical Psychology to Poetic Art*. In *Contributions* (1922).
—*Psychological Types, or, The Psychology of Individuation*. Trans. by H. G. Baynes. New York: Harcourt Brace, 1926 (1921).
—*Psychology and Religion*. New Haven, Conn.: Yale University Press, 1938.
—*Spirit and Life*. In *Contributions* (1926).
—*Two Essays on Analytical Psychology*. Trans. by H. G. and C. F. Baynes. New York: Dodd, Mead & Co., 1928 (1912).

NOTE:
Contributions to Analytical Psychology. Trans. by H. G. and C. F. Baynes. New York: Harcourt Brace, 1928.

JUSTINIAN (FLAVIUS ANICIUS JUSTINIANUS) (*c.* 482–565)
The Digest of Justinian. Trans. by C. H. Monro. 2 vols. Cambridge University Press, 1904–1909 (533).
—*The Institutes of Justinian*. Trans. by J. B. Moyle. Oxford: Clarendon Press, 1913 (533).

JUVENAL, DECIMUS JUNIUS (2d century A.D.)
The Satires of Juvenal. Trans. by W. Gifford. New York: Putnam's, 1906.

K

KAFKA, FRANZ (1883–1924)
The Castle. Trans. by E. and W. Muir. New York: A. A. Knopf, 1941.
—*The Trial*. Trans. by E. and W. Muir. New York: A. A. Knopf, 1937.

KALLEN, HORACE MEYER (1882–)
The Book of Job as Greek Tragedy. New York: Moffat, Yard & Co., 1918.

KAMES, LORD (HENRY HOME) (1696–1782)
Elements of Criticism. Ed. by A. Mills. New York: Sheldon & Co., 1871 (Edinburgh, 1762).
—*Sketches of the History of Man*. 3 vols. London: T. Cadell & W. Davies, 1807 (Edinburgh, 1774).

KANT, IMMANUEL (1724–1804)
Anthropologie in pragmatischer Hinsicht. In Vol. IV, *Sämtliche Werke* (Königsberg, 1798).
—*Cosmogony* [I, *Examination of the Question Whether the Earth Has Undergone an Alteration of Its Axial Rotation*; II, *Universal Natural History and Theory of the Heavens*]. Trans. by W. Hastie. Glasgow: J. MacLehose & Sons, 1900 (*Allgemeine Naturgeschichte und Theorie des Himmels*, Königsberg, 1755).
—[De Mundi Sensibilis] *Inaugural Dissertation and Early Writings on Space*. Trans, by J. Handyside. Chicago: Open Court, 1929 (*De Mundi Sensibilis Atque Intelligibilis Forma et Principiis*, Königsberg, 1770).
—*The Educational Theory of Immanuel Kant*. Trans. by E. F. Buchner. Philadelphia: Lippincott, 1904 (F. T. Rink, *Immanuel Kant Über Pädagogik*, Königsberg, 1803).
—*The Idea of a Universal History on a Cosmo-Political Plan*. Trans. by T. de Quincey. Hanover, N.H.: Sociological Press, 1927 (1784).
—*Introduction to Logic*. Trans. by T. K. Abbott. London: Longmans, Green & Co., 1885 (*Logik*, Königsberg, 1800).
—*Lectures on Ethics*. Trans. by L. Infield. New York: Century Co., 1930 (1780–1781).
—*Metaphysical Foundations of Natural Science*. See *Prolegomena* (*Metaphysische Anfangsgründe der Naturwissenschaften*, Riga, 1786).
—*On the First Grounds of the Distinction of Regions in Space*. See *Inaugural Dissertation* (1768).

—*Perpetual Peace, a Philosophical Essay.* Trans. by M. Campbell-Smith. New York: Columbia University Press, 1939. (*Zum ewigen Frieden, ein philosophischer Entwurf,* Königsberg, 1795).
—*The Principle of Progress.* In *Principles of Politics.* Ed. by W. Hastie. New York: Scribner's, 1891 (1794).
—*Prolegomena to Any Future Metaphysic* [includes *Metaphysical Foundations of Natural Science*]. Ed. and trans. by Paul Carus. Chicago: Open Court, 1929 (*Prolegomena zu einer jeden zukünftigen Metaphysik, die als Wissenschaft wird auftreten können,* Riga, 1783).
—*Religion Within the Limits of Reason Alone.* Trans. by T. M. Greene and H. H. Hudson. Chicago: Open Court, 1934 (*Die Religion innerhalb der Grenzen der blossen Vernunft,* Königsberg, 1794).
—*Untersuchung über die Deutlichkeit der Grundsätze der natürlichen Theologie und der Moral.* In Vol. I, *Sämtliche Werke* (Berlin, 1764).
NOTE:
Sämtliche Werke ("Akademieausgabe"). 22 vols. Berlin: F. Meiner, 1902–1920.

KAPTEYN, JACOBUS CORNELIUS (1851–1922)
Recent Researches in the Structure of the Universe. Smithsonian Institution, Annual Report (1908), Washington, D.C., 1909.

KASNER, EDWARD (1878–1955) and NEWMAN, JAMES (1907–1966)
Mathematics and the Imagination. New York: Simon & Schuster, 1940.

KEITH, SIR ARTHUR (1866–1955)
A New Theory of Human Evolution. New York: Philosophical Library, 1949.

KELSEN, HANS (1881–1973)
Der soziologische und der juristische Staatsbegriff, kritische Untersuchung des Verhältnisses von Staat und Recht. Tübingen: J. C. Mohr, 1928 (Tübingen, 1922).
—*General Theory of Law and State.* Trans. by A. Wedberg. Cambridge, Mass.: Harvard University Press, 1945.
—*Law and Peace in International Relations.* Cambridge, Mass.: Harvard University Press, 1942.
—*Society and Nature: A Sociological Inquiry.* University of Chicago Press, 1943.
—*Sozialismus und Staat, eine Untersuchung der politischen Theorie des Marxismus.* Leipsic: C. L. Hirschfeld 1920.
—*Staatsform und Weltanschauung.* Tübingen: J. C. Mohr, 1933.
—*Vom Wesen und Wert der Demokratie.* Tübingen: J. C. Mohr, 1929 (Tübingen, 1920).

KELSO, RUTH (1885–)
The Doctrine of the English Gentleman in the Sixteenth Century. Urbana, Ill.: University of Illinois Press, 1929 (1923).

KELVIN, BARON (SIR WILLIAM THOMSON) (1824–1907)
Lectures on Molecular Dynamics and the Wave Theory of Light. Baltimore, Md.: Publication Agency of the Johns Hopkins University Press, 1904 (1884).
—*Popular Lectures and Addresses.* 3 vols. New York: Macmillan, 1891–1894 (London, 1889–1894).

KENT, SHERMAN (1903–)
Writing History. New York: Crofts, 1941.

KEPLER, JOHANNES (1571–1630)
De Motibus Stellae Martis. In Vol. III, *Joannis Kepleri Astronomi Opera Omnia.* Ed. by C. Frisch. 8 vols. Frankfort: Heyder & Zimmer, 1858–1871 (1609).
—*Dioptrik.* Ed. and trans. by F. Plehn. Leipsic: W. Engelmann, 1904 (1611).
—*Harmonices Mundi.* In Vol. V, *Opera.* See *De Motibus* (1619).
—*Mysterium Cosmographicum.* In Vol. I, *ibid.* See *De Motibus* (1596).

KEYNES, JOHN MAYNARD (1883–1946)
The General Theory of Employment, Interest and Money. New York: Harcourt Brace, 1936.
—*A Treatise on Money.* 2 vols. New York: Harcourt Brace, 1935 (London, 1930).
—*A Treatise on Probability.* London: Macmillan, 1929 (London, 1921).

KEYNES, JOHN NEVILLE (1852–1949)
The Scope and Method of Political Economy. New York: Macmillan, 1904 (New York, 1891).
—*Studies and Exercises in Formal Logic, Including a Generalisation of Logical Processes in Their Application to Complex Inferences.* London: Macmillan, 1906 (London, 1884).

KIERKEGAARD, SÖREN AABYE (1813–1855)
Christian Discourses. Trans. by W. Lowrie. New York: Oxford University Press, 1939 (Copenhagen, 1848).
—*The Concept of Dread.* Trans. by W. Lowrie. Princeton University Press, 1944 (Copenhagen, 1844).
—*Concluding Unscientific Postscript.* Trans. by D. Swenson and W. Lowrie. Princeton University Press, 1941 (Copenhagen, 1846).
—*Edifying Discourses.* Trans. by D. and L. Swenson. Minneapolis, Minn.: Augsburg Publishing House, 1944 (Copenhagen, 1844).
—*Either/Or: A Fragment of Life.* Trans. by D. Swenson *et al.* 2 vols. Princeton University Press, 1944 (Copenhagen, 1843).
—*Of the Difference Between a Genius and an Apostle.* In *The Present Age and Two Minor Ethico-Religious Treatises.* Trans. by A. Dru and W. Lowrie. New York: Oxford University Press, 1940 (Copenhagen, 1849).
—*Philosophical Fragments; or, A Fragment of Philosophy.* Trans. by D. F. Swenson. Princeton University Press, 1936 (Copenhagen, 1844).
—*The Point of View, etc.* Trans. by W. Lowrie. New York: Oxford University Press, 1939 (1848).
—*The Sickness Unto Death.* Trans. by W. Lowrie. Princeton University Press, 1941 (Copenhagen, 1849).

—*Stages on Life's Way*. Trans. by W. Lowrie. Princeton University Press, 1940 (1845).
—*Works of Love: Some Christian Reflexions in the Form of Discourses*. Trans. by D. and L. Swenson. Princeton University Press, 1946 (Copenhagen, 1847).

KING, HENRY, BISHOP OF CHICHESTER (1592–1669)
The Exequy. In *The Poems of Bishop Henry King*. Ed. by J. Sparrow. London: Nonesuch Press, 1925 (London, 1657).

KINGSLEY, CHARLES (1819–1875)
Westward Ho! or, The Voyages and Adventures of Sir Amyas Leigh, Knt., of Burrough, in the County of Devon, in the Reign of Her Most Glorious Majesty Queen Elizabeth. Everyman's Library, New York: E. P. Dutton, 1934 (Cambridge, 1855).

KIRK, KENNETH ESCOTT (1886–1954)
Conscience and Its Problems: An Introduction to Casuistry. New York: Longmans, Green & Co., 1927.
—*Ignorance, Faith and Conformity: Studies in Moral Theology*. New York: Longmans, Green & Co., 1925.
—*The Vision of God: The Christian Doctrine of the Summum Bonum*. New York: Longmans, Green & Co., 1931.

KLEIN, CHRISTIAN FELIX (1849–1925)
Elementary Mathematics from an Advanced Standpoint. Trans. by E. R. Hedrick and C. A. Noble. New York: Macmillan, 1922 (*Elementarmathematik vom höheren Standpunkt aus*, Leipsic, 1908–1909).
—*Famous Problems of Elementary Geometry: The Duplication of the Cube, the Trisection of an Angle, the Quadrature of the Circle*. Trans. by W. W. Beman and D. E. Smith. New York: G. E. Stechert, 1930 (*Vorträge über ausgewählte Fragen der Elementargeometrie, ausgearbeitet von F. Tägert*, Leipsic, 1895).

KNOX, JOHN (*c.* 1505–1572)
An Answer to the Cavillations of an Adversarie Respecting the Doctrine of Predestination. In Vol. v, *The Works of John Knox*. Ed. by D. Laing. 6 vols. Edinburgh: J. Thin, 1895 (Geneva, 1560).

KOCH, ROBERT (1843–1910)
The Aetiology of Tuberculosis. New York: National Tuberculosis Association, 1932 (1882).

KOEHLER, WOLFGANG (1887–1967)
Gestalt Psychology. New York: Liveright, 1929.
—*The Mentality of Apes*. Trans. by E. Winter. New York: Harcourt Brace, 1925 (*Intelligenzprüfungen an Anthropoiden*, I, Berlin, 1917).

KOESTLER, ARTHUR (1905–)
Darkness at Noon. Modern Library, New York: Random House, 1949 (London, 1940).

KOFFKA, KURT (1886–1941)
Principles of Gestalt-Psychology. New York: Harcourt Brace, 1935.

KOHLER, JOSEF (1849–1919)
Philosophy of Law. Trans. by A. Albrecht. New York: Macmillan, 1921 (*Lehrbuch der Rechtsphilosophie*, Berlin, 1909).

KOHN, HANS (1891–1971)
The Idea of Nationalism: A Study in Its Origins and Background. New York: Macmillan, 1944.
—*Revolutions and Dictatorships; Essays in Contemporary History*. Cambridge, Mass.: Harvard University Press, 1939.

KONINCK, CHARLES DE (1906–)
Le problème de l'indéterminisme. Quebec, 1937.

KOVALEVSKY, MAXIM MAXIMOVITCH (1851–1916)
Modern Customs and Ancient Laws of Russia; Being the Illchester Lectures for 1889–90. London: D. Nutt, 1891.

KROPOTKIN, PETER ALEXEIVICH (1842–1921)
Anarchism: Its Philosophy and Ideal. London: Freedom Press, 1904 (*L'anarchie; sa philosophie—son idéal*, Paris, 1896).
—*The Conquest of Bread*. New York: Vanguard Press, 1926 (*La conquête du pain*, Paris, 1892).
—*Fields, Factories and Workshops; or, Industry Combined with Agriculture and Brain Work with Manual Work*. New York: Putnam's, 1913 (London, 1899).
—*Mutual Aid, a Factor of Evolution*. New York: A. A. Knopf, 1925 (1890–1896).
—*The State, Its Historic Role*. London: Freedom Press, 1903.

L

LA BOÉTIE, ÉTIENNE DE (1530–1563)
Anti-Dictator, the Discours de la servitude volontaire. Trans. by H. Kurz. New York: Columbia University Press, 1942 (1546?–1548?).

LA BRUYÈRE, JEAN DE (1645–1696)
The Characters. Ed. and trans. by H. Van Laun. London: G. Routledge, 1929 (*Les caractères de Théophraste traduits du Grec. Avec les caractères ou les moeurs de ce siècle*, Paris, 1688).

LACTANTIUS, LUCIUS CAECILIUS FIRMIANUS (260–330)
The Divine Institutes. In Vol. VII, *The Ante-Nicene Fathers*. Ed. by A. Roberts and J. Donaldson. 10 vols. New York: Christian Literature Co., 1885–1896 (*Institutionum Divinarum*, 304?–313?).

LAËNNEC, RENÉ THÉOPHILE HYACINTHE (1781–1826)
Translation of Selected Passages from Mediate Auscultation. New York: W. Wood, 1923 (*De l'auscultation médiate*, Paris, 1819).

LA FAYETTE, MARIE MADELEINE, COMTESSE DE (1634–1693)
The Princess of Cleves. Trans. by H. Ashton. New York: E. P. Dutton, 1925 (*La Princesse de Clèves*, Paris, 1678).

LA FONTAINE, JEAN DE (1621–1695)
The Fables of Jean de la Fontaine. Trans. by E. Marsh. London: W. Heinemann, 1933 (Paris, 1668–1694).

LAGERLÖF, SELMA OTTILIANA LOVISA (1858–1940)
The Ring of the Löwenskölds. Trans. by V. S. Howard and F. Martin. Garden City, N.Y.: Doubleday Doran, 1931 (*Löwensköldska Ringen, Charlotte Löwensköld, Anna Svärd,* Stockholm, 1925–1928).

LAGRANGE, JOSEPH LOUIS (1736–1813)
Mécanique analytique. 2 vols. Paris: Gauthier-Villars, 1888–1889 (Paris, 1788).

LAIRD, JOHN (1887–1946)
An Enquiry into Moral Notions. New York: Columbia University Press, 1936 (London, 1935).
—*Knowledge, Belief and Opinion.* New York: Century Co., 1930.

LAKE, KIRSOPP (1872–1946)
Immortality and the Modern Mind. Cambridge, Mass.: Harvard University Press, 1922.

LALO, CHARLES (1877–1953)
L'art et la morale. Paris: F. Alcan, 1934 (Paris, 1922).

LAMARCK, JEAN BAPTISTE PIERRE ANTOINE DE MONET (1744–1829)
Zoological Philosophy; an Exposition with Regard to the Natural History of Animals. Trans. by H. Elliot. London: Macmillan, 1914 (*Philosophie zoologique, ou Exposition des considérations relatives à l'histoire naturelle des animaux,* Paris, 1809).

LAMB, CHARLES (1775–1834)
The Essays of Elia. Everyman's Library, New York: E. P. Dutton, 1932 (London, 1823).
—*Hospita on the Immoderate Indulgences of the Pleasures of the Palate.* In Vol. IV, *The Works of Charles Lamb.* 5 vols. New York: T. Y. Crowell, 1881 (1810?).
—*On the Custom of Hissing at the Theatres; with Some Account of a Club of Damned Authors.* In Vol. V, *ibid.* (1811).

LAMETTRIE, JULIEN OFFROY DE (1709–1751)
Histoire naturelle de l'âme. The Hague: J. Néaulme, 1745.
—*Man a Machine.* Trans. by G. C. Bussey. Chicago: Open Court, 1912 (*L'homme machine,* Leyden, 1748).

LAMPRECHT, KARL (1856–1915)
What Is History? Five Lectures on the Modern Science of History. Trans. by E. A. Andrews. New York: Macmillan, 1905 (*Moderne Geschichtswissenschaft,* Freiburg, 1904).

LANDTMAN, GUNNAR (1878–1940)
The Origin of the Inequality of the Social Classes. University of Chicago Press, 1938.

LANG, ANDREW (1844–1912)
Custom and Myth. New York: Harper, 1885 (London, 1884).

LANGE, FRIEDRICH ALBERT (1828–1875)
The History of Materialism and Criticism of Its Present Importance. Trans. by E. C. Thomas. 3 vols. New York: Harcourt Brace, 1925 (*Geschichte des Materialismus und Kritik seiner Bedeutung in der Gegenwart,* Iserlohn, 1866).

LANGLAND, WILLIAM (*c.* 1330–*c.* 1400)
The Vision of Piers Plowman. Everyman's Library, New York: E. P. Dutton, 1945 (1362?–1392?).

LANGLOIS, CHARLES VICTOR (1863–1929) and SEIGNOBOS, CHARLES (1854–1942)
Introduction to the Study of History. Trans. by G. G. Berry. New York: Henry Holt, 1932 (*Introduction aux études historiques,* Paris, 1898).

LAPLACE, PIERRE SIMON (1749–1827)
Mécanique céleste (*Celestial Mechanics*). Trans. by N. Bowditch. 4 vols. Boston: Hillard Gray, 1829–1839 (Paris, 1799–1825).
—*A Philosophical Essay on Probabilities.* Trans. by F. W. Truscott and F. L. Ermory. New York: J. Wiley, 1917 (*Essai philosophique sur les probabilités,* Paris, 1814).
—*The System of the World.* Trans. by H. H. Harte. 2 vols. Dublin University Press, 1830 (*Exposition du système du monde,* Paris, 1796).

LARGE, ERNEST CHARLES
The Advance of the Fungi. New York: Henry Holt, 1940.

LASHLEY, KARL SPENCER (1890–1958)
Brain Mechanisms and Intelligence; a Quantitative Study of Injuries to the Brain. University of Chicago Press, 1929.

LASKI, HAROLD JOSEPH (1893–1950)
Authority in the Modern State. New Haven, Conn.: Yale University Press, 1927 (New Haven, 1919).
—*Democracy in Crisis.* Chapel Hill, N.C.: University of North Carolina Press, 1933.
—*Liberty in the Modern State.* New York: Harper, 1930.
—*Reflections on the Revolution of Our Time.* New York: Viking Press, 1943.
—*The State in Theory and Practice.* New York: Viking Press, 1935.

LASSALLE, FERDINAND JOHANN GOTTLIEB (1825–1864)
What Is Capital? Trans. by F. Keddell. New York: International Publishing Co., 1899 (from *Herr Bastiat Schultze von Delitzsch, der ökonomische Julian, oder Kapital und Arbeit,* Berlin, 1864).

LAW, WILLIAM (1686–1761)
An Appeal to All That Doubt, or Disbelieve the Truths of the Gospel. In Vol. VI, *The Works of the Reverend William Law, M.A.* 9 vols. London: G. Moreton, 1892–1893 (London, 1740).
—*A Practical Treatise upon Christian Perfection.* In Vol. III, *ibid.* (London, 1726).
—*A Serious Call to a Devout and Holy Life.* Everyman's Library, New York: E. P. Dutton, 1931 (London, 1729).

LAWRENCE, DAVID HERBERT (1885–1930)
Sons and Lovers. Modern Library, New York: Random House, 1940 (London, 1913).
—*Women in Love.* Modern Library, New York: Random House, 1937 (New York, 1920).

LAWRENCE, HENRY (1600–1664)
Of Our Communion and Warre with Angels. Amsterdam, 1646.

LAWRENCE, THOMAS EDWARD (1888–1935)
Seven Pillars of Wisdom. Garden City, N.Y.: Garden City Publishing Co., 1938 (New York, 1926).

LEA, CHARLES HENRY (1825–1909)
Materials Toward a History of Witchcraft. Ed. by A. C. Howland. Philadelphia: University of Pennsylvania Press, 1939.

LECKY, WILLIAM EDWARD HARTPOLE (1838–1903)
Democracy and Liberty. 2 vols. New York: Longmans, Green & Co., 1900 (London, 1896).
—*The Map of Life; Conduct and Character*. New York: Longmans, Green & Co., 1913 (London, 1899).

LEGNANO, GIOVANNI DA (d. 1383)
Tractatus De Bello, De Represaliis et De Duello (*On War, Reprisals, and the Duel*). Ed. by T. E. Holland, trans. by J. L. Brierly. New York: Oxford University Press, 1917 (*c.* 1360).

LEIBNITZ, GOTTFRIED WILHELM (1646–1716)
Characteristica (*Scientia Generalis*). In Vol. VII, *Philosophische Schriften*.
—*Correspondence with Clarke*. In *Philosophical Works*, *q.v.* (1715–1716).
—*Discourse on Metaphysics, Correspondence with Arnauld, and Monadology*. Ed. by P. Janet, trans. by G. R. Montgomery. Chicago: Open Court, 1931 (*Discours de le métaphysique*, 1686).
—*The Early Mathematical Manuscripts of Leibnitz*. Trans. by J. M. Child. Chicago: Open Court, 1920 (1673–1677).
—*Monadology*. See *Discourse on Metaphysics* (1714).
—*New Essays Concerning Human Understanding*. Trans. by A. G. Langley. Chicago: Open Court, 1916 (*Nouveaux essais sur l'entendement humain*, 1704).
—*Philosophical Works*. Ed. and trans. by G. M. Duncan. New Haven, Conn.: Tuttle, Morehouse, & Taylor, 1908 (1684–1714).
—[Theodicy] *Essais de Théodicée sur la bonté de Dieu, la liberté de l'homme, et l'origine du mal*. In Vol. VI, *Philosophische Schriften* (Amsterdam, 1710).
—*What Is "Idea"?* Appended to *New Essays*, *q.v.* (1678–1679).
NOTE:
Philosophische Schriften. Ed. by C. J. Gerhardt. 7 vols. Berlin: Weidmann, 1875–1890.

LENIN, VLADIMIR ILYICH (1870–1924)
Collected Works. 23 vols. New York: International Publishers, 1927. Vol. XVIII, *The Imperialist War* (1914–1916); Vol. XXI, *Toward the Seizure of Power* (1917).
—*Imperialism, the Highest Stage of Capitalism*. New York: International Publishers, 1939 (St. Petersburg, 1917).
—"*Left-Wing*" *Communism, an Infantile Disorder; A Popular Essay in Marxian Strategy and Tactics*. New York: International Publishers, 1940 (Moscow, 1920).
—*Materialism and Empiriocriticism*. Trans. by D. Kuitko and S. Hook. London: M. Lawrence, 1927 (Moscow, 1909).
—*Selected Works*. 12 vols. New York: International Publishers, 1943 (paper cited, 1915).
—*The State and Revolution*. New York: International Publishers, 1935 (St. Petersburg, 1918).

LENZEN, VICTOR FRITZ (1890–)
The Nature of Physical Theory; a Study in Theory of Knowledge. New York: J. Wiley, 1931.

LEO XIII, POPE (1810–1903)
[Rerum Novarum] *On the Condition of Labor*. In *Five Great Encyclicals*. New York: Paulist Press, 1939 (1891).

LEONARDO DA VINCI (1452–1519)
The Notebooks of Leonardo da Vinci. Trans. by E. MacCurdy. Garden City, N.Y.: Garden City Publishing Co., 1941.
—*A Treatise on Painting*. Trans. by J. F. Rigand. New York: G. Bell & Sons, 1892 (*Trattato della pittura*, 1485?–1500?).

LEOPARDI, COUNT GIACOMO (1798–1837)
Essays, Dialogues, and Thoughts. Ed. by B. Dobell, trans. by J. Thomson. New York: E. P. Dutton, 1905 (sel. from *Operette Morali*, Florence, 1827, and *Pensieri*).

LERMONTOV, MIKHAIL YUREVICH (1814–1841)
A Hero of Our Own Times. Trans. by E. and C. Paul. London: Allen & Unwin, 1940 (1840).

LE SAGE, ALAIN RENÉ (1668–1747)
The Adventures of Gil Blas. Trans. by Tobias Smollett. 2 vols. Everyman's Library, New York: E. P. Dutton, 1928 (*Histoire de Gil Blas de Santillane*, Paris, 1715–1735).

LESLIE, THOMAS EDWARD CLIFFE (1826–1882)
The Love of Money. In *Essays in Political Economy*. Dublin: Hodges, Figgis & Co., 1888 (1862).

LESSING, GOTTHOLD EPHRAIM (1729–1781)
The Education of the Human Race. Trans. by F. W. Robertson. London: C. K. Paul & Co., 1881 (*Die Erziehung des Menschengeschlechts*, Berlin, 1780).
—[How the Ancients Represented Death] *Laokoon, and How the Ancients Represented Death*. Trans. by H. Zimmern and E. C. Beasly. London: G. Bell & Sons, 1914 (*Wie die Alten den Tod gebildet; eine Untersuchung*, Berlin, 1769).
—*Laocoön, Nathan the Wise and Minna von Barnhelm*. Everyman's Library, New York: E. P. Dutton, 1930 (*Laokoon: oder über die Grenzen der Malerei und Poesie*, Berlin, 1766).
—*Minna von Barnhelm; or, Soldier's Fortune*. *Ibid*. (Berlin, 1767).
—*Nathan the Wise*. *Ibid*. (*Nathan der Weise*, Berlin, 1779).

LEVI-CIVITA, TULLIO (1873–1942)
Fragen der klassischen und relativistischen Mechanik. Berlin: J. Springer, 1924 (1921).

Lévy-Bruhl, Lucien (1857–1939)
Primitives and the Supernatural. Trans. by L. A. Clare. New York: E. P. Dutton, 1935 (*Le surnaturel et la nature dans la mentalité primitive*, Paris, 1931).

Lewes, George Henry (1817–1878)
The Principles of Success in Literature. Boston: Allyn & Bacon, 1894 (1865).
—*Problems of Life and Mind. First to Third Series*. 5 vols. New York: Houghton Mifflin, 1874–1891 (London, 1874–1879).

Lewis Carroll, pseud. for Charles Lutwidge Dodgson (1832–1898)
Alice's Adventures in Wonderland. In *Alice in Wonderland, Through the Looking-Glass, and Other Comic Pieces*. Everyman's Library, New York: E. P. Dutton, 1946 (London, 1865).
—*Euclid and His Modern Rivals*. London: Macmillan, 1885 (London, 1879).
—*Symbolic Logic, Part I, Elementary*. London: Macmillan, 1896.
—*Through the Looking-Glass and What Alice Found There*. See *Alice* (London, 1871).

Lewis, Clarence Irving (1883–1964)
An Analysis of Knowledge and Valuation. La Salle, Ill.: Open Court, 1947.
—*Mind and the World Order; Outline of a Theory of Knowledge*. New York: Scribner's, 1929.

Lewis, Clive Staples (1898–1963)
The Allegory of Love; a Study in Medieval Tradition. New York: Oxford University Press, 1938 (Oxford, 1936).
—*Out of the Silent Planet*. New York: Macmillan, 1943 (1938).
—*Perelandra*. New York: Macmillan, 1944.
—*The Problem of Pain*. New York: Macmillan, 1944 (London, 1940).
—*The Screwtape Letters*. New York: Macmillan, 1944 (London, 1942).

Lewis, Sir George Cornewall (1806–1863)
A Treatise on the Methods of Observation and Reasoning in Politics. 2 vols. London: J. W. Parker, 1852.

Lewis, Gilbert Newton (1875–1946)
The Anatomy of Science. New Haven, Conn.: Yale University Press, 1926.

Lewis, Sinclair (1885–1951)
Arrowsmith. Modern Library, New York: Random House, 1933 (New York, 1925).
—*Babbitt*. Modern Library, New York: Random House, 1942 (New York, 1922).

Lieber, Francis (1800–1872)
Manual of Political Ethics, Designed Chiefly for the Use of Colleges and Students at Law. Ed. by T. D. Woolsey. 2 vols. Philadelphia: Lippincott, 1911 (Boston, 1838–1839).

Liebknecht, Karl Paul August Friedrich (1871–1919)
Militarism. New York: B. W. Huebsch, 1917 (*Militarismus und Antimilitarismus*, Leipsic, 1907).

Lillie, Ralph Stayner (1875–1952)
Protoplasmic Action and Nervous Action. University of Chicago Press, 1923.

Lindsay, Alexander Dunlop (1879–1952)
The Modern Democratic State. New York: Oxford University Press, 1943.

Linnaeus (Carl von Linné) (1707–1778)
Caroli Linnei Systema Naturae—Regnum Animale. Leipsic: W. Engelmann, 1894 (*Systema Naturae, sive Regna Tria Naturae Systematice Proposita per Classes, Ordines, Genera et Species*, Leyden, 1735).

Lippmann, Walter (1889–)
Public Opinion. New York: Penguin Books, 1946 (1922).

Lipps, Theodor (1851–1914)
Ästhetik: Psychologie des Schönen und der Kunst. 2 vols. Leipsic: L. Voss, 1914–1920 (Leipsic, 1903–1906).

Livingstone, Sir Richard Winn (1880–1960)
On Education. Cambridge University Press, 1944 (originally pub. as *The Future in Education*, Cambridge, 1941, and *Education for a World Adrift*, Cambridge, 1943).

Lobachevski, Nicolas Ivanovich (1793–1856)
Geometrical Researches on the Theory of Parallels. Trans. by G. B. Halsted. Chicago: Open Court, 1942 (*Geometrische Untersuchungen zur Theorie der Parallellinien*, Berlin, 1840).

Locke, John (1632–1704)
Conduct of the Understanding. Ed. by T. Fowler. Oxford: Clarendon Press, 1901 (*c.* 1697).
—*A Discourse of Miracles*. In Vol. ix, *The Works of John Locke*. 10 vols. London: T. Tegg, 1823–1824 (1702–1703).
—*Four Letters on Toleration in Religion, Letters II–IV*. In Vol. vi, *ibid.* (*Second Letter*, London, 1690; *Third Letter*, London, 1692; *Fourth Letter*, posth., London, 1706).
—*The Reasonableness of Christianity as Delivered in the Scriptures*. In Vol. vii, *ibid.* (London, 1695).
—*A Second Vindication of the Reasonableness of Christianity*. *Ibid.* (London, 1697).
—*Some Considerations of the Consequences of Lowering the Interest, and Raising the Value of Money*. In Vol. v, *ibid.* (1691).
—*Some Thoughts Concerning Education*. In Vol. ix, *ibid.* (London, 1693).

Lods, Adolphe (1867–1948)
The Prophets and the Rise of Judaism. Trans. by S. H. Hooke. New York: E. P. Dutton, 1937 (*Les prophètes d'Israël et les débuts du judaïsme*, Paris, 1935).

Loeb, Jacques (1859–1924)
Comparative Physiology of the Brain and Comparative Psychology. New York: Putnam's, 1902 (*Einleitung in die vergleichende Gehirnphysiologie*

und vergleichende Psychologie, Leipsic, 1899).
—*Forced Movements, Tropisms and Animal Conduct*. Philadelphia: Lippincott, 1918.
—*The Mechanistic Conception of Life*. University of Chicago Press, 1912.
—*The Organism as a Whole, from a Physicochemical Viewpoint*. New York: Putnam's, 1916.

Löwith, Karl (1897–)
Meaning in History. University of Chicago Press, 1949.

Longinus (1st century A.D.?)
On the Sublime. Trans. by W. H. Fyfe. Loeb Library, Cambridge, Mass.: Harvard University Press, 1932.

Lorentz, Hendrik Antoon (1853–1928)
Lectures on Theoretical Physics. Trans. by L. Silberstein and A. P. H. Trivelli. London: Macmillan, 1927 (1907).
—*Problems of Modern Physics*. Ed. by H. Bateman. New York: Ginn & Co., 1927 (1922).

Lossky, Nikolai Onufrievich (1870–)
Freedom of Will. Trans. by N. Duddington. London: Williams & Norgate, 1932 (1927).

Lotze, Rudolf Hermann (1817–1881)
Grundzüge der Naturphilosophie. Diktate aus den Vorlesungen von Hermann Lotze. Leipsic: S. Hirzel, 1887 (1876).
—*Logic, in Three Books: Of Thought, of Investigation, and of Knowledge*. Ed. by B. Bosanquet, trans. by R. L. Nettleship *et al.* Oxford: Clarendon Press, 1884 (*Logik. System der Philosophie*, I, Leipsic, 1874).
—*Metaphysics, in Three Books, Ontology, Cosmology, and Psychology*. Ed. and trans. by B. Bosanquet. Oxford: Clarendon Press, 1884 (*Metaphysik. System der Philosophie*, II, Leipsic, 1879).
—*Microcosmos, an Essay Concerning Man and His Relation to the World*. Trans. by E. Hamilton and E. E. Constance Jones. 2 vols. Edinburgh: T. & T. Clark, 1885 (*Mikrokosmus, Ideen zur Naturgeschichte und Geschichte der Menschheit*, Leipsic, 1856–1858).
—*Outlines of a Philosophy of Religion*. Ed. by F. C. Conybeare. New York: Scribner's, 1916 (1875; 1878–1879).
—*Outlines of Encyclopedia of Philosophy*. See *Outlines of Logic*.
—*Outlines of Logic and of Encyclopedia of Philosophy: Dictated Portions of the Lectures of H. Lotze*. Ed. and trans. by G. T. Ladd. Boston: Ginn & Co., 1887.
—*Outlines of Metaphysic*. Ed. and trans. by G. T. Ladd. Boston: Ginn & Co., 1884.
—*Outlines of Psychology*. Ed. and trans. by G. T. Ladd. Boston: Ginn & Co., 1886 (*Grundzüge der Psychologie. Diktate aus den Vorlesungen von H. Lotze*, Leipsic, 1881).

Lovejoy, Arthur Oncken (1873–1962)
The Great Chain of Being; a Study of the History of an Idea. Cambridge, Mass.: Harvard University Press, 1936 (1933).
—*The Revolt Against Dualism: An Inquiry Concerning the Existence of Ideas*. New York: W. W. Norton, 1930.

Lowes, John Livingston (1867–1945)
The Road to Xanadu: A Study in the Ways of the Imagination. Boston: Houghton Mifflin Co., 1927.

Lubac, Henri De (1896–)
Surnaturel. Paris: Aubier, 1946.

Lucian (Lucianus Samosatensis) (2nd century A.D.)
Alexander the Oracle-Monger. In Vol. II, *The Works of Lucian of Samosata*. Trans. by H. W. and F. G. Fowler. 4 vols. Oxford: Clarendon Press, 1905 (180?).
—*The Fisher*. In Vol. I, *ibid.* (165?–175?).
—*The Gods in Council*. In Vol. IV, *ibid.* (165?–175?).
—*Icaromenippus: An Aerial Expedition*. In Vol. III, *ibid.* (165?–175?).
—*Of Sacrifice*. In Vol. I, *ibid.* (165?–175?).
—*Sale of Creeds*. *Ibid.* (165?–175?).
—*The Way to Write History*. In Vol. II, *ibid.* (165?).

Lull, Ramón (Lully) (1235–1315)
The Book of the Ordre of Chyvalry. Ed. by A. T. B. Byles, trans. by W. Caxton. London: H. Milford, 1926 (1276–1286).

Luther, Martin (1483–1546)
[Address to the German Nobility] *An Open Letter to the Christian Nobility of the German Nation*. In *Three Treatises* (Wittenberg, 1520).
—*Against the Robbing and Murdering Hordes of Peasants*. In Vol. IV, *Works* (*Wider die stürmenden Bauren*, Wittenberg, 1525).
—[The Babylonian Captivity] *A Prelude on the Babylonian Captivity of the Church*. In *Three Treatises* (Wittenberg, 1520).
—*The Magnificat*. In Vol. III, *Works* (*Das Magnificat verdeutscht und ausgelegt durch Martin Luther*, Wittenberg, 1520; 1521).
—*On Trading and Usury*. In Vol. IV, *ibid.* (*Von Kauffshandlung und Wucher*, Wittenberg, 1524).
—*The Schmalkald Articles*. In *The Christian Book of Concord*. Philadelphia: Jacob, 1882 (1537).
—*Secular Authority: To What Extent It Should Be Obeyed*. In Vol. III, *Works* (*Von weltlicher Oberkeit, wie weit man ihr Gehorsam schuldig sei*, Wittenberg, 1523).
—*The Table Talk of Martin Luther*. Ed. and trans. by W. Hazlitt. Philadelphia: United Lutheran Publication House, 1904 (1531–1546).
—*To the Councilmen of All Cities in Germany That They Establish and Maintain Christian Schools*. In Vol. IV, *Works* (Wittenberg, 1524).
—*A Treatise on Christian Liberty*. In *Three Treatises* (Wittenberg, 1520).
—*Trinity Sunday*. In Vol. IX, *The Precious and Sacred Writings of Martin Luther*. Ed. by J. N. Lenker, trans. by H. L. Burry. Minneapolis, Minn.: Lutherans in All Lands Co., 1903 (Wittenberg, 1535).

—*Whether Soldiers, Too, Can Be Saved*. In Vol. v, *Works* (*Ob Kriegsleute auch in seligem Stand sein können*, Wittenberg, 1526).

NOTE:

Three Treatises. Ed. and trans. by C. M. Jacobs *et al*. Philadelphia: Muhlenberg Press, 1947.

—*Works of Martin Luther*. Ed. by H. E. Jacobs. 6 vols. Philadelphia: A. J. Holman, 1915–1932.

LYELL, SIR CHARLES (1797–1875)

The Geological Evidences of the Antiquity of Man. Everyman's Library, New York: E. P. Dutton, 1914 (Philadelphia, 1863).

—*Principles of Geology; or, The Modern Changes of the Earth and Its Inhabitants Considered as Illustrations of Geology*. 2 vols. New York: D. Appleton, 1892 (London, 1830–1833).

LYLY, JOHN (*c.* 1554–1606)

Euphues: The Anatomy of Wit; Euphues and His England. Ed. by M. W. Croll and H. Clemons. New York: E. P. Dutton, 1916 (London, 1579; 1580).

M

MABLY, GABRIEL DE BONNOT (1709–1785)

Des droits et devoirs du citoyen. Paris: Bibliothèque Nationale, 1876 (Paris, 1758).

MACAULAY, THOMAS BABINGTON (1800–1859)

Miscellaneous Essays; the Lays of Ancient Rome. Everyman's Library, New York: E. P. Dutton, 1932 (essay cited, 1828).

MCDOUGALL, WILLIAM (1871–1938)

Modern Materialism and Emergent Evolution. New York: Van Nostrand, 1929.

MACH, ERNST (1838–1916)

The Analysis of Sensations and the Relation of the Physical to the Psychical. Ed. by S. Waterlow, trans. by C. M. Williams. Chicago: Open Court, 1914 (*Beiträge zur Analyse der Empfindungen*, Jena, 1886).

—*Erkenntnis und Irrtum: Skizzen zur Psychologie der Forschung*. Leipsic: J. A. Barth, 1905.

—*History and Root of the Principle of the Conservation of Energy*. Trans. by P. E. B. Jourdain. Chicago: Open Court, 1911 (1872).

—*Popular Scientific Lectures*. Trans. by J. McCormack. Chicago: Open Court, 1895.

—*The Science of Mechanics: A Critical and Historical Account of Its Development*. Trans. by T. J. McCormack. Chicago: Open Court, 1942 (*Die Mechanik in ihrer Entwicklung*, Leipsic, 1883).

—*Space and Geometry in the Light of Physiological, Psychological and Physical Inquiry*. Trans. by T. J. McCormack. Chicago: Open Court, 1906 (1901–1903).

MACHIAVELLI, NICCOLÒ (1469–1527)

The Art of War. In *Machiavelli*. Ed. by H. Cust, trans. by P. Whitehorne. 2 vols. London: D. Nutt, 1905 (*Dell' Arte della guerra*, Florence, 1521).

—*Belfagor*. In *Italian Novelists*. Ed. and trans. by T. Roscoe. London: F. Warne & Co., 1908.

—*Castruccio Castracani*. In *The Prince and Other Works*. Ed. and trans. by A. H. Gilbert. Chicago: Packard & Co., 1941 (1520).

—[The Discourses] *The Prince and the Discourses*. Trans. by C. E. Detmold. Modern Library, New York: Random House, 1940 (*Discorsi . . . sopra la prima deca di Tito Livio*, *c.* 1513).

—*Florentine History*. Trans. by W. K. Marriott. Everyman's Library, New York: E. P. Dutton, 1922 (*c.* 1520–1525).

MCILWAIN, CHARLES HOWARD (1871–)

Constitutionalism, Ancient and Modern. Ithaca: Cornell University Press, 1940 (1938–1939).

—*Constitutionalism and the Changing World; Collected Papers*. New York: Macmillan, 1939.

—*The Fundamental Law Behind the Constitution*. In *The Constitution Reconsidered*. Ed. by C. Read. New York: Columbia University Press, 1938.

MACIVER, ROBERT MORRISON (1882–1970)

Leviathan and the People. Baton Rouge, La.: Louisiana State University Press, 1939.

—*Society; Its Structure and Changes*. New York: Long & Smith, 1931.

—*The Web of Government*. New York: Macmillan, 1947.

MCLELLAN, JAMES ALEXANDER (1832–1907) and DEWEY, JOHN (1859–1952)

The Psychology of Number and Its Applications to Methods of Teaching Arithmetic. New York: D. Appleton, 1916 (New York, 1895).

MCTAGGART, JOHN MCTAGGART ELLIS (1866–1925)

The Nature of Existence. 2 vols. Cambridge University Press, 1921–1927.

—*Some Dogmas of Religion*. London: E. Arnold, 1906.

—*Studies in the Hegelian Dialectic*. Cambridge University Press, 1922 (Cambridge, 1896).

MADARIAGA, SALVADOR (1886–)

Anarchy or Hierarchy. New York: Macmillan, 1937 (Madrid, 1935).

MAHAN, ALFRED THAYER (1840–1914)

The Influence of Sea Power upon History, 1660–1783. Boston: Little, Brown & Co., 1915 (Boston, 1890).

MAIMONIDES (MOSES BEN MAIMON) (1135–1204)

The Eight Chapters of Maimonides on Ethics; a Psychological and Ethical Treatise. Ed. and trans. by J. I. Gorfinkle. New York: Columbia University Press, 1912 (1158–1168).

—*The Guide for the Perplexed*. Trans. by M. Friedlander. New York: E. P. Dutton, 1928 (1190?).

—*The Mishneh Torah*. Ed. and trans. by M. Hyamson. New York: Bloch Publishing Co., 1937 (1158–1190).

—*Regimen Sanitatis*. Facsimile of 1477(?) ed. Heidelberg: H. Grossberger, 1931 (1198?).

—*Treatise on Logic*. Ed. and trans. by I. Efros. New York: American Academy for Jewish Research, 1938 (1151).

MAINE, SIR HENRY JAMES SUMNER (1822–1888)
Ancient Law. Everyman's Library, New York: E. P. Dutton, 1931 (London, 1861).
—*Dissertations on Early Law and Customs, Chiefly Selected from Lectures Delivered at Oxford*. New York: Henry Holt, 1886 (London, 1883).
—*Lectures on the Early History of Institutions*. New York: Henry Holt, 1888 (London, 1875).
—*Popular Government; Four Essays*. London: J. Murray, 1897 (London, 1885).

MAINE DE BIRAN, PIERRE, pseud. for MARIE FRANÇOIS PIERRE GONTHIER (1766–1824)
The Influence of Habit on the Faculty of Thinking. Trans. by M. D. Boehm. Baltimore, Md.: Williams & Wilkins, 1929 (*Influence de l'habitude sur la faculté de penser*, Paris, 1803).

MAIRET, PHILIPPE (1886–)
Aristocracy and the Meaning of Class Rule: An Essay upon Aristocracy Past and Future. London: C. W. Daniel, 1931.

MAISTRE, JOSEPH MARIE DE (1753–1821)
Du pape. In *J. de Maistre*. Ed. by A. Crosnier. Paris: Desclée, de Brouwer, 1933 (Lyons, 1819).

MAITLAND, FREDERIC WILLIAM (1850–1906)
Justice and Police. London: Macmillan, 1885.

MALEBRANCHE, NICOLAS (1638–1715)
De la recherche de la vérité. Ed. by F. Bouillier. 2 vols. Paris: Garnier, 1879 (Paris, 1674–1675).
—*Dialogues on Metaphysics and Religion*. Trans. by M. Ginsberg. New York: Macmillan, 1923 (*Entretiens sur la métaphysique et la religion*, Rotterdam, 1688).

MALINOWSKI, BRONISLAW KASPER (1884–1942)
Crime and Custom in Savage Society. New York: Harcourt Brace, 1932 (New York, 1926).
—*Freedom and Civilization*. Ed. by A. V. Malinowska. New York: Roy Publishers, 1944.
—*The Sexual Life of Savages in North-Western Melanesia. An Ethnographic Account of Courtship, Marriage and Family Life Among the Natives of the Trobriand Islands, Brit. New Guinea*. New York: Liveright, 1929.

MALLOCK, WILLIAM HURRELL (1849–1923)
Aristocracy and Evolution: A Study of the Rights, the Origin and the Social Functions of the Wealthier Classes. New York: Macmillan, 1898.
—*Social Equality: A Short Study in a Missing Science*. London: R. Bentley, 1882.

MALORY, SIR THOMAS (*fl.* 1470)
Le morte d'Arthur. 2 vols. Everyman's Library, New York: E. P. Dutton, 1934–1935.

MALRAUX, ANDRÉ (1895–)
Man's Fate. Trans. by H. M. Chevalier. Modern Library, New York: Random House, 1936 (*La condition humaine*, Paris, 1933).
—*Man's Hope*. Trans. by S. Gilbert and A. Macdonald. Modern Library, New York: Random House, 1941 (*L'espoir*, Paris, 1937).

MALTHUS, THOMAS ROBERT (1766–1834)
An Essay on Population. 2 vols. Everyman's Library, New York: E. P. Dutton, 1933 (London, 1798).
—*Principles of Political Economy Considered with a View to Their Practical Application*. London: W. Pickering, 1836 (London, 1820).

MANDEVILLE, BERNARD DE (*c.* 1670–1733)
An Enquiry into the Origin of Honor, and the Usefulness of Christianity in War. London: J. Brotherton, 1732.
—*The Fable of the Bees; or, Private Vices, Publick Benefits*. Ed. by F. B. Kaye. Oxford: Clarendon Press, 1924 (originally pub. as *The Grumbling Hive; or, Knaves Turn'd Honest*, London, 1705).

MANN, THOMAS (1875–1955)
Buddenbrooks. Trans. by H. T. Lowe-Porter. New York: Garden City Publishing Co., 1940 (Berlin, 1901).
—*Joseph and His Brothers*. Trans. by H. T. Lowe-Porter. New York: A. A. Knopf, 1936 (Berlin, 1933).
—*Joseph in Egypt*. Trans. by H. T. Lowe-Porter. 2 vols. New York: A. A. Knopf, 1938 (*Joseph in Agypten*, Vienna, 1936).
—*The Magic Mountain*. Trans. by H. T. Lowe-Porter. Modern Library, New York: Random House, 1932 (*Der Zauberberg*, Berlin, 1924).
—*Tonio Kröger*. In *Stories of Three Decades*. Trans. by H. T. Lowe-Porter. New York: A. A. Knopf, 1936 (Berlin, 1903).
—*Young Joseph*. Trans. by H. T. Lowe-Porter. New York: A. A. Knopf, 1935 (*Der junge Joseph*, Berlin, 1934).

MANSEL, HENRY LONGUEVILLE (1820–1871)
Prolegomena Logica. An Inquiry into the Psychological Character of Logical Processes. Oxford: H. Hammans, 1851.

MANZONI, ALESSANDRO FRANCESCO TOMMASO ANTONIO (1785–1873)
The Betrothed (I promessi sposi): A Milanese Story of the Seventeenth Century. Trans. by D. J. Connor. New York: Macmillan, 1937 (Milan, 1825–1827).

MARÉCHAL, JOSEPH (1878–1944)
Le point de départ de la métaphysique: leçons sur le développement historique et théorique du problème de la connaissance. 3 vols. Bruges: C. Beyaert, 1922–1923.

MARETT, ROBERT RANULPH (1866–1943)
Head, Heart and Hands in Human Evolution. New York: Henry Holt, 1935.

MARIANA, JUAN DE (1536–1624)
The King and the Education of the King. Trans. by G. A. Moore. Washington: Country Dollar Press, 1948 (*De Rege et Regis Institutione*, 1599).

MARITAIN, JACQUES (1882–)
Art and Scholasticism, with Other Essays. Trans. by J. F. Scanlan. New York: Scribner's, 1937 (*Art et scholastique*, Paris, 1920).
—*Christianity and Democracy*. Trans. by D. C. An-

son. New York: Scribner's, 1944 (*Christianisme et démocratie*, New York, 1943).
—*De la philosophie chrétienne*. Paris: Desclée, de Brouwer, 1933 (1931).
—*The Degrees of Knowledge*. Trans. by B. Wall and M. R. Adamson. New York: Scribner's, 1938 (*Distinguer pour unir, ou les dégrés du savoir*, Paris, 1932).
—*Education at the Crossroads*. New Haven, Conn.: Yale University Press, 1943.
—*Existence and the Existent*. New York: Pantheon Press, 1948.
—*Freedom in the Modern World*. Trans. by R. O'Sullivan. New York: Scribner's, 1936 (*Du régime temporel et de la liberté*, Paris, 1933).
—*An Introduction to Logic*. Trans. by G. Choquette. New York: Sheed & Ward, 1937 (*L'ordre des concepts: I, Petite logique*, Paris, 1923).
—*An Introduction to Philosophy*. Trans. by E. I. Watkin. London: Longmans, Green & Co., 1930 (*Introduction générale à la philosophie*, Paris, 1920).
—*The Person and the Common Good*. Trans. by J. J. Fitzgerald. New York: Scribner's, 1947.
—*A Preface to Metaphysics, Seven Lectures on Being*. New York: Sheed & Ward, 1939 (*Sept leçons sur l'être et les premiers principes de la raison spéculative*, Paris, 1934).
—*Principes d'une politique humaniste*. New York: Éditions de la Maison Française, 1944.
—*Ransoming the Time*. Trans. by H. L. Binsse. New York: Scribner's, 1941.
—*Réflexions sur l'intelligence et sur la vie propre*. Paris: Desclée, de Brouwer, 1921.
—*Religion and Culture*. Trans. by J. F. Scanlan. New York: Sheed & Ward, 1931 (*Religion et culture*, Paris, 1930).
—*The Rights of Man and Natural Law*. Trans. by D. C. Anson. New York: Scribner's, 1943 (*Les droits de l'homme et la loi naturelle*, New York, 1942).
—*Saint Thomas and the Problem of Evil*. Trans. by Mrs. G. Andison. Milwaukee, Wis.: Marquette University Press, 1942.
—*Scholasticism and Politics*. Ed. by M. J. Adler. New York: Macmillan, 1940.
—*Science and Wisdom*. Trans. by B. Wall. London: Centenary Press, 1940 (*Science et sagesse, suivi d'éclaircissements sur la philosophie morale*, Paris, 1935).
—*Theonas, Conversations of a Sage*. Trans. by F. J. Sheed. New York: Sheed & Ward, 1933 (*Théonas, ou Les Entretiens d'un sage et de deux philosophes sur diverses matières inégalement actuelles*, Paris, 1921).
—*The Things That Are Not Caesar's*. Trans. by J. F. Scanlan. New York: Scribner's, 1930 (*Primauté du spirituel*, Paris, 1927).
—*True Humanism*. Trans. by M. R. Adamson. London: Centenary Press, 1938 (*Problemas espirituales y temporales de una nueva cristiandad*, Madrid, 1934).

Mark Twain, pseud. for Samuel Langhorne Clemens (1835–1910)
The Adventures of Huckleberry Finn. In *Tom Sawyer and Huckleberry Finn*. Everyman's Library, New York: E. P. Dutton, 1944 (London, 1884).
—*The Adventures of Tom Sawyer*. *Ibid*. (Hartford, Conn., 1876).
—*What Is Man? And Other Essays*. New York: Harper, 1917 (title essay, New York, 1906).

Marlowe, Christopher (1564–1593)
Edward the Second. In *The Plays of Christopher Marlowe*. Everyman's Library, New York: E. P. Dutton, 1947 (1592 or 1593).
—*Tamburlaine the Great*. *Ibid*. (1587 or 1588).
—*The Tragical History of Doctor Faustus*. *Ibid*. (1589?).

Marriott, Sir John Arthur Ransome (1859–1945)
Dictatorship and Democracy. Oxford: Clarendon Press, 1935.

Marshall, Alfred (1842–1924)
Principles of Economics. London: Macmillan, 1936 (London, 1890).

Marshall, Henry Rutgers (1852–1927)
Instinct and Reason, an Essay Concerning the Relation of Instinct to Reason, with Some Special Study of the Nature of Religion. New York: Macmillan, 1898.

Marsilius of Padua (*c*. 1270–1342)
[Defensor Pacis] *The Defender of Peace*. Trans. by A. Gewirth. New York: Columbia University Press, 1950 (1324).

Martianus Capella (5th century)
De Nuptiis Philologiae et Mercurii. In *Martianus Capella*. Ed. by A. Dick. Leipsic: B. G. Teubner, 1925 (430?).

Martin du Gard, Roger (1881–1958)
The Thibaults. Trans. by S. Gilbert. New York: Viking Press, 1939 (Paris, 1922–1929).

Martineau, James (1805–1900)
A Study of Religion, Its Sources and Contents. 2 vols. Oxford: Clarendon Press, 1900 (Oxford, 1888).

Marvell, Andrew (1621–1678)
Dialogue Between the Soul and the Body. In Vol. 1, *The Poems and Letters of Andrew Marvell*. Ed. by H. M. Margoliouth. 2 vols. Oxford: Clarendon Press, 1927 (1681).
—*To His Coy Mistress*. *Ibid*. (1681).

Marx, Karl (1818–1883)
The Civil War in France. New York: International Publishers, 1937 (1871).
—*A Contribution to the Critique of Political Economy*. Trans. by N. I. Stone. New York: International Library Publishing Co., 1904 (*Zur Kritik der politischen Oekonomie*, 1, Berlin, 1859).
—*A Criticism of the Hegelian Philosophy of Right*. In *Selected Essays*. Trans. by H. J. Stenning. New York: International Publishers, 1926 (*Zur Kritik der Hegelschen Rechtsphilosophie*, in *Deutsch-Französische Jahrbücher*, Paris, 1844).

—*Critique of the Gotha Programme*. Ed. by C. P. Dutt. New York: International Publishers, 1938 (1875).

—*The Eighteenth Brumaire of Louis Bonaparte*. Trans. by E. and C. Paul. London: Allen & Unwin, 1926 (1852).

—*The Poverty of Philosophy*. Trans. by H. Quelch. Chicago: C. H. Kerr, 1910 (*Misère de la philosophie. Réponse à La philosophie de la misère de M. Proudhon*, Paris, 1847).

—*Über die Differenz der demokritischen und epikureischen Naturphilosophie*. Vol. I, First Series. *Historisch-Kritische Gesamtausgabe*. Ed. by D. Rjazanov. Frankfort: Marx-Engels Archiv, 1927 (1841).

MARX, KARL and ENGELS, FRIEDRICH (1820–1895)
The German Ideology. Ed. by R. Pascal. New York: International Publishers, 1939 (Parts I and III, *Die deutsche Ideologie*, Moscow, 1932 [1846]).

MASON, OTIS TUFTON (1838–1908)
Woman's Share in Primitive Culture. New York: D. Appleton, 1914 (New York, 1894).

MATTHEW OF AQUASPARTA (*c.* 1234–1302)
Ten Disputed Questions on Knowledge. In Vol. II, *Selections from Medieval Philosophers*. Ed. and trans. by Richard McKeon. 2 vols. New York: Scribner's, 1929–1930.

MAUDSLEY, HENRY (1835–1918)
Responsibility in Mental Disease. New York: D. Appleton, 1901 (London, 1874).

MAURICE, FREDERICK DENISON (1805–1872)
The Conscience: Lectures on Casuistry, Delivered in the University of Cambridge. London: Macmillan, 1883 (London, 1868).

MAURON, CHARLES
Aesthetics and Psychology. Trans. by R. Fry and C. John. London: Hogarth Press, 1935.

MAURRAS, CHARLES (1868–1952)
Enquête sur la monarchie. Paris: A. Fayard, 1937 (Paris, 1900–1909).

MAXWELL, JAMES CLERK (1831–1879)
Matter and Motion. Ed. by J. Larmor. London: Society for Promoting Christian Knowledge, 1920 (London, 1876).

—*The Scientific Papers of James Clerk Maxwell*. Ed. by W. D. Niven. 2 vols. Cambridge University Press, 1890 (1846–1879).

—*Theory of Heat*. Ed. by Lord Rayleigh. New York: Longmans, Green & Co., 1916 (London, 1871).

—*A Treatise on Electricity and Magnetism*. Ed. by J. J. Thomson. 2 vols. Oxford: Clarendon Press, 1892 (Oxford, 1873).

MAYR, ERNST (1904–)
Systematics and the Origin of Species from the Viewpoint of a Zoologist. New York: Columbia University Press, 1942.

MAZZINI, GIUSEPPE (1805–1872)
The Duties of Man, and Other Essays. Everyman's Library, New York: E. P. Dutton, 1936 (*Dei doveri dell'uomo*, Genoa, 1851).

—*From the Council to God*. *Ibid*. (Letter to the Members of the Oecumenical Council, London, 1870).

MEAD, GEORGE HERBERT (1863–1931)
The Philosophy of the Present. Ed. by A. E. Murphy. Chicago: Open Court, 1932 (1930).

MEIKLEJOHN, ALEXANDER (1872–1964)
Education Between Two Worlds. New York: Harper, 1942.

MELANCHTHON, PHILIP (1497–1565)
Commentarius de Anima. In Vol. XIII, *Philipi Melanthonis Opera . . . Omnia* (*Corpus Reformatorum*). Ed. by C. G. Bretschneider. 28 vols. Halle: C. Schwetschke, 1834–1840 (Strasbourg, 1540).

—[Dialectica] *Compendiaria Dialectices Ratio*. *Ibid*. (Wittenberg, 1520).

—*The Loci Communes of Philip Melanchthon*. Trans. by C. L. Hill. Boston: Meador Publishing Co., 1944 (Wittenberg, 1521).

MELVILLE, HERMAN (1819–1891)
Omoo: A Narrative of Adventures in the South Seas. Everyman's Library, New York: E. P. Dutton, 1925 (New York, 1847).

—*Pierre; or, The Ambiguities*. New York: E. P. Dutton, 1929 (New York, 1852).

—*Typee: A Narrative of the Marquesas Islands*. Everyman's Library, New York: E. P. Dutton, 1930 (New York, 1846).

MENDEL, GREGOR JOHANN (1822–1884)
Experiments in Plant Hybridization. Cambridge, Mass.: Harvard University Press, 1941 (1866).

MENDELEYEV, DMITRI IVANOVICH (1834–1907)
The Principles of Chemistry. Ed. by T. H. Pope, trans. by G. Kamensky. 2 vols. London: Longmans, Green & Co., 1905 (St. Petersburg, 1869–1871).

MENDELSSOHN, MOSES (1729–1786)
Phädon; oder Ueber die Unsterblichkeit der Seele. Berlin: Nicolai, 1868 (Berlin, 1767).

MENGER, KARL (1840–1921)
Grundsätze der Volkswirtschaftslehre. Vienna: W. Braumüller, 1871.

MEREDITH, GEORGE (1828–1909)
The Amazing Marriage. New York: Scribner's, 1915 (Westminster, 1895).

—*Diana of the Crossways*. Modern Library, New York: Random House, 1931 (London, 1885).

—*Earth and Man*. In *The Poetical Works of George Meredith*. New York: Scribner's, 1912 (London, 1883).

—*The Egoist: A Comedy in Narrative*. Modern Library, New York: Random House, 1947 (London, 1879).

—*An Essay on Comedy and the Uses of the Comic Spirit*. New York: Scribner's, 1918 (1877).

—*Modern Love.* In *Poetical Works.* See above (London, 1862).
—*The Ordeal of Richard Feverel.* Everyman's Library, New York: E. P. Dutton, 1935 (London, 1859).

MERRIAM, CHARLES EDWARD (1874–1953)
The Making of Citizens; a Comparative Study of Methods of Civic Training. University of Chicago Press, 1931.
—*The New Democracy and the New Despotism.* New York: McGraw-Hill, 1939.
—*Systematic Politics.* University of Chicago Press, 1945.
—*What Is Democracy?* University of Chicago Press, 1941.
—*The Written Constitution and the Unwritten Attitude.* New York: R. R. Smith, 1931.

MERSCH, EMILE
Love, Marriage and Chastity. New York: Sheed & Ward, 1939 (1928).

MEYERSON, ÉMILE (1859–1933)
De l'explication dans les sciences. 2 vols. Paris: Payot, 1927 (Paris, 1921).
—*Du cheminement de la pensée.* 3 vols. Paris: F. Alcan, 1931.
—*Identity and Reality.* Trans. by K. Loewenberg. New York: Macmillan, 1930 (*Identité et réalité,* Paris, 1908).

MICHEL, VIRGIL GEORGE (1890–1938)
Christian Social Reconstruction; Some Fundamentals of the Quadragesimo Anno. Milwaukee, Wis.: Bruce Publishing Co., 1937.

MICHELANGELO BUONARROTI (1475–1564)
The Sonnets of Michael Angelo Buonarroti, Now for the First Time Translated into Rhymed English. Trans. by J. A. Symonds. London: J. Murray, 1926 (1531).

MICHELET, JULES (1798–1874)
Introduction à l'histoire universelle. In Vol. XXXV, *Oeuvres Complètes.* 40 vols. Paris: E. Flammarion, 1893–1899 (1831).
—*L'amour.* Paris: Calmann-Lévy, 1884 (Paris, 1858).
—*The People.* Trans. by C. Cocks. London: Longman, Brown, Green & Longmans, 1846 (*Le peuple,* Paris, 1846).
—*Satanism and Witchcraft: A Study in Medieval Superstition.* Ed. and trans. by A. R. Allinson. New York: Walden Publications, 1939 (*La sorcière,* Paris, 1862).

MICHELS, ROBERT (1876–1936)
Economia e felicità. Milan: F. Vallardi, 1918.
—*Political Parties: A Sociological Study of the Oligarchical Tendencies of Modern Democracy.* Trans. by E. & C. Paul. Glencoe, Ill.: The Free Press, 1949 (*Zur Soziologie des Parteiwesens in den modernen Demokratien,* German ed., 1910).

MILL, JAMES (1773–1836)
Analysis of the Phenomena of the Human Mind. Ed. by J. S. Mill. 2 vols. London: Longmans & Dyer, 1878 (London, 1829).
—*Elements of Political Economy.* London: H. G. Bohn, 1844 (London, 1821).
—*An Essay on Government.* Ed. by E. Barker. Cambridge University Press, 1937 (reprinted from the Supplement to the 5th ed., *Encyclopaedia Britannica,* 1824).

MILL, JOHN STUART (1806–1873)
Autobiography. Ed. by J. J. Cross. New York: Columbia University Press, 1944 (London, 1873).
—*Dissertations and Discussions: Political, Philosophical and Historical.* 4 vols. London: J. W. Parker, 1859–1875 (1833–1873).
—*An Examination of Sir William Hamilton's Philosophy, and of the Principal Philosophical Questions Discussed in His Writings.* New York: Longmans, Green & Co., 1889 (London, 1865).
—*Inaugural Address, Delivered to the University of St. Andrews, Feb. 1st, 1867.* London: Longmans, Green, Reader, & Dyer, 1867.
—*Principles of Political Economy, with Some of Their Applications to Social Philosophy.* Ed. by W. J. Ashley. London: Longmans, Green & Co., 1936 (London, 1848).
—*Socialism.* Chicago: Belfords, Clarke & Co., 1879 (1872–1873).
—*The Subjection of Women.* Everyman's Library, New York: E. P. Dutton, 1929 (Philadelphia, 1869).
—*A System of Logic, Ratiocinative and Inductive, Being a Connected View of the Principles of Evidence and the Methods of Scientific Investigation.* London: Longmans, Green & Co., 1930 (London, 1843).
—*Thoughts on Parliamentary Reform.* London: J. W. Parker, 1859.
—[Three Essays on Religion] *Nature; the Utility of Religion; and Theism.* New York: Longmans, Green & Co., 1923 (1850–1858; *Theism,* 1868–1870).

MILLAR, JOHN (1735–1801)
Observations Concerning the Distinction of Ranks in Society. London: J. Murray, 1781 (London, 1771).

MILNE, EDWARD ARTHUR (1896–1950)
Kinematical Relativity. Reprinted from the *Journal of the London Mathematical Society,* London, 1940.

MILTON, JOHN (1608–1674)
[Defence of the People of England] *John Milton an Englishman His Defence of the People of England Against Claudius Anonymous, Alias Salmasius, His Defence of the King.* In Vol. VII, *The Works of John Milton.* Ed. by F. A. Patterson. 18 vols. New York: Columbia University Press, 1931–1938 (*Joannis Miltoni Angli pro Populo Anglicano Defensio,* London, 1650).
—*The Doctrine and Discipline of Divorce: Restor'd to the Good of Both Sexes, etc.* In Vol. III, *ibid.* (London, 1643).

—[Grammar] *Accedence Commenc't Grammar, Supply'd with Sufficient Rules, etc.* In Vol. VI, *ibid.* (London, 1669).
—*Of Education.* In Vol. IV, *ibid.* (London, 1644).
—*The Readie and Easie Way to Establish a Free Commonwealth.* In Vol. VI, *ibid.* (London, 1660).
—*The Reason of Church-Government Urg'd Against Prelaty.* In Vol. III, *ibid.* (London, 1641).
—*The Tenure of Kings and Magistrates.* In Vol. V, *ibid.* (London, 1649).

MISES, RICHARD VON (1883–1953)
Probability, Statistics, and Truth. Trans. by J. Neyman *et al.* New York: Macmillan, 1939 (*Wahrscheinlichkeit, Statistik, und Wahrheit,* Vienna, 1928).

MITCHELL, SILAS WEIR (1829–1914)
Doctor and Patient. Philadelphia: Lippincott, 1904 (Philadelphia, 1888).

MITCHELL, WESLEY CLAIR (1874–1948)
Business Cycles: The Problem and Its Setting. New York: National Bureau of Economic Research, 1927 (Berkeley, Cal., 1913).

MOLIÈRE, pseud. for JEAN BAPTISTE POQUELIN (1622–1673)
La critique de l'école des femmes (The School for Wives Criticised). In Vol. I, *Comedies.* Trans. by H. Baker and J. Miller. 2 vols. Everyman's Library, New York: E. P. Dutton, 1935 (1663).
—*L'avare (The Miser). Ibid.* (1668).
—*Le bourgeois gentilhomme (The Cit Turned Gentleman).* In Vol. II, *ibid.* (1670).
—*Le malade imaginaire (The Hypochondriac). Ibid.* (1673).
—*Le médecin malgré lui (The Mock-Doctor).* In Vol. I, *ibid.* (1666).
—*Le misanthrope (The Man-Hater). Ibid.* (1666).
—*L'école des femmes (The School for Wives). Ibid.* (1662).
—*L'école des maris (The School for Husbands). Ibid.* (1661).
—*Tartuffe, or The Impostor.* In Vol. II, *ibid.* (1664).

MONTALEMBERT, CHARLES FORBES RENÉ DE TRYON, COMTE DE (1810–1870)
On Constitutional Liberty: A Picture of England Painted by a Frenchman. London: E. Wilson, 1858.

MONTESQUIEU, CHARLES DE SECONDAT, BARON DE (1689–1755)
Considerations on the Causes of the Grandeur and Decadence of the Romans. Trans. by J. Baker. New York: D. Appleton, 1894 (*Considérations sur la grandeur des Romains et de leur décadence,* Paris, 1734).
—*The Persian Letters.* Trans. by J. Davidson. New York: Dial Press, 1929 (*Lettres persanes,* Cologne, 1721).

MONTESSORI, MARIA (1870–1952)
The Montessori Method: Scientific Pedagogy as Applied to Child Education in the "Children's Houses." Trans. by A. E. George. New York: F. A. Stokes, 1912 (Turin, 1909).

MOORE, GEORGE EDWARD (1873–1958)
Ethics. New York: Henry Holt, 1912.
—*Philosophical Studies.* New York: Harcourt Brace, 1922.
—*Principia Ethica.* Cambridge University Press, 1903.

MORE, HENRY (1614–1687)
An Account of Virtue. Trans. by E. Southwell. New York: Facsimile Text Society, 1930 (*Enchiridion Ethicum, Praecipua Moralis Philosophiae Rudimenta Complectens, etc.,* London, 1667).
—*The Antidote Against Atheism.* In *Philosophical Writings of Henry More.* Ed. by F. I. MacKinnon. New York: Oxford University Press, 1925 (London, 1652).
—*The Immortality of the Soul. Ibid.* (London, 1659).

MORE, LOUIS TRENCHARD (1870–1944)
The Dogma of Evolution. Princeton University Press, 1925.

MORE, PAUL ELMER (1864–1937)
Aristocracy and Justice. Boston: Houghton Mifflin Co., 1915.

MORE, SAINT THOMAS (1478–1535)
Utopia. Ed. by H. Goitein, trans. by R. Robinson and F. Bacon. Everyman's Library, New York: E. P. Dutton, 1928 (Louvain, 1516).

MORGAN, CONWAY LLOYD (1852–1936)
Animal Life and Intelligence. London: E. Arnold, 1890–1891.
—*Emergent Evolution.* New York: Henry Holt, 1922.
—*Habit and Instinct.* London: E. Arnold, 1896.
—*Instinct and Experience.* New York: Macmillan, 1912.

MORGAN, LEWIS HENRY (1818–1881)
Ancient Society; or, Researches in the Lines of Human Progress from Savagery Through Barbarism to Civilization. New York: Henry Holt, 1907 (New York, 1877).
—*Systems of Consanguinity and Affinity of the Human Family.* Washington, D.C.: Smithsonian Institution, 1870 (1868).

MORGAN, THOMAS HUNT (1866–1945)
Evolution and Genetics. Princeton University Press, 1925 (originally pub. as *A Critique of the Theory of Evolution,* Princeton, 1916).
—*The Physical Basis of Heredity.* Philadelphia: Lippincott, 1919.
—*The Scientific Basis of Evolution.* New York: W. W. Norton, 1935 (New York, 1932).
—*The Theory of the Gene.* New Haven, Conn.: Yale University Press, 1928 (New Haven, Conn., 1926).

MORGANN, MAURICE (1726–1802)
Morgann's Essay on the Dramatic Character of Sir John Falstaff. Ed. by W. A. Gill. London: H. Frowde, 1912 (London, 1777).

MORLEY, JOHN (1838–1923)
Notes on Politics and History; a University Address. London: Macmillan, 1913.

—*On Compromise*. London: Macmillan, 1923 (London, 1874).

MORRIS, WILLIAM (1834–1896)
The Aims of Art. In *Signs of Change: Seven Lectures, Delivered on Various Occasions*. London: Longmans, Green & Co., 1903 (London, 1887).
—*Art and Socialism: The Aims and Ideals of the English Socialists of Today*. In *Architecture, Industry and Wealth: Collected Papers by William Morris*. London: Longmans, Green & Co., 1902 (London, 1884).
—*Hopes and Fears for Art*. London: Longmans, Green & Co., 1929 (London, 1882).

MOSCA, GAETANO (1858–1941)
The Ruling Class. Ed. by A. Livingston, trans. by H. D. Kahn. New York: McGraw-Hill, 1939 (*Elementi di scienze politica*, Turin, 1896).

MOUNIER, EMMANUEL (1905–1950)
A Personalist Manifesto. Trans. by monks of St. John's Abbey. New York: Longmans, Green & Co., 1938 (*Manifeste au service du personnalisme*, Paris, 1936).

MÜLLER, FRIEDRICH MAX (1823–1900)
Comparative Mythology. In Vol. II, *Chips from a German Workshop*. 5 vols. New York: Scribner's, 1889–1891 (1856).
—*The Languages of the Seat of War in the East. With a Survey of the Three Families of Language, Semitic, Arian, and Turanian*. London: Williams & Norgate, 1855 (London, 1854).
—*The Science of Language, Founded on Lectures Delivered at the Royal Institution in 1861 and 1863*. 2 vols. New York: Scribner's, 1891 (London, 1861–1863).

MUIR, EDWIN (1887–1959)
The Structure of the Novel. New York: Harcourt Brace, 1929 (London, 1928).

MUIRHEAD, JOHN HENRY (1855–1940)
Rule and End in Morals. New York: Oxford University Press, 1932.

MUMFORD, LEWIS (1895–)
Technics and Civilization. New York: Harcourt Brace, 1934.

MUN, THOMAS (1571–1641)
A Discourse of Trade from England unto the East Indies; Answering to Diverse Objections Which Are Usually Made Against the Same. New York: Facsimile Text Society, 1930 (London, 1621).

N

NAGEL, ERNEST (1901–)
On the Logic of Measurement. New York, 1930.

NEEDHAM, JOSEPH (1900–)
Order and Life. New Haven, Conn.: Yale University Press, 1936.

NEFF, EMERY EDWARD (1892–)
The Poetry of History. New York: Columbia University Press, 1947.

NEWMAN, GEORGE (1870–1948)
Citizenship and the Survival of Civilization. New Haven, Conn.: Yale University Press, 1928.

NEWMAN, JOHN HENRY (1801–1890)
Apologia Pro Vita Sua. Everyman's Library, New York: E. P. Dutton, 1934 (London, 1864).
—*Callista; A Sketch of the Third Century*. New York: Sheed & Ward, 1941 (London, 1856).
—*An Essay in Aid of a Grammar of Assent*. London: Longmans, Green & Co., 1939 (London, 1870).
—*An Essay on the Development of Christian Doctrine*. London: Longmans, Green & Co., 1920 (London, 1845).
—*Essays and Sketches*. 3 vols. New York: Longmans, Green & Co., 1948.
—*The Idea of a University Defined and Illustrated*. Ed. by D. O'Connor. New York: America Press, 1941 (originally pub. as *The Scope and Nature of University Education*, Dublin, 1852).
—*Lectures on the Doctrine of Justification*. London: Longmans, Green & Co., 1900 (London, 1838).
—*Lectures on the Prophetical Office of the Church Viewed Relatively to Romanism and Popular Protestantism*. London: Rivington, 1837.
—*A Letter to His Grace the Duke of Norfolk*. London: B. M. Pickering, 1875.
—*Parochial and Plain Sermons*. Ed. by W. J. Copeland. 8 vols. New York: Longmans, Green & Co., 1900–1902 (London, 1837–1842).
—*University Sketches*. New York: Walter Scott Publishing Co., 1902 (1854).

NEWTON, SIR ISAAC (1642–1727)
Daniel and the Apocalypse. Ed. by Sir W. Whitla. London: J. Murray, 1922 (*c.* 1693).
—*Letters of Sir Isaac Newton on Various Subjects in Natural Philosophy*. In Vol. IV, *Isaaci Newtoni Opera Quae Extant Omnia*. Ed. by S. Horsley. 5 vols. London: J. Nichols, 1779–1785 (1672–1676).
—*The Method of Fluxions and Infinite Series*. Ed. and trans. by J. Colson. London: H. Woodfall, 1736 (*Geometrica Analytica*, 1671).
—*Universal Arithmetic; or, A Treatise of Arithmetical Composition and Resolution*. Trans. by Ralphson. London: W. Johnston, 1769 (*Arithmetica Universalis; Sive de Compositione et Resolutione Arithmetica Liber*, London, 1707).

NEXÖ, MARTIN ANDERSEN (1869–1954)
Pelle the Conqueror. Trans. by J. Muir and B. Miall. 2 vols. New York: Henry Holt, 1917 (Copenhagen, 1906–1910).

The Nibelungenlied. Trans. by D. B. Shumway. Boston: Houghton Mifflin Co., 1937 (1190?–1205?).

NICOD, JEAN (1893–1924)
Foundations of Geometry and Induction. Trans. by P. P. Wiener. New York: Harcourt Brace, 1930 (*Le problème logique de l'induction*, Paris 1923, and *La géométrie dans le monde sensible*, Paris, 1924).

NICOLAS OF CUSA (1401–1464)
De Docta Ignorantia. In Vol. I, *Nicolai de Cusa Opera Omnia*. Ed. by E. Hoffman *et al.* 14 vols. Leipsic: F. Meiner, 1932–1939 (1440).
—*De Venatione Sapientiae*. In Vol. XII, *ibid.* (1463).
—*The Idiot*. Ed. by P. Radin. San Francisco: California State Library, 1940 (*Idiota*, 1450).
—*The Vision of God*. Ed. and trans. by E. G. Salter. New York: E. P. Dutton, 1928 (*De Visione Dei*, 1453).

NIEBOER, HERMAN JEREMIAS (1873–)
Slavery as an Industrial System; Ethnological Researches. The Hague: M. Nijhoff, 1900.

NIEBUHR, REINHOLD (1892–)
The Nature and Destiny of Man, a Christian Interpretation. 2 vols. New York: Scribner's, 1941–1943.

NIETZSCHE, FRIEDRICH WILHELM (1844–1900)
Beyond Good and Evil. Trans. by H. Zimmern. In *Philosophy of Nietzsche* (*Jenseits von Gut und Böse, Vorspiel einer Philosophie der Zukunft*, Leipsic, 1886).
—*The Birth of Tragedy from the Spirit of Music*. Trans. by C. P. Fadiman. *Ibid.* (*Die Geburt der Tragödie aus dem Geist der Musik*, Leipsic, 1872).
—*The Dawn of Day*. Trans. by J. M. Kennedy. Vol. IX, *Complete Works* (*Morgenröte. Gedanken über moralische Vorurteile*, Chemnitz, 1881).
—*The Genealogy of Morals*. Trans. by H. B. Samuel. In *Philosophy of Nietzsche* (*Zur Genealogie der Moral*, Leipsic, 1887).
—*Human, All-Too-Human, A Book for Free Spirits*. Trans. by H. Zimmern. Vols. VI–VII, *Complete Works* (*Menschliches, Allzumenschliches*, Chemnitz, 1878).
—*The Joyful Wisdom*. Trans. by T. Common. Vol. X, *ibid.* (*Die fröhliche Wissenschaft*. Chemnitz, 1882).
—*On the Future of Our Educational Institutions*. Trans. by J. M. Kennedy. Vol. III, *ibid.* (1872).
—*Thus Spake Zarathustra*. Trans. by T. Common. In *Philosophy of Nietzsche* (*Also sprach Zarathustra*, Chemnitz, 1883–1891).
—*The Use and Abuse of History*. Trans. by Adrian Collins. New York: The Liberal Arts Press, 1949 (*Vom Nützen und Nachteil der Historie für das Leben*, in *Unzeitgemässe Betrachtungen*, Leipsic, 1873–1876).
—*The Will to Power, an Attempted Transvaluation of All Values*. Trans. by A. M. Ludovici. Vols. XIV–XV, *Complete Works* (1883–1889).
NOTE:
The Complete Works of Friedrich Nietzsche. Ed. by Dr. O. Levy. 18 vols. London: T. N. Foulis, 1909–1915.
—*The Philosophy of Nietzsche*. Modern Library, New York: Random House, 1937.

[Njalssaga] *The Story of Burnt Njal; or Life in Iceland at the End of the Tenth Century*. Trans. by G. W. Dasent. Everyman's Library, New York: E. P. Dutton, 19—? (late 13th century).

NOCK, ALBERT JAY (1873?–1945)
The Theory of Education in the United States. New York: Harcourt Brace, 1932.

NORTHROP, FILMER STUART CUCKOW (1893–)
Science and First Principles. New York: Macmillan, 1931.

NYGREN, ANDERS THEODOR SAMUEL (1890–)
Agape and Eros; A Study of the Christian Idea of Love. Trans. by A. G. Hebert and P. S. Watson. 2 vols. New York: Macmillan, 1932–1939 (Stockholm, 1930; 1936).

O

OCKHAM, WILLIAM OF (*c.* 1290–*c.* 1349)
Expositio Aurea et Admodum Utilis Super Artem Veterem. Bologna: Benedictus Hectoris, 1496.
—*Studies and Selections*. Ed. and trans. by S. C. Tornay. Chicago: Open Court, 1938.
—*Summa Totius Logicae*. Venice, 1508 (*c.* 1322).

O'CONNOR, WILLIAM RICHARD (1897–)
The Eternal Quest. New York: Longmans, Green & Co., 1947.

OGDEN, CHARLES KAY (1889–1957)
Opposition. London: K. Paul, Trench, Trübner, 1932.

OGDEN, CHARLES KAY and RICHARDS, IVOR ARMSTRONG (1893–)
The Meaning of Meaning; a Study of the Influence of Language upon Thought and of the Science of Symbolism. New York: Harcourt Brace, 1944 (New York, 1923).

O'NEILL, EUGENE GLADSTONE (1888–1953)
Desire Under the Elms. In *Nine Plays by Eugene O'Neill*. Modern Library, New York: Random House, 1941 (1925).
—*The Emperor Jones*. *Ibid.* (1920).
—*Mourning Becomes Electra*. *Ibid.* (1931).
—*Strange Interlude*. *Ibid.* (1928).

OPPENHEIMER, FRANZ (1864–1943)
The State, Its History and Development Viewed Sociologically. Trans. by J. M. Gitterman. New York: Vanguard Press, 1926 (*Der Staat*, Frankfort, 1907).

ORÊME, NICOLE (NICOLAS ORESME) (1320–1382)
An Abstract of Nicholas Orême's Treatise on the Breadth of Forms. Ed. and trans. by C. G. Wallis. Annapolis, Md.: St. John's Press, 1941 (from *De Latitudinibus Formarum*, before 1370).

ORTEGA Y GASSET, JOSÉ (1883–1955)
The Dehumanization of Art. Princeton University Press, 1948 (1925).
—*Mission of the University*. Trans. by H. L. Nostrand. Princeton University Press, 1944 (*Misión de la universidad*, Madrid, 1930).
—*The Revolt of the Masses*. New York: W. W. Norton, 1932 (*La rebelión de las masas*, Madrid, 1929).
—*Toward a Philosophy of History*. Trans. by H. Weyl. New York: W. W. Norton, 1941.

OSLER, SIR WILLIAM (1849–1919)
Aequanimitas, with Other Addresses to Medical Students, Nurses and Practitioners of Medicine. Philadelphia: Blakiston Co., 1942 (London, 1904).
—*A Way of Life.* London: Constable & Co., 1914.

OSTROGORSKI, MOISEI Y. (1854–1919)
Democracy and the Organization of Political Parties. Trans. by F. Clarke. 2 vols. New York: Macmillan, 1902.

OSTWALD, WILHELM (1853–1932)
Natural Philosophy. Trans. by T. Seltzer. New York: Henry Holt, 1910 (*Vorlesungen über Naturphilosophie*, Leipsic, 1902).

OTTO, RUDOLPH (1869–1937)
The Idea of the Holy; an Inquiry into the Non-Rational Factor in the Idea of the Divine and Its Relation to the Rational. Trans. by J. W. Harvey. New York: Oxford University Press, 1923 (*Das Heilige. Über das Irrationale in der Idee des Göttlichen und sein Verhältnis zum Rationalen*, Breslau, 1917).

OVID (PUBLIUS OVIDIUS NASO) (43 B.C.–*c.* 18 A.D.)
[Amores] *Heroides and Amores.* Trans. by G. Showerman. Loeb Library, Cambridge, Mass.: Harvard University Press, 1925 (2 A.D.?).
—*The Art of Love and Other Poems.* Trans. by J. H. Mozley. Loeb Library, Cambridge, Mass.: Harvard University Press, 1929 (*Ars Amatoria*, 2 A.D.?).
—*Metamorphoses.* Trans. by F. J. Miller. 2 vols. Loeb Library, New York: Putnam's, 1916 (7 A.D.).

P

PAINE, THOMAS (1737–1809)
The Age of Reason; Being an Investigation of True and Fabulous Theology. In Vol. IV, *The Writings of Thomas Paine.* Ed. by M. D. Conway. 4 vols. New York: Putnam's, 1894–1908 (Paris, 1794).
—*Common Sense.* Ed. by M. van der Weyde. New York: Rimington & Hooper, 1928 (Philadelphia, 1776).
—*Dissertation on First Principles of Government.* In Vol. III, *Writings.* See above (Paris, 1795).
—*Rights of Man; Being an Answer to Mr. Burke's Attack on the French Revolution.* Everyman's Library, New York: E. P. Dutton, 1915 (London, 1791).

PAINLEVÉ, PAUL (1863–1933)
Les axiomes de la mécanique, examen critique; note sur la propagation de la lumière. Paris: Gauthier-Villars, 1922 (partly from *La méthode dans les sciences*, Paris, 1909, and *Bulletin de la Société Française de Philosophie*, Paris, 1905).

PALEY, WILLIAM (1743–1805)
Moral Philosophy. Ed. by R. Whately. London: J. W. Parker, 1859 (from *Principles of Moral and Political Philosophy*, London, 1785).
—*Natural Theology; or, Evidences of the Existence and Attributes of the Deity Collected from the Appearances of Nature.* Ed. by J. Ware. Boston: Gould & Lincoln, 1854 (London, 1802).
—*A View of the Evidences of Christianity.* Ed. by R. Whately. New York: J. Miller, 1860 (London. 1794).

PARACELSUS (THEOPHRASTUS VON HOHENHEIM) (*c.* 1490–1541)
The Diseases That Deprive Man of His Reason. In *Four Treatises.* Ed. by H. Sigerist. Baltimore, Md.: Johns Hopkins University Press, 1941 (1525?).
—*On the Miners' Sickness and Other Miners' Diseases. Ibid.* (1533?).
—*Seven Defensiones. Ibid.* (1538).

PARETO, VILFRIDO (1848–1923)
The Mind and Society. Ed. by A. Livingston, trans. by A. Bongiorno. 4 vols. New York: Harcourt Brace, 1935 (*Trattato di sociologia generale*, Florence, 1916).

PARSONS, SIR JOHN HERBERT (1868–1957)
An Introduction to the Theory of Perception. New York: Macmillan, 1927.

PASCAL, BLAISE (1623–1662)
Discours sur les passions de l'amour, attribué à Pascal. Ed. by É. Faguet. Paris: B. Grasset, 1911 (*c.* 1650–*c.* 1653).

PATER, WALTER HORATIO (1839–1894)
[Essay on Style] *Appreciations; with An Essay on Style.* London: Macmillan, 1931 (1888).
—*Marius the Epicurean.* Everyman's Library, New York: E. P. Dutton, 1934 (London, 1885).

PATMORE, COVENTRY KERSEY DIGHTON (1823–1896)
Mystical Poems of Nuptial Love. Ed. by T. L. Connolly. Boston: B. Humphries, 1938.

PAULI, WOLFGANG (1900–1958)
Relativitätstheorie. Leipsic: B. G. Teubner, 1921.

PAVLOV, IVAN PETROVICH (1849–1936)
Lectures on Conditioned Reflexes. Ed. and trans. by W. H. Gantt. 2 vols. New York: International Publishers, 1928–1941 (Moscow, 1923).

PEACOCK, GEORGE (1791–1858)
A Treatise on Algebra. 2 vols. New York: Yeshiva College, 1940 (London, 1842–1845).

PEACOCK, THOMAS LOVE (1785–1866)
Four Ages of Poetry. Ed. by H. F. B. Brett-Smith. Oxford: Blackwell, 1921 (1820).

PEANO, GIUSEPPE (1858–1932)
Arithmetica generale e algebra elementare. Turin: G. B. Paravia, 1902.
—*Arithmetices Principia.* Turin: Bocca, 1889.
—*Formulaire de mathématique.* 5 vols. Turin: Bocca, 1895–1908.

PEARL, RAYMOND (1879–1940)
The Biology of Death. Philadelphia: Lippincott, 1922.

PEARSON, KARL (1857–1936)
The Chances of Death, and Other Studies in Evolution. 2 vols. New York: E. Arnold, 1897.
—*The Grammar of Science.* Everyman's Library, New York: E. P. Dutton, 1937 (London, 1892).

PÉGUY, CHARLES PIERRE (1873–1914)
Basic Verities. Prose and Poetry. Trans. by A. and J. Green. New York: Pantheon Books, 1943 (from *Cahiers de la quinzaine*, Paris, 1900–1914).
—*Men and Saints. Prose and Poetry.* Trans. by A. and J. Green. New York: Pantheon Books, 1944 (from *Cahiers de la quinzaine*, Paris, 1900–1914).

PEIRCE, BENJAMIN (1809–1880)
An Elementary Treatise on Curves, Functions, and Forces. 2 vols. Boston: J. Munroe, 1846–1852.

PEIRCE, CHARLES SANDERS (1839–1914)
Collected Papers. Ed. by C. Hartshorne and P. Weiss. 6 vols. Cambridge, Mass.: Harvard University Press, 1931.

PENIDO, MAURILIO TEIXEIRA-LEITE (1895–)
Le rôle de l'analogie en théologie dogmatique. Paris: J. Vrin, 1931.

PENN, WILLIAM (1644–1718)
An Essay Towards the Present and Future Peace of Europe. In *The Peace of Europe: The Fruits of Solitude, and Other Writings.* Everyman's Library, New York: E. P. Dutton, 1916 (London, 1693).
—*Primitive Christianity Revived, in the Faith and Practice of the People Called Quakers. Ibid.* (London, 1696).

PENTY, ARTHUR JOSEPH (1875–1937)
A Guildsman's Interpretation of History. New York: Sunrise Turn, 1920.

PEPYS, SAMUEL (1633–1703)
The Diary of Samuel Pepys. 2 vols. Everyman's Library, New York: E. P. Dutton, 1930–1934 (1660–1669).

PERKINS, WILLIAM (1558–1602)
The Whole Treatise of the Cases of Conscience. London: T. Pickering, 1651 (*A Case of Conscience, the Greatest That Ever Was; How a Man May Know Whether He Be the Child of God or No. Resolved by the Word of God*, London, 1592).

PERRY, RALPH BARTON (1876–1957)
The Hope for Immortality. New York: Vanguard Press, 1945.
—*Puritanism and Democracy.* New York: Vanguard Press, 1944.

PESTALOZZI, JOHANN HEINRICH (1746–1827)
How Gertrude Teaches Her Children; an Attempt to Help Mothers to Teach Their Own Children. Ed. by E. Cooke, trans. by L. E. Holland and F. C. Turner. Syracuse, N.Y.: C. W. Bardeen, 1915 (*Wie Gertrude ihre Kinder lehrt*, Bern, 1801).

PETER LOMBARD (*c.*1100–*c.* 1164)
The Four Books of Sentences. In Vol. I, *Selections from Medieval Philosophers.* Ed. and trans. by Richard McKeon. 2 vols. New York: Scribner's, 1929–1930 (1145–1151).

PETRARCH, FRANCESCO (1304–1374)
On His Own Ignorance. In *The Renaissance Philosophy of Man.* Ed. by E. Cassirer *et al.* University of Chicago Press, 1948 (1368).
—*The Sonnets.* Trans. by J. Auslander. New York: Longmans, Green & Co., 1931 (1327–1361).
—*The Triumph of Love.* In *Sonnets, Triumphs, and Other Poems.* London: G. Bell & Sons, 1890 (1352).

PETRIE, WILLIAM MATTHEW FLINDERS (1853–1942)
The Revolutions of Civilization. New York: Peter Smith, 1941 (New York, 1911).

PETRUS ALPHONSI (1062–*c.* 1110)
Disciplina Clericalis. Trans. by W. H. Hume. Cleveland: Western Reserve Studies, 1919.

PETRUS HISPANICUS (JOHN XXI) (*c.* 1210–1277)
The Summulae Logicales of Peter of Spain. Ed. and trans. by Joseph Patrick Mullally. Notre Dame, Ind.: Notre Dame University Press, 1945.

PHILO JUDAEUS OF ALEXANDRIA (b. 20–10 B.C.)
On the Cherubim (*De Cherubim*). In Vol. II, *Philo, An English Translation.* Trans. by F. H. Colson and G. H. Whitaker. 10 vols. Loeb Library, Cambridge, Mass.: Harvard University Press, 1929–1941.
—*On the Creation of the World* (*De Opificio Mundi*). In Vol. I, *ibid.*
—*On the Eternity of the World* (*De Aeternitate Mundi*). In Vol. IX, *ibid.*

PHILODEMUS OF GADARA (1st century B.C.)
Philodemus: On Methods of Inference; a Study in Ancient Empiricism. Ed. and trans. by P. H. and E. A. DeLacy. Philadelphia: American Philological Association, 1941 (54? B.C.).

PHILOSTRATUS, FLAVIUS (*c.* 170–245 A.D.)
Philostratus and Eunapius; the Lives of the Sophists. Trans. by W. C. Wright. Loeb Library, New York: Putnam's, 1922 (230–238 B.C.?).

PICO DELLA MIRANDOLA, GIOVANNI (1463–1494)
Of Being and Unity. Ed. and trans. by V. M. Hamm. Milwaukee, Wis.: Marquette University Press, 1943 (*De Ente et Uno*, *c.* 1492).
—*Oration on the Dignity of Man.* In *The Renaissance Philosophy of Man.* Ed. by E. Cassirer *et al.* University of Chicago Press, 1948 (1488?).
—*A Platonick Discourse upon Love.* Ed. by E. G. Gardner, trans. by T. Stanley. Boston: Merrymount Press, 1914 (*Canzone dello Amore secondo la mente e opinione de' Platonici*, 1487).

PICO DELLA MIRANDOLA, GIOVANNI FRANCESCO (1470–1533)
On the Imagination. Trans. by H. Caplan. New Haven, Conn.: Yale University Press, 1930 (*De Imaginatione*, Rome, 1500).

PIÉRON, HENRI (1881–)
Thought and the Brain. Trans. by C. K. Ogden. New York: Harcourt Brace, 1927 (*Le cerveau et la pensée*, Paris, 1923).

Pirandello, Luigi (1867–1936)
The Old and the Young. Trans. by C. K. Scott-Moncrieff. 2 vols. New York: E. P. Dutton, 1928 (*I vecchi e i giovani*, 1909).
—*The Outcast: A Novel*. Trans. by L. Ongley. New York: E. P. Dutton, 1935 (*L'esclusa*, Rome, 1901).

Pirke Aboth; the Tractate 'Fathers,' from the Mishnah, Commonly Called 'Sayings of the Fathers.' Ed. and trans. by R. T. Herford. New York: Bloch Publishing Co., 1930 (70 A.D.?–200 A.D.?).

Pius XI, Pope (1857–1939)
[Casti Connubii] *Christian Marriage*. In *Five Great Encyclicals*. New York: Paulist Press, 1939 (1930).
—[Divini Illius Magistri] *Christian Education of Youth*. *Ibid*. (1929).
—[Quadragesimo Anno] *Reconstruction of the Social Order*. *Ibid*. (1931).

Planck, Max Karl Ernst Ludwig (1858–1947)
Das Prinzip der Erhaltung der Energie. Leipsic: B. G. Teubner, 1887.
—*The Origin and Development of the Quantum Theory*. Trans. by H. T. Clarke and L. Silberstein. Oxford: Clarendon Press, 1922 (*Die Entstehung und bisherige Entwicklung der Quantentheorie*, Leipsic, 1920).
—*The Philosophy of Physics*. Trans. by W. H. Johnstone. New York: W. W. Norton, 1936 (from *Wege zur physikalischen Erkenntnis*, Leipsic, 1933).
—*Scientific Autobiography and Other Papers*. New York: Philosophical Library, 1949.
—*A Survey of Physics*. Trans. by R. Jones and D. H. Williams. New York: E. P. Dutton, 1923 (*Physikalische Rundblicke*, Leipsic, 1922).
—*Treatise on Thermodynamics*. Trans. by A. Ogg. London: Longmans, Green & Co., 1945 (*Vorlesungen über Thermodynamik*, Leipsic, 1897).
—*Where Is Science Going?* Trans. by J. Murphy. New York: W. W. Norton, 1932 (from *Wege zur physikalischen Erkenntnis*, Leipsic, 1933).

Plekhanov, Georgi Valentinovich (1857–1918)
Essays in the History of Materialism. Trans. by R. Fox. London: J. Lane, 1934 (*Beiträge zur Geschichte des Materialismus*, Stuttgart, 1896).
—*Fundamental Problems of Marxism*. Ed. by D. Ryasanov, trans. by E. and C. Paul. New York: International Publishers, 1930 (1897).
—*In Defense of Materialism*. Trans. by A. Rothstein. London: Lawrence & Wishart, 1947 (1894).

Pliny the Elder (Gaius Plinius Secundus) (23/4 A.D.–79 A.D.)
Natural History. Trans. by J. Bostock and H. T. Riley. 6 vols. London: G. Bell & Sons, 1855–1890.

Plutarch (*c*. 46–*c*. 120 A.D.)
[Moralia] *Plutarch's Morals*. Ed. by W. Goodwin. 5 vols. Boston: Little, Brown & Co., 1871.

Poe, Edgar Allan (1809–1849)
The Poetic Principle. In *Edgar Allan Poe: Representative Selections*. Ed. by M. Alterton and H. Craig. New York: American Book Co., 1935 (1849).

Pohle, Joseph (1852–1922)
Eschatology; or, The Catholic Doctrine of the Last Things, a Dogmatic Treatise. Ed. and trans. by A. Preuss. St. Louis, Mo.: Herder Book Co., 1929 (*Lehrbuch der Dogmatik in sieben Büchern*, German ed., 1902).

Poincaré, Henri (1854–1912)
Science and Hypothesis. In *The Foundations of Science*. Trans. by G. B. Halsted. New York: Science Press, 1929 (*La science et l'hypothèse*, Paris, 1902).
—*Science and Method*. *Ibid*. (*Science et méthode*, Paris, 1908).
—*The Value of Science*. *Ibid*. (*La valeur de la science*, Paris, 1905).

Poinsot, Louis (1777–1859)
Élémens de statique. Paris: Bachelier, 1848 (1803).

Pollock, Sir Frederick (1845–1937)
Essays in Jurisprudence and Ethics. London: Macmillan, 1882.
—*The Expansion of the Common Law*. London: Stevens & Sons, 1904.

Polybius (*c*. 204–122 B.C.)
The Histories of Polybius. Trans. by W. R. Paton. 6 vols. Loeb Library, New York: Putnam's, 1922–1925 (132?–122).

Pomerius, Julianus (*fl*. 498 A.D.)
The Contemplative Life. Trans. by M. J. Suelzer. Westminster, Md.: Newman Bookshop, 1947.

Pomponazzi, Pietro (1462–1524)
On the Immortality of the Soul. In *The Renaissance Philosophy of Man*. Ed. by E. Cassirer *et al*. University of Chicago Press, 1948 (1516).

Poncelet, Jean Victor (1788–1867)
Cours de mécanique appliquée aux machines. 2 vols. Paris: Gauthier-Villars, 1874–1876 (1826).

Ponsonby, Arthur (1871–1946)
The Decline of Aristocracy. London: T. F. Unwin, 1912.

Pope, Alexander (1688–1744)
An Essay on Criticism. In *Selected Works of Alexander Pope*. Modern Library, New York: Random House, 1948 (London, 1711).
—*An Essay on Man*. *Ibid*. (London, 1733).

Porphyry (233–*c*. 301 A.D.)
Introduction to Aristotle's Predicaments: A Translation of Porphyrio's Eisagoge. Trans. by C. G. Wallis. Annapolis, Md.: St. John's Press, 1938.

Poulton, Edward Bagnall (1856–1943)
Essays on Evolution, 1889–1907. Oxford: Clarendon Press, 1908.

Pound, Roscoe (1870–1964)
The Spirit of the Common Law. Boston: Marshall Jones Co., 1921.

Powys, John Cowper (1872–1963)
In Defence of Sensuality. New York: Simon & Schuster, 1930.

PRICE, HENRY HABBERLEY (1899–)
Perception. London: Methuen, 1932.

PRICHARD, HAROLD ARTHUR (1871–1947)
Duty and Interest. Oxford: Clarendon Press, 1920.

PRIESTLEY, JOSEPH (1733–1804)
Experiments and Observations on Different Kinds of Air. 3 vols. Birmingham: T. Pearson, 1790 (London, 1774–1786).
—*Experiments and Observations Relating to Various Branches of Natural Philosophy*. 3 vols. London: J. Johnson, 1779–1786.

PRIESTLEY, JOSEPH and PRICE, RICHARD (1723–1791)
A Free Discussion of the Doctrine of Materialism and Philosophical Necessity, in a Correspondence Between Dr. Price and Dr. Priestley. London: J. Johnson & T. Cadell, 1778.

PROCLUS LYCIUS DIADOCHUS (410–485 A.D.)
The Elements of Theology. Trans. by E. R. Dodds. Oxford: Clarendon Press, 1933 (432? A.D.).

PROUDHON, PIERRE JOSEPH (1809–1865)
De la justice dans la révolution et dans l'église (*Essais d'une philosophie populaire*). 6 vols. Paris: Marpon & Flammarion, 1870 (Paris, 1858).
—*General Idea of the Revolution in the Nineteenth Century*. Trans. by J. B. Robinson. London: Freedom Press, 1923 (*Idée générale de la révolution au XIXe siècle*, Paris, 1851).
—*La guerre et la paix: Recherches sur le principe et la constitution du droit des gens*. Paris: M. Rivière, 1927 (Paris, 1861).
—[Philosophy of Misery] *System of Economic Contradictions; or, The Philosophy of Misery*. Trans. by B. R. Tucker. Boston, 1888 (*Système des contradictions économiques, ou, Philosophie de la misère*, Paris, 1846).
—*What Is Property; an Inquiry into the Principle of Right and of Government*. Trans. by B. R. Tucker. London: W. Reeves, 1902 (*Qu'est-ce que la propriété? Ou, Recherches sur le principe du droit et du gouvernement*, Paris, 1840–1841).

PROUST, MARCEL (1871–1922)
Remembrance of Things Past. Trans. by C. K. Scott-Moncrieff. 2 vols. New York: Random House, 1941 (*À la recherche du temps perdu*, Paris, 1913–1927).

PRYNNE, WILLIAM (1600–1669)
The Soveraigne Power of Parliaments and Kingdomes. London: M. Sparke, 1643.

PTOLEMY (CLAUDIUS PTOLEMAEUS) (2nd century A.D.)
Tetrabiblos. Trans. by F. E. Robbins. Loeb Library, Cambridge, Mass.: Harvard University Press, 1940.

PUFENDORF, SAMUEL (1632–1694)
De Jure Naturae et Gentium. Trans. by C. H. and W. A. Oldfather, English text in Vol. II. New York: Oxford University Press, 1934 (Lund, 1672).
—*De Officio Hominis et Civis Juxta Legem Naturalem*. Trans. by F. G. Moore, English text in Vol. II. New York: Oxford University Press, 1927 (Lund, 1673).

PUSHKIN, ALEXANDER SERGYGYEVICH (1799–1837)
Boris Godunov. Trans. by A. Hayes, in *The Poems, Prose and Plays of Pushkin*. Ed. by A. Yarmolinsky. Modern Library, New York: Random House, 1943 (1831).
—*The Captain's Daughter*. Trans. by N. Duddington, *ibid.* (1836).
—*The Queen of Spades*. Trans. by T. Keane, *ibid.* (1834).

Q

QUINTILIAN (MARCUS FABIUS QUINTILIANUS) (*c.* 35–*c.* 95 A.D.)
Institutio Oratoria. Trans. by H. E. Butler. 4 vols. Loeb Library, Cambridge, Mass.: Harvard University Press, 1921 (after 88? A.D.).

R

RACINE, JEAN BAPTISTE (1639–1699)
Andromaque. In *The Best Plays of Racine*. Trans. by Lacy Lockert. Princeton University Press, 1936 (1667).
—*Athalie*. *Ibid.* (Paris, 1691).
—*Britannicus*. *Ibid.* (1669).
—*Phèdre*. *Ibid.* (Paris, 1677).

RADESTOCK, PAUL
Habit and Its Importance in Education: An Essay in Pedagogical Psychology. Trans. by F. A. Caspari. Boston: D. C. Heath, 1908 (*Die Gewöhnung und ihre Wichtigkeit für die Erziehung. Eine psychologisch-pädagogische Untersuchung*, Berlin, 1882).

RAGLAN, FITZ ROY RICHARD SOMERSET, BARON (1885–1964)
The Hero; a Study in Tradition, Myth, and Drama. New York: Oxford University Press, 1937 (London, 1936).

RAMAZZINI, BERNARDINO (1633–1714)
De Morbis Artificum (*The Diseases of Workers*). Ed. and trans. by W. C. Wright. University of Chicago Press, 1940 (1713).

RAMUS, PETRUS (PIERRE DE LA RAMÉE) (1515–1572)
Dialecticae Institutiones. Paris: J. Bogardus, 1543.

RANK, OTTO (1884–1939)
Art and Artist; Creative Urge and Personality Development. Trans. by C. F. Atkinson. New York: A. A. Knopf, 1932 (*Der Künstler und andere Beiträge zur Psychoanalyse des künstlerischen Schaffens*, Leipsic, 1925).
—*Modern Education; a Critique of Its Fundamental Ideas*. Trans. by M. E. Moxon. New York: A. A. Knopf, 1932.
—*The Myth of the Birth of the Hero: A Psychological Interpretation of Mythology*. Trans. by F. Robbins

and Smith E. Jeliffe. New York: Nervous and Mental Disease Publishing Company, 1914 (*Der Mythos von der Geburt des Helden*, Vienna, 1909).

RANKE, LEOPOLD VON (1795–1886)
Über die Epochen der neueren Geschichte. In Vol. IX, Part II, *Weltgeschichte.* Ed. by Alfred Dove. 9 vols. Leipsic: Duncker & Humblot, 1881–1888 (1854).

RANSOM, JOHN CROWE (1888–)
The World's Body. New York: Scribner's, 1938.

RANULPH DE GLANVILLE (1130–1190)
The Laws and Customs of the Kingdom of England. Trans. by J. Beames. Washington: J. Byrne, 1900 (1188?).

RAVAISSON-MOLLIEN, JEAN GASPARD FÉLIX LACHER (1813–1900)
De l'habitude. Paris: F. Alcan, 1933 (Paris, 1838).

RAYLEIGH, JOHN WILLIAM STRUTT, BARON (1842–1919)
The Theory of Sound. 2 vols. New York: Dover Publications, 1945 (London, 1877–1878).

READ, CARVETH (1848–1931)
The Metaphysics of Nature. London: A. & C. Black, 1905.

READ, HERBERT EDWARD (1893–1968)
Form in Modern Poetry. New York: Sheed & Ward, 1932.

READE, CHARLES (1814–1884)
The Cloister and the Hearth. Everyman's Library, New York: E. P. Dutton, 1933 (London, 1861).

REICHENBACH, HANS (1891–1953)
Theory of Probability. Berkeley, Calif.: University of California Press, 1949 (1935).

REID, LEGH WILBER (1867–)
The Elements of the Theory of Algebraic Numbers. New York: Macmillan, 1910.

REID, THOMAS (1710–1796)
An Essay on Quantity; Occasioned by Reading a Treatise in Which Simple and Compound Ratios Are Applied to Virtue and Merit. In *The Works of Thomas Reid, D.D.* Ed. by Sir W. Hamilton. Edinburgh: MacLachlan & Stewart, 1852 (1748).
—*Essays on the Active Powers of the Human Mind. Ibid.* (Edinburgh, 1788).
—*Essays on the Intellectual Powers of Man. Ibid.* (Edinburgh, 1785).
—*An Inquiry into the Human Mind, on the Principles of Common Sense. Ibid.* (Edinburgh, 1764).

RENAN, JOSEPH ERNEST (1823–1892)
Caliban: A Philosophical Drama Continuing "The Tempest" of William Shakespeare. Trans. by E. G. Vickery. New York: Shakespeare Press, 1896 (*Caliban, suite de "La tempête," drame philosophique*, Paris, 1878).
—*De l'origine du langage.* Paris: Michel-Lévy, 1864 (Paris, 1858).
—*The Future of Science; Ideas of 1848.* Trans. by A.D. Vandam. London: Chapman & Hall, 1891 (*L'avenir de la science; pensées de 1848*).
—*The Life of Jesus.* Everyman's Library, New York: E. P. Dutton, 1934 (*La vie de Jésus*, Paris, 1863).
—*Philosophical Dialogues and Fragments.* Trans. by R. B. Mukharji. London: Trübner & Co., 1883 (*Dialogues et fragments philosophiques*, Paris, 1876).

RENOUVIER, CHARLES BERNARD (1815–1903)
Essais de critique générale. 3 vols. Paris: A. Colin, 1912 (Essay II, *L'homme: La raison, la passion, la liberté, la certitude, la probabilité morale*, Paris, 1859; Essay IV, *Introduction à la philosophie analytique de l'histoire*, Paris 1864).
—*Uchronie* (*l'Utopie dans l'histoire*). *Esquisse historique apocryphe du développement de la civilisation Européenne tel qu'il n'a pas été, tel qu'il aurait pu être.* Paris: F. Alcan, 1901 (Paris, 1876).

REULEAUX, FRANZ (1829–1905)
The Kinematics of Machinery. Outlines of a Theory of Machines. Ed. and trans. by A. B. Kennedy. London: Macmillan, 1876 (*Lehrbuch der Kinematik*, I, Brunswick, 1875).

REYNOLDS, JOHN (1667–1727)
Inquiries Concerning the State and Economy of the Angelical Worlds. London: J. Clark, 1723.

REYNOLDS, SIR JOSHUA (1723–1792)
Discourses on Art, Delivered to the Students of the Royal Academy. London: G. Routledge, 1909 (1769–1790).

RHETICUS (GEORG JOACHIM VON LAUCHEN) (1514–1576)
Narratio Prima. In *Three Copernican Treatises.* Trans. by E. Rosen. New York: Columbia University Press, 1939 (1540).

RIBOT, THÉODULE ARMAND (1839–1916)
Diseases of Memory. Trans. by W. H. Smith. New York: D. Appleton, 1893 (*Les maladies de la mémoire*, Paris, 1881).
—*The Diseases of the Will.* Trans. by Merwin-Marie Snell. Chicago: Open Court, 1894 (*Les maladies de la volonté*, Paris, 1883).
—*Essay on the Creative Imagination.* Trans. by A. H. Baron. Chicago: Open Court, 1906 (*Essai sur l'imagination créatrice*, Paris, 1900).
—*The Evolution of General Ideas.* Trans. by F. A. Welby. Chicago: Open Court, 1899 (*L'évolution des idées générales*, Paris, 1897).
—*The Psychology of the Emotions.* London: W. Scott, 1911 (*La psychologie des sentiments*, Paris, 1896).

RICARDO, DAVID (1772–1823)
The Principles of Political Economy and Taxation. Everyman's Library, New York: E. P. Dutton, 1937 (London, 1817).

RICHARDS, IVOR ARMSTRONG (1893–)
Interpretation in Teaching. New York: Harcourt Bracc, 1938.

—*Mencius on the Mind; Experiments in Multiple Definition*. New York: Harcourt Brace, 1932.
—*The Philosophy of Rhetoric*. New York: Oxford University Press, 1936.
—*Principles of Literary Criticism*. New York: Harcourt Brace, 1930 (New York, 1924).
—*Science and Poetry*. London: K. Paul, Trench, Trübner, 1935 (London, 1926).

RICHARDSON, SAMUEL (1689–1761)
Clarissa; or, The History of a Young Lady. 4 vols. Everyman's Library, New York: E. P. Dutton, 1932 (London, 1747–1748).
—*Pamela*. 2 vols. New York: E. P. Dutton, 1933 (London, 1740–1741).

RIEMANN, GEORG FRIEDRICH BERNHARD (1826–1866)
Über die Hypothesen welche der Geometrie zu Grunde liegen. Ed. by H. Weyl. Berlin: J. Springer, 1923 (1854) [trans. by W. K. Clifford in *Nature*, Vol. VIII, May, 1873].

RIEZLER, KURT (1882–1955)
Physics and Reality; Lectures of Aristotle on Modern Physics at an International Congress of Science. New Haven, Conn.: Yale University Press, 1940.

RITCHIE, DAVID GEORGE (1853–1903)
Natural Rights, a Criticism of Some Political and Ethical Conceptions. London: Swan Sonnenschein, 1903 (London, 1895).

RIVERS, WILLIAM HALSE (1864–1922)
Instinct and the Unconscious; a Contribution to a Biological Theory of the Psycho-Neuroses. Cambridge University Press, 1920.

ROBB, ALFRED ARTHUR (1873–1936)
A Theory of Time and Space. Cambridge University Press, 1914.

ROMAINS, JULES, pseud. for LOUIS FARIGOULE (1885–1972)
Doctor Knock; a Comedy in Three Acts. Trans. by H. Granville-Barker. London: E. Benn, 1925 (1923).
—*Verdun* [Vol. VIII, *Men of Good Will*]. Trans. by G. Hopkins. New York: A. A. Knopf, 1939 (*Prélude à Verdun* and *Verdun*, Paris, 1938).

The Romance of the Rose. Trans. by F. S. Ellis. Temple Classics, London: J. M. Dent, 1900 (13th century).

ROMANES, GEORGE JOHN (1848–1894)
Animal Intelligence. New York: D. Appleton, 1890 (London, 1881).
—*A Candid Examination of Theism*. London: K. Paul, Trench, Trübner, 1892 (London, 1878).
—*Mental Evolution in Animals*. New York: D. Appleton, 1891 (London, 1883).

ROSS, WILLIAM DAVID (1877–)
The Right and the Good. Oxford: Clarendon Press, 1930.

ROSSETTI, DANTE GABRIEL (1828–1882)
The House of Life, a Sonnet-Sequence. Cambridge, Mass.: Harvard University Press, 1928 (in *Ballads and Sonnets*, London, 1881).

ROSSITER, CLINTON L. (1917–1970)
Constitutional Dictatorship. Princeton University Press, 1948.

ROSTAND, EDMOND (1868–1918)
Cyrano de Bergerac. Modern Library, New York: Random House, 1949 (1897).
—*L'Aiglon: A Drama in Six Acts in Verse*. Trans. by B. Davenport. New Haven, Conn.: Yale University Press, 1927 (Paris, 1900).

ROUGEMONT, DENIS DE (1906–)
Love in the Western World. Trans. by M. Belgion. New York: Harcourt Brace, 1940 (*L'amour et l'Occident*, Paris, 1939).

ROUSSEAU, JEAN JACQUES (1712–1778)
[A Discourse on the Arts and Sciences] *The Social Contract and Discourses*. Trans. by G. D. H. Cole. Everyman's Library, New York: E. P. Dutton, 1913 (*Discours sur la question proposée par l'Academie de Dijon, etc.*, 1750).
—*Eloisa; a Series of Original Letters*. 3 vols. London: J. Harding, 1810 (*Julie, ou la nouvelle Héloïse*, Amsterdam, 1761).
—*Émile*. Trans. by B. Foxley. Everyman's Library, New York: E. P. Dutton, 1933 (The Hague, 1762).
—*Essai sur l'origine des langues*. In Vol. I, *Oeuvres complètes de J. J. Rousseau*. 13 vols. Paris: Hachette, 1909–1912 (1755).
—*A Lasting Peace Through the Federation of Europe*. In *A Lasting Peace and The State of War*. Trans. by C. E. Vaughan. London: Constable, 1917 (1756).

ROUTH, HAROLD VICTOR (1878–1951)
God, Man, and Epic Poetry, a Study in Comparative Literature. 2 vols. Cambridge University Press, 1927.

ROYCE, JOSIAH (1855–1916)
The Conception of God: An Address Before the Union. New York: Macmillan, 1902 (Berkeley, Cal., 1895).
—*The Conception of Immortality*. Boston: Houghton Mifflin Co., 1900.
—*The Philosophy of Loyalty*. New York: Macmillan, 1936 (New York, 1908).
—*The Principles of Logic*. Trans. by B. E. Meyer. In Vol. I, *Encyclopedia of the Philosophical Sciences*. London: Macmillan, 1913 (*Prinzipien der Logik*, 1912).
—*The Problem of Christianity*. 2 vols. New York: Macmillan, 1913.
—*Studies of Good and Evil; a Series of Essays upon Problems of Philosophy and of Life*. New York: D. Appleton, 1915 (New York, 1898).
—*The World and the Individual*. First and Second Series. 2 vols. New York: Macmillan, 1904 (New York, 1900–1901).

RUEFF, JACQUES (1896–)
From the Physical to the Social Sciences; Introduction to a Study of Economic and Ethical Theory. Trans. by H. Green. Baltimore, Md.: Johns

Hopkins University Press, 1929 (*Des sciences physiques aux sciences morales*, Paris, 1921).

RUMFORD, BENJAMIN THOMPSON (1753–1814)
An Experimental Inquiry Concerning the Source of the Heat Which Is Excited by Friction. In Vol. II, *Essays, Political, Economical and Philosophical.* 3 vols. Boston: D. West, 1798–1804 (London, 1796–1802).

RUSKIN, JOHN (1819–1900)
Fors Clavigera; Letters to the Workmen and Labourers of Great Britain. 4 vols. New York: J. W. Lovell Co., 1886 (New York, 1871–1884).
—*Modern Painters.* 5 vols. Everyman's Library, New York: E. P. Dutton, 1929–1935 (London, 1843–1860).
—*Munera Pulveris: Six Essays on the Elements of Political Economy.* New York: C. E. Merrill, 1891 (London, 1872).
—*Sesame and Lilies. The Two Paths. The King of the Golden River.* Everyman's Library, New York: E. P. Dutton, 1934 (London, 1865).
—*The Stones of Venice.* 3 vols. New York: E. P. Dutton, 1921–1927 (London, 1851–1853).
—*Time and Tide, etc.* Everyman's Library, New York: E. P. Dutton, 1921 (London, 1867).

RUSSELL, BERTRAND ARTHUR WILLIAM (1872–1970)
The Analysis of Matter. New York: Harcourt Brace, 1927.
—*The Analysis of Mind.* New York: Macmillan, 1921.
—*Education and the Good Life.* New York: Boni & Liveright, 1926.
—*An Essay on the Foundations of Geometry.* Cambridge University Press, 1897.
—*Freedom Versus Organization, 1814–1914.* New York: W. W. Norton, 1934.
—*Human Knowledge, Its Scope and Limits.* New York: Simon & Schuster, 1948.
—*An Inquiry into Meaning and Truth.* New York: W. W. Norton, 1940.
—*Introduction to Mathematical Philosophy.* London: Allen & Unwin, 1938 (New York, 1919).
—*Mysticism and Logic, and Other Essays.* New York: W. W. Norton, 1929 (London, 1918).
—*Our Knowledge of the External World.* New York: W. W. Norton, 1929 (Chicago, 1914).
—*Philosophical Essays.* New York: Longmans, Green & Co., 1910.
—*Power, a New Social Analysis.* New York: W. W. Norton, 1938.
—*The Principles of Mathematics.* New York: W. W. Norton, 1938 (Cambridge, 1903).
—*The Problems of Philosophy.* London: T. Butterworth, 1929 (New York, 1912).
—*Proposed Roads to Freedom: Socialism, Anarchism, and Syndicalism.* New York: Blue Ribbon Books, 1931 (New York, 1919).
—*Religion and Science.* New York: Henry Holt, 1935.
—*The Scientific Outlook.* New York: W. W. Norton, 1931.
—*Skeptical Essays.* New York: W. W. Norton, 1928.
—*What I Believe.* New York: E. P. Dutton, 1925.

RUSSELL, GEORGE WILLIAM, pseud., Æ (1867–1935)
The Hero in Man. London: Orpheus Press, 1909.

RUSSELL, HENRY NORRIS (1877–1957)
The Solar System and Its Origin. New York: Macmillan, 1935.

RUTHERFORD, ERNEST RUTHERFORD (1871–1937)
Radio-active Substances and Their Radiations. New York: Macmillan, 1930 (1912).

S

SAADIA GAON (*c.* 892–942)
The Book of Beliefs and Opinions. Trans. by S. Rosenblatt. New Haven, Conn.: Yale University Press, 1948 (933).

SACCHERI, GIOVANNI GIROLAMO (1667–1733)
Girolamo Saccheri's Euclides Vindicatus. Ed. and trans. by G. B. Halsted. Chicago: Open Court, 1920 (*Euclides ab Omni Naevo Vindicatus*, Milan, 1733).

SAINT-GERMAN, CHRISTOPHER (1460–1540)
Doctor and Student; or, Dialogues Between a Doctor of Divinity and a Student in the Laws of England. London: S. Sweet, 1815 (*Dialogus de Fundamentis Legum Angliae et de Conscientia*, London, 1523).

SAINT-PIERRE, CHARLES IRÉNÉE CASTEL DE (1658–1743)
Scheme for Lasting Peace. Selections from the Second Edition of the Abrégé du projet de paix perpétuelle. Trans. by H. Hale Bellot. London: Peace Book Co., 1939 (*Projet pour rendre la paix perpétuelle en Europe*, Utrecht, 1713–1717).

SAINT-SIMON, LOUIS DE ROUVROY (1675–1755)
The Memoirs of the Duke of Saint-Simon on the Reign of Louis XIV and the Regency. Trans. by B. St. John. 4 vols. New York: J. Pott, 1901 (1740–1743?).

SALEILLES, RAYMOND (1855–1912)
The Individualisation of Punishment. Trans. by R. Szold. Boston: Little, Brown & Co., 1913 (*L'individualisation de la peine; étude de criminalité sociale*, Paris, 1898).

SALLUST (C. SALLUSTIUS CRISPUS) (86–35/34 B.C.)
The War with Catiline. In *Sallust.* Trans. by J. Rolfe. Loeb Library, New York: Putnam's, 1931 (*Bellum Catilinae*, *c.* 40 B.C.).

SANDERSON, ROBERT (1587–1663)
De Obligatione Conscientiae. Ed. by W. Whewell, trans. anon. London: J. W. Parker, 1851 (London, 1660).

SANTAYANA, GEORGE (1863–1952)
Dialogues in Limbo. New York: Scribner's, 1925.
—*The Genteel Tradition at Bay.* New York: Scribner's, 1931.
—*The Idea of Christ in the Gospels; or, God in Man, a Critical Essay.* New York: Scribner's, 1946.

—*Interpretations of Poetry and Religion*. New York: Scribner's, 1900.
—*The Realm of Essence*. In *Realms of Being*. New York: Scribner's, 1942 (New York, 1927).
—*The Realm of Matter*. *Ibid*. (New York, 1930).
—*The Realm of Spirit*. *Ibid*. (New York, 1940).
—*The Realm of Truth*. *Ibid*. (London, 1937).
—*Reason in Art*. Vol. IV, *The Life of Reason; or, The Phases of Human Progress*. New York: Scribner's, 1928–1929 (New York, 1905–1906).
—*Reason in Common Sense*. Vol. I, *ibid*. (New York, 1905–1906).
—*Reason in Religion*. Vol III, *ibid*. (New York, 1905–1906).
—*Reason in Science*. Vol. V, *ibid*. (New York, 1905–1906).
—*Reason in Society*. Vol. II, *ibid*. (New York, 1905–1906).
—*Scepticism and Animal Faith; Introduction to a System of Philosophy*. New York: Scribner's, 1923.
—*The Sense of Beauty; Being the Outlines of Aesthetic Theory*. New York: Scribner's, 1926 (New York, 1896).
—*Soliloquies in England and Later Soliloquies*. I, *Soliloquies 1914–1918*; II, *Later Soliloquies 1918–1921*. New York: Scribner's, 1922.
—*Some Turns of Thought in Modern Philosophy*. Cambridge University Press, 1933.

Sapir, Edward (1884–1939)
Language, an Introduction to the Study of Speech. New York: Harcourt Brace, 1939 (New York, 1921).

Sarton, George Alfred Léon (1884–1956)
The Life of Science. New York: H. Schuman, 1948.
—*The Study of the History of Science*. Cambridge, Mass.: Harvard University Press, 1936.

Sartre, Jean-Paul (1905–)
Existentialism. Trans. by B. Frechtman. New York: Philosophical Library, 1947 (*L'existentialisme est un humanisme*, Paris, 1946).
—*L'être et le néant. Essai d'ontologie phénoménologique*. Paris: Nouvelle Revue Française, 1943.
—*What Is Literature?* New York: Philosophical Library, 1948.

Savigny, Friedrich Karl von (1779–1861)
Jural Relations, or, The Roman Law of Persons as Subjects of Jural Relations. Trans. by W. Rattigan. London: Wildy & Sons, 1884 (Vol. I, *System des heutigen römischen Rechts*, Berlin, 1840).
—*Vom Beruf unserer Zeit für Gesetzgebung und Rechtswissenschaft*. Heidelberg: J. Mohr, 1914 (Heidelberg, 1815).

Sayce, Archibald Henry (1845–1933)
Introduction to the Science of Language. 2 vols. London: K. Paul, Trench, Trübner, 1900 (London, 1880).

Scheler, Max Ferdinand (1874–1928)
Der Formalismus in der Ethik und die materiale Wertethik. Halle: M. Niemeyer, 1927 (1913–1916).
—*Vom Ewigen im Menschen*. 2 vols. Leipsic: Neuer Geist Verlag, 1933 (Leipsic, 1921).
—*Wesen und Formen der Sympathie*. Bonn: F. Cohen, 1923 (originally pub. as *Zur Phänomenologie und Theorie der Sympathiegefühle und von Liebe und Hass*, Halle, 1913).

Schelling, Friedrich Wilhelm von (1775–1854)
The Ages of the World. Ed. and trans. by F. de Wolfe Bolman, Jr. New York: Columbia University Press, 1942 (1811).
—*Ideen zu einer Philosophie der Natur*. In Vol. II, First Series, *Sämtliche Werke* (Leipsic, 1797).
—*Of Human Freedom*. Trans. by J. Gutmann. Chicago: Open Court, 1936 (*Philosophische Untersuchungen über das Wesen der menschlichen Freiheit und die damit zusammenhängenden Gegenstände*. In *Philosophische Schriften*, Landshut, 1809).
—*Philosophie der Kunst*. In Vol. V, First Series, *Sämtliche Werke* (1802–1805).
—*Von der Weltseele*. In Vol. II, *ibid*. (Hamburg, 1798).
NOTE:
Sämtliche Werke. Ed. by K. A. F. Schelling. 24 vols. Stuttgart: Cotta, 1856–1861.

Schiller (Johann Christoph) Friedrich von (1759–1805)
Don Carlos. Trans. by R. D. Boylan, in Vol. III, *Works* (Leipsic, 1787).
—*Letters upon the Esthetic Education of Man*. In *Literary and Philosophical Essays*. "The Harvard Classics," New York: P. F. Collier, 1910 (1795).
—*On Simple and Sentimental Poetry*. In Vol. VI, *Works* (1795).
—*The Stage as a Moral Institution*. In *Literary and Philosophical Essays*. See above (1785).
—*Wallenstein*. Trans. by S. T. Coleridge, in Vol. VII, *Works* (Tübingen, 1800).
—*William Tell*. Trans. by T. Martin, *ibid*. (Tübingen, 1804).
NOTE:
Schiller's Works. 7 vols. London: G. Bell & Sons, 1897–1903.

Schlegel, August Wilhelm von (1767–1845)
Lectures on Dramatic Art and Literature. Ed. by A. J. Morrison, trans. by J. Black. London: G. Bell & Sons, 1902 (*Über dramatische Kunst und Literatur*, Heidelberg, 1809–1811).

Schlegel, (Karl Wilhelm) Friedrich von (1772–1829)
Lucinde. Trans. by P. B. Thomas. In Vol. IV, *The German Classics of the Nineteenth and Twentieth Centuries*. Ed. by K. Francke and W. Howard. 20 vols. New York: German Publications Society, 1913–1915 (Berlin, 1799).
—*The Philosophy of History. A Course of Lectures Delivered at Vienna*. Trans. by J. B. Robertson. London: G. Bell & Sons, 1915 (*Philosophie der Geschichte*, Vienna, 1829).

SCHLEICHER, AUGUST (1821–1868)
Darwinism Tested by the Science of Language. Trans. by A. V. W. Bikkers. London: Hotten, 1869 (*Die Darwinsche Theorie und die Sprachwissenschaft*, Weimar, 1863).

SCHLEIERMACHER, FRIEDRICH ERNST DANIEL (1768–1834)
The Christian Faith. Ed. by H. R. Mackintosh and J. S. Stewart. Edinburgh: T. & T. Clark, 1928 (*Der Christliche Glaube nach den Grundsätzen der Evangelischen Kirche*, Berlin, 1821–1822).
—*Dialektik.* Ed. by J. Halpern. Berlin: Mayer & Müller, 1903 (1810–1831).
—*On Religion; Speeches to Its Cultured Despisers.* Trans. by J. W. Oman. London: K. Paul, Trench, Trübner, 1893 (*Über die Religion. Reden an die Gebildeten unter ihren Verächtern*, Berlin, 1799).
—*Soliloquies.* Trans. by H. L. Friess. Chicago: Open Court, 1926 (*Monologen*, Berlin, 1800).

SCHLICK, MORITZ (1882–1936)
Philosophy of Nature. New York: Philosophical Library, 1949.

SCHOPENHAUER, ARTHUR (1789–1860)
The Complete Essays of Arthur Schopenhauer. New York: Willey Book Co., 1936 (from *Parerga und Paralipomena*, Berlin, 1851).
—*Die beiden Grundprobleme der Ethik:* I, *Über die Freiheit des menschlichen Willens;* II, *Über das Fundament der Moral.* Leipsic: F. H. Brockhaus, 1908 (Frankfort, 1841).
—*On Human Nature. Essays (Partly Posthumous) in Ethics and Politics.* Ed. and trans. by T. Bailey Saunders. New York: Macmillan, 1897. Reprinted in *Complete Essays, q.v.* (largely from *Parerga und Paralipomena*, Berlin, 1851).
—*On the Doctrine of the Indestructibility of Our True Nature by Death.* In *Philosophy of Arthur Schopenhauer.* Trans. by B. Bax and B. Saunders. New York: Tudor Publishing Co., 1933 (in *Parerga und Paralipomena*, Berlin, 1851).
—*On the Fourfold Root of the Principle of Sufficient Reason, and On Will in Nature.* Trans. by Mme. Karl Hillebrand. London: G. Bell & Sons, 1891 (*Über die vierfache Wurzel des Satzes vom zureichenden Grunde*, Rudolstadt, 1813).
—*Studies in Pessimism.* Trans. by T. Bailey Saunders. London, 1898. Reprinted in *Complete Essays, q.v.* (from *Parerga und Paralipomena*, Berlin, 1851).
—*Transcendent Speculations on Apparent Design in the Fate of the Individual.* Trans. by D. Irvine. London: Watts & Co., 1913 (in *Parerga und Paralipomena*, Berlin, 1851).
—*The World as Will and Idea.* Trans. by R. B. Haldane and J. Kemp. 3 vols. London: K. Paul, Trench, Trübner, 1907–1909 (*Die Welt als Wille und Vorstellung*, Leipsic, 1819).

SCHRECKER, PAUL (1889–1963)
Work and History. Princeton University Press, 1948.

SCHRÖDINGER, ERWIN (1887–1961)
Collected Papers on Wave Mechanics. Trans. by J. F. Shearer and W. M. Deans. London: Blackie & Son, 1928 (*Abhandlungen zur Wellenmechanik*, Leipsic, 1927).
—*Four Lectures on Wave Mechanics.* London: Blackie & Son, 1928.
—*What Is Life?* New York: Macmillan, 1945 (1943).

SCHWANN, THEODOR (1810–1882)
Microscopical Researches into the Accordance in the Structure and Growth of Animals and Plants. Trans. by H. Smith. London: Sydenham Society, 1847 (*Mikroskopische Untersuchungen über die Uebereinstimmung in der Struktur und dem Wachsthum der Thiere und Pflanzen*, Berlin, 1839).

SCOTT, DUKINFIELD HENRY (1854–1934)
The Evolution of Plants. New York: Henry Holt, 1911.

SCOTT, SIR WALTER (1771–1832)
Ivanhoe; a Romance. New York: Dodd, Mead & Co., 1944 (Edinburgh, 1820).
—*Letters on Demonology and Witchcraft, Addressed to J. G. Lockhardt.* New York: G. Routledge, 1885 (London, 1830).

SENECA, LUCIUS ANNAEUS (*c.* 4 B.C.–*c.* 65 A.D.)
De Beata Vita. In Vol. II, *Moral Essays, q.v.* (58–59 A.D.).
—*De Beneficiis.* Vol. III, *ibid.* (59–62 A.D.).
—*De Consolatione ad Marciam.* In Vol. II, *ibid.* (*c.* 40 A.D.).
—*De Constantia Sapientis.* In Vol. I, *ibid.* (41–42 A.D.).
—*Moral Essays.* Trans. by J. W. Basore. 3 vols. Loeb Library, New York: Putnam's, 1928–1935.
—*Moral Letters.* Ed. and trans. by R. M. Gummere. 3 vols. Loeb Library, New York: Putnam's, 1920 (63–65 A.D.).

SERTILLANGES, ANTONIN GILBERT (1863–1948)
La famille et l'état dans l'éducation. Paris: V. Lecoffre, 1907.

SÉVIGNÉ, MARIE DE RABUTIN-CHANTAL, MARQUISE DE (1626–1696)
The Letters of Madame de Sévigné. Sel. and ed. by J. A. Harrison. Boston: Ginn & Co., 1899 (1647–1696).

SEXTUS EMPIRICUS (2nd century A.D.)
Against the Ethicists. In *Sextus Empiricus.* Trans. by R. G. Bury. 3 vols. Loeb Library, Cambridge, Mass.: Harvard University Press, 1933.
—*Against the Logicians. Ibid.*
—*Against the Physicists. Ibid.*
—*Outlines of Pyrrhonism. Ibid.*

SHAFTESBURY, ANTHONY ASHLEY COOPER, THIRD EARL OF (1671–1713)
Characteristics of Men, Manners, Opinions, Times. Ed. by J. M. Robertson. 2 vols. New York: E. P. Dutton, 1900 (London, 1711).

SHAPLEY, HARLOW (1885–1972)
Starlight. New York: G. H. Doran, 1926.

SHAW, GEORGE BERNARD (1856–1950)
Arms and the Man. In Vol. II, *Plays: Pleasant and Unpleasant* (1894).
—*Back to Methuselah: A Metabiological Pentateuch.* London: Constable & Co., 1931 (London, 1921).
—*Candida.* In Vol. II, *Plays: Pleasant and Unpleasant* (1895).
—[Crude Criminology] *Doctors' Delusions, Crude Criminology, and Sham Education.* London: Constable & Co., 1932 (London, 1931).
—*Doctors' Delusions. Ibid.* (London, 1931).
—*Dramatic Opinions and Essays, with an Apology by Bernard Shaw.* 2 vols. New York: Brentano's, 1907–1913 (New York, 1906).
—*The Intelligent Woman's Guide to Socialism and Capitalism.* London: Constable & Co., 1928.
—*Major Barbara.* New York: Dodd, Mead & Co., 1941 (1905).
—*Man and Superman: A Comedy and a Philosophy.* New York: Dodd, Mead & Co., 1939 (Westminster, 1903).
—*Pygmalion.* New York: Dodd, Mead & Co., 1939 (London, 1913).
—*The Revolutionist's Handbook and Pocket Companion by John Tanner, M.I.R.C.* Appended to *Man and Superman, q.v.*
—*The Sanity of Art: An Exposure of the Current Nonsense About Artists Being Degenerate.* New York: B. R. Tucker, 1908 (1895).
—*Socialism and Superior Brains: A Reply to Mr. Mallock.* New York: J. Lane, 1910 (London, 1909).
—*Widowers' Houses.* In Vol. I, *Plays: Pleasant and Unpleasant* (1892).
NOTE:
Plays: Pleasant and Unpleasant. 2 vols. New York: Dodd, Mead & Co., 1940.

SHELDON, WILMON HENRY (1875–)
Strife of Systems and Productive Duality; an Essay in Philosophy. Cambridge, Mass.: Harvard University Press, 1918.

SHELLEY, PERCY BYSSHE (1792–1822)
Adonais. An Elegy on the Death of John Keats. In *Poetical Works* (1821).
—*A Defense of Poetry.* Ed. by Mrs. Shelley. Indianapolis, Ind.: Bobbs Merrill Co., 1904 (1821).
—*Preface to Alastor.* In *Poetical Works* (1816).
—*Prometheus Unbound; A Lyrical Drama in Four Acts. Ibid.* (1820).
NOTE:
John Keats and Percy Bysshe Shelley: Complete Poetical Works. Modern Library, New York: Random House, 1932.

SHERIDAN, RICHARD BRINSLEY BUTLER (1751–1816)
The Rivals. In *Plays by Richard Brinsley Sheridan.* Everyman's Library, New York: E. P. Dutton, 1931 (1775).
—*The School for Scandal. Ibid.* (1777).

SHERRINGTON, SIR CHARLES SCOTT (1857–1952)
The Brain and Its Mechanism. Cambridge University Press, 1933.
—*The Integrative Action of the Nervous System.* New Haven, Conn.: Yale University Press, 1923 (New York, 1906).
—*Man on His Nature.* New York: Macmillan, 1941 (Cambridge, 1940).

SHOLOKHOV, MIKHAIL ALEKSANDROVICH (1905–)
The Silent Don. Vol. I, *And Quiet Flows the Don;* Vol. II, *The Don Flows Home to the Sea.* Trans. by S. Gary. New York: A. A. Knopf, 1942 (1928–1938).

SHOTWELL, JAMES THOMSON (1874–1965)
The History of History. New York: Columbia University Press, 1939 (*An Introduction to the History of History,* New York, 1922).

SIDGWICK, ALFRED (1850–1943)
Distinction and the Criticism of Beliefs. New York: Longmans, Green & Co., 1892.
—*Fallacies. A View of Logic from the Practical Side.* London: K. Paul, Trench, Trübner, 1901 (London, 1883).
—*The Use of Words in Reasoning.* London: A. & C. Black, 1901.

SIDGWICK, HENRY (1838–1900)
The Methods of Ethics. Ed. by E. Jones. London: Macmillan, 1913 (London, 1874).
—*Philosophy, Its Scope and Relations.* New York: Macmillan, 1902 (1886?–1900).
—*Practical Ethics: A Collection of Addresses and Essays.* New York: Macmillan, 1909 (New York, 1898).

SIDNEY, ALGERNON (1622–1683)
Discourses Concerning Government. 2 vols. Philadelphia: M. L. Weems, 1805 (1680–1681?).

SIDNEY, SIR PHILIP (1554–1586)
An Apology for Poetry. In *The Portable Elizabethan Reader.* New York: Viking Press, 1946 (1581).
—*Astrophel and Stella. Ibid.* (1575–1583).
—*The Countess of Pembroke's Arcadia.* New York: E. P. Dutton, 1921 (1580–1583).

SIEYÈS, JOSEPH EMMANUEL (1748–1836)
[Discours] *Les discours de Sieyès dans les débats constitutionnels de l'an III.* Ed. by Paul Bastid. Paris: L. Hachette, 1939 (1795).
—*An Essay on Privileges, and Particularly on Heredity.* Trans. anon. London: J. Ridgeway, 1791 (*Essai sur les privilèges,* first pub., 1789).

SIGWART, CHRISTOPH VON (1830–1904)
Logic. Trans. by Helen Dendy. 2 vols. New York: Macmillan, 1895 (Tübingen, 1873–1878).

SIMON, YVES (1903–1961)
Community of the Free. Trans. by W. R. Trask. New York: Henry Holt, 1947.
—*Introduction à l'ontologie du connaître.* Paris: Desclée, de Brouwer, 1934.
—*Nature and Functions of Authority.* Milwaukee, Wis.: Marquette University Press, 1940.

—*Trois leçons sur le travail*. Paris: Téqui, 1938.

SINCLAIR, UPTON BEALL (1878–1968)
The Jungle. New York: Vanguard Press, 1927 (New York, 1906).

Sir Gawain and the Green Knight. Modern English by S. O. Andrew. New York: E. P. Dutton, 1929 (1375?).

SITTER, WILLEM DE (1872–1934)
Kosmos: A Course of Six Lectures on the Development of Our Insight into the Structure of the Universe. Cambridge, Mass.: Harvard University Press, 1932.

SKIDMORE, THOMAS (?–1832)
The Rights of Man to Property! Being a Proposition to Make It Equal Among the Adults of the Present Generation, etc. New York: A. Ming, 1829.

SMILES, SAMUEL (1812–1904)
Life and Labor: or, Characteristics of Men of Industry, Culture and Genius. New York: Harper, 1888 (London, 1887).

SMITH, ADAM (1723–1790)
A Dissertation on the Origin of Languages. See *Theory of Moral Sentiments* (in 3rd ed., *Theory of Moral Sentiments*, London, 1767).
—*Essays Philosophical and Literary*. London: Ward, Lock & Co., 1880.
—*The History of Astronomy*. In *Essays Philosophical and Literary, q.v.* (before 1773?).
—*Lectures on Justice, Police, Revenue and Arms, Delivered in the University of Glasgow*. Ed. by E. Cannan. Oxford: Clarendon Press, 1896 (1766).
—*The Theory of Moral Sentiments*. Ed. by D. Stewart. London: G. Bell & Sons, 1892 (London, 1759).

SMITH, WILLIAM ROBERTSON (1846–1894)
The Prophets of Israel and Their Place in History to the Close of the Eighth Century B.C. London: A. & C. Black, 1907 (Edinburgh, 1882).

SMOLLETT, TOBIAS GEORGE (1721–1771)
The Expedition of Humphry Clinker. Everyman's Library, New York: E. P. Dutton, 1943 (London, 1771).

SMUTS, JAN CHRISTIAAN (1870–1950)
Holism and Evolution. New York: Macmillan, 1936 (New York, 1926).

SMYTH, HENRY DE WOLF (1898–)
Atomic Energy for Military Purposes. Princeton University Press, 1945.

SODDY, FREDERICK (1877–1956)
The Interpretation of the Atom. London: J. Murray, 1932.

The Song of Roland. Trans. by A. S. Way. Cambridge University Press, 1913 (late 11th century).

SOREL, GEORGES (1847–1922)
Les illusions du progrès. Paris: M. Rivière, 1927 (Paris, 1908).
—*Reflexions on Violence*. Trans. by T. E. Hulme. London: Allen & Unwin, 1925 (*Réflexions sur la violence*, Paris, 1908).

SOTO, DOMINGO DE (1494–1560)
Libri Decem de Justitia et Jure. 2 vols. Salamanca, 1553–1554.

SOUTHEY, ROBERT (1774–1843)
Essays, Moral and Political. Vol. I, London: J. Murray, 1832 (1810–1816).

SPEARMAN, CHARLES EDWARD (1863–1945)
The Abilities of Man; Their Nature and Measurement. New York: Macmillan, 1927.

SPENCER, HERBERT (1820–1903)
Essays on Education and Kindred Subjects. New York: E. P. Dutton, 1928 (1854–1859).
—*The Man Versus the State*. New York: D. Appleton, 1884.
—*The Principles of Ethics*. 2 vols. New York: D. Appleton, 1914 (London, 1892–1893. Part I pub. as *Data of Ethics*, New York, 1879).
—*The Principles of Psychology*. 2 vols. New York: D. Appleton, 1914 (London, 1855).
—*Progress: Its Law and Cause*. In *Essays on Education, q.v.* (in *Essays, Scientific, etc*., London, 1858).

SPENGLER, OSWALD (1880–1936)
The Decline of the West. Trans. by C. F. Atkinson. 2 vols. New York: A. A. Knopf, 1939 (*Der Untergang des Abendlandes*, Munich, 1918–1922).

SPENSER, EDMUND (*c*. 1552–1599)
Epithalamion. New York: Crofts, 1926 (London, 1595).
—*The Faerie Queene: Disposed into Twelve Books Fashioning Twelve Moral Virtues*. 2 vols. Everyman's Library, New York: E. P. Dutton, 1931–1933 (London, 1590–1596).
—*An Hymne of Heavenly Love*. In *Spenser's Minor Poems*. Ed. by E. De Sélincourt. Oxford: Clarendon Press, 1910 (London, 1596).

SPINOZA, BENEDICT DE (1632–1677)
Cogita Metaphysica. In Vol. III, *Benedicti de Spinoza Opera Quotquot Reperta Sunt*. Ed. by J. Van Vloten and J. P. N. Land. 3 vols. The Hague: M. Nijhoff, 1895 (first pub. with *Renati Descarti Principiorum Philosophiae, Pars i et ii, More Geometrico Demonstratae*, Amsterdam, 1663).
—*The Correspondence of Spinoza*. Ed. and trans. by A. Wolf. New York: Dial Press, 1927 (1661–1676).
—*Of the Improvement of the Understanding*. In Vol. II, *The Chief Works of Baruch Spinoza*. Ed. by R. H. M. Elwes. 2 vols. London: G. Bell & Sons, 1906 (*Tractatus de Intellectus Emendatione*. In *Opera Posthuma*, Amsterdam, 1677).
—*Tractatus Politicus*. In *Writings on Political Philosophy*. New York: D. Appleton-Century, 1937 (1677).
—*Tractatus Theologico-Politicus*. In Vol. I, *Chief Works*. See *Of the Improvement of the Understanding* (Amsterdam, 1670).

STALLO, JOHN BERNHARD (1823–1900)
Concepts and Theories of Modern Physics. New York: D. Appleton, 1897 (New York, 1882).

STAMMLER, RUDOLF (1856–1938)
The Theory of Justice. Ed. by F. Geny and J. C. H. Wu, trans. by I. Husik. New York: Macmillan, 1925 (*Theorie der Rechtswissenschaft*, Halle, 1911).

STEFFENS, JOSEPH LINCOLN (1866–1936)
The Autobiography of Lincoln Steffens. 2 vols. New York: Harcourt Brace, 1931.

STEINBECK, JOHN ERNST (1902–1968)
The Grapes of Wrath. Modern Library, New York: Random House, 1941 (New York, 1939).

STENDHAL, pseud. for MARIE HENRI BEYLE (1783–1842)
The Charterhouse of Parma. Trans. by C. K. Scott-Moncrieff. Modern Library, New York: Random House, 1937 (*La chartreuse de Parme*, Paris, 1839).
—*On Love*. Ed. by P. S. and C. N. Woolf. London: Duckworth, 1915 (*De l'amour*, Paris, 1822).
—*Racine et Shakespeare*. Ed. by P. Martino. 2 vols. Paris: É. Champion, 1925 (Paris, 1823–1825).
—*The Red and the Black*. Modern Library, New York: Random House, 1949 (*Le rouge et le noir*, Paris, 1831).

STEPHEN, SIR JAMES FITZJAMES (1829–1894)
Liberty, Equality, Fraternity. London: Smith, Elder & Co., 1873.

STEPHEN, SIR LESLIE (1832–1904)
An Agnostic's Apology, and Other Essays. London: Smith, Elder & Co., 1893 (title essay, London, 1876).
—*The Science of Ethics*. London: Smith, Elder & Co., 1907 (London, 1882).
—*Social Rights and Duties. Addresses to Ethical Societies*. 2 vols. London: Swan Sonnenschein, 1896.

STERNE, LAURENCE (1713–1768)
A Sentimental Journey Through France and Italy. Everyman's Library, New York: E. P. Dutton, 1947 (London, 1768).

STEVENSON, ROBERT LOUIS (1850–1894)
Across the Plains, with Other Memories and Essays. New York: Scribner's, 1912 (London, 1892).
—*Virginibus Puerisque, Familiar Studies of Men and Books*. Everyman's Library, New York: E. P. Dutton, 1929 (London, 1881).

STEVIN, SIMON (1548–1620)
L'art ponderaire, ou la statique. In Vol. IV, *Oeuvres mathématiques*. 6 vols. Leyden: B. & A. Elsevier, 1634 (1585).

STEWART, BALFOUR (1828–1887)
The Conservation of Energy. New York: D. Appleton, 1900 (New York, 1874).

STEWART, DUGALD (1753–1828)
Elements of the Philosophy of the Human Mind. Vols. II–IV, *The Collected Works of Dugald Stewart*. Ed. by Sir W. Hamilton. 11 vols. Edinburgh: T. & T. Clark, 1877 (Edinburgh, 1792; 1814; 1827).
—*Outlines of Moral Philosophy*. Vols. IV and VI, *ibid*. (Edinburgh, 1793).
—*Philosophical Essays*. Vol. V, *ibid*. (Edinburgh, 1810).
—*Philosophy of the Active and Moral Powers of Man*. Vols. VI–VII, *ibid*. (Edinburgh, 1828).

STIRLING, JAMES HUTCHISON (1820–1909)
Philosophy and Theology. Edinburgh: T. & T. Clark, 1890.

STOUT, GEORGE FREDERICK (1860–1944)
Analytic Psychology. 2 vols. London: Allen & Unwin, 1918 (London, 1896).
—*A Manual of Psychology*. London: University Tutorial Press, 1938 (London, 1898).
—*Mind and Matter*. Cambridge University Press, 1931 (1919–1921).

STRANATHAN, JAMES DOCKING (1898–)
The "Particles" of Modern Physics. Philadelphia: Blakiston Co., 1942.

STRAUS, ERWIN (1891–)
Vom Sinn der Sinne: Ein Beitrag zur Grundlegung der Psychologie. Berlin: J. Springer, 1935.

STRAUSS, LEO (1899–1973)
On Tyranny. New York: Political Science Classics, 1948.

STRINDBERG, AUGUST (1849–1912)
The Dance of Death. In *Plays. First Series*. Trans. by E. Björkman. New York: Scribner's, 1928 (Stockholm, 1901).
—*The Father: A Tragedy*. Trans. by N. Erichsen. Boston: J. W. Luce, 1907 (Helsingborg, 1887).

STURZO, LUIGI (1871–1959)
Church and State. Trans. by B. B. Carter. New York: Longmans, Green & Co., 1939 (London, 1937).
—*The Inner Laws of Society: A New Sociology*. Trans. by B. B. Carter. New York: P. J. Kenedy, 1944 (1935).
—*The International Community and the Right of War*. Trans. by B. B. Carter. New York: R. R. Smith, 1930 (London, 1929).

SUÁREZ, FRANCISCO (1548–1617)
De Religione. In Vol. XIII, *Opera Omnia*. Ed. by M. André and C. Berton. 28 vols. Paris: L. Vivès, 1856–1878 (1609).
—*Disputationes Metaphysicae*. In Vols. XXV–XXVI, *ibid*. (Salamanca, 1597).
—*On the Various Kinds of Distinctions*. Trans. by C. Vollert. Milwaukee, Wis,: Marquette University Press, 1947 (*Disputationes Metaphysicae, Disputatio VII, De Variis Distinctionum Generibus*).
—*On War*. In Vol. I, *Selections from Three Works of Francisco Suárez, S.J.* Ed. by J. B. Scott, trans. by G. L. Williams *et al*. 2 vols. Oxford: Clarendon Press, 1944.
—*A Treatise on Laws and God the Lawgiver*. In Vol. II, *ibid*. (*De Legibus ac Deo Legislatore in Decem Libros Distributus*, Coimbra, 1612).

SULLY, JAMES (1842–1923)
Illusions: A Psychological Study. New York: D. Appleton, 1888 (London, 1881).

SUMNER, WILLIAM GRAHAM (1840–1910)
The Absurd Effort to Make the World Over. In *War, q.v.* (1894).
—*Folkways; a Study of the Sociological Importance of Usages, Manners, Customs, Mores, and Morals*. Ed. by A. G. Keller. Boston: Ginn & Co., 1940 (Boston, 1907).
—*War and Other Essays*. Ed. by A. G. Keller. New Haven, Conn.: Yale University Press, 1911 (title essay, 1903).

SWEDENBORG, EMANUEL (1688–1772)
Angelic Wisdom Concerning the Divine Providence. In Vol. XXV, *Theological Works*. Rotch ed., 32 vols. Boston: Houghton Mifflin Co., 1907 (*Sapientia Angelica de Divina Providentia*, Amsterdam, 1764).
—*Heaven and Its Wonders and Hell, from Things Heard and Seen*. Everyman's Library, New York: E. P. Dutton, 1909 (*De Coelo et Ejus Mirabilibus, et de Inferno, ex Auditis et Visis*, London, 1758).

SWIFT, JONATHAN (1667–1745)
An Argument to Prove That the Abolishing of Christianity in England, May. . . . Be Attended with Some Inconveniences, and Perhaps not Produce those Many Good Effects Propos'd Thereby. In Vol. III, *The Prose Works of Jonathan Swift*. Ed. by T. Scott. 12 vols. London: G. Bell & Sons, 1900–1914 (London, 1708).
—*The Battle of the Books*. See *Tale of a Tub* (London, 1704).
—*An Essay on Modern Education*. In Vol. XI, *Prose Works*. See *An Argument* (1732).
—*A Modest Proposal for Preventing the Children of Poor People from Being a Burthen to Their Parents or Country, and for Making Them Beneficial to the Public*. In *The Portable Swift*. New York: Viking Press, 1948 (Dublin, 1729).
—*A Tale of a Tub, The Battle of the Books and Other Satires*. Everyman's Library, New York: E. P. Dutton, 1948 (London, 1704).

SYNGE, JOHN MILLINGTON (1871–1909)
Deirdre of the Sorrows. Boston: J. W. Luce, 1911 (1908–1909).
—*Riders to the Sea*. Boston: J. W. Luce, 1911 (1903).

T

TACITUS, CORNELIUS (*c.* 55–*c.* 120 A.D.)
[A Dialogue on Oratory] *Dialogus, Agricola, Germania*. Trans. by W. Peterson. Loeb Library, New York: Putnam's, 1925 (*Dialogus de Oratoribus*, 78–81 A.D.).
—*Germania*. *Ibid* (*c.* 98 A.D.).

TAINE, HIPPOLYTE ADOLPHE (1828–1893)
Essais de critique et d'histoire. Paris: Hachette, 1887 (Paris, 1858).
—*On Intelligence*. Trans. by T. D. Haye. New York: Henry Holt, 1889 (*De l'intelligence*, Paris, 1870).
—*The Philosophy of Art*. Trans. by John Durand. New York: Henry Holt, 1875 (*Philosophie de l'art*, Paris, 1865).

[Talmud] *New Edition of the Babylonian Talmud*. Trans. by M. L. Rodkinson. 20 vols. New York: New Talmud Publishing Co., 1896–1903 (3rd–5th centuries A.D.).

TARDE, GABRIEL DE (1843–1904)
The Laws of Imitation. Trans. by E. C. Parsons. New York: Henry Holt, 1903 (*Les lois de l'imitation; Étude sociologique*, Paris, 1890).

TARSKI, ALFRED (1902–)
Introduction to Logic and to the Methodology of Deductive Sciences. Trans. by O. Helmer. New York: Oxford University Press, 1941 (Polish ed., 1936).

TASSO, TORQUATO (1544–1595)
Jerusalem Delivered. Ed. by H. Morley, trans. by E. Fairfax. New York: Colonial Press, 1901 (*Gerusalemme Liberata*, Casalmaggiore, 1581).

TATE, JOHN ORLEY ALLEN (1899–)
Reactionary Essays on Poetry and Ideas. New York: Scribner's, 1936.

TAWNEY, RICHARD HENRY (1880–1962)
The Acquisitive Society. New York: Harcourt Brace, 1928 (London, 1920).
—*Equality*. New York: Harcourt Brace, 1931.
—*Religion and the Rise of Capitalism, a Historical Study*. New York: Harcourt Brace, 1926.

TAYLOR, ALFRED EDWARD (1869–1945)
The Christian Hope of Immortality. London: Unicorn Press, 1938.
—*Does God Exist?* New York: Macmillan, 1947 (1945).
—*Elements of Metaphysics*. London: Methuen, 1903.
—*The Faith of a Moralist*. 2 vols. London: Macmillan, 1937 (London, 1930).
—*Philosophical Studies*. London: Macmillan, 1934.
—*The Problem of Conduct; a Study in the Phenomenology of Ethics*. London: Macmillan, 1901.

TAYLOR, JEREMY (1613–1667)
Θεολογία Ἐκλεκτική, *or, A Discourse of the Liberty of Prophesying, with Its Just Limits and Temper*. In Vol. II, *The Whole Works of the Right Rev. Jeremy Taylor*. 3 vols. London: H. G. Bohn, 1851–1867 (London, 1647).
—*A Discourse of the Nature, Offices and Measures of Friendship*. In Vol. III, *ibid*. (London, 1657).
—*Ductor Dubitantium; or, The Rule of Conscience in All Her General Measures. Ibid*. (London, 1660).
—[Of Holy Dying] *The Rule and Exercises of Holy Dying*. In Vol. I, *ibid*. (London, 1651).
—(Of Holy Living] *The Rule and Exercises of Holy Living. Ibid*. (London, 1650).
—*Twenty-Five Sermons Preached at Golden Grove. Ibid*. (originally pub. as *A Course of Sermons for All the Sundaies of the Year*, London, 1653–1655).

TEGGART, FREDERICK JOHN (1870–1946)
Theory of History. New Haven, Conn.: Yale University Press, 1925.

TENNANT, FREDERICK ROBERT (1866–1957)
The Concept of Sin. Cambridge University Press, 1912.
—*Philosophical Theology*. 2 vols. Cambridge University Press, 1928–1930.
—*Philosophy of the Sciences, or, The Relations Between the Departments of Knowledge*. Cambridge University Press, 1932.

TENNYSON, ALFRED (1809–1892)
Crossing the Bar. In *Tennyson's Poems*. Everyman's Library, New York: E. P. Dutton, 1950 (1889).
—*In Memoriam*. *Ibid*. (1850).
—*Locksley Hall*. *Ibid*. (1842).
—*Ulysses*. *Ibid*. (1842).

TERESA OF JESUS, SAINT (1515–1582)
Book of the Foundations. In Vol. III, *The Complete Works of Saint Teresa of Jesus*. Ed. and trans. by E. Allison Peers. 3 vols. New York: Sheed & Ward, 1946 (*Libro de las fundaciones*, 1573–1582).
—*Interior Castle* (*The Mansions*). In Vol. II, *ibid*. (*Las moradas o Castillo interior*, 1577).
—*The Way of Perfection*. *Ibid*. (*Camino de perfección*, 1565–1566).

TERTULLIAN (QUINTUS SEPTIMIUS FLORENS TERTULLIANUS) (*c*. 155–*c*. 222 A.D.)
Apology and De Spectaculis. Trans. by T. R. Glover. Loeb Library, Cambridge, Mass.: Harvard University Press, 1931 (*Apologeticus*, 197?).
—*De Spectaculis*. See *Apology* (after 197?).
—*On Idolatry*. In Vol. III, *The Ante-Nicene Fathers*. Ed. by A. Roberts and J. Donaldson. 10 vols. New York: Christian Literature Co., 1885–1896 (*De Idolatria*, 212?).
—*The Prescription Against Heretics*. *Ibid*. (*De Praescriptione Haereticorum*).
—*A Treatise on the Soul*. *Ibid*. (*De Anima*, 203?).

THACKERAY, WILLIAM MAKEPEACE (1811–1863)
The History of Henry Esmond, Esq. Modern Library, New York: Random House, 1936 (London, 1852).
—*Vanity Fair, a Novel without a Hero*. Modern Library, New York: Random House, 1949 (London, 1847–1848).

Theologia Germanica: Which Setteth Forth Many Fair Lineaments of Divine Truth, and Saith Very Lofty and Lovely Things Touching a Perfect Life. Ed. by F. Pfeiffer, trans. by S. Winkworth. London: Macmillan, 1937 (*c*. 1375).

THEOPHRASTUS OF ERESOS (*c*. 372–*c*. 286 B.C.)
The Characters. Trans. by J. M. Edmonds. Loeb Library, Cambridge, Mass.: Harvard University Press, 1929 (319 B.C.?).
—*Enquiry into Plants*. Trans. by A. Hort. 2 vols. Loeb Library, Cambridge, Mass.: Harvard University Press, 1916 (315 B.C.?).
—*On the Senses*. In G. M. Stratton, *Theophrastus and the Greek Physiological Psychology*. New York: Macmillan, 1917.

THOMAS Á KEMPIS, SAINT (*c*. 1380–1471)
The Imitation of Christ. Trans. by Richard Whitford, ed. by E. J. Klein. New York: Harper, 1941 (*Imitatio Christi*, 1421?–1434?).

THOMAS OF ERFURT (14th century)
Grammatica Speculativa (*Liber Modorum Significandi*). Ed. by M. F. Garcia. Florence: Tipographia Collegii S. Bonaventurae, 1902.

THOMPSON, SIR D'ARCY WENTWORTH (1860–1948)
On Growth and Form. Cambridge University Press, 1942 (Cambridge, 1917).

THOMPSON, FRANCIS (1859–1907)
The Hound of Heaven. New York: Dodd, Mead & Co., 1922 (1893).

THOMPSON, WILLIAM ROBIN (1887–1972)
Science and Common Sense, an Aristotelian Excursion. New York: Longmans, Green & Co., 1937.

THOMSON, GEORGE PAGET (1892–)
The Atom. New York: Home University Library, 1947 (1930).

THOMSON, SIR WILLIAM (BARON KELVIN) (1824–1907) and TAIT, PETER GUTHRIE (1831–1901)
Elements of Natural Philosophy. Cambridge University Press, 1879 (Oxford, 1873).
—*Treatise on Natural Philosophy*. 2 vols. Cambridge University Press, 1895–1896 (Oxford, 1867).

THOREAU, HENRY DAVID (1817–1862)
Civil Disobedience. In *Walden and Other Writings of Henry David Thoreau*. Ed. by B. Atkinson. Modern Library, New York: Random House, 1937 (1849).
—*A Plea for Captain John Brown*. *Ibid*. (in James Redpath ed., *Echoes of Harper's Ferry*, Boston, 1860).
—*Walden*. *Ibid*. (Boston, 1854).
—*A Week on the Concord and Merrimack Rivers*. *Ibid*. (Boston, 1849).

THORNDIKE, EDWARD LEE (1874–1949)
Man on His Works. Cambridge, Mass.: Harvard University Press, 1943.

THURSTONE, LOUIS LEON (1887–1955)
The Vectors of Mind; Multiple-Factor Analysis for the Isolation of Primary Traits. University of Chicago Press, 1935.

TIRSO DE MOLINA, pseud. for GABRIEL TÉLLEZ (*c*. 1570–1648)
The Love Rogue; a Poetic Drama in Three Acts. Trans. by H. Kemp. New York: Lieber & Lewis, 1923 (*El Burlador de Sevilla*. In *Doze Comedias Nuevas de Lope de Vega, etc*., Barcelona, 1630).

TITCHENER, EDWARD BRADFORD (1867–1927)
Lectures on the Elementary Psychology of Feeling and Attention. New York: Macmillan, 1908.
—*Lectures on the Experimental Psychology of the Thought-Processes*. New York: Macmillan, 1909.

TOCQUEVILLE, ALEXIS CHARLES HENRI MAURICE CLEREL DE (1805–1859)
Democracy in America. Ed. by P. Bradley, trans.

by H. Reeve. 2 vols. New York: A. A. Knopf, 1945 (*De la démocratie en Amérique*, Brussels, 1835–1840).
—*L'ancien régime*. Trans. by M. W. Patterson. Oxford: Blackwell, 1933 (Paris, 1856).

TODHUNTER, ISAAC (1820–1884)
History of the Mathematical Theory of Probability from the Time of Pascal to That of Laplace. New York: G. E. Stechert, 1931 (Cambridge, 1865).

TÖNNIES, FERDINAND (1855–1936)
Fundamental Concepts of Sociology. Trans. by C. P. Loomis. New York: American Book Co., 1940 (*Gemeinschaft und Gesellschaft. Abhandlung über den Communismus und den Socialismus als empirische Culturformen*, Leipsic, 1887).

TOLMAN, RICHARD CHACE (1881–1948)
Relativity, Thermodynamics, and Cosmology. Oxford: Clarendon Press, 1934.

TOLSTOY, COUNT LEO NIKOLAEVICH (1828–1910)
Anna Karenina. Trans. by R. S. Townsend. 2 vols. Everyman's Library, New York: E. P. Dutton, 1935 (1875–1877).
—*Christianity and Patriotism*. In *War-Patriotism-Peace*. Ed. by S. Nearing. New York: Vanguard Press, 1926 (Geneva, 1895).
—*The Cossacks, and Other Tales of the Caucasus*. Trans. by L. and A. Maude. World's Classics, New York: Oxford University Press, 1929 (Moscow, 1863).
—*The Death of Ivan Ilyitch, and Other Stories*. Trans. by C. Garnett. New York: Dodd, Mead & Co., 1927 (1886).
—*The Gospel in Brief*. New York: T. Y. Crowell, 1896 (1883).
—*The Kingdom of God, with Peace Essays*. Trans. by A. Maude. New York: Oxford University Press, 1936 (Berlin, 1893).
—*The Law of Love and the Law of Violence*. New York: Boni & Gaer, 1948.
—*Memoirs of a Madman*. In *Ivan Ilych and Hadji Murad*. Trans. by L. and A. Maude. World's Classics, New York: Oxford University Press, 1935 (1883).
—*Notes for Soldiers*. In *What Is Religion? and Other New Articles and Letters by Leo Tolstoy*. Trans. by V. Tchertkoff and A. C. Fifield. New York: T. Y. Crowell, 1902 (1901).
—*On Life, and Essays on Religion*. Trans. by A. Maude. World's Classics, New York: Oxford University Press, 1934 (Geneva, 1891).
—*Resurrection*. Trans. by L. Maude. World's Classics, New York: Oxford University Press, 1928 (1899).
—*Three Deaths*. In *The Death of Ivan Ilyitch, and Other Stories, q.v.* (1859).
—*What Is Art? and Essays on Art*. Trans. by A. Maude. New York: Oxford University Press, 1932 (1897–1898).
—*What Men Live By*. In *Twenty-three Tales*. Trans. by L. and A. Maude. World's Classics, New York: Oxford University Press, 1930 (1881).
—*What Then Must We Do?* Trans. by A. Maude. World's Classics, New York: Oxford University Press, 1925 (originally pub. as *What To Do?*, London, 1887).

TOOKE, JOHN HORNE (1736–1812)
Ἔπεα Πτερόεντα, or The Diversions of Purley. London: W. Tegg, 1860 (London, 1786).

TOYNBEE, ARNOLD (1852–1883)
Lectures on the Industrial Revolution of the Eighteenth Century in England, Popular Addresses, Notes, and Other Fragments. New York: Longmans, Green & Co., 1937 (1879–1882).

TOYNBEE, ARNOLD JOSEPH (1889–)
Civilization on Trial. New York: Oxford University Press, 1948.
—*A Study of History*. Abr. ed. by D. C. Somervell. New York: Oxford University Press, 1947 (London, 1934).

TREITSCHKE, HEINRICH VON (1834–1896)
Politics. Trans. by B. Dugdale and T. Bille. 2 vols. New York: Macmillan, 1916 (*Politik*, Leipsic, 1897–1898).

TRENCH, RICHARD CHENEVIX (1807–1886)
On the Study of Words. Everyman's Library, New York: E. P. Dutton, 1936 (London, 1851).

TRENDELENBURG, FRIEDRICH ADOLF (1802–1872)
Naturrecht auf dem Grunde der Ethik. Leipsic: S. Hirzel, 1868 (Leipsic, 1860).

[Tristan and Iseult] *The Romance of Tristan and Iseult*. Trans. by H. Belloc and P. Rosenfeld. New York: Pantheon Books, 1945 (1210).

TROELTSCH, ERNST (1865–1923)
Der Historismus und seine Überwindung. Berlin: R. Heise, 1924.
—*Gesammelte Schriften*. 4 vols. Tübingen: Mohr, 1912–1925.
—*The Social Teaching of the Christian Churches*. Trans. by Olive Wyon. 2 vols. New York: Macmillan, 1931 (*Die Soziallehren der Christlichen Kirchen und Gruppen*, Tübingen, 1912).

TROLLOPE, ANTHONY (1815–1882)
Barchester Towers. Garden City, N.Y.: Doubleday Doran, 1945 (London, 1857).

TROTSKY, LEO DAVIDOVICH (1877–1940)
The Defense of Terrorism (*Terrorism and Communism*)*: A Reply to Karl Kautsky*. London: Allen & Unwin, 1921 (St. Petersburg, 1920).
—*The History of the Russian Revolution*. Trans. by M. Eastman. New York: Simon & Schuster, 1936 (Berlin, 1931–1933).
—*Literature and Revolution*. Trans. by R. Strumsky. New York: International Publishers, 1925 (Moscow, 1923).

TSANOFF, RADOSLAV ANDREA (1887–)
The Nature of Evil. New York: Macmillan, 1931.

TURGENEV, IVAN SERGEYEVICH (1818–1883)
Fathers and Sons. Trans. by C. J. Hogarth. Everyman's Library, New York: E. P. Dutton, 1934 (1862).

—*Liza*. Trans. by W. R. S. Ralston. Everyman's Library, New York: E. P. Dutton, 1923 (1858).
—*Virgin Soil*. Trans. by R. S. Townsend. Everyman's Library, New York: E. P. Dutton, 1929 (1877).

TURGOT, ANNE ROBERT (1727–1781)
Reflections on the Formation and Distribution of the Riches. New York: Macmillan, 1898 (1769–1770).

TYLOR, SIR EDWARD BURNETT (1832–1917)
Primitive Culture: Researches into the Development of Mythology, Philosophy, Religion, Language, Art, and Custom. 2 vols. New York: Brentano, 1924 (London, 1871).

TYNDALL, JOHN (1820–1893)
The Belfast Address. In Vol. II, *Fragments of Science* (London, 1874).
—*Light and Electricity: Notes of Two Courses of Lectures Before the Royal Institution of Great Britain*. New York: D. Appleton, 1895 (London, 1870).
—*On the Study of Physics*. In Vol. I, *Fragments of Science* (1854).
—*Scientific Use of the Imagination*. In Vol. II, *ibid*. (London, 1870).
NOTE:
Fragments of Science. A Series of Detached Essays, Addresses, and Reviews. 2 vols. New York: D. Appleton, 1897.

U

UEXKÜLL, JAKOB JOHANN VON (1864–1944)
Theoretical Biology. Trans. by D. L. MacKinnon. New York: Harcourt Brace, 1926 (*Theoretische Biologie*, Berlin, 1920).

UNAMUNO Y JUGO, MIGUEL DE (1864–1936)
Mist: A Tragicomic Novel. Trans. by W. Fite. New York: A. A. Knopf, 1928 (*Niebla*, Madrid, 1914).
—*The Tragic Sense of Life*. Trans. by J. E. C. Flitch. London: Macmillan, 1931 (*Del sentimiento trágico de la vida*, Madrid, 1913).

UNDSET, SIGRID (1882–1949)
Kristin Lavransdatter: The Bridal Wreath, The Mistress of Husaby, The Cross. Trans. by C. Archer and J. S. Scott. New York: A. A. Knopf, 1930 (Christiania, 1920–1922).

URBAN, WILBUR MARSHALL (1873–1952)
Language and Reality: The Philosophy of Language and the Principles of Symbolism. London: Allen & Unwin, 1939.

URE, PERCY NEVILLE (1879–1950)
The Origin of Tyranny. Cambridge University Press, 1922.

V

Valentine and Orson. Ed. by A. Dickson, trans. by H. Watson. New York: Oxford University Press, 1937 (*c*.1475–*c*.1489).

VALÉRY, PAUL AMBROISE (1871–1945)
Introduction à la poétique. Paris: Gallimard, 1938.
—*Variety*. Trans. by M. Cowley. New York: Harcourt Brace, 1927 (*Variété*, Paris, 1924).

VALLA, LORENZO (1406–1457)
Dialogue on Free Will. In *The Renaissance Philosophy of Man*. Ed. by E. Cassirer *et al*. University of Chicago Press, 1948 (1439).

VANDERPOL, ALFRED (1854–1915)
Le droit de guerre d'après les théologiens et les canonistes du moyen-âge. Paris: T. Tralin, 1911.

VAN DOREN, MARK ALBERT (1894–1972)
Liberal Education. New York: Henry Holt, 1943.
—*The Noble Voice, a Study of Ten Great Poems*. New York: Henry Holt, 1946.

VAN GOGH, VINCENT (1853–1890)
The Letters of Vincent Van Gogh to His Brother, 1872–1886. Trans. by J. Van Gogh-Bonger. 2 vols. New York: Houghton Mifflin Co., 1927.

VANN, GERALD (1906–1963)
Morality and War. London: Burns, Oates, & Washbourne, 1939.
—*Morals Makyth Man*. New York: Longmans, Green & Co., 1938.
—*On Being Human: St. Thomas and Mr. Aldous Huxley*. New York: Sheed & Ward, 1933.

VATTEL, EMMERICH DE (1714–1767)
The Law of Nations, or the Principles of Natural Law Applied to the Conduct and to the Affairs of Nations and of Sovereigns. Trans. by C. G. Fenwick. Washington, D.C.: Carnegie Institution, 1916 (*Le droit des gens, ou, Principes de la loi naturelle appliquées à la conduite et aux affaires des nations et des souverains*, Neuchâtel, 1758).

VAUGHAN, HENRY (1622–1695)
The Retreate. In Vol. II, *The Works of Henry Vaughan*. Ed. by L. C. Martin. 2 vols. Oxford: Clarendon Press, 1914 (in *Silex Scintillans*, London, 1650).

VAUVENARGUES, LUC DE CLAPIERS, MARQUIS DE (1715–1747)
Introduction à la connaissance de l'esprit humain. In *Oeuvres de Vauvenargues*. Paris: Furne & Cie., 1857 (Paris, 1746).

VEBLEN, OSWALD (1880–1960) and LENNES, NELS JOHANN (1874–)
Introduction to Infinitesimal Analysis; Functions of One Real Variable. New York: G. E. Stechert, 1935 (New York, 1907).

VEBLEN, OSWALD and YOUNG, JOHN WESLEY (1879–1932)
Projective Geometry. 2 vols. Boston: Ginn & Co., 1910–1918.

VEBLEN, THORSTEIN BUNDE (1857–1929)
The Higher Learning in America; a Memorandum on the Conduct of Universities by Business Men. New York: B. W. Huebsch, 1918.
—*An Inquiry into the Nature of Peace and the Terms of Its Perpetuation*. London: Macmillan, 1917.
—*The Instinct of Workmanship, and the State of the Industrial Arts*. New York: Viking Press, 1943 (New York, 1914).

—*The Place of Science in Modern Civilization, and Other Essays.* New York: Viking Press, 1932 (1892–1913).
—*The Theory of Business Enterprise.* New York: Scribner's, 1904.
—*The Theory of the Leisure Class. An Economic Study of Institutions.* Modern Library, New York: Random House, 1934 (New York, 1899).
—*The Vested Interests and the State of the Industrial Arts.* New York: B. W. Huebsch, 1919.

VECCHIO, GIORGIO DEL (1878–)
The Formal Bases of Law. Trans. by J. Lisle. Boston: Boston Book Co., 1914 (*I presupposti filosofici della nozione del diritto*, Bologna, 1905; *Il concetto del diritto*, Bologna, 1906; *Il concetto della natura e il principio del diritto*, Milan, 1908).

VENDRYÈS, JOSEPH (1875–1960)
Language; a Linguistic Introduction to History. Trans. by P. Radin. New York: A. A. Knopf, 1931 (*Le langage*, Paris, 1921).

VENN, JOHN (1834–1923)
The Logic of Chance. An Essay on the Foundations and Province of the Theory of Probability, with Especial Reference to Its Logical Bearings and Its Application to Moral and Social Science, and to Statistics. New York: Macmillan, 1888 (London, 1866).
—*On Some of the Characteristics of Belief, Scientific and Religious. Being the Hulsean Lectures for 1869.* London: Macmillan, 1870.
—*The Principles of Empirical or Inductive Logic.* London: Macmillan, 1907 (London, 1889).
—*Symbolic Logic.* London: Macmillan, 1894 (London, 1881).

VERLAINE, PAUL MARIE (1844–1896)
Art poétique. In Vol. 1, *Oeuvres complètes de Paul Verlaine.* 5 vols. Paris: Messein, 1926–1930 (1882).

VÉRON, EUGÈNE (1825–1889)
Aesthetics. Trans. by W. H. Armstrong. London: Chapman & Hall, 1879 (*L'esthétique*, Paris, 1878).

VESALIUS, ANDREAS (1514–1564)
The Epitome. Trans. by L. R. Lind. New York: Macmillan, 1949 (1543).

VICO, GIOVANNI BATTISTA (1668–1744)
Il diritto universale. Ed. by F. Nicoloni. 3 vols. Bari: G. Laterza, 1936 (*De Uno Universi Juris Principio et Fine Uno* and *De Constantia Jurisprudentis*, Naples, 1720; 1721).
—*The New Science.* Trans. by T. G. Bergin and M. H. Fisch. Ithaca, N.Y.: Cornell University Press, 1948 (1725).

VIGNY, COMTE ALFRED VICTOR DE (1797–1863)
Military Servitude and Grandeur. Trans. by F. W. Huard. New York: G. H. Doran, 1919 (*Servitude et grandeur militaires*, Paris, 1835).

VILLON, FRANÇOIS (1431–*c.* 1463)
The Debate of the Heart and Body of Villon. In *The Complete Works of François Villon, Including the Poems Long Attributed to Him.* Trans. by J. U. Nicolson. New York: Covici-Friede, 1931 (1458?).

VINOGRADOFF, SIR PAUL GAVRILOVITCH (1854–1925)
Common Sense in Law. New York: Henry Holt, 1913.
—*Custom and Right.* Cambridge, Mass.: Harvard University Press, 1925.
—*The Growth of the Manor.* London: Allen & Unwin, 1932 (London, 1905).

VIRCHOW, RUDOLF LUDWIG KARL (1821–1902)
Cellular Pathology as Based upon Physiological and Pathological Histology. Trans. by F. Chance. New York: R. M. DeWitt, 1860 (*Die Cellularpathologie in ihrer Begründung auf physiologische und pathologische Gewebelehre*, Berlin, 1858).

VITORIA, FRANCISCO DE (*c.* 1480–1546)
De Indis et De Jure Belli Relectiones. Trans. by J. P. Bate. Washington, D.C.: Carnegie Institution, 1917 (1532?).

VITRUVIUS POLLIO, MARCUS (*fl.* late 1st century B.C.)
On Architecture. Ed. and trans. by F. Granger. 2 vols. Loeb Library, New York: Putnam's, 1931–1934.

VIVES, JUAN LUIS (1492–1540)
A Fable About Man. In *The Renaissance Philosophy of Man.* Ed. by E. Cassirer *et al.* University of Chicago Press, 1948.
—*On Education.* Ed. and trans. by F. Watson. Cambridge University Press, 1913 (*De Tradendis Disciplinis*, Antwerp, 1531).

Völsung Saga: The Story of the Volsungs and Niblungs, with Certain Songs from the Elder Edda. Ed. by H. H. Sparling, trans. by W. Morris and E. Magnússon. London: W. Scott, 1888 (*c.* 1140–1220).

VOLTAIRE, pseud. for FRANÇOIS MARIE AROUET (1694–1778)
Candide, or Optimism. Modern Library, New York: Random House, 1930 (Geneva, 1759).
—[Essay on Toleration] *Toleration and Other Essays.* Trans. by J. McCabe. New York: Putnam's, 1912 (*Traité sur la tolérance*, Geneva, 1763).
—*The Huron, or Pupil of Nature.* In *Best Known Works* (*L'ingénue*, Utrecht, 1767).
—*The Ignorant Philosopher. Ibid.* (*Le philosophe ignorant*, Geneva, 1766).
—*Letters on the English.* In *French and English Philosophers*, Vol. XXXIV, "The Harvard Classics," ed. by C. W. Eliot. New York: P. F. Collier, 1910 (London, 1733).
—*Micromegas.* In *Zadig and Other Romances.* Trans. by I. H. Woolf. New York: E. P. Dutton, 1923 (London, 1752).
—*A Philosophical Dictionary.* Ed. by W. F. Fleming. 10 vols. New York: E. R. DuMont, 1901 (*Dictionnaire philosophique portatif*, London, 1764).
—*The Philosophy of History.* In *Best Known Works* (from *La philosophie de l'histoire*, Geneva, 1765).

—*The Sage and the Atheist. Ibid.* (*Histoire de Jenni, ou le sage et l'athée*, Geneva, 1775).

—*The Study of Nature, Ibid.* (*Les singularités de la nature*, Basel, 1768).

—*Zadig.* See *Micromegas* (*Zadig, ou la destinée*, Paris, 1747).

NOTE:

The Best Known Works of Voltaire. New York: Blue Ribbon Books, 1931.

VONIER, ANSCAR (1875–1938)
The Angels. New York: Macmillan, 1928.

—*The Human Soul and Its Relations with Other Spirits.* London: B. Herder, 1925 (London, 1913).

VON NEUMANN, JOHN (1903–1957) and MORGENSTERN, OSKAR (1902–)
Theory of Games and Economic Behavior. Princeton University Press, 1944.

VON WEIZSÄCKER, CARL FRIEDRICH (1912–)
The History of Nature. Trans. by F. D. Wieck. University of Chicago Press, 1949.

VRIES, HUGO DE (1848–1935)
The Mutation Theory: Experiments and Observations on the Origin of Species in the Vegetable Kingdom. Trans. by J. B. Farmer and A. D. Darbishire. 2 vols. Chicago: Open Court, 1909–1910 (*Die Mutationstheorie. Versuche und Beobachtungen über die Entstehung von Arten im Pflanzenreich*, Leipsic, 1901–1903).

W

WALLACE, ALFRED RUSSELL (1823–1913)
Contributions to the Theory of Natural Selection. A Series of Essays. New York: Macmillan, 1871 (1855–1870).

WALLAS, GRAHAM (1858–1932)
The Great Society: A Psychological Analysis. New York: Macmillan, 1923 (New York, 1914).

WALLIS, JOHN (1616–1703)
Mechanica: sive, De Motu. 3 vols. London, 1670–1671.

WARD, JAMES (1843–1925)
Naturalism and Agnosticism. 2 vols. New York: Macmillan, 1899.

—*The Realm of Ends, or Pluralism and Theism.* Cambridge University Press, 1911.

WARE, HENRY (1794–1843)
The Law of Honor. A Discourse Delivered 1838. Cambridge: Folsom, Wells, & Thurston, 1838.

WASSERMANN, JACOB (1873–1934)
The World's Illusion. Trans. by L. Lewisohn. New York: Harcourt Brace, 1920 (*Christian Wahnschaffe*, Berlin, 1919).

WATSON, W. H. (1899–)
On Understanding Physics. Cambridge University Press, 1938.

WATTS, ROBERT (1820–1895)
The Reign of Causality: A Vindication of the Scientific Principle of Telic Causal Efficiency. Edinburgh: T. & T. Clark, 1888.

WEBB, SIDNEY JAMES (1859–1947) and WEBB, BEATRICE (1858–1943)
Industrial Democracy. 2 vols. New York: Longmans, Green & Co., 1919 (London, 1897).

WEBER, MAX (1864–1920)
[Essays in Sociology] *From Max Weber: Essays in Sociology.* Sel. and trans. by H. H. Gerth and C. Wright Mills. New York: Oxford University Press, 1946.

—*Politics as a Vocation.* In *Essays in Sociology, q.v.* (*Politik als Beruf*, Munich, 1919).

—*The Protestant Ethic and the Spirit of Capitalism.* Trans. by T. Parsons. London: Allen & Unwin, 1930 (1904).

—*Science as a Vocation.* In *Essays in Sociology, q.v.* (*Wissenschaft als Beruf*, Munich, 1919).

WEDGWOOD, HENSLEIGH (1803–1891)
On the Origin of Language. London: Trübner & Co., 1866.

WEININGER, OTTO (1880–1903)
Sex and Character. New York: Putnam's, 1906 (*Geschlecht und Charakter*, Vienna, 1903).

WEISMANN, AUGUST (1834–1914)
Essays upon Heredity and Kindred Biological Problems. Ed. by E. P. Poulton, trans. by S. Schönland and A. E. Shipley. Oxford: Clarendon Press, 1889 (*Aufsätze über Vererbung und verwandte Fragen*, Jena, 1892).

—*The Germ-Plasm, a Theory of Heredity.* Trans. by W. N. Parker and H. Rönnfeldt. New York: Scribner's, 1902 (*Das Keimplasma. Eine Theorie der Vererbung*, Jena, 1892).

—*Studies in the Theory of Descent.* Ed. and trans. by R. Meldola. 2 vols. London: Low, Marston & Co., 1882 (*Studien zur Descendenztheorie*, Leipsic, 1875–1876).

WEISS, PAUL (1901–)
Nature and Man. New York: Henry Holt, 1946.

—*Reality.* Princeton University Press, 1938.

WELBY-GREGORY, LADY VICTORIA (1837–1912)
Significs and Language; the Articulate Form of Our Expressive and Interpretative Resources. London: Macmillan, 1911.

—*What Is Meaning? Studies in the Development of Significance.* London: Macmillan, 1903.

WELLS, HERBERT GEORGE (1866–1946)
The New Machiavelli. New York: Duffield & Co., 1919 (1910).

—*The New World Order; Whether It Is Attainable, How It Can Be Attained, and What Sort of World a World at Peace Will Have to Be.* New York: A. A. Knopf, 1940.

—*The World of William Clissold: A Novel at a New Angle.* 2 vols. New York: G. H. Doran Co., 1926.

WELLS, HERBERT GEORGE, HUXLEY, JULIAN SORELL and WELLS, GEORGE PHILIP
Reproduction, Genetics and the Development of Sex. Garden City, N.Y.: Doubleday Doran,

1932 (reprinted from *The Science of Life*, New York, 1929).

WENDELL, BARRETT (1855–1921)
The Privileged Classes. New York: Scribner's, 1908.
—*Stelligeri and Other Essays*. New York: Scribner's, 1893.

WERTHEIMER, MAX (1880–1943)
Productive Thinking. Ed. by S. E. Asch *et al.* New York: Harper, 1945 (1943).

WESTERMARCK, EDVARD ALEXANDER (1862–1939)
Ethical Relativity. London: K. Paul, Trench, Trübner, 1932.
—*The History of Human Marriage*. 3 vols. New York: Allerton Book Co., 1922 (London, 1891).
—*The Origin and Development of the Moral Ideas*. 2 vols. New York: Macmillan, 1924–1926 (New York, 1906–1908).

WEYL, HERMANN (1885–1955)
The Open World; Three Lectures on the Metaphysical Implications of Science. New Haven, Conn.: Yale University Press, 1932.
—*The Philosophy of Mathematics and Natural Science*. Princeton University Press, 1948.
—*Space—Time—Matter*. Trans. by H. L. Brose. London: Methuen, 1922 (*Raum, Zeit, Materie. Vorlesungen über allgemeine Relativitätstheorie*, Berlin, 1918).

WHARTON, EDITH NEWBOLD (1862–1937)
Ethan Frome. New York: Scribner's, 1938 (New York, 1911).

WHATELY, RICHARD (1787–1863)
Elements of Logic. New York: Sheldon & Co., 1873 (London, 1826).
—*Elements of Rhetoric*. New York: Sheldon & Co., 1871 (Oxford, 1828).

WHEELER, WILLIAM MORTON (1865–1937)
Foibles of Insects and Men. New York: A. A. Knopf, 1928.

WHEWELL, WILLIAM (1794–1866)
Astronomy and General Physics Considered with Reference to Natural Theology. London: H. G. Bohn, 1852 (London, 1833).
—*The Elements of Morality, Including Polity*. Cambridge: Deighton, Bell, 1864 (London, 1845).
—*Of a Liberal Education in General; and with Particular Reference to the Leading Studies of the University of Cambridge*. London: J. W. Parker, 1880 (London, 1845–1852).
—*On the Philosophy of Discovery, Chapters Historical and Critical*. London: J. W. Parker, 1860.
—*The Philosophy of the Inductive Sciences, Founded upon Their History*. 2 vols. London: J. W. Parker, 1840.
—*The Plurality of Worlds*. Boston: Gould & Lincoln, 1861 (London, 1853).
—*Six Lectures on Political Economy Delivered at Cambridge in Michaelmas Term, 1861*. Cambridge University Press, 1862.

WHITEHEAD, ALFRED NORTH (1861–1947)
Adventures of Ideas. New York: Macmillan, 1933.
—*The Aims of Education and Other Essays*. New York: Macmillan, 1929 (1912–1928).
—*The Concept of Nature*. Cambridge University Press, 1930 (Cambridge, 1920).
—*An Enquiry Concerning the Principles of Natural Knowledge*. Cambridge University Press, 1925 (Cambridge, 1919).
—*The Function of Reason*. Princeton University Press, 1929.
—*An Introduction to Mathematics*. London: T. Butterworth, 1931 (London, 1911).
—*Modes of Thought*. New York: Macmillan, 1938.
—*The Organization of Thought, Educational and Scientific*. Philadelphia: Lippincott, 1917.
—*The Principle of Relativity with Applications to Physical Science*. Cambridge University Press, 1922.
—*Process and Reality, an Essay in Cosmology*. New York: Macmillan, 1929.
—*Religion in the Making*. New York: Macmillan, 1926.
—*Science and the Modern World*. New York: Macmillan, 1937 (New York, 1925).
—*Symbolism, Its Meaning and Effects*. New York: Macmillan, 1927.
—*A Treatise on Universal Algebra, with Applications*. Cambridge University Press, 1898.

WHITEHEAD, ALFRED NORTH and RUSSELL, BERTRAND (1872–1970)
Principia Mathematica. 3 vols. New York: Macmillan, 1925–1927 (Cambridge, 1910–1913).

WHITMAN, WALT (1819–1892)
Democratic Vistas, and Other Papers. London: W. Scott, 1888 (Washington, D.C., 1871).
—*Leaves of Grass*. New York: Doubleday Doran, 1945 (New York, 1855).

WHITNEY, WILLIAM DWIGHT (1827–1894)
Oriental and Linguistic Studies. 2 vols. New York: Scribner's, 1893 (New York, 1873–1874).

WHITTAKER, EDMUND TAYLOR (1873–1956)
A History of the Theories of Aether and Electricity from the Age of Descartes to the Close of the Nineteenth Century. London: Longmans, Green & Co., 1910.
—*Space and Spirit*. New York: T. Nelson, 1947.
—*A Treatise on the Analytical Dynamics of Particles and Rigid Bodies, with an Introduction to the Problem of Three Bodies*. New York: Dover Publications, 1944 (Cambridge, 1904).

WHITTAKER, THOMAS (1856–1935)
Prolegomena to a New Metaphysic. Cambridge University Press, 1931.

WHITWORTH, WILLIAM ALLEN (1840–1905)
Choice and Chance, with 1000 Exercises. New York: G. E. Stechert, 1927 (Cambridge, 1867).

WIENER, NORBERT (1894–1964)
Cybernetics. New York: John Wiley & Son, 1949.

Wilde, Oscar (1854–1900)
The Picture of Dorian Gray. Modern Library, New York: Random House, 194–? (London, 1891).

Wilder, Thornton Niven (1897–)
The Bridge of San Luis Rey. New York: A. & C. Boni, 1927.

William of Saint-Thierry (1085–*c*.1148)
De Natura et Dignitate Amoris. In Vol. clxxxiv, *Patrologia Latina*.

Williams, Charles (1886–1945)
The Place of the Lion. London: Gollancz, 1947 (1931).

Willoughby, Westel Woodbury (1867–1945)
Social Justice; a Critical Essay. New York: Macmillan, 1900.

Wilson, Edmund (1895–1972)
To the Finland Station; a Study in the Writing and Acting of History. New York: Harcourt Brace, 1940.

Wilson, Francis Graham (1901–)
The Elements of Modern Politics: An Introduction to Political Science. New York: McGraw-Hill, 1936.

Wilson, James (1742–1798)
Works, Being His Public Discourses upon Jurisprudence and the Political Science. Ed. by J. De Witt Andrews. Chicago: Callaghan & Co., 1896.

Wilson, John Cook (1849–1915)
Statement and Inference, with Other Philosophical Papers. Ed. by A. S. L. Farquharson. 2 vols. Oxford: Clarendon Press, 1926 (1874–1914).

Wilson, Richard Albert (1874–1949)
The Miraculous Birth of Language. New York: Philosophical Library, 1948 (1937).

Wilson, Thomas (*c*.1525–1581)
[Arte of Rhetorique] *Wilson's Arte of Rhetorique (1560)*. Ed. by G. H. Mair. Oxford: Clarendon Press, 1909 (London, 1553).
—*A Discourse upon Usury, by Way of Dialogue and Orations for the Better Variety and More Delight of All Those That Shall Read This Treatise*. Ed. by R. H. Tawney. New York: Harcourt Brace, 1925 (London, 1572).

Wilson, Woodrow (1856–1924)
Congressional Government. Boston: Houghton Mifflin Co., 1913 (1885).
—*The State: Elements of Historical and Practical Politics. A Sketch of Institutional History and Administration*. Boston: D. C. Heath, 1918 (Boston, 1889).

Wittgenstein, Ludwig (1889–1951)
Tractatus Logico-Philosophicus. Trans. anon. New York: Harcourt Brace, 1922 (1921).

Wolff, Christian von (1679–1754)
[Ontologia] *Philosophia Prima, sive Ontologia, Methodo Scientifica Pertracta qua Omnis Cognitionis Humanae Principia Continentur*. Frankfort: Officina Libraria Rengeriana, 1729.

Wollstonecraft, Mary (Mrs. Godwin) (1759–1797)
The Rights of Woman. Everyman's Library, New York: E. P. Dutton, 1929 (London, 1792).

Woodbridge, Frederick James Eugene (1867–1940)
An Essay on Nature. New York: Columbia University Press, 1940.
—*Nature and Mind, Selected Essays*. New York: Columbia University Press, 1937 (1894–1936).
—*The Realm of Mind: An Essay in Metaphysics*. New York: Columbia University Press, 1926.

Woodger, Joseph Henry (1894–)
Biological Principles: A Critical Study. New York: Harcourt Brace, 1929.

Woodworth, Robert Sessions (1869–1962)
Psychological Issues; Selected Papers of Robert S. Woodworth . . . with a Bibliography of His Writings. New York: Columbia University Press, 1939 (1897–1920).

Woolman, John (1720–1772)
The Journal, with Other Writings of John Woolman. Everyman's Library, New York: E. P. Dutton, 1922 (1772).

Wordsworth, William (1770–1850)
Intimations of Immortality from Recollections of Early Childhood. In *The Poems of Wordsworth*. Ed. by T. Hutchinson. New York: Oxford University Press, 1926 (1807).
—*Michael. A Pastoral Poem. Ibid*. (1800).
—*Ode to Duty. Ibid*. (1807).
—*Preface to the Lyrical Ballads. Ibid*. (1800).
—*The Prelude; or, Growth of a Poet's Mind. Ibid*. (1805).
—[Tintern Abbey] *Lines Composed a Few Miles Above Tintern Abbey, on Revisiting the Banks of the Wye During a Tour. Ibid*. (1798).

Wright, Quincy (1890–1970)
A Study of War. 2 vols. University of Chicago Press, 1942.

Wundt, Wilhelm Max (1832–1920)
Die Prinzipien der mechanischen Naturlehre. Stuttgart: F. Enke, 1910 (originally pub. as *Die physikalischen Axiome und ihre Beziehung zum Kausalprincip*, Erlangen, 1866).
—*Ethics: An Investigation of the Facts and Laws of the Moral Life*. Trans. by E. B. Titchener *et al*. 3 vols. New York: Macmillan, 1897–1901 (*Ethik. Eine Untersuchung der Thatsachen und Gesetze des sittlichen Lebens*, Stuttgart, 1886).
—*Outlines of Psychology*. Trans. by C. H. Judd. New York: G. E. Stechert, 1907 (*Grundriss der Psychologie*, Leipsic, 1896).
—*Principles of Physiological Psychology*. Trans. by E. B. Titchener. New York: Macmillan, 1910 (*Grundzüge der physiologischen Psychologie*, Leipsic, 1874).

Wycliffe, John (*c*.1320–1384)
Tractatus de Officio Regis. Ed. by A. W. Pollard

and C. Sayle. London: Trübner & Co., 1887 (*c.*1379).

X

Xenophon (*c.*430–*c.*355 B.C.)
The Education of Cyrus (*Cyropedia*). Trans. by H. G. Dakyns. Everyman's Library, New York: E. P. Dutton, 1914 (394?–370? B.C.).
—*The Oeconomicus*. Ed. by A. H. N. Sewell. Cambridge University Press, 1925.

Xirau, Joaquin (1895–)
Amor y mundo. Mexico, D. F.: Colegio de México, 1940.

Y

Yeats, William Butler (1865–1939)
Letters on Poetry from W. B. Yeats to Dorothy Wellesley. New York: Oxford University Press, 1940 (1935–1938).

Yerkes, Robert Mearns (1876–1956) and Yerkes, Ada W. (1873–)
The Great Apes: A Study of Anthropoid Life. New Haven, Conn.: Yale University Press, 1929.

Young, John Wesley (1879–1932)
Lectures on Fundamental Concepts of Algebra and Geometry. New York: Macmillan, 1920 (New York, 1911).

Young, Thomas (1773–1829)
Miscellaneous Works. London: J. Murray, 1855.
—[Natural Philosophy] *A Course of Lectures on Natural Philosophy and the Mechanical Arts*. 2 vols. London: Taylor & Walton, 1845 (London, 1807).

Z

Zilboorg, Gregory (1890–1959)
The Medical Man and the Witch During the Renaissance. Baltimore, Md.: Johns Hopkins University Press, 1935.

Zola, Émile (1840–1902)
Germinal. Trans. by Havelock Ellis. Everyman's Library, New York: E. P. Dutton, 1933 (Paris, 1885).
—*Les Rougon Macquart*. 20 vols. Paris, 1871–1893.
—*Letter to M. Félix Faure* [*J'accuse*]. In *The Dreyfus Case, Four Letters to France*. London: J. Lane, 1898 (*Lettre à M. Félix Faure, président de la République*, 13 janvier, 1898).
—*Nana*. Trans. anon. Modern Library, New York: Random House, 1928 (Paris, 1880).

Zwingli, Huldreich (1484–1531)
Commentary on True and False Religion. In Vol. III, *The Latin Works of Huldreich Zwingli*. Ed. by C. N. Heller, trans. by H. Preble. 3 vols. Philadelphia: Heidelberg Press, 1929 (*Commentarius de Vera et Falsa Religione*, Zurich, 1525).

APPENDIX II

INVENTORY OF TERMS

The Inventory of Terms is designed to facilitate the use of the Syntopicon as a reference book. By means of the terms here listed in alphabetical order, it directs the reader to the relevant topics in the 102 chapters, and thus enables him to discover what the great books have to say on the 3000 topics which represent the themes of the great conversation. The titles of the 102 chapters are included in this alphabetical list because each of the great ideas is also a term in topics of chapters other than the one devoted to its consideration.

In order to see the particular topic in the context of related topics, the reader should turn first to the Outline of Topics in which the particular topic occurs. Immediately following the Inventory (p. 732), a table lists the pages in Volumes I and II of *The Great Ideas* on which each Outline of Topics appears. The Outline of Topics in each chapter directs the reader to the pages of its Reference section where the particular topic is treated.

EACH TERM IN THE INVENTORY is accompanied by references to the chapters and topics in which it is a significant element. The terms are the words or phrases printed in bold face type. Whole chapters are cited by both chapter number and name; for example, *see* CH 4: ART. Individual topics are cited by the name of the chapter and the number of the topic in the Outline of Topics of that chapter; for example, *see* ART 5a.

In each entry, topics are cited in the alphabetical order of the chapters in which they appear. However, whole chapters, when cited, always precede individual topics. In some entries, the citations are divided into two groups, those of primary and those of secondary significance. The first group is separated from the second by a diagonal line.

SOME WORDS CARRY A QUALIFIER in parentheses to indicate the sense in which they are being used. For example, **Balance** (*phys.*) stands for the term *balance* as used in physics; **Crisis** (*med.*) stands for the term *crisis* as used in medicine. When the same word is used in two or more senses, qualifiers indicate the distinct terms it represents. For example, **Function** (*biol.*) stands for the term *function* as it is used in biology, and **Function** (*math.*) stands for the term *function* as it is used in mathematics.

Terms which are the names of particular sciences, such as logic or biology, may be related to topics which treat the nature of the science itself, or they may be related to topics concerned with the subject matter of that science. The words "science of" or "subject matter of," following words like "logic" and "biology," indicate which sort of topic is being cited. For a small number of such words, the qualifying phrase is not needed to determine the meaning.

Phrases are sometimes necessary to express a single term or to make its meaning definite; for example, **Law of contradiction, Military strategy and tactics.** The same purpose is served by pairing related or similar words; for example, **Appearance and reality, Franchise or suffrage,** and **History, historian.**

FOR COMMENT ON THE USE of the Inventory of Terms, see the Preface in Volume I.

A

***A priori* and *a posteriori*:** *see* EXPERIENCE 2d; JUDGMENT 8c; KNOWLEDGE 6c(4); REASONING 5b(3) / *see also* MATHEMATICS 1c; MEMORY AND IMAGINATION 1a; SPACE 4a–4b; TIME 6c

Abilities (*psychol.*): *see* LIFE AND DEATH 3; MAN 4–5a; SOUL 2c–2c(3) / *see also* ANIMAL 1a(1)–1a(4); HABIT 2b, 5–5d; KNOWLEDGE 6b; MAN 6a; QUALITY 2a; SOUL 2a; VIRTUE AND VICE 2a

Abiogenesis: *see* EVOLUTION 4c / *see also* ANIMAL 8b; EVOLUTION 4a

Abnormal and normal: *see* NATURE 2e

Abnormality (*psychol.*): *see* DESIRE 6b–6c; DUTY 4b; EMOTION 3a, 3c–3c(4); LOVE 2a(2)–2a(4); MAN 5b; MEDICINE 6a–6c(2); MEMORY AND IMAGINATION 2e(2)–2e(4), 5c; MIND 8–8c; ONE AND MANY 3b(5); OPPOSITION 4c; PLEASURE AND PAIN 8c; PUNISHMENT 6; SIGN AND SYMBOL 6c; SIN 5; WILL 9b

Absolute: *see* ONE AND MANY 1; OPPOSITION 2e / *see also* HISTORY 4a(3); IDEA 1f; MIND 10f–10f(2); PROGRESS 1a

Absolute and limited government: *see* CONSTITUTION 1; LAW 7a; MONARCHY 1a–1a(2); TYRANNY 5–5c / *see also* CITIZEN 2b; CONSTITUTION 3a;

B

C

D

F

G

H

I

M

N

O

Q

R

S

T

U

U

Y

Z

LOCATION OF OUTLINES OF TOPICS

Volume I

Volume II

PRINTED IN THE U.S.A.

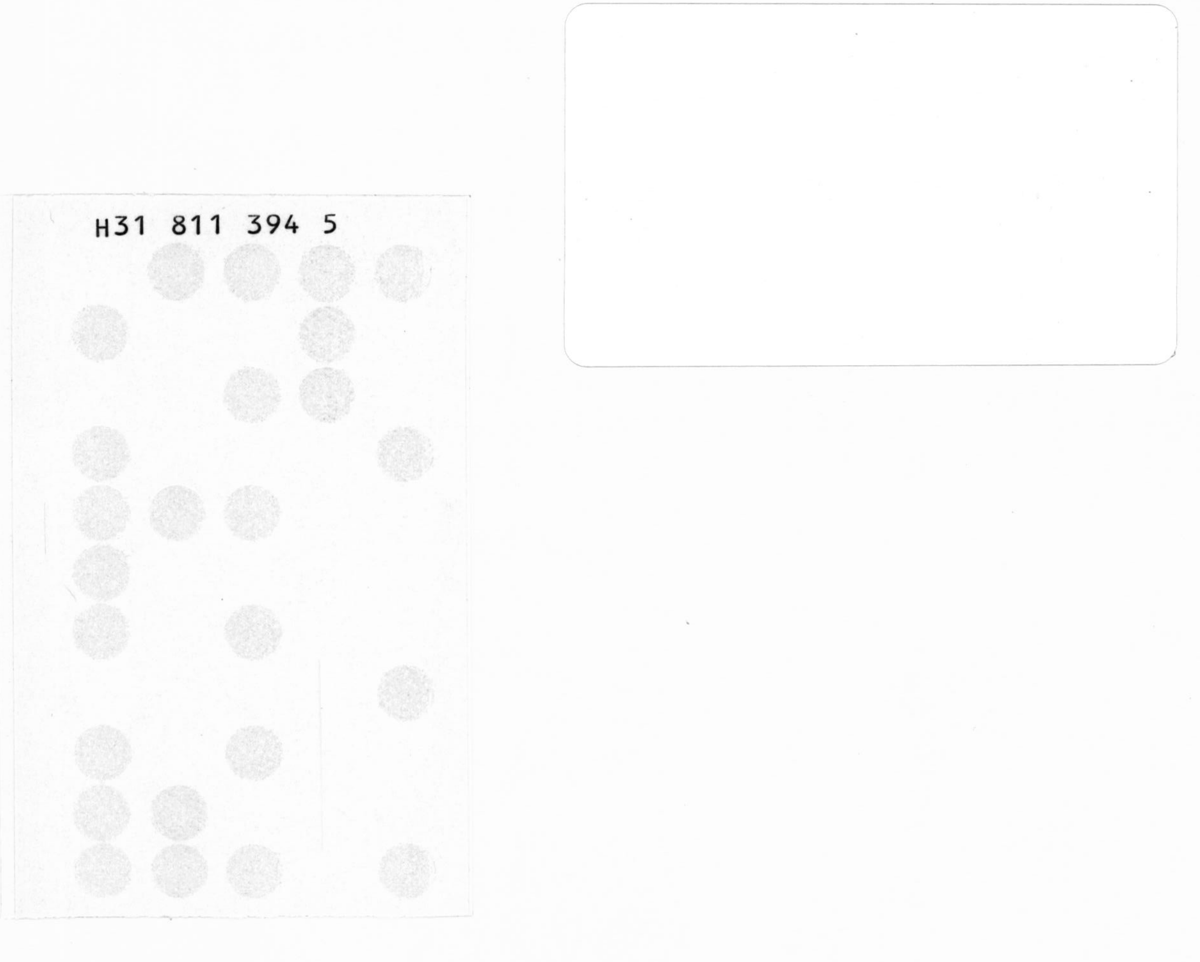
H31 811 394 5

THE GREAT IDEAS, Volumes 2 and 3

ANGEL
ANIMAL
ARISTOCRACY
ART
ASTRONOMY
BEAUTY
BEING
CAUSE
CHANCE
CHANGE
CITIZEN
CONSTITUTION
COURAGE
CUSTOM AND CONVENTION
DEFINITION
DEMOCRACY
DESIRE
DIALECTIC
DUTY
EDUCATION
ELEMENT
EMOTION
ETERNITY
EVOLUTION
EXPERIENCE
FAMILY
FATE
FORM
GOD
GOOD AND EVIL
GOVERNMENT
HABIT
HAPPINESS
HISTORY
HONOR
HYPOTHESIS
IDEA
IMMORTALITY
INDUCTION
INFINITY
JUDGMENT
JUSTICE
KNOWLEDGE
LABOR
LANGUAGE
LAW
LIBERTY
LIFE AND DEATH
LOGIC
LOVE
MAN
MATHEMATICS